The Panhandle
p417

Northeast
Florida
p318

Orlando &
Walt Disney
World
p227

The Space
Coast
p305

Tampa Bay &
Southwest Florida
p361

Southeast
Florida
p186

The Everglades
p136

Miami
p48

Florida Keys
& Key West
p153

PAGE 493 **SURVIVAL GUIDE**

VITAL PRACTICAL INFORMATION TO
HELP YOU HAVE A SMOOTH TRIP

Transportation

GETTING THERE
& AWAY

THIS EDITION WRITTEN AND RESEARCHED BY

Jeff Campbell, Jennifer Denniston, Adam Karlin,
Emily Matchar

welcome to Florida

Seaside Fantasy

Maybe there's no mystery to what makes the Florida peninsula so intoxicating. Beaches as fine and sweet as powdered sugar, warm teal waters, rustling mangroves: all conspire to melt our workaday selves. We come to Florida to be soothed, to let go – of worries and winter, of inhibitions and reality. For many, it's merely the desire for an indulgent beachy getaway of naps, swimming, seafood and rosy sunsets. Others seek the more excitable hedonism of South Beach, Spring Break and Key West. Still more hope to lose themselves within the perfected phantasmagorical realms of Walt Disney World and Orlando's theme parks. As for Ponce, he traipsed the peninsula seeking mermaids and the legendary fountain of youth, and in a thousand and one ways, Florida still nurtures these alluring, ever-hopeful fantasies.

Sexy Swamps

Exaggeration comes naturally to Florida. Within its hot, seductive, semitropical wilderness, alligators prowl beside every waterway, egg-white herons strut through reedy ponds, lovable manatees winter in crystal springs and sea turtles nest in summer. Osprey and eagles, dolphins and mighty tarpon, flocks of roseate spoonbills, coral-reef forests, oceans of sawgrass: despite the best efforts of 21st-century humans, overwhelming portions of Florida remain untamed, sometimes disconcert-

MARK LEWIS / PHOTOLIBRARY ©

Ever since Ponce de León, Florida has cast a sensual spell over travelers, and its surreal landscape, heavenly beaches and prehistoric beasts still quicken the pulse and inflame the imagination.

(left) The beach at sunrise, Fort Lauderdale (p190)
(below) An American alligator (p488)

DOUGLAS STEAKLEY / LONELY PLANET IMAGES ©

ingly so. We come to Florida to experience this taste of wildness, to paddle so close to our toothsome Jurrasic-era friends that our palms tingle. To meet loggerheads and manatees underwater, eye to eye. To look up and see a single precious jewel-like orchid clinging magically to the trunk of an ancient, moss-draped bald cypress.

Latin-Spiced Culture

Miami is one of America's great immigrant-rich cities, and its mix of Caribbean and Latin American cultures is led by its Cuban community, which long ago carved its own Spanish-speaking city within the city. These Latin flavors spice up everything: the dance floor, the kitchen, the cocktail glass, the dress code. In Miami and throughout South Florida, this indelible influence has given the state a temperament to match its temperature: the semitropical peninsula is also a cultural transition zone straddling the hot southern latitudes and the cooler northern ones. Wealth and celebrity also play a role in South Florida's cultural life: preserving South Beach's art-deco confections and the grandiose palaces of Florida's railroad tycoons, and supporting a flourishing arts scene brimming with the bold and the beautiful.

In the end, Florida promises escape – whether into the Magic Kingdom, into the swamp, into status-drenched excess, or merely into the calm turquoise ocean that surrounds you on nearly every side.

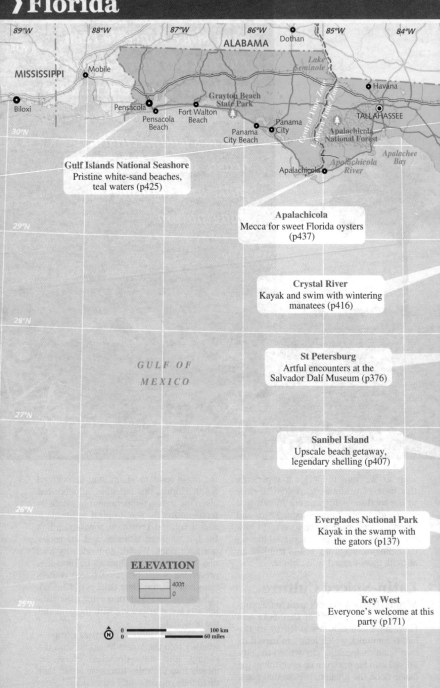

ALABAMA

Dothan

MISSISSIPPI

Mobile

Biloxi

Pensacola

Pensacola Beach

Fort Walton Beach

Grayton Beach State Park

Panama City Beach

Panama City

Lake Seminole

Havana

TALLAHASSEE

Apalachicola National Forest

Apalachicola River

Apalachee Bay

Apalachicola

Gulf Islands National Seashore
Pristine white-sand beaches,
teal waters (p425)

Apalachicola
Mecca for sweet Florida oysters
(p437)

Crystal River
Kayak and swim with wintering
manatees (p416)

GULF OF
MEXICO

St Petersburg
Artful encounters at the
Salvador Dalí Museum (p376)

Sanibel Island
Upscale beach getaway,
legendary shelling (p407)

Everglades National Park
Kayak in the swamp with
the gators (p137)

ELEVATION

400ft
0

Key West
Everyone's welcome at this
party (p171)

0   100 km
0   60 miles

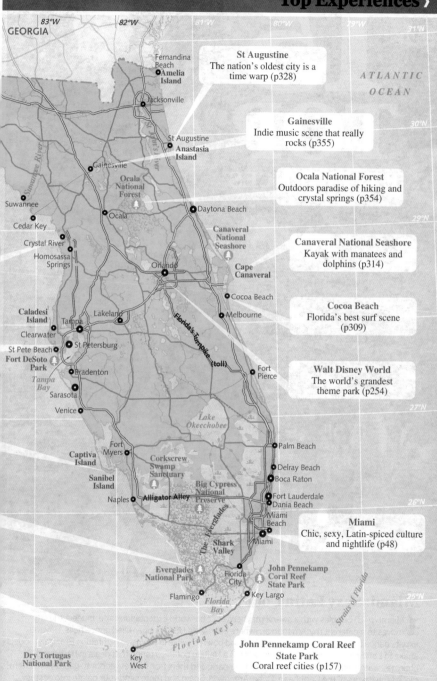

St Augustine
The nation's oldest city is a time warp (p328)

Gainesville
Indie music scene that really rocks (p355)

Ocala National Forest
Outdoors paradise of hiking and crystal springs (p354)

Canaveral National Seashore
Kayak with manatees and dolphins (p314)

Cocoa Beach
Florida's best surf scene (p309)

Walt Disney World
The world's grandest theme park (p254)

Miami
Chic, sexy, Latin-spiced culture and nightlife (p48)

John Pennekamp Coral Reef State Park
Coral reef cities (p157)

15 TOP EXPERIENCES

Miami: Sexy Latin Cool

1 Miami (p48) bubbles with a swank mayhem of Latin-world expectations and, indeed, the city moves to a different rhythm than anywhere else in the USA. In cigar-filled dance halls, Havana expats dance to *son* (a type of Cuban salsa) and boleros, while in exclusive nightclubs Brazilian models shake to Latin hip-hop. Improve your love life in a Haitian *botanica* (shop that deals in herbs and charms), watch old men clack dominoes in the park, and then, from street vendor to gastronomic temple, let the flavors of the Caribbean, Cuba, Argentina, Spain and more send your palate into ecstasy.

The Magic of Disney

2 Want to set the bar of expectations high? Call yourself 'The Happiest Place on Earth.' Walt Disney World (p254) does, and then pulls out all the stops to deliver the exhilarating sensation that you are the most important character in the show. Despite all the frantic rides, entertainment and nostalgia, the magic is watching a child swell with belief after they have made Goofy laugh, been curtsied to by Cinderella, guarded the galaxy with Buzz Lightyear and battled Darth Maul like a Jedi knight.

Kayaking the Everglades

3 The Everglades (p136) are unnerving. They don't reach majestically skyward or fill your heart with the aching beauty of a glacier-carved valley. They ooze, flat and watery, a river of grass mottled by hammocks, cypress domes and mangroves. You can't hike them, not really. To properly explore the Everglades – and meet its prehistoric residents up close – you must leave the safety of land. You must push a canoe or kayak off a muddy bank, tamp down your fear and explore the shallow waterways on the Everglades' own, unforgettable terms.

The Conch Republic

4 Florida is not one place but many, each nearly a self-contained world unto itself. Or so wish the Conchs (p171) of Key West, a separate island untethered from the nation, the state and even the rest of the island chain, except by a flimsy bridge one hurricane away from being swallowed by the Gulf. A bring-on-the-night crazy party animates Mallory Sq and Duval St nightly, part drunken cabal and part authentic tolerance for the self-expression of every impolite, noncomformist impulse known to humanity.

Canaveral National Seashore

5 If you've been to Florida's Atlantic Coast before, you know it is one extremely built-up and crowded stretch of sand. This is partly why the 24 miles of Canaveral National Seashore's (p314) unspoiled barrier island are so special. Here, virtually in the shadow of Kennedy's shuttle launchpad, the dunes, lagoons and white-sand beaches look much as they did 500 years ago when the Spaniards landed. Kayak among the mangroves with bottlenose dolphins and manatees, observe nesting sea turtles, swim on pristine beaches and camp in solitude.

Coral Reef Symphony

6 Florida's most breathtaking scenery is underwater. The bowl of the peninsula's spoon is edged by more coral reefs than anywhere else in North America, and their quality and diversity rival Hawaii and the Caribbean. The prime protected areas are Biscayne National Park, John Pennekamp Coral Reef State Park and Looe Key. Not only can you see the reefs and their rainbow-hued denizens by glass-bottom boat, snorkeling and diving, you can spend the night with the fishes (at John Pennekamp) if you just can't bear to surface.

7 According to legend, the USA's oldest city possesses Ponce de León's elusive fountain of youth. Though no doubt apocryphal, this anecdote indicates the breadth of the historic legacy so lovingly and atmospherically preserved along St Augustine's (p328) cobblestoned streets. Tour magnificent Spanish cathedrals and forts, and Henry Flagler's ludicrously ornate resorts; take spooky ghost tours and join scurvy-dog pirate invasions. Watch costumed re-enactors demonstrate blacksmithing, cannon firing, and how to shackle and chain prisoners. Then sip a cup of eternal youth, 'cause you never know.

Surfing Cocoa Beach

8 From the time that surfing hit pop culture, Florida's surf scene was overshadowed by California and Hawaii, but that changed in 1992 when 21-year-old phenom and Cocoa Beach–native Kelly Slater won the first of 10 (and counting) world titles and revolutionized the sport. Slater has said he believes the Space Coast's waves are the best place to learn, and if they're good enough for surfing's top competitor, who's to argue? Rent (or bring) a board and hit Cocoa Beach (p309) waves while spinning your own world-title fantasies.

VERONICA GARBUTT / LONELY PLANET IMAGES ©

Sanibel Island: 'Stooping' to Shell

9 Gorgeous Sanibel Island (p407) is famous for the bounty of colorful and exotic shells that wash up along its beaches; the 'Sanibel stoop' is the name for the distinctive profile of avid shellers (who these days save their backs with long-handled scoops). But the dirty little secret is this: like fishing and golf, shelling is just an excuse to do nothing but let the mind wander the paths of its own reckoning. Yet delightfully, when you awake, you're rewarded with a handful of spiral calcium treasures.

BILL LOZANSKY / ALAMY ©

MICHAEL AW / LONELY PLANET IMAGES ©

Swimming with Manatees

10 Is there any giant mammal as lovable, approachable and altogether nonthreatening as Florida's West Indian manatees? These lumbering, intelligent creatures seek Florida's warm-water springs and rivers each winter, and many places offer the chance to snorkel beside them as they chew sea grass and nuzzle their children. Top of the list, though, is Kings Bay (p416), near Crystal River on the Gulf Coast, where upwards of 500 may gather on a cold January day. But while manatees sometimes approach swimmers with their own curious wonder, one thing to avoid is touching them.

Gulf Islands National Seashore

STEVE BOWER / SHUTTERSTOCK ©

11 Near Pensacola, the Panhandle's barrier islands occupy about as much real estate as a string bikini, particularly the sensual stretches that form the Gulf Islands National Seashore (p425). While the region is well known for its activity-fueled beach towns, these are quickly left behind along the park's almost-pure-white quartz-sand beaches, gleaming like new snow. If you really need an activity, tour the moody, crumbling wreckage of historic Fort Pickens or hike the sand-floored woods, but really, isn't this why you came, to nap and tan in paradise?

Hiking the Ocala National Forest

M. TIMOTHY O'KEEFE / ALAMY ©

12 We love the Everglades. But there are moments within the subtropical forests, cypress stands, sinkholes and crystal springs of the Ocala National Forest (p354) and its adjacent state parks that are just as otherworldly and strange. You can get lost for weeks along hundreds of miles of forested trails, and among countless lakes, while hopping between dozens of campgrounds and soaking up oodles of Old Florida atmosphere. It's easy enough to dabble, but for dedicated outdoor enthusiasts, draw a big circle around Florida's heart and come here.

Surreal Encounters: Salvador Dalí Museum

13 It's all too easy to overuse the adjective 'surreal' when discussing Florida. In the case of the Salvador Dalí Museum (p377), surreal is exactly right. Dalí has no connection to Florida whatsoever; this magnificent collection of 96 oil paintings and an overwhelming slew of ephemera landed in St Petersburg almost by chance. Yet Dalí's and Florida's surrealism complement each other, and the museum's stunning new home has transformed this cultural institution into a must-visit destination and a crown jewel among Florida's art museums.

Stone Crabs, Scallops & Oysters

14 Florida enjoys the cornucopia of the sea in countless ways. Yet three seasonal events command the attention of seafood lovers: sweet stone crab claws (below) from October to April, Steinhatchee scallops from July to September and flavorful Apalachicola oysters from November to April. Apalachicola (p437) supplies 90% of Florida's oysters, and it is also the last place in the US where 'tongers' still harvest them wild. In Steinhatchee (p449), anyone is allowed to collect scallops, and for bivalve fanatics, what could be better than gathering your own?

Gainesville Rocks

15 If local boy Tom Petty and transplant Bo Diddley are the patron saints of Gainesville's rock-music scene (p355), the University of Florida – the nation's second-largest university campus – is the engine that keeps it going strong. Bands span about every iteration of rock, from Florida's own gator-swamp rockabilly to postpunk industrial, but blues, bluegrass, reggae and hip-hop get their due on any given night. Lots of Florida cities get loud, but Gainesville has the state's hungriest, most vibrant music scene.

need to know

Currency
» US dollars ($)

Language
» English, also Spanish in Miami and South Florida

When to Go

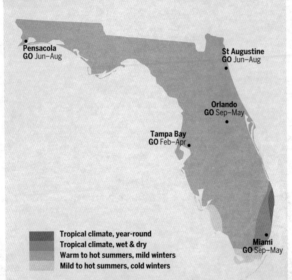

Pensacola
GO Jun–Aug

St Augustine
GO Jun–Aug

Orlando
GO Sep–May

Tampa Bay
GO Feb–Apr

Miami
GO Sep–May

Tropical climate, year-round
Tropical climate, wet & dry
Warm to hot summers, mild winters
Mild to hot summers, cold winters

High Season
(Mar–Aug)
» South Florida beaches peak with Spring Break.

» Panhandle and northern beaches peak in summer.

» Orlando theme parks peak in summer.

» Summer wet season hot and humid (May to September).

Shoulder
(Feb & Sep)
» In South Florida, February has ideal dry weather, but no Spring Break craziness.

» With school in September, northern beaches/theme parks less crowded, still hot.

» Prices drop from peak by 20% to 30%.

Low Season
(Oct–Dec)
» Beach towns quiet until winter snowbirds arrive.

» Hotel prices can drop from peak by 50%.

» November to April dry season is best time to hike/camp.

» Holidays spike with peak rates.

Your Daily Budget

Budget less than
$100
» Dorm beds/camping: $20–30

» Supermarket self-catering and cheap eats

» Beaches are free

» Avoid a car; stick to one place and bike

Midrange
$150–250
» Budget to midrange hotels: $80–150

» Mix of in-room meals and seafood feasts

» Target theme park/beach shoulder seasons

» Rental car: $40–50

Top End over
$300
» High-season beach hotel/resort: $250–400

» Miami gourmet dinner (for two): $150–300

» All-inclusive, four- to seven-day theme-park blowout: $1500–4000

Money

» ATMs widely available everywhere.

Visas

» Nationals qualifying for Visa Waiver Program allowed a 90-day stay without a visa; all others need visa.

Cell Phones

» Europe and Asia's GSM 900/1800 standard is incompatible with USA's cell-phone systems. Confirm phone can be used before arriving.

Driving

» Drive on the right; steering wheel is on the left side of the car.

Websites

» **Visit Florida** (www .visitflorida.com) Official state tourism website.

» **My Florida** (www .myflorida.com) Links to state parks.

» **Florida Smart** (www .floridasmart.com) Comprehensive Florida links.

» **Miami Herald** (www .miamiherald.com) Main daily newspaper.

» **Lonely Planet** (www.lonelyplanet .com/florida) Pretrip planning and fellow-traveler advice.

Exchange Rates

Australia	A$1	$1.06
Canada	C$1	$1.02
Europe	€1	$1.45
Japan	Y100	$1.24
New Zealand	NZ$1	$0.81
UK	UK£1	$1.63

For current exchange rates see www.xe.com.

Important Numbers

Country code	1
International access code	011
Emergency	911
Directory assistance	411

Arriving in Florida

» **Miami International Airport**
Metrobus – Every 30 minutes 6am-11pm; Miami Beach 35 minutes
Shuttle vans – $20–26
Taxis – $38 to South Beach

» **Orlando International Airport**
Lynx bus – Every 30 minutes 6am-10:30pm; downtown 40 minutes, Walt Disney World 70 minutes
Shuttle vans – $20–30
Taxis – $33–60. More to Walt Disney World.

Green Florida

Until recently, Florida wasn't known for conservation, sustainable lifestyles and eco-tourism, but that's changing fast. Use these resources to get in touch with local issues and to help do your part by traveling with a light footprint.

» **Department of Environmental Protection** (DEP; www.dep.state.fl.us) State-run agency tackles ecological and sustainability issues; a wealth of practical information.

» **Green Lodging Program** (www.dep.state.fl.us/greenlodging) DEP-run program recognizes lodgings committed to conservation and sustainability.

» **Florida Sierra Club** (http://florida.sierraclub.org) Outdoors and advocacy group.

» **Florida Surfrider** (http://florida.surfrider.org) Grassroots surfer-run nonprofit dedicated to protecting America's beaches; 11 Florida chapters.

» **Greenopia** (www.greenopia.com) Rates ecofriendly businesses in Miami, Orlando, Tampa, Jacksonville, Fort Myers and Fort Lauderdale.

» **Creative Loafing, Green Community** (http:cltampa.com/tampa/green) Tampa's alternative weekly tracks green issues and promotes eco-events.

» **Going Green Tampa** (www.goinggreentampa.com) Farmers' markets, alternative transportation and more around Tampa.

what's new

For this new edition of Florida, our authors have hunted down the fresh, the transformed, the hot and the happening. These are some of our favorites. For up-to-the-minute recommendations, see lonelyplanet.com/florida.

Tampa Riverwalk

1 Tampa has completely transformed its downtown waterfront with this undulating, scenic green space beside the Hillsborough River. Along Riverwalk, major cultural institutions have christened dazzling new homes – the Tampa Museum of Art, Tampa Bay History Center, Glazer Children's Museum – all connected by bridges and walking paths to downtown's other prominent attractions. And Tampa isn't done. Riverwalk will one day thread a breathable, soothing path northward to Tampa's Heights (p364).

Wizarding World of Harry Potter

2 Expelliarmas, Magic Kingdom! Universal Orlando has cast its spell and conjured the truly magical realm of Hogwarts, Quidditch and the Boy Who Lived. More fizzing whizbies, please (p291).

Salvador Dalí Museum

3 In 2011 the Salvador Dalí Museum unveiled its splendid new home, which presents as comprehensive and enlightening a survey of this 20th-century master as you could ever wish for (p377).

Legoland

4 Florida's newest theme park, christened in 2011, is based on the cleverest building system ever devised. Rides, shows, re-creations of Florida and pirate battles, and oh yes, build-your-own extravaganzas (p238).

Pirate & Treasure Museum

5 In St Augustine, this brand-new museum devoted to all things pirate – stuffed with real treasure chests, gold ingots, maps and cannons – has us wondering: what took so long? (p331)

Kennedy Space Center

6 In 2011 the US space-shuttle program ended, bringing to a close a magnificent 30-year era of watching manned spacecraft lift off from Kennedy, which remains a must-see attraction (p307).

Hollywood Beach Hotel & Hostel

7 Bright, modern, relaxed and just plain cool, this boutique-y hostel-slash-motel is a welcome budget addition to Hollywood's Venice Beach–like scene (p187).

Señora Martinez

8 Michelle Bernstein is one of Miami's culinary stars, and her latest restaurant, Senora Martinez, dishes gourmet Spanish cuisine and cocktails that have created serious buzz (p117).

Gansevoort South Hotel

9 It's hard to be an upscale boutique hotel in South Beach. So much competition! The Gansevoort delivers understated luxury and a rooftop pool of uncommon perfection (p106).

Everglades International Hostel

10 This is no ordinary hostel, but a newly renovated masterpiece, with gorgeous rooms and unforgettable gardens. It's hosteling...with style (p147).

if you like...

Secluded Islands

The Florida peninsula is ringed with barrier islands and mangrove-fringed keys. Many are accessible by causeways and bridges, but to really leave the crowds behind, you gotta go by boat. That's the only way to get to these beauties.

Cayo Costa Island Undeveloped and majestic; for real solitude, book a cabin or campsite and spend the night (p406).

Caladesi Island A 20-minute ferry ride to 3 miles of sugary, seashell-strewn goodness (p388).

St Vincent Island Just off the Panhandle coastline, with great hikes, wildlife and beaches (p439).

Cedar Keys National Wildlife Refuge Cedar Key is like a frontier town, with kayaking among dozens of tiny wildernesses (p450).

Dry Tortugas Far off Key West in the middle of the sea: camp, stargaze, snorkel coral reefs, and barter beers with fishermen for lobster (p178).

Roadside Attractions

Florida is strange enough without embellishment. Yet it boasts mermaids, Hogwarts, Haitian *botanicas* (shops that deal in herbs and charms), and at least three alleged fountains of youth, making Florida like a roadside attraction hall of fame. For these, you needn't travel north of I-75.

Coral Castle In Homestead, this monument to unrequited love defies explanation and belief. Who gets *this* upset? (p146).

Robert Is Here Also in Homestead, it's just a farmstand with a petting zoo, but feels like...an event (p147).

Skunk Ape Research Headquarters Apparently, Bigfoot's relatives live in the swamp, and they don't smell too good (p143).

Ochopee Post Office Not just the tiniest post office in the USA, the world's most patient postal worker (p143).

Key West Cemetery 'I told you I was sick' and other legendary epitaphs among the eerie mausoleums (p175).

Stiltsville Roadside attraction? Maybe not. In the middle of Biscayne Bay, seven bright-colored houses sit on stilts. Heck of a commute (p85).

Cars

Floridians love their cars, and they like to drive 'em fast. For a taste of the Floridian need for speed, watch *Smokey and the Bandit,* starring Florida-boy-madegood Burt Reynolds, and visit these shrines to automotive adoration.

Daytona International Speedway A mecca for Nascar race fans. Tour the track, then ride shotgun with a professional driver (p319).

Don Garlits Museums 'Big Daddy' Garlits floored his 'Swamp Rat' race cars into dragracing and pop-culture history (p353).

Palm Beach International Raceway Don't just come for the twice-weekly drag-race tune-ups; race your own wheels against the pros (p221).

Ragtops Motorcars Museum In West Palm Beach, a collection of automotive rarities (p216).

Fort Lauderdale Antique Car Museum Most of these ancient eternally cool machines would be hard-pressed to do 60mph (p192).

Classic Car Museum In Sarasota, with sexy beasts like Ringling's 'Silver Ghost,' John Lennon's Mercedes, concept cars and prototypes (p393).

RICHARD CUMMINS / LONELY PLANET IMAGES ©

» Orlando Museum of Art (p232)

Modern Art

Miami has a world-class gallery scene that's at least as self-consciously entertaining and dislocatingly postmodern as any bright-painted, pop-culture-ironic theme park. Yet Miami doesn't hold a monopoly on compelling modern-art museums. Seek out these standouts.

Museum of Contemporary Art In Greater Miami, inscrutably monumental works and installations are accompanied by special exhibits (p91).

Norton Museum of Art In West Palm Beach, Norton is truly huge, overwhelmingly diverse and provocatively stunning (p213).

Museum of Art In Fort Lauderdale, an eclectic mix of modern masters and diverse cutting-edge works (p192).

Naples Museum of Art Both modern and postmodern, both American and Mexican, plus some splendid Chihuly glass (p412).

Orlando Museum of Art More than just the moderns, with a great graphics collection and lots of pop (p232).

Manatees

From November through March, Florida's West Indian manatees seek the warmth of the peninsula's fresh-water rivers, its 72°F crystal springs and the warm-water discharge canals of power plants. Yeah, it's bizarre, but these canals are now protected sanctuaries. That's our modern world.

Crystal River Kings Bay is perhaps the best place to swim with these magnificent mammals (p416).

Homosassa Springs The state park's underwater observatory gets you nose-to-prehensile-nose with them (p415).

Lee County Manatee Park Manatees can crowd this Fort Myers discharge canal thick and almost close enough to touch (p401).

Space Coast Manatees like the intercoastal waters of Canaveral National Seashore, Mosquito Lagoon, Indian River Lagoon and more (p305).

Manatee Observation Center In Fort Pierce, a good educational center next to one of those irresistible power-plant canals (p225).

Blue Spring State Park This spring near Jacksonville can draw over 100 manatees during cold spells (p350).

Live Music

With loud, fist-pumping rock, gator-swamp rocka-billy and sweaty blues, Florida's northern cities flex their Southern roots. The state has a rich, diverse musical heritage, with lots of great venues.

Jacksonville Freebird Live is a shrine to Lynyrd Skynyrd and one of the nation's best small music venues (p344).

Gainesville Tom Petty's hometown has a first-rate and extensive college-music scene (p358).

Tallahassee The city is known for blues; just head for the Bradfordville Blues Club, a local legend (p446).

St Petersburg Recently refurbished, Jannus Live is a beloved, cozy outdoor venue where national acts perform intimate shows (p382).

West Palm Beach Perhaps surprisingly, West Palm Beach really rocks; its several venues include a BB King's blues outpost (p219).

Miami Yes, Miami is mainly about its DJ-driven nightclubs, but rock and Latin bands still pump up the volume (p125).

If you like...cigars, the humidors and history of Tampa's Ybor City await. Learn to roll your own in the former cigar capital of the world (p368).

Locavore Gourmet

The recent explosion of Florida's gourmet food scene has led, naturally, to an increasing embrace of today's locavore ethics and the arrival of accomplished chefs passionate about using products grown no further away than the charge of an electric car.

Michelle Bernstein's Bernstein is becoming a Florida gourmet icon, and her Palm Beach restaurant specializes in the state's own nouvelle Floridian palette (p211).

Sustain This Miami eatery seems hell-bent on finally destroying the notion that organic, local vegetarianism can't be chic, inventive and delicious. It appeals to carnivores, too, and anyone seeking gourmet swank (p117).

Refinery If there's such a thing as blue-collar locavore cuisine, Tampa's Refinery is it: a no-BS gourmet haven with sass and a Pabst-punk attitude (p371).

Mad Hatter Restaurant Urbanites vacationing on Sanibel Island get their gourmet locavore fix here (p410).

Floridian Farm-to-table freshness gets a neo-Southern makeover at this coolio St Augustine restaurant (p336).

Baseball

Major League Baseball's March spring training – with almost daily exhibition games – is a long-standing Florida tradition drawing hordes of fans. The 'grapefruit league' (www.floridagrapefruitleague.com) has 13 pro teams, and two stay when the season starts: the Tampa Bay Rays and Florida Marlins.

Tampa Bay area The Tampa Bay Rays play the regular season in St Petersburg at Tropicana Field (p382), and the New York Yankees have spring training in Tampa at Steinbrenner Field (p372).

Fort Myers Both the Boston Red Sox and Minnesota Twins hold spring training here (p402).

Jupiter The St Louis Cardinals have spring training at Roger Dean Stadium, and then the Marlins' minor-league team plays (p221).

Orlando area The Atlanta Braves play within Walt Disney World, and the Houston Astros hold court in nearby Kissimmee (p253).

Miami In 2012 the Florida Marlins will become Miami Marlins when they move into their new stadium near Little Havana (see www.floridamarlins.com).

The Circus

Sarasota is no longer the winter home of the Ringling Bros and Barnum & Bailey Circus, but it once was, and this has left a circus legacy in Florida that is equal parts nostalgia, palm-tingling performance and DIY thrills.

Ringling Circus Museum Truly, this shrine to Ringling's showmanship and the wonder of the circus is as entertaining and thrilling as the thing itself (p390).

PAL Sailor Circus Performed entirely by kids, and focusing on acrobatics, this may be the country's most unique circus. It's certainly the most heart-warming (p392).

South Florida Circus Arts School Weren't those kids amazing? Now you try the flying trapeze. Seriously. Climb the ladder. Stand on the platform. Graaaab the bar... (p97).

Cirque du Soleil La Nouba Walt Disney World designed the intimate theater to house this Cirque show, which, not surprisingly, is the best live entertainment Disney offers (p252).

If you like...military aircraft

Pensacola's National Museum of Naval Aviation displays all types of warcraft, from biplanes to fighter jets, with cockpit simulators (p423).
Near Fort Walton Beach, the US Air Force Armament Museum has an F-16, a B-17 Flying Fortress, and serious weaponry (p430).

Gay Nightlife

As much as Manhattan, San Francisco and LA, Florida is a destination for gay travelers. It hosts some of the wildest parties and has some of the best organized gay communities in the country.

Key West The Conch Republic is all about letting your freak flag fly. How established is gay life here? There's even a gay trolley tour (p183).

Miami In South Beach especially, gay nightlife is almost synonymous with 'nightlife.' Be as out as you like among the fashionistas and celebrities (p125).

Fort Lauderdale The Lauderdale scene is less snooty-patootie than South Beach, and welcomes hordes of sun-seeking gay travelers with B&Bs and bars (p197).

West Palm Beach Palm Beach's hipper sister has a notable and noticeable gay scene (p213).

Orlando Orlando is gay-friendly year-round, but everyone comes out for Gay Days in early June (p251).

Pensacola Surprise! Attend Pensacola's Memorial Day party, and you might not recognize the Panhandle (p428).

Cracker Cooking

Cracker cooking is Florida's unique take on Southern cuisine. Just combine amphibians and reptiles, a dash of Creole spices, a good-size fryer basket, sweet tea, corn bread and Key lime pie.

Yearling Restaurant At once the most historic and authentic experience, in Marjorie Kinnan Rawlings Historic State Park, near Micanopy. Don't miss the sour orange pie (p359).

Clark's Fish Camp Near Jacksonville, dine on gator, eel, snake and frog amid taxidermy beyond your imagination (p342).

Indian Pass Raw Bar On the Panhandle, come for famous Apalachicola oysters in a true Southern fish shack (p437).

Joannie's Blue Crab Café In the Everglades along the Tamiami Trail, see 'em, then eat 'em: get gator nuggets, plus frog's legs, stone crabs and fried green tomatoes (p144).

Key Largo Conch House In the Keys, Crackers (backwoods Florida pioneers) are called Conchs; head here to experience stylishly authentic Conch cuisine and Key lime pie (p159).

Wreck Diving

Skrrriiiitch! What was that sound? Just another ocean-going vessel striking reef and going down off Florida's coast. A few are even shallow enough for snorkelers.

Panama City Beach The 'Wreck Capital of the South' boasts over a dozen boats, barges, tugs and a WWII Liberty ship, plus natural reefs (p435).

Pensacola Dive a 900ft-long aircraft carrier, the *Oriskany*, deliberately sunk in 2007 (p425).

Fort Pierce Snorkel a Spanish galleon, the *Urca de Lima*, under only 10ft to 15ft of water (p226).

Fort Lauderdale Freighters, steamers, tugs and barges litter the sea floor near Fort Lauderdale (p192).

Biscayne National Park The Maritime Heritage Trail has six ships, and a two-masted schooner is shallow enough for snorkelers (p152).

Florida Keys History of Diving Museum Not a dive, just a must-stop for anyone who digs diving itself (p161).

month by month

Top Events

1 **Carnaval Miami**, March

2 **Fantasy Fest**, October

3 **SunFest**, May

4 **Goombay Festival**, June

5 **Gay Days**, June

January

January is smack in the middle of Florida's 'dry' season, winter. In northern Florida, cool temps make this off-season. In southern Florida, after the New Year's holidays, January becomes a beach resort shoulder season.

☆ College Football Bowl Games

On January 1, New Year's Day, Floridians go insane for college football. Major bowls are played in Orlando (Capital One Bowl), Tampa (Outback Bowl) and Jacksonville (Gator Bowl), while Miami's Orange Bowl (January 3) often crowns the collegiate champion.

February

Ideal month for less-crowded South Florida beaches; high season ramps up. Still too cool for tourists up north.

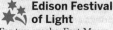 Edison Festival of Light

For two weeks, Fort Myers celebrates the great inventor Thomas Edison with a block party, concerts and a huge science fair. February 11, Edison's birthday, culminates with an incredible Parade of Light (www.edisonfestival.org).

☆ Speed Weeks

During the first two weeks of February, up to 200,000 folks rev their engines for two major car races – the Rolex 24 Hour Race and Daytona 500 – and party full throttle.

☆ Florida State Fair

Over a century old, Tampa's Florida State Fair is classic Americana: two mid-February weeks of livestock shows, greasy food, loud music and old-fashioned carnival rides.

🍴 South Beach Wine & Food Festival

No paper-plate grub-fest, this late-February event is a Food Network–sponsored culinary celebration of food, drink and celebrity chefs (www.sobefest.com).

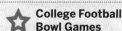 Mardi Gras

Whether it falls in late February or early March, Fat Tuesday inspires parties statewide, yet Pensacola Beach, closest to New Orleans, is Florida's best.

March

Beach resort high season all over, due to Spring Break. Modest temps, dry weather make ideal time to hike and camp. Last hurrah for manatees.

🍷 Spring Break

Throughout March to mid-April, American colleges release students for one-week 'spring breaks.' Coeds pack Florida beaches for debaucherous drunken binges – but hey, it's all good fun. The biggies? Panama City Beach, Pensacola, Daytona and Fort Lauderdale.

☆ Baseball Spring Training

Through March, Florida hosts Major League Baseball's spring training 'Grapefruit League' (www.floridagrapefruitleague.com): 13 pro teams train and play exhibition games in the Orlando area, the Tampa Bay area, and the Southeast.

Carnaval Miami

Miami's premier Latin festival takes over for nine days in early March: there's a Latin drag-queen show, in-line-skate competition, domino tournament, the immense Calle Ocho street festival, Miss Carnaval Miami and more (www .carnavalmiami.com).

Bike Week

Enjoy doing 12oz curls while admiring hogs and tatts? Join bikers for Daytona's Bike Week, a fortnight in early March. Everyone returns in mid-October for Biketoberfest.

Florida Film Festival

In Winter Park, near Orlando, this March celebration of independent films is fast becoming one of the largest in the southeast.

Captain Robert Searle's Raid

St Augustine re-creates Robert Searle's infamous 1668 pillaging of the town in March (p335). Local pirates dress up again in June for Sir Francis Drake's Raid. Volunteers are welcome!

St Patrick's Day

Ireland's patron saint gets his due across Florida on March 17 (any excuse to drink, right?). Miami turns the greenest.

Winter Music Conference

For five days in late March, DJs, musicians, promoters and music-industry execs converge on Miami to party, strike deals, listen to new dance music and coo over the latest technology (www .wmcon.com).

April

As Spring Break madness fades, prices drop. Last hurrah for the winter dry season.

Interstate Mullet Toss

In late April on Perdido Key (p429), near Pensacola, locals are famous for their annual ritual of tossing dead fish over the Florida–Alabama state line. Distance trumps style, but some have lots of style.

May

Summer 'wet' season begins: rain, humidity, bugs all increase with temperatures. Northern beach season ramps up; southern beaches enter off-season.

Sea Turtle Nesting

Beginning in May and extending through October, sea turtles nest on Florida beaches; after two months (from midsummer through fall), hatchling runs see the kids totter back to sea.

Isle of Eight Flags Shrimp Festival

On May's first weekend, Amelia Island celebrates shrimp, art and pirates, with an invasion and lots of scurvy pirate talk – aaarrrrgh!

SunFest

Over five days in early May, West Palm Beach holds South Florida's largest waterfront music and arts festival (www.sunfest.com).

Memorial Day Circuit Party

For late May's Memorial Day weekend, Pensacola (p428) becomes one massive three-day gay party, with lots of DJs, dancing and drinking.

Palatka Blue Crab Festival

For four late-May days, Palatka (p338) celebrates the blue crab and hosts the state championship for chowder and gumbo. That's some serious bragging rights.

June

Oh my it's getting hot. It's also the start of hurricane season, which peaks in September-October. School's out for summer, so theme parks become insanely crowded.

Gay Days

Starting on the first Saturday of June, and going for a week, upwards of 40,000 gays and lesbians descend on the Magic Kingdom and other Orlando theme parks, hotels and clubs. Wear red (www.gaydays.com).

Goombay Festival

In Miami's Coconut Grove, this massive four-day, early-June street party draws over 300,000 to celebrate the city's Bahamian culture with music, dancing and parades; it's one of America's largest black-culture festivals (www.goombayfestival coconutgrove.com).

July

Northern beach and theme park high season continues. Swamp trails are unbearably muggy and buggy; stick to crystal springs and coastlines.

Fourth of July

America's Independence Day is the cause

for parades and fireworks, large and small, across the state. Miami draws the biggest crowd for the best fireworks and laser show.

 ### Steinhatchee Scallop Season
The opening day of scallop season in Steinhatchee (p449) can draw a thousand folks, who take to the waters to harvest this delectable bivalve by hand. Anyone can join the following two-month treasure hunt.

August

Floridians do nothing but crank the air-con inside while foolish tourists swelter and burn on the beaches – and run from afternoon thundershowers.

Miami Spice
Miami's restaurants join together in August to offer prix-fixe lunches and dinners in an attempt to draw city residents from their apartments.

September

 ### Mickey's Not-So-Scary Halloween Party
At Disney World on select evenings over two months (starting in September), kids can trick or treat in the shadow of Cinderella's Castle, with costumed Disney favorites and a Halloween-themed parade (p275).

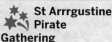
October

Temperatures drop, rains abate, school returns, crowds leave. Prices dip all over. The last hurricanes strike.

Fantasy Fest
Key West pulls out all the stops for this weeklong costumed extravaganza culminating in Halloween (p179). Everyone's even crazier than usual, and Key West's own Goombay Festival competes for attention the same week.

MoonFest
West Palm Beach throws a rockin', riotous block party for Halloween, October 31. Guests are encouraged to come in costume, and dozens of the best local bands play for free.

November

Florida's 'dry' winter season begins. Northern 'snowbirds' start flocking to their Florida condos. It's safe to hike again. Thanksgiving holidays spike tourism for a week.

White Party
A raucous gay and lesbian celebration (and HIV/AIDS fundraiser), the White Party is actually a series of parties and nightclub events in Miami Beach and Fort Lauderdale over a week in late November (www.whiteparty.net). And yes, wear white.

Tampa Cigar Heritage Festival
Tampa's Ybor City has a long history as the cigar-making capital of the US. That heritage, and the cigars themselves, are celebrated in this one-day festival (www.cigarheritage festival.com).

St Arrrgustine Pirate Gathering
Put on an eye patch and dust off your pirate lingo for this hokey celebration of scurvy dogs and seafaring rascals in St Augustine for three days in mid-November.

December

High season begins for South Florida beaches. Manatees arrive in warm-water springs.

Art Basel Miami Beach
Very simply, early December sees one of the biggest international art shows in the world, with over 150 art galleries represented and four days of parties (www.artbaselmiamibeach.com).

Victorian Christmas Stroll
The landmark 1891 Tampa Bay Hotel (now a museum) celebrates Christmas, Victorian-style, for three weeks in December, with folks in period costume acting out fairy tales.

King Mango Strut
Miami's Coconut Grove rings in the New Year with this wacky, freak-alicious, after-Christmas parade, which spoofs current events and local politics (www.kingmangostrut.org).

itineraries

Whether you've got five days or five weeks, these itineraries provide a starting point for the trip of a lifetime. Want more inspiration? Head online to lonelyplanet.com/thorntree to chat with other travelers.

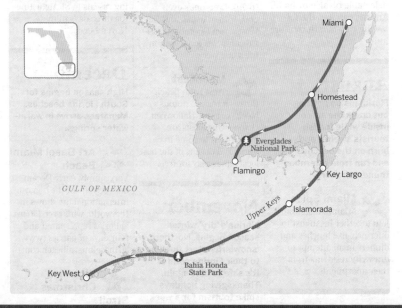

Seven to 10 Days
Iconic Florida

Florida offers much more, but for sheer iconic box-ticking, you can't do better than spending a week taking in Miami, the Everglades and the Florida Keys. First off, explore **Miami** for three solid days (more if you can). South Beach's pastel art-deco hotels and hedonistic beach culture? Check. Cuban sandwiches, Haitian *botanicas,* modern art? Check. Charming the velvet ropes, Latin hip-hop, mojitos? Hey, we're doing good.

Then take one day and visit the sunning alligators (check) of **Everglades National Park**. On the way, **Homestead** has some prime Florida roadside attractions (Coral Castle, Robert Is Here – check and check!), and the **Flamingo** visitor center offers great opportunities to kayak among the mangroves (check).

Now spend three days (or more) in the Florida Keys. Stop first in **Key Largo**, for Key lime pie, conch fritters and jaw-dropping coral reefs (check x3). Enjoy tarpon fishing in **Islamorada** (check), beach napping at **Bahia Honda State Park** (check), and finally, hit **Key West**. Pet Papa Hemingway's six-toed cats (check), ogle the Mallory Sq freak show (check) and raise a libation as the tangerine sun drops into an endless ocean – *salut!*

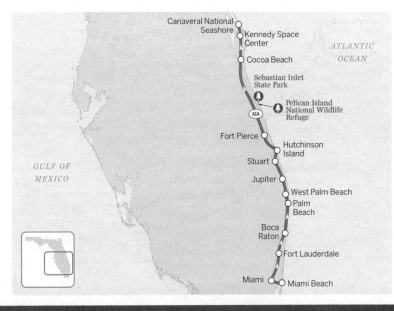

A1A: The Southern Atlantic Coast

Florida's southern Atlantic Coast is a symphony of beaches and barrier islands, of mangroves and sea turtles, of nostalgic Old Florida and nip-and-tucked celebrity Florida, of the wealthy and the you've-got-to-be-kidding-me obscenely rich. Three driving routes can be mixed and matched (I-95, Hwy 1 and A1A), but scenic, two-lane A1A knits the islands together and edges the sands as much as any road can.

A1A starts in **Miami Beach**, within the art-deco historic district. Naturally, you'll want to spend three days or so soaking up all that **Miami** offers. Then, rent a convertible, don your Oakley sunglasses, and nest a Dior scarf around your neck: it's time to road trip.

Whoops! There already? First stop is **Fort Lauderdale**. Preen along the promenade among the Rollerblading goddesses and be-thonged gay men, ride a romantic gondola in the canals, enjoy fine art and gourmet cuisine: it's a suite of pleasures the Gold Coast specializes in.

After two or three days, stagger on. Pause for a quiet interlude on the gorgeous beaches of **Boca Raton**, then repeat your Lauderdale experience in **Palm Beach**. Ogle the uber-wealthy as they glide between mansion and Bentley and beach, stop by the Flagler Museum to understand how this all got started, and each day decamp in **West Palm Beach**, the hipper, more happening sister city.

After several days, it's time to detox. Heading north, the Treasure Coast is known for unspoiled nature, not condos and cosmopolitans. Stop first in **Jupiter**; among its pretty parks, don't miss the seaside geyser at Blowing Rocks Preserve.

Even better, spend several days in **Stuart**. From here, you can kayak the Loxahatchee River, book a fishing charter, snorkel the reefs at St Lucie Inlet, and escape the crowds on nearby **Hutchinson Island** beaches.

If you only have two weeks, then you may have to skip the next offerings. At **Fort Pierce**, admire manatees in winter and snorkel a Spanish galleon. Surfers should pause at **Sebastian Inlet State Park**, and birders detour to the nation's first national wildlife refuge, **Pelican Island**.

Either way, spend your last two to three days in **Cocoa Beach**. The beaches here offer Florida's best surfing, and nearby **Kennedy Space Center** and **Canaveral National Seashore** are both must-visit Florida highlights. We've come a long way from Miami, yes? To continue on A1A, see Summer Farewell.

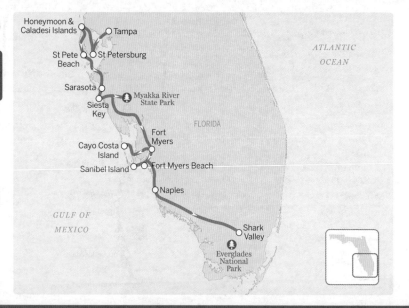

Two to Three Weeks
Gulf Coast Swing

Many prefer Florida's Gulf Coast: the beaches aren't as built up, soporifically warm waters lap blindingly white sand, and the sun sets (rather than rises) over the sea. Plus, it's easy to mix urban sophistication with seaside getaways and swampy adventures – just like around Miami, only even more family- (and budget-) friendly.

On this trip, spend your first three to four days in **Tampa** and **St Petersburg**. Stroll the museums and parks along Tampa's sparkling Riverwalk, and spend a day enjoying historic Ybor City's Spanish cuisine, cigars and nightclubs. St Pete offers similar city fun, but above all, don't miss its Salvador Dalí Museum.

Now head west for the barrier islands. Take their full measure by spending one day on unspoiled **Honeymoon and Caladesi Islands**, then enjoy the hyper, activity-fueled atmosphere of **St Pete Beach**.

Next, drive down to **Sarasota** for three days. You'll need that long to take in the magnificent Ringling Museum Complex, the orchid-rich Marie Selby Botanical Gardens, perhaps catch the opera and still allow plenty of time to build sandcastles on the amazing white-sand beaches of **Siesta Key**. If you have extra time, visit **Myakka River State Park** and kayak among the alligators.

Then skip down to **Fort Myers** for two days of regional exploring: if it's winter or spring, visit the local manatees, and take the ferry to **Cayo Costa Island** for a beach of unforgettable solitude. Families and coeds love the crowded strands of **Fort Myers Beach**; consider even more days here if you're staying longer.

However, you need to save at least two days for **Sanibel Island**. World famous for its shelling, it's also a bike-friendly island stocked with great eats and wildlife-filled bays ripe for kayaking.

Finally, end with two to three days in **Naples**, the quintessence of Gulf Coast beach towns: upscale, artistic, and warmly welcoming of every age demographic, with perhaps all of Florida's most pristine city beach. You can eat and shop to your heart's content, and no question: fit in a day trip to the **Everglades**. It's easy – zip along the Tamiami Trail to **Shark Valley**, and take a tram tour or bike ride among the sawgrass plains and sometimes countless alligators.

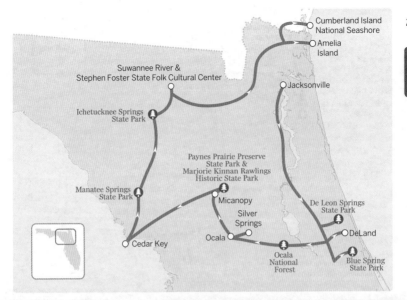

Two to Three Weeks
North Florida Backroads

North Florida appeals to outdoor-lovers who prefer that days be filled with forests and springs and rivers and fishing, and that evenings be spent reliving these adventures around campfires. This trip also includes beaches and museums and fine sit-down meals – and it's absolutely dripping in Southern charm and flavor – but the length and itinerary is particularly open to interpretation. These wildernesses allow you to dabble for an afternoon or immerse yourself for days; it's up to you.

Fly into **Jacksonville**, and spend the first day embracing the Atlantic Ocean on Jax beaches. For a full dose of Florida's Southern personality, have dinner at Clark's Fish Camp and see a show at Freebird Live.

Then drive south to small-town-idyllic **DeLand**. Base yourself for a few days or a week and explore **Blue Spring State Park**, which attracts manatees in winter and allows St John's River trips, while **De Leon Springs State Park** also has great crystal-springs kayaking. The big daddy down here, though, is the **Ocala National Forest**, with epic hiking and biking through Florida's fascinating limestone karst terrain and abundant camping.

Next, scoot over to **Ocala**. Here, the Old Florida glass-bottom boat tours of **Silver Springs** and high-revving dragster energy of the Don Garlits Museums beckon. Then go north to **Micanopy**, 'the town that time forgot,' for more eerie hikes at **Paynes Prairie Preserve State Park** and a taste of Cracker history at **Marjorie Kinnan Rawlings Historic State Park**.

For the next two to four days, string together these outdoor highlights: drive west to **Cedar Key**, where you can kayak among seabirds and manatees and unspoiled mangrove-fringed islands. Just north is **Manatee Springs State Park**, for more kayaking, hiking and camping along the Suwannee River. North again is **Ichetucknee Springs State Park**, which warrants a half day of tubing.

Save at least a day for a river trip along the **Suwannee River**, a muddy-brown moss-draped meander that's North Florida all over. Reserve ahead for a multiday river-camping trip, and visit the **Stephen Foster State Folk Cultural Center**.

Nothing personal, but it's clean-up time. Drive back to Jacksonville, and spend a final day or three on **Amelia Island**. Spoil yourself with a Victorian B&B and some gourmet seafood. Or, sneak into Georgia for one final adventure on the **Cumberland Island National Seashore**.

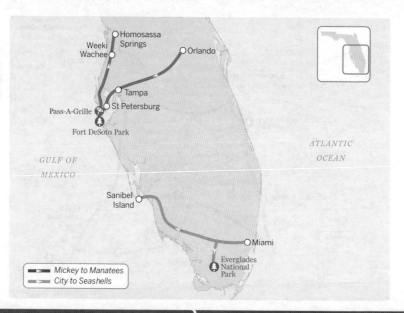

Mickey to Manatees
City to Seashells

One Week
Mickey to Manatees

Geez, the kids will kill you if you don't go to Walt Disney World, but Mom and Dad want some beach time, and maybe even a good meal, some authentic culture and a taste of that kitschy Old Florida atmosphere. Oh, and you've only got a week.

Presto change-o – here you go! For the first three or four days, stay in **Orlando**. Rather than give in entirely to **Walt Disney World**, spend two days there and another day at **Universal Orlando**, particularly if, you know, you've read any of those Harry Potter books.

For the next three or four days, hit the Tampa Bay Area. One day in **Tampa** choose between its tremendous zoo and aquarium and its fantastic museums (for kids and art), then end in historic Ybor City, for Spanish cuisine with a side of flamenco. In **St Petersburg**, even the kids will find the Salvador Dalí Museum intriguing. On the barrier islands, **Pass-A-Grille** and **Fort DeSoto Park** are perfectly relaxing family getaways. Then squeeze in a day trip north for the mermaid shows at **Weeki Wachee** and the manatees of **Homosassa Springs**. Everybody's happy!

One Week
City to Seashells

Geez, you really don't want to miss sexy, high-energy Miami, but if you don't get some sandy, leave-me-alone-with-my-mystery downtime you'll never make it when you return to work in [insert name of major metropolis here]. Oh, and you've only got a week.

Presto change-o – here you go! Spend the first three days in **Miami** and have a party. Tour the art-deco-district hotels, enjoy the sophisticated art museums, shop for tailored shirts and racy designer dresses, and prance past the velvet ropes to celebrity-spot and dance all night to Latin hip-hop.

Next, spend one day peering at alligators through dark sunglasses in the **Everglades**, just so everyone back home won't be all 'What? You went to Florida and didn't even go?'

For the last three days, chill on **Sanibel Island**. Get a hotel on a private stretch of beach and do nothing but sun, sleep, read and collect handfuls of beautiful seashells as you kick along. Maybe take a bike ride and have a gourmet dinner. But each night, dig your toes in the sand and enjoy the setting sun in romantic solitude.

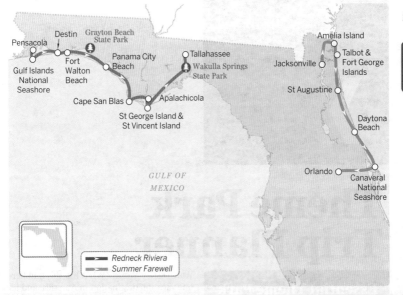

Redneck Riviera
Summer Farewell

Redneck Riviera

Sure, Florida's Panhandle gets rowdy, yet there's family-friendly warmth and unexpected sophistication along with its spectacular bone-white beaches.

Start your tour with a few days in **Pensacola**. Relax on the beaches of the **Gulf Islands National Seashore**, and enjoy Pensacola's historic village and its naval aviation history. The Blue Angels may even put on a show.

Spend another two days in the tourist towns of **Destin** and **Fort Walton Beach**, but don't miss the world-class sand of **Grayton Beach State Park**. If you have kids, a day among the hyperactive boardwalk amusements of **Panama City Beach** is virtually a must.

Afterward, shuffle along to the secluded wilderness of **Cape San Blas** and quaint **Apalachicola**, whose romantic historic village is perhaps not what you were expecting. The local specialty? Delectably fresh oysters.

St George and **St Vincent Islands** provide more secluded getaways, but if time is short, spend your last day around **Tallahassee**. Take a glass-bottom-boat tour at **Wakulla Springs State Park**, home of the *Creature from the Black Lagoon,* and get rowdy yourself at Tallahassee's Bradfordville Blues Club.

Summer Farewell

For argument's sake, let's say you want the warmest weather but the fewest people. Hello, September! Sure, this trip is good anytime, but Florida's north is particularly sweet as school starts and summer fades.

Fly into **Jacksonville**, but don't hesitate: go straight to **Amelia Island** for several days of romantic B&Bs, luscious food and pretty sand. The good vibes continue as you kayak and explore the undeveloped beaches of **Talbot and Fort George Islands**, just south.

Then spend two to three days in **St Augustine**. America's oldest city preserves its heritage very well, with plenty of pirate tales enlivening the Spanish forts and basilicas.

When you've had enough of fine dining and costumed re-enactors, spend a few days in **Daytona Beach**. High-octane thrills include the speedway, as well as the activity-filled beach scene. Perhaps you will even spy nesting sea turtles.

At this point, you've filled a week, but a few more days means more kayaking in **Canaveral National Seashore**, and perhaps a day or two in **Orlando** theme parks. Where aren't the kids when they're in school? In line.

Got even more time? Keep going south; see AIA: The Southern Atlantic Coast.

Theme Park Trip Planner

Essential Theme Park Strategies

Book multiple days and be flexible Allow for more park days than you'll need, and plan for partial days, not all-day ride-a-thons. If kids melt down, call it quits, hit the hotel pool, return later for evening entertainment, and tackle more rides tomorrow.

Arrive early Come before park gates open, hit top rides first, and consider leaving by lunch, when crowds are worst. You'll see more in less time and avoid wilting in the midday heat.

Pack snacks Theme park fast food is disappointing and overpriced; sit-down lunches are time-killers. Parks rarely allow picnics, but pack a small soft cooler with nonperishable snacks and nibble constantly.

Factor travel time When planning each day, carefully consider travel to and within the parks. At Disney, between-park logistics can waste hours.

Walt Disney World (WDW) is the number-one vacation destination in America, and its flagship property, the Magic Kingdom, is the most popular theme park in the world. Well over half of Florida's visitors make Disney a part of their trip, if not its sole purpose entirely. It's no exaggeration to say that Disney's 'happiest place on earth' is equivalent to a city-state, and more ink has probably been spilled dissecting its parks and plotting the best strategies for visiting than has been used in all of Disney's animated movies.

Yet Disney isn't Florida's only theme park – oh no. There is upstart Universal Orlando, as well as a host of smaller theme, water and wildlife parks, most in and around Orlando, that find all sorts of clever ways to combine rides, roller coasters, zoos, animal shows, high-fiving costumed characters, simulations, 4D movies and splash-tastic fun.

In fact, Florida invented the theme park in the 1930s – with Cypress Gardens and Silver Springs – and a few of those nostalgic Old Florida parks are still around, harkening back to the good old days of tin can tourism.

So you have some decisions to make. Destination chapters have detailed ride and theme-park descriptions, while this chapter overviews Florida's panoply of options. Here are the logistics to consider before arriving to skip merrily behind Mickey through Disney's magical gates.

Florida's Theme Parks

Walt Disney World

Today, WDW includes four completely separate theme parks: the **Magic Kingdom**, **Epcot**, **Hollywood Studios** and **Animal Kingdom**. There are also two huge water parks (**Typhoon Lagoon** and **Blizzard Beach**), a sports complex (Disney's Wide World of Sports), 23 hotels, almost 100 restaurants, and two shopping and nightlife districts (Downtown Disney and Disney's Boardwalk), as well as five golf courses, two miniature golf courses and lagoons with water sports, all connected by a complicated system of free buses, boats and monorails. Just to get from one end of Disney to the other is a $30 cab ride!

For sheer heart-warming nostalgia, nothing can match the Magic Kingdom, which is Disney at its finest. Disney's mythology touches everyone, from toddlers to grandparents. No one beats Disney's parades and fireworks, and the staff are legendary for being unfailingly friendly and kind.

Green, garden-filled, relaxing Epcot is another favorite; dedicated to technology, the future and the countries of the world, it lacks the crowded, hyperactive atmosphere of other theme parks. Trading Snow White for Buzz Lightyear, Hollywood Studios is dedicated to modern, hip Disney movies and icons; it can be a mixed bag and not the best park for the under-10 set. As the name implies, Animal Kingdom is a ride-and-show-filled wildlife park that emphasizes safari-like animal interactivity.

Universal Orlando Resort

In contrast to WDW, Universal Orlando is a more intimate, personal and walkable complex with two excellent theme parks – **Islands of Adventure** and **Universal Studios** – three first-rate resorts, and a carnival-like restaurant and nightlife district (CityWalk) connected by lovely gardened paths and a quiet wooden-boat shuttle.

Universal's theme parks offer shamelessly silly, snazzy pop-culture shenanigans for the whole family. Islands of Adventure is masterfully designed so that each section has its own distinctive tone and vibe. The Dr Seuss-themed area is fantastic and, unveiled in 2010, the truly phenomenal **Wizarding World of Harry Potter** has proven a runaway hit.

Emphasizing comic book superheroes and modern fare like *Shrek*, Universal Studios is primarily movie- and TV-themed rides and scheduled shows, but it also has one of Orlando's best children's play areas and a sweet Barney show.

Other Orlando Parks

In Orlando, about equidistant from Disney and Universal, are three major parks, all owned by the same parent company:

» **SeaWorld** An aquatic park with fantastic animal shows (particularly dolphins and killer whales), a handful of rides and animal-interaction programs.

» **Aquatica** A straight-up water park that matches Disney's water parks in popularity.

» **Discovery Cove** Limits number of guests, who enjoy quietude on a private beach, swimming with dolphins (for more on the practice, see p164) and lazy river floats through a bird aviary.

Other Orlando parks include:

» **Gatorland** Old Florida throwback that's an extravaganza of alligators – including alligator wrestling – and other only-in-Florida nuttiness.

» **Holy Land Experience** Re-creates biblical times in all earnestness, thus qualifying as a theme park, but without the roller coasters and 21st-century irony.

» **Wet 'n Wild** Another extremely popular Orlando water park.

Around Orlando

Within an hour or so of Orlando are three worthy destinations.

» **Legoland** In Winter Haven on the site of the old Cypress Gardens (RIP), Florida's newest theme park aims at the 12-and-under set. Legoland rebuilds the world brick by brick, but to scale; don't worry, the rides are *mostly* made of steel.

» **Kennedy Space Center** One of Florida's top attractions. On the Atlantic Coast, it has only one bona fide ride – the Shuttle Launch Simulator – but the complex, movies and astronaut presentations make it a fascinating all-day immersion in space and the US space program.

» **Silver Springs** One of the last remaining Old Florida theme parks. Near Ocala, Silver Springs invented the glass-bottom boat tour: be amazed by the world's largest crystal spring, riverboat rides through ancient cypress, and albino alligators, plus a small water park.

WHEN TO GO

Ignore the weather. If US schools are on break, kids are packing Orlando's theme parks. If schools are in session, kids are at desks, not bouncing in ride lines.

Despite the heat, summer is the busiest season, from June through August. Crowds are also surreal around July 4, Thanksgiving weekend, the week between Christmas and New Year's and throughout Spring Break (March through April).

The slowest times are September through October and mid-January through February. The few weeks in between Thanksgiving and Christmas are also a quiet window.

Two extended Disney events worth planning for are Mickey's Not-So-Scary Halloween Party (mid-September to October) and Mickey's Very Merry Christmas Party (November to mid-December). See p275 for more on these events.

Tampa Bay Area

» Busch Gardens In Tampa, Florida's largest theme park outside of Orlando offers a trifecta: African-themed wildlife encounters, various shows and musical entertainment, and some of the state's wildest roller coasters. Busch Gardens is a far-distant third behind Disney and Universal for themed quality, but it still rates for pure adrenaline; a worthy substitute if you won't be visiting Orlando.

» Adventure Island This top-notch water park is adjacent to and owned by Busch Gardens.

» Weeki Wachee Springs North of Tampa, this kitschy Old Florida original is world-famous for its spangly-tailed, long-haired mermaid shows. Little girls will go gaga. Plus, there's a small water park, animal presentations and river canoeing.

Tickets & Packages

Ticketing options are extremely varied, bewilderingly so. To make the most of your money, it's best to decide up front how many days you want to dedicate to theme parks, and to which ones.

For resorts, the longer you stay, the less you pay. Per-day ticket costs drop dramatically the more days you buy. Combination tickets that include several theme and water parks save cash as well. Then there are myriad add-ons and hotel/dining packages to consider.

Prices below are without tax. For more detailed price information, see the destination chapters.

Walt Disney World

Called **Magic Your Way**, tickets range from one to 10 days (adult $90 to $291, child three to nine a bit less), and allow unlimited entry to any one of Disney's four parks per day. To give a sense of the savings differential as you increase ticket length: by six days, the per-day cost is 50% of the one-day ticket, and the *total* cost difference between a four-day ticket and a 10-day ticket is $30. To this, you can *add* options:

» Water Park Fun & More For each day of your Magic Your Way ticket, this gives one pass to your choice of Disney's two water parks, the golf course, DisneyQuest Indoor Interactive Theme Park or ESPN Wide World of Sports. You pay only once ($56) no matter the number of days/passes, and you can use passes in any combination.

» No Expiration All multiday tickets expire 14 days after the first use. Purchase this option ($11 to $21 per day)and unused days never expire.

» Park Hopper Allows you to 'hop' between all four WDW parks within one day and for the length of your base ticket. Again, a one-time cost ($56). This is a very convenient and often-recommended option.

Peruse the Disney website (www.disneyworld.disney.go.com) for the dizzying array of packages that include park tickets, lodging and dining, as well as entertainment and recreation. For customized itinerary planning, premium dining and show reservations, consider the **Magic Your Way Platinum Package** and the **VIP Tour**. Note that if you buy a package, you may not get a full refund if you need to cancel. If you only book accommodation, and buy park tickets and dining options at the last minute, you can cancel up to 48 hours in advance with no penalty. An **Annual Pass** (adult/child $499/450) allows admission to all four parks, any time, for 365 days from the date of purchase.

» (above) Big Thunder Mountain Railroad (p259) at Walt Disney World
» (left) Killer whales at the Shamu show, SeaWorld (p300)

Universal Orlando Resort

Universal Orlando tickets are just called tickets, and they come in two main flavors: one or both parks per day. One-park tickets range from one to four days (adult $82 to $140, child three to nine $74 to $123); 'park-to-park' tickets range from one to seven days (adult $112 to $175, child $104 to $155). The savings differential is similar to Disney, with the per-day cost of a four-day ticket being less than 50% of a single day. If you buy at the gate, you pay $10 more per day. To this you can *add:*

» **Wet 'n Wild** To three- to seven-day tickets only, you can add access to this nearby water park. This is a one-time fee ($27.50).

» **Express Plus** This pass allows you to skip lines at certain designated rides; see website (www.universalorlando.com) for ride list. Limited number available each day. Price ($20 to $60) varies depending on days and parks included. Resort hotel guests automatically receive an Express Plus pass.

» **Meal Deal** Pay one price ($10 to $24) and eat unlimited times at select restaurants for lunch and dinner. Drinks not included. Price varies depending on age and parks.

Universal has three resort hotels, and additional room/dining/ticket packages are offered for guests. An **annual pass** ($219) allows unlimited park-to-park access, 365 days from date of purchase, plus other perks and discounts.

Orlando Flex Ticket

The **Orlando Flex Ticket** (adult/child $275/255), available online at many websites, gives 14-day unlimited entry to five parks: Universal Orlando's Universal Studios and Islands of Adventure, Wet 'n Wild, SeaWorld and Aquatica, as well as Universal's CityWalk. Add Tampa's Busch Gardens for about $40 more.

SeaWorld, Aquatica, Discovery Cove & Busch Gardens Tampa

Each of these four parks can be combined in almost every variation with the other three parks. Combo tickets that include Busch Gardens offer a free shuttle to the park. At SeaWorld, Aquatica and Busch Gardens,

you can add one-time per ride or unlimited Quick Queue ($15 to $36) line skipping.

» **SeaWorld** A one-day ticket ($72) allows a second day free within seven days. A two-park combo with SeaWorld and either Aquatica or Busch Gardens (from adult/child $110/107) allows unlimited access for 14 days. Or combine all three parks ($130/122) for 14 days.

» **Aquatica** The single day rate is $42.

» **Discovery Cove** Rates vary by day, season and demand, like airline tickets. The Day Resort Package ($129 to $169) includes everything but the dolphin interaction, which is included in the Dolphin Swim Package ($169 to $319; for more on the practice, see p164). Both tickets include unlimited 14-day admission to any one of the other three parks, or include all three for $50.

» **Busch Gardens** A one-day ticket ($70) allows a second day free within seven days. The Adventure Island water park ($43/39) can be combined with Busch Gardens ($93/85).

Staying in the Resorts

Put simply, Disney and Universal provide great perks for their hotel guests (and tons of package deals), so if you'll be spending several days exploring their parks, there's no compelling reason not to stay on-site. SeaWorld also has partner hotels that offer nice perks and packages.

If, however, you want to make only one-day visits to several different parks, then staying in an Orlando hotel can work well. Convenient locations to Disney theme parks are Lake Buena Vista, Kissimmee and the town of Celebration. International Drive is more convenient for Universal Studios and SeaWorld. That said, off-site hotel park shuttles can be a pain: they leave at prearranged times, make lots of stops and often require advance booking.

See the destination chapters for specific hotel reviews.

Walt Disney World Hotels

With two dozen hotels, Disney has lodgings for every budget, including camping. For the most amenities, choose a roomy villa, the only properties with full kitchen and in-room washer/dryer. You're paying for convenience and theming; quality-wise, except for the very best deluxe resorts, rooms are no better than good midrange chains elsewhere.

After price, location is the main consideration. Staying on the monorail is very convenient to the Magic Kingdom, but less so to the other parks (which require shuttle buses or two modes of transportation). Many prefer the deluxe resorts in Epcot (Disney's Boardwalk Inn, Disney's Yacht Club Resort and Disney's Beach Club Resort, and Walt Disney World Swan & Dolphin Resorts); these are walking distance to Epcot, Hollywood Studios and Disney's Boardwalk.

Hunting Disney hotel bargains is a favorite pastime. For websites, see Discounts & Discussion Boards (below). Also, practice good-old relentlessness: call again and again. Prices can change within 24 hours. Orlando rates vary wildly by demand, so calling same-day or just before arrival can yield amazing bargains.

Guest Perks

» **Extra Magic Hours** One theme park opens early and closes late for guests at Disney hotels only.

» **Disney transportation** Despite the frustration of tackling Disney buses, boats and monorails, they're far more convenient than off-site hotel shuttles.

» **Free parking** No fee at theme parks or hotels.

» **Disney's Magical Express** Complimentary deluxe bus transport from Orlando International Airport. Before you arrive, Disney sends special bag labels; check your bags before boarding your plane, and they'll be waiting for you at the hotel. No hassle of shuttles, baggage claim, car rental or costly taxis.

» **Baggage transfer** If you change to a different Disney hotel during your stay, leave your bags in the morning and they'll be at your new hotel by evening.

» **Dining plans** Only resort guests have access to the meal plans, which can save over 30%.

Universal Orlando Resort Hotels

Universal has only three resort hotels, but they are top quality, extremely well situated within their more intimate resort, and highly recommended.

Guest Perks

» **Universal Express** Guests at Universal's three resort hotels automatically receive access to the Express Plus lines, practically eliminating the hassle of waiting in line.

» **Universal transportation** Small boats run between the parks and both CityWalk and resort

---

DISCOUNTS & DISCUSSION BOARDS

There's only one thing people like more than a discount, and that's sharing their park tips. Most websites facilitate both, while specializing in one or the other.

Ticket Discounts

» **MouseSavers.com** (www.mousesavers.com) Bargains and discounts at Disney only.

» **Undercover Tourist** (www.undercovertourist.com) Authorized ticket reseller for Disney and other Orlando parks; good apps.

» **Ticket Mania** (www.ticketmania.com) Theme park tickets.

Online Forums & Advice

» **Theme Park Insider** (www.themeparkinsider.com) Covers all theme parks, rides, resort hotels etc.

» **Mouse Planet** (www.mouseplanet.com) Disney news and advice.

» **AllEars.Net** (http://allears.net) General Disney advice; great dining info, all menus online.

» **DIS** (www.wdwinfo.com) All things Disney and Universal.

» **DISboards.com** (www.disboards.com) Fantastic, active discussion boards.

» **Moms Panel** (http://disneyworldforum.disney.go.com) Disney-sponsored discussion boards run by and for moms.

hotels, making it extremely easy to get back and forth. There are well-lit paved walking trails as well.

» **Extra park hours** Like Disney, Universal's two theme parks open early or close late for resort guests only, particularly useful for the wildly popular Wizarding World of Harry Potter.

» **Airport transportation** For a fee, Universal will pick up and drop off guests at Orlando Airport.

Dining & Character Meals

Food service within the theme parks ranges from mediocre to awful, but there is plenty of it. The best meals are always at table-service resort restaurants; for these, *always* make advance reservations (which they call 'priority seating'). Cancellations are typically penalty-free, so reserve as soon as you know your dates; at minimum, plan and call a day ahead. Particularly at Disney, a sit-down meal can be virtually impossible to get without a reservation.

Disney allows restaurant reservations 180 days in advance, and for a Disney character meal or dinner show, reserve the moment your 180-day window opens. Seriously. Disney offers over 15 character meals, and some book up instantly. The most popular is Cinderella's Royal Table, where little girls are as elaborately costumed as the visiting princesses. Chef Mickey's at Disney's Contemporary Resort is a great start to a visit. For more, see Meeting Disney Characters, p274.

Universal has much more limited character dining. There is a daily character breakfast in the park, and characters visit a few hotel restaurants one or two nights a week. See park websites for specifics.

Want to prepare your own meals? Shop ahead online and have groceries delivered to any Disney or Universal resort hotel with **Garden Grocer** (www.gardengrocer.com).

Travel with Children

Best Regions for Kids

Orlando
Two words: theme parks. No, seven words: the theme park capital of the world.

Tampa Bay & Gulf Coast
Top-flight zoos, aquariums and museums, plus some of Florida's prettiest, most family-friendly beaches.

Florida Keys
Active families with older kids will adore the snorkeling, diving, fishing, boating and all-around no-worries vibe.

Daytona & Space Coast
Surfing, sandcastles, four-wheeling on the beach, kayaking mangroves: all ages love this stretch of Atlantic coastline.

Panhandle Beaches
Frenetic boardwalk amusements, family-friendly resorts, stunningly white sand: Panama City and Pensacola Beaches aim to please everyone.

Miami
Kid-focused zoos and museums, plus amazing beaches, but also Miami itself, one of the USA's great multicultural cities.

Florida does two things better than just about any place in the USA – beaches and theme parks. If you're traveling with kids, stop reading right now: that's your itinerary. Indeed, a Florida family trip can easily achieve legendary status with just a few well-placed phone calls. That's why so many families return year after sandy, sunburned year.

Florida for Kids

Every tourist town in Florida has already anticipated the needs of every age demographic in your family. With increasing skill and refinement, nearly every Florida museum, zoo, attraction, restaurant and hotel aims to please traveling families of all stripes.

Your only real trouble is deciding what to do. Florida offers so much for kids and families that planning can be tough. That simple beach-and-theme-park itinerary can suddenly become a frantic dawn-to-dusk race to pack it all in. We can't help you there. In fact, we can't even fit everything in this book, so don't try to fit everything in one trip.

Eating Out

Most midrange Florida restaurants have a dedicated kids' menu, along with high chairs, crayons for coloring and changing tables in restrooms. And most restaurants, even high-end ones, are typically happy to make a kid's meal by request. As a rule, families with infants or toddlers will get better service earlier in the dinner hour (by 6pm).

Only a few truly snooty big-city gourmet temples will look askance at young diners; if you're unsure, simply ask when making reservations.

Theme Parks

Walt Disney World, Universal Studios, SeaWorld, Discovery Cove, Busch Gardens: Florida's biggest theme parks are verily worlds unto themselves. You can visit for a day, or make them your sole destination for a week, even two. To do them justice, they have their own chapter (p30). This chapter focuses on all the *other* things families can do in Florida.

Beaches

The prototypical Florida family beach is fronted by or near very active, crowded commercial centers with lots of water sports and activities, tourist shops, grocery stores and midrange eats and sleeps. Some may be known for Spring Break–style party scenes, but all have family-friendly stretches and usually only get rowdy in the late evening. The beaches listed under highlights below are particularly popular destinations with all ages.

Zoos, Museums & Attractions

Up-close animal encounters have long been a Florida tourist staple, and the state has some of the best zoos and aquariums in the country. Florida's native wildlife is truly stunning, and it's easy to see. Florida's cities also have an extremely high number of top-quality hands-on children's museums, and there's a wealth of smaller roadside attractions and oddities designed for, or that appeal to, kids.

Getting into Nature

Don't overlook unpackaged nature. Florida is exceedingly flat, so rivers and trails are frequently ideal for short legs and little arms. Raised boardwalks through alligator-filled swamps make perfect pint-size adventures. Placid rivers and intercoastal bays are custom-made for first-time paddlers, adult or child. Never snorkeled a coral reef or surfed? Florida has gentle places to learn. Book a sea-life cruise, a manatee swim or nesting-sea-turtle watch. At Oleta River State Park (Miami) and most every state park we review in the Keys, there's family-accessible kayaking and boating.

Children's Highlights

Believe it or not, these extensive highlights merely cherry-pick the best of the best.

Family Beach Towns

» Amelia Island – Easygoing and upscale, a relaxed but very comfy family destination.

» St Augustine – Pirates, forts, jails, re-enactors and a nice beach too.

» Daytona – Tons of activities and amusements, ATVs on the beach, water park.

» Cocoa Beach – Ideal for water-sports-focused teens; learn to surf.

» Vero Beach – Homey small-town vibe.

» Lauderdale-by-the-Sea – Less snooty than the rich towns just south; water-ski park and butterfly world.

» Stuart – For outdoors-eager families, plus getaway beaches and an aquarium on Hutchinson Island.

» Florida Keys – The whole island chain is an all-ages activity-stuffed toy box.

» Naples – Upscale downtown bustles each evening; soothing beach scene.

» Sanibel Island – Bike, kayak and shell the days away; undeveloped beaches, great restaurants.

» Siesta Key – powdery white sand, plenty of activities, lively village scene at night.

» Fort Myers Beach – Party atmosphere, lots to do, yet quieter beaches just south.

» St Pete Beach – Activity-filled social epicenter of Tampa Bay area.

» Pensacola Beach – Great mix of unspoiled strands and low-key tourist center.

» Destin & Fort Walton Beach – For quieter getaways amid unforgettable beauty.

» Panama City Beach – Crazy seaside amusements and carnival atmosphere.

Zoos

» Lowry Zoo – In Tampa; a fantastic zoo with up-close encounters.

» Homosassa Springs Wildlife State Park – Old Florida staple, emphasizes Florida wildlife, underwater manatee observatory.

» Metrozoo – In Miami; extensive and wide ranging, all the big-ticket species.

» Monkey Jungle – In Miami; the tagline 'Where humans are caged and monkeys run wild' says it all. Unforgettable.

» Jungle Island – In Miami; tropical birds and exotic species like the liger, a tiger-and-lion crossbreed.

» Lion Country Safari – In West Palm Beach; an enormous drive-through safari park and rehabilitation center.

Aquariums

» Miami Seaquarium – On Key Biscayne; one of the state's biggies, various swim-with-the-fishes programs.

» Florida Aquarium – In Tampa; another stellar aquarium, excellent re-created swamp, swim programs and sealife tours.

» Mote Marine Laboratory – Center for shark study; visit sharks, manatees, dolphins and sea turtles up close.

» Clearwater Marine Aquarium – Intimate rehabilitation center with marvelous animal presentations.

» Florida Oceanographic Coastal Science Center – On Hutchinson Island near Stuart; great tanks and a sea-turtle-spotting program.

Nature Centers

» Marjory Stoneman Douglas Biscayne Nature Center – On Key Biscayne; kid-friendly intro to subtropical South Florida, great hands-on programs.

» Naples Nature Center – Premiere conservation and rehabilitation center; immersive experience of South Florida ecology.

» Florida Keys Eco-Discovery Center – In Key West; fantastic, entertaining displays pull together Florida Keys ecology.

» JN 'Ding' Darling National Wildlife Refuge – On Sanibel Island; the park's education center is tops; combine with easy tram tours.

Children's Museums

» Glazer Children's Museum – In Tampa; brand-new and utterly charming interactive and role-playing extravaganza.

» Museum of Science & Industry – In Tampa; huge hands-on realm treats science as play; IMAX and planetarium.

» Miami Children's Museum – Huge and extensive role-playing environments.

» Playmobil FunPark – In West Palm Beach; a wonderland of toys and play sets.

Wildlife Encounters: on Land

» Everglades National Park – Bike or take a tram tour along Shark Valley's paved road, or short boardwalk trails around the Royal Palm Visitor Center.

» National Key Deer Refuge – On Big Pine Key in Florida Keys; kids love spotting these cute-as-Bambi mini deer.

» Bill Baggs Cape Florida State Recreation Area – Accessible island-ecology walks.

» John D Macarthur State Park – For sea turtles and ranger-led watches.

» Corkscrew Swamp Sanctuary – West of Naples; maybe the most diverse and rewarding swampy boardwalk trail.

» Myakka River State Park – Tram tours, short hikes for birds and alligators; don't miss fun Canopy Trail.

» Lee County Manatee Park – In Fort Myers; easy way to see wintering manatees.

» Six Mile Cypress Slough Preserve – In Fort Myers; another ideal, shady boardwalk trail often packed with wildlife.

» Paynes Prairie Preserve State Park – Near Gainesville; chance upon wild horses, bison, alligators and sandhill cranes.

» Leon Sinks Geological Area – In Apalachicola National Forest; bizarre sinkhole terrain is bound to make an impression.

» St George Island State Park – Near Apalachicola; seabirds and loggerhead nesting.

RULES OF THE ROAD

Florida car-seat laws require that children under three must be in a car seat, and children under five in at least a booster seat (unless they are over 80lb and 4ft 9in tall, allowing seat belts to be positioned properly). Rental-car companies are legally required to provide child seats, but *only if you reserve them in advance;* they typically charge $10 to $15 extra. Avoid surprises by bringing your own.

Wildlife Encounters: by Water

» Everglades National Park – Visit Everglades City and Flamingo centers for family-friendly kayaking.

» Biscayne National Park – Glass-bottom boat tours, snorkeling over epic reefs.

» John Pennekamp Coral Reef State Park – Same great coral reefs, by snorkel or glass-bottom boat tour.

» Loxahatchee River – Near Jupiter, river and alligator adventure.

» Canaveral National Seashore – Easy intercoastal paddling, pontoon boats, sea-turtle watches.

» Myakka River State Park – Airboat tours and kayaking among hundreds of alligators.

» Weeki Wachee Springs – Watch mermaid show, then canoe the crystal-clear fish-and-manatee-filled river.

» Crystal River – Legendary manatee spot; boat and swim among them.

» Blue Spring State Park – Near Deland; canoe and cruise among manatees.

» Suwannee River – Great muddy river dotted with crystal-clear springs for swimming.

Planning

If you're a parent, you already know that luck favors the prepared. But in Florida's crazy-crowded, overbooked high-season tourist spots, planning can make all the difference. Before you come, plot your trip like a four-star general: pack everything you might need, make reservations for every place you might go, schedule every hour. Then, arrive, relax and go with the flow.

What to Bring

If you forget something, don't sweat it. Just bring yourself, your kids and any of their can't-sleep-without items. Florida can supply the rest, from diapers to clothes to sunscreen to boogie boards.

That said, here are some things to consider.

☐ For sleeping, a pack-and-play for infants and/or an inflatable mattress for older kids can be handy, especially if you're road-tripping or sticking to amenity-poor, budget-range motels.

☐ For potty-training infants, a waterproof pad protects against hotel-bed accidents.

☐ For mealtimes, pack a collapsible cooler with plastic cups, bowls, utensils and zippable plastic bags, along with food you know your kids will eat. You'll be self-sufficient if your kids don't like a restaurant's offerings, or whenever hunger strikes.

☐ Bring light rain gear and umbrellas; it *will* rain at some point.

☐ Bring water sandals, for beach, water parks and play fountains.

☐ Bring sunscreen (a daily necessity) and mosquito repellent.

☐ Prepare a simple first-aid kit; the moment unexpected cuts or fevers strike is not the time to run to the drugstore.

Accommodations

The vast majority of Florida hotels stand ready to aid families: they have cribs (often pack-and-plays) and rollaway beds (perhaps charging extra); they have refrigerators and microwaves (but ask to confirm); and they have adjoining rooms and suites.

FLORIDA-THEMED BOOKS FOR KIDS

Get reading-age kids in a Florida mood with these great books.

» *Hoot* (2002) by Carl Hiaasen: Hiaasen's same zany characters, snappy plot twists and environmental message, but PG-rated. If you like it, pick up *Flush* (2005) and *Scat* (2009).

» *Because of Winn-Dixie* (2000) by Kate DiCamillo: heartwarming coming-of-age tale about a 10-year-old girl adjusting to her new life in Florida.

» *The Yearling* (1938) by Marjorie Kinnan Rawlings: Pulitzer Prize–winning literary classic about a boy who adopts an orphaned fawn in Florida's backwoods.

» *The Treasure of Amelia Island* (2008) by MC Finotti: historical fiction that re-creates Spanish-ruled Florida through the eyes of an 11-year-old.

» *Bad Latitude* (2008) by David Ebright: unabashed pirate adventure for tween boys, with a dash of historical realism.

DATE NIGHT

Traveling with kids doesn't necessarily mean doing *everything* as a family. Want a romantic night on the town? Several child-care services offer in-hotel babysitting by certified sitters; a few run their own drop-off centers. Most focus on the Orlando, Miami and Tampa areas. Rates vary based on the number of children, and typically they require a four-hour minimum (plus a $10 travel surcharge). Hourly rates generally range from $14 to $20. For more resources while staying at Walt Disney World resorts, see p286.

» **Kid's Nite Out** (www.kidsniteout.com)

» **Sittercity** (www.sittercity.com)

» **Sunshine Babysitting** (www.sunshinebabysitting.com) Statewide.

Particularly in beach towns, large hotels and resorts can go toe-to-toe with condos for amenities, including partial or full kitchens, laundry facilities, pools and barbecues, and various activities. Properties catering specifically to families are marked by a family icon (🏠).

The only places that discourage young kids (they aren't allowed to discriminate) are certain romantic B&Bs and high-end boutique hotels. If you're unsure, ask, and they'll tell you what minimum age they prefer.

Travel Advice & Baby Gear

If you prefer to pack light, several services offer baby-gear rental (high chairs, strollers, car seats etc), while others sell infant supplies (diapers, wipes, formula, baby food etc), all delivered to your hotel; book one to two weeks in advance. These and other websites also provide family-centered travel advice. Most focus on Orlando, Miami and Tampa, but a few are statewide.

» **Babies Travel Lite** (www.babiestravellite .com) Sells baby supplies for delivery; also offers general and Florida-specific family-travel advice.

» **Baby's Away** (www.babysawayrentals.com) Rents baby gear.

» **Family Vacation Critics** (www.family vacationcritics.com) Trip Advisor–owned, parent-reviewed hotels, sights and travel.

» **Go City Kids** (http://gocitykids. parentsconnect.com) Nickelodeon-sponsored family travel in Miami, Orlando and Tampa.

» **Jet Set Babies** (www.jetsetbabies.com) Sells baby supplies, plus general infant-travel advice.

» **Travel for Kids** (www.travelforkids.com) Florida-specific family travel; helpful planning advice.

» **Traveling Baby Company** (www.traveling babyco.com) Rents baby gear.

regions at a glance

Miami

Museums ✓✓✓
Nightlife ✓✓✓
Food ✓✓✓

Museums & the Arts

Culture vultures circle Miami day and night, which is almost a real-time performance-art piece. There are the major cultural institutions – the Bass, the Adrienne Arsht Center, the Lowe, the Museum of Contemporary Art – as well as vibrant gallery and arts districts, like Wynwood and the Design District. There is architecture, from South Beach's art-deco hotels to the extravagant Biltmore Hotel. Then there are odd-balls like the World Erotic Art Museum. Whatever else, you'll get an eyeful.

p48

Nightlife

Welcome to *Lifestyles of the Rich & Famous*, where the tagline 'champagne wishes and caviar dreams' doesn't come close to capturing the indulgent, profligate love of beauty, youth, sexy DJs, sweet mojitos and good times that is Miami nightlife. Of course, it's not all glam celebrity-spotting, drag shows and bottle service. Authentic Cuban dancehalls and hipster-free dive bars keep things somewhat real.

Ethnic/Gourmet

Purely in culinary terms, Miami is the perfect storm, the ideal mix of wealth, immigrants and agricultural abundance to produce a world-class foodie scene. At one end are the trendy, celebrity-chef-driven laboratories of gourmet perfection, and at the other are the hole-in-the-wall ethnic eateries where something as simple as rice and beans can leave you devastated and babbling for years to come.

The Everglades

Wildlife-watching ✓✓✓
Activities ✓✓✓
Old Florida ✓✓

Wildlife-watching

There are 1.5 million alligators in Florida, and in the Everglades, sometimes nearly half of them seem to be within a 100yd dash of you. More than that, the Everglades can turn anyone into an avid amateur birder: over 350 species call the swamps home, including earth's most dramatic species.

Outdoor Adventures

Even a ramble along the raised wooden boardwalks near the visitor centers can feel like an adventure. Jump into a kayak or canoe and let yourself be swallowed by the Everglades' watery wilderness for an unforget-table, yet surprisingly easy, experience of a lifetime.

Roadside Attractions

Around here, life just isn't the same-old, same-old, and it shows. Bizarre food, strange legends of mythical beasts, offbeat roadside stands, monuments to scorned love? Yep, all here and then some.

p136

Florida Keys & Key West

Activities ✓✓✓
Beaches ✓✓
Nightlife ✓✓✓

Outdoor Activities

Except for drinking and partying (see below), people come to the Keys to do stuff: fish, snorkel, dive, kayak, hike, bike, fish some more, snorkel again, swim with dolphins (but see p164), feed tarpon, spot Key deer. North America's best coral reefs provide brag-worthy expeditions.

Beaches

Except for Bahia Honda, which often makes Florida's 'best beach' lists, Keys beaches aren't as uniformly perfect as elsewhere in the state, and yet they provide all that most need: a comfortable place to sleep off the night before.

Crazy Key West

No nightlife scene in Florida matches Key West's peculiar mix of offbeat craziness, self-conscious performance, gay humor and drunken loutishness. For some, like Hemingway and Jimmy Buffett, it's the port at the end of the world they were searching for.

p153

Southeast Florida

Beaches ✓✓✓
Activities ✓✓✓
Entertainment ✓✓

Beaches

With monikers like the Gold Coast and the Treasure Coast, you know where the money's at. Some of these towns – Palm Beach, Boca Raton, Fort Lauderdale – are so wealthy it's nearly obscene. But do they take care of their beaches? Very well, thank you very much.

Activities

Canal and gondola tours around Fort Lauderdale, river trips on the Loxa-hatchee, epic wreck diving, snorkeling Spanish galleons, good surfing, sport-fishing charters, turtle watches: many of Florida's most fun activities are experienced here at their best.

Entertainment

Southeast beach towns are simply good fun, whether people-watching along the Hollywood Broadwalk, partying in Fort Lauderdale bars, watching drag racing in Jupiter, catching blues in West Palm Beach, or simply gaping at the mansions of Palm Beach.

p186

Orlando & Walt Disney World

Theme Parks ✓✓✓
Entertainment ✓✓✓
Activities ✓✓

Theme Parks

If theme parks truly are worlds, then Orlando contains a galaxy. Walt Disney World is itself a veritable solar system of amusements; Universal Orlando may be smaller but is equally entertaining. Then there is SeaWorld, Discovery Cove, Gatorland, Holy Land, amusement parks, water parks...

Entertainment

Orlando specializes in enter-tainment. Start with Disney, which packs each night with a magical light parade, Cirque de Soleil, House of Blues shows and much more. Universal dishes up a luau, the Blue Man Group and Hard Rock shows. Or-lando itself is rife with bars, movies and live music.

Activities

In and around Orlando are plentiful opportunities to bike, golf, kayak, go river tubing and even 'skydive' indoors, not to mention all the water play the park resorts offer.

p227

The Space Coast

Activities ✓✓✓
Beaches ✓✓✓
History ✓✓

Surfing & Kayaking

Surfing and kayaking are the Space Coast's unbeatable one-two punch. All the surfing is good here, but Cocoa Beach is the scene's epicenter. Meanwhile, the wildlife to be seen among the protected, unspoiled lagoons and intercoastal waterways includes manatees, dolphins and more.

Beaches

Oh right, and Space Coast beaches are truly swell also, and much more relaxed and low-key than the beach communities just north and south. Seek out cute Vero Beach and escape on beautiful Apollo Beach.

Kennedy Space Center

Kennedy is reason enough to come to the Space Coast. The shuttle launches may have ended, but the space center is still a top-notch, immersive experience in the US space program and the life of an astronaut.

p305

Northeast Florida

Activities ✓✓✓
Old Florida ✓✓✓
Beaches ✓✓

Outdoor Adventures

First and foremost, the Ocala National Forest beckons with a veritable wealth of forested hikes, crystal springs, rivers and tons of camping. But the region's interior state parks are all prime, and then there's splendid kayaking among the waterways of the northeast coast.

Old & Oldest Florida

Old Florida can be found in Micanopy and Cross Creek, where Cracker (backwoods Florida pioneer) life is lovingly preserved in Marjorie Kinnan Rawlings Historic State Park. 'Oldest' Florida means Spanish-founded St Augustine, a splendid time warp to the days of Spanish explorers and missionaries and those dreaded pirates.

Beaches

For romantic getaways, choose Amelia Island; for high-octane, amusement-rich family fun, pick Daytona. These beach towns bookend a string of great beaches, though they do get overshadowed among Florida's tremendous sandy selections.

p318

Tampa Bay & Southwest Florida

Beaches ✓✓✓
Food ✓✓
Museums ✓✓✓

Beaches

The Gulf Coast from Tampa south enjoys some of Florida's best white-sand beaches and some of its best beach towns. There's really too much to choose from, but Siesta Key, Fort Myers Beach, Honeymoon Island, Naples, Fort DeSoto, St Pete Beach and Sanibel are all great.

Food

Tampa has a big-city foodie scene, with several gourmet destinations, and St Petersburg is no slouch. The sophisticated towns of Sarasota, Naples and Sanibel also provide their fare share of excellent cuisine.

Museums

The region has two of Florida's best museums – the Salvador Dalí Museum and the Ringling Museum complex – and each are worth trekking from Miami and Orlando to see. Yet sophisticated art and cultural institutions are highlights in Tampa, St Petersburg, Sarasota, Fort Myers and Naples, too.

p361

The Panhandle

Beaches ✓✓✓
Activities ✓✓✓
Entertainment ✓✓

Beaches

The Panhandle, dubbed the 'Redneck Riviera,' could just as easily be called 'pristine snow-white sands lapped by gentle emerald waters.' The beaches are unbelievably beautiful, and the sometimes raucous beach towns can be sought out or avoided as you wish.

Activities

Kayaking the waterways around Cedar Key is wonderful, and canoeing the Suwannee River is classic Florida. Meanwhile, there's swimming, snorkeling and diving in crystal springs, and great hiking and biking in the Apalachicola National Forest. Seek out the sinkholes of Leon Sinks Geological Area.

Entertainment

Enjoy the blues clubs of Tallahassee, the frantic boardwalk amusements of Panama City Beach, the glass-bottom boat tours of nature-as-entertainment Wakulla Springs State Park, and Pensacola's Blue Angels and beach-bar nightlife.

p417

Look out for these icons:

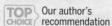 Our author's recommendation

 A green or sustainable option

FREE No payment required

See the Index for a full list of destinations covered in this book.

On the Road

Miami

Includes »

Best Places to Eat

» Señora Martinez (p117)

» Osteria Del Teatro (p112)

» Tap Tap (p111)

» Michy's (p118)

» Steve's Pizza (p114)

Best Places to Sleep

» The Standard (p104)

» Shore Club (p105)

» Circa 39 (p108)

» Pelican Hotel (p102)

» Hotel St Augustine (p102)

Why Go?

Miami is so many things, but to most visitors, it's mainly glamour, condensed into urban form.

They're right. The archaic definition of 'glamour' is a kind of spell that mystifies a victim. Well, they call Miami the Magic City. And it is mystifying. In its beauty, certainly: the clack of a model's high heels on Lincoln Rd, the teal sweep of Biscayne Bay, flowing cool into the wide South Florida sky; the blood-orange fire of the sunset, setting the Downtown skyline aflame.

Then there's less-conventional beauty: a Haitian dance party in the ghetto attended by University of Miami literature students, or a Venezuelan singing Metallica *en español* in a Coral Gables karaoke bar, or the passing *shalom/buenas días* traded between Orthodox Jews and Cuban exiles.

Miami is so many things. All glamorous, in every sense of the word. You could spend a fun lifetime trying to escape her spell.

When to Go

Miami

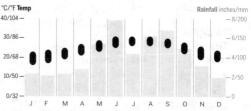

| **Jan–Mar** Warm and dry, with lots of tourists; snowbirds from the northeast and Europeans. | **Apr–Jun** Not as muggy as deep summer, but lusher and greener than winter. | **Jul–Oct** Prices plummet. When it's not as hot as an oven, there's storms: it's hurricane season. |

History

It's always been the weather that's attracted Miami's two most prominent species: developers and tourists. But it wasn't the sun per se that got people moving here – it was an ice storm. The great Florida freeze of 1895 wiped out the state's citrus industry; at the same time, widowed Julia Tuttle bought out parcels of land that would become modern Miami, and Henry Flagler was building his Florida East Coast Railroad. Tuttle offered to split her land with Flagler if he extended the railway to Miami, but the train man didn't pay her any heed until north Florida froze over and Tuttle sent him an 'I-told-you-so' message: an orange blossom clipped from her Miami garden.

The rest is a history of boom, bust, dreamers and opportunists. Generally, Miami has grown in leaps and bounds following major world events and natural disasters. Hurricanes (particularly the deadly Great Miami Hurricane of 1926) have wiped away the town, but it just keeps bouncing back and building back better than before. In the late 19th and early 20th centuries, Miami earned a reputation for attracting design and city-planning mavericks such as George Merrick, who fashioned the artful Mediterranean village of Coral Gables, and James Deering, designer of the fairy-tale Vizcaya mansion.

Miami Beach blossomed in the early 20th century when Jewish developers recognized the potential American Riviera in their midst. Those hoteliers started building resorts that were branded with a distinctive art-deco facade by daring architects willing to buck the more staid aesthetics of the northeast. The world wars brought soldiers who were stationed at nearby naval facilities, many of whom liked the sun and decided to stay. Latin American and Caribbean revolutions introduced immigrants from the other direction, most famously from Cuba. Cuban immigrants arrived in two waves: first, the anti-Castro types of the '60s, and those looking for a better life since the

MIAMI IN...

Two Days

There's more to Miami than South Beach, but we're assuming you're starting – and sleeping – here. Have breakfast at **Puerto Sagua** (p111) and, gorged, waddle to the **Wolfsonian-FIU** (p52) to get some background on the surrounding art-deco architecture. Now stroll around **Lincoln Road** (p61), hotel-spot on Collins Ave or check out South Beach's most flamboyant structures, like the **Delano Hotel** (p106), **Tides** (p106) and the **Shore Club** (p105).

Get in some beach time and as evening sets in consider an excellent deco district tour with the **Art Deco Welcome Center** (p133). For a nice dinner try **Osteria del Teatro** (p112) or **Tap Tap** (p111). When you're ready to hit the town (and the rails), we suggest early cocktails at **B Bar** (p122).

The next day potter around either of the excellent ethnic enclaves of **Little Haiti** (p79) or **Little Havana** (p85) before dining in the trendy **Design District** (p79). End your trip rocking out in one of Midtown's excellent venues, like **Bardot** (p125) or **Electric Pickle** (p124).

Four Days

Follow the two-day itinerary and visit whichever one of the 'Littles' (Haiti or Havana) you missed the first time round. If you can, visit Coral Gables, making sure not to miss the **Biltmore Hotel** (p89), the **Venetian Pool** (p89) and a shopping stroll down Miracle Mile. If all that isn't opulent enough for you, see what happens when Mediterranean revival, baroque stylings and a lot of money gets mashed together at the **Vizcaya Museum & Gardens** (p86). Top off a visit to these elegant manses with dinner at one of the best restaurants in Miami in, no kidding, a gas station at **El Carajo** (p120).

On day four, head downtown and take a long ride on the free **Metromover** (p135), hopping on and off to see the excellent **HistoryMiami** (p76) and the gorgeous **Adrienne Arsht Center for the Performing Arts** (p73). Have your last meal at **Michy's** (p118) on emergent N Biscayne Blvd and please, before you leave, guzzle a beer and pick at some smoked fish on the couches of **Jimbo's** (p84).

Miami Highlights

1 Catch a show in South Beach at the incredible **New World Center** (p61)

2 Go out for drinks and a stumble through Wynwood and the Design District on an **art walks gallery night** (p125)

3 Cigar smoke, dominoes and *guayaberas* (linen dress shirts); say *bienvenido a* Little Havana in **Máximo Gómez Park** (p85)

4 Take a free tour of downtown Miami via the old-school **Metromover** (p135)

5 Smoked fish, beer, La-Z-Boys and a mangrove swamp – aw, yeah – get to **Jimbo's** (p84)

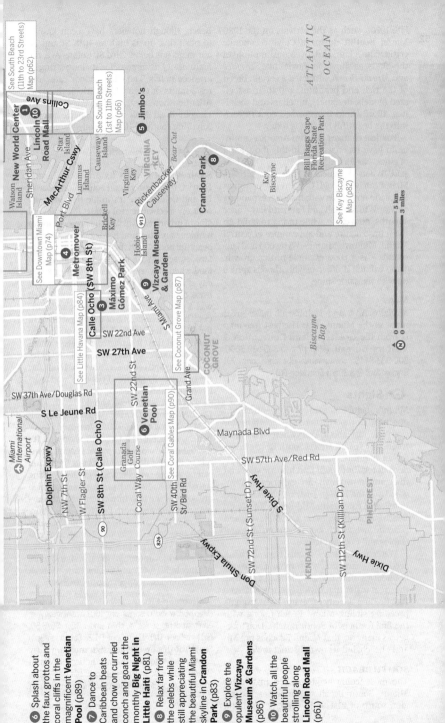

See South Beach (11th to 23rd Streets) Map (p62)

1 **New World Center**

10 **Lincoln Road Mall**

Collins Ave

Watson Island

Sheridan Ave

Star Island

Causeway Island

Lummus Island

See South Beach (1st to 11th Streets) Map (p66)

5 **Jimbo's**

MacArthur Cswy

Port Blvd

Virginia Key

Brickell Key

Rickenbacker Causeway

Bear Cut

Key Biscayne

VIRGINIA KEY

8 **Crandon Park**

Bill Baggs Cape Florida Recreation Park

See Key Biscayne Map (p82)

ATLANTIC OCEAN

See Downtown Miami Map (p74)

4 **Metromover**

3 **Máximo Gómez Park**

Calle Ocho (SW 8th St)

See Little Havana Map (p84)

Hobie Island

913

9 **Vizcaya Museum & Garden**

Miami Ave

SW 22nd Ave

SW 27th Ave

See Coconut Grove Map (p87)

Grand Ave

COCONUT GROVE

Biscayne Bay

Miami International Airport

SW 37th Ave/Douglas Rd

SW 22nd St

S Le Jeune Rd

6 **Venetian Pool**

See Coral Gables Map (p90)

Granada Golf Course

Dolphin Expwy

NW 7th St

W Flagler St

SW 8th St (Calle Ocho)

Coral Way

SW 40th St/Bird Rd

90

Maynada Blvd

SW 57th Ave/Red Rd

SW 72nd St (Sunset Dr)

S Dixie Hwy

826

Don Shula Expwy

KENDALL

SW 112th St (Killian Dr)

Dixie Hwy

PINECREST

N

0   5 km
0   3 miles

6 Splash about the faux grottos and coral cliffs in the magnificent **Venetian Pool** (p89)

7 Dance to Caribbean beats and chow on curried conch and goat at the monthly **Big Night in Little Haiti** (p81)

8 Relax far from the celebs while still appreciating the beautiful Miami skyline in **Crandon Park** (p83)

9 Explore the opulent **Vizcaya Museum & Gardens** (p86)

10 Watch all the beautiful people strolling along **Lincoln Road Mall** (p61)

late 1970s, such as the arrivals on the 1980 Mariel Boatlift during a Cuban economic crisis. The glam and overconsumption of the 1980s, as shown in movies like *Scarface* and *Miami Beach,* attracted a certain breed of the rich and beautiful, and their associated models, designers, hoteliers and socialites, all of whom transformed South Beach into the beautiful beast it is today.

Political changes in Latin America continue to have repercussions in this most Latin of cities – as former mayor Manny Diaz once said, 'When Venezuela or Argentina sneezes, Miami catches a cold.' Current mayor Tomas Regalado now deals with his town expanding outwards to Kendall and Palmetto Bay – once suburbs, now city – while trying to build up the infrastructure and appearance of central Miami. Midtown Miami – Wynwood and surrounds – is a good example of this growth. Time will tell if other neighborhoods spruce up with the same shine.

Maps

McNally, AAA and Dolph's all make great maps of the Miami area. The best free map is from the **Greater Miami Convention & Visitors Bureau** (Map p74; ☎305-539-3000, 800-933-8448; www.miamiandbeaches.com; 701 Brickell Ave; ☺8:30am-5pm Mon-Fri).

◉ Sights

Miami's major sights aren't concentrated in one neighborhood; there is something for everyone just about everywhere. The most frequently visited area is South Beach, home to hot nightlife, beautiful beaches and art-deco hotels, but you'll find historic sites and museums downtown, art galleries in Wynwood and the Design District, old-fashioned hotels and eateries in Mid-Beach (in Miami Beach), more beaches on Key Biscayne, and peaceful neighborhood attractions in Coral Gables and Coconut Grove.

Water and income – canals, bays and bank accounts – are the geographic and social boundaries that divide Miami. Of course, the great water that divides here is Biscayne Bay, holding the city of Miami apart from its preening sibling Miami Beach (along with the fine feathers of South Beach). Don't forget, as many do, that Miami Beach is not Miami's beach, but its own distinct town.

SOUTH BEACH

The most iconic neighborhood in Greater Miami, South Beach encompasses the region south of 21st St in the city of Miami

Beach, though hoteliers have been known to push that up as high as 40th St and on our maps it is below 23rd St. Collins Ave, the main artery, is famous for its long string of art-deco hotels. The chic outdoor cafes and restaurants of Ocean Dr overlook the wide Atlantic shorefront, while pedestrian-only Lincoln Road Mall is a shopper's heaven. Anything south of 5th St is called 'SoFi.'

TOP CHOICE / Art Deco Historic District
NEIGHBORHOOD

South Beach's heart is its Art Deco Historic District, from 18th St and south along Ocean Dr and Collins Ave. It's ironic that in a city built on speculative real estate, the main engine of urban renewal was the preservation of a unique architectural heritage. See, all those beautiful hotels, with their tropical-Americana facades, scream 'Miami.' They screamed it so loud when they were preserved they gave this city a brand, and this neighborhood a new lease on life. Back in the day, South Beach was a ghetto of vagrants, druggies and retirees. Then it became one of the largest areas in the USA on the National Register of Historic Places, and then it attracted models, photographers, hoteliers, chefs and...well, today it's a pastel medina of cruisers, Euro-fashionistas, the occasionally glimpsed celebrity, and tourists from Middle America.

Your first stop here should be the **Art Deco Welcome Center** (Map p62; ☎305-531-3484; 1200 Ocean Dr; ☺9:30am-7pm daily). To be honest, it's a bit of a tatty gift shop, but it's located in the old beach-patrol headquarters, one of the best deco buildings out there. You can book some excellent $20 guided walking tours (plus audio and private tours), which are some of the best introductions to the layout and history of South Beach on offer. Tours depart at 10:30am daily, except on Thursday when they leave at 6:30pm. No advance reservations required; just show up and smile. Call ahead for information on walking tours of Lincoln Rd (p61) and Collins Park, the area that encompasses upper South Beach.

Wolfsonian-FIU
MUSEUM

(Map p66; www.wolfsonian.org; 1001 Washington Ave; adult/student, senior & child under 12yr $5/3.50; ☺11am-9pm Thu, 11am-6pm Fri & Sat, noon-5pm Sun) Visit this excellent design museum early in your stay to put the aesthetics of Miami Beach into fascinating context. It's one thing to see how wealth, leisure and the pursuit of

continued on p61

Art Deco Miami

South Beach is called the American Riviera thanks to celebrity glam and glitz. Yet its cachet owes less to Paris Hilton than the Paris *Exposition Internationale des Arts Décoratifs et Industriels Modernes*. Held in 1925, this design fair birthed the art-deco movement, the architectural and aesthetic backbone of South Beach. Remember, in Miami Beach, cross streets can be determined by building number. Two zeroes after the first number means the building is at the base of the block. So 700 Ocean Dr is at 7th St and Ocean, while 1420 Ocean Dr is at 14th St & Ocean, just north of the intersection.

South Beach's Ocean Drive

Classical Deco South Beach Structures

In the past, South Beach architects distinguished themselves through decorative finials, parapets and neon signage. Miami Beach deco relies on 'stepped-back' facades that disrupt the harsh, flat Florida light and contribute to a rhythmical feel. Cantilevered 'eyebrows' jut out above windows to protect interiors from unrelenting sun.

Cardozo Hotel

1 This lovely building (p105), along with the neighboring Carlyle Hotel, was the first to be rescued by the original Miami Beach Preservation League when developers threatened to raze South Beach's deco buildings in the 1980s. It's owned by Gloria Estefan.

Carlyle Hotel

2 Located at 1250 Ocean Dr, the Carlyle comes with futuristic styling, triple parapets, a *Jetsons* vibe and some cinematic cachet: *The Birdcage* was filmed here.

Essex House Hotel

3 Porthole windows lend the feel of a grand cruise ship, while its spire looks like a rocket ship, recalling art deco's roots as an aesthetic complement to modernism and industrialism. Terrazzo floors also cool the lobby (p103).

Lifeguard Stations on South Beach

4 Besides being cubist-inspired exemplars of the classical deco movement, with their sharp, pleasing geometric lines, these stations are painted in dazzling colors. They're found along the beach from 1st St to 17th St.

Jerry's Famous Deli

5 Housed in the Hoffman Cafeteria Building, this spacious 1939 gem has a front that resembles the prow of a *Buck Rogers*–inspired ship. The carved owls on the roof scare off pigeons – and their poo (p113).

Clockwise from top left
1. Cardozo Hotel 2. Carlyle Hotel 3. Essex House Hotel
4. A colorful lifeguard station on South Beach

The CARLYLE

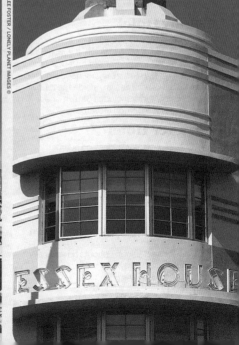

ESSEX HOUSE

Deco Elements & Embellishments

As individualized as South Beach's buildings are, they share quirks and construction strategies. Canopy porches give residents a cool place to sit. To reflect heat, buildings were originally painted white, then pastels, with accent colors highlighting smaller elements. Some hotels resemble Meso-American temples; others evoke cruise liners.

Crescent Hotel

1 Besides having one of Miami Beach's most recognizable neon facades, the Crescent (at 1420 Ocean Dr) has signage that draws the eye down into its lobby (the better to pack guests in), rather than up to its roof.

Waldorf Towers Hotel

2 Deco guru L Murray Dixon designed the tower of this hotel (at 860 Ocean Dr) to resemble a lighthouse, surely meant to illuminate the way home from drunken Ocean Drive revels.

Colony Hotel

3 The Colony, at 736 Ocean Dr, is the oldest deco hotel in Miami Beach. It was the first hotel in Miami, and perhaps in America, to incorporate its sign (a zigzagging neon wonder) as part of its overall design. Inside the lobby, a space-age interior includes Saturn-shaped lamps and *Flash Gordon* elevators.

Cavalier Hotel

4 The step-pyramid sides and geometric carvings that grace the front of this classic are some of the best examples of the 'Mayan/Incan temple-as-hotel' school of design (p106).

Wolfsonian-FIU

5 The lobby of this museum contains a phenomenally theatrical example of a 'frozen fountain.' The gold-leaf fountain, formerly gracing a movie-theater lobby, shoots up vertically and flows downward symmetrically (p52).

Clockwise from top left
1. Crescent Hotel 2. Waldorf Towers Hotel 3. Colony Hotel
4. Cavalier Hotel

'New' Deco Hotels

Hoteliers like Ian Schrager combine faith in technology – flat-screen TVs, Lucite 'ghost chairs,' computer-controlled lobby displays – with an air of fantastical glamour. Newer hotels like the W and Gansevoort South have deco roots, but have expanded the architectural sense of scale, integrating deco style into Miami Modern's (enormous) proportions.

Hotel Victor

1 Forward-thinking management (who give a nod to the past) have done an excellent job of turning this L Murray Dixon original into an undersea wonderland of jellyfish lamps and sea-green terrazzo floors (p102).

Delano Hotel

2 The top tower evokes old-school deco rocket-ship fantasies, but the theater-set-on-acid interior is a flight of pure modern fancy. The enormous backyard pool mixes Jazz Age elegance with pure Miami muscular opulence (p106).

Tides

3 The biggest deco structure of its day was a temple to the deco movement. Today, the lobby of the Tides feels like Poseidon's audience chamber, while rooms exemplify modern boutique aesthetics (p106).

Royal Palm Hotel

4 There's no better place to feel a sense of sea-borne movement than the *Titanic*-esque, ocean-liner back lobby of this massive and beautifully restored hotel. The mezzanine has enormous modern dimensions but classic deco styling (p107).

Surfcomber

5 One of the best deco renovations on the beach is offset by sleek, transit-lounge lines in the lobby and a lovely series of rounded shades over room windows (p107).

Clockwise from top left
1. Hotel Victor 2. Delano (left) and National Hotels
3. View across to the Tides hotel

Quirky Deco Delights

Tropical deco is mainly concerned with stimulating the imagination. Painted accents lifted from archaeology sites might make a passer-by think of travel, maybe on a cruise ship, and hey, isn't it funny the windows here resemble portholes? Almost all of the preserved buildings here still inspire this childlike sense of wonder.

Berkeley Shore Hotel

1 One of the older hotels in South Beach, the Berkeley Shore, at 1610 Collins Ave, has a striking exterior set off by a cylindrical 'prow' rising out of candy-colored, shade-providing 'eyebrows', plus elegant exterior friezes.

Bas-Relief & Friezes

2 Although art deco was inspired by stripped-down modernist aesthetics, it also rebelled against utilitarianism. Its fantastically embellished bas-relief and frieze work is noticeable on the exterior of many South Beach hotels.

Avalon Hotel

3 The exterior of the Avalon, at 700 Ocean Dr, is a fantastic example of classical art-deco architecture – clean lines, old-school signage lit up in tropical green, with a 1950s Oldsmobile parked outside.

11th Street Diner

4 It doesn't get much more deco than dining in a classical Pullman train car. Many buildings on Miami Beach evoke planes, trains and automobiles – this diner is actually in one (p112).

Portholes

5 The deco movement came about in the early 20th century, when affordable travel became a reality for the developed world. Sea journeys represented the height of luxury and many deco buildings are decorated with nautical porthole windows.

Right

1. Berkeley Shore Hotel 2. Art-deco bas-relief detail

continued from p52

beauty manifests in Miami Beach, it's another to understand the roots and shadings of local artistic movements. By chronicling the interior evolution of everyday life, the Wolfsonian reveals how these trends were architecturally manifested in SoBe's exterior deco. Which reminds us of the Wolfsonian's own noteworthy facade. Remember the Gothic-futurist apartment complex-cum-temple of evil in *Ghostbusters*? Well, this imposing structure, with its grandiose 'frozen fountain' and lionhead-studded grand elevator, could serve as a stand-in for that set.

Lincoln Road Mall   ROAD

Calling Lincoln Rd a mall, which many do, is like calling Big Ben a clock: it's technically accurate but misses the point. Yes, you can shop, and shop very well here. But this outdoor pedestrian thoroughfare between Alton Rd and Washington Ave is really about seeing and being seen; there are times when Lincoln feels less like a road and more like a runway. We wouldn't be surprised if you developed a slight crick in your neck from whipping around to check out all the fabulously gorgeous creatures that call 'the road' their natural environment. Carl Fisher, the father of Miami Beach, envisioned the road as a '5th Ave of the South'. Morris Lapidus, one of the founders of the loopy, neo-Baroque Miami-Beach style, designed much of the mall, including several shady overhangs and waterfall structures, traffic barriers that look like the marbles a giant might play with, plus the wonderfully deco **Colony Theatre** (p128) and the currently empty **Lincoln Theatre** (541 Lincoln Rd). There's also an excellent **farmers' market** (⊗9am-6pm Sun) and the **Antique & Collectible Market** (⊗9am-5pm, every 2nd Sun Oct-May; www.antiquecollectiblemarket.com), both held along Lincoln.

1111 Lincoln Rd

(Map p62; www.1111lincolnroad.com) The West Side of Lincoln Rd is anchored by what may be the most impressive parking garage you'll ever lay eyes on, a geometric pastiche of sharp angles, winding corridors and incongruous corners that looks like a lucid fantasy dreamed up by Pythagoras after a long night out. In fact, the building was designed by Swiss architecture firm Herzog & de Meuron, who describe the structure as 'all muscle without cloth'.

ArtCenter/South Florida

(Map p62; www.artcentersf.org; 924 Lincoln Rd) Established in 1984 by a small but forward-thinking group of artists, this compound is the creative heart of South Beach. In addition to some 52 artists' studios (many of which are open to the public), ArtCenter offers an exciting lineup of classes and lectures. The residences are reserved for artists who do not have major exposure, so this is a good place to spot up-and-coming talent. Monthly rotating exhibitions keep the presentation fresh and pretty avant-garde.

Miami Beach Community Church

(Map p62; www.mb-communitychurch.org; 1620 Drexel Ave) In rather sharp and refreshing contrast to all the uber-modern structures muscling their way into the art-deco design of South Beach, the community church puts one in mind of an old Spanish mission – humble, modest and elegantly understated in an area where overstatement is the general philosophy. Fourteen stained-glass windows line the relatively simple interior, while the exterior is built to resemble coral stone in a Spanish Revival style.

New World Center   CULTURAL BUILDING

(Map p62; ☑305-673-3330; www.nws.edu; 500 17th St) Miami has a penchant for sumptuous performing-arts venues and the New World Center is certainly competing with the Arsht Center (p73) for most-impressive concert hall in the city. The New World Center, designed by Frank Gehry, rises majestically out of a manicured lawn just above Lincoln Rd, looking somewhat like a tissue box (note the 'fluttering' stone waves that pop out of the exterior) from the year 3000 with a glass facade. The grounds form a 2½-acre public

---

HAVE YOUR SAY

Found a fantastic restaurant that you're longing to share with the world? Disagree with our recommendations? Or just want to talk about your most recent trip?

Whatever your reason, head to lonelyplanet.com, where you can post a review, ask or answer a question on the Thorn Tree forum, comment on a blog, or share your photos and tips on Groups. Or you can simply spend time chatting with like-minded travelers. So go on, have your say.

South Beach (11th to 23rd Streets)

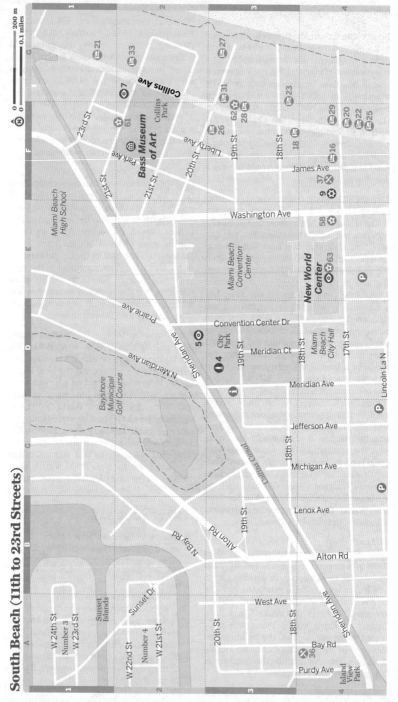

MIAMI

0 ——— 200 m
0 ——— 0.1 miles

MIAMI

ATLANTIC OCEAN

South Beach

Art Deco Historic District

A1A

16th St

15th St

Ocean Dr

14th La

The Promenade

Lummus Park

10

39 34 15

17

30

12th St

Ocean Ct

Collins Ave

24

32 13

43

45 56 53 41

14

54

42

Collins Ct

60

11

Washington Ave

Lincoln Rd

P

P

P

65 12

47

49

6

59

70

68 38

19

3

50

52 8

Old City Hall

11th St

Drexel Ave

Drexel Ave

12th St

13th St

14th St

Pennsylvania Ave

Española Way

Euclid Ave

14th Pl

Meridian Ave

15th St

16th St

Meridian Ave

12th St

55

64 69 44 40

Lincoln Rd Mall

2

48 67

46

66

Courtyard

35

Lincoln La S

57

Jefferson Ave

Michigan Ave

Flamingo Park

MIAMI BEACH

Jefferson Ave

11th St

51

Lenox Ave

14th St

13th St

12th St

1

Sun Trust Bank

907

Alton Rd

P

15th Tce

15th St

14th Ct

Alton La

See South Beach (1st to 11th Streets) Map (p66)

Alton Ct

Alton Ct

Lincoln Rd

Alton Ct

West Ave

Flamingo Way

14th Tce

13th Tce

Bay Rd

South Beach (11th to 23rd Streets)

park; performances inside the center are projected to those outside via a 7000-sq-ft projection wall (like you're in the classiest drive-in movie theater in the universe). Inside, the folded layers of white walls feel somewhere between organic and origami. The venue is the home of the acclaimed New World Symphony (p130); to get inside you generally need tickets to a show, but if you call ahead you may be able to organize a free guided walking tour of the interior, a program that was just beginning at the time of research.

Ocean Drive ROAD

(Map p66; runs from 1st to 11th St) Yar, here be the belly of the South Beach beast. It's just a road, right? No, it's the great cruising strip of Miami; an endless parade of classic cars, testosterone-sweating young men, peacock-like young women, street performers, vendors, those guys who yell unintelligible crap at everyone, celebrities pretending to be tourists, tourists who want to play celebrity, beautiful people, ugly people, people people

and the best ribbon of art-deco preservation on the beach. Say 'Miami.' That image in your head? Probably Ocean Drive.

South Pointe Park PARK

(Map p66; 1 Washington Ave; ☉sunrise-10pm) The very southern tip of Miami Beach has been converted into a lovely park, replete with manicured grass for lounging; views over a remarkably teal and fresh ocean; a restaurant; a refreshment stand; warm, scrubbed-stone walkways; and lots of folks who want to enjoy the great weather and views sans the South Beach strutting. That said, we saw two model photo shoots go off here in under an hour, so it's not all casual relaxation.

A1A ROAD

'Beachfront Avenue!' The A1A causeway, coupled with the Rickenbacker Causeway in Key Biscayne, is one of the great bridges in America, linking Miami and Miami Beach via the glittering turquoise of Biscayne Bay. To drive this road in a convertible or with the windows down, with a setting sun behind you, enormous cruise ships to the side, the palms swaying in the ocean breeze and, let's just say 'Your Love' by the Outfield on the radio, is basically the essence of Miami.

Bass Museum of Art   MUSEUM
(Map p62; www.bassmuseum.org; 2121 Park Ave; adult/student & senior $8/6; ☉noon-5pm Wed-Sun) The best art museum in Miami Beach has a playfully futuristic facade, a crisp interplay of lines and bright, white wall space – like an Orthodox church on a space-age Greek isle. All designed, by the way, in 1930 by Russell Pancoast (grandson of John A Collins, who lent his name to Collins Ave). The collection isn't shabby either: permanent highlights range from 16th-century European religious works to northern European and Renaissance paintings. The Bass forms one point of the Collins Park Cultural Center triangle, which also includes the three-story Miami City Ballet and the lovingly inviting Miami Beach Regional Library, which is a great place for free wi-fi.

Española Way Promenade   PROMENADE
(Map p62; btwn 14th & 15th Sts) Española Way is an 'authentic' Spanish promenade...in the

Florida theme-park spirit of authenticity. Oh, whatever; it's a lovely, terra-cotta and cobbled arcade of rose-pink and Spanish-cream architecture, perfect for browsing art (it was an arts colony in the 1920s and today houses the studios of several local artists), window-shopping, people-watching and cafe-sipping. A craft market operates here on weekend afternoons.

Jewish Museum of Florida   MUSEUM
(Map p66; www.jewishmuseum.com; 301 Washington Ave; adult/student & senior $6/5, Sat admission free; ☉10am-5pm Tue-Sun, closed Jewish holidays) Housed in a 1936 Orthodox synagogue that served Miami's first congregation, this small museum chronicles the rather large contribution Jews have made to the state of Florida, especially this corner of Florida. After all, it could be said that while Cubans made Miami, Jews made Miami Beach, both physically (in a developer's sense) and culturally (in an 'anyone is welcome' attitude of tolerance). Yet there were times when Jews were barred from the American Riviera they carved out of the sand, and this museum tells that story, along with some amusing anecdotes (like seashell Purim dresses). The mainstay is

South Beach (1st to 11th Streets)

Ô 0   200 m
0   0.1 miles

See South Beach (11th to 23rd Streets)
Map (p62)

Lummus
Park

South
Beach

The Promenade

Lummus Park &
Public Beach

Playground

South
Beach

ART DECO
HISTORIC DISTRICT

Wolfsonian-FIU

Ocean Dr

Ocean Ct

Ocean
Drive

Collins Ave

Collins Ct

Washington Ave

Old City
Hall

Pennsylvania Ave

Euclid Ave

Meridian Ave

Jefferson Ave

Michigan Ave

Lenox Ave

Alton Rd

Alton Ct

West Ave

Flamingo Park

Miami Beach Dr (5th St)

12th St
11th St
10th St
9th St
8th St
7th St
6th St
5th St

12th St
11th St
10th St
9th St
8th St

12th St
11th St
10th St

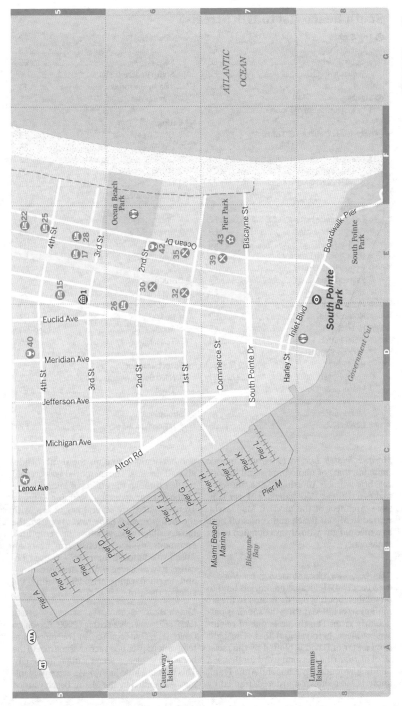

ATLANTIC
OCEAN

Ocean Beach
Park

Pier Park

Biscayne St

4th St
22 25

3rd St
17 28

Ocean Dr
2nd St
42
35
43
39

Euclid Ave
15
1

30
32

26

40

Meridian Ave

4th St 3rd St 2nd St 1st St

Jefferson Ave

Commerce St

South Pointe Dr

Michigan Ave

South Pointe
Park

Inlet Blvd

South Pointe Park

Boardwalk Pier

Harley St

Government Cut

Alton Rd

4

Lenox Ave

Pier A

Pier B

Pier C

Pier D

Pier E

Pier F

Pier G

Pier H

Pier J

Pier K

Pier L

Pier M

Miami Beach
Marina

Biscayne Bay

Causeway
Island

Lummus
Island

A1A

41

South Beach (1st to 11th Streets)

Mosaic: Jewish Life in Florida, a mosaic (imagine that) of photographs and historical bric-a-brac. Amusingly, the museum makes a whitewash of gangster Meyer Lansky – architect of the modern Mafia, who retired to Miami Beach and comes off here as a nice old guy who always donated to his synagogue.

Holocaust Memorial   MEMORIAL
(Map p62; www.holocaustmmb.org; cnr Meridian Ave & Dade Blvd) Holocaust memorials tend to be somber, but this one dedicated to the six million Jews killed during the *shoah* is particularly grim. The theme is one of relentless sadness, betrayal and loss. The light from a Star of David is blotted by the racist label of *Jude* (the German word for 'Jew'); a family surrounded by a hopeful Anne Frank quote is later shown murdered, framed by

another Frank quote on the death of ideals and dreams. The memorial was created in 1984 through the efforts of Miami Beach Holocaust survivors and sculptor Kenneth Treister. There are several key pieces, with the *Sculpture of Love and Anguish* the most visible to passers-by. The sculpture's enormous, oxidized bronze arm bears an Auschwitz tattooed number – chosen because it was never issued at the camp – and terrified camp prisoners scaling the sides of the arm.

Miami Beach Botanical Garden   GARDEN
(Map p62; www.mbgarden.org; 2000 Convention Center Dr; ☺9am-5pm Tue-Sat) For more contemplation space head across the street to the botanical garden, a secret garden in the city. This lush but little-known 4½ acres of plantings is operated by the Miami Beach Garden

Conservancy, and is an oasis of palm trees, flowering hibiscus trees and glassy ponds.

The Promenade
PROMENADE

(Map p62; Ocean Ave) This beach promenade, a wavy ribbon sandwiched between the beach and Ocean Dr, extends from 5th St to 15th St. A popular location for photo shoots, especially during crowd-free early mornings, it's also a breezy, palm-tree-lined conduit for in-line skaters, cyclists, volleyball players (there's a net at 11th St), dog walkers, yahoos, locals and tourists. The beach that it edges, called Lummus Park, sports six floridly colored lifeguard stands. There's a public bathroom at 11th St; heads up, the sinks are a popular place for homeless bathing.

Post Office
HISTORIC BUILDING

(Map p62; 1300 Washington Ave) Make it a point to mail a postcard from this 1937 deco gem of a post office, the very first South Beach renovation project tackled by preservationists in the '70s. This Depression moderne building in the 'stripped classic' style was constructed under President Roosevelt's reign and funded by the Works Progress Administration (WPA) initiative, which supported artists who were out of work during the Great Depression. On the exterior, note the bald eagle and the turret with iron railings, and inside, a large wall mural of Florida's Seminole Wars.

Temple Emanu El
RELIGIOUS

(Map p62; Washington Ave at 17th St) An art-deco temple? Not exactly, but the smooth, bubbly dome and sleek, almost aerodynamic profile

THE CAMPTON

If you're walking around Miami Beach enjoying the eye candy of all the beautiful people, hotels and restaurants, make a small detour to 1451 Washington St to see the old roots of South Beach. The Campton is a small residential condo complex (you may recognize it as the place where Jim Carrey lived in *Ace Ventura: Pet Detective*) occupied by older folks leading regular lives in one of the most unique neighborhoods in Florida. The condos themselves, with their swooping curves and shady, semicircular buttresses, are gems of art-deco design. This is what South Beach used to be, a collection of fading architectural treasures occupied by quiet retirees, before it became an international playground. The Campton is a residential building, so don't just wander in, but feel free to admire the exterior of the buildings.

of this Conservative synagogue, established in 1938, fits right in on SoBe's deco parade of moderne this and streamline that. Sabbath services are on Friday at 6:30pm and on Saturday at 8:45am.

World Erotic Art Museum
MUSEUM

(Map p62; WEAM; www.weam.com; 1205 Washington Ave; adult/student/senior $15/13.50/14, over 18yr only; ☺11am-10pm, to midnight Fri & Sat) In

THE CORAL CASTLE OF MANY NAMES

On a street full of fairly opulent buildings, 1114 Ocean Drive, a cream-colored Mediterranean revival castle built of hewn coral and exposed timber that should rightly be the center set piece of a *Pirates of the Caribbean* movie, stands out. The three-story palace, built in the 1930s, was modeled after the Governor's House in Santo Domingo, where Christopher Columbus' son once laid his head. For years it was known as the Amsterdam Palace – until one day, in the early 1980s, it caught the eye of a certain fashion designer named Gianni Versace. Versace bought the property, renamed it the Versace Mansion and promptly locked horns with local preservationists after announcing plans to tear down a neighboring hotel so he could build a pool. After a battle, the moneyed designer won – but also struck a deal that would allow for law changes, saving more than 200 other historic hotels in the process.

None of it mattered in 1997, when stalker Andrew Cunanan gunned Versace down in front of the beloved mansion. For years after, the house was known as Casa Casuarina and operated as a members-only club. Currently it is the site of the grand Villa by Barton G Hotel (p104). Ironically, the death of a European fashion guru here has attracted lots of, well, European fashion gurus. Tourists still shuffle by, armed with morbid curiosity and a thirst for celebrity-related photos of any kind.

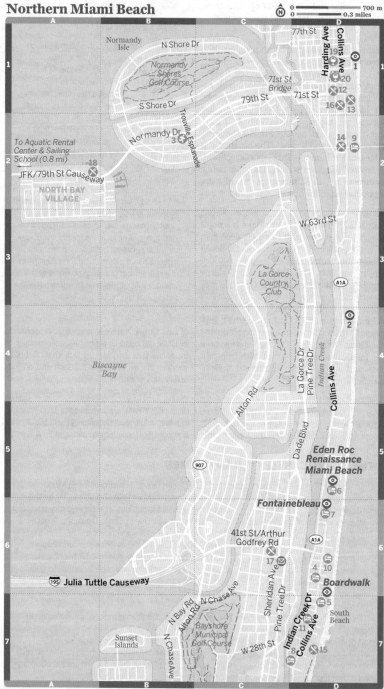

MIAMI

Northern Miami Beach

◉ Top Sights

◉ Sights

◉ Activities, Courses & Tours

◉ Sleeping

◉ Eating

◉ Drinking

a neighborhood where no behavior is too shocking, the World Erotic Art Museum screams, 'Hey! We have a giant golden penis!' We'll sound like nerds if we analyze the historical merits of an old lady's smut collection (the museum was founded by 70-year-old Naomi Wilzig, who turned her 5000-piece private erotica collection into a South Beach attraction in 2005), but here goes. WEAM's exhibits are a lot more seriously minded than its marketing material, which definitely tries to rope in anyone interested in the smutty. The collection is actually full of fascinating erotica through the ages, from ancient sex manuals to Victorian peep-show photos, to centuries of sex toys to, yes, a big golden phallus by the exit.

Maps refer to the area above South Beach as Miami Beach, but locals use the jargon Mid-Beach (around the 40th streets) and North Beach (70th St and above). Communities like Surfside, Bal Harbour, Sunny Isles and Aventura are further north and can be included in spirit. Indian Creek waterway separates the luxury hotels and high-rise condos from the residential districts in the west. Keep in mind the separate city of North Miami Beach (as opposed to the *region* of Northern Miami Beach) is not, technically, on the spit of land known as Miami Beach – it's on the mainland. Confused? So are most residents.

MIAMI SIGHTS

Fontainebleau   HISTORIC BUILDING

(Map p70; www.fontainebleau.com; 4441 Collins Ave) As you proceed north on Collins, the condos and apartment building grow in grandeur and embellishment until you enter an area nicknamed Millionaire's Row. The most fantastic jewel in this glittering crown is the Fontainebleau hotel. You may remember the old lobby from the final scene from *Scarface,* where Al Pacino snorts a small hill of cocaine and guns down a small army of Colombians. This iconic 1954 leviathan is a brainchild of the great Miami Beach architect Morris Lapidus and has undergone many renovations; in some ways, it is utterly different from its original form, but it retains that early glamour. Note the spectacular trompe l'oeil mural on the southern exterior, designed by Richard Haas and painted over an eight-week period by Edwin Abreu.

Eden Roc Renaissance
Miami Beach   HISTORIC BUILDING

(Map p70; www.edenrocmiami.com; 4525 Collins Ave) The Eden Roc Resort was the second groundbreaking resort from Morris Lapidus, and it's a fine example of the architecture known as MiMo (Miami Modern). It was the hangout for the 1960s Rat Pack – Sammy Davis Jr, Dean Martin, Frank Sinatra and crew. Extensive renovation has eclipsed some of Lapidus' style; the Ocean Tower, for example, is a completely new addition. But with that said, the building is still an iconic piece of Miami Beach architecture, and an exemplar of the brash beauty of Millionaire's Row.

Boardwalk   BEACH

(Map p70; 21st St to 46th St) What's trendy in beachwear this season? Seventeenth-century Polish gabardine coats, apparently. There are plenty of skimpily dressed hotties on the Mid-Beach boardwalk, but there are

THE FULL MOON DRUM CIRCLE

If there's a full moon, check out the beach between 79th and 85th street – a big, boisterous **drum circle** is held here that doubles as a full-moon party. The beat tends to start between 8:30pm and 9:30pm, and can run well into the wee hours. That said, drinking (and the consumption of other substances) is technically illegal on the beach, and police have broken up the event before. Still, it tends to be a pretty fun party that shouldn't be missed if you're in the area and want to see an incredible moonset. Check www.miamidrums.com for more information.

also Orthodox Jews going about their business in the midst of gay joggers, strolling tourists and sunbathers. Nearby are numerous condo buildings occupied by middle-class Latinos and Jews, who walk their dogs and play with their kids here, giving the entire place a laid-back, real-world vibe that contrasts with the nonstop glamour of South Beach.

Arthur Godfrey Road (41st Street)   ROAD

(Map p70; 41st St) It's no *shtetl*, but Arthur Godfrey Rd is a popular thoroughfare for the Jewish population of Miami Beach, and possibly the best place in Florida to enjoy a good reuben sandwich (and the only place outside Tel Aviv with kosher sushi houses). Just as Jews have shaped Miami Beach, so has the beach shaped its Jews: you can eat lox *y arroz con moros* (salmon with rice and beans) and while the Orthodox men don *yarmulkes* and the women wear head-scarves, they've all got nice tans and drive flashy SUVs.

Normandy Isle & Ocean Terrace   NEIGHBORHOOD

(Map p70; 71st St west of Collins Ave) A few years ago Normandy Isle was dubbed Little Argentina, and it's still one of the best places outside Mendoza to people-watch with a *cortada* (Argentine espresso) before digging into traditional pasta and steak dishes. But today the Argentines compete with their neighbors the Uruguayans, their rivals the Brazilians, and even a big crop of Colombians, for first place in the Normandy Isle ethnic-enclave stakes. Not that there's tension; this is as prosperous and pleasant as

Miami gets. On Saturday mornings the small village green hosts a lovely farmers' market. Just across Collins Ave is Ocean Tce, which evokes an old-Miami main street (note the colorfully tiled facade of Walgreens) with oceanfront cafes, MiMo apartment buildings and a strong Argentine flavor.

Haulover Beach Park   PARK

(www.miamidade.gov/parks/parks/haulover_park.asp; 10800 Collins Ave; per car $4; ☼sunrise-sunset) Where are all those tanned men in gold chains and Speedos going? That would be the clothing-optional beach in this 40-acre park hidden from condos, highway and prying eyes by vegetation. There's more to do here than get in the buff, though; most of the beach is 'normal' (there's even a dog park) and is one of the nicer spots for sand in the area (also note the colorful deco-ish shower 'cones'). The park is located on Collins Ave about 4.5 miles north of 71st St.

Oleta River State Park   PARK

(www.floridastateparks.org/oletariver; 3400 NE 163rd St; per person $2, per car $6; ☼8am-sunset) Tequesta people were boating the Oleta River estuary as early as 500 BC, so you're just following in a long tradition if you canoe or kayak in this park. At almost 1000 acres, this is the largest urban park in the state and one of the best places in Miami to escape the maddening throng. Boat out to the local mangrove island, watch the eagles fly by, or just chill on the pretension-free beach. On-site **Blue Moon Outdoor Center** (☎305-957-3040; www.bluemoonmiami.com) offers single kayaks ($18 per 1½ hours, $25 per three hours), tandem kayaks ($25.50 per 1½ hours, $40 per three hours) and bike rental ($18 per 1½ hours, $25 per three hours). The park is off 163rd St NE/FL-826 in Sunny Isles, about 8 miles north of North Miami Beach.

Arch Creek Park   PARK

(www.miamidade.gov/parks/parks/arch_creek.asp; 1855 NE 135 St; ☼9am-5pm Wed-Sun) This compact-and-cute park, located near Oleta River, encompasses a cozy habitat of tropical hardwood species that surrounds a pretty, natural limestone bridge. Naturalists can lead you on kid-friendly ecotours of the area, which includes a lovely butterfly garden, or visitors can peruse a small but well-stocked museum of Native American and pioneer artifacts. Call ahead to book into ghost tours (also fun for the kids), held on Wednesdays and Saturdays. The park is just off North

Biscayne Blvd, 7 miles north of the Design District.

DOWNTOWN MIAMI

Downtown Miami is the city's international financial and banking center, but also boasts new condos and high-rise luxury hotels in the area known as Brickell (or 'the Brick'), which includes the very posh Brickell Key. The lazy, gritty Miami River divides Downtown into north and south. Many of Miami's homeless gather here at night (and sometimes by day).

TOP CHOICE **Adrienne Arsht Center for the Performing Arts** CULTURAL BUILDING
(Map p74; www.arshtcenter.com; 1300 N Biscayne Blvd) The largest performing-arts center in Florida (and second largest, by area, in the USA) is Miami's beautiful, beloved baby. It is also a major component of Downtown's urban equivalent of a facelift and several regimens of Botox. Designed by Cesar Pelli (the man who brought you Kuala Lumpur's Petronas Towers), the center has two main components: the Ziff Ballet Opera House and Knight Concert Hall, which span both sides of Biscayne Blvd. The venues are connected by a thin, elegant pedestrian bridge, while inside the theaters there's a sense of ocean and land sculpted by wind; the rounded balconies rise up in spirals that resemble a sliced-open seashell. If you have the chance, catch a show here (see p128); the interior alone is easily a highlight of any Miami trip.

Bayfront Park PARK
(Map p74; www.bayfrontparkmiami.com; 301 N Biscayne Blvd) Few American parks can claim to front such a lovely stretch of turquoise (Biscayne Bay), but Miamians are lucky like that. Lots of office workers catch quick naps under the palms at a little beach that does you the favor of setting out 'sit and chill' chairs. Notable park features are two performance venues: the Klipsch Amphitheater, which boasts excellent views over Biscayne Bay, is a good spot for live-music shows, while the smaller 200-seat (lawn seating can accommodate 800 more) Tina Hills Pavilion hosts free springtime performances. Look north for the JFK Torch of Friendship, and a fountain recognizing the accomplishments of longtime US congressman Claude Pepper. There's a huge variety of activities here, including yoga classes, trapeze classes and, we hear, flying-trapeze yoga classes (seriously); check out the Activities section of this chapter for details (p98).

Sculptures

Noted artist and landscape architect Isamu Noguchi redesigned much of Bayfront Park in the 1980s and dotted the grounds with three sculptures. In the southwest corner is the Challenger Memorial, a monument designed for the astronauts killed in the 1986 space-shuttle explosion built to resemble both the twisting helix of a human DNA chain and the shuttle itself. The Light Tower is a 40ft, somewhat abstract allusion to Japanese lanterns and moonlight over Miami. Our favorite is the Mantra Slide, a twisting spiral of marble that doubles as a playground piece for the kids.

American Airlines Arena CULTURAL BUILDING
(Map p74; www.aaarena.com; 601 N Biscayne Blvd) Just north of the park, and resembling a massive spaceship that perpetually hovers at the edge of Biscayne Bay, this arena has been the home of the Miami Heat basketball team since 2000. The Waterfront Theater, Florida's largest, is housed inside; throughout the year it hosts concerts, Broadway

DOWNTOWN'S INTERNATIONAL BAZAARS

Downtown Miami has a reputation for being a bit rough around the edges. We think this is a bit undeserved; the area is dodgy at night but safe by day, if a little down-at-heel. Part of this ratty atmosphere is due to large amounts of cheap, knock-off electronics, fashion and jewelry shops that cluster in half-abandoned malls and shopping arcades. These stores are almost all run by immigrants, from West Africa, East Asia, South America and the Middle East (did we cover all the directions?). While we doubt you need cheap consumer goods of dubious origin, we do think it's fun to check out one of these markets, like the 777 International Mall (145 E Flagler St). This may be as close as you'll get to the messy, shouting, sweaty and exciting bazaars of the developing world, where folks yell at you to seal a deal and haggling is often an option. It's not as pretty as shopping in Miami Beach or the Design District, but it's a fascinating slice of this city's life.

Downtown Miami

400 m
0.2 miles

MacArthur Causeway

A1A

Intracoastal Waterway

Port Blvd

Lummus Island

Herald Plaza

Omni

Adrienne Arsht Center for the Performing Arts

Bicentennial Park

Bicentennial Park

Bayside Marketplace

Marina

14

38

8

Biscayne Blvd

31 34

Park West

1

7

Bayfront Park

School Board

NE 14th St
NE 13th St
NE 12th St

11th St

NE 2nd Ave

Freedom Tower

5

Biscayne Blvd

College/Bayside

1st St

NE 1st St

N Miami Ave

36

35

NE 10th St
NE 9th St
NE 8th St
NE 7th St
NE 6th St
NE 5th St

College North

SE 1st Ave

NE 4th St
NE 3rd St
NE 2nd St

12

30

37

3

NW 1st Ave

Overtown

NW 1st Ave

NW 1st Ct

NW 2nd Ave

NW 1st Ave

9

Arena/State Plaza

Metromover

Government Center

NW 3rd St
NW 2nd St

Government Center

Greyhound Station (Downtown)

95th St

NW 3rd Ct

Gibson Park

NW 12th St

NW 4th Ave

NW 10th St
Reeves Park

NW 9th St

NW 8th St

NW 5th Ave
NW 6th St

NW 5th St

Lummus Park

SW N River Dr

20

North-South Expwy

NW 7th St

24

Miami River

SW S River Dr

NW 3rd St
NW 2nd St

Culmer

NW 7th Ave

NW 10th St

NW 7th St
NW 6th Ave

NW 7th St

SW 6th Ave

NW 7th St

Biscayne Blvd

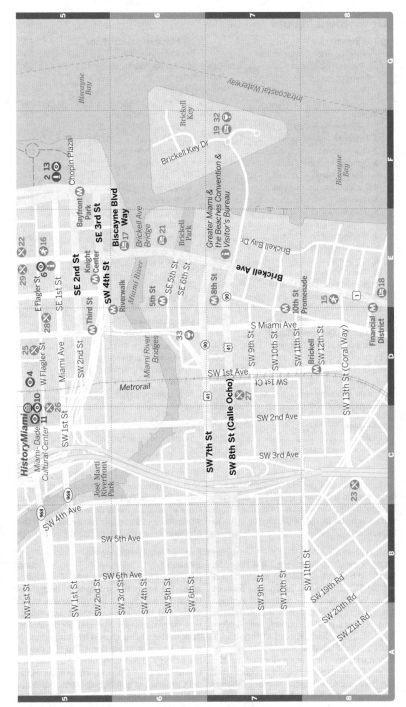

Biscayne Bay

Intracoastal Waterway

Brickell Key

19 32

Brickell Key Dr

Chopin Plaza

2 13

Biscayne Bay

Greater Miami & the Beaches Convention & Visitor's Bureau

Bayfront Park

SE 3rd St

Biscayne Blvd

17 Way

Brickell Ave Bridge

Knight Center

SE 2nd St

SE 4th St

SE 1st St

21

Brickell Park

Brickell Ave Bridge

E Flagler St

29 22

6 i

16

28

Third St

SW 4th St

Riverwalk

Miami River

5th St

SE 5th St

SE 6th St

8th St

Brickell Ave

Brickell Bay Dr

10th St Promenade

15

Financial District

18

HistoryMiami

Miami-Dade Cultural Center

4

25

10

26

W Flagler St

Miami Ave

SW 2nd St

SW 1st St

Metrorail

Miami River Bridges

33

S Miami Ave

SW 9th St

SW 10th St

SW 11th St

Brickell

SW 12th St

SW 13th St (Coral Way)

SW 1st Ave

SW 1st Ct

SW 1st St

José Martí Riverfront Park

SW 7th St

SW 8th St (Calle Ocho)

27

SW 2nd Ave

SW 3rd Ave

23

NW 1st St

SW 1st St

SW 2nd St

SW 3rd St

SW 4th St

SW 5th St

SW 6th St

SW 4th Ave

SW 5th Ave

SW 6th Ave

SW 9th St

SW 10th St

SW 11th St

SW 19th Rd

SW 20th Rd

SW 21st Rd

Downtown Miami

performances and the like. A giant airplane is painted on top of the arena; you may spot it (it looks like the shadow of a plane from afar) when you fly out of the city, or if you're Superman.

HistoryMiami   MUSEUM
(Map p74; www.historymiami.org; 101 W Flagler St; adult/child 6-12 yr/senior $8/5/7, combined ticket to MAM $10; ⊙10am-5pm Tue-Fri, noon-5pm Sat & Sun) South Florida – a land of escaped slaves, guerilla Native Americans, gangsters, land grabbers, pirates, tourists, drug dealers and alligators – has a special history, and it takes a special kind of museum to capture that narrative. This place, located in the Miami-Dade Cultural Center, does just that, weaving together the stories of the region's successive waves of population, from

Native Americans to Nicaraguans. It's interesting for kids and manages to explain the story of Miami's many demographic groups while still feeling tightly focused. Get off the Metromover at the Government Center stop.

Brickell Avenue Bridge &
Brickell Key   ISLAND
(Map p74; Brickell Ave) Crossing the Miami River, the lovely Brickell Avenue Bridge between SE 4th St and SE 5th St was made wider and higher several years ago, which was convenient for the speedboat-driving drug runners being chased by Drug Enforcement Administration agents on the day of the bridge's grand reopening! Note the 17ft bronze statue by Cuban-born sculptor Manuel Carbonell of a Tequesta warrior and his family, which sits atop the towering Pillar

of History column. Walking here is the best way to get a sense of the sculptures and will allow you to avoid one of the most confusing traffic patterns in Miami. Brickell Key looks more like a floating porcupine with glass towers for quills than an island. To live the life of Miami glitterati, come here, pretend you belong, and head into a patrician hangout like the Mandarin Oriental Hotel Miami, where the lobby and intimate lounges afford sweeping views of Biscayne Bay.

Metromover   TRAIN
(Map p74; www.miamidade.gov/transit/mover.asp) This elevated, electric monorail is hardly big enough to serve the mass-transit needs of the city, and has become something of a tourist attraction. Whatever its virtues as a commuting tool, the Metromover is a really great (and free!) way to see central Miami from a height (which helps, given the skyscraper-canyon nature of Downtown). Because it's gratis, Metromover has a reputation as a hangout for the homeless, but at the time of research a fair few folks were using it to commute as well, a number the media reported was climbing due to the price of gas.

Miami River   RIVER
(Map p74) For a taste of a seedy Old Florida that reeks of Humphrey Bogart in shirtsleeves and a fedora, come to the lazy, sultry and still kinda spicy Miami River. Much of the shore feels abandoned, and is lined with makeshift warehouses, where you-can-only-imagine-what is loaded and unloaded onto small tugboats bound for you-can-only-imagine-where. Fisherfolk float in with their daily catch, fancy yachts 'slumming it' dock at restaurants, nonconformists hang out on their houseboats and all in all, it just seems like a matter of time before the music from *Buena Vista Social Club* starts drifting over the scene.

Gusman Center for the
Performing Arts   CULTURAL BUILDING
(Map p74; www.gusmancenter.org; 174 E Flagler St) The Arsht Center is modernly pretty, but the Olympia Theater at the Gusman Center for the Performing Arts is vintage-classic beautiful. You know how the kids at Hogwarts can see the sky through their dining-hall roof? Well the Olympia re-creates the whole effect sans Dumbledore, using 246 twinkling stars and clouds cast over an indigo-deep, sensual shade of a ceiling, frosted with classical Greek sculpture and Vienna Opera House–style embellishment. The theater

first opened in 1925; today the lobby serves as the Downtown Miami Welcome Center (p133), doling out helpful visitor information and organizing tours of the historic district; at night you can still catch theater and music performances (p128).

Miami Art Museum   MUSEUM
(Map p74; MAM; www.miamiartmuseum.org; 101 W Flagler St; adult/child under 12 yr & students/senior $8/free/4, 2nd Sat of month free, combined ticket to HistoryMiami $10; ⊙10am-5pm Tue-Fri, noon-5pm Sat & Sun) Located within the Miami-Dade Cultural Center, this museum is ensconced in spectacular Philip Johnson–designed digs. Without having a permanent collection, its fine rotating exhibits concentrate on post-WWII international art. MAM is scheduled to move a new waterfront location at Bicentennial Park in 2013; check the website for details on the impressive design schematics for the new digs. The museum is open late (noon to 9pm) on the third Thursday of the month.

Miami-Dade Public Library   LIBRARY
(Map p74; www.mdpls.org; 101 W Flagler St; ⊙9am-6pm Mon-Wed & Fri, 9am-9pm Thu, 1-5pm Sun) The main branch of the Miami-Dade library system is a lovely escape from Downtown's bustle. To learn more about Florida (especially

---

RESURRECTING THE LYRIC

Hallowed names Duke Ellington and Ella Fitzgerald once walked across the stage of the **Lyric Theater** (Map p74; 819 NW 2nd Ave), a major stop on the 'Chitlin' Circuit' – the black live-entertainment trail of preintegration USA. But as years passed both the theater and the neighborhood it served, Overtown, fell into disuse. Then the **Black Archives History & Research Center of South Florida** (p133) kicked in $1.5 million for renovations and overhauled everything. The phoenix reopened its doors in 1999 to general appreciation, but at the time of research the theater's doors were closed due to accusations of fraud and financial mismanagement against contractors renovating the building. We expect this situation to be cleared by the time you read this, when hopefully the Lyric will be hosting performances that match the glamour of its heyday.

DON'T MISS

LITTLE HAITI

If you haven't been to Port-au-Prince, then Little Haiti (La Petite Haïti), one of the most evocative neighborhoods in Miami, is the next best thing. Young men in tank tops listen to Francophone rap, while broad-necked women wearing bright wraps gossip in front of the *botanicas* – which, by the way, are not selling plants. A *botanica* here is a *vodou* shop. The neighborhood is one of Miami's poorest and it's not advisable to walk around here alone after dark, but by day or if visiting the Little Haiti Cultural Center (p81) you'll be fine.

Botanicas are perhaps the most 'foreign' sight in Little Haiti. Storefronts promise to help in matters of love, work and sometimes 'immigration services,' but trust us, there are no marriage counselors or INS guys in here. As you enter you'll probably get a funny look, but be courteous, curious and respectful and you should be welcomed. Before you browse, forget stereotypes about pins and dolls. Like many traditional religions, *vodou* recognizes supernatural forces in everyday objects, and powers that are both distinct from and part of one overarching deity. Ergo, you'll see shrines to Jesus next to altars to traditional *vodou* deities. Notice the large statues of what look like people; these actually represent *loa* (pronounced lwa), intermediary spirits that form a pantheon below God in the *vodou* religious hierarchy. Drop a coin into a *loa* offering bowl before you leave, especially to Papa Legba, spirit of crossroads and, by our reckoning, travelers. Two good *botanicas* are **Vierge Miracle & St Phillipe** (Map p80; 5910 NE 2nd Ave) and **3×3 Santa Barbara Botanica** (Map p80; 5700 NE 2nd Ave).

For a more cerebral taste of Haitian culture, peruse the shelves at **Libreri Mapou** (Map p80; www.librerimapou.com; 5919 NE 2nd Ave), bursting with thousands of titles (including periodicals) in English, French and Creole, as well as crafts and recorded music.

South Florida), take a browse through the extensive Florida Department, or ask to see the Romer Collection, an archive of some 17,500 photos and prints that chronicle the history of the city from its early years to the 1950s.

Freedom Tower HISTORIC BUILDING
(Map p74; 600 Biscayne Blvd) Designed by the New York architectural firm of Shultz & Weaver in 1925, this tower is one of two surviving towers modeled after the Giralda bell tower in Spain's Cathedral of Seville (the second is at the Biltmore Hotel in Coral Gables). The 'Ellis Island of the South,' it served as an immigration processing center for almost half a million Cuban refugees in the 1960s. Placed on the National Register of Historic Places in 1979, it was also home to the *Miami Daily News* for 32 years.

Old US Post Office HISTORIC BUILDING
(Map p74; 100 NE 1st Ave; ⊗9am-5pm Mon-Fri) Constructed in 1912, this post office and county courthouse served as the first federal building in Miami. The building, which features a low-pitched roof, elaborate doors and carved entryways, was purchased in 1937 to serve as the country's first savings and loan (funny, considering S&Ls helped build Miami in the

1980s). Check out Denman Fink's 1940 mural *Law Guides Florida Progress* in the main courtroom on the 2nd floor.

Cisneros Fontanal Arts Foundation MUSEUM
(Map p74; CIFO; ✆305-455-3380; www.cifo.org; 1018 N Miami Ave; ⊗10am-4pm Thu-Sun) The arts foundation is one of the best spots in Miami to catch the work of contemporary Latin American artists, and has an impressive showroom to boot. Even the exterior blends postindustrial rawness with a lurking, natural ambience, offset by the extensive use of Bisazza tiles to create an overarching tropical motif. Similar to the Arsht Center, CIFO was built near the rattier edge of Downtown with the intention of revitalizing this semiblighted area with fresh arts spaces. The opening hours only apply during exhibition showings, although informal tours can be arranged if you call ahead.

Dade County Courthouse HISTORIC BUILDING
(Map p74; 73 W Flagler St) If you end up on trial here, at least you'll get a free tour of one of the most imposing courthouses in the USA. When Miami outgrew its first courthouse it moved legal proceedings to this neoclassical icon, built between 1925 and 1929 for $4 million. It's a very...appropriate building:

if structures were people, the courthouse would definitely be a judge. Some trivia: back in the day, the top nine floors served as a 'secure' prison, from which more than 70 prisoners escaped.

WYNWOOD, DESIGN DISTRICT & LITTLE HAITI

Now rebranded as 'Midtown', Wynwood and the Design District are Miami's official arts neighborhoods, plus the focal points of new art, food and nightlife in Greater Miami. This area still abuts some of the city's poorer 'hoods, and if you come here via city streets instead of the highway you'll see the rough edges that once characterized the vicinity. The Midtown mall is the area's natural center of gravity. Wynwood is the place for dedicated art galleries, while the small collection of posh retail outlets in the Design District are filled with things as beautiful as any canvas. Between the Italian-designed chairs, Russian Romanov-era cabinets and Dale Chihuly–esque chandeliers, the Design District tends to be expensive (we're talking thousands for a single item), although there are some relative bargains to be found if you look.

Unlike Wynwood, the Design District is pretty compact and walkable. Little Haiti is not to be missed and sits above the Design District. In between the two lies the leafy, lovely residential neighborhood of Buena Vista, where restaurants, bars, gay hot spots and gentrification are rapidly spreading.

Rubell Family Art Collection MUSEUM
(Map p80; www.rfc.museum; 95 NW 29th St, Wynwood; adult/student & under 18yr $10/5; ☺10am-6pm Wed-Sat Dec-Aug) The Rubell family – specifically, the niece and nephew of the late Steve, better known as Ian Schrager's Studio 54 partner – operates some top-end hotels in Miami Beach, but they've also amassed an impressive contemporary art collection that spans the last 30 years. The most admirable quality of this collection is its commitment to not just displaying one or two of its artists' pieces; the museum's aim is to showcase a contributor's entire career.

FINDING ART IN WYNWOOD

There is a plethora of art galleries in Wynwood, with new spaces opening on what sometimes feels like a weekly basis. The stomping grounds of 'Wypsters' (Wynwood hipsters, those who enjoy, staff and provide content for the neighborhood's galleries) shift month by month as 'guerilla' galleries, new murals, graffiti, cafes, restaurants and studio spaces spread across Midtown. In general, art galleries can be found in a square bound by NW 20th and NW 37th streets to the south and north, and N Miami Ave and NW 3rd Ave to the east and west. It's difficult for us to recommend one specific set of galleries given the diversity of what's on offer, but the following are some of our favorites.

» **Artopia** (Map p80; ☑305-374-8882; 1753 NE 2nd Ave) Proves the extents for Wynwood we mention above are flexible – Artopia is physically in Overtown, but culturally part of the gallery circuit. This was the old studio space of the late, renowned self-taught artist Purvis Young, who grew up near the studio. His folk-arty works and similar pieces are often displayed, as are pieces by up-and-coming artists local or otherwise. Call for opening hours.

» **PanAmerican Art Projects** (Map p80; ☑305-573-2400; www.panamericanart.com; 2450 NW 2nd Ave; ☺9:30am-5:30pm Tue-Fri, noon-5:30pm Sat) Despite the name, PanAmerican also showcases work from European and Chinese artists. But much of what is on display comes from fine artists representing Latin America, the Caribbean and the USA.

» **Art Modern Gallery** (Map p80; www.artmoderngallery.com; 175 NW 23rd St; ☺noon-4:30pm Mon-Sat) Curators here unsurprisingly focus on modern, contemporary and pop art drawn from both domestic and international talent.

» **Curator's Voice Art Projects** (Map p80; www.curatorsvoiceartprojects.com; 2509 NW 2nd Ave; ☺9:30am-5:30pm Mon-Fri, from noon Sat) Another large, elegant showing space that prides itself on displaying some of the most avant-garde work in Wynwood.

There are literally dozens of other galleries to check out; a nice way of seeing them and getting some drinking is attending the famous **Wynwood Art Walks** (see p125). Check out websites like www.beachedmiami.com and www.miamiartguide.com for more information.

Wynwood, Design District & Little Haiti

0 — 400 m
0 — 0.2 miles

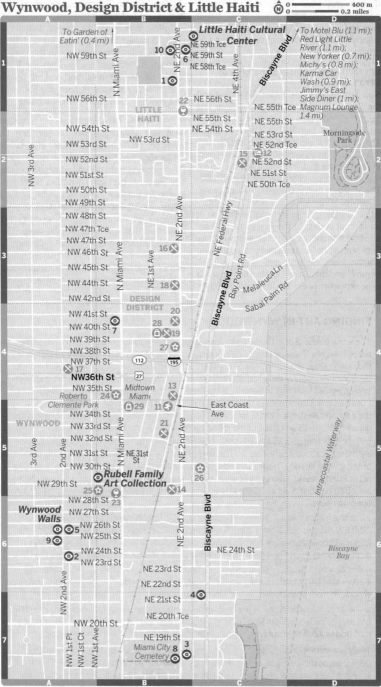

MIAMI

To Garden of
Eatin' (0.4 mi)
NW 59th St

10

Little Haiti Cultural
Center

6
NE 59th Tce
NE 59th St
NE 58th Tce

1

NW 56th St

NE 56th St

22

NE 55th St
NE 54th St

Biscayne Blvd

To Motel Blu (1.1 mi);
Red Light Little
River (1.1 mi);
New Yorker (0.7 mi);
Michy's (0.8 mi);
Karma Car
Wash (0.9 mi);
Jimmy's East
Side Diner (1 mi);
Magnum Lounge
1.4 mi)

LITTLE
HAITI

NW 54th St

NW 53rd St

NW 53rd St

NW 52nd St

NW 51st St

NW 50th St

NW 49th St

NW 48th St

NW 47th Tce

NW 47th St

NW 46th St

NW 45th St

NW 44th St

NW 42nd St

NW 41st St

NW 40th St

NW 39th St

NW 38th St

NW 37th St

17

NE 55th Tce
NE 55th St

NE 53rd St
NE 52nd Tce

15   12
NE 52nd St
NE 51st St
NE 50th Tce

Morningside
Park

NE 2nd Ave

NE 1st Ave

16

18

DESIGN
DISTRICT

20

28
19

27

N Miami Ave

NE Federal Hwy

Biscayne Blvd

Bay Point Rd

Melaleuca Ln

Sabal Palm Rd

7

112   195

27

NW36th St

NW 35th St

Roberto   24
Clemente Park

WYNWOOD

NW 34th St

NW 33rd St

NW 32nd St

NW 31st St

NW 30th St

NW 29th St

NW 28th St

NW 27th St

NW 26th St

NW 25th St

NW 24th St

NW 23rd St

Midtown
Miami

13

29   11

East Coast
Ave

21

NW 31st
St

NE 2nd Ave

26

14

25
23

Wynwood
Walls

5

9

2

3rd Ave

2nd Ave

N Miami Ave

NE 31st St

Rubell Family
Art Collection

NE 2nd Ave

Biscayne Blvd

NE 24th St

Intracoastal Waterway

Biscayne
Bay

NE 23rd St

NE 22nd St

NE 21st St   4

NE 20th Tce

NW 20th St

NE 19th St

Miami City
Cemetery

8   3

6

NW 1st Pl
NW 1st Ct
NW 1st Ave

NW 2nd Ave

Wynwood, Design District & Little Haiti

Little Haiti Cultural Center GALLERY
(Map p80; www.miamigov.com/lhculturalcenter; 212 NE 59th Tce; ⊙9am-5pm, plus evenings during events) Miami has the largest community of Ayisyens (Haitians) in the world outside Haiti, and this is the place to learn about their story. The cultural center is a study in playful island designs and motifs that houses a small but vibrant art gallery, crafts center and activities space – dance classes, drama productions and similar events are held here year-round. The best time to visit is for the **Big Night in Little Haiti** (www.bignightlittlehaiti.com), a street party held on the third Friday of every month from 6pm to 10pm. The celebration is rife with music, mouth-watering Caribbean food and beer, and is one of the safest, easiest ways of accessing the culture of Haiti outside of that island.

Wynwood Walls PUBLIC ART
(Map p80; www.thewynwoodwalls.com; NW 2nd Ave btwn 25th & 26th St; ⊙noon-8pm Wed-Sat) Not a gallery per se, Wynwood Walls is a collection of murals and paintings laid out over an open courtyard in the heart of Wynwood. What's on offer tends to change with the coming and going of major arts events like Art Basel (one of the US's major annual art

shows); when we visited the centerpiece was a fantastic portrait of Aung San Suu Kyi by artist Shepard Fairey.

Miami City Cemetery CEMETERY
(Map p80; 1800 NE 2nd Ave; ⊙7am-3:30pm Mon-Fri, 8am-4:30pm Sat & Sun) This quiet graveyard, the final resting place of some of Miami-Dade's most important citizens, is a sort of narrative of the history of the Magic City cast in bone, dirt and stone. The dichotomy of the past and modernity gets a nice visual representation in the form of looming condos shadowing the last abode of the Magic City's late, great ones. More than 9000 graves are divided into separate white, black and Jewish sections. Buried here are mayors, veterans (including about 90 Confederate soldiers) and the godmother of South Florida, Julia Tuttle, who purchased the first orange groves that attracted settlers to the area.

Living Room PUBLIC ART
(Map p80; cnr NW 40th St & N Miami Ave) Just to remind you that you're entering the Design District is a big, honking, public art installation of, yep, a living room – just the sort of thing you're supposed to shop for while you're here. Actually this Living Room, by

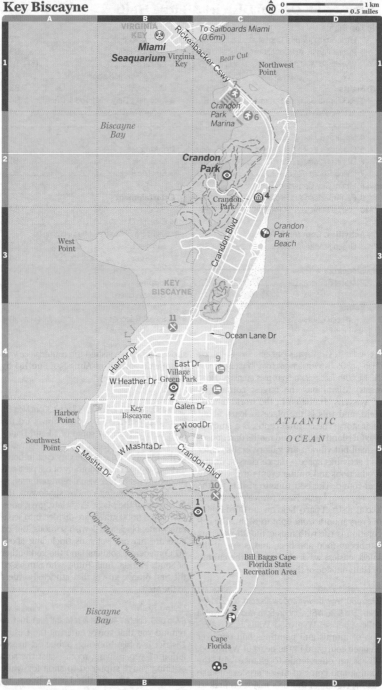

N 0 _____ 1 km
0 _____ 0.5 miles

MIAMI

VIRGINIA KEY

Miami Seaquarium

Virginia Key

Rickenbacker Cswy

To Sailboards Miami (0.6mi)

Bear Cut

Northwest Point

Biscayne Bay

Crandon Park Marina

Crandon Park

Crandon Park

Crandon Park Beach

West Point

KEY BISCAYNE

Crandon Blvd

Ocean Lane Dr

Harbor Dr

East Dr
Village Green Park

W Heather Dr

Galen Dr

Key Biscayne

E Wood Dr

Harbor Point

Southwest Point

S Mashta Dr

W Mashta Dr

Crandon Blvd

ATLANTIC OCEAN

Cape Florida Channel

Bill Baggs Cape Florida State Recreation Area

Biscayne Bay

Cape Florida

Argentine husband-and-wife team Roberto Behar and Rosario Marquardt, is an 'urban intervention' meant to be a criticism of the disappearance of public space, but we think it serves as a nice metaphor for the Design District as a whole: a contemporary interior plopped into the middle of urban decay.

Bacardi Building   ARCHITECTURE
(Map p80; 2100 Biscayne Blvd; admission free; ⊙9am-3:30pm or 4pm Mon-Fri) You don't need to down 151 to appreciate the striking Miami headquarters of the world's largest family-owned spirits company, Bacardi. The main event is a beautifully decorated tower that looks like the mosaic pattern of a tropical bathhouse on steroids. There used to be a small art gallery and museum inside dedicated to the famously anti-Castro Bacardis (think about what 'Cuba Libre' actually means the next time you order one) but it was indefinitely closed at time of research.

KEY BISCAYNE
The scenic drive along the Rickenbacker Causeway leads first to small Virginia Key, then over to Key Biscayne, an island that's just 7 miles long with unrivalled views of the Miami skyline. As you drive over the causeway, note the small public beaches, picnic areas and fishing spots arranged around on its margins. The road turns into Cranda Blvd, the key's only real main road, which runs to the Cape Florida Lighthouse at the island's southernmost tip.

Miami Seaquarium   AQUARIUM
(Map p82; www.miamiseaquarium.com; 4400 Rickenbacker Causeway; adult/child $39/30, parking $8; ⊙9:30am-6pm) This 38-acre marine-life park excels in preserving, protecting and educating about aquatic creatures, and was one of the country's first places dedicated to sea life. There are dozens of shows and exhibits, including a tropical reef; the Shark Channel, with feeding presentations; and Discovery Bay, a natural mangrove habitat that serves as a refuge for rehabilitating rescued sea turtles. Check out the Pacific white-sided dolphins or West Indian manatees being nursed back to health; some are released. Frequent shows put gorgeous animals on display, including a massive killer whale, some precious dolphins and sea lions. The Seaquarium's newly opened Dolphin Harbor is an especially fun venue for watching marine mammals play and show off; it also offers swim-with-the-cetacean fun via its Encounter (adult/child five to nine years $139/99), Odyssey ($199) and, for total dolphin-lovers only, Trainer for a Day ($495). Note that children under five cannot participate in the Encounter, people under 5ft 2in cannot participate in the Odyssey and children under three cannot enter the observation area. Read about the pros and cons of swimming with dolphins (see p164) before committing to these programs. Last entry is at 4:30pm.

Crandon Park   PARK
(Map p82; www.miamidade.gov/parks/parks/crandon_beach.asp; 6747 Crandon Blvd; per car $5; ⊙sunrise-sunset) This 1200-acre park boasts Crandon Park Beach, a glorious but crowded beach that stretches for 3 miles. Much of the park consists of a dense coastal hammock (hardwood forest) and mangrove swamps. Pretty cabanas at the south end of the park can be rented by the day for $37.45. The 2-mile-long beach here is clean, uncluttered with tourists, faces a lovely sweep of teal goodness and is regularly named one of the best beaches in the USA.

Marjory Stoneman Douglas Biscayne Nature Center
(Map p82; www.biscaynenaturecenter.org; Crandon Park, 6767 Crandon Blvd; admission free; ⊙10am-4pm) Marjory Stoneman Douglas was a beloved environmental crusader (see p144)

the simple things that make life worth living, and sometimes their simplicity is even ore elegant in the face of life's complexity. To wit: come to Jimbo's (Map p82; www. jimbosplace.com; Duck Lake Rd; ☺sunrise-sunset) in Virginia Key. In a city of unfettered development, this bar...no, shrimp shack...no, smoked-fish house...no, 24-hour trailer park bonfire...well, whatever. A series of dilapidated river shacks and a boccie court has been, for decades, its own version of everything that once was right in Florida. Of course, even here the vibe is a little artificial; all those rotting fish houses were set pieces for the 1980 horror movie *Island Claws*. Other flicks filmed here include *Ace Ventura: Pet Detective*, *True Lies* and the cinematic masterpiece, *Porky's 2*. But today the shacks have been claimed as the set pieces of the Jimbo show. Oh – the last time we were here, we went swimming off the dock and a manatee popped up. A manatee! To find Jimbo's, go to the end of Arthur Lamb Jr Rd.

and a worthy namesake of this child-friendly nature center. The structure is a perfect introduction and exploration of the continental USA's own subtropical ecosystem: South Florida. There are weekend hikes and nature lessons that let kids wade into the water with nets and try to catch sea horses, sponges and other marine life (released after a short lesson); check the website for a full breakdown of the many activities on offer, most of which cost $12 per person.

Bill Baggs Cape Florida State Park PARK
(Map p82; www.floridastateparks.org/capeflorida; 1200 S Crandon Blvd; per car $8, pedestrian $2; ☺8am-sunset) If you don't make it to the Florida Keys, come to this park for a taste of their unique island ecosystems. The 494-acre space is a tangled clot of tropical fauna and dark mangroves – look for the 'snorkel' roots that provide air for half-submerged mangrove trees – all interconnected by sandy trails and wooden boardwalks,

and surrounded by miles of pale ocean. A concession shack rents kayaks, bikes, in-line skates, beach chairs and umbrellas.

Cape Florida Lighthouse
At the state recreation area's southernmost tip, the 1845 brick lighthouse is the oldest structure in Florida (it replaced another lighthouse that was severely damaged in 1836 by during the Second Seminole War). Free tours run at 10am and 1pm Monday to Thursday.

FREE **Biscayne Community Center & Village Green Park** PARK
(Map p82; ☎305-365-8900; www.keybiscayne. fl.gov/pr; Village Green Way, off Crandon Blvd; ☺Community Center 6am-10pm Mon-Fri, 8am-8pm Sat & Sun; ♿) An unmissable park for kids: there's a swimming pool, jungle gyms, an activity room with a playset out of a child's happiest fantasies and an

Little Havana

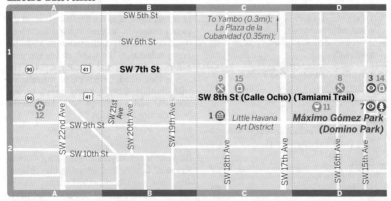

African baobab tree that's over a century old and teeming with tropical birdlife. Did we mention it's free?

Stiltsville   HISTORIC BUILDINGS
(Map p82; www.stiltsville.org) This collection of seven houses that stand on pilings out in Biscayne Bay has been around since the early '30s. You can view them, way out in the distance, from the southern shore of the Bill Baggs park, or take a boat tour (☎305-379-5119; www.islandqueencruises.com /stiltsville.htm; tours $49) out there with the illustrious historian Dr Paul George. In 2003, the nonprofit Stiltsville Trust was set up by the National Parks Service to rehabilitate the buildings into as-yet-unknown facilities; proposals include a National Parks Service visitor center, artist-in-residence colony or community center. Not much work seems to have progressed towards this idea, but if you'd like more information, check www .stiltsvilletrust.org.

LITTLE HAVANA

Little Havana's main thoroughfare, Calle Ocho (SW 8th St), doesn't just cut through the heart of the neighborhood; it is the heart of the neighborhood. In a lot of ways, this is every immigrant enclave in the USA – full of restaurants, mom-and-pop convenience shops and phonecard kiosks. Admittedly, the Cubaness of Little Havana is slightly exaggerated for visitors, and many of the Latin immigrants here are actually from Central America. With that said, this is an atmospheric place with a soul that's rooted outside the USA. Be on the lookout for the Cuban Walk of Fame, a series of sidewalk-implanted stars emblazoned with the names of Cuban celebrities that runs up and much of 8th St.

TOP CHOICE Máximo Gómez Park   PARK
(Map p84; SW 8th St at SW 15th Ave; ⏰9am-6pm) Little Havana's most evocative reminder of Old Cuba is Máximo Gómez Park, or 'Domino Park,' where the sound of elderly men trash-talking over games of chess is harmonized by the quick clak-clak of slapping dominoes. The jarring backtrack, plus the heavy smell of cigars and a sunrise-bright mural of the 1993 Summit of the Americas, combine to make Máximo Gómez one of the most sensory sites in Miami.

Cuban Memorials   MONUMENTS
(Map p84) The two blocks of SW 13th Ave south of Calle Ocho contain a series of monuments to Cuban and Cuban-American heroes, including those that died in the Cuban War of Independence and anti-Castro conflicts. The memorials include the Eternal Torch in Honor of the 2506th Brigade for the exiles who died during the Bay of Pigs

---

Little Havana

SW 6th St
SW 13th Ave
To Miami Hispanic Ballet (0.7 mi)

SW 7th St
16

SW 13th Ct
SW 14th Ave
Cuban Memorial Blvd
SW 12th Ct
SW 12th Ave
10   4   6   13   2   5
933
◎ **Cuban Memorials**

N   0 — 200 m   0 — 0.1 miles

MIAMI

...e **Cuba brass relief** depict-
...Cuba, dedicated to the 'ideals
...will never forget the pledge
...heir Fatherland free'; a **José**
...orial; and a **Madonna statue**,
...supposedly illuminated by a shaft
...at every afternoon. Bursting out of
the island in the center of the boulevard is
a massive ceiba tree, revered by followers of
Santeria. The tree is an unofficial reminder of
the poorer *Marielitos* (those who fled Cuba
in the 1980 Mariel Boatlift) and successive
waves of desperate-for-work Cubans, many of
whom are *santeros* (Santeria practitioners)
who have come to Miami since the 1980s.

Just away from the main drag are a fountain and monument, collectively entitled **La
Plaza de la Cubanidad** (Map p84; cnr W Flagler
St & NW 17th Ave), which is a tribute both to
the Cuban provinces and to the people who
were drowned in 1994 while trying to leave
Cuba on a ship, *13 de Marzo,* which was
sunk by Castro's forces just off the coast.

Cuba Ocho   GALLERY
(Map p84; www.cubaocho.com; 1465 SW 8th St;
⊘9am-6pm) The jewel of the Little Havana
Art District, Cuba Ocho functions as a community center, art gallery and research
outpost for all things Cuban. The interior
resembles a cool old Havana cigar bar, yet
the walls are decked out in artwork that
references both the classical past of Cuban

**VIERNES CULTURALES
(CULTURAL FRIDAYS)**

The Little Havana Arts District may not
be Wynwood, but it does constitute
an energetic little strip of galleries and
studios (concentrated on 8th St between SW 15th Ave & SW 17th Ave) that
house some of the best Latin American
art in Miami. Rather than pop into each
gallery, look around and feel pressure
to buy, why not visit on the last Friday
of each month for **Viernes Culturales**
(www.viernesculturales.org). No wine-
sipping art walk this; Cultural Fridays
in Little Havana are like little carnival
seasons, with music, old men in *guayaberas* (Cuban dress shirts) crooning to
the stars and more booty-shaking than
brie. Although there is also brie, and
plenty of time to appreciate local art
as all the Little Havana galleries throw
open their doors.

---

art and its avant-garde future. Frequent live
music, film, drama performances, readings
and other events go off every week. The
center opens during the evening for these
events; check online for more information.

FREE **Bay of Pigs Museum &
Library**   LIBRARY
(Map p84; 1821 SW 9th St; ⊘10am-5pm Mon-Fri)
This small museum is more of a memorial
to the 2506th Brigade, otherwise known as
the crew of the ill-fated Bay of Pigs Invasion.
Whatever your thoughts on Fidel Castro
and Cuban-Americans, pay a visit here to
flesh out one side of this contentious story.
You'll likely chat with survivors of the Bay of
Pigs, who like to hang out here surrounded
by pictures of comrades who never made it
back to the USA.

Tower Theater   HISTORIC BUILDING
(Map p84; www.mdc.edu/culture/tower.htm; 1508
SW 8th St) This renovated 1926 landmark
theater has a proud deco facade and a newly
done interior, thanks to support from the
Miami-Dade Community College. In its
heyday, it was the center of Little Havana
social life, and via the films it showed served
as a bridge between immigrant society and
American pop culture. Today the space frequently shows independent and Spanish-
language films (sometimes both) and hosts
varied art exhibitions in the lobby.

COCONUT GROVE
Coconut Grove, which attracts a mix of old
hippies, middle-class and mall-going Miami
and college students, unfolds along S Bayshore Dr as it hugs the shoreline. US Hwy 1
(S Dixie Hwy) acts as the northern boundary
for the Grove.

TOP
CHOICE **Vizcaya Museum &
Gardens**   HISTORIC BUILDING
(www.miamidade.gov/vizcaya; 3251 S Miami Ave;
adult/child $12/5; ⊘museum 9:30am-4:30pm Wed-
Mon) They call Miami the Magic City, and if it
is, this Italian villa, the housing equivalent of
a Fabergé egg, is its most fairy-tale residence.
In 1916, industrialist James Deering started
a long and storied Miami tradition by making a ton of money and building some ridiculously grandiose digs. He employed 1000
people (then 10% of the local population) for
four years to fulfill his desire for a pad that
looked centuries old. He was so obsessed
with creating an atmosphere of old money
that he had the house stuffed with 15th- to

19th-century furniture, tapestries, paintings and decorative arts; had a monogram fashioned for himself; and even had paintings of fake ancestors commissioned. The 30-acre grounds are full of splendid gardens and Florentine gazebos, and both the house and gardens are used for the display of rotating contemporary-art exhibitions. It's located between Downtown and Coconut Grove, roughly where SW 32nd Rd intersects with Dixie Hwy and S Miami Ave.

Barnacle Historic State Park PARK
(Map p87; www.floridastateparks.org/thebarnacle; 3485 Main Hwy; admission $2, house tours $3; ☉park 9am-4pm Fri-Mon, house tours 10am, 11:30am, 1pm, 2:30pm Fri-Mon) In the center of the village is the 1891, 5-acre pioneer residence of Ralph Monroe, Miami's first

Coconut Grove

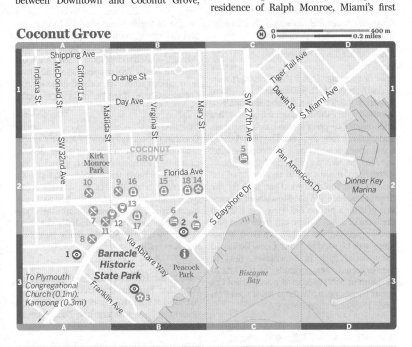

Coconut Grove

honorable snowbird. The house is open for guided tours, led by folks who are quite knowledgeable and enthusiastic about the park – which is, by the way, a lovely, shady oasis for strolling. Barnacle hosts frequent (and lovely) moonlight concerts, from jazz to classical. A little way down Main Hwy, on the other side of the road, there's a small Buddhist temple shaded by large groves of banyan trees, which gives it an authentically Southeast Asian feel (although it's a Tibetan Buddhist temple, so perhaps not).

Miami Museum of Science & Planetarium   MUSEUM
(www.miamisci.org; 3280 S Miami Ave; adult/child, student & senior $15/11; ⊙10am-6pm) The Miami Museum of Science is a dedicated if small institution with exhibits ranging from weather phenomena to creepy crawlies, coral reefs and vital-microbe displays. The planetarium hosts space lessons and telescope-viewing sessions, as well as old-school laser shows with trippy flashes set to the music of the Beatles and Pink Floyd. That said, at the time of research the old Museum of Science was getting a bit too old. Help has come in the form of a $35 million gift from local philanthropists Patricia and Phillip Frost. Those funds will be used to build a new facility in Bicentential Park in Downtown, next to the (expected) new grounds for the Miami Museum of Art. It's located northeast of Coconut Grove, near SW 32nd Rd if you're on Dixie Hwy or S Miami Ave.

Kampong   HISTORIC SITE, GARDENS
(Map p87; ☑305-442-7169; 4013 Douglas Rd; www.ntbg.org/gardens/kampong.php; ⊙tours by appointment only 10am-2pm Mon-Fri) If you speak Malay or Indonesian, then yes, this Kampong is named for the Bahasa word for village. David Fairchild, Indiana Jones of the botanical world and founder of Fairchild Tropical Gardens (p92), came up with the title, undoubtedly after a long Javanese jaunt. This was where the adventurer would rest in-between journeys in search of beautiful and economically viable plant life. Today it's listed on the National Register of Historic Places and the lovely grounds serve as a classroom for the National Tropical Botanical Garden. Free self-guided tours (allow at least an hour) are available by appointment, as are $20 two-hour guided tours. It's located in southwest Coconut Grove; if you're following the grid, Douglas Rd is also SW 37th Ave.

Arts Precinct   GALLERY
Coconut Grove, like many of Miami's neighborhoods, has been making a big deal of promoting its homegrown art galleries. You can walk among them, concentrated near CocoWalk and Streets of Mayfair malls (with a few exceptions), on the first Saturday night (from 7pm) of every month; the Coconut Grove Art Walk is decidedly the most family friendly of Miami's many neighborhood art walks.

AC Fine Art   GALLERY
(www.acfineartsite.com; 2911 Grand Ave; ⊙10am-6pm) One our favorite galleries, AC Fine Art specializes in limited editions and originals (!) of masters like Dalí, Picasso, Lautrec, Warhol, Basquiat and Lichtenstein.

Plymouth Congregational Church   CHURCH
(Map p87; www.plymouthmiami.com; 3400 Devon Rd; ⊙8:30am-4:30pm Mon-Fri) This 1917 coral church is striking, from its solid masonry to a hand-carved door from a Pyrenees monastery, which looks like it should be kicked in by Antonio Banderas carrying a guitar case full of explosives and Salma Hayek on his arm. Architecturally, this is one of the finest Spanish Mission–style churches in a city that does not lack for examples of the genre.

Ermita de la Caridad   MONUMENT
(☑305-854-2404;   www.ermitadelacaridad.org; 3609 S Miami Ave) The Catholic diocese purchased some of the bayfront land from Deering's Villa Vizcaya estate and built a shrine here for its displaced Cuban parishioners. Symbolizing a beacon, it faces the homeland, exactly 290 miles due south. There is

---

EVA MUNROE'S GRAVE

Tucked into a small gated area near the Coconut Grove Library (Map p87; 2875 McFarlane Rd), you'll find the humble headstone of one Ms Eva Amelia Hewitt Munroe. Eva, who was born in New Jersey in 1856 and died in Miami in 1882, lies in the oldest American grave in Miami-Dade County (a sad addendum: local African American settlers died before Eva, but their deaths were never officially recorded). Eva's husband Ralph entered a deep depression, which he tried to alleviate by building the **Barnacle** (p87), now one of the oldest historic homes in the area.

RESURRECTING THE COCONUT GROVE PLAYHOUSE

Miami's oldest theater is the Coconut Grove Playhouse, which sits at 3500 Main Hwy in the heart of the Grove (Map p87). Back in the day this was a grand dame of a building, with a snazzy marquee and celebrity vibe balanced by a good deal of artsy cred; Samuel Beckett's *Waiting for Godot* had its US premiere here in 1956 (the show was apparently a disaster). Sadly, the theater was shut down during its 50th-anniversary season due to major debt issues and still sits, today, like a sad shell over Main Hwy. Now the theater's board, in conjunction with Miami-Dade's Department of Cultural Affairs, is trying to resurrect the theater; at the time of research, backing for the project was shuttling between several nonprofits.

also a mural that depicts Cuban history. After visiting Vizcaya or the science museum, consider picnicking at this quiet sanctuary on the water's edge.

CORAL GABLES

The lovely city of Coral Gables, filled with Mediterranean-style buildings, is bordered by Calle Ocho to the north, Sunset Dr to the south, Ponce de León Blvd to the east and Red Rd to the west. The main campus of the University of Miami is located just south of the enormous Coral Gables Biltmore Golf Course and the main pedestrian drag is Miracle Mile – heaven for the shopping obsessed.

Biltmore Hotel   HISTORIC BUILDING

(Map p90; www.biltmorehotel.com; 1200 Anastasia Ave) In the most opulent neighborhood of one of the showiest cities in the world, the Biltmore peers down her nose and says, 'hrmph'. It's one of the greatest of the grand hotels of the American Jazz Age, and if this joint were a fictional character from a novel, it'd be, without question, Jay Gatsby. Al Capone had a speakeasy on-site, and the Capone Suite is still haunted by the spirit of Fats Walsh, who was murdered here (for more ghost details, join in the weekly storytelling in the lobby, 7pm Thursday). Back

in the day, imported gondolas transported celebrity guests like Judy Garland and the Vanderbilts around because, of course, there was a private canal system out the back. It's gone now, but the largest hotel pool in the continental USA, which resembles a sultan's water garden from *One Thousand & One Nights,* is still here. The lobby is the real kicker: grand, gorgeous, yet surprisingly not gaudy, it's like a child's fantasy of an Arabian castle crossed with a Medici villa.

Lowe Art Museum   MUSEUM

(www.lowemuseum.org; 1301 Stanford Dr; adult/student $10/5; ⊙10am-4pm Tue-Sat, from noon Sun) Your love of the Lowe, located on the campus of the University of Miami, depends on your taste in art. If you're into modern and contemporary works, it's good. If you're into the art and archaeology of cultures from Asia, Africa and the South Pacific, it's great. And if you're into pre-Columbian and Meso-American art, it's simply fantastic; the artifacts are stunning and thoughtfully strung out along an easy-to-follow narrative thread. That isn't to discount the lovely permanent collection of Renaissance and baroque art, Western sculpture from the 18th to 20th centuries, and paintings by Gauguin, Picasso and Monet – they're also gorgeous. To get here, look for the entrance to the University of Miami at Stanford Dr off Dixie Hwy.

Venetian Pool   HISTORIC SITE

(Map p90; www.coralgablesvenetianpool.com; 2701 De Soto Blvd; adult/child $11/7.35; ⊙10am-4:30pm; 👪) Just imagine: it's 1923, tons of rock have been quarried for one of the most beautiful neighborhoods in Miami, but now an ugly gash sits in the middle of the village. What to do? How about pump the irregular hole full of water, mosaic and tile up the whole affair, and make it look like a Roman emperor's aquatic playground? Result: one of the few pools listed on the National Register of Historic Places, a wonderland of coral rock caves, cascading waterfalls, a palm-fringed island and Venetian-style moorings. Take a swim and follow in the footsteps (finsteps?) of stars like Esther Williams and Johnny 'Tarzan' Weissmuller. Opening hours vary depending on the season, so check the website for details.

Merrick House   HISTORIC BUILDING

(Map p90; ☎305-460-5361; 907 Coral Way; adult/child/senior $5/1/3; ⊙tours 1pm, 2pm & 3pm Sun & Wed) It's fun to imagine this simple homestead, with its little hints of Med-style, as the

MIAMI

core of what would eventually become the gaudy Gables. When George Merrick's father purchased this plot, site unseen, for $1100, it was all dirt, rock and guavas. The property is now used for meetings and receptions, and you can tour both the house and its pretty organic garden. The modest family residence looks as it did in 1925, outfitted with family photos, furniture and artwork.

Entrances & Watertower   LANDMARKS
(Map p90) Coral Gables designer George Merrick planned a series of elaborate entry gates to the city, but the real-estate bust meant that projects went unfinished. Among the completed gates worth seeing, which resemble the entrance pavilions to grand Andalucian estates, are the Country Club Prado; the Douglas Entrance; the Granada Entrance (cnr Alhambra Circle & Granada Blvd); the Alhambra Entrance (cnr Alhambra Circle & Douglas Rd) and the Coral Way Entrance (cnr Red Rd & Coral Way). The Alhambra Watertower

(Alhambra Circle), where Greenway Ct and Ferdinand St meet Alhambra Circle, resembles a Moorish lighthouse.

Coral Gables City Hall   HISTORIC BUILDING
(Map p90; 405 Biltmore Way) This grand building has housed boring city-commission meetings since it opened in 1928. It's impressive from any angle, certainly befitting its importance as a central government building. Check out Denman Fink's *Four Seasons* ceiling painting in the tower, as well as his framed, untitled painting of the underwater world on the 2nd-floor landing. There's a small farmers' market on-site from 8am to 1pm, January to March.

Coral Gables Congregational Church   CHURCH
(Map p90; www.coralgablescongregational.org; 3010 De Soto Blvd) George Merrick's father was a New England Congregational minister, so perhaps that accounts for him donating the

land for the city's first church. Built in 1924 as a replica of a church in Costa Rica, the yellow-walled, red-roofed exterior is as far removed from New England as…well, Miami. The interior is graced with a beautiful sanctuary and the grounds are landscaped with stately palms.

Coral Gables Museum   MUSEUM
(Map p90; www.coralgablesmuseum.org; 285 Aragon Ave) Set to open by the time you read this (although delays have slowed the project in the past), this museum, based on its sample exhibition, should be a well-plotted introduction to the oddball narrative of the founding and growth of the City Beautiful (Coral Gables). The collection will include historical artifacts and mementos from succeeding generations in this tight-knit, eccentric little village. The main building is the old Gables police and fire station, itself a lovely architectural blend of Gables' Mediterranean revival and a more Miami Beach–esque, muscular Depression-moderne style.

GREATER MIAMI – NORTH

Museum of Contemporary Art   MUSEUM
(MoCA; www.mocanomi.org; 770 NE 125th St; adult/student & senior $5/3; ☺11am-5pm Tue & Thu-Sat,

1-9pm Wed, noon-5pm Sun) Located up in North Miami, a rapidly evolving neighborhood and real-estate magnet for hipsters who have tired of the South Beach scene, the Museum of Contemporary Art has long been a reason to hike up to this stretch of Miami. Its galleries feature excellent rotating exhibitions of contemporary art by local, national and international artists. Open late on the last Friday of every month (7pm to 10pm) for a jazz concert.

Ancient Spanish Monastery   CHURCH
(☑305-945-1461; www.spanishmonastery.com; 16711 W Dixie Hwy; ⊙10am-4pm Mon-Sat, 11am-4pm Sun) The Episcopal Church of St Bernard de Clairvaux is a stunning early-Gothic and Romanesque building. Constructed in 1141 in Segovia, Spain, it was converted to a granary 700 years later, and eventually bought by newspaper tycoon William Randolph Hearst. He had it dismantled and shipped to the USA in more than 10,000 crates, intending to reconstruct it at his sprawling California estate. But construction was never approved by the government, and the stones sat in boxes until 1954, when a group of Miami developers purchased the dismantled monastery from Hearst and reassembled it. Now it's a lovely, popular (especially for weddings, so call before going) oasis and allegedly the oldest building in the western hemisphere. Church services are held at 8am, 10:30am and noon on Sunday, and a healing service is held at 10am on Wednesday. You can get here easily via North Biscayne Blvd; it's about 10 miles north of the Design District.

Hialeah Park   PARK
(www.hialeahparkracing.com; 2200 E 4th Ave; ⊙9am-5pm Mon-Fri) Hialeah is more Havanan than Little Havana (more than 90% of the population speak Spanish as a first language), and the symbol and center of this working-class Cuban community is this grand but endangered former racetrack. Seabiscuit and Seattle Slew once raced here, but in 2001 this gem was in danger of being paved over. A public campaign ensued to preserve the park; in 2008, the song 'Save Hialeah Park' by Los Primeros, a Hialeah-based Latin boy band, became a major local hit. Thanks to the passage of a controversial gambling and gaming bill, the park was saved from destruction. Today a walk through the grounds is recommended, if only to gaze at the grand staircases and pastel-painted concourse, and imagine the thunder of racing hooves. Look for the caps, boots and saddle carved into the window below the administration building, and the oft-photographed central fountain. You can get here by heading west on NW 79th St, just north of Little Haiti.

GREATER MIAMI – SOUTH
Fairchild Tropical Garden   GARDENS
(www.fairchildgarden.org; 10901 Old Cutler Rd; adult/child/senior $25/12/18; ⊙9:30am-4:30pm) If you need to escape Miami's madness, consider a green day in the country's largest tropical botanical garden. A butterfly grove, jungle biospheres, and gentle vistas of marsh and keys habitats, plus frequent art installations from folks like Roy Lichtenstein, are all stunning. In addition to easy-to-follow, self-guided walking tours, a free 40-minute tram tours the entire park on the hour from 10am to

HIBISCUS, PALM & STAR ISLANDS

Floating off the edge of the A1A, in the heart of Biscayne Bay (and posh exclusivity), Hibiscus Island, Palm Island and Star Island are little floating Primrose Hills. There aren't many famous people living here – just wealthy ones – although Star Island is home to Gloria Estefan and for a short time Al Capone lived (and died) on Palm Island. In the 1970s and '80s a mansion on Star Island was the headquarters of the Ethiopian Zion Coptic Church (EZCC; www.ethiopianzioncopticchurch.org), a Rastafari sect eventually convicted of smuggling large amount of marijuana into the US. That incident prompted a media circus that focused on both the indictments and neighborly disputes between the long-haired, bearded white Rastas and their aristocratic Star Island neighbors, who complained about the fog of cannabis smoke constantly emanating from the EZCC's compound.

Today the drives for the islands are guarded by a security booth, but the roads are public, so if you ask politely and don't look sketchy, you can get in. Star Island is little more than one elliptical road lined with royal palms, sculpted ficus hedges and fancy gates guarding houses you can't see.

3pm. Located 5 miles south of Coral Gables; Old Cutler Rd is accessible via SW 57th Ave.

Charles Deering Estate LANDMARK

(www.deeringestate.org; 16701 SW 72nd Ave; adult/child under 14yr $12/7; ☺10am-5pm) The Deering estate is sort of 'Vizcaya lite', which makes sense as it was built by Charles, brother of James Deering (of Vizcaya fame). The 150-acre grounds are awash with tropical growth, an animal-fossil pit of bones dating back 50,000 years and the prehistoric remains of Native Americans who lived here 2000 years ago. There's a free tour of the grounds included in admission, and the estate often hosts jazz evenings under the stars. Last tickets sold at 4pm.

Metrozoo ZOO

(www.miamimetrozoo.com; 12400 SW 152nd St; adult/child $16/12; ☺9:30am-5:30pm) Miami's tropical weather makes strolling around the Metrozoo almost feel like a day in the wild. Look for Asian and African elephants, rare and regal Bengal tigers prowling an evocative Hindu temple, pygmy hippos, Andean condors, a pack of hyenas, cute koalas, colobus monkeys, black rhinoceroses and a pair of Komodo dragons from Indonesia. Keep your eyes peeled for informative zookeeper talks in front of some exhibits. For a quick overview (and because the zoo is so big), hop on the Safari Monorail; it departs every 20 minutes. There's a glut of grounds tours available, and kids will love feeding the Samburu giraffes ($2). Last admission at 4pm.

Jungle Island ZOO

(www.jungleisland.com; 1111 Parrot Jungle Trail, off MacArthur Causeway, Watson Island; adult/child/senior $33/25/31; ☺10am-5pm, to 6pm Sat & Sun) Jungle Island, packed with tropical birds, alligators, orangutans, chimps, lemurs, a (wait for it, *Napoleon Dynamite* fans) liger (a cross between a lion and a tiger) and a Noah's Ark of other animals, is a ton of fun. It's one of those places kids (justifiably) beg to go, so just give up and prepare for some bright-feathered, bird-poopie-scented fun in this artificial, self-contained jungle. The waterfront facility, lushly landscaped and using a minimum of pesticides, is pretty impressive, thanks in part to the flamingos, macaws, cockatoos and other parrots, flying about in outdoor aviaries. The Cape Penguin colony is especially cute.

Monkey Jungle ZOO

(www.monkeyjungle.com; 14805 SW 216th St; adult/child/senior $30/24/28; ☺9:30am-5pm) The

Monkey Jungle brochures have a tag line: 'Where humans are caged and monkeys run free.' And, indeed, you'll be walking through screened-in trails, with primates swinging freely, screeching and chattering all around you. It's incredibly fun, and just a bit odorous, especially on warm days (well, most days). In 1933, animal behaviorist Joseph du Mond released six monkeys into the wild. Today, their descendants live here with orangutans, chimpanzees and lowland gorilla. The big show of the day takes place at feeding time, when crab-eating monkeys and Southeast Asian macaques dive into the pool for fruit and other treats. There's also a lovely aviary for clouds of beautiful rescued parrots. Last admission at 4pm.

Pinecrest Gardens PARK

(www.pinecrest-fl.gov/gardens; 11000 SW 57th Ave; adult/child $3/2; ☺9am-5pm fall & winter, to 6pm spring & summer) When Parrot Jungle (now Jungle Island) flew the coop for the big city, the village of Pinecrest, which is the community that hosted the Jungle's former location, purchased the lovely property in order to keep it as a municipal park. It's now a quiet oasis with some of the best tropical gardens this side of the Gulf of Mexico; biomes include cypress hammocks, tropical hammocks, banana groves, rubber trees and a gorgeous centerpiece banyan tree. Outdoor movies and jazz concerts are held here, and in all this is a total gem that is utterly off the tourism trail.

Fruit & Spice Park PARK

(www.fruitandspicepark.org; 24801 SW 187th Ave; adult/child $8/2; ☺9am-5pm) Set just on the edge of the Everglades, this 35-acre tropical public park grows all those great tropical fruits you usually have to contract dysentery to enjoy. The park is divided into 'continents' (Africa, Asia etc) and admission to the pretty grounds includes a free tour; you can't pick the fruit, but you can eat anything that falls to the ground. If you're coming down this far, you may want to consider taking a day trip into Everglades National Park (p137).

Gold Coast Railroad Museum MUSEUM

(www.gcrm.org; 12450 SW 152nd St; adult/child 3-11yr $6/4; ☺10am-4pm Mon-Fri, from 11am Sat & Sun) Primarily of interest to serious train buffs, this museum was set up in the 1950s by the Miami Railroad Historical Society. It displays more than 30 antique railway cars, including the Ferdinand Magellan presidential car, where President Harry Truman famously brandished a newspaper with the erroneous headline 'Dewey Defeats Truman.' On weekends the museum offers 20-minute rides on old cabooses ($6), standard gauge cabs ($12) and, for kids, on a small 'link' train ($2.50). It's advised you call ahead to make an appointment to ride. It's located about 13 miles southwest of Coral Gables near the Miami Zoo.

Miami Children's Museum CHILDREN'S MUSEUM
(www.miamichildrensmuseum.org; 980 MacArthur Causeway, Watson Island; admission $15; ⊙10am-6pm) This museum, located between South Beach and downtown Miami, isn't exactly a museum. It feels more like an uberplayhouse, with areas for kids to practice all sorts of adult activities – banking and food shopping, caring for pets, reporting scoops as a TV news anchor in a studio, and acting as a local cop or firefighter. Be forewarned, this place is a zoo on rainy days.

Matheson Hammock Park PARK
(www.miamidade.gov/parks/parks/matheson _beach.asp; 9610 Old Cutler Rd; per car $5; ⊙sunrise-sunset) This 100-acre county park is the city's oldest and one of its most scenic. It offers good swimming for children in an enclosed tidal pool, lots of hungry raccoons, dense mangrove swamps and (pretty rare) crocodile-spotting.

Wings Over Miami MUSEUM
(www.wingsovermiami.com; Kendall-Tamiami Executive Airport, 14710 SW 128th St; adult/child under 12yr/senior $10/6/7; ⊙10am-5pm Wed-Sat, from noon Sun) Plane-spotters will be delighted by this Kendall-Tamiami Executive Airport museum, which chronicles the history of aviation. Highlights include a propeller collection, J47 jet engine, a Soviet bomber from Smolensk and the nose section of a B-29 called *Fertile Myrtle,* the same type of aircraft used to drop atomic bombs on Hiroshima and Nagasaki. An impressive exhibit on the Tuskegee Airmen features videos of the African American pilots telling their own stories. Historic bombers and other aircraft drop in for occasional visits, so you can never be sure what you'll see.

🏃 Activities

Biking

🖉 **Miami-Dade County Parks & Recreation Department** CYCLING
(📞305-755-7800; www.miamidade.gov/parksmaster plan/bike_trails_map.asp) Leads frequent eco-bike tours through parklands and along waterfront paths, and offers a list of traffic-free cycling paths on its website. For less strenuous rides, try the side roads of South Beach or the shady streets of Coral Gables and Coconut Grove. Some good trails:

Old Cutler Bike Path Starts at the end of Sunset Dr in Coral Gables and leads through Coconut Grove to Matheson Hammock Park and Fairchild Tropical Garden.

Rickenbacker Causeway This route takes you up and over the bridge to Key Biscayne for an excellent workout combined with gorgeous water views.

Oleta River State Park (3400 NE 163rd St) Has a challenging dirt trail with hills for off-road adventures.

Bowling

Bowlmor Lanes BOWLING
(www.bowlmor.com/miami; 11401 NW 12th St; ⊙4pm-1am Mon-Thu, noon-3am Fri, 11am-3am Sat, 11am-1am Sun) In the Dolphin Mall, this is a good example of what happens when Miami's talent for glitz and glamour (they post pics of Lindsay Lohan bowling here on the website) meets some humble 10-pins.

Lucky Strike BOWLING
(www.bowluckystrike.com; 1691 Michigan Ave; ⊙11:30am-1am Mon-Thu, to 2am Fri, 11am-2am Sat, 11am-1am Sun) Just off Lincoln Rd, this is Miami Beach's answer to high-end bowling, full of house and hip-hop music, electric-bright cocktails and beautiful club kids.

Day Spas

As you may have guessed, Miami offers plenty of places to get pampered. Some of the most luxurious spas in town are found at high-end hotels, where you can expect to pay $300 to $400 for a massage and/or acupressure, and $200 for a body wrap. Notable spas:

Spa at Viceroy SPA
(Map p74; 📞305-503-0369; www.viceroyhotel sandresorts.com; 485 Brickell Ave)
Philippe Starck–designed with an enormous gym, a cardio theater and (wow) a floating library.

Spa Internazionale SPA
(📞800-537-3708; www.fisherislandclub.com; Inn at Fisher Island) The most exclusive spa in the city, with a huge range of massage, yoga and body treatments, shouldn't be missed if you're staying on private Fisher Island.

Spa at the Setai SPA
(Map p62; 📞305-520-6900; www.setai.com/ thespa; 101 20th St) A silky Balinese haven in one of South Beach's most beautiful hotels.

Just because you enjoy a good back rub doesn't mean you need to go to some glitzy spa where they constantly play soft house music on a repetitive loop. Right? Why not head to a favorite 'hot' spot among folks who want a spa experience without the glamour, the **Russian & Turkish Baths** (Map p70; ☑305-867-8316; www.russianandturkishbaths.com; 5445 Collins Ave; ⊙noon-midnight). Enter this little labyrinth of *banyas* (steam rooms) and there's a plethora of spa choices. You can be casually beaten with oak-leaf brooms (for $40) called *venik* in a lava-hot spa (it's actually really relaxing...well, interesting anyway). There's Dead Sea salt and mud exfoliation ($50), plus, the on-site cafe serves delicious borscht, blintzes, dark bread with smoked fish and of course, beer. The crowd is interesting too: hipsters, older Jews, model types, Europeans and folks from Russia and former Soviet states, some of whom look like, um, entirely legitimate businessmen and we're leaving it at that.

Diving & Snorkeling

Head to the Keys or Biscayne National Park (p150), in the southeastern corner of Dade county. Operators in Miami:

Divers Paradise   DIVING
(Map p82; ☑305-361-3483; www.keydivers. com; 4000 Crandon Blvd; dive trip $60) In Key Biscayne, one of the area's most reliable outfits.

South Beach Divers   DIVING
(Map p66; ☑305-531-6110; www.southbeach divers.com; 850 Washington Ave, South Beach; dive trip $100) Runs regular excursions to Key Largo and around Miami, plus offers three-day classes.

Fishing

Places to drop a line:

South Pointe Park (Map p66)

Rickenbacker Causeway (Map p82)

Key Biscayne Beach (Map p82)

Fishing charters are commonplace but expensive; expect to pay at least $1000 for a day of sport fishing:

Yacht Charters Miami (☑305-490-0049; www.yachtchartersinmiami.com)

Ace Blue Waters Charters (Map p74; ☑305-373-5016; www.fishingmiami.net; Bayside Marketplace, 401 Biscayne Blvd, Downtown Miami)

Kelley Fleet (☑305-945-3801; www.miami beachfishing.com; Haulover Beach Park, 10800 Collins Ave, Bal Harbour).

Golf

At high-end resorts, expect to pay between $150 and $350 to tee off, depending on the season and time of day (it's more expensive in winter and daylight hours).

Biltmore Donald Ross Golf Course   GOLF
(Map p90; ☑305-460-5364; www.biltmorehotel. com/golf; 1210 Anastasia Ave, Coral Gables) Designed by the golfer of that name and boasts the immaculate company of the Biltmore Hotel.

Doral Golf Course   GOLF
(☑305-592-2000; www.doralresort.com; 4400 NW 87th Ave) Very highly rated, which may explain why it's difficult to get in and also why it once hosted the PGA Ford Championship.

Crandon Golf Course   GOLF
(Map p82; ☑305-361-9129; 6700 Crandon Blvd, Key Biscayne; daylight Dec-Apr $140, twilight May-Nov $30) Overlooks the bay from its perch on Key Biscayne.

Haulover Golf Course   GOLF
(Map p70; ☑305-940-6719; 10800 Collins Ave, Bal Harbour; $21-43) A nine-hole, par-three course that's great for beginners.

CRICKET – IT'S A PITCH

Cricket in South Florida? Oh yes. Really? There's a huge West Indian and Jamaican community in South Florida, plus a very sizable British expat population. As such cricket is actually quite popular in these parts. The **South Florida Cricket Alliance** (☑954-805-2922; www.southfloridacricket.com) is one of the largest cricket clubs in the US, the **Cricket Council of the USA** (www. cricketcouncilusa.com) is based in Boca Raton, and the first dedicated cricket pitch in the country opened in Lauderhill (where the population is 25% West Indian), north of Fort Lauderdale, in 2008. Contact any of the above if you'd like to watch a test or join a team.

Art Deco Miami Beach
Walking Tour

❯ Start at the **1 Art Deco Welcome Center**, at the corner of Ocean Dr and 10th St (named Barbara Capitman Way here after the founder of the Miami Design Preservation League). Step in for a permanent exhibit on art-deco style, then head out and go north along Ocean Dr; between 12th St and 14th St you'll see three examples of deco hotels: the **2 Leslie**, a boxy shape with eyebrows (cantilevered sun shades) wrapped around the side of the building; the **3 Carlyle**, featured in the film *The Birdcage* and boasting modernistic styling; and the graceful **4 Cardozo Hotel**, built by Henry Hohauser, owned by Gloria Estefan and featuring sleek, rounded edges. At 14th St, peek inside the sun-drenched **5 Winter Haven Hotel** to see its fabulous floors of ubiquitous terrazzo, made of stone chips set in mortar that is polished when dry. Turn left and head down 14th St to Washington Ave and the **6 US Post Office**, at 13th St. It's a curvy block of white deco in the stripped classical style. Step inside to admire the wall mural, domed ceiling and marble stamp tables. Stop for lunch at the **7 11th Street Diner**, a gleaming aluminum Pullman car that was imported in 1992 from Wilkes-Barre, Pennsylvania. Get a window seat and gaze across the avenue to the corner of 10th St and the stunningly restored **8 Hotel Astor**, designed in 1936 by T Hunter Henderson. After your meal, walk half a block east to the imposing **9 Wolfsonian-FIU**, an excellent museum of design, formerly the Washington Storage Company. Wealthy snowbirds of the '30s safely stashed their pricey belongings before heading back up north. Continue walking Washington Ave and turn left on 7th St and then continue north along Collins Ave to the **10 Hotel**, featuring an interior and roof deck by Todd Oldham. L Murray Dixon designed the hotel as the Tiffany Hotel, with a proud deco spire, in 1939. Turn right on 9th St and go two blocks to Ocean Dr, where you'll spy nonstop deco beauties, such as the 1935 **11 Edison Hotel**, another beautiful creation of deco legend Henry Hohauser.

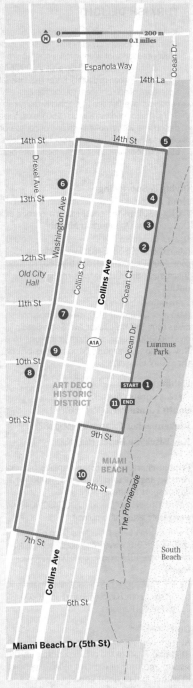

In-Line Skating

Serious crowds have turned promenades into obstacle courses for anyone crazy enough to strap on some blades. Leave the crowded strips to experts and try the ocean side of Ocean Ave, or Lincoln Rd before the shoppers descend.

Rent your wheels from Fritz's Skate Shop (Map p62; ☎305-532-1954; www.fritzs miamibeach.com; 1620 Washington Ave; ⏱10am-10pm), which also offers free lessons on Sunday at 10:30am – just about the only time there's ever room on the mall any more.

Kayaking & Windsurfing

Kayaking through mangroves, one of the coolest ecosystems on Earth, is magical: all those slender roots kiss the water while the ocean breeze cools your flanks. Try these places:

Haulover Beach Park (10800 Collins Ave)

Bill Baggs Cape Florida State Park (Map p82; www.floridastateparks.org/capeflorida; 1200 S Crandon Blvd)

Oleta River State Park (3400 NE 163rd St)

You can rent gear from the following:

Blue Moon Miami   WATER SPORTS
(☎305-957-3040; www.bluemoonmiami.com) Offers single kayaks ($18 per 1½ hours, $25 per three hours), tandem kayaks ($25.50 per 1½ hours, $40 per three hours) and bike rental ($18 per 1½ hours, $25 per three hours).

Sailboards Miami   WATER SPORTS
(☎305-361-7245; www.windsurfingmiami.com; 1 Rickenbacker Causeway; per hr s/tandem $15/20) Also rents kayaks. You can purchase 10 hours' worth of kayaking for $90. This is also a good spot to rent (and learn how to operate) windsurfing gear (lessons from $35, gear per hour $30).

Aquatic Rental Center and Sailing School   WATER SPORTS
(off Map p70; ☎305-751-7514, evening 305-279-7424; 1275 NE 79th St; sailboats per 2hr/3hr/4hr/day $85/125/150/225) If you're a bona-fide seaworthy sailor, this place will rent you a sailboat. If you're not, it can teach you how to operate one (sailing courses $400, $500 for two people).

Rodeo

Rodeo in South Florida? You just have to head a little way out of Miami. Check the below websites or call ahead for specific rodeo

SOUTH FLORIDA CIRCUS ARTS SCHOOL

Admit it: you always wanted to fly on the trapeze, clamber out of the clown car, tame a lion. Well, we can't really help you with those last two activities, but if you want to learn some circus-worthy acrobatics, contortion and flexibility skills, come to the South Florida Circus Arts School (SFCAS ☎954-540-1344; www.sfcas.com; 15161 NE 21st Ave) in North Miami, off North Biscayne Blvd, about 8 miles north of the Design District. SFCAS claims to be the only institution of its kind offering all-levels accessible education in the skills of the circus. It's a ton of fun and pretty unique; classes include aerial fitness, trapeze skills and the extremely popular flying yoga course (just try it), with fees ranging from $15 to $75 for an hour of instruction. See you in the center ring...

times. If the idea of performing animals and spurs in the same arena makes you ill at ease, you may want to avoid local rodeos.

Bergeron Rodeo Grounds   RODEO
(☎954-680-3555; www.davie-fl.gov/gen/daviefl _spclprjcts/bergeronrodeo; 4271 Davie Rd, Fort Lauderdale) In Davie, about 20 miles north of downtown Miami.

Homestead Rodeo   RODEO
(☎305-247-3515; www.facebook.com/pages/ Homestead-Rodeo/277924761912; 1034 NE 8th St, Homestead) In Homestead, about an hour south of Downtown.

Running

Running is quite popular, and the beach is very good for jogging, as it's flat, wide and hard-packed (apparently with amazingly hot joggers). A great resource for races, special events and other locations is the Miami Runners Club (☎305-255-1500; www.miami runnersclub.com).

Some good places for a run include the Flamingo Park track, located east of Alton Rd between 11th St and 12th St, for serious runners; Promenade in South Beach for its style; the boardwalk on Mid-Beach for great people-watching and scenery; and South Bayshore Drive in Coconut Grove for its shady banyan trees.

Surfing

Miami is not a good place for surfing. The Bahamas block swells, making the water very calm; many will tell you it's best to head about 100 miles north to Jupiter or Palm Beach to catch decent waves (not big waves, just surf consistent enough to hold a board upright). Plus, Miami surfers have worse reputations than Miami drivers when it comes to aggressive, territorial behavior. If you want to ride waves here, the best surfing is just north of South Pointe Park (Map p66), where you can sometimes find 2ft to 5ft waves and a nice, sandy bottom. Unfortunately it's usually closer to 2ft than 5ft, it can get a little mushy (so longboards are the way to go), and it's swamped with weekend swimmers and surfers. Conditions are better further north, near Haulover Beach Park (10800 Collins Ave, Bal Harbour) or anywhere north of 70th St, like Sunny Isles Beach (Sunny Isles Causeway). Check in with Island Water Sports (305-944-0104; www.iwsmiami.com; 16231 Biscayne Blvd) for gear, SoBe Surf (786-216-7703; www.sobesurf.com) for lessons (private instructors will meet with you somewhere on the beach) and www.dadecosurf.com for general information.

Swimming

All of the following pools have lap lanes, but call the Venetian beforehand, as their lap hours change often.

Venetian Pool (p89)

Flamingo Park Swimming Pool (Map p66; 305-673-7750; 999 11th St, South Beach; adult/child $10/6; laps 6:45-9am & 7-9pm)

Normandy Isle Park & Pool (Map p70; 305-673-7750; 7030 Trouville Esplanade; adult/child $10/6; laps 6:45-9am & 7-9pm)

Yoga

The beach is definitely not the only place to salute the sun in Miami. All of the following studios offer a large range of classes; bring your own mats.

Green Monkey Yoga (Map p80; 305-669-5959; www.greenmonkey.net; 3301 NE 1st Ave, Miami; classes from $20) Midtown, also has branches in South Beach and South Miami.

Brickell Hot Yoga (Map p74; 305-856-1387; www.brickellyoga.com; 301 SW 17th Rd, Brickell; 1/5/10-class pass $19/85/160) Downtown.

Prana Yoga Center (Map p90; 305-567-9812; www.pranayogamiami.com; 247 Malaga Ave, Coral Gables; 1/2/5-class pass $18/34/50) In Coral Gables.

MIAMI FOR CHILDREN

Well really, it's Florida, folks; your kids will be catered to. Many of the attractions run toward animal experiences, starting with the **Miami Seaquarium** (p83), which boasts a large collection of crocodiles, dolphins and sea lions and a killer whale, most of which perform. Next comes the **Metrozoo** (p93), a 740-acre zoo with plenty of natural habitats (thank you, tropical weather). Should your little ones like colorful animal shows, the outdoors and the smell of animal poo in all its myriad varieties, Miami shall not disappoint. **Monkey Jungle** (p93) acts as a habitat for endangered species and is everything you'd expect: screeching primates, covered pathways and a grand finale show of crab monkeys diving for fruit. **Jungle Island** (p93), on the other hand, tends to entertain with brilliant bird shows. Next door is the new **Miami Children's Museum** (p94), an indoor playland where youngsters can try out the roles of TV anchor, banker and supermarket customer, among others. Coral Gables draws the water-wise to its way-fun, lagoonlike **Venetian Pool** (p89). For a more educational experience, let your kids explore the **Marjorie Stoneman Douglas Environmental Center** (p83) on Key Biscayne. Coconut Grove is probably the most child-friendly neighborhood in Miami, with its malls, easy-to-digest (on every level) mainstream dining and thanks to events put on at places like **Barnacle Historic State Park** (p87).

Child Care

When it's time to head out for some adult time, check with your hotel, as many offer child-care services – any larger resort worth its salt should be able to provide child-care services. Or call the local Nanny Poppinz (305-607-1170; www.nannypoppinz.com). For more information, advice and anecdotes, read Lonely Planet's *Travel with Children*.

Bikram Yoga Miami Beach (Map p66; 305-448-3332; www.bikramyogamiami.com; 235 11th St, Miami Beach; per day/week $25/50) South Beach.

There's a lovely 'yoga by the sea' course offered at the **Barnacle Historic State Park** (p87; ☺classes 6-7:15pm Mon & Wed; per class $13) in Coconut Grove. If you don't feel like breaking out your wallet, try the free yoga classes at **Bayfront Park** (p73; ☺ ☺classes 6-7:15pm Mon & Wed, 9-10:15am Sat), held outdoors at Tina Hills Pavilion, at the south end of the park, three times a week.

🖝 Tours

Art Deco Welcome Center   WALKING
(Map p66; 305-531-3484; 1001 Ocean Dr, South Beach; guided tour per adult/child/senior $20/free/15; ☺tours 10:30am Fri-Wed, 6:30pm Thu) Tells the stories and history behind the art-deco buildings in South Beach, either with a lively guide from the Miami Design Preservation League, or a well-presented recording and map for self-guided walks (try the guides). Tours last 90 minutes.

Dr Paul George   WALKING
(305-375-1621; www.historymiami.org/tours/walking-tours; tours $25-42) For great historical perspective, call the lively Dr George, a historian for HistoryMiami (p76). George leads several popular tours – including those that focus on Stiltsville, Miami crime, Little Havana and Coral Gables at twilight – between September and late June; hours vary. Dr George also offers private tours by appointment.

Miami Food Tours   WALKING
(Map p74; 800-838-3006; www.miamifoodtours.com; 429 Lennox Ave; adult/child $45/30; ☺tours 11am-2pm Mon-Sat) You'll be visiting five of South Beach's best restaurants, but hey, it's a walking tour – you're burning calories, right?

Urban Tour Host   WALKING
(Map p74; 305-416-6868; www.miamicultural tours.com; 25 SE 2nd Ave, ste 1048; tours from $20) Has a rich program of custom tours that provide face-to-face interaction in all of Miami's neighborhoods. A deluxe city tour includes Coral Gables, South Beach, downtown Miami and Coconut Grove.

Captain Jimmy's Fiesta Cruises   BOAT
(Map p74; 305-371-3033; www.fiestacruises.com; 401 Biscayne Blvd; adult/child from $17/10) Fun, fantastic boat tours coordinated by a small, family-run operation. Try the

tarpon-feeding extravaganza (tarpon are basically very big fish) for $20.

Eco-adventure Bike Tours   BICYCLE
(305-365-3018; www.miamidade.gov/ecoadventures; from $28) The Dade County parks system leads excellent bike tours through peaceful areas of Miami and Miami Beach, including along beaches, on Key Biscayne and into the Everglades.

Island Queen   BOAT
(Map p74; 305-379-5119; www.islandqueencruises.com; 401 Biscayne Blvd; adult/child from $26/18) Boat tours of Millionaire's Row, the Miami River and Stiltsville, among other locations.

HMC Helicopters   HELICOPTER
(305-233-8788; www.hmchelicopters.com; Watson Island; flights $89-250) Runs scenic helicopter jaunts over the skyscrapers of Downtown and the waters of Biscayne Bay and Government Cut.

Miami Nice Tours   BUS
(305-949-9180; www.miaminicetours.com; 17030 Collins Ave; $25-99) Has a wide range of guided bus excursions to the Everglades, the Keys and Fort Lauderdale, as well as trips around Miami.

✯ Festivals & Events

There's something special happening year-round in Miami, with well-touted events bringing in niche groups from serious DJs (Winter Music Conference) to obsessed foodies (Miami Spice Restaurant Month). Addresses are given where there is a fixed festival location.

January

The beginning of the new year also happens to be the height of the tourist season in these parts. Expect fair weather, crowds of visitors, higher prices than usual and a slew of special events. New Year's Eve brings fireworks and festivals to South Beach and downtown Miami's bayfront.

Orange Bowl   FOOTBALL
(www.orangebowl.org; Sun Life Stadium, 2269 Dan Marino Blvd, Miami Gardens) Hordes of football fans descend on Miami for the Super Bowl of college football.

Art Deco Weekend   CULTURAL
(www.artdecoweekend.com; Ocean Dr btwn 1st St & 23rd St) This weekend fair featuring guided tours, concerts, classic-auto shows, sidewalk cafes, arts and antiques is held in mid-January.

NORTHERN CAPITAL OF THE LATIN WORLD

Miami may technically be part of the USA, but it's widely touted as the 'capital of the Americas' and the 'center of the New World.' That's a coup when it comes to marketing Miami to the rest of the world, and especially to the USA, where Latinos are now the largest minority. Miami's pan-Latin mixture makes it more ethnically diverse than any Latin American city. At the turn of the 21st century, the western suburbs of Hialeah and Hialeah Gardens were numbers two and one respectively on the list of US areas where Spanish is spoken as a first language (over 90% on the population).

How did this happen? Many of Miami's Latinos arrived in this geographically convenient city as political refugees – Cubans fleeing Castro starting around the '60s, Venezuelans fleeing President Hugo Chávez (or his predecessors), Brazilians and Argentines running from economic woes, Mexicans and Guatemalans arriving to find work. And gringos, long fascinated with Latin American flavors, can now visit Miami to get a taste of the pan-Latin stew without having to leave the country.

This has all led to the growth of Latin American businesses in Miami, which has boosted the local economy. Miami is the US headquarters of many Latin companies, including Lan Chile, a Chilean airline; Televisa, a Mexican TV conglomerate; and Embraer, a Brazilian aircraft manufacturer. Miami is also home to Telemundo, one of the biggest Spanish-language broadcasters in the US, as well as MTV Networks Latin America and the Latin branch of the Universal Music Group. Miami is the host city of the annual Billboard Latin Music Conference & Awards.

Cubans have a strong influence on local and international politics in Miami. Conservative exile groups have often been characterized as extreme, many refusing to visit Cuba while Castro remains in power. A newer generation, however – often referred to as the 'YUCAs' (Young Urban Cuban Americans) – are more willing to see both sides of issues in Cuba.

While many of the subtleties may escape you as a visitor, one thing is obvious: the Latino influence, which you can experience by seeking it out or waiting for it to fall in your lap. Whether you're dining out, listening to live music, overhearing Spanish conversations, visiting Little Havana or Little Buenos Aires, or simply sipping a chilled mojito at the edge of your hotel pool, the Latin American energy is palpable, beautiful and everywhere you go.

Miami Jewish Film Festival   FILM
(www.miamijewishfilmfestival.com; 4200 Biscayne Blvd) A great chance to cinematically *kvetch* with one of the biggest Jewish communities in the USA.

February

The last hurrah for northerners needing to escape the harsh winter, February brings arts festivals and street parties, as well as warm days and cool nights.

Coconut Grove Arts Festival   CULTURAL
(www.coconutgroveartsfest.com; Biscayne Blvd btwn NE 1st St & 5th St, Coconut Grove) One of the most prestigious arts festivals in the country, this late-February fair features more than 300 artists.

**Original Miami Beach
Antiques Show**   ANTIQUES
(www.originalmiamibeachantiqueshow.com; Miami Beach Convention Center) One of the largest events of its kind in the USA, with over 800 dealers from more than 20 countries.

South Beach Wine & Food Festival   FOOD
(www.sobefest.com) A festival of fine dining and sipping to promote South Florida's culinary image. Expect star-studded brunches, dinners and barbecues.

March

Spring arrives, bringing warmer weather, world-class golf and tennis, outdoor festivals and St Patrick's Day. Expect some Spring Breakers to behave badly on the beach.

Miami International Film Festival   FILM
(www.miamifilmfestival.com) This event, sponsored by Miami-Dade College, is a two-week festival showcasing documentaries and features from all over the world.

South Beach Comedy Festival   COMEDY
(www.southbeachcomedyfestival.com) Some of the best comedic talent in the world does stand-up in venues across the city.

Miami Fashion Week   FASHION
(www.miamifashionweek.com; Miami Beach Convention Center) Models are as abundant

as fish in the ocean as designers descend on the city and catwalks become ubiquitous.

Winter Music Conference MUSIC
(www.wmcon.com) Party promoters, DJs, producers and revelers come from around the globe to hear new artists, catch up on technology and party the nights away.

April
Welcome to the shoulder season, bringing quieter days, lower prices, balmier temperatures and a few choice events.

Billboard Latin Music Awards MUSIC
(www.billboardevents.com) This prestigious awards show in late April draws top industry execs, star performers and a slew of Latin music fans.

Miami Gay & Lesbian Film Festival FILM
(www.mglff.com) Held in late April to early May, this annual event features shorts, feature films and documentaries screened at various South Beach theaters.

May & June
May and June boast increased heat, fewer visitors and several cultural events.

Sweatstock MUSIC
(www.sweatrecordsmiami.com) Sweat Records puts on an annual music festival aimed at locals, with headline acts performing indie rock, punk and electronica.

Goombay Festival CULTURAL
(Grand Ave, Coconut Grove) A massive festival, held on the first week of June, which celebrates Bahamian culture.

Miami Museum Month CULTURAL
(www.miamimuseummonth.com) An excellent chance to see and hang out in some of the best museums in the city in the midst of happy hours, special exhibitions and lectures.

July & August
The most beastly, humidity-drenched days are during these months, when locals either vacation elsewhere or spend their days melting on the beach.

Independence Day Celebration HOLIDAY
(Bayfront Park, downtown Miami) July 4 is marked with excellent fireworks, a laser show and live music that draw more than 100,000 people to breezy Bayfront Park.

Miami Spice Restaurant Month FOOD
(www.ilovemiamispice.com) Top restaurants around Miami offer prix-fixe lunches and dinners to try to lure folks out during the heat wave.

September & October
The days and nights are still steamy and the start of school brings back college students.

International Ballet Festival DANCE
(www.internationalballetfestival.org) Some of the most important ballet talent in the world performs at venues across the city.

The Great Grove Bed Race RACE
(www.thegreatgrovebedrace.com) Between the pajama pub crawl and drag-racing beds through Coconut Grove, this is one of Miami's wackier celebrations.

November
Tourist season kicks off at the end of the month, bringing more crowds and slightly cooler days.

Miami Book Fair International CULTURAL
(www.miamibookfair.com; 401 NE 2nd Ave) Occurring in mid- to late November, this is among the most important and well-attended book fairs in the USA. Hundreds of nationally known writers join hundreds of publishers and hundreds of thousands of visitors.

White Party MUSIC
(www.whiteparty.net) If you're gay and not here, there's a problem. This weeklong extravaganza draws more than 15,000 gay men and women for nonstop partying at clubs and venues all over town.

December
Tourist season is in full swing, with northerners booking rooms so they can bask in the sunshine and be here for holiday festivities.

Art Miami ART
(www.art-miami.com) Held in January or December, this massive fair displays modern and contemporary works from more than 100 galleries and international artists.

Art Basel Miami Beach ART
(www.artbaselmiamibeach.com) One of the most important international art shows in the world, with works from more than 150 galleries and a slew of trendy parties.

King Mango Strut PARADE
(www.kingmangostrut.org; Main Ave & Grand Ave, Coconut Grove) Held each year just after Christmas since 1982, this quirky Coconut Grove parade is a politically charged, fun freak that began as a spoof on current events and the now-defunct Orange Bowl Parade.

🛏 Sleeping

It's in this category, more than any other, where all the hype surrounding Miami, and particularly South Beach, is justified. What sets South Beach apart – what defines it as a travel destination – is the deco district, and the deco district's backbone is hotels. This is one of the largest concentrations of boutique hotels in the country. And the Beach's glam only grows with every new accommodation lauded by the travel glossies, which brings the designers, which brings the fashionistas, which brings the models, which brings the tourists, which brings the chefs and...well, you get the idea.

South Beach hotels are some of the most expensive in Florida. Also, if you opt for hotel parking, expect to be charged $25 to $40 a day for the privilege. It may be easier to park in the large public garages scattered all around South Beach.

SOUTH BEACH (1ST TO 11TH STREETS)

TOP CHOICE **Pelican Hotel**   BOUTIQUE HOTEL $$$
(Map p66; ☎305-673-3373; www.pelicanhotel.com; 826 Ocean Dr; r $225-345, ste from $1500; ❀⊚) When the owners of Diesel jeans purchased the Pelican in 1999, they started scouring garage sales for just the right ingredients to fuel a mad experiment: 30 themed rooms that come off like a fantasy-suite hotel dipped in hip. From the cowboy-hipster chic of 'High Corral, OK Chaparral' to the jungly electric tiger stripes of 'Me Tarzan, You Vain,' all the rooms are completely different (although all have beautiful recycled-oak floors), fun and even come with their own 'suggested soundtrack'.

TOP CHOICE **Hotel St Augustine**   BOUTIQUE HOTEL $$
(Map p66; ☎305-532-0570; www.hotelstaugustine.com; 347 Washington Ave; r $180-280; ⓟ❀⊚) Wood that's blonder than Barbie and a crisp-and-clean deco theme combine to create one of SoFi's most elegant yet stunningly modern sleeps. Color schemes blend beige, caramel, white and cream – the sense is the hues are flowing into one eye-smoothing palette. The familiar, warm service is the cherry on top for this hip-and-homey standout, although the soothing lighting and glass showers – that turn into personal steam rooms at the flick of a switch – are pretty appealing too.

TOP CHOICE **Sense South Beach**   BOUTIQUE HOTEL $$$
(Map p66; ☎305-538-5529; www.sensesobe.com; 400 Ocean Dr; r $240-280; ⓟ❀⊚❋⛵) The Sense is fantastically atmospheric – smooth white walls disappearing behind melting blue views of South Beach, wooden paneling arranged around lovely sharp angles that feel inviting, rather than imposing, and rooms that contrast whites and dark grays into straight duochromatic cool. Pop art hangings and slender furnishings round out the MacBook-esque air. The staff are extremely helpful – warm even – which is eminently refreshing.

Lords Hotel   BOUTIQUE HOTEL $$
(Map p66; ☎877-448-4754; www.lordsouthbeach.com; 1120 Collins Ave; r $120-240, ste $330-540; ⓟ❀⊚) The epicenter of South Beach's gay scene is this cream puff of a hotel, with rooms decked out in lemony yellow and whites offset by graphic and pop art. A giant polar bear stands to greet you in the lobby, while out the back the boys gather around a pool and prepare to party. As hip as the Lords is, it doesn't affect any attitude; you'll be at ease here, unless you sit the wrong way on the weird studded chairs situated around the bar.

Hotel Victor   BOUTIQUE HOTEL $$$
(Map p66; ☎305-428-1234; www.hotelvictorsouthbeach.com; 1144 Ocean Dr; r $370-820; ⓟ❀⊚❋) The Victor wins – the 'hot design' stakes, that is. And the 'fishtanks full of jellyfish' competition. And the 'damn that room is fly' pageant too. Designed by L Murray Dixon in 1938, the redone Victor was opened in 2005 to much acclaim; these days, Shaquille O'Neal is famous for throwing parties in the $6000-a-night penthouse.

Kent Hotel   BOUTIQUE HOTEL $$
(Map p66; ☎305-604-5068; www.thekenthotel.com; 1131 Collins Ave; r $79-220; ⓟ❀⊚) Young party types will probably get a kick out of this lobby, filled with fuchsia and electric-orange geometric furniture plus bright Lucite toy blocks, which makes for an aggressively playful welcome. The special Lucite Suite is almost entirely constructed of the see-through material, giving it an icy playground feel. Take refuge in a side garden with Indonesian-style tables, bamboo and hammocks. One of the beach's better deals.

Hotel Astor   BOUTIQUE HOTEL $$
(Map p66; ☎305-531-8081; www.hotelastor.com; 956 Washington Ave; r $140-290; ⓟ❀⊚❋) They lay the retro-punk on thick in the Astor lobby, glamorizing and exaggerating the Age of Transportation into a hip caricature of itself:

a gigantic industrial fan blows over a ceiling studded with psychedelic 'lamp balls,' all suspended over a fanciful daydream of an old-school pilots' club. The earth-toned rooms are relaxing, and the small pool gets covered at night to make room for clubgoers who bop on the back-patio lounge.

Fashionhaus
BOUTIQUE HOTEL **$$**

(Map p66; 305-673-2550; www.fashionhaushotel.com; 534 Washington Ave; r $130-250; P❋ ☎☎) The Fashionhaus doesn't just sound like a Berlin avant-garde theater; it kinda feels like one, with its smooth geometric furnishings, 48 individualized rooms decked out in original artwork – from abstract expressionism to washed out photography – and its general blending of comfort, technology and design. Popular with Europeans, fashionistas, artists (and European fashionista artists) and those who just want to emulate that lifestyle.

Hotel
BOUTIQUE HOTEL **$$$**

(Map p66; 305-531-2222; 801 Collins Ave; www.thehotelofsouthbeach.com; r $260-425; P❋ ☎☎) This place is stylin' – and why shouldn't it be, when Todd Oldham designed the boldly beautiful rooms? The themed palette of 'sand, sea and sky' adds a dash of eye candy to the furnishings, as do the mosaic doorknobs and brushed-steel sinks. The Hotel boasts one of the best rooftop pools in South Beach, overshadowed only by a lovely deco spire (which says 'Tiffany,' because that was the name of this place before the blue-box jewelry chain threatened a lawsuit).

Chesterfield Hotel
BOUTIQUE HOTEL **$$**

(Map p66; 305-531-5831; www.thechesterfieldhotel.com; 855 Collins Ave; r $140-220, ste $280-520; P❋☎) Hip-hop gets jiggy with zebra-stripes on the curtains and cushions in the small lobby, which turns into the site of one of the hoppin'-est happy hours on Collins when the sun goes down. Leave a tip for the giant African statue while you're draining that mojito. Rooms mix up dark wood furniture overlaid with bright-white beds and vaguely tropical colors swathed throughout.

Clinton Hotel
BOUTIQUE HOTEL **$$**

(Map p66; 305-938-4040; www.clintonsouthbeach.com; 825 Washington Ave; r $140-396; P❋☎☎) Washington Ave is the quietest of the three main drags in SoBe, but the Clinton doesn't mind. This joint knows it would be the hottest girl in the most crowded party, with her blue velveteen banquettes and ubercontemporary metal

ceiling fans. The tiny sunporches in the Zen rooms are perfect for breakfast or an evening cocktail.

Essex House Hotel
BOUTIQUE HOTEL **$$**

(Map p66; 305-534-2700, 800-553-7739; www.essexhotel.com; 1001 Collins Ave; r $154-204, ste $354-404; ❋☎☎) When you gaze at this lobby, one of the best-preserved interiors in the deco district, you're getting a glimpse of South Beach's glorious gangster heyday. Beyond that the Essex has helpful staff, rooms furnished with soft, subdued colors and a side veranda filled with rattan furnishings that's a particularly pleasant people-watching perch.

Hotel Shelley
BOUTIQUE HOTEL **$$**

(Map p66; 305-531-3341; www.hotelshelley.com; 844 Collins Ave; r $120-260; ❋☎) Gossamer curtains, a lively lounge and a sublimely relaxing violet-and-blue color scheme combines with orblike lamps that look like bunched-up glass spider webs. The rooms are as affordably stylish as the rest of the offerings in the South Beach Group selection of hotels (see www.southbeachgroup.com).

Dream South Beach
BOUTIQUE HOTEL **$$$**

(Map p66; 305-673-4747; www.dreamsouthbeach.com; 1111 Collins Ave; r $190-240, ste $300-570; P❋☎) How to explain the Dream? From the outside it looks like an ice-cube box of clean white lines, but come inside and it feels like a cross between the interior of an Indian palace, an electric-blue tube of toothpaste and one of those hip European ice hotels – not the construction material, mind, but the way it seems to resemble a glittering arctic palace plucked from, well, your dreams. The rooftop bar is a perfect place to kick back and pretend you're some kind of film-industry mogul, before returning to your room and pretending to be a futuristic Mughal.

Miami Beach International Travelers Hostel
HOSTEL **$**

(Map p66; 305-534-0268; www.hostelmiamibeach.com; 236 9th St; dm from $25, r from $29; ❋@☎) The rooms are a tad worn, but security is good, the staff friendly and the lobby cheerful (at night it sort of resembles a club). Half the 100 rooms are private; the others are four-bed dorms, all clean and even vaguely deco-ish. Strictly speaking, to get a room you'll need an out-of-state university ID, HI card and a US or foreign passport with a recent entry stamp or an onward ticket, but these rules are only enforced when it's crowded. There's a good social vibe throughout.

South Beach Hostel
HOSTEL $

(Map p66; ☎305-534-6669; www.thesouthbeach hostel.com; 235 Washington Ave; dm from $23, r from $60; ❄@🛜) On a quiet end of SoFi (the area south of 5th St, South Beach), this hostel has a happening common area and spartan rooms. It may not be too flashy, but the staff are friendly and the on-site bar (open to 5am) seems to stay busy. The property is split between six-bed dorms and private rooms; regarding the latter, couples are probably better off in midrange hotel rooms elsewhere, which are probably twice as nice for the same price.

The Villa by Barton G
RESORT $$$

(Map p66; ☎305-576-8003; www.thevillabybar tong.com; 1116 Ocean Dr; r from $900; P❄🛜⛱) Formerly the Versace Mansion, it has been turned into one of South Beach's most upscale resorts by Barton G, replete with a mosaic pool plucked from Ancient Rome, marble bathrooms, linen spun from angel's hair and rooms that resemble the guest wing of a minor South American oligarch's personal compound.

Mondrian
RESORT $$$

(Map p66; ☎305-514-1500; www.mondrian-miami. com; 1100 West Ave; r $250-500, ste $550-750; P❄🛜⛱) Morgan Hotel Group hired Dutch design star Marcel Wanders (whose name they'll drop till it falls through the floor) to basically crank it up to 11 at the Mondrian. The theme is inspired by *Alice in Wonderland* (if it had been penned by Crockett from *Miami Vice*) – columns carved like giant table legs, chandelier showerheads, imported Delft tiles with beach scenes and magic walls with morphing celebrity faces (perhaps because the morphing nature of celebrity is what fuels South Beach's glamour?). Oh, and there's a private island (naturally).

Casa Grande Hotel
BOUTIQUE HOTEL $$$

(Map p66; ☎866-420-2272; www.casagrandesuit ehotel.com; 834 Ocean Dr; r $315-575; P❄🛜⛱) Fall colors and a splash of bright citrus start the show in the lobby, but the main event is the snow-white elegance of the 35 so-chic rooms, each one an ultramodern Scandinavian designer's dream – although we've got to say the big, marble Virgin Mary in the room we visited was way out of place. We do

like the flowers on the pillow, though – nice touch, guys.

Wave Hotel
BOUTIQUE HOTEL $$

(Map p66; ☎305-673-0401, 800-501-0401; www. wavehotel.com; 350 Ocean Dr; r $100-250; P❄🛜) Dark-blue, plush molded furniture and curving, cool lines give the lobby a sense of tidal momentum. There's a space-race theme (as in '50s Sputnik-era retro chic) going on in the rooms; you have to love the lamps, which look like cartoon bubble helmets from *Buck Rogers*. Book early enough and you can get a room here for an absolute steal.

Ocean Five Hotel
BOUTIQUE HOTEL $$

(Map p66; ☎305-532-7093; www.oceanfive.com; 436 Ocean Dr; r/ste from $130/200; P❄🛜) This boutique hotel is all pumpkin-bright; deco dressed up on the outside, with cozy, quiet rooms that reveal a maritime-meets-vintage theme on the inside, with a dash of Old West ambience on top. Think mermaid murals on pale stucco walls. There are no balconies here, but the attached restaurant is a warm, friendly spot to have a drink and a fine Italian meal before strolling up Ocean Dr.

Ohana Hostel
HOSTEL $

(Map p66; ☎305-534-2650; 750 Collins Ave; dm from $33; ❄@🛜) Rooms are kept sparkly clean, an international crowd chills in the lounge, and all is basically well in this corner of the budget-travel world.

Jazz on South Beach
HOSTEL $

(Map p66; ☎305-672-2137; www.jazzhostels. com/jazzsouthbeach; 321 Collins Ave; ❄@🛜) A nice addition to the expanding SoBe backpacker scene. The hip vibe attracts lots of scenesters and club kids.

SOUTH BEACH (11TH TO 23RD STREETS)

TOP CHOICE **The Standard**
BOUTIQUE HOTEL $$$

(☎305-673-1717; www.standardhotels.com/miami; 40 Island Ave; r $170-280, ste from $480; P❄🛜⛱) Look for the upside-down 'Standard' sign on the old Lido building on Belle Island (between South Beach and downtown Miami) and you'll find the Standard – which is anything but. This excellent boutique blends hipster funk with South Beach sex, and the result is a '50s motel gone glam. There are organic wooden floors, raised white beds, and gossamer curtains, which open onto a courtyard of earthly delights, including a heated hammam (Turkish bath). The crowd, which feels like the Delano kids with a bit more maturity, gathers to flirt and gawk.

Shuttles ferry guests to the Sagamore every 30 minutes, so you're never too isolated from the scene – unless you want to be, and given the grace of this place, we'd totally understand why. Show up on Sunday afternoons for the coolest outdoor bingo-bar-barbecue experience in the city.

TOP CHOICE Shore Club BOUTIQUE HOTEL $$$

(Map p62; ☑305-695-3100; www.shoreclub.com; 1901 Collins Ave; r $270-470, ste from $1400; P※@≋) Imagine a Zen ink-brush painting; what's beautiful isn't what's there, but what gets left out. If you could turn that sort of art into a hotel room, it might look like the stripped-down yet serene digs of the Shore Club. Yeah, yeah: it has the 400-thread-count Egyptian cotton sheets, Mexican sandstone floors etc; a lot of hotels in SoBe lay claim to similar luxury lists. What the Shore Club does like no other hotel is arrange these elements into a greater whole that's impressive in its understatement; the aesthetic is compelling because it comes across as an afterthought.

Cardozo Hotel BOUTIQUE HOTEL $$$

(Map p62; ☑305-535-6500, 800-782-6500; www.cardozohotel.com; 1300 Ocean Dr; r $220-290, ste $320-460; P※☎) The Cardozo and its neighbor, the Carlyle, were the first deco hotels saved by the Miami Design Preservation League, and in the case of the Cardozo, we think they saved the best first. Owner Gloria Estefan, whose videos are looped on flat-screen mini-TVs in the lobby, likely agrees. It's the combination of the usual contemporary sexiness (white walls, hardwood floors, high-thread-count sheets) and playful embellishments: leopard-print details, handmade furniture and a general sense that, yes, you are cool if you stay here, but you don't have to flaunt it. Oh – remember the 'hair gel' scene in *There's Something About Mary*? Filmed here.

Sagamore BOUTIQUE HOTEL $$$

(Map p62; ☑305-535-8088; www.sagamorehotel.com; 1671 Collins Ave; r $260-320, ste $400-680; P※@≋) Spencer Tunick got 600 people to pose nude in massive structured photo shoots set all around the Sagamore in 2007. Nude art installation – that's hot, but also expected at this hotel-cum-exhibition space, which likes to blur the boundaries between interior decor, art and conventional hotel aesthetics. Almost every space within this hotel, from the lobbies to the rooms, doubles

as an art gallery thanks to a talented curator and an impressive roster of contributing artists.

Cadet BOUTIQUE HOTEL $$

(Map p62; ☑305-672-6688; www.cadethotel.com; 1701 James Ave; r $170-280, ste $340-530; P※☎) The Cadet wins our award for most creative embellishments in its rooms. From paper lanterns hanging from ceilings to furry throw rugs; from clamshell designs encapsulating large mirrors to classical Asian furniture and, as always, a great art-deco facade, this spot has the aesthetics right. Check out the shaded veranda at the back, lifted from a fantasy idea of what a plantation should feel like.

Betsy Hotel BOUTIQUE HOTEL $$$

(Map p62; ☑305-531-6100; www.thebetsyhotel.com; 1440 Ocean Dr; r from $330; P※☎≋) The Betsy's 63 rooms present a sort of blend of Caribbean plantation and modern Ikea store; pastel and tropical color schemes blot into the usual South Beach monochrome white, which makes for an elegant but friendly vibe. The exterior suggests much the same spirit, but given the elite set this hotel attracts, areas like the lobby and the pool feel more exclusive and self-assured. The shutter-style doors that frame the windows within the rooms are a nice touch, as are the walnut floors and bath mirrors with inbuilt LCD TVs.

Townhouse Hotel BOUTIQUE HOTEL $$

(Map p62; ☑305-534-3800; www.townhousehotel.com; 150 20th St at Collins Ave; r $145-195, ste from $350; ※☎≋) You'd think the Townhouse was designed by the guy who styled the iPod but no, it was Jonathan Morr and India Mahdavi who fashioned a cool white lobby and igloo-like rooms with random scarlet accents and a breezy, white rooftop lounge. Who needs mints on pillows when the Townhouse provides beach balls?

Setai BOUTIQUE HOTEL $$$

(Map p62; ☑305-520-6000; www.setai.com; 101 20th St; ste $900-6000; P※☎≋⊕) There's a *linga* in the lobby – nothing says high-end luxury like a Hindu phallus. It's all part of the aesthetic at Miami's most expensive sleep, where a well-realized theme mixes Southeast Asian temple architecture, Chinese furniture, contemporary luxury and an overarching Anywhere Asia concept. Each floor is staffed by teams of 24-hour butlers, while rooms are decked out in chocolate teak wood, clean lines, and Chinese and Khmer embellishments. Note: the studio is small for four figures. Service is outstanding and surprisingly down-to-earth, and the Setai, hip as it is, is quite family-friendly.

W Hotel
RESORT $$$

(Map p62; ☎305-938-3000; www.starwoodhotels. com; 2201 Collins Ave; r $460-510, ste $660-1100; P❋🛜⛲) There's an astounding variety of rooms available at the South Beach outpost of the famous W chain, which brings the whole W-brand mix of luxury, hipness and overblown cool to Miami Beach in a big way. The 'spectacular studios' balance long panels of reflective glass with cool tablets of *cippolino* marble; the Oasis suite lets in so much light you'd think the sun had risen in your room; the Penthouse may as well be the setting of an MTV video (and given the sort of celebrities who stay here, that assessment might not be far off). The attendant bars, restaurants, clubs and pool built into this complex are some of the most well regarded on the beach.

Delano Hotel
BOUTIQUE HOTEL $$$

(Map p62; ☎305-672-2000; www.delano-hotel. com; 1685 Collins Ave; r $380-540, ste $885-1400; P❋🛜⛲) The Delano opened in the 1990s and immediately started ruling the South Beach roost. If there's a quintessential 'I'm too sexy for this song' South Beach moment, it's when you walk into the Delano's lobby, which has all the excess of an overbudgeted theater set. 'Magic mirrors' in the halls disclose weather info, tide charts and inspirational quotes. The pool area resembles the courtyard of a Disney princess' palace and includes a giant chess set; there are floor-to-ridiculously-high-ceiling curtains in the two-story waterfront rooms; and the bedouin tent cabanas are outfitted with flat-screen TVs. Rooms are almost painfully white and bright; all long, smooth lines, reflective surfaces and sexy, modern, luxurious amenities.

Gansevoort South
RESORT $$$

(Map p62; ☎866-932-6694; www.gansevoortmiam ibeach.com; 2377 Collins Ave; r $300-500, ste from $550; P❋🛜⛲) The Gansevoort has been aggressively pushing the glamour bar higher and higher in South Beach, which is a quite an accomplishment given neighbors like the W, Delano and Shore Club. Nonetheless the Gansevoort delivers, from its lobby where a small shark swims through a fuchsia-backlit aquarium, to one of the best rooftop pools

in Miami, to rooms that drip luxury but are surprisingly understated (if still posh).

Aqua Hotel
BOUTIQUE HOTEL $$

(Map p62; ☎305-538-4361; www.aquamiami. com; 1530 Collins Ave; r $150-180, ste from $200; P❋🛜⛲) A front desk made of shiny surfboard sets the mellow tone at this former motel – the old, family kind where the rooms are set around a pool. That old-school vibe barely survives under the soft glare of aqua spotlights and an alfresco lounging area, popular with the mostly gay clientele. The sleekness of the rooms is offset by quirky furniture, like a sumptuous chair made of spotted cowhide.

Tides
BOUTIQUE HOTEL $$$

(Map p62; ☎305-604-5070, 800-439-4095; www. tidessouthbeach.com; 1220 Ocean Dr; r $320-625, ste $1000-4000; P❋🛜⛲) The 50 ocean-fronting rooms are icy cool, with their jumbled vintage, ocean organic and indie vibe. The pure-white bedding is overlaid by beige, tan and shell, and offset with cream accents. Rooms come with telescopes for planetary (or Hollywood) stargazing, and the lobby, bedecked with nautical embellishments, looks like a modern sea god's palace. You can't miss this place; it's one of the biggest buildings fronting Ocean Dr.

Clay Hotel & Miami Beach International Hostel
HOSTEL $

(Map p62; ☎305-534-2988, 800-379-2529; www. clayhotel.com; 1438 Washington Ave; dm $25-29, r $60-120; ❋@🛜) How many HI hostels are located in a 100-year-old Spanish-style villa? The Clay has clean and comfortable rooms, from single-sex, four- to eight-bed dorms to decent private rooms, many of which are located in a medinalike maze of adjacent buildings. Staff are harassed due to sheer volume, but are friendly and helpful. This is yet another Miami place where Al Capone got some shut-eye.

Cavalier Hotel
BOUTIQUE HOTEL $$

(Map p62; ☎305-531-3555, 800-688-7678; www. cavaliermiami.com; 1320 Ocean Dr; r $129-155, ste $229; P❋🛜) The exterior is a rare Ocean Dr example of the Mayan/Incan inspiration that graced some deco facades (look for Meso-American details like the step pattern on the sides of the building). Inside? The Cavalier sacrifices ultrahip for Old Florida casualness, which is refreshing. We love the earthy touches in the rooms, like batik fabrics in tones of brown and beige.

MIAMI'S BEST HOTEL POOLS

Miami has some of the most beautiful hotel pools in the world, and they're more about seeing and being seen than swimming. Most of these pools double as bars, lounges or even clubs. Some hotels have a guests-only policy when it comes to hanging out at the pool, but if you buy a drink at the poolside bar you should be fine.

» **Delano Hotel** (p106)
» **Shore Club** (p105)
» **Gansevoort South** (p106)
» **Epic Hotel** (p109)
» **Biltmore Hotel** (p89)
» **Raleigh Hotel** (p107)
» **Fontainebleau** (p108)

Beachcomber Hotel   HOTEL $$
(Map p62; ☑305-531-3755, 888-305-4683; www.beachcombermiami.com; 1340 Collins Ave; r $89-189; ✳@) Green takes center stage at this deco classic, with a green-banana-colored facade, a soothing mint-green lobby, green-flecked terrazzo floor, sea-foam-green couches and a chartreuse bar, all floating beneath sleek aluminum ceiling fans. The rooms, while not quite as seductive as the entrance, are basic, cozy and clean.

Winter Haven Hotel   BOUTIQUE HOTEL $$
(Map p62; ☑305-531-5571; www.winterhavenhotelsobe.com; 1400 Ocean Dr; r $149-259; P✳☎☀) Al Capone used to stay here; maybe he liked the deco ceiling lamps in the lobby, with their sharp, retro sci-fi lines and grand-Gothic proportions, and the oddly placed oriental mirrors (which have nothing to do with art deco whatsoever). A young but laid-back crowd hangs at the Haven, which sits on the pretty-people end of Ocean Dr. The rooms, with their dark-wood accents and ice-white bedspreads, are a bit warmer than your average South Beach digs.

Surfcomber   HOTEL $$$
(Map p62; ☑305-532-7715; www.surfcomber.com; 1717 Collins Ave; r $310-560; P✳☎☀) Simply one of the best classical deco structures in Miami, the Surfcomber is (sh) actually owned by Doubletree. Well, more power to 'em; the chain has renovated this property into an immaculate state. Note the movement-suggestive lines on the exterior and semi-circular, shade-providing 'eyebrows' that jut out of the windows. Also especially note the lobby – the rounded, aeronautical feel of the space suggests you're entering a 1930s airline lounge but no, you're just going to your room. Parking is $39 per day.

Royal Palm Hotel   HOTEL $$$
(Map p62; ☑305-604-5700; www.royalpalmmiamibeach.com; 1545 Collins Ave; r $169-369, ste $299-689; P✳☎☀) Even the trolleys here have a touch of curvy deco flair, to say nothing of the chunky staircase and mezzanine, which are the best South Beach examples of the building-as-cruise-liner deco theme. Note the porthole windows, wire railings and general sense of oceanic space; you can almost hear waves slapping the side of the building. There's a glut of pop art by Romero Britto in the lobby (and even a Britto-themed restaurant); rooms are full of sharp, square-ish angles and modern furnishings.

National Hotel   HOTEL $$
(Map p62; ☑305-532-2311; www.nationalhotel.com; 1677 Collins Ave; r $240-420, ste from $450; P✳☎☀) The National is an old-school deco icon, with its bell-tower–like cap and slim yet muscular facade. Inside the hotel itself you'll find off-white rooms fashioned to fit more traditional, as opposed to uber-modern, tastes – a departure from the South Beach norm. The lobby and halls are riots of geometric design, while outside a lovely infinity pool beckons guests and visitors. The decadent cabana suites are exercises in luxury, offering unfettered access to said pool, private terraces and on-site tropical gardens.

Raleigh Hotel   BOUTIQUE HOTEL $$$
(Map p62; ☑305-534-6300, 800-848-1775; www.raleighhotel.com; 1775 Collins Ave; r $360-470, ste $560-740; P✳☎☀) While everyone else was trying to get all modern, the Raleigh painstakingly tried to restore itself to prewar glory. It succeeded in a big way. Celebrity hotelier André Balazs has managed to capture a tobacco-and-dark-wood men's club ambience and old-school elegance while simultaneously sneaking in modern design elements and amenities. Have a swim in the stunning pool; Hollywood actress Esther Williams used to.

Catalina Hotel   BOUTIQUE HOTEL $$
(Map p62; ☑305-672-4554; www.catalinahotel.com; 1732 Collins Ave; r $160-250; P✳☎☀) The Catalina is a lovely example of midrange

deco style. Not too flashy, like the uber-resorts further up Collins, yet also not too ratty like many of the cheaper properties in the area, this is a great middle of the road option that nonetheless knows how to lay on the luxury should the need present itself. The back pool, concealed behind the main building's crisp white facade, is particularly attractive and shaded by a large grove of tropical trees.

Tropics Hotel & Hostel   HOTEL $

(Map p62; ☎305-531-0361; www.tropicshotel.com; 1550 Collins Ave; dm $27, r from $59; ✸☒) The surprisingly nice Tropics (which looks a bit tacky from the outside) sports a big swimming pool and a patio area that seems consistently packed with chatting travelers. The clean four-bed dorms have attached bathrooms; private rooms are basic and serviceable.

Santa Barbara   HOSTEL $

(Map p62; ☎305-538-4411; www.miami-santa-barbara.hostel.com; 230 20th St; dm from $22, r from $55; ✸@☎) This hostel is located in a classical old deco apartment building. The rooms are all clean and well-tended, although the eight-bed dorms can get a little cramped. The rooms front a large courtyard that becomes a default social area for guests, making this place feel like *Melrose Place* for backpackers.

NORTHERN MIAMI BEACH

TOP CHOICE Circa 39   BOUTIQUE HOTEL $

(Map p70; ☎305-538-3900; www.circa39.com; 3900 Collins Ave; r $90-150; ✸@☒) If you love South Beach style but loathe South Beach attitude, Circa has got your back. The lobby, with its multicolored light board, molded furniture and wacky embellishments, is one of the funkiest in Miami. The hallways are low-lit under sexy red lamps and the icy-blue-and-white rooms are hip enough for the most exclusive scenesters (although Circa frowns on folk who act like snobs). Be you a family, a gay person or just someone who loves laid-back fun, this hotel welcomes all. The buy-in-advance web rates are phenomenal – you can find deals here for under $80.

Indian Creek Hotel   BOUTIQUE HOTEL $

(Map p70; ☎305-531-2727; www.indiancreekhotel.com; 2727 Indian Creek Dr; from r $90; ✸☒☒) Get your room key – attached to a plastic alligator – and walk through the old Miami lobby, spruced up with souvenir-stand schlock, to your comfortable, earthy-warm digs. Or

wander out to the surprisingly modern pool, where happy, sexy people are ready to have a good time. Mix in friendly staff and an easy stroll to the boardwalk, and you've got a classic boutique hotel.

Red South Beach   BOUTIQUE HOTEL $$

(Map p70; ☎800-528-0823; www.redsouthbeach.com; 3010 Collins Ave; r $130-200; ✸☎☒) Red is indeed the name of the game, from the cushions on the sleek chairs in the lobby to the flashes dancing around the marble pool to deep, blood-crimson headboards and walls wrapping you in warm sexiness in the small but beautiful guest rooms. The Red is excellent value for money and come evening the pool-bar complex is a great place to unwind and meet fellow guests.

Fontainebleau   RESORT $$$

(Map p70; ☎800-548-8886; www.fontainebleau.com; 4441 Collins Ave; r $369-461, ste $551-861; P✸☎☒) The 1200-room Fontainebleau opened in 1954, when it became a celeb-sunning spot. Numerous renovations have added beachside cabanas, seven tennis courts, a grand ballroom, a shopping mall and a fabulous swimming pool. The rooms have a midcentury-modern vibe and are surprisingly bright and cheerful – we expected more hard-edged attempts to be cool, but the sunny disposition of these chambers is a welcome surprise.

Eden Roc Renaissance   RESORT $$$

(Map p70; ☎305-531-0000, 800-327-8337; www.edenrocmiami.com; 4525 Collins Ave; r from $310, ste from $430; P✸☎☒☒) The Roc's immense inner lobby draws inspiration from the Rat Pack glory days of Miami Beach cool, and rooms in the New Ocean Tower boast lovely views over the Intracoastal Waterway. All the digs here have smooth, modern embellishments and amenities ranging from MP3 players to HDTV, ergonomic furniture and turn-down service, among others.

Daddy O Hotel   BOUTIQUE HOTEL $$

(☎305-868-4141; www.daddyohotel.com; 9660 E Bay Harbor Dr; r $150-260; P✸☎☒) The Daddy O is a cheerful, hip option that looks, from the outside, like a large B&B that's been fashioned for MTV and Apple employees. This vibe continues in the lobby and the rooms: cool, clean lines offset by bright, bouncy colors, plus a nice list of amenities: flat-screen TVs, custom wardrobes, free wi-fi and the rest. It's located about 3 miles north of North Miami Beach.

Claridge Hotel
HOTEL $$

(Map p70; ☑305-604-8485, 888-422-9111; www.
claridgefl.com; 3500 Collins Ave; r $120-215;
❋@≋) This 1928 Mediterranean-style pal-
ace feels like a (Americanized) Tuscan villa,
with a honey-stone courtyard enclosing a
sparkling pool, framed by palms, frescoed
walls and gleaming stone floors. The sooth-
ing, old-world rooms are set off by rich earth
tones and staff are eager to please.

Mimosa
BOUTIQUE HOTEL $$

(Map p70; ☑305-867-5000; www.themimosa.
com; 6525 Collins Ave; r from $210; ❋☎≋) The
Mimosa is decked out in mid-20th-century
modern furniture, offset by deco embellishment like portico-style mirrors, dark-and-
light room color schemes and a tangerine-
and-cream lobby with a citrus-bright vibe.
The pool is smallish, but overlooks a lovely
stretch of the Atlantic Ocean.

Palms South Beach
HOTEL $$$

(Map p70; ☑305-534-0505; www.thepalmshotel.
com; 3025 Collins Ave; r $140-289, ste $320-550;
P❋@≋) The lobby of the Palms manages
to be imposing and comfortable all at once;
the soaring ceiling, cooled by slow-spinning
giant rattan fans, makes for a colonial-villa-
on-convention-center-steroids vibe. Upstairs
the rooms are perfectly fine, a mix of pastel
colors and comfortable, if slightly bland, fur-
nishings.

DOWNTOWN MIAMI

Miami River Inn
B&B $$

(Map p74; ☑305-325-0045, 800-468-3589;
www.miamiriverinn.com; 119 SW South River Dr; r
$99-300; P❋≋) Cute mom-and-pop B&Bs
stuffed full of antique furniture, pretty-as-
lace gardens and a general 'Aw, thanks for
breakfast' vibe are comparatively rare in Miami. The River Inn, listed on the National
Register of Historic Places, bucks this trend,
with charming New England-style rooms,
friendly service and one of the best libraries of Miami literature in the city. In a place
where every hotel can feel like a loud experi-
ment in graphic design, this relaxing watercolor invites you onto the back porch.

Epic
HOTEL $$$

(Map p74; ☑305-424-5226; www.epichotel.com;
270 Biscayne Blvd; r $250-510; P❋☎≋) Epic in-
deed! This massive Kimpton hotel is one of
the more attractive options downtown and
it possesses a coolness cred that could match
any spot on Miami Beach. Of particular note
is the outdoor pool and sun deck, which

overlooks a gorgeous sweep of Brickell and
the surrounding condo canyons. The rooms
are outfitted in designer-chic furnishings
and some have similarly beautiful views of
greater Miami-Dade. There's an on-site spa
and bar that gives this spot a bit of youthful
energy that's lacking in other corporate-style
downtown hotels.

Mandarin Oriental Miami
HOTEL $$$

(Map p74; ☑305-913-8288, 866-888-6780; www.
mandarinoriental.com/miami; 500 Brickell Key Dr; r
$480-750, ste from $900; P❋☎≋) The Mandarin shimmers on Brickell Key, which is actually annoying – you're a little isolated from
the city out here. Not that it matters; there's
a luxurious world within a world inside this
exclusive compound, from swank restaurants to a private beach and skyline views
that look back at Miami from the far side of
Biscayne Bay. Rooms are good in a luxury-
chain kind of way, but nothing sets them
apart from other sleeps in this price range.

Four Seasons Miami
HOTEL $$$

(Map p74; ☑305-358-3535, 305-381-3381; www.
fourseasons.com/miami; 1435 Brickell Ave; r $350-
580, ste $750-1500; P❋☎≋) The marble com-
mon areas double as art galleries, a massive
spa caters to corporate types and there are
sweeping, could-have-been-a-panning-shot-
from-*Miami-Vice* views over Biscayne Bay
in some rooms. The 7th-floor terrace bar, Ba-
hia, is pure mojito-laced, Latin-loved swank-
iness, especially on Thursdays and Fridays
from 6pm to 8pm, when ladies drink free.

KEY BISCAYNE

Silver Sands Beach Resort
RESORT $$

(Map p82; ☑305-361-5441; www.silversandsbeach
resort.com; 301 Ocean Dr; r $169-189, cottages
$279-349; P❋≋) Silver Sands: aren't you
cute, with your one-story, stucco tropical
tweeness? How this little, Old Florida–style
independent resort has survived amid the
corporate competition is beyond us, but
it's definitely a warm, homey spot for those
seeking some intimate, individual attention
– to say nothing of the sunny courtyard, garden area and outdoor pool.

Ritz-Carlton Key Biscayne
RESORT $$$

(Map p82; ☑305-365-4500; www.ritzcarlton.com;
455 Grand Bay Dr; r from $330, ste $1200-3000;
P❋☎≋☻) Many Ritz-Carlton outposts
feel a little cookie-cuttered, but the Key Bis-
cayne outpost of the empire is pretty unique.
There's the magnificent lobby, vaulted by
four giant columns lifted from a Cecil B

MIMO ON BIBO

That cute little phrase means "Miami Modern on Biscayne Boulevard", and refers to the architectural style of buildings on north Biscayne Blvd past 55th Street. Specifically, there are some great roadside motels here with lovely, Rat Pack–era '50s neon beckoning visitors in. This area was neglected for a long time, and some of these spots are seedy (when we asked one owner why she advertised rooms for only $25, she smiled and said, '*Por hora*' – by the hour). But north BiBo is also one of Miami's rapidly gentrifying areas, and savvy motel owners are cleaning up their act and looking to attract the hipsters, artists and gay population flocking to the area. There's already exciting food here (see p118). Now the lodgings are getting stimulating too. All these hotels provide South Beach comfort at half the price.

» **New Yorker** (off Map p80; ☑305-759-5823; www.hotelnewyorkermiami.com; 6500 Biscayne Blvd; r $75-130; P✷☎) This hotel has been around since the 1950s and it shows – in a good way. If you could turn a classic Cadillac into a hotel with a modern interior and hipster cred, then bam, there's the New Yorker in a nutshell. Staff are friendly and rooms – done up with pop art, geometric designs and solid colors – would make Andy Warhol proud.

» **Motel Blu** (off Map p80; ☑877-784-6835; www.motelblumiami.com; 7700 Biscayne Blvd; r $52-150; P✷☎≋) Situated above Miami's Little River, the Blu may not look like much from the outside, but inside you'll find freshly-done-up rooms with a host of modern amenities. Rooms are comfortable and have a soothing lime-and-lemon interior.

» **Motel Bianco** (Map p80; ☑305-751-8696; www.motelbianco.com; 5255 Biscayne Blvd; r $80-110; P✷☎) The Bianco situates several orange-and-milky-white rooms around a glittery courtyard where coffee is served and guests can get to know each other. Contemporary art designs swirl through the larger rooms and wicker furniture abounds throughout.

DeMille set – hell, the whole hotel is lifted from a DeMille set. Tinkling fountains, the view of the bay and the marble grandeur speak less of a chain hotel and more of early-20th-century glamour. Rooms and amenities are predictably excellent.

COCONUT GROVE

Mutiny Hotel   HOTEL $$$
(Map p87; ☑305-441-2100, 866-417-0640; www.providenceresorts.com/mutiny-hotel; 2951 S Bayshore Dr; ste $190-390; P✷☎≋) This small, luxury bayfront hotel, with 120 one- and two-bedroom suites featuring balconies, boasts an indulgent staff, high-end bedding, gracious appointments, fine amenities and a small heated pool. Although it's on a busy street, you won't hear the traffic once inside. The property boasts fine views over the water.

Ritz-Carlton Coconut Grove   RESORT $$$
(Map p87; ☑305-644-4680; www.ritzcarlton.com; 3300 SW 27th Ave; r & ste $270-399; P✷☎≋✿☀) Another member of the Ritz-Carlton organization in Miami, this one overlooks the bay, has immaculate rooms and offers butlers for every need, from shopping and web-surfing to dog-walking and bathing. The massive spa is stupendous.

Sonesta Hotel & Suites Coconut Grove   HOTEL $$
(Map p87; ☑305-529-2828; www.sonesta.com/coconutgrove; 2889 McFarlane Rd; r $140-400, ste $210-660; P✷☎≋✿) The Coco Grove outpost of this luxury chain of hotels has decked its rooms out in almost all white with a splash of color (South Beach style). The amenities, from flat-screen TVs to mini-kitchenettes, add a layer of luxury to this surprisingly hip big-box. Make your way to the top of the building to enjoy a wonderful outdoor deck pool.

Grove Isle Club & Resort   RESORT $$$
(☑305-858-8300, 800-884-7683; www.groveisle.com; 4 Grove Isle Dr; r $250-529, ste $389-879; P✷☎≋) One of those 'I've got my own little island' type places, Grove Island is off the coast of Coconut Grove. This stunning boutique hotel has colonial elegance, lush tropical gardens, its own jogging track, decadent pool, sunset views over Biscayne Bay, amenities galore and the cachet of staying in your own floating temple of exclusivity.

CORAL GABLES

TOP CHOICE Biltmore Hotel
HOTEL $$$

(Map p90; ☑305-913-3158, 800-727-1926; www.
biltmorehotel.com; 1200 Anastasia Ave; r $240-
400, ste from $1200; P❄︎🅿︎❄︎🛏︎🐾) Though the
Biltmore's standard rooms can be small, a
stay here is a chance to sleep in one of the
great laps of US luxury. The grounds are so
palatial it would take a solid week to explore
everything the Biltmore has to offer – we
highly recommend reading a book in the
Romanesque/Arabian-nights opulent lobby,
sunning underneath enormous columns
and taking a dip in the largest hotel pool in
the continental USA.

Hotel St Michel
HOTEL $$

(Map p90; ☑305-444-1666; www.hotelstmichel.
com; 162 Alcazar Ave; r $125-220; P❄︎🅿︎🛏︎) The
Michel is more Metropole than Miami,
and we mean that as a compliment. The
old-world wooden fixtures, refined sense of
tweedy style and dinner-jacket ambience
don't get in the way of friendly service. The
lovely restaurant and cool bar-lounge are as
elegant as the hotel they occupy.

Wishes
MOTEL $

(Map p90; ☑305-566-9871; 4700 SW 8th St; r from
$60; P❄︎🅿︎) The Wishes is a cute motel lo-
cated in a strong of seedy flophouses; while
the neighbors may not look the best, Wishes
itself is excellent. The rooms are surprisingly
large and comfortable, clean if a little dark,
with TVs and good hot water. Their main
draw is they're on offer for quite a bargain.

GREATER MIAMI

Inn at the Fisher Island Club
RESORT $$$

(☑305-535-6080, 800-537-3708; www.fisherisland
club.com; r $600-2250; ❄︎🅿︎❄︎) If you're not
Jeb Bush (who lives here), the only way to
glimpse Fisher Island is to stay at this luxu-
rious resort. Whether in 'simple' rooms or
Vanderbilt-era cottages, your money will be
well spent: one of the best-rated spas in the
country is here, as well as eight restaurants
(this seems like overkill given the size of the
island) and enough royal perks to please a
pharaoh.

✖️ Eating

Miami is a major immigrant entrepôt and
a place that loves showing off its wealth.
Thus you get a good mix of cheap ethnic
eateries and high-quality top-end cuisine
here. There's admittedly a lot of dross too,
especially on Miami Beach, where people
can overcharge tourists and get away with
it. The best new spots for dining are in the
Wynwood, Midtown and Design District
area, a trend started by the famed Michelle
Bernstein; Coral Gables is also an estab-
lished foodie hot spot. Note that new hotels
often try to market themselves with new res-
taurants and big-name celebrity chefs.

SOUTH BEACH (1ST TO 11TH STREETS)

TOP CHOICE Tap Tap
HAITIAN $$

(Map p66; ☑305-672-2898; www.taptaprestaurant.
com; 819 5th St; mains $9-20; ⊙noon-11pm Mon-
Thu, to midnight Fri & Sat) In Haiti, tap-taps are
brightly colored pickup trucks turned public taxis, and their tropi-psychedelic paint
scheme inspires the decor at this excellent
Haitian eatery. No Manhattan-style South
Beach Lounge, this – here you dine under
bright murals of Papa Legba, guardian of the
dead, emerging from a Port-au-Prince cemetery. Meals are a happy marriage of West African, French and Caribbean: spicy pumpkin
soup, snapper in a scotch-bonnet lime sauce,
curried goat and charcoal-grilled Turks and
Caicos conch. Make sure you try the *mayi
moulen*, a signature side of cornmeal smoth-
ered in a rich bean sauce – bloody delicious!
If you need some liquid courage, shoot
some Barbancourt rum, available in several
grades (all strong).

Grazie
ITALIAN $$$

(Map p66; ☑305-673-1312; www.grazieitalian
cuisine.com; 702 Washington Ave; mains $19-34;
⊙noon-3pm Mon-Fri, 6pm-midnight daily) Thanks
indeed; Grazie is top class and comfort-
ably old-school Northern Italian. There's a
distinct lack of gorgeous, clueless waitstaff
and unwise menu experimentation. Instead
there's attentive service, solid and delicious
mains, and extremely decent prices given
the quality of the dining and high-end na-
ture of the location. The porcini risotto is
simple in construction yet deeply complex
in execution – one of the best Italian dishes
on the beach.

Puerto Sagua
CUBAN $

(Map p66; ☑305-673-1115; 700 Collins Ave; mains
$6-17; ⊙7:30am-2am) There's a secret colony
of older working-class Cubans and construc-
tion workers hidden among South Beach's
sex-and-flash, and evidently, they eat here
(next to a Benetton). Puerto Sagua challenges
the US diner with this reminder: Cubans can
greasy-spoon with the best of them. Portions
of favorites such as *picadillo* (spiced ground

beef with rice, beans and plantains) are stupidly enormous. The Cuban coffee here is not for the faint of heart – strong stuff.

11th Street Diner
DINER $

(Map p66; www.eleventhstreetdiner.com; 1065 Washington Ave; mains $8-15; ⊙24hr) You've seen the art-deco landmarks. Now eat in one: a Pullman-car diner trucked down from Wilkes-Barre, Pennsylvania, as sure a slice of Americana as a *Leave It to Beaver* marathon. If you've been drinking all night, we'll split a three-egg omelet with you and the other drunkies at 6am – if there's a diner where you can replicate Edward Hopper's *Nighthawks,* it's here.

Pizza Rustica
PIZZERIA $

(Map p66; www.pizza-rustica.com; 863 Washington Ave; slices $3-5; ⊙11am-3am Sun-Thu, 11am-6am Fri & Sat) South Beach's favorite pizza place has several locations to satisfy the demand for crusty Roman-style slices topped with an array of exotic offerings. A slice is a meal unto itself and goes down a treat when you need something to soak up the beer.

Taverna Opa
GREEK $$

(Map p66; ☑305-673-6730; www.tavernaoparest aurant.com; 36 Ocean Dr; mains $11-29; ⊙4pm-midnight, to 1am weekends) Cross Coyote Ugly Saloon with a big fat Greek wedding and you get this tourist-oriented restaurant and ouzo fest, where the meze are decent and the vibe resembles something like a Hellenic frat party. Seriously, who knew feta, lamb and bachelorette parties went together? By the end of the night, table dancing is pretty much mandatory, and this may be the only Greek dining experience you have that ends with a sloppy make-out session.

Spiga
ITALIAN $$

(Map p66; ☑305-534-0079; www.spigarestaurant. com; Impala Hotel, 1228 Collins Ave; mains $15-26; ⊙6pm-midnight) This romantic nook is a perfect place to bring your partner and gaze longingly at one another over candlelight, before you both snap out of it and start digging into excellent traditional Italian such as lamb in olive oil and rosemary, and baby clams over linguine.

Big Pink
DINER $

(Map p66; ☑305-532-4700; 157 Collins Ave; mains $11-23; ⊙8am-midnight Sun-Wed, to 2am Thu, to 5am weekends) Big Pink does American comfort food with a joie de vivre and a dash of whimsy. We're more impressed with the

lunch offerings than the dinner options; in the former, pulled Carolina pork holds the table next to a nicely done reuben. In the evening, expect seared tuna and roasted ribeye. The interior is somewhere between a '50s sock hop and a South Beach club; expect to be seated at a long communal table.

Nemo
FUSION $$$

(Map p66; ☑305-532-4550; www.nemorestaurant. com; 100 Collins Ave; mains $29-44; ⊙noon-3pm & 6:30pm-midnight Mon-Sat, 11am-3pm & 6:30pm-midnight Sun) Raw bars and warm, copper sconces are a good sign; the nudge into greatness comes when Asian elegance graces Latin-American exuberance. Fish with chimichurri sauce and kiss-the-grill nori-dusted tuna are a few jewels plucked from this fusion gem mine.

Prime 112
STEAKHOUSE $$$

(Map p66; ☑305-532-8112; www.prime112.com; 112 Ocean Dr; mains $29-68; ⊙noon-3pm Mon-Fri, 5:30pm-midnight Sun-Thu, to 1am weekends) Sometimes, you need a steak: well aged, juicy, marbled with the right bit of fat, served in a spot where the walls sweat testosterone, the bar serves Manhattans and the hostesses are models. Chuck the above into Miami Beach's oldest inn – the beautiful 1915 Browns Hotel – and there's Prime 112. Prime can definitely be said to attract celebrities; one night in 2008 it is rumored Enrique Iglesias, Anna Kournikova, Alonzo Mourning, LL Cool J, Mike Piazza and the King of Jordan all ate here...on the same night. On that note, don't come dressed in shorts and sandals. The steak, incidentally, is very good, although the service can leave something to be desired – some wait staff are lovely, but others behave with unwarranted pretension (hey, our money is as good as LL Cool J's).

News Cafe
AMERICAN $

(Map p66; www.newscafe.com; 800 Ocean Dr; mains $7-17; ⊙24hr) News Cafe is an Ocean Dr landmark that attracts thousands of travelers. We find the food to be pretty uninspiring, but the people-watching is good, so take a perch, eat some over-the-average but not-too-special food and enjoy the anthropological study that is South Beach as she Rollerblades, salsas and otherwise shambles by.

SOUTH BEACH (11TH TO 23RD STREETS)

TOP CHOICE Osteria del Teatro
ITALIAN $$

(Map p62; ☑305-538-7850; www.osteriadelteatro miami.com; 1443 Washington Ave; mains $16-31;

⊘6-11pm Mon-Thu, to 1am weekends) There are few things to swear by but the specials board of Osteria, one of the oldest and best Italian restaurants in Greater Miami, ought to be one. When you get here, let the gracious Italian waiters seat you, coddle you and then basically order for you off the board. They never pick wrong.

Burger & Beer Joint   BURGERS $
(Map p62; ☑305-531-1200; www.bnbjoint.com; 450 Lincoln Rd; mains $5.50-9; ⊘11:30am-midnight; ⚐) Gourmet burgers. Microbrew beer. Clearly, the folks at B&B did their marketing research. Because who doesn't love both? Oh yes, vegetarians, you're catered to as well; the 'Dear Prudence', a mix of portobello, red pepper, walnut pesto and zucchini fries will keep herbivores happy. Oh, there's a turkey and stuffing burger with gravy served *between turkey patties,* an ahi tuna burger, a patty of wagyu beef with foie gras…you get the idea. Did we mention the microbrew beer?

Jerry's Famous Deli   DELI $$
(Map p62; ☑305-532-8030; www.jerrysfamousdeli. com; 1450 Collins Ave; mains $9-17; ⊘24hr) Important: Jerry's delivers. Why? Because when you've gorged on the pastrami on rye, turkey clubs and other mile-high sandwiches at this enormous Jewish deli (housed in what used to be the Warsaw nightclub), you'll be craving more of the above 24/7.

Casa Tua   ITALIAN $$$
(Map p62; ☑305-673-1010; www.casatualifestyle. com/restaurant; 1700 James Ave; mains $23-58; ⊘11:30am-3pm Mon-Fri, 6:30-11pm daily) Casa Tua is way too cool to have a sign out front. You'll know it by the oh-so-fabulous crowd streaming in, the hovering limos and what you can see of the beautiful building itself (much of it hidden behind a high hedge). If you manage to get a table in the magnificent, 1925 Mediterranean-style villa, you can linger over delicious prosciutto, Dover sole, risotto with lobster and veal cheeks.

Grillfish   SEAFOOD $$
(Map p62; ☑305-538-9908; www.grillfish.com; 1444 Collins Ave; mains $13-28; ⊘11:30am-11pm, to 12:30pm weekends) Sometimes it's all in a name. They grill here. They grill fish. They could call it 'Grillfish Awesome' because that's what this simple yet elegant restaurant, with its cutely mismatched plates and church-pew benches, serves: fresh seafood, done artfully, simply and joyfully.

Mr Chow   CHINESE $$$
(Map p62; ☑305-695-1695; www.mrchow.com; 2201 Collins Ave; mains $30-45; ⊘6pm-midnight) Located in the W Hotel, Mr Chow takes Chinese-American comfort food to gourmet heights. The setting is almost intimidatingly cool, with dangling moderne-style chandeliers and an enormous bar plucked out of *Sex and the City*, yet service is friendly and the food lovely: velvet chicken served with diced chilies; stinky, spicy tofu; squid sautéed with asparagus.

Van Dyke Cafe   FUSION $$
(Map p62; ☑305-534-3600; www.thevandykecafe .com; 846 Lincoln Rd; mains $10.50-26; ⊘8am-2am) One of Lincoln Rd's most touristed spots, the Van Dyke is an institution akin to the News Cafe, serving adequate food in a primo spot for people-watching. It's usually packed and takes over half the sidewalk. Service is friendly and efficient, and you get free preening models with your burgers and eggplant Parmigiana. There's excellent nightly jazz upstairs.

Guru   INDIAN $$
(Map p62; ☑305-534-3996; www.gurufood.com; 232 12th St; mains $15-23; ⊘noon-11:30pm) A sexy, soft-lit interior of blood reds and black wood sets the stage for this Indian eatery, where local ingredients like lobster swim into the korma. Goan fish curry goes down a treat but the service often seems rushed and the kitchen can be inconsistent. Try coming at lunchtime for the *thali* special, an assemble-your-own meal extravaganza that's a steal at $9.

Balans   FUSION $$
(Map p62; ☑305-534-9191; www.balans.co.uk; 1022 Lincoln Rd; mains $13-36; ⊘8am-midnight) Kensington, Chiswick…South Beach? Oi, give this Brit-owned fusion favorite a go. Where else do veal saltimbocca and lamb *jalfrezi* share a menu? After you down the signature lobster club, you'll agree tired stereotypes about English cooking need to be reconsidered.

Nexxt Cafe   FUSION $$
(Map p62; ☑305-532-6643; 700 Lincoln Rd; mains $7-23; ⊘11:30am-11pm Mon-Thu, to midnight weekends, 11am-11pm Sun) There's a lot of cafes arranged around Lincoln Rd that offer good people-watching along one of Miami Beach's most fashionable stretches. Many of these spots are of questionable quality. Nexxt is the best of the bunch, with a huge menu that jumps between turkey chili, gourmet

BUILDING A CUBAN SANDWICH

The traditional Cuban sandwich, also known as a *sandwich mixto*, is not some slapdash creation. It's a craft best left to the experts – but here's some insight on how they do it. Correct bread is crucial – it should be Cuban white bread: fresh, soft and easy to press. The insides (both sides) should be buttered and layered (in the following order) with sliced pickles, slices of roast Cuban pork, ham (preferably sweet-cured ham) and baby Swiss cheese. Then it all gets pressed in a hot *plancha* (sandwich press) until the cheese melts. Mmmm.

burgers and low-cal salads the size of your face. Speaking of which, the menu is simply enormous, and though nothing is really excellent, everything is pretty good.

Yuca   LATIN $$$

(Map p62; ☑305-532-9822; www.yuca.com; 501 Lincoln Rd; mains $22-42; ☺noon-11:30pm) This was one of the first Nuevo Latino hot spots in Miami and it's still going strong, even if locals say it has lost a little luster over the years. The Yuca *rellena* (a mild chili stuffed with truffle-laced mushroom *picadillo*) and the tender guava ribs still make our mouth water.

Gelateria Parmalat   ICE CREAM $

(Map p62; 670 Lincoln Rd; mains $3.85-8; ☺9am-midnight Sun-Thu, to 1:30am Fri & Sat) It's hot. You've been walking all day. You need ice cream, stat. Why hello, tamarind-and-passionfruit homemade gelato! This is an excellent spot for creamy, pillowy waves of European-style frozen goodness, and based on the crowds it's the favorite ice cream on South Beach.

Pasha's   MEDITERRANEAN $

(Map p62; ☑305-673-3919; www.pashas.com; 900 Lincoln Rd; meals $4-12; ☺8am-midnight, to 1am weekends) Pasha's is a serious self-promoter judging by this place, a sleek, two-level, healthy fast-food emporium that has its name everywhere you look. No matter; the food at Pasha's rocks. Have some delicious *labneh* (thick yogurt), a plate of hummus and grilled chicken served over rice. Pasha's has started expanding as a chain and now has locations across Miami.

Flamingo Restaurant   NICARAGUAN $

(Map p62; ☑305-673-4302; 1454 Washington Ave; mains $2.50-7; ☺7am-9pm Mon-Sat) This tiny Nicaraguan storefront-cafe serves the behind-the-scenes laborers who make South Beach function. You will very likely be the only tourist eating here. Workers devour hen soup, pepper chicken and cheap breakfasts prepared by a meticulous husband-and-wife team.

Paul   BAKERY $

(Map p62; 450 Lincoln Rd; mains $5.50-9; ☺8:30am-8pm; ☑) Paul sells itself as a 'Maison de Qualite', which in other words means you can get some very fine bread here, the sort of crusty-outside and pillow-soft-inside bread you associate with a Parisian *boulangerie*. Gourmet sandwiches and light pastries make for a refreshing Lincoln Rd lunch stop.

Front Porch Cafe   AMERICAN $$

(Map p62; www.frontporchoceandrive.com; 1418 Ocean Dr; mains $10-18; ☺7am-11pm) A blue-and-white escape from the madness of the cruising scene, the Porch has been serving excellent salads, sandwiches and the like since 1990 (eons by South Beach standards). Weekend brunch is justifiably mobbed; the big omelets are delicious, as are the fat pancakes and strong coffees.

NORTHERN MIAMI BEACH

TOP CHOICE Steve's Pizza   PIZZA $

(☑305-233-4561; www.stevespizzas.net; 18063 Dixie Hwy; pizzas from $10; ☺10:30am-11pm, to midnight weekends, 11am-11pm Sun) So many pizza chains compete for the attention of tourists in South Beach, but ask a Miami Beach local where to get the best pizza and they'll tell you about Steve's. This is New York–style pizza, thin crust and handmade with care and good ingredients. New branches of Steve's are opening elsewhere in Miami, all in decidedly nontouristy areas, which preserves that feeling of authenticity.

Indomania   INDONESIAN $$

(Map p70; ☑305-535-6332; www.indomaniarestaurant.com; 131 26th St; mains $17-28; ☺6pm-10:30pm Tue-Sun) There's a lot of watered-down Asian cuisine in Miami; Indomania bucks this trend with an authentic (and welcome) execution of dishes from the largest country in Southeast Asia. Dishes reflect Indonesia's diversity, ranging from chicken in coconut curry to snapper grilled in banana leaves to gut-busting rijsttafel, a sort of buffet of small, tapas-style dishes that reflects the culinary character of particular Indonesian regions. Indomania is delicious, unique and decidedly off the tourist trail, and the service is enthusiastically friendly to boot.

Roasters' n Toasters   DELI $

(Map p70; www.roastersntoasters.com; 525 Arthur Godfrey Rd; mains $8-16; ⊙6:30am-3:30pm) Miami Beach has one of the largest Jewish populations in the US, so people here expect a lot out of their delis. Given the crowds and the satisfied smiles of customers, Roasters' n Toasters meets the demanding standards of its target demographic thanks to juicy deli meat, fresh bread, crispy bagels and warm latkes. Sliders (mini-sandwiches) are served on Jewish challah bread, an innovation that's as charming as it is tasty.

Cafe Prima Pasta   ARGENTINE $$

(Map p70; ☑305-867-0106; www.primapasta. com; 414 71st St; mains $13-24; ⊙5pm-midnight Mon-Sat, from 4pm Sun) We're not sure what's better at this Argentine-Italian place: the much-touted pasta, which deserves every one of the accolades heaped on it (try the gnocchi), or the atmosphere, which captures the dignified sexiness of Buenos Aires. Actually, it's no contest: you're the winner, as long as you eat here.

Fifi's Place   SEAFOOD $$

(Map p70; ☑305-865-5665; www.fifisseafood.com; 6934 Collins Ave; mains $13-30; ⊙noon-midnight) Latin seafood is the name of the game here – Fifi's does delicious seafood paella, a dish that mixes the supporting cast of *The Little Mermaid* with Spanish rice, and an equally good seafood *parrillada*, which draws on the same ingredients and grills them with garlic butter. Awesome.

Shuckers   AMERICAN $

(Map p70; ☑305-866-1570; www.shuckersbarand grill.com; 1819 79th St Causeway; mains $8-19; ⊙11am-late) With excellent views overlooking the waters from the 79th St Causeway, Shuckers has to be one of the best-positioned restaurants around. This is as much a bar as it is a grill, and as such the food is pub grub: burgers, fried fish and the like. We come here for one reason: the chicken wings. They're basted in several mouthwatering sauces, deep-fried and then grilled again, which results in what we can only describe as small pieces of heaven on a bone. We could sit here and devour a flock

of poultry if our willpower was low. Kitchen closes around 9pm.

El Rey del Chivito   URUGUAYAN $

(Map p70; ☑305-864-5566; www.elreydelchivito. com; 6987 Collins Ave; mains under $15; ⊙11am-midnight) Heart, meet the 'King of Chivitos' and his signature dish: a sandwich of steak, ham, cheese, fried eggs and mayonnaise (there may have been lettuce, peppers and tomatoes too, but the other ingredients just laughed at them). Now run, heart, run away! That's just the basic, by the way, and it comes with fries. We've never heard of Uruguayan restaurants in the US, and now we know why: anyone who could have spread the word died of a coronary long ago. El Rey also serves Uruguayan pizza; try it topped with *faina,* long strips of bread mixed with cheese and peppers.

La Perrada de Edgar   HOT DOGS $

(Map p70; 6976 Collins Ave; hot dogs from $5; ⊙10am-2am) Back in the day, Colombia's most (in)famous export to Miami was cocaine. But seriously, what's powder got on La Perrada and its kookily delicious hot dogs that were devised by some Dr Evil of the frankfurter world? Don't believe us? Try an *especial,* topped with plums, pineapple and whipped cream. How about shrimp and potato sticks? Apparently these are normal hot-dog toppings in Colombia. The homemade lemonade also goes down a treat.

DOWNTOWN MIAMI

Emily's Restaurante   LATIN AMERICAN $

(Map p74; ☑305-375-0013; 204 NE 1st St; mains $4-8; ⊙7am-4:30pm) A few bucks gets you two eggs, toast and coffee here; $5 gets you one of the best buffet deals in town. There are daily specials of Colombian, Cuban and Spanish cuisine: chicken soup, oxtail and *lengua en salsa* (marinated tongue).

La Moon   COLOMBIAN $

(Map p74; www.lamoonrestaurantmiami.com; 144 SW 8th St; meals $6-15) Nothing – and we're not necessarily saying this in a good way – soaks up the beer like a Colombian hot dog topped with eggs and potato sticks. Or fried pork belly and pudding. These delicacies are the preferred food and drink of Miami's 24-hour party people, and the best place for this wicked fare is here, within stumbling distance of bars like Tobacco Road. To really fit in, order a *refajo:* Colombian beer (Aguila) with Colombian soda (preferably the red one).

KEEP ON TRUCKIN'

The food-truck craze has rumbled into Miami with a vengeance. If you're not familiar with the trend, mobile kitchens drive around a city, perching on select spots where they serve ready-to-go, restaurant-quality fare for cheap – like fast food, except it's fast but not crap. Food trucks tend to have favored target destinations, but there are ways to track them down, with Twitter being the most popular. There are now more than 25 food trucks in Miami, and many congregate at **Tobacco Road** (626 S Miami Ave) on Sunday from 1pm to 5pm. Here's some of our favorite purveyors of mobile cuisine; we've included Twitter handles so you can follow their locations online:

» **Purple People Eatery** (@purpleppleatery; www.purpleppleatery.com; mains $4-8) Battered mahimahi, herb-crusted mac 'n' cheese and gourmet bison burgers.

» **Cheese Me** (@cheesememobile; www.cheeseme.com; mains $4-12) Gourmet grilled cheese, shoestring fries, braised short ribs and artisanal breads.

» **Miso Hungry** (@misohungryFT; www.misohungrymobile.com; mains $3-8) Asian-fusion options from curry to a pork burger with cilantro mayo, to vegan tofu with soy sauce.

» **Slow Food Truck** (@SlowFoodTruck; www.slowfoodtruck.com; mains $4-8) Seasonal, local food – a changing menu ensures variety and straight deliciousness.

Soya e Pomodoro   ITALIAN $

(Map p74; 305-381-9511; www.soyaepomodoro miami.com; 120 NE 1st St; mains $9-16; 11:30am-4pm Mon-Fri, 7-11:30pm Thu-Sat) S&P is a nickname that sounds suspiciously corporate, but Soya e Pomodoro is anything but. Instead, this feels like a bohemian retreat for Italian artists and filmmakers, who can dine on bowls of fresh, mouth-watering pasta under vintage posters, glittery accoutrements and rainbow paintings and wall-hangings. Think what would happen if hippies were dropped into the set of *Casablanca*. As per this vibe, readings, jazz shows and other arts events take place here on select evenings.

Fresco California   MEDITERRANEAN $

(Map p74; 305-858-0608; 1744 SW 3rd Ave; mains $9-15; 11:30am-3:30pm Mon-Fri, 5-10:30pm Mon-Thu, to 11pm Fri, 11am-11pm Sat) Fresco serves all kinds of West Coast takes on the Mediterranean palate. Relax in the candlelit backyard dining room, which feels like an Italian porch in summer when the weather is right (ie almost always). Pear and walnut salad and portobello sandwiches are lovely, while the pumpkin-stuffed ravioli is heaven on a platter. The prices are fairly low, but you'll inevitably be tempted to get wine, have multiple courses and turn a meal here into a long night out.

Azul   FUSION $$$

(Map p74; 305-913-8358; Mandarin Oriental Miami, 500 Brickell Key Dr; mains $30-72; 7-11pm Mon-Sat) Falling-water windows, clean metallic spaces and curving copper facades complement one of the nicest views of the city. The Scandi-tastic decor works in harmony with a menu that marries the Mediterranean to Asia; try the oysters wrapped in beef and *hamachi* carpaccio.

La Cocotte   CARIBBEAN $

(Map p74; 305-377-6515; www.lacocottemiami. com; 150 W Flagler St, Suite 175; mains under $10; 7:30am-3pm Mon-Fri) French Caribbean fare? Yes please! This innovative spot was sorely needed to spice up the otherwise slightly bland lunchtime fare usually found Downtown. The plantains Creole, served with scotch-bonnet slaw (hot!) and pulled pork or shrimp, or hearty brown stew chicken with carrots, onion and rosemary, are all as rich and tasty as they sound. Expect to leave lunch with a slightly expanded paunch.

Garcia's   SEAFOOD $

(Map p74; 305-375-0765; 398 NW River Dr; mains $8-18; 11am-9:30pm) Crowds of Cuban office workers lunch at Garcia's, which feels more like you're in a smugglers' seafood shack than the financial district. Expect occasionally spotty service (a bad thing), freshly caught-and-cooked fish (a good thing) and pleasantly seedy views of the Miami River.

Mini Healthy Deli   DELI $

(Map p74; 305-523-2244; Station Mall, 48 E Flagler St; mains $6-10; 11am-3pm;) This excellent cafe, tucked into a half-vacant mini-mall, is where chef Carlos Bedoya works solo and churns out remarkably fresh and delicious specials such as grilled tilapia, fresh salad, and rice and beans. There are only two little tables, but it's worth waiting – or standing while you eat.

Granny Feelgoods
HEALTH FOOD $

(Map p74; ☑305-377-9600; 25 W Flagler St; mains $9-15; ☺7am-4pm Mon-Fri; ☑) If you need karmic balance (or just tasty vegetarian fare), try this neighborhood health-food staple. Located next to the courthouse, Granny's must have the highest lawyer-to-beansprouts ratio in the USA. Try simple, vegetarian dishes such as tofu sandwiches and spinach lasagna. Carnivores are catered for too – there's a turkey burger.

WYNWOOD, DESIGN DISTRICT & LITTLE HAITI

TOP CHOICE Señora Martinez
AMERICAN $$$

(Map p80; ☑305-424-9079; www.sramartinez. com; 3252 NE 1st Ave; mains $13-30; ☺noon-3pm Tue-Fri, 6-11pm Tue-Thu, to midnight Fri & Sat, to 10pm Sun; ☑) At the time of our research, Señora Martinez was the most exciting top-end restaurant in Miami, pushing the boundaries of experimentation and plain good food. The menu is eclectic, with no one overriding regional influence, besides perhaps Miami, entrepôt that it is. Squidink risotto comes with chimichurri sauce; roasted bone marrow is scooped out next to pickled onions; duck sausage swims in port wine. The cocktail menu is as exciting as the food; with bartenders mixing up stuff like espresso tequila, fernet and honey, or rum, allspice, cider and maple syrup. Eat up, drink up, revel in your own decadent excess and hit the town.

Sustain
AMERICAN $$$

(Map p80; ☑305-424-9079; www.sustainmiami. com; 3252 NE 1st Ave; mains $13-30; ☺11:30am-3pm, 5-10:30pm; ☑) Sustain is one of the leading – and more affordable – purveyors of locally sourced, organically grown, raised and caught food in the Miami area. The lovely dining room blends smooth white walls with warm wood paneling and rounded metallic edges. The food is fantastic; try the bright, meltingly textured fish sandwich or fired chicken swimming in creamy kale and barbecued beans. The menu changes with the season. Vegetarians and vegans are always catered to, although carnivores will find plenty to enjoy as well.

Michael's Genuine Food & Drink
AMERICAN $$$

(Map p80; ☑305-573-5550; www.michaelsgenu ine.com; Atlas Plaza, 130 NE 40th St; mains $16-36; ☺11:30am-3pm Mon-Fri, 5:30-11pm Mon-Thu, to midnight Fri & Sat, 11am-2:30pm & 5:30-10pm Sun; ☑) The 'genuine' in Michael Schwartz' restaurant name refers to its use of locally sourced ingredients and healthy dose of innovation, moderated by its respect for the classics. Hence, the pork shoulder in parsley sauce and cheese grits that taste as though your grandma has just became a cordonbleu chef. The chocolate-and-red interior feels cheerful and welcoming rather than snobbish and intimidating, and that goes for the attentive waitstaff as well.

Cheese Course
CHEESE $

(Map p80; ☑786-220-6681; www.thecheesecourse. com; 3451 NE 1st Ave; mains under $16; ☺10:30am-9pm Sun-Wed, to 10pm Thu, 10:30am-11pm Fri & Sat; ☑) We love the idea at this place – pick out a few cheeses with the help of the staff and have them assemble a platter for you with fresh bread, candied walnuts, cornichons or whatever other accoutrement you so desire. There are also nice sandwiches, spreads and preserves, but for our money you can't beat a perfect lunch here of fermented dairy goodness.

Mandolin
GREEK $$

(Map p80; ☑305-576-6066; www.mandolinmiami. com; 4312 NE 2nd Ave; mains $12-26; ☺noon-11pm Mon-Sat; ☑) Mandolin doesn't just provide good Greek food – although that is present in the form of fresh fish grilled in lemon and olive oil, tomato and Turkish chorizo sandwiches and light meze like smoked eggplant and creamy yogurt. What Mandolin also provides is excellent Greek atmosphere. It's all Aegean whites and blues, colors that come to life under the strong, melting Miami sun, especially if you sit in the back courtyard, shaded by the same trees that stretch over the surrounding Buena Vista neighborhood.

Lemoni Café
CAFE $

(Map p80; ☑305-571-5080; www.mylemonicafe. com; 4600 NE 2nd Ave; mains under $10; ☺11am-10:30pm; ☑) Lemoni is as bright as its name suggests, a cute, cozy hole in the wall that serves up superlative sandwiches, wraps and salads. The salami sandwich with greens and olive oil is a simple revelation, and we'd probably rob a bank to get another slice of its Key lime pie. Located in the pretty Buena

NORTH BISCAYNE BOULEVARD

As North Biscayne Blvd continues to gentrify, better and better restaurants are opening up. Here are some winners from this foodie find:

Michy's (🖉305-759-2001; 6927 Biscayne Blvd; meals $28-43; 🕙6-10:30pm, 5:30-11pm Fri & Sat, Tue-Fri, 5:30-10pm Sun; 🖋) Blue-and-white pop decor. Organic, locally sourced ingredients. A stylish, fantastical bar where Alice could drink before painting Wonderland red. Welcome to Michelle 'Michy' Bernstein's culinary lovechild – one of the brightest stars in Miami's culinary constellation. The emphasis is on good food and fun. The 'half plates' concept lets you halve an order and mix up delicious gastronomic fare, such as foie gras on corn cakes, chicken pot pie with wild mushrooms, white almond gazpacho, and blue-cheese croquettes.

Red Light Little River (🖉305-757-7773; 7700 Biscayne Blvd; mains $14-28; 🕙Tue-Thu 6-11pm, to midnight Fri & Sat) New Orleans comfort food gets mixed up with Florida ingredients in this laid-back, excellent-value eatery perched above its namesake, Little River. The result is cuisine both clean and rich; sour oranges with sea scallops and hearty lentils; spicy shrimp-grilled-cheese sandwiches; and skirt steak in decadent rosemary and gorgonzola demiglace.

Karma Car Wash (🖉305-759-1392; www.karmacarwash.com; 7010 Biscayne Blvd; sandwiches & tapas $4.50-8; 🕙8am-8pm) This ecofriendly car wash also serves soy chai lattes, organic tapas and good microbrews. The idea could have been be precocious in execution, but it ends up being fun – more fun than your average wash 'n' wait, anyway. Of course, hybrid drivers get a 25% discount, and the bar becomes a lounge at 8pm, with DJs spinning as you wonder, 'Should I have gotten the wax finish?'

Honey Tree (Map p80; 🖉305-756-1696; 5138 Biscayne Blvd; mains under $10; 🕙8am-8pm Mon-Thu, to 7pm Fri, 9am-6pm Sat; 🖋) The Honey Tree is a health-food store that happens to serve excellent juices, smoothies and what many consider to be Miami's best vegan lunch. What's on offer varies day by day, but rest assured it will be cheap (it's priced by weight) and delicious. Lunch is usually served from noon to 2pm, but keep in mind that food often runs out due to high demand.

Jimmy's East Side Diner (🖉305-754-3692; 7201 Biscayne Blvd; mains $5-13; 🕙6:30am-4pm) Come to Jimmy's, a classic greasy spoon (that happens to be very gay-friendly; note the rainbow flag out front), for big cheap breakfasts of omelets, French toast or pancakes, and turkey clubs and burgers later in the day.

Vista neighborhood, this is a perfect place to grab a sidewalk alfresco lunch or dinner.

Enriqueta's   LATIN $
(Map p80; 🖉305-573-4681; 186 NE 29th St; mains $5-8; 🕙6:30am-3:45pm Mon-Fri, to 2pm Sat) Back in the day, Puerto Ricans, not installation artists, ruled Wynwood. Have a taste of those times in this perpetually packed roadhouse, where the Latin-diner ambience is as strong as the steaming shots of *cortadito* (Cuban-style coffee) served at the counter. Balance the local gallery fluff with a steak-and-potato-stick sandwich.

Lost & Found Saloon   MEXICAN $
(Map p80; 🖉305-576-1008; www.thelostandfound saloon-miami.com; 185 NW 36th St; mains $10-17; 🕙11am-3am; 🖋) The service is as friendly as the omelets and burritos are awesome (which is to say, very) at this little Wynwood spot, the sort of saloon where microbrews

are on tap and the wine list reads like a year abroad. Come the evening, this turns into a fun hipster kind of bar.

Garden of Eatin'   VEGAN $
(Map p80; 🖉305-754-8050; 136 NW 62nd St; mains under $10; 🕙11am-9pm Mon-Sat; 🖋) The Garden of Eatin' is run by a Rastafarian Haitian that serves up *i-tal* (sort of like Rastafarian kosher – invariably vegetarian and in this case, vegan-friendly) food for customers. The menu changes a lot, and can include anything from soy fish to tofu and greens to brown rice in pea sauce. The Garden is a one-man show and located in a fairly tough part of Little Haiti, so you may want to call ahead to see if it's open. Cash only. A drum circle is held here on Monday evenings.

Lester's   CAFE $
(Map p80; 🖉305-456-1784; www.lestersmiami. com; 2519 NE 2nd Ave; mains under $5; 🕙9am-

10pm Tue-Thurs, 9am-midnight Fri & Sat) Lester's is the first of what will doubtless be the model for many future cafes in Wynwood: studiolike wide interior, pop art (for some reason focused on mustaches), graphic-design bookshelves and of course, wi-fi, coffees and snacks.

KEY BISCAYNE

Boater's Grill   SEAFOOD $$

(Map p82; ☑305-361-0080; 1200 S Crandon Blvd; mains $14-34; ⊗9am-9pm) Located in Crandon Park, this waterfront restaurant (actually there's water below and all around) feels like a Chesapeake Bay sea house from up north, except the menu is packed with South Florida maritime goodness: stone crabs, ma-himahi and lobster paella.

Rusty Pelican   SEAFOOD $$

(☑305-361-3818; 3201 Rickenbacker Causeway; mains $18-30; ⊗9am-sundown) More than the fare itself, it's the panoramic skyline views – among the best in Miami – that draw the faithful and romantic to this airy, tropical restaurant. But if you do come for a sunset drink, the fresh air could certainly seduce you into staying for some of the surf 'n' turf menu, which is good enough considering the setting and lack of options.

Oasis   CUBAN $

(Map p82; 19 Harbor Dr; mains $5-12; ⊗8am-8pm) This excellent Cuban cafe has a customer base that ranges from the working poor to city players, and the socioeconomic barriers come tumbling down fast as folks sip high-octane Cuban coffee. Between the super-strong coffee and *masas de puerco* – marinated pork chunks, which go great with hot sauce – we're in hole-in-the-wall heaven.

LITTLE HAVANA

Hy Vong Vietnamese
Restaurant   VIETNAMESE $

(☑305-446-3674; www.hyvong.com; 3458 SW 8th; mains $7-22; ⊗6-11pm Wed-Sun, closed mid-late Aug) In a neighborhood full of exiles from a communist regime, it makes sense to find a Vietnamese restaurant. And it's telling that despite all the great Latin food around, Little Havanans still wait hours for a seat here. Why? Because this great Vietnamese food (with little touches of Florida, like Florida-style mango marinade) combines quality produce with Southeast Asian spice and a penchant for rich flavors inherited from the French colonial past. Just be prepared to

wait a long time for your culinary reward. Check the website to learn about Hy Vong's cooking classes. Hy Vong is on 8th St, located about 2 miles west of the heart of Calle Ocho.

Islas Canarias   CUBAN $

(☑305-649-0440; 285 NW 27th Ave; mains $8-19; ⊗7am-11pm) Islas may not look like much, sitting in a strip mall, but it serves some of the best Cuban in Miami. The *ropa vieja* (shredded beef) is delicious and there are nice Spanish touches on the menu (the owner's father is from the Canary Islands, hence the restaurant's name). Don't pass up the signature homemade chips, especially the ones cut from plantains.

El Cristo   CUBAN $

(Map p84; ☑305-643-9992; 1543 SW 8th St; mains $6-18; ⊗7am-11pm) A popular hangout among locals, the down-to-earth El Cristo has options from all over the Spanish-speaking world. Lots of people say it's as good as Calle Ocho gets. The menu has daily specials, but the standout is fish – try it fried for a local version of fish & chips, or take away some excellent fish empanadas and *croquetas* (deep-fried in breadcrumbs). The outdoor area is an excellent perch for enjoying 8th St eye candy.

Versailles   CUBAN $

(☑305-444-0240; 3555 SW 8th St; mains $5-20; ⊗8am-2am) Versailles (ver-*sigh*-yay) is an institution, and a lot of younger Cubans will tell you it's an overrated institution. We disagree – the food may not be the best Cuban in Miami, but it's certainly quite good (the ground beef in a gratin sauce is particularly good). And besides, older Cubans and Miami's Latin political elite still love coming here, so you've got a real chance to rub elbows with a who's who of Miami's most prominent Latin citizens. It's located 2 miles west of central Calle Ocho.

Yambo   LATIN AMERICAN $

(off Map p84; 1643 SW 1st St; mains under $10; ⊗24 hr) If you're a bit drunk in the middle of the night and can find a cab or a friend willing to drive all the way out to Little Havana, direct them to Yambo. We've never actually been here during the day, although the restaurant is surely a pretty place for lunch or breakfast. At night Yambo does a roaring stock in trade selling trays and take-away boxes about to burst with juicy slices of carne asada, piles of rice and beans and sweet fried plantains. If you're going to soak up beer, this is a great sponge.

Los Pinareños Frutería   FRUIT STAND $
(Map p84; 1334 SW 8th St; snacks & drinks $2-4; ⏰7am-7pm, to 2pm Sun) Nothing says refreshment on a sweat-stained Miami afternoon like a long, cool glass of fruit smoothie at this popular juice and veggie stand – try the sugarcane juice for something particularly sweet and bracing. The produce is pretty fresh and flavorful too.

El Rey de Las Fritas   BURGERS $
(Map p84; www.reydelasfritas.com; 1821 SW 8th St; snacks $2-3; ⏰8am-10:30pm Mon-Sat) If you've never had a *frita* (Cuban-style burger) make your peace with McDonald's and come down to El Rey with the lawyers, developers, construction workers and every other slice of Miami's Latin life. These *fritas* are big, juicy and served under a mountain of shoestring fries. Plus, the *batidos* (Latin American milkshakes) definitely brings the boys to the yard.

COCONUT GROVE

Xixon   SPANISH $$
(☎305-854-9350; 1801 SW 22nd St; tapas $8-15; ⏰11am-10pm Mon-Thu, to 11pm Fri & Sat, closed Sun) It takes a lot to stand out in Miami's crowded tapas-spot stakes. Having a Basque-country butcher-and-baker-turned-hip interior is a good start. Bread that has a crackling crust and a soft center, delicate explosions of *bacalao* (cod) fritters and the best eels cooked in garlic we've ever eaten secures Xixon's status as a top tapas contender. The *bocadillo* (sandwiches), with their blood-red Serrano ham and salty Manchego cheese, are great picnic fare. This place is a few miles north of the central Coconut Grove area.

Lulu   AMERICAN $$
(Map p87; ☎305-447-5858; 3105 Commodore Plaza; mains $9-25; ⏰11:30am-1am Mon & Tue, to 2am Wed, to 3am Thu & Fri, 9am-3am Sat, 9am-midnight Sun; 🍴) Lulu is the Grove's exemplar of using local, organic ingredients to provide gourmet versions of comfort food in a nice outdoor setting. Well, there is an interior dining space, and it is lovely, but the outdoor seating, shaded by the spreading boughs of Coconut Grove's many trees, is where we prefer to be. The truffle mac 'n' cheese is rich and immensely satisfying, while the Lulu burger is to die for.

Green Street Cafe   AMERICAN $$
(Map p87; ☎305-567-0662; 3468 Main Hwy; mains $10-23; ⏰7:30am-1am) Sidewalk spots don't get more popular (and many say more delicious) than Green Street, where the Grove's young and gorgeous congregate at sunset. There's an excellent mix of lamburgers with goat cheese, salmon salads, occasional art shows and general indie defiance of Grove gentrification, which makes for an idiosyncratic dining experience.

Jaguar   LATIN $$
(Map p87; ☎305-444-0216; www.jaguarspot.com; 3067 Grand Ave; mains $17-32; ⏰11:30am-11pm Mon-Thu, to 11:30 Fri & Sat, 11am-11pm Sun) The menu spans the Latin world, but really, everyone's here for the ceviche 'spoon bar.' The idea: pick from six styles of ceviche (raw, marinated seafood), ranging from swordfish with cilantro to corvina in lime juice, and pull a culinary version of DIY. It's novel and fun, and the $2 ceviche varieties are pretty damn delicious. Other mains include different kinds of grilled meats and fish – endearing in their simplicity, but lacking the tasty complexity of the ceviche.

George's in the Grove   FRENCH $$
(Map p87; ☎305-444-7878; 3145 Commodore Plaza; mains $13-29; ⏰10am-11pm, Mon-Fri, from 8am Sat & Sun) George's has a manically over-the-top menu that throws in everything from French to Italian to Latin plus the kitchen sink. This all comes packaged with manic, over-the-top decor that looks like a cozy attic just exploded all over Coconut Grove. Mains are rich in the best rural French culinary tradition; standbys include steak frites, duck confit and grilled branzino.

Last Carrot   VEGETARIAN $
(Map p87; ☎305-445-0805; 3133 Grand Ave; mains $6; ⏰10am-6:30pm Mon-Fri, to 4pm Sat, closed Sun; 🍴) Folks of all walks, corporate suits included, come here for fresh juice, delicious wraps (veggie options are great but the tuna melt is divine) and old-Grove neighborliness. The Carrot's endurance next to massive CocoWalk is testament to the quality of its good-for-your-body food served in a good-for-your-soul setting.

CORAL GABLES

TOP CHOICE El Carajo   SPANISH $$
(☎305-856-2424; www.elcarajointernationaltapas andwines.com; 2465 SW 17th Ave; tapas $3.50-15; ⏰11:30am-10pm Mon-Thu, to midnight Fri & Sat,

1-8pm Sun) Pass the Penzoil please. We know it is cool to tuck restaurants into unassuming spots, but the Citgo station on SW 17th Ave? Really? Really. Walk past the motor oil into a Granadan wine cellar and try not to act too fazed. And now the food, which is absolutely incredible: chorizo in cider blends burn, smoke and juice; frittatas are comfortably filling; and *sardinas* and *boquerones...* wow. These sardines and anchovies cooked with a bit of salt and olive oil are dizzyingly delicious. It is tempting to keep El Carajo a secret, but not singing its praises would be lying and we're not going to lie: if there's one restaurant you shouldn't miss in Miami, it's this one.

La Palme d'Or   FRENCH $$$

(Map p90; ☑305-913-3201; www.biltmorehotel. com/dining/palme.php; Biltmore Hotel, 1200 Anastasia Ave; fixed menus $39-89; ☺6:30-10:30pm Tue-Thu, to 11pm Fri & Sat) One of the most acclaimed French restaurants in the USA, Phillipe Ruiz' Palme is the culinary match for the Jazz Age opulence that ensconces it. With its white-gloved, old-world class and US attention to service, unmuddled by pretensions of hipness, the Palme captures, in one elegant stroke, all the exclusivity a dozen South Beach restaurants could never grasp. The menu shifts seasonally but remains consistently magnificent at one of Miami's best splurges.

Matsuri   JAPANESE $

(Map p90; ☑305-663-1615; 5759 Bird Rd; mains $7-20; ☺11:30am-2:30pm Tue-Fri, 5:30-10:30pm Tue-Sat) Note the customers here: Matsuri, tucked into a nondescript shopping center, is consistently packed with Japanese people. They don't want scene; they want a taste of home, although many of the diners are actually South American Japanese who order *unagi* (eels) in Spanish. Spicy *toro* (fatty tuna) and scallions, grilled mackerel with natural salt, and an ocean of raw fish are all *oishi* (delicious). The excellent $8 bento lunch makes the rest of the day somewhat disappointing in comparison.

Seasons 52   FUSION $$

(Map p90; ☑305-442-8552; 321 Miracle Mile; mains $14-32; ☺11:30am-11pm, to midnight Fri & Sat, to 10pm Sun) We love the concept and the execution at Seasons 52. The concept? A menu that partially rotates on a weekly basis depending on what is seasonally available (now the title makes sense). The execution?

Warm flatbreads overlaid with sharp melted cheese and steak; tiger shrimp tossed in a light pasta and chili that manages elegance and heartiness all at once.

Pascal's on Ponce   FRENCH $$$

(Map p90; ☑305-444-2024; www.pascalmiami. com; 2611 Ponce de León Blvd; mains $34-40; ☺11:30am-2:30pm Mon-Fri, 6-10pm Mon-Thu, to 11pm Fri & Sat) They're fighting the good fight here: sea scallops with beef short rib, crème brûlée and other French fine-dining classics set the elegant stage at this neighborhood hangout, a favorite night out among Coral Gables foodies who appreciate time-tested standards. The menu and the atmosphere rarely changes, and frankly we think this a good thing: if it ain't broke...

Caffe Abbracci   ITALIAN $$

(Map p90; ☑305-441-0700; www.caffeabbracci. com; 318 Aragon Ave; mains $17-37; ☺11:30am-3:30pm Mon-Fri, 6pm-midnight daily) Perfect moments in Coral Gables come easy. Here's a simple formula: you, a loved one, a muggy Miami evening, some delicious pasta and a glass of red at a sidewalk table at Abbracci – one of the finest Italian restaurants in the Gables.

GREATER MIAMI

Lots of Lox   DELI $

(www.originallotsoflox.com; 14995 S Dixie Hwy; mains $4-13; ☺8am-2:30pm) In a city with no shortage of delis, especially in mid-Miami Beach, who would have thought some of the best chopped liver on rye could be found in this unassuming place all the way down in Palmetto Bay? It is bustling, friendly and the excellent lunch meats sneer at their cousins over on Arthur Godfrey Rd, secure in their dominance of Greater Miami's deli ranks.

Graziano's   STEAKHOUSE $$

(☑305-225-0008; www.parrilla.com; 9227 SW 40th St; mains $14-34; ☺11am-11pm) People love to argue over who does the best South American steak in Miami, but among the Argentinian population the general consensus seems to be this very traditional *parilla* (grill), located on a strip of gas stations on Bird Rd. Everything is plucked out of Buenos Aires: the quebracho wood on the grill, the Argentinian customers and, most of all, the racks of *lomo* (steak), sweetbreads and blood sausage, gristly bits beloved by *portenos* (Buenos Aires natives), which are tough to find in more Yankee-friendly establishments.

SOUTH BEACH SIPPIN'

Starbucks has a pretty iron grip on the Miami coffee scene (we don't count stand-up Cuban coffee counters, as you can't sit there and read a book or work on your laptop, although if you speak Spanish, they're a good place for hearing local gossip). That said, there are some options besides Starbucks in Miami Beach.

» **A La Folie** (Map p62; www.alafoliecafe.com; 516 Española Way; mains $5-15; ⊙11am-8pm; ⊘) A *tres* French cafe where the waiters have great accents. Why yes, we would like 'zee moka.'

» **Segafredo L'Originale** (Map p62; 1040 Lincoln Rd; mains $5-15; ⊙10:30am-1am; ⊘) Immensely popular with Europeans and South Americans, this chic cafe always seems packed with gorgeous people. Credited with being the first Lincoln Rd business to open its trade to the outside street.

» **Nespresso** (Map p62; 1111 Lincoln Rd; mains $5-15; ⊙10:30am-11pm; ⊘) This futuristic cafe, all done up in geometric swirls and shapes, has excellent (if overpriced) coffee.

 Drinking

Too many people assume Miami's nightlife is all about being superattractive, super-rich and supersnooty. Disavow yourself of this notion, which only describes a small slice of the scene in South Beach. Miami has an intense variety of bars to pick from that range from grotty dives to beautiful – but still laid-back – lounges and nightclubs. Not to say you can't spot celebrities if you want to...

Dedicated gay nightlife in Miami consists largely of some South Beach clubs (and club nights) and a string of bars in the area around North Biscayne Blvd.

SOUTH BEACH

TOP CHOICE **Abraxas**   BAR

(Map p66; 407 Meridian Ave) Abraxas is open, uncrowded, located in a classical deco building, serves fantastic beer from around the USA and the world, and has clientele and staff who are the friendly sort, the types who will quickly make friends with a stranger and then keep said stranger entertained and inebriated until closing time. It's tucked away in a residential area; take your traveling friends here and they'll wonder how you ever found it.

TOP CHOICE **Room**   BAR

(Map p66; www.theotheroom.com; 100 Collins Ave) The Room's a gem: a crowded, dimly lit boutique beer bar where you can guzzle the best (brew) Miami has to offer and gawk at the best (hotties) South Beach has to show off. It's hip as hell, but the attitude is as low-key as the sexy mood lighting. Just beware, it gets crowded and it can be tough to find seats as the night goes on.

Abbey Brewery   BAR

(Map p62; www.abbeybrewinginc.com; 1115 16th St) The only brew-pub in South Beach is on the untouristed end of South Beach (near Alton Rd). It's friendly and packed with folks listening to the Grateful Dead and slinging back some excellent homebrew: give Father Theo's stout or the Immaculate IPA a shot.

Jazid   LOUNGE

(Map p62; www.jazid.net; 1342 Washington Ave) While the downstairs caters to folks seeking a mellow, candlelit spot to hear live jazz, soul and funk bands, the upstairs lounge has DJs spinning soul, funk and hip-hop to a cool, multiculti crowd. By being cool and not trying to be, this place has remained popular while places all around it have come and gone.

Zeke's   BAR

(Map p62; 625 Lincoln Rd) Zeke's is a great beer bar and one of the few nightspots on Lincoln Rd where it feels like the focus is more on having fun than looking prettier than anyone else. The beer selection is pretty awesome – they have Beer Lao, from Laos! That's a find in the USA, as are the dozens of other brews.

Ted's Hideaway   SPORTS BAR

(Map p66; 124 2nd St) Somewhere in the Florida panhandle is a bumpin', fabulous gay club, which clearly switched places with Ted's, a no-nonsense, pool table and sports-showin' 'lounge' smack in the middle of SoFi's elegance.

B Bar   BAR

(Map p62; Betsy Hotel, 1440 Ocean Ave) This smallish basement bar, tucked under the Betsy Hotel, has two salient features. One is a crowd of the beautiful, in-the-know SoBe-tastic types you expect at South Beach nightspots. The other is an odd, low-hanging reflective ceiling, built out of a sort of wobbly material that sinks in like soft Jell-o and ripples like a stone in a pond when you touch it. It's a pretty cool thing to witness, especially when all sorts of drunk, beautiful people try to (literally) raise the roof.

Lost Weekend   BAR
(Map p62; 218 Española Way) The Weekend is a grimy, sweaty, slovenly dive, filled with pool tables, cheap domestics and – hell yeah – Golden Tee arcade games and Big Buck Hunter. God bless it. Popular with local waiters, kitchen staff and bartenders.

Sagamore Bar   BAR
(Map p62; www.sagamorehotel.com; 1671 Collins Ave) Should you need a more refined vibe than the madness at the Delano (p106), walk into this cool white lobby, sit across from the rotating art projects and have a drink.

Mac's Club Deuce Bar   BAR
(Map p62; 222 14th St) The oldest bar in Miami Beach (established in 1926), the Deuce is a real neighborhood bar and hype-free zone. It's just straight-up seediness, which depending on your outlook can be quite refreshing. Plan to see everyone from trans-gendered ladies to construction workers – some hooking up, some talking rough, all having a good time.

Chesterfield Hotel Bar   BAR
(Map p66; Chesterfield Hotel, 855 Collins Ave) Perch on some prime Collins people-watching real estate and get crunk on the hip-hop and zebra-stripe theme they've got going. You'd think this would be a start-the-night-out sort of place, but the setting's so fly, folks end up stationary, sipping on mad martinis until they stumble into their rooms.

Dewey's Tavern   BAR
(Map p66; 852 Alton Rd) Dewey's is an art-deco dive (really; the exterior is a little gem of the genre) and it's as unpretentious as the best sordid watering holes get. Come here to get wasted and menace the crowds seeking serenity on quiet Alton Rd (just kidding – behave yourself!).

Bond Street Lounge   LOUNGE
(Map p62; www.townhousehotel.com/bond.asp; Townhouse Hotel, 150 20th St) The crowd in this white-and-red candy-cane-striped hotel bar like their litchitinis (lychee martinis) over sushi. Throw yourself over a white couch or cylindrical white ottoman, order up, sip and stare at the crowd.

NORTHERN MIAMI BEACH

Circa 39 Bar   LOUNGE
(Map p70; 3900 Collins Ave) Tucked off to the back of Circa 39's moody front lobby, the designer dream bar has a warm, welcoming feel to it. Definitely stop in for a cosmopolitan if you're up this way, before sauntering across the street and checking out the nighttime ocean.

Cabana Beach Club   BAR
(Map p70; 4525 Collins Ave) The back-porch bar at the Eden Roc is a surprisingly laid-back place for a drink. That's not to say the folks here aren't a beautiful bunch – they are – but the vibe is more 'chill out and enjoy the ocean view' (or the view into the pool via underwater porthole windows) than 'act like you're at a five-star resort'.

Boteco   BAR
(www.botecomiami.com; 916 NE 79th St) If you're missing São Paolo, come to Boteco on Friday evening to see the biggest Brazilian expat reunion in Miami. *Cariocas* (Rio natives) and their countrymen flock here to listen to samba and bossa nova, and chat each other up over the best caipirinhas in town.

Lou's Beer Garden   PUB
(Map p70; www.lousbeergarden.com; 7337 Harding Ave) We're frankly surprised it took so long for a beer garden to open in Miami. The weather's perfect, right? Nonetheless, this is the first beer garden to open in the Magic City in anyone's memory. Gather around long tables under tropical trees, order a cheese plate or a Kobe beef burger and down pints of Belgian craft ales. What could be better?

On the Rocks   SPORTS BAR
(Map p70; ☎305-531-0000; 217 71st St) Deep in mid-Miami Beach, this may be the only Cuban-Sports-Seedy-Dive-Bar we've visited in the USA.

DOWNTOWN MIAMI

Bar Black   LOUNGE
(Map p74; 28 NW 14th St) Bar Black is one of Miami's prime hipster hot spots – the sort of place that attracts artsy types with thick-framed glasses who mingle amid rotating art installations. This is still Miami, so folks are beautiful and there's a lovely backyard

court area to boot. But there's no cover and drinks are pretty cheap.

Tobacco Road · BAR
(Map p74; www.tobacco-road.com; 626 S Miami Ave) Miami's oldest bar has been on the scene since the 1920s. These days it's a little touristy, but it has stayed in business for a reason: old wood, blue lights, cigarette smoke and sassy bartenders greet you like a buddy. Cold beers are on tap and decent live acts crank out the blues, jazz and rock. The staff proudly reminds you its liquor license was the first one issued in a city that loves its mojitos. Tobacco Road has been here since the 1920s when it was a Prohibition-era speakeasy; today it remains a great place to order a drink or listen to live music. Film buffs may recognize it as the place where Kurt Russell has a drink in *The Mean Season* (1985).

D.R.B. · BAR
(Map p74; www.drbmiami.com; 255 NE 14th St) The acronym stands for Democratic Republic of Beer, and that's what's on offer here: a good variety of microbrews and hard-to-score imports, served in a small, understated bar area or outside on comfy couches within view of the Adrienne Arsht Center.

Kyma · LOUNGE
(Map p74; Epic Hotel, 270 Biscayne Blvd Way) Circle the round bar in the Epic Hotel, then wander past the Euro crowd onto a terrace that juts out over the slow-moving Miami river. Wander back in under 30ft ceilings for a drink, jam out to the soft pumping house music, and revel in this posh take on *Miami Vice*.

Level 25 · BAR
(Map p74; Conrad Miami, 1395 Brickell Ave) When Neo buys Morpheus a drink, they probably meet at this Conrad Miami spot (guess which floor), where it's all long white lines, low black couches, pin-striped gorgeousity and God's-eye views over Biscayne Bay.

M Bar · BAR
(Map p74; Mandarin Oriental Miami, 500 Brickell Key Dr) The high-class lobby bar here may be tiny, but its martini menu – more than 250 strong – isn't. The views aren't bad either.

WYNWOOD, DESIGN DISTRICT & LITTLE HAITI

Electric Pickle · BAR
(Map p80; www.electricpicklemiami.com; 2826 N Miami Ave) Miami can work its magic on anyone, even Wynwood's angst-ridden

artists and hipsters (Wypsters). Like Cinderella touched by a fairy godmother (or a very good DJ), they become glamorous club kids in this two-story hepcat hot spot. The Pickle is as sexy and gorgeous as Miami gets, but with its modish library and (semi)literati clientele, it's also intelligent enough to hold a conversation...though you should expect it to be a sloppy, fun drunk by midnight.

Churchill's · PUB
(Map p80; www.churchillspub.com; 5501 NE 2nd Ave, Little Haiti) Churchill's is a Brit-owned, East End–style pub in the midst of what could be Port-au-Prince. There's a lot of live music here, mainly punk, indie and more punk – expect a small cover charge if a show is on when you visit. Not insipid modern punk either: think the Ramones meets the Sex Pistols. While everyone's getting their ya-yas off, Haitians are waiting outside to park your car or sidle in and enjoy the gig and a beer with you. Brits, this is the place to watch your sports.

Magnum Lounge · GAY & LESBIAN
(709 NE 79th St) This gay piano lounge is... wait a second. Let's go over those three words again: "Gay piano lounge." Do we need to tell you more? Oh, fine: Magnum is located on the edge of gentrification, so it feels cool to 'discover' this spot. The interior is all dark shadows and deep reds but not to the point you're blind, and the clientele is a nice mix: gays, lesbians, straights on dates or just looking for something different – and by the way, the drinks are stiff, the prices are reasonable and the piano music is quite good.

LITTLE HAVANA

Casa Panza Bar · TAVERNA
(Map p84; 1620 SW 8th St) It doesn't get cornier than this 'authentic' Spanish taverna where the live shows, flamenco dancers, Spanish guitarists and audience participation reach new heights of sangria-soaked fun. Drop your cynicism, enter and enjoy.

COCONUT GROVE
Everything here closes at 3am.

Taurus · BAR
(Map p87; 3540 Main Hwy) The oldest bar in Coconut Grove is a cool mix of wood-paneling, smoky leather chairs, about 100 beers to choose from and a convivial vibe – as neighborhood bars go in Miami, this is one of the best.

ART WALKS: THE NEW CLUBBING?

It's hipsters gone wild! Or to put it another way: it's free wine! And artsy types, and galleries open till late, and the eye candy of a club, and the drunken momentum of a pub crawl and – best of all – no red ropes. The free Wynwood & Design District Art Walk is one of the best nightlife experiences in Miami. And we're not (just) being cheapskates. The experience of strolling from gallery to gallery ('That piece is *gorgeous*. Pour me another'), perusing the paintings ('No, I don't think there's a bathroom behind the performance artist') and delving into the nuances of aesthetic styles ('The wine's run out? Let's bounce') is as genuinely innovative as...well, the best contemporary art. Just be careful, as a lot of galleries in Wynwood are separated by short drives (the Design District is more walkable). Art Walks take place on the second Saturday of each month, from 7pm to 10pm (some galleries stretch to 11pm); when it's all over, lots of folks repair to Electric Pickle (p124) or Bardot (p125). Visit www.artcircuits.com for information on participating galleries.

Tavern in the Grove   BAR
(Map p87; 3416 Main Hwy) To say this sweatbox is popular with University of Miami students is like saying it rains sometimes in England. More of a neighborhood dive on weekdays.

Barracuda   BAR
(Map p87; 3035 Fuller St) The other place in the Grove to get overloaded on backwards baseball caps and coeds in miniskirts.

CORAL GABLES

Seven Seas   BAR
(Map p90; 2200 SW 57th Ave) Seven Seas is a genuine Miami neighborhood dive, decorated on the inside like a nautical theme park and filled with University of Miami students, Cuban workers, gays, straights, lesbians and folks from around the way. The best times to come are on Tuesday, Thursday and Saturday for the best karaoke in Miami – there's plenty of Spanish-language music, which adds some Latin spice.

The Bar   BAR
(Map p90; 172 Giralda Ave) All in a name, right? Probably the best watering hole in the Gables, The Bar is just what the title says (which is unusual in this neighborhood of extravagant embellishment). If you're in the 'hood on Friday, come here for happy hour (5pm to 8pm), when the young Gables professionals take their ties off and let loose long into the night.

Titanic   BAR
(305-668-1742; www.titanicbrewery.com; 5813 Ponce de León Blvd) By day, it's an All-American-type bar and grill, but at night Titanic turns into a popular University of Miami watering hole. Thursday tends to

be a big night. Located by the University entrance near Dixie Hwy and Red Rd (SW 57th Ave).

☆ Entertainment

Miami's artistic merits are obvious, even from a distance. Could there be a better creative base? There's Southern homegrown talent, migratory snowbirds bringing the funding and attention of northeastern galleries, and immigrants from across the Americas. These disparate cultures communicate their values via the language of expression. Creole, Spanish and English, after all, are poor languages compared to dance, music and theater.

Gay and lesbian nightlife used to be the province of South Beach, but today the scene is pretty integrated into straight Miami. Some clubs are still found in South Beach, while more casual gay bars are in Midcity, North Biscayne Blvd and Northern Miami Beach.

Clubs

Expect a cover charge at all of the following unless otherwise noted. In South Beach, covers range from $20 to $25 (sometimes higher!); elsewhere in the city you'll be paying around $5 to $10.

Bardot   CLUB
(Map p80; 305-576-5570; 3456 N Miami Ave) If you can't stand lines and crowds, we recommend visiting Bardot, in Wynwood, on a weekday. This could be said of any club in Miami, but you really should see the interior of Bardot before you leave the city. It's all sexy French vintage posters and furniture seemingly plucked from a private club

that serves millionaires by day, and becomes a scene of decadent excess by night. There are a lot of gorgeous Miamians here and we stress: the crowd is local, so while it's a glam scene, it's a much more friendly, laid-back one than the ridiculous posturing you might see in South Beach (not that there's no posturing going on). The entrance looks to be on N Miami Ave, but it's actually in a parking lot behind the building (indicated on our map).

Vagabond
CLUB

(Map p74; ✆305-379-0508; www.thevagabondmiami.com; 30 NE 14th St) If the South Beach Clubs are Manhattan and Hollywood, then the Vagabond scene is Brooklyn or Silver Lake, which is a travel writer's way of saying: if you tire of the lame Top 40, plastic and mediocre big-name clubs in Miami Beach, come to the Vagabond, a cool club in a rough part of Overtown. The folks are still fine, but they're funkier, definitely more local and the music is more experimental. The animal-print furniture and flying, loopy lines and curves are made to be gawked at, which is possible as no one keeps the Vagabond too dimly lit. Friday night, hosted by indie record shop Sweat, is a blast.

La Covacha
LIVE MUSIC

(✆305-594-3717; www.lacovacha.com; 10730 NW 25th St, Doral) Drive out about halfway to the Everglades (just kidding, but only just) and you'll find Covacha, the most hidden, most hip Latin scene in Miami. Actually, it's not hidden; all the young Latinos know about Covacha and love it well, and we do too. It's an excellent spot to see new bands, upcoming DJs (almost all local), an enormous crowd and few tourists. Covacha is out in Doral, a good 14 miles west of Downtown Miami.

The Stage
LIVE MUSIC

(Map p80; ✆305-576-9577; www.thestagemiami.com; 170 NE 38th St) The Stage is many things: edgy art gallery, live music venue, arts and crafts bazaar, occasional bar, and sometimes all of these things at once. Check the website to see what shows are playing and try to catch a party here – you may see a more bohemian, creative side of Miami than you initially expected (on our last visit a one-man folk-bluegrass-punk band played for a crowd dressed in rockabilly chic). On Sunday afternoon The Stage hosts family-friendly all-ages shows starting at 2pm.

Skybar
CLUB

(Map p62; ✆305-695-3900; Shore Club, 1901 Collins Ave) Skybar is one of those SoBe spots that is so impossibly full of beautiful people you wonder if you've walked into a dream – and it's not just the clientele who are gorgeous. The setting: the Moroccan garden of delights that is the courtyard of the Shore Club hotel. Chill alfresco in a sultan's pleasure garden under enormous, wrought-iron lanterns, gaze at the patricians lounging around the pool, or try (and fail, if you're an unlisted travel writer) to get into the all-crimson, all-A-list Red Room.

White Room
CLUB

(Map p74; ✆305-995-5050; www.whiteroomshows.com; 1306 N Miami Ave) Sitting as it does in edgy Overtown, it already feels like you're in on some secret when you find the White Room. Then the beautiful artists, hipsters and scenesters flock in, drinking, dancing and chatting as the requisite weird movies play on open-air projectors, near Lawrence of Arabia tents curving around an exposed-industrial main-stage. What we're saying is: hot hipsters get drunk and dance with other hot hipsters. You go, White Room.

Twist
GAY

(Map p66; ✆305-538-9478; www.twistsobe.com; 1057 Washington Ave) Never a cover, always a groove, and right across from the police station, this two-story gay club has some serious staying power and a little bit of something for everyone: six different bars; go-go dancers; drag shows; lounging areas and a small dance floor.

Nikki Beach Miami
CLUB

(Map p66; ✆305-538-1111; www.nikkibeach.com; 1 Ocean Dr) Get your groove on outdoors, wandering from immaculate gossamer beach cabana to cabana at Nikki's, which feels like an incredibly upscale full-moon party. On Sunday (Sunday?!), starting around 4pm, it's the hottest party in town, as folks clamor to get in and re-live whatever it was they did the night before.

Florida Room at the Delano
CLUB

(Map p62; ✆305-672-2000; 1685 Collins Ave) Framed posters of Snoop Dogg looking ghetto-fabulous line the entrance to The Florida Room, which should give you an idea of the atmosphere here. This is as exclusive as clubs get – plus, there's a popular dancehall-samba piano lounge for local scenesters who eschew the tourist trap megaclubs further

If you're going out in Miami, ask yourself: what do I want? Do I want to dance? Hear good tunes? Score? See celebrities? If you answered yes to the first two questions, the downtown Miami and Wynwood scene might be more to your liking. If you answered yes to the last two questions, you may want to stay in South Beach.

Also, ask yourself another question: What do I bring? If it's good looks, money or promoter connections, the world is your oyster. If you have none of the above you can still party, but be prepared for some ego-crushing. Best overheard conversation in the course of this research:

Guy A: [Looking at model] 'How do you approach a girl like that?'

Guy B: 'In a Mercedes.'

Here's how it breaks down: the South Beach club scene plays on the appeal of celebrity. More famous customers equal more regular customers. Eventually, a strange equilibrium works out where enough regular customers make people assume famous people are there, even if they're not. But those regular customers can't appear too regular, so a little social engineering is committed by club owners and the titans of the cultural scene (bouncers) in the form of the red rope. How do you get by it?

» **Be polite** Don't be skittish, but don't act like you're J Lo either. And whatever you do, don't yell at the doorman – or touch him or yank on his clothing – to try to get his attention.

» **Get guest-listed** Ask the concierge at your hotel to help you out, or simply call the club and leave your name; it's often that simple.

» **Remain confidently aloof** Don't stare at the doorman. Look elsewhere – but look hot doing it.

» **Be aggressive. Failing that, be rich** If there's a clamoring crowd, standing at the back of it and hoping it'll part is about as effective as being meek when you need a seat on the New York subway. Push your way through to the front. Or order bottle service (an overpriced bottle of spirits), which usually guarantees you a pass to the front.

» **Come correct** For women, showing a sophisticated amount of skin is effective, although 'sophisticated' depends on the wearer. We've seen chic women in barely-there tops look less trashy than folks sporting a standard miniskirt ensemble. Men, don't wear T-shirts and jeans, unless you're one of those guys who can and still look put together. In which case, we're jealous, dude. Also, this is Miami – be a little more daring than a button-up shirt and slacks if you want to stand out.

» **Get there early** Do you want to be cool or do you want to get in? From 10:30pm to 11pm is a golden time for bouncer leniency, but you can't club-hop with this strategy.

» **If you're a man, bring a woman** A man alone is not worth much (unless you're at a gay club, natch); up your value by having a beautiful woman – or two or three – on your arm.

Though our listings represent the hottest parties as of press time, we urge you to do some follow-up research when you arrive: talk to friends and your concierge, and pick up a copy of the local arts weekly, *Miami New Times,* or a free monthly such as *Miami Living Magazine* or the pint-sized *Ego Miami Magazine*.

down the beach. Show up before 11pm or be on the list (or be Lenny Kravitz – who helped design this place) to get in.

Louis CLUB
(Map p62; ☎305-531-4600; www.louismiami.com; 2325 Collins Ave) The resident club at the Gansevoort South is dark, crowded, expensive and loud, the music is meh and a 17% gratuity is automatically added to your bill, so the bartenders have little incentive to be nice to you. But Louis, whose interior resembles Marie Antoinette's boudoir after it collided with a Sex Pistols party, is located in the aforementioned Gansevoort, and as such this is the sort of place where you may well rub shoulders with a celebrity. It's Miami Beach; you came here to drink with models

and superstars, right? Well, here's a place to do just that.

Cameo CLUB

(Map p62; ☑305-532-2667; www.cameomiami.com; 1445 Washington Ave) This enormous, touristy club, where Gwen Stefani tracks get smooshed into Oakenfold, is where the sexy times are to be had – if by sexy time you mean thumping music, a packed crowd and sweat to slip on. Sunday's gay night (the specific party name frequently changes) is one of the best in town.

Hoy Como Ayer LIVE MUSIC

(Map p84; ☑305-541-2631; 2212 SW 8th St; cover $8-25) This Cuban hot spot – with authentic music, unstylish wood paneling and a small dance floor – is enhanced by cigar smoke and Havana transplants. Stop in nightly for *son* (a salsalike dance that originated in Oriente, Cuba), *boleros* (a Spanish dance in triple meter) and modern Cuban beats.

Mansion CLUB

(Map p62; ☑305-532-1525; www.mansionmiami.com; 1235 Washington Ave) Every night the lines stretch around the block as plebs beg, cajole and strut in a vain attempt to get past that damned red rope. Inside? Well, they don't call it 'Mansion' for nothing. Expect megaclub grandiosity, plenty of attitude, waiting in line for hours and the chance to see young celebs do something tabloid-worthy.

Mynt CLUB

(Map p62; ☑305-532-0727; www.myntlounge.com; 1921 Collins Ave) Join the partying stars – Justin Timberlake, Vin Diesel, Britney Spears etc – by bottle servicing yourself into the VIP section. Otherwise, make friends with the red rope until you can order a drink and then try not to spill it, which is tough in the sweaty scrum of models, Moët and mojitos.

Score GAY

(Map p62; ☑305-535-1111; www.scorebar.net; 727 Lincoln Rd) Muscle boys with mustaches, glistening six-packs gyrating on stage, and a crowd of men who've decided shirts really aren't their thing: do we need to spell out the orientation of Score's customer base? It's still the best dedicated gay bar on the beach, and the addition of the more mature Crème Lounge upstairs will undoubtedly raise the cachet of this perennial favorite.

Space CLUB

(Map p74; ☑305-375-0001; www.clubspace.com; 34 NE 11th St) This multilevel warehouse is Miami's main megaclub. With 30,000 sq ft to fill, dancers have room to strut, and an around-the-clock liquor license redefines the concept of after-hours. DJs usually pump each floor with a different sound – hip-hop, Latin, heavy trance – while the infamous rooftop lounge is the place to be for sunrise.

Performing Arts

Adrienne Arsht Center for the Performing Arts THEATER

(Map p74; ☑305-949-6722, 786-468-2000; www.arshtcenter.org; 1300 Biscayne Blvd) This magnificent venue manages to both humble and enthrall visitors. Today the Arsht is where the biggest cultural acts in Miami come to perform; a show here is a must-see on any Miami trip. Get off the Metromover at Omni stop.

Colony Theatre THEATER

(Map p62; ☑305-674-1040; www.colonytheatremiamibeach.com; 1040 Lincoln Rd, South Beach) The Colony is an absolute art-deco gem, with a classic marquee and Inca-style crenellations, which looks like the sort of place where gangsters would go to watch *Hamlet*. Built in 1935, this used to be the main cinema house in upper South Beach before it fell into disrepair in the mid-20th century. It was renovated and revived in 1976 and now boasts 465-seats and great acoustics. This treasure now serves as a major venue for performing arts – from comedy and occasional musicals to theatrical dramas, off-Broadway productions and ballet – as well as hosting movie screenings and small film festivals.

Gusman Center for the Performing Arts THEATER

(Map p74; ☑305-374-2444; www.gusmancenter.org; 174 E Flagler St) This elegantly renovated 1920s movie palace services a huge variety of performing arts including film festivals, symphonies, ballets and touring shows. The acoustics are excellent.

Fillmore Miami Beach/Jackie Gleason Theater THEATER

(Map p62; ☑305-673-7300; www.fillmoremb.com/index; 1700 Washington Ave, South Beach) Built in 1951, South Beach's premier showcase for touring Broadway shows, orchestras and other big musical productions has 2700 seats and excellent acoustics. Jackie Gleason chose to make the theater his home for the long-running 1960s TV show, but now you'll find an eclectic lineup of shows – Elvis Costello or

Albita one night, the Dutch Philharmonic or an over-the-top musical the next.

Light Box Theatre/Miami Light Project
THEATER

(Map p80; 305-576-4350; www.miamilightproject.com; 3000 Biscayne Blvd) The Miami Light Project is a nonprofit cultural foundation that represents innovative shows from theater troupes and performance artists from around the world. Shows are performed across the city, but the project is housed at Light Box Theatre.

THEATER

See www.southfloridatheatre.com for a comprehensive directory of playhouses in greater South Florida.

Actors Playhouse
THEATER

(Map p90; 305-444-9293; www.actorsplayhouse. org; Miracle Theater, 280 Miracle Mile, Coral Gables; tickets $20-50) Housed within the 1948 deco Miracle Theater, this three-theater venue stages musicals and comedies, children's theater on its kids stage and more avant-garde productions in its small experimental black-box space. Recent productions have included *Footloose* and *The Wizard of Oz* for the little ones.

Gablestage
THEATER

(Map p90; 305-446-1116; www.gablestage.org; 1200 Anastasia Ave, Coral Gables; tickets $15-40) Founded as the Florida Shakespeare Theatre in 1979 and now housed on the property of the Biltmore Hotel, this company still performs an occasional Shakespeare play, but mostly presents contemporary and classical pieces; recent productions have included *Frozen, Bug* and *The Retreat from Moscow*.

Jerry Herman Ring Theatre
THEATER

(305-284-3355; www.miami.edu/ring; University of Miami, 1321 Miller Dr; tickets $8-15) This University of Miami troupe stages musicals, dramas and comedies, with recent productions including *Falsettos* and *Baby*. Alumni actors include Sylvester Stallone, Steven Bauer, Saundra Santiago and Ray Liotta.

Miami Improv
COMEDY

(Map p87; 305-441-8200; www.miamiimprov. com; 3390 Mary St, Coconut Grove; tickets $10-70) Part of a national chain, this 3rd-floor club has the usual club-circuit suspects plus monthly Miami Comics, open-mic shows and Urban Nights, which feature stars from

MIAMI ENTERTAINMENT

Comedy Central's Showtime, HBO's Def Comedy Jam and BET's Comic View.

DANCE

Miami City Ballet
DANCE

(Map p62; 305-929-7000; www.miamicityballet. org; 2200 Liberty Ave, South Beach) Formed in 1985, this troupe is guided by artistic director Edward Villella, who studied under the great George Balanchine at the NYC Ballet. So it's no surprise Balanchine's works dominate the repertoire, with shows held at a lovely three-story headquarters designed by famed local architectural firm Arquitectonica. The facade allows passers-by to watch the dancers rehearsing through big picture windows, which makes you feel like you're in a scene from *Fame,* except the weather is better and people don't spontaneously break into song.

Ifé-Ilé Afro-Cuban Dance
DANCE

(305-476-0832; www.ife-ile.org) Ifé-Ilé is a nonprofit organization that promotes cultural understanding through dance and performs in a range of styles – traditional Afro-Cuban, mambo, rumba, conga, chancleta, son, salsa and ritual pieces. Call for further information.

Miami Hispanic Ballet DANCE
(☑305-549-7711; www.miamihispanicballet.org; 900 SW 1st St) Directed by Cuban-trained Pedro Pablo Peña, this troupe presents mainly classical ballets based out of the lovely Manuel Artime Theater, the 'largest small venue' in the city. It's located on SW 1st St between Downtown and Little Havana.

CLASSICAL

Miami Chamber Symphony ORCHESTRA
(☑305-858-3500, 305-284-6477; Gusman Concert Hall & University of Miami, 1314 Miller Dr; tickets $15-30; ⏰performances Nov-May) Its yearly series features world-renowned soloists at shows held at the University of Miami's Gusman Concert Hall (not to be confused with the Downtown Gusman Center for the Performing Arts).

New World Symphony ORCHESTRA
(NWS; ☑305-673-3330; www.nws.edu; 500 17th St) Housed in the New World Center (p61) – a funky explosion of cubist lines and geometric curves, fresh white against the blue Miami sky – the acclaimed New World Symphony holds performances from October to May (tickets $20 to $70). The deservedly heralded NWS serves as a three- to four-year preparatory program for very talented musicians who have already graduated from prestigious music schools.

Sports

Miami Heat BASKETBALL
(☑786-777-1000; www.nba.com/heat; tickets $22-375; ⏰season Nov-Apr) At the time of research, the Heat were (forgive us) one of the hottest teams in the NBA. The team plays at American Airlines Arena (p73).

Miami Dolphins FOOTBALL
(☑305-943-8000; www.miamidolphins.com; Sun Life Stadium, 2269 Dan Marino Blvd, Miami Gardens; tickets $35-8500; ⏰season Aug-Dec) 'Dol-fans' are respectably crazy about their team, even if a Super Bowl showing has evaded them since 1985. Games are wildly popular and the Dolphins are painfully successful, in that they always raise fans' hopes but never quite fulfill them. Sun Life Stadium is in Miami Gardens, 15 miles north of Downtown.

University of Miami Hurricanes FOOTBALL
(☑800-462-2637; www.hurricanesports.com; tickets $22-60; ⏰season Aug-Dec) The Hurricanes were once undisputed titans of university football, but experienced a slow decline in 2004. They've recovered a bit as of research,

and attending a game surrounded by UM's pack of fanatics is lots of fun.

University of Miami Hurricanes BASKETBALL
(☑800-462-2637; www.hurricanesports.com; tickets $20; ⏰season Nov-Apr) Catch the beloved college Hurricanes shooting hoops at the BankUnited Center at the University of Miami.

 Shopping

There are two main shopping strips in South Beach – Lincoln Road Mall, a pedestrian road lined with a great mix of indie shops and chain stores; and the southern end of Collins Ave, below 9th St. Here you'll find mostly high-end chains like A/X, Ralph Lauren and Barney's Co-op. Shooting way north of here, you'll find two extremely popular shopping malls: the **Aventura Mall** (www.shopaventuramall.com; 19501 Biscayne Blvd, Aventura), a mainstream collection including JC Penney and Bloomingdale's, and the chichi **Bal Harbour Shops** (www.balharbourshops.com; 9700 Collins Ave, Bal Harbor), a classy scene boasting Prada, Gucci, Chanel and Saks Fifth Avenue outposts. Bal Harbour is located about 3 miles north of North Miami Beach; Aventura is 9 miles north of North Miami Beach.

Move over to the mainland and there are a few options, the hippest being the Design District where you'll find a glut of art and homewares plus clothing and accessories hawkers. You'll have an easier time at the touristy, chain-store-drenched **Bayside Marketplace** (Map p74; www.baysidemarketplace.com; 401 Biscayne Blvd), on the shores of downtown Miami. Find more outdoor malls in Coconut Grove, at the ever-popular **CocoWalk** (Map p87; 3015 Grand Ave) and **Streets of Mayfair** (Map p87; www.mayfairinthegrove.net; 2911 Grand Ave); Coral Gables meanwhile, has the **Village of Merrick Park** (www.villageofmerrickpark.com; 358 San Lorenzo Ave), located a mile south of Coral Gables' Miracle Mile, near the intersection of S Le Jeune Rd and Dixie Hwy, anchored by the classy department stores Neiman Marcus and Nordstrom.

Art, Furniture & Home Design

Miami Mid Century ANTIQUES
(Map p80; ☑305-572-0558; 3404 N Miami Ave; ⏰10am-7pm) Miami Mid Century has a playful approach to antiques and retro homewares – big sunglasses, old stacks of magazines, cool geometric lamps – sorely

lacking in the more snooty shops of the Design District.

Española Way Art Center ART
(Map p62; ☑305-673-0946; 405 Española Way) There are three levels of studios here, plus excellent original work and prints for sale, all by local artists. Hours vary by studio.

Clothing & Accessories

Consign of the Times VINTAGE
(Map p62; ☑305-535-0811; www.consignofthe times.com; 1635 Jefferson Ave; ☺11am-9pm) Cute vintage boutique that carries labels as lovely as Gucci (patent-leather shoes!), Von Furstenberg (leather slingbacks!) and Versace (silver bustier!).

C Madeleine's VINTAGE
(☑305-945-7770; 13702 Biscayne Blvd; ☺11am-6pm Mon-Sat, noon-5pm Sun) The undisputed queen of vintage Miami, C Madeleine's is more than your standard used-clothes write-off. This is a serious temple to classical style, selling Yves Saint Laurent couture and classic Chanel suits. Come here for the sort of timeless looks that are as beautiful now as when they first appeared on the rack. Located on North Biscayne Blvd about 7.5 miles north of the Design District.

Hip.e CLOTHING
(Map p90; ☑305-445-3693; 359 Miracle Mile; ☺11am-7pm Mon-Sat) A bit more hip than hippie, the clothes and jewelry here manage to mix up indie and hip-hop aesthetics in an admirably wearable way. Think Lucite bangles just slightly embellished by bling and you've got an idea of the vibe.

Alchemist CLOTHING
(Map p62; ☑305-531-4653; www.shopalchemist. com; 438 Lincoln Rd; ☺10am-9pm) This high-end boutique eschews bling and snootiness for friendly attitude, minimalism and simply beautiful clothes – standout labels include Zara and Proenza Schouler. Has another location on the 5th floor of the 1111 Lincoln Rd garage

Pepe Y Berta CLOTHING
(Map p84; ☑305-266-1007, 305-857-3771; 1421 SW 8th St; ☺10am-6:30pm, 9am-7pm Sat) The most gorgeous collection of *guayaberas* in Miami can be found in this family-run shop, where the friendly owner will hand measure you and tailor a shirt to your tastes.

Boy Meets Girl CHILDREN
(Map p90; ☑305-445-9668; 355 Miracle Mile; ☺10am-7pm Mon-Fri, 11am-6pm Sat) Fantastically upscale and frankly expensive

clothing for wee ones – if the kids are getting past puberty, look elsewhere, but otherwise they'll be fashionable far before they realize it.

Olian MATERNITY
(Map p90; ☑305-446-2306; 356 Miracle Mile; ☺10am-7pm Mon-Fri) Flagship of the Olian empire and Miami's premier maternity boutique, this is where expecting mommies can outfit themselves to look as glam as any South Beach model.

Hiho Batik CLOTHING
(Map p70; ☑305-892-7733; www.hihobatik.com; 2174 NE 123rd St; ☺11am-6pm Mon-Sat) Hiho is a neat little shop where you can design your own batik (wax-and-dyed artwork); here they usually put it on T-shirts) with a friendly staff of artsy types. Located about 7 miles north of the Design District.

U Rock Couture CLOTHING
(Map p62; ☑305-538-7625; 928 Ocean Dr; ☺10am-1am, to 2am Sat) U Rock is the quintessential Miami Beach clothing store. Loud, flashy and in your face, it resembles a mangled clash of rhinestones, tight clothes, revealing dresses, deep tans, euro accents and the cast of *Jersey Shore*. Somehow, this is all strangely appealing... rather like Lincoln Rd itself.

Gifts

Books and Books BOOKS
(Map p90; ☑305-442-4408; 265 Aragon Ave St; ☺10am-11pm, to midnight Fri & Sat) The best indie bookstore in South Florida is a massive emporium of all things literary. Hosts frequent readings and is generally just a fantastic place to hang out. Has other outposts on Lincoln Rd (☑305-532-3222; 927 Lincoln Rd) and the Bal Harbour shops.

🖉 Metta Boutique GIFTS
(Map p87; ☑305-648-0250; 3435 Main Hwy; ☺9am-5pm) A cute store that exemplifies the evolution of the Grove from hippie hangout to massive market, in that it sells consumer goodies – clothes, journals, accessories, gifts and tchotchkes – that are decidedly green/ organic/sustainable/fair trade.

Celestial Treasures GIFTS
(Map p87; ☑305-461-2341; 3444 Main Hwy; ☺noon-8pm, to 10pm Fri & Sat) Your one-stop shop for spiritual and metaphysical needs, this shop has accoutrement, books, cards and components for those interested in Zen, Kabbalah, Wicca, Yoga, Buddhism

and Hinduism. Also has staff psychics on hand.

Bookstore in the Grove BOOKS
(Map p87; ☑305-483-2855; 3399 Virginia St; ⊙7am-10pm, from 8am Sat & Sun) Coconut Grove's independent bookstore is a good spot for all kinds of lit, and has a great cafe (try the empanadas) to boot.

Taschen BOOKS
(Map p62; ☑305-538-6185; 1111 Lincoln Rd; ⊙11am-9pm Mon-Thu, to 10pm Fri & Sat, noon-9pm Sun) Ridiculously cool, well-stocked collection of art, photography, design and coffee-table books to make your hip home look that much smarter.

Ricky's NYC GIFTS
(Map p62; ☑305-674-8511; 536 Lincoln Rd; ⊙10am-midnight, to 1am Sat) This South Beach standby boasts hundreds of tacky gifts (boxing-nun puppets), pop art paraphernalia and, well, 'adult' accoutrements of sex toys, games, costumes and other unmentionables.

El Crédito Cigars TOBACCONIST
(Map p84; ☑305-858-4162; 1106 SW 8th St; ⊙8am-6pm Mon-Fri, to 4pm Sat) In one of the most popular cigar stores in Miami, and one of the oldest in Florida, you'll be treated as a venerated member of the stogie-chomping club.

Little-Havana-To-Go SOUVENIRS
(Map p84; ☑305-857-9720; www.littlehavanatogo.com; 1442 SW 8th St) This is Little Havana's official souvenir store, and has some pretty cool items, from Cuban-pride T-shirts to posters, flags, paintings, photo books, cigar-box purses and authentic clothing.

M&N Variedades BOTANICA
(Map p84; ☑305-649-3040; 1753 SW 8th St; ⊙9am-8pm) This *Santeria botanica* offers spell components, magic candles, *consultas espirituales* (spiritual consultation) and computer repair.

Eyes on Lincoln EYEWEAR
(Map p62; ☑305-532-0070; 708 Lincoln Rd; ⊙10am-8pm) The most sexy, impressive collection of glasses, sunglasses and optical accoutrement we've seen in South Florida.

Genius Jones TOYS
(Map p80; ☑866-436-4875; 49 NE 39th St; ⊙noon-8pm Tue-Sun, to 10pm Fri & Sat) High-end toys, dolls and gear for babies and toddlers and their parents. Fatboy 'bean-bag' chairs, Primo Viaggio car seats and Bugaboo strollers – geek out, parents.

Music

Sweat Records MUSIC
(Map p80; ☑786-693-9309; 5505 NE 2nd Ave; ⊙noon-10pm Tue-Sat, to 5pm Sun) Sweat's almost a stereotypical indie record store – there's funky art and graffiti on the walls, it has big purple couches, it sells weird Japanese toys and there are skinny guys with thick glasses arguing over LPs and EPs you've never heard of, and of course, there's coffee and vegan snacks.

ℹ Information

Dangers & Annoyances

There are a few areas considered by locals to be dangerous: Liberty City, in northwest Miami; Overtown, from 14th St to 20th St; Little Haiti and stretches of the Miami riverfront. In these and other reputedly 'bad' areas you should avoid walking around alone late at night, use common sense and travel in groups. If in doubt, it's best to take a taxi and to know your address.

Deserted areas below 5th St in South Beach are more dangerous at night, but your main concerns are aggressive drunks or the occasional strung-out druggie, rather than muggers. In downtown Miami, use caution near the Greyhound station and around causeways, bridges and overpasses where homeless people and some refugees have set up shanty towns.

Natural dangers include the strong sun (use a high-SPF sunscreen), mosquitoes (use a spray-on repellent) and hurricanes (between June and November). There's a hurricane hotline (☑305-229-4483), which will give you information about approaching storms, storm tracks, warnings and estimated time to touchdown – all the things you will need to make a decision about if and when to leave.

Emergency

Ambulance (☑911)
Beach Patrol (☑305-673-7714)
Hurricane Hotline (☑305-468-5400)
Poison Information Center (☑305-585-5250)
Rape Hotline (☑305-585-7273)
Suicide Intervention (☑305-358-4357)

Internet Access

Most hotels and hostels (and increasingly, even camping grounds) offer wi-fi access. Free wi-fi is also available in libraries, Starbucks and McDonald's.

Media

Beach Channel (www.thebeachchannel.tv) Local 24-hour TV station on channel 19, like a quirky infomercial about goings-on in Miami Beach.

Diario Las Americas (www.diariolasamericas.com) Spanish-language daily.

El Nuevo Herald (www.elnuevoherald.com) Spanish-language daily of the *Herald*.

Miami Herald (www.miamiherald.com) Major daily covering local, national and international news.

Miami New Times (www.miaminewtimes.com) Free alternative weekly paper.

Miami Sun Post (www.miamisunpost.com) In-depth news and lifestyle coverage.

Sun-Sentinel (www.sun-sentinel.com) Daily covering South Florida.

WLRN (www.wlrn.org) Local National Public Radio affiliate, at 91.3FM on the dial.

Medical Services

Beach Dental Center (☑305-532-3300; 1680 Michigan Ave, South Beach) For dental needs.

Coral Gables Hospital (☑305-445-8461; 3100 Douglas Rd, Coral Gables) A community-based facility with many bilingual doctors.

Eckerd Drugs (☑305-538-1571; 1421 Alton Rd, South Beach; ☺24hr) One of many 24-hour Eckerd pharmacies.

Miami Beach Community Health Center (☑305-538-8835; 710 Alton Rd, South Beach) Walk-in clinic with long lines.

Mount Sinai Medical Center (☑305-674-2121; 4300 Alton Rd, Miami Beach) The area's best emergency room. Beware that you must eventually pay, and fees are high.

Visitor's Medical Line (☑305-674-2222; ☺24hr) For physician referrals.

Money

Bank of America has branch offices all over Miami and Miami Beach. To get currency exchanged you can go to **Amex** (☑305-358-7350; www.amex.com; 100 N Biscayne Blvd, downtown Miami; ☺9am-5pm Mon-Fri).

Post

The following branches have hours extended until evening thanks to self-serve machines in the lobbies:

Post office Mid-Beach (Map p70; 445 W 40th St; ☺8am-5pm Mon-Fri, 8:30am-2pm Sat); South Beach (Map p62; 1300 Washington Ave; ☺8am-5pm Mon-Fri, 8:30am-2pm Sat)

Tourist Information

Art Deco Welcome Center (Map p66; ☑305-672-2014; www.mdpl.org; 1001 Ocean Dr, South Beach; ☺10am-7:30pm Mon-Sat, to 6pm Sun) Run by the Miami Design Preservation League (MDPL); has tons of art-deco district information and organizes excellent walking tours.

Black Archives History & Research Center of South Florida (☑305-636-2390; www.theblackarchives.org; 5400 NW 22nd Ave,

ste 101, Liberty City) Information about black culture.

Coconut Grove Chamber of Commerce (Map p87; ☑305-444-7270; www.coconutgrovechamber.com; 2820 McFarlane Rd, Coconut Grove; ☺9am-5pm Mon-Fri)

Coral Gables Chamber of Commerce (Map p90; ☑305-446-1657; www.coralgableschamber.org; 224 Catalonia Ave, Coral Gables; ☺9am-5pm Mon-Fri)

Downtown Miami Welcome Center (Map p74; ☑786-472-5930; www.downtownmiami.com; 900 S Miami Ave; ☺9am-5pm Mon-Fri) Provides maps, brochures and tour information for the downtown area.

Greater Miami Convention & Visitors Bureau (Map p74; ☑305-539-3000, 800-933-8448; www.miamiandbeaches.com; 701 Brickell Ave; ☺8:30am-5pm Mon-Fri) Located in an oddly intimidating high-rise building.

Miami Beach Chamber of Commerce (Map p62; ☑305-672-1300; www.miamibeachguest.com; 1920 Meridian Ave, South Beach; ☺9am-5pm Mon-Fri)

Websites

Art Circuits (www.artcircuits.com) The best insider info on art events; includes excellent neighborhood-by-neighborhood gallery maps.

Mango & Lime (www.mangoandlime.net) The best local food blog is always ahead of the curve on eating events in the Magic City.

Meatless Miami (www.meatlessmiami.com) Vegetarians in need of an eating guide, look no further.

Miami Beach 411 (www.miamibeach411.com) A great guide for Miami Beach visitors, covering just about all concerns.

Miami Nights (www.miaminights.com) Get a good, opinionated lowdown on Miami's ever-shifting after-dark scene.

Beached Miami (www.beachedmiami.com) The best independent arts website in Miami.

Miami Favs (www.miamifavs.tumblr.com) A great list of the best of Miami.

❶ Getting There & Away

Air

Miami is served by all major carriers via two main airports: Miami International Airport (MIA) and the Fort Lauderdale-Hollywood International Airport (FLL), half an hour north of MIA. **MIA** (Map p50; ☑305-876-7000; www.miami-airport.com) is the third-busiest airport in the country. Just 6 miles west of downtown Miami, the airport is open 24 hours and is laid out in a horseshoe design. There are left-luggage facilities on two concourses at MIA, between B and C, and on G; prices vary according to bag size.

The **Fort Lauderdale-Hollywood Internation-al Airport** (☑954-359-6100, 866-435-9355; www.broward.org/airport; 320 Terminal Dr), about 15 miles north of Miami just off I-95, often serves as a lower-cost alternative to MIA, especially because it's serviced by popular, cut-rate flyers including Southwest Airlines and JetBlue.

Boat

Though it's doubtful you'll be catching a steamer to make a trans-Atlantic journey, it is quite possible that you'll arrive in Miami via a cruise ship, as the **Port of Miami** (☑305-347-4800; www.miamidade.gov/portofmiami), which received nearly four million passengers in 2003, is known as the 'cruise capital of the world.' Arriving in the port will put you on the edge of downtown Miami; taxis and public buses to other local points are available from nearby Biscayne Blvd. See p185 for details on the Key West Express ferry to Key West from Miami.

Bus

Greyhound (☑800-231-2222; www.grey hound.com) is the major carrier in and out of town. There are four major terminals: **Airport terminal** (☑305-871-1810; 4111 NW 27th St); **Main Downtown terminal** (Map p74; ☑305-374-6160; 1012 NW 1st Ave); **Northern Miami terminal** (Map p70; ☑305-945-0801; 16560 NE 6th Ave); and the **Southern Miami terminal** (☑305-296-9072; Cutler Ridge Mall, 20505 S Dixie Hwy). There are several buses daily that head both up the East Coast and across the panhandle through the Gulf Coast.

Train

The main Miami terminal of **Amtrak** (☑305-835-1222, 800-872-7245; www.amtrak.com; 8303 NW 37th Ave) connects the city with the rest of continental USA and Canada. Travel time between New York and Miami is a severe 27 to 30 hours and costs $99 to $246 one-way. The Miami Amtrak station has a left-luggage station, which costs $2 per bag.

ⓘ Getting Around

To/From the Airport

MIAMI INTERNATIONAL AIRPORT It's a cinch to get from the airport to just about anywhere in Miami, especially Mid-Beach. If you're driving, follow Rte 112 from the airport, then head east on the Julia Tuttle Causeway or the I-195 to get to South Beach. Other options include the free shuttles offered by most hotels or a taxi ($38 flat rate from the airport to South Beach). Alternatively, catch the Airport Owl night-only public bus, or the SuperShuttle (☑305-871-8210; www.supershuttle.com) shared-van service, which will cost about $26 to South Beach. Be sure to reserve a seat the day before.

FORT LAUDERDALE HOLLYWOOD INTERNATIONAL AIRPORT Put the money you save on flights toward getting to Miami once you land; either rent a car at one of the many Fort Lauderdale agencies (see p508), or take the free shuttle from terminals 1 and 3 to the airport's **Tri-Rail station** (☑800-874-7245; www.tri-rail.com; one-way $2-5.50) you can ride this commuter train into Miami. The schedule is infrequent, though, so you may want to opt for the **GOShuttle** (☑954-561-8888; http://floridalimo.hudsonltd.net), which will cost about $40 to South Beach.

Bicycle

A bike-share program on Miami Beach makes cycling around the beaches, at least, a cinch.

The Miami area may be as flat as a pancake, but it's also plagued by traffic backups and speedy thoroughfares, so judge the bikeability of your desired route carefully.

The city of Miami Beach offers the **DecoBike** (☑305-532-9494; www.decobike.com; 1-/3-day access $14/30) bike-share program. Bike stations are located in dozens of spots around Miami Beach (there's a map on the website, plus a link to an iPhone app that tells you where the nearest station is).

Places that rent bicycles:

BikeAndRoll (☑305-604-0001; www.bikeand roll.com; 401 Biscayne Blvd; ☉10am-6pm; per hr/day from $5/15) Also does bike tours.

Mangrove Cycles (☑305-361-5555; 260 Crandon Blvd, Key Biscayne; ☉10am-6pm Tue-Sun; per 2hr/day/week from $20/25/75)

Highgear Cycling (☑305-444-2175; www.highgearcycling.com; 3423 Main Hwy, Coconut Grove; ☉10am-7pm Mon-Fri, to 6pm Sat, noon-5pm Sun; per hr/day from $12/35)

Bus

The local bus system is called **Metrobus** (☑305-891-3131; www.miamidade.gov/transit/routes.asp; tickets $2). An easy-to-read route map is available online. You may spend more time waiting for a bus than you will riding on one.

In South Beach, an excellent option is the **South Beach Local Circulator** (☑305-891-3131; $0.25), a looping shuttle bus that operates along Washington between South Pointe Dr and 17th St and loops back around on Alton Rd on the west side of the beach. Rides come along every 10 to 15 minutes.

Car & Motorcycle

If you drive around Miami there are a few things to keep in mind. Miami Beach is linked to the mainland by four causeways built over Biscayne Bay. They are, from south to north: the MacArthur (the extension of US Hwy 41 and Hwy A1A);

Venetian ($1.50 toll); Julia Tuttle and John F Kennedy.

The most important north–south highway is I-95, which ends at US Hwy 1 south of downtown Miami. US Hwy 1, which runs from Key West all the way north to Maine, hugs the coastline. It's called Dixie Hwy south of downtown Miami and Biscayne Blvd north of downtown Miami. The Palmetto Expressway (Hwy 826) makes a rough loop around the city and spurs off below SW 40th St to the Don Shula Expressway (Hwy 874, a toll road). Florida's Turnpike Extension makes the most western outer loop around the city. Hwy A1A becomes Collins Ave in Miami Beach.

Miami has an annoying convention of giving major roads multiple names. So for example, Bird Rd is both SW 40th St and Hwy 976. Hwy 826 is the Palmetto Expressway. US 1 is the Dixie Hwy – except in Downtown, when it becomes Biscayne Blvd. Hwy 836 is the Dolphin Expressway, while in Miami Beach 5th St becomes A1A. Calle Ocho is SW 8th St, as well as the Tamiami Trail, and US 41 (phew), and Hwy 959 is Red Rd, except when it's SW 57th St. Somehow, this isn't as confusing as it reads on paper – most signage indicates every name a route may have, but it can be frustrating to first-time Miami drivers.

Besides the causeways to Miami Beach, the major east–west roads are SW 8th St; Hwy 112 (also called Airport Expressway); and Hwy 836 (also called Dolphin Expressway), which slices through downtown Miami and connects with I-395 and the MacArthur Causeway, and which runs west to the Palmetto Expressway and Florida's Turnpike Extension.

Miami drivers are...how can we put this delicately?...aggressive, tailgating jerks who'd cut off their grandmother if they could figure out how to properly change lanes. We are, of course, kidding. Not all Miami drivers fit the above description, but there are enough of these maniacs about to make driving here a nightmare.

PARKING Parking is pretty straightforward. Regulations are well signposted and meters are plentiful (except perhaps on holiday-weekend evenings in South Beach). Downtown, near the **Bayside Marketplace**, parking is cheap but a bit confusing: you must find a place in the head-on parking lots (backing into the parking space not allowed), buy a ticket from a central machine, and display it in your windshield.

On South Beach there's metered street parking along most streets (except Lincoln Rd and residential areas). Meters are enforced from 9am to as late as 3am in some parts of South Beach. Most allow you to pay for up to three hours, although some have increased that range to 12 hours. Most Miami Beach meter machines include a credit-card option; parking rates vary, but it rarely costs more than $1.50 per hour.

There are many **municipal parking garages**, which are usually the easiest and cheapest option – look for giant blue 'P' signs. You'll find several located along Collins Ave and Washington Ave. If you park illegally or if the meter runs out, parking fines are about $30, but a tow could cost much more.

Taxi
Central Cabs (☑305-532-5555)
Dispatch Service (☑305-525-2455)
Flamingo Taxis (☑305-759-8100)
Metro (☑305-888-8888)
Sunshine (☑305-445-3333)
Yellow (☑305-400-0000)

Train
Around Miami the **Metromover** (www.miami dade.gov/transit), which is equal parts bus, monorail and train, is helpful for getting around downtown Miami. It offers visitors a great perspective on the city and a free orientation tour of the area.

Metrorail (www.miamidade.gov/transit) is a 21-mile-long heavy-rail system that has one elevated line running from Hialeah through downtown Miami and south to Kendall/Dadeland. Trains run every five to 15 minutes from 6am to midnight. The fare is $2, or $1 with a Metromover transfer.

The regional **Tri-Rail** (☑800-874-7245; www .tri-rail.com) double-decker commuter trains run the 71 miles between Dade, Broward and Palm Beach counties. Fares are calculated on a zone basis; the shortest distance traveled costs $4.40 round-trip, the most you'll ever pay is for the ride between MIA and West Palm Beach ($11.55 round-trip). No tickets are sold on the train, so allow time to make your purchase before boarding. All trains and stations are accessible to riders with disabilities. For a list of stations, log on to the Tri-Rail website.

The Everglades

Includes »

Best Places to Eat

Best Places to Stay

Why Go?

The Everglades truly make South Florida unique, even more so than Miami. Called the 'River of Grass' by its initial Native American inhabitants, this is not just a wetland, or a swamp, or a lake, or a river or a prairie, or a grassland – it is all of the above, twisted together into a series of soft horizons, long vistas, sunsets that stretch across your entire field of vision and the creeping grin of a large population of dinosaur-era reptiles.

When you watch anhinga flexing their wings before breaking into a corkscrew dive, or the slow, Jurassic flap of a great blue heron gliding over its domain, or the sun kissing miles of unbroken saw grass as it sets behind humps of skeletal cypress domes, you'll have an idea of what we're speaking of. In a nation where natural beauty is measured by its capacity for drama, the Everglades subtly, contentedly flows on.

When to Go

Everglades City

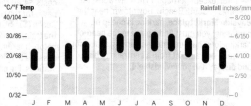

Dec–Mar Dry season: top wildlife viewing along watercourses, but some kayaking will be difficult.	**Apr–Jun** Although the weather gets pretty hot, there's a good mix of water and wildlife.	**Jul–Nov** Lots of heat, lots of bugs and (except October and November) chances of hurricanes.

EVERGLADES NATIONAL PARK

Although the grassy waters – the Everglades ecosystem – extend outside Everglades National Park (the third-largest in continental USA), you really need to enter the park to experience it. There are three main entrances and three main areas of the park: one along the southeast edge near Homestead and Florida City (Ernest Coe section); at the central-north side on the Tamiami Trail (Shark Valley section); and a third at the northwest shore (Gulf Coast section), past Everglades City. The Shark Valley and Gulf Coast sections of the park come one after the other in geographic succession, but the Ernest Coe area is entirely separate. At all of these entrances you'll pay $10 for a vehicle pass, or $5 if you're a cyclist, both of which are good for entrance for seven consecutive days into any entrance in the park.

These entrances allow for two good road trips from Miami. The first choice is heading west along the Tamiami Trail, past the Miccosukee reservation and Shark Valley, all the way to Everglades City, the Gulf Coast and the crystal waters of the 10,000 Islands.

The other option is to enter at Ernest Coe and take Hwy 9336 to Flamingo through the most 'Glades-y' landscape in the park, with unbroken vistas of wet prairie, big sky and long silences.

❶ Getting There & Away

The largest subtropical wilderness in the continental USA is easily accessible from Miami. The Glades, which comprise the 80 southernmost miles of Florida, are bound by the Atlantic Ocean to the east and the Gulf of Mexico to the west. The Tamiami Trail (US Hwy 41) goes east–west, parallel to the more northern (and less interesting) Alligator Alley (I-75).

❶ Getting Around

You need a car to properly enter the Everglades and once you're in, wearing a good pair of walking boots is essential to penetrate the interior. Having a canoe or kayak helps as well; these can be rented from outfits inside and outside of the park, or else you can seek out guided canoe and kayak tours. Bicycles are well suited to the flat roads of Everglades National Park, particularly in the area between Ernest Coe and Flamingo Point, but they're useless off the highway. In addition, the road shoulders in the park tend to be dangerously small.

Tamiami Trail

Calle Ocho, in Miami's Little Havana (p85) happens to be the eastern end of the Tamiami Trail/US 41, which cuts through the Everglades to the Gulf of Mexico. So go west, young traveler, along US 41, a few dozen miles and several different worlds away from the city where the heat is on. This trip leads you onto the northern edges of the park, past long landscapes of flooded forest, gambling halls, swamp-buggy tours, roadside food shacks and other Old Florida accoutrements.

Past Hialeah, Miami fades like a trail of diminishing Starbucks until...*whoosh*...it's all huddled forest, open fields and a big canal off to the side (evidence of US 41's diversion of the Glades' all-important sheet flow). The surest sign the city is gone and the Glades have begun is the Confederate flag decals on **Pit BBQ** (p144). The empty road runs past the **Miccosukee Resort & Convention Center** (☑305-925-2555, 877-242-6464; www .miccosukee.com; 500 SW 177th Ave; r Dec-Mar/Apr-Nov $150/120; ❀☎). It's essentially a casino-hotel complex full of slot machines and folks chunking coins into them – not really an ecological wonderland. Rooms have attractive geometric Native American designs worked into the furniture, but again, there's no need to stay here unless you're gambling.

As you head west you'll see fields and fields of pine forest and billboards advertising swamp tours. Airboats tours are an old-school way of seeing the Everglades (and there is something to be said for getting a tour from a raging Skynyrd fan with killer tatts and better camo), but there are other ways of exploring the park as well.

SHARK VALLEY
❍ Sights & Activities

Shark Valley   PARK
(☑305-221-8776; www.nps.gov/ever/planyourvisit/svdirections; car/cyclist $10/5; ❂8:30am-6pm) Shark Valley sounds like it should be the headquarters for the villain in a James Bond movie, but it is in fact a slice of National Park Service grounds heavy with informative signs and knowledgeable rangers. Shark Valley is located in the cypress-and-hardwood-and-riverine section of the Everglades, a more traditionally jungly section of the park than the grassy fields and forest domes surrounding the Ernest Coe visitor center. A 15-mile/24km paved trail takes you past

continued on p142

THE EVERGLADES TAMIAMI TRAIL

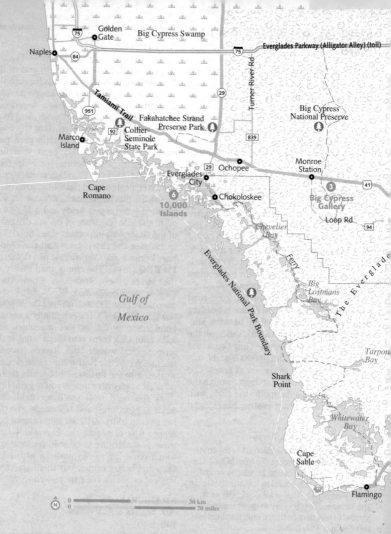

Everglades Highlights

1 Watching the sun set over the ingress road to **Pa-hay-okee Overlook** (p148) from the roof of your car

2 Canoeing or kayaking into **Hell's Bay Paddling Trail**

(p148), a tangled morass of red creeks, slow blackwater and the heavy vegetative curtain of a preserved marsh

3 Checking out some of the best photography of the

surrounding swamps, forests, beaches and sea at **Big Cypress Gallery** (p142)

4 Helping support the animal rescue operations

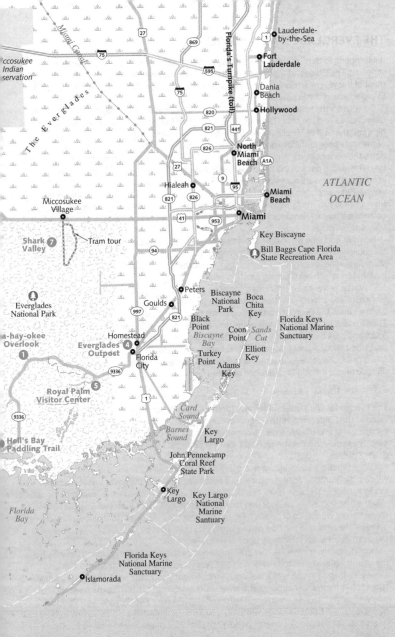

Lauderdale-
by-the-Sea

Fort
Lauderdale

Dania
Beach

Hollywood

North
Miami
Beach

Hialeah

Miami
Beach

Miami

**ATLANTIC
OCEAN**

Miami Canal

Florida's Turnpike (toll)

iccosukee
Indian
servation

The Everglades

Miccosukee
Village

Shark
Valley

Tram tour

Everglades
National Park

Goulds

Peters

Biscayne
National
Park

Boca
Chita
Key

*Sands
Cut*

Florida Keys
National Marine
Sanctuary

Key Biscayne

Bill Baggs Cape Florida
State Recreation Area

a-hay-okee
Overlook

Homestead
Everglades
Outpost
Florida
City

Black
Point

*Biscayne
Bay*

Coon
Point

Turkey
Point

Adams
Key

Elliott
Key

Royal Palm
Visitor Center

Hell's Bay
Paddling Trail

*Card
Sound*

*Barnes
Sound*

Key
Largo

John Pennekamp
Coral Reef
State Park

*Florida
Bay*

Key
Largo

Key Largo
National
Marine
Santuary

Florida Keys
National Marine
Sanctuary

Islamorada

underway at the **Everglades
Outpost** (p147)

5 Spotting alligators at
night at the **Royal Palm
Visitor Center** (p148)

6 Riding your bicycle or the
excellent public tram at **Shark
Valley** (p137)

7 Canoeing or kayaking
through the scattered islands
of **10,000 Islands** (p146).

THE EVERGLADES: AN OVERVIEW

It's tempting to think of the Everglades as a swamp, but 'prairie' may be a more apt description. The Glades, at the end of the day, are grasslands that happen to be flooded for most of the year: visit during the dry season (winter) and you'd be forgiven for thinking the Everglades was the Everfields.

So where's the water coming from? Look north on a map of Florida, all the way to Lake Okeechobee and the small lakes and rivers that band together around Kissimmee. Florida dips into the Gulf of Mexico at its below-sea-level tip, which happens to be the lowest part of the state geographically and topographically. Run-off water from central Florida flows down the peninsula via streams and rivers, over and through the Glades, and into Florida Bay. The glacial pace of the flood means this seemingly stillest of landscapes is actually in constant motion. Small wonder the Calusa Indians called the area Pa-hay-okee (grassy water). Beloved conservationist Marjory Stoneman Douglas (1890–1998) called it the River of Grass; in her famous book of the same title, she revealed that Gerard de Brahm, a colonial cartographer, named the region the River Glades, which became Ever Glades on later English maps.

So what happens when nutrient-rich water creeps over a limestone shelf? The ecological equivalent of a sweaty orgy. Beginning at the cellular level, organic material blooms in surprising ways, clumping and forming into algal beds, nutrient blooms and the ubiquitous periphyton, which are basically clusters of algae, bacteria and detritus (ie stuff). Periphyton ain't pretty: in the water they resemble puke streaks and the dried version looks like hippo turds. But you should kiss them when you see them (well, maybe not), because in the great chain of the Everglades, this slop forms the base of a very tall organic totem pole. The smallest tilt in elevation alters the flow of water and hence the content of this nutrient soup, and thus the landscape itself: all those patches of cypress and hardwood hammock (not a bed for backpackers; in this case, hammock is a fancy Floridian way of saying a forest of broadleaf trees, mainly tropical or subtropical) are areas where a few inches of altitude create a world of difference between biosystems.

Fight for the Green Grassy Waters

The Everglades were utter wilderness for thousands of years. Even Native Americans avoided the Glades; the 'native' Seminole and Miccosukee actually settled here as exiles escaping war and displacement from other parts of the country. But following European settlement of Florida, some pioneers saw the potential for economic development of the Grassy Waters.

Cattle ranchers and sugar growers, attracted by mucky waters and Florida's subtropical climate (paradise for sugarcane), successfully pressured the government to make land available to them. In 1905, Florida governor Napoleon Bonaparte Broward personally dug the first shovelful of a diversion that connected the Caloosahatchee River to Lake Okeechobee. Hundreds of canals were cut through the Everglades to the coastline to 'reclaim' the land, and the flow of lake water was restricted by a series of dikes. Farmland began to claim areas previously uninhabited by humans.

Unfortunately, the whole 'River of Grass' needs the river to survive. And besides being a pretty place to watch the birds, the Everglades acts as a hurricane barrier and kidney. Kidney? Yup: all those wetlands leeched out pollutants from the Florida Aquifer (the state's freshwater supply). But when farmland wasn't diverting the sheet flow, it was adding fertilizer-rich wastewater to it. Result? A very sweaty (and well-attended) biological orgy. Bacteria, and eventually plant life, bloomed at a ridiculous rate (they call it fertilizer for a reason), upsetting the fragile balance of resources vital to the Glades' survival.

Enter Marjory Stoneman Douglas, stage left. Ms Douglas gets the credit for almost single-handedly pushing the now age-old Florida issue of Everglades conservation; for more on this titan of the US environmental movement, see the boxed text, p144.

Despite the tireless efforts of Douglas and other environmentalists, today the Florida Aquifer is in serious danger of being contaminated and drying up. In 2011, the water level in Okeechobee was almost 2.7 inches below normal level. The number of wading birds nesting has declined by 90% to 95% since the 1930s. Currently, there are 67 threatened and endangered plant and animal species in the park.

The diversion of water away from the Glades and run-off pollution are the main culprits behind the region's environmental degradation. This delicate ecosystem is the neighbor of one of the fastest-growing urban areas in the US. The current water-drainage system in South Florida was built to handle the needs of two million people; the local population topped six million in 2010. And while Miami can't grow north or south into Fort Lauderdale or Homestead, it can move west, directly into the Everglades. At this stage, scientists estimate the wetlands have been reduced by 50% to 75% of their original size.

Humans are not the only enemy of the Everglades. Nature has done its share of damage as well. During 2055's Hurricane Wilma, for example, six storm-water treatment areas (artificial wetlands that cleanse excess nutrients out of the water cycle) were lashed and heavily damaged by powerful winds. Without these natural filtration systems, the Glades are far more susceptible to nutrient blooms and external pollution. In 2011, wildfires caused by drought incinerated huge patches of land near the Tamiami Trail.

Restoration of the Everglades

Efforts to save the Everglades began in the late 1920s, but were sidelined by the Great Depression. In 1926 and 1928, two major hurricanes caused Lake Okeechobee to overflow; the resulting floods killed hundreds. The Army Corps of Engineers did a really good job of damming the lake. A bit too good: the Glades were essentially cut off from their source, the Kissimmee watershed.

In the meantime, conservationists began donating land for protection, starting with 1 sq mile of land donated by a garden club. The Everglades was declared a national park in 1947, the same year Marjory Stoneman Douglas' *The Everglades: River of Grass* was published.

By draining the wetlands through the damming of the lake, the Army Corps made huge swaths of inland Florida inhabitable. But the environmental problems created by shifting water's natural flow, plus the area's ever-increasing population, now threaten to make the whole region uninhabitable. The canal system sends, on average, over 1 billion gallons of water into the ocean every day. At the same time, untreated runoff flows unfiltered into natural water supplies. Clean water is disappearing from the water cycle while South Florida's population gets bigger by the day.

Enter the **Comprehensive Everglades Restoration Project** (CERP; www.everglades plan.org). CERP is designed to address the root of all Everglades issues: water – where to get it, how to divert it and ways to keep it clean. The plan is to unblock the Kissimmee, restoring remaining Everglades lands to predevelopment conditions, while maintaining flood protection, providing freshwater for South Florida's populace and protecting earmarked regions against urban sprawl. It sounds great, but political battles have significantly slowed the implementation of CERP. The cost of the project has bloomed from around $7.8 billion to $15 billion, and rather than sharing a 50-50 split, as of research Florida has footed 79% of the CERP bill. In the meantime, Florida funding has fallen from $200 million during the Jeb Bush years to $17 million under Rick Scott.

Bringing back the Everglades is one of the biggest, most ambitious environmental restoration projects in US history, one that combines the needs of farmers, fishers, urban residents, local governments and conservationists. The success or failure of the program will be a bellwether for the future of the US environmental movement.

AIRBOATS & SWAMP BUGGIES

Airboats are flat-bottomed skiffs that use powerful fans to propel themselves through the water. Their environmental impact has not been determined, but one thing is clear: airboats can't be doing much good, which is why they're not allowed in the park. Swamp buggies are enormous balloon-tired vehicles that can go through wetlands, creating ruts and damaging wildlife.

Airboat and swamp-buggy rides are offered all along US Hwy 41 (Tamiami Trail). Think twice before going on a 'nature' tour. Loud whirring fanboats and marsh jeeps really don't do the quiet serenity of the Glades justice. That said, many tourists in the Everglades are there (obviously) because of their interest in the environment, and they demand environmentally knowledgeable tours. The airboat guys are pretty good at providing these – their livelihood is also caught up in preservation of the Glades, and they know the back country well. We recommend going with the guys at Cooperstown (305-226-6048; www.cooperstownairboats.com; 22700 SW 8th St; adult/child $22/11;), one of the first airboat operators you encounter heading west on 41. Just expect a more touristy experience than the National Park grounds.

continued from p137

small creeks, tropical forest and 'borrow pits' (manmade holes that are now basking spots for gators, turtles and birdlife). The pancake-flat trail is perfect for bicycles, which can be rented at the entrance for $7.50 per hour. Bring water with you.

Tram Tour

(305-221-8455; www.sharkvalleytramtours.com; adult/child under 12yr/senior $18.25/11.50/17.25; departures 9:30am, 11am, 1pm, 3pm May-Dec, 9am-4pm every hour on the hour Jan-Apr) If you don't feel like exerting yourself, the most popular and painless way to immerse yourself in the Everglades is via the two-hour tram trip that runs along Shark Valley's entire 15-mile trail. If you only have time for one Everglades activity, this should be it, as guides are informative and witty, and you'll likely see gators sunning themselves on the road. Halfway along the trail is the 50ft-high Shark Valley Observation Tower, an ugly concrete tower that offers dramatically beautiful views of the park.

Trails

At the park entrance, the easy Bobcat Boardwalk makes a loop through a thick copse of tropical hardwoods before emptying you out right back into the Shark Valley parking lot. A little ways past is the Otter Cave Trail, which heads over a limestone shelf that has been Swiss-cheesed into a porous sponge by rainwater. Animals now live in the eroded holes (although it's not likely you'll spot any) and Native Americans used to live on top of the shelf.

Miccosukee Village
PARK

(www.miccosukee.com; village/airboat ride $8/10; 9am-5pm) Just across the road from Shark Valley, this 'village' is an informative, entertaining open-air museum that showcases the culture of the Miccosukee via guided tours of traditional homes, a crafts gift store, dance and music performances, an airboat ride into a hammock-cum-village of raised 'chickee' (wooden platforms built above the waterline) huts and (natch) gator wrestling. There's a somewhat desultory on-site restaurant if you get hungry. The on-site art gallery and the handmade crafts make a good souvenir.

BIG CYPRESS & OCHOPEE

The better part of the Tamiami Trail is fronted on either side by long cypress trees overhung with moss and endless vistas of soft prairie, flooded in the wet season into a boggy River of Grass.

Sights & Activities

Big Cypress Gallery
GALLERY

(941-695-2428; www.clydebutcher.com; Tamiami Trail; 10am-5pm Wed-Mon) The highlight of many Everglades trips, this gallery showcases the work of Clyde Butcher, an American photographer who follows in the great tradition of Ansel Adams. His large-format black-and-white images elevate the swamps to a higher level. Butcher has found a quiet spirituality in the brackish waters and you might, too, with the help of his eyes. Every Labor Day (first weekend in September), the gallery holds a gala event, which includes a fun $20 swamp walk onto his 30-acre property; the party attracts swamp-stompers from across the state. At the time of writing, the gallery was setting up two homes located in the cypress woods as guesthouses – the properties look pretty nice, can sleep from four to six people and will cost around $200 per night.

Big Cypress National Preserve PARK
(☎239-695-4758; 33000 Tamiami Trail E; ⏱8:30am-4:30pm) The 1139-sq-mile Big Cypress Preserve (named for the size of the park, not its trees) is the result of a compromise between environmentalists, cattle ranchers and oil-and-gas explorers. The area is integral to the Everglades' ecosystem: rains that flood the Preserve's prairies and wetlands slowly filter down through the Glades. About 45% of the cypress swamp (actually a group of mangrove islands, hardwood hammocks, slash pine, prairies and marshes) is protected. Great bald cypress trees are nearly gone, thanks to pre-Preserve lumbering, but dwarf pond cypress trees (more impressive than the name suggests) fill the area with their own understated beauty. The **Oasis Visitor Center** (☎941-695-1201; ⏱8am-4:30pm Mon-Fri;♿), about 20 miles west of Shark Valley, has great exhibits for the kids and an outdoor, water-filled ditch popular with alligators.

Florida National Scenic Trail
(www.nps.gov/bicy/planyourvisit/florida-trail.htm) There are some 31 miles of the Florida National Scenic Trail within Big Cypress National Preserve. From the southern terminus, which can be accessed via Loop Rd, the trail runs 8.3 miles north to US 41. The way is flat, but it's hard going: you'll almost certainly be wading through water, and you'll have to pick your way through a series of solution holes (small sinkholes) and thick hardwood hammocks. There is often

no shelter from the sun, and the bugs are... *plentiful.* There are three primitive campsites with water wells along the trail; pick up a map at the visitor center. Most campsites are free, and you needn't register. **Monument Lake** (May-Dec 14 free, Dec 15-Apr $16) has water and toilets.

Ochopee VILLAGE
(GPS 25.901529, -81.306023) Drive to the hamlet of Ochopee (population about four)...no... wait...turn around, you missed it! Then pull over and break out the cameras: Ochopee's claim to fame is the country's smallest **post office**. It's housed in a former toolshed and set against big park skies; a friendly postal worker patiently poses for snapshots.

Skunk Ape Research Headquarters PARK
(☎239-695-2275; www.skunkape.info; 40904 Tamiami Trail E; ⏱7am-7pm, 'zoo' closes around 4pm) Sometimes we think Florida needs to change its state motto to 'Florida; You Can't Make This Stuff Up.' To whit: the Skunk Ape Research Center, topped by a giant panther statue, dedicated to tracking down Southeastern USA's version of Bigfoot, the eponymous Skunk Ape (a large gorilla-man who supposedly stinks to high heaven). We never saw a Skunk Ape here, but you can see a corny gift shop and, in the back, a reptile and bird zoo run by a true Florida eccentric, the sort of guy who wraps albino pythons around his neck for fun. Donate a few bucks at the entrance.

Everglades Adventure Tours TOURS
(EAT; ☎800-504-6554; www.evergladesadventuretours.com; tours from $69) We already like the guys at EAT for being based out of the same headquarters as the Skunk Ape people; we like them even more for offering some of the best private tours of the Everglades

DETOUR: LOOP ROAD

Loop Rd, off Tamiami Trail (Hwy 41), offers some unique sites. One: the homes of the Miccosukee, some of which have been considerably expanded by gambling revenue. You'll see some traditional chickee-style huts and some trailers with massive add-on wings that are bigger than the original trailer – all seem to have shiny new pickup trucks parked out front. Two: great pull-offs for viewing flooded forests, where egrets that look like pterodactyls perch in the trees. Three: houses with large Confederate flags and 'Stay off my property' signs; these homes are as much a part of the landscape as the swamp. And four: the short, pleasantly jungly Tree Snail Hammock Nature Trail. Be warned the Loop is a rough, unpaved road; you'll need a 4WD vehicle (there has been talk of repaving the road, so it may have improved by the time you read this). True to its name, the road loops right back onto the Tamiami; expect a good long jaunt on the Loop to add two hours to your trip.

we've found. Swamp hikes, 'safaris,' airboats and, best of all, being poled around in a canoe or skiff by some genuinely funny guys with genuine local knowledge of the Grassy Waters; it's an absolute treat. The Eat guys have set up a campsite at Skunk Ape HQ; it costs $30 to camp here, and there's wi-fi throughout the camp.

✗ Eating

Joannie's Blue Crab Café   AMERICAN $
(joaniesbluecrabcafe.com; Tamiami Trail; mains $9-17; ⊙9am-5pm) This quintessential shack, east of Ochopee, with open rafters, shellacked picnic tables and alligator kitsch, serves delicious food of the 'fried everything' variety on paper plates. There's live music most days.

Pit BBQ   AMERICAN $
(16400 SW 8th St, btwn Miami & Shark Valley; mains $4-9; ⊙11am-11:30pm) The barbecue is decent and served on picnic tables with a side of country music and Confederate-flag accoutrement. It is as cheesy as a dairy, so if you can't arm yourself with irony, drive on.

EVERGLADES CITY

The end of the track is an old Florida fishing village of raised houses, turquoise water and scattershot emerald-green mangrove islands. Hwy 29 runs south through town into the peaceful residential island of Chokoloskee, past a great psychedelic mural of a gator on a shed. 'City' is an ambitious name for Everglades City, but this is a friendly fishing town where you can easily lose yourself for a day or three.

◉ Sights & Activities

Gulf Coast Visitor Center   PARK
(☑239-695-3311; Hwy 29, Everglades City, 815 Oyster Bar Ln; ⊙9am-4:30pm May-Oct, from 8am Nov-Apr; tours from $25, boat rentals per hr from $13) This is the northwestern-most ranger station for Everglades National Park, and provides access to the 10,000 Islands area. Boat tours depart from the downstairs marina into the mangrove flats and green islands – if you're lucky you may see dolphins springing up beside your craft. This tangled off-shore archipelago was a major smuggling point for drugs into the mainland USA

GLADES GUARDIAN

In a state known for iconoclasts, no one can hold a candle to Marjory Stoneman Douglas. Not just for her quirks, but for her drive. A persistent, unbreakable force, she fueled one of the longest conservation battles in US history.

Born in 1890, Douglas moved to Florida after her failed first marriage. She worked for the *Miami Herald* and eventually as a freelance writer, producing short stories that are notable for both the quality of the writing and their progressive themes: *Plumes* (1930) and *Wings* (1931), published in the *Saturday Evening Post*, addressed the issue of Glades bird-poaching when the business was still immensely popular (the feathers were used to decorate ladies' hats).

In the 1940s, Douglas was asked to write about the Miami River for the Rivers of America Series and promptly chucked the idea in favor of capturing the Everglades in her classic, *The Everglades: River of Grass*. Like all of Douglas' work the book is remarkable for both its exhaustive research and lyrical, rich language.

River of Grass immediately sold out of its first print-run, and public perception of the Everglades shifted from 'nasty swamp' to 'national treasure.' Douglas went on to be an advocate for environmental causes ('It is a woman's business to be interested in the environment. It's an extended form of housekeeping.'), women's rights and racial equality, fighting, for example, for basic infrastructure in Miami's Overtown.

Today she is remembered as Florida's favorite environmentalist. Always immaculately turned out in gloves, dress, pearls and floppy straw hat, she would bring down engineers, developers, politicians and her most hated opponents, sugar farmers ('They should go at any time, now, as far as I'm concerned. Pick up and go. Any minute. We won't miss them a bit.') by force of her oratory alone. She kept up the fight, speaking and lecturing without fail, until she died in 1998 at the age of 108.

Today it seems every environmental institution in Florida is named for Douglas, but were she around, we doubt she'd care for those honors. She'd be too busy planting herself in the CERP office, making sure everything was moving along on schedule, and playing the disappointed older woman if it weren't.

during the late 1970s and early '80s; bales of marijuana were nicknamed 'square grouper' by local fishermen. It's great fun to go kayaking and canoeing around here; boats can be rented from the marina, but make sure to take a map with you (they're available for free in the visitor center).

Museum of the Everglades   MUSEUM
(NACT; www.evergladesmuseum.org; 105 W Broadway; ☺9am-5pm Tue-Fri, to 4pm Sat) This small museum, located in an old library, has some placards and information on the settlement of the Everglades – the focus is far more concerned with the human history of the area than the natural environment. It's a decidedly community museum, with the feel of an attic full of everyone's interesting stuff and heirlooms, but charming for all that as well.

If you're up for a tour, try Everglades Adventure Tours (p143) or the guys at North American Canoe Tours (NACT; ☎941-695-3299/4666; www.evergladesadventures.com; Ivey House Bed & Breakfast, 107 Camellia St; ☺Nov–mid-Apr) rent out camping equipment and canoes for full/half-days ($35/$25) and touring kayaks ($45 to $65). You get 20% off most of these services and rentals if you're staying at the Ivey House Bed & Breakfast (below), which runs the tours. Tours shuttle you to places like Chokoloskee Island, Collier Seminole State Park, Rabbit Key or Tiger Key for afternoon or overnight excursions (from $99).

🛏 Sleeping

All lodging is family-friendly, and comes with air-conditioning and parking.

🔝 Everglades City Motel   MOTEL $$
(☎239-695-4244, 877-567-0679; www.everglades citymotel.com; 310 Collier Ave; r from $80; ✳🛜🚗) With large renovated rooms that have flat-screen TVs, arctic air-conditioning and a fantastically friendly staff that will hook you up with whatever tours your heart desires, this is an exceptionally good-value lodge for those looking to spend some time near the 10,000 Islands.

Ivey House Bed & Breakfast   B&B $$
(☎239-695-3299, 877-567-0679; www.iveyhouse .com; 107 Camellia St; lodge $74-120, inn $99-209; ✳🛜🚗) This family-run tropical inn serves good breakfasts in its small Ghost Orchid Grill. Plus it operates some of the best nature trips around (North American Canoe Tours).

Ivey offers an entire range of package vacations (www.iveyhouse.com/package-vacation. htm), from day trips to six-day excursions including lodging, tours and some meals; trips run from $300 to $2290.

Rod & Gun Club Lodge   B&B $$
(☎239-695-2101; www.evergladesrodandgun.com; 200 Riverside Dr; r July–mid-Oct $95, mid-Oct-Jun $110-140; P✳🚗) Built in the 1920s as a hunting lodge by Barron Collier (who needed a place to chill after watching workers dig his Tamiami Trail), this masculine place, fronted by a lovely porch, has a restaurant that serves anything that moves in them thar waters.

Parkway Motel & Marina   MOTEL $
(☎239-695-3261; 1180 Chokoloskee Dr; www. parkwaymotelandmarina.com; r $99-120; P✳🚗) An extremely friendly owner (and an even friendlier dog) runs this veritable testament to the old-school Floridian lodge: cute small rooms and one cozy apartment in a one-story motel building.

✗ Eating

JT's Island Grill & Gallery   AMERICAN $
(238 Mamie St, Chokoloskee; mains $5-16; ☺11am-3pm late Oct-May) Just a mile or so past the edge of town, this awesome cafe-cum-art-gallery sits in a restored 1890 general store. It's outfitted with bright retro furniture and piles of kitschy books, pottery, clothing and maps (all for sale). But the best part is the food (lunch only) – fresh crab cakes, salads, fish platters and veggie wraps, made with locally grown organic vegetables.

Oyster House   SEAFOOD $
(on Chokoloskee Causeway; mains $8-22; ☺10am-11pm) Besides serving the Everglades staples of excellent fried seafood and burgers, Oyster House has a friendly bar with a screened-in porch where you can drink, slap mosquitoes and have a chat with friendly local boozehounds.

Seafood Depot   SEAFOOD $
(102 Collier Ave; mains $14-33; ☺10:30am-9pm) Don't totally sublimate your desire for fried food, because the gator tail and frog's legs here offer an excellent way to honor the inhabitants of the Everglades: douse them in Tabasco and devour them.

ℹ Information
Everglades Area Chamber of Commerce
(☎239-695-3941; cnr US Hwy 41 & Hwy 29; ☺9am-4pm)

CANOE CAMPING ON 10,000 ISLANDS

One of the best ways to experience the serenity of the Everglades – somehow desolate yet lush, tropical and foreboding – is by paddling the network of waterways that skirt the northwest portion of the park. The 10,000 Islands consist of many (but not really 10,000) tiny islands and a mangrove swamp that hugs the southwestern-most border of Florida. The Wilderness Waterway, a 99-mile path between Everglades City and Flamingo, is the longest canoe trail in the area, but there are shorter trails near Flamingo.

Most islands are fringed by narrow beaches with sugar-white sand, but note that the water is brackish, and very shallow most of the time. It's not Tahiti, but it's fascinating. You can camp on your own island for up to a week.

Getting around the 10,000 Islands is pretty straightforward if you religiously adhere to National Oceanic & Atmospheric Administration (NOAA) tide and nautical charts. Going against the tides is the fastest way to make a miserable trip. The Gulf Coast Visitor Center (p144) sells nautical charts and gives out free tidal charts. You can also purchase charts prior to your visit – call ☑305-247-1216 and ask for chart numbers 11430, 11432 and 11433.

EVERGLADES CITY TO NAPLES

Fakahatchee Strand Preserve PARK
(www.floridastateparks.org/fakahatcheestrand/; Coastline Dr, Copeland; admission free; ⊙8am-sunset) The Fakahatchee Strand, besides having a fantastic name, also houses a 20-mile by 5-mile estuarine wetland that could have emerged directly out of the *Jurassic Park* franchise. A 2000ft boardwalk traverses this wet and wild wonderland, where panthers still stalk their prey amid the black waters. While it's unlikely you'll spot any, there's a great chance you'll see a large variety of bird life and reptiles ranging in size from tiny skinks to grinning alligators.

Homestead to Flamingo Point

Head south of Miami to drive into the heart of the park and the best horizons of the Everglades. Plus, there are plenty of side paths and canoe creeks to detour onto. You'll see some of the most quietly exhilarating scenery the park has to offer on this route, and have better access to an interior network of trails for those wanting to push off the beaten track into the buggy, muggy solar plexus of the wetlands.

HOMESTEAD & FLORIDA CITY

Homestead is not the prettiest town in the USA. After getting battered into rubble by Hurricane Andrew in 1992 and becoming part of the expanding subdivisions of South Miami, it's been poorly planned around fast-food stops, car dealerships and gas stations. A lot of Mexicans have moved here seeking farm work (or moved here providing services for farm laborers), and as a result, if you speak Spanish, it's impossible not to notice the shift in accent as Cuban Spanish gives way to Mexican. Radio stations also shift from Cuban reggaeton and hip-hop to brass-style mariachi music.

You could pass a mildly entertaining afternoon walking around Homestead's almost quaint Main Street (www.homesteadmainstreet.org) which essentially comprises a couple of blocks of Krome Ave extending north and south of Old Town Hall (41 N Krome Ave). It's a good effort at injecting some character into 'downtown' Homestead.

With that said, let us give Homestead huge props: it houses two of the great attractions of the Florida roadside, one of its best hostels and an incredible farmers' market. Yup: four 'top picks' in one town.

◉ Sights

TOP CHOICE Coral Castle CASTLE
(www.coralcastle.com; 28655 S Dixie Hwy; adult/child 7-18yr $12/7; ⊙8am-6pm, to 8pm Sat & Sun) 'You will be seeing unusual accomplishment,' reads the inscription on the rough-hewn quarried wall. That's an understatement. There is no greater temple to all that is weird and wacky about South Florida than the legend: a Latvian gets snubbed at the altar. Comes to the US. Moves to Florida. Hand carves, unseen, in the dead of night, a monument to unrequited love: a rock compound that includes a 'throne room,' a sun dial, a stone stockade (his intended's 'timeout area') and a revolving boulder gate that engineers around the world, to this day, cannot

explain. Oh, and there are audio stations situated around the place that explain the site in a replicated Latvian accent, so it feels like you're getting a narrated tour by Borat.

TOP CHOICE **Everglades Outpost** WILDLIFE SANCTUARY (www.evergladesoutpost.org; 35601 SW 192nd Ave; recommended donation $20; ⊙10am-4pm Sat & Sun, by appointment Mon-Fri) If the Coral Castle is amusing, the Everglades Outpost is moving and heart-warming. An effort cobbled together by a dedicated family and friends, all animal-lovers to the core, the outpost houses, feeds and cares for wild animals that have been seized from illegal traders, abused, neglected or donated by people who could not care for them. Residents of the outpost include gibbons, a lemur, wolves, cobras, alligators and a pair of majestic tigers (one of whom was bought by an exotic dancer who thought she could incorporate it into her act). Your money goes into helping the outpost's mission; we can think of few better causes in the area. During the week, just call ahead to visit.

🛏 **Sleeping**

There are plenty of chains like Best Western, the Days Inn and similar hotels and motels all along Rt 1 Krome Ave.

TOP CHOICE **Everglades International Hostel** HOSTEL $ (☎305-248-1122, 800-372-3874; www.everglades hostel.com; 20 SW 2nd Ave, Florida City; camping $18, dm $28, d $61-75; P ❉ 🕸 ⊛ ⊠) Located in a cluttered, comfy 1930s boarding house, this friendly hostel has good-value dorms, private rooms and 'semi-privates' (you have an enclosed room within the dorms and share a bathroom with dorm residents). But what

they've done with their back yard – wow. It's a serious garden of earthly delights. There's: a tree house; a natural rock-cut pool with a waterfall; a Bedouin pavilion that doubles as a dancehall; a gazebo; an open-air tented 'bed room'; an oven built to resemble a tail-molting tadpole. It all needs to be seen to be believed, and best of all you can sleep anywhere in the back for $18. Sleep in a tree house! We think that's an amazing deal. We should add the crowd is made up of all those funky international traveler types that made you fall in love with backpacking in the first place, and the hostel conducts some of the best tours into the Everglades around.

Redland Hotel HOTEL $$ (☎305-246-1904; www.redlandhotel.com; 5 S Flagler Ave, Homestead; r $83-150; P 🕸) This historic inn has clean, individualized rooms with a distinct doily vibe. The building served as the town's first hotel, mercantile store, post office, library and boarding house (for real!) and is now favored by folks who want more of a personal touch than you can get from the chains.

🍴 **Eating**

TOP CHOICE **Robert Is Here** MARKET $ (www.robertishere.com; 19200 SW 344th St, Homestead; ⊙8am-7pm Nov-Aug) More than a farmer's stand, Robert's is an institution. This is Old Florida at its kitschy best, in love with the Glades and the agriculture that surrounds it. There's a petting zoo for the kids, live music at night, plenty of homemade preserves and sauces, and while everyone goes crazy for the milkshakes – as they should – do not leave without having the fresh orange juice. It's the best in the world. What's up with the funny name? Well, back in the day

---

AH-TAH-THI-KI MUSEUM

If you want to learn about Florida's Native Americans, come to this **Seminole museum** (☎877-902-1113; www.ahtahthiki.com; Big Cypress Seminole Indian Reservation, Clewiston; adult/child/senior $9/6/6; ⊙9am-5pm), 17 miles north of I-75. All of the excellent educational exhibits on Seminole life, history and the tribe today were founded on gaming proceeds, which provide most of the tribe's multimillion-dollar operating budget.

The museum is actually located within a cypress dome cut through with an interpretive boardwalk, so from the start it strikes a balance between environmentalism and education. The permanent exhibit has several dioramas with life-sized figures depicting various scenes out of traditional Seminole life, while temporary exhibits have a but more academic polish (past ones have included lengthy forays into the economic structure of the Everglades). There's an old-school 'living village' and recreated ceremonial grounds as well. Overall, the Ah-tah-thi-ki is making an effort to not be a cheesy Native American theme park, and the Seminole tribe is to be commended for its effort in this regard.

the namesake of the pavilion was selling his daddy's cucumbers on this very spot, but no traffic was slowing down for the produce. So a sign was constructed that announced, in big red letters, that Robert was, in fact, here. He has been ever since, too.

Rosita's
MEXICAN $

(☎ 305-246-3114; 199 W Palm Dr, Florida City; mains under $10; ⊙ 8:30am-9pm) There's a working-class Mexican crowd here, testament to the sheer awesomeness of the tacos and burritos. Everyone is friendly, and best of all, they'll give you a takeaway plate if you're staying at the next-door Everglades International Hostel.

Farmers Market Restaurant
AMERICAN $

(☎ 305-242-0008; 300 N Krome Ave, Florida City; lunch mains $8-13, dinner mains $12-16; ⊙ 5:30am-9pm) This restaurant's as fresh and hardy as the produce in the next-door farmers' market and its rural-worker clientele. It's a bit barebones on the inside, but the food will fill you up, and nicely too.

🔒 Shopping

ArtSouth
GALLERY

(☎ 305-247-9406; www.artsouthhomestead.org; 240 N Krome Ave, Homestead; ⊙ 10am-6pm Tue-Fri) This colony of artists' studios is a good place to see local talent and pick up Glades-inspired artwork. It's also a nice sight in and of itself. Outdoor exhibits make the compound feel like a dreamy sculpture garden (or at least a decent free museum), and provide a good aesthetic anchor to the north side of Homestead's main-street project.

ℹ️ Information

Chamber of Commerce (☎ 305-247-2332; www.chamberinaction.com; 455 N Flagler Ave, Homestead; ⊙ 9am-noon & 1-5pm Mon-Fri)

ERNEST COE & ROYAL PALM TO FLAMINGO

Drive past Florida City, through miles of paper-flat farmland and past an enormous, razor-wired jail (it seems like an escapee heads for the swamp at least once a year) and turn left when you see the signs for Robert Is Here (p147) – or stop in so the kids can pet a donkey at Robert's petting zoo.

👁️ Sights & Activities

Ernest Coe Visitor Center
PARK

(☎ 305-242-7700; www.nps.gov/ever; 40001 State Rd 9336; ⊙ 8am-5pm) As you go past Homestead and Florida City, the farmland loses its uniformity and the flat land becomes more tangled, wild and studded with pine and cypress. After a few more miles you'll enter Everglades National Park at this friendly visitor center. Have a look at the excellent exhibits, including a diorama of 'typical' Floridians (the fisherman looks like he should join ZZ Top).

Royal Palm Visitor Center
PARK

(☎ 305-242-7700; State Rd 9336; ⊙ 8am-4:15pm) Four miles past Ernest Coe Visitor Center, Royal Palm offers the easiest access to the Glades in these parts. Two trails, the **Anhinga** and **Gumbo Limbo** (the latter named for the gumbo-limbo tree, also known as the 'tourist tree' because its bark peels like a sun-burned Brit), take all of an hour to walk and put you face to face with a panoply of Everglades wildlife. Gators sun on the shoreline, anhinga spear their prey and wading birds stalk haughtily through the reeds. Come at night for a ranger walk on the boardwalk and shine a flashlight into the water to see one of the coolest sights of your life: the glittering eyes of dozens of alligators prowling the waterways.

Kayaking & Canoeing
BOATING

The real joy here in this part of the park is canoeing into the bracken heart of the swamp. There are plenty of push-off points, all with names that sound like they were read off Frodo's map to Mordor, including **Hell's Bay**, the **Nightmare**, **Snake Bight** and **Graveyard Creek**. Our favorite is Hell's Bay. 'Hell to get into and hell to get out of,' was how this sheltered launch was described by old Gladesmen, but damn if it isn't heaven inside: a capillary network of mangrove creeks, saw-grass islands and shifting mudflats, where the brambles form a green tunnel and all you can smell is sea salt and the dark organic breath of the swamp. Three chickee sites are spaced along the trail.

Hiking Trails
HIKING

State Rd 9336 cuts through the soft heart of the park, past long fields of marsh prairie, white, skeletal forests of bald cypress and dark clumps of mahogany hammock. There are plenty of trails to detour down; all of the following are half a mile (800m) long. **Mahogany Hammock** leads into an 'island' of hardwood forest floating on the waterlogged prairie, while the **Pinelands** takes you through a copse of rare spindly swamp pine and palmetto forest. Further on, **Pa-hay-okee Overlook** is a raised platform that

Gators

Alligators are common in the park, although not so much in the 10,000 Islands, as they tend to avoid saltwater. If you do see an alligator, it probably won't bother you unless you do something overtly threatening or angle your boat between it and its young. If you hear an alligator making a loud hissing sound, get the hell out of Dodge. That's a call to other alligators when a young gator is in danger. Finally, never feed an alligator – it's stupid and illegal.

Crocs

Crocodiles are less common in the park, as they prefer coastal and saltwater habitats. They are more aggressive than alligators, however, so the same rules apply. With perhaps only a few hundred remaining in the USA, they are also an endangered species.

Panthers

The Florida panther is critically endangered, and although it is the state's official animal its survival in the wild is by no means assured. There are an estimated 100 panthers left in the wild, and although that number has increased from around 20 to 30 since the 1980s, it's not cause for big celebration either. As usual, humans have been the culprit behind this predator's demise. Widespread habitat reduction (ie the arrival of big subdivisions) is the major cause of concern. In the past, poor data on panther populations and the approval of developments that have been harmful to the species' survival have occurred; environmental groups contend the shoddy information was linked to financial conflicts of interest. Breeding units, which consist of one male and two to five females, require about 200 sq miles of ground to cover, and that often puts panthers in the way of one of Florida's most dangerous beasts: drivers. Sixteen panthers were killed by cars in 2010.

If you're lucky enough to see one (and you gotta be pretty damn lucky), Florida panthers are rather magnificent brown hunting cats (they are, in fact, cougars). They are extremely elusive and only inhabit 5% of their historic range. Many are relatively concentrated in **Big Cypress National Preserve** (p143).

Weather

Thunderstorms and lightning are more common in summer than in winter. But in summer the insects are so bad you won't want to be outside anyway. In emergency weather, rangers will search for registered campers, but under ordinary conditions they won't unless they receive information that someone's missing. If camping, have a friend or family member ready to contact rangers if you do not report back by a certain day.

Insects

You can't overestimate the problem of mosquito and no-see-ums (tiny biting flies) in the Everglades; they are, by far, the park's worst feature. While in most national parks there are warning signs showing the forest-fire risk, here the charts show the mosquito level (call ☎305-242-7700 for a report). In summer and fall, the sign almost always says 'extremely high.' You'll be set upon the second you open your car door. The only protections are 100% DEET or, even better, a pricey net suit.

Snakes in a Glade!

There are four types of poisonous snake in the Everglades: diamondback rattlesnake *(Crotalus adamanteus);* pigmy rattlesnake *(Sistrurus miliarius);* cottonmouth or water moccasin *(Agkistrodon piscivorus conanti),* which swims along the surface of water; and the coral snake *(Micrurus fulvius).* Wear long thick socks and lace-up boots – and keep the hell away from them. Oh, and now there are Burmese pythons prowling the water too. Pet owners who couldn't handle the pythons (this happens with depressing frequency) have dumped the animals into the swamp, where they've adapted like...well, a tropical snake to a subtropical forest. The python is an invasive species that is badly mucking up the natural order of things.

WILDERNESS CAMPING

Three types of backcountry campsites are available: beach sites, on coastal shell beaches and in the 10,000 Islands; ground sites, which are basically mounds of dirt built up above the mangroves; and 'chickees,' wooden platforms built above the waterline where you can pitch a free-standing (no spikes) tent. Chickees, which have toilets, are the most civilized – there's a serenity found in sleeping on what feels like a raft levitating above the water. Ground sites tend to be the most bug-infested.

Warning: if you're just paddling around and see an island that looks pleasant for camping but isn't a designated campsite, beware – you may end up submerged when the tides change.

From November to April, camping permits cost $10, plus $2 per person per night; from May to October sites are free, but you must still self-register at Flamingo and Gulf Coast Visitor Centers or call ☑239-695-2945.

Some backcountry tips:

» Store food in a hand-sized, raccoon-proof container (available at gear stores).

» Bury your waste at least 10in below ground, but keep in mind some ground sites have hard turf.

» Use a backcountry stove to cook. Ground fires are only permitted at beach sites, and you can only burn dead or drowned wood.

peeks over one of the prettiest bends in the River of Grass. The **West Lake Trail** runs through the largest protected mangrove forest in the Northern Hemisphere. Further down you can take a good two-hour, 1.8-mile (2.9km) hike to **Christian Point**. This dramatic walk takes you through several Glades environments: under tropical forest, past columns of white cypress and over a series of mudflats (particularly attractive on grey, cloudy days), and ends with a dramatic view of the windswept shores of Florida Bay.

Flamingo Visitor Center PARK
(☑239-695-2945; State Rd 9336; ☺8am-4:15pm)
The most isolated portion of the park is a squat **marina** (☑239-696-3101, 239-695-2591) where you can go on a backcountry boat tour or rent boats, but facilities were shut down for renovations during our visit. In the past, boat tours ran for around $20/10 for adult/child, while canoes (one hour/half-day/full day $8/22/32) and sea kayaks (half-/full day $35/45) were available for rental. You're largely left to explore the channels and islands of Florida Bay on your own. Be careful in coastal areas here during rough weather, as storm surges can turn an attractive spread of beach into a watery stretch of danger fairly quickly.

🛏 Sleeping

**National Park Service
Campsites** CAMPGROUND $
(NPS; ☑800-365-2267; www.nps.gov/ever/plan yourvisit/camping; sites May-Oct free, Nov-Apr $16)

There are campgrounds run by the NPS located throughout the park. Sites are primitive and do not have hookups. Depending on the time of year, cold-water showers are either bracing or a welcome relief. The NPS information office at Royal Palm can provide a map of all campsites, as does the park website.

Long Pine Key Campground CAMPGROUND $
(☑305-242-7873; May-Oct free, Nov-Apr $16)
This is a good bet for car campers, just west of Royal Palm Visitor Center.

Flamingo Campground CAMPGROUND $
(☑877-444-6777; May-Oct free, Nov-Apr $30)
There are 41 car camping sites at the Flamingo Visitor Center that have electrical hookups.

BISCAYNE NATIONAL PARK

Just to the east of the Everglades is Biscayne National Park, or the 5% of it that isn't underwater. Let us explain: a portion of the world's third-largest reef sits here off the coast of Florida, along with mangrove forests and the northernmost Florida Keys. Fortunately this unique 300-sq-mile park is easy to explore independently with a canoe, or via a glass-bottom boat tour.

A bit unfairly shadowed by the Everglades, Biscayne is unique as national parks go, requiring both a little extra planning and a lot more reward for your effort. The offshore keys, accessible only by boat, offer pristine opportunities for camping. Generally, summer and fall are the best times to visit the park; you'll want to snorkel when the water is calm. This is some of the best reef-viewing and snorkeling you'll find in the US, outside Hawaii and nearby Key Largo.

◉ Sights

Biscayne National Park   PARK
(☑305-230-7275, 305-230-1100; www.nps.gov/bisc, www.biscayneunderwater.com; 9700 SW 328th St) The park itself offers canoe rentals, transportation to the offshore keys, snorkeling and scuba-diving trips, and glass-bottom boat viewing of the exceptional reefs. All tours require a minimum of six people, so call to make reservations. Three-hour glass-bottom boat trips ($45) depart at 10am and are very popular; if you're lucky you may spot some dolphins or manatees. Canoe

rentals cost $12 per hour and kayaks $16; they're rented from 9am to 3pm. Three-hour snorkeling trips ($45) depart at 1:15pm daily; you'll have about 1½ hours in the water. Scuba trips depart at 8:30am Friday to Sunday ($99). You can also arrange a private charter boat tour around the park for $300.

Offshore Keys   ISLANDS
Long Elliott Key has picnicking, camping and hiking among mangrove forests; tiny Adams Key has only picnicking; and equally tiny Boca Chita Key has an ornamental lighthouse, picnicking and camping. These little islands were settled under the Homestead Act of 1862, which gave land freely to anyone willing to take five years at turning a scratch of the tropics into a working pineapple and Key-lime farm. No-see-ums are invasive, and their bites are devastating. Make sure your tent is devoid of minuscule entry points.

MANATEES' BIGGEST THREAT

Manatees are shy, utterly peaceful mammals that are, for all intents, the poster children of Floridian environmentalism. They look like obese seals with vaguely elephantine noses. Back in the day, sailors apparently mistook them for mermaids and sirens, which suggests these guys had been at sea for entirely too long.

Jokes aside, the manatee is a major environmental concern for Florida. Pollution is a problem for these gentle giants, but their biggest killers are boaters, and of those, the worst offenders are pleasure boaters.

Manatees seek warm, shallow water and feed on vegetation. South Florida is surrounded by just such an environment, but it also has one of the highest concentrations of pleasure boats in the world. Despite pleas from environmental groups, wildlife advocates and the local, state and federal governments, which have declared many areas 'Manatee Zones', some pleasure boaters routinely exceed speed limits and ignore simple practices (see p491) that would help protect the species.

After grabbing a bite, manatees come up for air and often float just beneath the surface, chewing and hanging around. When speedboats zoom through the area, manatees are hit by the hulls and either knocked away or pushed under the boat, whose propeller then gashes the mammal as the boat passes overhead. Few manatees get through life without propeller scars, which leave slices in their bodies similar to the diagonal slices on a loaf of French bread.

There are several organizations throughout the state that rescue and rehabilitate injured manatees, but they're fighting what would appear to be a losing battle. Some of these organizations include Save the Manatee (www.savethemanatee.org) and the Miami Seaquarium (p83). Divers, animal experts and veterinarians of Seaquarim's Marine Mammal Rescue Team patrol South Florida waters, responding to reports of stranded manatees, dolphins and whales. While the Seaquarium's program has been successful, pleasure boaters still threaten the manatees' survival. In 2010, the Florida Fish & Wildlife Commission reported that 83 manatees were killed by watercraft.

In February of 2011, a man was charged with killing a nursing manatee mother while speeding his boat through a slow-water area. He was put on probation for a year and had his boat seized by authorities. The ruling was welcomed by conservationists, but decisions like this are few and far between – the speeder was caught in the act of killing the manatee, but most such incidents are not reported.

One of the only trails of its kind in the USA, the Maritime Heritage Trail was still technically under development at the time of research, but already taking 'hikers'. If you've ever wanted to explore a sunken ship, this may well be the best opportunity in the country. Six are located within the park grounds; the trail experience involves taking visitors out, by boat, to the site of the wrecks where they can swim and explore among derelict vessels and clouds of fish – there are even waterproof information site cards placed among the ships. Five of the vessels are suited for scuba divers, but one, the *Mandalay,* a lovely two-masted schooner that sank in 1966, can be accessed by snorkelers.

🏃 Activities

Boating and fishing are naturally very popular and often go hand in hand, but to do either you'll need to get some paperwork in order. Boaters will want to get tide charts from the park (or from www.nps.gov/bisc/planyourvisit/tide-predictions.htm). And make sure you comply with local slow-speed zones, designed to protect the endangered manatee (see p151).

The slow zones currently extend 1000ft out from the mainland, from Black Point south to Turkey Point, and include the marinas at Black Point and Homestead Bayfront Parks. Another slow zone extends from Sands Cut to Coon Point; maps of all of the above can be obtained from rangers, and are needed for navigation purposes in any case.

Although Biscayne is a national park, it is governed by state law when it comes to fishing, so if you want to cast a line, you'll need a state license. These come in varieties many and sundry, all of which can be looked up at http://myfwc.com/fishing, which also provides a list of places where licenses can be obtained. At the time of writing, nonresi-dent seven-day salt- and freshwater fishing permits cost $50 each.

For information on boat tours and rental, contact Biscayne Underwater (www.biscayneunderwater.com), which can help arrange logistics.

The water around Convoy Point is regarded as prime windsurfing territory. Windsurfers may want to contact outfits in Miami (p97)

🛏 Sleeping

Primitive camping on Elliott and Boca Chita Keys costs $15 per tent, per night; you pay on a trust system with exact change on the harbor (rangers cruise the Keys to check your receipt). Bring all supplies, including water, and carry everything out. There's no water on Boca Chita, only saltwater toilets, and since it has a deeper port, it tends to attract bigger (and louder) boats (and boaters). Bring your own water to the island. There is potable water on the island, but it always pays to be prepared. It costs $20 to moor your boat overnight at Elliott or Boca Chita harbors, but that fee covers the use of one campsite for up to six people and two tents.

ℹ Information

Dante Fascell Visitor Center (☑305-230-7275; www.nps.gov/bisc; 9700 SW 328th St; ⊙8:30am-5pm) Located at Convoy Point, this center shows a great introductory film for an overview of the park and has maps, information and excellent ranger activities. The grounds around the center are a popular picnic grounds on weekends and holidays, especially for families from Homestead. Also showcases local artwork.

ℹ Getting There & Away

To get here, you'll have to drive about 9 miles east of Homestead (the way is pretty well signposted) on SW 328th St (North Canal Dr) into a long series of green-and-gold flat fields and marsh.

Florida Keys & Key West

Includes »

Best Places to Eat

» Café Solé (p181)
» Keys Fisheries (p166)
» Seven Fish (p181)
» Midway Cafe (p162)
» Key Largo Conch House (p159)

Best Places to Stay

» Deer Run Bed & Breakfast (p169)
» Curry Mansion Inn (p180)
» Mermaid & Alligator (p180)
» Casa Morada (p162)
» Bahia Honda State Park Campground (p169)

Why Go?

The Keys are a place separate from mainland USA. They march to the beat of their own drum, or Alabama country band, or Jimmy Buffett single, or Bahamanian steel calypso set...whatever. The point is, this is a place where those who reject everyday life in the Lower 48 escape to. What do they find? About 113 mangrove-and-sandbar islands where the white sun melts over tight fists of deep green mangroves, long, gloriously soft mudflats and tidal bars, water as teal as Arizona turquoise and a bunch of people often like themselves: freaks, geeks and lovable weirdoes all.

Key West is still defined by its motto, which we love – One Human Family – an ideal that equals a tolerant, accepting ethos where anything goes and life is always a party (or at least a hungover day after). The color scheme: watercolor pastels cooled by breezes on a sunset-kissed Bahamian porch. Welcome to the End of the USA.

Have a drink.

When to Go

Key West

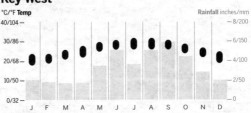

Dec–Mar It's dry, the sun is out, weather is grand and lodging is at its most expensive.

Apr–Jun Sea breezes help to keep the summer heat down, and hotel rates drop precipitously.

Jul–Nov There's some rain (and maybe even some hurricanes), but plenty of festivals happening too.

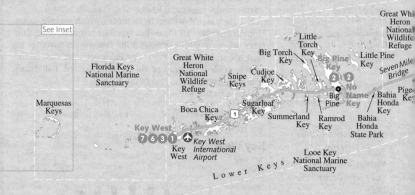

Gulf of
Mexico

Everglades National Park Boundary

Shark
Point

Hospital
Key
Middle
Key
East
Key
Loggerhead
Key
Bush Key
Garden Key
Long Key
10 Dry Tortugas
National Park

Marquesas
Keys

Note: Same scale as main map

Great White
Heron
National
Wildlife
Refuge

See Inset

Florida Keys
National Marine
Sanctuary

Marquesas
Keys

Great White
Heron
National
Wildlife
Refuge

Little
Torch
Key

Big Torch
Key

Snipe
Keys

Cudjoe
Key

Big Pine
Key

Little Pine
Key

Seven Mile
Bridge

2 **2**
No
Name
Key

Pige
Ke

Sugarloaf
Key

Boca Chica
Key

Summerland
Key

Big
Pine
Key

Bahia
Honda
Key

Ramrod
Key

Bahia
Honda
State Park

Key West
7 6 3 1
Key
West

Key West
International
Airport

Looe Key
National Marine
Sanctuary

Lower Keys

Florida Keys & Key West Highlights

1 Getting friendly with the
locals as you down drinks at
the oldest bar in Key West, the
Green Parrot (p182).

2 Spotting Key deer while
you wander on Big Pine and

No Name Keys at the **National
Key Deer Refuge** (p168)

3 Watching the sun set
over the ocean as you sit and
take in the raucous show at
Mallory Square (p171).

4 Diving around the rainbow
reefs of **John Pennekamp
Coral Reef State Park** (p157).

5 Paddling out to eerie,
lonely, beautiful **Indian Key
State Historic Site** (p161)

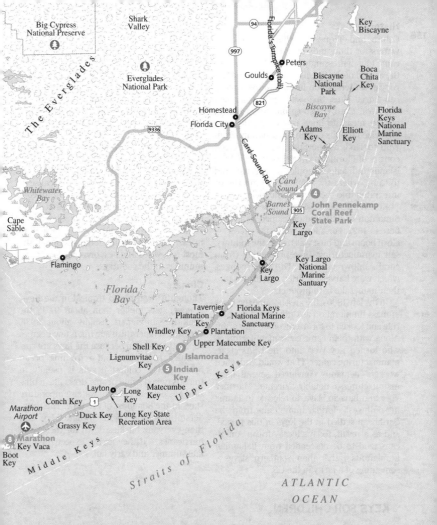

Big Cypress
National Preserve

Shark
Valley

94

997

Peters

Key
Biscayne

Goulds

Biscayne
National
Park

Boca
Chita
Key

Everglades
National Park

821

The Everglades

Homestead

Florida City

9336

Card Sound Rd

Biscayne
Bay

Adams
Key

Elliott
Key

Florida
Keys
National
Marine
Sanctuary

Whitewater
Bay

Cape
Sable

Card
Sound

Barnes
Sound

905

Key
Largo

4 John Pennekamp
Coral Reef
State Park

Flamingo

Florida
Bay

Key
Largo

Key Largo
National
Marine
Sanctuary

Tavernier
Plantation
Key

Florida Keys
National Marine
Sanctuary

Windley Key

Plantation

Shell Key

9

Upper Matecumbe Key

Lignumvitae
Key

Islamorada

5 Indian
Key

Layton

Long
Key

Matecumbe
Key

Upper Keys

Conch Key

1

Marathon
Airport

Duck Key

Long Key State
Recreation Area

Grassy Key

Middle Keys

8 Marathon
Key Vaca

Boot
Key

Straits of Florida

ATLANTIC

OCEAN

6 Donning a purple and
green crocodile costume and
partying in the streets at Key
West's **Fantasy Fest** (p179)

7 Scratching Papa's six-toed
cats behind their ears at the

lovely **Hemingway House**
(p175)

8 Strolling through the palm
hammock and pineland scrub
at eco-educational **Crane
Point Museum** (p165)

9 Feeding the giant tarpon
swimming in circles at
Robbie's Marina (p160)

10 Making an island-hopping
daytrip and detour to **Dry
Tortugas National Park** (p178)

History

Calusa and Tequesta Indians plied these waters for thousands of years, but that era came to a depressingly predictable end with the arrival of the Spanish, the area's first European settlers. Upon finding Native American burial sites, Spanish explorers named Key West Cayo Hueso (pronounced kah-ya way-so, meaning Bone Island), a title since anglicized into its current incarnation. From 1760 to 1763, as the Spaniards transferred control of Florida to Great Britain, all of the islands' indigenous peoples were transferred to Cuba, where they either died in exile or integrated into the local ethnic mélange.

Key West itself was purchased by John Simonton in 1821, and developed as a naval base in 1822. For a long while, the area's cycle of boom and bust was tied to the military, salt manufacturing, lime production (from coral), shipwrecks (see p179) and sponges, which were harvested, dried and turned into their namesake bath product.

In the late 1800s, the area became the focus of mass immigration as Cubans fled Spanish rule and looked to form a revolutionary army. Along with them came cigar manufacturers, who turned Key West into the USA's cigar-manufacturing center. That would end when workers' demands convinced several large manufacturers, notably Vicente Martínez Ybor and Ignacio Haya, to relocate to Tampa in southwest Florida. Immigrants from the Caribbean settled in the Keys in this period, and as a result, today's local African Americans tend to be descended from Bahamian immigrants rather than Southern slaves – something of a rarity in the US.

During the Spanish-American War (1898), Key West was an important staging point for US troops, and the military presence lasted through to WWI. In the late 1910s, with Prohibition on the horizon, Key West became a bootlegging center, as people stocked up on booze. The Keys began to boom around 1938 when Henry Flagler constructed his Overseas Hwy, replacing the by-then defunct Overseas Railroad.

Key West has always been a place where people buck trends. A large society of artists and craftspeople congregated here at the end of the Great Depression because of cheap real estate, and that community continues to grow (despite today's pricey real estate). While gay men have long been welcomed, the gay community really picked up in earnest in the 1970s; today it's one of the most renowned and best organized gay communities in the country.

Climate

Though it's warm and tropical in the Keys, it never gets higher than about 97°F; the peak in summer is usually about 89°F, with the temperature staying a few degrees cooler than Miami because the Keys are surrounded by ocean (and refreshing ocean breezes). The coldest it gets is usually in the 50s (when some people dress like a blizzard has descended), and water temperature stays in the 80s most of the time. The thunderstorm season begins by late May, and then everyone buckles down for the feared hurricanes – if they arrive, expect them in late summer and early fall.

KEYS FOR CHILDREN

Check out some of the following options to entertain the kids:

» **Florida Keys Eco-Discovery Center** (p175) Get an understanding of the region's environment.

» **Glass-bottom boat tours at John Pennekamp Coral Reef State Park** (p157) Your own window to the underwater world.

» **Key West Butterfly & Nature Conservatory** (p176) Pretty flying things.

» **Turtle Hospital** (p165) Save (or watch) the turtles.

» **Conch Tour Train** (p179) Kitschy, corny, enjoyable tour.

» **Ghost tours** (p179) Only slightly spooky; younger kids may find this one a bit scary.

» **Key-deer spotting** (p168) Kids go crazy for cute mini-deer.

» **Key West Cemetery** (p175) Get Gothic with these often humorus tombs.

» **Robbie's Marina** (p160) All sorts of activities, including the ever-popular tarpon (giant fish) feeding frenzy.

ℹ Information

The Monroe County Tourist Development Council's **Florida Keys & Key West Visitor's Bureau** (☑800-352-5397; www.fla-keys.com) runs an excellent website, which is packed with information on everything the Keys has to offer.

Check www.keysnews.com for good daily online news and information about the islands.

ℹ Getting There & Away

Getting here can be half the fun – or, if you're unlucky, a whopping dose of frustration. Imagine a tropical-island hop, from one bar-studded mangrove islet to the next, via one of the most unique roads in the world: the Overseas Hwy (US Hwy 1). On a good day, driving down the Overseas with the windows down, the wind in your face and the twin sisters of Florida Bay and the Atlantic stretching on either side, is the US road trip in tropical perfection. On a bad day, you end up sitting in gridlock behind some fat guy who is riding a midlife-crisis Harley.

Greyhound (☑800-229-9424) buses serve all Keys destinations along US Hwy 1 and depart from downtown Miami and Key West; you can pick up a bus along the way by standing on the Overseas Hwy and flagging one down. If you fly into Fort Lauderdale or Miami, the **Keys Shuttle** (☑888-765-9997) provides door-to-door service to most of the Keys ($70/80/90 to the Upper and Middle Keys/Lower Keys/Key West). Reserve at least a day in advance.

See also p185.

UPPER KEYS

No, really, you're in the islands!

It is a bit hard to tell when you first arrive, as the huge, rooty blanket of mangrove forest that forms the South Florida coastline spreads like a woody morass into Key Largo. In fact, the mangroves become Key Largo, which is more famous for its underwater than aboveground views. Keep heading south and the scenery becomes more archipelagically pleasant as the mangroves give way to wider stretches of road and ocean, until – bam – you're in Islamorada and the water is everywhere. If you want to avoid traffic on US 1, you can try the less trafficked FL 997 and Card Sound Rd to FL 905 (toll $1), which passes Alabama Jack's (p160).

Key Largo & Tavernier

We ain't gonna lie: Key Largo (both the name of the town and the island it's on) is slightly underwhelming at a glance. 'Under'

is the key word, as its main sights are under the water, rather than above. As you drive onto the islands, Key Largo resembles a long line of low-lying hammock and strip development. But that's Key Largo from the highway. Head down a side road and duck into this warm little bar, or that converted Keys plantation house, and the island idiosyncrasies become more pronounced.

The 33-mile long Largo, which starts at MM 106, is the longest island in the Keys, and those 33 miles have attracted a lot of marine life, all accessible from the biggest concentration of dive sites in the islands. The town of Tavernier (MM 93) is just south of the town of Key Largo.

⊙ Sights & Activities

John Pennekamp Coral Reef State Park

PARK

(www.pennekamppark.com, www.floridastateparks.org/pennekamp; MM 102.5 oceanside; car/motorcycle/cyclist or pedestrian $8/4/2; ⊘8am-sunset; ⌖) John Pennekamp has the singular distinction of being the first underwater park in the USA. There's 170 acres of dry parkland here and over 48,000 acres (ie 75 sq miles) of wet: the vast majority of the protected area is the ocean. Before you get out in that water, make sure to dig around some pleasant beaches and stroll over the nature trails. The **Mangrove Trail** is a good boardwalk introduction to this oft-maligned, ecologically awesome arboreal species (the trees, often submerged in water, breathe via long roots that act as snorkels – neat). Stick around for nightly campfire programs and ranger discussions.

The visitor center is well run and informative and has a small, cute **aquarium** (⊘8am-5pm) that gives a glimpse of what's under them thar waters. To really get beneath the surface of this park (pun intended), you should take a 2½-hour **glass-bottom boat tour** (☑305-451-6300; adult/child $24/17; ⊘tours 9:15am, 12:15pm & 3pm). You won't be ferried around in some rinky-dink fishing boat; you're brought out in a safe, modern 38ft catamaran from which you'll ooh and aah at filigreed flaps of soft coral, technicolor schools of fish, dangerous-looking barracudas and massive, yet ballerina-graceful sea turtles. Besides the swirl of natural coral life, interested divers can catch a glimpse of the *Christ of the Abyss,* an 8.5ft, 4000lb bronze sculpture of Jesus – a copy of a similar sculpture off the coast of Genoa, Italy, in the Mediterranean Sea.

DIVER DOWN

If you go diving in the Keys, Florida state law requires you to raise a 'Diver Down' flag whenever you are underwater. If you don't have one, they can be bought at any Keys dive shop.

If you want to go even deeper, try straight-up **snorkeling trips** (☑305-451-6300; adult/child $29.95/24.95) or **diving excursions** (☑305-451-6322, 877-727-5348; dive excursions with/without own gear $60/90). DIYers may want to take out a canoe ($12 per hour) or kayak (single/double per hour $12/$17) to journey through a 3-mile network of trails. Call ☑305-451-6300 for boat-rental information.

To learn more about the reef in this area, go to www.southeastfloridareefs.net.

Florida Keys Wild Bird Rehabilitation Center   WILDLIFE SANCTUARY

(www.fkwbc.org; 93600 Overseas Hwy, MM 93.6; suggested donation $5; ⊘sunrise-sunset) This sanctuary is the first of many animal hospitals you'll come across built by critter-loving Samaritans throughout the Keys. You'll find an alfresco bird hospital that cares for birds that have swallowed fish hooks, had wings clipped in accidents, been shot by BB pellets etc. A pretty trail leads back to a nice vista of Florida Bay and a wading bird pond. Just be warned, it does smell like bird doo back here.

Harry Harris Park   PARK

(MM 93.5; ⊘sunrise-sunset; 🚼) This small park is a good place to take the kids – there's a small playground, picnic table and other such accoutrements, and (rare for the Keys) a good patch of white sand fronting a warm lagoon that's excellent for swimming. There are good boat ramps here as well.

Jacob's Aquatics Center   PARK

(☑305-453-7946; 320 Laguana Ave, MM 99.6; ⊘11am-6pm Mon-Fri, 10am-7pm Sat & Sun; adult/child/student $8/5/6 Mon-Fri, $10/6/8 Sat & Sun; 🚼) Jacob's is a complex of all kinds of aquatic fun. There's an eight-lane pool for lap and open swimming, a therapy pool with handicapped access, courses on water aerobics and a small waterpark for the kids with waterslides, a playground and of course, kiddie-sized pools.

Caribbean Club Bar   FILM LOCATION

(MM 104 bayside; ⊘7am-4am) Here's one for the movie fans, particularly Bogie buffs: the Caribbean Club Bar is, in fact, the only place in Key Largo where *Key Largo,* starring Humphrey Bogart and Lauren Bacall, was filmed (the rest of the island was a Hollywood soundstage). If that's not enough, the original *African Queen,* of the same-titled movie, is docked in a channel at the Holiday Inn at MM 100 – just walk around the back and there she is.

Crocodile Lake National Wildlife Refuge   WILDLIFE SANCTUARY

(www.fws.gov/nationalkeydeer/crocodilelake; FL 905) If you approach Key Largo from FL 905, you'll be driving through one of the last wild sanctuaries for the threatened American crocodile, indigo snake and Key Largo woodrat – the latter is an enterprising fellow who likes to build 4ft by 6ft homes out of forest debris. Unfortunately, this really is a refuge; the wildlife areas are closed to the public, and your chances of seeing the species we've mentioned from the road are negligible.

🛏 Sleeping

Key Largo House Boatel   HOTEL $$

(☑305-766-0871; www.keylargohouseboatel.com; Shoreland Dr, MM 103.5 oceanside; houseboat small/medium/large from $75/100/150) If you can't afford to sleep underwater at Jules' Undersea Lodge, why not sleep on it here? There are five houseboats available, and they're a steal. The largest one is incredibly spacious and fairly well decorated for the Keys, with minimal sea-themed decor and enough room to sleep six people comfortably. The boats are right on the docks (and across from a bar), so no possibility of being isolated from land (or booze). Call ahead for directions, as the 'boatel' is a little off the beaten track.

Largo Lodge   HOTEL $$

(☑305-451-0424, 800-468-4378; www.largolodge .com; MM 102 bayside; winter apt/cottages $150/195, summer apt $95-115, cottages $125-155; 🅿) The manager of the property couldn't be friendlier, and his six hidden cottages, tucked into a glimmery secret tropical garden with a private swimming cove, couldn't be cozier. And, as a side note, there couldn't be more squirrels having the run of the joint. The interior of the rooms get lots of soothing green light thanks to that strong Keys sunshine slashing in over the copses of trees in the back.

KEY LIME PIE

Many places claim to serve the original Key lime pie, but no one knows who discovered the tart treat. Types of crust vary, and whether or not the pie should be topped with meringue is debated. However, the color of Key lime pie is not open to question. Beware of places serving green Key lime pie: Key limes are yellow, not green. Restaurants that add green food coloring say that tourists expect it to be green. Steer clear.

Kona Kai Resort & Gallery　　HOTEL **$$$**
(☑305-852-7200, 800-365-7829; www.konakairesort.com; MM 97.8 bayside; r $199-369, ste $249-975; P♠☎) This intimate hideaway features 11 airy rooms and suites (with full kitchens). They're all bright and comfortable, with good natural light and linoleum floors, but some feel a little too old-fashioned. Kona Kai also happens to house one of the better galleries in this corner of the Keys and extensive botanical gardens; guided tours are offered Tuesday and Thursday at 9:30am and 4:30pm, and on Saturdays at 9:30am, for $15. There's plenty to do otherwise – from tennis, kayaking and paddleboating to lounging in one of the hammocks that dot the palm-strewn, white-sand beach.

Hilton Key Largo Resort　　HOTEL **$$**
(☑888-871-3437; www.keylargoresort.com; MM 102 bayside; summer apt $95-115, cottage $170-230, ste from $315; P♠☎🐾) For an enormous outpost of a largely impersonal hotel chain, the Hilton Key Largo has a lot of friendliness and character. Folks just seem to get all laid back when lounging in clean, designer rooms outfitted in blues, greens and (why not?) blue-green. Throw in some beiges and you've got a supremely soothing sleeping experience. The grounds are enormous and include an artificial waterfall-fed pool and frontage to a rather large stretch of private white-sand beach.

Jules' Undersea Lodge　　HOTEL **$$$**
(☑305-451-2353; www.jul.com; 51 Shoreland Dr, MM 103.2 oceanside; per person $400-500) For a while, it seemed like some fancy hotel in Dubai was going to supplant tiny, kitschy Jules as the world's only underwater hotel. But then there was a financial crisis, the Dubai hotel tanked and bam! Key Largo: 1; Dubai: 0. Jules' Undersea Lodge, the world's

only underwater hotel is still the only place you and your significant other can join the 'five-fathom club' (we're not elaborating). Once a research station, this module has been converted into a delightfully cheesy Keys motel, but wetter. In addition to two private guest rooms (there's just the *teensiest* nautical theme – everywhere), there are common rooms, a fully stocked kitchen-dining room, and a wet room with hot showers and gear storage. Telephones and an intercom connect guests with the surface. Guests must be at least 10 years old and you gotta dive to get here – plus, there's no smoking or alcohol. If you just want to visit, sign up for a three-hour mini-adventure ($125), which also gives access to breathing hookahs (120ft-long air hoses for tankless diving). There's a good variety of PADI certification courses here (an open-water course runs $595).

John Pennekamp Coral Reef State Park　　CAMP GROUND **$**
(☑800-326-3521, ☑305-451-1202; www.pennekamppark.com; MM 102.5 oceanside; per night $31.49, hire of pavilion $32.25-53.75; P) You don't even have to leave Pennekamp at closing time if you opt for tent or recreational vehicle (RV) camping, but be sure to make a reservation, as the sites fill up fast.

Stone Ledge Paradise Inn　　HOTEL **$**
(☑305-852-8114; www.stoneledgeparadiseinn.com; 95320 Overseas Hwy; r winter $88-118, summer $78-98, villas winter $250-300, summer $185-250; P) This is a pink palace (well, squat bunch of motel blocks) of old-school US seaside kitsch. The wooden fish hung on every door are only the tip of the nautical-tack iceberg, but the real joy is the sweeping view over Florida Bay at the back of the property. Rooms are pretty simple on the inside.

✖ Eating

TOP CHOICE **Key Largo Conch House**　　FUSION **$$**
(☑305-453-4844; MM 100.2 oceanside; lunch $8-14, dinner $13-25; ⊙7am-9:30pm Sun-Thu, to 10pm Fri & Sat; ♠) A wi-fi hotspot, coffeehouse and innovative kitchen that likes to sex up local classics (conch in a lime and white-wine sauce, or in a vinegar sauce with capers), set in a restored old-school Keys mansion wrapped in a *Gone With the* Wind veranda? Yes please, and more of it. It's hard not to love the way the period architecture blends in seamlessly with the local tropical fauna. A justifiably popular spot with tourists and locals. The fish tacos are intensely good.

DETOUR: FLORIDA KEYS OVERSEAS HERITAGE TRAIL

One of the best ways to see the Keys is by bicycle. The flat elevation and ocean breezes are perfect for cycling, and the Florida Keys Overseas Heritage Trail (FKOHT; www.dep.state.fl .us/gwt/state/keystrail) will connect all the islands from Key Largo to Key West. At the time of writing about 70 miles of the trail were paved, but there have been significant delays to its completion.

If you are keen to ride, it's currently possible to bike through the Keys by shoulder riding (it takes three days at a good clip). There are particularly pleasant rides around Islamorada, and if you're uncomfortable riding on the shoulder, you can contact the FKOHT through its website for recommended bike excursions.

Mrs Mac's Kitchen AMERICAN $

(MM 99.4 bayside; breakfast & lunch $7-11, dinner $9-18; ⊙7am-9:30pm Mon-Sat) When Applebee's stuffs its wall full of license plates, it's tacky. When Mrs Mac's does it, it's homey. Probably because the service is warm and personable, and the breakfasts are delicious. Plus, the food packs in the locals, tourists, their dogs and pretty much everyone else on the island (plus, admittedly, a fair few calories, but that's why it tastes good).

Fish House SEAFOOD $$

(✆305-451-4665; 1024021 Overseas Hwy; mains $12-28; ⊙11:30am-10pm) The Fish House delivers on the promise of its title – very good fish, bought whole from local fishermen and prepared fried, broiled, jerked, blackened or char-grilled. This sort of cooking lets you taste the fish, which is as it should be. Because the Fish House only uses fresh fish, the menu changes daily based on what is available. We prefer the original Fish House over the more sushi-centered next door Fish House Encore.

DJ's Diner AMERICAN $

(99411 Overseas Hwy; mains $6-14; ⊙7am-9pm, to 3pm Sat & Sun) You're greeted by a mural of Humphrey Bogart, James Dean *and* Marilyn Monroe – that's a lot of Americana. It's all served with a heapin' helpin' of diner faves, vinyl-boothed ambience, and South Florida staples like *churrasco* (skirt steak) and conch.

Drinking & Entertainment

Alabama Jack's BAR

(58000 Crad Sound Rd; ⊙11am-7pm) Welcome to your first taste of the Keys: zonked-out fishermen, exiles from the mainland, and Harley heads getting drunk on a mangrove bay. This is the line where Miami-esque South Florida gives way to the country-fried American South. Wildlife-lovers: you may spot the rare mulleted version of *Jacksonvillia Redneckus!* But seriously, everyone raves about the conch fritters, and the fact they have to close because of nightly onslaughts of mosquitoes means this place is as authentically Florida as they come. Country bands take the stage on weekends from 2pm to 5pm.

Tavernier Towne Cinemas CINEMA

(✆305-853-7003; MM 92) This multiplex, showing new releases, is a perfect rainy-day option.

ⓘ Information

Key Largo Chamber of Commerce (✆305-451-1414, 800-822-1088; www.keylargo.org; MM 106 bayside; ⊙9am-6pm) Helpful office; has area-wide information.

Key Largo post office (✆305-451-3155; MM 100 bayside)

Mariner Hospital (✆305-434-3000; www .baptisthealth.net; Tavernier, MM 91.5 bayside)

ⓘ Getting There & Away

The Greyhound bus stops at MM 99.6 oceanside.

Islamorada

Islamorada (eye-luh-murr-*ah*-da) is also known as 'The Village of Islands.' Doesn't that sound pretty? Well, it really is. This little string of pearls (well, keys) – Plantation, Upper and Lower Matecumbe, Shell and Lignumvitae (lignum-*vite*-ee) – shimmers as one of the prettiest stretches of the islands. This is where the scrubby mangrove is replaced by unbroken horizons of ocean and sky, one perfect shade of blue mirroring the other. Islamorada stretches across some 20 miles, from MM 90 to MM 74.

◉ Sights & Activities

TOP CHOICE **Robbie's Marina** MARINA

(✆800-979-3370, 305-664-9814; www.robbies. com; MM 77.5 bayside; tours from $35; ⊙8am-6pm; ⑭) Robbie's really may be the happiest dock on Earth. More than a boat launch, Robbie's is a local flea market, tacky tourist shop (all the shells you ever wanted), sea pen for tarpons (very big-ass fish) and jump-off for excellent fishing expeditions, all wrapped into one driftwood-laced compound. There's a glut of boat-rental and tour options here. The party boat (half-day/night/full-day trips $35/40/60) is just that: a chance to drink, fish and basically achieve Keys Zen. Or, for real Zen (ie the tranquil kind as opposed to drunken kind), take an ecotour ($35) on an electrically propelled silent boat deep into the mangroves, hammocks and lagoons. Snorkeling trips are a good deal; for adult/child $35/20 you get a few hours on a very smooth-riding Happy Cat vessel and a chance to bob amid some of the USA's only coral reefs. If you don't want to get on the water, at least feed the freakishly large tarpons from the dock ($2.79 per bucket, $1 to watch).

Indian Key State Historic Site   ISLAND
(http://floridastateparks.org/indiankey; ⊘8am-sunset) You may have encountered spooky abandoned houses, mansions, even towns in your travels – but how about a derelict island? In 1831, renegade wrecker (shipwreck salvager) Jacob Housman turned this quiet island into a thriving city, complete with a warehouse, docks, streets, hotel and about 40 to 50 permanent residents. By 1836, Indian Key was the first seat of Dade County, but four years later the inhabitants of the island were killed or scattered by a Native American attack during the Second Seminole War. There's not much left at the historic site – just foundation, some cisterns, Housman's grave and jungly tangle. There are trails that follow the old layout of the city streets, and there is an observation tower, or you can walk among ruins and paddle around spotting rays and dolphins in utter isolation in a canoe or kayak – which, by the way, is the only way out here. Robbie's used to bring boats this way, and still does boat rental (single/double/glass-bottom kayak/canoe per hour $20/27.50/30/30). You can also see the island from the water on an ecotour with Robbie's ($35).

Lignumvitae Key State Botanical Site   ISLAND
(☑305-664-2540; http://floridastateparks.org/lignumvitaekey; ⊘9am-5pm Thu-Mon) This key, only accessible by boat, encompasses a 280-acre island of virgin tropical forest and is home to roughly a zillion jillion mosquitoes. The official attraction is the 1919 **Matheson**

House, with its windmill and cistern; the real draw is a nice sense of shipwrecked isolation. Strangler figs, mastic, gumbo-limbo, poisonwood and lignum vitae trees form a dark canopy that feels more South Pacific than South Florida. Guided walking tours (1¼ hours) are given at 10am and 2pm Friday to Sunday. You'll have to get here via Robbie's Marina (p160); boats depart for the 15-minute trip (adult/child $20/12) about 30 minutes prior to each tour and reservations are recommended.

Florida Keys History of Diving Museum   MUSEUM
(☑305-664-9737; www.divingmuseum.org; MM 83; adult/child $12/6; ⊘10am-5pm, to 7pm Wed) You can't miss the diving museum – it's the building with the enormous mural of swimming manatees on the side – and we mean that in every sense of the phrase. In other words, don't miss this museum, a collection of diving paraphernalia from around the world, including diving 'suits' and technology from the 19th century. This is the sort of charmingly eccentric museum that really reflects how many quirks live in the Keys. The hall of dozens of variations of the diving helmet from around the world, from Denmark to Japan, is particularly impressive. Folks in the museum can also provide information on diving in a vintage Mark V diving suit (the ones with the bulbous onion-heads connected to surface pumps), or you can call ☑305-394-1706 for more information.

Anne's Beach   BEACH
(MM 73) Anne's is one of the best beaches in these parts. The small ribbon of sand opens upon a sky-bright stretch of tidal flats and a green tunnel of hammock and wetland. Nearby mudflats are a joy to get stuck in, and will be much loved by the kids.

Windley Key Fossil Reef Geological State Park   PARK
(☑305-664-2540; www.floridastateparks.org/windleykey; MM 85.5; per person $2.50). To get his railroad built across the islands, Henry Flagler had to quarry out some sizable chunks of the Keys. The best evidence of those efforts can be found at this former quarry-cum-state-park. Besides having a mouthful of a name, Windley has leftover quarry machinery scattered along an 8ft former-quarry wall. The wall offers a cool (and rare) public peek into the stratum of coral that forms the substrate of the Keys. Ranger tours are offered at 10am and 2pm Friday to Sunday for $3.

Rain Barrel
ARTS CENTER

(305-852-8935; 86700 Overseas Hwy; 9am-5pm) We want to tell you the Rain Barrel, Islamorada's local artists' village, strikes a balance between the beautiful and the tacky. But you're more likely to find souvenir-y tourist tat here than a truly striking work of art. That said, strolling around the seven studios and galleries that make up the Rain Barrel is a nice way to pass about an hour of your time, and who knows, you may find the piece of your dreams, or at least a handpainted sign that says 'It's always 5 o'clock somewhere.'

Sleeping

Casa Morada
HOTEL $$$

(305-664-0044, 888-881-3030; www.casamorada .com; 136 Madeira Rd, off MM 82.2; ste winter $299-659, summer $239-459; P) Contemporary chic comes to Islamorada, but it's not gentrifying away the village vibe. Rather, the Casa adds a welcome dab of sophistication to Conch chill: a Keystone standing circle, freshwater pool, manmade lagoon, plus a *Wallpaper* magazine-worthy bar that overlooks Florida Bay; all make this boutique hotel worth a reservation. It's a bit of South Beach style over the usual Keys-style Jimmy Buffett blah. The slick back bar is one of our favorite places to catch a drink and a sunset in the Keys.

La Siesta Resort & Marina
RESORT $$$

(305-664-2132; www.lasiestaresort.com; MM 80.5 oceanside; ste $190-340; P) This pretty option consists of renovated suites and apartments that let in generous amounts of light and are decorated to feel modern and classy, but are still refreshingly un-hip and family-friendly. Service is amiable, the pool is busy and the ocean views are lovely.

Ragged Edge Resort
RESORT $$

(305-852-5389; www.ragged-edge.com; 243 Treasure Harbor Rd; apt $69-259; P) This low-key and popular efficiency and apartment complex, far from the maddening traffic jams, has 10 quiet units and friendly hosts. The larger studios have screened-in porches, and the entire vibe is happily comatose. There's no beach, but you can swim off the dock and at the pool.

Conch On Inn
MOTEL $

(305-852-9309; conchoninn.com; MM 89.5, 103 Caloosa St; apt $59-129; P) A simple motel popular with yearly snowbirds, Conch On Inn has basic rooms that are reliable, clean and comfortable.

Eating

Midway Cafe
CAFE $

(305-664-2622; 80499 Overseas Hwy; mains under $5; 7am-3pm Thu-Tue, to 2pm Sun) The lovely folks who run this cafe – stuffed with every variety of heart-warming art the coffee shop trope can muster – roast their own beans, make baked goods that we would swim across the Gulf for, and are friendly as hell. You're almost in the Middle Keys: celebrate making it this far with a cup of joe.

Pierre's
FRENCH $$$

(305-664-3225; www.pierres-restaurant.com; MM 81.6 bayside; mains $28-42; 5-10pm Sun-Thu, to 11pm Fri & Sat) Why hello two-story waterfront plantation – what are you serving? A tempura-ed spiny lobster tail...good, decadent start. Hogfish meunière? Well, that's rich enough to knock out a rhino. A filet mignon with black truffle mash potatoes? Splurge, traveler, on possibly the best food between Miami and Key West.

Morada Bay
AMERICAN $$

(305-664-0604; MM 81.6 bayside; lunch $10-15, dinner $21-29; 11:30am-11pm Sun-Thu, to midnight Fri & Sat) If you can ignore the service from staff who can get overwhelmed by customers and the awful bands that occasionally 'headline' the lunch rush, this is a lovely, laid-back Caribbean experience, complete with imported powder-white sandy beach, nighttime torches, tapas and fresh seafood.

Spanish Gardens Cafe
SPANISH $

(305-664-3999; MM 80.9 oceanside; mains $9.50-19; 11am-9pm Tue-Sun) A great option for those sick of fried everything, this pink, Barcelona-esque cafe serves sandwiches and salads dripping with manchego cheese, chorizo, *piquillo* peppers and other Iberian foodstuffs that get foodies going.

Bob's Bunz
CAFE $

(www.bobsbunz.com; MM 81.6 bayside; mains $6-12; 6am-2pm) The service at this cute cafe is energetic and friendly in an only-in-America kinda way, and the food is fine, filling and cheap. Key lime pie is a classic Keys dish and Key-lime anything at this bakery is highly regarded, so buy that souvenir pie here.

Drinking

Hog Heaven
BAR

(305-664-9669; MM 85 oceanside) We're tempted to place this joint in the eating section, as the seafood nachos are so good. But it deserves pride of place in Drinking thanks to huge crowds that trip all the way down from Fort Lauderdale for back-porch, alfresco imbibing.

Morada Bay BAR
(☑305-664-0604; MM 81.6 bayside) In addition to its excellent food (p162), the Bay holds monthly full-moon parties that attract the entire party-people population of the Keys. The whole shebang typically starts around 9pm and goes until whenever the last person passes out; check www.moradabay -restaurant.com for dates.

ⓘ Information

Islamorada Chamber of Commerce (☑305-664-4503, 800-322-5397; www.islamorada chamber.com; MM 83.2 bayside; ☺9am-5pm Mon-Fri, 10am-3pm Sat & Sun) Located in an old caboose.

Post office (☑305-664-4738; MM 82.9 oceanside)

ⓘ Getting There & Away

The Greyhound bus stops at the Burger King at MM 82.5 oceanside.

Long Key

The 965-acre **Long Key State Recreation Area** (☑305-664-4815; www.floridastateparks. org/longkey; MM 67.5 oceanside; per car/motorcycle/cyclist $5/4/2) takes up much of Long Key. It's about 30 minutes south of Islamorada, and comprises a tropical clump of gumbo-limbo, crabwood and poisonwood trees; a picnic area fronting a long, lovely sweep of teal water; and lots of wading birds in the mangroves. Two short nature trails head through distinct plant communities. The park also has a 1.5-mile canoe trail through a saltwater tidal lagoon and rents out canoes (per hour/day $5/10) and ocean-going kayaks (per two/four hours $17.20/32.25).

If you want to stay here, make reservations this minute: it's tough to get one of the 60 sites at the **campground** (☑305-326-3521, 888-433-0287; www.reserveamerica.com; MM 67.5 oceanside; sites $38.50; Ⓟ). They're all waterfront, making this the cheapest (and probably most unspoiled) ocean view – short of squatting on a resort – you're likely to find in Florida.

As you truck down the Keys, the bodies of water get wider until you reach the big boy: Seven Mile Bridge, one of the world's longest causeways and a natural divider between the Middle and Lower Keys. In this stretch of islands you'll cross specks like Conch Key and Duck Key, green, quiet Grassy Key, and finally Key Vaca (MM 54 to MM 47), where Marathon, the second-largest town and most Key-sy community in the islands, is located.

Grassy Key

At first blush Grassy Key seems pretty sedate. Well spotted; Grassy is very much an island of few attractions and lots of RV lots and trailer parks. These little villages were once the heart of the Keys, where retirees, escapists, fishermen and the wait staff who served them lived, drank and dreamed (of a drink). Some of these communities remain, but development is relentless, and so, it seems, is the migration of the old Conch trailer towns.

◉ Sights & Activities

Dolphin Research Center WILDLIFE RESERVE
(☑305-289-1121; www.dolphins.org; MM 59 bayside; adult/child under 4yr/child 4-12yr/senior $20/ free/15/17.50, swim program $180-650; ☺9am-4pm) By far the most popular activity on this island is swimming with the descendants of Flipper. Of all the dolphin swimming spots in the Keys, we prefer this one; the dolphins are free to leave the grounds and a lot of marine-biology research goes on behind the (still pretty commercial) tourist activities, such as getting a dolphin to paint your T-shirt or playing 'trainer for a day' ($650).

Curry Hammock State Park PARK
(☑305-289-2690; http://floridastateparks.org/ curryhammock; MM 56.2 bayside; per car/motorcycle/cyclist $5/4/2; ☺8am-sunset) This park is small but sweet and the rangers are just lovely. Like most parks in the Keys, it's a good spot for preserved tropical hardwood and mangrove habitat – a 1.5-mile hike takes you through both environments. Local waters are blissfully free of power boats, which is a blessing down here. Rent a kayak (single/double for two hours $17.20/21.50) or, when the wind is up, join the crowds of windsurfers and kiteboarders. You can also

SHOULD YOU SWIM WITH DOLPHINS?

There are four swim-with-the-dolphin (SWTD) centers in the Keys, and many more arguments for and against the practice.

For

» While SWTD sites are commercial, they are also research entities devoted to learning more about their charges.

» The dolphins raised on-site are legally obtained and have not been not captured from the wild.

» The dolphins are used to humans and pose a negligible danger to swimmers, especially when overseen by expert trainers.

» Dolphin swim programs increase our knowledge of dolphins and promote conservation.

» At places such as the **Dolphin Research Center** (p163), the dolphins can actually swim out of their pens into the open water, but choose not to.

Against

» Dolphins are social creatures that require interaction, which is impossible to provide in captivity.

» SWTD tourism encourages the capture of wild dolphins in other parts of the world.

» Dolphin behavior is never 100% predictable. Dolphins can seriously injure a human, even while playing.

» SWTD centers encourage customers to think of dolphins as anthropomorphized 'friends,' rather than wild animals.

» Dolphins never appreciate captivity. Those that voluntarily remain in SWTD sites do so to remain close to food.

SWTD Centers

If you decide to swim or see dolphins in the Keys, you can contact one of the following:

Theater of the Sea (☎305-664-2431; www.theaterofthesea.com; Islamorada, MM 84.5 bayside; swim programs $175; ☻9:30am-4pm) has been here since 1946. Structured dolphin swims and sea-lion programs ($135) include 30 minutes of instruction and a 30-minute supervised swim. You can also swim with stingrays ($55).

Dolphins Plus (☎305-451-1993, 866-860-7946; www.dolphinsplus.com; off MM 99.5 bayside; swim programs $135-220), a Key Largo center, specializes in recreational and educational unstructured swims. They expect you know a good deal before embarking upon the swim, even though a classroom session is included.

There is also dolphin swimming at Grassy Key's **Dolphin Research Center** (p163) and **Hawk's Cay Resort** (p164).

---

camp at the park for $36 per night – sites have toilets and electric hookups.

🛏 Sleeping & Eating

Hawk's Cay Resort　　　　　　　RESORT $$$
(☎888-395-5539; 305-743-7000; www.hawkscay
.com; 61 Hawk's Cay Blvd, Duck Key, off MM 61
oceanside; r & ste winter $350-1600, summer $150-
500; 🅿🛜🏊🐾) Now, if after one dolphin
swim center and fish ranch you're thinking,
Man, I *still* want to play with some sealife...,
don't worry: Hawk's Cay Resort is there
for you. The Cay is an enormous luxury
compound that could well have its own
zip code, and besides a series of silky-plush
rooms and nicely appointed townhouses, it
has more activities than you can shake a...
flipper at. Which is to say, the Cay has its
own dolphin pool where you can swim with
the dolphins – plus a sailing school, snorkeling, tennis and boat rentals.

Rainbow Bend　　　　　　　　　HOTEL $$$
(☎800-929-1505; www.rainbowbend.com; MM 58
oceanside; r $150-270; 🅿🏊) You'll be experiencing intensely charming Keys-kitsch in

these big pink cabanas, where the apartments and suites are bright, the tiki huts are shady, the bedsheets are ghastly, the beach swing is...um, swing-y and the ocean is (splash)...right there. Half-day use of the Bend's Boston whalers (motorboats), kayaks and canoes is complimentary.

Wreck Galley & Grill   AMERICAN $$
(☑305-743-8282; MM 59 bayside; mains $10-25; ◷11am-10pm) The Wreck is a Keys classic, where fisherman types knock back brew and feast on wings – but it's definitely a local haunt, where island politicos like to tongue wag about the issues (fishing). The food is excellent; it grills one of the best burgers in the Keys, and the aforementioned wings go down a treat with a tall beer.

Marathon

Marathon sits right on the halfway point between Key Largo and Key West, and is a good place to stop on a road trip across the islands. It's perhaps the most 'developed' key outside Key West (that's really pushing the definition of the word 'developed') in the sense that it has large shopping centers and a population of a few thousand. Then again it's still a place where exiles from the mainland fish, booze it up and have a good time, so while Marathon is more family-friendly than Key West, it's hardly G-rated.

◉ Sights & Activities

Crane Point Museum   PARK
(www.cranepoint.net; MM 50.5 bayside; adult/child over 5yr/senior $12.50/8.50/11; ◷9am-5pm Mon-Sat, noon-5pm Sun; 🛦) This is one of the nicest spots on the island to stop and smell the roses. And the pinelands. And the palm hammock – a sort of palm jungle (imagine walking under giant, organic Japanese fans) that only grows between MM 47 and MM 60. There's also Adderly House, a preserved example of a Bahamian immigrant cabin (which must have *baked* in summer) and 63 acres of green goodness to stomp through. This is a great spot for the kids, who'll love the pirate exhibits in an on-site museum and yet another bird hospital.

Turtle Hospital   WILDLIFE SANCTUARY
(☑305-743-2552; www.theturtlehospital.org; 2396 Overseas Hwy; adult/child $15/7.50; ◷9am-6pm 🛦) Be they victims of disease, boat propeller strikes, flipper entanglements with fishing lines – whatever, really – any injured

sea turtle in the Keys will hopefully end up in this motel-cum-sanctuary. We know we shouldn't anthropomorphize animals, but these turtles just seem so sweet, so it's sad but heartening to see the injured and sick ones well looked after. The whole setup is a labor of love by Richard Moretti, who's quite the Keys character himself. Tours are educational and fun, and offered at 10am, 1pm and 4pm. It's recommended you call ahead before visiting, as hospital staff may be away 'on call' at any moment.

Pigeon Key   ISLAND
(☑305-289-0025, 305-743-5999; www.pigeon key.net; MM 47; adult/child $12/9; ◷tours 10am, 11:30am, 1pm & 2:30pm) For years, tiny Pigeon Key, located 2 miles west of Marathon (basically below the Old Seven Mile Bridge) housed the rail workers and maintenance men who built the infrastructure that connected the Keys. Today you can tour the historic structures of this National Historic District or just relax on the beach and get in some snorkeling. Ferries leave from Knight's Key (to the left of the Seven Mile Bridge if you're traveling south) to Pigeon; the last one returns at 4pm. The **Old Seven Mile Bridge**, meanwhile, is closed to traffic and now serves as 'the World's Longest Fishing Bridge'; park at the northeastern foot of the bridge and have a wander.

Marathon Community Park & Marina   MARINA
(12222 Overseas Hwy) Has athletic fields and a skate park for disaffected adolescents. The marina, better known as **Boot Key Harbor** (☑305-289-8877; www.bootkeyharbor.com; VHF 16), is one of the best maintained working waterfronts in the Keys, and an excellent spot to book charter-fishing and diving trips. Come during Christmas to see a 'boat parade' of boats decked out with Christmas lights.

Sombrero Beach   BEACH
(Sombrero Beach Rd, off MM 50 oceanside) One of the few white-sand, mangrove-free beaches in the Keys. It's a good spot to lay out or swim, and it's free.

Marathon Kayak   KAYAKING
(☑305-395-0355; www.marathonkayak.com; 6363 Overseas Hwy) Does guided mangrove ecotours, sunset tours and boat rentals starting from around $45.

Sombrero Reef Explorers (☑305-743-0536; www.marathoncharters.com; 19 Sombrero Rd, off MM 50 oceanside) and **Tilden's Scuba Center**

It's easy to think of the Keys, environmentally speaking, as a little boring. The landscape isn't particularly dramatic (with the exception of those sweet sweeps of ocean visible from the Overseas Hwy); it tends toward low brush and...well, more low brush.

Hey, don't judge a book by its cover. The Keys have one of the most unique, sensitive environments in the US. The difference between ecosystems here is measured in inches, but once you learn to recognize the contrast between a hammock and a wetland, you'll see the islands in a whole new tropical light. Some of the best introductions to the natural Keys can be found at **Crane Point Museum** (p165) and the **Florida Keys Eco-Discovery Center** (p175).

But here, we want to focus on the mangroves, the coolest, if not most visually arresting habitat in the islands. They rise from the shallow shelf that surrounds the Keys (which also provides that lovely shade of Florida teal), looking like masses of spidery fingers constantly stroking the waters. Each mangrove traps the sediment that has accrued into the land your tiki barstool is perched on. That's right, no mangroves = no Jimmy Buffett.

The three different types of mangrove trees are all little miracles of adaptation. Red mangroves, which directly front the water, have aerial roots, called propagules, which allow them to 'breathe' even as they grow into the ocean. Black mangroves, which grow further inland, survive via 'snorkel' roots called pneumatophores. Resembling spongy sticks, these roots grow out from the muddy ground, gasping in fresh air. White mangroves grow furthest inland and actually sweat out the salt they absorb through air and water to keep healthy.

The other tree worth a prop here isn't a mangrove, but the lignum vitae, which is restricted to the Keys in the US, is just as cool. Its sap has long been used to treat syphilis, hence the tree's Latin name, which translates to 'tree of life.'

(☎305-743-7255; www.tildensscubacenter.com; 4650 Overseas Hwy) both offer snorkeling and diving expeditions through nearby sections of the coral reef.

🛏 Sleeping

Seascape   B&B $$
(☎305-743-6212; 1275 76th St, between MM 51 & 52; r from $125; P❖☎❄❀) The classy, understated luxury in this B&B manifests in the nine rooms, which all have a different feel, from old-fashioned cottage to sleek boutique. Seascape also has a waterfront pool, kayaks for guests to use and a lovely lobbylounge where you'll find breakfast, and afternoon wine and snack (all included).

Tranquility Bay   RESORT $$$
(☎888-755-7486; www.tranquilitybay.com; MM 48.5 bayside; r $280-650; P❖☎❄❀) If you're serious about going upscale, you should be going here. Tranquility Bay is a massive condotel resort with plush townhouses, high-thread-count sheets and all-in-white chic. The rooms really do have a dollhouse effect going on – between shades of eggwhite and sea blue they resemble nothing so much as pieces of delicate china. The grounds are enormous and activity-filled; they really don't want you to leave.

Siesta Motel   MOTEL $
(☎305-743-5671; www.siestamotel.net; MM 51 oceanside; r $75-105; P❖❀) Head here for one of the cheapest, cleanest flops in the Keys, located in a friendly cluster of cute Marathon homes – and it's got great service, to boot.

Seadell Motel   MOTEL $$
(☎305-743-5161; 5000 Overseas Hwy; r $79-180; P@) The Seadell is a Keys classic: low-slung huts containing linoleum-floored rooms that sport tropical bedspreads. The rooms are more or less self-sufficient small apartments, and can comfortably accommodate small families.

🍴 Eating

TOP CHOICE Keys Fisheries   SEAFOOD $
(3502 Gulf View Ave; mains $7-16; ⏱11am-9pm) The lobster reuben is the stuff of legend here. Sweet, chunky, creamy, so good it's making us leave unsightly drool all over our keyboard. But you can't go wrong with any of the excellent seafood here, all served with

sass (to order you have to identify your favorite car, color, etc; a question that depends on the mood of the guy behind the counter). Expect pleasant levels of seagull harassment as you dine on a working waterfront.

Hurricane
AMERICAN $$

(☎305-743-2200; MM 49.5 bayside; mains $12-19; ☺11am-midnight) Besides being our favorite bar in Marathon, the Hurricane also serves an excellent menu of creative South Florida–inspired goodness. Snapper stuffed with crabmeat comes after an appetizer of conch sliders (miniburgers) jerked in Caribbean seasoning. Save room for the chicken wings, an amazing blend of hot, sweet and plain delicious. The $5 lunch specials are a hell of a deal.

Wooden Spoon
AMERICAN $

(MM 51 oceanside; mains $3-9; ☺7am-3pm) It's the best breakfast around, served by sweet Southern women who know their way around a diner. The biscuits are fluffy, but they drown so well in that thick, delicious sausage gravy, and the grits are the most buttery soft starch you'll ever have the pleasure of seeing beside your eggs.

Villa Blanca
CUBAN $

(2211 Overseas Hwy; mains $7-12; ☺7am-8pm Mon-Sat) Villa Blanco's roast pork is a superlative example of the genre (of Cuban pork – a method cuisine with many practitioners in South Florida). It's pillowy soft, luscious, citrus tangy – yet comforting. It's also freakishly huge, as you will be if you eat in this friendly, barebones cafeteria too often.

Dion's
FRIED CHICKEN $

(MM 51 bayside; fried-chicken dinner $4-6; ☺24hr) Hold on – it's a gas station. Well, gas stations treated you right in Miami, didn't they (see El Carajo, p120)? Dion's serves our favorite fried chicken in South Florida: crisp but juicy, plump and rich, with gooey, melty mac and cheese and sweet fried-but-just-firm-enough plantains on the side…Oh man, we'll be right back.

Drinking & Entertainment

TOP CHOICE Hurricane
BAR

(☎305-743-2200; MM 49.5 bayside) The staff is sassy, sarcastic and warm. The drinks will kick your ass out the door and have you back begging for more. The ambience is: locals, tourists, mad fishermen, rednecks and the odd journalist saddling up for endless

Jägerbombs before dancing the night away to any number of consistently good live acts. It's the best bar before Key West, and it deserves a visit from you.

Island Fish Company
BAR

(☎305-743-4191; MM 54 bayside) The Island's got friendly staff pouring strong cocktails on a sea-breeze-kissed tiki island overlooking Florida Bay. Chat with your friendly Czech or Georgian bartender, tip well, and they'll top up your drinks without you realizing it. The laid-back by-the-water atmosphere is quintessentially Keys.

Brass Monkey
BAR

(☎305-743-4028; Marathon, MM 52) When Colonel Kurtz whispered, 'The horror, the horror,' in *Apocalypse Now* he was probably thinking about the night he got trashed in this scuzziest of dives, the preferred watering hole for off-the-clock bar and wait staff in Marathon.

Marathon Cinema & Community Theater
CINEMA

(☎305-743-0408; www.marathontheater.org; 5101 Overseas Hwy) A good, old-school, single-stage theater that shows movies and plays in big reclining seats (with even bigger cup-holders).

ℹ Information

Fisherman's Hospital (☎305-743-5533; www.fishermanshospital.com; 3301 Overseas Hwy) Has a major emergency room.

Marathon Visitors Center Chamber of Commerce (☎305-743-5417, 800-262-7284; www.floridakeysmarathon.com; MM 53.5 bayside; ☺9am-5pm) Sells Greyhound tickets.

ℹ Getting There & Away

You can fly into the **Marathon Airport** (☎305-289-6060; MM 50.5 bayside) or go Greyhound, which stops at the airport.

LOWER KEYS

The Lower Keys are fierce bastions of Conch Keys native culture. Some local families have been Keys castaways for generations, and there are bits of Big Pine that feel more Florida Panhandle than Overseas Hwy. It's an odd contrast, the islands get at their most isolated, rural and quintessentially 'Keez-y' before opening onto (relatively) cosmopolitan, heterogeneous (yet strongly homosexual) Key West.

> **DON'T MISS**
>
> ## KEY DEER
>
> While we can't guarantee you'll spot one, if you head down the side roads of Big Pine Key, there's a pretty good chance you'll spot the Key deer, roughly the size of a large dog. Once mainland dwellers, the Key deer were stranded on the islands during the formation of the Keys. Successive generations grew smaller and had single births, as opposed to large litters, to deal with the reduced food resources in the Keys. While you won't see thundering herds of dwarfish deer, the little cuteballs are pretty easy to spot if you're persistent and patient. In fact, they're so common you need to pay careful attention to the reduced speed limits. Note: speed limits drop further at night, because cars are still the biggest killer of Key deer.
>
> To visit the official Key deer refuge (although the deer can be spotted almost anywhere on Big Pine) take Key Deer Blvd (it's a right at the lights off the Overseas Hwy at the southern end of Big Pine) north for 3.5 miles from MM 30.5.

Big Pine, Bahia Honda & Looe Key

Big Pine is home to endless stretches of quiet roads, Key West employees who found a way around astronomical real-estate rates, and packs of wandering Key deer. Bahia Honda has got everyone's favorite sandy beach, while the coral-reef system of Looe offers amazing reef-diving opportunities.

⊙ Sights & Activities

Bahia Honda State Park   PARK
(☑305-872-3210; www.bahiahondapark.com; MM 36.8; per car/motorcycle/cyclist $5/4/2; ☺8am-sunset; ⓓ) This park, with its long, white-sand (and seaweed-strewn) beach, named Sandspur Beach by locals, is the big attraction in these parts. As Keys beaches go, this one is probably the best natural stretch of sand in the island chain, but we wouldn't vote it best beach in the continental USA (although Condé Nast did...in 1992). As a tourist, the more novel experience is walking a stretch of the **old Bahia Honda Rail Bridge**, which offers nice views of the surrounding islands. Or check out the nature trails (ooh, butterflies!) and science center, where helpful park employees help you identify stone crabs, fireworms, horseshoe crabs and comb jellies.

The **park concession** (☑305-872-3210; MM 36.8 oceanside) offers daily 1½-hour snorkeling trips at 9:30am and 1:30pm (adult/child $30/25). Reservations are a good idea in high season.

Looe Key National Marine Sanctuary   MARINE PARK
(☑305-292-0311; floridakeys.noaa.gov) Looe (pronounced 'loo') Key, located five nautical miles off Big Pine, isn't a key at all but a reef, part of the Florida Keys National Marine Sanctuary. This is an area of some 2800 square nautical miles of 'land' managed by the National Oceanic & Atmospheric Administration. The reef here can only be visited through a specially arranged charter-boat trip, best arranged through any Keys diving outfit, the most natural one being **Looe Key Dive Center** (☑305-872-2215; www.diveflakeys.com; snorkel/dive $44/84). The marine sanctuary is named for an English frigate that sank here in 1744, and the Looe Key reef contains the 210ft *Adolphus Busch*, used in the 1957 film *Fire Down Below* and then sunk (110ft deep) in these waters in 1998.

National Key Deer Refuge Headquarters   WILDLIFE RESERVE
(☑305-872-2239; www.fws.gov/nationalkeydeer; Big Pine Shopping Center, MM 30.5 bayside; ☺8am-5pm Mon-Fri; ⓓ) What would make Bambi cuter? Mini Bambi. Introducing: the Key deer, an endangered subspecies of white-tailed deer that prance about primarily on Big Pine and No Name Keys. The folks here are an incredibly helpful source of information on the deer and all things Keys. The refuge sprawls over several islands, but the sections open to the public are on Big Pine and No Name. The headquarters also administers the Great White Heron National Wildlife Refuge, 200,000 acres of open water and mangrove islands north of the main Keys that is only accessible by boat; there is no tourism infrastructure in place to get out here, but you can inquire about nautical charts and the heron themselves at the office.

Blue Hole
POND

(off MM 30.5; ⊘24hr) This little pond (and former quarry) is now the largest freshwater body in the Keys. That's not saying much, but the hole is a pretty little dollop of blue (well, algal green) surrounded by a small path and information signs. The water is home to turtles, fish, wading birds and two alligators, including a hefty sucker named 'Bacardi.' Apparently people have taken to (illegally) feeding the wildlife here; please don't follow in their footsteps. A quarter mile further along the same road is **Watson's Nature Trail** (less than 1 mile long) and **Watson's Hammock**, a small Keys forest habitat.

No Name Key
ISLAND

Perhaps the best named (or lack thereof) island in the Keys gets few visitors, as it's basically a residential island. It's one of the most reliable spots for Key deer watching. From Overseas Hwy, go on to Watson Blvd, turn right, then left onto Wilder Blvd. Cross Bogie Bridge and you'll be on No Name.

Veterans Memorial Park & Beach
PARK

(MM 39 oceanside; ⊘sunrise-sunset; ♿) This small park has covered picnic tables and good access to the mudflat and mangrove habitat that makes up most of the Keys' coastline. The views onto the ocean are pristine.

Big Pine Flea Market
MARKET

(MM 30.5 oceanside; ⊘8am-sunset Sat & Sun) This market, which attracts folks from across the Keys, rivals local churches for weekly attendance. You know how we keep harping on about how weird Keys residents are? Well, imagine rummaging through their closets and seeing their deepest, darkest secrets – on sale for 50¢?!

Strike Zone Charters
SNORKELING, DIVING

(☎305-872-9863, 800-654-9560; www.strikezonecharter.com; MM 29.5 bayside) Runs snorkeling ($35) and diving trips ($45) aboard glass-bottom boats, in which you can explore the thousands of varieties of colorful tropical fish, coral and sea life in the Looe Key sanctuary.

🛏 Sleeping

🔝 Deer Run Bed & Breakfast
B&B $$$

(☎305-872-2015; www.deerrunfloridabb.com; 1997 Long Beach Dr, Big Pine Key, off MM 33 oceanside; r $235-355; Ⓟ❄) This state-certified green lodge and vegetarian B&B is isolated on a lonely, lovely stretch of Long Beach Dr. It's a garden of quirky delights, complemented by assorted love-the-earth paraphernalia, street signs and four simple but cozily scrumptious rooms with names such as Eden, Heaven and Utopia. The helpful owners will get you out on a boat or into the heated pool for some chillaxation, while they whip up organic, vegetarian meals. We should add: the vibe is decidedly not self-righteous vegetarian. You could take home a steak-and-bacon sandwich and the staff wouldn't mind.

🔝 Bahia Honda State Park Campground
CAMP GROUND $

(☎305-872-2353; www.reserveamerica.com; MM 37, Bahia Honda Key; sites $36, cabins $160; Ⓟ) Bahia Honda has the best camping in the Keys. There's nothing quite like waking up to the sky as your ceiling and the ocean as your shower (Ow! Damned sand flies. OK, it's not paradise...). The park has six cabins, each sleeping six people, and 200 sites a short distance from the beach. Reserve well in advance.

Barnacle Bed & Breakfast
B&B $$

(☎305-872-3298; www.thebarnacle.net; 1557 Long Beach Dr, Big Pine Key; r $145-195; Ⓟ❄) Another great Keys B&B, the Barnacle welcomes you into its atrium with the promise of fresh ocean breezes. Wander around the pool and Jacuzzi, past the swinging hammocks, into highly individualized rooms that nonetheless all share a lovingly crazy design sense: tropical knickknacks and big windows that let in lots of Keys sunlight are standard. Meals should be enjoyed on the excellent deck, which overlooks a gorgeous clean sweep of the sea.

Big Pine Key Fishing Lodge
HOTEL $

(☎305-872-2351; MM 33 oceanside, Big Pine Key; sites with/without electricity $40/35, motel apt $80-120; Ⓟ❄♿) This tidy canalside spot has a loyal clientele of snowbirds who wouldn't call anywhere else their Keys home. Key deer wander the clean grounds, staff is friendly and there are plenty of activities for the kids. The lodge, geared toward fishing and diving types, does boat rental.

Parmer's Place Guesthouse
HOTEL $$

(☎305-872-2157; www.parmersresort.com; 565 Barry Ave, Little Torch Key, off MM 28.5 bayside; r winter $134-294, summer $99-209; 🛜❄) Appearing deceptively small from the outside, this 5-acre property takes up a nice chunk of Little Torch Key and fills it with inviting rooms that overlook local cuts and channels. The rooms are spacious, although you'd be mad not to step outside them and enjoy a view of the islands from your balcony.

Little Palm Island Resort & Spa   RESORT $$$
(☎305-872-2524, 800-343-8567; www.littlepalmis land.com; ste $1091-2072; @☎) How do you get here? By boat or by plane, accompanied by a big wad of money. If you can afford to get here you can afford to spoil yourself, and this exclusive island, with its Zen gardens, blue lagoons and general Persian-empire air of decadent luxury, is very good at spoiling you.

✕ Eating

No Name Pub   PIZZA $
(☎305-872-9115; N Watson Blvd, Big Pine Key, off MM 30.5 bayside; mains $7-18; ⏲11am-11pm) The No Name's one of those off-the-track places that everyone seems to know about. It feels isolated, it looks isolated, yet somehow, the tourists are all here – and this doesn't detract in the slightest from the kooky ambience, friendly service, excellent locally brewed beer and primo pizzas served up at this colorful semidive. Note, the name of this place implies that it is located on No Name Key, but it is on Big Pine Key, just over the causeway.

Coco's Kitchen   DINER $
(Big Pine Key Shopping Center, MM 30.5 bayside; mains & sandwiches $10.50; ⏲7am-2pm & 4-7pm Tue-Sat) Enter through the oddly mirrored storefront into this tiny luncheonette, where local fishers join shoppers from the Winn Dixie next door for diner fare and local gossip. Serves a good mix of American standards and Cuban diner fare such as *picadillo* (ground beef cooked in Cuban spices).

Good Food Conspiracy   VEGETARIAN $
(Big Pine Key, MM 30 oceanside; mains under $10; ⏲9:30am-7pm Mon-Sat, 11am-5pm Sun; ⚐) This place serves pork-fat and baby-seal tacos. Just kidding! Rejoice, health-food nuts, all the greens, sprouts, herbs and tofu you've been dreaming about during that long, fried-food-studded drive down the Overseas are for sale in this friendly little macrobiotic organic shop. There is a good smoothie and fresh-juice bar on site. Note the big pink shrimp out front – Keezy kitsch as its best.

❶ Information

Lower Keys Chamber of Commerce (☎305-872-2411; www.lowerkeyschamber.com; MM 31

oceanside; ⏲9am-5pm Mon-Fri, 9am-3pm Sat) Stocked with brochures and tourist information.

Sugarloaf & Boca Chica Keys

This is the final stretch before the holy grail of Key West. There's not much going on – just a few good eats and a thoroughly batty roadside attraction.

This lowest section of the Keys goes from about MM 20 to the start of Key West.

◉ Sights

Perky's Bat Tower   TOWER
(Sugarloaf Key, MM17) It resembles an Aztec-inspired fire lookout, but this wooden tower is actually one real-estate developer's vision gone utterly awry. In the 1920s Richter C Perky had the bright idea to transform this area into a vacation resort. There was just one problem: mosquitoes. His solution? Build a 35ft tower and move in a colony of bats (he'd heard they eat mosquitoes). He imported the flying mammals, but they promptly took off, leaving the tower empty. Perky never built in this area again.

Sheriff's Animal Farm   ZOO
(☎305-293-7300; 5501 College Rd, Stock Island; ⏲1-3pm every other Sun or by appt; ⚐) Just before you hit Key West, you may be tempted to stop into this farm, located near the Monroe County Sheriff's Office and Detention Center (seriously). This shelter for Monroe County animals that have been abandoned or given up is a lovely place to take the kids (call ahead to visit and farmer Jeanne Selander will be happy to show you around). There are tortoises, South American cavvies (a kind of rodent), birds, llamas, an albino python – it's a zoo, folks, and a fun one at that.

🛏 Sleeping

Sugarloaf Key Resort KOA   CAMP GROUND $
(☎305-745-3549, 800-562-7731; www.koa.com/campgrounds/sugarloaf-key; 251 County Rd, off MM 20 oceanside; sites tent/RV from $55/72; ᴾ☎☎) This highly developed KOA (Kampground of America) has about 200 tent sites and 200 RV sites, with amenities including beachfront volleyball, swimming pool, minigolf and sunset cruises.

Sugarloaf Lodge   HOTEL $$
(☎800-553-6097; www.sugarloaflodge.net; Sugarloaf Key, MM 17; r $115-165; ᴾ☎) The 55 motel-

Conchs (pronounced 'conk' as in 'bonk,' not 'contsh' as in 'bunch') are people who were born and raised in the Keys. It's a rare title to achieve. Even transplants can only rise to the rank of 'freshwater Conch.' You will hear reference to, and see the flag of, the Conch Republic everywhere in the islands, which brings us to an interesting tale.

In 1982 US border patrol and customs agents erected a roadblock at Key Largo to catch drug smugglers and illegal aliens. As traffic jams and anger mounted, many tourists disappeared. They decided they'd rather take the Shark Valley Tram in the Everglades, thank you very much. To voice their outrage, a bunch of fiery Conchs decided to secede from the USA. After forming the Conch Republic, they made three declarations (in this order): secede from the USA; declare war on the USA and surrender; and request $1 million in foreign aid. The roadblock was eventually lifted, and every February, Conchs celebrate the anniversary of those heady days with nonstop parties, and the slogan 'We Seceded Where Others Failed.'

Today the whole Conch Republic thing is largely a marketing gimmick, but that doesn't detract from its official motto: 'One Human Family.' This emphasis on tolerance and mutual respect has kept the Keys' head and heart in the right place, accepting gays, straights, and peoples of all colors and religions.

like rooms are nothing special, though every single one has a killer bay view. There is also an on-site restaurant, a tiki bar, a marina and an airstrip, from which you can charter a seaplane tour or go skydiving.

Eating

Sugarloaf Food Company AMERICAN $
(MM 24 bayside; breakfast $2.25-4.25, lunch $5-9; ⏰6:30am-3pm Tue-Sat) A cozy, airy alternative to fried dullness, the Food Company specializes in excellent sandwiches and salads, plus some cute handcrafted postcards. An almost impossibly cute artsy retreat-cum-restaurant.

Mangrove Mama's CARIBBEAN $$
(MM 20 oceanside; lunch $10-15, dinner $19-29; ⏰11:30am-3:30pm & 5:30-10pm) This groovy roadside eatery serves Caribbean-inspired seafood – coconut shrimp, spicy conch stew, lobster – best enjoyed on the backyard patio and accompanied by a little live reggae.

Baby's Coffee CAFE $
(☎800-523-2326; MM 15 oceanside; ⏰7am-6pm Mon-Fri, 7am-5pm Sat & Sun) This very cool coffeehouse has an on-site bean-roasting plant and sells bags of the aromatic stuff along with excellent hot and cold java brews – many locals consider this to be some of the best coffee in the islands. Other essentials are sold, from yummy baked goods to Dr Brommer's liquid soap.

KEY WEST

The Keys, like any frontier, have always attracted two 'E's': edges and eccentrics. And when it came to the far frontier, the very edge, the last outpost of America – out here, only the most eccentric would dare venture. And thus, Key West, is the most beautifully strange (or is it strangely beautiful?) island in the US. This place is seriously screwy, in a (mostly) good way. There's no middle separating the high and low brow, that's for sure. On one side of the road, literary festivals, Caribbean villas, tropical noir and expensive art galleries. On the other, an S&M fetishist parade, frat boys vomiting on their sorority girlfriends and 'I Love to Fart' T-shirts (seriously).

Where the other Keys are a bit more country-fried, Key West, a historical haven for homosexuals and artists, remains a little more left of center. The locals revel in their funky nonconformity here, probably because weirdness is still integral to the Key West brand. But past these idiosyncrasies is simply a beautiful tropical island, where the moonflowers bloom at night and the classical Caribbean homes are so sad and romantic it's impossible not to sigh when you see them.

Sights

Mallory Square SQUARE
(⏰sunset;) Take all those energies, subcultures and oddities of Keys life – the hippies, the rednecks, the foreigners and, of course, the tourists – and focus them into one

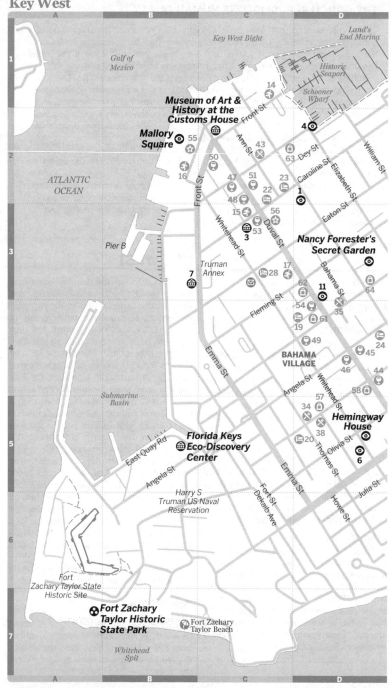

Key West Bight

Gulf of Mexico

Land's End Marina

Historic Seaport

Schooner Wharf

Museum of Art & History at the Customs House

Mallory Square 55

14

4

63 Dey St

43

Front St

Ann St

Caroline St

William St

Elizabeth St

ATLANTIC OCEAN

16

50

47 51

48

23

1

Eaton St

Bahama St

64

Front St

15

22

56

53

3

Whitehead St

Duval St

Nancy Forrester's Secret Garden

Pier B

7

Truman Annex

17

28

62

11

35

Fleming St

54

61

19

49

24

45

BAHAMA VILLAGE

46

44

58

Submarine Basin

Emma St

Angela St

Whitehead St

34

57

Hemingway House

Florida Keys Eco-Discovery Center

East Quay Rd

Angela St

38

20

Olivia St

Thomas St

6

Julia St

Harry S Truman US Naval Reservation

Emma St

Fort St

Dekalb Ave

Howe St

Fort Zachary Taylor State Historic Site

Fort Zachary Taylor Historic State Park

Fort Zachary Taylor Beach

Whitehead Spit

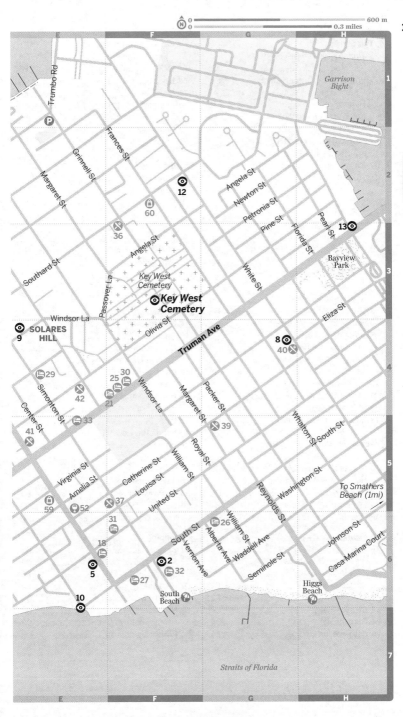

0
0

600 m
0.3 miles

N

Garrison Bight

Trumbo Rd

Grinnell St

Frances St

Margaret St

Southard St

P

12

60

36

Angela St

Newton St

Petronia St

Pine St

Angela St

Passover La

Key West Cemetery

◉ Key West Cemetery

White St

Florida St

Pearl St

13 ◉

Bayview Park

Windsor La

Olivia St

Truman Ave

Eliza St

◉ SOLARES HILL
9

8 ◉
40 ✕

Simonton St

Center St

29

25 30
42
21

33

41

Windsor La

Margaret St

Packer St

39 ✕

Whalton St   South St

Virginia St

Amelia St

59

52

37 ✕

31

18

Catherine St

Louisa St

William St

Royal St

United St

South St

Vernon Ave

Alberta Ave

William St

Waddell Ave

Reynolds St

Washington St

To Smathers Beach (1mi)

26

Johnson St

Seminole St

Casa Marina Court

5

10 ◉

◉ 2
32

27

South Beach

Higgs Beach

Straits of Florida

Key West

torchlit, family-friendly (but playfully edgy), sunset-enriched street party. The child of all these raucous forces is Mallory Sq, one of the greatest shows on Earth. It all begins as the sun starts to set, a sign for the madness that it's OK to break out. Watch a dog walk a tightrope, a man swallow fire, British acrobats tumble and sass each other. Have a beer. And a conch fritter. And wait for the sun to dip behind the ocean and for the carnival to really get going.

Duval Street   STREET
Key West locals have a love-hate relationship with the most famous road in Key West (if not the Keys). Duval, Old Town Key West's main drag, is a miracle mile of booze, tacky everything and awful behavior (and not awful in an awfully good way either). It's more like awful in a loud, belligerently drunk, omigodthatshirtsays 'Put some lipstick on my dipstick' *really*? kinda way). But it's fun. The 'Duval Crawl' is one of the best pub crawls in the country. The mix of live music drink-o-ramas, T-shirt kitsch, local theaters, art studios and boutiques is more charming than jarring. And the experience is quintessentially Key West ('Keezy'). Have some perspective, have a laugh, and appreciate Duval for her pimples-and-all, to see why this street continues to be the island's tipsy heart.

Hemingway House   HISTORIC SITE
(www.hemingwayhome.com; 907 Whitehead St; adult/child 6-12yr $12.50/6; ☺9am-5pm) Key West's biggest darling, Ernest Hemingway, lived in this gorgeous Spanish colonial house from 1931 to 1940. Papa moved here in his early 30s with wife No 2, a *Vogue* fashion editor and (former) friend of wife No 1. *The Short Happy Life of Francis Macomber* and *The Green Hills of Africa* were produced here, but Hemingway didn't just work; like all writers he wasted a lot of time, specifically by installing Key West's first saltwater swimming pool. The construction project set him back so badly he pressed his 'last penny' into the cement on the pool's deck. It's still there today, along with the evil descendants of his famous six-toed cat, who basically rule the house and grounds. The author's old studio is preserved as he left it – when he ran off in 1940 with wife No 3.

FREE Florida Keys
Eco-Discovery Center   MUSEUM
(eco-discovery.com/ecokw.html; 35 East Quay Rd, Truman Annex; ☺9am-4pm Tue-Sat; P) So,

you've been making your way down the Keys, visiting all these lovely state parks and nature reserves, thinking, Gosh, could there be a place that ties all the knowledge of this unique ecological phenomenon into one fun, well-put-together educational exhibit? OK, maybe those weren't your exact thoughts, but this is exactly what you get at this excellent center. This place does a marvelous job of filling in all the wild details of the natural Keys. The kids love it, and by the way, it's free *and* has free parking, an abnormality around here.

Fort Zachary Taylor
Historic State Park   PARK
(☎305-292-6713; www.floridastateparks.org/fort taylor; Truman Annex; per car/motorcycle/pedestrian & cyclist $6/4/2; ☺8am-sunset) 'America's Southernmost State Park,' this park is oft-neglected by authorities and visitors, which is a shame as it's a nice place to while away a quiet afternoon. The actual fort walls are still standing, and within the compound those most-blessed of nerds – historical re-enactors – put on costumes and act out scenes from Civil War and pirate days (we have yet to see a Civil War soldiers vs pirates fight here. But we can hope). Butterflies flit over the grounds, and the **beach** here is the best one Key West has to offer – it's got white sand to lounge on, deep enough water to swim in and tropical fish under the waves. Beach divers who head about 20ft from shore may spot some decent fish life.

Key West Cemetery   CEMETERY
(Margaret & Angela St; ☺sunrise-sunset;) A darkly alluring Gothic labyrinth beckons (rather incongruously) at the center of this pastel town. Built in 1847, the cemetery crowns Solares Hill, the highest point on the island (with an elevation of all of 16ft). Some of the oldest families in the Keys rest in peace – and close proximity – here. With body space at a premium, the mausoleums stand practically shoulder to shoulder. Island quirkiness penetrates the gloom: seashells and green macramé adorn headstones with inscriptions like, 'I told you I was sick.' Get chaperoned by a guide from the **Historic Florida Keys Foundation** (☎305-292-6718), with guided tours for $10 per person at 9:30am on Tuesday and Thursday; departs from the main gate at Margaret and Angela Sts.

Key West Butterfly & Nature Conservatory   WILDLIFE SANCTUARY

(☎305-296-2988; www.keywestbutterfly.com; 1316 Duval St; adult/child/seniors & military $12/8.50/9; ⊙9am-5pm; ⊞) This vast domed conservatory lets you stroll through a magic garden of flowering plants, colorful birds and up to 1800 fluttering butterflies, all live imports from around the globe.

Nancy Forrester's Secret Garden   GARDEN

(www.nfsgarden.com; 1 Free School Lane; admission $10; ⊙10am-5pm) Nancy, a local artist and fixture of the Keys community, invites you to bring lunch (but no cell phones!) into her oasis of lush palms, orchids, and chatty caged parrots and macaws. Although the place is called a secret garden, Nancy considers it to be a piece of art in and of itself – the last acre of undeveloped (although tended and cared for by human hands) natural space within the heart of Key West. The garden-artwork becomes a bridge between the natural world and the Key West that surrounds it. However you choose to interpret it, most agree this is a serene, near-magical place.

Museum of Art & History at the Customs House   MUSEUM

(www.kwahs.com/customhouse; 281 Front St; adult/child/senior $7/5/6; ⊙9:30am-4:30pm) There is art at the end of the road, and you'll find the best at this museum, which is worth a look-see if only for its gorgeous home – the grand Customs House, long abandoned until its impressive renovation in the '90s. Actually, this place is worth a look-see for any number of reasons, including a permanent display of massive portraits and some of the best showcases of international (particularly Caribbean) art in the region. The raw, almost cartoonish paintings of Key West done on wood by Mario Sanchez are a particular draw.

Fort East Martello Museum & Gardens   MUSEUM

(www.kwahs.com/martello.htm; 3501 S Roosevelt Blvd; adult/child/senior $7/5/6; ⊙9:30am-4:30pm) This old fortress was built to resemble old Italian Martello-style coastal watchtowers (hence the name), a design that quickly became obsolete with the advent of the explosive shell. Now the fort serves a new purpose: preserving the old. That is to say, the historical memorabilia, artifacts, the folk art of Mario Sanchez and 'junk' sculptor Stanley Papio, who worked with scrap metal and (cue ominous music)...Robert the Doll. Perhaps the most haunted thing in Key West, Robert is a genuinely creepy looking child's doll from the 19th century who reportedly causes much misfortune to those who question his powers. Honest, he looks like something out of a Stephen King novel; see www.robertthedoll.org for more information.

Studios of Key West   GALLERY

(TSKW; ☎305-296-0458; www.tskw.org; 600 White St; ⊙10am-6pm) This nonprofit showcases about a dozen artists' studios in a gallery space located in the old Armory building, which includes a lovely sculpture garden. Besides its public visual-arts displays, TSKW hosts readings by local authors like Robert Stone, literary and visual workshops, concerts, lectures and community discussion groups. Essentially, it has become the accessible heart of this city's enormous arts movement, and offers a good point-of-entry for visitors who want to engage in Key West's creative scene but don't have a clue where to start. You may want to call ahead before you visit in case exhibits are being installed.

Little White House   HISTORIC BUILDING

(☎305-294-9911; www.trumanlittlewhitehouse. com; 111 Front St; adult/child 5-12yr/senior $16/5/13.50; ⊙9am-4:30pm) While we were first tempted here by the prospect of a Lego-sized execution of the presidential digs, this is in fact the spot where ex-president Harry S Truman used to vacation when he wasn't molding post-WWII geopolitics. It is as lushly luxurious as you'd expect and open only for guided tours, although you are welcome to walk around the surrounding botanical **gardens** (⊙7am-6pm) for free. Plenty of Truman's possessions are scattered about, but the real draw is the guides, who are intensely intelligent, quirky and helpful.

Heritage House   HISTORIC BUILDING

(☎305-296-3573; www.heritagehousemuseum.org; 410 Caroline St; admission $5; ⊙10am-4pm Mon-Sat) Of all the many historic Key West homes open to visitors, this Caribbean-Colonial house is among the most wonderful to walk through. That's because it's rarely crowded, has passionate guides, and contains original furnishings and antiques, from a piano from the court of Marie Antoinette to a set of dining chairs from the 1600s. All have been collected and preserved by seven generations of a local family. The Robert Frost Cottage, where the poet stayed for 16 winters, is out back, along with another wonderful garden.

Numerous lectures, readings, writers' workshops and weddings are held here.

San Carlos Institute   HISTORIC BUILDING
(www.institutosancarlos.org; 516 Duval St) Founded in 1871 by Cuban exiles, the San Carlos is a gorgeous building constructed in classical Spanish mission style. The current structure dates from 1924 and received an extensive overhaul in 1992. The interior is spackled with Cuban tile work, Italian marble and statues of Cuban luminaries, including Jose Marti, who spoke here and dubbed the building 'La Casa Cuba.' Today the building serves as a library, art gallery, lecture hall, theater and general multipurpose building; it is only open during events, but these occur pretty often.

Bahama Village   NEIGHBORHOOD
Bahama Village was the old Bahamian district of the island, and in days past it had a colorful Caribbean feel about it – which is resurrected a bit during the **Goombay Festival** (p179). But today the village is pretty gentrified; many areas have been swallowed into a sort of pseudo-Duval periphery zone, but some retain their old Caribbean charm. At the **Office of the Secretary General of the Conch Republic** (☏305-296-0213; 613 Simonton St) you can see all manner of Conch Republic tat – flags, souvenirs and such.

Casa Antigua   HISTORIC BUILDING
(314 Simonton St; ☺10am-6pm) This was technically Hemingway's first house in Key West and the spot where he wrote *A Farewell to Arms,* but it isn't all that notable, except for a lush garden in the back and one of the kitschiest 'guided tours' in the US. Here's how it breaks down: go to the **Pelican Poop Gift Shoppe** (www.pelicanpoop.com; 314 Simonton St), which now occupies the Casa, pay the $2 garden entrance fee and let the kitsch begin! Go into the peaceful green area out the back, then a recorded tape plays at the volume God uses whenever he says anything that begins with 'Let there be...' At this ear-splitting volume, a man with a voice that can only be described as Big Gay Al raised in Dixie lays down the history of the Casa for you. It's gloriously hilarious.

Strand Building   HISTORIC BUILDING
(527 Duval St) The historic Strand Theater was one of the Key West's great old-time movie houses, and was used to stand in as a movie house in the 1993 film *Matinee.* Today it's a Walgreens pharmacy, but the exterior is as romantic as ever.

Key West Lighthouse   LIGHTHOUSE
(www.kwahs.com; 938 Whitehead St; adult/student over 7yr/senior $10/5/9; ☺9:30am-4:30pm) You can climb up 88 steps to the top of this lighthouse, built in 1846, for a decent view. But honestly, it's just as enjoyable to gaze up at the tower from the leafy street below.

Southernmost Point   LANDMARK
(cnr South & Whitehead Sts) The most photographed spot on the island, this red-and-black buoy isn't even the southernmost point in the USA (that's in the off-limits naval base around the corner). The most overrated attraction in Key West.

🏃 Activities

Beach Going   BEACH
Key West is *not* about beach going. In fact, for true sun 'n' surf, locals go to Bahia Honda (p168) whenever possible. Still, the three city beaches on the southern side of the island are lovely and narrow, with calm and clear water. **South Beach** is at the end of Simonton St. **Higgs Beach**, at the end of Reynolds St and Casa Marina Ct, has barbecue grills, picnic tables, and a big crowd of gay sunbathers and Key West's Eastern European seasonal workforce. **Smathers Beach**, further east off S Roosevelt Blvd, is more popular with jet-skiers, parasailers, teens and college students. The best local beach, though, is at Fort Zachary Taylor (p175); it's worth the admission to enjoy the white sand and relative calm.

Boating
Check www.charterboatkeywest.com for a directory of the many fishing and cruising charters offered in Key West.

🔝 Jolly II Rover   BOAT TOUR
(☏305-304-2235; www.schoonerjollyrover.com; cnr Greene & Elizabeth Sts, Schooner Wharf; cruises $39) This outfit has a gorgeous tanbark (reddish-brown) 80ft schooner that embarks on daily sunset cruises under sail. It looks like a pirate ship and has the cannons to back the image up.

Reelax Charters   KAYAKING
(☏305-304-1392, 305-744-0263; www.keyskayaking.com; MM 17 Sugarloaf Key Marina; kayak trips $200) Get your paddle on and slip silently into the surrounding mangroves and mudflats of the Lower Keys with Andrea Paulson. Based on Sugarloaf Key.

DETOUR: DRY TORTUGAS NATIONAL PARK

After all those keys, connected by all that convenient road, the nicest islands in the archipelago require a little extra effort. Ponce de León named them Las Tortugas (The Turtles) for the sea turtles that roamed here. A lack of freshwater led sailors to add a 'dry.' Today the Dry Tortugas are a national park under the control of the **National Park Service** (☎305-242-7700; www.nps.gov/drto; admission $5) and are accessible by boat or plane.

Originally the Tortugas were the US's naval perch into the Gulf of Mexico. But by the Civil War, **Fort Jefferson**, the main structure on the islands, had become a prison for Union deserters and at least four people, among them Dr Samuel Mudd, who had been arrested for complicity in the assassination of Abraham Lincoln. Hence, a new nickname: Devil's Island. The name was prophetic; in 1867 a yellow-fever outbreak killed 38 people, and after an 1873 hurricane the fort was abandoned. It reopened in 1886 as a quarantine station for smallpox and cholera victims, was declared a national monument in 1935 by President Franklin D Roosevelt, and was upped to national-park status in 1992 by George Bush Sr.

The park is open for day trips and overnight camping, which provides a rare phenomenon: a quiet Florida beach. Garden Key has 13 campsites ($3 per person, per night), which are given out on a first-come, first-served basis. Reserve early by calling the National Park office. There are toilets, but no freshwater showers or drinking water; bring everything you'll need. The sparkling waters offer excellent snorkeling and diving opportunities. A **visitor center** is located within fascinating Fort Jefferson.

If you're hungry, watch for Cuban-American fishing boats trolling the waters. They'll happily trade for lobster, crab and shrimp; you'll have the most leverage trading beverages. Just paddle up and bargain for your supper. In March and April, there is stupendous bird-watching, including aerial fighting. Star-gazing is mind-blowing any time of the year.

Getting There

If you have your own boat, the Dry Tortugas are covered under National Ocean Survey chart No 11438. Otherwise, the **Yankee Freedom II** (☎305-294-7009, 800-634-0939; www.yankeefreedom.com; Historic Seaport) operates a fast ferry between Garden Key and the Historic Seaport (at the northern end of Margaret St). Round-trip fares cost $165/120 per adult/child. Reservations are recommended. Continental breakfast, a picnic lunch, snorkeling gear and a 45-minute tour of the fort are all included.

Key West Seaplanes (☎305-294-0709; www.seaplanesofkeywest.com) can take up to 10 passengers (flight time 40 minutes each way). A four-hour trip costs $250/free/160/190 per adult/child under two years/child two to six years/child under 12 years; an eight-hour trip costs $515/free/320/365. Again, reserve at least a week in advance.

The $5 park admission fees are included in the above prices.

Diving & Snorkeling

The diving is better in Key Largo and Biscayne National park, but there is some decent wreck diving near Key West.

The website of the **Keys Association of Dive Operators** (http://divekeys.com; 3128 N Roosevelt Blvd) is a clearing house for information on diving opportunities in the islands; it also works on enhancing local sustainable underwater activities by creating artificial reefs and encouraging safe boating and diving practices.

Subtropic Dive Center   DIVING
(☎305-296-9914, 800-853-3483; www.subtropic.com; 1605 N Roosevelt Blvd) Reliable operator

with a good reputation. Does open-water certification for $499, and offers numerous other levels of PADI certification.

Dive Key West   DIVING
(☎305-296-3823, 800-426-0707; www.divekeywest.com; 3128 N Roosevelt Blvd) Largest dive facility on the island. Wreck-diving trips cost $144 with all equipment and air provided.

☞ Tours

Worth noting is *Sharon Wells' Walking & Biking Guide to Historic Key West*, a booklet of self-guided walks available free at inns and businesses around town, written by a local. See www.seekeywest.com.

Old Town Trolley Tours
TROLLEY
(☑305-296-6688; www.trolleytours.com/key-west; adult/child under 13yr/senior $29/free/26; ⊙tours 9am-4:30pm; 🐾) These tours are a great introduction to the city. The 90-minute, hop-on, hop-off narrated tram tour starts at Mallory Sq and makes a large, lazy loop around the whole city, with nine stops along the way. Trolleys depart every 15 to 30 minutes from 9am to 4:30pm daily. The narration is hokey, but you'll get a good overview of Key West, its history, and gossipy dirt about local issues and people in the news.

Conch Tour Train
TRAIN
(☑305-294-5161; www.conchtourtrain.com; adult/child under 13yr/senior $29/free/26; ⊙tours 9am-4:30pm; 🐾) Run by the same company as trolley tours, though this one seats you in breezier linked train cars with no on/off option. Offers discounted admission to sights like the Hemingway House.

Historic Key West Walking Tour
WALKING
(☑800-844-7601; 1 Whitehead St; www.trusted tours.com; adult/child $18/9) A walking tour that takes in some of the major architecture and historical sights of the island. Takes about two hours. You need to book in advance.

Ghosts & Legends of Key West
GHOST
(☑305-294-1713; www.keywestghosts.com; Porter House Mansion, 429 Caroline St; adult/child $18/10; ⊙tours 7pm & 9pm) Promises to take you 'off the beaten track' to places 'only a Conch could show you,' including the old city morgue and a small cemetery.

Original Ghost Tours
GHOST
(☑305-294-9255; www.hauntedtours.com; 423 Fleming St; adult/child $15/10; ⊙tours 8pm & 9pm) Stories about souls who inhabit locations that include about half the bars and hotels on the island.

✯ Festivals & Events

Contact the **Key West Art & Historical Society** (☑305-295-6616; www.kwahs.com) to get the skinny on upcoming studio shows, literary readings, film festivals and the like.

Annual Key West Literary Seminar LITERARY
(http://keywestliteraryseminar.org/lit) Now in its 23rd year, draws top writers from around the country each January (although it costs hundreds of dollars to attend).

Robert Frost Poetry Festival LITERARY
(www.robertfrostpoetryfestival.com) Held in April.

Hemingway Days LITERARY
Held in late July, brings parties, a 5km run and an Ernest look-alike contest.

WomenFest LESBIAN & TRANSEXUAL
(www.womenfest.com) Nothing says dignified sexiness like this festival, held in early September, which attracts thousands of lesbians who just want to party.

Fantasy Fest CULTURAL
You gotta see this festival held throughout the week leading up to Halloween in late October. It's when all the inns get competitive about decorating their properties, and everyone gets decked out in the most outrageous costumes they can cobble together (or decked down in daring body paint).

Goombay Festival CULTURAL
(www.goombay-keywest.org) Held during the same out-of-control week as Fantasy Fest, this is a Bahamian celebration of food, crafts and culture.

Parrot Heads in Paradise Convention MUSIC
(www.phip.com/motm.asp) This festival in November is for, you guessed it, Jimmy Buffett fans (rabid ones only, natch).

🛏 Sleeping

There's a glut of boutique hotels, cozy B&Bs and four-star resorts here at the end of the USA, so sleepers won't want for accommodations. Although we've labeled some options as more central than others, the fact is that any hotel in Old Town will put you within walking distance of all the action. Though all people, gay and straight, are welcome just about anywhere, there are some exclusively gay inns, noted here.

All of the following properties have aircon. Lodgings have higher rates during the high season (mid-December to April). In addition, many properties add a 'shoulder' (midseason) that runs from May to June; rates may fall somewhere between low (July to November) and high during midseason. Many hotels (especially smaller properties) enforce two-night minimum stays. Expect rates to be extremely high during events such as New Year's and Fantasy Fest, when some places enforce up to seven-night minimum stays.

Curry Mansion Inn
HOTEL $$$

(☎800-253-3466, 305-294-5349; http://curry mansion.com; 511 Caroline St; r low season $195-285, high season $240-365; P❄@🤶🏊) In a city full of stately 19th-century homes, the Curry Mansion is especially handsome. All the elements of an aristocratic American home come together here, from plantation-era Southern colonnades to a New England–style widow's walk and, of course, bright Floridian rooms with canopied beds. Enjoy bougainvillea and breezes on the veranda.

Mermaid & Alligator
GUESTHOUSE $$

(☎305-294-1894, 800-773-1894; www.kwmermaid .com; 729 Truman Ave; r low season $148-198, high season $218-298; P❄@🏊) It takes a real gem to stand out amid the jewelry store of Keys hotels, but this place, located in a 1904 mansion, more than pulls off the job. Each of the nine rooms is individually designed with a great mix of modern comfort, Keys Colonial ambience and playful laughs. The treetop suite, with its exposed beams and alcoved bed and bathroom, is our pick of this idiosyncratic litter.

La Mer & Dewey Hotel
BOUTIQUE HOTEL $$$

(☎305-296-6577; www.southernmostresorts.com /lamer; 504 South St; r $200-350; ❄🤶) Nineteen rooms are spread across two historic homes, one Victorian, the other fashioned like an old-school Keys cottage. Inside, the rooms come equipped with a lovely mix of European twee antiques and sleek modern amenities. Your porch basically looks out onto the Atlantic Ocean, whose breezes make for nice natural air-conditioning (not that you can't crank up the A/C in your room).

Santa Maria
BOUTIQUE HOTEL $$$

(☎305-600-5165; www.santamariasuites.com; 1401 Simonton St; r $300-450; P❄🤶🏊) The Santa Maria looks like it took a wrong turn on South Beach, Miami, and ended up in Key West. First, it's an incredible deco edifice. The exterior should rightly be studied by architecture students looking to identify the best of deco design. Second, the interior rooms are an airy, luxurious dream, each one calling to mind the leisure lounge of a businessman from the 1950s. Finally, this place boasts in its central courtyard one of the finest hotel pools in Key West. Go ahead – splurge and let yourself go.

Gardens Hotel
HOTEL $$$

(☎305-294-2661, 800-526-2664; www.gardensho tel.com; 526 Angela St; r & ste low season $165-420, high season $325-645; P❄@🏊) Would we be stating the obvious if we mentioned this place has really nice gardens? In fact, the 17 rooms are located in the Peggy Mills Botanical Gardens, which is a longish way of saying 'tropical paradise.' Inside, Caribbean accents mesh with the fine design to create a sense of green-and-white-and-wood space that never stops massaging your eyes.

L'habitation
GUESTHOUSE $$

(☎800-697-1766, 305-293-9203 www.lhabitation. com; 408 Eaton St; r $109-179; ❄🤶) A beautiful classical Keys cottage with cute rooms kitted out in light tropical shades, with lamps that look like contemporary art pieces and skittles-bright quilts. The friendly bilingual owner welcomes guests in English or French. The front porch, shaded by palms, is a perfect place to post and engage in Keys people-watching.

Cypress House
HOTEL $$$

(☎800-525-2488, 305-294-6969; www.cypress housekw.com; 601 Caroline St; r $165-305; P❄🤶🏊) This plantationlike getaway has wrap-around porches, leafy grounds, a secluded swimming pool and spacious, individually designed bedrooms with four-poster beds. It's lazy, lovely luxury in the heart of Old Town, and one of the most extensively renovated and converted mansions we've seen anywhere. We'd recommend rooms in the Main House and Simonton House over the blander guest studios. Parking costs $10 per day.

Truman Hotel
HOTEL $$$

(☎866-487-8626; www.trumanhotel.com; 611 Truman Ave; r low season $195-285, high season $240-365; P❄🤶🏊) Close to the main downtown drag, these playful rooms have huge flat-screen TVs, kitchenettes, zebra-print throw rugs and midcentury modern furniture. The bouncy fluff-erific beds will serve you well after the inevitable Duval Crawl (which is only steps from your door). Make sure to grab a drink by the lovely courtyard pool at the bar, seemingly carved from a single stone.

Big Ruby's Guesthouse
HOTEL $$

(☎305-296-2323, 800-477-7829; www.bigrubys. com; 409 Applerouth Lane; r $193-305; P❄🤶🏊) This gay-only place looks like a refined Conch mansion on the outside, but once you get to your room, you'll see it's all contemporary, white and sleeker than a designer's decadent dreams. The clothing-optional lagoon pool is capped by a treetop walkway, elegant decking and tropical palms; plus there are fine linens and lots of privacy.

Caribbean House
GUESTHOUSE $

(☎305-296-0999; www.caribbeanhousekw.com; 226 Petronia St; r incl breakfast from $85; Ⓟ❋@) This is a cute, canary-yellow Caribbean cottage in the heart of Bahama Village. The 10 small, brightly colored guest rooms aren't too fancy, but it's a happy, cozy bargain.

Avalon Bed & Breakfast
B&B $$

(☎305-294-8233; www.avalonbnb.com; 1317 Duval St; r low season $89-189, high season $169-289; ❋◈▣) A cute, restored Victorian house on the quiet end of Duval blends attentive service with stately old ceiling fans, tropical lounge-room rugs, and black-and-white photos of olde-timey Key West. Music the cat likes to greet guests at reception.

Pearl's Rainbow
B&B $$

(☎305-292-1450, 800-749-6696; www.pearlsrainbow.com; 525 United St; r incl breakfast $99-200; ❋◈▣) Pearl's is one of the best low-key lesbian resorts in the country, an intimate garden of tropical relaxation and enticing rooms scattered across a few cottages. A clothing-optional backyard pool bar is the perfect spot for alfresco happy hour, or to enjoy your brekkie.

Chelsea House
HOTEL $$

(☎305-296-2211; www.historickeywestinns.com/the-inns/chelsea-house; 707 Truman Ave; r low season $120-180, high season $200-250; Ⓟ❋@◈▣) This perfect pair of Victorian mansions beckons with large vaulted rooms and big comfy beds, with the whole shebang done out in floral, but not dated, chic. The old-school villa ambience clashes – in a nice way – with the happy vibe of the guests and the folks at reception.

Merlin Inn
GUESTHOUSE $$

(☎305-296-3336, 800-642-4753; 811 Simonton St; low season $89-225, high season $135-300; Ⓟ❋@▣) Set in a secluded garden with a pool and elevated walkways, everything here is made from bamboo, rattan and wood. Throw in the rooms' high ceilings and exposed rafters, and this hotel oozes Colonial-tropical atmosphere.

Key Lime Inn
HOTEL $$

(☎800-559-4430; www.historickeywestinns.com; 725 Truman Ave; r $99-229; Ⓟ❋◈▣) These cozy cottages are all scattered around a tropical

hardwood backdrop. Inside, the blissfully cool rooms are greener than a jade mine, with wicker furniture and tiny flat-screens on hand to keep you from ever leaving.

Key West Youth Hostel & Seashell Motel
HOSTEL $

(☎305-296-5719; www.keywesthostel.com; 718 South St; dm from $44, motel r from $75; Ⓟ❋) This isn't our favorite hostel, but it's about the only youth-oriented budget choice on the island. That said, both dorms and motel rooms are overpriced.

✕ Eating

For such a small island, Key West has a superlative range of places to eat, from delicious neighborhood joints in the wall to top-end purveyors of haute cuisine that could easily compete with the best restaurants in Miami.

TOP CHOICE Café Solé
FRENCH $$$

(☎305-294-0230; www.cafesole.com; 1029 Southard St; lunch $5-11, dinner $25-32; ⊙5:30-10pm) Conch carpaccio with capers? Yellowtail fillet and foie gras? Oh yes. This locally and critically acclaimed venue is known for its cozy back-porch ambience and innovative menus, cobbled together by a chef trained in southern French techniques who works with island ingredients. The memory of the anchovies on crostini makes us smile as we type. It's simple – fish on toast! – but it's the sort of simple yet delicious that makes you feel like Mom's whipped up something special for Sunday dinner.

Seven Fish
SEAFOOD $$

(☎305-296-2777; www.7fish.com; 632 Olivia St; mains $17-20; ⊙6-10pm Wed-Mon) This simple yet elegant tucked-away storefront is the perfect place for a romantic feast of homemade gnocchi or sublime banana chicken. All that said, the way to go here is to order the fresh fish of the day. The dining room might be the Zen-est interior in the islands. In point of fact, the entire experience here is one of minimalism (except for the flavors, which are abundant in the extreme).

Nine One Five
FUSION $$$

(☎305-296-0669; www.915duval.com; 915 Duval St; mains $18-34; ⊙6pm-midnight; ✒) Classy Nine One Five certainly stands out from the nearby Duval detritus of alcoholic aggression and tribal band tattoos. Ignore all that and enter this immaculate, modern and elegant space, which serves a creative, New

American-dips-into-Asia menu. It's all quite rich – imagine a butternut squash and almond risotto, or local lobster accompanied by duck confit potatoes.

Mo's Restaurant
CARIBBEAN $

(http://salsalocakeywest.com; 1116 White St; mains $11-16; ☺11am-10pm Mon-Sat) The words 'Caribbean,' 'home' and 'cooking', when used in conjunction, are generally always enough to win over. But it's not just the genre of cuisine that wins us over at Mo's – it's the execution. The dishes are mainly Haitian, and they're delicious – the spicy pickles will enflame your mouth, which can get cooled down with a rich vegetable 'mush' over rice, or try the incredible signature snapper.

Camille's
FUSION $$

(1202 Simonton St; breakfast $3-13, lunch $4-13, dinner $14-25; ☺8am-10pm; 🖉) This healthy and tasty neighborhood joint is the kind of place where players on the Key West High School softball team are served by friends from their science class, and the hostess is the pitcher's mom – when Conchs head out for a casual meal, they often come here. For 20 years the homey facade of Camille's has concealed a sharp kitchen that makes a mean chicken-salad sandwich, stone crab claws with Dijon mayo and a macadamia-crusted yellowtail we shudder (with pleasure) to recall.

Blue Heaven
AMERICAN $$

(☎305-296-8666; http://blueheavenkw.homestead .com; 729 Thomas St; dinner mains $19-38; ☺8am-10:30pm Mon-Sat, from 9am Sun) Proof that location is *nearly* everything, this is one of the quirkiest venues on an island of oddities. Customers and a local chicken flock dine in the spacious courtyard where Hemingway once officiated boxing matches; restrooms are in the adjacent former brothel. This place gets packed with customers who wolf down Southern-fried takes on Keys cuisine – the barbecued shrimp, drunk in a spicy sauce, are gorgeous.

Conch Town Café
SEAFOOD $

(801 Thomas St; mains $5-18; ☺11:30am-7:30pm) Too many people ignore this walk-up/carry-out, with its plastic patio furniture and scruffy island vibe. It's a shame, as it serves conch – good for more than listening to the ocean – deliciously 'cracked' (deep-fried) with a lip-puckeringly sour-lime marinade. You'll be tempted to wash it down with

the homemade smoothies, but be warned: they're more milky than refreshing.

Café
VEGETARIAN $

(509 Southard St; mains $7-17; ☺11am-10pm Mon-Sat; 🖉) The Café is the only place in Key West that exclusively caters to herbivores (OK, they have one fish dish). By day, it's a cute, sunny, earthy-crunchy luncheonette; by night, with flickering votive candles and a classy main dish (grilled, blackened tofu and polenta cakes), it's a sultry-but-healthy dining destination.

Thai Cuisine
THAI $$

(513 Greene St; lunch $10-12, dinner $15-24; ☺11:30-10pm) There's surprisingly good Thai to be had here near the top of Duval. It's not Bangkok, but the weather's just as nice and there are no *tuk-tuk* drivers or ladyboys interrupting your meal. There's sushi on the premises as well, although we don't think it's much compared to the curry and noodles.

Mathieson's 4th of July
AMERICAN $

(1110 White St; ice cream $3.50-6, mains $7-12; ☺11am-10pm Tue-Thu, to 11pm Fri & Sat, to 9pm Sun) The poodle skirts, ponytails and even the occasional pair of roller skates lay the '50s Americana diner vibe on as thick as they douse the excellent ice cream in toppings like gorgeous hot melted chocolate. The menu of burgers and such is really good, but we come to Mathieson's mainly for the ice cream, which is perfect relief from the heat of a Key West day.

El Siboney
CUBAN $

(Catherine St; mains $9.50-16; ☺11am-9:30pm) This is a rough-and-ready Cuban joint where the portions are big and there's no screwing around with either high-end embellishment or bells and whistles. It's rice, it's beans, it's shredded beef and roasted pork, it's cooked with a craftman's pride, and it's good.

🍷 Drinking

Basically, Key West is a floating bar. 'No, no, it's a nuanced, multilayered island with a proud nautical and multicultural histo...' *bz-zzt!* Floating bar. Make your memories (or lack thereof) at one of the following. Bars close at 3am; for gay venues, see p183.

TOP CHOICE Green Parrot
BAR

(601 Whitehead St) The oldest bar on an island of bars, this rogues' cantina opened in the late 19th century and hasn't closed yet. The

owner tells you the parachute on the ceiling is 'weighed down with termite turds,' while a blues band howls through clouds of smoke. Defunct business signs and local artwork litter the walls and, yes, that's the city attorney showing off her new tattoo at the pool table. Men: check out the Hieronymus Bosch–like painting *Proverbidioms* in the restroom, surely the most entertaining urinal talkpiece on the island.

Porch
BAR

(429 Caroline St) If you're getting tired of the frat-boy bars on the Duval St strip, head to the Porch. It's a friendly little artisan beer bar that's more laid back (but hardly civilized) than your average Keys watering hole. The knowledgeable bartenders will trade jokes with you and point you in the right direction for some truly excellent brew. Then sit on the porch of the Porch and watch the Keys stumble on by.

Garden of Eden Bar
BAR

(224 Duval St) Go to the top of this building and discover Key West's own clothing-optional drinking patio. Lest you get too excited, cameras aren't allowed, most people come clothed, and those who do elect to flaunt their birthday suits are often...erm...older.

Captain Tony's Saloon
BAR

(428 Greene St) Propagandists would have you believe the nearby megabar complex of Sloppy Joe's was Hemingway's original bar, but the physical place where the old man drank was right here, the original Sloppy Joe's location (before it was moved onto Duval St and into frat-boy hell). Hemingway's third wife (a journalist sent to profile Papa) seduced him in this very bar, wallpapered with business cards from around the world (including this travel writer's).

Irish Kevin's
BAR

(211 Duval St) One of the most popular megabars on Duval, Kevin's has a pretty good entertainment formula pinned down: nightly live acts that are a cross between a folk singer, radio shock jock and pep-rally cheerleader. The crowd consistently goes ape-poo for acoustic covers of '80s favorites. Basically, this is a good place to see 50 women from New Jersey do tequila shots, scream 'Livin' on a Prayer' at the top of their lungs and then inexplicably sob into their Michelob. It's more fun than it sounds.

Hog's Breath
BAR

(400 Front St) A good place to start the infamous Duval Pub Crawl, the Hog's Breath is a rockin' outdoor bar with good live bands and better cold Coronas.

GAY & LESBIAN KEY WEST

Key West's position at the edge of the USA has always attracted artists and eccentrics, and with them a refreshing dose of tolerance. The island had one of the earliest 'out' communities in the USA, and though less true than in the past, visiting Key West is a rite of passage for many LGBT (lesbian, gay, bisexual and transgender) Americans. In turn, this community has had a major impact on the local culture. Just as there is a straight trolley tour, you can hop aboard the **Gay & Lesbian Trolley Tour of Key West** (☑305-294-4603; tour $25), departing from the corner of South St and Simonton St at 11am on Saturday. The tour provides commentary on local gay lore and businesses (you'll also see the sites of the infamous Monster club). It's organized by the Key West Business Guild, which represents many gay-owned businesses; the guild is housed at the **Gay & Lesbian Community Center** (☑305-292-3223; www.glcckeywest.org; 513 Truman Ave), where you can access free internet on one of the few computers, plus pick up loads of information about local gay life. For details on gay parties and events, log onto www.gaykeywestfl.com.

Gay nightlife, in many cases, blends into mainstream nightlife, with everybody kind of going everywhere these days. But the backbone of the gay bar scene can be found in a pair of cruisey watering holes that sit across the street from one another, **Bourbon St Pub** (724 Duval St) and **801 Bourbon Bar** (801 Duval St), and can be summed up in five words: drag-queen-led karaoke night. For a peppier scene that includes dancing and occasional drag shows, men and women should head to **Aqua** (☑305-294-0555; 711 Duval St), while women will enjoy the backyard pool bar at the women's inn **Pearl's Rainbow** (☑305-292-1450; 525 United St).

☆ Entertainment

La Te Da CABARET
(www.lateda.com; 1125 Duval St) While the outside bar is where locals gather for mellow chats over beer, you can catch high-quality drag acts – big names come here from around the country – upstairs at the fabulous Crystal Room on weekends. More low-key cabaret acts grace the downstairs lounge.

Virgilio's JAZZ
(524 Duval St) This bar-stage is as un-Keys as they come, and frankly, thank God for a little variety. This town needs a dark, candlelit martini lounge where you can chill to jazz and get down with some salsa, and Virgilio's handsomely provides. Enter on Applerouth Lane.

Red Barn Theatre THEATER
(☑305-296-9911; www.redbarntheatre.org; 319 Duval St) An occasionally edgy and always fun, cozy little local playhouse.

Tropic Cinema CINEMA
(☑877-761-3456; www.tropiccinema.org; 416 Eaton St) Great art-house movie theater with deco frontage.

Key West Players THEATER
(☑305-294-5015; www.waterfrontplayhouse.com; Waterfront Playhouse, Mallory Sq) Catch high-quality musicals and dramas from the oldest-running theater troupe in Florida. The season runs November through April.

Key West Symphony Orchestra OPERA
(☑305-292-1774; www.keywestsymphony.com; Tennessee Williams Theatre, 5901 Collage Rd) This critically acclaimed orchestra performs classics from Debussy, Beethoven and Mendelssohn from December through April.

🛍 Shopping

Bright and breezy art galleries, excellent cigars, leather fetish gear and offensive T-shirts – Key West, what don't you sell?

Montage SOUVENIRS
(512 Duval St; ☺9am-10pm) Had a great meal or wild night at some bar or restaurant in the Keys? Well, this store probably sells the sign of the place (along with lots of Conch Republic tat), which makes for a nice souvenir.

Peppers of Key West FOOD
(602 Greene St; ☺10am-8pm Mon-Sat) For a downright shopping party, you should bring your favorite six-pack with you into this store and settle in at the tasting bar, where the entertaining owners use double

entendres to hawk seriously mouth-burning hot sauces, like their own Right Wing Sauce (use Liberally).

Project Lighthouse ARTS & CRAFTS
(418 Eaton St) Lighthouse is a community organization that runs programs for street kids (Key West is a popular runaway destination); it partly supports itself by selling arts and crafts made by its charges.

Bésame Mucho GIFTS
(315 Petronia St; ☺10am-6pm, to 4pm Sun) This place is well stocked with high-end beauty products, eclectic jewelry, clothing and housewares.

Dogs on Duval PETS
(800 Duval St; ☺10am-9pm) Pet accoutrement, like university sports jerseys for dogs, is on the rack behind – puppies! Heart-wrenchingly cute puppies.

Leather Master LEATHER
(415 Applerouth Lane; ☺11am-10pm, to 11pm Fri & Sat, noon-5pm Sun) Besides the gladiator outfits, studded jockstraps and S&M masks, they do very nice bags and shoes here. Which is what you came for, right?

Frangipani Gallery ARTS & CRAFTS
(1102 Duval St; ☺10am-6pm) One of the best galleries of local artists' work.

Haitian Art Co ARTS & CRAFTS
(600 Frances St; ☺9am-5pm Mon-Fri) Haitian arts and crafts.

ℹ Information

Media

Keeping up with local goings-on is easy, as this well-read town has nearly 10 newspapers (though some are entertainment-only rags). Also among the following are Key West's most accessible medical services.

Bank of America (☑305-296-1204; 510 Southard St, Key West)

Citizen (www.keysnews.com) A well-written, oft-amusing daily.

Key West Chamber of Commerce (☑305-294-2587; www.keywestchamber.org; 510 Greene St; ☺8:30am-6:30pm Mon-Sat, to 6pm Sun) An excellent source of information.

Lower Keys Medical Center (☑305-294-5531, 800-233-3119; www.lkmc.com; 5900 College Rd, Stock Island, MM 5) Has a 24-hour emergency room.

National Public Radio (NPR) Tune into 91.3FM.

Post office (400 Whitehead St; ☺8:30am-9pm Mon-Fri, 9:30am-noon Sat)

Solares Hill (www.solareshill.com) Weekly, slightly activist take on community interests.

South Med (☎305-295-3838; www.southmed. us; 3138 Northside Dr) Dr Scott Hall caters especially to the gay community, but serves all visitors.

❶ Getting There & Around

Key West International Airport (EYW) is off S Roosevelt Blvd on the east side of the island. You can fly into Key West from some major US cities such as Miami or New York. Flights from Los Angeles and San Francisco usually have to stop in Tampa, Orlando or Miami first. **American Airlines** (☎800-433-7300) and **US Airways** (☎800-428-4322) have several flights a day. **Cape Air** (☎305-352-0714, 800-352-0714; www.flycapeair.com) flies between Key West and Fort Myers. From the Key West airport, a quick and easy taxi ride into Old Town will cost about $15.

Greyhound (☎305-296-9072; www.grey hound.com; 3535 S Roosevelt Blvd) has two buses daily between Key West and downtown Miami. Buses leave Miami for the 4¼-hour journey at 12:35pm and 6:50pm and Key West at 8:55am and 5:45pm going the other way (from US$40 each way).

You can boat from Miami to the Keys on the **Key West Express** (☎888-539-2628; www .seakeywestexpress.com; adult/child round-trip $146/81, one-way $86/58), which departs from Fort Myers beach daily at 8:30am and does a 3½-hour cruise to Key West. Returning boats depart the seaport at 6pm. You'll want to show up 1½ hours before your boat departs. During winter and fall the Express also leaves from Marco Island (adult/child round-trip $125/81, one-way $86/58).

Once you're in Key West, the best way to get around is by bicycle (rentals from the Duval St area, hotels and hostels are about $10 a day). Other options include the **City Transit System** (☎305-292-8160; tickets 75¢), with color-coded buses running about every 15 minutes; mopeds, which generally rent for $35 for four hours ($50 for a six-hour day); or the ridiculous electric tourist cars, or 'Conch cruisers,' which travel at 35mph and cost about $50/200 per hour/day.

Southeast Florida

Best Places to Eat

» Le Tub (p189)

» Gran Forno (p195)

» Sheila's Bahamian Conch & BBQ (p207)

» Michelle Bernstein's (p211)

» Rhythm Cafe (p217)

» Little Moir's Food Shack (p222)

Best Places to Stay

» Hollywood Beach Hotel & Hostel (p187)

» Pillars (p194)

» Sundy House Inn (p204)

» Crane's Beach House (p204)

» Breakers (p210)

Why Go?

Zooming north from Miami's tanned and diamond-draped clutches, you'll find an endearing collection of beach towns – some classy, others quirky, all unique. From activity-packed, gay- and family-friendly Fort Lauderdale to quiet, exclusive, semireclusive Palm Beach; from laid-back Lauderdale-by-the-Sea to the rugged coast of Jupiter, you'll find more culture and nightlife than you can handle. This chunk of coast includes some of Florida's wealthiest enclaves – enjoy gawking at the castle-like beachfront mansions, but don't rear end that $350,000 Bentley when parallel parking in front of the Gucci store in Palm Beach!

For those looking for a more, er, down-to-earth setting, the region's numerous natural gems – secluded islands, moss-draped mangrove swamps, wild rivers, empty dunes – will surely satisfy your demands for nonmaterial pleasures.

So please, whatever you do, don't skip over this region on your journey from Miami to Disney World.

When to Go
Palm Beach

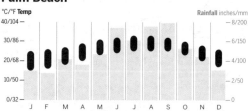

Mar & Apr Spring Break madness hits, packing the beaches with party-happy twentysomethings.

Jun–Nov Atlantic hurricane season, plus steamy summer weather, means a major tourism slowdown.

Dec–Apr Chilly temperatures up north bring vacationers and second home owners down in droves.

History

Two words: Henry Flagler. If it weren't for this deep-pocketed visionary, southeast Florida may still be overrun with cabbage palms, bloodthirsty mosquitos and territorial gators snapping at trembling canoers. After transforming northeastern Florida into a winter wonderland in the 1870s, Flagler set his sights further south, and by the mid-1890s had already completed two world-class hotels (including the 1100-room Royal Poinciana Hotel in Lake Worth, at the time the largest wooden structure in the world), established both Palm Beach and West Palm Beach and began pushing on to Miami and the Keys.

GOLD COAST

Though the 70-or-so miles of sparkling Atlantic shoreline from Hollywood to Jupiter earned its nickname from the gold salvaged from area shipwrecks, it could easily have come from the mix of sapphire skies, cinnamony sands and wealthy residents bejeweling the region.

Here, the coastline has a split personality. First, there's slow-going, ocean-fronting Rte 1, a pleasant drive revealing infinite vistas and unspoiled beaches...though occasionally it feels like driving through the valley of a high-rise condo-canyon. Second, there's wizened, wrinkled Dixie Hwy, running parallel to Rte 1 but further inland, past dive bars, hole-in-the-wall eateries and diverse, working-class communities that sometimes forget the ocean's just a shell's throw away. Drive both stretches; each is rich with divergent offerings.

Hollywood & Dania Beach

954 / HOLLYWOOD POP 143,000 /
DANIA BEACH POP 28,000

Two 'suburban Fort Lauderdale' communities have managed to make names for themselves. Hollywood, a bustling, varied waterfront town that positions itself as a gateway to Fort Lauderdale, has earned a sizable wedge of the Spring Break market since Lauderdale gave revelers the boot. The resulting influx brings with it concerts in the sand, beach-volleyball tourneys and assorted debauchery each March. These days, the city's trying to glam up its image with several new South Beach–style developments.

In contrast, Dania (dane-ya) remains a mellow little town, with a fledgling antiques district and a breezy fishing pier.

◉ Sights & Activities

Hollywood Beach & Broadwalk   BEACH
Reminiscent of California's famed Venice Beach, this beach and adjacent promenade teem with scantily clad Rollerbladers, fanny pack–wearing tourists and local families speaking a rainbow of languages. Standing guard over the walk are tacky T-shirt shops, ice-cream vendors, snack shacks and bars. This ain't no snooty Palm Beach, and that's why it's so much fun. The Broadwalk itself is a 2.2-mile, six-person-wide cement path, regularly clogged with skaters, strollers, and entire families pedaling enormous group bikes. If you feel like rolling along it, a dozen or so Broadwalk vendors rent bikes, Rollerblades and other gear by the hour or the day.

Kayaking   KAYAKING
Once an important stop for Prohibition-era bootleggers, lush Whiskey Creek (get it?), nestled inside John U Lloyd Beach State Park (www.floridastateparks.org/lloydbeach; per vehicle $6; ☉8am-sundown), is now a kayaking hot spot. The dense mangrove-lined route, roughly 2.5 miles long, is shallow, calm, ideal for beginners and just 15 minutes from downtown Dania. Full Moon Kayak Co (☎954-597-3040; www.fullmoonkayak.com; tours from $35; ☉10am-6pm Mon-Sat) runs day trips here and to other local paddling places. No guarantees, but they have spotted manatees.

🛏 Sleeping

Both Hollywood and Dania abound with character-ful motels and guesthouses, many seemingly unchanged from the 1940s.

TOP CHOICE **Hollywood Beach**
Hotel & Hostel   HOTEL, HOSTEL $
(☎954-391-9441; www.hollywoodbeachhostel.com; 334 Arizona St, Hollywood; dm from $17, r from $59; ✱@☎) Part of Hollywood's wave of hip new businesses, this slick complex combines dorms with a warren of whitewashed, vaguely Moroccan-looking motel units. Friendly staff, a clean and bright common kitchen, bike and surfboard rentals, and a deck with hammock chairs add sociability, but this is generally a quiet place which appeals to families as well as the traditional backpacker types. Those who do want to live

Southeast Florida Highlights

1 Throw self-consciousness to the wind and rent an absurd-looking six-person bike to pedal along the delightfully raucous Hollywood Beach **Broadwalk** (p187)

2 Glide along the Intracoastal, listening to tales of celebrity gossip and white-collar crime aboard the **Carrie B** (p193), a lifestyles-of-the-rich-and-famous boat tour

3 Sip matcha green tea at the monthly tea ceremony at Delray Beach's serene **Morikami Museum and Japanese Gardens** (p204)

4 Goggle at the gazillion-dollar mansions along **Ocean Blvd** (p210) in ritzier-than-ritzy Palm Beach, then window shop on **Worth Avenue** (p213), Florida's answer to Rodeo Dr

5 Dig West Palm Beach's **Clematis By Night** (p219), a free event held every Thursday under the stars, with rockin' musicians and loads of tasty street food

6 Press the shutter at sunrise as the tide rushes in at **Blowing Rocks Preserve** (p221), Jupiter Island

7 Kayak Jupiter's 'Wild and Scenic' **Loxahatchee River** (p222), for close-up views of cypress knees, mangrove forests and sunning alligators

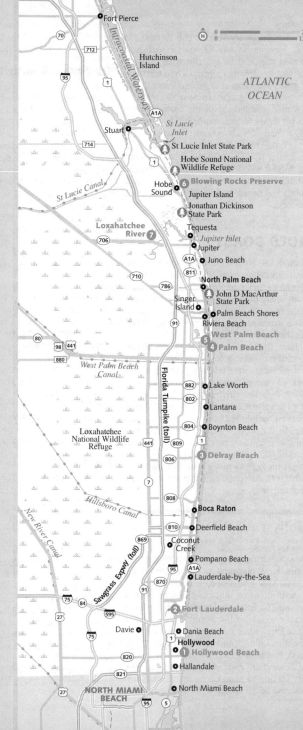

it up can head to the adjacent Taco Beach Shack.

Villa Sinclair
GUESTHOUSE **$$**

(📞954-450-0000; www.villa-sinclair.com; 317 Polk St, Hollywood; studios from $99, apt from $149; 🅿❄🛜) Like the lair of some eccentric 1940s movie star, this under-the-radar little guesthouse combines glamour with quirk. The 1941 villa is carved into intimate studios and apartments, all decorated with rich jewel tones and funky local art, with oddball touches like teddy bears on the beds. The deck, tricked out with a sauna, hot tub and multiple Moroccan-style lounges, will make walking to the beach seem frankly unnecessary. Guests gather here for nightly movie screenings. If you're not sold yet, listen to this: all rooms come with a free pineapple. Gay-friendly.

Seminole Hard Rock Hotel & Casino
HOTEL **$$$**

(📞866-502-7529; www.seminolehardrockholly wood.com; 1 Seminole Way, Hollywood; r $149-400; ❄🛜🏊) This Mediterranean-style monster provides everything you'd ever need under one massive roof. In this case, it's casinos, eateries, theaters, a day spa, 500 swank guest rooms and some of the most alluring concert bills in the state. It's all very Vegas. Except for the 4.5-acre lagoon-style pool totally surrounding a bar – *that's* out of this world.

✖ Eating & Drinking

Unless you find yourself starving in the middle of your inline-skating session, give most of the Broadwalk restaurants a miss – they're overpriced, overcrowded and mediocre. There are better eats to be found along Ocean Dr, or inland in downtown Hollywood.

TOP CHOICE Le Tub
BURGERS, AMERICAN **$$**

(www.theletub.com; 1100 N Ocean Dr, Hollywood; mains $9-27; ❄noon-4am; 🚼) Decorated exclusively with flotsam collected over four years of daybreak jogs along Hollywood Beach, this quirky Intracoastal-side institution features multiple tiers of outdoor seating, plus bathtubs and toilet bowls (!) sprouting lush plants. The thing to order here is the sirloin burger – it's bigger than your head (seriously) and is routinely named 'Best in America' by the likes of *GQ*. Expect a wait, both for seating and for cooking time. It's worth it.

Jaxson's Ice Cream Parlor
ICE CREAM **$**

(www.jaxsonsicecream.com; 128 S Federal Hwy, Dania; ice cream from $4; ❄11:30am-11pm, to midnight Fri & Sat; 🚼) Originally opened in 1956, this place has 80-plus flavors of homemade ice cream. Come hungry and try one of the signature gourmet concoctions like the meant-to-be-shared Kitchen Sink – several *gallons* of ice cream served in a real kitchen sink!

Taco Beach Shack
MEXICAN **$**

(www.tacobeachshack.com; 334 Arizona St, Hollywood; tacos $4-10; ❄11:30am-10pm Mon-Thu, to midnight Fri & Sat) Hipsters and hangers-on lounge around on wicker chaises at this new open-air taqueria, the brainchild of the former chef for the Miami Heat. The menu (written on a surfboard) has a very of-the-moment mix of ethnic flavors – try the Korean short rib and kimchi tacos. You'll feel cooler just by eating one.

🛍 Shopping

Josh's Organic Garden
FOOD

(cnr Harrison & S Broadwalk, Hollywood; ❄9am-5:30pm Sun) Under tents overlooking the ocean, Josh sells 100% certified organic fruits, veggies, nuts and juices in PLA cups (made from corn, so it's compostable, like the bags he provides). Buy lots, because it's good for you, but don't feel compelled to spend: whatever remains is donated to a homeless shelter. An adjacent juice stand whips up killer smoothies.

Sawgrass Mills Mall
FASHION

(12801 W Sunrise Blvd, Sunrise; ❄10am-9:30pm Mon-Sat, 11am-8pm Sun) America's sixth-largest mall, Sawgrass features 350-plus name-brand stores and outlets, so budget a whole day.

ℹ Information

Greater Dania Beach Chamber of Commerce (📞954-926-2323; www.greaterdania.org; 102 W Dania Beach Blvd; ❄9am-5pm) Lots of local info.

Hollywood Office of Tourism (📞954-672-2468; www.visithollywood.org; 1100 N Broadwalk; ❄9am-5pm) Info. And some more info.

ℹ Getting There & Around

An old-fashioned trolley travels between downtown Hollywood and the beach from 10am to 10pm Wednesday through Sunday. Fares are $1; bright-colored signs mark the stops.

Broward County Transit (www.broward.org/bct) serves Hollywood and Dania, connecting them with Fort Lauderdale. Fares are $1.75.

From either city, get to the Fort Lauderdale/Hollywood Airport (BCT bus 1 takes you) and jump on **Tri-Rail** (www.tri-rail.com; 200 Terminal Dr), which'll shoot you north to West Palm Beach or south to Miami.

Parking at the beach in Hollywood is hellacious – if you can't find on-street parking, try the parking deck on Johnson St.

Fort Lauderdale

🕿954 / POP 185,000

After years of building a reputation as *the* destination for beer-swilling college students on raucous Spring Breaks, Fort Lauderdale now angles for a slightly more mature and sophisticated crowd – think martinis rather than tequila shots, jazz concerts instead of wet T-shirt contests (don't worry, there's still plenty of carrying-on within the confines of area bars and nightclubs).

Few visitors venture far inland – except maybe to dine and shop along Las Olas Blvd; most spend the bulk of their time on the coast, frolicking at water's edge. It's understandable. Truly, it's hard to compete with beautiful beaches, a system of Venicelike waterways, an international yachting scene,

spiffy new hotels, top-notch restaurants and gay hot spots.

The city's Port Everglades is one of the busiest cruise-ship ports in the world, with megaships departing daily for the Caribbean, Mexico and beyond. So if you get tired of life on land, hop aboard.

⊙ Sights

Fort Lauderdale Beach & Promenade   BEACH, PROMENADE

In the mid-1990s, this promenade received a $26-million renovation, and boy-oh-boy, does it show. A magnet for runners, inline skaters, walkers and cyclists, the wide, brick, palm tree–dotted pathway swoops along the beach, running parallel to A1A. You can also surf at Fort Lauderdale beach.

And what a beach it is, stretching from the southern edge of South Beach Park (Map p193), where the cruise ships pass, north 7 miles to Lauderdale-by-the-Sea (see p198). Thirty public-parking facilities – expect to pay about a buck an hour, if you can find a meter – serve the smooth, white beaches here, recently declared among the nation's cleanest, safest and most accessible. The park's 27.5-acre South Beach is the most family friendly, regularly hosting basketball games, beach-volleyball tourneys and fam-

Fort Lauderdale

ily reunions at the on-site grills and picnic tables. Further north, the stretch across from E Las Olas Blvd is less for recreation and more for, um, sightseeing. Expect olive-skinned, oiled-up saline queens and European guys in banana hammocks strutting their stuff.

Even further north, dog-friendly **Canine Beach** (Map p193; cnr Sunrise Blvd & N Atlantic Blvd; weekend permits $7; ⊙3-7pm winter, 5-9pm summer) is the 100yd swath running from E Sunrise Blvd to lifeguard station 5.

Riverwalk & Las Olas Riverfront WALKING

Curving along the New River, the meandering **Riverwalk** (Map p190; www.goriverwalk.com) runs from Stranahan House to the Broward Center for the Performing Arts. Host to culinary tastings and other events, the walk connects a number of sights, restaurants and shops. **Las Olas Riverfront** (Map p190; cnr SW 1st Ave & Las Olas Blvd) is basically a giant alfresco shopping mall with stores, restaurants and live entertainment nightly; it's also the place to catch many river cruises (see p193).

Museum of Discovery & Science MUSEUM
(Map p190; www.mods.org; 401 SW 2nd St; adult/child $11/9; ⊙10am-5pm Mon-Sat, noon-6pm Sun;

⛵) Fronted by the intricate 52ft Great Gravity Clock, Florida's largest kinetic-energy sculpture, this environmentally oriented museum is a treat for kids of all ages, with hands-on exhibits on rocket ships, the Everglades and coral reefs (it's got the world's largest indoor Atlantic coral reef). The on-site IMAX theater (adult/child $9/7) screens nature- and science-oriented documentaries in the morning, and 3D Hollywood blockbusters in the afternoon and evening.

Bonnet House HISTORIC BUILDING
(Map p190; www.bonnethouse.org; 900 N Birch Rd; adult/child 6-18yr $20/16, grounds only $10; ⊙10am-4pm Tue-Sat, 11am-4pm Sun) Hugh Taylor Birch, after being blown ashore in a freak accident in 1893, believed this part of the world was where God wanted him. Subsequently, he purchased 3 miles of beachfront property (for $1 per acre) and developed it. Today, the picturesque Bonnet House stands as a tribute to Birch and features 35 subtropical acres overflowing with native and imported plants, including a vast orchid collection. Seeing the art-filled house requires a guided tour (and 1¼ hours), but you're free to wander the grounds and nature trails on your own.

SOUTHEAST FLORIDA FORT LAUDERDALE

Fort Lauderdale

OUT TITANIC-ING THE TITANIC

Think the *Titanic* was big? Well, two new mega-jumbo cruise ships, both of which call Fort Lauderdale's Port Everglades home, make the legendary vessel look like a bathtub toy – they're literally five times as large! The MS *Allure of the Seas* and the MS *Oasis of the Seas*, both owned by Royal Caribbean (www.royalcaribbean.com), are the largest and most expensive cruise ships the world has ever seen – each top out at 1181ft long, with 16 decks. Seen from their specially built dock, they look more like high-rise condos than boats; each can hold more than 8000 people. The ships are veritable floating cities of amusement park–style pleasures: each contains several dozen restaurants and bars, rock-climbing walls, skating rinks, fake beaches with surfable waves, nine-story-high zip lines, and a vast central park with more than 12,000 plants. Whether this sounds like heaven or hell for you is a matter of taste. Seven-night cruises start at about $800 and sail for Haiti's heavily guarded (and highly controversial) Labadee port, as well as Jamaica, Yucatán and other Caribbean destinations.

Museum of Art
MUSEUM

(Map p190; www.moaflnsu.org; 1 E Las Olas Blvd; adult/child $10/7; ⊙11am-6pm, to 8pm Wed, noon-5pm Sun) Vigorously reinventing itself, this curvaceous museum is one of Florida's standouts. The impressive permanent collection includes works by Picasso, Matisse, Dalí and Warhol, plus a growing and impressive collection of Cuban, African and South American art. Its temporary exhibitions range freely across time and genre, covering everything from Catholic religious art to 20th-century fashion photography.

Stranahan House
HISTORIC BUILDING

(Map p190; www.stranahanhouse.org; 335 SE 6th Ave; adult/child $12/7; ⊙tours 1pm, 2pm & 3pm) Constructed from Dade County pine, grand Stranahan House is a fine example of Florida vernacular design and one of the state's oldest homes. It served as both home and store for Ohio transplant Frank Stranahan, who built a small empire trading with the Seminoles before committing suicide by jumping into the New River after real-estate and stock-market losses in the late 1920s. The house, with many original furnishings, is open for three daily hour-long tours.

Hugh Taylor Birch State
Recreation Area
PARK

(Map p193; 3109 E Sunrise Blvd; per vehicle $6; ⊙8am-sunset) This fragrant, lusciously tropical park contains one of the last significant maritime hammocks in Broward County. There are mangroves and a freshwater lagoon system (great for birding) and several endangered plants and animals (including the gopher tortoise and golden leather fern). You can fish, picnic, stroll the short Coastal Hammock Trail or bike the 1.9-mile park drive. Canoe rentals, to be used on the half-mile trail, cost about $6 per hour.

Fort Lauderdale Antique
Car Museum
MUSEUM

(www.antiquecarmuseum.org; 1527 Packard Ave; adult/child $8/5; ⊙9am-3pm Mon-Fri) Auto buffs will dig this quirky car museum, showcasing the history of the Packard (a now-defunct line of American luxury cars), from a 1909 Model 18 Speedster through WWII-era touring sedans. The museum is between downtown and the airport.

🏃 Activities

Everything from Waverunners to parasailing to deep-sea fishing charters is available at the beach. If you want to tool around in your own boat, try **Best Boat Club** (Map p193; ☑954-779-3866; www.fortlauderdaleboatrentals.com; per day from $100), which rents everything from single-engine 21ft Bowriders to luxurious 27ft Crownlines.

Fort Lauderdale Parasail
PARASAILING

(Map p193; ☑954-543-2938; www.ftlauderdaleparasail.com; 1005 Seabreeze Blvd; flights $70-95) If you're curious how mansions along Miracle Mile look from above, sign up for a trip to soar between 600ft and 1000ft above the waves while strapped securely to an enormous smiley-face parachute.

Sea Experience
BOATING, SNORKELING

(Map p193; ☑954-467-6000; www.seaxp.com /departures.html; 801 Seabreeze Blvd; adult/child $35/21; ⊙10:15am & 2:15pm daily; ⊕) Takes guests in a 40ft glass-bottom boat along the Intracoastal and into the ocean to snorkel on a natural reef, thriving with marine life, in 10ft to 20ft of water. Also offers scuba trips.

Fort Lauderdale Beach

Pro Dive DIVING

(Map p193; ☎954-776-3483; www.prodiveusa .com; 429 Seabreeze Blvd; 2-tank dives $75) Get underwater with this well-rated dive shop and school, offering daily two-tank wreck and reef dives, as well as the full gamut of PADI courses.

Fish Lauderdale FISHING

(Map p193; ☎954-764-8723; www.fishlauderdale .com; 801 Seabreeze Blvd; up to 6 people per hr $125; ☺8am-sunset) The waters off Fort Lauderdale are rich with marlin, sailfish, snapper, tarpon, wahoo and more. Naturally, there are plenty of fishing charters available – this outfit has four boats to take you trolling for dinner.

☞ Tours

Fort Lauderdale's miles of canals make it one of the top spots in Florida for boat tours.

TOP CHOICE **Carrie B** BOAT TOURS

(Map p190; ☎954-768-9920; www.carriebcruises .com; tours adult/child $20/13) Hop aboard this replica 19th-century riverboat for a narrated

Fort Lauderdale Beach

BAHAMAS DAY TRIPS

Just 55 miles east of Florida, the Bahamian island of Grand Bahama is close enough for day-trip or overnight cruises. Two operators ply the 'quickie cruise' territory: **Discovery Cruise Line** (☎800-259-1579; www.discoverycruiseline.com; trips from $99) does a popular one-day party cruise from the Port Everglades cruise dock, with all-you-can-eat breakfast and dinner buffets, free booze and casino gambling. The trip is about four hours each way, which leaves time for an afternoon of shopping and sun in the Grand Bahama port of Freeport/Lucaya. You can also elect to stay overnight and cruise back a day or two later. **Bahamas Celebration** (☎800-314-7735; www.bahamascelebration.com; trips from $99) leaves Palm Beach in the afternoon, spends the night at sea, then docks in Grand Bahama the following morning for a day of island activities before returning that evening. More upscale and family-friendly than the party-hearty *Discovery*, it's got a spa and a kids' club onboard and cabins ranging from bare-bones to luxe. For a longer stay, choose a two- or four-night add-on at a Grand Bahama luxury hotel. Yes, you need a passport.

90-minute 'lifestyles of the rich and famous' tour of the ginormous mansions along the Intracoastal and New River. Because Florida's infamous 'homestead exemption' law prevents houses from being seized by creditors, some of these homes are used as money shelters for white-collar criminals ('to your left, note the Spanish-style villa of notorious tax evader Richie McRicherson'). Tours leave at 11am, 1pm and 3pm from Las Olas at SE 5th Ave.

Gondola Man   GONDOLA RIDES
(Map p190; ☎877-926-2467; www.gondolaman .com; rides $125) With over 300 miles of navigable inland waterways, Fort Lauderdale is known as 'the Venice of the Americas.' And what do you do in Venice? A gondola tour, of course! Float around the canals as an authentically dressed gondolier narrates the sights (or keeps quiet while you sip champagne – your choice). Rides depart from the canal adjacent to 1109 E Las Olas Blvd.

Jungle Queen Riverboat   BOAT TOURS
(Map p193; www.junglequeen.com; 801 Seabreeze Blvd; adult/child $17/13) Runs three-hour tours along the waterfront, Millionaires' Row and part of the Everglades on a Mississippi-style paddle-wheeler; four-hour evening excursions include all-you-can-eat shrimp or BBQ dinners and entertainment (adult/child $40/21).

🛏 Sleeping

The splashiest hotels are found along the beach. Of course, those places are also the priciest. Meander inland, and you'll discover some wonderful inns with Old Florida charm, many of which exclusively welcome gay guests (these are noted below).

TOP CHOICE Pillars   B&B $$$
(Map p193; ☎954-467-9639, 800-800-7666; www.pillarshotel.com; 111 N Birch Rd; r $179-520; P❄✳☎) From the harp in the sitting area to the private balconies to the intimate pre-arranged dinners for two, this tiny boutique hotel radiates hushed good taste. Sun-soaked rooms, done up in natural fibers and elegant botanical prints, look torn from the pages of *Coastal Living* magazine. It's a block from the beach, half a mile from E Las Olas Blvd and facing one of the best sunsets in town. If you want to get as far away as possible from liquor-fueled beach culture, this is your spot.

TOP CHOICE Pineapple Point   GUESTHOUSE $$$
(☎888-844-7295; www.pineapplepoint.com; 315 NE 16th Terrace; r $199-279, ste $299-399; P✳@ ☎✉) Tucked away behind a tall fence in a quiet residential neighborhood, this intimate guesthouse complex caters to a loyal gay male clientele. Suites and apartments are bright and beachy (with the occasional tasteful erotic photo), all clustered around a handful of pools, hot tubs and tree-shaded sitting areas. Daily happy hours ensure mingling, and the super-friendly staff know all the best restaurants and gay bars in town. Pineapple Point is a few blocks northeast of the main drag of Las Olas, inland from the beach.

Alhambra Beach Resort   HOTEL $$
(Map p193; ☎954-525-7601; 3021 Alhambra St; r $99-200; P✳✉☎) Beloved for its reasonable prices and warm-hearted owners, this charming little 1930s-era inn has modest-but-immaculate rooms and suites painted in cheerful buttercup yellow, and a pleasant

pool deck amid a manicured garden of palms and hibiscus. A gate adds a private feel, though the beach is only half a block away. Scads of return guests mean the place books up quickly!

Riverside Hotel
HOTEL $$
(Map p190; ☑954-467-0671, 800-325-3280; www .riversidehotel.com; 620 E Las Olas Blvd; r $143-200; P✦❄@☎≋) This 1936 hotel, smack in the middle of downtown and fronted by stately columns, oozes an old-fashioned, Old Florida charm. Save some money by opting for a 'Traditional' room – they're older, and have slightly creaky furniture and odd coffered ceilings, but those features only add character, in our opinion. 'Standard' rooms are plush and classic. The lobby, all Spanish tile and potted ferns, has a stately charm, and the hotel restaurant, the Golden Lyon, is prime for people-watching, with outdoor tables right on Las Olas.

W
HOTEL $$$
(Map p193; ☑954-414-8200; 401 N Fort Lauderdale Beach Blvd; r $219-529; P✦@☎≋) With an exterior resembling two giant sails and an interior that looks like the backdrop for a J Lo video, this is where the glitterati stay – bust out your stiletto heels/skinny ties and join them. The massive lobby is built for leisure, with a silver-and-aqua lounge area, a moodily lit bar with mod sea urchin–shaped tables, and a deck lined with wicker chaises. Swank, modern rooms are done up in a monochromatic palate of sand, silver and cream.

Shell Motel
MOTEL $
(Map p193; ☑954-463-1723; www.sableresorts .com; 330 Bayshore Dr; r from $85, ste from $150; P✦☎≋⛵) One of six modest motels owned by the same company, this sweet little Old Florida–style spot has two stories of bright, clean rooms surrounding a small pool and hibiscus-shaded shuffleboard court. We'd advise splashing out for a suite – they're much larger and nicer.

Lago Mar Resort
RESORT $$$
(☑800-524-6627, 954-523-6511; www.lagomar .com; 1700 S Ocean Lane; r $158-560; P✦@≋) On the south end of South Beach, this wonderfully noncorporate resort has it all: a private beach, over-the-top grand lobby, massive island-style rooms, a full-service spa, on-site eateries and the personal touch of family ownership.

Schubert Resort
MOTEL $$
(☑866-763-7435, 954-763-7434; www.schubertre sort.com; 855 NE 20th Ave; r summer $105-225, winter $169-339; P✦☎≋) One of the area's many gay inns, this retro place is housed in the shell of a 1953 motel but has sleek and thoroughly modern rooms, and a well-trafficked (clothing-optional) pool area. The resort is inland from the beach, north of Fort Lauderdale's main downtown.

Ritz-Carlton
HOTEL $$$
(Map p193; ☑954-465-2300; www.ritzcarlton .com; 1 N Fort Lauderdale Beach Blvd; r $200-900; P✦☎≋) This art deco–style palace of swank has an opulent marble-and-cream lobby, skywalk to the beach, a chichi restaurant, a 8500-sq-ft full-service spa, and large rooms blessed with both ocean and Intracoastal views.

Sea Club Resort
MOTEL $
(Map p193; ☑954-564-3211; www.seaclubresort .com; 619 Fort Lauderdale Beach Blvd; r from $80; P✦☎≋) It ain't a resort, and it ain't fancy, but this beachfront motel has a funky charm, with a faux-stone grotto in the lobby, a resident parrot named Touki, and a popular nautical-themed pub.

✗ Eating

Fort Lauderdale has a great food scene, heavily influenced by the area's large Italian-American population. Las Olas Blvd in downtown Fort Lauderdale has the bulk of the nicer eating places, especially the stretch between 5th and 16th Aves.

TOP CHOICE Gran Forno
ITALIAN, BAKERY $$
(Map p190; www.granforno.com; 1235 E Las Olas Blvd; mains $6-12; ⏱7:30am-7pm Tue-Sun) At midday, follow the hordes of businesspeople to the best lunch spot in downtown Fort Lauderdale. A delightfully old-school Milanese-style bakery and cafe, Gran Forno ('big oven' in Italian) turns out warm, crusty pastries, bubbling pizzas and fat, golden loaves of ciabatta, which they stuff with ham, roast peppers, pesto and other delicacies for some of the area's best sandwiches. Seating is limited – crowd into one of the banquettes in the black-and-white tiled interior, or sip your Peroni under a big red umbrella on the sidewalk. Finish it up with a thimble of hot, strong espresso and a sliver of homemade biscotti.

Johnny V's
MODERN AMERICAN $$$

(Map p190; ☎954-761-7020; 625 E Las Olas Blvd; mains $28-42; ☺11am-3pm daily, 5-11pm Thu, to midnight Fri & Sat) Despite the vaguely mafioso-sounding name (it's actually named after the chef, Johnny Vinczencz), this perennially popular bistro is Nouvelle American all the way – modern brick-and-slate dining room, menu full of witty takes on regional classics (wild-mushroom 'pancakes' with balsamic 'syrup,' braised short ribs with haute onion rings). The late-afternoon happy hour is a daily event among well-heeled Fort Lauderdale-ites.

Rustic Inn
SEAFOOD $$$

(☎954-584-1637; www.rusticinn.com; 4331 Ravenswood Rd; mains $14-45; ☺10:30am-10:45pm Mon-Sat, to 9pm Sun) Don't wear your Sunday best to this place – or bring a date you want to whisper sweet nothings to. Hungry locals at this messy, noisy crab house use wooden mallets at long, newspaper-covered tables to get at the good stuff served here. The house specialty is crabs – choose from Dungeness, blue or golden – drenched in garlic and a secret family recipe (think: butter). Not in a crabby mood? This hearty, happy family-style restaurant has schools of seafood and pasta options. The restaurant is a short drive north of downtown Fort Lauderdale.

Casablanca Cafe
MEDITERRANEAN $$$

(Map p193; ☎954-764-3500; www.casablancacafe online.com; 3049 Alhambra St; mains $13-38; ☺11:30am-late daily) Wednesday to Sunday this sophisticated bar grooves with night-time entertainment, but the real attraction at this romantic, hibiscus-ringed cafe is the delightful Mediterranean-inspired dishes; try the twisted hummus or the fennel-infused steamed mussels. Order a sublime frozen mojito, head up to the oceanfront balcony and watch cruise ships inch along the horizon.

11th Street Annex
AMERICAN, FUSION $

(twouglysisters.com; 14 SW 11th St; lunch mains $9; ☺11:30am-2pm Mon-Fri) You don't get more off-the-beaten path than this tiny peach cottage, on a residential side street just off busy S Andrews Ave. Inside, Jonny Altobell and Penny Sanfilippo – both culinary-school grads who call themselves 'the two ugly sisters' – serve up whatever strikes their fancy on a given day. Brie mac 'n' cheese, chicken confit and sour-cream chocolate cake have all made appearances in the past. There's always a veggie option, much of which comes from the cottage's garden.

Cafe Sharaku
ASIAN FUSION $$$

(☎954-563-2888; www.cafesharaku.com; 2736 N Federal Hwy; mains $25-32; ☺11:30am-3pm Tue-Fri, 5:30-10pm Tue-Sun) Local foodies only whisper about this place, unwilling to allow the exquisite little 18-seat bistro to be trampled by the masses. Well, sorry, but the cat's out of the bag: Sharaku is fabulous. Chef Iwao Kaita treats fish with the utmost respect, crafting gemlike plates of miso bass or sesame-crusted salmon. The restaurant is a short drive north of downtown Fort Lauderdale.

Eduardo de San Angel
MEXICAN $$$

(☎954-772-4731; www.eduardodesanangel.com; 2822 E Commercial Blvd; mains $24-34; ☺5:30am-10pm Mon-Sat) Dreamy upscale Mexican food full of romantic ingredients (squash blossoms! Chocolate-chili! Guava syrup!), served in a warmly elegant dining room full of Mexican folk art. The restaurant is north of downtown, nearly in Lauderdale-by-the-Sea.

Lester's Diner
DINER $

(250 SE 24th St; mains $4-17; ☺24hr; 🚗) Hailed endearingly as a greasy spoon, campy Lester's Diner has been keeping folks happy since the late 1960s. Everyone makes their way here at some point, from business types on cell phones to clubbers to blue-haired ladies with third husbands. Lester's is between downtown Fort Lauderdale and the airport.

Drinking & Entertainment

Fort Lauderdale bars can stay open until 4am on weekends and 2am during the week. A handful of bars and pubs are found in the Himmarshee Village area on W 2nd St, while the beach offers plenty of open-air boozing. For gay and lesbian venues, see p197.

Elbo Room
BAR

(Map p193; www.elboroom.com; 241 N Fort Lauderdale Beach Blvd) Open since 1938, this dive achieved immortality thanks to the '60s classic 'Where the Boys Are.' It hit its stride during the Spring Break years but keeps going with drink specials and great music that attracts the young, beer-swilling, hipshaking set.

Mai-Kai
DINNER SHOW

(www.maikai.com; 3599 N Federal Hwy) This old-school Polynesian joint is pure kitsch, with Vegas-style dinner shows and froofy tiki cocktails (try the potent 'mystery drink'). Mai-Kai

Sure, South Beach is a mecca for gay travelers, but lately, Fort Lauderdale has been nipping at the high heels of its southern neighbor. Compared to South Beach, Lauderdale is a little more rainbow-flag oriented and a little less exclusive. And for the hordes of gay boys who flock here, either to party or to settle down, therein lies the charm. You don't need to be A-list to feel at home at any of the many gay bars, clubs or restaurants, and you won't have any trouble finding 'the scene.'

Fort Lauderdale is home to several dozen gay bars and clubs, as many gay guesthouses, and a couple of way-gay residential areas including **Victoria Park**, the established gay hub just northeast of downtown Fort Lauderdale, and, a bit further north, **Wilton Manors**, more recently gay-gentrified and boasting endless nightlife options, including **Bill's Filling Station** (www.billsfillingstation.com; 2209 Wilton Dr), a friendly 'bear' bar, **Matty's** (www.mattysonthedrive.com; 2426 Wilton Dr), a low-key neighborhood watering hole, and **Georgie's Alibi** (www.georgiesalibi.com; 2266 Wilton Dr), which is best for its Wednesday comedy night with Cashetta, a fabulous female impersonator. There's even a gay sports bar, **Sidelines** (www.sidelinessports.com; 2031 Wilton Dr), with a super-fun Wednesday dart tournament, and a leather/bear/cowboy club, **Ramrod** (www.ramrodbar.com; 1508 Wilton Dr).

Gay guesthouses are plentiful; see p194 for some suggestions, or visit www.gayftlauderdale.com. Consult the glossy weekly rag *Hot Spots* (www.hotspotsmagazine.com) to keep updated on gay nightlife. For the most insanely comprehensive list of everything gay, log on to www.jumponmarkslist.com.

is a short drive north of downtown Fort Lauderdale toward Lauderdale-by-the-Sea.

Lulu's Bait Shack
BAR
(Map p193; www.lulusbaitshack.com; 17 S Fort Lauderdale Beach Blvd, Suite 212) A great view of the beach can be seen over the rims of the fishbowl cocktails this place serves.

Bourbon on 2nd
BAR
(Map p190; bourbonon2nd.wordpress.com; 201 SW 2nd St) Fun new Cajun restaurant and bar, with live music and a boozy New Orleans vibe.

Side Bar
BAR
(Map p190; 210 SW 2nd St) A sleek, grown-up bar for the wine-sipping set, with a popular happy hour.

Voodoo Lounge
CLUB
(Map p190; www.voodooloungeflorida.com; 111 SW 2nd Ave; ☺10pm-4am Wed-Sun) A massive club with 50,000 watts of booty-shaking sound – look for Sunday drag nights, Latin nights and other themed events.

🛍 Shopping

Fort Lauderdale Beach Blvd has a gaggle of T-shirt shops and sunglass huts, while Las Olas is lined with swanky boutiques and antiques shops. For outlet shopping, head to massive **Sawgrass Mills Mall** (p189) in nearby Hollywood.

Swap Shop
MARKET
(www.floridaswapshop.com; 3291 W Sunrise Blvd; ☺9am-6pm) Perhaps the most fun shopping in town, the state's biggest flea market has acres of stalls selling everything from underwear to antique cookie jars to pink lawn flamingos, and a carnival atmosphere of mariachi music, hot-dog trucks and a 14-screen drive-in movie theater. The flea market is slightly northwest of downtown.

ℹ Information

Convention & Visitors Bureau (Map p190; ✆954-765-4466; www.sunny.org; 100 E Broward Blvd, Suite 200) Has an excellent array of visitor information about hotels and attractions in the greater Fort Lauderdale region.

Post office (Map p190; 1404 E Las Olas Blvd, Suite B) Not the main one, but well located.

ℹ Getting There & Away

Air

Fort Lauderdale-Hollywood International Airport (FLL; ✆954-359-1200; www.fll.net) is easy to reach from I-95 or US 1 and sandwiched about halfway between Lauderdale and Hollywood. The airport is served by more than 35 airlines, including some with nonstop flights from Europe. There's also free wi-fi throughout the terminal. In fact, FLL is so hassle-free and accessible that many Miami visitors choose to fly from here. From the airport, it's a short 20-minute drive to downtown, or a $20 cab ride.

Boat

The **Port Everglades Authority** (www.porteverglades.org) runs the enormous Port Everglades cruise port (the second busiest in the world after Miami). From the port, walk to SE 17th St and take bus 40 to the beach or to Broward Central Terminal.

If you're heading to Fort Lauderdale in your own boat (not that unlikely here), head for the **Bahia Mar Resort & Yacht Center** (Map p193; www.bahiamarhotel.com).

Bus

The **Greyhound station** (www.greyhound.com; 515 NE 3rd St at Federal Hwy) is about four blocks from Broward Central Terminal (below), the central transfer point for buses in the area.

Train

Tri-Rail (www.tri-rail.com) runs between Miami and Fort Lauderdale (one way $5, 45 minutes). A feeder system of buses has connections at no charge. Free parking is provided at most stations. Provide ample cushion for delays. **Amtrak** (800-872-7245; www.amtrak.com; 200 SW 21st Tce) also uses Tri-Rail tracks.

Getting Around

If you're driving here, I-95 and Florida's Turnpike run north–south. I-595, the major east–west artery, intersects I-95, Florida's Turnpike and the Sawgrass Expressway. It also feeds into I-75, which runs to Florida's west coast.

Sun Trolley (www.suntrolley.com; fare $0.50) runs between Las Olas and the beaches. **Broward County Transit** (BCT; www.broward.org/bct; fare $1.75) operates between downtown, the beach and Port Everglades. From **Broward Central Terminal** (Map p190; 101 NW 1st Ave), take bus 11 to upper Fort Lauderdale Beach and Lauderdale-by-the-Sea; bus 4 to Port Everglades; and bus 40 to 17th St and the beaches.

The fun, yellow **Water Taxi** (www.watertaxi.com; 651 Seabreeze Blvd; all-day pass adult/child $20/12) travels the canals and waterways between 17th St to the south, Atlantic Blvd/Pompano Beach to the north, the Riverfront to the west and the Atlantic Ocean to the east.

Lauderdale-by-the-Sea & Deerfield Beach

954 / LAUDERDALE-BY-THE-SEA POP 5900 / DEERFIELD BEACH POP 75,000

Just north of Fort Lauderdale, the highrises and mega-hotels thin out, giving way to these two sleepy, family-oriented vacation communities. If your idea of fun is less about clubbing and high-end dining, and more about chilling out on the beach with a picnic, this might be the spot for you.

Sights & Activities

Quiet Waters Park — WATER PARK
(401 S Powerline Rd, Deerfield Beach; admission $1.50;) Hardly quiet, this 430-acre county park rings with the squeals of kids (and grown-ups) enjoying all kinds of wet 'n' wild fun. There's **Splash Adventure** (admission $5), a kiddie water playground with a shallow pool and fountains spraying every which way. Then there's the **Ski Rixen** (www.skirixenusa.com; per hr/day $20/40; 10am-7pm Tue-Fri), a super-cool cable water-ski system. Using an innovative cabling system suspended from towers surrounding a half-mile course, waterskiers (and wake-boarders) are pulled over a wake-free watercourse. Obstacles are available for advanced tricksters; otherwise, riders can perfect their water-skiing techniques without the hassle of a boat. For lower-octane adventures, the park has fishing, hiking trails, kayak rental and a mountain-bike trail.

Butterfly World — ANIMAL PARK
(www.butterflyworld.com; 3600 W Sample Rd, Coconut Creek; adult/child $25/20; 9am-5pm Mon-Sat, from 11am Sun;) The first indoor butterfly park in the US, this is one of the largest butterfly exhibits anywhere, featuring thousands of live, exotic species, such as the bright-blue morphos or camouflaged owl butterfly. Various exhibits, each highlighting different creatures – from butterflies to hummingbirds – make Butterfly World an excellent place to spend the better part of a day, especially with wide-eyed children or trigger-happy shutterbugs.

South Florida Diving Headquarters — DIVING
(954-783-2299; www.southfloridadiving.com; 101 N Riverside Dr, Pompano Beach; 2-tank dives $55, snorkeling $30) Dive natural and artificial reefs, or float along one of the area's famous drift dives with this PADI-certified company. Forty-five-minute snorkeling trips will keep nondivers happy.

Anglin's Pier — FISHING
(Commercial Blvd, Lauderdale-by-the-Sea) Score bait in the 24-hour tackle shop and rent a rod for $5. Lit for night fishing, the pier is an easy shuffle from the rest of town. Don't expect to hook a 300lb grouper here, though it has been done!

Deerfield Beach Fishing Pier   FISHING
(200 NE 21st Ave, Deerfield Beach) Further north, this pier is known for large catches like king mackerel on west winds. Rods rent for $16.

🛏 Sleeping

Both towns have no shortage of sweet, family-run motels and guesthouses. **Quiet Waters Park** (☑955-357-5100; tents $35) offers 'rent-a-tent' tepees for camping.

Courtyard Villa   HOTEL $$
(☑954-489-9870; www.buenavistacorp.com; 4312 El Mar Dr, Lauderdale-by-the-Sea; r $109-359; ❀🛜❄) This Mediterranean-style quartet of courtyard suites and apartments is infused with a breezy style with its ceiling fans, parquet floors and four-poster beds. Overnighters get free use of the bikes, grills, tennis courts and rooftop patio. It's no wonder rooms here go fast.

High Noon Resort   MOTEL $$
(☑954-776-1121; www.highnoonresort.com; 4424 El Mar Dr, Lauderdale-by-the-Sea; r/cabana $130/387; ❀@🛜❄🛏) Spilling onto the beach, this ultraclean motel-resort includes two sister properties, the Sea Foam (apartment-style stays) and the Nautilus (for those seeking seclusion). Guests can enjoy the property's seven tiki huts, two pools and shuffleboard court. Steps from bars and restaurants, nothing says Florida like relaxing under this property's numerous palm trees and listening to the sea breeze rustle the leaves.

A Little Inn by the Sea   HOTEL $$
(☑954-772-2459; alittleinnhotel.com; 4546 El Mar Dr, Lauderdale-by-the-Sea; r $119-159; ❀@🛜❄) In a funky atomic-age building, this friendly little guesthouse is architecturally odd – rooms wrap around an indoor atrium, like a motel folded in on itself. But newly renovated rooms, a sociable common living area and beachfront access make this popular with loyal repeat guests.

🍴 Eating & Drinking

Da Campo Osteria   ITALIAN $$$
(☑954-226-5002; www.dacamporestaurant.com; 3333 NE 32nd St, Fort Lauderdale; meals $26-45; ⊙lunch 11:30am-2:30pm Tue-Sat, dinner 5:30-10pm Mon-Sat) Technically in Fort Lauderdale, though much closer to the center of Lauderdale-by-the-Sea, this new spot by celebrity chef Todd English has been drawing no shortage of crowds and buzz, despite its awkward setting in an ugly gray hotel tower

at the end of a shoddy commercial strip. Reserve well in advance to enjoy divine housemade pastas and homey-yet-exquisite mains like oxtail ragu and jumbo meatballs. Don't miss the pièce de résistance – homemade mozzarella prepared tableside with your choice of spices and seasonings.

Aruba Beach Cafe   CARIBBEAN $$
(www.arubabeachcafe.com; 1 Commercial Blvd, Lauderdale-by-the-Sea; mains $10-22; ⊙11am-11pm Mon-Sat, 9am-11pm Sun; 🛜) The food isn't the only reason people flock here (though the conch fritters *are* divine). There's also live music nightly, daily drink specials served from three separate bars and only a bank of sliding glass doors separating you and the beach.

La Spada's Original Hoagies   SANDWICHES
(www.laspadashoagies.com; 4346 Sea Grape Dr, Lauderdale-by-the-Sea; ⊙10am-8pm) This strip-mall spot is a hush-hush cult favorite for crazy-good Philly-style hoagies and a staff of fun-loving jokers who can toss a slice of turkey like a Frisbee and make it land on your bread. Pssst: try the Monster.

Village Pump   BAR
(www.villagegrille.com; 4404 El Mar Dr, Lauderdale-by-the-Sea) Serving sturdy drinks in a nautical wood-paneled room since 1949.

ℹ Information
Deerfield Beach Chamber of Commerce (☑954-427-1050; www.deerfieldchamber.com; 1601 E Hillsboro Blvd)
Lauderdale-by-the-Sea Chamber of Commerce (☑954-776-1000; www.lbts.com; 4201 Ocean Dr) Info on businesses throughout the area.

ℹ Getting There & Around
Tri-Rail (www.tri-rail.com) heads north from Fort Lauderdale. If you're driving, try to take A1A (sometimes called Ocean Blvd): the drive's glorious.

Boca Raton
☑561 / POP 86,000
The name Boca Raton may mean 'mouth of the rat,' but there's nothing ratty about this proud-to-be-posh coastal town. What began as a sleepy residential community was transformed in the mid-1920s by architect Addison Mizner, who relied on his love of Spanish architecture to build the place into

a fancy-pants town. His fingerprints remain on numerous structures throughout the area, though his name is most often invoked when talking about the popular anchor of town – the alfresco mall, Mizner Park. The rest of Boca is a mostly mainstream collection of hoity-toity chain stores and restaurants and, as you near the ocean, some peaceful beaches and parks. Most people don't come to Boca on vacation unless they have family here, as there are almost no beachfront hotels – and that suits residents just fine.

◉ Sights & Activities

TOP CHOICE Gumbo Limbo Nature Center PARK
(www.gumbolimbo.org; 1801 N Ocean Blvd; admission by donation; ◎9am-4pm Mon-Sat, noon-4pm Sun;) Boca's best asset is not its collection of retail, cultural or culinary treats, but this condo-free stretch of waterfront parkland. The crown jewel of the system is this wild preserve of tropical hammock and dunes ecosystems, a haven for all manner of sea creatures and birds. Dedicated to educating the public about sea turtles and other local fauna, the natural-history displays include fascinating saltwater tanks full of critters – fed with leftover seafood scraps donated by local businesses. The highlight is the brand-new sea-turtle rehabilitation center, which cares for sick and injured turtles, and is open for 90-minute tours at 10am and 1pm Monday through Saturday, and 1pm Sunday.

The preserve also has a number of secluded hikes along elevated boardwalks through tropical foliage and along an artificial mangrove wetland, reclaimed using filtered wastewater from the city. A native-flower garden attracts a slew of gemstone-colored butterflies.

Red Reef Beach BEACH
(1 N Ocean Blvd; per vehicle Mon-Fri $16, Sat & Sun $18; ◎8am-sunset;) Thanks to a unique artificial reef just offshore, this beach is tops for water-lovers, offering lifeguards in swimming areas, and great shallow pools for beginner snorkelers. Together with neighboring South Beach Park, the beaches encompass some 60 acres of wild shores.

Mizner Park PLAZA
(www.miznerpark.com) This Spanish-style outdoor shopping mall, bookended on one side by the Boca Raton Museum of Art, has valet parking and a slew of chichi restaurants and upscale chain stores. At the north end, the

Count de Hoernle Amphitheater accommodates over 4000 people for symphonies, ballet, rock concerts and other cultural events. Since Boca lacks a cohesive downtown, Mizner Park generally serves as the city's center.

Boca Raton Museum of Art MUSEUM
(www.bocamuseum.org; 501 Plaza Real; adult/child $8/4; ◎10am-5pm Tue-Fri, noon-5pm Sat & Sun) In Mizner Park, this elegant museum showcases the minor works of modern masters like Picasso, Chagall and Modigliani, and has a genuinely worthwhile collection of pieces by 20th- and 21st-century American and European painters, sculptors and photographers.

Boca Raton Historical Society MUSEUM, TOURS
(☎561-395-6766; www.bocahistory.org; 71 N Federal Hwy) The main reason to visit this tiny museum is to check out the building, the former Boca Raton town hall (1927), topped by a glimmering gold dome.

The society runs a guided **trolley tour** on the second Thursday of the month from January through May (tickets $20). The 1½-hour docent-led trip takes you to the **Florida East Coast Railway Depot**, a Mediterranean Revival train station built in the 1930s for Flagler's railroad, as well as the **Old Floresta Historic District**, a 1920s-era residential neighborhood. Alternatively, take

Boca Raton

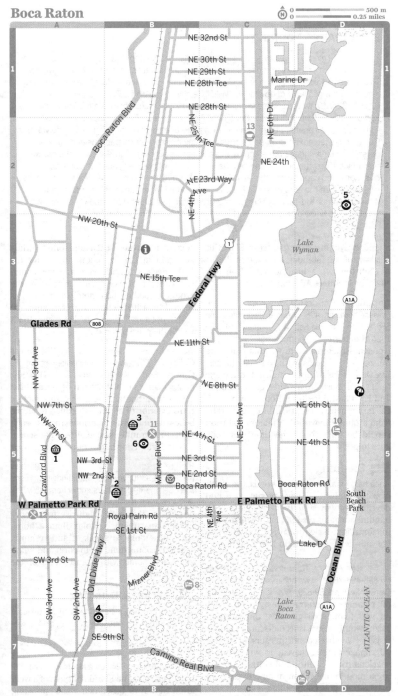

0 — 500 m
0 — 0.25 miles

NE 32nd St
NE 30th St
NE 29th St
NE 28th Tce
NE 28th St
NE 25th Tce
Marine Dr
NE 6th Dr
13
NE 24th
NE 23rd Way
NE 4th Ave
5
Lake Wyman
Boca Raton Blvd
NW 20th St
NE 15th Tce
Federal Hwy
1
Glades Rd
808
NE 11th St
A1A
NE 8th St
7
NE 6th St
10
3
11
NE 4th St
NE 4th St
NW 3rd Ave
6
Mizner Blvd
NE 3rd St
NE 2nd St
Boca Raton Rd
Boca Raton Rd
NW 7th St
NW 7th St
1
NW 3rd St
NW 2nd St
2
E Palmetto Park Rd
South Beach Park
W Palmetto Park Rd
12
Crawford Blvd
Royal Palm Rd
SE 1st St
NE 4th Ave
NE 5th Ave
Lake D
SW 3rd St
Mizner Blvd
Old Dixie Hwy
8
Ocean Blvd
SW 3rd Ave
SW 2nd Ave
4
Lake Boca Raton
A1A
ATLANTIC OCEAN
SE 9th St
Camino Real Blvd
9

SOUTHEAST FLORIDA GOLD COAST

EVERGLADES TOURS

Boca isn't all glossy development and glitzy malls. The western edge of town borders the northern reach of the Everglades (see p136), the only subtropical park in North America. To explore this time-forgotten area, filled with swamp ferns and nodding nixies, you need a guide. Ten miles west of downtown, Wild Lyle's **Loxahatchee Everglades Tours** (☑561-482-6107; www.evergladesairboattours.com; 15490 Loxahatchee Rd; adult/child under 12yr $44/22; ☺10am-5pm) offers hourly eco explorations of the Everglades on one of eight custom airboats (a boat using a fan instead of a propeller to push it over the water). Guests enjoy an adventure ride through swampy marsh, around papyrus and hurricane grass, past long-winged birds and turtles and gators sunning themselves. At the halfway point, Lyle stops the boat, discusses the importance of the Everglades and answers questions. You can't stump this guy. A crusty old bugger with nearly 40 years' experience, Lyle's explored the area thoroughly and even conducted rescue missions recovering downed planes. Kid-friendly but science-drenched, an airboat ride with Lyle is a great way to get to know a part of the world that most people don't understand.

a guided **walking tour** (per person $15; ☺Tue Dec-May) of the fabulous Boca Raton Resort & Club (below), a historic hotel from the 1920s by architect Addison Mizner.

Boca Raton Children's Museum MUSEUM
(www.cmboca.org; 498 Crawford Blvd; admission $5; ☺noon-4pm Tue-Sat; 🖐) Housed in the 1925 'Singing Pines' home, one of the oldest wooden structures in town, this children's museum has rooms with various themes, like Oscar's Post Office (where kids can make their own postcards), KidsCent's banking and FACES Multicultural Room (with musical instruments, try-on clothing and crafts from around the world). A major expansion should be finished by the time this book goes to press.

🛏 Sleeping

Boca has a startling lack of hotels, the result of zoning laws that have privileged condo development over tourism. There are a handful of chains off I-95, but if you're looking for unique beachfront digs, you'll have to lay your head just north in Deerfield Beach.

TOP CHOICE **Boca Raton Resort & Club** RESORT $$$
(☑888-498-2622; www.bocaresort.com; 501 E Camino Real; r $169-629; ❄🐾🏊) A collection of palatial Mediterranean-style buildings on vast manicured grounds, this Addison Mizner–built resort is as old-school glam as it gets. Well-heeled northerners make the pilgrimage here each year to winter in its spacious rooms, suites and cottages, enjoying a modern collection of amenities, from two 18-hole golf courses and a 32-slip ma-

rina to a private beach and otherworldly spa. Add in the five pools, 10 restaurants and priceless historic vibe and you'll find you can stay a week and never leave the grounds. Foodies, take note: the resort has several top-rated celeb-run restaurants (see p203), open only to guests. For some, that's worth the price of a room.

Ocean Lodge MOTEL $$
(☑561-395-7772; www.oceanlodgeflorida.com; 531 N Ocean Blvd; r winter/summer from $169/109; ❄🐾🏊) On a hushed stretch of Ocean Blvd across from South Beach Park, this motel's retro exterior of atomic-era concrete lattice belies its modern, luxurious rooms, each with full granite kitchenettes, flat-screen TVs and travertine bathrooms.

Bridge Hotel HOTEL $$
(☑561-368-9500; www.bocaratonbridgehotel.com; 999 E Camino Real; r winter/summer from $159/109; ❄🐾) Hidden in plain sight among the condo towers, this beige high-rise feels more like an apartment complex than a hotel, with little lobby to speak of and tranquil, spacious rooms done up in coral and white and aqua, some with grand views of the Intracoastal.

🍴 Eating & Drinking

Mizner Park has a half dozen or so upscale restaurants with outdoor seating and a see-and-be-seen vibe.

Ben's Kosher Deli DELI $
(www.bensdeli.net; 9942 Clint Moore Rd; mains $5-12; ☺11am-9pm) The Florida outpost of a well-loved New York–based deli, Ben's sprawling

menu covers all the Jewish classics – corned-beef sandwiches, knishes (potato-stuffed pastries), sweet-and-sour beef tongue, eggs with smoked salmon. If you're under 60, you may be the only one! The deli is about 20 minutes' drive northwest of Mizner Park.

Saporissimo   ITALIAN $$$
(☎561-750-2333; 366 Palmetto Park Rd; mains $15-50; ◷5:30-10:30pm daily) Translating as 'extremely delicious,' this Italian restaurant is simultaneously romantic and shabby-chic, unlike many of its frou-frou neighbors. Choose from unusual Tuscan treats – wild boar, truffles, rabbit and elk – or more traditional options like ravioli or veal. Finish it off with a rustic Italian dessert like *torta della nonna* (custard cake with pine nuts), or apple strudel.

Max's Grille   MODERN AMERICAN $$
(www.maxsgrille.com; 404 Plaza Real, Mizner Park; mains $14-28; ◷8am-2am) In tony Mizner Park, Max's sleek, slightly corporate slate-and-mahogany dining room is always packed with shoppers, wine-sippers and ladies (and gentlemen) who lunch. The likeable 'New American bistro' menu has everything from Asian duck tacos to Cobb salads to skirt steak, and the lovely outdoor bar is excellent for people-watching.

Funky Buddha Lounge   PUB
(www.thefunkybuddha.com; 2621 N Federal Hwy; ◷5pm-2am) Choose from 110 microbrews, dozens of organic wines and teas, fair-trade coffees and over 40 shisha flavors to smoke in the on-site hookahs.

❶ Information

Boca Raton News (www.bocanews.com) is published daily.
Chamber of Commerce (☎561-395-4433; www.bocaratonchamber.com; 1800 N Dixie Hwy) Helpful, with racks of pamphlets and the best map in town.
Library (200 NW Boca Raton Blvd; ◷9am-9pm Mon-Thu, to 6pm Fri & Sat, noon-8pm Sun) Free internet access.
Post office (170 NE 2nd St)

❶ Getting There & Around

Boca Raton is about 50 miles north of Miami and sprawls several miles east and west of I-95. You can also get there from points north and south on Hwy A1A or US 1. The town is more or less equidistant from Fort Lauderdale-Hollywood International Airport (FLL; p197) and Palm Beach International Airport (PBI; p220).

MEMBERS ONLY: MORIMOTO

Fans of Iron Chef will recognize the name – **Morimoto** (☎561-447-3640; www.bocaresort.com/dining; Boca Resort; rolls & appetizers $6-38; ◷noon-3pm & 5-10pm) is celebrity chef Masaharu Morimoto's latest endeavor, inside the Boca Raton Resort. Though, annoyingly, you have to be a resort guest or member to enjoy his exquisite creations – octopus carpaccio, soft-shell-crab rolls, fresher-than-fresh cuts of sashimi – plenty of foodies have shelled out for an overnight just for the chance to eat here.

The Boca Raton **Tri-Rail station** (www.tri-rail.com; 680 Yamato Rd) has shuttle services to both airports. PalmTran bus 94 connects downtown Boca with the Tri-Rail station.

PalmTran (www.palmtran.org) serves southeast Florida from North Palm Beach to Boca Raton. It costs $1.50 to ride. From the Tri-Rail station, bus 2 takes you to PBI and bus 94 to FAU, where you can transfer to bus 91 to Mizner Park. From Mizner Park, take bus 92 to South Beach Park.

Boca Taxi (☎561-392-2727; www.bocataxi.com) serves the area. Cabs to the Fort Lauderdale or West Palm airports are $55; the Miami airport is $95.

Delray Beach

☎561 / POP 65,000
Founded by Seminole Indians, and further settled by newly freed slaves and Japanese agriculturists, this melting pot retooled itself for the tourist trade when the railroads chugged through Delray Beach, and never looked back. Local hotels and clubs turned a blind eye to prohibition laws and accommodated everyone. Perhaps this eclectic mix of early residents – from the industrious to the lawless – is why Delray today so effortlessly juggles a casual seaside vibe and a suave urban sophistication. Look for cute beachy shops, high-end antiquaries, thoughtful cultural attractions and wide-ranging restaurant options. Atlantic Ave, the town's main drag, is lined with boutiques, bistros, hotels and more. A few blocks away, a stretch of NE 2nd Ave known as Pineapple Grove has a lower-key hipster vibe.

◉ Sights & Activities

TOP CHOICE Morikami Museum & Japanese Gardens MUSEUM, GARDEN

(www.morikami.org; 4000 Morikami Park Rd; adult/child $12/7; ◎10am-5pm Tue-Sun) West of the beach, away from the hubbub of downtown, is this serene cultural landmark. The initial aim of the so-called Yamato settlement was to attract Japanese families to Florida, where they would introduce new and profitable agricultural techniques to the region. There was one big problem when it opened in 1905: only single Japanese men came; the stable families that founders had hoped for were uninterested. The group soon disbanded, though one settler, Sukjei 'George' Morikami, stuck around and planted some gardens.

Today his plantings skirt the edge of the 200-acre property – with more than a mile of trails – highlighting traditional Japanese landscaping techniques from intricate bonsai to authentic koi-filled ponds, all with monuments favored by Japanese gardeners of various eras. The outstanding Morikami Museum has a collection of 5000 Japanese antiques and objects, including textiles, tea-ceremony items and works of fine art. There are tea ceremonies in the **Seishin-An teahouse** (with museum admission $5) on the third Saturday of the month from October to June.

The museum's **Cornell Cafe** (mains $7-10; ◎11am-3pm), which, despite its Anglo name, serves neo-Japanese cuisine like sweet potato tempura, ginger-roasted duck and sushi rolls, is considered one of the best museum restaurants in the country.

Beaches BEACHES

Among the best sandy spits are the **Atlantic Dunes Beach** (1600 Ocean Blvd), with 7 acres of shorefront sporting clean restroom facilities, volleyball courts and picnic areas, and the **public beach** (Ocean Blvd at Atlantic), a hip gathering spot for young locals and visitors, with excellent surf for swimming. Coin-operated meters charge $1.25 per hour.

Old School Square Cultural Arts Center MUSEUM

(www.oldschool.org; 51 N Swinton Ave) This historic and cultural center, a collection of preserved buildings on 4 acres, injects a dose of culture into Delray. For example, the **Cornell Museum of Art & History** (adult/child $6/free; ◎10:30am-4:30pm Tue-Sat, from 1pm Sun), a restored 1913 elementary-school building with four galleries, shows rotating exhibits of masters and locals and also houses a tearoom and the Delray Historical Archives.

Delray Yacht Cruises BOAT TOURS

(☎561-243-0686; www.delraybeachcruises.com; launching from 777 Atlantic Plaza; adult/child $22/19) The Intracoastal from Delray Beach south to Boca Raton is pretty swanky. Get to know the area better with a narrated sightseeing cruise aboard the 105ft luxury *Lady Atlantic*. Choose from chipper day trips (Wednesday to Sunday at 1:30pm) or romantic sunset cruises (Saturday only, 7pm to 9pm). Departs from the canal side of Veterans Park.

🛏 Sleeping

Delray has tons of sleeping options, from family-run motels to swanky B&Bs – most visitors to nearby Boca Raton crash here.

TOP CHOICE Sundy House Inn B&B $$$

(☎561-272-5678; www.sundyhouse.com; 106 S Swinton Ave; r winter $275-650, summer $139-575; ❄️🐾❅) It's just off Atlantic Ave, but stepping through the front gate at this sumptuous B&B feels like being transported to Bali. Pathways twine through a dense 1-acre garden of trumpet flowers, hibiscus and coconut palms, the vegetation occasionally parting to reveal treasures like vintage bird cages or Chinese lion statues. Guest rooms are British-colonial chic, with heavy wood furniture and dark shutters. But the true highlight is the freshwater pool, designed to look like a jungle pond, complete with darting fish. Even if you sleep elsewhere, don't miss the on-site Sundy House Restaurant (p205).

Crane's Beach House GUESTHOUSE $$

(☎561-278-1700; www.cranesbeachhouse.com; 82 Gleason St; r & ste $150-350; ❄️@❅❅) Through a jasmine-entwined arch, this hidden garden guesthouse has 27 spacious rooms and suites, brightly appointed in colorful Key West style with loads of funky local art. Palm-shaded grotto swimming pools, guest hammocks and a weekend tiki bar add a fun, sociable spirit, and the ultra-friendly staff love to chat and help out with tips and restaurant recommendations.

Colony Hotel & Cabana Club HOTEL $$

(☎561-276-4123, 800-552-2363; www.thecolonyhotel.com; 525 Atlantic Ave; r from $109; ❄️❅)

If you dig historical detail, you'll love this 1926 Atlantic Ave classic, complete with an attendant-operated cage elevator. Rooms are more simple than grand, with hardwood floors and old-fashioned white-tiled bathrooms. Though it's in the center of downtown Delray, its private oceanfront Cabana Club is only 2 miles away by free shuttle.

Seagate Hotel & Spa
HOTEL $$$

(☑561-330-3775; www.theseagatehotel.com; 100 E Atlantic Ave; r winter/summer from $320/150; ❄🏖🛏) Delray's newest hotel would fit right in in elegant, moneyed Boca Raton. Oversized fish tanks serve as decor in the glamorous white-on-white lobby, and the beach-chic theme continues upstairs in the 156 guest rooms, all done up with crisp white linens, rattan furniture and colonial-style shutters. There's a 24-hour gym, a spa, two pools and a free shuttle to the hotel's private beach club.

Wright by the Sea
HOTEL $$

(☑561-278-3355; www.wbtsea.com; 1901 S Ocean Blvd; r winter/summer from $320/150; ❄🏖🛏👪) With a spiffy green lawn and retro blue shutters, this shipshape little seaside hotel recalls the glory days of American family travel. Suites are spacious and clean, with pullout couches and private hallways leading from the living room to the bathroom, a boon for those traveling with children.

✗ Eating

Delray's got one of the area's best eating scenes, with everything from Parisian-style cafes to funky lunch counters to swanky seafood bistros.

TOP CHOICE Bamboo Fire
CARIBBEAN $$

(www.bamboofirecafe.com; 149 NE 4th Ave; mains $9-15; ☉6-10:30pm Wed-Thu, to 11:30pm Fri, noon-11:30pm Sat) On a quiet shopping street a few blocks from the main Delray action, this arty little hole-in-the-wall is a cult favorite for authentic Caribbean fare like conch fritters, jerk chicken and oxtail stew. Veggies and vegans will be in tofu heaven – try it curried, grilled or fried.

Lemongrass
ASIAN $$

(☑561-247-7077; www.lemongrassasianbistro.com; 420 E Atlantic Ave; mains $8-25; ☉11am-3pm & 5:30-10:30pm Mon-Thu, to 11:30pm Fri & Sat, to 10pm Sun) Buddhist art, soothing earth tones and sleek, calming lines in this modern Asian bistro almost make up for the abso-

lute always-totally-packed franticness of it all. The food, though, is divine; hence, the always-totally-packed franticness. Authentic Thai curries, one-off sushi creations (like Sex on the Moon) and Vietnamese noodles are some of the many offerings here.

Sundy House Restaurant
MODERN AMERICAN $$$

(☑561-272-5678; 106 S Swinton Ave; mains $25-41; ☉11:30am-2:30pm Tue-Sat, 6-10pm Tue-Sun, brunch 10:30am-2pm Sun) Nibble goat-cheese salads and fennel-pollen seared salmon at Delray's most romantic restaurant, overlooking the primeval Taru Gardens at the Sundy House Inn. Sunday brunch, complete with made-to-order crepes and a prime rib-carving station, is an extravaganza.

Tryst
PUB $$

(☑561-921-0201; www.trystdelray.com; 4 E Atlantic Ave; mains $12-26; ☉11:30am-10pm Mon-Fri, 5:30-11pm Fri & Sat, 4-10pm Sun, late-night menu 10pm-late) Cashing in on the local-seasonal-organic trend to great success, this upmarket gastropub is a hit for casual bistro food with modern twists: fish 'n' chips with smoked sea salt, steak frites with blue cheese.

Doc's All-American
BURGERS, AMERICAN $

(10 N Swinton Ave; mains $6-15; ☉11am-11pm Sun-Thu, to 1am Fri & Sat; 👪) Great, greasy burgers and thick, frosty shakes are summertime classics at this beloved open-air '50s-style walk-up counter.

🍷 Drinking & Entertainment

Most hipsters head to West Palm to party, but there are a few places worth haunting right here in town.

TOP CHOICE Dada
PUB, CAFE

(www.dada.closermagazine.com; 52 N Swinton Ave) Join the cool cats lounging in this two-story bungalow to sip cocktails, hear poetry readings or live bands and nibble on fare like ravioli, salads and hummus. The front porch, outdoor lanterns and boho vibe all add to the romantic charm.

Falcon House
BAR, CAFE

(www.thefalconhouse.com; 116 NE 6th Ave) Small plates (all $8.88, or $4.44 for half portions) and classic cocktails like sidecars draw the hipsters to this historic bungalow, a few blocks from the bustle of Atlantic Ave. Try to snag an outdoor seat.

TOP SUNRISE SPOTS

Florida has some of the most magical sunrises anywhere. Those pale pinks, lavenders and blues can really invigorate and set the tone for the entire day. When preparing for a sunrise, be sure to set out a few things the night before. The more prepared you are, the easier it'll be to drag yourself out of bed. Be sure to bring warm clothes (early mornings can be surprisingly cool) and bug spray, especially if you are near mangroves. You might also consider packing your camera, sunglasses, a chair or blanket to sit on – and a chilled bottle of champagne and a jug of Florida OJ, for fun.

Almost any spot will do, as long as it faces east. Here's a short list to get the brain working:

» Overlooking the inlet at Fort Lauderdale's South Beach (p190)

» Palm Beach's municipal beach, just off Barton Ave (p210)

» Your Peanut Island campsite (p217)

» Blowing Rocks Preserve (p221)

» Wide, peaceful – and dog-friendly! – Juno Beach (p221)

» Any of the sandy, empty beaches on Hutchinson Island (p223)

Boston's on the Beach   BAR, MUSIC
(www.bostonsonthebeach.com; 40 S Ocean Blvd) This perennial beachfront favorite has nightly live music, great sea views and a party-happy vibe.

🔒 Shopping

Atlantic Ave is one of South Florida's best shopping districts. Look for everything from doggie gift shops to vintage thrift stores to jewelry shops selling necklaces made from shells and sea glass. Antique-lovers should head to the **Delray Beach Antique and Consignment Mall** (www.delraybeachantique mall.com; 695 E Atlantic Ave; ⏰10am-6pm) for 17,000 sq ft of antiques and collectibles.

ℹ Information

Chamber of Commerce (☑561-278-0424; www.delraybeach.com; 64 SE 5th Ave) For maps, guides and local advice.

Library (100 W Atlantic Ave; ⏰9am-8pm Mon-Wed, to 5pm Thu-Sat, 1-5pm Sun) Free internet access in this brand-new facility.

ℹ Getting There & Around

Delray Beach is about 20 miles south of West Palm Beach and 45 miles north of Miami on I-95, US Hwy 1 or Hwy A1A.

The **Greyhound station** (☑561-272-6447; 402 SE 6th Ave) is served by PalmTran. Bus 2 takes you to PBI or Boca Raton; bus 81 services the Tri-Rail station, Amtrak and downtown Delray. **Amtrak** (☑800-872-2745; 345 S Congress Ave), half a mile south of Atlantic Ave, shares a station with **Tri-Rail** (☑800-874-7245; www .tri-rail.com).

Lake Worth

☑561 / POP 36,000

Billing itself as 'Where the tropics begin,' this bohemian community sits further east than any place in South Florida. Meanwhile, just offshore, the Gulf Stream flows further west than anywhere along the coast. This geographical good fortune means Lake Worth has warm weather year-round – but it also enjoys near-constant breezes, especially at night.

With a distinct artsy vibe, this down-to-earth, ragtag beach town boasts a cool collection of eateries and nightspots – not to mention a robust local music scene. Take a stroll along Lake Ave and you'll see a healthy mix of unpretentious visitors and locals milling about; cross over the causeway and you'll find a spectacular sliver of public-access beachfront.

👁 Sights & Activities

Lake Worth is light on sights; most people come here for the beach, or use the town as a budget-priced jumping-off point to explore nearby Delray Beach, Boca Raton or Palm Beach.

Lake Worth Beach   BEACH
This stretch of sand is universally agreed to be the finest beach between Fort Lauderdale and Daytona. Surfers come from miles to tame the waves; everyone else comes to enjoy the fine, white sand. If you're looking for a laid-back place to get sunburned – er...to relax on the beach – this is a great place to do it.

Wet Pleasures DIVING
(☎561-547-4343; www.wetpleasuresfla.com; 312 W Lantana Rd) Thanks to its unspoiled beaches and tranquil waters, Lake Worth enjoys some excellent snorkeling and diving opportunities. Head to this (unfortunately named) dive shop for lessons, equipment and advice. They'll also hook you up with charters to take you diving as far south as the Keys.

Bar Jack Fishing FISHING
(☎561-588-7612; barjackfishing.com; 314 E Ocean Ave; 4hr trips $37) Deep-sea-fishing day trips aboard the *Lady K*, with departures at 8am, 1:30pm and 6:30pm. All gear included.

🛏 Sleeping

Mango Inn B&B $$
(☎561-533-6900; www.mangoinn.com; 128 N Lakeside Dr; r $109-150, ste $190-250; P☀️🛜♨️) All three buildings composing the Mango Inn were built between 1915 and 1920 in a residential area. As a result, this lushly landscaped inn today boasts one of the most secluded settings around. Only three blocks from town and a 15-minute walk to the beach, accommodation ranges from single rooms (many with private entrances) to an adorable cottage with French doors opening on to the heated pool.

Sabal Palm B&B B&B $$
(☎561-582-1090; www.sabalpalmhouse.com; 109 N Golfview Rd; r winter $159-249, summer $115-199; P☀️🛜) A classic, knickknack-and-floral-print B&B, this 1936 house has rooms named after artists (to escape the frilliness, try the Dali Room, with an art deco-y modern vibe).

🍴 Eating

TOP CHOICE Sheila's Bahamian
Conch & BBQ BAHAMIAN $
(US 1 & S 12th Ave; mains $6-13; ⏰11:30am-late) As authentic a Bahamian conch shack as you'll find this side of the Gulf Stream, this concrete bunker hunkers down on a stretch of bare asphalt on the corner of the Dixie Hwy. Smoke pouring from the back chimney attests to the ribs being slow-smoked inside – the sweet-savory smell travels for miles. Order from a window in the wall and sit down at a picnic table in the screened-in porch to wait. Cracked conch (a battered and fried Caribbean sea snail, which tastes like calamari) is crisp and tender, while sides like collards and plantains taste just like granny's Nassau kitchen. Expect a line

at lunch and dinner – sip a cold Bahamas-brewed Kalik beer while you wait.

Cottage FUSION $$
(www.thecottagelw.com; 522 Lucerne Ave; mains $7-16; ⏰11am-2am) The prettiest spot in Lake Worth, the Cottage offers multicultural small plates (hummus, sliders, ahi-tuna tartar) and a dynamic bar featuring local and regional microbrews and wines. Dine alfresco under a twinkling canopy, surrounded by thick weeping figs and in sight of the projector screening classic films, or inside by the light of candles and the one-of-a-kind rainbow-splashed stained-glass bar back.

Pelican DINER, INDIAN $
(610 Lake Ave; mains $3-10; ⏰6:30am-2pm; 🥗) This early-risers' place offers hearty portions of perfectly prepared breakfast, plus a carnival of vegetarian-friendly specials, many with Mediterranean or Middle Eastern flavors (the owners are Pakistani). It also offers divine Indian dinners on Friday from 6pm to 10pm with a range of potent curries and masalas.

Fiorentina ITALIAN $$
(☎561-588-9707; 707 Lake Ave; mains $10-25; ⏰11:30am-midnight) This sleek new Italian joint on Lake Worth's main drag serves up made-for-sharing nibbles like calamari, mint-infused lamb chops and pizzas – don't miss the decadent, oozy *insalata caprese*.

🍷 Drinking & Entertainment

Nightlife is where Lake Worth truly shines, with an outsized wealth of great bars and music venues.

TOP CHOICE Havana Hideout BAR
(www.havanahideout.com; 509 Lake Ave) The most happening place in town, open-air, palm-fringed Havana has live music most nights, a thoughtful draft-beer selection and an on-site taqueria that fills countless stomachs on Taco Tuesdays, when tacos are $1.50 apiece.

Bamboo Room LIVE MUSIC
(☎561-585-2583; www.bamboorm.com; 25 S J St) This favorite spot with an intimate road-house feel features regional and internationally known blues, rockabilly, alt-country and jam bands, drawing music lovers from miles around.

Bar LESBIAN
(2211 N Dixie Hwy) This cozy lesbian-centric pub has a dance floor and hosts regular Pride parties and other events.

Lake Worth Playhouse   THEATER
(☑561-586-6410; www.lakeworthplayhouse.org; 713 Lake Ave; tickets $15-32) Housed in a restored 1924 vaudeville venue, this intimate spot stages classic community theater. The attached Stonzek Studio Theatre screens independent films (tickets $6 to $8).

Lake Worth Drive-In   CINEMA
(☑561-965-4517; 3438 Lake Worth Rd) When was the last time you went to the drive-in?! Screening first-run movies under the stars seven nights a week – drive in, tune in and sit back. Coolers are welcome; dogs are not.

ℹ Information

Chamber of Commerce (☑561-582-4401; www.lwchamber.com; 501 Lake Ave)
Post office (Lucerne Ave btwn J & K Sts)
Public library (15 N M St) Free internet access.

ℹ Getting There & Around

The **Tri-Rail Station** (1703 Lake Worth Rd) is at the intersection of A St. PalmTran bus 61 connects the station to downtown.

Palm Beach

☑561 / POP 9,600

The third-wealthiest city in America, Palm Beach looks every inch the playground for the rich and famous that it is. Palatial Greco-Roman mansions line the shore, Bentleys and Porsches cruise the wide avenues of downtown, streets look clean enough to eat off. Life here revolves around charity balls, Beverly Hills–style shopping and wine-soaked three-hour lunches. Though all the bling may feel a bit intimidating, fear not – much of Palm Beach is within the reach of even the brokest budget traveler. Stroll along the truly gold Gold Coast beach, ogle the massive gated compounds on A1A or window-shop in uber-ritzy Worth Ave – all free.

◉ Sights

TOP CHOICE **Flagler Museum**   MUSEUM
(www.flagler.org; 1 Whitehall Way; adult/child $18/10; ⊙10am-5pm Tue-Sat, noon-5pm Sun) The only true museum on Palm Beach is probably the county's most fascinating. Housed in the spectacular 1902 mansion built by Henry Flagler as a gift for his bride, Mary Lily Keenan, the beaux arts–styled Whitehall Mansion is beyond belief. Built in 18 months, the elaborate 55-room palace was the first residential home to feature both a heating system and an air-con system; features pink aluminum-leaf wallpaper (more expensive, at the time, than gold); impresses with a 4750-sq-ft Grand Hall, the largest single room of any gilded-age private residence; and sports a drool-worthy billiards room. Don't expect many details about Flagler the Railroad Mogul, however, as the emphasis here is on the couple's opulent lifestyle. Gruesome tip: Flagler died as a result of injuries sustained from tumbling down the Grand Staircase, so watch your step.

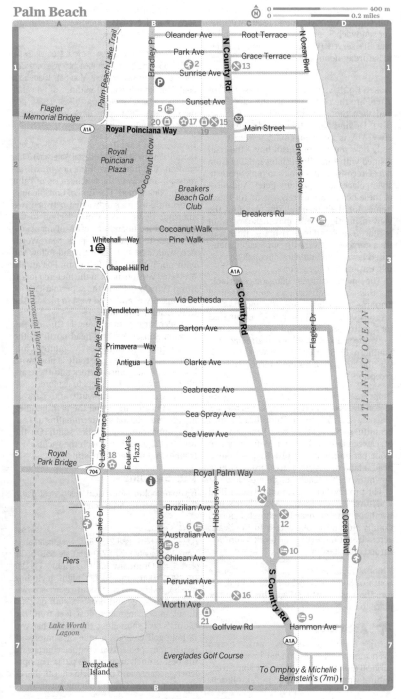

The **Café des Beaux-Arts** treats you to a full 'Gilded Age-Style' lunch ($36), with finger sandwiches, scones and custom-blended teas. It's served 11:30am to 2:30pm Tuesday to Saturday, noon to 3pm on Sunday. Pinkies out!

Ocean Boulevard   SCENIC DRIVE
There are the rich, there are the super-rich, and then there are the denizens of Ocean Blvd. Driving along this seaside stretch of Hwy A1A is an eye-popping lesson in exactly how much money can buy – the road is lined with sprawling estates ranging from faux Greco-Roman temples to pink Spanish-style palaces as big as any hotel. And most of these houses are merely second (or third) homes for their owners! You may find the view inspirational, or it may make you want to start a proletarian uprising – either way, it's a gorgeous drive, with impeccably manicured lawns and snatches of cobalt sea visible through the hedgerows.

The most famous mansion overlooking this stretch of surf and sand is Donald Trump's predictably over-the-top **Mar-a-Lago** (1100 S Ocean Blvd), purchased in 1985 for a paltry $8 million and soon turned into a private club. Best glimpsed driving over Southern Blvd Bridge from West Palm, it was the location of his most recent wedding reception.

Palm Beach Municipal Beach   BEACH
(Ocean Blvd btwn Royal Palm Way & Hammon Ave; ☺sunrise-sunset) One of Palm Beach's two beautiful public beaches, both kept pleasantly seaweed-free by the town. Metered beachfront parking is an absurd $5 per hour – head inland to snag free street-front parking downtown. This beach can get crowded.

For privacy, head north on S Ocean Blvd and turn left on Barton Ave. There's free two-hour parking near the church before S County Rd and public access to the beach across from Clarke Ave, one block before you turned onto Barton.

Phipps Ocean Park   BEACH
South of Southern Blvd on Ocean Blvd, before the Lake Worth Bridge, this is another place to catch rays.

🏃 Activities

Nature Trails & Bike Paths   WALKING, CYCLING
Even among all the artificial luxuries and surgical enhancements, there are some truly natural wonders to be found in Palm Beach.

It's common to see walkers, joggers, inline skaters and cyclists enjoying the fresh air and unmatched views.

Palm Beach Bike Shop BICYCLE, SCOOTER RENTAL
(☑561-659-4583; www.palmbeachbicycle.com; 223 Sunrise Ave; ☺9am-5:30pm Mon-Sat, 10am-5pm Sun) This shop rents all manner of wheeled transportation, including bikes ($39 per day), skates ($39 per day) and scooters ($100 per day).

Palm Beach Lake Trail   WALKING
(Royal Palm Way at the Intracoastal Waterway) This smooth, flat trail runs from downtown almost all the way to the northern tip of Palm Beach. Nicknamed 'The Trail of Conspicuous Consumption,' it's sandwiched between two amazing views: Lake Worth lagoon to the west, and an unending series of mansions to the east. To get here, park near Worth Ave, walk west to S Lake Dr and follow the path north to the Sailfish Club. For an abbreviated version, park in the metered lot off Royal Palm Way (or in the supermarket's lot on Sunset Ave) and head west to pick up the trail. Head north. Gawk.

A nice stretch runs along **N County Rd**. Park on Sunset Ave and head north on the path running to Palm Beach Country Club. At just under 2 miles, the route is lined with houses and magnificent trees and there are plenty of exotic side streets to explore.

You can also head south and park at Phipps Ocean Park. Stroll the path paralleling the Intracoastal and terminating at Lantana, approximately 3 miles south. On the way, try to guess how much the yachts cost. Double that figure; you're still low.

🛏 Sleeping

If you're looking for a deal, head west. Palm Beach properties aren't cheap.

 Breakers   RESORT $$$
(☑561-655-6611, 888-273-2537; www.thebreakers .com; 1 S County Rd; r $270-1250, ste $510-5500; ❋@☎☜) Originally built by Henry Flagler (in 1904 rooms ran $4 per night, including meals), today this 550-room resort sprawls across 140 acres and boasts a staff of 2300 fluent in 56 languages. Just feet from the county's best snorkeling, this palace has two 18-hole golf courses, a mile of semiprivate beach, four pools, two croquet courts and the best brunch around (see p211). For opulence, elegance and old-world charm, there's no other choice. Green Lodging certified.

Omphoy
TOP CHOICE RESORT $$$

(☑561-540-6440; www.omphoy.com; 2842 S Ocean Blvd; r $220-440; ❋@🛜🏊) The first new oceanfront hotel to open in Palm Beach in nearly two decades, the Omphoy debuted in 2010 to the delight of design lovers everywhere. Sleek and moody, all mod wood paneling and smoked glass, it's a hit with a slightly younger crowd of glitterati who find grande dames like the Breakers a bit...old-fashioned. Hip amenities include a yoga studio, a meditation garden and a yummy infinity pool lined with private cabanas. The hotel restaurant, Michelle Bernstein's, draws foodie pilgrims all the way from Miami.

Chesterfield
HOTEL $$$

(☑561-659-5800; www.chesterfieldpb.com; 363 Cocoanut Row; r $159-520, ste $250-945; ❋🛜🏊) From its old-fashioned room keys to the cookie jar in the lobby, this hotel aims for an old-world elegance that's much appreciated by its loyal guests, many of whom have been returning for decades. Room decor is very 'Great White Hunter,' with English plaid wallpaper and murals of monkeys gamboling around the jungle. The hotel's Leopard Lounge, with its painted ceilings and tiger-print banquettes, is a perennial favorite for long lunches and evening piano music.

Brazilian Court
HOTEL $$$

(☑561-655-7740; 301 Australian Ave; www.thebraziliancourt.com; r $205-370, ste $450-2500; ❋🛜🏊) Built in 1926, this swanky resort is an excellent choice for those who want pampering but not obsequiousness. Trendy but timeless, it's got a lovely Mediterranean style, a romantic courtyard and fashionable suites effortlessly blending sleek lines and soft comfort. The on-site Frédéric Fekkai salon and renowned (and ultra-romantic) French **Café Boulud** are major draws, too.

Colony
HOTEL $$$

(☑561-655-5430; www.thecolonypalmbeach.com; 155 Hammon Ave; r $190-450, ste $250-1100; ❋🛜🏊) Like much of Palm Beach, this 90-room hotel recently received a face-lift. Super-stylish – as it should be, towering over Worth Ave – the pale-yellow and hunter-green rooms have hosted the likes of President Clinton and Zsa Zsa Gabor. The beach is a block away, which can be tricky, considering how alluring the alfresco poolside court is. A certified Green Lodging.

Palm Beach Historic Inn
B&B $$

(☑561-832-4009; www.palmbeachhistoricinn.com; 365 S County Rd; r $79-279, ste $129-329; ❋🛜) Housed on the 2nd floor of a landmark building brimming with character, this intimate European-style hotel has well-lit rooms with hardwood floors and brightly painted walls. Best of all: it's two blocks to Worth Ave and less than a block to the beach.

Bradley Park Hotel
HOTEL $$

(☑561-832-7050; www.bradleyparkhotel.com; 2080 Sunset Ave; r $89-200; ❋🛜) Another good midrange choice, this hotel has no lobby to speak of but features plushly comfortable rooms done up in golds and neutrals just a short walk from the shops and restaurants of Royal Poinciana Way.

🍴 Eating

Dining out in Palm Beach is pretty much a high-end affair, though there is a pleasant selection of budget bites. After all, just because you can afford to eat foie gras and kobe beef every night doesn't mean you never crave a big, greasy burger with fries, right? Right?

Michelle Bernstein's
TOP CHOICE MODERN AMERICAN $$$

(☑561-540-6440; www.omphoy.com; 2842 S Ocean Blvd; mains $29-38; ⊙5:30-10pm) Miami celebrity chef Michelle Bernstein riffs on Nouvelle Floridian cuisine at this new restaurant in the trendy Omphoy hotel, drawing on her own Jewish and Latin American heritage, and on the rich produce and seafood offerings of South Florida. Start, for example, with foie gras and tangerine compote, move on to shrimp *tiradito* (a Japanese-Peruvian raw-fish dish), then dig into a main of local cobia fish with shiitakes and Spanish ham. If the homemade donuts are on the dessert menu, we must insist you order them – you'll thank us later. There's the odd grumble about slow service, so come here when you're plenty relaxed.

Circle
AMERICAN, EUROPEAN $$$

(☑561-659-8440, 888-273-2537; www.thebreakers.com; 1 S County Rd; per person $90; ⊙11am-2:30pm Sun) Sure, it's steep, but brunch at the Breakers' storied restaurant will certainly rank among the most amazing you'll ever enjoy. Beneath soaring 30ft frescoed ceilings, surrounded by ocean views and entertained by a roving harpsichordist, guests begin their feast at the breakfast bar, featuring homemade donuts, tropical fruits and an on-demand omelette chef. Next, swing through the carving station, past the cheese table brimming with exotic goat cheeses and more, and make your way to the 4ft-tall ice sculpture standing vigil over the seafood bank overflowing with tiger shrimp, king-crab legs and mussels. Hit the hot-foods banquette and as you weave back to your seat, grab a treat from the caviar station (featuring both American sturgeon and salmon). Gorge. Repeat.

Green's Pharmacy
DINER $
(151 N County Rd; mains $4-13; ⊙breakfast & lunch) This place, housed inside a working pharmacy, hasn't changed since John F Kennedy, looking to slip away from the Secret Service, would stroll across the mint-green linoleum and grab a bite. Choose between a table or a stool at the Formica counter and order from the paper menu just like everyone else, from the trust-fund babies slumming it to the college girls headed to the beach.

Ta-boo
MODERN AMERICAN $$$
(☎561-835-3500; www.taboorestaurant.com; 221 Worth Ave; mains $16-45; ⊙11:30am-10pm Mon-Fri, to 11pm Fri & Sat) If you believe the legend, the Bloody Mary was invented here, mixed to soothe the hangover of Woolworth heiress Barbara Hutton. Today, with the most coveted window seats on Worth Ave, competition is as stiff as her drinks from the previous night. But get past the intricate woodwork and jungle murals, and you'll enjoy a well-executed US bistro meal.

Nick & Johnnie's
FUSION $$
(☎561-655-3319; www.nickandjohnniespb.com; 207 Royal Poinciana Way; mains $14-35; ⊙11am-3am Mon-Sat, from 7am Sun) With a younger, hipper vibe than the average Palm Beach establishment, this stylish California-inspired spot serves everything from kosher hot dogs to ahi-tuna tacos. With its robin's-egg-blue and chocolate walls, abundant mirrors and slick local art, this gargantuan see-and-be-seen spot nails sophisticated fun.

Hamburger Heaven
BURGERS $
(314 S County Rd; mains $6-14; ⊙7am-3pm Mon-Sat) Delightfully frills-free, this bright diner is a locals-magnet. Slip into a vinyl booth and order a burger the way you like it; you may just spot a makeup-free, baseball-hat-hidden celeb while you're chewing.

Bice
ITALIAN $$$
(☎561-835-1600; www.palmbeach.bicegroup.com; 313 1/2 Worth Ave; mains $21-35; ⊙12:30-10:30pm) Be a member (temporarily at least) of the lunching class at this courtyard trattoria, a favorite for white wine–soaked lunches that blend seamlessly into happy hour. Fancy salads and pasta dishes will help soak up the booze.

Cafe L'Europe
EUROPEAN $$$
(☎561-655-4020; www.cafeleeurope.com; 331 S County Rd; mains $30-46; ⊙11am-2:30pm Tue-Fri, 5-10pm Tue-Sun) Reservations are essential if you hope to sample the fab caviar, poached salmon, lamb chops or snapper. The dining room is transcendent, the owners friendly.

Drinking & Entertainment
Palm Beach doesn't party much (must be tired from all that shopping and afternoon wine-sipping), but all the large hotels have swanky bars. If you want to get wild, head across the bridge to West Palm.

Cucina Dell'arte
CLUB
(cucinadellarte.com; 257 Royal Poinciana Way; ⊙7am-3am) Reminiscent of a Florentine cafe, this high-end eatery overflows with warm colors, art and some of the finest glitterati in Palm Beach. Around 10pm they shove the tables out of the way and blast the music. Expect to see dancing botox queens, beautiful visiting fashionistas, desperate old guys and totally normal people soaking it all in. Pretentious enough to be fun; if you arrive wearing a serious face, you'll be sorry.

O Bar
BAR
(www.omphoy.com; Omphoy Hotel, 2842 S Ocean Blvd) Moneyed hipster types sip 'Aum-Foys' (Lillet Blanc, ruby grapefruit, sparkling white wine), guava margaritas and other chic cocktails at this sleek, moodily lit bar in the trendalicious Omphoy hotel.

Leopard Lounge
LOUNGE, LIVE MUSIC
(www.chesterfieldpb.com/dining/bar/; 363 Cocoanut Row; ⊙6:30pm-1am) This swanky fresco-and-leopard-print place attracts a mature crowd and the occasional celeb (neither photos nor autograph hounds are allowed). Live music nightly.

Society of the Four Arts
PERFORMING ARTS
(www.fourarts.org; 2 Four Arts Plaza) The concert series here includes cabaret, the Palm Beach Symphony, chamber orchestras, string quartets and piano performances.

Shopping

The quarter-mile, palm-tree-lined strip along Worth Avenue (www.worth-avenue .com) is Florida's answer to Rodeo Dr. You can trace its history to the 1920s, when the now-defunct Everglades Club staged weekly fashion shows and launched the careers of designers from Bonwit Teller to Elizabeth Arden. Today you'll find more than 200 shops, representing every exclusive brand known: Cartier, Armani, Gucci, Chanel, Dior, Jimmy Choo, Ann Gish, Loro Piana, Emilo Pucci and Hermes are just the beginning. Half the shops close for summer, but it's fun to stroll and window-shop (and celeb-spot), whether you want to lay down your plastic or not. Royal Poinciana Way is another shopping hot spot, with a slightly more accessible price range.

Deja Vu Consignment   FASHION
(219 Royal Poinciana Way; ⊙10am-6pm Mon-Sat, noon-5pm Sun) Palm Beachers don't like to be seen multiple times in the same outfit, so this immaculate secondhand store overflows with very gently used clothes. Most of the items are grandma-friendly, but a little digging can yield fantastic results. The boutique is a bit hidden in a courtyard shopping complex.

Tropical Fruit Shop   FOOD
(www.tropicalfruitshop.com; 261 Royal Poinciana Way) Since 1915, this dim little storefront has been shipping the finest Indian River oranges and grapefruits to friends and family of Palm Beach vacationers. Stop in to pick out a gift basket for a deserving loved one, or just to buy some retro orange candies.

ℹ Information

Note that many shops and restaurants are only open Thanksgiving to Easter. For 'normal' needs, such as internet cafes and laundries, head to West Palm Beach.

Chamber of Commerce (☑561-655-3282; www.palmbeachchamber.com; 400 Royal Palm Way) Excellent maps, racks of pamphlets and several gratis glossy magazines, including *Worth Avenue, Palm Beach Illustrated, Palm Beach Society* and *Vive,* all of which offer convincing arguments for indulgence at every level.

Post office (95 N County Rd)

ℹ Getting There & Around

PalmTran (www.palmtran.org) bus 41 covers the bulk of the island, from Lantana Rd to Sunrise Ave; transfer to bus 1 at Publix to go north or

south along US 1. To get to Palm Beach International Airport in West Palm Beach, take bus 41 to the downtown transfer and hop on bus 44.

Though it's a fairly compact city, the two major downtown neighborhoods, centered on Royal Poinciana Way and Worth Ave, are a fair hike apart.

West Palm Beach
☑561 / POP 100,000

When Henry Flagler decided to develop what is now West Palm Beach, he knew precisely what it would become: a working-class community for the labor force that would support his glittering resort town across the causeway. And so the fraternal twins were born – Palm Beach, considered the fairer of the two, and West Palm Beach, working hard, playing harder and simply being cooler.

West Palm is a groovy place to explore, despite the seemingly never-ending condo construction going on downtown and along the waterfront. It's a community with a surprisingly diverse collection of restaurants, friendly inhabitants (including a strong gay community) and a gorgeous waterway that always seems to reflect the perfect amount of starlight. If you ask most people where to go, they'll send you to CityPlace – the massive alfresco mall that's practically taken over town – so be sure to ask where *else* you should go. CityPlace is cool, but this city has much more to offer.

⊙ Sights

Norton Museum of Art   MUSEUM
(www.norton.org; 1451 S Olive Ave; adult/child $12/5; ⊙10am-5pm Tue-Sat, to 9pm Thu, 11am-5pm Sun) The largest museum in Florida, the Norton opened in 1941 to display the enormous art collection of industrialist Ralph Hubbard Norton and his wife Elizabeth. The Nortons' permanent collection of more than 5000 pieces (including works by Matisse, Warhol and O'Keeffe) is displayed alongside important Chinese, pre-Columbian Mexican and US Southwestern artifacts, plus some wonderful contemporary photography and regular traveling exhibitions. Don't miss the Nessel Wing, consisting of an oval atrium, 14 galleries and a colorful crowd-pleaser: a ceiling made from nearly 700 pieces of handblown glass by Dale Chihuly. Lie back on one of the corner couches and get lost in his magical creation.

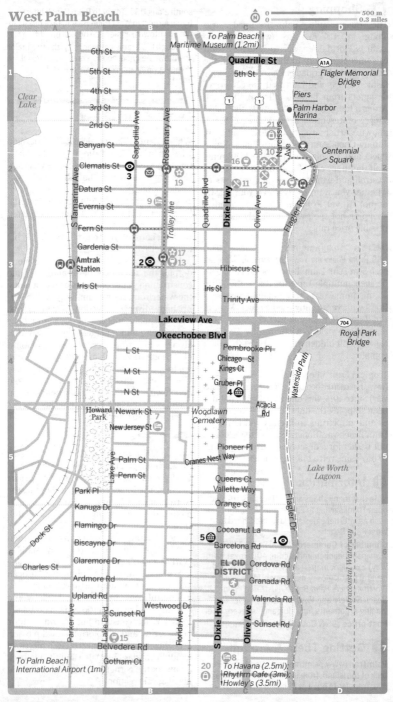

N
0   500 m
0   0.3 miles

Clear Lake

6th St
5th St
4th St
3rd St
2nd St
Banyan St
Clematis St
Datura St
Evernia St
S Fern St
Gardenia St
Iris St

Quadrille St
5th St
To Palm Beach Maritime Museum (1.2mi)

Flagler Memorial Bridge
Piers
Palm Harbor Marina
Centennial Square

Sapodilla Ave
Rosemary Ave
Quadrille Blvd
Dixie Hwy
Olive Ave
Narcissus Ave
Flagler Rd
S Tamarind Ave

Trolley line

Amtrak Station

Hibiscus St
Iris St
Trinity Ave

Lakeview Ave
Okeechobee Blvd

Royal Park Bridge
Waterside Path

L St
M St
N St
Howard Park
Newark St
New Jersey St

Pembrooke Pl
Chicago St
Kings Ct
Gruber Pl
Woodlawn Cemetery
Acacia Rd

Lake Worth Lagoon

Pioneer Pl
Cranes Nest Way
Queens Ct
Vallette Way
Orange Ct

Lake Ave
Palm St
Penn St
Park Pl
Kanuga Dr
Flamingo Dr
Biscayne Dr
Claremore Dr
Charles St
Ardmore Rd
Upland Rd

Cocoanut La
Barcelona Rd
EL CID DISTRICT
Cordova Rd
Granada Rd
Valencia Rd
Sunset Rd

Flagler Dr

Intracoastal Waterway

Dock St

Parker Ave
Lake Blvd
Sunset Rd
Westwood Dr
Florida Ave
S Dixie Hwy
Olive Ave
Belvedere Rd
Gotham Ct

To Palm Beach International Airport (1mi)

To Havana (2.5mi); Rhythm Cafe (3mi); Howley's (3.5mi)

Ann Norton Sculpture Garden
SCULPTURE GARDEN

(www.ansg.org; 253 Barcelona Rd; admission $7; ⊘10am-4pm Wed-Sun) This serene collection of sculptures is a real West Palm gem. The historic house, verdant grounds and enormous sculptures are all the work of Ralph Norton's second wife, Ann. After establishing herself as an artist in New York in the mid-1930s, she became the first sculpture teacher at the Norton School of Art in West Palm and soon married Ralph. When planning the garden, she intended to create a soothing environment for the public to relax in. She succeeded.

After poking through Norton's historic, but simple, antique-filled home, you can wander the grounds and uncover her soaring feats of granite, brick, marble and bronze. Perhaps most awe-inspiring is the 1965 *Cluster*, a collection of seven burka-clad Islamic women done in pink granite. Before leaving, be sure to peek into Norton's light-filled studio, where unfinished pieces and dusty tools lie just as she left them.

CityPlace
PLAZA

(www.cityplace.com; 701 S Rosemary Ave) This massive outdoor shopping and entertainment center is the crown jewel of West Palm Beach's urban-renewal initiative; locals love telling visitors how this area was formerly filled with crack houses. A mix of boutiques and chain stores, CityPlace is a one-stop destination for diners, moviegoers, trendy-shop shoppers and anyone who wants a reason to take a stroll. Its 600,000 sq ft comprise a slew of stores, about a dozen restaurants, a 20-screen movie theater, the Harriet Himmel Theater and 570 private residences – not to mention free concerts in the outdoor plaza. Beautiful but vaguely sterile, CityPlace has nevertheless been immensely successful in bringing all types together in one spot, from tourist families looking for fun on a rainy day to clutches of local ladies out for a day of shopping – and everyone in between.

Clematis Street
STREET

Long before CityPlace came along, there was Clematis St, a hip, bohemian strip bustling with locals doing their shopping, diners looking for a foodie scene, and scads of bar-hoppers come nightfall. In short, this stretch is the most eclectic strip in town – and much of it's also a historic district with a jumbled collection of architecture – Greek Revival, Venetian Revival, Mediterranean Revival and art deco.

Every Thursday night, Clematis plays host to West Palm's signature event, Clematis by Night (p219).

Lion Country Safari
ANIMAL PARK

(www.lioncountrysafari.com; 2003 Lion Country Safari Rd; adult/child $26.50/19.50; ⊘9:30am-5:30pm; ⊞) The first cageless drive-through safari in the country, this incredible animal park puts you in the cage (ie your car) as 900 creatures roam freely, staring at *you*. Equal parts conservation area and safari, the park's 500 acres are home to bison, zebra, white rhinos, chimpanzees and, of course, lions. You tour the safari section in your car (unless it's a convertible; short-term rentals are available), driving slowly, hoping the animals approach the vehicle. The best time to go is when it rains, because the animals are more active when it's cool.

After experiencing this backward-zoo, you can enjoy the aviaries, reptile exhibits, petting zoo, water park and daily educational presentations. The safari is an official rehabilitation facility, taking in injured animals and nursing them back to health before returning them either to the wild or to a more appropriate (less touristy) home. It's a surreal combo of tacky tourism gone wild and animal-loving kindness – but for many people, this is as close as they'll come to seeing wild animals 'in the wild.'

The park is about half an hour's drive west of downtown West Palm.

Peanut Island PARK
(www.pbcgov.com/parks/peanutisland) Plopped right off the northeastern corner of West Palm, Peanut Island was created in 1918 by dredging projects. Originally named Inlet Island, the spit was renamed for a peanut oil–shipping operation that failed in 1946. It has long been a popular spot for boaters to moor and party by day, and in 2005 the county plunked $13 million into island rehabilitation, resulting in Peanut Island Park, which includes a pier, an artificial reef and some pretty sweet campsites.

The island also features a blast shelter built in secret for President John F Kennedy shortly after his 1960 election. Kennedy never used the facility – other than as a jumping-off point for water skiing – but today, the **Palm Beach Maritime Museum** (www.pbmm.org; admission $10; ⊘11am-4pm) offers guided tours of the red-roofed facility.

There are no roads to the island. Visitors must either have their own boats or take the water taxi.

WEST PALM BEACH FOR CHILDREN

For just $1, your kiddos can play to their hearts' content at **Playmobil FunPark** (playmobilusa.com; 8031 N Military Trail, Palm Beach Gardens; admission $1; ⊘10am-6pm Mon-Sat, noon-5pm Sun; ☒), a 20,000-sq-ft indoor play land filled with all the Playmobil figurines and toys in the known universe. Ever think your kid would be jealous of your six-year-old? The FunPark is about 20 minutes' drive northwest of downtown West Palm.

Palm Beach Zoo ZOO
(www.palmbeachzoo.com; 1301 Summit Blvd; adult/child $17/12; ⊘9am-5pm; ☒) The highlight of this compact zoo is the Tropics of the Americas exhibit, a 3-acre recreation of a rainforest, stocked with jaguars, monkeys, snakes, macaws and other tropical creatures. Gator feedings occur regularly and are advertised. The zoo's also home to a few of the last remaining Florida panthers, North America's rarest mammal. Other unusual residents include Komodo dragons (the largest lizard in the world), capybaras (the largest rodent in the world) and red kangaroos, which can hop at speeds of up to 40mph. The zoo is a brief drive south of downtown.

Ragtops Motorcars Museum MUSEUM
(www.ragtopsmotorcars.com; 2119 S Dixie Hwy; adult/child $8/4; ⊘10am-5pm Mon-Sat) This spot was originally a classic-car dealership with three convertible Mercedes, but Ty Houck's incredible automobile collection grew quickly, compelling area automotive enthusiasts to stop by for a look-see. Today, you can test-drive many of the vehicles on display, though it helps to have serious intent to buy. Otherwise, you're free to browse the rarities displayed, including an amphibious 1967 Triumph, a regal 1935 Bentley and a 1959 Edsel station wagon.

🏃 Activities

You'll find several parks around town, many equipped with paved trails suitable for cycling, blading or running.

Okeeheelee County Park OUTDOORS
(7715 Forest Hill Blvd) Five miles south of town, this park has a 6-mile paved path – not to mention a BMX track, a golf course, a water-ski park, a nature center and an equestrian trail.

The most scenic walk – a smooth, waterside path wide enough for all sorts of active folk – is the one that edges the Intracoastal Waterway along Flagler Dr. From Okeechobee Blvd heading north, notable waymarkers include aging but impressive Trump Tower and secluded Palm Harbor Marina.

El Cid District WALKING
Heading south from Okeechobee, you'll enter this lovely neighborhood, packed with multimillion-dollar homes – ranging from Mediterranean Revival to classic Florida bungalow – offering numerous tantalizingly distracting side streets.

STICKY WICKET! THE NATIONAL CROQUET CENTER

Get a real taste of the upper-crusty Palm Beach lifestyle at the **National Croquet Center** (www.nationalcroquet. com; 700 Florida Mango Rd, West Palm Beach), the largest croquet facility in the world (who knew?). Here, genteel sportsmen and women dressed in crisp whites hit balls through wickets on 12 of the world's biggest, greenest, most manicured lawns. It's members-only, but the public is invited to free lessons on Saturday mornings at 9:45am. The pro shop, inside the 19,000-sq-ft plantation-style clubhouse, has all the latest in mallets and croquet wear. The center is about a 10-minute drive southwest of downtown West Palm.

☞ Tours

Palm Beach Water Taxi　　　BOAT TOURS
(☑561-683-8294; www.sailfishmarina.com; 98 Lake Dr, Singer Island) Water taxis run between downtown West Palm and Singer Island ($15), as well as to Peanut Island (round-trip $10), leaving from Singer Island. Additionally, the outfit offers guided tours along the Intracoastal, including 90-minute narrated tours of Palm Beach mansions ($28).

Diva Duck　　　BUS-BOAT TOURS
(☑561-844-4418; www.divaduck.com; adult/child $25/15; 🚗) This hybrid bus-boat gives quacky 75-minute narrated tours of downtown's historic district, CityPlace, the surrounding waterways and the shores of Peanut Island. Yes, the bus really does float in the water. Tours start at CityPlace.

🛏 Sleeping

Skip the depressing chain hotels near the airport and try one of these cool spots.

TOP CHOICE Casa Grandview　　B&B, COTTAGE **$$$**
(☑561-313-9695; www.casagrandview.com; 1410 Georgia Ave; r $175-325; ❄🛜🐕🚗) Hidden behind hedgerows in the historic Grandview Heights neighborhood, this intimate little compound has five B&B rooms, seven cottages and five suite apartments. B&B rooms are in the main house, which has a charming-if-odd medieval-Spanish feel, with a nar-

row stone staircase and elf-sized wooden doors in the walls (where do they go? You'll have to find out for yourself). We love the cozy Library Suite – small but plush. Luxurious cottages have a stylized 1940s beach chic, with vintage signs and bright tiled kitchens – great for families.

🏖 Hotel Biba　　　MOTEL **$$**
(☑561-832-0094; www.hotelbiba.com; 320 Belvedere Rd; r winter/summer $129/79; ❄🛜🏊) Funky, retro Hotel Biba has injected an ordinary motel with pop-art flair. This groovy spot has lots going for it – spare-chic decor in vibrantly colored rooms; a leafy little courtyard with hidden-away pool; and a hip, sexy bar where you'll find the complimentary continental breakfast (featuring local Cuban pastries) in the morning and a thriving lounge scene at night. A block from the Intracoastal, the Biba is perched on the edge of the beautiful El Cid district.

Palm Beach Hibiscus　　　B&B **$$**
(☑561-833-8171; www.palmbeachhibiscus.com; 213 S Rosemary Ave; r $110-280; ❄🛜) Fabulously located just a block from CityPlace, this pair of 1917 homes has four-poster beds, floral prints, abundant light and a cool front porch with wicker chairs. Take a load off and watch the world – including the city trolley, which stops out front – roll by. Reserve ahead for lunch and dinner in the shady tiki bar lounge.

Peanut Island　　　CAMPGROUND **$**
(☑561-845-4445; www.pbcgov.com/parks/peanut island/; sites $23) This tiny island has 20 developed campsites by reservation only and a host of primitive sites right on the sand on a first-come, first-served basis. There are some restrictions, so call or hit the website.

🍴 Eating

The food scene here is an eclectic affair – ethnic eats mixed with quirky spaces and quaint tearooms – and lots of affordable options. Here's where you'll find the antidotes to the fancy fest across the waterway.

TOP CHOICE Rhythm Cafe　　　FUSION **$$**
(☑561-833-3406; www.rhythmcafe.cc; 3800 S Dixie Hwy; mains $15-30; ⏱5:30-10pm Tue-Sat, to 9pm Sun) There's no lack of flair at this colorful, upbeat bistro, in a converted drugstore in West Palm's antiques district, strung with Christmas lights and hung with bright,

bobbing paper lanterns. The menu is equally vibrant, bopping happily from goat-cheese pie to 'the best tuna tartar ever' to pomegranate-infused catch of the day. Dessert's a star – the chocolate butter-cream cake is advertized as 'so good you'll slap your momma!' We don't advise that, but do taste the cake.

Rocco's Tacos & Tequila Bar   MEXICAN $$
(www.roccostacos.com; 224 Clematis St; mains $12-19; ⊙11:30am-11pm Sun & Mon, to midnight Tue & Wed, to 1am Thu-Sat) This saucy Nuevo Mexican restaurant, in the heart of West Palm's Clematis St, is not your typical taqueria. Under the warm twinkle of funky chandeliers enjoy guacamole prepared tableside, fresh-made ceviche, or a range of tacos from pork to mushroom to cactus paddle. And, oh yeah, there are 175 different kinds of tequila to choose from. Just remember the immortal words of George Carlin: one tequila, two tequila, three tequila, floor!

Grease Burger Bar   BURGERS $
(greasewpb.com; 213 Clematis St; burgers $8-12; ⊙11am-late) This buzz-worthy new Clematis St spot is easy to find – just look for the life-sized cow statue on the roof. These are 21st-century burgers – massive, sloppy monsters topped with 'burger bling' like truffled ketchup or 'nuclear relish.' Fancy salads, bratwursts, sweet-potato fries and a full complement of microbrews round out the menu. The dining room, all warm wood and twinkly pub lights, is more neighborhood bistro than fast-food joint.

Havana   CUBAN $$
(www.havanacubanfood.com; 6801 S Dixie Hwy; dinner mains $12-18; ⊙11am-11pm Sun-Thu, to 1am Fri & Sat) Biting into this Cuban restaurant's tender *ropa vieja* (shredded beef in a spicy sauce) is like stepping into Cuba, c 1955. Added bonus: the walk-up window, serving the full menu, is open round the clock. When you need a pick-me-up, nothing works faster or tastes better than the steaming *café con leche* here.

Sunset Bar & Grill   SEAFOOD $$
(eatatsunset.com; 2500 W Broadway; mains $9-28; ⊙11am-2pm Tue-Fri, 5:30-9pm Tue-Thu, to 10pm Fri & Sat) Arty and out-of-the-way, this is the kind of neighborhood cafe we all wish we had on our block. Go for bistro classics like strip steak or crab cakes, or choose from a menu of lighter fare like burgers, gazpacho and Key lime chicken salad. The early-bird special – $15 for three courses, Wednesday, Thursday and Friday before 6:30pm – alone is worth the trip. The restaurant is a five-minute drive north of downtown.

Leila   MIDDLE EASTERN $$$
(☑561-659-7373; www.leilawpb.com; 120 S Dixie Hwy; mains $20-35; ⊙11:30am-2:30pm Mon-Fri, dinner from 5:30pm nightly) Translating as 'exotic night,' cosmopolitan Leila offers mouthwatering starters like grilled Syrian cheeses; main dishes include zesty plates of lamb, beef or veggies. Cap dinner with a muscular Turkish coffee or a post-meal puff from a hookah.

DETOUR: SINGER ISLAND

To reach Singer from West Palm Beach, take Olive Ave north over the bridge (where it's called Broadway) until you hit Blue Heron Blvd; cross the causeway, turn right on Lake Dr and follow it to the **Sailfish Marina** (☑561-42-8449; www.sailfishmarina.com; 98 Lake Dr), which serves brunch on weekends between 8am and 1pm. Grab a seat close to the water, slowly chew your smoked salmon, tropical fruit or fresh Belgian waffles and watch the resident pelicans paddle around the yachts, searching for their own breakfast.

Full? Good. Get in the car and head east to S Ocean Ave, then head north to Beach Rd and scoot into the parking lot. Park and head past the surf shop and gently rolling dunes. You're probably thinking, 'Where are all the people?' Yup, that's why we're here. Pick a spot, spread your towel, lie down and let breakfast digest. Read a magazine. Stroll the beach. Take a dip.

Holy cow, where did the time go? If you're thirsty, nearby **Tiki Waterfront Sea Grill** (200 E 13th St; mains $10-30; ⊙11am-10pm Mon-Fri, from 8am Sat & Sun), a dive teeming with sunburned boaters, has a loud, fun bar, great fish tacos and regular live music. To get there, head back along Blue Heron to Broadway, turn left (south) and then left on E 13th St. The Tiki Grill is at the end of the street. Enjoy your tacos; dance awhile. You're in Florida.

Howley's

AMERICAN $$

(4700 S Dixie Hwy; mains $14-25; ⊙11am-2pm Mon-Thu, to 5am Fri & Sat) Open almost all night, this mint-green 1950s diner's tagline is 'cooked is right, must be right.' The food, which might be described as 'upscale retro' (shake 'n' bake pork chops, crab hash, tiki-style tuna burgers, banana pancakes), certainly tastes right – especially at 2am!

🍷 Drinking & Entertainment

Clematis and CityPlace have a revolving door of ultrachic bar-lounges and late-night dance clubs; they're also home to a couple of great, casual, stalwart hangouts. Fancypants Palm Beach types cross the bridge to party here.

Respectable Street

LIVE MUSIC

(www.respectablestreet.com; 518 Clematis St) Respectables has kept South Florida jamming to great bands for two decades; it also organizes October's MoonFest, the city's best block party. Great DJs, strong drinks and a breezy chill-out patio are added bonuses. See if you can find the hole that the Red Hot Chili Peppers' Anthony Kiedis punched in the wall when they played here.

Feelgood's

CLUB

(www.drfeelgoodswestpalmcom; 219 Clematis St) Co-owned by Mötley Crüe frontman Vince Neil, this 8500-sq-ft rock bar–dance club has shiny choppers, rock memorabilia and a mammoth snake slithering into the rafters. Heads up: the place is packed with girls, from bartenders in skimpy outfits, to dancers on the poles, to customers coming to get wild – some visitors will love it and some will loathe it; bypass this place if you are of the latter variety. Not enough big '80s hair, but it's still good, cheesy fun.

ER Bradley's Saloon

BAR

(www.erbradleys.com; 104 S Clematis St) Mostly a restaurant until about 10pm, at which point the music cranks up, the rum starts flowing, and the mixed-age crowd starts grooving on the multiple decks and bar areas. If you find yourself, um, a little peaky in the morning, come right back for 8am steak and eggs! Great views of the Intracoastal make this a nice happy-hour spot as well.

Roxy's

BAR

(www.roxyspub.com; 309 Clematis St) Home to the county's first liquor license, this joint has changed hands (and locations) several times, but the 42ft mahogany and brass Brunswick Bar has remained since 1935. With 55 beers on tap, a great pub menu and frequent live music, it's still a West Palm favorite.

BB King's

LIVE MUSIC

(www.bbkingclubs.com; 550 S Rosemary Ave) One of bluesman BB King's stable of clubs, this Mississippi Delta–themed nightspot in City-Place has a menu of (mediocre) Southern soul food and an excellent lineup of blues and jazz bands.

HG Roosters

BAR

(www.hgroosters.com; 823 Belvedere Rd) A mainstay of West Palm's thriving gay community, this bar has been offering wings, bingo and hot young male dancers since 1984.

Blue Martini

BAR

(www.bluemartinilounge.com; 550 S Rosemary Ave) This chic CityPlace lounge, known to attract its share of celebs, has three full bars, an extensive martini menu and live music nightly. Dress to impress – it's required.

Florida's largest waterfront music and art festival, **SunFest** (www.sunfest.com) rocks for five days in early May, attracting more than 250,000 visitors and raising money for scholarships for art students. In addition to giving up-and-comers a stage, international acts have ranged from Sheryl Crow to Ziggy Marley.

Every Thursday from 6pm to 9:30pm, the city shuts down the eastern terminus of Clematis St, brings in food carts and crafts vendors and stages a free outdoor music festival under the stars. The kid- and dog-friendly **Clematis by Night** (www.clematisbynight.net) spotlights great local and national acts playing everything from rock to swing. Drink up: proceeds from the beer truck are split between the city and the nonprofit group pouring drinks that night.

On Friday and Saturday, CityPlace hosts **free outdoor concerts** (www.cityplace.com) from 6pm to 10pm in front of the gorgeous CityPlace Fountain. Bands stick to familiar rock, R&B and occasionally country sounds.

🛍 Shopping

Clematis St and CityPlace have tons of both chain and nonchain boutiques, home-decor shops and more.

Greenmarket MARKET

On Saturday morning, just north of the plaza at 2nd St and Narcissus Ave (where local schoolkids frolic in the fountains on hot afternoons), this delightful market offers treats ranging from locally grown avocados and orchids to organic coffee and dog treats.

Antiques Row ANTIQUES

(S Dixie Hwy) Just south of town, this peerless market has more than 50 antiquaries. You're sure to unearth an incredible find from a Palm Beach estate.

ⓘ Information

The *Palm Beach Post* (www.palmbeachpost. com) is the largest paper. The visitor center publishes several vacation-planning guides, available online (www.palmbeachfl.com).

Library (100 Clematis St) Free internet access.

Post office (640 Clematis St)

Visitor center (☎800-554-2756; www.palm beachfl.com; 1555 Palm Beach Lakes Blvd)

ⓘ Getting There & Around

Palm Beach International Airport (PBI; ☎561-471-7420; www.pbia.org) is the king of medium-sized airports, refreshingly small and hassle-free. PBI is served by most major airlines and car-rental companies. It's about a mile west of I-95 on Belvedere Rd. **PalmTran** (www.palmtran .org) bus 44 runs between the airport, the train station and downtown ($1.25).

In a brilliant display of civil engineering, **Greyhound** (☎561-833-9636; 215 S Tamarind Ave), **Tri-Rail** (☎800-875-7245; 203 S Tamarind Ave) and **Amtrak** (☎561-832-6169; 201 S Tamarind Ave) share the same building, the historic Seaboard Train Station. PalmTran serves the station with bus 44 (from the airport).

Once you're settled, driving and parking is a cinch, plus a cute and convenient (and free!) trolley runs between Clematis St and CityPlace starting at 11am.

TREASURE COAST

If you ask people to describe Florida, many would probably mention Miami's art-deco scene, Fort Lauderdale's party scene, Palm Beach's mansion scene…and skip straight to Disney. While the area north of West Palm – dubbed the Treasure Coast – doesn't have many party strips or flashy mansions, it does have much to offer.

The Treasure Coast gets its name from the same source from which the Gold Coast gets its moniker – for being the site of numerous treasure-laden shipwrecks over the years. In fact, today the Treasure Coast is where you'll find Florida's true jewels, in the form of unspoiled paradise.

Industrialist billionaire and philanthropist John D MacArthur once owned almost everything from Palm Beach Gardens to Stuart, and he kept it mostly pristine during his life. Over time, he grew concerned that Florida's real-estate bonanza would compromise – or destroy – what he considered paradise. Therefore, in his will, he stated that thousands of acres would be kept wild, and the rest would be deeded out incrementally, in order to save the oceanfront property from Miami's fate. And you know what? His plan worked.

John D Macarthur State Park

While this **state park** (www.macarthurbeach .org; 10900 Jack Nicklaus Dr; admission per vehicle $5; ☺8am-sunset) is one of the smallest in the region, it has among the best turtle-watching programs around, as loggerhead, green and leatherback turtles nest along the beach in June and July. It's home to several aquariums and a spectacular 1600ft boardwalk spanning the mangroves of Lake Worth Cove. The on-site nature center offers guided (single/double $20/35) and unguided (single/double $10/15 per hour) **kayak trips**.

In June and July, lucky visitors might catch a glimpse of hatching baby sea turtles during the ranger-led turtle walks, led nightly at 8:30pm.

Jupiter & Jupiter Island

☎561 / JUPITER POP 50,600 / JUPITER ISLAND POP 670

Jupiter is largely ritzy-residential (it's one of the wealthiest communities in America). For visitors, it's best seen as a jumping-off point for exploring the area's fantastic parks, nature preserves and beaches. Unlike those of its southerly neighbors Palm Beach and Boca Raton, the beaches around here are largely untouched by condo development.

◉ Sights & Activities

Jonathan Dickinson State Park PARK

(16450 SE Federal Hwy; admission per vehicle $6; ☺8am-sunset) With almost 11,500 acres to explore, this is an excellent state park between US Hwy 1 and the Loxahatchee River. There's no ocean access in the park, but its attraction lies in its several habitats: pine flatwoods, cypress stands, swamp and increasingly endangered coastal sand-pine scrub. Ranger-led nature walks leave at 9am Sunday from the Cypress Creek Pavilion, and campfire programs are offered Saturday at dusk next to the Pine Grove campground.

You can rent canoes and kayaks from the **concession stand** ([☎]561-746-1466; www.florida parktours.com; ⊙9am-5pm). Canoes cost $16 for two hours; kayaks cost $15 for two hours. You can also rent motorboats at $50 for two hours, but mind the manatees. Guided-tour boat rides of the Loxahatchee River are available throughout the day (adult/child $19/12).

There are also several short-loop **hiking and bicycle trails**, the most popular of which is the Kitching Creek Trail, just north of the boat landing, walkable in about 1½ hours. Visit www.clubscrub.org for details on cycling options.

Jupiter Inlet Lighthouse   LIGHTHOUSE
(www.jupiterlighthouse.org; intersection Capt Armour's Way, US Hwy 1 & Beach Rd; adult/child $9/5; ⊙10am-5pm Tue-Sun) Built in 1860, this historic lighthouse hasn't missed a night of work in more than 100 years and is among the oldest lighthouses on the Atlantic coast. Visitors can climb the 108 steps and see the surrounding area (including the ocean). Tours to the lighthouse depart every half hour. There's some interesting Seminole and pioneer Florida memorabilia in the small (and woefully disorganized) museum.

Hobe Sound National
Wildlife Refuge   WILDLIFE REFUGE
(US 1) A 1035-acre federally protected nature sanctuary, Hobe Sound National Wildlife Refuge has two sections: a small slice on the mainland between Hobe Sound and US Hwy 1, opposite the Jonathan Dickinson State Park; and the main refuge grounds at the northern end of Jupiter Island.

The Jupiter Island section has 3½ miles of beach (it's a favorite sea-turtle nesting ground), mangroves and sand dunes, while the mainland section is a pine scrub forest. In June and July, nighttime turtle-watching walks occur on Tuesday and Thursday (reservations necessary), and birding trips can be arranged through the Hawley Education Center at Blowing Rocks Preserve. There's also a leafy bike path.

WOOF! DOG-FRIENDLY BEACH   221

Traveling with a four-legged companion? The county's only dog-friendly beach is in nearby Juno Beach. To get there, follow Indiantown Rd east to A1A and turn right (south). The dog-friendly stretch begins across from Xanadu Lane and stretches 2 miles south, to Marcinski Rd. Good luck finding more delighted grins anywhere along the east coast.

Blowing Rocks Preserve   NATURE RESERVE
(admission $2; ⊙9am-4:30pm) This preserve encompasses a mile-long limestone outcrop riddled with holes, cracks and fissures; when the tide is high and there's a strong easterly wind (call for conditions), water spews up as if from a geyser. Bring a tripod and an empty memory card. Even when seas are calm, you can hike through four coastal biomes: shifting dune, coastal strand, interior mangrove wetlands and tropical coastal hammock.

Finding the refuge is a little tricky, as there's no signage: from US Hwy 1, take Bridge St (708 east) to Hobe Sound. Turn left on Beach St (707). Travel about 3 miles; the refuge is on your right.

Palm Beach International
Raceway   RACETRACK
(www.racepbir.com; 17047 Bee Line Hwy) Located on 200 acres of wooded property, this motorsports park has a 2.25-mile 10-turn course and regular race events of all stripes. But the real fun here is the twice-weekly 'Test & Tune' on the NHRA-sanctioned 0.25-mile drag strip. Every Wednesday and Friday from 6pm to 11pm, you're allowed to race your beater against another vehicle on the track. Just slip on the helmet you brought (mandatory if you plan to drive over 13.99mph), stage and burn rubber. After your run, pick up your time slip to see how your vehicle performed. It's $25 to race, $10 to watch.

Roger Dean Stadium   STADIUM
(www.rogerdeanstadium.com; 4751 Main St) It may not be a 'nature' activity, but an afternoon here will get you outdoors. This small but immaculate stadium is home to spring-training action for the Florida Marlins, the St Louis Cardinals and various minor-league teams. Ticket prices vary; call for details.

WHAT THE? BURT REYNOLDS & FRIENDS MUSEUM

Does Burt Reynolds' moustache drive you wild? Do you envy/adore his famously luxurious chest hair? If so, you simply must make the pilgrimage to this delightfully oddball museum (www.brift.org; 100 N US Hwy 1; admission $5; ☺10am-4pm Thu-Sun), housing all manner of personal memorabilia belonging to the 1970s star (and Jupiter resident). Highlights include boots once belonging to cowboy actor Roy Rogers, letters from Elizabeth Taylor and a baseball autographed by Mickey Mantle.

Jupiter Outdoor Center   KAYAKING
(☑561-747-0063; www.jupiteroutdoorcenter.com; 1000 Coastal A1A) The center rents kayaks and standup paddleboards ($35/40 per half day) and organizes themed kayak trips (from $45) in the area, like languid moonlight excursions and exploratory trips around Jupiter Inlet's mangroves.

🍴 Sleeping & Eating

Jupiter Waterfront Inn   HOTEL $$
(☑561-747-9085; www.jupiterwaterfrontinn.com; 18903 SE Federal Hwy; r from $99; ❄🐾🗺) As sunny and friendly as can be, this spick-and-span new highway-side inn has huge rooms with flat-panel TVs, Intracoastal views and a marina for boaters. Decor is beachy, with Spanish-tile floors and cheerful yellow walls. For romance, ask for a room with an in-suite Jacuzzi tub. The inn's own 240ft fishing pier is a big hit with anglers.

Jupiter Beach Resort   HOTEL $$$
(☑561-746-2511; www.jupiterbeachresort.com; 5 N A1A; r & ste $199-900; ❄🐾🗺🛏) This elegant, slightly stuffy Key-lime-and-chocolate destination offers rooms (and over-the-top penthouse suites) sporting British-colonial style and million-dollar views. Inside, the floors are lined with Turkish marble; outside, the resort provides 1000ft of secluded beach, tennis courts and a heated swimming pool with a poolside bar.

Jonathan Dickinson State Park   CAMPGROUND $
(☑772-546-2771; 16450 SE Federal Hwy; sites $26) This state park has campgrounds with hot showers, plus rustic cabins, which have a minimum two-night stay on weekends.

TOP CHOICE **Little Moir's Food Shack**   CARIBBEAN, SEAFOOD $$
(www.littlemoirsfoodshack.com; 103 S US Hwy 1; mains $9-24; ☺11am-9pm Mon-Sat) If you didn't know to look, you'd walk right past this strip-mall hole-in-the-wall, its windows covered by bamboo curtains. But then you'd miss out on one of Florida's genuine foodie finds, a neo-Caribbean cafe serving a mouth-exploding blend of global flavors: sweet potato–crusted fish, Jamaican pepperpot soup, lobster egg rolls. The seafood is as fresh as you'd expect (but so rarely find) from a seaside town, and the microbrew list is sure to please. Sound awesome? It is, and the secret's out – this humble food shack has already been raved about in the national media as far away as Boston.

Square Grouper   AMERICAN $
(www.squaregrouper.net; 1111 Love St; snacks $1-7; ☺noon-midnight Sun-Thu, to 1am Fri & Sat) If this

---

DETOUR: KAYAKING THE LOXAHATCHEE RIVER

One of two federally designated 'Wild and Scenic' rivers in the state, the free-flowing Loxahatchee River is home to a wide range of habitats, from tidal marsh riverines and dense mangrove communities to tidal flats and oyster bars. Translated as 'River of Turtles,' the coffee-colored river, which flows north, is home to countless shelled reptiles, as well as herons, ospreys, otters, raccoons, the occasional bobcat – and lots of alligators. For a great day exploring the various aquatic preserves here, no one beats Riverbend Park's Canoe Outfitters (☑561-746-7053; www.canoeskayaksflorida.com; 9060 W Indiantown Rd; 2-person canoes/single kayaks $50/40), which provides access to this lush waterway. From the launch, paddle to the right for thick, verdant waterways overhung with fallen branches and a small but thumping rapid; paddle to the left for open vistas and plentiful picnic areas. Canoes are good for families, but difficult to maneuver in this narrow waterway, so choose wisely. This terrific day out is gentle enough to be kid-friendly but eye-popping enough to appeal to the discerning adventurer.

Old Florida dive looks familiar, it's because the video for the Alan Jackson-Jimmy Buffett tune 'It's Five O'Clock Somewhere' was shot here. Perched on the water, with an ample (sandy) dance floor, this place is an ultracasual gem in an otherwise well-heeled town. It's a bit hard to find – drive to the end of Love St and turn right.

ⓘ Getting There & Around

Though I-95 is the quickest way through this area, do yourself a favor and get off the freeway. US Hwy 1 runs consistently up the coastline, and Hwy A1A jumps back and forth between the mainland (where it's the same as US Hwy 1) and various barrier islands.

Stuart & Around

☑772 / POP 16,000

Often overlooked in favor of its more famous southern neighbors, Stuart has long been a hush-hush destination for sporty millionaires and their gleaming yachts. Fishing is tops here, which explains Stuart's nickname: 'Sailfish Capital of the World.' It wasn't until the late 1980s, however, that Stuart got its first exit off I-95, which is when the wave of rich folk, leaving places like Boca, started coming by in earnest.

Though Stuart's retro, sherbet-colored downtown has some cute restaurants and boutiques, the real draws of the region are the adjacent beach areas of Jensen Beach and Hutchinson Island. Jensen Beach, on the mainland facing the Indian River Lagoon, caters to fishermen and arty types, with a tiny-but-adorable downtown lined with craft shops and tackle stores. Just across the water by the bridge, narrow Hutchinson Island is where visitors go for sun and fun.

◉ Sights & Activities

Hutchinson Island   ISLAND
This long, skinny barrier island, which begins in Stuart and stretches north to Fort Pierce, features a stunning array of unspoiled beaches, all with free access, excellent for walking, swimming and even some snorkeling. Most of the access roads and parking lots are dirt, but barring a 40-day flood, you're unlikely to get stuck. The beaches get less touristed the further north you go.

If you've got your four-footed friends with you, be sure to head to the only dog-friendly beach in St Lucie County, Walton Rocks, across from the St Lucie Power Plant (6501 Hwy A1A).

Elliott Museum
(☑407-225-1961; www.elliottmuseumfl.org; 825 NE Ocean Blvd, Hutchinson Island; adult/child $8/4; ⊙10am-4pm Mon-Sat, 1-4pm Sun) If you need a break from the sun, stop at this quirky museum, dedicated to inventor Harmon Elliott. In this eclectic collection of old Americana exhibits you'll see a fabulous miniature circus, recreations of old-time shops (an apothecary, a barber shop), a Victorian parlor and a typical 18th-century girl's bedroom. It's a strange and diverse collection that's a fun switch from the rest of town. Note: the Elliott Museum is currently closed while they build a newer, bigger facility, slated for a 2013 opening.

Florida Oceanographic Coastal Science Center
(☑772-225-0505; www.floridaoceanographic.org; 890 NE Ocean Blvd; adult/child $10/5; ⊙10am-5pm Mon-Sat, noon-4pm Sun) Right across from the Elliott Museum, this center is great for kids, who'll be mesmerized by the four 300-gallon tropical-fish aquariums, a worm reef and touch tanks with crabs, sea cucumbers and starfish. They've got an excellent menu of guided tours and nature programs, from guided nature walks at 10:15am (except Sunday) to daily stingray feedings (10:30am and 2pm Monday to Saturday, 1pm Sunday) to summer sea turtle–spotting expeditions. Check out the website for a full schedule.

St Lucie Inlet State Park   PARK
(4810 SE Cove Rd; admission per boat $3) Accessible only by boat, the main part of this park protects 6 sq miles of reef in the Atlantic Ocean just off Jupiter Island. Twelve species of hard and soft coral inhabit the reef, so anchor on the sandy bottom. Snorkeling and scuba diving are permitted; depths range from 5ft to 35ft. Complementing the 2.7 miles of beaches are toilets and running water, piers and hiking trails. From the mainland at the eastern end of Cove Rd, a 3300ft boardwalk runs from dock to beach.

If you want to explore the miles of tidal creek this park has to offer, rent a kayak from Island Water Sports (☑772-334-1999; www.iwsjensen.com; 3291 B NE Indian River Dr; singles/tandems per day $50/60). In most cases, you can arrange delivery of the kayaks to your hotel, but if you're headed here, collect the boats yourself.

Lady Stuart
FISHING

(☑772-286-1860; www.ladystuart.com; 555 NE Ocean Blvd, Stuart; adult/child $40/30) The crew will take you out, bait your hook, and clean and fillet any fish you catch. There are no guarantees of hooking dinner, but they know where to sink their lines.

Hot Tuna Charters
FISHING

(☑772-334-0401; www.hottunacharters.com; half-/full day $450/650) Run by native Floridian Captain Wakeman – boasting over 20 years' experience and holding 10 world records on both fly and conventional tackle – Hot Tuna will help you find and catch stuff that swims.

Snook Nook
FISHING

(☑772-334-2145; www.snooknook.net; 3595 NE Indian River Dr; per day $7.50; ⏰6am-8pm Mon-Sat, to 6pm Sun) If you don't feel like leaving shore, check the fishing report at www.snooknook.net/Fishing_Reports.html, rent a rod and head to the water.

🛏 Sleeping

Hutchinson Island has a handful of upscale resorts (the Marriott is the pick of the litter), while Jensen Beach caters to anglers. You'll find mid-price chains and family-run budget motels on Federal Hwy in Stuart.

TOP CHOICE River Palm Cottages & Fish Camp
COTTAGE $$

(☑772-334-0401; www.riverpalmcottages.com; 2425 NE Indian River Dr, Jensen Beach; winter $139-429, summer $89-299; ❄🐾🛜🏊) Perched on Indian River, this paradisiacal complex has adorable cottages with kitchens, some with waterfront views and all sporting cool tiled floors and a breezy, Caribbean style. The peaceful grounds are lush with grassy patches, palm trees and other flowering and fruit-bearing varieties, including guava and the exotic praying-hands banana tree. There's a private beach, a ping-pong table and a pier for watching sunsets. Pets are welcome, too.

Jensen Beach Bed & Breakfast
B&B $$

(☑772-225-2272; www.jensenbeachbb.com; 1899 NE Jensen Beach Blvd; r $99-109; ❄🛜) This old-fashioned B&B reminds us of classic European above-the-pub corner hotels, situated on the 2nd floor over an Irish restaurant in arty downtown Jensen Beach. With wood-paneled walls and chenille bedspreads, the six rooms have an appealing lodgelike feel.

Inn Shepard's Bed & Breakfast
B&B $$

(☑772-781-4244; www.innshepard.com; 601 SW Ocean Blvd; r $125-185; ❄🛜) Overlooking a waterfront park just off a busy road near downtown Stuart, this sweet lavender cottage has four comfortable rooms and a communal hot tub and fire pit on the back patio. Decor is homey and feminine, with pale watercolor walls and white quilts.

Savannas Recreation Area
CAMPGROUND $

(☑772-464-7855; www.stlucieco.gov/parks/savannas.htm; 1400 Midway Rd; tent sites $15; ⏰Nov-May) Covering 550 acres and five distinct biological communities – pine flatwoods, wet prairie, marsh, lake and scrub – the Savannas features both primitive and developed campsites.

🍴 Eating

TOP CHOICE Harry & the Natives
AMERICAN $$

(www.harryandthenatives.com; 11910 SE Federal Hwy, Hobe Sound; mains $8-19; ⏰7am-9pm Tue-Sat; 🚹) 'Practice Safe Lunch: Use Condiments' proclaims the sign, one of many, many goofy puns and jokes that adorn the walls and the menu of this Old Florida roadhouse a few miles south of Stuart. The food – egg breakfasts, quesadillas, jambalaya, Key lime pie – is likeable, but the vibe's what's unforgettable. Music on the outdoor stage ranges from aging Jimmy Buffett types to hip young singer-songwriters.

Crawdaddy's
CAJUN $$

(☑772-225-3444; www.crawdaddysrestaurant.org; 1949 NE Jensen Beach Blvd, Jensen Beach; mains $13-20; ⏰11am-10pm Sun-Wed, to 11pm Thu-Sat) With a menu drenched in a Louisiana tradition – think rum-soaked shrimp and the New Orleans picnic (for hungry seafood lovers) – and a twinkling courtyard hosting live music on weekends, this place is a sliver of the French Quarter right near the beach.

11 Maple St
MODERN AMERICAN $$$

(☑772-334-7714; www.11maplestreet.net; 3224 NE Maple St, Jensen Beach; mains $32-45; ⏰6-10pm Wed-Sun) This romantic spot, a series of rooms inside a historic cottage, has a daily changing menu of eclectic large and small plates, from roasted pompano with saffron essence to grilled elk tenderloin. For special-occasion dinners, this is your best bet short of driving south to Palm Beach.

Mulligan's Beach House
AMERICAN, PUB $$

(www.mulligansrestaurant.net; 2019 Jensen Beach Blvd, Jensen Beach; mains $7-18; ⏰8am-11pm

Mon-Wed, to 1am Thu-Sat, to 10pm Sun) Hawaiian shirts meet Irish pub at this popular casual dining spot, serving a crowd-pleasing menu of conch fritters, burgers, pizzas and fish. It ain't gourmet, but it's a fun spot for a drink and some nibbles, right in downtown Jensen Beach.

Conchy Joe's   CARIBBEAN, AMERICAN **$$**
(www.conchyjoes.com; 3945 NE Indian River Dr, Jensen Beach; mains $10-22; ⏱11:30am-10pm) Overlooking St Lucie River, drinks and pub grub at the palm tree–filled bar are a surefire blast, especially when the band's jamming.

Fredgie's Hot Dog Wagon   HOT DOGS **$**
(3595 NE Indian River Dr, Jensen Beach; hot dogs from $2; ⏱11am-4pm Wed-Sun) This vending cart has been dishing dogs for nearly two decades.

🛍 Shopping

Historic downtown Stuart overflows with cute shops and antique stores. Jensen Beach is also tops for shopping, especially for arts and crafts – check out the galleries on Jensen Beach Blvd and Maple St.

ℹ Information

The **chamber of commerce** (☎772-287-1088; www.stuartmartinchamber.org; 1650 S Kanner Hwy; ⏱8:30am-5pm Mon-Thu, to 4pm Fri) is about a mile south of town.

ℹ Getting There & Away

Though I-95 is the quickest way to and from this area, if you've got some time, treat yourself and explore the local roads. South of Stuart, US Hwy 1 runs up the coastline and then jogs west, into and through town. If you're headed between Stuart and Fort Pierce, the best route is the slow-but-scenic NE Indian River Dr, with gorgeous waterfront homes to the west and the water to the east.

Fort Pierce

☎772 / POP 42,600
Fort Pierce may not have as many millionaires as its neighbors, but it does have plenty to recommend it: a nice, sleepy feel, top sport fishing and some great beaches. Downtown, though newly renovated, often feels like a ghost town, with lots of vacancies and few people. Orange Ave is the main drag, far more vibrant than adjoining blocks.

◉ Sights & Activities

Manatee Observation Center   NATURE CENTER
(www.manateecenter.com; 480 N Indian River Dr; admission $1; ⏱10am-5pm Tue-Sat, noon-4pm Sun Oct-Jun, 10am-5pm Thu-Sat Jul-Sep; 🚼) Right downtown, this center educates the public on the plight of the manatee. Videos, exhibits and even the gift shop teach boaters how to avoid hurting the creatures – and the rest of us how our lifestyle has indirectly eradicated most of the manatee population. Manatee sightings are common-ish in winter, however, when waters along the museum's observation deck, warmed by the nearby power plant, are home to between eight and 20 of the precious creatures.

Florida Dolphin Watch   ANIMAL WATCHING
(☎772-466-4660; www.floridadolphinwatch.com; up to 6 people $175) Wild dolphins are spotted routinely in the Indian River Lagoon, occasionally from the riverbank. If you want to increase your chances of seeing them, you need to get on the water. This outfitter offers two-hour dolphin-spotting tours aboard its comfortable 25ft 'tri-toon.' With a cap of six passengers, the 15-mile charter comes complete with a wildlife library, binoculars, water and soda. It also does all kinds of other nature tours – just ask.

**Fort Pierce Inlet State
Recreation Area**   PARK
(905 Shorewinds Dr; admission per vehicle $6; ⏱8am-sunset) This 3400-acre park has everything you'd want in a waterfront recreation spot: sandy shores, verdant trails, mangrove swamps with a beautiful bird population and a family-friendly picnic area. It's also home to endangered beach stars, a low-lying sedge growing on the dunes and near the boardwalks, so stick to the sand, Bigfoot.

Heathcote Botanical Gardens   GARDENS
(www.heathcotebotanicalgardens.org; 210 Savannah Rd; adult/child $6/2; ⏱9am-5pm Tue-Sat, from 1pm Sun) Beginning as a Japanese-style garden in 1955, today this small but lovely botanical garden features a rainforest, a collection of palm trees from around the world and a historic garden with century-old bonsai trees.

UDT-SEAL Museum   MUSEUM
(www.navysealmuseum.com; 3300 Ocean Blvd; adult/child $8/4; ⏱10am-4pm Mon Jan-Apr only, to 4pm Tue-Sat, noon-4pm Sun) The world's only museum dedicated to the elite warriors of Naval Special Warfare, this Hutchinson Island exhibit features once-top-secret tools

SNORKEL A SPANISH GALLEON

In 1715, a Spanish flotilla was decimated in a hurricane off the Florida coast. One of the ships, the **Urca de Lima** went down (relatively) intact. Today, the wooden-hulled ship is partly exposed within snorkeling distance from the beach. To get here, exit Ocean Blvd (Hwy A1A) at Pepper Park and walk north along the beach about 1000yd from the park boundary. The wreck is about 200yd from shore on the first offshore reef, under 10ft to 15ft of water.

and weapons used by the most elite combat forces of the US.

🛏 Sleeping & Eating

Stuart and Jensen Beach offer way more sleeping options. For eating, there are a handful of waterfront places on Seaway Dr, and more on downtown's Orange Ave.

Sandhurst   HOTEL **$**
(☎866-395-7263; www.thesandhurst.com; 1230 Seaway Dr; r from $85; P✳🛜🏊) This big sherbet-colored box doesn't have a whole heck of a lot of personality, but it's one of the nicer options in town – rooms are clean and bright, management friendly.

TOP CHOICE ⟩ **Archie's Seabreeze**   PUB **$**
(www.archiesseabreeze.com; 401 S Ocean Dr; mains $5-10; ⊙9am-midnight, kitchen closes 10pm) This open-air biker-friendly bar has been partying since 1947. Look for big ol' picnic tables, raw-oyster shooters, pool tables and the coolest handmade floor ever. Karaoke night is Wednesday – time to polish up your Guns 'n' Roses repertoire?

Tiki Bar & Restaurant   AMERICAN, CARIBBEAN **$$**
(www.originaltikibar.com; 2 Ave A; mains $9-22; ⊙11am-10pm) Adjacent to the Fort Pierce Marina, a huge thatched roof covers two bars and dozens of tables. The waffle fries are supreme, as are the 360-degree water views (look for dolphins and manatees cruising past). Dockage available.

❶ Information

Seven Gables House (☎772-468-9152; 482 N Indian River Dr; ⊙9am-5pm Mon-Fri, 10am-4pm Sat) The visitor center in this historic building has loads of maps.

❶ Getting There & Around

From Stuart, take I-95 or US Hwy 1 (a gorgeous drive that's highly recommended as a trip unto itself!) about 25 miles north. To get downtown from I-95, take the Orange Ave exit east, crossing US Hwy 1 (here called N 4th St).

Orlando & Walt Disney World

Best Places to Eat

» Ravenous Pig (p240)

» Yellow Dog Eats (p249)

» Dandelion Communitea Café (p249)

» Jiko (p282)

» Dessert Lady Café (p247)

Best Places to Stay

» Grande Lakes Orlando (p245)

» Celebration Hotel (p247)

» Portofino Bay (p295)

» Park Plaza Hotel (see boxed text, p241)

» Omni Orlando Resort at Championsgate (p246)

Why Go?

Play quidditch with Harry Potter, disappear into the Twilight Zone in a haunted elevator, whip through the air on a sea monster. In Orlando, the Theme Park Capital of the World, it's all about high-adrenaline fun wrapped up in the mystyique of storytelling and fantasy – Walt Disney World, Universal Orlando Resort (including the Wizarding World of Harry Potter), SeaWorld, Discovery Cove and the water-park Aquatica cluster within 15 miles of one another, and Legoland is an hour's drive. Their carefully constructed worlds, dripping with illusion and magic and filled with rides, shows and parades, promise escape from the everyday, the ordinary, the real, and folks flock here by the thousands looking for just that.

Yes, Orlando has a quieter side, with world-class museums and excellent parks, but as wonderful as it may be, the city will always lie in the shadow of Cinderella's Castle and Hogwarts School of Witchcraft.

When to Go
Orlando

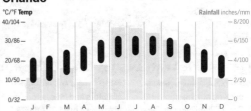

Fall Theme-park crowds thin, accommodation rates drop and summer sizzle fades.

May Warm, a lull between Spring Break and summer vacation peaks, and before the rains.

Thanksgiving–mid-Dec Avoid soaring holiday prices; enjoy over-the-top seasonal festivities.

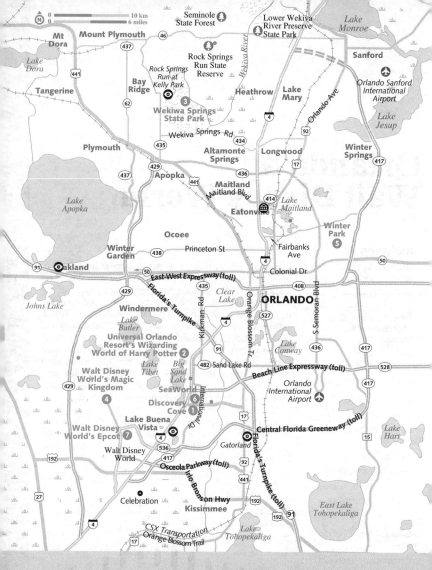

Orlando & Walt Disney World Highlights

1 Interacting with dolphins, snorkeling among tropical fish and floating on the lazy river through the bird aviary at **Discovery Cove** (p302)

2 Wandering Hogsmeade's cobblestone streets and zipping through Hogwarts at Universal Orlando Resort's **Wizarding World of Harry Potter** (p291)

3 Paddling quietly past alligators and blue herons on the Wekiva River at **Wekiwa Springs State Park** (p244)

4 Watching Magic Kingdom's **SpectroMagic parade** and sticking around for **Wishes Nighttime Spectacular fireworks** (p263) over Cinderella's Castle

5 Poking through art museums and boutique shops in **Winter Park** (p241)

6 Feeding rays and watching sea-lion and orca shows at **SeaWorld** (p299)

7 Meeting Sleeping Beauty after sipping wine in Italy and watching the Beatles in England at Disney's **Epcot** (p263)

History

In 1824, three years after Florida became a US territory, swampy Mosquito County was established. The first US settlers arrived in 1837, and in 1838 the US military built Fort Gatlin as a base for the Seminole Indian Wars (p457). Upon Florida statehood in 1845, Mosquito County changed to the far more alluring Orange County. Orlando grew as a cow town, with lots of gamblin', fightin' and womanizin', and in 1875 the 2-sq-mile city (population 85) was officially incorporated. With the arrival of the railroad in 1880, Indian fighting and cows gave way to orange growing and tourists. WWII brought air bases and missile building, but it was the 1971 opening of Walt Disney World's Magic Kingdom that paved the way to the city's contemporary reputation as the theme-park capital of the US.

State & Regional Parks

Lake Louisa State Park (☎352-394-3969; www.floridastateparkr.org/lakelouisa; 7305 US 27; admission $5, primitive camping per person $5, hookups $24, cabins $120; ☉8am-sundown), with six lakes and 20 miles of hiking trails, sits about a half-hour from Walt Disney World. Take Hwy 192 west from I-4 about 9 miles, head north 8 miles on Hwy 27 and follow the signs.

At the 14,000-acre **Rock Springs Run State Reserve** (☎407-884-2008; www.florida stateparks.org/rockspringsrun; 30601 CR 433, Sorrento; admission $3; ☉8am-6pm), about 15 miles northwest of downtown Orlando, you'll find 17 miles of hiking trails through pine flatland, and guided horseback riding (see p242). For details on canoeing the Wekiva River, which flows through the reserve, see Wekiwa Springs State Park (p244).

ℹ️ Getting There & Away

AIR Orlando is serviced by two international airports: **Orlando International Airport** (Map p228; www.orlandoairports.net), 12 miles east of downtown Orlando, and the much smaller **Sanford International Airport** (Map p228; www.orlandosanfordairport.com), 30 miles north.

BUS A Greyhound bus originating in New York City, with stops including Washington, DC and Daytona Beach, Florida, terminates in Orlando (one way $80 to $200, 24 hours from NY City).

CAR Orlando lies 285 miles from Miami; the fastest and most direct route is a 4½-hour road trip via the Florida Turnpike. From Tampa it is an easy 60 miles along I-4. Both the Beachline Expressway and Hwy 50 will take you east to beaches on the Space Coast in just under an hour; the expressway has frequent tolls, but may shave some time off the drive.

TRAIN Amtrak's 97 *Silver Meteor* and 91 *Silver Star* from New York to Miami stop at Winter Park, downtown Orlando and Kissimmee. It's about a 22-hour ride from New York City ($200 to $230, more for a sleeper car). A daily auto

ORLANDO IN...

Two Days

Buy an Express Plus pass in advance, and get to **Islands of Adventure** before the gates open. Head straight to the **Wizarding World of Harry Potter**. Have dinner out of the park at **Yellow Dog Eats**, and hit **Magic Kingdom** the next morning. Take the monorail for dinner at **'Ohana** or **Narcoossee's** and return to the park for **Disney's SpectroMagic parade** and **Wishes Nighttime Spectacular**.

Four Days

Breakfast at **White Wolf Café**, canoe and swim at **Wekiwa Springs State Park**, float an inner tube at **Kelly Park** and eat dinner at **Ravenous Pig**. Spend a day at **Discovery Cove**, and take in Downtown Disney's **Cirque du Soleil La Nouba**.

Seven Days

Spend a morning at **Hollywood Studios**, lunch at **50's Prime Time Café** and take a boat to **Epcot**. Pick up a FastPass for **Soarin'**, eat, drink and shop your way around the world, and catch **Illuminations**. After a full day at **SeaWorld**, go to dinner outside the gates at **Thai Thani** or head to **Celebration**. Hit **Typhoon Lagoon** first thing the next morning, and head to **Winter Park** for lunch. Go to **Charles Hosmer Morse Museum of American Art**, take a **boat tour** and browse the gift shops. Finish the day with dinner and a movie at the **Enzian Theater**.

train from Lorton, Virginia terminates at Sanford, 30 miles north of downtown Orlando.

ℹ Getting Around

CAR & MOTORCYCLE

Highway I-4 is the main north–south thoroughfare, though it's labeled east–west: to go north, take the I-4 east (toward Daytona Beach) and to go south, hop on the I-4 west (toward Tampa). Just about every place you'd want to be located through an I-4 exit number. From south to north, exit 62 through exit 87, you will find Walt Disney World, SeaWorld, Aquatica and Discovery Cove, Universal Studios, downtown Orlando and Thornton Park, Loch Haven Park and Winter Park.

Both airports, Walt Disney World and many hotels have car-rental agencies. If you have a motorcycle endorsement on your license or valid proof of a motorcycle license, you can rent a Harley from **Orlando Harley-Davidson** (☏877-740-3770; www.orlandoharley.com; 3770 37th St; per day $100-140).

PUBLIC TRANSPORTATION

In Walt Disney World, complimentary buses, boats and monorails service attractions and restaurants at the more than 20 hotels, four theme parks, two water parks and two dining and entertainment districts; at Universal Orlando Resort, boats connect the three hotels, two theme parks and one dining and entertainment district.

Lynx (☏route info 407-841-8240; www.golynx.com; single ride/day/week pass $2/4.50/16, transfers free) Orlando's public bus covers greater Orlando.

Lynx Central Station (Map p234; ☏407-841-2279; www.golynx.com; 455 Garland Ave;

ORLANDO FOR CHILDREN

The challenge for families vacationing in the theme park capital of the world is digging through the overwhelming options and inflated rhetoric to find what best suits your time, budget and family. For an overview of Orlando's major theme and water parks, see p30. But if time is limited, stick to Disney's iconic **Magic Kingdom** and Universal Orlando Resort's edgier **Islands of Adventure**, boasting the marvelously themed **Wizarding World of Harry Potter**.

Though part of the Disney magic is how it magically makes your money disappear, there are plenty of inexpensive highlights in and around Orlando. State parks north of town and the lovely **Historic Bok Sanctuary** make perfect day trips. Catch a free outdoor movie at Disney's Fort Wilderness **Chip 'n' Dale Campfire Singalong** (see Meeting Disney Characters, p274) and head to the **Peabody Orlando** (p245) for the famous march of the mallard ducks through the lobby (10am and 5pm). If you call in advance, you may be able to arrange for your kids to be an official **Duck Master**, helping the birds waddle through the lobby.

Everything in Orlando is an opportunity to attract tourists, and eating is no exception. There are **character meals** both inside the parks and at resort hotels, **dinner shows** at Walt Disney World, Universal Orlando Resort and venues around town, and **themed restaurants** offering everything from dining next to sharks to burgers and milkshakes in a mock drive-in theater.

You may be ready for bed once the sun sets, obsessively checking your watch to see if it's time yet to collapse, but there's more fun to be had. With the exception of Animal Kingdom, all of Disney's theme parks offer **light shows** or **fireworks**; Orlando's performing-arts scene includes excellent **children's theater** (see p252), and Downtown Disney's **Cirque du Soleil La Nouba** performs nightly. **Downtown Disney**, **Disney's Boardwalk** and Universal Orlando Resort's **CityWalk** all make for a festive evening, with street performers and plenty of eye candy, but if you've had enough adrenaline for one day kick back in small-town **Celebration** or **Winter Park**. Kids appreciate the slow pace, and on a summer evening, after a day slogging through parks, sitting with a glass of wine while the children play in Celebration's lakefront fountain just may be heaven.

Sprinkle in the big bang high-energy fun judiciously. Yes, you might ride the Winnie the Pooh seven times in a row, and yes, you may never make it to the Finding Nemo muscial in Animal Kingdom. If only we had gotten up earlier, if only we hadn't waited in line for that Mickey ice cream, if only we had scurried out of the park after the fireworks, if only, if only, if only, we'd have been able to see this, that and the other thing.

Forget it. There's too much, and you'll never win that game. In the end it's what you do that kids remember, not what you missed.

⊙6am-8pm Mon-Fri, 8am-5:30pm Sat & Sun) Tickets & maps.

TAXI

Fares are $3.85 for the first mile plus $2.20 for each additional mile – and those miles can add up! A ride from the Disney area to downtown Orlando, for example, costs roughly $50. Cabs sit outside the theme parks, Downtown Disney, resorts and other tourist centers, but otherwise you'll need to call to arrange a pickup.

Star Taxi (☑407-423-5566)
Yellow Cab (☑407-422-5151)

WHEELCHAIR & SCOOTER

Orlando's theme parks rent wheelchairs and Electronic Convenience Vehicles (ECV), but they don't all take advance reservations. Reserve one in advance at **Walker Mobility** (☑888-727-6837; www.walkermobility.com; scooters per day $30-45, wheelchairs per day $30, each additional day $6). It offers free delivery and pickup, and can have one ready for you at the airport.

ORLANDO & AROUND

☑407 / POP 1.8 MILLION

While it's quite easy to get caught up in the isolated worlds of Disney or Universal Orlando, squeezing in one more ride, one more parade, one more show and never venturing beyond their constructed environments designed precisely to keep you there, Orlando has so much more. Lovely pockets of tree-lined neighborhoods, established communities with an entrenched sense of history and community, a rich performing-arts scene and several fantastic gardens, parks and museums in and around the city encourage a slower, lazier pace often passed over by tourists. Even if you're coming to Orlando for the theme parks, take a few days to jump off their spinning wheels of adrenaline-pumped fantasy to explore the quieter, gentler side of Orlando. You may be surprised to find that you enjoy the theme parks all that much more because of the time you spend away from them.

Orlando's theme parks – Walt Disney World, Universal Orlando, and SeaWorld, Aquatica and Discovery Cove – are detailed in their own sections in this chapter.

⊙ Sights

DOWNTOWN ORLANDO

Lake Eola & Thornton Park   NEIGHBORHOOD
(Map p234) A gathering point for the downtown community, Lake Eola makes a pretty,

Shave expenses with an Orlando Magi-card, a discount book with coupons for attractions, entertainment, transportation, hotels and restaurants. Download it at www.orlandoinfo.com or pick one up at Orlando's Official Visitor Center on International Drive.

shaded backdrop on a hot day. A flat, paved sidewalk, about 1 mile long, circles the water, a playground sits on its eastern shore and you can toot around the lake on a swan paddleboat (per 30min $15). Fashionable Thornton Park, an admirable example of urban revitalization, borders the lake to the east. Remodeled historic homes line its narrow brick streets, and giant Spanish oaks weave their gnarly branches into natural green canopies. Though it's only a few blocks, and there's a slight sense that the economic slump halted development just as it was hitting its stride, this neighborhood off the tourist track is where you'll find an excellent independent urban hotel, several good restaurants and a handful of neighborhood bars. To get here from downtown Orlando, head east 0.4 miles from Lake Eola's western shore on Central Blvd or Robinson St to Sumerlin Ave, Thornton Park's main drag.

Orange County Regional
History Center   MUSEUM
(Map p234; www.thehistorycenter.org; 65 E Central Blvd; adult/child 3-12/senior $10/3.50/6.50; ⊙10am-5pm Mon-Sat, from noon Sun) Permanent exhibits cover prehistoric Florida, European exploration and settlement, and citrus production, among other things.

Wells' Built Museum of African
American History and Culture   MUSEUM
(Map p234; www.pastinc.org; 511 W South St; adult/child 4-14/senior $15/2/3; ⊙9am-5pm Mon-Fri) Dr Wells, one of Orlando's first black doctors, came to Orlando in 1917. In 1921 he built a hotel for African Americans barred from Florida's segregated hotels, and soon after he built South Street Casino, an entertainment venue for black entertainers. Together, they became a central icon of the African American music community. This small museum of African American history is housed in the original hotel.

ORLANDO & AROUND SIGHTS

Gallery at Avalon Island GALLERY
(Map p234; www.galleryatavalonisland.com; 39 S
Magnolia Ave; ⏰11.30am-6pm Thu-Sat) Housed
in the oldest commercial building in Orlando, this gallery features paintings, photography, sculpture and other mediums by
local artists. On the third Thursday of every
month, the gallery hosts free art receptions
with live music from 6pm to 9pm.

City Arts Factory GALLERY
(Map p234; www.cityartsfactory.com; 29 S Orange
Ave; ⏰11am-7pm Mon-Sat) Six handsome art
galleries with changing exhibits.

LOCH HAVEN PARK

Picturesque Loch Haven Park (Map p232),
with 45 acres of parks, huge shade trees and
three lakes, is home to several museums and
theaters concentrated within walking distance. To get here, take I-4 east to Princeton
St (exit 85), turn right; from Thornton Park,
head north a few miles on Mills Ave, and
turn left onto Princeton.

TOP CHOICE **Orlando Museum of Art** MUSEUM
(☏407-896-4231; www.omart.org; 2416 N Mills Ave;
adult/child 6-18 $8/5; ⏰10am-4pm Tue-Fri, from
noon Sat & Sun) Founded in 1924, Orlando's
grand and blindingly white center for the

Greater Orlando

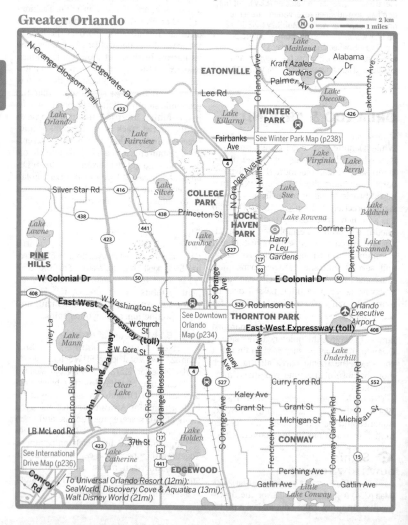

ORLANDO & WALT DISNEY WORLD ORLANDO & AROUND

arts boasts a fantastic collection. The museum provides family guides, runs week-long day-camps and hosts **Art Adventures** ($10; ☉9:30am 2nd Tue of month). Each session looks at a particular element within the art (eg brushstrokes) and offers hands-on activities for kids. On the first Thursday of every month, **First Thursday** ($10; ☉6-9pm) celebrates local artists with regional work, live music, a cash wine bar and food from local restaurants.

Mennello Museum of American Folk Art
MUSEUM

(www.mennellomuseum.org; 900 E Princeton St; adult/child under 12 $4/free; ☉10:30am-4:30pm Tue-Sat, from noon Sun) A tiny but excellent lakeside art museum featuring the work of Earl Cunningham, whose brightly colored images, a fusion of pop and folk art, leap off the canvas.

Orlando Science Center
CHILDREN'S MUSEUM

(☑407-514-2000; www.osc.org; 777 E Princeton St; adult/child 3-11 $15/10; ☉10am-5pm, closed Wed) Changing exhibits on dinosaurs, the human body, the solar system and more offer candy-coated science education. Unfortunately, many displays are too complicated to teach anything and too educational to be fun, and the result is a lot of kids just running around punching buttons. A giant tree grows through the four-story atrium, at the base of which you'll find alligators and a natural science discovery room. Check the website for screenings at the giant Cinedome Theater, as well as Science Live events like stingray feeding and science experiments.

INTERNATIONAL DRIVE

I-Drive, packed with chain restaurants, hotels, dinner theaters and a handful of minor Orlando attractions, parallels I-4 to its east, directly across the interstate from Universal Orlando Resort and stretching from the Prime Outlets International mall southeast to SeaWorld. The couple miles between the convention center and Sand Lake Rd is a divided road, with palm trees, museums and a relatively pleasant walking district. From Sand Lake Rd north to the dead end at Prime Outlets International, however, it's a strip of asphalt, souvenir shops and parking lots. This is Orlando tourist hell at full throttle, with $5.99 Disney T-shirts, an ice-cream stand shaped like a soft-serve cone and a miniature golf course advertising the opportunity to 'feed our live alligators.'

WonderWorks
MUSEUM

(Map p236; ☑407-351-8800; www.wonderworks online.com; 9067 International Dr; adult/child 4-12 $25/20; ☉9am-midnight) Housed in a hard-to-miss, upside-down building, this bright, loud, frenetic landmark is a cross between a children's museum, a video arcade and an amusement park. It offers high-speed, multisensory education with several stories of wall-to-wall hands-on exhibits. You can lie on a bed of nails, sit inside a hurricane simulator, and measure how high you can jump. Younger children may find the pulse disorienting and frightening, but older ones will probably enjoy the cool stuff to do. Plus there's a 36ft indoor ropes course, a 4D theater with changing shows, laser tag and the **Outta Control Magic Show** (dinner show incl unlimited pizza, beer, wine & dessert adult/child $25/17; ☉9am & midnight), pairing pizza with illusions.

Wet 'n' Wild
WATER PARK

(Map p236; ☑407-351-1800; www.wetnwildorlando. com; 6200 International Dr; adult/child 3-9 $48/42, half-price afternoon admission; ☉call for opening hours) Of the four water parks in Orlando, Wet 'n' Wild caters primarily to teenagers who don't mind blaring music, bad food and stretching their towels out on pavement. While there is a small wave pool, a lazy river and a kids' play area, this park is about high-speed water thrills; if you can tolerate the lines, their dives, twists and turns won't disappoint. Attractions include **Mach 5**, a superslick mat ride; **Black Hole: The Next Generation**, enclosed for maximum disorientation; **Disco H2O**, a four-person ride with music and lights; and the **Bomb Bay**, where a trapdoor drops you sliding nearly vertical for 73ft to the pool below. From May through September, noon to dusk, the **Wake Zone** lets you wake ski, 'knee skate' and tube around a half-mile lake (helmets required, added fee).

Wet 'n' Wild participates in the Orlando FlexTicket program. Check the website for multiday passes and call ☑800-992-9453 for hours and weather closings. Parking is $10.

Ripley's Believe It Or Not
MUSEUM

(Map p236; www.orlando.ripleys.com; 8201 International Dr; adult/child 4-12 $19/12; ☉9:30am-midnight) The 1933 World's Fair in Chicago introduced Ripley's collection of 'oddities and unusual people' to the public. While it may today offend 21st-century politically correct sensibilities, this 'odditorium' offers

ORLANDO & WALT DISNEY WORLD ORLANDO & AROUND

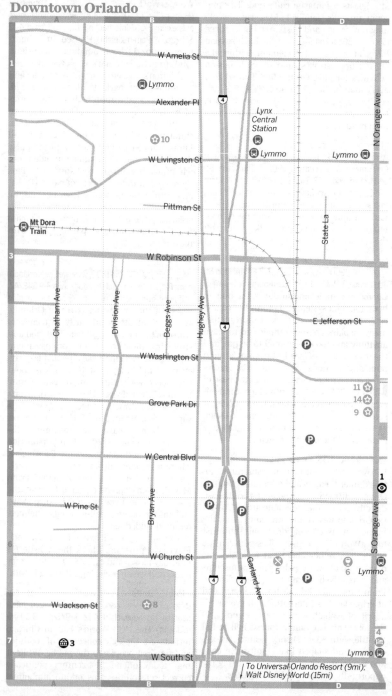

W Amelia St

Lymmo

Alexander Pl

I-4

Lynx Central Station

Lymmo

Lymmo

☆10

W Livingston St

N Orange Ave

Pittman St

Mt Dora Train

State La

W Robinson St

Chatham Ave

Division Ave

Beggs Ave

Hughey Ave

I-4

E Jefferson St

P

W Washington St

11 ☆
14 ☆
9 ☆

Grove Park Dr

P

W Central Blvd

Bryan Ave

P

P

1 ◉

W Pine St

P

P

S Orange Ave

W Church St

Garland Ave

I-4   I-4

✗ 5

6 🚻 *Lymmo*

P

W Jackson St

☆ 8

4 🚻
Lymmo

🏛 3

W South St

To Universal Orlando Resort (9mi);
Walt Disney World (15mi)

Ripley's vision with no holds barred. A short documentary film chronicles his search for the 'strange, exotic and incredible,' and TVs throughout the museum screen footage of classic Ripley, including exotic food customs, the man with the 'strongest eyes in the world' and a snake slithering through a guy's nose and out his mouth. Twenty-first-century additions tend to focus on the creation of odd, like a dog sculpture made out of clothes pins, rather than the finding of odd.

I Fly Orlando   THRILL RIDE
(Map p236; ☑407-903-1150; www.iflyorlando. com; 8501 International Dr; adult/child 3-7/child 7-12 $35/7/20, family package $240; ☉10:30am-9pm Mon-Fri) Think you may like to jump out of a moving plane? Or does the thought give you the heebie-jeebies? Either way, this indoor skydiving experience, in which you soar free-form in a vertical wind tunnel, gives folks as young as three the chance to skydive.

Downtown Orlando

◎ Top Sights
Orange County Regional History
    Center..E5

◎ Sights
1 City Arts Factory.................................D5
2 Gallery at Avalon Island....................E5
3 Wells' Built Museum of African
    American History and
    Culture...A7

◎ Sleeping
4 Westin Grand Bohemian....................D7

◎ Eating
5 Dessert Lady Café..............................C6

◎ Drinking
Bösendorfer Lounge ....(see 4)
6 Latitudes..D6
7 Wall Street Plaza E5

◎ Entertainment
8 Amway Center....................................B7
9 Beacham...D5
10 Bob Carr Performing Arts
    Center...B2
11 Independent Bar.................................D4
12 Mad Cow Theater...............................E6
13 Plaza Cinema Café 12........................E6
SAK Comedy Lab.........................(see 1)
14 Social..D4

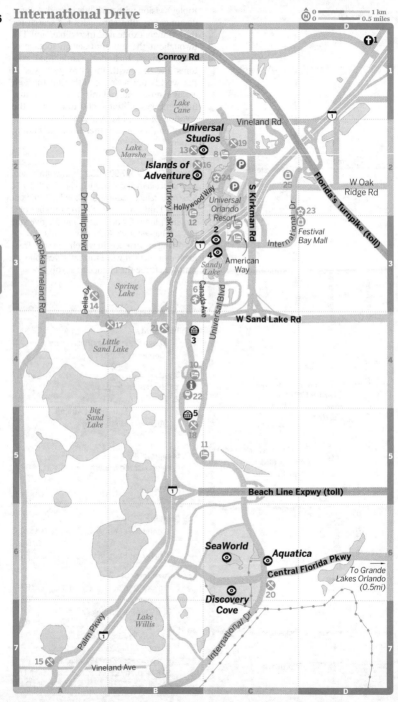

N 0 ——————— 1 km
0 ——————— 0.5 miles

Conroy Rd

Lake Cane

Vineland Rd

Universal Studios
13 × 8
19 ×

Islands of Adventure 16 ×

Turkey Lake Rd

Hollywood Way

Universal Orlando Resort
12

S Kirkman Rd

25

Florida's Turnpike (toll)

W Oak Ridge Rd

International Dr

23
Festival Bay Mall

9
2 ×
7
4 ×
American Way

Sandy Lake

Dr Phillips Blvd

Apopka Vineland Rd

Spring Lake

Della Dr
14

6
Canada Ave

Universal Blvd

W Sand Lake Rd

17 ×
21 ×
3

Little Sand Lake

Big Sand Lake

10
22
5
18

11

Beach Line Expwy (toll)

SeaWorld   *Aquatica*
Central Florida Pkwy
To Grande
Lakes Orlando
(0.5mi)
20 ×

Discovery Cove

Palm Pkwy

Lake Willis

International Dr

15 ×
Vineland Ave

GREATER ORLANDO

TOP CHOICE Gatorland   ANIMAL PARK

(Map p228; www.gatorland.com; 14501 S Orange Blossom Trail; adult/child 3-12 $23/15; ⊙9am-5pm) With no fancy roller coasters or drenching water rides, this mom-and-pop park harkens back to Old Florida. It's small, it's silly and it's kitschy with, you guessed it, plenty of gators. Allow time to see all the rather tongue-in-cheek shows, charmingly free of special effects, dramatic music and spectacular light design. At the **Jumparoo Show** 10ft-long alligators leap almost entirely out of the water to grab whole chickens from the trainer, and after the **Gator Wrestling Show** you can go on down to get a photo of yourself sitting on a gator. The best is **Up-close Encounters**, where mysterious boxes hold animals the public has sent to the park. The trainers are too scared to open 'em, so they drag audience members down to help. A splintery wooden boardwalk winds past the hundreds of alligators in the **breeding marsh**, and you can buy hot dogs to feed to them.

Sign up in advance for the two-hour **Trainer for a Day** (incl park admission $125) program. After some safety demonstrations you may get to wrestle a gator, feed them chickens and hold one of the adorable babies. Kids must be at least 12 years old to participate, but little ones get a kick just from watching.

Fun Spot USA   AMUSEMENT PARK

(Map p256; www.skycoaster.com; 2850 Florida Plaza Blvd; admission & parking free, unlimited

International Drive

all-day rides adult/child under 5 $35/15; ⏱10am-midnight) Plenty of whirling, swinging and twisting on old-time carnival rides, including four go-kart tracks and a handful of kiddy rides, give this alternative to the major theme parks an old-school vibe. In addition to the classics, you'll find the Skycoaster, one of the most adrenaline-pumped experiences in Florida. Picture this: you and up to two other people are hooked onto a long rope, which pulls you for more than a minute straight up into the air. You dangle helplessly for a few moments, release and shoot down head first, 120ft free fall at speeds of up to 85mph. At the last second before impact, you're suddenly soaring over the water. One person flies for $40, two for $70; repeat flight $25. There's a sister park called Fun Spot Action Park, without the Skycoaster and with fewer thrills, on International Drive.

Legoland
AMUSEMENT PARK

(http://florida.legoland.com) In October 2011, a spanking new 150-acre Legoland opened in Winter Haven, 45 minutes' drive south of Walt Disney World. Apart from its miniature city built out of Lego, it has rides, shows, restaurants and offers vacation packages.

Audubon Center for Birds of Prey
BIRD REHABILITATION

(☎407-644-0190; 1101 Audubon Way, Maitland; adult/child 3-12 $5/4; ⏱10am-4pm Tue-Sun) Centered at a cool old house and very much off the beaten track, this lovely lakeside rehabilitation center for hawks, bald eagles, screech owls and other talon-toed feathered friends treats nearly 700 birds per year. It's small and low-key, with opportunities to see the birds up close, just hanging out on the trainers' arms, and in aviaries for those unable to return to the wild. A boardwalk leads to a gazebo by the water. The center can be difficult to find; it's located in a residential area along Lake Sybelia in Maitland, immediately north of Winter Park (I-4, exit 88).

FREE Zora Neale Hurston National Museum of Fine Arts
MUSEUM

(www.zoranealehurstonmuseum.com; 227 E Kennedy Blvd, Eatonville; ⏱9am-4pm Mon-Fri, 11am-1pm Sat) Novelist Zora Neale Hurston, a pillar of America's Harlem Renaissance and best known for her novel *Their Eyes Were Watching God*, was born in Eatonville. Changing exhibits of African American artists honor her memory and spirit. The museum is about 5 miles northeast of downtown Winter Park; take Fairbanks Ave west to

Orlando Ave, turn right and go 1.6 miles to Lake Ave. Lake Ave turns into Kennedy Blvd.

Green Meadows Petting Farm FARM
(☎407-846-0770; www.greenmeadowsfarm.com; 1368 S Poinciana Blvd; adult/child over 2yr $21/17; ☺9:30am-4pm) Take a day in the country at this farm about 30 minutes' drive from Disney. You can pet the farm animals, milk a cow, ride a pony and the little train. It's certainly a pleasant spot with plenty of shade and grass, a picnic area and a playground, but unfortunately you can't just wander around – you must go on a more than two-hour tour. They run continuously until 3pm, but there's no regular schedule and if there aren't enough people, the tour is cancelled. If you arrive after 3pm, you may not be allowed in. Call for directions.

Maitland Art Center ARTS CENTRE
(www.maitlandartcenter.org; 231 W Packwood Ave, Maitland; admission free; ☺11am-4pm Tue-Sun) Founded as an art colony in 1937, this little spot provides classes and studio space to area artists, as well as lovely galleries where they can display their work. The facilities, listed on the National Register of Historic Places and one of the few remaining examples of Mayan Revival architecture in Florida, boast lovely gardens. Take I-4 east to Maitland Blvd; head right, then right onto Maitland Ave and right onto Packwood Ave.

Old Town AMUSEMENT PARK
(Map p256; ☎407-396-4888, 800-843-4202; www.old-town.com; 5770 W Irlo Bronson Memorial Hwy; admission & parking free; rides each $2-6; ☺10am-11pm, rides & bars stay open later) At this complex of rides, shopping, dining and live music, 'county fair' meets 'boardwalk,' plopped among the exhaust, chain motels and the treeless landscape of Hwy 192. There's live rock 'n' roll and car cruises Wednesday, Friday and Saturday (8:30pm), and line-dancing lessons at the Little Darlin' Street Party (7:30pm Wednesday).

Holy Land Experience AMUSEMENT PARK
(Map p236; 4655 Vineland Rd; adult/child 6-12 $35/20; ☺10am-6pm Mon-Sat) A self-proclaimed not-for-profit Christian organization, this theme park off I-4 is designed to look like Jerusalem c AD 33. Staff members wear flowing bedouin robes and hawk Middle Eastern food treats such as mint tea, tabbouleh and falafel, as well as Goliath burgers and chicken fajitas (that famous culinary

Founded in 1858, this cozy college town concentrates some of Orlando's best-kept secrets, including an outstanding museum and an excellent historic hotel, into a few shaded, pedestrian-friendly streets.

Charles Hosmer Morse Museum of American Art (Map p239; www.morsemuseum .org; 445 N Park Ave; adult/child under 12/student $5/free/1; ⊙9:30am-4pm Tue-Sat, from 1pm Sun, to 8pm Fri Nov-Apr), internationally famous as the world's most comprehensive collection of Tiffany leaded-glass lamps, windows, jewelry, blown glass, pottery and enamel, is stunningly delightful. A centerpiece is the chapel interior Louis Comfort Tiffany designed for the World's Columbian Exposition in Chicago (1893), and in 2011 the new 12,000-sq-ft Laurelton Hall opened to house architectural and art objects from Tiffany's Long Island home. Tours are given Tuesdays and Thursdays 2:30pm to 4:30pm, first-come, first-served. In addition to Tiffany's work, you'll find a broad selection of objects from the late-19th-century Arts and Crafts movement as well as US paintings. Free admission Fridays 4pm to 8pm November through April.

A sweet one-hour **Scenic Boat Tour** (Map p239; www.scenicboattours.com; 1 E Morse Blvd; adult/child 2-11 $8/4; ⊙10am-4pm, every hr) floats through 12 miles of tropical canals and lakes. The enthusiastic tour guide talks about the mansions, Rollins College and other sites along the way. Boats are small pontoons, holding about 10 people each.

Scattered through the grounds of the stately **Albin Polasek Museum & Sculpture Gardens** (Map p239; www.polasek.org; 633 Osceola Ave; adult/child under 12/senior $5/free/4; ⊙10am-4pm Tue-Sat, from 1pm Sun) are the works of Czech sculptor Albin Polasek. The small yellow villa, listed on the National Register of Historic Places and perched on the shore of Lake Osceola, was the artist's home.

The tiny **Cornell Fine Arts Museum** (Map p239; www.rollins.edu/cfam; Rollins College, 1000 Holt Ave; adult/child 2-11 $5/free; ⊙10am-4pm Tue-Fri, noon-5pm Sat & Sun), on the campus of lovely Rollins College, houses an eclectic collection of historic and contemporary art. It's worth a peek, but don't expect to go through inch by inch looking at a wealth of displays. Excellent changing exhibits range from documentary photography to Japanese printmaking to senior art student projects.

As far back as 1881, Hannibal Square was home to African Americans employed as carpenters, farmers and household help in the Winter Park region. The small **Hannibal Square Heritage Center** (Map p239; www.hannibalsquareheritagecenter.org; 642 W New England Ave; admission free; ⊙noon-4pm Tue-Thu, to 5pm Fri, 10am-2pm Sat), home to the Heritage Collection: Photographs and Oral Histories of West Winter Park, preserves the community's culture and history with a collection of photographic and oral histories.

Particularly stunning January through March, when the azaleas burst into bloom, the 11-acre **Kraft Azalea Gardens** (Map p232; 1363 Alabama Dr) on the shores of Lake Maitland promises tranquility. Stroll along the paths and relax by the water with a book. Take Park Ave north past the golf course and turn right onto Stoven Ave. Stoven Ave merges into Palmer Ave; take Palmer east a few blocks and turn left onto Alabama.

Brick walls, clean-lined wood furniture, antiques and luscious white cotton bedding give every room at the historic two-story **Park Plaza Hotel** (Map p239; ☏407-647-1072, 800-228-7220; www.parkplazahotel.com; 307 S Park Ave; r $180-220, ste $260-320; 🅿@🛜) a simple elegance and a distinct Arts and Crafts sensibility. Rooms lining Winter Park's main strolling drag share a thin balcony, each with a private entrance and a few wicker chairs hidden from the street by hanging ferns, and are well worth the extra money. Bring up a bottle of wine and cheese, and watch the Park Ave activity.

One of the most talked-about foodie destinations in Orlando, the bustling **Ravenous Pig** (off Map p239; ☏407-628-2333; www.theravenouspig.com; 1234 Orange Ave; mains $14-29; ⊙11:30am-2pm & 5:30-9:30pm Tue-Sat) lives up to its reputation for creative, fresh and delicious food. Start off with a Kumquat and Jalapeno Margarita or Umatilla Smash (whiskey, muddled orange and mint with house-spiced syrup) and try the shrimp and grits or lobster taco. Black-and-white photos hang from exposed pipes in the ceiling and there are a handful of sidewalk tables. Reservations highly recommended.

Four Rivers Smokehouse Deli & Bakery (off Map p239; ☑407-474-8377; http://4rsmokehouse.com; 2103 Fairbanks Ave; mains $5-10; ⊙11am-9pm), a tiny walk-up shack just east of I-4 on Fairbanks, has lines that wind out the door. Try snagging seats at one of the few picnic tables in the back, or take your pulled pork to the car like most folks. Mains include ribs, briskets and sandwiches, with sides of Southern classics like sweet potato casserole and fried okra, but save room for a banana foster cupcake. Swallow it down with a bottle of old-school soda. Call in an order to the pickup window.

Clean decor, solid fare and reasonable prices make **Bosphorous Turkish Cuisine** (Map p239; ☑407-644-8609; www.bosphorousrestaurant.com; 108 S Park Ave; mains $8-21; ⊙11:30am-10pm Mon-Thu, to 11pm Sat & Sun) a standout in a town of great restaurants. Try the *lahmacun* (Turkish pizza) or the Hunkar Begendi, an Ottoman dish with beef and eggplant. Kids love the chicken kebab. Linger on the sidewalk over Turkish coffee and baklava and, if you're a smoker, exotic tobacco in the long and elaborate hookah.

Orchid (Map p239; ☑07-331-1400; www.orchidparkavenue.com; 305 N Park Ave; mains $8-15; ⊙11am-3pm & 5-9pm Mon-Thu, 11am-10pm Fri & Sat, noon-9pm Sun) is a tasty Thai restaurant with contemporary style, friendly service and classic dishes. Don't miss the delectable Golden Thai Doughnuts, dough balls fried with a sweet condensed-milk dressing and sprinkled with crushed peanuts.

Eola Wine Company (Map p239; www.eolawinecompany.com; 136 S Park Ave; ⊙4-11pm Mon-Fri, from noon Sat & Sun) features a California-style menu of light foods designed to pair with wine or quirky independent-label beers. How about a buffalo-chicken wrap with a bottle of Dogfishhead Ale, or roasted garlic with a flight of Take a Cab? You can also get a flight of beer or bubbly, and the cheese plate includes a choice from 16 Spanish, French, Italian and US cheeses.

Purchase a wine card when you enter the **Wine Room** (270 S Park Ave; ⊙3pm-midnight Mon-Thu, 11am-1:30am Fri & Sat, 1-9pm Sun), and then simply slide your card into the auto-mated servers of whatever wine looks good, press the button for a taste or a full glass, and enjoy. Wines are organized according to region and type, and prices range upwards from $2.50 for a taste. If you purchase a bottle to enjoy on the premise, there is a whopping $10 corkage fee, but the corkage fee is waived Sundays and Mondays.

At **Popcorn Flicks in the Park** (☑407-629-1088; www.enzian.org), bring a picnic and a blanket, and kick back under the stars for an outdoor film classic perfect for the whole family. Screenings are usually held on the second Thursday of each month and are free. Just north of Winter Park is **Regal Winter Park Village 20** (off Map p239; ☑407-628-0035; 510 N Orlando Ave; adult/child $10/7). While not in downtown Winter Park, it's within an outdoor mall with a bustling restaurant scene, many with outdoor seating.

Winter Park supports an eclectic mix of shops, with everything from upscale chains, like Williams Sonoma and Lucky Jeans, to not one but two specialty spice shops and several gift shops.

Consignment-shop junkies will love the overstuffed racks of vintage and designer fash-ions at **Cida's Consignment** (Map p239; 535 N Park Ave; ⊙10am-5:30pm Mon-Sat). There are adorable children's clothes, books and toys at **Tugboat and the Bird** (Map p239; 433 W New England Ave; ⊙10am-7pm Tue-Sat, to 5pm Sun).

The **Cheese Shop** (Map p239; 329 N Park Ave; ⊙10am-7pm Tue-Sat, to 5pm Sun) special-izes in traditional artisan cheeses, many locally produced and organic, and offers wine by the glass. Ask for a taste of its Guinness- or whiskey-infused cheddar. Alternatively, grab a bucket and select your favorite retro candy, including candy cigarettes and Razzles, at **Sassafras Sweet Shoppe** (Map p239; 114 E Morse Blvd; ⊙10:30am-6pm Mon-Fri, 11am-5pm Sat & Sun).

The **Farmers' Market** (Map p239; 200 W New England Ave, Winter Park; ⊙7am-1pm Sat) is housed in a former train station – hit it early for freshly baked croissants and local goodies.

To get to Winter Park, take I-4 east to Fairbanks Ave, head east 2 miles to Park Ave and turn left.

ORLANDO & AROUND SIGHTS

delight from 1st-century Jerusalem). Even more prevalent are the shops selling Holy Land Experience gear, carved wooden camels, Jesus-fish neckties, bibles and the like. Most of the attractions are proselytizing live presentations designed 'to bring the bible to life...and bring the gospel of Jesus Christ to the world,' so if you want to cover the park you're going to need at least a half-day. Parking costs $5.

⚡ Activities

Biking

Several resorts at Walt Disney World run their own cycling programs, including rentals and trails. One of the prettiest paths is between Disney's Boardwalk and Beach Club resorts – try it on a tandem candy-striped bike. Orlando's bike trails are in flux as the city develops a vast interconnected system of trails. **Outdoor Travels** (www.outdoortravels.com/biking_fl_overview_orlando.php) has descriptions of greater Orlando's bike trails. **Metro Plan Orlando** (www.metroplanorlando) has updated pdf maps.

West Orange Trail Bikes & Blades   BIKING
(☎407-877-0600; www.orlandobikerental.com; 17914 State Rd 438, Oakland, Florida Turnpike exit 272; bikes hr $6-10, day $30-50, week $99-149; ☺11am-5pm Mon-Fri, 9am-5pm Sat & Sun) There is a $40 delivery/pickup charge, and rates include a car rack.

WORTH A TRIP

SADDLE UP

Slow down, relax and unwind with a day on the trails. **Rock Springs Riding Ranch** (☎352-735-6266; www.rsrranch.com; 3700 County Rd 33, Sorrento; 1/2/3hr rides $37/60/80) features one-, two- and three-hour and all-day rides through meadows, pine-scrub swampland and dense forests in the 14,000-acre Rock Springs Run State Reserve (Map p228). Complete the getaway with a night at the ranch's **Hammock House** (☎353-383-7657; 6 people $250), a three-bedroom riverfront cabin. The ranch lies 8 miles west of I-4 exit 101C, about 45 minutes' drive north of downtown Orlando; alternatively, it's a four-hour canoe float from Wekiwa Springs State Park to Hammock House.

Water Sports

Orlando may be landlocked, but its 300-plus lakes provide plenty of water playgrounds. For water sports at Walt Disney World, see p274.

Buena Vista Watersports   WATER SPORTS
(☎407-239-6963; www.bvwatersports.com; 13245 Lake Bryan Dr; water skiing, tubing & wakeboarding per hr $145; ☺9am-6:30pm) Just outside the Disney gates, with similar things for slightly less and a more low-key and bucolic feel. From I-4, take exit 68 (Hwy 535).

Fishing

Central Florida is famous for its freshwater fishing (especially largemouth bass), and the canals and lakes in and around Orlando offer some of the best.

Lake Tohopekaliga   FISHING
(Map p228) Just south of Kissimmee, this lake, known locally as Lake Toho, is particularly favored with anglers looking for trophy-sized catches and has hosted several fishing tournaments. Half- and full-day guide services range from $150 to $350.

Kissimmee Boat Rentals   FISHING
(☎407-580-8458; www.kissimmeeboatrentals.com; 101 Lake Shore Blvd, Kissimmee; half day $120-150, full day $205-250) Offers pontoon and fishing-boat rental.

Golf

Golfpac Orlando (☎800-486-0948; www.golfpacorlando.com) is the go-to source for information on the area's more than 100 championship golf courses. Call individual golf courses for details on specials, club rental and twilight times. Hours vary seasonally.

For golf at Walt Disney World, see p273. For golf in the town of Celebration, see p247.

Dubsdread Golf Course   GOLF
(☎407-246-2551; 549 W Par St; with cart 9 holes $32-40, 18 holes $40-65) Low-key old-school Orlando course dating to 1923. Dubsdread lies north of downtown Orlando; take I-4 east, exit 86 (Par Ave) and head west on Par Ave about 1 mile.

Grand Cypress Golf Club   GOLF
(Map p256; ☎407-239-4700; www.grandcypress.com/golf_club; 1 Grand Cypress Blvd; 18 holes $120-175) Beautiful golf resort villas and an 18-hole Scottish links-style course.

Ritz Carlton (Grande Lakes Orlando)   GOLF
(off Map p236; ☎407-393-4900; www.grandelakes.com; 4040 Central Florida Pkwy; 18 holes Jan-May 7am-1:30pm $175, 1:30-4pm $115, after

Rain ruins a day at the beach, but it doesn't have to dampen your fun in Orlando. It can be the best time to hit the theme parks, as most folks don't want to tackle roller coasters with umbrellas, so lines can be blissfully short or nothing at all, and there are plenty of indoor rides and shows (particularly in Epcot). DisneyQuest's five stories of interactive and classic video games is perfect for waiting out a stormy day, or catch a matinee at Universal Orlando Resort's CityWalk, Walt Disney World's Downtown Disney or cineplexes around town. Museums in Loch Haven Park and along International Drive are fun for kids and adults alike, the **World Bowling Center at Dowdy Pavilion** (Map p236; www. worldbowlingcenter.com; 7540 Canada Ave; adult/child $4/3; ⊙noon-11pm Mon-Sun, to 2am Fri & Sat) has 32 lanes, and adrenaline junkies love the ramps and courses at **Van's Skatepark** (Map p236; Festival Bay Mall, 5150 International Dr; admission $15; ⊙10am-10pm). One-hour lessons (6 years and older) cost $40 and are offered Monday through Thursday from noon to 7pm.

4pm $75, call for off-season rates) Has won environment awards for conservative water use. Ask about no-charge family golf specials.

✪ Festivals & Events

Walt Disney World (p275), Universal Orlando Resort (p295) and SeaWorld (check www .seaworld.com/orlando to see what's on) cele-brate the holidays with seasonal shows and parades.

Capital One Bowl SPORTS
(www.capitalonebowl.com) Football fans decked out in their university's colors crowd into hotels for the parade and New Year's Day game; formerly called Citrus Bowl.

**Zora Neale Hurston Festival
of the Arts and Humanities** CULTURAL
(www.zoranealehurstonfestival.com) The Zora Neale Hurston Museum hosts this annual celebration in late January featuring African American music, art and culture.

Spring Training SPORTS
(www.springtrainingonline.com) Atlanta Braves and Houston Astros start playing in mid-February.

Winter Park Sidewalk Art Festival CULTURAL
(www.wpsaf.org) Artists display work in the streets in mid-March.

Florida Film Festival FILM
(www.floridafilmfestival.com) Celebrate all things Florida with Indie movies and food at the Enzian in April.

Gay Days GAY & LESBIAN
(www.gaydays.com) Events in the theme parks and venues throughout town in May.

Orlando Film Festival FILM
(www.orlandofilmfest.com) Screened at the cineplex downtown in October.

🛏 Sleeping

Rack rates vary dramatically according to demand, change within the course of a week or even a day, and plummet for no apparent reason. Rates outside theme park hubs are lowest from June through September and highest between Christmas and New Year, and in March and April. Rates quoted below are a range during high season. You'll find every conceivable motel and hotel chain in every nook and cranny of greater Orlando and plenty of cheap independent motels, particularly along Hwy 192 east of I-4. Most hotels offer complimentary shuttles to the theme parks, but if you plan on using this service always ask about details when selecting a room, as many require advance reservations, fill up easily and only run a couple of times a day. They can be miserably inconvenient.

DOWNTOWN
EO Inn & Spa BOUTIQUE HOTEL $$
(☎407-481-8485; www.eoinn.com; 227 N Eola Dr, Thornton Park; r $139-229; ❋🛜🏊🐾) This little hotel sits across the street from the east shore of Lake Eola, blocks from the restaurants and bars of leafy Thornton Park. Soothing beige-and-white rooms evoke a sense of serenity that feels miles away from the hustle of the city.

Westin Grand Bohemian LUXURY HOTEL $$$
(Map p234; ☎407-313-9000; www.grandbohemian hotel.com; 325 S Orange Ave; r $179-299, ste $299-499; ❋@🛜🏊) Downtown's most

BEYOND THE PAVEMENT

After a few days of rides and lines, fried food, loud music, traffic and shopping, a jaunt beyond the pavement can soothe and rejuvenate even the most harried of spirits.

Wekiwa Springs State Park

Explore this 42,000-acre **park** (Map p228; ⊠407-884-2008; www.floridastateparks.org; 1800 Wekiwa Circle; car $6, RV or tent site $24; ☺8am-6pm) by paddling along the tranquil waters of the Wekiva River, a federally designated 'Wild and Scenic River.' **Nature Adventures** (⊠407-884-4311; www.canoewekiva.com; 2hr $15-20) rents kayaks and canoes; arrange at least 24 hours in advance to float the 9 miles to **Katie's Landing** (2-3 people $30-40, child under 6 free; ☺9:30am departure, 3:30pm shuttle return) and hop a shuttle 37 miles back. There's a three-boat minimum, so they'll call to let you know if the minimum has been filled. To really get away, book a riverbank campsite through the state park. Two days and one night, including canoe or kayak, tent, sleeping bags, stoves, lanterns and cooler, costs $132. The park also has 13 miles of wooded hiking trails and a fantastic swimming hole.

Rock Springs Run at Kelly Park

Pick up an inner tube ($5) at the roadside bar about a half-mile before the entrance to the **park** (Map p228; ⊠407-889-4179; 400 E Kelly Park Rd, Apopka; per vehicle $5; ☺8am-8pm Mar-Oct, to 6pm Nov-Feb, water closes 1hr before park closing) and float the shallow, 1-mile stream formed by Rock Spring. On the weekends and during the summer the park fills with locals, creating a raucous party atmosphere, but during the winter your only company might be the otter swimming along beside you, the turtles lounging on the rocks and the deer grazing along the creek's edge. Kelly Park is about a 40-minute drive northwest of Orlando, a quarter mile east of County Rd 434 on Kelly Rd.

Historic Bok Sanctuary

Frederick Law Olmstead Jr designed these spectacular **gardens** (www.boktowergardens.org; 1151 Tower Blvd, Lake Wales; adult/child 5-12 $10/3; ☺8am-6pm, last admission 5pm) and in 1929 President Calvin Coolidge dedicated them to the US people. The centerpiece of the 250-acre property is the meticulously carved 205ft stone bell tower. Pick up special paper at the entry and make a treasure hunt out of looking for the iron rubbing posts, each with a different animal to rub. Children can also borrow a readers' backpack, with puppets, books and a blanket. Also on-site is a small cafe, a museum and the beautiful 20-room Mediterranean-style Pinewood Estates. Check the website for a schedule of outdoor classical music concerts ($25). Take I-4 west to exit 55. Proceed south on Hwy 27 for 23 miles and follow the signs.

Nature Conservancy's Disney Wilderness Preserve

Hidden within Orlando's sprawl, this 12,000-acre **preserve** (www.nature.org/florida; 2700 Scrub Jay Trail; adult/child 6-17 $3/2; ☺9am-5pm Mon-Fri) is the result of wetland laws that required Walt Disney World to compensate for the company's impact on (and devastation of) wetlands and sensitive natural habitats. Home to gopher tortoises, bald eagles, sandhill cranes and hundreds of other wildlife species, the park features short walking trails through the scrub, fields and woods. The park is located about 20 minutes' drive from Walt Disney World, just south of Kissimmee. Take Poinciana Blvd south off Hwy 192 several miles and turn right on Pleasant Hill Rd/Cypress Parkway. Drive 0.5 miles and turn left onto Old Pleasant Hill Rd. Follow signs 0.7 miles to the preserve.

Harry P Leu Gardens

Lovely **gardens** (Map p232; www.leugardens.org; 1920 N Forest Ave; adult/child $7/2; ☺9am-5pm, last admission 4pm) encompass 50 acres and include camellias, orange groves and desert plants along the shores of Lake Rowena. Tours of Leu House, an 18th-century mansion, run every half-hour from 10am to 3:30pm. There's an outdoor movie the first Friday of every month from March to November (except July), as well as storytelling and live music. From I-4, take exit 85 to Princeton St.

luxurious and elegant option has marble floors, a stunning art-deco bar with massive black pillars, weekend jazz and handsome urban rooms. The small rooftop pool echoes 1950s Miami Beach.

Courtyard at Lake Lucerne B&B $$
(☑407-648-5188, 800-444-5289; www.orlando historicinn.com; 211 Lucerne Circle NE; r & ste $99-225; ▣ ☎ ♨ ☀) This lovely historic inn (c 1883), with its enchanting gardens, romantic fountains, complimentary cocktails and genteel breakfast, sits directly under two highway overpasses. The art-deco suites, housed in Orlando's first apartment building (c 1946), have small kitchens and plenty of room, and there are handsome antiques throughout. But you can hear the trucks rumble overhead and it's an ugly, unpleasant walk to the restaurants and bars in downtown Orlando and Thornton Park. In a better location, this place would be a favorite. From downtown, head south one block from South St, turn east on W Anderson St and follow it a couple blocks under the toll road, where it becomes Delaney Ave. The inn is at the end of the road, on Lake Lucerne.

Veranda Bed & Breakfast B&B $$
(☑407-849-0321; www.theverandabandb.com; 707 E Washington St, Thornton Park; r $109-189, ste $209-269; ▣ ☎ ♨) Simple and low-key, with several good restaurants and neighborhood bars within blocks. It sits just off Summerlin Ave, about a block east of Lake Eola and two blocks south of Robinson St.

INTERNATIONAL DRIVE (AROUND UNIVERSAL ORLANDO RESORT & SEAWORLD)

Grande Lakes Orlando LUXURY HOTEL $$$
(off Map p236; ☑JW Marriott 407-206-2300, Ritz 407-206-2400; www.grandelakes.com; 4012 Central Florida Pkwy; r $299-400, ste from $350; ▣ @ ☎ ♨ ♨) Two properties, one a Ritz and the other a Marriott, share facilities. The grounds, peaceful and elegant, with plenty of greenery and the best lazy river pool in Orlando, sit in a sheltered oasis of quiet and luxury. The spa is divine, the service impeccable, the food outstanding and most rooms have balconies overlooking the free-form pool and the 18-hole golf course. Excellent for honeymooners and families alike, this hotel is the rare gem that seamlessly combines child-friendly with adult-friendly. Rates at the Marriott are generally about $50 less.

Peabody Orlando RESORT $$$
(Map p236; ☑407-352-4000, 800-732-2639; www.peabodyorlando.com; 9801 International Dr; r & ste $250-500; ▣ ☎ ☎ ♨ ♨) This first-rate hotel has all the amenities you'd expect at these prices, plus one famous extra: the March of the Peabody Ducks. At 11am a line of ducks waddles down a red carpet into the lobby fountain and at 5pm they march back to their palatial nighttime digs. Unlike its sister hotel in Memphis, this is a decidedly modern and massive facility. Service is absolutely top-notch, rooms are spacious, beds are scrumptious. TVs blend into the bathroom mirror! Last-minute and off-season rates drop to $120.

**Holiday Inn Resort Orlando –
The Castle** HOTEL $$
(Map p236; ☑407-345-1511, 800-952-2785; www.thecastleorlando.com; 8629 International Dr; r $120-160, ste $217-250; ▣ @ ☎ ☎ ♨ ☀) You can't miss the castle-like exterior of this International Drive landmark, as distinctive inside as it is out. A whimsical purple 'castle creature' greets guests in the peach-walled lobby, which is adorned with gilt and chandeliers; outside the small pool features a fish-shaped fountain. An intimate breakfast room serves grab-and-go breakfast, and handsome rooms are nothing like the Holiday Inn you may expect. Take a picnic or a bottle of wine to the gardened rooftop terrace and catch Disney's distant fireworks. Rates plummet to $69 during slow times.

TOP CHOICE Hilton Garden Hotel MOTEL $$
(Map p236; ☑407-351-2100, 800-327-1366; www.hiltongardenorlando.com; 5877 American Way; r $95-124; ▣ @ ☎ ♨ ♨) Handsome rooms with Florida pastels, free internet and parking, a little tiki bar by the pool, and an on-site restaurant, this newly built chain is an excellent midrange option, particularly if you're going to Universal Orlando. It's less than a mile to the parks and though it sits on I-4, it's set apart from the chaos of International Drive.

HOME AWAY FROM HOME

If you want to be close to the theme parks, most vacation home rentals will be in gated housing developments, many with pools. For Old Florida small-town and lakefront digs, rent in Winter Park.

All Star Vacation Homes (www .allstarvacationhomes.com)

Emerald Island (www.emerald-island .com)

Vacation Rental By Owner (www .vrbo.com)

Hilton Homewood Suites   MOTEL $$
(Map p236; ☑407-226-0669; http://homewood suites1.hilton.com; 5893 American Way; ste $120-160; ❉@☎☒♠) An all-suite hotel across from the Hilton Garden Inn that is perfect for families. Beds are super comfy, suites are spacious and each one has a fully equipped kitchen. Fill in your grocery list when you check in, and they'll do the shopping for you with no extra fee. There's complimentary daily breakfast and hot snacks and drinks (including beer) Monday through Thursday, and a warm and quiet feel at both Hiltons that is lacking at comparable chain hotels in Orlando.

Four Points by Sheraton
Orlando Studio City   HOTEL $$
(Map p236; ☑407-351-2100, 800-327-1366; www. sheratonstudiocity.com; 5905 International Dr; r & ste $65-150; ❉☎☒♠) The art-deco motif starts at the driveway arch and spills into the small checkerboard-floored and mirrored lobby of this tall, skinny building in the middle of International Drive mayhem. Nothing special, but a solid choice conveniently located close to the parks with good value.

AROUND WALT DISNEY WORLD

Hotels in Lake Buena Vista, Kissimmee and Celebration (all on Map p228) lie within a few miles of Walt Disney World. In addition to these recommended options, there's an excellent selection of chain motels along grassy Palm Parkway just outside Disney's gates and a cluster of seven upscale chain hotels (www. downtowndisneyhotels.com) across from Downtown Disney.

Omni Orlando Resort at
Championsgate   RESORT $$
(☑407-390-6664, 800-843-6664; www.omni hotels.com; 1500 Masters Blvd; r $175-300; ❉@☎☒♠) Because the hotel is buffered from noise and congestion by two Greg Norman–designed golf courses, wetlands and plenty of green space, it's easy to forget you're so close to the theme parks. There's an adult-only pool, with a lovely hot tub, and a pleasantly landscaped family pool boasting a waterslide and an 850ft lazy river. Unfortunately, the on-site Japanese restaurant is expensive and mediocre. Two- and three-bedroom villas sleeping six to eight people cost $560 to $750. From Disney, take I-4 west to exit 58 and bear right.

TOP
CHOICE **Hyatt Regency Grand**
Cypress Resort   RESORT $$
(Map p256; ☑407-239-1234, 800-233-1234; www. hyattgrandcypress.com; 1 Grand Cypress Blvd, Lake Buena Vista; r $169-350; ❉@☎☒♠♠) The villas here are some of the nicest accommodations in Orlando. Considering the proximity to Disney (just outside the gates) and SeaWorld, and the quality of the rooms, the service, the grounds and the amenities, this is one of the better-value top-end resorts in Orlando.

Waldorf Astoria   LUXURY HOTEL $$$
(Map p256; ☑407-597-5500; www.waldorfastoria orlando.com; 14200 Bonnett Creek Resort Lane; $200-400, ste $450-560; ❉@☎☒♠) This elegant newcomer doesn't offer the sheltered-oasis feel of its competitors, but the quality of its rooms, amenities and service is impeccable and it's the closest luxury resort to Disney. The excellent buffet breakfast includes several stations, and two grandly styled pools border the golf course. Between the Guerlain spa and absolutely divine beds, it's hard to drag yourself to the parks. Luxury bus shuttle to Disney is complimentary but undependable – it may make several stops on the way to or from your destination, stretching what should be a 15-minute ride closer to an hour and rendering the benefit of close proximity to Disney irrelevant. **Hilton Orlando Bonnet Creek** (☑407-597-3600; www.hilton. com/bonnetcreek), with a lazy river and pool slide, shares amenities with the Waldorf, and rooms and packages are a bit less.

TOP
CHOICE **Mona Lisa Suite Hotel**   HOTEL $$
(Map p256; ☑407-647-1072, 800-228-7220; www. monalisasuitehotel.com; 225 Celebration Pl, Celebration; ste $180-320; ❉@☎☒♠) You can't miss this distinctive round, stone building floating oddly out of place next to the hospital, just off I-4 on Hwy 192. Inside, it's stylishly contemporary, with a circular pool

Built by Disney from the swamps in 1994, the New Urbanism–style town of Celebration (Map p228) is small-town America like you imagine it may have once been...before David Lynch, *Desperate Housewives* and John Cheever introduced irony, before strip malls, before leaf blowers. We could wonder what goes on behind closed doors, but why? Just let it go, and fall into the 20th-century Beverly Cleary–*Father Knows Best* vibe that defines Celebration. Relax over coffee, play in the fountain and watch the ducks. Sure, maybe it doesn't sound that exciting, but wasn't that day at Universal's Islands of Adventure exciting enough?

Celebration, no longer part of Disney, sits off Hwy 192, east of I-4 and a few miles from Walt Disney World. The main attraction is the small lake, with a perfectly manicured promenade circling its length, palm trees dotting the banks, and sidewalk cafes along the few blocks of downtown. The **Celebration Golf Club** (407-939-4653; www.celebrationgolf.com; 701 Golf Park Dr; 18 holes $89; 6am-8pm) is a lovely course suitable for all levels.

On New Year's Eve, the town is transformed into a winter wonderland, with 'snow' falling from the lights and 'ice' skating in the street, and there are amazing midnight fireworks. It makes for a charming night, particularly for families looking for a quieter, gentler alternative to the big bang New Year celebrations in Orlando and the theme parks.

Celebration Hotel (407-566-6000, 888-499-3800; www.celebrationhotel.com; 700 Bloom St; r $150-275, ste $250-350;) is quiet and genteel, with what has to be the city's smallest pool perched on the patio next to the lake. Celebration's only downtown hotel, it offers excellent service, handsome rooms, and a relaxing and friendly alternative to the impersonality of a large resort and the chaos of bars, nightly entertainment and programmed children's activities. Best of all, it's an easy drive to all the parks but feels years and miles away. Note that this is one of the few places that charges a hefty extra for a shuttle to Disney.

The handful of pubs and restaurants in town, all within walking distance of the Celebration Hotel, serve up a surprising variety of cuisine, including Thai, Italian and excellent Japanese: at the intimate, modern **Seito Sushi** (www.seitosushi.com; 671 Front St; mains $8-23; 8am-10pm) you'll find the usual, including *yakisoba* (yellow egg noodles), bento boxes and tempura, and the sushi is quite good. There are a few more locations around Orlando.

surrounding an island of palm trees, and earth-toned suites with fully equipped kitchens. A golf cart shuttles folks to downtown Celebration.

Barefoot'n in the Keys MOTEL **$**
(Map p256; 407-397-1144; www.barefootn.com; 2750 Florida Plaza Blvd; ste 1-bedroom $80-120, 2-bedroom $125-170, 3-bedroom $207-300;) Clean, bright and spacious suites in a yellow six-story building across the road from Old Town – each with an exterior entrance, a kitchen and a patio – face a quiet stretch of grass and trees. Low-key, friendly, close to Disney and set back from the Hwy 192 strip, this makes an excellent alternative to generic chain hotels and fancy resorts.

Eating

Restaurant Row, a half-mile stretch of W Sand Lake Rd just west of Whole Foods and inside the strip mall Plaza Venezia (Map p236), offers a concentration of diverse restaurants and high-end chains more popular with locals than tourists.

DOWNTOWN
All but the Dessert Lady Café lie in Thornton Park (off Map p234), on the eastern shore of Lake Eola and about a half-mile from downtown Orlando on Central Blvd or Robinson St.

Dessert Lady Café CAFE **$**
(Map p234; 407-999-5696; www.dessertlady.com; 120 W Church St; mains $5-10; 11:30am-11pm Tue-Thu, to midnight Fri, 4pm-midnight Sat) Ask Patti Schmidt how she became Orlando's first and only Dessert Lady and she'll tell you that it all started with a carrot cake. Now enjoy desserts from fruit cobbler to bourbon pecan pie over a glass of wine. Rich reds and draping silks give the tiny interior a bordello atmosphere, and a bistro menu serves pulled-pork sliders, excellent chicken salad sandwiches and a handful of other soups, quiches and salads. A slice of cake costs as much as the

sandwich ($10), which should tell you something about that slice of cake!

Graffiti Junktion American Burger Bar
BURGERS $$

(900 E Washington St, Thornton Park; mains $12-25; ⏱11am-1am, to midnight Sun) Massive painted guitars greet folks at this neon graffiti-covered happenin' hangout in a residential district. Sure, there's a handful of sandwiches and salads, but come for the burgers washed down with a Graffiti-tini. The Green Mountain is topped with Canadian bacon, fried egg and cheddar, and you can add artichoke hearts, chili or avocado to any burger for a dollar.

Shari Sushi
JAPANESE $$

(☎407-420-9420; www.sharisushilounge.com; 621 E Central Blvd, Thornton Park; mains $14-24; ⏱11am-10pm Tue-Sat, 10am-3pm Sun) Black and white contemporary minimalist decor, huge sidewalk windows and excellent sushi.

Aroma Italian Café and Wine Bar
ITALIAN $$

(☎407-426-8989; www.aromaitaliancafe.com; 712 E Washington St, Thornton Park; mains $9-18; ⏱4:30pm-late Wed-Sun, noon-6pm Sun) Father and son play guitar several nights a week at this intimate family-owned spot serving Italian classics. Check the website for special events like wine tasting for AIDS fundraising.

Hue
AMERICAN $$

(☎407-849-1800; www.huerestaurant.com; 629 E Central Blvd, Thornton Park; mains $12-20; ⏱4-11pm Sun-Wed, to midnight Thu-Sat, 8am-3pm Sun) Another favorite with the 20-somethings of Thornton Park, with sidewalk seating and bustling weekend brunch. The name refers to hue of color, not the city in Vietnam.

INTERNATIONAL DRIVE (AROUND UNIVERSAL ORLANDO RESORT & SEAWORLD)

Five Guys Burgers and Fries
BURGERS $

(Map p236; www.fiveguys.com; 4821 New Broad St; mains $5-10; ⏱8am-11pm Mon-Sat, to 9pm Sun) Sure, it's a chain. Sure, you can find them scattered through Florida and beyond. Sure, it's nothing more than a fast-food burger joint. But hands down, this Obama favorite is the best burger and fries in town. It's an easy drive from Universal Orlando Resort, with a retro vibe and dozens of framed awards and rave reviews plastering the walls. Other Orlando locations include one in Prime Outlet Mall.

Thai Thani
THAI $$

(Map p236; www.thaithani.net; 11025 International Dr; mains $9-22; ⏱11:30am-11pm) Just past the gates to SeaWorld, Discovery Cove and Aquatica, this dark little place makes an ideal dinner choice after a day of dolphin shows and waterslides. It's friendly, cool and quiet, with gilded Thai decor and traditional Thai seating on the floor. Expect a dramatically watered down spice level, but it's fresh and tasty. There's a second location in Celebration.

Taverna Opa
GREEK $$

(Map p236; www.opaorlando.com; Pointe Orlando; mains $12-25; ⏱11am-midnight; ✎) The waitstaff at this high-ceilinged Greek eatery crush up fresh hummus table-side and serve it with warm pita rather than just plopping down a basket of bread. While it can get kind of crazy at night, when the belly dancer shimmers and shakes from table to table and it isn't unusual for folks to climb onto those solid tables and kick up their heels, the rest of the time it's a pleasant, simple place for solid and tasty Greek classics, including plenty of vegetarian options

Melting Pot
FONDUE $$

(Map p236; www.meltingpot.com/orlando; 7549 W Sand Lake Rd; mains $12-25; ⏱5-10pm Mon-Thu, to 11pm Fri & Sat, 4-10pm Sun; ✎) Kids in particular love the novelty of a fondue dinner (cheese, beef, chicken, seafood and, of course, chocolate).

B-Line Diner
DINER $$

(Map p236; www.peabodyorlando.com/dining; Peabody Orlando, 9801 International Dr; mains $8-20; ⏱24hr) A retro diner cafe serving basic diner food 24-7.

Johnny Rockets
DINER $

(Map p236; www.johnnyrockets.com; Pointe Orlando; mains $6-10; ⏱11:30am-11pm Sun-Thu, to 2am Fri & Sat) Straight out of *Happy Days*, with red vinyl seating, lots of chrome and flip-style jukeboxes on the tables. The Fonz would feel right at home.

AROUND WALT DISNEY WORLD

In addition to the following, you'll find plenty of restaurants catering to the Walt Disney World tourist in Lake Buena Vista and Kissimmee (both on Map p228), but it's mostly chains. If you're looking for a quiet evening away from the Walt Disney World spinning wheel of eye candy and sensory overload, head to Celebration. Several restaurants and bars line the small lake, and they all have patio dining.

Hemmingways
SEAFOOD $$$

(Map p256; 407-239-1234; www.grandcypress. hyatt.com; Hyatt Regency Grand Cypress Resort, 1 Grand Cypress Blvd, Lake Buena Vista; mains $29-40; 5-10pm) Located inside the luxurious grounds of the Hyatt Grand Cypress, this quiet spot serves up Key West fare. Crab cakes with big chunks of lump crab and very little filler pair perfectly with a salad and a glass of wine. Simple seafood dishes are clean, fresh and delicious. Ask to sit on the screened-in porch, nestled among the greenery and watched over by a bronze Buddha.

Habibi
MIDDLE EASTERN $$

(Map p236; www.habibiusa.com; 8607 Palm Parkway, Lake Buena Vista; mains $19-27; 5-10pm;) Quiet outdoor patio, Lebanese wine and good food, just outside Disney and close to motels along Palm Parkway.

GREATER ORLANDO

Yellow Dog Eats
BARBECUE $

(407-296-0609; www.yellowdogeats.com; 1236 Hempel Ave, Windermere; mains $10-20; 11:30am-10pm Mon-Thu, to 11pm Fri, noon-11pm Sat, 3-8pm Sun;) Housed in what was once a general store, with a tin roof, an old boys' school locker filled with bottled beer, and an eclectic mix of quirky and dog-inspired decor, this laid-back Orlando gem serves up excellent barbecue. Massive homes, including that of Tiger Woods, have replaced the orange groves that once surrounded the site, and it feels like a drive to get here, but don't be deterred. Menu offerings range from Florida Cracker (pulled pork with Gouda, bacon and fried onions) to the recommended Puppy Love (peanut butter, strawberries, bananas, chocolate shavings, chopped roast peanuts) and excellent Cuban-style black beans. Call in advance for pickup orders.

Yellow Dog Eats sits about 6 miles northwest of Universal Orlando Resort. Take Turkey Lake Rd (which borders the park on the west) for about a mile and turn left at the T onto Conroy Rd. In 2 miles turn right onto S Apopka Vineland Rd, then left at the church onto Windy Ridge Rd and right onto Hempel Ave.

Dandelion Communitea Café
VEGETARIAN $

(407-362-1864; http://dandelioncommunitea.com; 618 N Thornton Ave; mains $5-10; 11am to 10pm Mon-Sat, to 5pm Sun;) Unabashedly crunchy and definitively organic, this pillar of the

Celebrating a birthday? Or just looking for a decadently delicious sweet something? Head to tiny **Bluebird Bakery** (407-228-3822; 3122 Corrine Dr; pastries $2-4; 7am-5pm Tue-Sat, 10am-4pm Sun, closes early if cupcakes run out) for daily baked cupcakes and organic java. Flavors range from classic chocolate to quirky vanilla black pepper or sweet potato. Named after the favorite bird of the owner's grandma, it's located on Corrine Dr, 0.6 miles east of Harry P Leu Gardens.

'sprouts and tofu, green tea and soy milk' crowd serves up creative and excellent vegetarian fare in a refurbished old house that invites folks to sit down and hang out. The focus is on Florida-grown produce and locally blended teas, and it is 100% green. If it all sounds too healthy, try a Fluffer Nutter (wheat bread with almond butter, bananas and ricemallow fluff), its nod to junk food. There's an informal fire-pit, tables in the yard, and microbrew beer; check the website for details on art openings, poetry readings and live music. From downtown Orlando head north on Magnolia Ave, turn right at E Colonial Dr and then right in 0.7 miles onto Thornton Ave.

Bikes, Beans & Bordeaux
CAFE $

(www.b3cafe.com; 3022 Corrine Dr; mains $6-12; 8am-3pm Tue-Sat, 7am-2pm Sun) Organic fare with a contemporary cafe vibe, couches for lounging and bold red walls featuring local art. Try the hot feta dip and delicious quiche, or create your own flatbread concoction. The wine and beer list follows the international cycling season, with French Bordeaux during the Tour de France and so on, and there's weekend live music and cyclists' happy hour specials. From Harry P Leu Gardens, head east on Corrine Dr for 0.6 miles, and look for the tiny strip mall on the right.

White Wolf Café
DINER $$

(www.whitewolfcafe.com; 1829 N Orange Ave; mains $14-29; 7am-9pm Mon-Fri, 8am-10pm Sat, 8am-3pm Sun) Tiffany-styled chandeliers, a massive wooden bar and an eclectic mix of antiques offer a welcomed respite from the plethora of chains and themed restaurants that define Orlando eateries. Simple but excellent basics like burgers, pastas and piz-

ORLANDO & AROUND EATING

zas, as well as stick-to-your bones breakfasts. From downtown take I-4 exit 85 (Princeton St) and turn right; take the first right onto N Orange Ave and look for White Wolf on the left. Alternatively, head north on Magnolia Ave and right on N Orange.

Greek Corner Restaurant   GREEK $
(www.thegreekcorner.net; 1600 N Orange Ave; mains $6-14; ⊙11am-10pm Mon-Sat, to 8pm Sun) A simple cafe with white walls and a small patio, this little place across from Lake Ivanhoe serves delicious gyros, moussaka and other Greek specialties. Located a few blocks south of White Wolf Café.

Ethos Vegan Kitchen   VEGETARIAN $
(www.ethosvegankitchen.com; 1235 N Orange Ave; mains $6-10; ⊙11am-10pm Tue-Sat, 10am-3pm Sun;) The 100% vegan menu includes pizzas with broccoli, banana peppers, zucchini and seitan, pecan-encrusted eggplant, homemade soups and various sandwiches with names like A Fungus Among Us and the Hippie Wrap. Look for Ethos a few blocks south of White Wolf Café.

🍷 Drinking

Orlando likes to drink, so whether tastes lean toward a flight of wine at a sidewalk cafe, a Pabst Blue Ribbon in a dark and smoky dive or shots of tequila at a pulsing nightclub, Orlando satisfies. The downtown Orlando drinking scene can be a crazy *Girls Gone Wild* meets Spring Break scene, particularly on the weekends and late at night, with thumping music blaring into the streets and burly bouncers manning the doors. The significant police presence keeps drunken brawls and other unseemly behavior to a minimum.

Neighborhood bars in Celebration, Winter Park and Thornton Park (which is just east of downtown Orlando's Lake Eola; listed in the following Downtown section) offer an altogether different vibe, with wine bars, acoustic live music and outdoor cafes sporting water bowls for canine companions. Walt Disney World's Downtown Disney (p285) and Universal Studio Orlando's CityWalk (p297) both have plenty of drinking and live music as well.

DOWNTOWN

Latitudes   BAR
(Map p234; www.churchstreetbars.com; 33 W Church St; ⊙4:30pm-2am) Low-key island-inspired rooftop bar with tiki torches and potted palms. It's completely outside, three stories above street level, perfect for balmy Orlando nights. Latitudes is on the 3rd floor of Church Street Bars – look for Chillers on the 1st floor – and there's a microbrewery with pool tables on the 2nd floor.

Bösendorfer Lounge   LOUNGE
(Map p234; ☏407-313-9000; Westin Grand Bohemian, 325 S Orange Ave; ⊙11am-midnight Sun-Wed, to 1am Thu, to 2am Fri & Sat) With zebra-fabric chairs, gilded mirrors, massive black pillars and marble floors, this hotel bar with a circular bar oozes pomp and elegance. Popular with Orlando residents, who pop on over for an after-work drink, the lounge picks up with live jazz at 7pm. The name stems from the lounge's rare Bösendorfer piano.

Dexters of Thornton Park   WINE BAR
(808 E Washington St, Thornton Park; ⊙11am-10pm Mon-Thu, to 11pm Sat, 10am-10pm Sun) Neighborhood restaurant with outdoor seating, live local music and wine by the flight, glass or bottle. There's a second location in Winter Park.

Burtons   BAR
(801 E Washington St, Thornton Park; ⊙noon-2am) A neighborhood corner bar that's been around for almost 70 years. Expect forgettable wine but plenty of cheap cold beer, a jukebox with REM and the like and a couple of pool tables.

Wall Street Plaza   THEME BAR
(Map p234; ☏407-420-1515; www.wallstplaza.net; 25 Wall St Plaza) Eight bars, with live music and every imaginable kind of theme night, cluster together in a downtown Orlando pedestrian mall and define downtown Orlando's party drinking scene. Festivals include Martini Fest, Margarita Fest, Rum Fest and Beer Fest – you get the idea. Most have outdoor seating and food, and there's plenty of, shall we say, mingling. Hours vary; call for details.

INTERNATIONAL DRIVE

Funky Monkey   WINE BAR
(Map p236; Pointe Orlando; ⊙4-10pm Mon-Thu, 11am-midnight Fri & Sat, 4-9pm Sun) A sophisticated wine bar with a simple menu (mains $7 to $17), plenty of windows and modern decor. Funky Monkey sits in the hub of tourist traps on International Drive and offers relative quiet.

Howl at the Moon   THEME BAR
(Map p236; 8815 International Dr; cover $5-10; ⊙11:30am-2am Mon-Sat, 7pm-2am Sun) The au-

In 1991 Orlando gay activist Doug Swallow and a handful of friends encouraged gays and lesbians to 'wear red and be seen' when visiting the Magic Kingdom. Some 2500 made it. Ever since, an estimated 40,000 to 50,000 red-shirted gay and lesbian visitors descend on Cinderella's Castle on the first Saturday in June for what is now an entrenched Florida tradition, and events extend throughout the city for the week. Though it explodes during Gay Days, there is a solid gay and lesbian community in Orlando year-round. Go to www. orlandogaycities.com for a thorough listing and reviews of bars and clubs, events, hotels, bathhouses and more.

Gay, Lesbian & Bisexual Community Center (☑407-228-8272; www.glbcc.org; 946 N Mills Ave; ☺9am-4pm Mon & Thu, to 8pm Tue, Wed & Fri, noon-8pm Sat, noon-5pm Sun) General resource center, with tips on local hot spots and social events.

Parliament House (☑407-425-7571; www.parliamenthouse.com; 410 N Orange Blossom Trail; r $60-120, Gay Day $155; ☎☒) This legendary gay resort and an Orlando institution sits on Rock Lake and features several clubs and bars, a restaurant and some of the best drag shows south of the Mason–Dixon Line. From downtown, take I-4 east to exit 80B (Hwy 441 N) and head west about 3 miles.

Ritzy Rags (www.ritzyrags.com; 928 N Mills Ave, Thornton Park; ☺from 11am Mon-Sat, closing hour varies) Owner and performer Leigh Shannon offers makeup and wardrobe tips for making the most of what you were born with and sells everything a drag queen could want.

Pulse (☑407-649-3888; www.pulseorlando.net; 1912 S Orange Ave; $5) Three nightclubs, each with its own distinct vibe but all ultramodern and sleek. Call for directions and hours.

dience sings along at the rock-and-roll dueling piano show. It's popular with tourists staying at the area's many hotels.

GREATER ORLANDO
Wally's Mills Ave Liquors   BAR
(1001 N Mills Ave; ☺7:30pm-2am) It's been around since the early '50s, before Orlando became Disney, and while its peeling naked-women wallpaper could use some updating, it wouldn't be Wally's without it. Nothing flashy, nothing loud, just a tiny windowless old-school bar with a jukebox and cheap drinks, as much a dark dive as you'll find anywhere. Wednesday night is $3 microbrews, and the attached package store sells beer, wine and liquor. From Thornton Park, head north a couple miles on Mills Ave.

☆ Entertainment
Clubs & Live Music
Social   LIVE MUSIC
(Map p234; ☑407-246-1419; www.thesocial.org; 54 N Orange Ave; cover varies; ☺7pm-2am) Matchbox 20 got their start at this Orlando favorite for live music on stage. Vaulted ceilings, an enormous bar and VIP lounges give it a South Beach flair. Note that the smoking policy is determined by the band, allowed on some nights and not allowed others.

Beacham   CLUB
(Map p234; ☑407-246-1419; www.thebeacham .com; 46 N Orange Ave; cover varies; ☺9pm-3am) Connected to The Social and owned by the same folk, this cornerstone of Orlando's nightclubs blasts hip-hop, reggae, salsa and old-school rock during the week and has live music on the weekend.

Will's Pub   LIVE MUSIC
(☑407-898-5070; 1040 N Mills; ☺4pm-2am Mon-Sat, from 6pm Sun) With $2 Pabst on tap, a permanent layer of smoke hovering over the pool tables, Ms PacMan and pinball and vintage pin-ups on the walls, this is Orlando's less polished music scene. It's an established institution as the spot to catch local and nationally touring indie music. Will's is on Mills Ave, just over a mile north of Thornton Park.

Independent Bar   CLUB
(Map p234; ☑407-839-0457; 70 N Orange Ave; cover $10; ☺10pm-3am Sun, Wed & Thu, from 9:30pm Fri & Sat) Hip, crowded and loud, with DJs spinning underground dance and alternative rock until the wee hours.

Cinemas
Go to www.buildabettermousetrip.com/activity-outdoormovie.php for a schedule of free outdoor screenings of Disney movies at Disney hotels. There are also cinemas

ON THE STAGE & UNDER THE STARS

There's more to Orlando than theme parks and techno-club hopping. In addition to the following, Walt Disney World, Universal Orlando Resort and SeaWorld all have an island-inspired luau, Disney offers three dinner shows, and several Disney resorts screen classic Disney films outdoors (free). There's also a free classic movie on the second Thursday of every month in Winter Park.

Cirque du Soleil La Nouba (Map p256; ☎407-939-7600; www.cirquedusoleil.com; Downtown Disney; adult $76-132, child 3-9 $61-105; ⊙6pm & 9pm Tue-Sat) Disney's best live show features mind-boggling acrobatic feats expertly fused to light, stage and costume design to create a cohesive artistic vision. And of course, there's a silly Disney twist involving a princess and a frog. This is a small horseshoe theater, with only about 20 rows from the stage to the top, no balcony and designed by Disney specifically to house La Nouba. There are no bad seats.

Blue Man Group (Map p236; ☎407-258-3626; www.universalorlando.com; Universal Orlando Resort CityWalk; adult $59-74, child 3-9 $49-64) Originally an off-Broadway phenomenon in 1991, this high-energy and multisensory fun show features three bald men painted blue engaging in all kinds of craziness involving percussion 'instruments,' paintballs, marsh-mallows and modern dancing.

Mad Cow Theatre (Map p234; ☎407-297-8788; www.madcowtheatre.com; 105 S Magnolia Ave; tickets $18-30) A model of regional theater, with classic and modern performances in downtown space.

Theatre Downtown (☎407-841-0083; www.theatredowntown.net; 2113 N Orange Ave; tickets $16-22) Repertory theater featuring original works from local playwrights, regional actors and classic productions. Located two blocks west of Loch Haven Park.

Sak Comedy Lab (Map p234; ☎407-648-0001; www.sak.com; 29 S Orange Ave; tickets $15; ⊙9pm shows Tue & Wed) Improv comedy in 200-seat downtown theater; 9pm shows Tuesday and Wednesday cost $3. Reservations recommended. Check website for other show times.

John and Rita Lowndes Shakespeare Center (☎407-447-1700; www.orlandoshakes .org; 812 E Rollins St, Loch Haven Park; tickets $20-35) Set on the shores of Lake Estelle in grassy Loch Haven Park, this lovely theater includes three intimate stages hosting classics like *Pride and Prejudice* and *Beowulf* and excellent children's theater.

Orlando Repertory Theater (☎407-896-7365; www.orlandorep.com; 1001 E Princeton St, Loch Haven Park; tickets $10-25) Performances for families and children run primarily in the afternoon or early evening. Shows stretch the gamut of styles and content, including *Anne Frank and Me, Hairspray* and *James and the Giant Peach*.

Dinner Theater (www.dinnertheaterorlando.com; adult $25-45, child 3-9 $19-35) Orlando loves its dinner theater, so if you're looking for over-the-top kitschy fun you'll find something to tickle your fancy. Shows, spread at venues south of downtown Orlando and close to the theme parks, include *Arabian Nights,* with decked-out horses prancing on stage, and the swashbuckling *Pirates*. Prices include dinner, beer, wine and soft drinks.

Orlando Venues (☎407-849-2000; www.orlandovenues.net; prices vary) City-owned corporation sells tickets for theater and live-music events ranging from Taylor Swift to *The Lion King*, at the Bob Carr Performing Arts Center, Citrus Bowl, Amway Center and other smaller venues.

at Downtown Disney (p284), Universal Orlando Resort (p298) and Winter Park (p241).

TOP CHOICE **Enzian Theater** CINEMA (☎407-629-0054; www.enzian.org; 1300 S Orlando Ave, Maitland; adult/child $7/5, weekend matinees $5; ⊙5pm-midnight Tue-Fri, noon-midnight Sat

& Sun; Ⓟ) The envy of any city or college town, this fantastic clapboard-sided theater screens independent and classic films and has an excellent restaurant featuring primarily local and organic fare. Have a veggie burger and a beer on the patio underneath the cypress tree, or opt for table service in the theater. Instead of traditional rows of seats, the theater has tables and comfie chairs. From Friday through Sunday, the Eden Bar serves lunch, with noodles and seafood salad, sandwiches and flatbread, and soup, everything for under $10. On the second Thursday of every month, the Enzian teams up with Winter Park to present Popcorn Flicks (free), a series of classic movies like *Casablanca* screened outside in the park. The Enzian is in Maitland, just north of Winter Park.

Regal Point Orlando Stadium and IMAX
CINEMA

(Map p236; ☑407-248-9045; 9101 International Dr; adult/child $10/7) Just north of the Peabody Hotel on International Drive.

Plaza Cinema Café 12
CINEMA

(Map p234; ☑407-248-9045; www.cobbtheatres.com/plazacinema12.aspx; 155 S Orange Ave; adult/child $10.75/7.50) Downtown Orlando.

Cinemark at Festival Bay
CINEMA

(Map p236; ☑407-352-1042; 5150 International Dr, Festival Bay Mall; adult/child $10/7) Inside Festival Bay Mall, on the north end of International Drive.

Sports

Even if you're not a baseball fan, spring training in Orlando is a great way to wile away an afternoon or evening. Bring a blanket, grab the Cracker Jacks and watch baseball like it was meant to be. Ticket prices vary, but expect to pay about $23. The Atlanta Braves train at the ESPN Wide World of Sports Complex (p284) in Walt Disney World.

Osceola County Stadium
BASEBALL

(☑407-697-3200; 631 Heritage Park Way) The Houston Astros play at the Grapefruit League's smallest ballpark, in Kissimmee (Map p228).

Amway Center
BASKETBALL, FOOTBALL

(Map p234; ☑tickets 800-653-8000; www.orlandovenues.net; 400 W Church St) The Orlando Magic (www.nba.com/magic) National Basketball Association team and the Orlando Predators (www.orlandopredators.com) Arena Football League team both play at the Amway Center.

Citrus Bowl
SOCCER

(☑tickets 800-653-8000; www.orlandovenues.net; 1610 W Church St) Founded in 2010, the professional Orlando City (www.orlandocitysoccer.com) soccer team plays here. From the Amway Center, head west on W Church St about 1 mile.

For University of Central Florida Knights football games, go directly to their website, http://ucfathletics.cstv.com.

🛍 Shopping

Head to Celebration or Winter Park for pleasant browsing, small-town American style, or to Downtown Disney for shopping on steroids.

Prime Outlets International
MALL

(Map p236; ☑407-354-0126; International Dr & I-4; ⊙10am-9pm Mon-Sat, to 6pm Sun) Particularly popular with overseas travelers, this outlet mall offers the usual discount-mall suspects as well as a few surprises, like the ultrachic Barneys.

Farmers Market Lake Eola
MARKET

(off Map p234; Lake Eola; ⊙10am-4pm Sun) Local produce, cheese and handicrafts, live music and a beer and wine garden on the shores of downtown Orlando's Lake Eola.

Mall At Millenia
MALL

(www.mallatmillenia.com; I-4 Exit 78/Conroy Rd; ⊙10am-9pm Mon-Sat, 11am-7pm Sun) Big hitters at this pricey high-end mall include Anthropologie, Bloomingdales, Crate & Barrel and J Crew.

Orange World
FOOD

(off Map p256; 407-239-6031; www.orangeworld192.com; 5395 W Irlo Bronson Memorial Hwy; ⊙8am-10:45pm) When in Florida, send an orange. Or a tangelo, whatever.

ℹ Information

Emergency

Call ☑911 in an emergency.

Police (☑407-246-2470, 321-235-5300; 100 S Hughey Ave) Central police office downtown.

Media

Axis (www.axismag.com) *Orlando Sentinel's* magazine covers the music, movie and bar scene.
Orlando Sentinel (www.orlandosentinel.com) Daily city paper.
Orlando Weekly (www.orlandoweekly.com) Free weekly.

Medical Services

Arnold Palmer Hospital for Children (☑407-649-9111; 1414 Kuhl Ave; ⊙24hr) The city's primary children's hospital. Located just east of I-4 at exit 81 (Kaley Ave).
Centra Care Walk-In Medical (☑407-934-2273; www.centracare.org; 12500 S Apopka Vineland Rd/SR 535, Lake Buena Vista; ⊙8am-midnight Mon-Fri, to 8pm Sat & Sun) A walk-in medical center offering adult and pediatric

care. Located near Downtown Disney, on SR 535 south of Palm Parkway; see website or call for other locations.

Doctors on Call Services (☑407-399-3627; ⊙24hr) House and hotel-room calls to greater Orlando, including Walt Disney World and Universal Orlando Resort, and hotline for regional medical facilities.

Dr P Phillips Hospital (☑407-351-8500; 9400 Turkey Lake Rd; ⊙24hr) Closest hospital to SeaWorld and International Drive. From SeaWorld, take Central Florida Parkway west about 0.5 miles and turn right onto Turkey Lake Rd for just over 1 mile.

Florida Hospital Celebration Health (☑407-303-4000; 400 Celebration Pl; ⊙24hr) Located just east of I-4 off Hwy 192; the closest hospital to Walt Disney World.

Lakeside Medical Center (☑407-370-4881; 8723 International Dr; ⊙8am-8pm Mon-Thu, to 9pm Fri, 9am-9pm Sat, 9am-5pm Sun) A walk-in clinic, which costs $130 a visit. Call for other locations.

Money

Bank of America (☑407-244-7041; 390 N Orange Ave; ⊙9am-4pm Mon-Thu, to 6pm Fri) Right downtown, but there are branches everywhere.

Mall at Millenia Concierge (www.mallat millenia.com; I-4 exit 78/Conroy Rd; ⊙10am-6:30pm Mon-Sat) There's a currency exchange at Guest Services.

Post

Post office (Map p234; ☑407-425-6464; 51 E Jefferson St; ⊙7am-5pm Mon-Fri)

Tourist Information

Orlando's Official Visitor Center (Map p236; ☑407-363-5872; www.visitorlando.com; 8723 International Dr; ⊙8:30am-6:30pm) Sells legitimate discount attraction tickets. You'll find a handful of walk-up tourist-information kiosks along International Drive, dozens of rinky-dink operations on Hwy 192, and plenty of information at your hotel.

Websites

Orlando Sentinel (www.orlandosentinel.com /travel) Travel page of the city paper.

ReserveOrlando (www.reserveorlando.com) Central booking agency.

VisitOrlando (www.visitorlando.com) Orlando Visitors Center.

❶ Getting Around

TO/FROM THE AIRPORT Many hotels and motels run complimentary airport shuttles.

Disney's Magical Express (☑407-939-6244) If you're staying at a Walt Disney World hotel

and are arriving into the Orlando airport (as opposed to Sanford), arrange in advance for complimentary luggage handling and deluxe bus transportation.

Legacy Towncar of Orlando (☑888-939-8227; www.legacytowncar.com) Services both airports; from Sanford International Airport to the Disney area, it's $185 round-trip for a town car (seats four) and $245 for a van (seats nine). Prices include a convenient 20-minute grocery-store stop on the way from the airport.

Mears Transportation (☑407-423-5566; www.mearstransportation.com) Expect to pay $20 to $30 one way to Disney World or Universal Studios areas, a bit less to downtown Orlando and bit more to Winter Park.

PUBLIC TRANSPORTATION **I-Ride Trolley** (www.iridetrolley.com; rides adult/child under 12yr $1/free) Runs along two routes along International Drive from 8am to 10:30pm. Buy one-ride tickets on board (exact change only) or a multiday pass (one-/three-/five-/seven-/14-day pass $3/5/7/9/16) at hotels and stores along I-Drive.

Lymmo Free bus service circles downtown Orlando.

WALT DISNEY WORLD

> Here in Florida, we have something special we never enjoyed at Disneyland...the blessing of size. There's enough land here to hold all the ideas and plans we can possibly imagine.
>
> *Walt Disney*

Minutes before the Magic Kingdom opens, Alice in Wonderland, Cinderella, Donald Duck and others stand where all can see them, sing 'Zippidee Doo Dah' and throw sparkly Mickey Mouse confetti into the crowds. They dash off on an open-windowed train, the gates open, and children, adults, honeymooners, grandparents and everyone in between enter the park, some strolling, others dashing down the impeccably clean Main Street toward Cinderella's Castle. That iconic image is as American as the Grand Canyon, a place as loaded with myth and promises of hope as the Statue of Liberty. If only for these few minutes, this is indeed the Happiest Place on Earth.

Yes, there will be lines with seemingly endless waiting and sure, you'll spend more money than you intended on a Mickey Mouse sweatshirt that you wouldn't have dreamed of buying before you came. That Pirates of the Caribbean ride may not be everything everyone said it'd be, and you

It takes a little bit of planning to coordinate your schedule to hit Disney's parades and nighttime spectaculars. Note that times vary according to season and you won't be able to catch both the SpectroMagic and the Electrical Parade on the same trip; Disney offers one or the other for years at a stretch. In addition to the following cornerstones, check www.disneyworld.disney.go.com for holiday celebrations and specialty parties.

» **Celebrate a Dream Come True** (parade, Magic Kingdom, 3pm) Elaborate floats and dancing characters from classic Disney, including Snow White, Cinderella and Alice in Wonderland.

» **Main Street Electrical Parade** (parade, Magic Kingdom) Tinkerbell leads this nostalgic favorite with floats made of thousands of twinkling lights.

» **SpectroMagic** (parade, Magic Kingdom) A night version of Celebrate a Dream Come True.

» **Fantasmic!** (light show, Hollywood Studios) Mickey Mouse faces Disney's assembled dark side. Limited seating for the 25-minute show begins 90 minutes in advance.

» **Wishes Nighttime Spectacular** (fireworks, Magic Kingdom) Jiminy Cricket narrates this classic Disney display over Cinderella's Castle.

» **Illuminations** (light show, Epcot) Fiery interpretation of the history of the earth explodes from the center of the lagoon. If you're exiting via foot or boat from the park's International Gateway, watch the fireworks from the UK or France to minimize mass exodus crowds at the end.

» **Pixar Pals Countdown to Fun** (parade, Hollywood Studios, 3pm) A must for fans of more contemporary hits, including *Ratatouille, Toy Story, Up* and *Monsters Inc*.

» **Jammin' Jungle** (parade, Animal Kingdom, 3pm) Huge folk-art animal puppets, African dancing and Disney characters in safari motif.

WALT DISNEY WORLD

may get stuck behind the guy who spreads his shopping bags and empty stroller parallel to the curb so your kids can't sit down to see the parade ('I got here first,' he growls). You'll return to the hotel exhausted and aching, vaguely dissatisfied with the day's meals, carrying your sleeping Belle, her face painted with now-smudging sparkles and her poofy yellow dress stained with ice cream, cotton candy and that green punch so tantalizingly named Tinker Bell and Friends. You swear that next time you'll take a real vacation... Until those last minutes before you fall asleep, when everything you need to do is done and you're finally relaxing in bed, your eyes closed. You see your child's face staring adoringly at Winnie the Pooh as he gives a big ol' bear hug, your child's arms reaching out to grab the Donald Duck that pops out from the 3D movie. And it's OK. That beach vacation can wait.

Walt Disney World itself is like a child. One minute, you think you can't take another cafeteria-style restaurant serving fried food and bad coffee or another second in an overstuffed shuttle bus. There's no magic here, you mutter. And the next, she does something

right – maybe it's the fireworks, maybe it's a particular turn in a particular ride, maybe it's the corny joke of the guy who drives the horse-drawn carriage down Main Street.

And all is forgiven.

History

When Disneyland opened in southern California, it took off in a huge way, fundamentally transforming the concept of theme parks. Walt Disney, however, was irritated at the hotels and concessions that were springing up in a manner that he felt was entirely parasitic. In 1965, after a secret four-year search, he bought 27,000 acres of swamp, field and woodland in central Florida. His vision was to create a family vacation destination and he wanted to control every aspect – hotels, restaurants, parking and transportation. Sadly, he would never see the realization of his dreams; in 1966, at age 65, Walt Disney died of lung cancer and his brother Roy took over responsibility for development. Walt Disney World's Magic Kingdom opened in 1971, and three months later Roy died of a brain hemorrhage. Epcot opened in 1982, Hollywood Studios in 1989 and Animal Kingdom in 1998.

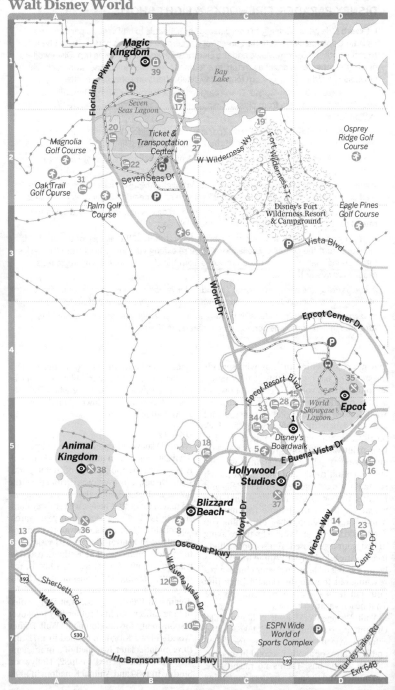

⊙ Sights

Walt Disney World covers over 40 sq miles, and includes four separate theme parks and two water parks, all connected by a complicated system of monorail, boat and bus and intersected by highways and roads. Sights, primarily in the form of rides, movies and shows, are spread out among the six parks and, to a far lesser extent, two entertainment districts. You must purchase tickets to enter the theme and water parks, but sights, activities and entertainment at resort hotels and Disney's entertainment districts do not require park admission.

Magic Kingdom (p257) Low on thrills and high on nostalgia, with Cinderella's Castle and nightly fireworks.

Epcot (p263) A handful of rides on one side, country-based food, shopping and attractions to the other.

Animal Kingdom (p266) Part zoo and part county fair, with a heavy dusting of Disney-styled Africa.

Hollywood Studios (p268) Movie-based attractions and Pixar characters.

Typhoon Lagoon (p271) Water park particularly excellent for families.

Blizzard Beach (p271) Water park with high-speed twists and turns.

Disney's Boardwalk (p272) Intimate waterfront boardwalk with a handful of shops, restaurants and entertainment; no admission fee.

Downtown Disney (p272) Outdoor pedestrian mall with shops, bars, live music and entertainment; no admission fee.

MAGIC KINGDOM

When most people think of Walt Disney World, they're thinking of the Magic Kingdom (Map p256). This is Disney of commercials, Disney of princesses and pirates, Disney of dreams come true and Tinkerbell, quintessential old-school Disney with classic rides like It's a Small World and Space Mountain. Enter the park under the railroad station and continue on to Main Street, USA, past the small-town America storefronts toward that most iconic of all things Disney, Cinderella's Castle. A horse-drawn carriage runs continuously from the park entrance to the castle, and from there paths lead to the six 'lands.' Each land is listed below, in rough geographic order from the park entrance.

WALT DISNEY WORLD SIGHTS

Main Street, USA LANDMARK

Fashioned after Walt's hometown of Marceline, Missouri, bustling Main Street, USA is best experienced with an aimless meander. Peruse the miniature dioramas of Peter Pan and Snow White in the street windows, pop in to catch the black-and-white movie reels of old Disney cartoons and browse the hundreds of thousands of must-have Disney souvenirs.

Adventureland RIDES, SHOWS

Adventure Disney style means pirates and jungles, magic carpets and tree houses, whimsical and silly representations of the exotic locales from storybooks and imagination. Don't miss Pirates of the Caribbean – the slow-moving indoor boat tour through the dark and shadowy world of pirates remains one of the most popular at Disney, but there's no FastPass so lines can quickly get very long. Drunken pirates sing pirate songs, sleep among the pigs and sneer over their empty whiskey bottles, but unless you're scared of the dark or growling pirates, it's a giggle not a scream. And that Jack Sparrow looks so incredibly lifelike that you'll swear it's Johnny Depp himself! The silliness continues at Jungle Cruise (FastPass), but this time the captain takes you past fake crocodiles, elephants and monkeys, all the while throwing out the cheesiest jokes in all of Disney World.

Kids love flying around and around, up and down on Magic Carpets of Alladin, and its popularity rivals Dumbo, but skip the slow train of folks climbing 116 steps at Swiss Family Treehouse, a replica tree house of the shipwrecked family from the book and movie *The Swiss Family Robinson*. Iago, the scurrilous parrot from Disney's *Aladdin,* and Zazu, the bossy hornbill from *The Lion King,* sing and crack jokes at the Enchanted Tiki Room, a two-bit attraction that enjoys curious cult attraction.

Frontierland   RIDES, SHOWS
This is Disney's answer to the Wild West. Splash Mountain (FastPass), based on the movie *Song of the South,* depicts the misadventures of Brer Rabbit, Brer Bear and Brer Fox, complete with chatty frogs, singing ducks and other critters. The 40mph drop into the river makes for one of the biggest thrills in the park, and you will get very wet!

With no steep drops or loop-dee-loops, mild Big Thunder Mountain Railroad (FastPass) coaster is a great choice for little ones. The 'wildest ride in the wilderness' takes you through the desert mountain and a cave of bats, past cacti and hot-spring geysers.

Dubbed by many as a peaceful escape, Tom Sawyer Island is a disappointment. This was originally designed for California's Disneyland in 1955, and in its day, when Disney was smaller and children's expectations were lower, it was a place for adventure.

DOWN TIME: MAGIC KINGDOM

The covered waterside pavilion in the rose garden just off the bridge to the right of Cinderella's Castle makes a perfect place to pull out those goldfish snacks you brought along and take a quiet rest. Pictured but not labeled on Walt Disney World's Magic Kingdom map, look for this quiet treasure on your way into Tomorrowland.

WALT DISNEY WORLD SIGHTS

Disney expectations run high, and the reality of things can be disappointing. That pirate cruise with Captain Hook that sounded so, well, magical, on the website involves a long time hanging out in a hotel lounge eating Oreos, and getting jostled and tugged through the crowds and lines leaves little Anna staring sadly, exhausted and deflated. But you have some Disney magic of your own, and it's simple. Plan ahead with scrupulous attention to detail, making dinner reservations, planning when to go where based on parade and show schedules and deciding what attractions to tackle once you're there, and then throw all those plans out the window when the kids decide they want to sleep late and go down the hotel pool's slide again and again and again. Plan like a general, travel like a gypsy. Beyond that number-one mantra, follow some simple tips.

» **Buy a ticket that covers more days in the parks than you think you'll need** It's less expensive per day, and it gives the freedom to break up time at the theme parks with down time in the pool or at low-key attractions beyond theme-park gates.

» **Stay at a Walt Disney World resort hotel** While it's tempting to save money by staying elsewhere, the value of staying at a Walt Disney World resort lies in the conveniences they offer. Don't expect the quality of the room and amenities to match the price: you're paying for Walt Disney World, not for Ritz-like luxury. See p34 for more on staying in the resorts.

» **Stock up on snacks** Even if it's nothing more than a loaf of bread and a jar of peanut butter, you'll save the irritation of waiting in line for overpriced bad food.

» **Get to the park at least 30 minutes before gates open** Don't window-shop or dawdle – just march quickly to the rides, and then kick back for the afternoon. If you can only manage this on one day of your trip, make it the day you're going to Magic Kingdom. Watch the opening ceremony and be one of the first into the park.

» **Speed up, slow down** Yes, there's a time to hurry, as 10 minutes of pushing the pedal to the metal could save two hours waiting in line, but allow days to unfold according to the ebbs and flows of your children's moods.

» **Program Disney Dining into your cell phone** While you'll want to make some plans well in advance, once you have a sense of where you'll be at meal time, call 407-939-3463 to make reservations at table-service restaurants at all four theme parks, Disney resort hotels and at Disney's two shopping districts. Also, check for last-minute cancellations to dinner shows or character meals. Just keep interrupting the recorded message by pressing '0' until you get a real human voice.

Today, people mill about, not sure what to do and wondering why they waited so long in line to take a boat out here. Some kids may enjoy exploring Injun Joe's Cave and the rustic (at best) playground, but most seem as puzzled as the adults.

In the odd and strangely dated Country Bear Jamboree, stuffed bears emerge from the stage and sing corny country songs.

Liberty Square   RIDES, SHOWS
The ramblin' 19th-century mansion houses Haunted Mansion, another classic favorite low on thrill and high on silly fun and the only real ride in Liberty Sq. Cruise slowly past the haunted dining room, where apparitions dance across the stony floor, but beware of those hitchhiking ghosts – don't be surprised if they jump into your car unin-vited! While mostly it's lighthearted ghosty goofiness, kids may be frightened by spooky pre-ride dramatics where everyone gathers in a small room with strange elongated paintings on the wall and an eerie voice warns guests that there are no doors, no windows and no escape. All sorts of presidential memorabilia decorate the waiting area of the Hall of Presidents. Folks are herded into a theater to watch a super-patriotic flick on US history, ending with every US president before you on stage.

A paddle-wheel Liberty Belle Riverboat toots around Tom Sawyer Island on an underwater track.

Fantasyland   RIDES, SHOWS
Quintessential Disney, Fantasyland is the highlight of any Disney trip for both the

eight-and-under crowd and grown-ups looking for a nostalgic taste of classic Disney, though tweens too cool for fairy tales and teens looking for thrills may turn up their noses. Look for big changes here as Disney plans a major overhaul with a new Snow White and the Seven Dwarfs roller coaster and expanded opportunities to mingle with princesses. Check www.disneyworld.disney.go.com for updated information.

Without a doubt the best 3D show in Disney, **Mickey's PhilharMagic (FastPass)** takes Donald Duck on a whimsical adventure through classic Disney songs and movies. Ride with him through the streets of Morocco on Aladdin's carpet and feel the champagne on your face when it pops open during *Beauty and the Beast*'s 'Be Our Guest.' Fun, silly and lighthearted, this is Disney at its best.

It's A Small World, a sweet boat trip around the globe, has captivated children since the song and ride debuted at the 1964 New York World's Fair. Small boats gently glide through country after country, each decked out floor to ceiling with elaborate and charmingly dated sets and inhabited by hundreds of animated dolls dressed in clothes appropriate to their country. They sing 'It's a Small World' as they dance and play in their native environments. While snide comments about how the song sticks irritatingly in your head for weeks have become a Disney cliché, there's something poignantly endearing, almost melancholy, in this simple ride. Little ones love it and the wait is rarely longer than 10 minutes.

Board a pirate ship and fly through fog and stars over London to Never Never Land on **Peter Pan's Flight (FastPass)**, take a sweet journey through the Hundred Acre Wood on the **Many Adventures of Winnie the Pooh (FastPass)** and ride through *Snow White and the Seven Dwarfs* on **Snow White's Scary Adventures**. While all three are delightful, some children may be afraid of the dark and the pirates on Peter Pan, and the Snow White ride is more about the scary witch than the sweet, animal-loving girl. Rumor has it that once the Seven Dwarfs roller coaster is up and running, Snow White's Scary Adventures will close. At **Dumbo the Flying Elephant**, toddlers love jumping on a Dumbo and riding slowly around and around, up and down, and thrill at the chance to control how high they go. Lines here can be unbelievably long and slow, and

the ride is incredibly short – hit this when the park gates open.

Wait until your last meal is well digested before venturing out on the **Mad Tea Party**, especially if you think your kids have it in for you. It's a basic spinning ride, and you and others in the teacup decide just how much you'll be twirling.

Dream Along with Mickey is a high-octane musical performance that brings the villains, princesses, Mickey and Donald to the steps of Cinderella's Castle for dancing and dramatic twists. See the *Times Guide* for show times.

The gilded **Cinderella's Golden Carousel** has plenty of horses, so lines rarely get too long or too slow.

BEST OF MAGIC KINGDOM

With the exception of Space Mountain, Splash Mountain and the scary introduction to the Haunted Mansion, these are all Disney Perfect for children.

Mickey's Philharmagic 3D movie perfection.

Space Mountain Indoor roller coaster in the dark.

Pirates of the Caribbean Cruise through the world of pirates.

Haunted Mansion Slow-moving ride past lighthearted spooks.

Celebrate a Dream Come True Daytime parade.

Dream Along With Mickey Outdoor show in front of Cinderella's Castle.

Dumbo the Flying Elephant A favorite with toddlers.

Mad Tea Party Quintessential Disney spinning.

It's a Small World Boat ride through the world – you know the song.

Many Adventures of Winnie the Pooh A must for fans of that honey-loving bear.

Peter Pan's Flight Gentle flight through the story and over London.

Jungle Cruise Disney silliness at its best.

Splash Mountain Classic water ride.

Monsters, Inc Laugh Floor Interactive comedy show.

WALT DISNEY WORLD SIGHTS

QUICK EATS: MAGIC KINGDOM

You certainly won't starve, as there are snacks, fast-food eateries and table-service restaurants at every turn, but there's little here worth seeking out.

Sleepy Hollow   FAST FOOD $
(Liberty Sq; snacks $3-6; ⊙9am-park closing) The best snack in the park is this walk-up window's ice-cream sandwich with oozing vanilla ice cream squished between fresh-baked warm chocolate-chip cookies. Also try the tasty Mickey Mouse waffles sprinkled with powdered sugar.

Columbia Harbour House   FAST FOOD $
(Liberty Sq; mains $7-12; ⊙11am-park closing) Decent vegetarian chili, unusually tasty chicken nuggets and a Garden Galley Salad with mixed greens, chicken, pecans, pineapple and feta cheese.

Meet *Tangled*'s Rapunzel and Flynn Ryder at the little stone grotto of **Fairytale Garden**, and keep an eye out for Cinderella and her stepsisters, Mary Poppins, Alice in Wonderland and other favorites throughout Fantasyland.

Tomorrowland   RIDES, SHOWS
Space Mountain (FastPass) hurtles you through the darkness of outer space. This indoor roller coaster is the most popular ride in the Magic Kingdom, so come first thing and if the line is already excruciating, get a FastPass.

Monsters, Inc Laugh Floor picks up where the movie left off – monsters are no longer interested in harnessing screams but instead they must capture human laughter. This hilarious interactive movie, different every time and incorporating audience members projected on the big screen, is all about trying to make you laugh and it's very silly in the very best sense of the word.

A cross between a ride and a video game, **Buzz Lightyear's Space Ranger Spin (FastPass)** puts you inside the spin-off video game for *Toy Story II*. Cruise along and let loose with your laser cannon at almost anything that moves and see how many points you can rack up. Speed Racer fantasies come to life when kids can put the pedal to the metal on grand-prix-style cars around the huge figure-eight track at **Tomorrowland Indy Speedway**. The cars themselves are affixed to the track and you don't control the steering. Note that kids must be 52in tall to 'drive' on their own, which pretty much eliminates this ride's target audience. Strangely, plenty of childless adults wait in long lines to squish into a car for what can best be described as a 'poke' around a track. **Astro Orbiter** is a revolving rocket ride with nice views of Tomorrowland, and the **Tomorrowland Transit Authority** people mover makes a great break from the chaos of the park. The best time to ride this is when it's really hot or at night, when the area is lit up like a futuristic neon city.

ⓘ Getting There & Around

The only direct way to get to Magic Kingdom is by boat or monorail from the Magic Kingdom resorts of Disney's Grand Floridian, Disney's Grand Polynesian Resort, Disney's Contempo-

TOP FIVE DISNEY ATTRACTIONS TO SKIP

Plenty of rides and just about every show and parade are worth the wait and crowds, some for their thrills, some for their silly kitsch and some for their nostalgic charm, but others leave folks muttering disappointedly.

» **Drew Carey Sounds Dangerous – Starring Drew Carey** For seven minutes of this 30-minute show, the audience sits in complete darkness listening on individual headphones as detective Drew Carey clumsily chases down bad guy Lefty Moreno.

» **Journey into Narnia: Prince Caspian** Surround screen preview for the movie.

» **Honey, I Shrunk the Audience** 3D movie with random and disconnected special effects.

» **Journey into the Imagination with Figment** Figment the purple dragon takes you on a snooze cruise.

» **Stitch's Great Escape** You're harnessed tightly to a chair and forced to endure strange smells, smoke and sound for a truly painful 20 minutes.

The best place to catch Magic Kingdom's nighttime parade is on the curb of Main Street, just past the entrance gates. You're perfectly situated to watch the postparade Wishes Nighttime Spectacular fireworks over the castle and can beat the crowds out of the park and to the lines for the boats and monorail afterwards. Settle someone with a book and their cell phone to save a spot at least one hour before the parade starts. Alternatively, skip the parade, escape the crowds and watch the sky from a distance.

» **Boat** Bring a bottle of wine on a private **Specialty Fireworks Cruise** (☑407-939-7529; up to 10 people $225-300) or, for a more swashbuckling experience, with songs, storytelling and a pirate captain, take the **Pirates and Pals Fireworks Voyage** (☑407-939-7529; per person $54). Rates include photo op with Mr Smee and Captain Hook inside Disney's Contemporary Resort and dockside photo op with Peter Pan; pontoon-styled boats hold about 50 people.

» **Disney's Contemporary Resort** Make advance reservations for a meal at the rooftop California Grill or head up for a drink on its terrace. You'll want to get there an hour or more before the show though, as they close the elevator to anyone without dinner reservations when the bar is full.

» **Disney's Grand Floridian Resort & Spa** Grab a glass of wine at Narcoossee's and sit on the pier; for real seclusion, walk over to the grassy area in front of the lagoon-side rooms.

» **Lagoon-view room** Several deluxe Disney hotels, including Disney's Grand Floridian, Disney's Contemporary Resort and Disney's Polynesian Resort, offer rooms with a view of Magic Kingdom.

» **Disney's Polynesian Resort** Sip a pink umbrella drink on the beach.

rary Resort, Disney's Fort Wilderness Resort or Disney's Wilderness Lodge, or by 600-passenger ferry or monorail from the Transportation & Ticket Center. There is no parking, so if you drive, you have to park at the Transportation & Ticket Center and then take the monorail or the ferry to the park. With its massive parking lot and endless lines for bus shuttles, the Transportation & Ticket Center, however, can be unbearable. Grown men knock down toddlers in their efforts to catch the bus, harried parents scream at exhausted children, and it's a depressing and miserable way to end a magical day.

Instead, consider hopping the monorail or water launch to Disney's Contemporary Resort, Disney's Grand Floridian or Disney's Polynesian Resort, and then taking a cab to your hotel; in the morning, do the reverse. If you coordinate reserved breakfast or dinner at one of these resorts, and many offer character meals, this works particularly nicely. Note that you can get to Magic Kingdom via monorail from Epcot, but you must switch trains at the Transportation & Ticket Center.

The open-air Walt Disney World Railroad follows the perimeter of the park and stops at Main Street, USA and Frontierland. A horse-drawn carriage carries folks back and forth down Main Street, USA, from the entrance gate to Cinderella's Castle.

EPCOT

With no roller coasters screeching overhead, no parades, no water rides, and plenty of greenery, things here run a bit slower, with a bit less va-voom, than in the rest of Walt Disney World. Slow down and enjoy. Smell the incense in Morocco, listen to the Beatles in the UK and sip miso in Japan.

Epcot (Map p256) is divided into two sections. Future World is composed of eight pavilions, each holding rides and attractions and separated by grass, fountains and gardens. World Showcase, arranged country by country around the lagoon, offers shops, restaurants and a handful of movies. Staff members from the nations represented come here on one-year contracts, and operate authentic-feeling villages that offer some of the most interesting shopping and food in Walt Disney World.

Note that though Disney's Epcot map shows only one entrance, there are two. The main entrance, next to the bus and monorail stations, sits at the landmark geodesic dome of Spaceship Earth in Future World – look for the giant golf ball towering overhead. Guest Services is to your left as you enter the park. The back entrance, labeled International Gateway, brings visitors into the UK.

Both entrances have lockers, strollers and wheelchair rental.

In addition to the following attractions (ordered below in rough geographical order beginning at the main entrance gate), each nation in the World Showcase has live music, comedy or dancing shows; check the *Times Guide*. Little ones can cool off in the fountain just before the central bridge from Future World to World Showcase. The fountain is pictured but not labeled on Disney's Epcot map.

Future World   RIDES, SHOWS
Epcot's only two thrill rides are immediately left from the main entrance.

Mission: Space (FastPass)
You're strapped into a tiny four-person spaceship cockpit and launched into space. While this is not a high-speed ride, the special effects can be nauseating and the dire warnings are enough to scare away even the most steel-bellied folk. There are two options, one with less intensity than the other.

Test Track (FastPass)
The rather disturbing shtick for this is that that you are a living crash-test dummy. Ride a General Motors car through heat, cold, speed, braking and crash tests – at one point a huge semi with blinding lights heads right for you, its horn blaring. When testing the acceleration, the car speeds up to 60mph within a very short distance, and while it's fast and fun, there are few turns and no ups and downs like a roller coaster. If you don't have a FastPass, take the line for solitary riders. At the exit, climb around a Hummer, a Saab convertible and other models, talk to a GM representative, and pick up that perfect Disney souvenir, a T-shirt with a pink-sequin Hummer.

Ellen's Energy Adventure
This 45-minute ride is arguably the oddest ride in all of Orlando, perhaps in the entire state of Florida. It begins with a movie during which Ellen DeGeneres dreams that she is playing *Jeopardy!* with Jamie Lee Curtis. Determined to outsmart her know-it-all opponent, Ellen joins the Bill Nye the Science Guy on a trip through history to learn about energy sources. At this point, you enter a 96-passenger vehicle and lurch slowly through the darkness into the Cretaceous period (the root of today's fossil fuels). Giant dinosaurs stomp about menacingly and, in one particularly surreal display, a mannequin Ellen battles a ferocious one. After this jaunt through dinosaur-land, the movie preaches wind energy, hydro-energy and other alternative fuel sources, and concludes with Ellen's *Jeopardy!* victory. The whole thing is just very weird.

Spaceship Earth
Inside the giant golf ball landmark at the park's entrance is Spaceship Earth, a strange, kitschy slow-moving ride through time that enjoys a cult following.

Innovations East & West
The two semicircular glass buildings behind Spaceship Earth house these two pavilions filled primarily with corporate-sponsored interactive exhibits. Expect to see lots of kids pressing buttons randomly or playing video games, and adults wandering aimlessly wondering what they're supposed to be doing. At the **Sum of All Thrills** you can design your own simulator ride, deciding how fast you want to go, how high you want to spin and so on and then 'ride' your creation as a 4D experience. It's pretty crazy and a lot of

FASTPASS

A FastPass is a free paper ticket that allows you to return to an attraction during a designated time window, thereby jumping the mind-numbingly long lines and hopping right on. This is the lowdown: if a ride has a FastPass option (noted next to each attraction description on the park map and within this chapter), there will be automated ticket machines at the ride entrance. Swipe your park ticket and out pops your FastPass with your return time. Return to the ride within the designated time frame, show your paper FastPass ticket at the FastPass line, and zip right onto the ride with no more than a 15-minute wait. The catch? Check the bottom of your FastPass to find out when you are eligible to swipe your card for another FastPass – the crowd level determines whether or not you can get a second one before your allocated time to use the first one, and you are never allowed more than two at a time. FastPasses for the most popular attractions can run out by midday, and don't be surprised if your return time isn't for upwards of five hours from the time you get your pass. If you really want to see something, get your FastPass as soon as possible.

fun, so go ahead and test out that wild ride you've always imagined would be so perfect.

Seas with Nemo & Friends Pavilion

Kids under 10 won't want to miss the two Nemo-themed attractions inside this pavilion. Board a clamshell at the **Seas with Nemo & Friends**, and gently wind through the ocean looking for Nemo. It follows in the footprints of Disney rides like Winnie the Pooh and Peter Pan, where you ride through the story, and though it may lack the old-school creative energy of those classics, kids love it. From here, head to **Turtle Talk with Crush**, an Epcot highlight. We don't know how they do it, but hey, that's the Disney magic. A small blue room with a large movie screen holds about 10 rows of benches with sitting room for kids in front. Crush talks to the children staring up at him, interacting with and taking questions from the 'dude in the dark-blue shell' and cracking jokes about how sea grass gives him the bubbles. Dory shows up and gets squished against the screen by the whale. It's a fantastic and funny interactive show.

Soarin' (FastPass)

Simulates hang gliding over California. Soar up and down, hover and accelerate as the giant screen in front of you takes you over citrus groves, golf courses, mountains, coasts, rivers and cities and, finally, into the fireworks over Cinderella's Castle at Disney Lane. You smell the oranges and your feet almost touch those surfers below. While not at all scary in terms of speed or special effects, folks with agoraphobia may feel a bit uneasy. You'll want to hit this as soon as you get to Epcot, as it's one of the best rides at Disney for everyone from toddlers to grandpas. Lines can be excruciating and FastPasses either run out quickly or have return times upwards from five hours. When you finally do get to the front of the line, ask for a front-row seat. Otherwise, feet dangling in front of you can ruin the effect.

Living with the Land (FastPass)

A boat ride past laboratory-like greenhouses. A narrator talks about growing food in and under water, which is actually more interesting than it may sound. Look for vegetables grown into Disney shapes.

The Circle of Life

This short film, featuring Simba and his buddies from *The Lion King,* addresses the fragile relationship between the environment and the creatures that live within it.

Near Innovations West but not on the map, Club Cool offers free samples of soft drinks from other countries that aren't sold in the USA. Try Smart Watermelon from China, Vegitabeta from Japan and Beverley from Italy, among others. Particularly fun for kids, and for a fee you can put together your own cup.

Character Spot

Mickey Mouse, Minnie Mouse, Goofy and other Disney characters, each with an appropriate backdrop, line up at Character Spot so you can go through and catch them all, one after the other. Perfect for filling those autograph books, and it's air-conditioned.

World Showcase   RIDES, SHOWS

Who needs the hassle of a passport and jetlag when you can travel the world right here at Walt Disney World? Watch belly dancing in Morocco and buy personally engraved bottles of perfume in France before settling down to watch fireworks about world peace and harmony. Disney was right. It truly is a small world after all. Sure, this is quite a sanitized and stereotypical vision of the world, but so what? This is, after all, a theme park. The featured countries from left to right around the water are Mexico, Norway, China, Germany, Italy, the USA (The American Adventure), Japan, Morocco, France, the UK and Canada. Each section has architecture unique to that country, restaurants serving national cuisine, and gift shops with country-specific merchandise.

The best way to experience the World Showcase is to simply wander as the mood moves you, poking through stores and restaurants and catching what amounts to Bureau of Tourism promotional films and gentle rides at some of the countries. Who knows, it might just inspire you to hop a plane and check out the real thing, and it certainly is a great way to show kids a little something about the world.

Gran Fiesta Tour Starring the Three Caballeros

A boat takes you through Mexico with Donald Duck and his comrades from the 1994 Disney film *The Three Caballeros.*

KIM POSSIBLE

Pick up a 'Kimmunicator,' an interactive cell-phonelike device available at Team Possible Recruitment Centers marked 'KP' on Disney's Epcot map, and head through seven countries of World Showcase in a self-paced treasure-hunt-styled effort to defeat supervillians. Make the beer steins in Germany sing, hidden mummies glow, and activate surprises from China to the UK.

Maelstrom (FastPass)

Tucked away in the Norway pavilion, this cute little boat ride meanders past Vikings, trolls and waterfalls. Skip the film put out by a Norway tourism company.

Reflections of China

A 20-minute film screened on a 360-degree screen focuses on China's stunning landscape and exotic cities.

American Adventure

Benjamin Franklin and Mark Twain host a cacophony of audio-animatronic figures in this simplified interpretation of US history, from the Pilgrims to Charles Lindbergh, from Susan B Anthony to Magic Johnson.

Impressions de France

Spectacularly beautiful 18-minute film, screened in an air-conditioned sit-down theater, celebrates France's natural countryside.

O'Canada

Martin Short dispels the myth of Canada as the place of 24-hour snow and showcases the beauty of the country. The 10-minute film screens in a 360-degree theater.

❶ Getting There & Around

A pleasant, well-lit paved waterfront path or boat shuttle connects Epcot to Hollywood Studios, Disney's Boardwalk and the following Epcot resorts: Walt Disney World Swan & Dolphin, Disney's Yacht Club and Disney's Beach Club, and Disney's Boardwalk Inn. The monorail runs a direct line between Epcot and the Transportation & Ticket Center; from there, catch a monorail or ferry to Magic Kingdom. Disney buses depart from outside Epcot to Disney resorts, Hollywood Studios and Animal Kingdom.

Within the park, a boat shuttles folks to and from Morocco and Germany from two boat docks at Showcase Plaza, just outside Future World.

ANIMAL KINGDOM

Set apart from the rest of Disney both in miles and in tone, Animal Kingdom (Map p256) attempts to blend theme park and zoo, carnival and African safari, all stirred together with a healthy dose of Disney characters, storytelling and transformative magic. The result is, at times, quite odd. Enter the park at the Oasis and walk either direction toward the bridge to Discovery Island. Here, a road lined with food outlets and shops circles the landmark Tree of Life and four more bridges cross the water into Camp Minnie-Mickey, Africa, Asia and DinoLand

---

QUICK EATS: EPCOT

The following places can all be found at World Showcase.

Cantina de San Angel   MEXICAN $
(Mexico; mains $4-8; ⊙11am-park closing) One of the best fast-food places in the park. Try the tacos, served with surprisingly tasty pico de gallo and fresh avocado.

Boulangerie Patisserie   FRENCH $
(France; pastries & sandwiches $2-6; ⊙park hours) Sidewalk cafe near the back of France with two cases filled with cakes, éclairs and cookies. Most folks come for sweet things, but it also sells ham-and-cheese croissants, quiche, and those baguette sandwiches that are ubiquitous in the real France. If the few outdoor tables fill up or it's too hot to eat outside, head next door to the air-conditioned Souvenir de France shop. Designed to look like a railroad station, the store has several bistro-styled tables.

Yorkshire County Fish Shop   FISH & CHIPS $
(UK; mains $7-12; ⊙11am-park closing) Crispy fish with vinegar at the walk-up window outside the pub in UK.

Yakitori House   JAPANESE $
(Japan; mains $4-8; ⊙11am-park closing) Next to the lavish temples of Japan, with miso soup, teriyaki chicken and noodle dishes.

USA. Raffi's Planet is accessible by train from Africa. The two most popular rides are Kilimanjaro Safari and Expedition Everest, located at opposite ends of the park.

Oasis
ZOO

Lovely gardens hide all kinds of cool critters, including a giant anteater, but it's best to move along to other attractions before the lines get too long. Pause to enjoy on your way out.

Discovery Island
RIDES, SHOWS

This is the park's hub, and like Cinderella Castle at Magic Kingdom, Spaceship Earth at Epcot and the Sorcerer's Hat at Hollywood Studios, the huge, ornate Tree of Life serves as the best landmark for orienting yourself in Animal Kingdom. It's 14 stories tall, holds more than 100,000 nylon leaves, and has over 325 animal images carved into its trunk.

The 3D It's Tough to Be a Bug! (Fast-Pass) is more than a movie, with periods of darkness, dry-ice and flashing lights. It's a lot of fun, but if your kids are terrified of darkness or creepy crawlies keep them out of this extravaganza. Even though it's very cute much of the time, you will definitely hear children crying by the end.

Camp Minnie-Mickey
SHOW, CHARACTER GREETING

One of the most overrated attractions at Disney, the 30-minute theater-in-the-round Festival of the Lion King features acrobats, dancing, singing and fire theatrics. *The Lion King* music is fun, and actors decked out in full African garb involve the audience in all kinds of silly animal sounds, but there's no narrative structure to hold it all together. The best part is the massive floats, each a different animal.

Four huts at Greeting Trails in Camp Minnie-Mickey each house a Disney character, and you can wait in individual lines to get your photo taken with them. Mickey and Minnie (in safari garb) each have their own spot, but the other two huts could have anyone from Pluto to friends from *The Lion King* or *The Jungle Book*.

Africa
RIDES, ZOO

With live animals and that Disney touch, Kilimanjaro Safaris (FastPass) gives just about any zoo in the country some healthy competition! Board a rickety jeep and ride through the African Savannah. But beware. Just as you're barreling down rutted roads, past zebras, lions and more, the driver gets word that poachers are on the loose! Local law enforcement can't do it alone, so you've got to help but, oh no! The bridge that's been causing so much trouble seems worse today and it might just give out on you. Unless your kids are frightened of lions, there's nothing scary here at all.

Pass gorillas, hippos, a great bat display and a hive of naked mole rats on the lush Pagani Forest Exploration Trail. Nothing more than you'd find in any zoo, but those mole rats sure are cute.

Asia
RIDES, SHOWS

If you're looking for thrills, Expedition Everest (FastPass) won't disappoint. Wait (and wait, and wait) in a reconstructed Nepalese village, made to make you feel that you are indeed about to take a train to the top of Mt Everest. A mini-museum focusing on the mountain's climbers also contains copious evidence of a mysterious mountain creature, but you pay no attention as you board the steam train. It's only as you climb, up and up and up into the glaciers, that you begin to worry. Like so much of Disney the ride is as much about the narrative shtick and set design as the ride itself. This is a roller coaster. It goes backwards, it plummets at high speeds, it zooms around turns, with eerie hints (and more) of that Yeti.

Kali River Rapids, the park's second thrill ride (and there are only two), starts out pleasant enough, as you drift free-form on a circular 12-person raft through bamboo, rainforests and temple ruins. But this ain't no float trip – be prepared for rapids, sharp turns and other surprises.

Owls and peregrine falcons dazzle audiences at Flights of Wonder, a live bird show. It's got some cheesy dialogue, but the animals are spectacular as they zoom around over your head. Afterwards you can approach the trainers and their birds to ask questions and take photos.

WALT DISNEY WORLD SIGHTS

DOWN TIME: NATURE TRAILS

Short trails around Discovery Island lead to quiet spots along the water, where a handful of benches make a great place to relax with a snack. Keep your eye out for animals such as tortoises and lemurs in and around the water.

DON'T MISS

FINDING NEMO – THE MUSICAL

Arguably the best show at Walt Disney World, this sophisticated theater performance wows children and adults alike. The show is directed by Peter Brosius, artistic director of the Children's Theater Company of Minneapolis, and the spectacular puppets were created by Michael Curry, who helped design the puppets for Broadway's *The Lion King*. The music is fun, the acting is phenomenal, and narrative structure follows the vision and spirit of the movie. Make a lunch reservation for the Tusker House buffet between 1pm and 1:45pm and you'll be given reserved seating to the 3:15pm performance, thus avoiding the lines. There's no extra fee, but be sure to ask when you make your lunch reservation. Oddly, Disney doesn't clump the Nemo-themed attractions in one park: Turtle Talk with Crush and the Seas with Nemo & Friends, both Disney highlights for little ones, are in Epcot.

Walk past Bengal tigers, huge fruit bats and Komodo dragons on the **Maharajah Jungle Trek**, a self-guided path past habitats designed to look like Angkor Wat.

Dinoland USA
GAMES, RIDES

This strange carnival-like area seems more like a local fair in rural Midwest America than part of Disney's magic, and it's a bit odd to plop the garish plastic dinosaurs of Dinoland right along with the live animals of Asia and Africa. Everything is oh-so-cleverly tied into the dinosaur theme. Buy fast-food snacks at 'Trilo-Bite' or at 'Restaurantosaurus' and play the usual midway games at **Fossil Fun Games**. The kids' coaster at **Primeval Whirl (FastPass)** is a particularly whirly-twirly good time, but it's not superbarfy like the tea-cup ride in Magic Kingdom. The coaster on the left is identical to the one on the right. If you're looking for bigger thrills, head to **Dinosaur (FastPass)**. It takes you back in time to the Cretaceous period, where you've got to rescue a huge and scary dinosaur specimen before a meteor hits... This is definitely not for little kids, unless yours is tough as nails.

Rafiki's Planet Watch
ZOO

The **Wildlife Express Train** you take to get here might just be the best part of this Disney enigma. The **Habitat Habit** features a few adorable, fist-sized tamarinds, and the **Affection Section** is a pleasant enough petting zoo with sheep and goats. Veterinarians care for sick and injured animals at the **Conservation Station**, the park's veterinary and conservation headquarters, and sometimes they have animal interactions.

ⓘ Getting There & Away

Disney buses stop at Animal Kingdom, but note the ride here can be up to 45 minutes, maybe longer. There is parking just outside the park gates.

HOLLYWOOD STUDIOS

The least charming of Walt Disney World's theme parks, Hollywood Studios (Map p256) offers none of the nostalgic charm of Magic Kingdom, the sophisticated delights of Epcot or the kitschy fun of Animal Kingdom. It's meant to conjure the heydays of Hollywood, with a replica of Graumann's Chinese Theatre and Hollywood Brown Derby, but most of the attractions find their inspiration from unabashed 21st-century energy. Hannah Montana souvenirs line store shelves, screams from the Tower of Terror echo through the park and *American Idol* wannabes line up daily to strut their stuff.

The 122ft Sorcerer's Hat serves as the park's primary focal point. Make a right onto Sunset Blvd to hit the roller coasters, the Beauty and the Beast show and Fantasmic (a nighttime spectacular), and left toward New York for the movie-based attractions, primarily in the form of shows and movies. Several meet-and-greet spots feature favorites from *Cars, Up, Toy Story, The Incredibles* and *Monsters Inc*. Check *Show Times* for times and location.

You won't need a whole day here – the best plan is to come first thing in the morning to avoid lines at two of Disney's most popular roller coasters, linger for lunch, relax elsewhere for the afternoon and return for Fantasmic.

Sunset Boulevard
RIDES, SHOWS

Two of Disney's most talked about rides are conveniently located right next to each other. At **Rock 'n' Roller Coaster Starring Aerosmith (FastPass)** the shtick is that you're hurrying off in a limo to catch the Aerosmith concert. 'Dude (Looks Like a Lady)' cranks through headrest speakers as the coaster twists and turns in darkness, but there are no steep drops that send your belly through your mouth. Some claim this is one of the best rides in Disney, but just as many say it's high on hoopla and short on thrill.

Follow the screams to the **Twilight Zone Tower of Terror (FastPass)**, one of the best thrills at any Disney park. The preride spiel explains how the building, once a bustling Hollywood hotel, came to be so ramshackle and empty, and then, Rod Serling invites you into...The Twilight Zone. Enter an elevator and slowly climb up through the eerie old hotel, past the lurking ghosts. Clatter, clatter, clatter, until suddenly and without warning the elevator free falls. Clatter up, crash down, again and again, all in total darkness. Every ride is different.

Both the Rock 'n' Roller Coaster and Tower of Terror are hugely popular – get a FastPass for the coaster first thing in the morning, and then hop into the line for the tower; alternatively, take advantage of the single-rider line for Rock 'n' Roller Coaster.

The simple and sweet outdoor theater performance of **Beauty and the Beast – Live on Stage** follows the storyline, incorporates the classic songs, and doesn't fall back on any special effects or crazy shenanigans. It's a rock-solid hit with the Disney-princess-loving crowd.

Pixar Place, Animation Courtyard & Mickey Avenue   RIDES, SHOWS
At **Toy Story Mania! (FastPass)**, one of Disney's newest attractions, folks don 3D glasses and shoot their way through midway games trying to score points. FastPasses are usually gone within three hours of the park opening.

Beautifully executed but disappointingly short, **Voyage of the Little Mermaid (Fast-Pass)** is an indoor live performance. Black lighting creates utter darkness so that the fluorescent sea critters (handled by puppeteers swathed in black) pop out in a brilliant flash of color. Bubbles descend from the ceiling to complete the underwater effect, and Ariel croons classic songs from the film. Unfortunately, huge narrative holes confuse even the most die-hard of *Little Mermaid* fans. We meet Ariel under the sea with her fish friends, we see her make a deal with the nefarious Sea Witch and then, next scene, Ariel is happily married to the prince!

Familiar faces from the Playhouse Disney TV channel, including Mickey and Winnie the Pooh, sing and dance at the 20-minute **Playhouse Disney – Live on Stage**. With carpeted floor seating and plenty of interactive action, it's a favorite with toddlers.

When Hollywood Studios opened as MGM Studios in 1989, the park served as a working studio, and you could watch animation artists at work at the **Magic of Disney Animation**. Animation for modern classics like *Beauty and the Beast, The Lion King* and *Alladin* were drawn here. Today, however, this attraction has been reduced to a short film about the animation process, usually featuring the latest Disney movie. Skip

WALT DISNEY WORLD SIGHTS

BEST OF HOLLYWOOD STUDIOS

Several jewels sparkle through the filler and fluff at Hollywood Studios, and a little strategizing will save you hours in lines and the irritation of wandering aimlessly through a mishmash of mediocrity. Within hours of the park opening, FastPass return times for Tower of Terror and Rock 'n' Roller Coaster can be after dark, so get to the park when the gates open and turn right at the Sorcerer's Hat. Immediately pick up a FastPass to one, and get in line for the other.

» **Twilight Zone Tower of Terror** Elevator free fall through a haunted hotel, this is classic Disney thrills.

» **Rock 'n' Roller Coaster** Indoor roller coaster and one of the most popular at any park.

» **Beauty and the Beast – Live on Stage** Outdoor stage show of the princess tale.

» **Voyage of the Little Mermaid** Charming black light live performance, but frustratingly short.

» **Toy Story Mania!** Ride-through video game.

» **Pixar Pals Countdown to Fun parade** Pixar characters dance through the streets.

» **Sci-Fi Dine-In Theater** Burgers and glow-in-the-dark drinks served drive-in movie style (p282).

» **50's Prime Time Café** Disney theme dining at its absolute best (p281).

ANIMATION 101

In this day of Photoshop and computer-driven animation, it's hard to imagine the painstaking process behind classic Disney animation. Try your hand at drawing a Disney character at Hollywood Studio's **Animation Academy**, a short course hosted by a Disney animator. There are about 40 drafting tables, equipped with paper and pencil, and your drawing may be one of the best souvenirs of the trip! Classes start at 10:30am and are held every half-hour at the Magic of Disney Animation.

the show and head to the interactive exhibits at the end, where you'll also find original celluloids from Disney films.

Anyone even vaguely interested in the story behind Walt Disney won't want to miss **Walt Disney: One Man's Dream**. The biographical exhibit, with enough eye candy (TV monitors with cartoon clips and miniature set replicas) to keep little ones amused, ends with a short documentary movie. You can see the museum but skip the movie if you want.

Hollywood Boulevard & Echo Lake
RIDES, SHOWS

Cruise slowly past animatronic stars of some of the world's most beloved movies, including *The Wizard of Oz, Casablanca* and *Raiders of the Lost Ark,* on the **Great Movie Ride**. Yes, it's strikingly dated, but that's part of the charm.

At **American Idol**, pre-selected contestants (see www.disneyworld.disney.go.com for details on how to audition) compete several times daily, belting out their best for the audience members to judge – winners compete in the end-of-the-day finale. At the **Indiana Jones Epic Stunt Spectacular** (FastPass), performed in a huge outdoor theater, professional stunt people show the audience how stunts are created. Indiana Jones falls into a vat of steam and fire, is chased by a boulder and leaps out of tall buildings. Audience volunteers, chosen about a half-hour before each show, don costumes to become extras in the Cairo market scene.

Streets of America
RIDES, SHOWS

The massive 30-minute stunt-show **Lights, Motors, Action! Extreme Stunt Show** (FastPass) features cars, motorcycles and characters from the Pixar movie *Cars* engaged in all kinds of speeding, crashing and jumping. The auditorium seats more than 2500 people, so it's usually easy to get a seat. The idea of the **Studio Backlot Tour** is that you're taken behind the scenes to see how movies are made, but in practice it's a lot of waiting for nothing. Ride a tram through staff parking lots past the Mickey Mouse–eared water tower, planes used in *Pearl Harbor,* props from different movies and Walt Disney's private plane. The best part is the stop at Catastrophe Canyon, a movie set canyon where you see how they produce special effects for an out-of-control disaster. A gas tank explodes and 70,000 gallons of water come crashing through the canyon walls straight for the shuttle. The 3D technology of **Muppet Vision 3-D**, helped along with animatronic hecklers in the audience, *becomes* rather than enhances the story. With no driving narrative and aging special effects, it's truly ho-hum.

❶ Getting There & Away

A paved waterfront walkway or a boat shuttle connects Hollywood Studios to Disney's Boardwalk and the following Epcot resorts: Walt Disney World Swan & Dolphin, Disney's Yacht Club and Disney's Beach Club, and Disney's Boardwalk Inn. Disney buses provide transportation to other parks and hotels, sometimes requiring a transfer.

QUICK EATS: HOLLYWOOD STUDIOS

See p281 for table-service restaurants that take advance reservations, including Sci-Fi Dine-In Theater and 50's Prime Time Café, two of Disney's most creatively themed experiences.

ABC Commissary INTERNATIONAL $
(Commisary Lane; mains $6-12; ⊙11am-park closing) Surprisingly interesting choices include tabbouleh wraps, Cuban sandwiches and even a children's vegetable noodle stir-fry.

Writer's Stop DESSERTS $
(Commisary Lane; mains $6-12; ⊙park hours) Decent coffee, cookies and muffins in a small shop designed to look like an independent bookstore. If it's not too crowded, the few comfy chairs around a TV screening Disney cartoons and shelves of books make this a good place to rest your weary bones.

TYPHOON LAGOON & BLIZZARD BEACH

In addition to the four theme parks, Disney boasts two distinctly themed water parks. Of the two, Blizzard Beach boasts the better thrills and speed, but Typhoon Lagoon has the far superior wave pool, a fantastic lazy river and tots' play area, and plenty of room to splash on the beach.

Be prepared to spend upwards of a half-hour in line for a ride that's over in less than a minute and take those wait times seriously – if it says the wait is 60 minutes, it's 60 minutes. Yes, 60 minutes for *one* slide. Come in the morning to beat the crowds, and head straight to the high-speed slides. Both parks have fast-food restaurants and an outdoor pool bar.

Typhoon Lagoon

WATER PARK

(Map p256; ☑407-560-4141; adult/child 3-9 $49/43 or incl in Water Park Fun & More ticket; ☺call for hours) Perhaps the most beautiful water park in the country, Typhoon Lagoon boasts an abundance of palm trees, a zero-entry pool with a white sandy beach, and the best wave pool in Orlando. Twice the size of a football field, the pool generates a massive 10ft wave every 90 seconds. First you hear the low rumble as the wave is generated, then the ripples of delighted anticipatory squeals as swimmers see the wave approach, and finally the laughing and screams of joy as everyone dives into and rides the wave. Again and again. And the best part is, no line. A few islands along the lagoon's shore break the waves and create a calm, shallow inlet for tots.

The center point of the park is Mt Mayday, with a wrecked shrimp boat on its peak. Several slides emanate from the peak, including the ultrasteep crazy-fast Humunga Kowabunga and Mayday Falls, where you zip down a winding slide on an inner tube. For more relaxing thrills, float through dense rainforest, rocky gorges and tropical flowers on Castaway Creek. The aptly named Ketchakiddee Creek attracts the little ones with a leaky tugboat, bubbly fountains, warm-water pools and family-friendly slides.

Typhoon Lagoon has two particularly unique attractions that set it apart from the other water parks. First is the Crush 'n' Gusher water coaster, a combination log flume and roller coaster with jets of water that propel your tube up snaking hills and down through dark tunnels. The second is Shark Reef, where you can jump in and snorkel (free rentals) for an up-close look at rays, sharks and tropical fish. Sounds cool, but be warned that the water is very cold, you're not allowed to leave the surface or kick your feet, and the sharks are tiny and hang out down at the bottom. To spend more time with the fishes, take the Supplied Air Snorkeling (SAS) Adventure (per 30min $20), which uses a regulator like in scuba diving; sign up at Hammer Head Fred's Dive Shop.

Blizzard Beach

WATER PARK

(Map p256; ☑407-560-3400; adult/child 3-9 $49/43 or incl in Water Park Fun & More ticket; ☺call for hours) Though the newer of Disney's two water parks, Blizzard Beach is the 1980s Vegas Strip hotel to Typhoon Lagoon's Bellagio. At its center sits the snowcapped Mt Gushmore, from which the waterslides burst forth. You can choose several options for your descent, but because the wooden-bench chairlift that transports riders to the top rarely works you'll have to huff it up before you can zoom down. But don't worry – the lines are usually so long you'll have plenty of time to relax on the way up! The fastest and craziest ride down is Summit Plummet, with a 12-story drop; alternatively, try the slightly less intense Slush Gusher or race your friends down the eight-lane Toboggan Racer.

ⓘ Information

Swimsuits with buckles or metal parts aren't allowed on most of the rides. Hours vary by day and by season; call the individual parks for current hours. From October through March, only

---

WATER PARKS 101

Orlando's water parks can be a blast for all ages, but remember the basics.

» **Bring beach towels** The ones they rent in the park are postage-stamp sized.

» **Keep cash and a credit card with you at all times in a small water-proof container** Sold at the parks (about $4).

» **Do not leave valuables unattended** Store everything but essentials in on-site lockers ($5 to $10).

» **Life jackets are available throughout the parks** Keep kids safe.

» **Wear water shoes or flip-flops** You don't want to pick up nasty fungus or cut your feet.

» **Parks keep fickle hours** Call for seasonal and weather-related closings.

one Disney water park is open at a time. Disney's two water parks are included in the price of a Water Park Fun & More ticket.

❶ Getting There & Away

Disney buses stop at both Typhoon Lagoon and Blizzard Beach, and there is complimentary self-parking at both parks.

DISNEY'S BOARDWALK

Far less harried and crowded than Downtown Disney, the very small Disney's Boardwalk (Map p256) area across from Epcot and along Crescent Lake echoes waterfront boardwalks of turn-of-the-century New England seaside resorts. On Thursday to Saturday evening street performers like magicians, jugglers and musicians give a festive vibe. Pick up a doughnut or cute lil' Mickey Mouse cakes at the bakery and toot around on a two-passenger surrey-with-the-fringe-on-top bike.

For drinking and entertainment options at Disney's Boardwalk, see p284.

❶ Information

Public areas at Disney's Boardwalk are open from 8am to 2am.

❶ Getting There & Away

A well-lit paved walking path and small boats connect Disney's Boardwalk to Epcot and Hollywood Studios, as well as to the following Epcot resorts: Walt Disney World Swan & Dolphin and Disney's Yacht Club and Disney's Beach Club. Disney buses stop at the Boardwalk Resort, a low-lying clapboard hotel at the center of the boardwalk.

DOWNTOWN DISNEY

Stretching along the water, Downtown Disney (Map p256) is an outdoor mall that lures tourists with three districts of shops, restaurants, music venues and more shops: **West Side** is home to a multiplex dine-in theater and the stage show Cirque du Soleil La Nouba, **Marketplace** features the largest Disney store in the world, and **Pleasure Island** has several restaurants, bars and clubs. There's a Disney-styled party atmosphere here, particularly on the weekends, with folks walking around sipping margaritas from paper cups, street performers dancing on stilts and parents pushing strollers loaded down with Disney shopping bags. For details on select stores, see p285; for table-service restaurants that take advanced reservations, see p282. For drinking and entertainment options, see p284.

Disney is in the midst of completely overhauling Downtown Disney, and in 2013 Pleasure Island will reopen as **Hyperion Wharf**. Call ☎407-827-2281 or check www.disneyworld.disney.go.com for updated information.

QUICK EATS: DOWNTOWN DISNEY

Ghiradelli Soda Fountain & Chocolate Shop   ICE CREAM $
(Map p256; ice cream $2-8; ◷9am-11:30pm, to midnight Fri & Sat) Decadent ice-cream concoction involving entire chocolate bars blended into milkshakes.

Fresh-A-Peel   HEALTH FOOD $
(Map p256; mains $5-12; ◷9:30am-11:30pm, to midnight Fri & Sat) If your tastes lean more toward fruit smoothies than triple chocolate sundaes, head to the rusty orange building next to the Lego store. With nitrate-free hot dogs served on whole-grain buns, veggie burgers, turkey burgers and 'popped chips,' this is the closest to health food you'll find at Disney.

Earl of Sandwich   SANDWICHES $
(Map p256; sandwiches $5-8; ◷7:30am-10pm) Surprisingly good toasted sandwiches range from basic to exotic. One of the most satisfying lunches at Disney, with plenty of bang for your buck.

Babycakes NYC   BAKERY $
(Map p256; desserts $3-6; ◷8am-11pm; ✐) Vegan, gluten-free and organic bakery (with sister stores in New York City's Soho and Los Angeles) that uses agave rather than sugar in most of its baked goods. Try the tasty baked donuts, or choose from a quirky selection of cupcakes and cookies. It's tucked into a corner of the Pollo Campero building.

Pollo Campero   LATIN AMERICAN $
(Map p256; mains $6-12; ◷8am-11pm) This 2011 newcomer serves fried chicken, sweet plantains and black beans, a welcome change to the usual fast-food options.

DisneyQuest Indoor Interactive
Theme Park   ARCADE

(Map p256; Downtown Disney; 1 day $36-42; ☺11:30am-10pm Sun-Thu, to 11pm Fri & Sat) With five dizzying floors of exhibits designed to indulge video-game addicts, this 'interactive theme park' makes the perfect place to while away a rainy or hot afternoon. Virtual-reality attractions include a trip on Alladin's magic carpet over Agrabah and a float down a river into the Mesozoic Age. You can design and 'ride' your own roller coaster, which is a lot of fun, and lose yourself for hours in old-school video games and pinball machines. All kinds of technological delights satisfy folks with even the most limited attention spans.

Characters in Flight   SCENIC FLIGHT

(Map p256; Downtown Disney; 10min experience adult/child 3-9 $18/12; ☺9am-midnight, weather permitting) Silhouettes of Mary Poppins, Alladin, Peter Pan and other iconic Disney characters pop out from the glowing yellow orb of this massive tethered gas balloon. Guests climb on board the basket and ascend 400ft into the air for 360-degree views. Depending on the weather, up to 29 guests can go up at a time.

ℹ Information

Public areas at Downtown Disney are open from 8am to 2am.

ℹ Getting There & Around

Downtown Disney is accessible by boat from Downtown Disney resorts and by bus from everywhere else. There is complimentary self-parking, but no direct Disney transportation to any of the theme parks. You can walk from one end of Downtown Disney to the other, or catch a boat shuttle that stops at each district.

🏃 Activities

In addition to the theme parks, water parks and entertainment districts, Disney offers a dizzying array of recreational activities, many based at Disney hotels and none requiring park admission. Call Walt Disney World Recreation (☎407-939-7529) for reservations and details on everything from water-skiing lessons to bike rental; for general information on activities at Walt Disney World, check www.disneyworld.disney.go.com.

Golf

Walt Disney World has four 18-hole championship courses and one family-friendly nine-hole course. Call ☎407-939-4063 to reserve tee-times up to 90 days in advance for resort

STAR WARS AT DISNEY

Kids aged four to 12 can participate in **Jedi Training Academy** shows, in which 15 little ones don brown robes, pledge the sacred Jedi oath and grab a light saber for on-stage training by a Jedi Master. But it's first-come, first-served, so you need to get to Hollywood Studios when gates open and sign up at Backlot. Look for it on the eastern edge of the park, left just past the giant green dinosaur ice-cream stand on Echo Lake – it's not labeled on the map. The updated Star Wars–themed 3D experience **Star Tours: The Adventure Continues** promises to be a huge improvement over the old Star Wars attraction, but hadn't opened at the time of writing. In June, the park launches **Star Wars Weekends**, with all kinds of themed events. See www.disneyworld.disney.go.com for details.

guests, 60 days in advance for nonresort guests ($109 to $164).

Winter Summerland Miniature Golf   GOLF

(Map p256; ☎407-560-3000; adult/child 3-9 $12/10; ☺10am-11pm) Holiday-inspired miniature golf next to Blizzard Beach.

Fantasia Gardens Miniature Golf   GOLF

(Map p256; ☎407-560-4870; adult/child 3-9 $12/10; ☺10am-11pm) Sweet miniature golf with fairyland theme across from the Walt Disney World Dolphin Resort.

Tennis

Several resorts and the ESPN Wide World of Sports offer hard and clay courts, but the only place that rents rackets and balls is the ESPN Wide World of Sports. Call ☎407-621-1991 to reserve a court anywhere in Walt Disney World. Rates are $12.50 per person per hour, or $90 for 90 minutes for one to four people, including rackets and balls.

Biking

Trails along the shores of Disney's lagoons and past woods, resorts and golf courses make for some lovely family-friendly biking, and several Disney hotels rent two-wheel bikes (hour/day $9/18) and old-fashioned surreys ($22 per half-hour), with a covered top and seating two to four people. Bike helmets are free with rental, and most locations offer training wheels and baby seats.

Fort Wilderness Bike Barn BICYCLE RENTAL
(Map p256; ☑407-824-2742; Fort Wilderness Resort & Campground)

Barefoot Bay Marina BICYCLE RENTAL
(Map p256; ☑407-934-2850; Disney's Caribbean Beach Resort)

Surrey Bikes at the Boardwalk BICYCLE RENTAL
(Map p256; ☑407-560-8754; Disney's Boardwalk)

Disney's Coronado Springs Resort BICYCLE RENTAL
(Map p256; ☑407-939-1000; Disney's Coronado Springs Resort)

Horseback Riding

Carriage rides are also available at Disney's Port Orleans Resort.

Fort Tri-Circle-D Ranch HORSEBACK RIDING
(Map p256; ☑407-824-2832; Disney's Fort Wilderness Resort & Campground) Has guided trail, pony and carriage rides.

Water Sports

More than 10 Disney hotels rent kayaks, canoes, jetskis and pontoons, among other things.

Typhoon Lagoon SURFING
(Map p256; ☑407-939-7873; $150; ☉6:45am Tue & Thu, but call to confirm) No, Orlando is not

MEETING DISNEY CHARACTERS

Folks of all ages pay a lot of money and spend a lot of time in line to get their photo taken with Winnie the Pooh, Snow White, Donald Duck and other Disney favorites. It doesn't make much sense on paper, but somehow, once at Disney, even the most hard-hearted swoon. Note that any character experiences in the resort hotels do *not* require theme-park tickets.

Free Meetings

In addition to permanent character greeting locations in Epcot and Animal Kingdom, look on individual maps for the pointing white finger and check the *Times Guide* for details. Each theme park has specific places where characters hang out, and you can simply hop in line to meet them and have your photo taken. Not all parks, however, have the same characters. Mickey, Minnie, Pluto, Donald and Goofy are everywhere, but meet Pixar characters (*The Incredibles, Monsters Inc, Cars* and *Toy Story*) at Hollywood Studios, which is also where you're most likely to find any new folk, and your best bet to catch a princess is at Magic Kingdom. Lines at Epcot's World Showcase are usually shorter than at other parks, as are lines for lesser-known characters.

Over at Disney's Fort Wilderness Resort & Campground, one of Disney's best offerings is the intimate and low-key **Chip 'n' Dale Campfire Singalong** (free; ☉winter/summer 7pm/8pm) followed by an outdoor screening of a Disney film. Purchase s'more supplies or bring your own, and don't forget a blanket to stretch out on. Cars are not allowed in Fort Wilderness; park at the first left after the entry gate or take a Disney bus or boat to the hotel, and catch a campground shuttle to the campfire.

Character Dining

Make reservations up to six months (yes, six!) either online or by calling **Walt Disney World Dining** (☑407-939-3463) for any of the many character-dining meals in the theme parks and resort hotels. Disney's Grand Floridian Resort features a buffet breakfast with Winnie the Pooh, Mary Poppins and Alice in Wonderland, as well as lunch, tea or dinner with the princesses; there's a jam-packed breakfast and dinner with Goofy and pals at Chef Mickey's in Disney's Contemporary Resort; and the 100-Acre-Wood folk come to Magic Kingdom's Crystal Palace for three meals a day. Probably the most coveted seat is **Cinderella's Royal Table** (adult $33-45, child $24-28) inside Cinderella's Castle at Magic Kingdom. Cinderella greets guests and sits for a formal portrait (included in the price), and a sit-down meal with the princesses is served upstairs. Note that character meals are not fine-dining experiences, nor are they intimate affairs – they can be rather loud and chaotic. Characters rotate around the room, stopping for a minute or so at each table to pose for a photograph and sign autograph books. Check www.disneyworld.disney.go.com for character-dining options.

on the ocean, but that doesn't stop Disney. Typhoon Lagoon gives surf lessons before the water park opens to the public. Price includes a half-hour on land and two hours in the water, and nonpaying family and friends are welcome to come watch. If you stick around after the park opens, you must purchase admission tickets.

Sammy Duvall's Watersports Centre   WATER SPORTS
(Map p256; ☑407-939-0754; www.sammyduvall .com; Disney's Contemporary Resort, 4600 N World Dr; water skiing, tubing & wakeboarding incl instructors for up to 5 people for 2hr $165; ☺10am-5pm) Zip around Seven Seas Lagoon and Bay Lake, in the shadow of Magic Kingdom. This centre rents boats and equipment and offers lessons. It also offers fishing cruises and parasailing.

Other

Richard Petty Driving Experience   DRIVING
(Map p256; ☑800-237-3889; Walt Disney World Speedway; prices vary; ☺9am-4pm) Nascar wannabes can race Winston Cup–style cars around a real track. The Ride Along Program ($105) puts you shotgun in a stock car (riders must be at least 16) and three other options allow you to drive on your own.

☞ Tours

Walt Disney World offers at least a dozen guided tours (☑407-939-8687). The five-hour Keys to the Kingdom ($78; ☺8:30am, 9am & 9:30am) takes you through the Magic Kingdom's underground tunnels (no children allowed, so as not to destroy the magic). Check www.disneyworld.disney.go.com for a full listing; attendance is limited, prices vary widely and advanced reservations are required.

★✯ Festivals & Events

On select nights from September through October 31, Mickey's Not-So-Scary Halloween Party (adult/child $49/43) features characters decked out in costumes, trick-or-treating and Halloween-inspired fireworks, parade and events.

In November and December, millions of lights and hundreds of Christmas trees, specialty parades and holiday shows celebrate the season throughout Walt Disney World. There's Holidays Around the World – Candlelight Procession at Epcot, and the Osborne Family Spectacle of Dancing Lights at Hollywood Studios. Magic Kingdom's Mickey's Very Merry Christmas

FANTASTIC FANTASMIC   **275**

Book Fantasmic Dining Package (☑407-939-3463; adult $26-58, child $13-20) up to 180 days in advance for a fixed-price meal at one of three restaurants within Hollywood Studios and reserved priority-seating for the park's nighttime spectacular Fantasmic. Dining times are generally between 1pm and 5pm; your best bet is to hit the park gates when they open, eat at 1pm, lounge by your hotel pool for the afternoon and return for the show.

Party ($52-63; ☺7pm-midnight) goes all out, with a Christmas parade, snowfall on Main Street and seasonal shows.

The Disney topiary and garden displays at the annual Epcot International Flower and Garden Festival (March to June) are spectacular, and folks return annually for Epcot's Food and Wine Festival (October).

Check www.disneyworld.disney.go.com for details on these and other special events at Walt Disney World.

🛏 Sleeping

Disney resort hotels are divided according to location, and Disney-provided transportation to *that* location is indicated in the hotel details below. It is important to take note of what transport is available to/from your chosen resort when planning your trip, as you can use Disney transportation to reach any attraction from any resort but not everything is directly connected.

Prices vary drastically according to season, and there are 20 (yes, 20!) different seasons; to further complicate it, deluxe resorts can have upwards of 10 different 'room types' that vary according to location and amenities, and rooms that sleep five or more aren't necessarily more expensive than suites. There's an easy-to-use chart at www.disneyworld.disney .go.com that describes the exhausting selection of room options at each resort, and a drop-down menu that gives exact prices for each season. Prices given here are for value/peak weekends; note that weekdays will be a bit less. Most rooms sleep up to five, with no extra charge for children; check the website for details on concierge-level rooms.

While deluxe resorts are the best Disney has to offer, don't expect the same bang for

DISNEY'S VALUE RESORTS

Value resorts, the least expensive Disney properties available (not including camping), have thousands of motel-style rooms, are garishly decorated according to the theme, connect to the parks by bus only and cater to families and traveling school groups (expect cheerleading teams practicing in the courtyard or a lobby of teenagers wearing matching jerseys). You will definitely feel the difference in price: instead of proper restaurants, there are only food courts and snack bars, and things are particularly bright, hectic and loud. Rates for a double room range from $82 to $110 during value season and from $119 to $150 during peak season.

Disney's Art of Animation Resort (Map p256; 407-939-6000; ❄️✈️📶) Inspired by four animated Disney classics, this resort was not yet open at the time of writing. The *Lion King*, *Cars* and *Finding Nemo* buildings, each with their own thematically designed courtyards, offer family suites, with two bathrooms, a master bedroom and three separate sleeping areas. The *Little Mermaid* buildings have basic rooms. Scheduled to open summer 2012.

Disney's All-Star Movies Resort (Map p256; 407-939-7000; ❄️✈️📶) Icons from Disney movies including *Toy Story* and *101 Dalmatians*.

Disney's All-Star Music Resort (Map p256; 407-939-6000; ❄️✈️📶) Family suites and motel rooms surrounded by giant instruments.

Disney's All-Star Sports Resort (Map p256; 407-939-5000; ❄️✈️📶) Five pairs of three-story buildings divided thematically by sport.

Disney's Pop Century Resort (Map p256; 407-939-6000; ❄️✈️📶) Each section pays homage to a different decade of the late 20th century, with massive bowling pins extending beyond the roof and giant Play Doh.

your buck as you'd get elsewhere. They do, however, offer multiroom suites (many with bunk-bed options), upscale restaurants, children's programs and incredibly easy access to theme parks. You're paying for convenience and Disney theming, not luxury. Epcot resorts offer easy walking access and boat transport to restaurants and entertainment at Disney's Boardwalk, Hollywood Studios and Epcot, while Magic Kingdom resorts are an easy boat or monorail ride to its gates. If you have little ones, you'll want to stay at a Magic Kingdom resort.

In a category all its own, **Shades of Green Resort** (Map p256; 407-824-3400; www.shadesofgreen.org; 1950 W Magnolia Palm Dr, Lake Buena Vista; r $90-150, ste $250-275; ❄️✈️; bus transportation) sits within Walt Disney World but is owned by the Armed Forces Recreation Center. Only active and retired members of the US Armed Services (including members of the National Guard) and their widows and widowers can stay here, and rates are divided into three categories determined according to rank.

Disney Vacation Club

Disney Vacation Club is Disney's version of a timeshare, and many of the properties we list participate in the program. Go to www .disneyvacationclub.com for details.

MAGIC KINGDOM

The number-one advantage to staying at one of these hotels on Bay Lake is that they are one easy monorail or boat ride from Magic Kingdom – they're the only hotels at Walt Disney World where you can get to classic Disney with no need for transfers. This may not sound like much, but when you're slogging home with three exhausted children or are desperate for a quick afternoon dip in the pool, it makes a world of difference. You can also take the monorail to Epcot, though you have to transfer at the Transportation & Ticket Center, and there are nonstop buses to Animal Kingdom and Hollywood Studios.

TOP CHOICE **Disney's Fort Wilderness Resort & Campground** CAMPGROUND $ (Map p256; 407-824-2900; campsites value $51-82, peak $80-118, cabins value/peak $300/405; ❄️📶✈️🏊🐾; boat transportation) Located in a huge shaded natural preserve, Fort Wilderness caters to kids and families with hayrides, fishing and nightly campfire singalongs. Cabins sleep up to six and are hardly rustic, with cable TV and full kitchens, and while cars aren't allowed within the gates, you can rent a golf cart to toot around in. Campsites have partial or full hookups. Staff keep a strict eye on after-hours noise, the grounds are meticulously maintained, and there's a wonderfully casual and friendly state-parklike tone to the entire resort. Boats depart regularly to Magic Kingdom, and buses service the rest of Disney.

TOP CHOICE Disney's Grand Floridian Resort & Spa
RESORT $$$

(Map p256; ☑407-824-3000; r value $495-820, peak $655-1075, ste value $1235-2345, peak $1600-2944; ❄ 🛜 ⛱ 🛗; boat & monorail transportation) Just one easy monorail stop from Magic Kingdom, the Grand Floridian rides on its reputation as the grandest, most elegant property in Disney World, and it does indeed exude a welcomed calm and charm. The four-story lobby, with a grand piano, formal seating areas and huge flower arrangements, has all the accoutrements of Old Florida class and style, but at its heart this is Disney. Sparkling princesses ballroom-dance across the oriental rugs, exhausted children sit entranced by classic Disney cartoons and babies cry. In contrast to the massive ferries from the Transportation & Ticket Center, small wooden boats shuttle folks back and forth to Magic Kingdom.

TOP CHOICE Disney's Wilderness Lodge
RESORT $$$

(Map p256; ☑407-824-3200; r value $260-435, peak $425-605, ste value $435-995, peak $640-1405; ❄ 🛜 ⛱ 🛗; boat transportation) The handsome lobby's low-lit tepee chandeliers, hand-carved totem pole and dramatic 80ft fireplace echo national-park lodges of America's ole West. Though it's meant to feel as if you're in John Muir country, with its wooded surrounds and hidden lagoon-side location, the fake geyser and singing waiters in the lobby restaurant dispel the illusion mighty quick.

Disney's Polynesian Resort
RESORT $$$

(Map p256; ☑407-824-2000; r value $435-750, peak $585-985, ste value $710-2335, peak $930-3000; ❄ 🛜 ⛱ 🛗; boat & monorail transportation) With faux-bamboo decor, a jungle motif in the lobby, and coconut-shell cups and shell necklaces in the store, you just may think you're in the South Pacific. The rounded lagoon-side pool features a slide, a zero entrance perfect for little ones and an excellent view of Cinderella's Castle.

Disney's Contemporary Resort
RESORT $$$

(Map p256; ☑407-824-1000; r value $340-655, peak $435-835, ste value $765-1105, peak $955-1405; ❄ 🛜 ⛱ 🛗; boat & monorail transportation) The granddaddy of Disney resorts, the Contemporary's futuristic A-frame opened Walt Disney World in 1971 but feels uninspired and disappointing by today's standards. Yes, it's cool to see the monorail zip silently through the lobby and its withering grandeur evokes melancholy sentimental attachment, but the years have faded this iconic hotel's sparkle. Balcony rooms front Magic Kingdom, an excellent top-floor restaurant lures folks with its drop-dead views of Disney's fireworks and streamlined rooms have a decidedly modern vibe. Vacation Club suites in Bay Lake Towers (added in 2009) are some of the most handsome at Disney.

EPCOT

One of the best parts about this cluster of hotels on the shore of Crescent Lake is their easy access to restaurants and entertainment in Epcot, Hollywood Studios and Disney's Boardwalk. The area is particularly pedestrian-friendly, and it's a pleasant walk or an easy boat ride to Epcot's International Gateway (back entrance) and to Hollywood Studios. To get to Magic Kingdom, however, you must walk through Epcot and catch the monorail from the front gate, or take a bus from any hotel to the Transportation & Ticket Center, and then connect to a monorail or boat from there to the park entrance.

TOP CHOICE Disney's Boardwalk Inn
RESORT $$$

(Map p256; ☑407-939-5100; r value $370-655, peak $515-845, 1 & 2 bedroom cottages & ste value $720-2295, peak $900-2830; ❄ 🛜 ⛱ 🛗; boat & foot transportation) This resort embodies the seaside charm of Atlantic City in its heyday, with a waterfront the color of saltwater taffy, tandem bicycles with candy-striped awnings, and a splintery boardwalk. The lovely lobby features sea-green walls, hardwood floors and soft floral vintage seating areas. Elegant rooms have terrace or balcony. The resort is divided into two sections, the Inn and the Villas; the Inn, with cute picket-fenced suites, quiet pools and plenty of grass, is far nicer and subdued. Accommodations range from rooms sleeping up to five, to two-bedroom cottages sleeping up to nine.

WALT DISNEY WORLD SLEEPING

TOP CHOICE Walt Disney World Swan & Dolphin Resorts RESORT $$$

(Map p256; ☎888-828-8850, 407-934-3000; www .swandolphin.com; r $140-380; ❄ 🛜 ☒ 🛁; boat & foot transportation) These two high-rise hotels, which face each other on Disney property and share a gym and pool facilities, are actually owned by Westin and Sheraton respectively, and there's a distinct toned-down Disney feel here. The cushy feather beds at the Dolphin arguably offer the best night's sleep in Disney, and there's a full-size lap pool along the lagoon. Character breakfasts and other Disney perks, including Disney transportation and extra Magic Hours (where a theme park opens early and closes late for guests at Disney hotels only), are available at both. These are the only non-Disney hotels next to a theme park, and online and last-minute deals can save literally hundreds of dollars.

Disney's Yacht Club Resort and Disney's Beach Club Resort RESORT $$$

(Map p256; ☎Yacht Club 407-934-7000, Beach Club 407-934-8000; r value $360-580, peak $505-755, ste value $650-1955, peak $840-2455; ❄ 🛜 ☒ 🛁; boat & foot transportation) These handsome sister resorts, pleasantly located along the wa-

ter and a five-minute walk from Epcot, strive for old New England beachside charm. The pools, boasting sandy shores and a slide off the mast of a ship, earn rave reviews, but we found them cramped and in need of a face-lift.

Disney's Caribbean Beach Resort RESORT $$

(Map p256; ☎407-934-3400; r value $174-229, peak $224-279; ❄ 🛜 ☒ 🛁; bus transportation only) A Disney taste of the islands means painted beds, pastel rooms, a food court that looks like a street festival during Carnival and a pool with a vague resemblance to ancient temple ruins. Disney gave some rooms here a much-needed update in 2009, and almost 400 rooms now boast a swashbuckling pirate theme. Unlike other Epcot resorts, this hotel does not sit along Crescent Lake and does not have convenient boat transportation to Epcot and Hollywood Studios.

ANIMAL KINGDOM

Along with Disney's value resorts, these are the most inconveniently located of all Disney resorts. To get from these hotels to Epcot, Hollywood Studios, Animal Kingdom, Downtown Disney and Disney's Boardwalk, you must take a bus (or drive) and to get to Magic Kingdom you'll need to take a bus and then a monorail or boat.

TOP CHOICE Disney's Animal Kingdom Lodge RESORT $$$

(Map p256; ☎407-938-3000; r value $285-425, peak $425-580, ste value $800-2420, peak $1070-2960; ❄ 🛜 ☒ 🛁; bus transportation only) With an abutting 33-acre savannah parading a who's who of Noah's Ark past hotel windows and balconies, park rangers standing ready to answer questions about the wildlife, a distinctly tribal decor and African-inspired food served at the recommended restaurants, this resort succeeds better than any other in creating a themed environment. Ask about intimate tours through the animal park and storytelling and singing around the fire. If you want to see giraffes and ostriches out your room window, you'll have to reserve the more expensive savannah-view rooms, but anyone can enjoy animals from the deck out back. Even if you're not staying here, swing by for a drink after an afternoon at Animal Kingdom.

Disney's Coronado Springs Resort RESORT $$$

(Map p256; ☎407-939-1000; r value $169-209, peak $219-254, ste value $375-1033, peak $555-

HIDDEN MICKEYS

Mickey Mouse is hiding. He's hiding in the rug in the hotel lobby, in the giant snowflakes of the parade, in the bricks outside Magic Kingdom. Yes, those iconic ears are everywhere, and some folks can become downright obsessive about finding them. Hidden Mickeys started during the construction of Epcot, some say as an inside joke among Disney Imagineers, others say in defiance to official Disney policy that restricted characters to Magic Kingdom only. Whatever the reason, they took off and today there are books, websites and chatrooms all dedicated to identifying Hidden Mickeys at Walt Disney World.

While the most prevalent Hidden Mickey form is the tri-circle frontal silhouette, with a big circle for the face and two circles as ears, other designs include full body silhouette, handprints or even just initials. Get started at www .hiddenmickeysguide.com.

1220; ✳@🛜☒♿; bus transportation only) The Southwestern theme, evidenced in the warm pink-and-yellow guest rooms, the colored lights strung across the Pepper Market and the adobe-colored buildings, creates a low-key tone that sets this resort apart from other Disney hotels. Several pleasantly landscaped two-story buildings, some with their own private and quiet pools, sit along a central lake. There's plenty of grass, and little beaches with hammocks hung between the palm trees sprinkle the shore. At the central pool, an open-air slide zooms down a Maya pyramid. Suites and casitas sleep up to six, and the hotel is popular for conventions.

DOWNTOWN DISNEY

While these hotels offer easy and pleasant boat access to Downtown Disney, the only Disney transportation to the theme parks and Disney's Boardwalk is by bus.

Disney's Old Key West Resort RESORT $$$
(Map p256; ☑407-827-7700; 1- & 2-bedroom villas value $415-570, peak $540-830; ✳🛜☒♿; boat transportation) Victoriana oozes from every gingerbread-accented corner, palm-tree enclave and the azure-blue waters. This is an 'all villa' resort, meaning accommodation options are studios sleeping up to four, one- and two-bedroom villas sleeping up to eight, and three-bedroom villas sleeping up to 12.

Disney's Port Orleans French Quarter and Riverside Resorts RESORT $$$
(Map p256; ☑French Quarter 407-934-5000, Riverside 407-934-6000; r value $174-204, peak $214-244; ✳🛜☒♿; boat transportation) These sister resorts, combined to create one of the largest at Walt Disney World, offer plenty of activities. There's a pool with a sea-serpent waterslide, several quiet pools, boat rental, fishing and evening horse-drawn-carriage rides. Lush gardens and a jubilant Mardi Gras motif blend in an effort to create a Louisiana feel, but the result falls flat and the simple rooms, some with rough-hewn beds and sleeping up to five, are showing their age; request one without a parking-lot view. A boat connects the two properties, or it's a 15-minute walk.

Disney's Saratoga Springs Resort & Spa RESORT $$$
(Map p256; ☑407-827-1100; 1- & 2-bedroom villas value $425-580, peak $540-830, tree-house villas $580/830; ✳🛜☒♿; boat transportation) Set on 16 acres and modeled on an upstate New York resort spa, this grassy complex of three-

and four-story units attracts families looking for plenty of space. Studio, one-, two- and three-bedroom villas surround a family-friendly zero-entry pool with a Donald Duck fountain play area. Rooms feel a bit dated, but the 2009-renovated tree-house villas, nestled in the woods 10ft above the ground, boasting spacious decks and sleeping up to nine, are particularly fun. Three-bedroom villas sleep up to 12.

✗ Eating

Expect lots of mediocre fast food, bad coffee and cafeteria cuisine at premium prices. Yes, it's difficult to find a decent meal at Disney, despite the fact that there are more than 100 restaurants here, and it gets frustrating paying a lot of money for disappointing meals. Table-service restaurants, listed below according to location, accept 'priority seating' reservations up to 180 days in advance unless otherwise noted. Call Disney Dining at ☑407-939-3463 or go to www.disneyworld .disney.go.com to peruse menus and make reservations at these and dozens more. For a more complete selection of menus to peruse in advance, go to www.wdwinfo.com. If you don't have a reservation and the line is long, try the bar – many places have great bars with limited menus.

MAGIC KINGDOM

Three of the five table-service restaurants here are buffet, and none are anything to recommend. You're better off bringing something into the park or hopping the monorail to Epcot or a Magic Kingdom resort hotel. Cinderella's Royal Table, inside Cinderella's Castle, is one of the most popular character-dining options at Disney; see Meeting Disney Characters, p274.

SPECIALTY DINING

In addition to character meals (p274), check www.disneyworld.disney.go.com for specialty dining offerings ranging from a private safari followed by an African dinner to dessert and reserved seating for Magic Kingdom's Wishes Nighttime Spectacular. One of the most popular is chatting with the folk behind Disney magic at **Dine With a Disney Imagineer** (☑407-939-3463; Hollywood Brown Derby, Hollywood Studios; adult/child 3-9 $70/35; ⊙11:30am).

DISNEY DINNER SHOWS

The park's three **dinner shows** (☑407-939-3463; adult $57-65, child $28-34) sell out early, so make your reservation for these up to 180 days in advance; you can cancel up to 48 hours in advance with no penalty.

» **Hoop-Dee-Doo Musical Revue** (Map p256) Nineteenth-century vaudeville show at Disney's Fort Wilderness Resort, with ribs delivered to your table in metal buckets, corny jokes, and the audience singing along to 'Hokey Pokey' and 'My Darling Clementine.' This is one of Disney's longest-running shows and great fun, once you grab your washboard and get into the spirit of it all.

» **Spirit of Aloha Show** (Map p256) Lots of yelling and pounding on drums while hula-clad men and women leap around stage, dance and play with fire in this South Pacific–style luau at Disney's Polynesian Resort.

» **Mickey's Backyard Barbecue** (Map p256) The only dinner theater with Disney characters; expect country-and-western singin', ho-down style stompin', fried chicken and goofy Mickey antics at this Disney favorite at Disney's Fort Wilderness Resort.

EPCOT

Eating at Epcot is as much about the experience as the food, and many of the restaurants go overboard to create an atmosphere characteristic of their country. You can savor a glass of champagne or a flight of wine in France, order a stein at the tavern in Germany, or indulge in a blood-orange margarita in Mexico before heading to China for wonton soup. As one visitor said, perusing the menu of a fast-food eatery in Future World, 'I'm gonna wait and try something exotic over in Morocco.' None of the food is going to knock your socks off, but it's a lot of fun.

La Hacienda de San Angel   MEXICAN $$
(Map p256; Mexico; mains $23-30; ⊙4pm-park closing; 🎵) Authentic Mexican rather than Tex Mex, this Epcot newcomer features corn tortillas made daily, mango and chipotle salsas and on-the-rocks margaritas ranging from rose-infused Rosita to a classic with cactus lemongrass salt on the rim. Or stick to the basics with a flight of tequila. Massive windows face the lagoon, perfect for watching Illuminations.

La Cava del Tequila   MEXICAN $
(Map p256; Mexico; tapas $6-12; ⊙noon-park closing; 🎵) Pop in for a cucumber, passion fruit or blood orange margarita. Can't decide? Try a flight of margaritas or shots. The menu features more than 70 types of tequila and a limited tapas menu, and it's a cozy, dark spot, with tiled floors, Mexican-styled murals and a beamed ceiling. La Cava is connected to San Angel Inn, a full-service sit-down restaurant, but does not take reservations.

Rose & Crown   ENGLISH $$
(Map p256; UK; mains $13-21; ⊙11am-park closing; 🎵) Housed in a classic British pub, this little spot serves up ploughman's lunch, steak, fish & chips and a tasty vegetable curry. Wash it down with Bass on tap and head across the path for a garden concert of the Fab Four, or settle on the patio for the nightly light show Illuminations.

Bistro de Paris   FRENCH $$$
(Map p256; France; mains $29-43; ⊙11am-park closing; 🎵) The most upscale option in the park, and one of the few with a dress code, this elegant 2nd-floor restaurant, decorated in muted earth tones and self-consciously fancy, serves upmarket French food. A multicourse meal with wine pairings costs $89 ($59 without wine), an excellent choice for an upscale Disney experience, and if you're lucky you can score a window seat, with lovely views of the lagoon. There is no children's menu.

Le Cellier Steakhouse   STEAKHOUSE $$$
(Map p256; Canada; mains $21-35; ⊙11am-park closing; 🎵) If you love meat, this place is for you. Try the buffalo. Dark and cavernous, with stone walls and lanterns, it makes a good spot to escape the heat, but the dense sauces and decadent desserts might not be the best fuel to get you through the day. Come here if your afternoon promises nothing more than lazing by the pool, or for a hearty dinner.

Chefs de France   FRENCH $$
(Map p256; France; mains $19-35; ⊙11pm-park closing; 🎵) Bright yellow and with lovely big windows, this bustling French brasserie

features steak *frites* and other standards of a French bistro. Four times a day, from Monday to Saturday, *Ratatouille*'s Remy makes an appearance. He won't stop at every table, like a traditional character meal, but he dances about, stopping randomly to visit with folk.

Via Napoli   PIZZERIA **$$**
(Map p256; Italy; pizzas $13-22; ⊘11am-park closing; 🖶) Grab pizza by the slice at the walk-up window outside on the stoops of the piazza. Inside, thin-crust pizza cooked in a wood-burning stove is quite tasty, and the toppings take things beyond run-of-the-mill pepperoni.

Biergarten   GERMAN **$$**
(Map p256; Germany; buffet adult/child lunch $20/11, dinner $27/13; ⊘11am-park closing; 🖶) Satisfy a hearty appetite with traditional German foods (don't miss the pretzel bread) and a massive stein of cold brew. The restaurant interior is made to look like an old German village, with cobblestone, trees and a Bavarian oompah band in the evening.

Teppan Edo   JAPANESE **$$**
(Map p256; Japan; mains $16-29; ⊘11am-park closing; 🖶) Chefs toss the chicken, fling the chopsticks and frenetically slice and dice the veggies in this standard cook-in-front-of-you eatery next to Japan's lovely gardens.

Restaurant Marrakesh   MEDITERRANEAN **$$$**
(Map p256; Morocco; mains $21-36; ⊘11am-park closing; 🖶) Sparkling belly dancers shimmer and shake past the massive pillars and around the tables of the Sultan's Palace, magnificently decorated with mosaic tiles, rich velvets and sparkling gold. While the lamb kebabs, vegetable couscous and other basics are disappointing, the windowless elegance is a fun escape from the searing sun and kids love to join in the dancing.

ANIMAL KINGDOM
Plenty of quick counter-service joints disguised behind African names and offering nods to a somewhat tribal feel define eating options at Animal Kingdom.

Yak and Yeti   ASIAN **$$**
(Map p256; Asia; mains $14-29; ⊘11am-park closing; 🖶) Sharing the name of Kathmandu's most exclusive digs in the real Nepal and serving pan-fried noodles, pot stickers and tempura, this getaway at the base of Mt Everest is a welcome respite from burgers and chicken nuggets. With a little imagina-

tion, the vaguely Nepalese-infused decor and the icy Tsing Tao transports you from Disney to the Himalayas. And yes, chilled sake is technically Japanese, but hey, it's close enough to Nepal's traditional Raksi, right? An adjacent quick-service option serves beer and basics.

Rainforest Café   THEME RESTAURANT **$$**
(Map p256; 📞407-938-9100; mains $12-24; ⊘8:30am-1hr after Animal Kingdom closes; 🖶) Just outside the park entrance.

HOLLYWOOD STUDIOS
[TOP CHOICE] **50's Prime Time Café**   AMERICAN **$$**
(Map p256; Echo Lake; mains $13-21; ⊘11am-park closing; 🖶) Step into a quintessential 1950s home for a home-cooked meal, including Grandma's Chicken Pot Pie, Aunt Liz's Golden Fried Chicken and Mom's Old-Fashioned Pot Roast, served up on a Formica tabletop. Waitresses in pink plaid and white aprons banter playfully and admonish folks who don't finish their meals and put their elbows on the table with a sassy 'shame, shame, shame.'

BEST OF DISNEY DINING

Sip on a glowing Lunar Landing in a mock drive-in theater, dine on wild boar next to the Serengeti, munch on oak-fire skewers of chicken while kids do the limbo and roll coconuts, or simply sit by the water and take a load off those weary feet. Call 📞407-939-3463 for reservations up to 180 days in advance.

» **Themed** – Sci-Fi Dine-In Theater (p282) and 50's Prime Time Café (p281), both at Hollywood Studios.

» **Buffet** – Boma (p283), at Disney's Animal Kingdom Lodge.

» **For Families** – 'Ohana (p283), at Disney's Polynesian Resort.

» **View** – California Grill (p283), at Disney's Contemporary Resort.

» **Peace and Quiet** – Narcoossee's (p283), at Disney's Grand Floridian Resort.

» **Waterfront** – La Hacienda de San Angel (p280), at Epcot.

» **Romantic Special Occasion** – Victoria & Albert's (p283), at Disney's Grand Floridian Resort.

» **General** – Jiko (p282), at Disney's Animal Kingdom Lodge.

Sci-Fi Dine-In Theater
TOP CHOICE | AMERICAN **$$**

(Map p256; Commissary Lane; mains $11-21; ⏰11am-park closing; 🍴) A 'drive-in' where you eat in abbreviated Cadillacs and watch classic sci-fi flicks. It's dark in here, and the sky twinkles with stars.

Hollywood Brown Derby
AMERICAN **$$**

(Map p256; Hollywood Blvd; mains $18-32; ⏰11:30am-park closing; 🍴) Semi-upscale surroundings modeled after the LA original, with an odd selection of gourmet eats ranging from a noodle bowl with wok-fried coconut tofu to Sam Adams–braised short ribs and, of course, that Derby classic, the Cobb Salad. This is heavy fare, not the place for a quick light lunch.

Mama Melrose's Ristorante Italiano
ITALIAN **$$**

(Map p256; Streets of America; mains $12-22; ⏰11am-park closing; 🍴) Wash down flatbread pizzas, risotto and pasta with a carafe of sangria.

DISNEY'S BOARDWALK

Flying Fish
SEAFOOD **$$$**

(Map p256; mains $26-39; ⏰5-10pm; 🍷🍴) This airy waterfront eatery offers fresh seafood as well as a handful of vegetarian and hearty meat dishes. A multicourse wine-pairing menu is a particularly good value, by Disney standards.

Kouzzina by Cat Cora
GREEK **$$**

(Map p256; mains $15-35; ⏰7-10:30am & 5-10:30pm; 🍴) Though it can be very loud and hectic, with an open kitchen and high ceilings, Kouzzina boasts an interesting menu and pleasant waterfront location, a great place for a breakfast of blueberry orange pancakes and chicken sausage before walking to Hollywood Studios. Top off a classic Mediterranean dinner with some chilled ouzo or a flight of Greek wine.

DOWNTOWN DISNEY

Paradiso 37
SOUTH AMERICAN **$$**

(Map p256; ☎407-934-3700; mains $15-25; ⏰11:30am-11pm Sun-Thu, to midnight Fri & Sat; 🍴) This waterfront newcomer claims to represent 37 countries of North, South and Central America. A tequila-themed chandelier hangs from the ceiling, and there's 37 kinds of tequila, a 2nd-floor wine bar, pages of specialty drinks and live music on the weekend. Family-friendly, with an excellent 'little tykes' menu (with tacos, grilled chicken and a 'triple stack pb & j'), although the mood becomes decidedly barlike as the night progresses. Call directly for reservations, as it often has more flexibility and openings than Disney Dining.

RESORT HOTELS

Jiko
AFRICAN **$$$**

(Map p256; Disney's Animal Kingdom Lodge; mains $24-35; ⏰5-10pm; 🍴) Excellent food, with plenty of grains, vegetables and creative twists, a tiny bar and rich African surrounds make this a Disney favorite for both quality and theming. For a less expensive option, enjoy an appetizer (the Taste of Africa features various dips and crackers) at the bar. Swing by for dinner, or at least a cocktail, after a

BUYING GROCERIES

Save bundles of time and money by stocking up on basics at a local grocery store and bringing a simple lunch into the parks. Most hotels have a small refrigerator and microwave, and the airport service of Legacy Towncar of Orlando (p254) includes a 20-minute grocery stop.

Whole Foods (Map p236; 8003 Turkey Lake Rd, Orlando; ⏰8am-10pm) Organic fruits, vegetables, meat, a salad bar, brick-oven pizza, deli sandwiches, pre-packaged dinners and more. It lies on the corner of Turkey Lake and Sand Lake Rds between Universal Orlando Resort and Walt Disney World, just west of International Drive and I-4. There's also a branch at 1989 Aloma Ave, Winter Park.

Publix Supermarket (8145 Vineland Ave; ⏰24hr) Statewide grocery chain. From Downtown Disney, go left on Hotel Plaza Blvd to Apopka Vineland Rd/SR 535, turn right and then left in less than a mile onto Vineland. The store is 3 miles on the left. From International Drive, head south until it dead-ends on Vineland Ave and turn right.

Goodings Supermarket (☎407-827-1200; www.goodings.com; SR 535 & I-4; ⏰8am-9pm) Local Orlando grocery with online shopping and delivery service from 4pm.

day at Animal Kingdom. You can relax with a glass of wine on the hotel's back deck, alongside the giraffes and other African beasts.

California Grill
AMERICAN $$$

(Map p256; Disney's Contemporary Resort; mains $15-38; ⊙5-10pm; ⛎) Earning consistent rave reviews from locals and repeat Disney guests, the rooftop California Grill offers everything from quirky sushi like the Double Crunch Rainbow Roll or Snake in the Grass to chicken and dumplings; from triple-cheese flatbread to spinach ravioli. The kids' menu is blessedly chicken-nugget free. Window views for Magic Kingdom's fireworks are the most coveted seats at Walt Disney World.

TOP CHOICE 'Ohana
KEBAB $$

(Map p256; Disney's Polynesian Resort; mains $15-30; ⊙character breakfast 7:30-11am, dinner 4:30-10pm; ⛎) The Polynesian's signature restaurant evokes a South Pacific feel with rock-art graphics of lizards, octopuses and other animals on the ceiling, a huge oak-burning grill cooking up massive kebabs of meat, and demonstrations of hula and limbo dancing, coconut racing and other Polynesian-themed shenanigans. Kids jump from their seats to join in the fun. The only thing on the menu is the all-you-can-eat family-style kebabs and veggies, slid off skewers directly onto the giant woklike platters on the table.

Narcoossee's
SEAFOOD $$$

(Map p256; Disney's Grand Floridian Resort; mains $19-37; ⊙4:30-10pm; ⛎) On the shores of the Seven Seas Lagoon and an easy boat ride from Magic Kingdom, this small muted dining room makes a convenient and pleasant respite if you've been at the park for the afternoon and want to return after dinner for the parade and fireworks. Though offering primarily seafood, there's also duck, filet mignon and free-range chicken.

Boma
AFRICAN $$

(Map p256; Disney's Animal Kingdom Lodge; buffet adult/child breakfast $17/10, dinner $27/13; ⊙7:30-11am & 4:30-10pm; ⛎) Several steps above Disney's usual buffet options, this African-inspired eatery offers wood-roasted meats, interesting soups like coconut curried chicken and plenty of salads. Handsomely furnished with dark woods, decorated with African art and tapestries, and enclosed on one side with plate-glass windows overlooking the garden, Boma offers not only good food but unusually calming and pleasant surrounds.

VICTORIA & ALBERT'S: NO-KIDS-ALLOWED DINING

When Disney announced that children under 10 would no longer be allowed at Victoria & Albert's (Map p256), crème de la crème of Orlando's dining scene, headlines roared with news of Disney's ban on children and the internet gaggle was nothing short of horrified indignation. But with almost 100 other restaurants to choose from, families should have no problem finding alternatives to this three-hour, seven-course dinner ($125 per person, wine pairing costs an additional $60). Indulge yourself with exquisite food and top-notch service in the Victorian-inspired decor of earthy creams. Along with Cinderella's Table, this place, located inside Disney's Grand Floridian Resort, books up months in advance; make reservations at ☎407-939-3463 the morning of the 180th day before you want to dine.

Blue Zoo
SEAFOOD $$$

(Map p256; ☎407-934-1111; Walt Disney World Dolphin Resort; mains $28-34; ⊙5pm-1am; ⛎) Floor-to-ceiling silver threads shimmer in columns at this flashy blue-infused hot spot, invoking a trendy, urban spin on the underwater theme. Excellent seafood makes this one of the few restaurants at Disney where you feel like maybe you've gotten your money's worth. A truncated menu in the bar offers less expensive choices.

Citrico's
MEDITERRANEAN $$

(Map p256; Disney's Grand Floridian Resort; mains $14-29; ⊙4:30-11pm; ⛎) An extensive wine list and handsome northern California ambience set this low-key spot apart from other Disney restaurants; it falls between the hectic family style and self-consciously upscale style, and serves up tasty and fresh eclectic fare. Try for a window seat, with views of Seven Seas Lagoon.

Kona Café
HAWAIIAN $$

(Map p256; Disney's Polynesian Resort; mains $16-25; ⊙7:30am-10pm; ⛎) A bright and intimate spot with pomegranate barbecue, coconut almond chicken and macadamia-crusted mahimahi. Ceiling fans and a carpet designed with huge Hawaiian flowers complete the Pacific Islands decor. Try the Tonga Toast (banana-stuffed French toast dusted with powdered sugar), perfect for fueling up before jumping the monorail to Magic Kingdom.

Artist Point
AMERICAN $$$

(Map p256; Disney's Wilderness Lodge; mains $21-43; ⊙4:30-10pm; 🅜) Arts and Crafts decor and dishes inspired by the Pacific Northwest, including roast venison and salmon, grilled buffalo and berry cobbler. Take your apple martini or Lodge Fizz (Grey Goose Vodka, Triple Sec, cranberry juice and Sprite) to the outdoor patio.

🍷 Drinking & Entertainment

Disney has enough drinking and entertainment options to keep you busy with something different every night of the week for a month straight. There's dueling pianos, nightclubs, margaritas to go, animal safaris, dinner with princesses, fireworks, light shows, vaudeville dinner theater, country-western dancing with Mickey, outdoor movies, parades, the list goes on and on and on, everywhere you turn. At Disney, the problem is never looking for something to do, but rather finding time to do nothing. Downtown Disney and the much smaller Disney's Boardwalk are Walt Disney World's designated shopping, drinking and entertainment districts, but you'll find bars and sometimes live music at most Disney resorts and within the theme parks. Magic Kingdom is the only place that does not sell alcohol.

Go to www.buildabettermousetrip.com/activity-outdoormovie.php for a schedule of free outdoor screenings of Disney movies at Disney hotels.

One of the best shows at Walt Disney World is Finding Nemo – The Musical in Animal Kingdom (p268).

TOP CHOICE Belle Vue Room
BAR

(Map p256; Disney's Boardwalk; ⊙5pm-midnight) On the 2nd floor of Disney's Boardwalk Resort, this is an excellent place for a quiet drink. It's more like a sitting room than a bar: you can relax and play a board game, listen to classic radio shows like *Lone Ranger,* or simply take your drink to a rocking chair on the balcony and watch the comings and goings along Disney's Boardwalk.

Raglan Road
PUB

(Map p256; ☑407-938-0300; Downtown Disney; ⊙11am-1.30am) Live music nightly from 8pm starts off with traditional Irish ditties and continues into the wee hours. An Irish dancer, solid Irish fare, and beer flights with Guinness, Harp, Smithwicks and Kilkenny complete the leprechaun mood. For counter-service, **Cookes of Dublin** serves good fish & chips and is owned by the same people.

Big River Grille & Brewing Works
BREWERY

(Map p256; Disney's Boardwalk; ⊙11:30am-11pm) Open-air microbrewery with outdoor seating along the water makes a pleasant spot to relax with a cold one, but don't expect much from the food.

ESPN Club
SPORTS BAR

(Map p256; Disney's Boardwalk; ⊙11:30am-1am Sun-Thu) Food, drinks and so many TVs screening the hottest game that even in the bathroom you won't miss a single play.

TOP CHOICE Cirque du Soleil
La Nouba
PERFORMING ARTS

(Map p256; ☑407-939-7600; www.cirquedusoleil.com; Downtown Disney's West Side; adult $76-132, child 3-9 $61-105; ⊙6pm & 9pm Tue-Sat) This mind-blowing acrobatic extravaganza is one of the best shows at Disney. See p252 for details.

ESPN Wide World of Sports
Complex
SPECTATOR SPORT

(http://espnwwos.disney.go.com; ⊙varied) This 220-acre sports complex hosts hundreds of amateur and youth events every year, as well as a handful of professional events including Atlanta Braves spring-training games. Equipped with lots of TVs and PS3 systems, the PlayStation Pavilion can kill hours on a rainy day.

AMC Downtown Disney 24
CINEMA

(Map p256; www.amctheatres.com/dinein; Downtown Disney's West Side; tickets $6-12) At this massive Cineplex several screens offer Fork and Screen theater, where you can order meals and have them delivered to your seat through a personal call button at your seat. The bar sells beer, wine and cocktails to take into the flick, and the Cinema Suites option, for guests 21 and over, includes luxury recliner seats.

House of Blues
LIVE MUSIC

(Map p256; ☑407-934-2583; www.houseofblues.com; Downtown Disney; ⊙11:30am-11pm Mon-Thu & Sun, to 1:30am Fri & Sat) Though you can swing by for some good ol' Southern cooking, the real reason to come to this national chain is the music. On Sundays, the **Gospel Brunch** (adult/child 3-9 $34/18; ⊙10:30am &

1pm Sun) features rockin' gospel with a buffet breakfast.

Jellyrolls
LIVE MUSIC

(Map p256; Disney's Boardwalk; admission $10; ⊙7pm-2am) Comedians tickle the keys of dueling pianos and encourage the audience to partake in all kinds of musical silliness.

Atlantic Dance Hall
CLUB

(Map p256; Disney's Boardwalk; ⊙9pm-2am) Blaring Top 40 tunes, dancing, and a massive screen with music videos by request. If you really want to shake your bootie, this is your only Disney option. Otherwise, no reason to come here.

🔒 Shopping

While there are endless stores throughout Walt Disney World, don't expect to find the same things in all the parks and resorts. Most stores are thematically oriented, so after the Star Wars ride you'll find lots of Star Wars stuff, after the Winnie the Pooh ride you'll find lots of Winnie the Pooh stuff, and after the Indiana Jones ride you'll find, well, an Indiana Jones fedora, of course. Unless you're looking for something related to a specific story, movie or character, the fun of shopping at Walt Disney World is browsing.

Call **Walt Disney World Merchandise Guest Services** (✆407-363-6200,877-560-6477; www.disneyparks.com/store) with any questions about shopping at Disney, including details on returning and exchanging items purchased at the parks or checking the status of something you had sent to your home.

THEME PARKS

For an international twist to your Disney souvenir, walk around the world at Epcot. Buy a belly-dancer kit (including a scarf, a hat, a CD and finger cymbals) in Morocco, tartan shawls and Mickey Mouse Shortbread cookies in the UK, and a pink bejeweled wine stopper in France. Japan has a store filled with Hello Kitty stuff, and in Germany you can buy Steiff animals and make your own doll. The wine shop in France offers a pretty extensive selection; with three hours' notice it will have your bottles waiting for you to pick up at the park exit.

Classic Disney shops, with mouse-ear Rice Crispies, crystal Donald Ducks and princess everything, line Magic Kingdom's Main Street leading up to Cinderella's Castle, mak-

ing this the best place for quintessential and off-the-radar shopping pleasures.

Bibbidee Bobbidee Boutique
CHILDREN

(Map p256) Inside Cinderella's Castle, fairy godmothers finalize your kid's transformation from shorts and T-shirt to bedazzling princess with fanciful hairstyling and makeup. Girls three and older can choose from the coach (hair and makeup, from $49), the crown (hair, makeup and nails, from $50) or the castle package (hair, makeup, nails, costume and photograph, $190). For boys, there's the Knight Package (hair, a sword and a shield, $15). Call ✆407-939-7895 for reservations. For just a plain trim, perhaps with some spiky green hair or a pink updo and Disney sequins ($10 to $20) go to the Harmony Barber Shop on Main Street, just as you walk into the Magic Kingdom. There's a second boutique in Downtown Disney.

DOWNTOWN DISNEY

Once Upon a Toy
CHILDREN

(Map p256; Downtown Disney; ⊙9am-11pm) Design a personalized My Little Pony, build your own light saber and create your own tiara at one of the best toy stores anywhere. You'll find old-school classics like Mr Potato Head and Lincoln Logs, board games, action figures, stuffed animals and more.

Lego Imagination Center
CHILDREN

(Downtown Disney; ⊙9am-11pm) Outside there are amazing life-size Lego creations, inside tables to create your own masterpieces and a wall of individually priced Lego pieces. The center is in the midst of a complete overhaul that promises even more Lego delights.

BUY IT NOW

After a while, Disney stores blur together, and the shelves of toys and racks of clothes all start to look the same. But if you see something perfect, don't make the mistake of thinking, as you stand hot, tired and in line yet again, that you'll just get it later, at another Disney store or online. You may not be able to find it anywhere else, and shops throughout Walt Disney World will ship your purchases to your home for a small fee or, if you're staying at a Disney hotel, they'll send them to your hotel at no extra charge.

Ridemakerz
CHILDREN

(Downtown Disney; ⊙9am-11pm) Select from hundreds of options to build your own customized model or remote-control car or truck, and then test it on the store's indoor track. Disney claims that that there are more than 649 million possible combinations of wheels, bodies, accessories etc. Even if you don't want to shell out the bucks to make one of your own, check out the eight full-size cars on display and watch other folks play with their creations.

World of Disney
SOUVENIRS

(Downtown Disney; ⊙9am-11pm) With room after room of Disney everything, this massive store is ideal for all things Disney.

❶ Information

Child Care

Baby-care centers are located in every park. They're air-conditioned, packed with toys, and some run Disney cartoons. You can purchase diapers, formula, baby powder and over-the-counter medicine. Walt Disney World uses **Kid's Nite Out** (☑800-696-8105; www.kidsniteout.com; per hr $14-21.50, depending on number of children) for private babysitting either in the hotel or in the parks. There is a four-hour minimum and a $10 travel fee is charged. Credit cards only; reservations accepted up to three months in advance.

Several Disney resorts offer excellent drop-off children's activity centers ($11.50 per hour per child including dinner; two-hour minimum) for children aged three to 12, with organized activities, toys, art supplies, meals and a Disney movie to end the evening. This is particularly handy if you'd like to enjoy a quiet, upscale meal at a Disney resort, as you do not have to be a guest at the hotel to use the centers.

Camp Dolphin (☑407-934-3000; Walt Disney World Dolphin Resort; ⊙5:30pm-midnight)
Cub's Den (☑407-824-1083; Disney's Wilderness Lodge; ⊙4:30pm-midnight)

---

❶ **HELP, I LOST MY TICKET**

Each person must use their own ticket, identified at theme-park gates by finger-print scan, so if you lose it, you're screwed. If, however, you photocopy or photograph the back of your ticket (the side with the magnetic strip), Guest Relations may be able use this to issue you a new one.

Mouseketeer Club (☑407-824-1000; Disney's Grand Floridian Resort; ⊙4:30pm-midnight)
Never Land Club (☑407-824-1639; Disney's Polynesian Resort; ⊙4pm-midnight)
Sandcastle Club (☑407-939-3463; Disneys Yacht Club Resort; ⊙4:30pm-midnight)
Simba's Clubhouse (☑407-938-4785; Disney's Animal Kingdom Lodge; ⊙4:30pm-midnight)

Internet Access

Disney hotels offer wi-fi or internet cable connection for a fee ($10 per day), but there is no access from the parks. Wi-fi is also available, for the same fee, in the lobbies of Disney's Contemporary Resort, Disney's Grand Floridian Resort, Disney's Coronado Springs Resort, and Disney's Yacht Club and Beach Club Resorts. You may be able to find free wi-fi hot spots, but it's changing and inconsistent.

Kennels

With the exception of select campsites at Disney's Fort Wilderness Resort & Campground, pets are not allowed anywhere at WDW. **Best Friends Pet Care at Walt Disney World** (☑877-493-9738; 2510 Bonnet Creek Pkwy; ⊙1hr before WDW parks open to 1hr after closing) offers overnight boarding and day care for dogs, cats and 'pocket pets.' Prices are a bit less for guests staying at a Disney hotel. Reservations and written proof of vaccination (DHLPP, rabies and Bordetella for dogs, FVRCP and rabies for cats) is required. Rates are $16 to $69 for day care and $37 to $76 for overnight boarding, depending on how many walks and extra perks you'd like. Best Friends is on Bonnet Creek Parkway, across the street from Disney's Port Orleans Resort.

Lost & Found

Walt Disney World Resort Lost & Found (☑407-824-4245) Check individual park's Guest Services for items lost same-day. Items found at Disney's four theme parks, Disney's two water parks, Downtown Disney and on Disney transportation are sent to this central location at the end of each day. For items lost at individual hotels, this number can connect you.

Maps

The free *Walt Disney World Resort Map,* available throughout the resort and at any Orlando visitor center, has a transportation-network chart. You'll get a free map of each individual park, color coded according to thematically divided lands, and a *Times Guide* with character greeting and show times when you enter each park – don't lose them because, strangely, they're not easily available beyond the entrance gate!

Medical Services

Medical facilities are located within each theme park and at both Disney water parks; see park maps for locations.

Money

You will find ATMs throughout Walt Disney World. Guest Services at each park offer limited currency exchange.

Park Hours

Theme park hours change not only by season, but day to day within any given month. Generally, parks open at 8am or 9am and close sometime between 6pm and 10pm. At Walt Disney World, one of the four theme parks stays open or closes late for guests of Walt Disney World hotels only – these 'Magic Hours' are a major perk of staying at a Disney hotel.

Parking

If you're staying at a Disney resort, parking at all the parks is free; otherwise, it costs $14 per day. You will find parking lots outside the gates of all the parks except for Magic Kingdom; if you're driving to Magic Kingdom, you have to park at the Transportation & Ticket Center and take a monorail or ferry to the park. Parking tickets bought at one park are good all day for all Disney parks. Parking at Downtown Disney, the water parks, ESPN Wide World of Sports and all the golf courses is free, but there is no transportation from these attractions to any of the four theme parks. Self-parking at Disney resort hotels is free; valet parking at deluxe hotels is $12.

Stroller Rental

Strollers (single/double per day $15/31, multi-day $13/27) are available on a first-come, first-served basis at Magic Kingdom, Epcot, Animal Kingdom, Hollywood Studios and Downtown Disney, and you can also purchase umbrella strollers (folding strollers). There is no stroller rental at Disney's two water parks, Disney's Boardwalk or at the resort hotels.

Tickets

Walt Disney World Tickets are called Magic Your Way. The minimal base ticket, which allows access to one theme park for one day, costs adult/child three to nine $90/84. From that, you can add days and options either when you first purchase your ticket or any time within the 14 days after the ticket is first used.

MULTIPLE DAYS UP TO 10 The per-day cost drops 50% if you buy a seven-day or longer base ticket. Multiple-day tickets allow unlimited admission to all four of Disney's theme parks (but not the water parks), so you can go in and out of a theme park as many times as

you'd like, *but you can only go to one theme park a day*. They can be used anytime within 14 consecutive days. Adult tickets for two/three/four/five/six/seven/eight/nine/10 days cost $168/232/243/251/259/267/275/283/291. Tickets for children aged 3 to 10 cost a bit less.

WATER PARK FUN & MORE ($56) Includes one admission per day to your choice of Blizzard Beach water park, Typhoon Lagoon water park, DisneyQuest Indoor Interactive Theme Park (at Downtown Disney), ESPN Wide World of Sports and Disney's Oak Trail Golf Course (with reserved tee time). You will be given one pass for each day of your Magic Your Way ticket, and you can use these passes to access whatever you'd like, whenever you'd like; if you have a five-day ticket and you add this option, you can go to a water park in the morning, golf in the afternoon and DisneyQuest in the evening, and you'll have used three of your five passes. The price for this option is the same regardless of how many days your Magic Your Way base ticket includes.

NO EXPIRATION Unused days of multiple-day tickets do not expire after 14 days. The price varies from $22 if added on to a two-day ticket, to $67 if added on to a four-day ticket, to $213 if added on to a 10-day ticket.

PARK HOPPER ($56) Allows unlimited access to any of the four theme parks during the course of one day, so you can spend the morning at Magic Kingdom, the afternoon at Animal Kingdom and head to Epcot for the evening. The cost is the same regardless of when you add this option and whether you are adding it to a one-day ticket or to a 10-day ticket.

DISNEY DINING Disney offers an incredibly complicated Disney Dining Plan available to guests staying at a Disney resort hotel; see www.disneyworld.disney.go.com for prices. If you decide to purchase a dining plan, do not do so when you make your room reservation. You may not get a full refund of your dining plan if you need to cancel, and you can add a dining plan anytime up until the day you check into your hotel.

Tourist Information

Guest Services are located at the entrance to each theme and water park, with maps and general information.

The front desk of Disney hotels can help with all things Disney, including transportation, dining and entertainment questions, and reservations.

Any time you call Disney, you'll be prompted to give all kinds of information they use for customer research. Keep pressing '0' – just cut them off mid-sentence – and you'll quickly get a real human being.

Disney Dining (☑407-939-3463) Dinner reservations, including dinner shows, up to 180 days in advance.

UK Guest Information (☑from UK 0870 24 24 900, from Florida 407-939-7718)

Walt Disney World (☑407-824-8000, 407-939-6244) Central numbers for all things Disney, including packages, resort, ticket and dining reservations and general questions about hours and scheduled events. While there are separate numbers for all of this, all you need is either of these. They'll connect you to whatever you need.

Travelers with Disabilities

The *Guidebook for Guests with Disabilities*, available at Guest Services at each park and on Disney's website, has maps and ride-by-ride guides with information on closed captioning and accommodating wheelchairs and seeing-eye dogs. On many rides, folks in wheelchairs will be waved to the front of the line. You can borrow braille guides and audiotape guides from Guest Services and rent wheelchairs ($12) and electronic convenience vehicles (ECV; $50) at each of Disney's theme parks and at Downtown Disney. All chairs are first-come, first-served; reservations are not possible.

Public transportation is wheelchair accessible and select resort hotels offer features and services for guests with disabilities. Call ☑407-824-4321 or 407-827-5141 for further information. For thorough information on navigating Disney in a wheelchair, go to www.themouseonwheels.com.

ORLANDO'S TOP 10 THEME PARK THRILLS

» **Incredible Hulk Coaster** (Islands of Adventure, p289)

» **Harry Potter and the Forbidden Journey** (Islands of Adventure, p291)

» **Kraken** (SeaWorld, p300)

» **Manta** (SeaWorld, p300)

» **Space Mountain** (Magic Kingdom, p262)

» **Expedition Everest** (Animal Kingdom, p267)

» **Hollywood Rip Ride Rockit** (Universal Studios, p292)

» **Revenge of the Mummy** (Universal Studios, p294)

» **Twilight Zone Tower of Terror** (Hollywood Studios, p269)

» **Dr Doom's Fearfall** (Islands of Adventure, p290)

Websites

Google absolutely anything to do with Disney, and you'll find pages of blogs and websites offering tips, advice and recommendations. Here are some comprehensive favorites.

AllEars.Net (www.allears.net) Updated information on attractions, schedules, menus and more.

DIS (www.wdwinfo.com) Particularly readable.

MouseSavers.com (www.mousesavers.com) Excellent tips for saving at Disney, as well as printable coupons.

Walt Disney World Resort (www.disneyworld.disney.go.com) Official Walt Disney World website is incredibly thorough and easy to navigate.

ℹ Getting There & Away

See p288 for information on trains, planes and buses to Orlando.

TO/FROM AIRPORT If you're flying into Orlando International Airport, are staying at a Disney resort hotel, and have no urge to visit Orlando or the surrounding area, you don't need to rent a car. Arrange in advance complimentary luxury bus transportation to and from the airport through **Disney's Magical Express** (☑866-599-0951). It'll send you baggage labels in advance, will collect your luggage at the airport, and if you transfer from one Disney hotel to another in the middle of your stay, the resort will transfer your luggage while you're off for the day.

BUS From Orlando's Lynx Central Station you can catch buses to the Disney parks, but it's about an hour's ride.

CAR & MOTORCYCLE Disney lies 25 minutes' drive south of downtown Orlando. Take I-4 to well-signed exits 64, 65 or 67. At the **Disney Car Care Center** (☑407-824-0976; 1000 W Car Care Dr, Lake Buena Vista; ☺7am-7pm Mon-Fri, to 4pm Sat), near the parking exit of Magic Kingdom, there is a full-service garage and an Alamo car-rental desk. A second Alamo desk is inside the Walt Disney World Dolphin Resort.

SHUTTLE Call one day in advance to arrange personalized transport to/from Universal Orlando Resort and SeaWorld with **Mears Transportation** (☑407-423-5566; www.mearstransportation.com). It costs $19 round-trip per person.

TAXI Taxicabs can be found at hotels, theme parks (except for Magic Kingdom, where there is no road access), the Transportation & Ticket Center, ESPN Wide World of Sports and Downtown Disney.

ℹ Getting Around

The Disney transportation system utilizes boats, buses and a monorail to shuttle folks to hotels, theme parks and other attractions within the resort. The Transportation & Ticket Center operates as the main hub of this system. Note that it can take up to an hour to get from point A to point B using the Disney transportation system, and there is not always a direct route. Pick up a copy of the *Walt Disney World Transportation Guide/Map* at the resorts or from Guest Relations at the parks, or download it from www.disneyworld.disney.go.com in advance.

BOAT Water launches connect Magic Kingdom directly to Disney's Grand Floridian Resort & Spa and Disney's Polynesian Resort; a second route connects Magic Kingdom to Disney's Fort Wilderness Resort & Campground and Disney's Wilderness Lodge; and a third route, utilizing 600-passenger ferries, connects Magic Kingdom to the Transportation & Ticket Center. Boats also connect Epcot and Hollywood Studios to Disney's Boardwalk Inn & Villas Resort, Disney's Yacht Club Resort and Disney's Beach Club Resort, and Walt Disney World Swan & Dolphin Resorts. Finally, boats connect Downtown Disney to Downtown Disney resort hotels.

BUS Everything but Magic Kingdom is accessible by bus (city-bus style) from other areas, but not all destinations are directly connected.

MONORAIL Three separate monorail routes service select locations within Walt Disney World. The Resort Monorail loops between the Transportation & Ticket Center, Disney's Polynesian Resort, Disney's Grand Floridian Resort & Spa, Magic Kingdom and Disney's Contemporary Resort. A second monorail route connects the Transportation & Ticket Center to Epcot, and a third route connects the Transportation & Ticket Center to Magic Kingdom.

UNIVERSAL ORLANDO RESORT

Smaller, easier to navigate and pedestrian friendly, Universal Orlando Resort is everything you wish Disney could be. Both resorts offer fantastic rides, excellent children's attractions and entertaining shows, but Universal does everything just a bit smarter, a bit funnier, a bit more smoothly. Instead of the seven dwarfs, there's the Simpsons. Instead of Donald Duck and Mickey Mouse, there's Spider-Man and Shrek. While Universal can never replace Disney, and it certainly lacks the sentimental charm of Snow White, Peter Pan and Winnie the Pooh, it offers pure, unabashed, adrenaline-pumped, full-speed-ahead fun for the entire family. Universal's got spunk, it's got spirit, it's got attitude.

The Universal Orlando Resort consists of two theme parks – Islands of Adventure, with incredibly designed themed areas and the bulk of the thrill rides, and Universal Studios, with movie-based attractions and shows – one entertainment and dining district (CityWalk) and three deluxe resort hotels. Small wooden shuttle boats and pleasant walking paths connect the entire resort. Characters roaming the parks include Spider-Man, the Incredible Hulk, SpongeBob SquarePants, and characters from *The Simpsons, Madagascar* and Dr Seuss books.

Universal is constantly updating and rethinking its attractions, pushing the limits of ride engineering and incorporating new movies and shows into its repertoire – rides close and new ones open at a regular pace. In 2010 Universal opened the Wizarding World of Harry Potter, a magnificently themed section within the Islands of Adventure theme park, and by 2011 engineers and art designers were already making plans for expansion. Which is a good thing, because the biggest criticism of this latest and best Orlando theme park hot spot is that there simply isn't enough of it!

◉ Sights & Activities

The main attractions are the rides, movies and shows within Islands of Adventure and Universal Studios theme parks. In addition, Universal Orlando Resort offers **Golf Universal Orlando** (☑407-503-3097), which includes preferred tee times, complimentary transportation and club-rental arrangements at several of Orlando's golf courses.

ISLANDS OF ADVENTURE
This place (Map p236) is just plain fun. Scream-it-from-the-rooftops, no-holds-barred, laugh-out-loud kind of fun. Superheroes zoom by on motorcycles, roller coasters whiz overhead, and plenty of rides will get you soaked.

Marvel Super Hero Island   RIDES
Techno music blares from the fake facades of superhero-covered buildings, the **Incredible Hulk Coaster (Express Plus)** rumbles and roars overhead and superheroes speed through on motorcycles. Bright, loud and fast-moving, Marvel Super Hero Island is sensory overload and a thrill-lover's paradise. Comic-book characters patrol this area, so keep an eye out for your favorites. Don't

miss the motion simulator **Amazing Adventures of Spider-Man (Express Plus)**, where super villains rendered in incredible 3D are on the loose, jumping on your car and chasing you around the streets of New York City. At **Dr Doom's Fearfall (Express Plus)**, you're sitting there, strapped, and out of the blue *zoom,* rocket 150ft up in the air and free fall down. **Storm Force Accelatron (Express Plus)** is another barf-o-rama.

Toon Lagoon
RIDES

Loud with kids' squeals, with lots of short buildings covered with primary-colored cartoon classics, this sparkly, lighthearted spot aims to transport visitors to the days when lazy weekends included nothing more than watching *Popeye* and the *Rocky and Bullwinkle Show* on a Saturday morning and afternoons running under the sprinkler. Most of the attractions here are for kids, but older folks will want to hit **Dudley Do-Right's**

Ripsaw Falls (Express Plus), a classic water ride with a short but steep fall that will absolutely get you soaked.

Jurassic Park
RIDES

Oddly quiet, with no screams or loud music, no neon colors or hawking vendors, this oasis of palm trees, greenery and ferns takes visitors into the days of dinosaurs. **Jurassic Park River Adventure (Express Plus)**, a water ride with a prehistoric twist, floats you past friendly vegetarian dinosaurs. All seems well and good until, you guessed it, things go wrong and grass-munchin' cuties are replaced with the stuff of nightmares. To escape the looming teeth of the giant T. Rex, you plunge in darkness 85ft to the water below. Children will be terrified by the creatures, the dark and the plunge.

Pteranodon Flyers floats gently over the lush landscape of Jurassic Park and all its robotic dinosaurs. You must be between 36in

BEST OF UNIVERSAL ORLANDO RESORT

Universal out-thrills and out-wows Disney hands down, and its top-notch ride engineers have designed some of the most incredible simulated rides you'll see anywhere. Technology and creativity combine with a sense of humor and a disarming childlike passion for fun and silliness to create attractions that leave you, quite simply, awed. On top of that, Universal's Express Plus system, far superior to Disney's FastPass system, minimizes line anxiety on all but a few.

Universal Studios

» **The Simpsons Ride** *The Simpsons* creators James Brooks and Matt Groening helped create this masterful simulated experience.

» **Hollywood Rip Ride Rockit** Hard-core coaster where you select your own soundtrack.

» **Revenge of the Mummy** Indoor coaster with fire and mummies.

» **Men in Black Alien Attack** Interactive ride puts you face-to-face with aliens.

» **Twister...Ride It Out** Special-effects show takes you into a frightening summer night in middle America.

» **Terminator 2: 3-D** Sensory overload performance combining 3D movie, live actors and 4D effects.

Islands of Adventure

» **Harry Potter and the Forbidden Journey** Ride through Hogwarts, past the cold chill of Dementors and into a Quidditch match.

» **Incredible Hulk Coaster** Screams from this crown-jewel coaster echo throughout the park.

» **Amazing Adventures of Spider-Man** Don 3D glasses and ride into New York City with Marvel Comics' classic superhero.

» **Dragon Challenge** Dueling coasters give illusion of head-on collision.

» **Dudley Do-Right's Ripsaw Falls** Quintessential water ride with steep drop and big splash.

WIZARDING WORLD OF HARRY POTTER

The hottest thing to hit Orlando since Cinderella's Castle, the magnificently whimsical Wizarding World of Harry Potter in Universal Orlando Resort's Islands of Adventure invites muggles into JK Rowling's imagination. Poke along the cobbled streets and impossibly crooked buildings of Hogsmeade, sip frothy Butter Beer, munch on Cauldron Cakes, and mail a card via Owl Post, all in the shadow of Hogwarts Caste. Alan Gilmore and Stuart Craig, art director and production designer for the films, collaborated closely with the Universal Orlando Resort engineers to create what is without exception the most fantastically realized themed experience in Florida. The detail and authenticity tickle the fancy at every turn, from the screeches of the mandrakes in the shop windows to the groans of Moaning Myrtle in the bathroom; keep your eyes peeled for magical happenings. Queue half an hour before the park gates open, and expect changes by 2013, as plans are already in the works to expand the 20-acre world into what is currently The Lost Continent.

Harry Potter and the Forbidden Journey Wind through the corridors of Hogwarts, past talking portraits, Dumbledore's office and other well-known locations, to one of the best rides in Orlando. You'll feel the cold chill of Dementors, escape a dragon attack, join a Quidditch match and soar over the castle with Harry, Hermione and Ron. Though it's not a fast-moving thrill ride, this is scary stuff. Little ones can enjoy the castle but sit out the ride with a parent in the Child Swap waiting room, where Harry Potter films run continuously.

Dragon Challenge Gut-churning dueling roller coasters twist and loop, narrowly avoiding each other; inspired by the first task of the Triwizard Tournament in *Harry Potter & the Goblet of Fire*.

Ollivander's Wand Shop Floor-to-ceiling shelves crammed with dusty wand boxes and a winding staircase set the scene for a 10-minute show that brings to life the iconic scene in which the wand chooses the wizard. Come first thing, as the line quickly extends upwards of an hour.

Flight of the Hippogriff (Express Plus) Family-friendly coaster passes over Hagrid's Hut; listen for Fang's barks and don't forget to bow to Buckbeak!

Honeydukes Sweet shop with Bertie Botts Every Flavor Beans, Chocolate Frogs, Rock Cakes and other Harry Potter–inspired goodies.

Zonkos Pick up Screaming Yo-Yos, Extendable Ears and more at this store stuffed with magical tricks and toys.

Owl Post & Owlery Buy Wizarding World stamps and send a card officially postmarked Hogsmeade.

Filch's Emporium of Confiscated Goods Souvenir shop featuring the Marauders Map on display.

Three Broomsticks & Hog's Head Tavern with surprisingly good Shepherd's Pie, Pumpkin Juice and Hogs Head Brew.

Dervish & Banges Magical supplies and Hogwarts robes for sale.

and 56in tall to fly. Waits can be upwards of an hour for the 80-second ride, and it's just not worth it. The kids' play area here, enticingly named **Jurassic Park Discovery Center**, is another thing to skip.

Lost Continent SHOWS
Magic and myth from across the seas and the pages of fantasy books inspire this mystical corner of the park. Here you'll find dragons and unicorns, psychic readings and fortune-tellers. And don't be startled if that fountain talks to you – yes you, the little girl in blue holding the cotton candy – as you walk past. The **Mystic Fountain** banters sassily, soaking children with his waterspouts when they least expect

it and engaging them in silly conversation. And no, no one is hiding with a remote control. This is a talking fountain.

At the **Eighth Voyage of Sinbad Stunt Show (Express Plus)** Sinbad and his sidekick Kabob must rescue Princess Amoura from the terrible Miseria, and of course, Sinbad has to tumble and jump around to do it. There's lots of swashbuckling shenanigans, with corny jokes, the audience warning the clueless Sinbad of lurking danger and hissing for the bad guys.

Don't waste your time at **Poseidon's Fury (Express Plus)**, one of those rare occasions when Universal just strikes out and one of the worst attractions in Orlando. Expect to be herded into and through a massive, dark structure for what seems like an eternity and forced to watch some sort of strange nonsensical story with lots of disconnected banging and special effects.

Seuss Landing
RIDES

Anyone who has fallen asleep to the reading of *Green Eggs and Ham* or learned to read with *Sam I Am* knows the world of Dr Seuss: the fanciful creatures, the lyrical names, the rhyming stories. Here, realized in magnificently designed three-dimensional form, is Dr Seuss' imagination. The Lorax guards his Truffula Trees, Thing One and Thing Two make trouble, and creatures from all kinds of Seuss favorites adorn the shops and the rides. Drink Moose Juice or Goose Juice, eat Green Eggs and Ham, and peruse shelves of Dr Seuss books before riding through *The Cat in the Hat* or around and around on an elephant bird from *Horton Hears a Who*. Seuss Landing, one of the best places for little ones in all of Orlando's theme parks, brings the spirit and energy of Dr Seuss' vision to life. So come on in, walk into his world and take a spin on a fish.

OH WHAT A RELIEF IT IS

If Universal's motion-simulator rides and twisting coasters leave you needing the help of your friendly neighborhood pharmacy, **Schwabs Pharmacy** (p296) keeps heartburn, headache and motion-sickness remedies on hand. But you have to ask for 'em, as they're kept under the counter.

UNIVERSAL STUDIOS

The silver screen inspired the majority of the rides at this quieter and more peaceful brother to the energy of Islands of Adventure. The park (Map p236) features elaborate New York and San Francisco backdrops, motion-simulator rides and audience-participation shows. You'll find two of Orlando's best roller coasters, Revenge of the Mummy and Hollywood Rip Ride Rockit, but adrenaline junkies should seek out the park's wilder sibling, Islands of Adventure. Less clearly defined by theme than other Orlando parks, Universal Studios consists of several geographical regions defined by region-specific architecture and ambience.

For some down time, a fenced-in grassy area with shade trees, flowers and views across the lagoon sits just across from the entrance to Woody Woodpecker's Kidzone. Spread out a blanket and enjoy a snack, or simply chill out. It makes an excellent meeting spot, and is a pleasant and quiet place to nurse an infant. The park map shows the park but does not label it.

Production Central
SHOWS, RIDES

A multisensory roller coaster, **Hollywood Rip Ride Rockit (Express Plus)** includes 21st-century special effects and Universal's trademark commitment to the interactive experience. You'll Rip up to 65mph, Ride 17 stories above the theme park and around a loop-dee-loop, and Rockit to customized music (chosen before you strap in).

Pick up where the movie *Shrek* left off at **Shrek 4-D (Express Plus)**. This 3D movie with 4D effects sends you zipping along with Shrek and Donkey in a desperate effort to save Princess Fiona from a fierce dragon. And that dragon is indeed fierce – it pops out at you with red eyes, spitting fire into your face. The dragon sneezes and you feel it, and your chair rocks when Shrek and the donkey chase the dragon. It's a lot of fun, but tiny tots will be scared.

Hollywood Boulevard
SHOWS, RIDES

With glorious 3D 360-degree film footage, live action stunts and 4D special effects, **Terminator 2: 3-D Battle Across Time (Express Plus)** is complete sensory overload, delicious fun for some, overwhelming and scary for others.

If you're really into horror makeup, **Universal Horror Make-Up Show (Express Plus)** may be a little too short and thin on substance. It's humorous, full of silly antics.

UNIVERSAL FOR LITTLE ONES

The word on the street says that Universal Orlando Resort is great for teens and adults but doesn't offer much for kids under seven. This is simply not true. No, it doesn't have as much as Walt Disney World and you won't find Disney's nostalgic charm, but Universal Orlando Resort is a master at blending attractions for all ages into one easily digestible and navigable package of fun, fun, fun. Animals from *Madagascar,* Dr Seuss' Grinch, superheroes and other Universal characters make appearances at both Universal Studios and Islands of Adventure, and Cat in the Hat, Spider-Man and Thing One and Thing Two join folks for a **character buffet breakfast** (☎407-224-4012; diningreservations@universalorlando.com; Islands of Adventure; adult/child 3-9 $18/12; ☺8-10am Sun & Thu) at Confisco Grille. Characters from *Scooby Doo, Shrek* and *Simpsons* swing by restaurants at the three resort hotels on Wednesday, Friday and Saturday nights. CityWalk is very family-friendly, despite its many bars and live music, and the Wantilan Luau (p297) at Portofino Bay Hotel gives folks of all ages a taste of the islands.

Most of the kid-friendly attractions cluster at Universal Studios Woody Woodpecker's Kid Zone and Islands of Adventure's Seuss Landing, the Wizarding World of Harry Potter and Toon Lagoon. You'll want to bring a change of clothes, as both parks have attractions designed to get kids wet!

Universal Studios

Dragon spits fire into your face at Shrek 4-D. It's fun for braver kids, but pretty scary for the six-and-under crowd.

» **Barney Show** Delightfully gentle theater-in-the-round live performance and sing-along.

» **Curious George Goes to Town** Best tiny tot water-play area in any of the theme parks and giant room of nerf balls to throw and shoot from cannons.

» **Woody Woodpecker's Nuthouse Coaster** Gentle coaster for kids three and up.

» **Animal Actors on Location!** Big-stage show that highlights exploits of animal actors.

» **ET Adventure** Board a bike and ride through the woods, the police in hot pursuit, before rising safely into the sky through outer space to ET's fanciful home planet. There are a few spooky spots – prepare kids for darkness, loud noises and steam – but there are no spins, speeds or plummets.

Islands of Adventure

» **One Fish, Two Fish, Red Fish, Blue Fish** Ride a Seussian fish around and around, slowly up and down.

» **Cara-Seuss-al** Hop on a fanciful storybook Seuss character.

» **High in the Sky Seuss Trolley Train Ride** Soar gently over the park.

» **If I Ran the Zoo** Colorful interactive play area with water-spurting triggers.

» **Me Ship, the Olive** Kids crawl, climb and squirt on Popeye's playground ship and zoom down tunnel waterslides.

» **Popeye & Bluto's Bilge-Rat Barges** Float, twist and bump along on a circular raft.

» **Hogwarts** Little ones too young for the scary Harry Potter and the Forbidden Journey ride can simply walk through the magical charms of the most famous school of witchcraft and wizardry. The separate line for this isn't marked, so ask – Universal folks are most accommodating. Other kid-friendly highlights in the Wizarding World of Harry Potter are Ollivander's Wand Shop (the 10-minute show is great fun) and family coaster the Flight of the Hippogriff.

Optical illusions could freak out kids if they're not really clear from the get-go that it's not real.

Fans of the famous redhead Lucille Ball will particularly enjoy **Lucy – A Tribute**, a biographical exhibit with *I Love Lucy* clips, costumes, photos and Lucy's letters. Keep an eye out for the loveable redhead herself walking the streets outside.

New York   SHOWS, RIDES

Just waiting in line for **Twister...Ride It Out (Express Plus)** is enough to frighten kids. Several TV screens show film clips from the movie *Twister*, including a child screaming as a tornado makes its way toward her home. Bill Paxton and Helen Hunt, the stars of the movie, talk in grave tones about the dangers of tornados and the perils of working on the film set, and they warn that this attraction will take you into the horror of their filmmaking experience. The attraction itself takes folks into a film set of a rather dilapidated, old-fashioned Midwest America town. There's a drive-in theater and an old gas station. A radio announces a severe storm warning, and slowly you see and feel the storm approach. A tornado develops in the distant sky, and it's coming, closer and closer, louder and louder... Anyone who has felt the fear of living through a real tornado, or children who already wake up scared of them thanks to sirens, hours in the basement and the eerie blanket of tornado-breeding green skies, should seriously think twice before going to this attraction.

One of the most thrilling coaster rides in Orlando, **Revenge of the Mummy (Express Plus)**, delves into ancient Egyptian catacombs in near pitch black – whatever you do, don't anger Imhotep the mummy or...well, too late for that. Incur his wrath as he flings you past fire, water and more in-your-face special effects.

World Expo   RIDES

Can you qualify for the most elite law-enforcement agency in the galaxy? **Men in Black Alien Attack (Express Plus)** gives you the chance to prove it, if you dare. Speed through the streets of New York City and aim your lasers at aliens of every size and description. Your car swings and spins through a danger-laden downtown, and those guys shoot back!

Even if you're not a fan of the TV cult favorite *The Simpsons,* you won't want to miss **The Simpsons Ride**. This combination ride and 3D film zip you through a Simpsons-inspired adventure with Krusty the Clown and Homer.

San Francisco/Amity   RIDES, SHOWS

Take a little boat for a scenic ride through Nantucket harbor on **Jaws (Express Plus)**. But beware. This is Jaws territory, and he just might be lurking below the surface. The captain does his best to keep everyone safe, with various weapons to stave off the great white beast, but it's no easy task. That shark lurches toward the boat, his huge mouth and sparkling teeth poised for attack, and gas tanks burst into flames.

The premise of **Disaster! (Express Plus)** is that you are the cast of a disaster movie entitled *Mutha Nature*. A fast-talking Hollywood casting agent chooses a handful of folks from the audience, gives the actors directions ('give me terror like Britney Spears is your babysitter'), and each volunteer is filmed for a second or so. Everyone then heads to the 'set' and boards a subway train in the incredibly authentic replica of a San Francisco BART (Bay Area Rapid Transit) station. Suddenly, the big one hits: tracks buckle, the place crumbles and general mayhem ensues. Hint: 65,000 gallons of water are released and recycled every six minutes, but you don't get wet. And yes, you do see the footage of those volunteers.

Beetlejuice, the Werewolf, Dracula, Frankenstein and his Bride rock out in the unbelievably corny and exceptionally loud **Beetlejuice's Graveyard Revue (Express Plus)**, something to skip if time is tight. At **Fear Factor Live (Express Plus)** pre-selected audience members compete to see who can best overcome their greatest fears. Think creepy-crawly bugs and jumps from high places.

GIVING YOUR TWO CENTS

Some folks are pulled from the crowds and asked to go the **Delancy Street Preview Center** to watch clips from a TV pilot or movie and give their opinions. It's a way of testing potential new shows, and the best part is participants are generally compensated for their time. As in money. They're looking for a particular demographic based on the material, and it's not always open, but if you stop by and ask you just may be what they want.

Woody Woodpecker's Kidzone RIDES, SHOWS
Rides, shows and a fantastic water-play area for little ones, this rivals Islands of Adventure's Seuss Landing as park favorite of the eight-and-under crowd. Though primarily geared toward little guys, the **Curious George Ball Room**, a giant room of nerf balls and cannons, is fun for all ages.

✦ Festivals & Events

From February to April Universal Orlando Resort celebrates **Mardi Gras** with parades, live music and Cajun food, and in September and October Universal Studios goes all out with magnificently spooky haunted houses and shows at **Halloween Horror Nights** – watch for goblins and monsters roaming the streets! During the Christmas season, Islands of Adventure hosts **Grinchmas**, featuring a live musical production of *How the Grinch Stole Christmas,* and Universal Studios features the **Macy's Holiday Parade.**

Go to www.universalorlando.com for details on these and other seasonal events.

🛏 Sleeping

Universal Orlando Resort boasts three excellent resorts. Generally less expensive than Walt Disney World's deluxe accommodation, they offer far superior service, food, decor, amenities and rooms. It's a pleasant gardened walk or a quiet boat ride to the parks, all guests receive Universal Express access to park attractions, kids get a free gift at check in and the Loews Loves Pets program welcomes Fido as a VIP (Very Important Pet). Ask about kids' suites with bunk beds and flat-screen TVs, including the new Jurassic Park–themed suites at Royal Pacific and whimsical Seuss suites at Portofino Bay. For reservations and package deals, call ☎888-273-1311.

Portofino Bay Hotel RESORT $$$
(Map p236; ☎407-503-1000; 5601 Universal Blvd; r & ste from $269; ❉@🐾🏊❖🐕) Sumptuous and elegant, with goose-down duvets, plenty of pillows and chenille throws in the earth-toned rooms, cobblestone streets, and sidewalk cafes around a central lagoon, this resort evokes the charm of seaside Italy. There are three pools, including a family pool and two quiet pools surrounded by grass, palm trees and a peaceful boccie court, the outstanding Mandara Spa and supervised children's activities.

Royal Pacific Resort RESORT $$$
(Map p236; ☎407-503-3000; 6300 Hollywood Way; r & ste from $325; ❉@🐾🏊❖🐕) The glass-enclosed Orchid Court, with its reflecting pool, Balinese fountains and carved stone elephants splashing in the water, sits at the center of the airy lobby at this friendly South Pacific–inspired resort. The grounds are lovely, with lots of grass, tropical plantings, flowers, bamboo and palm trees, and the on-site restaurants are excellent (see p295). Unfortunately, the over-the-top, family-friendly pool, with an interactive play area, real sand, volleyball, shuffleboard and Ping-Pong, is loud, chaotic and unsupervised, and rooms tend to be smaller than those at the other two Universal hotels.

Hard Rock Hotel RESORT $$$
(Map p236; ☎407-503-2000; 5800 Universal Blvd; r & ste from $310; ❉@🐾🏊❖🐕) From the grand lawn with the massive guitar fountain at its entrance to the shocking black-and-white bathrooms and pumped-in underwater music at the pool, the modern and stylized Hard Rock embodies the pure essence of rock and roll. Families mingle harmoniously alongside a young party crowd, but the loud live band sometimes playing in the lobby and rockin' energy may be overkill for older folk looking for a peaceful getaway.

🍴 Eating

Universal Orlando Resort offers the all-you-can-eat Universal Meal Deal (adult/child under nine, one park on one day $20/10, two parks on one day $24/12), which allows you to eat as much as you'd like from participating restaurants at Islands of Adventure and Universal Studios. It's good only from lunch through dinner. The only sit-down restaurants in the theme parks that take advance reservations are Universal Studio's Finnegan's Bar & Grill and Lombard's Seafood Grille, and Island of Adventure's Mythos Restaurant and Confisco Grille. Go to www.universalorlando.com for details on all restaurants at Universal Orlando Resort.

ISLANDS OF ADVENTURE
All the usual fast-food suspects are sold at premium prices throughout the park, but with a commitment to theme that you don't see elsewhere. Sip a Predator Rocks in the lush foliage of the Cretaceous period in Jurassic Park or grab a Hogs Head Brew in Hogsmeade.

BREAKFAST WITH SPIDER-MAN & DINNER WITH SCOOBY-DOO

The only character meal within the parks is Confisco Grille's **character breakfast** (☎407-224-9255; adult/child 3-10 $18/12; ☺8-10am Thu & Sun) with Spider-Man, Thing One and Thing Two, and the Cat in the Hat.

Several nights a week, one of the three resort hotels hosts Scooby-Doo and others at **character dinners** (☎407-503-3463 for reservations up to 3 months in advance). Call for details, as they appear at a different hotel each night and it varies seasonally.

TOP CHOICE Three Broomsticks   ENGLISH $
(Wizarding World of Harry Potter; mains $11-16; ☺11am-park closing; 🖮) Fast-food styled British fare inspired by Harry Potter, with Butter Beer, Cornish Pasties and rustic wooden benches. Look out for the growling hog's head at the adjacent Hogs Head Pub.

Mythos Restaurant   MEDITERRANEAN $
(Map p236; ☎407-224-4012; The Lost Continent; mains $8-15; ☺11am-5pm; 🖮) Housed in an ornate underwater grotto, this spot offers particularly tasty fare and is one of the best meals at Universal.

Confisco Grille   AMERICAN $
(Map p236; ☎407-224-4012; Port of Entry; mains $6-22; ☺noon-5pm; 🖮) Chase quesadillas, wood-oven pizza and panini with a cold beer. On Sundays and Thursdays, there's a character breakfast from 8am to 10am, with Spider-Man, Thing One and Thing Two, and Cat in the Hat.

UNIVERSAL STUDIOS

You'll find a plethora of snack and drink stands, most serving icy beer. Take one to the outdoor shows, or just settle back on the grass or a bench by the water and watch the crowds go by.

Finnegan's Bar & Grill   PUB $
(Map p236; ☎407-224-3613; New York; mains $8-20; ☺11am-park closing; 🖮) An Irish pub with live acoustic music plopped into the streets of New York serves up Cornish pasties and Scotch eggs, as well as Harp, Bass and Guinness on tap. Try the corned-beef sandwich

served on a yummy pretzel roll and warm bread pudding.

Schwab's Pharmacy   ICE CREAM $
(Hollywood Blvd; mains $5-10; ☺11am-park closing; 🖮) In the '30s two brothers bought what would become a favorite lunch-counter hangout for struggling movie-star wannabes in Hollywood. They say Ava Gardner worked the soda fountain, Harold Arlin composed 'Over the Rainbow' here, and regulars included Marilyn Monroe, Clark Gable and Orson Welles. The original is long gone, but Universal re-created the charm. Grab a sandwich and Ben and Jerry's.

Mel's Diner   BURGERS $
(Hollywood Blvd; mains $6-10; ☺11am-park closing; 🖮) Classic cars and rockin' bands outside, '50s diner style inside, and you half expect a roller-skating waitress to serve up that burger and fries. This is a fast-food eatery, not much different really than your standard McDonald's, but it's a lot more fun!

Lombard's Seafood Grille   SEAFOOD $$
(Map p236; ☎407-224-3613; San Francisco; mains $12-25; ☺11am-park closing; 🖮) The food is nothing special, but you can sit outside on the pleasant little deck overlooking the water and listen to the jingle-jangle of the boats on their buoys.

Classic Monsters Cafe   PIZZA $
(Production Central; mains $5-12; ☺11am-park closing; 🖮) Munch on wood-oven pizza, salad and pasta in a mad scientist's laboratory.

RESORT HOTELS

Call ☎407-503-3463 for reservations at other sit-down restaurants within the resort hotels.

Orchid Court Sushi Bar   JAPANESE $$
(Map p236; Royal Pacific Resort; sushi $4-8, mains $12-20; ☺11am-11pm; 🖮) Sip on a Cherry Blossom Saketini over first-rate sushi and sashimi. Located within the light and airy glass-enclosed lobby of the hotel, with cushioned couches and chairs, this informal restaurant makes a great place to relax.

Emeril's Tchoup Chop   SEAFOOD $$
(Map p236; ☎407-503-2467; Royal Pacific Resort; mains $15-30; ☺11:30am-2:30pm & 5:30-10pm; 🖮) Excellent island-inspired food, including plenty of seafood and Asian accents, prepared with the freshest ingredients. One of the best sit-down meals at the resort, but unfortunately the service is painfully slow.

Emack and Bolio's Marketplace ICE CREAM $
(Map p236; Hard Rock Hotel; ice cream $3-8;
⊙6:30am-11pm; ☑) Originally from Boston,
Emack and Bolio ice cream beats all the rest
hands down. And of course, only at this bastion
of rock and roll will you find Bye Bye
Miss American Mud Pie.

CITYWALK

Three massive themed restaurants draw
crowds all day long. They don't take reservations,
but call them directly to be put on a list
for priority seating – you'll be put at the top
of the list for a table, and given a pager so
you can walk around until your table is ready.

Hard Rock Café AMERICAN $$
(Map p236; ☑407-351-7625; mains $12-22; ⊙11am-
midnight; ☑) Excellent burgers and a rock-
and-roll theme. Priority seating taken up to
two weeks in advance or book online.

NBA City AMERICAN $$
(Map p236; ☑407-363-5919; mains $9-20;
⊙11am-1am; ☑) A giant basketball player
out front and endless basketball games on
screens throughout the restaurant. Come
for the theming fun, not for gourmet fare.

NASCAR Sports Grille AMERICAN $$
(Map p236; ☑407-224-2155; mains $9-18;
⊙11am-1am; ☑) Featuring Nascar simula-
tors and games and basic American fare

with a car racing twist – try the Daytona
Chiliburger or the Pit Crew Pulled Pork
Sandwich.

🍷 Drinking & Entertainment

TOP
CHOICE **Velvet Bar & Lobby Lounge** LOUNGE
(Map p236; ☑407-503-2401; www.hardrocklive
.com; Hard Rock Hotel; ⊙5pm-1am) Trendy
contemporary-styled bar with zebra-fabric
chairs, hardwood floors, floor-to-ceiling
windows and excellent martinis. On the last
Thursday of the month, the bar hosts Velvet
Sessions, a 'rock n' roll cocktail party' with
themed drinks, live music and finger food;
call for details on other live music events.

Blue Man Group PERFORMING ARTS
(Map p236; ☑407-528-3626; www.universalorlando
.com; CityWalk; adult/child 3-9 $59/74) Crazy out-
of-control stage performance featuring live
music and men painted blue. See p252 for
details.

Wantilan Luau DINNER SHOW
(Map p236; ☑407-503-3463; Royal Pacific Resort;
adult/child under 12yr $60/30; ⊙6pm Tue & Sat
May-Aug, call for Sep-Apr showtimes) Pacific Is-
land fire dancers shimmer and shake on
stage while guests enjoy a tasty buffet of
roast suckling pig, guava-barbecued short
ribs and other Polynesian-influenced fare.

UNIVERSAL ORLANDO RESORT DRINKING & ENTERTAINMENT

CITYWALK

Connecting the two theme parks is a pleasantly landscaped pedestrian mall (Map p236;
www.citywalkorlando.com; ⊙11am-2am) along the canal with themed restaurants, bars, a
multiplex movie theater, shops, a carousel and a fountain for kids to play in. Live music
and mucho alcohol sums up the entertainment options here and though it can be packed
with partying 20-somethings, particularly after the theme parks close, there's a distinct
family-friendly vibe and several bars have decent food. Individual bars charge nightly
covers ($5 to $9), or purchase a CityWalk Party Pass ($12, free with multiday theme-park
admission) for unlimited all-night club access. For a movie and clubbing, buy the CityWalk
Party Pass and Movie Ticket ($15), and for dinner and a movie, purchase the Meal and
Movie Deal ($15). Call or stop by CityWalk Guest Services Ticket Window (☑407-
224-2691) or pick them up at any resort. For dinner reservations, call ☑407-224-3663.

» **Bob Marley – A Tribute to Freedom** Jamaica-inspired food and music.

» **CityWalk's Rising Star** Karaoke to live music and talent contests.

» **the groove** Dance club with sleek blue neon walls and blaring music from the '70s
and '80s. Check website for select 'teen nights.'

» **Jimmy Buffett's Margaritaville** Three bars themed around Jimmy Buffett songs,
a full menu and live music after 10pm.

» **Pat O'Brien's** A homogenized slice of New Orleans with Cajun food, that strange
Orlando obsession, dueling pianos, and cocktails with a punch.

» **Red Coconut Club** Live bands, martini bar and rooftop balcony.

» **Latin Quarter** Latin American flair.

The Maori warrior's roar can be rather scary and that fire might be a bit close for comfort in the eyes of little ones, but there's a pleasant grassy area next to the open-air dining theater where kids can putz about. The atmosphere is wonderfully casual and, like everything at Universal Orlando, this is simple unabashed silliness and fun. Unlimited mai tais, beer and wine are included in the price.

Hard Rock Live   LIVE MUSIC
(Map p236; ☑407-351-5483; www.hardrocklive.com; CityWalk; tickets $20-30; ⊙box office 10am-9pm) With a hulking 3000-person capacity, this landmark between the parks draws some fairly big rock-and-roll names and comedy acts.

Universal Cineplex 20   CINEMA
(Map p236; ☑407-262-4386; Universal Orlando Resort CityWalk; adult/child $10/7) Park at Universal Orlando Resort.

Information

Child Care
Nursing facilities and companion bathrooms are located at the Health Services and First Aid facilities in each park. A baby-bottle icon next to select stores on the park map indicates which stores carry baby supplies (not on display). Gift shops at the resorts offer a wider selection. Each resort has a drop-off child-care center, with DVDs, arts and crafts, organized activities and games for children aged four to 14 available to hotel guests only. Per hour prices vary and hours are limited. For private babysitting services, see p286.

Kennels
Studio Kennel (☑407-224-9509; per pet per day $10), inside the parking structure, offers day boarding. You must provide food and occasionally return to walk your animal. The three Universal Orlando Resort resorts welcome pets.

Lockers
Available inside both theme parks for $5 per day.

Lost & Found
Inside Guest Services at both parks.
General (☑407-224-4233)
Islands of Adventure (☑407-224-4245)
Universal Studios (☑407-224-4244)

Maps
Pick up a free map and an *Attractions & Show Times* guide, with a schedule of events, show times and time and location of free character interactions, at each park entrance and at resort hotels.

Medical Services
Each theme park has medical facilities; see park maps for locations.

Park Hours
Theme park hours change not only by season, but day to day within any given month. Generally, parks open at 8am or 9am and close sometime between 6pm and 10pm. Guests at one of the three on-site hotels at Universal Orlando Resort can enter the Wizarding World of Harry Potter inside Islands of Adventure one hour before the park opens.

Parking
Parking for both theme parks and CityWalk is available inside a giant garage structure (car/RV $11/12); valet parking costs $18.

Stroller Rental
Single/double strollers cost $12/16 and are available at Guest Services inside both theme parks.

Tickets
A one-park one-/two-/three-/four-day ticket costs $82/115/130/140; a one-/two-/three-/four-/seven-day park-to-park ticket costs $112/135/145/150/175. Tickets for children three to nine cost about $10 less. Tickets are good for 14 consecutive days, and multiple-day tickets include admission to paid venues in CityWalk. Universal Orlando Resort participates in the Orlando Flex Ticket (p34).
EXPRESS PLUS This pass allows you to avoid the lines at designated Express Plus rides (identified on the map and in this book) by flashing your pass at the separate Express Plus line. You can go to any ride, any time you'd like. If you are staying at a Universal resort you automatically receive an Express Plus pass; otherwise, a limited number of passes per day are available online or at the park gate. Prices vary according to season, ranging from $20 to $60 for a one-day/one-park pass and from $26 to $60 for a one-day/two-park pass.
DINING PLAN See www.universalorlando.com for details on dining packages at select restaurants throughout Universal Orlando Resort.
WET 'N WILD Package prices include admission to Wet 'n Wild, a water park a few miles away. See www.universalorlando.com for pricing.

Tourist Information
Concierge services at the three hotels can help with all things Universal.
Dining CityWalk & Theme Parks (☑407-224-9255) Advanced priority seating for restaurants in CityWalk, Islands of Adventure and Universal Studios.
Dining Resort Hotels (☑407-503-3463) Advanced priority seating for restaurants at

Portofino Bay Hotel, Hard Rock Hotel and Royal Pacific Resort.

Guest Services (☎407-224-6350, 407-224-4233) Located at the entrance to each theme park. Foreign-language maps and brochures and a limited foreign-currency exchange; if you have any problems or questions, go here.

Resort Hotel Reservations (☎888-273-1311) Room-only reservations.

Universal Orlando Resort (☎407-224-4233, 407-363-8000, 800-232-7827; www.universal orlando.com; 1000 Universal Studios Plaza) For all questions, directions, hotel reservations and room reservations. A website prompt allows for email questions. See website or call for daily hours as these vary frequently.

Travelers with Disabilities

The free *Rider Safety and Guests With Disabilities* guidebook is available at Guest Services, and includes attraction scripts and detailed ride requirements. See the park map for details on the wheelchair accessibility of each attraction. There are also sign-language-interpreting, closed-captioning and assistive-listening devices available at no extra charge, and large-print and braille maps. TDD-equipped (Telecommunications Device for the Deaf) telephones are located throughout the park; an icon on the maps indicates location. Rent wheelchairs ($12) and Electric Convenience Vehicles ($40) at the entrance to each park.

Deaf or Hard of Hearing TDD (☎800-447-0672) Information on parks, rooms, entertainment and restaurants.

❶ Getting There & Around

See p288 for information on trains, planes and buses to Orlando and p254 for transport to/from the airport.

BOAT Water taxis, which leave each point about every 20 minutes, shuttle regularly between the three Universal hotels and CityWalk, just outside the gates of the parks. Service usually begins at 8:30am and ends at 2am.

CAR From the I-4, take exit 74B or 75A and follow the signs. From International Drive, turn west at Wet 'n Wild onto Universal Blvd.

SHUTTLE Most hotels just outside Universal Studios and along International Drive provide free shuttle service to the Universal Orlando Resort, but remember that many are first-come, first-served. If you intend to use hotel shuttles, always ask for details including how often they run and whether or not they take reservations. Unlike shuttles to Walt Disney World, shuttles to Universal Orlando Resort are direct – they will drop you off within a few minutes' walk of both parks and CityWalk. Resort hotels offer guests complimentary shuttle service to SeaWorld and

Wet 'n Wild. Call **Mears Transportation** (☎407-423-5566; www.mearstransportation.com; round-trip per person $19) one day in advance to arrange personalized shuttle service to Disney.

WALKING Universal Orlando's three resort hotels, two theme parks and CityWalk are linked by well-lit and landscaped pedestrian walkways.

SEAWORLD, DISCOVERY COVE & AQUATICA

Far more subdued than Disney or Universal, these animal-inspired theme parks strut a personal style that sets them apart from the rest of Orlando. SeaWorld is not only a stellar marine-animal facility, but boasts a few knuckle-whitening rides, an excellent kiddie-ride section and a full day's worth of outstanding animal shows. At the idyllic Discovery Cove you can swim with dolphins (but see p164 for arguments for and against the practice), feed exotic birds from the palm of your hand and enjoy the crowd-free atmosphere of a private beach and a winding lazy river nestled in a tropical Eden. It's quiet, relaxing and blissfully free of screams and loud music, roaming characters, long lines and flashy entertainment. Aquatica, which opened in 2008, is a water park.

The three theme parks, owned by the same parent company and located next to each other, are not a self-contained resort like Walt Disney World and Universal Orlando Resort.

SeaWorld

Beyond the handful of rides and the excellent shows, SeaWorld (Map p236) offers opportunities to feed stingrays, sea lions and other critters, is pleasantly landscaped with plenty of greenery and flowers, and has decent food. On top of the leaping dolphins, silly sea lions and splashing whales, SeaWorld is home to two of the biggest thrill rides in town.

◉ Sights & Activities

For priority seating for rides and shows, consider a SeaWorld VIP Tour (adult/child three to nine $100/75). This seven-hour tour includes premium reserved seating at One Ocean, Clyde and Seamore Take Pirate Island, and Blue Horizons, front-of-the-line access to Manta, Kraken and Journey to Atlantis, lunch, and the chance to feed dolphins, rays, seals and sea lions. Considering that express passes to the rides cost $20 to

ORLANDO & WALT DISNEY WORLD SEAWORLD

$35, lines to get into shows can eat an hour or more, and bucks spent on those dead fish you feed to sea creatures can add up, it's not a bad deal, particularly if you're coming during high season. Make reservations at www .seaworld.com/orlando or by phone at ☎888-800-5447.

Rides

Folks with little ones in tow should count on spending a couple of hours at **Shamu's Happy Harbor**, where six eye-candy rides, four stories of nets connected with slides and tunnels and a water-spewing playground delight the under-10 crowd. Ride a dolphin or another creature of the sea on the **Sea Carousel**, spin on **Jazzy Jellies** and board the **Shamu Express** for a gentle coaster thrill. Lines for everything but the carousel move incredibly slowly, and are particularly long just after lunch; come first thing when the park opens and during Shamu shows, when crowds are thinnest and lines can dwindle down to nothing.

The two sea-inspired roller coasters at Sea World push the thrill level up a notch with simple design twists. **Kraken**, a whiplash ride of twists, turns, inversion and plunges touted by aficionados as one of the most wicked coasters in Florida and beyond, has no floor so your feet dangle free. On **Manta**, you lie horizontally, face down, several to a row, so that the coaster vaguely resembles a manta ray, and dive and fly through the air in this position, reaching speeds of almost 60mph. Neither of these hard-core coasters is for the faint of heart or weak bellied! SeaWorld's third and last thrill is a water ride. **Journey to Atlantis** begins in darkness, moving gently through an underwater world of neon and fluorescent coral and fish. Things turn macabre when the creepy evil mermaid beckons you into her world and up, up, up you go, clackity-clack, through the steam, before the coaster plunges 60ft into the water. It doesn't twist upside down or plunge particularly fast, but the special effects will frighten little ones.

On **Wild Arctic**, an IMAX movie combines with a simulated ride to take viewers on a helicopter ride to Bas Station. A bad storm front moves in, and the pilot brings you very close to some polar bears before setting down on thin ice. Of course, after hearing an awful rumbling sound, you fall through the ice, and it's touch and go for a while, but... Afterwards, you see above- and below-water views of polar bears, walrus and other Arctic life.

For something more leisurely, head to the **Skytower**. Capsules take six minutes to slide up the 400ft pole, slowly rotating for a 360-degree panorama of the area, including points as far away as downtown Orlando.

Shows

This is why folks come to SeaWorld, and none of them disappoint. Shows vary, sometimes including a Sesame Street-themed option, an alternative sea-lion show and seasonal holiday specials. Shows run several times a day, and you'll need to take some time to plan your day if you want to see more than one or two. Check www.seaworld .com/orlando for a schedule or look on the park map when you arrive.

Blue Horizons SHOW
More than a dolphin show, this fantastic extravaganza of light, music, dolphins, birds and acrobats in spectacular costumes tells some sort of story of good and evil. But never mind the details of the narrative, as none of that matters. It's just a good ole show, with lots of splashing and drama.

Clyde & Seamore Take Pirate Island SHOW
Another must-see, this delightful show stars sea lion, otter and walrus 'comedians.' It's particularly fun for kids, who find its goofy and slapstick humor just hilarious, but great for the whole family.

A'Lure The Call of the Ocean SHOW
A bit like Cirque du Soleil on a much pared-down level, this unusual 30-minute circus performance combines acrobats, elaborate costumes and a heap of special effects to tell the story of the sea sirens, those mythical creatures who lured Odysseus. The gravity-defying stunts will have you holding your breath.

One Ocean SHOW
Killer whales are the stars at the newest Shamu show at SeaWorld, and it actually brings tears to some folks' eyes! The first 15 rows – sometimes more – of Shamu Stadium are the 'splash zone,' and both whales and trainers enjoy soaking the crowd with water.

Pets Ahoy SHOW
Featuring the talents of cats, birds, rats, pot-bellied pigs and others, this show tickles little ones' funny bones. Many of the stars were rescued from local animal shelters.

Reflections SHOW
During the holiday season and in the summer, the park closes with a fireworks and light show over the lagoon.

Other Attractions

Stingray Lagoon
STINGRAY FEEDING

Pick up a box of fish ($7) and feed the stingrays any time. Don't get frustrated if the stingrays don't take your fish, as there's a trick: hold the food between your index and middle finger, and place your hand in the water palm-up, with the lil' fishies swaying enticingly in the water. When the rays go by, they vacuum it right up. Pet their backs as they glide past – it feels just like the white of a hard-boiled egg.

Beluga Interaction Program
ANIMAL INTERACTION

(from $99; minimum age 10) There aren't that many places where you can feed and talk (via hand signals) to a beluga whale. Or any whale, for that matter.

Marine Mammal Keeper Experience
ANIMAL INTERACTION

(from $399; minimum age 13) Just what it sounds like: participants join animal trainers working with dolphins, beluga whales and sea lions.

Sharks Deep Dive
DIVING

(from $59; minimum age 10) Descend in a steel shark cage into a tank of sandtiger sharks, nurse sharks and schools of fish. You don't even need to know how to scuba dive, thanks to a 'water helmet.'

Dolphin Cove
ANIMAL INTERACTION

Here you can personally feed the dolphins rather than just watch 'em get fed. Scheduled regularly throughout the day.

Pacific Point Preserve
ANIMAL-WATCHING

California sea lions, fur seals and harbor seals make merry (and plenty of noise).

Shark Encounter
ANIMAL-WATCHING

Ride a conveyer belt through a 60ft-long Plexiglas tube surrounded by menacing sharks, rays, barracudas, lionfish and skates.

Penguin Encounter
ANIMAL-WATCHING

Watch these silly little birds waddle around, slide into the water, and swim like munchkin torpedoes in tanks made to look like the Arctic, with manufactured snow and ice.

Manatees: The Last Generation?
WILDLIFE SANCTUARY

The SeaWorld Orlando Animal Rescue Team rescues injured and sick manatees, and you can see the recuperating sweeties.

Jewel of the Sea Aquarium
AQUARIUM

A well-designed aquarium of brightly colored tropical fish sits next to Journey

to Atlantis and makes a good spot to keep little ones busy while everyone else is on the ride.

Manta Aquarium
AQUARIUM

Spectacular floor-to-ceiling tanks with more than 300 graceful rays gliding overhead, the adorably shy Pacific octopus and more.

☞ Tours

Make required reservations for this and a handful of others at www.seaworld.com/orlando or by phone at ☑888-800-5447.

Up-Close Tours
GUIDED TOUR

(adult/child 3-9 dolphins $50/30, penguins $40/20, sea lions $40/20) These 45- to 60-minute tours take you up close to penguins, dolphins or sea lions, well worth it if you're particularly enamored with a particular critter. If you're really looking to become personal with a dolphin, however, consider a day at Discovery Cove – an unlimited 14-day pass to SeaWorld is included in the price.

✖ Eating & Drinking

Eating at SeaWorld is mostly fast food and cafeteria-style options, though there's a pleasant selection of decent healthy alternatives. The park's All Day Dining Meal (adult/child three to 10 $30/15) allows for one main, one side or one dessert, and one nonalchoholic beverage each time you go through the cafeteria line at six eateries in the park. Note that the children's wristband allows for kids' meals only, and that Naked juices, hot drinks and bottled water are not included. Unless you expect to eat a lot of mediocre fast food it's not worth it. Only Sharks Underwater Grill takes priority seating reservations; go to www.seaworld.com/orlando for details on all the restaurants at SeaWorld.

Sharks Underwater Grill
SEAFOOD $$

(☑407-351-3600; mains $9-21; ⊙11am-park closing) Eat among the sharks in an underwater grotto. Cool, dark and particularly fun for kids; the bar is literally a tropical aquarium.

Voyager's Smokehouse
BARBECUE $

(Waterfront; mains $9-15; ⊙11am-park closing) Barbecue and corn on the cob.

Seafire Inn
FAST FOOD $

(Waterfront; mains $8-14; ⊙11am-park closing) Serves up a blend of flavors, and it's not unusual to see burgers flipped next to Mongolian woks.

WHEN YA GOTTA GO

The line of anxious kids hopping from one foot to the other at the bathrooms in Shamu's Happy Harbor can wind out the door. Instead, head to the bathroom inside the Baby Center (the cute house with rocking chairs on the porch) just next door.

Information

KENNELS Air-conditioned and staffed kennels for dogs only are located outside the main entrance of SeaWorld. They are open from park open until just after park close and cost $15 per day. You must have proof of vaccinations and return to walk your pet.

LOCKERS Can be rented for $7 to $12.

LOST & FOUND Located in Guest Services, at the front entrance.

PARK HOURS The park opens around 9am but park closing hours vary within the year and within the week, ranging from 6pm to 11pm. See www.seaworld.com/orlando for a calender of daily hours.

PARKING Costs $14.

STROLLERS & WHEELCHAIRS Go to www.seaworld.com/orlando to reserve strollers (single/double $13/18), wheelchairs ($12) and ECVs ($45) in advance, or pick one up first-come, first-served at the front gate.

TICKETS A two-day pass is sold as a 'one day pass, second day free' and costs $72; be sure to trade your ticket in for a return ticket when you leave the park, and you can come back for one day anytime within seven days at no extra charge. The Quick Queue Unlimited Pass includes all-day priority access to Kraken, Manta, Journey to Atlantis and Wild Arctic and costs an additional $20 to $35; a Quick Queue One-Time Access costs a bit less. Unlimited entrance over 14 consecutive days to both SeaWorld and Aquatica SeaWorld costs $115/107 for adult/children three to nine. SeaWorld participates in Orlando's Flex Ticket (p34). Go to www.seaworld.com/orlando for details on accommodation packages.

TOURIST INFORMATION Located in Guest Services, at the front entrance. Contact **Sea-World** (☑407-351-3600, 888-800-5447; www.seaworld.com/orlando; 7007 SeaWorld Dr; ☉from 9am) for all questions.

Getting There & Away

SeaWorld is located at the intersection of I-4 and FL 528 at the southern end of International Drive. From Walt Disney World take I-4 east toward Orlando to exit 71 and follow the signs; from Universal Orlando Resort and downtown Orlando, take I-4 west to exit 72 and follow the signs. Public buses do not stop at SeaWorld, but a free shuttle connects SeaWorld to Aquatica.

Discovery Cove

Walk into the lobby of Discovery Cove (Map p236), with its stone floor, turquoise dolphins suspended above, printed rattan furnishings and beamed ceiling, and you instantly feel that you're somewhere special. Inside, visitors spend the day in a tropical sanctuary of boldly colored flowers, white-sand beaches and warm pools surrounded by boulders. One of the most relaxing places in Orlando, the pace here is luxuriously slow, marvelously lazy, delightfully subdued. It's small, friendly and completely secured, with several lifeguards overseeing the lazy river and the swimming areas, and staff everywhere to help with anything you could possibly need. You won't find any high-speed thrills, catch any shows and parades, fight any crowds or see any princesses or superheroes, and the only reason you'll need to check the time is so you don't miss your dolphin swim. Schedule a day here between visits to theme parks to give everyone much-needed down time.

Discovery Cove allows only 1000 guests per day and you must make advance reservations. Once you're in the park, everything from wet suits to unlimited beer and snacks, from a family portrait to a buffet lunch, is included in the price.

◉ Sights & Activities

The most popular reason to come to the park is the 30-minute **Dolphin Swim Experience** (see 164 for arguments for and against the practice). When you arrive at the park at breakfast, you'll be assigned a time and place to meet your instructor. Groups of about 10 gather under a thatched-roof tiki hut, are given a brief orientation and a wet suit (choose between a vest or half-suit), and then head into the chilly lagoon with the dolphins. After some basic training and a little lesson on Dolphins 101, each group is assigned a dolphin for hands-on interaction and a short one-on-one glide through the water. The minimum age for a dolphin swim is six, and children under 12 must be accompanied by a paying adult. See www.discoverycove.com for details on **Trainer for the Day** (per person $458-538; advance reservations required, minimum age 13), a deeper dolphin interaction.

For the rest of the day, just relax. Wiggle your toes in the sand, pull on your mask and fins and snorkel among tropical rainbow fish and massive spotted eagle rays in the **Tropical Reef**, stretch out in the sun with a beer, snorkel some more. **Wind-away River**, a shallow and warm lazy river, curves around the entire cove, and an enormous waterfall empties **Serenity Bay**, a tropical swimming lagoon. Pick up a noodle and float along the gentle current, among the flowers and palm trees, pausing at the **Explorers Aviary**. Pick up a cup of food and watch the brightly colored feathered critters eat right out of your hand, and don't be surprised if they land on your shoulder! In 2011 Discovery Cove opened the 2.5-acre **Grand Reef**, a second tropical reef surrounded with paths and bridges and filled with rays, sharks and other sea creatures.

Make reservations in advance to walk along an underwater trail in **SeaVenture** (per person $59; minimum age 10). You'll don a 75-pound 'dive helmet' and join schools of saltwater fish, rays, sharks and other creatures, but don't worry – the more dangerous ones lie behind a glass barrier! The experience is limited to six people at a time, does not require scuba experience, and takes one hour, with 20 minutes of it underwater. This attraction had not yet opened at the time of writing.

✖ Eating & Drinking

Included in the cost of admission are a basic cafeteria breakfast and a more elaborate and tasty lunch, both served at a lovely beachside patio, and unlimited snacks (ice cream, Oreos and pretzels), beer and sodas.

❶ Information

PARK HOURS Discovery Cove is open from 8:30am to 5:30pm.

TICKETS All-day Resort Only Package costs $129 to $169 and includes breakfast, lunch, unlimited beer, soda and snacks, snorkel gear, a wet suit, a locker, shower facilities, towels and parking; the Dolphin Swim Package includes the same plus the dolphin interaction experience and costs $169 to $319. Both tickets include unlimited entrance over 14 consecutive days to your choice of SeaWorld, Aquatica or Busch Gardens; for $50 more you can add unlimited entrance to all three parks.

TOURIST INFORMATION Discovery Cove (407-370-1280, 877-434-7268; www

Discovery Cove prices tickets according to availability, like airlines; a dolphin-swim day package on one day could be $199, but weeks later when Uncle George decides to join you, the price has gone up to $299. You can change your date once you've made a reservation if they have availability, but you'll have to pay any price difference. Check www.discoverycove.com for a calendar with updated prices.

.discoverycove.com; ◷8:30am-5:30pm) For all questions.

TRAVELERS WITH DISABILITIES Specially designed wheelchairs, outfitted with oversized tires for easy maneuvering on the beach, can be reserved in advance by calling ☎877-557-7404. Note that if you're in one of these wheelchairs, you cannot operate them without assistance.

❶ Getting There & Away

Discovery Cove sits at the intersection of I-4 and FL 528 at the southern end of International Drive. From Walt Disney World take I-4 eastward Orlando to exit 71; from Universal Orlando Resort and downtown Orlando, take I-4 west to exit 72.

Aquatica

Orlando's latest water park (Map p236) opened with great fanfare in the spring of 2008, but for all intents and purposes, it's just another water park. It's newer, cleaner and prettier than the others, with better food, plenty of tropical greenery offering a vague taste of Polynesia, some cool animals to check out and little of the narrative shtick that defines Disney attractions. But in the end, come here to splash around in the water, laze in the sand, float along the lazy river and zoom down slides into water. That's what you do at water parks, and Aquatica is no different.

◉ Sights & Activities

Aquatica boasts that the **Dolphin Plunge** spits you through a glass-enclosed tube through a tank of Commerson's dolphins, and it does indeed do this; the problem, of course, is that perhaps a high-speed waterslide just isn't the best way to see dolphins.

You zoom through so fast and the stretch through the tank is so short that you're lucky if you catch a passing glance at the black-and-white cuties. Check 'em out at the Commerson's Dolphin Exhibit instead. Other animal encounters include rafting Loggerhead Lane through the grotto of tropical fish, and meeting macaws, anteaters, turtles and other critters that roam the park with their trainers. For high-speed thrills, try the HooRoo Run, a blessedly simple open-aired inner-tube slide, and its enclosed sister ride the Walhalla Wave; Tassie's Twisters, where you speed around and around and are then dropped into a pool below; Taumata Racer, the multilane toboggan run; and Whanau Way, a twisting, enclosed inner-tube slide. Two lagoon-inspired Wave Pools, lined with white sand and row upon row of beach chairs, make a good base to hunker down for the day.

The children's play areas here are excellent. At Walkabout Waters buckets of water dump regularly over all kinds of brightly colored climbing structures and fountains, while Kookaburra Cove offers tiny slides and shallow water perfect for toddlers.

✕ Eating & Drinking

Food at the park's three restaurants is better than what you'll find at Orlando's other water parks, and there's plenty of cold beer available throughout the park. Aquatica allows guests to bring a small cooler, but you won't be able to wheel in that family-sized one. Just outside the gates and next to the bus drop-off area, however, there are picnic tables and the park provides complimentary cooler-size lockers at Guest Services.

Banana Beach Cookout   BUFFET $$
(all-day pass adult/child 3-9 $16/10) If you've built up an appetite from all that slippin' and slidin', your best option is this all-you-can-eat cookout. The buffet includes veggie burgers, barbecue chicken, corn on the cob, hot dogs and salads. Purchase tickets at www.aquatica byseaworld.com in advance or at the park.

WaterStone Grill   FAST FOOD $
(mains $6-12; ⊙11am-park closing) Stick-in-your gut items like cheese-smothered

steak sandwiches and Cuban pork as well as a few hearty salads.

Mango Market   FAST FOOD $
(mains $5-13; ⊙park hours) Tasty wood-fired flat-bread pizza, grilled-chicken salad, veggie wraps and other grab-and-go options. You can also buy baby food here.

❶ Information

KENNELS Air-conditioned and staffed kennels for dogs only are located outside the main entrance of SeaWorld. They are open from park open until just after park close and cost $15 per day. You must have proof of vaccinations and return to walk your pet.

LOCKERS Cost $7 to $12.

LOST & FOUND Located in Guest Services, at the front entrance.

PARK HOURS During Spring Break Aquatica is open 10am to 5pm, with extended hours on weekends and in summer. Go to www.aquatica byseaworld.com for a calender that lists day by day hours.

PARKING Costs $14.

STROLLERS & WHEELCHAIRS Go to www .aquaticabyseaworld.com to reserve strollers (single/double $13/18), wheelchairs ($12) and ECVs (45) in advance, or pick one up first-come, first-served at the front gate.

TICKETS One-day pass costs $42. Unlimited entrance to Aquatica and SeaWorld over 14 consecutive days costs $115/107 for adult/children three to nine. Aquatica participates in Orlando's Flex Ticket (p34).

TOURIST INFORMATION Located in Guest Services, at the front entrance. Call ☏866-787-4307 for current park hours and weather-related closings. Contact **Aquatica** (☏407-351-3600; www.aquaticabyseaworld.com; 5800 Water Play Way; ⊙10am-5pm, extended hours on weekends & from Jun-Aug) for all questions.

❶ Getting There & Away

Aquatica is located just east of the intersection of I-4 and FL 528, at the southern end of International Drive. From Walt Disney World take I-4 east toward Orlando to exit 71; from Universal Orlando Resort and downtown Orlando, take I-4 west to exit 72. Public buses do not stop at Aquatica, but a free shuttle connects SeaWorld to Aquatica.

The Space Coast

Why Go?

More than 75 miles of barrier-island Atlantic Coast stretch from Canaveral National Seashore south to Vero Beach, encompassing undeveloped beaches of endless white sand, an entrenched surf culture and pockets of Old Florida.

The Kennedy Space Center and several small museums dedicated to the history, heroes and science of the United States' space program give the Space Coast its name, and the region's tourist hub of Cocoa Beach is the launching point for massive cruise ships. But beyond the 3D space movies and tiki-hut bars, chain motels and surf shops, the Space Coast offers quintessential Florida wildlife for everyone from grandmas to toddlers. Kayak with manatees, camp on a private island or simply stroll along nature trails – it's easy to find a quiet spot.

Best Places to Eat

» Maison Martinique (p317)

» Café Coconut Cove (p316)

» Fat Snook (p313)

» Slow and Low Barbecue (p313)

» El Ambia Cubano (p316)

Best Places to Stay

» Caribbean Court Boutique Hotel (p317)

» Beach Place Guesthouses (p311)

» Vero Beach Hotel and Spa (p317)

» Sea View Motel (p315)

» Windemere Inn (p315)

When to Go
Cocoa Beach

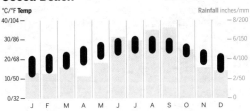

Jul Crowds diminish; prices plummet; loggerhead sea turtles nest along miles of sandy coastline.

Apr More sunny days than any other month, and most Spring Breakers have come and gone.

Fall Peak migratory-bird season.

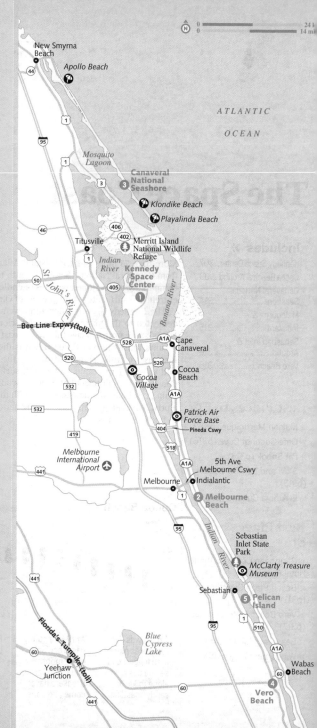

Space Coast Highlights

1 Catching a rocket launch from **Kennedy Space Center** (p307)

2 Watching the sun set over the Indian River at Melbourne Beach's **Café Coconut Cove** (p316)

3 Walking miles of beach and exploring historic sites at **Canaveral National Seashore** (p314)

4 Settling into the barefoot life in **Vero Beach** (p316), the quintessential beach escape with a small-town vibe

5 Strolling through peaceful **Pelican Island National Wildlife Refuge** (p316)

6 **Kayaking** among the mangroves alongside manatees and river dolphins

7 **Surfing** Florida's hottest waves or simply spreading a beach towel and soaking in the surfing scene

New Smyrna Beach

Apollo Beach

ATLANTIC

OCEAN

Mosquito Lagoon

Canaveral National Seashore

Klondike Beach

Playalinda Beach

Titusville

Merritt Island National Wildlife Refuge

Indian River

Kennedy Space Center

Bee Line Expwy (toll)

Cape Canaveral

St John's River

Cocoa Village

Cocoa Beach

Patrick Air Force Base

Pineda Cswy

Melbourne International Airport

5th Ave Melbourne Cswy

Melbourne

Indialantic

Melbourne Beach

Indian River

Sebastian Inlet State Park

McClarty Treasure Museum

Sebastian

Pelican Island

Blue Cypress Lake

Florida's Turnpike (toll)

Yeehaw Junction

Wabas Beach

Vero Beach

History

The arrival of the railroad at the end of the 18th century transformed the region into a center for citrus farming, and in 1949 President Harry S Truman established the Joint Long Range Proving Grounds at Cape Canaveral for missile testing.

The first rocket was launched on July 24, 1950, and in 1958 the National Aeronautics & Space Administration (NASA) was born here to 'carry out the peaceful exploration and use of space.' Though Soviet cosmonaut Yuri Gagarin took the honor of the first man in space on April 12, 1961, Alan Shepard became the first American one month later and in February 1962 John Glenn circled the earth three times in the world's first orbital flight. On July 16, 1969, a *Saturn V* rocket left Kennedy Space Center, and four days later Neil Armstrong spoke the immortal phrase: 'That's one small step for man, one giant leap for mankind.' America's manned space program, encompassing both great successes and tragic disasters, continued until 2011, when NASA closed its space shuttle program indefinitely.

National & State Parks

Miles of the Space Coast are dedicated to national and state parks and wildlife refuges, including **Canaveral National Seashore** (part of the national park system), **Merritt Island National Wildlife Refuge** and **Sebastian Inlet State Park**. The Atlantic Ocean pounds along the eastern edge, while the calm, brackish waters of the Banana and Indian Rivers and Mosquito Lagoon separate the barrier island from the mainland to the west. See www.spacecoasthiking.com for area trail maps and detailed descriptions. Consult www.spacecoastbirding.com for the region's birding hot spots.

ⓘ Getting There & Around

AIR **Melbourne International Airport** (☎321-723-6227; www.mlbair.com) services Delta, Spirit and Continental, as well as smaller carriers. Orlando International Airport and Sanford International Airport are about 50 minutes west of Cocoa Beach.

BUS **Space Coast Area Transit** (SCAT; ☎321-633-1878; www.ridescat.com) operates a local bus service including a mainland route from Merritt Island south to Melbourne Beach, a beach trolley in Cocoa Beach and a bus running along Hwy A1A from Cocoa Beach to Indialantic. **GoLineIRT** (☎772-569-0903; www.golineirt.com) services Sebastian Inlet south to Vero Beach, and **Greyhound buses** (☎321-723-4329; www.greyhound.com) stop along the mainland.

CAR Major car-rental agencies have offices in Cocoa Beach, Melbourne and Vero Beach.

TRAIN Amtrak trains run as far as Orlando.

Kennedy Space Center

One of Florida's most visited sights, the more than 140,000-acre Kennedy Space Center was once a working space-flight facility, where shuttles were built and astronauts rocketed into the cosmos. With the termination of NASA's shuttle program in the summer of 2011, however, the Kennedy Space Center began the shift from a living museum to a historical one. Expect exhibits, tours and programs to change during this transition. Admission includes attractions in the Visitor Complex, a guided bus tour to sights beyond the Visitor Complex, and entrance to the US Astronaut Hall of Fame, 6 miles down the road.

◉ Sights

Kennedy Space Center   MUSEUM
(☎321-449-4444; www.kennedyspacecenter.com; adult/child 3-11yr $43/33; ⊗9am-6pm) Only a tiny portion of the Kennedy Space Center

---

SPACE COAST FOR CHILDREN

Easily accessible wildlife, rocket launches and space museums combine with Atlantic beaches to one side and gentle river and lagoon waters to the other to make this stretch of barrier island one of the best family destinations in Florida. Make advanced reservations for a **kayak trip** among the mangroves and allow a few days in Cocoa Beach to see **Canaveral National Seashore**, **Merritt Island National Wildlife Refuge**, the **Kennedy Space Center** and **Brevard Zoo** before packing a cooler and hitting Hwy A1A south for a day of flip-flop life at its best. You'll want to stop at **Sebastian Inlet State Park**, **Mc-Clarty Treasure Museum** and **Pelican Island Wildlife Refuge**, but the best part of this 53-mile stretch is simply following your whim. And when you get to lovely, low-key **Vero Beach**, with its white sand, grassy playgrounds and small-town vibe, you'll want to spend plenty of time just being lazy.

THE SPACE COAST

KIDS' PLAY

Skip Kennedy Space Center's disappointing Children's Play Dome and cool off in the spurting fountain on the far corner of the Rocket Garden. It's on the map, but not labeled.

is open to the public. The Visitor Complex holds the bulk of the tourist attractions, and is the starting point for guided bus tours. Note that while a basic guided tour is included in price of admission, several more specialized tours and experiences require reservations and an added fee. Guests with disabilities can call ☏321-449-4364 (voice) or 321-454-4198 (TDD) to arrange special tours in advance. Strollers, wheelchairs and air-conditioned kennels are offered free of charge. Though there are no longer manned space shuttles launching from Kennedy Space Center, rockets continue, to launch satellites and exploratory missions. See www.spacecoastlaunches.com for the center's launch schedule.

Visitor Complex

The surprisingly small Visitor Complex, with several exhibits showcasing the history and future of US space travel and research, is the heart of the Kennedy Space Center. Here you'll find the Rocket Garden, featuring replicas of classic rockets towering over the complex; Space Shuttle Explorer, a shuttle replica that gives a firsthand feel for the cramped spaces astronauts endured; the Nature and Technology museum, with an easily digestible discussion of the local environment and the history of the US space program; and the hour-long Astronaut Encounter, where a real, live astronaut fields questions from the audience. Two delightful IMAX films, offering clear explanations of complicated science and cool footage of gravity-free life in space, delight folks of all ages. Astronauts pass tortillas through the air like Frisbees, toss M&Ms to each other and catch bubbles of water when they're thirsty. *Space Station 3D,* narrated by Tom Cruise, depicts the construction and operations of the International Space Station (ISS), and Leonardo DiCaprio narrates *Hubble 3D,* featuring truly awesome images (like actual star nurseries!) captured from the Hubble telescope.

Less impressive is the over-hyped $60-million Shuttle Launch Simulator, a virtual ride developed over three years with the help of astronauts, test pilots and NASA experts. Designed to give the impression of a vertical launch into orbit, this isn't much more fun than a particularly bumpy landing on a commercial jet. Die-hard *Star Trek* fans or folks looking for an escape from the sun may be the only ones who can sit through the silly interactive show Star Trek Live.

The stunningly beautiful Astronaut Memorial, a shiny granite wall standing four stories high, reflects both literally and figu-

CATCHING A WAVE

Ten-time surfing world champion Kelly Slater, born and raised in Cocoa Beach, learned his moves on the Space Coast surf, arguably the best place in Florida to catch a wave. Surfing culture thrives around here – you'll have no problem finding a place to rent a board, and there are surfing events year-round. The Ron Jon Easter Surf Festival, the country's second-oldest surf competition and the granddaddy of them all, attracts 30,000-plus cool surfer dudes, tan beach bunnies and sunburned college kids.

The long-running Ron Jon Surf School (☏321-868-1980; www.cocoabeachsurfing school.com; 3901 N Atlantic Ave, Cocoa Beach; per hr $50-65) offers lessons for everyone from groms (that's surf talk for beginners) to experts, and there are plenty of other schools. For children five to 17, Beach Place Guest House hosts week-long Surf Art Camps (☏321-799-3432; www.marymoonarts.com; per child $295; ☉9am-3pm Jun-Aug). A total of 12 kids are divided into two groups, with one getting down and dirty with the paints on the deck while the other tackles the surf; after lunch, they switch, and for one morning they take a kayaking trip in the calm waters of Indian Lagoon. Ask about pro-rated options for shorter or fewer days.

Finally, if you just want to get out there with your board, the 70 miles of Space Coast beach stretching from New Smyrna south to Sebastian Inlet lures folks of all ages and ability. Go to www.surfguru.com for details and conditions.

ratively on the personal and tragic stories behind the cheerleader rhetoric and theme-park energy that permeates the space center. Several stone panels display the photos and names of those who died during shuttle disasters, briefly noting the circumstances of their death.

Kennedy Space Center Tour
This two-hour bus tour is the only way to see beyond the Visitor Complex without paying for an add-on tour. The first stop is the LC 39 Observation Gantry, a 60ft observation tower with views of the twin launch pads. From here, the bus winds through the launch facilities to the Apollo/Saturn V Center, where you don't want to miss the multimedia show in the Firing Room. Video footage on three screens and a sound-and-light show depict America's first lunar mission, the 1968 launch of *Apollo VIII*. Finally, check out the astronauts' cramped living spaces at the International Space Station Center. Tours depart every 15 minutes from 10am to 2:45pm. Look for the coach buses and long lines to the right when you enter the Visitor Complex.

Add-on Experiences
The extended Cape Canaveral Then & Now (4hr tours adult/child $21/15; ⊙12:50pm) tour includes a visit to the Air Force Space & Missile Museum. The bus tour Discover KSC: Today and Tomorrow (3hr tours adult/child $21/15; ⊙multiple departures daily) stops at the massive Vehicle Assembly Building, but note that you stay with the group and on the bus for the entire tour. Great for kids, Lunch with an Astronaut (adult/child $44/33; ⊙12:15pm) offers a chance to hang out with a real astronaut and find out more about what it's like to shoot into space and live without gravity. The Astronaut Training Experience (ATX) (per person $145) is an action-oriented taste of astronaut training; families with kids aged seven to 14 need to sign up for the tamer ATX Family.

US Astronaut Hall of Fame   MUSEUM
(☑321-449-4444; www.kennedyspacecenter.com; admission incl in ticket to Kennedy Space Center, or for Hall of Fame only adult/child $20/16; ⊙noon-7pm; ⊕) Six miles from the Visitor Complex, this eye-candy museum features interactive exhibits and motion simulators dedicated to celebrating US astronauts. It is particularly fun for children, but families will need two days to cover attractions in both the Visitor Complex and the Hall of Fame.

❶ Getting There & Away
There is no public transport to the space center. Parking is available free of charge.

Cocoa Beach & Around
☑321 / POP 17,000
Driving east on Hwy 528, the main drag from Orlando, the first hint of Cocoa Beach is the neon signs announcing pier locations for cruise ships. When you see the larger-than-life sculptures of surfers outside Ron Jon's Surf Shop, you know you've arrived. Though still a company town for NASA and

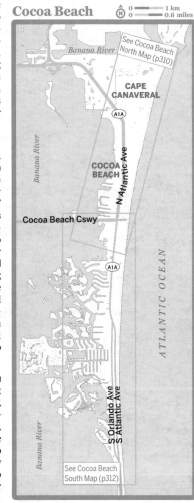

Cocoa Beach

THE SPACE COAST

the air-force base, folks waiting to catch a cruise and surfers looking to party dominate the Cocoa Beach scene.

Three causeways – Hwy 528, Hwy 520 and Hwy 404 – cross the Indian River, Merritt Island and the Banana River to connect Cocoa Beach to the mainland. At Ron Jon's, Hwy 528 (also Minutemen Causeway) cuts south and becomes Hwy A1A (also Atlantic Ave), a north–south strip with chain hotels and restaurants, tourist shops and condos. Hwy A1A divides into two one-ways (southbound Orlando Ave and northbound Atlantic Ave) for a couple miles, reconnects and continues south along the barrier-island coast 53 miles to Vero Beach and beyond.

⊙ Sights

In addition to these standouts – and Kennedy Space Center (p307) – space enthusiasts will want to see the handful of smaller museums dedicated to space and science surrounding Cocoa Beach.

From the blaring tunes and surfboard rentals around Ron Jon's southward to quieter and thinner stretches off the residential district, Cocoa Beach offers something for every kind of beach bum. In addition to the public beaches with seasonal lifeguards listed below, stub-end streets access the ocean south from Ron Jon's to the air-force base.

TOP CHOICE **Merritt Island**
National Wildlife Refuge WILDLIFE RESERVE
(www.merrittisland.com; I-95 exit 80; ⊙8am-4.30pm Mon-Fri, 9am-5pm Sat & Sun, closed Sun Apr-Oct) Bordering both the Kennedy

Space Center and Canaveral National Seashore, this spectacular 140,000-acre refuge includes brackish marshes, mangrove swamps, pine flatlands and coastal dunes. More than 500 species of wildlife make this their home, including thousands of waterfowl stopping along their north–south migrations, alligators, otters and armadillos. The 7-mile **Black Point Wildlife Drive** has a pull-out for the 5-mile **Cruickshank Trail**, and several other shorter trails can be found throughout the refuge. Stop at the visitor center, 4 miles east of Titusville on SR 402, for a park map.

| TOP |
| CHOICE | Brevard Zoo   ZOO

(www.brevardzoo.org; 8225 N Wickham Rd, Melbourne; adult/child 2-12yr $13.75/10.25, under 2yr free; ⊙9:30am-5pm) Hand-feed giraffes and lorikeets, who climb onto your head and arms in their enthusiasm, ride a train past camels and monkeys roaming free, and kayak through 22 acres of wetlands at this jewel of Old Florida zoos. Small, easily navigable, and boasting a great water-play area, this may just outshine the Kennedy Space Center for the under-10 crowd. Take I-95 exit 91 (Wickham Rd) 0.5 miles east.

Lori Wilson Park   BEACH

(Map p312; Hwy A1A) A 32-acre park with a small dog-play area and a mellow vibe.

Cocoa Village   VILLAGE

(off Map p310) This small, pedestrian-friendly historic downtown on the mainland off Hwy 520 is a pleasant alternative to the Cocoa Beach strip. Here you'll find several cafes and upscale restaurants, including the recommended **Café Margaux** (220 Brevard Ave; ⊙11am-3pm & 5-9pm Mon-Sat).

Sidney Fischer Park   BEACH

(Map p312; Hwy A1A; parking $5) A half-mile south of Shepard, this is crowded with surfers and cruise-ship crowds.

Cocoa Beach Pier   PIER

(Map p310; www.cocoabeachpier.com; ⊙11am-10pm) Souvenir shops, restaurants and bars stretch along one side and countless speakers blast music.

Shepard Park   BEACH

(Map p310; Hwy A1A; parking $10) At the end of Hwy 520, this beach is also crowded with surfers and cruise-ship crowds.

🏃 Activities

The Banana River, Indian River Lagoon and Mosquito Lagoon lure boaters of all kinds, from Spring Breakers to eco-tourists, and plenty of businesses in and around town cater to their needs.

Ron Jon's Watersports   WATER SPORTS

(Map p310; ☑321-799-8888; 4151 N Atlantic Ave; ⊙8am-8pm) Rents just about anything water-related from fat-tired beach bikes ($15 daily) to surfboards ($30 daily).

🛏 Sleeping

Of Cocoa Beach's many chain hotels, most located along a 2-mile stretch south from Ron Jon, the Doubletree sits directly on the beach and is separated a bit from the others.

Beach Place Guesthouses   APARTMENT **$$**

(Map p312; ☑321-783-4045; www.beachplace guesthouses.com; 1445 S Atlantic Ave; ste $195-350; ❄🐾🛜📶🐾) A little piece of heaven in the swirl of burned tourists and partying beach scene, this little two-story laid-back spot sits in a residential neighborhood. Suites sleeping up to six open onto grass, hammocks and a

---

DON'T MISS

KAYAKING THE INDIAN RIVER LAGOON

Even in Cocoa Beach proper, where you're more likely to hear tunes blasting than birds singing, you can paddle silently alongside dolphins and manatees through the mangroves of Indian River Lagoon. Tim and Cinnamon at **Fin Expeditions** (Map p312; ☑321-698-7233; www.finexpeditions.com; Ramp Rd; per person $30; 🚗) offer two-hour guided kayaking trips with a focus on wildlife. Linger to watch a cormorant dry his wings, coast gently over horseshoe crabs, pause as Cinnamon explains the differences between mangrove species. The calm waters, stable boats, and attentive and enthusiastic guides make this an excellent choice for families.

Consult www.spacecoastpaddling.com for maps, descriptions and directions for kayaking and canoeing along the entire Space Coast.

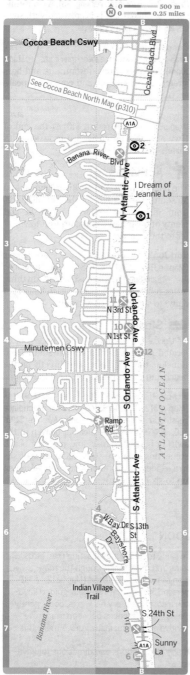

lovely deck, just steps away from the dunes and beach. A handful of rooms along the short driveway fill with long-term residents, and there's a common room with games and sometimes a movie screened on a sheet hanging from the wall.

Surf Studio
MOTEL $$

(Map p312; ☑321-783-7100; www.surf-studio.com; 1801 S Atlantic Ave; r & ste $115-160; ❋🤶🏊🛏🐾) Friendly old-school, single-story, family-owned motel that sits on the ocean and offers basic doubles and apartments surrounded by grass and palms. One-bedroom apartments sleeping six cost $195 to $225; no charge for children under 10.

Dolphin Inn
MOTEL $

(Map p312; ☑321-868-3701; 2902 S Atlantic Ave; r $50-80; ❋🤶🛏🐾) Spacious and simple rooms arc from the Banana River around a small lawn, with stone benches, palm trees and a community grill. Catch the sunset from the motel's private pier. Complimentary kayaks and an under-the-radar vibe.

Fawlty Towers
MOTEL $

(Map p310; ☑321-784-3870; www.fawltytowers resort.com; 100 E Cocoa Beach Causeway; r $90-114; ❋🤶🏊🐾) In the heart of downtown Cocoa Beach and across the street from Ron Jon's, this two-story mom-and-pop motel offers basic rooms surrounding a surprisingly quiet pool and tiki bar and caters to folks catching cruise ships; no charge for children under 12.

Jetty Park
CAMPGROUND $

(Map p310; 321-783-7111; www.jettypark.org; 400 Jetty Rd; campsites $20-40;) In nearby Cape Canaveral, with beach access and a fishing pier.

Eating

Fat Snook
SEAFOOD $$$

(Map p312; 321-784-1190; www.thefatsnook.com; 2464 S Atlantic Ave; mains $21-34; 5-10pm) Hidden inside an uninspired building and decorated in cool and calming blue and green hues with a minimalist and modern flair, tiny Fat Snook stands out as an oasis of fine cooking. Yes, there's a distinct air of food snobbery here, so don't even think about asking for any tweaks to what the chef is preparing. But it's so tasty, no one seems to mind.

Slow and Low Barbecue
BARBECUE $$

(Map p312; www.slowandlowbarbecue.com; 306 N Orlando Ave; mains $8-20; 11am-midnight) After a day on the beach, nothing satisfies better than a plate overflowing with barbecue ribs, fried okra, turnip greens and sweet fried potatoes. Away from the tourist mayhem around the pier, Slow and Low boasts a small patio and a loyal local following. There's a daily happy hour, live music Thursday through Sunday and 2am closing on the weekends.

Simply Delicious
CAFE $

(Map p312; 125 N Orlando Ave; mains $6-12; 8am-3pm Tue-Sat, to 2pm Sun) You can't miss this little yellow house on the southbound stretch of A1A. It's a homey Americana place – nothing fancy, nothing trendy, just solid food. One of the owners is Japanese, hence the bowl of rice on the breakfast menu. Grab some cookies for the road.

Silvestro's
ITALIAN $$$

(Map p312; 321-783-4853; www.silvestros.com; Banana River Sq, 2039 N Atlantic Ave; mains $15-30; 5-10pm) You won't find ocean-side romance, river sunsets or Florida charm at this Italian spot in a strip mall next to the Publix, but the food is excellent, the portions large, and the service warm and effusive. This is where the astronauts came to dine, or so the waiter says.

Drinking & Entertainment

Beach Shack
LIVE MUSIC

(Map p312; www.beachshackbar.com; 1 Minuteman Causeway; 10am-2am) With wobbly chairs and wood paneling that must be decades

From March through August manatees hang out in the shallow waters of Snug Harbor (Map p312) – follow the signs off S Orlando Ave and keep your eyes peeled!

old, this is a classic locals' bar. Two pool tables, a beach front patio, and blues Thursday to Sunday. Next to Coconuts.

Sunset Waterfront Grill & Bar
BAR

(Map p310; 500 W Cocoa Beach Causeway/Hwy 528; 11am-10pm) Sure, it serves food, but the main attraction is the sunset – you won't find a view this divine anywhere in Cocoa. But don't expect quiet or pristine at this river-front eatery just off the causeway.

Crackerjacks
BAR

(www.crackerjackstiki.com; 2A Max Brewer Parkway, Titusville; 3pm-close Mon, 11am-2am Tue-Sat, noon-midnight Sun) Stop at this tiki bar just off Hwy 1 underneath the bridge to Merritt Island National Wildlife Refuge for a drink after a day at the refuge or Canaveral National Seashore. There's live music on the small deck 6pm Friday, Saturday and Sunday and $3 margaritas all day.

Mai Tiki Bar
BAR

(Map p310; www.cocoabeachpier.com; Cocoa Beach Pier; 11am-10pm) Kick back at this bar at the very tip of Cocoa Beach Pier and soak up the surfing-town mood.

Cocoa Village Playhouse
PERFORMING ARTS

(321-636-5050; www.cocoavillageplayhouse.com; 300 Brevard Ave, Cocoa Village; tickets $15-22) Stages locally produced plays on the site of the ornate Aladdin Theatre (1924).

Shopping

Ron Jon Surf Shop
OUTDOOR EQUIPMENT

(Map p310; www.ronjons.com; 4151 N Atlantic Ave; 24hr) With live music, classic cars and a warehouse jammed with everything you could possibly need for a day at the beach, the massive 52,000-sq-ft Ron Jon is more than a store. And should you find yourself needing surf wax at 4am, no worries – it's open 24 hours a day.

Sunseed Food Co-op
FOOD & DRINK

(Map p310; www.sunseedfoodcoop.com; 6615 N Atlantic Ave; 10am-6pm Mon-Wed & Sat, to 7pm

DREAMING OF JEANNIE

Fans of the 1960s US sitcom *I Dream of Jeannie* will be sorely disappointed if they come expecting the show's idyllic beach town, as nothing in today's Cocoa Beach even hints at the life of Captain Nelson and his blonde in the bottle. The single tribute to the show is the name of the lane (Map p310) leading off A1A into Lori Wilson Park.

Thu & Fri) Swing by this healthy oasis for locally grown fruits, veggies, microbrew beers, wines and after-sun lotions.

Village Outfitters OUTDOOR EQUIPMENT
(✆321-633-7245; www.villageoutfitters.com; 229 Forrest Ave, Cocoa Village; ☺10:30am-5pm Mon-Fri, to 7pm Sat) Outdoor and camping gear, as well as kayak rental.

❶ Information

MEDICAL SERVICES **Cape Canaveral Hospital** (✆321-799-7111; 701 W Cocoa Beach Causeway) Emergency care.
Health First Physicians (✆321-868-8313; 105 S Banana River Blvd) Walk-in services.
TOURIST INFORMATION Go to www.cocoa beach.com and www.space-coast.com for events, accommodations and more.
Space Coast Office of Tourism (✆321-433-4470; 430 Brevard Ave, Cocoa Village; ☺8am-5pm Mon-Sat) Inside the Bank of America, one block south of the Village Playhouse.

Canaveral National Seashore

Part of America's national-park system, spectacular Canaveral National Seashore (✆386-428-3384, Playalinda Beach 321-867-4077; www.nps.gov/cana; admission $3, under 16yr free; ☺6am-6pm Oct-Mar, to 8pm Apr-Sep) includes 24 miles of undeveloped wide, white sand beach. Two roads squeeze along a skinny bridge of barrier island, one heading 6 miles south from the small beach town of New Smyrna Beach and another 6 miles north from Merritt Island National Wildlife Refuge. Each road dead-ends, leaving about 16 miles of wilderness beach between them, and it is a 1½-hour drive around Mosquito Lagoon from one entrance to the other.

◉ Sights

Inexpressibly beautiful, Canaveral's three Atlantic beaches each have a distinct character, and Mosquito Lagoon offers calm waters for kayaking and fishing as well as several historic sights. Pick up a map at the entrance gate, the visitors center or at Merrit Island Wildlife Refuge.

Apollo Beach BEACH
This 6-mile beach, at the north end of the park and immediately south of New Smyrna, attracts families. It has boardwalk access, and a longer stretch of road along the dunes with fewer parking lots than at Playalinda. There are several hiking trails to historic sites, overlooks and sandy shores along Mosquito Lagoon, and a small Visitor Information Center. It feels more isolated, and is perfect for cycling.

Klondike Beach BEACH
The stretch between Apollo and Playalinda is as pristine as it gets, with no roads and accessible only on foot or by bike (if you can ride on the beach).

Playalinda Beach BEACH
At the southern end, Playalinda is popular with surfers. Boardwalks provide beach access, but only 2 miles of park road parallel the dunes and there are more parking lots than at Apollo, with fewer opportunities to access the lagoon.

Mosquito Lagoon OUTDOORS
Hugging the west side of the barrier-island strip, the lagoon has islands and mangroves teeming with wildlife. Rent kayaks in Cocoa Beach, or simply splash in the calm shallows. There is one boat launch off each park road, as well as several off Hwy 3 on the east side of the lagoon, outside the fee area.

◎ Tours

Pontoon Boat Tours BOAT TOURS
(✆386-428-3384; per person $20) Rangers offer tours from the Visitor Information Center on most Sundays.

Sea-turtle Nesting Tours WILDLIFE WATCHING
(✆386-428-3384; adult/child 8-16yr $14/free; ☺7-11:30pm Jun-Aug) In summer, rangers lead groups of up to 30 people on these nightly tours, with about a 75% chance of spotting the little guys. Reservations are required (beginning May 15 for June trips, June 15 for July trips); children under eight are not allowed.

🛏 Sleeping

Required permits are available up to seven days in advance. Be sure to bring plenty of water.

Beach Camping   PRIMITIVE CAMPING
(sites $10, per 7 people or more $20) Two sites on Apollo Beach are available from November to late April.

Island Camping   PRIMITIVE CAMPING
(sites $10, per 7 people or more $20) Fourteen primitive campsites scattered throughout the islands in Mosquito Lagoon are available year-round. The park has canoes ($25 per day) available for rent to campers only from the Visitor Information Center.

❶ Information

The **Canaveral National Seashore Visitor Information Center** (☑386-428-3384; www.nps.gov/cana; ⊙8am-6pm Oct-Mar, to 8pm Apr-Sep) is located just south of the North District entrance gate. There is a fee station at both the North and South District entrances, but several boat launches and trails are accessible west of the lagoon at no fee. Lifeguards patrol Playalinda Beach Parking Area No 8 and Apollo Beach Parking Area No 1 from May 30 to September 1. There is a toilet at most beach parking areas, but the only vending machine for food or water is at the Visitor Information Center. Riptides can be particularly fierce here.

❶ Getting There & Around

To get to the North District take I-95 to SR 44 (exit 249), head east to New Smyrna, and south on A1A 7 miles to the entrance gate. Access to the South District is 12 miles east of Titusville, through Merritt Island National Wildlife Refuge (I-95 exit 220 to SR 406). There is no public transportation to or within the park, and no road access to Klondike Beach.

Melbourne & Indialantic

South from Cocoa Beach, Hwy A1A stretches along the barrier island 53 miles to Vero Beach, passing plenty of well-signed access to Atlantic beaches, state parks, small pockets of condos and long stretches of emptiness.

Indialantic, a blink and you miss it beach town 16 miles south of Cocoa Beach, isn't expansive, but it sure feels homey. You'll find a pizza place and a handful of other businesses, and the same surf and white sand, but it's worlds away from the Cocoa Beach rattle and hum.

BEST BEACHES

» **South Beach** (Vero Beach) Widest of this beach town's many great stretches; a boardwalk leads to a grassy area with picnic tables, showers and toilets.

» **Apollo Beach** (Canaveral National Seashore) Shines in a class of its own, offering miles of solitude and silence and, if you walk south from the southernmost dune parking lot, nude sun-bathing.

» **Indialantic Beach** (Indialantic) Small-town beach.

» **Lori Wilson Park** (Cocoa Beach) Nicest in town.

On the mainland a few minutes west of the beach town of Indialantic (look for signs on A1A), historic Melbourne offers a small-town feel with several good restaurants, coffee shops and bars.

🛏 Sleeping

Windemere Inn   B&B $$$
(☑321-728-9334, 800-224-6853; www.windemere inn.com; 815 Hwy A1A, Indialantic; r $155-274, ste $350-400; ❄🛜) An immaculate and low-key oceanside B&B with English antiques, afternoon tea and a full breakfast. If you can overlook the attitude, it's a lovely place.

Sea View Motel   MOTEL $$
(☑321-723-0566; www.seaviewmelbourne.com; 4215 S Hwy A1A, Melbourne Beach; r & ste $125-195; ❄🛜🐾🛁) Located directly on the beach along a quiet and undeveloped stretch of Hwy A1A, this renovated 1950s two-story motel attracts folks looking for a laid-back beach getaway. Eight simple, bright rooms with quilts, wood floors and fully equipped kitchens are available by the day, week or month, there's a shared beachfront patio, and one of the best spots on the Space Coast for a sunset drink is an easy walk across Hwy A1A.

Crane Creek Inn   B&B $$
(☑321-768-6416; www.cranecreekinn.com; 907 E Melbourne Ave, Melbourne; r $100-199; ❄@🛁) Two blocks from historic downtown Melbourne, this homey B&B sits in a residential district directly on Crane Creek, a tributary of Indian River.

Eating & Drinking

Café Coconut Cove   GERMAN $$$
(☏321-727-3133; www.cafecoconutcove.com; 4210 S Hwy A1A; mains $14-30; ☺11am-10pm) Owned and run by the Himmeroeder family for 24 years, this handsome restaurant on a quiet stretch of the Indian River serves goulash and schnitzel bratwurst to fans up and down the coast. Stop for a drink on the tiny waterfront patio. Look for it 15 minutes south of Melbourne Beach, about halfway between Cocoa Beach and Vero Beach.

El Ambia Cubano   CUBAN $
(www.elambiacubano.com; 950 E Melbourne Ave, Melbourne; mains $8-12; ☺11am-10pm Mon-Sat) Conga stools, weekend salsa, jazz and acoustic guitar, and tasty family cooking in a tiny spot across from Crane Creek. Linger over a sweet Cafecito and chocolate flan.

Sebastian Inlet & Around

Continuing south along Hwy A1A, development trickles beyond sleepy Melbourne Beach. You'll find plenty of access to beaches, hiking and birding along both the Atlantic Coast and the Indian River. Just south of Sebastian Inlet State Park, mile after mile of tidy hedges and bike paths line the highway, hiding upscale homes of northern Vero Beach.

Sights & Activities

The following recommended sights, all along Hwy A1A, are listed geographically from north to south.

Sebastian Inlet State Park   PARK
(☏321-984-4852; www.floridastateparks.org/sebastianinlet; Hwy A1A; admission $5; ☺10am-4:30pm) Stretching along a narrow strip of the barrier island 18 miles south of Indialantic, with the Indian River Lagoon to one side and the Atlantic on the other, this busy park popular with fishermen, surfers, boaters and families is divided into two sections by the inlet bridge. On the north is child-safe swimming in the calm-water lagoon; on the south you'll find a marina with boat rental, a small fishing museum and an uninspiring campground ($25 per site).

McClarty Treasure Museum   MUSEUM
(Hwy A1A; admission $2; ☺10am-4pm) In 1715 a Spanish ship carrying gold and treasures went down in a hurricane, and survivors built a makeshift camp. This small museum, featuring a 45-minute movie, dioramas and artifacts from the shipwreck, sits on the site of that wreck. Even today, folks looking for a pretty shell stumble upon treasures washed ashore, and treasure hunters moor offshore doing their thing. The museum's 1 mile south of Sebastian Inlet State Park.

TOP CHOICE / Pelican Island National Wildlife Refuge   WILDLIFE RESERVE
(www.fws.gov/pelicanisland; Hwy A1A; ☺7:30am-sunset) Established in 1903, Pelican Island was America's first federal bird reservation, the forerunner of today's national wildlife-refuge system. A paved path from the dusty parking lot leads to a watchtower with views of the island, and several trails offer delightful quiet. The reserve is 22 miles south of Indialantic.

Vero Beach

☏772 / POP 18,160
Dubbed 'zero beach' by action-hungry folks in Cocoa Beach, this carefully zoned coastal town, with lovely grassy parks, wide, white, lifeguarded beaches and a pedestrian-friendly downtown, feels like a step into the past.

Sights & Activities

Though most are happy to lose themselves in the lull of beach life, walking barefoot off the dunes for a slice of pizza and catching some bluegrass at the weathered Driftwood Resort, Vero boasts a rich commitment to both the arts and the environment. In addition to the following, there's a Smithsonian marine research station, botanical gardens, regular art walks and several small, regional museums worth a visit.

Vero Beach Museum of Art   MUSEUM
(www.vbmuseum.org; 3001 Riverside Park Dr; ☺10am-4:30pm Mon-Sat, from 1pm Sun) With changing fine-art exhibitions and regular outdoor jazz concerts, this sleek, white museum in Riverside Park could easily hold its own against any big-city heavy hitter. Look for signs on Hwy A1A.

Environmental Learning Center   OUTDOORS
(☏772-589-5050; www.discoverelc.org; 255 Live Oak Dr; admission $5, children under 12yr free; ☺10am-4pm Tue-Fri, 9am-noon Sat, 1-4pm Sun; ⊞) This 51-acre reserve, dedicated to educating folks about the fragile environment of the Indian River estuary, offers hands-on displays and a boardwalk through the

mangroves. Check the website for details on **EcoVentures**, guided nature trips including canoe and pontoon boat trips, and nature walks.

Sail Moonraker BOATING
(☎772-696-2941; www.sailmoonraker.com; 2-8hr cruises for up to 6 guests $300-800; ⏹) Captain Bruce offers customized dolphin-watching, swimming and sunset cruises in the Indian River Lagoon, excellent for children, grandparents and everyone in between, aboard his 40ft catamaran.

Orchid Island Bikes & Kayaks BICYCLE RENTAL
(☎772-299-1286; www.orchidislandrentals.com; 1175 Commerce Ave; per day/week/month $15/44/79, delivery & pickup $20) Vero Beach is the perfect place to ditch the car for a bike, as even kids can easily pedal to restaurants, hotels and the beach. Rent kayaks and toodle around Indian River Lagoon.

🛏 Sleeping

Caribbean Court
Boutique Hotel BOUTIQUE HOTEL $$
(☎772-231-7211; www.thecaribbeancourt.com; 1601 S Ocean Dr; r & ste $139-250; ❀🐾🛜🚹🐕) In a quiet residential area a block off South Beach, this lovely spot expertly blends understated elegance with a casual beach vibe. Bougainvillea and palm trees hide a small garden pool, and handsome white-walled rooms with earthy accents have rattan furnishings, tiled sinks, thick towels and a refrigerator stocked with imported beers ($3). Nestled under flowers and palms, the delightfully tiny private patios are the perfect spot for morning coffee. Ask about weekday discounts.

Vero Beach Hotel and Spa HOTEL $$$
(☎772-231-5666; www.verobeachhotelandspa.com; 3500 Ocean Dr; r & ste $230-500; ❀🐾@🛜🚹🐕) This beachfront resort offers all the amenities of a deluxe hotel with the intimate, low-key and friendly tone of a boutique inn, and is an easy walk to downtown Vero Beach. Note that the least expensive accommodation is an interior room with no windows.

South Beach Place MOTEL $$
(☎772-231-5366; www.southbeachplacevero.com; 1705 S Ocean Dr; ste per day $125-75, per week $700-1050; ❀🛜🚹🐕) Old Florida with a face-lift, this tasteful and bright two-story motel sits in a particularly quiet stretch across from South Beach. One-bedroom suites face the courtyard pool and have a full kitchen.

🍴 Eating

Maison Martinique FRENCH $$$
(☎772-231-5366; www.caribbeancourt.com; Caribbean Court Boutique Hotel, 1601 S Ocean Dr; mains $18-35; ⏱5-10pm) Outstanding French cuisine with first-rate service and intimate surrounds. On warm evenings, eat by the little pool. For something more casual but just as tasty, head to the piano bar upstairs.

Lemon Tree CAFE $$
(☎772-231-0858; 3125 Ocean Dr; mains $8-20; ⏱7am-9pm) Bright and busy, this cheerful downtown eatery is particularly popular for weekend brunch.

Island Cafe CAFE $
(www.islandcafevero.com; 3101 Ocean Dr; mains $3-10; ⏱7am-5pm, to 7pm Nov-Apr) Grab a tuna hoagie or burrito at the walk-up window across from the playground and beach.

South Beach Pizzeria PIZZERIA $
(☎772-231-1110; www.islandcafevero.com; 1621 S Ocean Dr; slices $2.50; ⏱10am-9pm Mon-Thu, to 10pm Fri & Sat, 11am-9pm Sun) Tiny quintessential beach-town pizza place serves excellent thin crust by the pie or slice, perfect for a midday break from South Beach.

🍷 Drinking & Entertainment

🏆TOP
CHOICE **Havanna Nights Piano Bar** BAR
(Caribbean Court Boutique Hotel, 1601 S Ocean Dr; ⏱from 5:30pm; 🅿) Romantic 2nd-story bar with cozy balcony, delicious tapas and nightly piano. Try the snapper for two, a local favorite.

Waldo's LIVE MUSIC
(Driftwood Resort, 3150 Ocean Dr; 🅿) A Vero Beach institution for dinner and music for everyone from twentysomethings to families to local retirees, with a small bar, an oceanside deck and a rustic feel.

ℹ Information

For tourist information, see www.verobeach.com. **Indian River Medical Center** (☎772-567-4311; 1000 36th St) Cross over to the mainland on Hwy 60 at Riverside Park, and head north on Hwy 1.

ℹ Getting There & Away

Vero Beach lies 53 miles south of Cocoa Beach on Hwy A1A. The closest international airports are in Orlando, 90 minutes to the northwest, West Palm Beach, 90 minutes to the south, and Melbourne, 30 minutes up the coast. **Vero Beach Shuttle** (☎772-267-0550; www.verobeach shuttle.com) provides airport shuttle service.

Northeast Florida

Best Places to Eat

» Floridian (p336)

» Singleton's Seafood Shack (p344)

» 29 South (p348)

» Satchel's Pizza (p357)

» Yearling Restaurant (p359)

Best Places to Stay

» At Journey's End (p334)

» St Francis Inn (p335)

» One Ocean Hotel, Resort & Spa (p344)

» Elizabeth Pointe Lodge (p347)

» Fairbanks House (p347)

Why Go?

Florida's already a diverse state in terms of geography and character, but the northeast truly takes things into multiple-personality-disorder territory. At the northeastern border, Amelia Island is a gracious Southern belle who will greet you with a glass of sweet tea on the porch of a Victorian B&B. Forty-five minutes south, Jacksonville is a macho banker type, all high-rises and steel-girded bridges. A stone's throw away resides cultured St Augustine, who can lecture you for hours about Spanish colonial–era architecture (but don't fear; she's got a wild pirate side as well). Then, of course, there's Daytona Beach, the proudly rednecky party king who just wants to whip his shirt off, down a beer and watch some Nascar.

If all those personalities are enough to give you whiplash, you can head inland for a slower pace: cute college towns and antiques villages, pristine springs, and miles of clover-green horse pastures.

When to Go
Daytona Beach

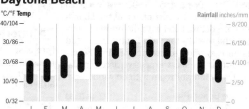

| Mar & Apr Spring Break: an influx of booze-happy college students, especially in Daytona Beach. | Jun–Sep Summer is high season on the beaches; temps range from balmy to sweltering. | Mar–Jun & Nov–Dec When weather's cooler, prices rise in non-beach places like St Augustine. |

ATLANTIC COAST

In 1902 speed catapulted Daytona into the national psyche when playboy race-car drivers Ransom Olds (of Oldsmobile fame) and Alexander Winston waged a high-profile race along the unusually hard-packed sandy shore, reaching an unheard of 57mph. The Florida East Coast Automobile Association was founded in 1903, and the Winter Speed Carnival (predecessor to today's Daytona 500) in 1904. For the next 30 years Daytona Beach was where speed records were made – and subsequently shattered. Stock-car racing came into vogue during the late 1930s; 'Race Weeks' packed beaches with fans. In 1947 Nascar was born here (see the boxed text below). In 1959, racing was relocated from the beach to the Daytona International Speedway.

Leaving 'The World's Most Famous Beach,' Daytona Beach, zoom north along Florida's Atlantic Coast to historic St Augustine, buzzing Jacksonville and charming Amelia Island, with plenty of picturesque islands, parks and places to explore en route.

Daytona Beach

📞 386 / POP 65,000

Known for expansive beaches, '50s retro carnival attractions, leather-clad biker culture and Spring Break madness, Daytona Beach's strongest association, however, is with supercharged speed. As home to the Daytona 500, its name is indelibly linked with the ultra-Southern sport of Nascar racing.

Anything but a wallflower, Daytona Beach has an overflowing dance card: it hosts one of the last Spring Breaks on the Atlantic Coast (tamer now than during its halcyon days); its population quintuples during Speed Weeks; and as many as half a million bikers roar into town for motorcycle events in spring and fall. There's also a tame side: Daytona is also home to a gentrified downtown, quality cultural attractions and nesting sea turtles.

Somehow, the thought of the racetrack and souped-up autos everywhere inspires drivers to push the pedal to the metal. Police know this, of course, and quickly curtail any need for speed.

⊙ Sights & Activities

Daytona International Speedway   RACETRACK
(📞800-748-7467; www.daytonaintlspeedway.com; 1801 W International Speedway Blvd; tickets from $15) This legendary 480-acre speedway boasts a more diverse race schedule than any other track in the world, hence its billing as the 'World Center of Racing.' Event ticket prices accelerate sharply for big races, but if nothing is going on, you can wander through the gift shop and into the grandstands for free.

Tram tours take you behind the scenes at the track and pits. The standard **Speedway Tour** (adult/child $15/10; ⊙11:30am, 1:30pm, 3:30pm & 4pm) is half an hour long and hits the main highlights, while the hour-long **All-Access Tour** (adult/child $17/22; ⊙hourly 10am-3pm) takes you to the driver's meeting room, the press box and other special areas. Both are first-come, first-served. Superfans

---

NASCAR & THE AMERICAN SOUTH

During Prohibition, production of moonshine (corn liquor with a lightning-bolt kick) was integral to the Southern economy, and renegades with cars speedy enough to outrun cops handled distribution. During their time off, they raced each other; when Prohibition was repealed the races continued. The most alluring venue was Daytona's Beach St track, where driver Bill France began promoting 'Race Weeks' that attracted thousands.

The sport exploded, though some automotive enthusiasts dismissed it as rednecks racing cars any mechanic could build. France knew better and in 1947 set about transforming his obsession into a world-class sport. The result was Nascar, which succeeded beyond his wildest dreams: Nascar is now the most watched sport in America after football.

The appeal of Nascar makes sense when you understand that dumping money at cars doesn't buy victory; winning relies on strategic driving skills and knowledge (when to pit, for example, or how many tires to change). Beneath those colorful product endorsements, the cars are everyday autos that conform to strict regulations to ensure the driver and pit crew – *not* the car – are tested.

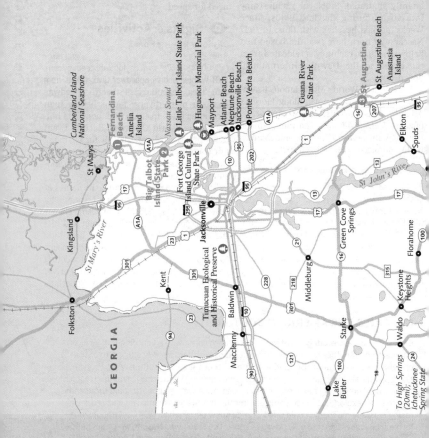

Northeast Florida Highlights

1 Chill on the porch of your 1890s B&B in **Fernandina Beach** (p346) on postcard-pretty Amelia Island

2 Stroll the forlorn beach at **Big Talbot Island State Park** (p346) and discover an eerie driftwood graveyard set against a barren bluff

3 Explore the Spanish-colonial houses, pirate museums, sweeping cathedrals and haunted pubs of **St Augustine** (p328), America's oldest city

4 Crack open a Bud and watch some racin' at **Daytona International Speedway** (p319), the spiritual home of Nascar

ATLANTIC OCEAN

GEORGIA

Cumberland Island National Seashore

St Marys

Kingsland

Folkston

Kent

Macclenny

Baldwin

Lake Butler

Starke

Waldo

Keystone Heights

Florahome

Elkton

Spuds

Middleburg

Green Cove Springs

Jacksonville

Timucuan Ecological and Historical Preserve

Fort George Island Cultural State Park

Big Talbot Island State Park

Little Talbot Island State Park

Huguenot Memorial Park

Mayport

Atlantic Beach

Neptune Beach

Jacksonville Beach

Ponte Vedra Beach

Guana River State Park

St Augustine

St Augustine Beach

Anastasia Island

Fernandina Beach

Amelia Island

Nassau Sound

St Mary's River

St John's River

To High Springs (20mi); Ichetucknee Spring State

30 km
20 miles

Cape Canaveral

Cape Canaveral

A1A

Kennedy Space Center

Canaveral National Seashore

Cocoa Village

New Smyrna Beach

1

Titusville

1

528

Bee Line Expressway (toll)

520

Port Orange

A1A

95

46

50

Washington Oaks Garden State Park

Flagler Beach

Ormond Beach

4 Daytona Beach

1

415

Osceola

Bunnell

1

40

92

44

Lake Woodruff National/ Wildlife Refuge

Cassadaga

Deltona

417

Pierson

11

De Leon Springs

92

DeLand

Orlando

17

De Leon Springs State Recreation Area

St John's River

Blue Spring State Park

4

528

Crescent Lake

20

Crescent City

17

Astor

42

44

46

436

441

Lake George

Fort Gates Ferry

Salt Springs

40

Ocala National Forest 6

Ocklawaha River

Eustis

19

Tavares

Lake Apopka

27

310

315

Silver Springs

441

27

Wildwood

Florida's Turnpike (toll)

50

33

Marjorie Kinnan Rawlings Historic State Park

Island Grove

325

Citra

Belleview

25

301

Bushnell

471

Micanopy

441

Orange Lake

75

Ocala

301

75

301

Ridge Manor

To 7 Troy Springs (70mi)

27

200

40

Withlacoochee River

44

Inverness

41

Brooksville

50

98

5 Down a few beers and check out a local band in **Gainesville** (p358), a college town with a thriving music scene

6 Hike, camp and canoe your way through the wildlife-rich **Ocala National Forest** (p354)

7 Dive or snorkel over the spooky ruins of a Civil War–era steamship at **Troy Springs** (p360)

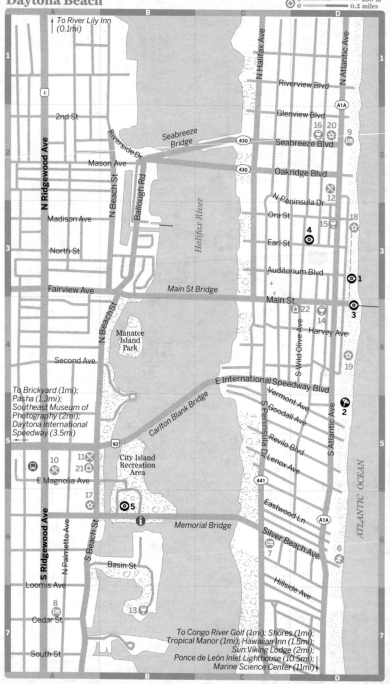

can opt for the all-access **VIP Tour** (per person $50; ⊙1pm Tue & Thu) aboard an air-conditioned bus, with up-close looks at Nascar icons like winning cars, trophies and more. By advance reservation only.

Daytona Beach   BEACH
(per car $5; ⊙8am-7pm May-Oct, sunrise-sunset Nov-Apr) One look at this perfectly planar stretch of sand and you can see why it served as the city's raceway. Today you can drive sections of the beach, tide permitting, to a strictly enforced top speed of 10mph. There are six well-signed beach entrances from Ormond Beach (Granada Blvd) to Ponce Inlet (Beach St); between Seabreeze Blvd and International Speedway Blvd it's traffic-free. Tired of your boring old ride? There are a few transport options from beach-side vendors: rent anything from an ATV tricked out

like a '58 'Vette convertible to fat-tired two-wheeled beach cruisers to recumbent trikes. If you're tired of wheels, beach-based vendors rent slick-bottomed boogie boards ($5 per hour) and 8ft surfboards ($10 per hour), and offer banana-boat rides and other types of splashy fun.

For an adrenaline rush that affords a bird's-eye view of the coast, try **Daytona Beach Parasail** (☑386-547-6067; www.daytonaparasailing.com; parasailing $65-100), on the beach to the left of the Silver Beach approach ramp.

Beyond the high-tide mark, looser sand creates a nesting environment for sea turtles to lay eggs at night from May to October. The eggs and hatchlings are monitored carefully by the Marine Science Center, which is a rehabilitation center for turtles.

Jackie Robinson Ballpark   STADIUM
(www.daytonacubs.com; 105 E Orange Ave; VIP/adult/child $12/7/6) On an island in the Halifax River, this ballpark is home to the Daytona Cubs, a Class A minor-league affiliate of the Chicago Cubs. In 1946, the Montreal Royals, Jackie Robinson's team, was in Florida to play an exhibition against their parent club, the Brooklyn Dodgers. Other Florida cities refused to let the game proceed due to segregation laws, but Daytona Beach cried, 'Play ball!' and Robinson later went on to be the first African American baseball player in the majors. The ballpark, seating 4200 people, was renamed in his honor in 1990.

Museum of Arts & Sciences   MUSEUM
(www.moas.org; 1040 Museum Blvd; adult/student $13/7; ⊙9am-5pm Tue-Sat, 11am-5pm Sun) Beat the heat at this diverse museum, featuring cultural collections ranging from Cuban to African to Chinese. In the Museum of Arts & Sciences you'll find the noteworthy Dow Gallery of American Art, showcasing early American paintings, and antique furniture and silver donated by a wealthy St Augustine benefactor. Root Museum, sponsored by the family that bottled Coca-Cola from day one, has a surreal assortment of relics from the soda's history, including ancient vending machines and 1920s delivery vans. The museum is in inland Daytona, just east of the airport.

Marine Science Center   AQUARIUM
(☑386-304-5545; www.marinesciencecenter.com; 100 Lighthouse Dr; adult/child $5/2; ⊙10am-4pm Tue-Sat, noon-4pm Sun; ☒) Despite the built-up environs at Daytona Beach, loggerheads,

VROOOM! DRIVE YOUR OWN RACE CAR

If merely watching Nascar drivers streak around the track isn't adrenaline pumping enough for you, you can actually get in the car yourself via the **Richard Petty Driving Experience** (☎800-237-3889; www.drivepetty.com). Choose from several levels of death-defying action, from the three-lap passenger-seat Race Ride ($135) to the daylong Experience of a Lifetime ($2200), which puts you behind the wheel for 30 white-knuckle laps. The experience is held on a rotating basis on Nascar tracks around the country; it usually lands in Daytona about three weekends out of the month – see the online calendar for details.

green turtles, Kemp Ridleys and occasionally leatherbacks are found in the area. A rehab center for injured sea turtles and birds, the Marine Science Center has a wet/dry lab, some great kid-friendly exhibits and a guided tour of the on-site turtle and seabird rehabilitation facilities (call ahead).

Boardwalk & Pier   WATERFRONT, PIER
Follow Main St E and you'll cross Daytona's sabal palm–lined, ocean-fronting Boardwalk. Look for ice-cream shops, arcade games and beachside patios where you can sip beer from plastic cups. It's good family fun with a side of sleaze to keep things hopping. Follow Main St further east and you'll stumble onto the long, coral-colored pier, once a summer-vacation icon. It's currently in a state of sad disrepair, but locals hope to have it up and running again in the near future.

Daytona Lagoon   WATER PARK
(daytonalagoon.com; 601 Earl St; waterpark admission $27, all-access admission $55, selected activities $6-12; ☺11am-11pm Sun-Thu, to midnight Fri & Sat; 🖰) Kids can burn off energy at this beachside water park, which has a tube float, a tidal-wave pool and a multilevel water playground, as well as arcade games, go-karts, laser tag, a climbing wall, an erupting volcano and a cannon blaster firing foam balls.

Ponce de León Inlet Lighthouse   LIGHTHOUSE
(ponceinlet.org; 4931 S Peninsula Dr; adult/child $5/1.50; ☺10am-5pm winter, to 9pm summer)

Climb the 203 steps to the top of Florida's tallest working lighthouse, then take your time checking out the museum and buildings dotting the grounds of what was once a remote, lonely outpost; displays include a restored 15ft Fresnel lens. The lighthouse is 10 miles south of Daytona; follow A1A to Beach St.

Congo River Golf   MINI GOLF
(www.congoriver.com; 2100 S Atlantic Ave; adult/child $11/9; ☺10am-11pm Sun-Thu, to midnight Fri & Sat; 🖰) Daytona's got plenty of mini-golf courses. But how many of them have live gators, dyed-blue waterfalls, a fake airplane and gem-panning?

FREE **Southeast Museum of Photography**   MUSEUM
(www.smponline.org; Daytona Beach Community College, 1200 W International Speedway Blvd, Bldg 37; ☺11am-5pm Tue-Fri, 1-5pm Sat & Sun) The only museum in Florida dedicated solely to photography, this vibrant gallery doesn't shy from provocative subjects like human rights in its rotating exhibitions.

⚝ Festivals & Events

Speed Weeks   CAR RACING
In the first two weeks of February the Rolex 24 Hour Race and Daytona 500 are held, and 200,000 people accomplish a *lot* of partying.

Bike Week   MOTORCYCLES
Over 10 days in early March, 500,000 bikers drool over each other's hogs and party round the clock. Locals run a 'death pool' predicting the number of casualties.

WORTH A TRIP

GAMBLE PLACE

Twenty minutes south of Daytona but a million miles away, the winter **estate** (919 Taylor Rd, Port Orange; adult/child $6/3; ☺10am-3pm Fri & Sat, tours 10am, noon & 2pm) of the Gamble family (of Procter & Gamble fortune) lies in a sun-dappled glade. The cracker-style house and several whimsically named cottages (including a replica *Snow White and the Seven Dwarfs* house) are open for weekend tours. An adjacent canoe company offers paddling trips down silent, moss-shrouded Cracker Creek. When you've OD'd on Daytona's neon and noise, this is the perfect antidote.

Spring Break   STUDENT PARTY

Currently with one-fifth of the attendance of peak years, 100,000 breakers do keg stands in March. Most of the action's at the beach.

Coke Zero 400   CAR RACING

Nascar fans fly the checkered flag at this 400-lap race during July 4 weekend.

Biketoberfest   MOTORCYCLES

Same as Bike Week, but in mid-October. More drinking.

🛏 Sleeping

Accommodations here run the gamut: you can find everything from filthy fleabaggers to cute B&Bs to luxury suites – with a range of price tags. Prices soar during events, so book well ahead if there is something on. The Daytona Convention and Visitors Bureau website (www.daytonabeach.com) has a great lodgings listing.

TOP CHOICE **August Seven Inn**   B&B **$$**

(☏386-248-8420; www.jpaugust.net; 1209 S Peninsula Dr; r $99-155; ❋🤶🏊) As elegant and refined as Daytona Beach is, well, *not,* this utterly charming Victorian house has eight guest rooms done up in a chic mix of period antiques, art-deco pieces and modern prints. Built in 1896 by James Gamble of Procter & Gamble riches, it sits atop a neatly manicured square of lawn just blocks from the bustle and neon of the beach. A stocked guest pantry and a slightly goofy 'Tranquility Room' with massage chairs will make you feel right at home, as will friendly innkeepers Peter and Joseph.

TOP CHOICE **River Lily Inn**   B&B **$$**

(☏386-253-5002; www.riverlilyinnbedandbreakfast.com; 558 Riverside Dr; r $125-220; ❋🤶🏊) There's a grand piano in the living room, a heart-shaped pool in the backyard, Belgian waffles for breakfast and a fridge full of free Klondike bars for snacks. What more could you want in a B&B? Add to that a quiet location on an oak-shaded property overlooking the river, elegant rooms with high ceilings (some with private balconies), and friendly-as-can-be owners, and you've got the recipe for a perfect getaway.

Tropical Manor   RESORT **$$**

(☏386-252-4920, 800-253-4920; www.tropicalmanor.com; 2237 S Atlantic Ave; r $88-315; ❋🤶🏊) With enormous painted hibiscuses splashed across the walls, miniature horse statues

Sure, the **park** (2099 N Beach St; per vehicle $6) itself is lovely, a bird-watchers' heaven of former indigo fields turned hardwood forests, but the drive here from Daytona Beach is even lovelier. A canopy of trees overhangs the two-lane road like a green tunnel, letting in only the stray dapple of sunlight. The park is about 20 minutes from downtown Daytona.

hidden hither and thither, and beachfront umbrellas colored from the dye of candy hearts, staying here is like sleeping inside a game of Candy Land. If you can survive the pastel overload, this immaculate beachfront place offers everything from one-room apartments for two people to three-bedroom and two-bathroom suites sleeping 11.

Coquina Inn B&B   B&B **$$**

(☏386-254-4969; www.coquinainn.com; 544 S Palmetto Ave; r $99-139; ❋🤶) Shaded by an ancient oak, this sweet yellow-and-stone cottage smells of homemade cookies and looks like your grandma's house – in a good way (painted flowers on the wall, snowy white quilts, holiday decorations). Friendly owners and a people-loving house dog named Godiva complete the homey vibe. It's located in a quiet residential neighborhood near downtown.

Shores   RESORT **$$$**

(☏386-767-7350; www.shoresresort.com; 2637 S Atlantic Ave; r $120-320; ❋🤶🏊) With a plush, intimate lobby of dark wood and burbling fountains, this is one of Daytona's most elegant options. Rooms are chic and airy, with canopy beds and a 1940s color palette of peaches and pale blues. Want to get away from the Spring Break crowd? This is the place.

Plaza Resort & Spa   RESORT **$$$**

(☏800-329-8662; www.plazaresortandspa.com; 600 N Atlantic Ave; r $120-600; ❋🤶🏊) Built in 1908, this glossy resort recently received a $70-million renovation – and every penny shows. From the miles of honey-colored marble lining the lobby to the 42in plasma TVs and cloud-soft beds in the rooms, to the 15,000-sq-ft spa, this resort coos luxury.

PARKING-LOT PREACHING

Back in 1954, when the old Neptune Drive-in Theater closed, this car-obsessed town devised a novel solution for increasing church attendance: services people could attend while remaining in their cars.

Daytona Beach Drive-In Christian Church (3140 S Atlantic Ave; ☉services 8:30am & 10am Sun) is a drive-in Protestant church. Pull up, hook a speaker to your car (or do as the locals do and tune to 680AM or 88.5FM) and listen to the Rev preach. He and the choir hold service on a balcony overlooking the sea of cars. There's free coffee and donuts between services. Only in Daytona.

Sun Viking Lodge
RESORT $$
(☎386-252-6252, 800-874-4469; www.sunviking.com; 2411 S Atlantic Ave; r $80-285; ❋☂☒⛟) The comfy rooms here could use a renovation, but the balcony views are divine. Moreover, the outdoor pool with a 60ft waterslide, the endless activities planned for kids, and the 2ft walk to the beach make the dated rooms seem like heaven. Oh, and there's shuffleboard!

Hawaiian Inn
HOTEL $
(☎800-922-3023; www.hawaiianinn.com; 2301 S Atlantic Ave; r $49-149; ❋☂☒) Don't be put off by the jaundice-yellow hallways; this beachfront budget spot actually has pleasant, spacious rooms, plus the kitsch value of a freaky-tiki luau dinner show in the lobby restaurant.

✖ Eating

It may feel like Daytona's a wasteland of fast food and biker bars, but there are quite a few restaurants that break out of the burgers-'n'-beer mold. The newly revitalized downtown has several good choices, while the beach remains fairly tourist trap-y.

Dancing Avocado Kitchen
VEGETARIAN, MEXICAN $
(110 S Beach St; mains $6-11; ☉8am-4pm Mon-Sat) Fresh and healthful, a meal here makes you feel better…or is it just the fresh air flowing through the custom-made air filters? Yummy Mexican dishes like extreme burritos and quesadillas dominate the menu at this vegetarian-oriented cafe, but the signature dancing avocado melt is tops. There's a juice and smoothie bar on-site, the salsa is made from scratch, and once a month all tips go to charity.

Rose Villa
EUROPEAN $$$
(☎386-615-7673; www.rosevillaormond.com; 43 West Granada Blvd, Ormond Beach; mains $6-11; ☉5-10pm Tue-Thu, to 11pm Fri & Sat) In-the-know local B&B owners frequently steer their guests to this lovely new under-the-radar bistro, in a renovated Victorian house a few miles north of Daytona. The menu is charmingly old-fashioned 'Continental' – veal chop in cream sauce, Scottish salmon with caper butter – and the setting (vintage wallpaper, heavy carpets, bone china) enchanting. If it's nice out, try for a table in the tree-shaded backyard gazebo.

Pasha
MIDDLE EASTERN $
(www.pashacafedaytona.com; 919 W International Speedway Blvd; mains $5-13; ☉10am-7:30pm Mon-Sat, noon-6pm Sun) Virtually unchanged since it opened in the '70s, this place combines an Aladdin's cave deli of imported Middle Eastern goods and a cafe with authentic dishes like Armenian breaded cheese pie and platters served with the owner's grandma's pita bread.

Cellar
ITALIAN $$$
(☎386-258-0011; www.thecellarrestaurant.com; 220 Magnolia Ave; mains $18-36; ☉5-10pm Tue-Sun) Now you can tell your friends that you've dined in the summer mansion of 29th US President Warren G Harding! Harding is consistently ranked as one of the worst presidents in history; the restaurant rates much better – its classic, upscale Italian fare and elegant ambience has made it Daytona's go-to spot for special-occasion dinners.

Aunt Catfish's on the River
SEAFOOD, SOUTHERN $$
(☎386-767-4768; www.auntcatfishontheriver.com; 4009 Halifax Dr, Port Orange; mains $8-23; ☉11:30am-9pm daily, brunch 9am-2pm Sun) Emphasis on meat, butter and fat – even the green beans are stewed…and locals love it. This insanely popular place also has fried, grilled and Cajun-style catfish. Sunday's endless Blue Jean Brunch features cinnamon rolls made to a 27-year-old family recipe.

Brickyard
AMERICAN $$
(www.brickyardlounge.com; 747 W International Speedway Blvd; mains $7-19; ☉11am-11pm Mon-Sat,

noon-8pm Sun) Sit cheek by jowl with bikers and speedway freaks at this beloved grease pit, in a bizarre A-frame building decked out with racing memorabilia. Burgers, wings and T-bones are done just right, and beer keeps flowing until you say 'uncle.'

Starlite Diner DINER $
(www.starlitedinerdaytona.com; 401 N Atlantic Ave; ⊗7am-midnight Mon-Thu, to 1am Fri & Sat, to 10pm Sun) Straight outta *Happy Days,* this gleaming chrome diner serves giant good 'n' greasy portions under assorted '50s memorabilia.

 Drinking & Entertainment

Daytona's entertainment scene skews pretty lowbrow – biker bars with rollicking live music (mostly along Main St), high-octane dance clubs (on or near Seabreeze Blvd – aka the 'Beachside Party District'), and some good kitschy retro places.

Froggy's Saloon BAR
(www.froggyssaloon.com; 800 Main St) Outside this train wreck of a bar, a bone chopper gleams in the window. Inside, a sign asks, 'Ain't drinking fun?' You better believe they mean it: opening at 7am, this is Party Central for bikers and others who want to go bonkers. Expect to see flashing chicks, smoky beards, orgasm contests and more leather than on an African safari.

Razzles CLUB
(www.razzlesnightclub.com; 611 Seabreeze Blvd; cover $5-10; ⊗8pm-3am) Clubs come and go, but this high-energy dance zone keeps on thumping. Twenty years after it opened, this cavernous warehouse features 10 bars, dazzling light shows, cutting-edge beats and more beads than Mardi Gras.

Blue Grotto CLUB
(www.bluegrottodaytona.com; 125 Basin St) A late-20 through 40-something crowd dances like nobody's watching at this underwater-themed waterfront club, with grotto rock walls, aquarium windows and a light-up blue bar. Avoid the food.

Ocean Deck BAR
(www.oceandeck.com; 127 S Ocean Ave) No woman? No cry! Live reggae nightly at this beachfront bar.

Oyster Pub PUB
(www.oysterpub.com; 555 Seabreeze Blvd) Perpetually crowded, this sporty pub has a zillion TVs, tons of outdoor seating and all the fresh Gulf oysters you can suck down.

Mai Tai Bar BAR
(www.maitaibar.com; 250 N Atlantic Ave) A party-happy crowd downs crayon-colored rum drinks at this fun Hawaiian-themed bar.

Daytona Beach Bandshell LIVE MUSIC
(www.daytonabandshell.com; 70 Boardwalk) Constructed in 1937 from coquina shell, this landmark beachfront venue stages a summer concert series and summer outdoor movies.

Cinematique of Daytona CINEMA
(www.cinematique.org; 242 S Beach St; tickets $7) Home to the Daytona Beach Film Festival, Cinematique screens independent and foreign films.

 Shopping

The Speedway gift shop hawks all things Nascar, as do plenty of beachfront gift emporiums.

Daytona Flea & Farmers Market MARKET
(www.daytonafleamarket.com; 2987 Bellevue Ave; ⊗9am-5pm Fri-Sun) With over 1000 booths and 600 vendors, this claims to be the world's biggest flea market. At the corner of US 92 at I-95, 1 mile west of the Speedway.

Chopper's World MOTORCYCLE GEAR
(www.choppersworld.com; 618 Main St) The best of the bike shops; browse brain buckets, deerskin dusters and studded saddlebags among more than 10,000 motorcycle parts.

FREE CHOCOLATE? YES, PLEASE

Get your cacao fix at **Angell & Phelps Chocolate Factory** (www.angelland phelps.com; 154 S Beach St; ⊗tours 10am, 11am, 1pm, 2pm, 3pm & 4pm Mon-Sat), a downtown Daytona tradition since 1925. Free 20-minute tours of the production area include a sweet taste of the goods. While you're here, snag a bag of chocolate-covered potato chips, chocolate gators or the factory's signature creation, a caramel, cashew and chocolate confection known as the HoneyBee. It's not high-end stuff, but only the grouchiest of food snobs will complain.

NORTHEAST FLORIDA DAYTONA BEACH

ⓘ Information

Backstage Pass (www.backpassmag.com) Details local entertainment.

Daytona Beach Area Convention & Visitors Bureau (☑386-255-0415; www.daytonabeach.com; 126 E Orange Ave; ⊙9am-5pm Mon-Fri) Very useful website.

Gaydaytona (www.gaydaytona.com) News and entertainment for the gay and lesbian community.

Library (105 E Magnolia Ave) Two hours' free internet access.

News-Journal (www.news-journalonline.com) The big daily paper.

ⓘ Getting There & Around

Daytona Beach International Airport (☑386-248-8030; www.flydaytonafirst.com; 700 Catalina Dr), just south of the Speedway, is served by Delta and US Airways, and all major car-rental companies.

Greyhound (www.greyhound.com; 138 S Ridgewood Ave) has bus service to everywhere.

Daytona is close to the intersection of two major interstates, I-95 and I-4. I-95 is the quickest way to Jacksonville (about 90 miles) and Miami (260 miles), though Hwy A1A and US Hwy 1 are more scenic. Beville Rd, an east–west thoroughfare south of Daytona proper, becomes I-4 after crossing I-95; it's the fastest route to Orlando (55 miles).

Votran (www.votran.com) runs buses and trolleys (adult/child under 6yr $1.25/free) throughout the city.

Flagler Beach & Around

☑386 / POP 5400

Just 30 miles north of Daytona, isolated Flagler Beach is far removed from the towering hotels, dizzying lights and tire-tracked sands of its rowdy neighbor. On a 6-mile stretch of beach, this string of modest residences and smattering of shops has a three-story cap on buildings, spectacular sunrises and an end-of-the-earth feel.

Rent a pole and fisher from the Flagler Beach Pier, try to catch some (small-ish) waves with a surfboard from Z Wave Surf Shop (www.zwavesurfshop.com; 400 S Hwy A1A; per hr/day $5/20), or use one of its rental bikes to glide along A1A. Have a picnic at Washington Oaks Gardens State Park (6400 N Oceanshore Blvd; per vehicle $5), with resplendent camellia- and bird-of-paradise-filled gardens.

Of several inexpensive motels, the standout is the Topaz Motel (☑386-439-3301; www

.topazflaglerbeachfl.com; 1224 Hwy A1A; r $70-160; ❄☀@🐾). It's got a slew of bright, beachy motel rooms, but kitsch lovers should ask for one of the creaky, vintage doll–filled rooms in the 1927 main house, a former coast-guard station. It may not be haunted, but it sure feels like it could be! Camp beachside at Gamble Rogers Memorial State Recreation Area (☑386-517-2086; 3100 Hwy A1A; per vehicle $5, camping $28), which straddles both sides of A1A; you can rent kayaks here.

For grub, High Tide at Snack Jacks (www.snackjacks.com; 2805 Hwy A1A; mains $10-15; ⊙11am-11pm) has valet parking, but only to squeeze everyone in for the fried and grilled fish at this laid-back, open-air place, a favorite since 1947. Cash only.

Fort Matanzas National Monument

This tiny, 1742-built fort (www.nps.gov/foma; 8635 Hwy A1A; admission free; ⊙9am-5:30pm) is located on Rattlesnake Island, near where Menéndez de Avilés executed hundreds of shipwrecked French soldiers and colonists when rations at St Augustine ran low. Today it makes a terrific excursion via a free five-minute ferry that launches every hour (at half-past) from 9:30am to 4:30pm, weather permitting. Once there, the ranger provides an overview and lets you wander.

From Daytona, take I-95 north to exit 289. Exit right and follow Palm Coast Parkway (a toll road) until you reach Hwy A1A. Turn left and follow A1A north to the monument, which will be on your left. The trip should take just under one hour.

To catch the 35-person ferry to the monument – the last free thing in Florida – go through the visitor center and out to the pier. The ferry ride lasts about 10 minutes.

St Augustine

☑904 / POP 13,000

The oldest continuously occupied European settlement in the US, St Augustine was founded by the Spanish in 1565. Today, tourists flock here to saunter along cobbled roads, linger at cute cafes, browse endearing shops, learn about the city's rich history at countless museums – and cap it all off with snug dinners at lamp-lit restaurants and brews at quaint pubs. Meanwhile, horse-drawn carriages clip-clop past townsfolk dressed in period costume wandering this 144-block National Historic Landmark District.

It could all add up to a theme park–style experience at best – traveler hell at worst – but for the most part, St Augustine eclipses tourist trappings and retains charm and integrity. Why? Many reasons. First, unlike theme parks, these centuries-old buildings, monuments and narrow lanes are authentic. Second, the charming, one-off cafes and restaurants are the real deal, too: there's plenty of good eating in this small town. Third, even though they may not be required to, many people dress in period costume for work, emphasizing the town's historic character – some settle here purely for this lifestyle. And fourth, there are still many gems to discover off the well-trodden trail.

◉ Sights & Activities

All of St Augustine's historic district feels like a museum; there are literally dozens of separate attractions to choose from. Narrow little **Aviles Street**, the oldest European-settled street in the country, and long, pedestrian-only **St George Street** are both lined with galleries, cafes, museums and pubs, and are attractions in and of themselves.

Museums

Spanish Quarter Museum   HISTORIC BUILDINGS
(entry via 53 St George St; adult/child $7/4; ☺9am-4:45pm) Spanning 2 acres, this multi-building complex is a recreation of 1740 St Augustine. Walled off from the street, you're encouraged to wander the garrison's restored buildings and speak to the craftspeople (re-enactors) who use 18th-century technology to operate recreated 'storefronts': a blacksmith, a leather shop and a carpentry studio. Explana-

CAT RUGS & MUMMY TOES: VILLA ZORAYDA

Looking like a faux Spanish castle from a medieval theme park, this odd gray edifice elicits 'huh?' reactions from tourists strolling downtown St Augustine. Built in 1883 by an eccentric millionaire who was obsessed with Spain's 12th-century Alhambra Palace, it's made from a mix of concrete and local coquina shells. Today, the building is newly reopened as the odd-but-engaging **Villa Zorayda Museum** (www.villa zorayda.com; 83 King St; admission $10; ☺10am-5pm Mon-Sat, 11am-4pm Sun). The Moorish-style atrium and rooms contain quirky antiques and archaeological pieces, the two highlights being the 2400-year-old mummy's foot, and an equally old Egyptian 'Sacred Cat Rug' made from real cat fur.

tions of the centuries-old procedures are in 21st-century vernacular, but the craftspeople live out their period roles, often camping for weeks in nearby wilderness areas using only materials available in the 1700s, road-testing the clothing and tools you see them make here.

Lightner Museum   MUSEUM
(www.lightnermuseum.org; 75 King St; adult/child $10/5; ☺9am-5pm) This brilliantly eclectic museum is in the restored Alcazar Hotel, one of Henry Flagler's two St Augustine resorts, which housed (at the time) the world's largest indoor pool. Museum founder Otto C Lightner started his career writing about

AMERICA'S OLDEST CITY

Timucuans settled what is now St Augustine about 1000 BC, hunting alligators and cultivating corn and tobacco. In 1513, Spanish explorer Juan Ponce de León sighted land, came ashore and claimed La Florida (Land of Flowers) for Spain. In 1565 his compatriot Don Pedro Menéndez de Avilés arrived on the feast day of Augustine of Hippo, and accordingly christened the town San Augustín. Menendez quickly established a military base against the French, who had established Fort Caroline near present-day Jacksonville. The French fleet did him the favor of getting stuck in a hurricane; Menendez' men butchered the survivors. By the time Spain ceded Florida to the US in 1821, St Augustine had been sacked, looted, burned and occupied by pirates and Spanish, British, Georgian and South Carolinian forces.

Today the city's buildings, made of coquina – a DIY concrete made of sedimentary rock mixed with crushed shells – lend an enchanting quality to the slender streets, and the city's long and colorful history is palpable.

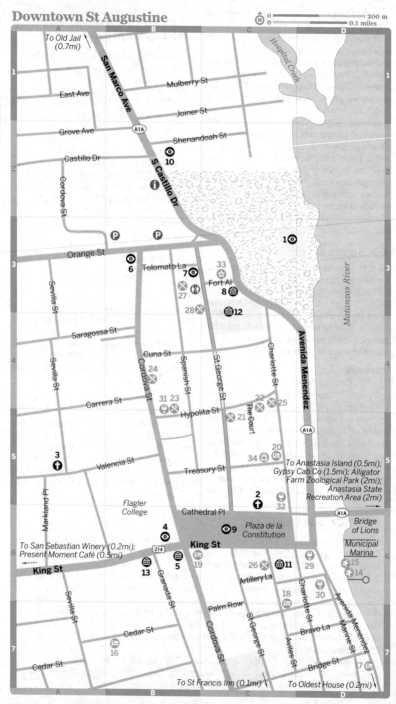

To Old Jail (0.7mi)

San Marco Ave

Mulberry St

East Ave

Joiner St

Grove Ave

A1A

Shenandoah St

Castillo Dr

S Castillo Dr

10

Cordova St

Orange St

6

Tolomato La

7

33

27

Fort Al

8

28

12

Saragossa St

Sevilla St

Cuna St

24

Spanish St

St George St

Charlotte St

Sevilla St

31 23

Carrera St

Hypolita St

21

The Court

22 25

Valencia St

Treasury St

34 20

A1A

To Anastasia Island (0.5mi);
Gypsy Cab Co (1.5mi); Alligator
Farm Zoological Park (2mi);
Anastasia State
Recreation Area (2mi)

Markland Pl

Flagler
College

3

Cathedral Pl

2

32

A1A

Bridge
of Lions

4

9

Plaza de la
Constitution

Municipal
Marina

To San Sebastian Winery (0.2mi);
Present Moment Café (0.5mi)

214

King St

5

19

King St

13

26

11

29

15

14

Granada St

Artillery La

Sevilla St

18

Charlotte St

30

Palm Row

St George St

Cedar St

Cordova St

Avilés St

Bravo La

Marine St

Avenida Menendez

16

Cedar St

Bridge St

17

To St Francis Inn (0.1mi)

To Oldest House (0.2mi)

Hospital Creek

Matanzas River

1

Avenida Menendez

collections for a hobby magazine and then started buying them – buttons, match safes, Renaissance art – becoming, essentially, a collector of collections. None of the exhibits seem to relate to each other, but that's part of the charm. Expect everything from antique musical instruments (played at 11am and 2pm; amazing acoustics make this a must-hear), to a shrunken head, to Egyptian-themed art-deco sculpture.

Pirate & Treasure Museum   MUSEUM

(www.thepiratemuseum.com; 12 S Castillo Dr; adult/child $12/7; ⊗9am-8pm;) An interactive treasure hunt, animatronic pirates (including a decapitated Blackbeard) and periodic cannonball blast noises make this brand-new spot seem halfway between theme park and museum. But don't be mistaken: there are plenty of historical treasures here, from a genuine treasure chest to 17th-century gold-and-silver plunder. It's all the private collection of Pat Croce, former Philadelphia 76ers owner and sports commentator.

Spanish Military Hospital Museum   MUSEUM

(www.spanishmilitaryhospital.com; 3 Aviles St; adult/child $5/3; ⊗10am-3pm Mon-Sat) Not for the faint of heart, guided tours of this museum discuss Colonial-era medical techniques in all their gory glory: amputations, leeching, the whole shebang. Housed in a reconstruction of the original hospital, the museum will make you very glad you're not a patient in 1791!

Ripley's Believe It or Not!   MUSEUM

(staugustine.ripleys.com; 19 San Marco Ave; adult/child $15/8; ⊗9am-7pm Sun-Thu, to 8pm Fri & Sat;) Inside the old (1887) Castle Warden, this is the first of the now-ubiquitous Ripley's 'Odditoriums.' Shrunken heads, a drum made from skulls, and goofy pirate displays are par for the course here.

Forts & Historic Buildings

Castillo de San Marcos National Monument   FORT

(www.nps.gov/casa; adult/child $6/free; ⊗8:45am-5:15pm, grounds closed midnight-5:30am;) Wandering from the clogged downtown streets onto the headland where this incredibly photogenic fort stands guard really amplifies its imposing scale. In 1672, after the British had burned the city around them one too many times, the Spanish began constructing this coquina citadel. Completed 23 years later, it's the oldest masonry fort in the

Downtown St Augustine

continental US. Rangers wearing Spanish colonial–era uniforms add to the medieval ambience and can answer questions as you take the fort's excellent self-guided tour. Cannon can be heard all over town when they're fired on the half-hour (10:30am to 3:30pm Friday to Sunday; cannon are not fired if fewer than four visitors are at the monument). The fort is located between San Marco Ave and Matanzas River.

Hotel Ponce de León   HISTORIC BUILDING
(74 King St; adult/child $7/1; ⊘tours hourly 10am-3pm summer) An 80ft domed rotunda and stained glass crafted by Louis Comfort Tiffany are the hallmarks of the Spanish Renaissance Revival hotel, Henry Flagler's flagship resort. Completed in 1888, it had to contend almost immediately with the vagaries of tourism: a yellow-fever epidemic and the worst freeze in Florida's history (1895). Nonetheless, this architectural wonder, the first major poured-concrete structure in the US, quickly became the country's most exclusive winter resort, before succumbing to a lack of guests in the 1960s, which led it to become part of the private Flagler College.

Oldest House   HISTORIC BUILDING
(www.oldesthouse.com; 14 St Francis St; adult/student $8/4; ⊘9am-5pm) Also known as the González-Alvarez House, this is the oldest surviving Spanish-era home in Florida, dating to the early 1700s and sitting on a site occupied since the 1600s. The house is part of a complex that also contains two small historical museums and a lovely ornamental garden.

Oldest Wooden School
House   HISTORIC BUILDING
(www.oldestwoodenschoolhouse.com; 14 St George St; adult/child $3/2; ⊘10am-4:30pm Mon-Sat, 11am-4:30pm Sun) Built from red cedar and cypress, the 200-year-old building is peopled by animatronic teachers and students, providing a glimpse into 18th-century life and education. Naughty kids may be frightened into civility when they see the Dungeon.

FREE Old Drugstore   HISTORIC BUILDING
(31 Orange St; ⊘9:30am-6pm) Built in 1739, this dusty pharmacy offers a unique collection of antique vials and tonics in sepia-colored bottles, as well as some other curiosities, like vintage suppository molds. Adjacent to the artifacts is an extensive assortment of herbal remedies for sale (from stevia leaf to lotus flowers) for homeopathic use.

Old Jail   HISTORIC BUILDING
(167 San Marco Ave; adult/child $9/5; ⊘8:30am-4:30pm) Built in 1891, this is the former town prison and residence of the town's first sheriff, Charles Joseph 'the terror' Perry (towering menacingly at 6ft 6in tall and weighing 300lb). Today, costumed 'deputies' escort visitors through cellblocks and detail the site's arresting history.

Plaza de la Constitución   SQUARE
In the heart of downtown, this grassy square, a former marketplace for food (and slaves), has a gazebo, some cannon and a Civil War memorial, as well as the remains of the town well.

Churches & Shrines

Cathedral Basilica of St Augustine   CHURCH
(www.thefirstparish.com; 38 Cathedral Pl) With its magnificent bell tower lording it over the Plaza de la Constitución, this Spanish mission–style cathedral is likely the country's first Catholic house of worship.

Flagler Memorial Presbyterian
Church   CHURCH
(32 Sevilla St) Henry Flagler, his daughter and her stillborn child lie in the mausoleum at this church, Flagler's own, magnificent Venetian-Renaissance edifice. The floor is Sienna marble, the wood is Santo Domingo mahogany and the pipe organ (played 8:30am and 11am Sunday) is colossal.

Mission of Nombre de Dios   CHURCH
(27 Ocean Ave) Just north of downtown on 1A, the mission dates back to the earliest days of Spanish settlement. Today, the peaceful memorial gardens feature a replica of the original altar, a tiny ivy-shrouded chapel and a small museum.

Beach-Area Attractions
Cross the Bridge of Lions and take Anastasia Blvd right out to the beach.

St Augustine Beach   BEACH
The 7-mile stretch of St Augustine Beach is a great place to soak up rays, and the road fronting it has a small handful of hotels, family restaurants and boisterous bars.

There's a visitor-information booth at the foot of St John's Pier, where you can rent a rod and reel ($3 for two hours, $1 for each additional hour).

About three blocks south of the pier, the end of A St has – as Florida goes – some fine waves. For late-breaking surf conditions, to rent or buy a board, or just to chill with your fellow surfer dudes and dudettes, stop at **Pit Surfshop** (www.pitsurfshop.com; 18 A St; boards per day $16).

Raging Water Sports (57 Comares Ave) rents kayaks ($20 per hour), sailboats ($40 per hour), jet skis ($90 per hour) and motorboats (starting at $75 per hour). Located at Conch House marina resort.

St Augustine Lighthouse   LIGHTHOUSE
(www.staugustinelighthouse.com; 81 Lighthouse Ave; adult/child $9.50/7.50; ☺9am-6pm) The light produced by this 1870s striped lighthouse beams all the way downtown. A great place to bring kids over six and more than 44in tall (since all climbers must be able to ascend and descend the tower under their own power), the lighthouse operates 'Dark of the Moon' paranormal tours on weekends at 8:30pm ($25/20 per adult/child).

Anastasia State Recreation Area   PARK
(1340 Hwy A1A; per vehicle $8) Escape the tourist hordes at Anastasia Island's recreation area, boasting a stunning beach, vibrant dunes, bike trails, a tidal salt marsh–fringed lagoon and a campground. Inside the park, **Anastasia Watersports** (☎904-460-9111; www.anastasiawatersports.com) rents kayaks, canoes and windsurfers.

Other Attractions

FREE **San Sebastian Winery**   WINERY
(www.sansebastianwinery.com; 157 King St; ☺10am-6pm Mon-Sat, 11am-6pm Sun) Free hour-long tours at this winery are capped with wine tastings and a video about Florida winemaking since the 1600s; there's wine and live jazz from 7pm to 11pm at the rooftop **Cellar Upstairs** (wine per glass $4-6; ☺4pm-midnight Fri, noon-midnight Sat & Sun). If you're around in August, join the squishy fun during the annual grape-stomping competitions.

Alligator Farm Zoological Park   ZOO
(www.alligatorfarm.us; 999 Anastasia Blvd; adult/child $22/11; ☺9am-5pm, to 6pm summer; 🏇) Maximo – a 1250lb, 15ft, 3in Australian saltwater crocodile – is the biggest of the reptiles at this gator-palooza, the world's only facility with every species of crocodilian in residence. Look for albino alligators, freaky gharials and seven different species of endangered monkey, including the world's smallest, the pygmy marmoset (the size of a mouse). There are talks and shows throughout the day; catch hungry alligators snapping their jaws at feeding times (noon and 3pm). The park is a five-minute drive from downtown St Augustine along Anastasia Blvd.

Fountain of Youth   PSEUDOHISTORICAL SITE
(www.fountainofyouthflorida.com; 11 Magnolia Ave; adult/child $10/6; ☺9am-5pm) When Ponce de León first came ashore here in 1513, the Timucuans are said to have shown

DETOUR: WORLD GOLF VILLAGE

The ultimate monument to a good walk spoiled, the **World Golf Village** (www.golfwgv.com; 1 World Golf Pl) is a massive golf resort, golf-course complex, golf museum and all-around golf-themed attraction.

Even non-fans will enjoy the village's centerpiece, the **World Golf Hall of Fame** (adult/child $20/5; ☺10am-6pm Mon-Sat, noon-6pm Sun). Featuring 18 exhibits (get it?), the front nine cover golf's history while the back nine examine modern pro golf. Separating them is the Hall of Fame itself, with multimedia exhibits on inductees. Admission includes 18 holes on a putting green designed to PGA specifications and an IMAX film.

Two legendary on-site courses, **King & Bear** and **Slammer & Squire**, are open for public tee times. If you're keen to improve your swing, two- to five-day **PGA Tour Golf Academy** (www.touracademy.com) packages start from $635; more expensive packages include accommodation at one of four on-site resorts. Private lessons start at $90 per hour.

Whether you're staying here or not, grab a burger from **Caddyshack** (455 S Legacy Trail; mains $7-14) restaurant and bar, named for the movie starring Bill Murray, who – along with his five brothers – owns it.

World Golf Village is just off I-95 via exit 323, about halfway between St Augustine and Jacksonville.

him a freshwater stream some believe to be the fabled Fountain of Youth. Today, you can take a kitschy 45-minute tour of the site, now an 'archaeological park,' and drink from the sulfur-tasting trickle, but we seriously doubt it'll have any anti-wrinkle powers! The park is about a mile north of downtown – just follow the signs.

Tours

St Augustine City Walks HISTORY TOUR
(☎904-540-3476; www.staugustinecitywalks.com; tours $14-45) Super-popular and extremely fun, these walking tours range from the Haunted Pub Crawl to the Savory Faire Food Tour (exploring the culture and history behind the city's cuisine) to the History, Mystery, Mayhem and Murder tour of the city's cemeteries, pirate hangouts and other dark spots.

Old Town Trolley Tours TROLLEY TOUR
(☎904-829-3800; www.trolleytours.com; 167 San Marco Ave; adult/child $23/10) These old-fashioned orange-and-green trolleys chug through town all day, letting visitors on and off at different sights, narrating as they go. They also do a fun Ghosts and Graves nighttime tour ($26/14).

St Augustine Eco Tours KAYAK TOUR
(☎904-377-7245; www.staugustineecotours.com; 111 Avenida Menendez; adult/child $45/35; ☺midmorning & dusk) This eco-outfitter has certified naturalists who take kayakers on 3-mile ecology trips. If you don't feel like paddling, its 1½-hour boat tours explore the estuary

and use hydrophones to search for bottlenose dolphins. A portion of profits goes to environmental organizations.

St Augustine Sightseeing Trains TRAIN TOUR
(☎904-829-6545; www.redtrains.com; 170 San Marco Ave; adult/child $22/9) Get around in distinctive fire-engine-red trains. You can get on and off as often as you like at any of 20 stops.

Victory III Scenic Cruises BOAT TOUR
(☎904-824-1806; www.scenic-cruise.com; adult/child $17/10; ☺11am, 1pm, 2:45pm & 4:30pm year-round, plus evening cruises spring-fall) Narrated 1¼-hour waterfront cruises, leaving from the Municipal Marina, just south of the Bridge of Lions.

🛏 Sleeping

The most atmospheric rooms are in historic downtown St Augustine, an area which boasts more than two dozen elegant B&Bs; check www.staugustineinns.com. The beach has some nice spots, too. St Augustine is a popular weekend escape for Florida residents, so expect room rates to rise about 30% on Friday and Saturday; often there's a required minimum two-night stay. Summer rates tend to be higher than winter rates.

Inexpensive motels and chain hotels dot San Marco Ave, near where it meets US Hwy 1.

At Journey's End B&B $$
(☎904-829-0076; www.atjourneysend.com; 89 Cedar St; r $129-219; ❄☎💻🐾) Free from the

---

ST AUGUSTINE FOR CHILDREN

So maybe visiting historical homes and shopping for antiques isn't quite your kids' cup of tea? Don't wait for a temper tantrum to happen – St Augustine's got plenty of diversions for the pint-sized traveler. Here are a few ideas:

» Shiver yer timbers at the **Pirate and Treasure Museum** (p331), though the scary animatronic pirates (like a cackling, decapitated Blackbeard) might scare the littlest travelers

» Ride the choo-choos with the cherry-red **St Augustine Sightseeing Trains** (p334)

» Go waaaay beyond cherry-orange-lime at the **Hyppo** (p336), a wild and wacky popsicle shop with flavors like lavender lemonade and the Elvis Presley (banana, peanut butter, honey)

» Watch the soldiers in costumes and listen to the cannons fire at **Castillo de San Marcos** (p331)

» Squeal at the shrunken heads and other 'true' oddities at **Ripley's Believe It or Not!** (p331)

» See the scary gators devour their lunches at the **Alligator Farm Zoological Park** (p333)

Notorious throughout the Caribbean and Americas, pirates routinely ransacked St Augustine, given its vulnerable seaside location. Laying in wait along the coast, pirates would pounce on silver- and gold-laden fleets returning to Europe from Mexico and South America. When ships weren't around, they'd simply raid the town (which was home to the Spanish Royal Treasurer for Florida, no less).

Among the many brutal attacks on St Augustine was Sir Francis Drake's raid in June 1586, when he and his cohort pillaged the township before burning it down. Perhaps even more violent was Jamaican pirate Robert Searle's attack in 1668. After capturing a Spanish ship, Searle and crew went on a plundering and killing spree. No one was safe: one of Searle's victims was a five-year-old girl, whose ghost, it's said, haunted him to madness and ultimately suicide.

Both these events are meticulously reenacted every year in St Augustine. Participants must conform to rigid requirements including no skull-and-crossbones emblems (they weren't used regularly by pirates until the early 1700s); no polyester or modern items of any kind, including eyeglasses and wristwatches; and no 'silly plumes.' If you're interested in participating, get thee to St Augustine in March (to reenact Searle's raid) or June (for Drake's). For more information, log on to www.searlesbucs.com.

Other local pirate activities include September's 'Talk Like a Pirate Day' (www.talk likeapirate.com), a global event that particularly shivers timbers in this place, and October/November's Saint Arrrgustine's Pirate Gathering (www.pirategathering.com).

granny-ish decor that haunts many St Augustine B&Bs, this pet-friendly, kid-friendly, gay-friendly spot was recently purchased by a pair of hospitable Bostonian gentlemen, who have outfitted it in a chic mix of antiques and modern furniture. Guests crowd around the rustic wooden breakfast table each morning for eggs Benedict and apple-toffee French toast, before taking off for sightseeing downtown, just a block away.

St Francis Inn INN $$$
(☎904-824-6068, 800-824-6062; www.stfrancisinn.com; 79 St George St; r $159-299; ❀🐾) Looking like something out of Chaucer, St Augustine's oldest inn has been in continuous operation since 1791. Crushed-coquina-shell and ancient wood-beam architecture create a Ye Olde Guesthouse ambience, abetted by open fireplaces, a maze of antique-filled nooks and crannies, beds with handmade quilts, and a lush walled courtyard. A short stroll from downtown, it's a good choice for those who crave quiet. Best of all? Free local wine and a full menu of complimentary desserts every evening.

🌿 Casa Monica HOTEL $$$
(☎904-827-1888, 800-648-1888; www.casamonica.com; 95 Cordova St; r $179-779; ❀🐾🏊) Built in 1888 and superbly restored in 1999, this colossal turreted landmark encompasses St Augustine's finest digs and is worth a stop even if you're not sleeping here. Through the grand carriage entrance are a spectacular lobby, expansive swimming pool, fountains, gourmet restaurants, shops...as well as richly appointed suites with wrought-iron beds, ceramic-tiled bathrooms, mahogany furnishings, imported feather duvets and every amenity you can imagine. It's also designated a Green Lodging by the state of Florida.

Casa de Solana B&B $$
(☎877-824-3555; www.casadesolana.com; 21 Aviles St; r $129-249; ❀🐾) Just off pedestrian-only Aviles St in the oldest and narrowest part of town, step through a jasmine-hung gateway into the courtyard of this utterly charming little inn. Built in the early 1800s, the inn remains faithful to its time period with a colonial blue-and-yellow color scheme, exposed beams and antique striped textiles. Rooms are a bit small and dim, but consider their price point and location.

Pirate Haus Inn HOSTEL $
(☎904-808-1999; www.piratehaus.com; 32 Treasury St; dm $20, r $50-95; ❀🐾🚲) Famed for its free all-you-can-eat 'pirate pancake' breakfast, this family-friendly hostel has light, bright rooms, a full kitchen, rooftop barbecue, bike rentals...all in what is arrrrghuably the best downtown location possible (parking is limited, however). Innkeeper 'Captain' Conrad is a wealth of local info, matey. Dig that staircase.

DON'T MISS

WORLD'S BEST POPSICLES

On steamy St Augustine afternoons, skip the mediocre ye olde ice-cream shops lining St George St and seek out the **Hyppo** (www.thehyppo.com; 15 Hypolita St; popsicles $3.50; ☺11am-10pm), a slip of a popsicle shop with an ever-changing whiteboard menu of outrageous flavors – pineapple-cilantro, rice pudding, Kick (an energising blend of espresso, green tea AND chocolate). Keep your eyes open for anything containing datil pepper, a high-octane local chili beloved by Spanish settlers (it goes great with strawberry).

Bayfront Marin House — INN $$$

(☎904-824-4301; www.bayfrontmarinhouse.com; 142 Avenida Menendez; r incl breakfast $119-299; ❋☂❂) Created by joining three old houses, this buttercup-yellow waterfront inn is dominated by a bi-level wraparound porch with a commanding view of Matanzas Bay. Rooms are plush and classic, with four-poster beds and lots of rich brocades – for character, choose a room in the 1700s-era wing, with cool crushed-coquina-shell walls.

Conch House — MOTEL $$

(☎904-829-8646; www.conch-house.com; 57 Comares Ave; r $95-275; ❋☂❂) Party-happy boaters love this festive Key West-y motel, with rooms facing the 200-slip marina, an always-packed patio bar, and a pool deck perfect for beer-sipping. It's minutes from either downtown or the beach.

Beachfront B&B — B&B $$$

(☎904-461-8727, 800-233-2746; www.beachfrontbandb.com; 1 F St; r $189-289; ❋☂❂) For people who like seasides more than cityscapes, this sunny modern beach house – with canopy beds, rich pine floors (in some rooms) and private heated pool – is perfect. Steps from the beach, most of the rooms have fireplaces and private entrances.

Anastasia State Recreation Area — CAMPGROUND $

(1340 Hwy A1A; sites $28) Beautiful campground, spotless facilities. It's five minutes' drive from downtown off Ocean Blvd.

Eating

St Augustine has one of the best eating scenes in Florida, providing you know where to go, and which overcrowded, over-priced tourist traps to avoid.

TOP CHOICE Floridian — MODERN AMERICAN $$

(☎904-829-0655; www.thefloridianstaug.com; 39 Cordova St; mains $12-20; ☺11am-3pm & 5-9pm Mon & Wed-Fri, to 10pm Sat & Sun, closed Tue) Though it oozes hipster-locavore earnestness, this new farm-to-table restaurant is so friggin' fabulous you won't even want to roll your eyes. The chef-owners scour every corner of North Florida for produce, meat and fish, which they turn into whimsical neo-Southern creations – fried-green-tomato bruschetta with local goat cheese, Vietnamese *bahn mi* sandwiches with acorn-fed pork, catch-of-the-day with Florida citrus–sweet potato salsa. The dining room is oh-so-cool, with vintage turquoise Formica tables, mismatched chandeliers and an old rowboat suspended from the ceiling like modern art.

TOP CHOICE Spanish Bakery — BAKERY $

(www.thespanishbakery.com; 42 1/2 St George St; mains $3-5.50; ☺9:30am-3pm) Through an arched gate, this diminutive stucco bakeshop (a reproduction of the 17th-century original) sits in the middle of a picnic table–filled courtyard. Get in line to order your empanada, sausage roll or other conquistador-era favorites, then sit down under the shady trees to eat your goodies slathered in hot sauce. Double back for a bag of lemon, almond or cinnamon cookies before you go. Hurry – when they're sold out, you're out of luck.

Present Moment Café — VEGAN $$

(www.thepresentmomentcafe.com; 224 W King St; mains $7-15; ☺10am-9pm Mon-Sat) Dishing up 'Kind Cuisine,' this folksy restaurant only serves vegan and raw food. Its organic dishes burst with flavor, live enzymes and nutrients and won't leave you feeling bloated – unless you order a second chocolate marble torte with drunken banana.

Casa Maya — MEXICAN $$

(17 Hypolita St; mains $6-18; ☺10am-3:30pm & 5:30-9pm Wed-Thu, 8am-3:30pm & 5:30-9pm Fri-Sun, 8am-3:30pm Mon; ☂) Snappy jazz wafts through the jasmine-shaded patio of this vegetarian-friendly Mayan (or Northern Central American) restaurant. The Mayan wrap features (oddly, but tastily) hummus and feta, and comes with organic chips.

Most dishes incorporate local ingredients. Don't miss the hibiscus sangria!

Collage INTERNATIONAL $$$
(📞904-829-0055; www.collagestaug.com; 60 Hypolita St; mains $26-36; ⊗5:30pm-close) Inside the cool, terracotta-walled dining room of this upscale eclectic spot, you'll feel a world away from the heat and bustle of touristy downtown. The seafood-heavy menu wins raves for its subtle touch with global flavors – hand-cut beef tenderloin with tamarind sauce, Mexican shrimp with garlic and chili. Service can be a bit hover-y, but otherwise lovely.

Local Heroes SANDWICHES $
(www.localheroescafe.com; 11 Spanish St; mains $3.50-8; ⊗11am-late Tue-Fri, from noon Sat & Sun) This blue 1820s bungalow has hot sandwiches, frosty brews, a cool back porch shaded by a massive oak and an awesome Curtis Mayfield collection. A fun way to jump from the 1570s to the 1970s.

Bunnery Café BAKERY $
(121 St George St; mains $4-7; ⊗8am-6pm) The friendly staff at this bakery pour frosting on your cinnamon rolls to your specs. Strudels, panini and fat, wedge-shaped scones are all hits. Expect major lines at midday.

Gypsy Cab Co FUSION $$
(📞904-824-8244; www.gypsycab.com; 828 Anastasia Blvd; mains $15-22; ⊗4:30-10pm Sun-Thu, to 11pm Fri & Sat, lunch 11am-3pm Mon-Sat, brunch 10:30am-3pm Sun) Across the bridge from downtown, this arty turquoise-and-purple bistro is a local fave for an eclectic menu spanning Italian pastas, French strip steaks, Asian tofu and Middle Eastern hummus platters.

Mango Mango's CARIBBEAN $$
(www.mangomangoesstaug.com; 700 A1A; mains $12-25; ⊗11am-10pm) It's hard not to be charmed by this cheery lime- and coral-colored beach bistro, with a menu of likeable Caribbean-fusion fare – crunchy coconut shrimp, chicken with mango sauce, tons of sandwiches and wraps.

La Herencia Café CUBAN $$
(www.laherenciacafe.com; 4 Aviles St; mains $12-25; ⊗9am-6pm, to 8pm Fri & Sat) On St Aug's oldest street, this brightly painted Cuban cafe serves breakfast all day and killer Cuban sandwiches. Relax here with a cup of *café con leche*, just like in Old Havana.

🍷 Drinking & Entertainment

🏆TOP CHOICE Taberna del Gallo BAR
(53 St George St; ⊗2-9:30pm Thu-Sat, noon-7pm Sun) Sans electricity, only flickering candles light this 1736 tavern, which serves beer and wine to guests in the stone-walled interior and outdoor courtyard. On weekend nights the Bilge Rats sing sea shanties that get progressively bawdier.

Scarlett O'Hara's PUB
(www.scarlettoharas.net; 70 Hypolita St; ⊗11am-1am) Good luck grabbing a rocking chair: the porch of this pine building is packed all day, every day. Built in 1879, today Scarlett's serves regulation pub grub, but it's got the magic ingredients – hopping happy hour, live entertainment nightly, hardworking staff, funky bar – that draw folks like spirits to a séance.

A1A Ale Works PUB
(www.a1aaleworks.com; 1 King St; ⊗11am-11:30pm Sun-Thu, to midnight Fri & Sat) Sidle up to the copper bar and order a Bridge of Lions Brown Ale or A Strange Stout (named for the founder's granddad). Though it lacks the historical ambience that makes St Augustine special, the beers brewed here are spectacular.

TradeWinds Lounge LOUNGE
(www.tradewindslounge.com; 124 Charlotte St; ⊗11am-1am) Tiny bathrooms and big hairdos rule this nautical-themed dive. Smelling sweetly of stale beer, this classic bar's survived two locations and six decades. Crowds tumble out the door during happy hour, and there's live music – mostly Southern rock or '80s music – nightly.

Mill Top Tavern LIVE MUSIC
(www.milltop.com; 19½ St George St; ⊗11:30am-1am) Grooving to live music at the open-air Mill Top, on the 2nd story of a 19th-century mill that's hugged by a huge oak, is like hanging out in a treehouse – one that has a full bar and kitchen.

Café Eleven LIVE MUSIC
(www.cafeeleven.com; 501 Hwy A1A; ⊗7am-9pm) At night, the tables of this slick beach cafe get shoved aside and the place transmogrifies into a theater for some of indie rock's biggest names.

JP Henley's PUB
(www.jphenleys.com; 10 Marine St; ⊗11am-1am) With 50 beers on tap, 120 more in the bottle and over 75 bottles of wine, this place will

WORTH A TRIP

PALATKA

In its heyday, the village of Palatka (pronounced puhl-*at*-kuh), about 30 miles west of St Augustine, was the furthest south you could travel by steamship and boasted more than 7000 hotel rooms for wealthy snowbirds. Today, visitors are trickling back to this sweet, sleepy-verging-on-comatose town for fishing, Memorial weekend's blue-crab festival, and simply to get away from the coastal crowds.

Spend a pleasant afternoon exploring the Bronson-Mulholland House (100 Madison St; noon-5pm Thu-Mon), an 1854 historic mansion turned house museum, or crossing the swinging suspension footbridge through Ravine Gardens State Park (1600 Twig St; per car $5).

Don't leave without a stop at deliciously retro Angel's Dining Car (209 Reid St; mains $2.50-8; 6am-8pm Sun-Thu, to midnight Fri), serving cheeseburgers and Pusalow (an only-in-Palatka drink of chocolate milk with vanilla syrup and crushed ice) directly to patrons' cars since 1932.

---

appeal to even the most discriminating beer or wine snob. Great music, too.

🛍 Shopping

Meandering through the town's antique shops could take days; contact Antique Dealers Association of St Augustine (www.adasta.org) for advice on collectibles.

St George Street   SHOPPING DISTRICT
This 11-block stretch of pedestrian shopping, eating and entertainment is the heart of Old Spanish St Augustine. Look for everything from souvenir shops hawking pirate shot glasses to elegant antiques stores.

Aviles Street   SHOPPING STREET
Opposite the plaza from St George St, this tiny pedestrian-only alleyway has some wonderfully dusty map shops and art galleries.

St Augustine Premium Outlets   OUTLET MALL
(www.premiumoutlets.com; 2700 State Rd; 9am-9pm Mon-Sat, to 6pm Sun) Name brands like Gap, Banana Republic, Nike and more, at steep discounts. The outlets are a 15-minute drive from downtown along FL-16.

St Augustine Outlets   OUTLET MALL
(www.staugoutlets.com; 500 Prime Outlets Blvd; 9am-9pm Mon-Sat, to 6pm Sun) Dozens of name brands, including Saks, BCBG and Kate Spade, just down the street from St Augustine Premium Outlets. The outlets are a 15-minute drive from downtown along FL-16.

Hot Stuff Mon   FOOD
(34 Treasury St; 10am-6pm) Dozens of types of hot sauce made from St Augustine's fa-

mous datil pepper and other great gifts for foodies.

ℹ Information

INTERNET ACCESS **Public Library** (1960 N Ponce de León Blvd; 10am-8pm Mon-Wed, to 6pm Thu & Fri, to 5pm Sat) Free internet access.

MEDIA The daily **St Augustine Record** (www .staugustinerecord.com) has good visitor information on its website. The free **Folio Weekly** (www.folioweekly.com) has events information, restaurant and bar listings every Tuesday.

TOURIST INFORMATION **Visitor Information Center** (904-825-1000; www.ci.st-augustine .fl.us; 10 Castillo Dr; 8:30am-5:30pm) Helpful, period-dressed staff sell tour tickets (see p334).

ℹ Getting There & Around

Driving from the north, take I-95 exit 318 and head east past US Hwy 1 to San Marcos Ave; turn right and you'll end up at the Old City Gate, just past the fort. Alternately, you can take Hwy A1A along the beach, which intersects with San Marco Ave, or US Hwy 1 south from Jacksonville. From the south, take exit 298, merge onto US 1 and follow it into town.

Cars are a nightmare downtown with one-way and pedestrian-only streets and severely limited parking; outside the city center, you'll need wheels.

If you're flying into Jacksonville, **Airport Express** (904-824-9400; www.airportexpress pickup.com) charges $65 to drop you downtown. For an additional $20, it'll take you to your hotel. Reservations required.

The **Sunshine Bus Company** (www.sunshinebus .net) runs approximately 7am to 6pm and serves downtown, the beaches and the outlet malls, as well as many points in between ($1 one way).

Try **Solano Cycles** (☏904-825-6766; www
.solanocycle.com; 32 San Marco Ave) for bikes
($18 per day) and scooters ($80 per day).

Jacksonville

904 / POP 813,500

At a whopping 840 sq miles, Jacksonville is
the largest city by area in the continental US
and the fourth largest in the world. Sprawling along three meandering rivers, with
sweeping bridges and twinkling city lights
reflected in the water, it's got a brash big-city
charm. While all the high-rises, corporate
banking offices and chain hotels sometimes
make Jacksonville feel a bit soulless, its
sweet Southern heart will reveal itself to the
patient explorer.

Though most visitors see the city as
merely a jumping-off spot for points further north or south, Jacksonville's museums
and restored historic districts are worth
a wander. The Five Points and San Marco
neighborhoods are both charming, walkable areas lined with bistros, boutiques and
bars, and feel worlds away from the buzzing downtown. The Jax beaches – a world
unto themselves – are a half-hour drive from
the city, much longer if there's traffic (and
there's ALWAYS traffic in Jacksonville), so if
the ocean's your main destination, plan on
staying there.

◉ Sights

⎡TOP⎤
⎣CHOICE⎦ **Cummer Museum of Art &**
Gardens   MUSEUM
(www.cummer.org; 829 Riverside Ave; adult/student
$10/6, 4-9pm Tue free; ⊙10am-9pm Tue, to 5pm
Wed-Sat, noon-5pm Sun) This handsome mu-

seum, Jacksonville's premier cultural space,
has a genuinely excellent collection of American and European paintings, Asian decorative art and antiquities. Look out for works
of local interest, including Thomas Moran's
'Ponce de León in Florida' painting, and
Winslow Homer's portrait of the St John's
River. The garden, draped with wisteria and
shaded by a massive, mossy oak so large it
needs supports for its limbs, is a grand place
to unwind after absorbing all the beauty inside. Both the museum and gardens are im-
pressively accessible, including a number of
Braille and audio guides.

Jacksonville Zoological Gardens   ZOO
(www.jacksonvillezoo.org; 370 Zoo Parkway; adult/
child $22/15; ⊙9am-5pm; ⓘ) Northeast Flori-
da's only major zoo opened in 1914 with one
deer; today, it's home to over 1800 exotic
animals. Jaguar football fans won't want to
miss jaguars prowling replicated Mayan-
temple ruins. Other highlights include the
wetlands of Wild Florida, with rare Florida
panthers, and an elevated viewing platform
that brings you face to nose with giraffes.
The zoo is about 15 minutes north of downtown off I-95.

Anheuser-Busch
Budweiser Brewery   BREWERY
(www.budweisertours.com; 111 Busch Dr; ⊙10am-
4pm Mon-Sat) Equal parts history and propa-
ganda, a tour at the brewery is nevertheless
a fascinating look at how this plant produces
8.4 million barrels (or 2.7 trillion bottles!) of
beer each year. Highlights include learning
about the factory's sustainable manufacturing practices and (if you're over 21) sampling
free Bud products while watching classic

JACKSONVILLE: ORIENTATION

As big as it is, Jacksonville can be a bit tricky to navigate. A few things to know:

» Jacksonville is trisected by a very rough T formed by the St John's River. Downtown
Jacksonville is on the west side of the St John's.

» I-95 comes in straight from the north to a junction just south of downtown with I-10.
Follow I-10 east into downtown, where a maze of state highways offers access to surrounding areas.

» Three bridges cross the river and will take you to San Marco: Fuller Warren (I-10),
Acosta (Hwy 13) and Main St Bridge.

» I-295 breaks off from I-95, forming a circle around the city.

» Though the city is enormous, most sites of interest to the visitor are concentrated
along the St John's River's narrowest point: downtown; Five Points, just south of downtown along the river; and the elegant San Marco Historical District along the southern
shore.

NORTHEAST FLORIDA ATLANTIC COAST

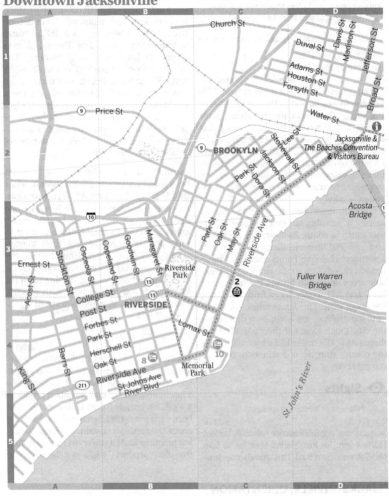

Bud commercials. Dude! Free tours depart on the half hour. The brewery is 15 minutes north of downtown off I-95.

Jacksonville Museum of Modern Art
MUSEUM

(www.mocajacksonville.org; 333 N Laura St; adult/senior $8/5; ⊘10am-4pm Tue-Sat, to 9pm Thu, noon-4pm Sun) The focus of this ultra-modern space extends beyond painting: in the cavernous white halls, you'll get lost in sculpture, prints, photography and film in excellent rotating exhibits of post-1945 creations.

Museum of Science & History   MUSEUM

(MOSH; www.themosh.org; 1025 Museum Circle; adult/child $10/8; ⊘10am-5pm Mon-Fri, to 6pm Sat, 1-6pm Sun; ⚐) Enlightening exhibits about Jacksonville's pre-Columbian history and Spanish, French and US settlements fill this museum, along with a comprehensive natural history of the St John's River system, one of the few rivers in the world that flow north.

Admission is also good for the **Brian Gooding Planetarium**, which shows your traditional sky and space fare, plus kids' movies and the occasional rock 'n' light show.

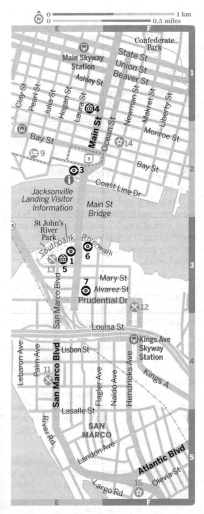

Downtown Jacksonville

this densely packed museum has an array of nautical artifacts, scale models and shipping logs.

Jacksonville Landing   PROMENADE
(www.jacksonvillelanding.com; 2 Independent Dr) At the foot of the high-rise downtown, this prominent shopping and entertainment district has about 40 mostly touristy shops surrounding a tip-top food court with outdoor tables and regular, free live entertainment.

🏃 Activities

With 72 golf courses in the greater area, there are plenty of opportunities to tee off. You can browse course summaries by visiting www.visitjacksonville.com and following the links to 'visitors,' then 'golf.'

🛏 Sleeping

Jacksonville's nontouristy status does mean a serious dearth of interesting nonchain hotels. You'll find the cheapest rooms along I-95 and I-10, where the lower-priced chains congregate. Nice mid-price chains crowd the top end of San Marcos, just across the river from downtown. Additional accommodations options, including camping and some swanky resorts, are available at the beaches.

Southbank Riverwalk   PROMENADE
This 1.2-mile boardwalk, on the south side of the St John's River, opposite downtown and Jacksonville Landing, has spectacular views of the city's skyline. Most nights yield head-shakingly beautiful scenes, but firework displays are a real blast. The Southbank Riverwalk connects the museums flanking Museum Circle and makes a pleasant promenade.

Jacksonville Maritime Museum   MUSEUM
(www.jaxmaritimemuseum.org; 2 Independent Dr; admission by donation; ☉10:30am-3pm Mon-Fri, 1-5pm Sat & Sun) For insight into how maritime history intertwines with this port city,

LOCAL ODDITY: THE TREATY OAK

At first glance, it looks like a small forest is growing in the middle of the concrete on Jacksonville's south side. But upon closer inspection you'll see that the 'forest' is really one single enormous tree, with a trunk circumference of 25ft and a shade diameter of nearly 200ft. According to local lore, the live oak tree is the oldest thing in Jacksonville – its age is estimated to be 250 years. You'll find the super-tree in Jesse Ball duPont Park (1123 Prudential Dr).

TOP CHOICE Inn at Oak Street   B&B **$$**

(☏904-379-5525; www.innatoakstreet.com; 2114 Oak St; r $120-165; ❋☎) This gabled three-story 1902 house, with views of the St John's River, is now a peaceful B&B with loads of upscale touches. Six individually decorated rooms are handsome and unfussy, with heart pine floors, understated antiques and personal wine cabinets (!). For a whimsical view, book the Treehouse Room, with a window looking right into the leaves of a grand live oak. Savor strawberry crepes and fresh scones for breakfast, then work off the carbs at the Snap Fitness gym across the street – all guests get a free pass.

Riverdale Inn   B&B **$$**

(☏904-354-5080; www.riverdaleinn.com; 1521 Riverside Ave; r $120-220; ❋☎) Elegant as can be, this tall, handsome Victorian has 10 rooms with tasteful antique furniture, vintage botanical prints and warm lighting. There's a clubby, English-style bar downstairs, and a full breakfast served in the light-drenched dining room. Since the inn caters mostly to business travelers, rates are cheaper on weekends.

Omni Jacksonville Hotel   HOTEL **$$**

(☏904-355-6664; 245 Water St; r from $150; ❋☎❄☎) Within sight of Jax Landing, this 354-room hotel has lavish, amenity-laden rooms (some with wheelchair access), acres of marble, a heated rooftop pool and, best of all, free video games – just perfect for decompressing. Small pets are allowed.

✖ Eating & Drinking

The Five Points neighborhood, southwest of downtown, and the San Marco neighborhood, across the river from downtown, both have tons of trendy cafes and bars with outdoor seating. The city's suit-and-tie financial industry means lots of steakhouses and upscale bistros.

TOP CHOICE Aix   MEDITERRANEAN, FRENCH **$$$**

(☏904-398-1949; www.bistrox.com; 1440 San Marco Blvd; mains $14-28; ☉11am-10pm Mon-Thu, to 11pm Fri, 5-11pm Sat, 5-9pm Sun) Bankers and Beautiful People dine on fashionably fusiony Mediterranean dishes at Aix, whose location – inside a nearly unmarked brick building in an ungentrified area of San Marco – adds to its charm. The menu bursts with global flavors – start with, say, Moroccan lamb meatballs, move on to white-truffle pizza, then finish with locally raised duck with mushroom bread pudding. Reservations recommended; service can be slow.

Casbah   MEDITERRANEAN, HOOKAH **$$**

(www.thecasbahcafe.com; 3628 St Johns Ave; mains $8-15; ☉11am-2am) Upon spying the swords,

WORLD'S WEIRDEST RESTAURANT: CLARK'S FISH CAMP

When we say the words 'America's largest private taxidermy collection,' do you A) cringe in disgust or, B), exclaim 'Seriously?! Where?!' If the answer is B, then head straight into the wilds of sub-suburban south Jacksonville to **Clark's Fish Camp** (www.clarks fishcamp.com; 12903 Hood Landing Rd; mains $13-22; ☉5:30-9:30pm Mon-Fri, from 11:30am Sat & Sun). The freakish love child of Tim Burton and Mr Kurtz from *Heart of Darkness*, this massive swamp-side wooden shack is presumably a restaurant, but, bizarre as the menu is (gator, smoked eel, fried snake and frogs' legs all make appearances amid more prosaic offerings like catfish and steak), its strangeness pales in comparison to the decor. Taxidermied monkeys prowl the ceiling. Leopards glare glassily from the corners. Bears and deer stand together in implausibly peaceful tableaus. Flayed gators decorate the bar. A white tiger stands in the center of the dining room, his mouth open in an eternal snarl. If this grotesque menagerie puts you off your food, you can always sit outside by the murky water. But a word to the wise: don't feed the gators.

camels and Moorish lanterns lining the walls, you'll wonder if a passport is required for entry. Featuring authentic Middle Eastern dishes, beer, music and belly dancing, the cafe doubles as a hookah lounge with dozens of flavorful tobacco concoctions. A favorite for young hipster types. Casbah is in the Avondale neighborhood, just southwest of the main downtown area.

bb's FUSION $$
(☎904-306-0100; www.bbsrestaurant.com; 1019 Hendricks Ave; mains $12-29; ☉11am-10:30pm Mon-Thu, to midnight Fri & Sat) With its molded-concrete bar, clean, modern lines and daily cheese selection, this Euro-staurant may initially feel hipper-than-thou. But pull up a seat, chat with the staff and discover they're just like you – only dressed entirely in black. The chocolate ganache cake alone is worth the trip.

River City Brewing Company SEAFOOD $$$
(☎904-398-2299; www.rivercitybrew.com; 835 Museum Circle; mains $18-30; ☉10am-3pm & 5-10pm Mon-Sat, 10:30am-2:30pm Sun) Panoramic river views compete with upscale, globally influenced seafood dishes at this restaurant-brewery. At night, the brewhouse draws an after-work crowd eager to unwind.

☆ Entertainment

Florida Theatre THEATER
(www.floridatheatre.com; 1128 E Forsyth St) Home to Elvis' first indoor concert in 1956, which a local judge endured to ensure Presley was not overly suggestive, this opulent 1927 venue is an intimate place to catch big-name musicians, musicals and movies.

San Marco Theatre CINEMA
(www.sanmarcotheatre.com; 1996 San Marco Blvd; adult/child $7/5) A landmark 1938 art-deco creation where you can order beer, wine, pizza and sandwiches while watching a flick.

❶ Information

Florida Times-Union (www.times-union.com) Conservative daily paper; Friday's *Weekend* magazine features family-oriented events listings.

Folio Weekly (www.folioweekly.com) Free; with club, restaurant and events listings. Found all over town.

Jacksonville Public Library (303 N Laura St; ☉9am-8pm Mon-Thu, to 6pm Fri & Sat, 1-6pm Sun) Free wi-fi.

Out in the City Covers Jacksonville's gay and lesbian scene. Found all over town.

GAY HOT SPOT: METRO

Metro (www.metrojax.com; 2929 Plum St), Jacksonville's top gay entertainment complex, has a disco, a cruise bar, a piano bar, a games room with pinball machines, a smoke-free chill-out loft, a leathery boiler room and a show bar. The club is a five-minute drive southwest of the main downtown.

Visit Jacksonville (☎904-798-9111, 800-733-2668; www.visitjacksonville.com; 550 Water St, Suite 1000; ☉8am-5pm Mon-Fri)

❶ Getting There & Around

Jacksonville International Airport (JAX; ☎904-741-4902; www.jia.aero;) is served by major and regional airlines as well as major car-rental companies. The airport's about 18 miles north of downtown on I-95, off the Airport Rd exit; a cab to downtown costs about $32.

The **Greyhound bus station** (10 Pearl St) is at the west end of downtown. The **Amtrak station** (3570 Clifford Lane) is 5 miles northwest of downtown.

The **Jacksonville Transportation Authority** (www.jtafla.com) runs buses and trolleys in town and the beaches (fare $1), as well as a scenic, if underused, river-crossing skyway.

Jacksonville Area Beaches

☎904 / POP 22,000

The stretches of beaches closest to Jacksonville are delightfully sparse. Moving from south to north, Ponte Vedra Beach is the posh home of the ATP and PGA tours, with golf resorts and courses. Urban Jacksonville Beach is where to go for a party, while cozy Neptune Beach is more subdued. And if you want some sand to yourself, Atlantic Beach, with several entrances off Seminole Beach Rd, is sublime.

❷ Sights & Activities

Most of the action is concentrated at Jacksonville Beach, which buzzes all summer (and most of the mild winter, too).

Constructed from removable planks, allowing it to be dismantled in the event of a hurricane, the 1300ft **pier** (www.jacksonville beachpier.com; 503 N 1st St; walk-on/fishing $1/4; ☉6am-10pm) has a bait shop, concessions and fish-cleaning stations. Bring drinks, cast your line and wait for a nibble.

FREEBIRD LIVE

Fans of local-boys-done-good Lynyrd Skynyrd will want to pay homage at **Freebird Live** (www.freebirdlive.com; 200 N 1st St, Jacksonville Beach; ⊙8pm-2am Wed-Sat), a two-story music venue with wide verandas owned by the Van Zant family. The band's founding lead singer, Ronnie Van Zant, and many of his bandmates died in a 1977 plane crash; his younger brother Johnny took his place when the band reformed a decade later.

With two original members still in the lineup, Skynyrd rocks this joint when they're not touring; there's plenty of memorabilia, too. But the Freebird is way more than a shrine. With an intimate stage and great acoustics, it has carved out a reputation as one of the nation's best small music venues. In addition to giving local talent a stage, past acts have included Willie Nelson, the Killers and George Clinton.

If the lure of the water is just too great, swing by **Atlantic Watersports** (☎904-270-0200; www.atlantic-watersports.com; 2327 Beach Blvd; all vessels 1/4/8hr $79/229/349), which rents 14ft fishing boats, 19ft bowriders, 24ft pontoon boats and three-person jet skis.

The roads are flat and the towns are small: why not rent a bike? In addition to various beach and water-sports equipment, **RentBeachStuff** (☎904-305-6472; www.rentbeachstuff.com) will deliver a 26in beach cruiser to your hotel for $30 per day.

🛏 Sleeping

TOP CHOICE **One Ocean Hotel, Resort & Spa** HOTEL $$$
(☎904-249-7402; www.oneoceanresort.com; 1 Ocean Blvd, Atlantic Beach; r $180-370; ❋🌐≋) New in 2008, the One Ocean rocks a flashy South Beach look – tons of white marble, rippling iridescent walls, mod installation art in the lobby. All-white rooms are classy and contemporary, shot through with touches of silver and pewter and sea green. Dig the blue-lit stone tunnel leading to Azurea Restaurant, consistently rated as one of the beach's top fine-dining spots. Oh, and the oceanfront spa...yummy.

Fig Tree B&B B&B $$
(☎904-246-8855; www.figtreeinn.com; 185 4th Ave, Jacksonville Beach; r $145-175; ❋🌐) This rustic cedar-shingle cottage conceals six rooms, including the quirky Bird Room, with a handmade willow-frame queen-size bed and willow reading chair. In addition to breakfast (fully cooked on weekends, self-serve weekdays), it does afternoon tea on the shady porch.

🌿 **Lodge at Ponte Vedra** RESORT $$$
(☎904-285-1111; www.pontevedra.com; 100 Ponte Vedra Blvd, Ponte Vedra; r $250-500; ❋🌐≋) Well-heeled families love this opulent Mediterranean-style resort, where kids play by the pool while the grownups enjoy a much-needed beachfront massage. Rooms and suites are plush and airy, with tasteful sage-and-sand decor and super-luxe granite-and-marble bathrooms.

Sea Horse Oceanfront Inn MOTEL $$
(☎800-881-2330; www.jacksonvilleoceanfronthotel.com; 120 Atlantic Blvd, Neptune Beach; r $119-199; ❋🌐≋) Each room in this Pepto Bismol–colored refurbished motel has a view of both the kidney-shaped pool and the ocean. This is definitely a cut above the average beach motel, with big flat-screen TVs and friendly management.

Casa Marina HOTEL $$
(☎904-270-0025; www.casamarinahotel.com; 691 N 1st St, Jacksonville Beach; r from $139; ❋🌐) Right on the beach, this restored 1925 building is a stunning example of Mediterranean architecture from the days when this stretch of coast was a playground for the rich (check the hallways' framed prints for proof). The jewel-toned rooms are a bit small and dark.

Kathryn Abbey Hanna Park CAMPGROUND $
(☎904-249-4700; 500 Wonderwood Dr, Atlantic Beach; sites $22) In Atlantic Beach, this place has a well-spaced, shady campground 200yd from the ocean with its own freshwater lake. Little Talbot Island State Park (p346) also has camping.

🍴 Eating & Drinking

TOP CHOICE **Singleton's Seafood Shack** SEAFOOD $$
(2728 Ocean St, Mayport; mains $10-19; ⊙10am-10pm) Wedged between a navy base and the mouth of the St John's River is the grubby, industrial fishing village of Mayport, first settled by the Spanish in the late 1500s. Why

come here? One reason: this fabulously divey Old Florida seafood shack, serving up perfectly fried shrimp, Spanish Minorcan chowder, and massive 'seafood boil' pots perfect for sharing. Decor looks like a beach-house rec room, all wood-paneled walls and decorative fishing nets. To get here, just take A1A north until it ends.

Beach Road Chicken Dinners   SOUTHERN $
(www.beachroadchickendinners.com; 4132 Atlantic Blvd; mains $4-11; ⏰take-out from 11am Tue-Sat, dining room from 4pm) When a place has been frying chicken since the 1930s, you can pretty much figure it's got its recipe down. Tear off a chunk of tender thigh meat and wrap it up in one of Beach Road's fluffy biscuits, and you'll understand why people line up every day at this much-loved shack.

European Street   DELI $
(www.europeanstreet.com; 992 Beach Blvd; mains $5-11; ⏰10am-10pm) Sneak away from the beaches at this combination chocolatier, deli, bar (boasting 150 imported beers) and gourmet market, with a huge menu of salads, sandwiches and German fare.

Beach Hut Café   SOUTHERN $
(1281 3rd St S; meals $3-8; ⏰6am-2:30pm) Don't let its strip-mall location deceive you: the food here is divine. Famous for its big, all-day Southern breakfasts, it draws *huge* lines – especially on weekends.

❶ Information

The **Beaches Visitor Center** (☑904-242-0024; www.jacksonvillebeach.org; 380 Pablo Ave, Jacksonville Beach; ⏰10am-4:30pm Tue-Sat) has information about the beaches.

❶ Getting There & Around

Traveling by car from Jacksonville, follow I-10 to Atlantic Beach, and Hwy 90 (Beach Blvd) directly to Jacksonville Beach. Coming from St Augustine, you follow Hwy A1A due north.

Jacksonville Transportation Authority (www.jtafla.com) operates buses from Jacksonville to the beaches ($1.50).

Talbot & Fort George Islands

☑900

Between Jacksonville's beaches and Amelia Island, coastal Hwy A1A laces together the Talbot and Fort George Islands. Shaded by flourishing vegetation, it's a scenic drive

even if you don't stop, but there are several reasons you'll want to: exceptional kayaking, distinctive state parks with natural and human-made wonders, and blissful beach and riverfront camping.

If you're heading north from the Jacksonville Beaches along the A1A, you'll have to jump on the St John's River Ferry (www.stjohnsriverferry.com; per car $5; ⏰every half-hour 6am-7pm).

◉ Sights & Activities

Kingsley Plantation   HISTORIC BUILDING
(www.nps.gov/timu; ⏰9am-5pm) Zephaniah Kingsley moved to this former cotton and citrus plantation in 1814, managing it with his wife, Anna Jai, whom he originally purchased as a slave and later married in a traditional African ceremony, subsequently freeing both her and their children.

Ensuing tussles with the government over racial laws forced Kingsley to send his family to Haiti in 1835. He died in 1843, never having joined them. In 1860 Jai returned to Florida in time to see the Emancipation Proclamation delivered.

Today, the main house is the oldest standing plantation house in Florida. While the main house is undergoing near-constant structural repairs necessitated by termites and humidity, you can tour portions of it as well as the remains of 23 tabby-construction slave cabins. Daily at 2pm, a ranger-led program discusses natural history, slavery and the Kingsleys' lives. It's a nice spot for a picnic.

Fort George Island Cultural State Park   PARK
(12157 Heckscher Dr; ⏰8am-sunset) Laden with history, this state park is part of the Timucuan Ecological and Historic Preserve, which also includes Fort Caroline National Memorial.

Enormous shell middens date the island's habitation by Native Americans to over 5000 years ago. In 1736 British General James Oglethorpe (the founder of Georgia) erected a fort in the area, though it's long since vanished and its exact location is uncertain.

Fort George raged in the '20s when flappers flocked to the ritzy Ribault Club for Gatsby-esque bashes with lawn bowling and yachting. Built in 1928 on top of an indigenous shell mound, this bone-white mansion flaunts grand archways and three dozen sets of cypress French doors. Meticulously restored, the club now hosts private events and houses a visitor center (⊙9am-5pm Wed-Sun). The island's 4.4-mile Saturiwa loop trail, which you can walk, bike or drive, begins and ends here. The visitor center has first-rate historical trail guides, both printed and on CD, allowing you to undertake a self-guided tour at your own pace.

Little Talbot Island State Park   PARK
(12157 Heckscher Dr; per vehicle $5; ⊙8am-sunset) This pristine island, the same size as Big Talbot Island, has 5 miles of unspoiled beaches, extraordinary wildlife (river otters, marsh rabbits, bobcats) and grand tidal fishing for mullet and sheepshead. Kayak Amelia rents kayaks and offers guided trips around the island.

Big Talbot Island State Park   PARK
(A1A N; per vehicle $3; ⊙8am-sunset) Deposit your fee in the blue envelope and pull into the lone parking lot at this stark but lovely park. Take your camera on the short trail to Boneyard Beach, where salt-washed skeletons of live oak and cedar trees litter the white sand, framed by a 20ft bluff of eroded coastline.

Kayak Amelia   NATURE TOURS
(☑904-251-0016; www.kayakamelia.com; 13030 Heckscher Dr; guided trips from $60, kayak rental per day from $47) This top-notch outfitter doles out easy-to-follow instructions, moral support and home-baked chocolate-chip cookies in equal measure. You can rent your own kayak or canoe, or join one of the many guided kayak, paddleboard or bike eco-tours. Of the half-day trips, the standout – tide and current permitting – follows the former trade route of the Fort George River to the Kingsley Plantation, with time to wander the estate during a break from paddling. Feeling starry-eyed? Moonlight paddles through the silvered marsh are a magical way to experience meditative waters. Kids are welcome, but call in advance to make arrangements.

🛏 Sleeping & Eating
Wake up to the waves rolling in at Little Talbot Island State Park campsite (beachfront sites with hookups $24).

Eating is limited to a handful of sandwich shops, or the Sandollar Restaurant & Marina (www.sanddollarrestaurantjax.com; 9716 Heckscher Dr; mains $9-19; ⊙11am-9pm), where you can dine on meat and seafood on a deck over the river.

The closest markets are near the ferry on Fort George Island or on Amelia Island.

Amelia Island
☑904 / POP 12,000

Just 13 miles from the Georgia border, this glorious sea island combines the moss-draped charm of the Deep South with the sun-'n'-fun beach culture of Florida. We can hardly think of a more charming spot, and we're not the only ones – vacationers have been flocking here since the 1890s, when Henry Flagler first tamed the wild east coast and helped convert the area into a playground for the rich. The legacy of that golden era remains visible today in Amelia's central town of Fernandina Beach, with 50 blocks of historic buildings, Victorian B&Bs, and restaurants housed in converted fishing cottages. Dotting the rest of the island are swanky resorts, endless green fairways and miles of shark-tooth-covered shoreline, sealed by a commanding Civil War–era fort surrounded by a quintessentially Southern oak-shaded state park.

⊙ Sights & Activities
Strolling Fernandina Beach's bistro- and boutique-packed historical downtown is one of the main attractions on the island, whose other draws include, of course, the beach, and several parks.

Fort Clinch State Park   PARK
(2601 Atlantic Ave; park pedestrian/car $2/6; ⊙park 8am-sunset, fort 9am-5pm) The US government began constructing Fort Clinch in 1847. State of the art at the time, rapid advancements in military technology rendered its masonry walls obsolete by the Civil War. A Confederate militia occupied the almost-complete fort early in the conflict but evacuated soon after. Federal troops again occupied the fort during WWII, when it served as a surveillance and communications station for the US Coast Guard. Today, the park offers a variety of activities. In addition to a 0.5-mile-long fishing pier, there are also serene beaches for shelling and 6 miles of peaceful, unpaved trails for hiking and cycling.

On the first weekend of the month, authentically outfitted troops perform a re-enactment of the Confederate evacuation that extends to cooking in the old kitchen's massive iron cauldron and sleeping on straw mats in the soldiers' barracks. A candlelight tour ($3) is a treat if you're here May to September; call for reservations.

Amelia Island Museum of History MUSEUM
(www.ameliamuseum.org; 233 S 3rd St; adult/student $7/4; ⊙10am-4pm Mon-Sat, 1-4pm Sun) Housed in the former city jail (1879–1975), Florida's only oral-history museum has tiny but informative exhibits exploring Native American history, the Spanish-mission period, the Civil War and historic preservation. There's also a good overview of the history of water, timber and tourism in the county. Most fun of all is the eight-flags tour, every day at 11am and 2pm, when guides provide lively interpretations of the island's intricate history: eight flags have flown over the island, starting with the French flag in 1562, followed by the Spanish, the English, the Spanish again, the Patriots, the Green Cross of Florida, the Mexican Rebels, the US, the Confederates, then the US again (1821 onward).

Kelly Seahorse Ranch HORSE RIDING
(☑904-491-5166; www.kellyranchinc.com; 1hr rides $60; ⊙10am, noon, 2pm & 4pm) This working ranch also does beachside horseback-riding tours; call in advance for longer trips. You don't need prior riding experience, but children must be at least 13 years old. The ranch is down the path that's the last left turn off Amelia Rd at the southern tip of the island.

Pipeline Surf Shop SURFING
(☑904-277-3717; 2022 1st Ave) From fall through spring when nor'easters bluster through, surfable beach breaks can be common, especially at Main Beach. Pipeline rents all kinds of boards and wetsuits, and gives surf lessons from beginner to advanced.

☞ Tours

Amelia River Cruises BOAT TOUR
(☑904-261-9972; www.ameliarivercruises.com; 1 N Front St, Fernandina Beach; tours from $26) Hop aboard a 33ft riverboat to explore Amelia and nearby Cumberland Island, Georgia, stopping to marvel at plantation ruins and dense tracts of Spanish moss covered–trees.

Old Towne Carriage Company CARRIAGE TOUR
(☑904-556-2662; www.ameliacarriagetours.com; adult/child $15/7.50) Horse carriages clip-clop through the historical downtown, offering hour or half-hour rides.

🛏 Sleeping

Fernandina Beach has a wealth of charming Victorian B&Bs, while beach resorts are scattered across the island. Room rates can rise by 50% during summer and special events.

TOP CHOICE Elizabeth Pointe Lodge INN $$$
(☑904-277-4851, 888-261-6161; www.elizabethpointelodge.com; 98 S Fletcher Ave; r $215-460; ❄☎) Expect fresh flowers, homemade cookies and shelves of worn board games and books in this eccentric old maritime inn. Constructed in an 1890s Nantucket shingle style, the towering lodge is perched on the ocean, yet is only 2 miles from downtown. Rocking chair–lined porches hug the main floor and all the bedrooms have oversized tubs (some have Jacuzzis). The lodge offers buffet breakfast, bike rental and the best seats on the island for beholding a sunrise…if you can struggle out of bed. Adjacent to the main lodge, the new Ocean House has four rooms done up in a luxe West Indian style – hardwood floors, white linens, botanical prints.

TOP CHOICE Fairbanks House B&B $$$
(☑904-277-0500; www.fairbankshouse.com; 227 S 7th St; r $175-265; ❄☎) You could imagine Indiana Jones retiring to a place like this grand, Gothic Victorian, stuffed to the gills with silk carpets, heavy leather-bound books and global knickknacks like a bronze bust of an Egyptian pharaoh. Guest rooms are so large they feel like suites; we especially like the downstairs room carved out of the house's original

DETOUR: CUMBERLAND ISLAND NATIONAL SEASHORE

The largest wilderness island in the US, Cumberland Island (www.nps.gov/cuis) lies just over the Georgia state line. At 17.5 miles long and 3 miles wide, almost half of its 36,415 acres is marshland, mudflats and tidal creeks. Only 300 visitors are allowed on the island, accessible by a 45-minute ferry ride.

Ashore, rangers lead free one-hour tours concluding at the ruins of Thomas and Lucy Carnegie's 1884 mansion, Dungeness. Along the way rangers interpret the rich bird and animal life – including sandpipers, ospreys, painted buntings, nesting loggerhead turtles, armadillos and deer – and detail 4000 years of human history that spans Timucuans, British colonists and Spanish missionaries.

After the Civil War, freed slaves purchased parcels of land at the island's northern end and founded the First African Baptist Church in 1893. The tiny, 11-pew, white-painted wooden church was rebuilt in the 1930s, and the late John Kennedy Jr and Carolyn Bessette were married in it in 1996. It's open to the public, but it's a hefty 15-mile hike from the ferry drop through moss-draped thickets.

The historic village of St Marys (www.stmaryswelcome.com) is the island's charming gateway. Accommodation options on the island range widely, from an opulent mansion to rugged camping. Check the St Marys website for details.

Ferries (912-882-4335; www.nps.gov/cuis; round-trip adult/child $20/14) depart at 9am and 11:45am, returning at 10:15am and 4:45pm (an additional ferry runs at 2:45pm Wednesday to Saturday March to November; no ferries run on Tuesday or Wednesday December to February). Reservations are recommended.

Be sure to come prepared: there are no shops on the island. Bring food, insect repellent and perhaps a camera...or maybe a canvas and paint palette.

From northern Florida, take I-95 north to St Marys Rd exit 1. Turn right onto GA-40/St Marys Rd E and follow it to the end.

1800s kitchen. The upstairs Tower Suite, with a wood-paneled log-cabin ambience, sleeps five, and allows you private use of the glass cupola overlooking the oaks. Other guests will have to make do with the small pool and butterfly garden in the backyard.

Addison   B&B $$
(904-277-1606, 800-943-1604; www.addisononamelia.com; 614 Ash St; r $145-220; ❄️📶) Built in 1876, the Addison has modern upgrades (whirlpool tubs, deluge showers, Turkish-cotton towels and wi-fi) that'll trick you into thinking it was finished last week. While many B&Bs in Florida seem to have been decorated by grannies, the Addison's white, aqua and sage color scheme is bright and totally un-stuffy. Enjoy daily happy hours overlooking a delightful courtyard with the friendliest (and funniest) innkeepers on Amelia. Eco-conscious guests take note: the inn's water- and energy-saving efforts have earned it a Green Lodging certification from the state.

Hoyt House   B&B $$
(904-277-4300, 800-432-2085; www.hoythouse.com; 804 Atlantic Ave; r $185-240; ❄️📶🏊) This tall Victorian, perched on the edge of downtown, boasts an enchanting gazebo that begs time with a cool drink. Ten rooms each have their own stylish mix of antiques and found treasures. Want a really unique stay? The owners will rent out their luxury yacht, *Nice Aft* (heh heh), for overnights!

Fort Clinch State Park   CAMPGROUND $
(904-277-7274; sites $26) Despite 62 campsites in the park – the oak-and-moss protected Amelia River sites are far more private than the exposed beach sites – be sure to make reservations well in advance.

✗ Eating

Downtown Fernandina Beach has dozens of cute cafes and bistros.

TOP CHOICE 29 South   SOUTHERN $$$
(904-277-7919; www.29southrestaurant.com; 29 S 3rd St; mains $18-28; ⏰11:30am-2:30pm Tue-Sat, 5:30-9:30pm Mon-Sat, 10am-2pm Sun) Lobster corn dogs. Sweet tea–brined pork chops. Homemade 'coffee and donuts' of donut bread pudding and coffee ice cream. Yes, yes and YES, please! In a pale-purple cottage, this newish neo-Southern bistro takes

Fernandina Beach dining to the next level. Many ingredients are local, from St Augustine honey to North Florida farm eggs.

Café Karibo & Karibrew FUSION, PUB $$
(www.cafekaribo.com; 27 N 3rd St; mains $8-24; ⊙11am-9pm Tue-Sun, to 3pm Mon) This funky side-street favorite serves a large and eclectic menu of burgers, enchiladas, Asian pasta dishes and more in a sprawling two-story space with a shady patio hung with twinkling Christmas lights. Have a crab-cake sandwich, or down a Sloppy Skip's Stout at the adjacent Karibrew brewpub, which has its own menu of global pub grub.

Merge MODERN AMERICAN $$$
(☑904-277-8797; 510 S 8th St; meals $20-26; ⊙from 5pm) Run by the former chef from the island's Ritz-Carlton resort, this new bistro is a bit off the beaten path on the side of busy 8th St. Local foodies rave about exquisite seafood dishes using local ingredients – think sea scallops over braised rhubarb, and cornmeal-breaded oysters in white cheddar cream.

Le Clos FRENCH $$$
(☑904-261-8100; www.leclos.com; 20 S 2nd St; meals $20-26; ⊙5:30-9:30pm Mon-Sat) Dine on classic French dishes with a light Florida twist – fish with citrus glazes, perfect steak frites, shatteringly crisp crème brûlée – at this almost-too-cute-for-words patio bistro.

T-Ray's Burger Station BURGERS $
(202 S 8th St; mains $3-6; ⊙7am-3pm Mon-Fri, 8am-1pm Sat) Hidden inside an Exxon station, this place looks more like an overflowing storage shed than a takeaway. The Big Breakfast, burgers and daily specials are revered by locals. Believe them – the line's there for a reason.

☕ Drinking & Entertainment

Many downtown restaurants double as bars.

TOP CHOICE Palace Saloon BAR
(www.thepalacesaloon.com; 113-117 Centre St) Push through the swinging doors at the oldest continuously operated bar in Florida (since c 1878), and the first thing you'll notice is the 40ft gas lamp-lit bar. Knock back the saloon's rum-laced Pirate's Punch in dark, velvet-draped surroundings, curiously appealing to both bikers and Shakespeare buffs.

Green Turtle Tavern BAR
(www.greenturtletavern.com; 14 S 3rd St) In a crooked little cottage decorated with license

plates, this long, skinny bar offers only wine and beer. Ask Chef Nori about his off-menu special bowl meals.

🛍 Shopping

Downtown Fernandina Beach is a shopper's delight – more than a dozen blocks lined with fudge shops, children's boutiques, candle stores and more. It's particularly noteworthy for antiques, especially nautical-themed goods. For one-stop antiques shopping, check out the **Eight Flags Antiques Mall** (605 Centre St), with three dozen dealers in one large indoor space.

ℹ Information

Historic Downtown Visitor Center (☑904-261-3248, 800-226-3542; 102 Centre St; ⊙11am-4pm Mon-Sat, noon-4pm Sun) Reams of useful information and maps in the old railroad depot. A fun stop in itself.

Library (25 N 4th St; ⊙10am-6pm Mon-Sat, to 8pm Mon & Thu) Free internet access.

Welcome Center (☑800-226-3542; www.ameliaisland.org; 961687 Gateway Blvd; ⊙9am-5pm Mon-Sat) Coming from the west, it's your first right-hand turn once you cross the bridge to the island.

ℹ Getting There & Around

Hwy A1A splits in two directions on Amelia Island, one heading west toward I-95 and the other following the coast; both are well marked.

To get to Amelia the fastest route from the mainland is to take I-95 north to exit 373 and head east about 15 miles straight to the island.

Want a prettier route? Heading from Jacksonville Beach to the town of Mayport, catch the **St Johns River Ferry** (www.stjohnsriverferry.com; cars $5; ⊙6am-8:30pm), which runs every 30 minutes to Fort George Island.

NORTH CENTRAL FLORIDA

Upon escaping Orlando's northern clutches, you enter what might be a different state, one conversely more Southern than South Florida. Sprinkled between the thoroughbred-horse studs, the sprawling forest of Ocala and the funky college town of Gainesville you'll find crystal-clear springs, meandering back roads and the small Victorian gingerbread towns that were the norm before mass tourism.

DETOUR: BARBERVILLE PRODUCE – KING OF THE ROADSIDE STANDS

On Rte 40, plunked halfway between Ocala and Daytona and roughly one-third the way between DeLand and Palatka, nestled cozily beneath a Spanish-moss canopy, sits the king of roadside stands, Barberville Roadside Yard Art & Produce (☑386-749-3562; Rte 40 at Hwy 17, Barberville). Offering more than just fruits, veggies and honey, this open-air market fills 3 acres with mounds of fountains, wrought-iron furniture, gazing balls, ceramic drop-in sinks and old-fashioned peanut brittle. There's even an 8ft-tall aluminum rooster. Who doesn't need one of those?

Blue Spring State Park

The largest spring on the St John's River, Blue Spring maintains a constant 72°F, and between November and March it serves as the winter refuge for between 25 and 50 West Indian manatees, though as many as 200 have been spotted here! The best time to see them is before 11am; there's a wheelchair-accessible path to the viewing platform. This tranquil state park (2100 W French Ave; per vehicle $6) is a revitalizing spot to swim (prohibited when manatees are present), snorkel or canoe (rent gear at the office). You can also spend two hours cruising the peaceful waters with St Johns River Cruises (☑386-917-0724; www.sjrivercruises.com; adult/child $22/16; ⊘tours at 10am & 1pm), whose nature tours offer a thoughtful insight into this fragile ecosystem.

There's a developed campground ($24 per night), as well as backcountry camping.

Cassadaga

In 1894, 27-year-old New Yorker George Colby was suffering from tuberculosis. Seneca, Colby's Native American spirit guide, told him to head south to a lake and found a spiritualist community, where he'd be healed. Colby did it, and Cassadaga (pronounced kassuh-*day*-guh) was born.

Today, Colby's camp – a collection of mainly 1920s Cracker cottages – is a registered historic district, the oldest active religious community in the US, and home to the Southern Cassadaga Spiritualist Camp Meeting Association (www.cassadaga.org). The association believes in infinite intelligence, the precepts of prophecy and healing, and that communication with the dead is possible. It's said the area is one of 20 places in the world with an energy vortex where the spirit and earth planes are exceptionally close, creating a 'portal' between the two. We've been to some weird places before, but Cassadaga really takes the cake.

You wouldn't find the town if you weren't looking for it. At a rural crossroads about 2 miles off the main drag, the tiny camp doesn't have an ATM or gas station. Scattered throughout the area are 30-some spiritual practitioners who offer readings – the main 'attraction' here – during which spirits gone from this plane speak through the practitioner, offering insight into your life. Readings start at around $50 for 30 minutes (see p351).

The camp's heart is the Cassadaga Camp Bookstore (☑386-228-2880; www.cassadaga.org; 1112 Steven St; ⊘10am-5pm Mon-Sat, 11.30am-5pm Sun), which sells New Age books, crystals and incense, and serves as the de facto visitor center for the town. Check out the whiteboard in the back room, which lists which psychics are working that day – you can use the courtesy phone to schedule your appointment. The store also organizes historical tours of the village (1pm and 3pm Saturday, $15) and orb tours (8pm Saturday, $25), where photographers shoot glowing balls of light – reportedly spirits from another world. A $1 donation gets you a camp directory, allowing you to make a pretty good self-guided tour. Mandatory stop: spooky, serene Spirit Lake, where residents scatter the ashes of the departed.

The original Cassadaga Hotel (☑386-228-2323; www.cassadagahotel.net; 355 Cassadaga Rd; r from $55; ✸) burned down in 1926. Today, ghosts reportedly lurk in the shadows (sniff for Jack's cigar smoke, and listen for two girls terrorizing the upstairs halls) of the rebuilt hotel. Looking like a rejected set from *The Shining,* the hotel is appropriately creepy and creaky – on the atmosphere scale, this place is off the charts! – but it's not terribly elegant.

DeLand

☑ 386 / POP 26,000

While much of Florida seems frantic to cover itself in neon and high-rises, stoic DeLand shrugs that off as nonsense. Development is coming, but locals, intimate with the area and acutely aware of what's needed, are bringing it. The quaint, walkable Woodland Blvd, bisecting the east side of town from the west, is home to independent shops and restaurants – modern yet thoroughly small-town. Ancient oaks lean in to hug each other over city streets and Spanish moss dribbles from their branches. Picture-perfect Stetson University, with one of the prettiest campuses in America, forms the town's heart. This is Old Town Florida, and it feels so cozy. Ironically, DeLand was the first town in Florida to enjoy electricity.

Despite all this hometown goodness, risk-taking flows through DeLand's blood. In the 1870s New York baking-soda magnate Henry DeLand traveled down the St John's River with a vision of founding the 'Athens of Florida.' That moniker has stuck, but these days, DeLand is most famous for skydiving – the tandem jump was invented here.

◉ Sights & Activities

Several historic buildings are open for tours. Check out the West Volusia Historical Society for info (www.delandhouse.com).

De Leon Springs State Park   PARK

(601 Ponce de Leon Blvd, Ponce de Leon; per car $6; ☺8am-sunset) Fifteen minutes north of town, these natural springs were used by Native Americans 6000 years ago and have been developed into a huge swimming area – great for kids.

Concessions rent canoes and kayaks to explore the springs, which flow into the Lake Woodruff National Wildlife Refuge, with 18,000 acres of lakes, creeks and marshes. Alternatively, Captain Frank takes passengers on 45- and 90-minute trips through **Fountain of Youth Tours** (☑386-837-5537; www.foytours.com; tours $18) and discusses both the area's ecology and the likelihood that this area – and not the spring in St Augustine (see p333) – is the fabled Fountain of Youth.

Experienced hikers can attack the 4.2-mile Wild Persimmon Trail, meandering through oak hammocks, floodplains and open fields. Marked with blue blazes, this hike is robust.

NORTHEAST FLORIDA DELAND

A LONELY PLANET WRITER VISITS A PSYCHIC *EMILY MATCHAR*

The woman who opens the cottage door looks like a wizardess straight out of Central Casting: waist-length iron-gray hair, prominent mole on one cheek, thousand-mile stare. She ushers me in to her dark, incense-clouded living room, where she motions for me to sit at a table covered in bottles of oils and potions.

'Your name and birth date, please,' she asks, and requests to hold my wedding ring to 'summon the spirits.' She closes her eyes, rubs my ring between her palms.

Then she opens her eyes, and – skeptic though I am – I feel a bit of a tingle. Am I about to hear my future? Fame? Fortune? A million-dollar book deal? But as the psychic begins to make pronouncements, it becomes increasingly clear that my future is, well, a bit... vague: My marriage is a love match and we will be together forever. I'm ambitious, and will be successful. I have a friend who is blondish who may need my support through 'a difficulty' in the coming months or years. I have a spirit guide who is either blonde or brunette, who recently died of cancer or a heart attack or something related to the chest area (grandma? Elizabeth Taylor?).

After each statement, she scans my face for agreement – if I nod or smile, she continues, but if I arch an eyebrow skeptically, she veers off on another course. In answer to direct questions, she is frustratingly vague.

'Will my husband get the job he's applied for?' I ask.

'I'm not sure, specifically, but he will do very well, ultimately,' she says.

'Will we have children?' I ask.

'Do you *want* children?' she replies.

Aren't you the psychic? I want to yell.

After half an hour, she's done. 'I'm not getting any more spirit communication,' she says.

I shake her hand and leave, $50 poorer, with a scent of patchouli incense in my hair that will linger for the rest of the day.

ROADSIDE ATTRACTION: US POSTAL MUSEUM & HOTEL

Philatelists (AKA 'stamp collectors') will marvel at the collection of 'fancy cancels' (interesting postage-cancellation stamps) and vintage decorative envelopes at this quirky museum, in the lobby of the pleasant **1876 Heritage Inn** (386-774-8849; www.1876heritageinn .com; 300 S Volusia Ave, Orange City; r $55; P), just down the road from DeLand in Orange City.

Overlooking the manicured grounds, the **Old Spanish Sugar Mill Grill & Griddle House** (all-you-can-eat pancakes $4.50; 9am-5pm Mon-Fri, 8am-5pm Sat & Sun) has a toasty open fireplace and great all-you-can-eat pancakes that you cook yourself on an electric griddle set into the center of the table.

Skydive DeLand   SKYDIVING
(386-738-3539; www.skydivedeland.com; 1600 Flightline Blvd; tandem jumps $179, freefall training & 1st jump $351) If plummeting toward earth at speeds of 120mph sounds like a whiz-bang time, you're in the right place. A short briefing and a seasoned professional strapped to your back is all it takes to experience the least-boring two minutes of your life above some glorious countryside with Skydive DeLand. Experienced skydivers can jump solo or advance their skills at this first-rate facility. It also offers freefall training so you can learn to jump on your own.

FREE **Deland Hospital Museums**   MUSEUMS
(www.delandhouse.com; 230 N Stone St; 10am-3pm Wed-Sat) Originally a hospital, today this quirky museum houses eight galleries and exhibits, ranging from a somewhat unsettling 1920s operating room to the Hawtense Conrad Elephant Fantasyland – a collection of more than 1000 elephants. Appreciators of the odd and kitschy will definitely want to check this place out.

🛏 Sleeping & Eating

Most of the cheap hotels are along Hwy 17 (Woodland Blvd), north of New York Ave. There's camping nearby in Ocala National Forest.

DeLand Country Inn   B&B $
(386-736-4244; www.delandcountryinn.com; 228 West Howrie Ave; r $89-99;) Popular with skydivers, this sweet B&B is run by a lovely English couple, and its six rooms have a cozy English auntie's feel – quilts, vintage china plates on the walls. A full English breakfast is fried up daily!

DeLand Artisan Inn   HOTEL $$
(386-626-2050; www.delandartisaninn.com; 215 S Woodland Blvd; r from $100;) The lobby's a bit smoky from the adjacent bar, but this small and centrally located yellow stucco hotel has rooms homey enough to make you feel like you're staying at a friend's house rather than a hotel.

TOP
CHOICE **Cress**   MODERN AMERICAN $$$
(386-734-3740; www.cressrestaurant.com; 103 W Indiana Ave; mains $19-32; 5:30pm-close Tue-Sat) Citified foodies trek all the way to sleepy DeLand just to eat at this cutting-edge bistro, whose chef, Hari Pulapaka, snagged an ultra-prestigious James Beard Award nomination this year for his fearless work with a rainbow of global ingredients. On any given day, the menu might offer such delights as local seafood *mofongo* (a classic Caribbean dish), Indonesian shrimp curry, and a salad of delicate pea tendrils with passion fruit emulsion. Look for lots of fiery Indian flavors – Pulapaka was born in Mumbai, and ditched a career as a math professor to follow his passion for food.

Buttercup Bakery   BAKERY $
(197 E Church St; snacks $2-7; 7am-5pm Mon-Fri, 8am-3pm Sat) Inside this sunny yellow cottage the pastry cases are stacked high with luscious sweets: lemon-curd bars, white-chocolate-apricot bars, chocolate-chip bread pudding, and more. It also serves organic coffee, tea and salad.

ℹ Information

Visitor information is available online at www .stjohnsrivercountry.com and at the town's **Welcome Center** (386-734-4331; www.deland chamber.org; 336 N Woodland Blvd; 8:30am-5pm Mon-Fri).

Ocala

352 / POP 56,000

Greater Ocala is blanketed by velvety emerald paddocks hemmed by wooden post-and-rail fences, and sleek-limbed horses neigh in the misty morning air. In short, the town's outskirts look like the (United States Department of Agriculture-certified) 'Horse Capital of the World' *should* look. There are about 1200 horse farms in Marion County, with more than 45 breeds represented.

Downtown Ocala, however, isn't as picture book pretty, though there's plenty of money in the historic properties southeast of town. The compact commercial district trots along at its own pace – there's a reason locals call it 'Slocala' – but live music at the local pub can spur things to a gallop.

Anxious to get out of town? This rural city is surrounded by beautiful clear springs and the best backyard in Florida, Ocala National Forest.

◎ Sights & Activities

TOP CHOICE **Silver Springs** THEME PARK
(www.silversprings.com; 5656 E Silver Springs Blvd; adult/child under 10yr $30/25; ⊙10am-5pm) Glass-bottomed boats were invented at this delightfully old-fashioned nature theme park in 1878 to show visitors the natural springs and stunningly clear Silver River; they're still the main attraction here today.

Peer down as you slowly cruise over eel grass and spring formations, before the grand finale: a pass over Mammoth Spring, which is the world's largest artesian limestone spring and gushes 550 million gallons of 99.8% pure spring water per day.

Other attractions include the Lost River Voyage, transporting guests into untamed Florida and winding among 500-year-old cypress stands; lofty views from the 80ft carousel-gondola lighthouse ride at the headwaters; and snake- and bear-filled wildlife shows. Keep your eyes peeled for the 'Swamp Ghosts' – a pair of rare albino alligators.

Big-name country music concerts held at Twin Oaks Mansion are included in admission. If you're starving, there are a couple ice cream parlors and pizza places on-site. Parking costs $6. Check out the website before you go – they almost always offer 2 for 1 ticket specials. The adjacent **Wild Waters Water Park** (adult/child $30/20, Silver Springs plus Wild Waters combo $45) is fun for kids.

Cactus Jack's Trail Rides HORSE RIDING
(☑352-266-9326; www.cactusjackstrailrides.com; 11008 S Hwy 475; 1/2/3hr rides $45/65/85) You're in the horse capital of America, so saddle up! Debbie and Jamie Zito will take you trotting through shady forests and clover-green fields on the backs of their handsome quarter horses and thoroughbreds.

DON GARLITS MUSEUMS

Fans will tell you straight up: Don 'Big Daddy' Garlits isn't just a legend of drag racing... Don Garlits *is* drag racing. Over four decades, his Swamp Rat series – 34 black, self-designed, hand-built racecars – saw him win 144 national events and 17 World Championship titles, shattering numerous records in his breakneck speedsters. One of them, his Swamp Rat XXX, is even enshrined in the Smithsonian.

Speaking of museums, Big Daddy, who doesn't do things by halves, has two of his own. Even if you're not into cars, the **Don Garlits Museums** (www.garlits.com; 13700 SW 16th Ave; adult/child $15/6; ⊙9am-5pm) are outstanding. If you like cars even a teeny bit, the museums are an essential pilgrimage.

First up: the **Museum of Drag Racing**, where you'll see engine collections and an impressive line-up of dragsters (about 150, arranged chronologically). Look for the 1969 Slingshot, the first dragster to successfully employ a planetary two-speed transmission. This car nearly cost Don his life. In 1970, Don lost part of his right foot in a freak explosion, but rather than let it get him down, he rebounded and developed rear engine cars that would go on to see even greater success.

Next door is a testament to Don's other great passion; the **Museum of Classic Cars** houses a phenomenal collection of more than 70 autos. Starting with a 1904 Orient Buckboard, there's a 1926 Model T, gleaming 1940s Studebakers, Don's red-and-white two-toned 1950 Mercury driven by the Fonz in *Happy Days,* and 1960s Mustangs and Chrysler Muscle Cars, some built to Nascar specifications. Now grandparents of five, Don and his wife Pat (who is a trophy-winning racer) live here.

Admission includes both museums; you'll want at least two hours to look around. Children under five must be hand-held, both for their safety and for the sake of Don's painstaking restoration of this impressive machinery.

🛏 Sleeping & Eating

There's a cluster of cheap lodgings just south of downtown Ocala on Hwy 441 (S Pine Ave) and more within walking distance of Silver Springs.

Silver River State Park   CAMP GROUND **$**
(☑352-236-7148; 1425 NE 58th Ave; sites $24, cabins $110; ❋🐾) Pets are welcome at any of the 59 campsites nestled among the woods at this 5000-acre park. If you want something more sumptuous (but canine-free), try the park's fully equipped luxury cabins, which sleep up to six.

Hilton Ocala   HOTEL **$$**
(☑352-854-1400; www.hiltonocala.com; 3600 SW 36th Ave; r from $139; ❋🐾🛜) Ocala's paddockside Hilton has its own Clydesdale horse, Buddy (and free horse cookies for you to feed him), who waits patiently to take guests on free carriage rides. There's a bi-weekly chocolate fountain and a jogging trail, too.

The Schnitzel Factory   GERMAN **$$**
(www.theschnitzelfactory.com; 1053 NE 14th St; mains $14-20; ⏲11am-8pm Tue-Sat) There's something about hearty, homemade German food that just feels right in sleepy, stodgy Ocala. So tuck into a plate of hand-cut veal or pork schnitzel with a side of buttery spaetzle and red cabbage, all washed down with a dark German beer. Atmosphere is very 'Bavarian strip mall.'

ℹ Information

Ocala & Marion County Visitors Center
(www.ocalamarion.com; 112 N Magnolia Ave; ⏲9am-5pm Mon-Fri)

ℹ Getting There & Around

Greyhound (☑352-732-2677; 529 NE 1st Ave) is in the Central Transfer Station, at the corner of NE 5th St, just a few blocks from downtown. The transfer station for **Amtrak** (☑352-629-9863; www.amtrak.com) is here, and so is **SunTran** (☑352-401-6999; www.suntran.com), whose buses can get you around town between roughly 6am and 7pm; bus trips $1.25.

Ocala National Forest

☑352

The oldest national forest east of the Mississippi River and the southernmost national forest in the continental US, the 400,000-acre Ocala National Forest is one of Florida's most important natural treasures.

An incredible ecological web, the park is a tangle of springs, biomes (sand-pine scrub, palmetto wilderness, subtropical forest) and endangered flora and fauna.

With 18 developed campgrounds and 24 primitive ones, 219 miles of trails and 600 lakes (30 for boating), there are endless opportunities for swimming, hiking, cycling, horseback riding, canoeing, bird- and wildlife-watching – or just meditating on how great it is that the government got here before the theme parks did.

Two highways cross the region: Hwy 19 runs north–south and Hwy 40 runs east–west.

⊙ Sights & Activities

Hiking & Cycling Trails   HIKING, CYCLING
Also referred to as the Ocala Trail, roughly 61 miles of the **Florida National Scenic Trail** spears the center of the forest north-south. Marked with orange blazes, pickup points include Juniper Springs, Alexander Springs and Clearwater Lake recreation areas. Outside hunting season, hikers can camp anywhere 200ft from the trail, but if you prefer to commune with others you'll find spur trails to developed campgrounds about every 10 to 12 miles.

Passing through prairies and live-oak domes, the popular 22-mile **Paisley Woods Bicycle Trail** is yellow blazed. Its end points are Alexander Springs to the north and Clearwater Lake to the south, but it's shaped like a figure eight so you can do either half as a loop. Be sure to bring both a bike that can handle off-road conditions and plenty of water (none is available along the trail).

The 8.5-mile **St Francis Trail** (blue blazes) winds through riverine and bayhead swamp to the abandoned 1880s pioneer town of St Francis on the St John's River. No buildings remain, but you'll see the old logging railroad bed and levee built for rice growing.

Juniper Springs
Recreation Area   LAKE, OUTDOORS
(☑352-625-3147; admission/campsites $5/21; ⏲8am-8pm) Developed in the mid-1930s, this is the forest's flagship recreation area. Concessions sell groceries and firewood, and rent kayaks and canoes ($33.50 per day, open 8am to 8pm) for making the 7-mile, palmetto- and cypress-lined run down Juniper Creek. There's a pickup and a return shuttle at the end of the creek between 1:30pm and 4:40pm ($6 per person and $6 per boat).

Swimming is sublime at Juniper Springs. It's chilly, though: the water is a crisp 72°F year-round.

Salt Springs Recreation
Area
LAKE, OUTDOORS

(🕿352-685-2048; admission $5.50, campsites with/without hookups $26/19; ⊙8am-8pm) Rumored to have curative powers, Salt Springs is a favorite with RV owners for its lovely shady area. Head to the marina (🕿352-685-2255; ⊙7am-4pm), about half a mile south of the recreation area in front of the doctor's office, where you can rent vessels to cruise enormous Lake Kerr: canoes ($20), pontoon boats ($70 for four hours, $110 daily plus gas) or a 16ft Carolina skiff ($27.50 for four hours, $45 daily plus gas).

Alexander Springs
Recreation Area
LAKE, OUTDOORS

(🕿352-669-3522; admission/campsites $5.50/21; ⊙8am-8pm) This picturesque recreation area has one of the last untouched subtropical forests left in Florida. The stunning sapphire-blue freshwater spring attracts wildlife, swimmers, scuba divers (extra $6.50 fee) and sunbathers. Canoe rental ($16/38 per two hours/daily) includes a welcome rehaul at the end of the 7-mile paddle.

❶ Information

Rangers serve most of the area and all campgrounds have resident volunteers who are good sources of information. There's no single admission fee and no one number to call; day-use areas are generally open 8am to 8pm. Pick up free literature and maps or buy a topographical version (around $7) at any of the visitor centers, all open 8am to 5pm.

Ocklawaha visitor center (🕿352-236-0288; 3199 NE Hwy 315, Silver Springs) Your first stop if you're coming from Ocala and Silver Springs.

Pittman visitor center (🕿352-669-7495; 45621 SR 19, Altoona) On the major throughway from Orlando and Mt Dora.

Salt Springs visitor center (🕿352-685-3070; 14100 N Hwy 19, Salt Springs) In Salt Springs, accessible from Jacksonville and Palatka.

❶ Getting There & Away

Several different entrances can be used to access Ocala National Forest. From Orlando take Hwy 441 north to the Eustis turnoff and continue north on Hwy 19 (about 40 miles); from Daytona take Hwy 92 west to DeLand, then head north on Hwy 17 to Barberville and west on SR 40 (about 30 miles); from Ocala take Silver Springs Blvd due west about 6 miles to the forest's main entry.

Gainesville

🕿352 / POP 117,000

Originally a whistle-stop along the Florida Railroad Company's line chugging from Cedar Key to Fernandina Beach, Gainesville soon thrived as a citrus-producing community until repeated frosts in the 1890s drove orange-growers south. Today, Gainesville is an energetic, upbeat city, routinely ranked among the country's best places to live and play. It's also home to the nation's second-largest university, the sprawling University of Florida (UF). The campus itself is 2 miles from downtown, but the student vibe infuses the entire city, with loads of economical eats, cool bars and fine galleries. The university also bequeathed the world Gatorade: the science department developed it to counteract the on-field dehydration of its football team, the Fightin' Gators, which has a huge following here (just try getting a room on game weekends).

The town is known for its thriving music scene – the most notable band to hail from Gainesville is Tom Petty and the Heartbreakers. Indie rock and punk rock rule clubs today, though audiophiles can find everything from bluegrass to hip-hop almost every night.

Gainesville is also a mecca for the outdoorsy. Surrounding the city are pristine wilderness areas and a succession of stunningly clear springs just aching to be tubed.

⊙ Sights & Activities

Gainesville has a unique citywide cell-phone audio tour – when you spot a placard, dial the number listed for information about historical and cultural sites.

Florida Museum of
Natural History
MUSEUM

(www.flmnh.ufl.edu; cnr SW 34th St & Hull Rd; museum admission free, Butterfly Rainforest adult/child $10.50/6; ⊙10am-5pm Mon-Sat, 1-5pm Sun) The highlight of this excellent natural-history museum is the expansive Butterfly Rainforest. Hundreds of butterflies from 55 to 65 species flutter freely in the soaring, screened vivarium. As you stroll among waterfalls and tropical foliage, peek at scientists preparing specimens in the rearing lab of this, the world's largest butterfly research facility.

Kanapaha Botanical
Gardens
BOTANICAL GARDEN

(www.kanapaha.org; 4700 SW 58th Dr; adult/child $6/3; ⊙9am-5pm Mon-Fri, to dusk Sat & Sun; 🐾)

NORTHEAST FLORIDA GAINESVILLE

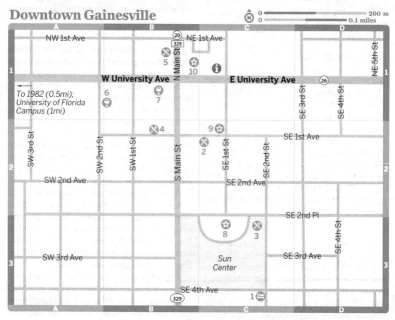

Downtown Gainesville

🛏 Sleeping
1	Zen Hostel	C3

🍴 Eating
2	Emiliano's	C2
3	Maude's Classic Café	C3
4	Paramount Grill	B2
5	Top	B1

🍷 Drinking
6	2nd Street Speakeasy	B1
7	Stubbies & Steins	B1

🎭 Entertainment
8	Hippodrome	C3
9	Lillian's Music Store	C2
10	University Club	B1

Central Florida's lush native plants – azaleas, rare double-crowned cabbage palms, southern magnolias – are on proud display at this highly rated 62-acre garden, with hiking paths, a labyrinth, a children's koi pond and special herb and ginger gardens. Especially cool is the dense bamboo garden, whose dark groves look like fairy homes. Dogs are welcome!

Devil's Millhopper State Geological Site   PARK
(4732 Millhopper Rd; per car $4; ⏰9am-5pm Wed-Sun) As the name indicates, this is not your average park. The site centers on a 120ft-deep, 500ft-wide funnel-shaped rainforest which you enter by descending a 232-step wooden staircase. Water trickles down the slopes from the surrounding springs; some

of it flows into a natural drain and ultimately to the Gulf of Mexico. Rangers lead tours every Saturday at 10am. The park is about 20 minutes northwest of downtown by car.

University of Florida   UNIVERSITY, MUSEUMS
(www.ufl.edu) The city is dominated by the UF campus, one of the largest in the country. Wander around to check out the student vibe, or peer in at ancient Indian sculptures and contemporary paintings at the free **Samuel P Harn Museum of Art** (cnr SW 34th St & Hull Rd).

🛏 Sleeping

Prices soar during football games and graduations, when a minimum stay may be required and rooms fill rapidly. Many inexpensive motels are just east of UF, along SW

13th St or on approach roads. Just east of downtown, the historic district has a handful of elegant B&Bs in restored Victorian homes.

TOP CHOICE Zen Hostel
HOSTEL $

(☑352-336-3613; www.zenhostel.com; 404 SE 2nd St; dm $25, r $35-40; ❄️📶) Look for the Tibetan prayer flags decorating the porch of this rambling yellow house, which feels like an old-school 1970s commune: chickens in the yard, barefoot children, kombucha tea fermenting in the shared kitchen. Popular among visiting students at nearby massage and acupuncture schools, it's got creaky-floored dorms and rooms decorated with thrift-store furniture, and a clean shared bathroom with a funky clawfoot tub. Toby, the owner, knows all the best bike trails and alternative bookshops.

Magnolia Plantation
B&B $$

(☑352-375-6653; www.magnoliabnb.com; 309 SE 7th St; r $120-155, cottages $200-380; ❄️📶) Lovingly restored, this French Second Empire–style mansion was unique to Gainesville when constructed by a woodworker in 1885. It's still unique today. The main house boasts five rooms, 10 fireplaces (check the detailing in those mantels!) and snacks around the clock. Outside, a tangled hidden garden has a pond and chairs for relaxing.

Laurel Oak Inn
B&B $$

(☑352-373-4535; www.laureloakinn.com; 221 SE 7th St; r $140-199; ❄️📶) The 1885 Lassiter House has been splendidly redone as a handsome yellow B&B, with high ceilings, velvet fainting couches and fresh flowers everywhere.

✖️ Eating

Downtown Gainesville has a solid selection of everything from Thai to Italian to old-fashioned Southern. The area around the Hippodrome is a mini food court, with a half dozen or so good lunch spots. For a real Gainesville experience, tuck into a free vegetarian lunch served up by chanting Hare Krishnas (www.krishnalunch.com; Plaza of the Americas; ⏱11:30am-1:30pm Mon-Fri during school session) on the UF campus.

TOP CHOICE Satchel's Pizza
PIZZERIA $

(www.satchelspizza.com; 1800 NE 23rd Ave; mains $2.75-13; ⏱11am-10pm Tue-Sat) Two miles northeast of downtown, this wacky place has the best pizza on Florida's east coast (and a darn good salad, to boot). Here, you can sit surrounded by funky outsider art and savor steaming build-your-own gourmet pies served on mismatched crockery. Grab a seat at a mosaic courtyard table or in the back of a gutted 1965 Ford Falcon. Most nights there's live music in the Back 40 Bar; there's bocce ball and a head-scratchingly eccentric junk museum featuring various bizarro collections. Satchel's doesn't take credit cards; the fees from the on-site ATM go to charity. Skip Satchel's and you miss Gainesville's soul. Expect a wait.

Paramount Grill
MODERN AMERICAN $$$

(☑352-378-3398; www.paramountgrill.com; 12 SW 1st Ave; mains $16-28; ⏱11am-2pm & 5:30-9:30pm Mon-Thu, to 10:30pm Fri & Sat, 5:30-9:30pm only Sun) Very Scandinavian chic, with minimalist wood tables and apple-green walls decorated with vintage sailor photos, this is the top spot for innovative upscale-casual eats in Gainesville. A globally influenced menu spans crab cakes, duck dishes and homemade ravioli.

Top
FUSION, BAR $$

(☑352-376-1188; 15 N Main St; mains $8-24; ⏱5pm-2am Tue-Sat, 11am-2:30pm & 5-10pm Sun) Combining 1950s kitsch, hunter-lodge decor

---

DETOUR: WINGED FURY AT THE BAT HOUSE

Across from Gainesville's little Lake Alice, adjacent to a student garden, stands what appears to be an oversized birdhouse. However, this gabled gray house on stilts is actually the **Bat House**, home to a family of Mexican free-tailed bats. Built in 1991 after the flying mammals' poop began stinking up the campus, the population has since exploded to 60,000. Each night just after sundown, the bats drop from their roost – at the amazing rate of 100 bats per second! – and fly off to feed.

If you want to witness this winged fury for yourself, follow University Ave west to Gale Lamerand Dr, turn left and head south to Museum Rd. Turn right (west) and follow Museum Rd around a bend. The Bat House will be on your right. It's situated between two permitted lots, but at this time of day, you should be good. If anyone hassles you, just tell 'em you're a vampire coming to see your blood brothers.

and giant owl art, this place is both hip and comfortable. Vegetarians will thrill at the options here and everyone will appreciate the working photo booth in the back ($2). Just as popular for nightlife as it is for food.

Emiliano's   CUBAN $$
(www.emilianoscafe.com; 7 SE 1st Ave; mains $9-20; ☺11am-10pm) A Gainesville standby, Emiliano's rocks a mid-century Cuban-Floridian vibe, with striped awnings, rattan chairs and salsa in the background. Go for Cuban classics like *ropa vieja* (pulled skirt steak) or fried plantains, or pick something a little more contemporary off the tapas menu.

Maude's Classic Café   CAFE $
(101 SE 2nd Pl; mains $8-11; ☺7am-11pm, to 1am Fri & Sat, from 9am Sat, from 10am Sun) Bohemian hangout, serving tea and coffee, as well as movie-named sandwiches and salads ('When Harry Met Salad').

Drinking & Entertainment

Live music is to Gainesville what mouse ears are to Orlando, and many bars double as music venues. For an up-to-the-minute overview of local music, visit www.gainesville bands.com.

Stubbies & Steins   PUB
(☎352-384-1261; www.stubbiesandsteins.com; 9 W University Ave; ☺5pm-2am) When Berkeley Hoflund visited Australia, she fell in love with the beer. Upon returning, she opened this awesomely quirky Australia-meets-Germany pub and restaurant, with a doorstopper beer menu of 400-plus brews representing 16 countries, and classic Bavarian chow like sausages and schnitzels.

2nd Street Speakeasy   BAR
(21 SW 2nd St) If you're not paying attention, you'll cruise right past the dark door leading into Gainesville's chillest bar. Fringe-tipped crimson lamps, a mellow azure aquarium and cushy burgundy sofas are some of the cool features here. What's coolest, though, is that the volume of the lounge music is set so you can actually chat with people.

Swamp   BAR
(www.swamprestaurant.com; 1642 W University Ave) A college bar for a college town, with cheap pitchers and drunken frat boys galore, plus a pretty darn nice patio for daytime boozing. Gets wild on weekends.

Lillian's Music Store   BAR, LIVE MUSIC
(112 SE 1st Ave; ☺2pm-2am Mon-Sat, 3-11pm Sun) The crowd's a little older than in the clubs along University, so they appreciate that elegant stained-glass partition and the 3ft-tall gorilla at the entrance. There's great live music every night, but the Monday night jam sessions really pack 'em in.

1982   LIVE MUSIC
(352-371-9836; 919 W University Ave) Cramped, dingy and musty, this sweet spot boasts both local and national bands, and a great beer selection. If the band sucks, you can play classic Nintendo games on one of four TVs behind the bar. Duck Hunt FTW!

University Club   CLUB
(www.ucnightclub.com; 18 E University Ave) Predominantly gay, but straight-friendly, this place is the hub of the local gay and lesbian scene and is famous for its drag shows. The entrance is around back. DJs spin most nights, though karaoke is also a popular draw.

Hippodrome   THEATER, CINEMA
(thehipp.org; 25 SE 2nd Pl) In an imposing historic edifice (1911), the Hippodrome is the city's main cultural center, with a diverse theater and independent-cinema program.

ℹ Information

You'll find free wi-fi coverage downtown around the Hippodrome.

Alachua County Visitors & Convention Bureau (☎352-374-5260, 866-778-5002; www.visitgainesville.come; 30 E University Ave; ☺9am-5pm Mon-Fri)

Library (401 E University Ave; ☺9:30am-9pm Mon-Thu, to 6pm Fri, to 5pm Sat, 1-5pm Sun) Offers free internet access.

Pride Community Center (☎352-377-8915; www.gainesvillepride.org; 3131 NW 13th St; ☺3-7pm Mon-Fri, noon-4pm Sat) For gay and lesbian info.

ℹ Getting There & Around

Gainesville Regional Airport (☎352-373-0249; www.gra-gnv.com), 10 miles northeast of downtown, is served by a handful of domestic carriers.

The **Greyhound bus station** (101 NE 23rd Ave) is a mile or so north of downtown.

Gainesville Regional Transit System (RTS; www.go-rts.com; fare $1.50) services the city with buses.

Around Gainesville

MICANOPY
🚗352 / POP 700

The oldest inland settlement in Florida, Micanopy (pronounced mickuh-noh-pee) started as an Indian trading post. A hundred and ninety years later, it's still a trading post of sorts – for antique hunters. Known as 'the town that time forgot,' the nickname may seem trite, but it's jaw-droppingly accurate. Hulking oaks festooned with Spanish moss line wide roads that wind lazily past stoic brick buildings. It looks like a movie set, and Hollywood has already come calling: *Doc Hollywood* was filmed here in 1991, and residents have never forgotten!

The 0.5-mile main drag, NE Cholokka Blvd, features half a dozen antique shops and the delightfully disheveled O Brisky Books (114 Cholokka Blvd; ⊙10am-5pm Tue-Sun), with a browse-worthy collection of vintage maps and prints.

Two miles north on Hwy 441, wild horses and bison roam the 21,000-acre Paynes Prairie Preserve State Park (100 Savannah Blvd; per vehicle $6; ⊙8am-sunset). This slightly eerie reserve's wet prairie, swamp, hammock and pine flatwoods have more than 34 trails, including the 16-mile Gainesville–Hawthorne Rail Trail, slicing through the northern section. The 3-mile La Chua Trail takes in the Alachua Sink and Alachua Lake, offering alligator- and sandhill crane-spotting opportunities. Just north of the visitor center, climb the 50ft observation tower for panoramas. Campsites cost $18, and include water and electricity.

For pure luxury, nothing beats Herlong Mansion (☎352-466-3322, 800-437-5664; www.herlong.com; 402 NE Cholokka Blvd; r $119-189), sitting on the northern edge of Micanopy like a king surveying his fiefdom. Impeccably manicured, the mansion's 2nd floor boasts two endless porches, perfect for relaxing with a cool drink.

CROSS CREEK

Near the rural hamlet of Cross Creek, 20 minutes east of Micanopy, swing by the Marjorie Kinnan Rawlings Historic State Park (18700 S CR 325, Cross Creek; per vehicle $3; ⊙9am-5pm). Rawlings (1896–1953) was the author of the Pulitzer Prize–winning novel *The Yearling,* a coming-of-age story set in what's now Ocala National Forest. Her career flourished only after Max Perkins, Rawlings' (and also Ernest Hemingway's and F

Scott Fitzgerald's) editor, told her that her letters about her friends and neighbors were more interesting than her gothic fiction, inspiring her to write *Cross Creek,* a book about her life in this area. Her former Cracker-style home is open for tours (adult/child $3/2; ⊙10am-4pm Thu-Sun, closed Aug & Sep) on the hour (except noon). You can stroll the orange groves, farmhouse and barn on your own – pick up a self-guided walking brochure from the car park.

Cross Creek's cedar-shingled Yearling Restaurant (www.yearlingrestaurant.net; 14531 Hwy 325; mains $6-15; ⊙5-10pm Thu & Fri, noon-10pm Sat, noon-8:30pm Sun) serves 'Cracker cuisine' like gator tail, hush puppies and catfish in an atmospheric wood-paneled dining room decorated with historical photos and paintings. It's worth a stop just to try its famous sour orange pie, one of our very most favorite treats in the entire state of Florida.

HIGH SPRINGS
🚗352 / POP 4700

Quaint High Springs, the 'friendliest town in Florida,' is a hub for antiquers, bikers and locals seeking a getaway. Main St, dotted with shops, galleries and restaurants, is the major north–south divider. Intersecting it, Hwy 441 (here called 1st Ave) is the east–west throughway.

The town is the gateway to superb natural springs, including Poe Springs (28800 NW 182nd Ave; admission $5; ⊙9am-sunset) and Ginnie Springs (www.ginniespringsoutdoors.com; 7300 NE Ginnie Springs Rd; adult/child $12/3; ⊙8am-7pm Mon-Sun, shorter hours winter, later on weekends), 2 miles further west on CR 340. Ginnie Springs is more developed, with kayaks and tubes for rent (kayaks/tubes $25/6 per day), and a handful of campsites ($20).

ROADSIDE ATTRACTION: THE ORANGE SHOP

Follow the billboards to the hamlet of Citra, just outside Cross Creek, where you'll find the Orange Shop (18545 US Hwy 301, Citra), a retro orange-themed souvenir shop hawking 10lb bags of Florida oranges, bottles of orange-blossom honey, orange marmalade, orange gel candies, novelty orange-shaped chewing gum and other kitschy Florida goodies. Visitors are treated to a free Dixie Cup of fresh-squeezed orange juice from the backyard grove.

WRECK DIVING IN TROY SPRINGS

At the bottom of crystalline Troy Springs is something unexpected: the wreck of a Civil War steamboat. The *Madison* was deliberately sunk in 1863 to prevent her capture by Union troops; though her owner intended to raise her after the war, when he returned he found her body stripped by scavengers. Today, divers float over the *Madison*'s ravaged skeleton, peering at her 150-year-old hull. Even snorkelers can have a gander – the water's so clear you can see straight down 70ft. Divers must be certified and bring a buddy. The springs are part of Troy Springs State Park, at 674 Troy Springs Rd in Branford, just east of Ichetucknee Springs. Park entry is $5 per car.

Grady House Bed & Breakfast (☎386-454-2206; www.gradyhouse.com; 420 NW 1st Ave; r $115-155; P 📶) has five rooms themed according to color: the Red Room has over 350 classic nudes gracing the walls; the Navy Room is styled nautically. **Great Outdoors Restaurant** (☎386-454-1288; greatoutdoorsdining.com; 65 N Main; mains $14-26; ⏲11am-close Tue-Sun) is a woodsy, lantern-lit steakhouse and saloon in the former downtown Opera House.

ICHETUCKNEE SPRINGS STATE PARK

Relax in a giant inner tube and float through gin-clear waters at this popular **park** (admission $6, canoes or tubes $5; ⏲8am-sunset), on the lazy, spring-fed Ichetucknee River.

Various water sports are available here, but tubing is certainly the most popular. Floats last from 45 minutes to 3½ hours, with scattered launch points along the river. The park runs regular trams bringing tubers to the river and also a free shuttle service (May to September) between the north and south entrances.

To minimize environmental impact, the number of tubers is limited to 750 a day; arrive early as capacity is often reached mid-morning. Use the south entrance: the shuttle service takes you to the launch points, allowing you to float back down to your car.

You'll see farmers advertising tube rental as you approach the park along Hwy 238 and 47 (the park itself does not rent tubes). Tubes are $5 and one- or two-person rafts cost $10 to $15. At the end of the day, leave your gear at the tube drop at the southern end of the park; it'll be returned.

Tampa Bay & Southwest Florida

Best Places to Eat

- » Refinery (p371)
- » Peg's Cantina (p386)
- » Cafe Lurcat (p413)
- » IM Tapas (p413)
- » Columbia Restaurant (p370)

Best Places to Stay

- » Dickens House (p379)
- » Postcard Inn (p384)
- » Hotel Ranola (p394)
- » Mango Street Inn (p404)
- » Gram's Place (p369)

Why Go?

To drive southwest Florida's Gulf Coast is to enter an impressionistic watercolor painting: first, there is the dazzling white quartz sand of its barrier-island beaches, whose illuminated turquoise waters darken to silver-mantled indigo as the fiery sun lowers to the horizon. Later, seen from the causeways, those same islands become a phosphorescent smear beneath the inky black, star-flecked night sky.

The Gulf Coast's beauty is surely its main attraction, but variety is a close second: from Tampa to St Petersburg to Sarasota to Naples, there is urban sophistication, passionate artistry and exquisite cuisine. There are secluded islands, family-friendly resorts and Spring Break–style parties, as at Clearwater and St Pete Beach.

Here, Ringling's circus and Salvador Dalí's melting canvases fit perfectly – both are bright, bold, surreal entertainments to match wintering manatees, roseate spoonbills, open-mouthed alligators, earthy Ybor City cigars in corrugated rows and the flamenco dancer's blood-red dress.

When to Go
Tampa Bay

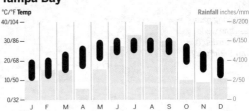

Mid-Feb–mid-Apr Peak season. Ideal weather, high prices. Best for camping, hiking, manatees.

Jun-Sep Very hot, muggy, rainy. Low season; some places close. Bargain-hunter's beach time.

Nov-Dec Snowbirds start arriving. Weather cools and dries, water still warm, great off-season prices.

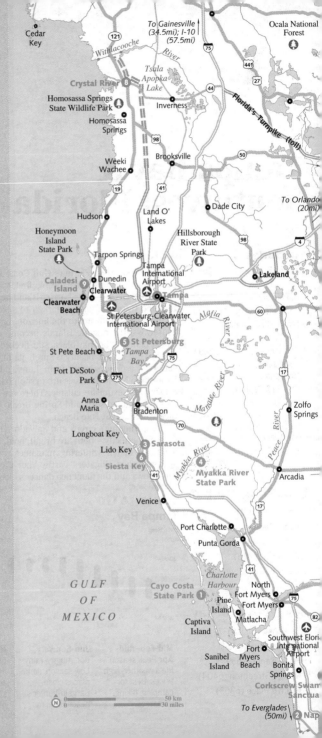

Tampa Bay & Southwest Florida Highlights

1 Getting lost on secluded Cayo Costa Island, mostly preserved as **Cayo Costa State Park** (p406)

2 Strolling après beach along 5th Ave in **Naples** (p411)

3 Juggling art and circus at Sarasota's **Ringling Museum Complex** (p390)

4 Kayaking with alligators at **Myakka River State Park** (p397)

5 Pondering *The Hallucinogenic Toreador* at St Petersburg's **Salvador Dalí Museum** (p377)

6 Building pure white sandcastles at **Siesta Key** (p391)

7 Smoking cigars, drinking mojitos in Tampa at **Ybor City** (p368)

8 Swimming with manatees at **Crystal River** (p416)

9 Sunning, shelling and solitude on **Caladesi Island** (p388)

10 Admiring bald cypress and wood storks at **Corkscrew Swamp Sanctuary** (p414)

History

First established as Fort Brooke in 1824, Tampa was little more than a yellow fever–plagued frontier outpost and minor port for most of its early history. Up until the 1880s, the town census never topped a thousand ragged souls.

Then Tampa's fortunes changed in a hurry. Phosphate was discovered and mining began. In 1883, Henry B Plant built a railroad connecting Tampa with Jacksonville. And in 1886, the first in a wave of cigar manufacturers relocated from Key West to Tampa, in large part because of the easy railroad transportation north.

As in Florida generally, railroads led to increased tourism by northern 'snowbirds.' In 1885, inventor Thomas Alva Edison became one of the most famous, building a winter home in Fort Myers. In another budding winter resort, Sarasota, John Ringling located the winter home of his traveling circus in 1911.

Immigrants from Cuba, Spain, Germany and Italy arrived by the thousands to work in Tampa's cigar factories, which by 1900 had made Tampa the 'Cigar Capital of the World.' For the next 30 years, cigars were Tampa's backbone, and well-paid workers enjoyed the good life of a genuine boom town. The polyglot city's population exploded, more than tripling from 1900 to 1920, to 51,000 people.

Florida's early-20th-century road-building frenzy encouraged new waves of 'tin-can tourists' to enjoy the Gulf's torpid waters. By the time the Tamiami Trail was completed in 1928 – connecting the region to Miami – Tampa and neighboring St Petersburg were Florida's third- and fourth-largest cities, respectively.

Then the Great Depression hit, and Tampa struggled. Undermined by the advent of machine-rolled cigarettes, the cigar industry steadily declined from its 1929 peak (folding entirely with the 1959 US embargo of Cuba). However, after WWII, GIs who'd served at Tampa's MacDill Field returned to settle down; new arrivals flooded Tampa again, and the city recovered.

The region's most recent decade has been defined by hurricanes and suburban sprawl. Two of the worst hurricanes in US history – 2004's Hurricane Charley and 2005's Hurricane Wilma – decimated the Gulf Coast just south of Tampa, causing over $35 billion in damage between them.

Then, residents and newcomers sparked a suburban building boom, and over 2000–10, Tampa grew by 17%. This expansion turned into contraction with the 2007–09 national recession. Today, the Tampa Bay area is glutted with foreclosed and abandoned homes and struggling with suddenly high levels of homelessness. As elsewhere in the Sunshine State, creating a sustainable balance has become the city's mantra.

National, State & Regional Parks

Wilderness and wildlife are in rich supply in this region, and an abundance of top-notch parks provide easy access to them.

For state parks protecting undeveloped island beaches, some accessible only by boat, visit Cayo Costa, Honeymoon & Caladesi Islands, Fort DeSoto and Lover's Key.

To see manatees, visit the Tampa Bay area's Manatee Viewing Center and Fort Myers' Lee County Manatee Park. To also swim with them, go to Crystal River.

Wildlife refuges highlight swamps, alligators and seabirds. Don't miss Corkscrew Swamp Sanctuary, Six Mile Cypress Slough Preserve and JN 'Ding' Darling National Wildlife Refuge.

Great camping is available at several state parks (particularly Fort DeSoto and Cayo Costa). Two more are Hillsborough River State Park and Myakka River State Park, which both offer fantastic canoeing as well.

❶ Getting There & Around

Tampa, the region's hub city, is an easy drive from Florida's other main cities. It's 84 miles due west of Orlando via I-4, and 130 miles due south of Gainesville via I-75. From Florida's capital, Tallahassee, it's 273 miles via I-10 and I-75. From Miami it's 255 miles; take I-95 north to I-75 and head west across 'Alligator Alley' to Naples, then continue north on I-75.

Within the region, I-75 skirts the eastern edge of Tampa Bay and I-275 skirts the western edge through St Petersburg. The congested Alt US 19 connects barrier beach communities from St Pete Beach to Tarpon Springs. Traffic light–heavy US 41 – also called the Tamiami Trail – parallels I-75 and connects Tampa with all major towns south to Naples (and on to Miami).

Greyhound buses serve the main towns in the region. The main international airport is in Tampa, but other far smaller international airports are St Petersburg-Clearwater, Sarasota-Bradenton and Southwest Florida International in Fort Myers.

TAMPA BAY AREA

Surrounding the gorgeous deep-water Tampa Bay are two major cities and a seemingly endless expanse of urban-suburban sprawl – forming the state's second-largest metropolitan area – which along the Gulf Coast is edged by some 35 miles of barrier-island beaches. Not many places in the country offer as much big-city sophistication mere minutes from so much dazzling sand. Yet since Miami is one of them, the bay area is rarely given its due. Both Tampa and St Petersburg burble with cultural and culinary excitement as they spruce up their historic districts and polish their arts institutions. The range of adventures on offer – from fine arts to world-class aquariums to hot nightclubs to roller coasters to dolphin cruises to unblemished islands to seafood feasts beneath lurid sunsets – make this a compelling region to explore.

Tampa Bay

813 / POP 335,700

Tampa Bay, particularly compared to Miami, seems to exemplify the dictionary definition of 'generic big city, American.' Sprawling and businesslike, Tampa lacks the iconic downtown skyline or cultural buzz that stamps other US cities with an indelible, distinct persona. For instance, the Tampa Bay area's most prominent landmark is the Sunshine Skyway Bridge. Though the bridge connects to St Petersburg, not Tampa, its two majestic harplike towers are the city in a nutshell: soaring yet plain, form stripped to functional essence.

Therefore, it's surprising to learn that locals take a perverse pride in their city's unofficial designation as the 'lap-dance capital of the world.' Really? *Tampa?* The city has no red-light district, yet scattered among the strip malls are somehow enough strip joints to warrant the claim. Indeed, Tampa

surprises: it's much more fun and intriguing than first meets the eye.

In fact, so many new museums, parks and gourmet South Tampa restaurants have popped up recently that the city is dangerously close to becoming stylish. In the heart of downtown, the revitalized Riverwalk along the Hillsborough River glitters with contemporary architecture and scenic green spaces. Plus, between the zoo and aquarium, the children's museums and theme parks, families have enough top-shelf entertainment to last a week.

Best of all, Tampa's influential, immigrant-rich history has never been better showcased. Historic Ybor City, the center of Tampa's turn-of-the-century Cuban community and cigar industry, is a compact neighborhood of handsome brick buildings where everyday life still moves to a Spanish beat. Then by evening Ybor's streets transform into Southwest Florida's hottest bar and nightclub scene.

As it turns out, Tampa's not so buttoned-down after all.

Sights

Tampa has two main sightseeing destinations: downtown and Ybor City. Downtown, the attractive Tampa Riverwalk (www .thetampariverwalk.com) connects most sights. Along the Hillsborough River, this undulating green space, with playgrounds and restrooms, makes a pretty walk from the museums edging Curtis Hixon Park, past the Convention Center, to the aquarium at the far end. Within downtown, the Franklin St Mall is a pedestrian-only corridor between Kennedy Blvd and Zack St that's lined with food carts and lunchtime eateries.

Ybor City is a short car or trolley ride northeast of downtown, and the Lowry Zoo and Busch Gardens are a short drive north of downtown.

Lowry Park Zoo
TOP CHOICE   ZOO

(813-935-8552; www.lowryparkzoo.com; 1101 W Sligh Ave; adult/child 3-11yr $24/19; 9:30am-5pm; P) When it comes to animal encounters, Florida sets the bar high, and Tampa's AZA-accredited zoo clears it with room to spare. The well-designed exhibits emphasize getting as close to the animals as possible, with several free-flight aviaries, a camel ride, giraffe feeding, a wallaby enclosure and a rhino 'encounter.' Not only does Lowry contain all the big-ticket African animals you'll

TAMPA DISCOUNTS

Looking to save a few bucks on museum admissions? The best bet is the **Destination Tampa Bay Tour Desk** (813-905-5202; 10am-4pm). It's at the cruise-ship terminal, directly across from the aquarium, with discounted tickets for Busch Gardens, the aquarium, MOSI, the History Center, Imax movies and various cruises.

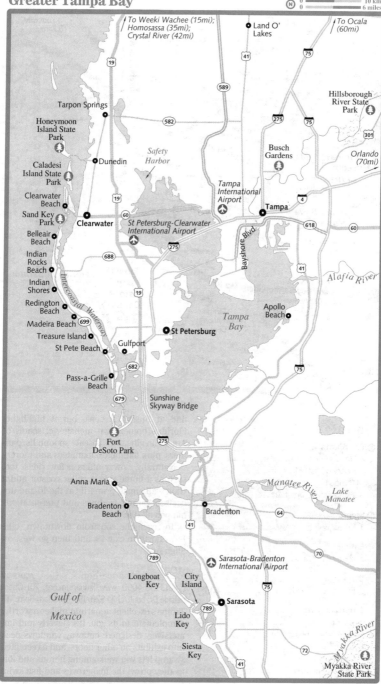

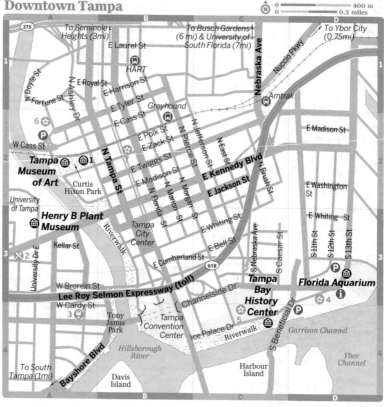

find at Busch Gardens, but it highlights Florida's homegrown menagerie: scores of American alligators, roseate spoonbills, panthers, pink flamingos, manatees and more.

Naturally, Lowry offers a few rides, too, such as a flume ride, a roller coaster and a train – all aimed primarily at the 10 and under set. Various feedings and presentations happen all day.

To reach the zoo from downtown, take I-275 north to exit 48, and then go west on Sligh Ave.

TOP CHOICE Florida Aquarium   AQUARIUM
(☎813-273-4000; www.flaquarium.org; 701 Channelside Dr; adult/child $20/15; ◎9:30am-5pm; ⊕) Tampa's excellent aquarium makes a worthy complement to its zoo. It's cleverly and immersively designed: cutaway windows peek into exhibits on other floors, and a recreated swamp lets you walk among herons and ibis as they prowl the mangroves and fish swim

past their legs. Stroke enormous manta rays, and wonder at giant grouper, tarpon, sea turtles and sharks gliding through coral reefs. But don't just watch. Two dive programs let you swim with the fishes: anyone aged six and up can plunge into the Coral Reef Gallery ($75), and certified divers aged 15 and up can join the sharks ($175). For details and reservations, call ☎813-239-4015.

An outdoor splash zone and playground lets kids run loose (bring swimsuits), and Ecotours (adult/child $22/18) aboard a 72ft catamaran cruise Tampa Bay, home to over 500 bottlenose dolphins, plus manatees and seabirds. Combination tickets are a good deal.

Glazer Children's Museum   CHILDREN'S MUSEUM
(☎813-443-3861; www.glazermuseum.org; 110 W Gasparilla Plaza; adult/child $15/9.50; ☺10am-5pm Mon-Fri, to 6pm Sat, 1-6pm Sun; ⊞) Oh, to be eight again. Creative play spaces for kids don't get any better than this bright, brand-new museum. Eager staff help children engage their limbs and imaginations among the plethora of interactive exhibits: the watery port of Tampa, a TV station with hidden cameras throughout the museum, a working theater stage, art lab, Lego building station, paper-airplane tester, supermarket, vet clinic and more. Best of all: it's adjacent to Curtis Hixon Park, a scenic grassy swath with its own playground.

Tampa Museum of Art   MUSEUM
(☎813-274-8130; www.tampamuseum.org; 120 W Gasparilla Plaza; adult/child 7-18yr $10/5, 4-8pm Fri free; ☺11am-7pm Mon-Thu, to 8pm Fri, to 5pm Sat & Sun) Reopened in February 2010 on Curtis Hixon Park in a glorious, dramatically cantilevered building sheathed in a silver-mesh skin, the Tampa Museum of Art now commands attention among the bay area's crowded art world. Six cavernous galleries balance their permanent collection – an unusual mix of Greek and Roman antiquities, contemporary photography and new media – with major traveling exhibitions. Enjoy a sandwich in the slow-food cafe, and no, no one has counted the number of holes.

Tampa Bay History Center   MUSEUM
(☎813-228-0097; www.tampabayhistorycenter.org; 801 Old Water St; adult/child 4-12yr $12/7; ☺10am-5pm) In a new three-story building along the Riverwalk, this first-rate history museum is the best place to learn about the region's Seminoles, Cracker pioneers and the legendary Cuban community and cigar industry that formed the cornerstone of turn-of-the-

century Tampa. Like maps? Its dazzling cartography collection covers 400 years of mapmaking, as conquistadors and tycoons tried to pin down Florida. An outpost of the Columbia Restaurant (☺11am-9pm) makes a delicious lunch stop.

Henry B Plant Museum   MUSEUM
(☎813-254-1891; www.plantmuseum.com; 401 W Kennedy Blvd; admission $10; ☺10am-5pm Tue-Sat, noon-5pm Sun) The silver minarets of the 1891 Tampa Bay Hotel glint majestically across the river from downtown. Built by railroad magnate Henry B Plant, the hotel is now a National Historic Landmark and part of the University of Tampa. In one section, this museum recreates the original hotel's luxurious, gilded late-Victorian world, capturing the life and times of one of Florida's most influential industrialists.

Museum of Science & Industry   MUSEUM
(MOSI; ☎813-987-6000; www.mosi.org; 4801 E Fowler Ave; adult/child 2-12yr $24/20; ☺9am-5pm Mon-Fri, to 6pm Sat & Sun; P⊞) All ages can find something intriguing at this interactive science museum. Younger kids: go straight to Kids in Charge, whose wealth of hands-on activities hides science beneath unadorned play. An extreme-weather exhibit recreates

---

TAMPA FOR CHILDREN

Families will find Tampa a compelling destination, and not just because of Busch Gardens (p375). Don't wait for the proverbial rainy day. These sights are worth seeking out any time.

» **Lowry Park Zoo** Great zoo that's every bit Busch Gardens' equal for animal encounters.

» **Florida Aquarium** Creative, extensive exhibits, plus sea-life cruises. Jump in the shark tank!

» **Glazer Children's Museum** New under-10 play museum is a treat.

» **Museum of Science & Industry** Bang, push, ride, puzzle, build all afternoon.

» **Hillsborough River State Park** A city escape with lazy river kayaks and huge swimming pool.

» **Columbia Restaurant** The whole family will enjoy the flamenco show and Spanish atmosphere.

the effects of hurricanes and tornadoes. However, the frank human body exhibit – with preserved fetuses and cautionary looks at pregnancy and health – is best for older kids. Don't miss the Imax movie; it's included with admission. From downtown, take I-275 north to exit 51, and go east on Fowler Ave.

FREE **Manatee Viewing**
Center   ANIMAL WATCHING
(☑813-228-4289; www.tampaelectric.com/mana tee; Big Bend Rd, Apollo Beach; ◷10am-5pm Nov 1-Apr 15) One of Florida's more surreal wildlife encounters is spotting manatees in the warm-water discharge canals of coal-fired power plants. Yet these placid mammals show up here so reliably from November through April that this is now a protected sanctuary. Look for tarpon, rays and sharks, too. A snack bar, small exhibit, bathrooms and picnic tables round out the sight. It's half an hour from downtown Tampa; take I-75 south to exit 246 and follow signs.

YBOR CITY

Like the illicit love child of Key West and Miami's Little Havana, Ybor City is a multiethnic, nostalgia-rich neighborhood that hosts the Tampa Bay area's hippest party scene. The cobblestone 19th-century historic district is a redolent mix of wrought-iron balconies and rustling palm trees, of globe streetlamps and brick buildings, that preserves a strong Cuban, Spanish and Italian heritage from its days as the epicenter of the Tampa cigar industry. Still, as you stroll Ybor (ee-bore) City's main drag, along 7th Ave (La Septima) between 14th and 21st Sts, it's clear this urban enclave remains in transition. Mingled among the packed restaurants, cigar stores and nightclubs are shuttered storefronts like knocked-out teeth, and the bustling historic district is bordered by run-down, neglected neighborhoods.

Yet despite time and troubles, a playful, Spanish-style embrace of life still animates the sidewalks. If Tampa grew up into a respectable American city, Ybor City retains the charming, rakish personality of its immigrant roots.

For a guided, 90-minute walking tour, reserve ahead with **Ybor City Historic Walking Tours** (☑813-505-6779; www.yborwalking tours.com; adult/child $15/5); they typically run twice daily.

TECO Streetcars make the quick, easy trip from downtown. Ybor City also has plenty of street parking; convenient lots are on 13th and 16th Aves.

Ybor City Museum State Park   MUSEUM
(☑813-247-6323; www.ybormuseum.org; 1818 9th Ave; admission $4; ◷9am-5pm) This somewhat dusty, old-school history museum preserves an authentic slice of a bygone era: tour immigrant cigar worker houses and poke your head into the massive, original bakery ovens. Fascinating photographs bring late-19th-century Ybor City to life. Best of all, the museum store is one of the best places to buy a cigar, and excellent **walking tours** (☑813-428-0854; per person $8) are conducted every Saturday at 10:30am, led by Wallace Reyes.

🎆 Festivals & Events

Gasparilla Pirate Festival   CULTURAL
(www.gasparillapiratefest.com) On the last Saturday in January, pirates invade and parade in Tampa's version of Mardi Gras.

Florida State Fair   CULTURAL
(www.floridastatefair.com; Florida State Expo) Classic Americana for over 100 years; enjoy rides, food and livestock for two weeks in February.

Ybor City Heritage &
Cigar Festival   CULTURAL
(www.cigarheritagefestival.com) Ybor City pulls out the stops for its biggest cultural event, a street party of food, music and smokes in mid-November.

Victorian Christmas Stroll   CULTURAL
(www.plantmuseum.com) Hosted by the Henry B Plant Museum, this two-week December

---

GETTIN' NEKKID IN PARADISE

Those for whom getting naked is both philosophy and lifestyle shouldn't miss **Paradise Lakes Resort** (☑813-949-9327; www.paradiselakes.com; 2001 Brinson Rd, Land O' Lakes; r $105-135; ✳🛜🌊), one of America's largest 'clothing optional' resorts. An older, mature crowd lets it all hang out around three heated pools; the only thing they take seriously is the volleyball. Get a day pass or stay the night: condo-style rooms are simple, plain and functional, and there's a bar, restaurant and, naturally, a sexy **nightclub** (◷Thu-Sat). It's 17 miles north of downtown Tampa off Hwy 41; call for directions.

Tampa's revitalized historic cigar district has a rich heritage. But let's start further south. Due to its proximity to Cuba and its excellent tobacco, Key West had long been the cigar-making capital of the US. But when workers started organizing in Key West, the cigar barons figured that the only way to break the union's grip on their factories was to relocate them, and the only direction in which they could head was north. In 1886, when Vicénte Martínez Ybor and Ignacio Haya moved their considerable cigar factories – the Principe de Gales (Prince of Wales) and La Flor de la Sanchez y Haya, respectively – to present-day Ybor City, it marked a turning point. And as if to send a message to Key West that its cigar-making days were over, a fire broke out there on April 1, 1886, destroying several cigar factories, including a branch of Ybor's Principe de Gales. Over the next 50 years, as more Cuban cigar-makers moved into Tampa en masse, Ybor City turned into the cigar capital of the USA. From then on, Tampa became synonymous with quality, epitomized by brands like Tampa Sweethearts and Hav-a-Tampa.

Today, the old Tampa Sweethearts factory still stands (at 1301 N 22nd St), but the most personalized experience is the Ybor City Museum walking tour, run by PhD Wallace Reyes, who has his own cigar label and currently holds the world record for rolling the longest cigar, a whopping 196ft 3/8in. At tour's end he'll show you how to roll your own: a practiced hand can do the first or main roll in three to four minutes. Then, the cigar is pressed for 45 minutes before adding the final wrap leaves, which impart the flavor and are what distinguish different brands.

Several storefronts in Ybor City have demonstration rollers in their windows, but the most knowledgeable (and legitimate) places to buy cigars in Ybor City are the following:

Metropolitan Cigars (2014 E 7th Ave; ⊙9:30am-8pm Mon-Fri, 10:30am-5:30pm Sat) The store itself is actually a humidor; perhaps the best cigar shop in Tampa Bay.

King Corona Cigar Factory (www.kingcoronacigars.com; 1523 E 7th Ave; ⊙10am-6pm Mon, to 10:30pm Tue-Wed, to 1am Thu-Sat, noon-6pm Sun) The city's largest cigar emporium, complete with an old-fashioned cigar bar.

El Sol (www.elsolcigars.com; 1728 E 7th Ave; ⊙10:30am-5:30pm Mon-Sat) Established in 1929, and the oldest cigar store in Ybor City.

Gonzales y Martinez Cigar Company (2025 E 7th Ave; ⊙10am-9pm Mon-Thu, to 11pm Fri & Sat, noon-6pm Sun) Within the Columbia Restaurant gift store.

Finally, of course, anyone who loves cigars and Ybor City shouldn't miss the annual cigar festival in mid-November.

event evokes the Victorian holiday spirit with dramatizations in period costume.

🛏 Sleeping

Interesting, independent lodging isn't Tampa's strong suit. Business travelers tend to aim for the high-end chains (like Westin or Marriott) downtown, while travelers are best situated in Ybor City. An abundance of midrange chains are also north of downtown, close to Busch Gardens and the University of South Florida.

TOP CHOICE **Gram's Place**   HOSTEL $
(☎813-221 0596; www.grams-inn-tampa.com; 3109 N Ola Ave; dm $23, r $25-70; @) Named for Gram Parsons, this low-key hostel is as ram-

shackle as an aging country music star, and as charismatic. Genuine love infuses the music-themed rooms (the train-car dorm was inspired by Jimmy Rogers), and the owner, Bruce, creates a welcoming vibe for travelers of all ages, whether you're a middle-aged hippie or a Danish backpacker. Hostels aren't for everyone, but if you prefer personality over perfect linens, come here: relax around the in-ground hot tub, hang out for the Saturday-night jam session. Those songs about Key West life? This is what they're about.

Tahitian Inn   HOTEL $$
(☎813-877-6721; www.tahitianinn.com; 601 S Dale Mabry Hwy; r $100-170; P✳@🛜🏊♿) The highly recommended, family-owned Tahitian Inn performs a neat trick: it offers full-service,

boutique-hotel aspirations at midrange chain prices. The 81 rooms sport fresh-feeling Tommy Bahama–style decor, and in addition to the attractive pool, spa, fitness center, lounge and cafe-restaurant, it offers airport transportation.

Don Vicente de Ybor Historic Inn
HISTORIC HOTEL **$$**

(☎813-241-4545; www.donvicenteinn.com; 1915 Av República de Cuba; r $130-200; P❄☎) Though slightly faded, the 1895 Don Vicente is the most atmospheric stay in Tampa, harkening back to Ybor City's glory days – especially the elegant, old-world public rooms with their rose-tinted chandeliers, oil paintings and grand staircase. The 16 rooms are less dramatic and warm, but they feature antiques, sleigh beds, velvet drapes and Persian rugs. Balcony rooms facing Av de República are best situated. Hot breakfast is included. In Ybor City.

Hilton Garden Inn Ybor City
HOTEL **$$**

(☎813-769-9267, 877-367-4458; www.hiltongardeninn.com; 1700 E 9th Ave; r from $100-160; P❄☎≋🐾) Attractive, clean, reliable, ideally located chain digs. Nice pool. In Ybor City.

Hampton Inn & Suites Ybor City
HOTEL **$$**

(☎813-247-6700; www.hamptoninn.hilton.com; 1301 E 7th Ave; r $100-180; P❄@☎≋🐾) Very comfortable chain, walkable to the action. Pool is tiny. In Ybor City.

✕ Eating

Tampa has an excellent restaurant scene, though precious little is downtown. Ybor City is jam-packed with restaurants, particularly good Spanish and Italian, while the Seminole Heights neighborhood (along Florida Ave near Hillsborough Ave) is an up-and-coming hipster hangout. However, SoHo (South Howard Ave) in South Tampa has been dubbed 'restaurant row' for its plethora of chic eateries; the stretch between Kennedy and Bayshore Blvds is prime.

YBOR CITY

[TOP CHOICE] **Columbia Restaurant**
SPANISH **$$$**

(☎813-248-4961; www.columbiarestaurant.com; 2117 E 7th Ave; mains $17-28; ⊙11am-10pm Mon-Thu, to 11pm Fri & Sat, noon-9pm Sun) The Spanish atmosphere is so thick it feels like a schtick, but the Columbia's historic, original location is laudably authentic and truly memorable. Reserve ahead for the main dining room's 45-minute flamenco show (twice

nightly): it's an exuberant performance, with red dresses swishing beneath dusty iron chandeliers. The Spanish cooking is robust and traditional, rather than refined. Stick to the classics that made them famous: *arroz con pollo,* paella, *ropa vieja,* and the 1905 salad, spun tableside. At minimum hit the burnished bar for a mojito and garlicky tapa.

La Segunda Bakery
BAKERY **$**

(2512 N 15th St; items $1-8; ⊙6:30am-5pm Mon-Fri, 7am-3pm Sat, 7am-1pm Sun) At 15th Ave and 15th St, just outside Ybor's main drag, this authentic Spanish bakery cranks out delicious breads and pastries, rich Cuban coffee and maybe Tampa's best Cuban sandwich. Here since 1915, it bustles every AM with a cross-section of Tampa society.

Bunker
CAFE **$**

(www.yborbunker.com; 1907 19th St N; items $3-8; ⊙7:30am-6pm Mon, to 9pm Tue-Sat, 9am-3pm Sun) Ybor City's hipster contingent wake up at this relaxed community coffeehouse, which offers a range of breakfast burritos, soups and sandwiches all day. Come evening, it hosts open mics, movie nights and even GLBT speed dating.

Mema's Alaskan Taco
MEXICAN **$**

(1724 E 8th Avey; mains $5-9; ⊙noon-1am, to 3am Thu-Sat) The crispy and delicious pan-fried tacos at this funky Mexican hut (off Centennial Park) make a fun, quick meal. Try gator, chorizo and shrimp.

SOUTH TAMPA

[TOP CHOICE] **Bern's Steak House**
STEAKHOUSE **$$$**

(☎813-251-2421; www.bernssteakhouse.com; 1208 S Howard Ave; steaks $25-60; ⊙from 5pm) Bern's is legendary, a nationally renowned steakhouse that offers far more than a meal: dining here is an unforgettable event. The menu is an education in steaks and beef (dry-aged on the premises, naturally); sides are generous and often organic. There are dozens of caviars, and dessert is so overwhelming you relocate to a separate dining room; many reserve solely for dessert. Merely ask, and you may tour the kitchens and epic wine cellar. Jackets aren't required but won't feel out of place in this paean to old-world moneyed elegance.

🖋 Sidebern's
FUSION **$$$**

(☎813-258-2233; www.sideberns.com; 2208 W Morrison Ave; mains $29-40; ⊙5-10pm Mon-Thu, to 11pm Fri & Sat; ☎) Don't feel like steak? This trendy alternative to Bern's offers inventive, refined gourmet cuisine, locally sourced, that appeals to adventurous, big-city palates. The wine list is spectacular, the service impeccable, the interior contemporary and stylish. To avoid choosing, order the six-course tasting menu ($70).

🍴 **Restaurant BT** FUSION $$$
(☎813-258-1916; www.restaurantbt.com; 2507 S MacDill Ave; lunch $10-13, dinner $23-34; ⏱11:30am-2:30pm & 5:30-10pm Mon-Sat, to 11pm Fri & Sat) Chef Trina Nyugan-Batley has combined her high-fashion background and Vietnamese upbringing to create this ultra-chic temple to sustainable, locavore gourmet cuisine. While it freely raids the international cupboard, the backbone of BT's inventive menu is its distinctive French-Vietnamese hybrid. Lunch is a more low-key affair of *pho*, green-papaya salads and baguette sandwiches.

717 South ITALIAN $$$
(☎813-250-1661; www.717south.com; 717 S Howard Ave; mains $16-26; ⏱11:30am-2:30pm Mon-Fri, 5-10pm Mon-Thu, 5-11pm Fri & Sat) 717 perfectly encapsulates the cosmopolitan, young-professional South Tampa vibe. Start with a swank cocktail at the trendy bar, then shift to an intimate dining table amid art-deco paintings. The menu updates Italian classics along with a range of Asian-Floribbean seafood.

SEMINOLE HEIGHTS & AROUND

TOP CHOICE **Refinery** FUSION $$
(☎813-237-2000; www.thetamparefinery.com; 5137 N Florida Ave; mains $12-18; ⏱5-10pm Tue-Thu, 5-11pm Fri & Sat, 11am-3pm Sun; 🍴) A semifinalist for the 2011 James Beard award for best new restaurant, the Refinery marries a sustainability ethic with a punk attitude. The hyperlocal changing menu features small plates (and 'more than a small plate'), allowing chef Greg Baker extreme latitude for his clever creativity. At this blue-collar gourmet joint, they promise chipped plates, mismatched cutlery and no pretensions, just playful, delicious cuisine 'for folks like us.'

La Teresita SPANISH $
(www.lateresitarestaurant.com; 3246 W Columbus Ave btwn Himes & N MacDill Aves; mains $5-7; ⏱5am-midnight Mon-Wed, 24hr Thu-Sat, to 10pm Sun) At this Cuban cafeteria, grab a stool at a horseshoe-shaped counter (ignore the separate restaurant) and experience the 'real' Tampa. Locals from all walks of life get their

Spanish comfort food here: bay leaf–steeped black beans, neon-yellow rice, fried plantains, grilled steak with onions and peppers. Add a dash of hot sauce. Perfection.

DOWNTOWN

Mise en Place MODERN AMERICAN $$$
(☎813-254-5373; www.miseonline.com; 442 W Kennedy Blvd; lunch $10-15, dinner $20-35; ⏱11:30am-2:30pm Tue-Fri, 5:30-10pm Tue-Sat, to 11pm Fri & Sat) This landmark Tampa restaurant has been a destination for romantic, sophisticated dining for over 25 years. The menu emphasizes contemporary American cuisine with Floribbean accents; the two tasting menus ($30 to $50) are excellent deals. It's an ideal choice for a delicious yet affordable lunch while museum-hopping downtown.

🍷 Drinking & Entertainment

For nightlife, Ybor City is party central, though SoHo and Seminole Heights are also hip and happening. Tampa Bay's alternative weekly is *Creative Loafing* (www.cltampa .com), with event and bar listings. *Arts Tampa Bay* (www.artstampabay.com) maintains a regionwide cultural calendar.

Ybor City is also the center of Tampa's GLBT life; to connect with it, check out the **GaYbor District Coalition** (www.gaybor.com) and **Gay Tampa** (www.gaytampa.com).

Seminole Hard Rock Hotel & Casino CASINO
(www.seminolehardrocktampa.com; 5223 N Orient Rd, East Tampa; ⏱24hr; [P]) There's so much rock-and-roll memorabilia, it's as if the Hard Rock chain has mugged every famous musician for the last 50 years. This up-to-date casino is equivalent to Atlantic City standards but not Vegas overkill. The snazzy restaurant has live bands nightly. Free outdoor parking.

Channelside BAR, CINEMA
(www.channelsidebayplaza.com; 615 Channelside Dr) Next to the aquarium, this entertainment complex is an unapologetic tourist trap, with bars and restaurants, outdoor entertainment, an Imax theater, bowling and souvenir shops. Occasional big events draw crowds.

Bars & Clubs
Some weekend nights, Ybor City could pass for New Orleans' Bourbon St. Intense, festive crowds can keep clubs throbbing till the wee hours. (Most clubs are open 10pm to 3am Thursday to Saturday and charge a cover of $10 to $30.) It's easy enough to walk E 7th Ave and judge each venue's vibe for yourself:

do you fancy a hookah bar or a sports bar, a comedy club or Coyote Ugly? What's hard is getting past the bouncers, bikini-clad models and velvet ropes of the sexiest nightclubs if you aren't dressed like you mean business.

TOP CHOICE **Skipper's Smokehouse** LIVE MUSIC
(☎813-971-0666; www.skipperssmokehouse.com; cnr Skipper Rd & Nebraska Ave; cover $5-25; ⊙11am-midnight Tue-Sun) Did this place blow in from the Keys on a hurricane? No, for over 30 years Skipper's has been an unpretentious, beloved Old Florida institution and Tampa's best open-air venue for blues, funk, folk, reggae and gator-swamp rockabilly. Hell, it's so damn friendly you can bring the kids. The attached seafood restaurant is nothing special, but Skipper's certainly is. Take I-275 N to exit 52/Fletcher Ave.

Independent BAR
(www.independenttampa.com; 5016 N Florida Ave; ⊙from 4pm Mon-Fri, from 1pm Sat & Sun) If you appreciate craft brews, roll in to this converted gas station, now a low-key hip bar in Seminole Heights. You can count on one or more local Cigar City Brews, and they serve some mean pub grub.

Four Green Fields IRISH PUB
(www.fourgreenfields.com/tampa; 205 W Platt St; ⊙11am-3am Mon-Sat, noon-3am Sun) This thatch-roof, plaster-sided bit o' blarney looks like a traditional Irish cottage, and the gregarious Irish staff, football shirts, draft Guinness and Irish menu (items $11 to $13) will have you affecting your own Irish brogue.

Tampa Bay Brewing Company BREWERY
(www.tampabaybrewingcompany.com; 1600 E 8th Ave; ⊙11am-11pm, to midnight Fri & Sat) This fun brewpub in the heart of Ybor City makes a great start to an evening. Sample a flight of its own delicious beers. There's a full menu of standard pub-grub fare (items $9 to $14).

Ybor City nightclubs come and go, but these two have withstood the test of time: **Club Prana** (www.clubprana.com; 1619 E 7th Ave) has five floors, with different music on each floor; **Empire** (www.empirelive.com; 1902 E 7th Ave) has two levels dedicated to hip-hop.

Cinemas
Tampa Theatre CINEMA
(☎813-274-8981; www.tampatheatre.org; 711 N Franklin St; tickets $9) This historic 1926 theater in downtown is a gorgeous venue to see

an independent film, and before most movies they play the mighty Wurlitzer organ. Too bad showtimes are so limited: only one evening screening midweek and three on weekends. Look for special events.

Cinebistro CINEMA
(☎813-514-8300; www.cobbcinebistro.com; 1609 W Swann Ave, Hyde Park Village, South Tampa; mains $10-20) Cross a trendy South Beach nightclub with a plush arthouse cinema, and you get this: a snazzy, lobby cocktail bar, and upscale munchies to nosh at your seat while you watch. It's moviegoing... with style.

Performing Arts
Straz Center for the Performing Arts PERFORMING ARTS
(☎813-229-7827; www.strazcenter.org; 1010 MacInnes Pl; tickets $10-80) Beautifully sited on a riverside park, this is the largest performing-arts center south of the Kennedy Center in Washington, DC. With five venues, ranging from the 2600-seat Carol Morsani Hall to a 130-seat black box stage, it hosts the full gamut of fine-arts performances: major pops concerts, the Florida Orchestra, touring Broadway productions, cutting-edge dramas, the Tampa Ballet, Opera Tampa and more.

Improv Comedy Theater COMEDY
(☎813-864-4000; www.improvtampa.com; Centro Ybor, 1600 E 8th Ave; tickets $10-30; ⊙6pm-1am Wed-Sun) This 21+ comedy club brings the funny five nights a week with local and national acts.

Sports
The NFL's Tampa Bay Buccaneers play at **Raymond James Stadium** (☎813-879-2827; www.buccaneers.com; 4201 N Dale Mabry Hwy) from August (pre-season) to December, but single-game tickets are hard to come by; most games sell out.

The New York Yankees play spring-training baseball games in March at **Steinbrenner Field** (☎813-875-7753; www.steinbrennerfield .com; 3802 ML King Jr Blvd at N Dale Mabry Hwy), the 10,000-seat stadium modeled after the 'House that Ruth Built' (ie Yankee Stadium in New York). The Yankees' class-A minor-league team, the Tampa Yankees, plays at Legends Field from April to September.

The NHL's Tampa Bay Lightning play hockey at the **St Pete's Times Forum** (☎813-301-6600; www.lightning.nhl.com; 401 Channelside Dr) from October to March. The forum also hosts basketball games, concerts and ice shows.

As across Florida, college sports are followed avidly in Tampa: the **USF Bulls** (www.gousfbulls.com) field competitive football, baseball, basketball and other teams. Basketball teams play in the **Sun Dome** (www.sundome.com), and football games are held at Raymond James Stadium. Indeed, Tampa's biggest college-football event is definitely the **Outback Bowl** (☏813-874-2695; www.outbackbowl.com; Raymond James Stadium; tickets $75), an NCAA (National College Athletic Association) football game on New Year's Day.

🛍 Shopping

Inkwood Books   BOOKS
(www.inkwoodbooks.com; 216 S Armenia at Platt; ⊙10am-6pm Mon-Sat, to 9pm Thu, 1-5pm Sun) In a small house close to Hyde Park, Tampa's best independent bookstore has a fantastic selection of new Florida titles, both nonfiction and mysteries, and wonderful children's books.

The most interesting street shopping is definitely in Ybor City, from funky boutiques and trinket shops to cigars and fresh-roasted coffee. The Columbia Restaurant gift shop has a notable selection of hand-painted Spanish ceramics. On 8th Ave between 15th and 17th Sts, **Centro Ybor** (www.centroybor.com) is an attractive shopping, dining and entertainment complex. In addition, the **Ybor City Farmers Market** (Centennial Park, 8th Ave & 18th St; ⊙9am-3pm Sat) emphasizes arts and crafts.

Tampa has its share of malls, but for upscale trends and fashion, seek out **Hyde Park Village** (www.hydeparkvillage.net), in the lovely Old Hyde Park neighborhood in South Tampa. This outdoor mall is between Swann and Morrison Aves and Rome and Oregon Aves.

Finally, SoHo (South Howard St) south of Platt is another trendy stretch with cool finds and boutiques.

ℹ Information

Dangers & Annoyances

Tampa has big-city problems with homelessness, panhandlers and crime. Both downtown and Ybor City are safe in themselves, but they are bordered by tough neighborhoods; don't wander aimlessly. Panhandlers tend to gather on the median at stoplights and approach drivers; to end a solicitation, simply shake your head.

Internet Access

Federal Express Kinkos (www.fedexkinkos.com; 400 N Tampa St; per hr $12; ⊙7:30am-9pm Mon-Fri, 10am-6pm Sat)

Library (www.hcplc.org; 900 N Ashley Dr; ⊙10am-9pm Mon-Wed, to 8pm Thu, to 6pm Fri & Sat, 12:30-5pm Sun) Free internet access. Sells used books (50¢ mysteries).

Media

The Tampa Bay area has two major daily newspapers.
St Petersburg Times (www.tampabay.com)
Tampa Tribune (www.tampatrib.com)

Medical Services

Tampa General Hospital (☏813-844-7000; www.tgh.org; 1 Tampa General Circle, Davis Island; ⊙24hr) South of downtown on Davis Island.

Money

Bank of America (www.bankofamerica.com; 101 E Kennedy Blvd) Branches are everywhere.

Post

Post office (Commerce Retail Station; N Ashley Dr & E Kennedy Blvd) Most convenient downtown location.

Tourist Information

Tampa Bay Convention & Visitors Bureau (☏813-223-1111, 800-826-8358; www.visittampabay.com; 615 Channelside Dr; ⊙9:30am-5:30pm Mon-Sat, 11am-5pm Sun) This visitor center has good free maps and lots of information. The website links directly to hotels for booking.

Ybor City Visitor Center (☏813-241-8838; www.ybor.org; 1600 E 8th Ave; ⊙9am-5pm Mon-Sat, noon-5pm Sun) This VC is itself a small museum, with nice historic displays, a short video and the 'world's largest cigar box.'

Websites

Going Green Tampa (www.goinggreentampa.com) Find farmers markets and eco-friendly businesses.

Watermark (www.watermarkonline.com) Regional news and events for gays, lesbians and bisexuals.

ℹ Getting There & Around

Air

The region's major airport, and the state's third-busiest airport, is **Tampa International Airport** (TPA; www.tampaairport.com; 5503 W Spruce St; ⊙), about 13 miles west of downtown, off Hwy 589. It's an easy, pleasant airport to negotiate.

Hillsborough Area Regional Transit (HART) bus 30 picks up and drops off at the Red Arrival Desk on the lower level; exact change is required. From the airport, buses make the 40-minute trip downtown about every 15 minutes on weekdays, every half hour on weekends.

BUSCH GARDENS & ADVENTURE ISLAND

Orlando doesn't hold a monopoly on Florida theme parks. In Tampa, Busch Gardens presents two enormous thrill-seeker destinations: the Africa-themed Busch Gardens, with some of the country's best roller coasters, and the adjacent Adventure Island water park. If you'll be visiting both, get combo tickets. For general advice on theme park visits, see p30.

Both parks are about 7 miles north of downtown Tampa; take I-275 north to exit 50/ Busch Blvd and follow signs. Parking costs $13.

Busch Gardens

This **theme park** (☑813-987-5082, 866-353-8622; www.buschgardens.com; 10000 McKinley Dr; adult/child 3-9yr $80/70; ☺varies by day & season) has nine named African regions, but these flow together without much fuss. The entire park is walkable. Admission includes three types of fun: epic roller coasters and rides, animal encounters and various shows, performances and entertainment. All are spread throughout the park, so successful days require some planning: check show schedules before arriving and plan what rides/animals to visit around the shows. Coaster lines only get longer as the day goes on.

» **Egypt** In 2011, Busch Gardens unveiled its newest coaster: Cheetah Hunt, an epic, low-to-the-ground scream-fest meant to mimic a cheetah's acceleration. Another top-notch ride is Montu, the southeast USA's largest inverted steel roller coaster. The Moroccan Palace Theater presents the headliner shows (such as Cirque du Soleil). Also, get up close to lions, hippos and hyenas, and glimpse the Serengeti Plain.

» **Serengeti Plain** This 80-acre habitat mimics the African plains, with hundreds of free-roaming animals. You can view it from the Serengeti Railway train ride, but the main access is the Serengeti Safari Tour ($34 per person), which lets you out of the truck to feed giraffes, and so on. Several 'behind-the-scenes' tours are also offered ($20).

» **Morocco** Gwazi, a huge but traditional wooden coaster, is here, along with monkey and ape encounters. It's close to the other main animal exhibits in Egypt and Nairobi.

» **Nairobi** Devoted mostly to animals, Nairobi has reptiles and nocturnal creatures in Curiosity Caverns, and Jamba Junction lets you pet a flamingo and eyeball cute critters.

» **Timbuktu** Smaller, carnival-like rides and arcades dominate Timbuktu. The 4D theater shows are a hoot: shameless 'interactive' fun where the seats goose and douse you.

All major car agencies have desks at the airport. By car, take the I-275 to N Ashley Dr, turn right and you're in downtown.

Bus, Trolley & Streetcar

Greyhound bus station (☑813-229-2174, 800-231-2222; www.greyhound.com; 610 Polk St) Serves the region and connects Tampa with Miami, Orlando, Sarasota and Gainesville.

Hillsborough Area Regional Transit (HART; ☑813-254-4278; www.gohart.org; 1211 N Marion St) HART buses converge at the Marion Transit Center on Morgan St. Buses cost $1.75 one way, $3.75 for an all-day pass. Routes service the zoo, Busch Gardens, the Henry Plant Museum and Ybor City.

In-Town Trolley (fare 25¢; ☺6-9am & 3-6pm Mon-Fri, also 6pm-2am Fri & Sat) Within downtown, HART's inexpensive trolley runs up and down Florida Ave, Tampa St and Franklin St every 10 minutes.

TECO Line Streetcars (www.tecolinestreetcar .org; tickets $2.50; ☺11am-10pm Mon-Thu, 11am-2am Fri, 9am-2am Sat, noon-8pm Sun) HART's old-fashioned electric streetcars connect downtown's Marion Transit Center with Ybor City.

Car & Motorcycle

Between Tampa and Orlando, take I-4. The fastest route to Miami is via I-75 south, which turns east at Naples and meets I-95 south at Fort Lauderdale. Another option, with Everglades detours, is to pick up US 41 (Tamiami Trail) at Naples, and follow this directly to Miami.

Train

Amtrak (☑813-221-7600, 800-872-7245; www.amtrak.com; 601 Nebraska Ave) Operates several daily shuttles between Tampa and Orlando.

» **Congo** A long-standing favorite, the formidable Kumba is one of the best roller coasters anywhere. It features three gulp-inducing loops and a 360-degree spiral. Recover on the Congo River Rapids, a water ride.

» **Jungala** Designed for younger kids, Jungala has a fantastic climbing structure, a splash area and a zip-line ride, as well as encounters with tigers and orangutans.

» **Stanleyville** Another all-star coaster is SheiKra, North America's first dive coaster, which plunges straight down and even goes underground. Two fun if traditional flume rides cool you off.

» **Safari of Fun & Bird Gardens** Bring the wee ones to the *Sesame Street*–themed Safari of Fun and let them go: a fence prevents runaways, and the awesome play and climbing structures and splash zones will keep them busy for hours. Don't miss the Elmo and Friends show; reserve ahead to dine with costumed characters. Adjacent Bird Gardens (the seed of the modern park) has the quintessential flock of flamingos and a walk-in aviary.

Adventure Island

This 30-acre **water park** (☎813-987-5600; www.adventureisland.com; 10001 McKinley Dr; adult/child 3-9yr $43/39; ⊘daily mid-Mar–Aug, weekends only Sep–Oct, hours vary by day & season) has everything a modern, top-flight water park requires: long, lazy river, huge wave pool, bucket-dumping splash zones, swimming pool, sandy lounge areas and enough twisting, plunging, adrenaline-fueled waterslides to keep teens lining up till closing.

Sleeping & Eating

Within the park, cafes and food carts outnumber rides. They're merely adequate and get expensive; bring plenty of snacks, to save time and money.

Near Busch Gardens, at the corner of Busch Blvd and 30th St, are several midrange chain hotels: Holiday Inn Express, La Quinta and Days Inn. While they may advertise being 'walkable' to the park, it is an *extremely* long walk that isn't recommended (especially with young kids). Just north of Busch Gardens, and across from USF, Fowler Ave also is home to a string of dependable midrange chains; Wyngate by Windham is a good bet.

Hillsborough River State Park

When Tampa residents need a woodsy escape, they head to this fantastic 3400-acre **state park** (☎813-987-6771; www.floridastateparks.org/hillsboroughriver; 15402 US 301 N; per car $6; ⊘8am-sunset; 🚻), just 20 minutes northeast of Tampa. For visiting families, it provides easy, kid-friendly encounters with Florida's wilderness, and you'll find the region's best (nonbeach) camping.

In summer, no question, the biggest draw is the giant half-acre **swimming pool** (per person $4, campers free; ⊘Memorial Day–Labor Day). On weekends, arrive by 8am or it might already be full (then you can't enter till someone leaves). However, the flat, winding park roads make for scenic **cycling** (bike rental per hr $4), and there are over 10 miles of equally easy **hiking** trails through pine flatwoods and cypress swamps.

The most evocative and fun activity, though, is **canoeing** (canoe rental 1-4hr $11-27, kayak rental per hr $14.50). Despite some small riffles, the lazy Hillsborough River lends itself to little paddlers. Who doesn't thrill to spotting raptors, deer, foxes and alligators gliding beneath torn curtains of Spanish moss? Early morning is best; animals are more active (and rentals can sell out).

The pretty 112-site **campground** (sites $27) has good facilities and solar-heated hot water, but not a lot of privacy. Spots along the river are prime, and camping is best (and busiest) during the October–March dry season (book up to a year in advance). Midweek is always less busy, with less competition for rentals and campsites.

From Tampa, take Fowler Ave/Hwy 582 east to US 301 N; it's about 9 miles.

St Petersburg

📞727 / POP 244,700

St Petersburg – Tampa's more arty and youthful sibling – has a bawdy reputation as a party town, where they like to say the sun shines, on average, 361 days a year. But in fact, the bay area's two cities are more alike than they are different. For the last decade, both have been strained by unrelenting urban sprawl, and today both are working hard to revitalize and restore their historic neighborhoods and waterfront districts. Both are also succeeding admirably and are worth visiting.

The Salvador Dalí Museum is St Petersburg's headline attraction, yet the museum's world-renowned and dazzling new home is just the most high-profile addition to St Pete's lively cultural scene. In contrast to Tampa, St Pete's main sights form a single compact district, making it easy to explore on foot. Day or night, the historic downtown and waterfront is a delightful, communal place to stroll, and seemingly each step passes spiffy new museums, galleries, restaurants and bars.

Indeed, if you prefer sleeping in a city and making day trips to the beach, St Pete is a good choice, as it's a quick drive to the barrier islands, and it's also close to the cultural sights in Tampa and Sarasota.

◉ Sights & Activities

When taking in the sights, visitors can confine themselves to a walkable, T-shaped route: along Central Ave, mainly from 8th St to Bayshore Dr, and along Bayshore Dr from the Dalí Museum to the bayfront parks in the Old Northeast neighborhood. There is usually adequate street parking and numerous lots.

St Petersburg Museum of Fine Arts MUSEUM
(📞727-896-2667; www.fine-arts.org; 255 Beach Dr NE; adult/child 7-18yr $17/10; ⊙10am-5pm Mon-Sat, noon-5pm Sun) The Museum of Fine Arts collection is as broad as the Dalí's is deep, and the two make satisfyingly complementary experiences. Here, traverse the world's antiquities and follow art's progression with examples from nearly every era. Monet, O'Keeffe and George Inness highlight the Impressionists, and intriguing galleries are devoted to pewter, silver, Steuben glass and Wedgwood vases.

Florida Holocaust Museum MUSEUM
(📞727-820-0100; www.flholocaustmuseum.org; 55 5th St S; adult/child $14/8; ⊙10am-5pm, to 8pm Thu) The understated exhibits of this Holocaust museum, one of the country's largest, present these mid-20th-century events directly and plainly, connecting them to contemporary examples of prejudice and genocide worldwide. With the free audio tour and videos, you hear many survivors tell their stories, and you end contemplating an actual boxcar used to take prisoners to the death camps. It's incredibly moving, which is why last admission is 90 minutes before closing.

Chihuly Collection GALLERY
(📞727-896-4527; www.chihulycollectionstpete.com; 400 Beach Dr; adult/child $15/12; ⊙10am-6pm Mon-Sat, noon-6pm Sun) New in 2010, this paean to Chihuly's glass artistry has designed the galleries around the installations, making each delicate garden and too-intricate-to-comprehend chandelier its own swirling drama of color and light. There are guided tours (every half hour) and a short film.

FREE **Morean Arts Center** GALLERY
(📞727-822-7872; www.moreanartscenter.org; 719 Central Ave; ⊙9am-6pm Mon-Sat, noon-6pm Sun) This lively community arts center hosts in-

SUNSHINE SKYWAY BRIDGE

Supported by canary-yellow cables, the impressive, 4-mile Sunshine Skyway Bridge ($1 toll) spans Tampa Bay south of St Petersburg. It's worth the toll just to experience this dramatic arc over the bay. This bridge is actually a replacement for the original span, which was destroyed in 1980 when a boat, *Summit Venture*, rammed into its base, and bits of the old bridge now bookend the modern one and form what is proudly hailed as the 'world's largest fishing pier.' At about 2 miles, the South Skyway Fishing Pier is the longest stretch; both offer dramatic bay-and-bridge views, especially at sunset, and bait shops with rentals for the anglers crowding the railings. To enter the piers, sightseeing is $3 per car; fishing is $4 per car plus $4 per person. Just want a quick peek? Free public parks are situated at each pier's base.

SALVADOR DALÍ MUSEUM

Unveiled in 2011, the theatrical exterior of the new **Salvador Dalí Museum** (☑727-823-3767; www.thedali.org; 1 Dali Blvd; adult/child 6-12yr $21/7, after 5pm Thu $10; ☉10am-5pm Mon-Wed, to 8pm Thu, to 5:30pm Fri & Sat, noon-5:30pm Sun) augurs great things: out of a wound in the towering white shoebox oozes the 75ft geodesic atrium Glass Enigma. Even better, what unfolds inside is like a blueprint of what a modern art museum should be, or at least, one devoted to understanding the life, art and impact of a single revolutionary artist. Salvador Dalí is often trivialized as a foppish visual trickster, but he was a passionate, daring intellectual and a true 20th-century visionary. Even those who dismiss his dripping clocks and curlicue mustache are still swept away by this museum.

The Dalí's 20,000 sq ft of gallery space is designed specifically to display all 96 oil paintings in the collection, along with 'key works from every moment and in every medium': drawings, prints, sculptures, photos, manuscripts, even movies, everything arranged chronologically and explained in context. You get photographer Philippe Halsman's famous portraits (like *Dalí Atomicus*) and the sublimely absurd and still shocking 1929 film *Un Chien andalou*. The museum is so sharp it includes a 'contemplation area' with nothing but white walls and a window. Another great breather is the garden, which is small but, like everything, shot through with cleverness.

Excellent, free docent tours occur hourly (on the half hour); these are highly recommended to help crack open the rich symbolism in Dalí's monumental works. Audio guides are also free, but they get snapped up fast. Indeed, 3000 people have been known to come in a day, so get here early or suffer waits for everything. Topping this off, the Spanish cafe is first rate, and the gift store is the region's best, hands down. The only disappointments: the kid-focused 'DillyDally with Dali' activity room and the introductory film both feel perfunctory.

Later, adjusting to the over-bright sunshine outside, you recognize Dali's fingerprints all over the 21st century. His 'surrealism' was both precise and prescient, unlocking the hidden architecture of our hearts, minds and media.

teresting rotating exhibits in all media. If you love glass, don't miss Morean's attached **Hot Shop** (☑727-827-4527; adult/child $8/5; ☉1-5pm Mon-Sat, noon-5pm Sun): intimate, full-blast glassmaking demonstrations occur every half hour. Reserve ahead for a one-on-one 'hot glass experience' ($50) and take home your own creation.

St Petersburg Museum of History MUSEUM (www.spmoh.org; 335 2nd Ave NE; adult/child 7-17yr $9/5; ☉10am-5pm Wed-Sat, 1-5pm Sun) As city history museums go, St Pete's is intriguingly oddball: with a real 3000-year-old mummy, two-headed calf, life-size replica of a Benoist plane, plus Tampa Bay Rays baseball, bay ecology and more. Funny place, this town.

Coffee Pot Bayou & the Old Northeast NEIGHBORHOOD
North of downtown are the brick-lined streets of St Pete's most historic neighborhood, as well as a string of parks, recreation facilities, and a paved waterfront path that's perfect for **walking**, **jogging** or **cycling** on one of St Pete's 361 sunny days. The visitor center has a **driving-tour** brochure and map.

The Old Northeast, or Coffee Pot Bayou, begins around 9th Ave NE and goes to 30th Ave NE; it extends inland from the bay to about 4th St. Simply follow North Shore Dr NE from 5th Ave NE. At about 10th Ave NE is the **North Shore Aquatic Complex** (visitors $5; ☉9am-4pm Mon-Fri, 10am-4pm Sat, 1-4pm Sun), with three gorgeous swimming pools, including a kids' pool with waterslide. Adjacent are grassy public parks, which include the **Gizella Kopsick Palm Arboretum** (admission free; ☉sunrise-sunset), essentially an open, 2-acre garden of over 500 palms, all signed and lovingly landscaped. Also here are large parking lots, restrooms and a long, white-sand **swimming beach**. Or, keep going along the paved trail, past pretty homes and private docks, all the way to small **Coffee Pot Park**, where manatees are occasionally spotted.

Pier WATERFRONT
(☑727-821-6164; www.stpetepier.com; 800 2nd Ave NE; ☉10am-8pm Mon-Thu, to 9pm Fri & Sat,

TAMPA BAY & SOUTHWEST FLORIDA TAMPA BAY AREA

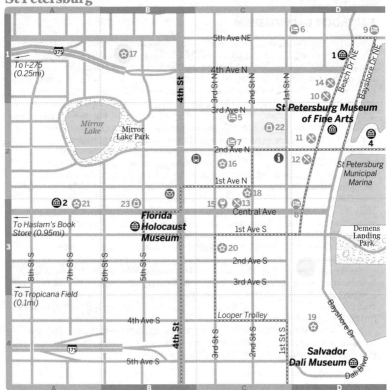

11am-7pm Sun) St Pete's tourist pier is a long, wide, aging landmark. It culminates in an inverted, primary-colored pyramid that looks like a 3D Mondrian painting and houses an uninspired tourist trap. There are shops, a tiny aquarium (www.pieraquarium.org; adult/child $5/4), a bait house with rod rentals, dolphin cruises, bike rentals, several gulf-view restaurants (the best is an outpost of Tampa's Columbia Restaurant), and brown pelicans awaiting fishy handouts. Plans are afoot to tear it down and start from scratch; expect changes.

Boyd Hill Nature Park   HIKING
(www.stpete.org; 1101 Country Club Way S; adult/child $3/1.50; ⏱10am-7pm Tue-Fri, 7am-6pm Sat, 10am-6pm Sun) A low-key, hidden oasis, Boyd Hill has nearly 4 miles of nature trails and boardwalks amid its 245 acres of pine flatwoods and swampy woodlands. Alligators, snowy egrets and bald eagles are among the wildlife you might see. From downtown, follow Martin Luther King Jr Blvd (9th St) south to 50th Ave and follow signs.

Pinellas Trail   CYCLING, RUNNING
(www.pinellascounty.org/trailgd) This 47-mile county-maintained trail calls to dedicated urban cyclists and runners. A converted railway, the paved path starts along 1st Ave S and Shore Dr in St Petersburg and continues, through town, country and suburb, north to Tarpon Springs. Download trail maps and route details online.

🎉 Festivals & Events

Crawfish Festival   FOOD
(www.cajunconnection.org) Down-home Cajun and zydeco food, music and dancing in early March.

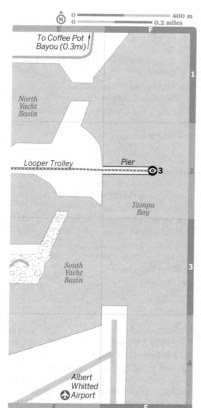

To Coffee Pot
Bayou (0.3mi)

North
Yacht
Basin

Looper Trolley   Pier
                              ●3

Tampa
Bay

South
Yacht
Basin

Albert
Whitted
✈ Airport

0 ———————— 400 m
0 ———————— 0.2 miles

Grand Prix   CULTURAL
(www.gpstpete.com) Grand Prix racing roars
through downtown St Pete for four days in
late March. Events are kicked off with the
all-American Festival of States Parade.

Tampa Bay Blues Festival   MUSIC
(www.tampabaybluesfest.com; Vinoy Park) Three
days of first-rate blues in early April.

International Folk Fair   CULTURAL
(www.spiffs.org) A three-day fair in early
November showcasing different cultures
through traditional foods, crafts and folk
dancing.

🛏 Sleeping

For southwest Florida, St Petersburg has a
notable selection of nice B&Bs; contact the
local Association of Bed & Breakfast Inns
(www.spaabbi.com).

⌖ Dickens House   B&B $$
(☎727-822-8622; www.dickenshouse.com; 335
8th Ave NE at Beach Dr NE; r $130-230; ✳@✿)
Once a decrepit rooming house and now
passionately restored into a Craftsman-
style dream, this charming B&B in the
historic Coffee Pot Bayou district has it all.
The five lushly designed rooms are cozy
romantic getaways that perfectly blend
modern comforts and idiosyncratic per-
sonality. Book the humorous Cracker Suite
for a headboard of raw tree limbs and your
TV on an ironing board. The gregarious,
gay-friendly owner knows St Pete well and
whips up a gourmet breakfast.

Ponce de Leon   BOUTIQUE HOTEL $$
(☎727-550-9300; www.poncedeleonhotel.com; 95
Central Ave; r $110-150; P✳@✿) For a bou-
tique hotel with Spanish flair in the heart
of downtown, there is one option, and it's a
good one: the Ponce. Hallways have splashy
murals of flamenco dancers, and rooms mix
blood-red chairs, glass sinks, teal walls and
hardwood floors; a few enjoy water views.
It's not perfect: some bathrooms await renovations, wall-mounted TVs are small and
parking is off-site. But for style, location
and its hot restaurant (Ceviche), it's hard
to beat.

Renaissance Vinoy Resort   LUXURY HOTEL $$$
(☎727-894-1000, 800-468-3571; www.vinoyrenais
sanceresort.com; 501 5th Ave NE; r $250-310;
P✳@✿≋) The coral-pink grande dame
of St Petersburg hotels, the 1925 Vinoy; is
such a landmark that the historical exhibit
on its 2010 renovation amounts to a history
of the city. That renovation also means this
full-service resort's 361 rooms are now spar-
kling, sumptuous concoctions, with leather
headboards, granite countertops and brand-
new furnishings. Guest Tower spa rooms
have Jacuzzis on private balconies. Facilities
include a gorgeous pool, spa and fitness cen-
ters, tennis courts, golf course and upscale
restaurants. Off-season and online deals
make for affordable luxury.

Pier Hotel   HISTORIC HOTEL $$
(☎727-822-7500; www.thepierhotel.com; 253 2nd
Ave N; r $100-200; P✳@✿) This historic ho-
tel needs a sugar daddy. Atmospheric period
and antique touches, and elegant public
rooms, provide an old-world European feel,
but scuffs show and some bathrooms are
small and awkward. Nevertheless, it's an
affordable, interesting sleep in the thick of

downtown. Continental breakfast is included; parking is $4. Web deals can be a steal.

Mansion House B&B B&B $$

(☎727-821-9391; www.mansionbandb.com; 105 5th Ave NE; r $130-250; P✳@☎≋) Two turn-of-the-century buildings with 12 rooms shelter a lovely courtyard with a small pool and hot tub on the edge of the Old Northeast. Rooms have hardwood floors, four-poster beds and an appealing mix-and-match aesthetic of antiques and funky modern pieces; lots of lounging and reading nooks make it hard to leave. Hot breakfast is made to order.

Hotel Indigo HOTEL $$

(☎727-822-4814; www.hotelindigo.com/stpete downtown; 234 3rd Ave N; r $150-210; P✳@☎≋👪) This upscale chain is a crisp, dependable choice that's walking distance to the waterfront. The 76 fresh-feeling, boutique-style rooms are designed to stand apart. They emphasize a sherbet-green and rose palette, wall-size murals, hardwood floors, flat-screen TVs and nice tiled bathrooms. The pool is small.

✕ Eating

Beach Dr along the waterfront is a warm, friendly scene lined with attractive mid-range restaurants; stroll at sunset and let your palate guide you.

TOP CHOICE Ceviche TAPAS $$

(☎727-209-2299; www.ceviche.com/1828; 95 Central Ave; tapas $5-13, mains $15-23; ⊙11am-10pm Sun-Mon, to midnight Tue-Thu, to 1am Fri & Sat) Panache counts, and Ceviche has it in spades, with its upbeat atmosphere, colorful tiled tables and wrought-iron railings. While you won't think you've stumbled into Madrid, order a pitcher of sangria and a handful of the flavorful, generously portioned tapas and you'll definitely have a good time. This is virtually guaranteed if you end the evening in the Flamenco Room, a sexy, cavernlike bar below with live flamenco music and dancing Thursday and Saturday nights. Every morning (from 8am), the attached cafe Pincho y Pincho dishes up tasty Spanish-influenced breakfasts and espresso coffees.

Bella Brava ITALIAN $$

(☎727-895-5515; www.bellabrava.com; 204 Beach Dr NE; lunch $7-10, dinner $14-20; ⊙11:30am-10pm, to 11pm Fri & Sat, 3-9pm Sun) Along with Cassis, Bella Brava anchors St Pete's prime intersection near the waterfront with breezy, attractive sidewalk dining. At Brava, the stylish, contemporary interior matches the cuisine, which specializes in updated northern Italian cooking. Thin-crust pizza, house-made gnocchi and comforting mains are satisfying and interesting.

Cassis

FRENCH $$$

(☎727-827-2927; www.cassisab.com; 170 Beach Dr NE; lunch $10-20, dinner $18-28; ⊙8-11am Mon-Fri, 11am-10pm daily) Doing its best imitation of a Parisian brasserie, with globe lights and banquettes inside and sidewalk tables outside, Cassis draws crowds for its affordable and well-executed French menu and its perfect waterfront location. It runs its own bakery next door. Service suffers when it gets hopping.

Moon Under Water

INDIAN $$

(☎727-896-6160; www.themoonunderwater.com; 332 Beach Dr NE; mains $9-17; ⊙11am-11pm, to midnight Fri & Sat) Sporting an upbeat, 19th-century British-colonial atmosphere, Moon Under Water serves admirably flavorful Indian curries; ask for a capsicum 'enhancer' to adjust the heat to your palate. The British side of the menu specializes in fish and chips, shepherd's pie and bangers and mash. Both imported British and local Cigar City brews on tap.

Garden

MEDITERRANEAN $$

(☎727-896-3800; www.thegardendtsp.com; 217 Central Ave; lunch $7-10, dinner $14-20; ⊙11am-10pm Mon-Sat, to 2am Fri & Sat, 10am-2pm Sun) With its cozy, hidden courtyard shaded by vine-draped trees and strung with lights, Garden is well named. The menu emphasizes light, Mediterranean-influenced salads and pastas, while live jazz music and DJs enhance the mood on Friday and Saturday, when a late bar menu is served till 2am.

AnnaStella Cajun Bistro

CAJUN $

(☎727-498-8978; www.annastellacajunbistro.com; 300 Beach Dr N; dishes $6-15; ⊙8am-10pm Sun-Thu, to 11pm Fri & Sat; ☝) A great breakfast or lunch choice along Beach Dr, Nola specializes in spicy Cajun and Creole dishes: red beans and rice, bisque, gumbo, and po' boy sandwiches. In the morning, relax over a national newspaper, chicory coffee and fresh powdered beignets.

Red Mesa Cantina & Lucha Bar

MEXICAN $$

(☎727-896-8226; www.redmesacantina.com; 128 3rd St S; mains $10-17; ⊙11am-10pm, to 11pm Fri & Sat) Rounding out St Pete's plethora of contemporary ethnic cuisine, Red Mesa dishes up tasty, updated Mexican entrees, plus a range of interesting ceviches and tacos. Its Lucha Bar specializes in high-end tequilas and strong margaritas; happy hour (3pm to 7pm Monday to Friday) promises good deals.

Biff-Burger

BURGERS $

(www.biffburgers.com; 3939 49th St N; mains $3-8; ⊙6am-10:30pm Mon-Thu, to midnight Fri & Sat, 7am-9:30pm Sun; ☝) Once a national drive-in chain, the last standing Biff-Burger has morphed into a down-home, blue-collar institution. Under a tin roof is an extremely long, double-sided bar and thick-lacquered picnic tables, where a wall of TV screens and various live musicians vie for your attention. For a buck and two bits (that is, $1.45), the Biff deluxe is the best burger around; go on, get two. The 'gourmet' is a super-sized feast, or order some sticky-sweet BBQ. Biker nights on Wednesday and Saturday are a scene. Biff-Burger is far from downtown, near 39th Ave N.

Coney Island Hot Dog

HOT DOGS $

(250 9th St N; items $2-3; ⊙10am-7pm Mon-Fri, to 3:30pm Sat) Collectors of Americana and hot-dog fanatics: order two delicious chili dogs, slaw and a milkshake and savor the vinyl-booth charm of this authentic, unvarnished old St Pete institution. Cash only. Near 3rd Ave N.

Drinking

Until recently, drinking in St Petersburg was mostly a beer-and-bourbon affair, but a flush of sleeker cocktail joints are elbowing in among the cigar bars and Irish pubs. The center of the action is Central Ave between 2nd and 3rd Sts, and within a block on all sides. Many restaurants also have lively bar scenes late, particularly Ceviche, Garden and Lucha Bar.

Kicking off each month, 'First Friday' is an evening block party and giant pub crawl with live music on Central Ave.

Central Cigars

CIGAR BAR

(www.centralcigars.com; 273 Central Ave; ⊙10am-10pm Mon-Thu, to midnight Fri & Sat, noon-5pm Sun) Enjoy a premium cigar and a classic cocktail at this stylish, popular watering hole. Perch at the long wooden bar or sink into a leather armchair; join the club and get your own humidor.

Ferg's Sports Bar & Grill

SPORTS BAR

(www.fergssportsbar.com; 1320 Central Ave; ⊙11am-2am Mon-Sat, noon-11pm Sun) Next to Tropicana Field, this huge sports bar with lots of outdoor and deck seating is the place to be before, during or after a Tampa Bay Rays baseball game, or really for any televised sporting event.

☆ Entertainment

For St Pete and some Tampa concert listings, check out **State Media** (www.statemedia.com). The **BayWalk** (www.newbaywalk.com) shopping complex also has a multiplex cinema. Many St Petersburg bars offer live music, but the town has few DJ-fueled nightclubs.

TOP CHOICE **Jannus Live** CONCERT VENUE
(📞727-565-0551; www.jannuslive.com; 16 2nd St N; tickets $15-30) The Tampa Bay area's most beloved concert venue received a welcome face-lift in 2009, improving the bathrooms and bar areas. Unchanged is the intimate stage hidden in a cozy open-air courtyard in the middle of the block, where national and local bands reverberate downtown.

Mahaffey Theater PERFORMING ARTS
(📞727-892-5767; www.mahaffeytheater.com; 400 1st St S; tickets $15-70) The gorgeous, 2000-seat Mahaffey Theater hosts a wide range of performing arts, from touring comedy acts to Broadway, dance, orchestra and more.

State Theatre CONCERT VENUE
(📞727-895-3045; www.statetheatreconcerts.com; 687 Central Ave; tickets $8-20) Up-and-coming bands of all stripes, and occasional national acts, play this restored art-deco theater (built in 1927).

Push Ultra Lounge DJ
(www.pushlounge.com; 128 3rd St S; ⊙9pm-3am Thu-Sat) In a three-story brick building above Red Mesa Cantina, Push is St Pete's premier hip-hop nightclub, where celebs like Danica Patrick and Paris Hilton have been spotted.

Coliseum Ballroom DANCE
(www.stpete.org/coliseum; 535 4th Ave N; tea dances $7-10) This old-fashioned, beautiful 1924 ballroom hosts occasional events and has regular 'Tea Dances' on the first and third Wednesday every month. Sessions run from 1pm to 3:30pm; dance lessons start at 11:30am. The classic ballroom was featured in the 1985 film *Cocoon*.

American Stage THEATER
(📞727-823-7529; www.americanstage.org; 163 3rd St N; tickets $25-47) One of the Tampa Bay area's most highly regarded regional theaters presents American classics and recent Tony winners (like *Red*). Its 'in the park' series presents Broadway musicals.

Florida Orchestra CLASSICAL MUSIC
(📞7272-892-3337; www.floridaorchestra.com; 163 3rd St N; tickets $20-70) The Florida Orchestra's box office is in St Petersburg, but it plays at Tampa's Straz Center as often as at Mahaffey downtown.

Tropicana Field STADIUM
(www.raysbaseball.com; cnr 1st Ave S & 16th St S; tickets $9-80; ⊙9am-5pm) Home to the major-league Tampa Bay Rays, who play baseball from April to September. Huge parking lots line 10th St S near 1st Ave S.

🛍 Shopping

The main shopping corridor is along Central Ave between 5th and 8th Sts and also between 10th and 13th Sts. This hip stretch doesn't lack for funky boutiques, art galleries, antique stores, vinyl records and cheap eats; it's an enjoyable afternoon ramble (though it's deserted at night).

Downtown, **BayWalk** (www.newbaywalk.com) is a troubled upscale shopping mall at 1st St N and 2nd Ave N that is, for the moment, mostly unoccupied; trendy shops may again fill it by the time you read this.

TOP CHOICE **Haslam's Book Store** BOOKS
(www.haslams.com; 2025 Central Ave; ⊙10am-6:30pm Mon-Sat, noon-5pm Sun) This bookstore is a bona fide attraction. A half-block long, with a tremendous selection of new and used books and a fantastic Florida section, Haslam's claims to be the largest independent bookstore in the US Southeast. Many beach days have been lost perusing its shelves.

Florida Craftsmen Gallery ARTS & CRAFTS
(📞727-821-7391; www.floridacraftsmen.net; 501 Central Ave; ⊙10am-5:30pm Mon-Sat) A nonprofit association runs this gallery-store dedicated to Florida craftspeople. Find unusual, unique, high-quality ceramics, jewelry, glass, clothing and art.

ℹ Information

All Children's Hospital (📞727-898-7451; www.allkids.org; 6th St S btwn 8th & 9th Aves; ⊙24hr)

Bayfront Medical Center (📞727-823-1234; www.bayfront.org; 701 6th St S; ⊙24hr)

Mirror Lake Library (www.splibraries.org; cnr 5th St & 3rd Ave N; ⊙9am-6pm Mon-Sat) Free internet access.

Post office (76 4th St N; ⊙8:30am-5pm Mon-Fri)

St Pete Downtown Arts Association (www.stpetearts.org)

St Petersburg Area Chamber of Commerce (📞727-821-4069; www.pleasure.stpete.com; 100 2nd Ave N; ⊙9am-5pm Mon-Fri) Helpful, staffed chamber office has good maps and a driving guide.

St Petersburg Times (www.tampabay.com)
St Petersburg/Clearwater Area Convention & Visitors Bureau (www.visitstpeteclearwater.com)

ℹ Getting There & Around

AIR **St Petersburg-Clearwater International Airport** (www.fly2pie.com; Roosevelt Blvd & Hwy 686, Clearwater) Served by several major carriers, but Tampa is main international airport.

BUS **Downtown Looper** (www.loopertrolley.com; fare 25¢; ⊙10am-5pm Sun-Thu, to midnight Fri & Sat) Old-fashioned trolley cars run a downtown circuit every 15 minutes; great for sightseeing.

Greyhound (☑727-898-1496; www.greyhound.com; 180 9th St N) Buses connect to Miami, Orlando and Tampa.

Pinellas Suncoast Transit Authority (PSTA; www.psta.net; 340 2nd Ave N; fare $2; ⊙5am-9pm Mon-Sat, 7am-5pm Sun) St Petersburg buses serve the barrier-island beaches, Clearwater and Tarpon Springs; unlimited-ride Go Cards are $4.50 per day.

CAR From Tampa, take I-275 south over the Howard Frankland Bridge. Reach downtown via either I-375 or I-175.

To Sarasota, continue on I-275 south over the Sunshine Skyway Bridge, which connects with I-75 and US 41 (Tamiami Trail).

To St Pete Beach, take I-275 to exit 17, and follow US 682/Pinellas Bayway. Or take Central Ave due west to Treasure Island Causeway or turn south on 66th St to the Corey Causeway.

To Clearwater Beach, go north on US 19 (34th St in St Petersburg) to Gulf to Bay Blvd; turn west and follow signs.

St Pete Beach & Barrier Island Beaches

☑727 / POP 9300

Ah, at last, the beach. In just 20 minutes from downtown St Petersburg, you can reach the legendary barrier-island beaches that are the sandy soul of the peninsula. This 30-mile-long stretch of sun-faded towns and sun-kissed azure waters is the perfect antidote to city life and the primary destination of most vacationers. Winter and spring are the high seasons, particularly January through March. During these months, readiness is all: book rooms far in advance, and get up early to beat the traffic and snag sometimes elusive parking spaces.

While St Pete Beach is the biggest town, a string of communities offers variations on a theme: of sand and Gulf waters, of seafood and radiant sunsets. This section covers the highlights from Fort DeSoto Park in the south all the way to Belleair Beach in the north; for Clearwater Beach, see p386.

◉ Sights & Activities

FREE **Fort DeSoto Park & Beach**   BEACH
(www.pinellascounty.org/park; 3500 Pinellas Bayway S; ⊙sunrise-sunset) Fort DeSoto's North Beach is unquestionably one of the Gulf Coast's, and even Florida's, top beaches – with the accolades to prove it. This long, silky stretch of dune-cradled white sand is accessed by huge parking lots and has excellent facilities, including grassy picnic areas and a cafe and gift store (⊙10am-4pm Mon-Fri, to 5pm Sat & Sun) with bike rentals. East Beach, meanwhile, is smaller and coarser, and consequently less crowded.

Fort DeSoto also offers terrific camping, two fishing piers (with bait shops and rentals) where you can spot dolphins, kayak rentals, and its namesake historic fort, which dates to 1898 and the Spanish-American War.

Fort DeSoto Park is signed off US 682/Pinellas Bayway (exit 17 off I-275).

Beaches   BEACH
Barrier-island beaches are almost uniformly excellent in terms of the quality of their white sand and the soporific, gentle warmth of their waters. Rather, they are distinguished by how amenable they are to day-trippers: some have much more public parking, access, commerce and hotels, while others are wholly residential and offer nary a parking space. Parking meters are $1.25 per hour; some lots have pay-and-display kiosks. The following are listed south to north.

The epic sliver of sand that is **Pass-a-Grille Beach** is almost idyllic, as it's backed only by beach houses and has by far the longest stretch of public parking. At the southernmost end, a cute, laid-back village center the size of a sand dollar provides T-shirts, eats and ice cream.

St Pete Beach is a long, double-wide strand with parasail booths and chair rentals seemingly every 50ft; big public parking lots. It's incredibly crowded with families and Spring Breakers, who appreciate all the restaurants, bars and motels just steps away.

Treasure Island is, if anything, even wider and more jam-packed with fun-seekers, concessions and motels than St Pete Beach; very built up, with lots of public access.

The string of 'towns' that is **Madeira, Redington & Indian Shores** is indistinguishable and offers very little public access. There are a few small lots in between the condos and vacation rentals.

A series of small lots and one larger lot with restrooms near 17th Ave make the quieter stretch of **Indian Rocks Beach** more appealing to day-trippers. Similar feel to Pass-a-Grille.

Limited public parking at **Belleair Beach** keeps day-trippers away, who are better served just north at Sand Key and Clearwater.

John's Pass Village   PIER

(☎727-391-7738; www.johnspass.com; 209 Boardwalk Pl E, Madeira Beach) For an industrial-strength concentration of Florida seaside tackiness, tie up the boat (er, park the car) at this former fishing village now transmogrified into an all-in-one, wharf-size nautical tourist trap. Any kind of rental or boat trip is available: Waverunners, pirate ships, dolphin cruises, parasailing, fishing charters, you name it. Watch pelicans scavenge below the fish-cutting stations. Wander the wooden boardwalk dripping ice cream. Navigate the culinary Scylla and Charybdis of Hooters and Bubba Gump. It's no-regrets holiday fun.

Suncoast Seabird Sanctuary   WILDLIFE SANCTUARY

(www.seabirdsanctuary.com; 18328 Gulf Blvd, Indian Shores; admission by donation; ☉9am–sunset) The largest wild-bird hospital in North America, this sanctuary has up to 600 sea and land birds for public viewing at any one time, including a resident population of permanently injured birds. Thousands of birds are treated and released back to the wild annually.

🛏 Sleeping

If you don't want a beach-based vacation, St Pete Beach is an easy day trip from St Petersburg. If, against all advice, you show up without a reservation, cruise Gulf Blvd in St Pete Beach and Treasure Island: the main drag is packed shoulder-to-shoulder with motels, hotels and condos; someone invariably will have a room. Low season nets steep discounts.

⎡TOP⎤ Fort DeSoto Park
CHOICE
Campground   CAMPGROUND $

(☎727-582-2267; www.pinellascounty.org/park; 3500 Pinellas Bayway S; tent/RV sites $35/40;

⎡🚗🏊⎤) For tent camping, the Gulf Coast hardly offers better than the more than 200 sites here. Well shaded by thick-growing palms, many face the water, and there are good facilities, hot showers, a grassy field and small camp store, in addition to other park concessions. Reserve ahead, but a few first-come, first-served sites are available daily.

PASS-A-GRILLE BEACH

Inn on the Beach   MOTEL $$

(☎727-360-8844; www.innonbeach.com; 1401 Gulf Way; r $125-250, cottages from $200; ✴@♿) For that quiet, relaxing seaside getaway, these 12 newly renovated rooms are unqualified gems. With bright coral and teal accents, wood-slat tables, functional kitchenettes and lovely tile bathrooms, these quarters are a pleasure to return to in the evening; a couple 2nd-floor rooms have luscious gulf views. Management is on the ball, and there are separate cottages, too.

Keystone Motel   MOTEL $$

(☎727-360-1313; www.keystonemotel.com; 801 Gulf Way; r $95-130; ✴🐾♿) This standard beach motel is well kept and in decent repair; it's the location and budget price that really get your attention. Keystone is right in Pass-a-Grille's tiny village, directly across from the beach. The pool is small.

ST PETE BEACH

⎡TOP⎤ Postcard Inn   BOUTIQUE MOTEL $$$
CHOICE
(☎727-367-2711; www.postcardinn.com; 6300 Gulf Blvd, near 64th Ave; r $160-260; P✴🏊) For its vintage 1950s hang-10 style alone, the Postcard Inn leads the pack in St Pete Beach. The long, double-armed shell of a 1957 Colonial Gateway has been transformed into a designer-chic surf shack: rooms are amusing concoctions of woven mats, wood-slat shutters, mod couches, standing surfboards and wall-size murals of wave riders in the curl. Some have outdoor hammocks, and all surround the spacious courtyard and sizable pool, with ping-pong tables, tiki bar and direct access to the beach. The young, hip crowd matches this fun place.

Don Cesar Beach Resort & Spa   RESORT $$$

(☎727-360-1881; www.loewshotels.com/doncesar; 3400 Gulf Blvd; r $270-400; P✴@🛜🏊♿) The magnificent, coral-pink Don Cesar shimmers like a mirage as you approach St Pete Beach from the causeway. Built in 1928, it's the sort of elegant seaside palace you imagine F Scott Fitzgerald spilling cocktails in, with chandelier-filled hallways and white cabanas by the glittering pool. Rooms are less refined, more relaxed roosts, and the full-service, four-diamond property has all you need: fine dining, European-style spa, kids' programs and, most of all, its own sultry beach far removed from the tourist madness.

Alden Beach Resort   RESORT $$$
(727-360-7081; www.aldenbeachresort.com; 5900 Gulf Blvd; r $140-300; P✳@☁⛹) This well-managed, well-kept property stands out as a great choice for families looking for a longer stay. The 143 good-size suites have standard decor, but are fresh, spotlessly clean, and come with nicely appointed full kitchens. Grounds include tennis and basketball courts, a kids' playground, a deck for grilling and direct beach access.

TREASURE ISLAND
Thunderbird Beach Resort   MOTEL $$
(727-367-1961; www.thunderbirdflorida.com; 10700 Gulf Blvd; r & apt $150-190; P✳@☁⛹) Since 1958, the art-deco sign has beckoned travelers, and the Thunderbird remains a reliable choice in the thick of the Treasure Island commercial corridor. Clean, standard decor eschews seaside kitsch for sage and coppery bronze hues. The real amenities, though, are the pool, tiki bar and beach.

INDIAN ROCKS BEACH
Laughing Lizard   B&B $$
(727-595-7006; www.laughinglizardbandb.com; 2211 Gulf Blvd; r $160-200; P✳@) Bill Ockunzzi, the gregarious former mayor of Indian Rocks, has whipped up a perfectly funky and festive south of the border–style B&B. The five rooms and one efficiency are each unique, filled with playful art, chunky crayon-colored tile, bright quilts and lizards everywhere. Full hot breakfast, afternoon sangria and loaner kites are included.

✗ Eating & Drinking
PASS-A-GRILLE BEACH
Black Palm   LATIN AMERICAN $$$
(727-360-5000; www.blackpalmrestaurant.com; 109 8th Ave; mains $17-32; from 5pm Tue-Sun) The most interesting meal in Pass-a-Grille is served on the Black Palm's delightful outdoor patio. The menu is a fusion of Latin cuisines, especially South America and the Caribbean. Tapas, ceviche, rib-eye with chimichurri sauce and grilled seafood mix perfectly with the salty breezes and live jazz music.

Wharf   SEAFOOD $$
(www.wharfrestaurant.org; 2001 Pass-a-Grille Way; mains $7-18; 11am-11pm, bar to 2am) For fried fish and chowder, and to rub elbows with local fishermen at the bar, head for this salty-dog shack on the harbor side. It has all the favorites, plus stone crab in season.

ST PETE BEACH
Ted Peter's Famous
Smoked Fish   SEAFOOD $$
(1350 Pasadena Ave; mains $6.50-19; 11:30am-7:30pm Wed-Mon) Ted Peter's is an only-in-St-Pete-Beach experience you gotta try once. Since the 1950s, they've been smoking fresh salmon, mackerel, mahimahi and mullet in the little smokehouse here, then dishing it up whole or in sandwich spreads. You eat at outdoor picnic tables; nothing fancy. The salmon is awesome; the mullet intense. Cash only. Pasadena Ave is actually on the mainland side of the Corey Causeway.

Wildwood BBQ   BARBECUE $$
(www.wildwoodbbq.com; 6300 Gulf Blvd; mains $8-18; 11:30am-9pm) A New York transplant attached to the Postcard Inn, Wildwood has an urban-industrial vibe and a menu offering a mix of BBQ styles, such as Texas, Memphis and St Louis. With your ribs, brisket, pulled pork and burgers you can also get Southern sides like collard greens and baked beans. The full bar specializes in bourbons and frozen drinks.

Undertow Bar   BAR
(www.undertowbeachbar.com; 3850 Gulf Blvd; noon-3am) Locals, bikers and coeds all mingle along the three flagstone-topped bars to booze it up and flirt day or night on the edge of the sand. When live reggae or DJs aren't playing, country music dominates the jukebox. It's friendly and casual.

REDINGTON BEACH & INDIAN SHORES
Salt Rock Grill   SEAFOOD $$$
(727-593-7625; www.saltrockgrill.com; 19325 Gulf Blvd, Indian Shores; mains $15-40; 4-10pm Mon-Thu, 4-11pm Fri & Sat, noon-10pm Sun) This contemporary, upscale harbor-side eatery puts everything on display: the basement wine cellar through a floor cutaway, the waterfront from sweeping windows and the outdoor deck, and the open kitchen's wood-fired grill, where seafood and steaks sizzle at a promised 1200°F. Or try lobster, the raw bar and pastas, but definitely reserve ahead.

GULFPORT

Don't tell anyone, but Gulfport is the cutest, quirkiest little beach town not on the barrier islands. Nestled at peninsula's end within Boca Ciega Bay, this overlooked artists community exudes that legendary, yet so often elusive, easygoing, fun-loving attitude Florida made famous. This hard-to-resist spell emerges on sultry evenings when the trees along Beach Blvd glow with lights and the outdoor restaurants burble with laughter.

It doesn't compare to the barrier islands, of course, but Gulfport does have a beach, one perfectly adequate for sunning and swimming, with a playground and shady picnic area. Beach Blvd, meanwhile, is a four-block stretch of funky boutiques, friendly locals, little cafes and surprisingly good restaurants. Get the full dose of wry local sensibilities during the twice-monthly art walk, essentially a low-key street party, every first Friday and third Saturday from 6pm to 10pm.

Peg's Cantina (☑727-328-2720; www.pegscantina.com; 3038 Beach Blvd; mains $10-16; ⊙5-10pm Tue-Fri, noon-9pm Sat & Sun) is ripe with Gulfport mojo. This brewpub in a woodsy bungalow perfectly pairs fanciful Mexican dishes with creamy handcrafted beers, ideally enjoyed in the wonderful gardens. Or, sit at the cozy bar and partake in a de facto beer class, sampling from the cornucopia of international selections from the beer fridge.

If you're tempted to spend the night, the historic **Peninsula Inn** (☑727-346-9800; www.innspa.net; 2937 Beach Blvd; r $130-180; ❀@🛜) has been renovated into a pretty, romantic choice. It also has a recommended restaurant with jazz music on weekends.

For more information, visit www.gulfportchamberofcommerce.com. To get there from St Petersburg, take I-275 exit 19 onto 22nd Ave S/Gulfport Blvd, and turn left onto Beach Blvd into town. From St Pete Beach, the Corey Causeway connects to Gulfport Blvd, or hop on the flamingo-festooned **Gulfport Trolley** (www.mygulfport.us; rides $2; ⊙8am-9:30pm). You'll be glad you did.

Lobster Pot
SEAFOOD $$$

(☑727-391-8592; www.lobsterpotrestaurant.com; 17814 Gulf Blvd, Redington Shores; mains $23-50; ⊙from 4:30pm) For a splash-out lobster feast, this is the place. The crustaceans hail from Maine, South Africa and the Caribbean, and preparations are classic. Indeed, stick to what they do best: whole steamed beasts served with candle-warmed butter just like in the movies. Reserve ahead.

INDIAN ROCKS BEACH

TOP CHOICE Guppy's
SEAFOOD $$

(☑727-593-2032; www.3bestchefs.com; 1701 Gulf Blvd; lunch $9-14, dinner $13-25; ⊙11:30am-10pm) For variety, quality and price, it's hard to beat Guppy's, which packs them in nightly. Preparations are diverse, skillfully spanning styles (and budgets), from Italian cioppino to Hawaiian seared-ahi and Caribbean spice-rubbed grouper. The only problem: it doesn't take reservations, though its 'call-ahead seating' gets your name on the wait list before arrival.

❶ Information

Easy Guide (www.easyguideonline.com) Listings for southern Gulf beaches.

St Petersburg/Clearwater Area Convention & Visitors Bureau (www.visitstpeteclearwater.com)

Tampa Bay Beaches Chamber of Commerce (☑727-360-6957; www.tampabaybeaches.com; 6990 Gulf Blvd at 70th Ave; ⊙9am-5pm Mon-Fri) Extremely helpful VC, excellent maps and advice.

❶ Getting There & Around

For information on driving to St Pete Beach, see p384. PSTA **Suncoast Beach Trolleys** (www.psta.net; rides $2; ⊙5:30am-9:30pm) ply the entirety of Gulf Blvd, from Pass-a-Grille north to Sand Key, and connect with other peninsula trolley and bus services.

Clearwater Beach

☑727 / POP 107,700

The psychological divide between the city of Clearwater and Clearwater Beach is wider than the harbor between them. A few details tell the story. First, the indefatigable Hooters restaurant chain was invented in Clearwater in 1983, and its burgers-and-babes dining concept certainly encapsulates the beach scene, which is the loudest, most crowded

Spring Break–style party this side of St Pete Beach.

Meanwhile, the city has a stuck-in-amber, gray-suited, 1950s-era downtown that's dominated by the international spiritual headquarters of the Church of Scientology. The Clearwater church, known as Flag Land Base, has occupied the historic Fort Harrison Hotel since the late 1970s, and they are currently constructing what will be the largest Scientology center in the world, the 'Super Power Building.' None of this is open to the public, and Clearwater itself remains deeply ambivalent about being home to the largest concentration of Scientologists outside of LA.

Finally: beach traffic is a nightmare. If you're coming for sun and fun, either cross the causeway as pink-tinged dawn arrives, or book a room, ditch the car and walk to the beach and the bars and back again.

⊙ Sights & Activities

TOP CHOICE Clearwater Marine
Aquarium   AQUARIUM
(☎727-447-1790; www.seewinter.com; 249 Windward Passage; adult/child 3-12yr $15/10; ⊙9am-5pm Mon-Thu, to 7pm Fri & Sat, 10am-5pm Sun) The home of Winter, this nonprofit aquarium is dedicated to rescuing and rehabilitating injured sea animals, such as dolphins, sea otters, fish, rays, and loggerhead and Kemp's ridley sea turtles. Though small, it provides unusually intimate encounters with these magnificent creatures, plus their

---

DON'T MISS

BOWLING BALL HOUSE

Aficionados of art houses should make the trek to Safety Harbor's 'bowling ball house.' Named for the painted orbs that line the front gardens, this is really two houses catercorner to each other, each a wild pastiche of tile murals, metal sculptures, upturned-bottle trees, tiki masks and twinkling, grinning sun mandalas. The carefree, creative spirit of artists Todd Ramquist and Kiaralinda, who've been futzing and fiddling for 20 years, is perfectly captured by the chimney, which spells out 'whimzey.'

To drive: from US 19, take Sunset Point Rd/Main St west toward Safety Harbor. Turn north on 12th Ave N; it's on the corner at 1206 3rd St N.

The most famous celebrity in Clearwater these days is Winter, a tailless dolphin who's the subject of the 2011 Hollywood movie *Dolphin Tale*. Filmed on location at the Clearwater Marine Aquarium, the movie co-stars Morgan Freeman and Ashley Judd, and it tells Winter's truly amazing, heartwarming story: as a baby she was found caught in a crab trap and injured so badly her tail flukes died and fell off. Yet Winter survived and has thrived despite her handicap. You can meet her in person every day of the week and even get in the water with her. Sure, the wade encounter is pricey ($250), but it's not every day you can swim with a movie star.

---

excellent, conservation-focused movies, animal shows and presentations are included with admission. On its recommended Sea Life Safari (adult/child $23/20), a marine biologist drags a net behind the boat and discusses the catch; other dolphin-interaction programs ($75 to $250) must be reserved ahead. It's located midway along the Memorial Causeway.

Clearwater Beach & Pier 60   BEACH
In high season, Clearwater's long, idyllic stretch of smooth, white sand becomes a scrum of sun-baked coeds and extended families, for whom sunning and swimming is almost secondary to one's social agenda. Hotels, resorts and raucous beach bars line the sand, particularly near Pier 60, where sunset is 'celebrated' each night with a festive, if eclectic, menagerie of musicians, magicians, performers, trinket stands and craftspeople hawking their wares. On Coronado Dr across from the pier, activity booths offer parasailing, fishing, cruises and so on.

FREE **Sand Key Park & Beach**   BEACH
(www.pinellascounty.org/park; 1060 Gulf Blvd; ⊙7am-sunset) If you want a less-crowded beach day free of commercial folderol, head to this 65-acre, family-friendly beach park. It's at the northern tip of the barrier island to the south, just over the Clearwater Pass Bridge. The sand isn't nearly as fine as at Clearwater Beach, but it's a wide strand with decent shelling that's popular with

local families. It has restrooms and outdoor showers, but bring lunch. Clearwater's Jolley Trolley stops here. Metered parking ($1.25 per hour) has a five-hour limit.

🛏 Sleeping

Chain lodgings dominate your choices. Reserve a year ahead for spring, but like St Pete Beach, so many hotels vie for your business, a cruise along Gulfview Blvd usually turns up something. Resorts along South Beach typically cordon off their own slice of sand.

TOP CHOICE Shephards   RESORT $$$

(☏727-442-5107; www.shephards.com; 601 S Gulfview Blvd; r $160-230; P✿@☀) In for a penny, in for a pound. Do Clearwater right at Shephards, a very popular resort that

keeps the beat with a lounge, nightclub and two tiki bars, all with live music and DJs, plus two restaurants and an all-you-can-eat buffet. Naturally, the pool and private beach are the sought-after spots to preen. In fact, the rooms are quite nice: all are recently renovated, stylishly done in copper and brick-red color schemes, with kitchenettes, tile floors, padded headboards and granite countertops. All have balconies facing the gulf, and above the 2nd floor, you hardly feel the music at all.

Best Western Sea Wake Beach Resort   RESORT $$

(☏727-443-7652; www.bestwestern.com/seawake beachresort; 691 S Gulfview Blvd; r $140-180; P✿@☀♨) Families who want all the fun Clearwater offers – without the hookups – will be happy with the Sea Wake, an ex-

---

DON'T MISS

HONEYMOON & CALADESI ISLANDS

Two of the best beaches in Florida (and thus, the nation) are just north of Clearwater: Honeymoon Island, which you can drive to, and the ferry-only Caladesi Island.

Honeymoon Island State Park (www.floridastateparks.org/honeymoonisland; 1 Dunedin Causeway; per car $8; ☉8am-sunset; 🐾) is graced with the Gulf Coast's legendary white sand and warm aquamarine waters, and Honeymoon has the state park system's only dog-friendly beach. Huge parking lots and convenient facilities make for easy public access, but while it gets crowded with all ages, it's never as packed or frenetic as Clearwater Beach. The only thing people come to pick up here are shells. On the beach, the **Island Cafe** (www.romantichoneymoonisland.com; ☉9am-5pm) serves sandwiches, snacks and beer, and offers bike, kayak and umbrella rentals. Best of all, the island is blissfully undeveloped. The park's **Nature Center** (www.honeymoonnaturecenter.org; ☉9am-5pm) has wildlife exhibits, and hiking trails lead through virgin slash pine and past nesting eagles and osprey in winter and spring. Check the 'skeeter meter,' though; outside winter, mosquitoes are ravenous inland.

To get to Honeymoon, take Alt Hwy 19 north to the town of Dunedin and go west on Curlew Rd/Hwy 586, or the Dunedin Causeway.

Honeymoon Island is where you catch the ferry to **Caladesi Island State Park** (www.floridastateparks.org/caladesiisland; admission free; ☉8am-sunset), which is just south of Honeymoon. Caladesi is today virtually as nature made it (and hurricanes have reshaped it): unspoiled and pristine. Consequently, it often tops national beach polls, and its three palm-lined miles of sparkling, sugar-sand beaches – as liberally strewn with shells as any strand north of Sanibel – should make the top of your list, too. Secluded, uncrowded, with limited access, it still boasts a 110-slip marina, kayak rentals, a tiny cafe, a gift shop, restrooms and showers – all the necessities. Though you can kayak *to* Caladesi from Honeymoon or Clearwater, it's far more relaxing to kayak the mangroves while *at* Caladesi.

Caladesi Island Adventure (☏727-734-1501; www.caladesiferry.org; adult/child $12/6) runs 20-minute ferries (longer if you spot dolphins) from Honeymoon every hour on the hour beginning at 10am and generally ending around 4pm. On busy weekends, trips might run every half hour and go later. Capacity is 62 people, and ferries often fill up; come midweek if you can. Also, officially you must catch a return ferry within four hours. If you're late, you won't have to walk the plank, but passengers with the correct return times board first, meaning you might have to wait.

tremely comfortable, clean, reliable sleep at the end of South Beach's resort row, with a much quieter private beach and pool. Decor is pleasing and fresh, if chain standard. Also has a restaurant and bar.

Parker Manor Resort   MOTEL $$
(☎727-446-6562; 115 Brightwater Dr; r $100, ste $120-165; [P][✱][☎][⌂]) Want even more quiet? On the harbor, but still walkable to the beach, this small, well-kept complex attracts an older crowd who enjoy playing billiards in the covered courtyard and lounging by the small pool. Suites are fully loaded for cooking and extended stays.

✖ Eating & Drinking

No one comes to Clearwater for the food, but rest assured, cheap to midrange meals are plentiful.

Frenchy's Original Cafe   SEAFOOD $$
(☎727-446-3607; www.frenchysonline.com; 41 Baymont at Mandalay Ave; mains $8-13; ⊙11am-11pm) This beach-bum-casual hole-in-the-wall serves grouper sandwiches you'll dream about months later. These crusty beauties on an onion roll go perfectly with its light-and-sweet pineapple coleslaw. As you'll notice, the bar is a popular local hangout. Well-loved Frenchy's has multiple Clearwater locations.

Island Way Grill   SEAFOOD $$$
(☎727-461-6617; www.islandwaygrill.com; 20 Island Way; mains $17-25; ⊙4-10pm Sun-Thu, to 11pm Fri & Sat; [⌂]) Eschew the beachfront seafood shacks and come to this contemporary restaurant overlooking the inner harbor. Wide windows and an expansive deck do justice to sunset, and the moderately priced Asian-influenced menu is bound to please everyone, with a raw bar, a sushi bar, crab cakes, pastas, steaks and wok-seared fresh fish. It's more casual than the decor, and easy to bring the kids.

ⓘ Information

At the base of Pier 60, there is a Clearwater Beach **information booth** (⊙11am-7pm); for more, visit www.beachchamber.com and www.visitclearwaterflorida.com.

ⓘ Getting There & Around

Driving from the peninsula, take Hwy 19 to Hwy 60/Gulf to Bay Blvd, and follow it west to Memorial Causeway and the beach.

Greyhound (www.greyhound.com; 2811 Gulf to Bay Blvd, Clearwater) Buses run between Tampa and Clearwater; take PSTA to the beach.

Jolley Trolley (www.clearwaterjolleytrolley .com; 483 Mandalay Ave; adult/child 5-18yr $2/1.25; ⊙10am-10pm) Toodles around Clearwater Beach and south to Sand Key.

Suncoast Beach Trolley (www.psta.net/beach trolley.html; 14840 49th Ave N; ⊙5am-10pm) PSTA's Suncoast Beach Trolley ($2) connects downtown Clearwater, Clearwater Beach and the barrier-island beaches south to Pass-a-Grille.

SOUTH OF TAMPA

People who prefer Florida's Gulf side over its Atlantic one generally fall in love with this stretch of sun-kissed coastline from Sarasota to Naples. These two affluent, cultured towns set the tone for the whole region, where visits sway gently between soporific beach days and stunning art museums, between boardwalk hikes through alligator-filled swamps and evenings of theater, fine dining and designer cocktails. With their rowdy bars and casual fun, Siesta Key and Fort Myers Beach are slight exceptions, but even they don't reach the same pitch of Spring Break hysteria just north. No, in this region you'll remember hunting prehistoric shark's teeth in Venice and jewel-like tulip shells in Sanibel, a night at the circus in Sarasota and buying art in Matlacha.

Sarasota

[☎]941 / POP 51,900
Entire vacations can be spent soaking up the sights and culture, and the egregiously pretty beaches, of sophisticated Sarasota. In fact, base your stay here, and the majority of the Tampa Bay area's highlights are within easy reach, while the region's urban bustle remains at a comfortable arm's length.

In 1911, when John Ringling decided to make this struggling town the winter home of his circus, he set Sarasota on the course to what it is today: a welcoming, well-to-do bastion of the arts, one with a performer's weakness for the theater's sodium lights. Ringling's mansion and museums – devoted to his fine art collection and his famous big top – are reason enough to come to Sarasota. And nearby, Siesta Key marries its dazzling beach with its friendly, lively village so well it epitomizes what a beach town should be. Head inland, and the alligators of Myakka River State Park provide even more thrills.

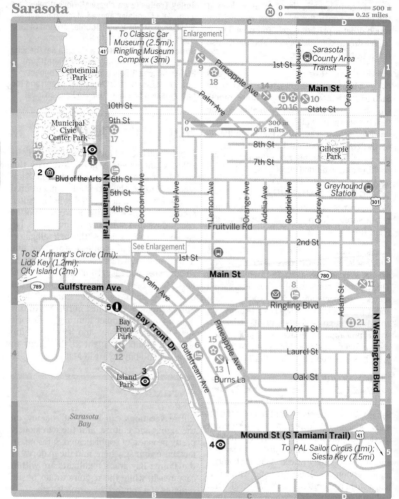

The only things you really need are a car and a good local map (ask at the VC). Sarasota isn't that big, but sights are spread out and not well served by public transportation.

⊙ Sights & Activities

TOP CHOICE Ringling Museum Complex   MUSEUM
(☏941-359-5700; www.ringling.org; 5401 Bayshore Rd; adult/child 6-17yr $25/10, Mon free; ☺10am-5pm, to 8pm Thu; ⊛) The 66-acre winter estate of railroad, real-estate and circus baron John Ringling and his wife, Mable, is one of the Gulf Coast's premier attractions. Indeed, this excellent museum complex has a lot to

see, and several ways to see it. For the complete experience, plan a full day or several shorter visits. For instance, the landscaped grounds and rose gardens are free to the public during open hours. The art museum (alone) is free Monday, while 5pm till 8pm Thursday both the art and circus museums are discounted (adult/child $10/5). Saturday from 1pm till 4pm is 'family day,' with activity carts and family-oriented guides. There are also two cafes and a good gift shop.

In addition to the sights below, the historic Asolo Theater shows a highly recommended, 30-minute PBS-produced film on Ringling's life (included with admission). The theater is itself an attraction – its ornate Italian interior dating to 1798 – and at night hosts a Hollywood film series and special events.

John & Mable Ringling Museum of Art

The Ringlings aspired to become serious art connoisseurs, and they amassed a vast, impressive collection of 14th- to 18th-century European tapestries and paintings. Like Rubens' tremendous *Triumph of the Eucharist* cycle, many are imposing works of passionate religious and mythological subjects from the late-medieval, baroque and Renaissance eras. One wing, though, presents rotating exhibits of contemporary art, and the sculpture garden is filled with replicas of Greek and Roman statuary. In 2012, the Searing Wing plans to open a new atrium, a stunning James Turrell–designed 'Sky Space.'

Cà d'Zan

Ringling was a showman, and his winter home Cà d'Zan (1924–26), or 'House of John,' displays an unmistakable theatrical flair. Even the patio's zigzag marble fronting Sarasota Bay dazzles. The home itself favors the Venetian Gothic style, but borrows Renaissance and baroque touches freely to overwhelming effect. Ceilings are painted masterpieces, especially Willy Pogany's *Dancers of Nations* in the ballroom. Self-guided tours include the 1st floor's kitchens, tap room and opulent public spaces, while guided tours ($5) add the 2nd floor's stupendous bedrooms and bathrooms. A pianist fills the halls with music Monday and Friday, 10am to 1pm, playfully evoking the home's Roaring Twenties heyday.

Circus Museum

This is actually several museums in one, and they are as delightful as the circus itself. One building preserves the hand-carved animal wagons, calliopes, silver cannons and artifacts from Ringling Bros' original traveling show. One highlight here is the Wisconsin, Ringling's personal railcar, restored to plush glory. Other exhibits present vintage circus posters and trace the evolution of the circus from sideshow to Cirque du Soleil. Yet in the center ring, so to speak, is the miniature Howard Bros Circus: a truly epic recreation at 1/12th scale of the entire Ringling Bros and Barnum & Bailey Circus in action, from the big tent's high wire to the stables, dressing areas and railway cars. This colossal, intricately detailed work occupies its own building, and is mostly the 50-year labor of love of one man, Howard Tibbels.

Sarasota Beaches   BEACH

Below the mouth of Tampa Bay, the string of Gulf Coast barrier islands continues. North to south, this section covers the beaches and public access on Anna Maria Island, Longboat Key, Lido Key and Siesta Key.

On Anna Maria Island, west of Bradenton (follow Hwy 684), the very popular family-focused **Bradenton Beach** has tons of public parking and a lively beachside stretch of shops and restaurants. The sand is great, just not Siesta Key perfect.

Upscale resorts and condos have claimed most of **Longboat Key** as their own. A few teeny-tiny public parking lots don't offer much access for day-trippers.

Due west of Sarasota's St Armand Circle, **Lido Beach** is an excellent, wide stretch of

CIRCUS KIDS

The only actual circus in Sarasota is performed by kids, and it's worth planning a trip around. The **PAL Sailor Circus** (☑941-361-6350; www.sailorcircus.org; 2075 Bahia Vista St; tickets $10-16; ⊙late Dec & Mar-Apr; 🖐) is truly unique: it's an extracurricular activity for Sarasota County students, who gear up for two big shows a year: during the December holidays, and for 10 days in late March and April. The Sailor Circus started in 1949, and like Cirque du Soleil, it focuses exclusively on acrobatics and clowning.

About 150 students aged 10 to 18 participate each year in what they call 'The Greatest Little Show on Earth,' and everyone performs, regardless of ability. But don't be misled: there is nothing little about this show. The moment the big top lights come up, and 50 performers in peacock-colored, sequined costumes bound across the center ring at once and start climbing ropes, you are treated to a spectacle of human daring and grace that is jaw dropping. You get it all: the high wire and trapeze, hand balancing and unicycles, juggling and clowning, and innumerable mid-air ballets while dangling from tissues, rings and bars. It is, in its way, even more thrilling than watching professionals; seeing their effort and occasional mistakes, your heart soars even more when they tumble and twirl and fly through the air with the greatest of ease.

If you miss the show, consider arranging a tour; customized individually, they include the big tent, costume shop, homey museum and – hopefully – attending practice. Please bring your own kids; just know they will nurture, forever after, running-away-to-the-circus dreams.

white sand. Street and lot parking is free, so expect crowds. A concession stand at the parking lot has food, restrooms and even a small lap **swimming pool** (adult/child 4-11yr $4/2; ⊙10am-4:45pm Tue-Sun). About a mile south is **South Lido Beach**, whose grills and grassy lawns are extremely popular with picnicking local families; this beach is almost too wide, and strong currents discourage swimming.

With pure quartz sand so fine it's like confectioner's sugar, **Siesta Key Beach** shimmers almost magically. The enormous parking lot (at the corner of Beach Rd and Beach Way) has an information booth dispensing info on all types of activities and water sports (parasailing, jet-ski rental, kayaks, bikes and more), plus nice facilities, a snack bar and covered eating areas. Eight volleyball courts beckon, as if the fluffy white sand weren't enough. SCAT bus 11 comes here from downtown Sarasota. Complete facility renovations are scheduled for 2013.

For quiet, come to **Turtle Beach**. The sun and teal waters are the same, but it's several miles south of the action, and the narrow ash-gray sand beach isn't half as fine, so few prefer it. Not so sea turtles, who nest here from May through October. Parking is free.

TOP CHOICE **Mote Marine Laboratory**   AQUARIUM
(☑941-388-4441; www.mote.org; 1600 Ken Thompson Pkwy, City Island; adult/child $17/12; ⊙10am-5pm) A research facility first and an aquarium second, the Mote is one of the world's leading organizations for shark study, and glimpsing its work is a highlight: marvel at seahorse 'fry' born that very day, and time your visit for **shark training** (⊙11am Mon, Wed & Fri). Above-average exhibits include a preserved giant squid (37ft long when caught), a stingray touch tank, a dramatic shark tank, and a separate building with intimate encounters with sea turtles, manatees and dolphins. An interactive immersion theater is perfect for kids. Also don't miss **Save Our Seabirds** (suggested donation $5; ⊙10am-5pm); adjacent to Mote, it displays a wide range of rescued seabirds in outdoor cages. Finally, Sarasota Bay Explorers (opposite) is based here. To get there, go to St Armands Circle, take John Ringling Blvd north to Ken Thompson Parkway and follow to the end.

Marie Selby Botanical Gardens   GARDENS
(☑941-366-5730; www.selby.org; 811 S Palm Ave; adult/child 6-11yr $17/6; ⊙10am-5pm) If you visit just one botanical garden in Florida, choose Selby, which has the world's largest scientific collection of orchids and bromeliads, over 20,000 species. Emblematic of Florida, these sideshow freaks of the plant kingdom propa-

gate in such bizarre fashion it boggles the mind. In addition, Selby's genteel outdoor gardens are exceptionally well landscaped and relaxing, with 80-year-old banyan trees, koi ponds and splendid bay views. Art exhibits, a cafe and an enticing plant shop complete the experience.

Classic Car Museum
MUSEUM

(☎941-355-6228; www.sarasotacarmuseum.org; 5500 N Tamiami Trail; adult/child $8.50/6; ☺9am-6pm) This sexy museum is an automotive voyeur's delight. There isn't much narrative or context, but ogling the collection's more than 80 automobiles is entertaining enough. Several Ringling cars include his 1924 Rolls-Royce 'Silver Ghost.' Drool over Don Garlitz' 1975 'Jungle' car, a 1981 stainless-steel DeLorean, various futuristic prototypes and Paul McCartney's 1965 Mini Cooper.

Art Center Sarasota
GALLERY

(☎941-365-2032; www.artsarasota.org; 707 N Tamiami Trail; donation $3; ☺10am-4pm Tue-Sat) This community-oriented nonprofit gallery has four exhibition spaces that mix local and out-of-town artists. It's a warm, friendly introduction to the local art scene. In winter, family days (per family $5; ☺1-4pm Sat) let kids get creative.

St Armand's Circle
SQUARE

(www.starmandscircleassoc.com) Conceived and initially developed by John Ringling in the 1920s, St Armand's Circle is essentially an upscale outdoor shopping mall surrounded by posh residences. Yet even more than downtown, this traffic circle is Sarasota's social center; it's where everyone strolls in the early evening, window shopping and buying souvenir T-shirts while enjoying a Kilwin's waffle cone. Numerous restaurants, from diners to fine dining, serve all day. The circle is also an unavoidable traffic chokepoint; mid-morning and late-afternoon beach commutes are worst.

Island Park
PARK

Sarasota's marina is notable for Island Park, an attractive green space poking into the harbor: it has a great playground and play fountain, restrooms, tree-shaded benches, a restaurant and tiki bar, and kayak, Waverunner and boat rentals. A short stroll north along the waterfront is *Unconditional Surrender,* a towering statue of WWII's most famous kiss.

G.Wiz
MUSEUM

(☎941-309-4949; www.gwiz.org; 1001 Blvd of the Arts; adult/child 3-16yr $10/7; ☺10am-5pm Mon-Sat, noon-5pm Sun) Though modest by current standards, this interactive kids' science museum remains a laudable family destination, particularly if you like the current traveling show. However, its latest exhibit, 'Fab Lab,' promises a unique treat: it's essentially a machine shop for the public, who can design and make prototypes (in metal, wood and plastic), or just personalize a souvenir (call for times/fees).

Siesta Sports Rentals
BICYCLE RENTAL, KAYAKING

(☎941-346-1797; www.siestasportsrentals.com; 6551 Midnight Pass Rd) South of Siesta Village, just south of the Stickney Point Bridge, this rental shop has bikes, kayaks, scooters, surreys, beach gear, baby equipment and more.

☞ Tours

Sarasota Bay Explorers
BOAT TOUR

(☎941-388-4200; www.sarasotabayexplorers.com; 1600 Ken Thompson Parkway, Mote Marine Laboratory) Under the supervision of marine biologists, boat cruises trawl a net and then examine the sponges, sea horses and various fish you catch. You also inspect rookeries and stop on an uninhabited island for a short nature walk; you may spot manatees and dolphins. The 1¾-hour ecotours (adult/child $26/22) depart from the Mote aquarium daily at 11am, 1:30pm and 4pm. They also offer guided kayak tours (adult/child $55/45).

★★ Festivals & Events

Art & Craft Festivals
CULTURAL

(www.artfestival.com) For two days in late March, an explosion of art and craft stalls dominates downtown Sarasota. The same happens in Siesta Village in late April.

Ringling International Arts Festival
CULTURAL

(www.ringlingartsfestival.org) For a week in mid-October, Ringling partners with NYC's Baryshnikov Arts Center to bring international dance, theater and music to Sarasota.

🛏 Sleeping

Sarasota is so close to Siesta Key, it's not critical you stay at the beach, though it avoids traffic. South of the airport along US 41/N Tamiami Trail are dependable midrange chains, such as Comfort Inn and La Quinta.

DOWNTOWN SARASOTA

TOP CHOICE Hotel Ranola   BOUTIQUE HOTEL $$
(941-951-0111; www.hotelranola.com; 118 Indian Pl, No 6; r $180-190; P✳@) For urban funk and livability, there's nothing like Hotel Ranola in the Tampa Bay area. It is the only hotel walkable to Sarasota's historic downtown. The nine rooms feel like a designer's actual brownstone apartment: free-spirited and comfortable, with hardwood floors, royal grape accent walls, glass-topped desks, bright paintings, leather armchairs and real working kitchens. Indeed, half of the 1926 building is occupied by tenants, so don't expect lots of amenities, just a big-city home away from home.

Cypress   B&B $$$
(941-955-4683; www.cypressbb.com; 621 Gulf Stream Ave S; r $260-290; P✳@☏) For a romantic getaway, Cypress is dreamy. Tucked on a quiet street, it feels secluded even though it's near downtown. The artistic owners have individualized each room, though a Victorian seaside mood prevails, with wicker bed frames, Oriental throw rugs over hardwood floors, palm-frond fans, antiques and modern art. A full hot breakfast and afternoon cocktails can bookend trips to the beach. Children are discouraged.

Hotel Indigo   HOTEL $$$
(941-487-3800; www.hotelindigo.com; 1223 Blvd of the Arts; r $180-235; P✳@☏☼✳) Boutique-style chain, reliable and attractive, close to downtown. Good off-season discounts.

SIESTA KEY

Sunsets on the Key   CONDO HOTEL $$$
(941-312-9797; www.sunsetsonthekey.com; 5203 Avenida Navarre; apt $230-340; P✳☏☼✳) On the backside of Ocean Blvd in the heart of Siesta Village, Sunsets' eight well-kept condo apartments are run like a hotel, with the same coral-and-blue seaside decor, full kitchens and rigorous cleanliness. The tree-shaded grass lawn and secluded pool with rock waterfall create a relaxing mood.

Tropical Breeze Resort   RESORT $$$
(941-349-1125; www.tropicalbreezeinn.com; 140 Columbus Blvd; r $170, apt $200-300; P✳☏✳✳) The biggest operation in Siesta Village, Tropical Breeze has 64 units spread among numerous buildings along several streets, all walkable to the village. The fully stocked apartments aren't memorable, but they are well managed, in good shape and designed for long stays. Only one of its three pools is lounge-worthy.

Turtle Beach Campground   CAMPGROUND $
(941-349-3839; www.scgove.net/turtlebeach campground/default.asp; 8862 Midnight Pass Rd; campsites $45-60; P☏) This park campground is small, caters to RVs, has zero privacy and doesn't allow campfires, but it's well worth camping here to be mere steps from Turtle Beach and a quick drive to Sarasota.

Siesta Beach Resort   MOTEL $$$
(941-349-3211; www.siestakeyflorida.com; 5311 Ocean Blvd; r $150-185, ste $200-255; P✳☏☼✳) The Siesta Village location is tops, but only the renovated rooms are recommended in this otherwise tired, standard motel.

✖ Eating

DOWNTOWN SARASOTA

TOP CHOICE Owen's Fish Camp   SOUTHERN $$
(941-951-6936; www.owensfishcamp.com; 516 Burns Lane; mains $9-20; ⏱4-10pm, to 11pm Fri & Sat) The actual house of Sarasota's founder has been turned into a swamp shack serving upscale interpretations of Florida-style Southern cuisine. Order cornmeal-crusted catfish, chicken-fried steak, collard greens, smooth cheesy grits and pecan pie. The delicious succotash is edamame, corn, chickpeas and peppers. The emphasis is on seafood, and the energy is high.

Main Bar Sandwich Shop   SANDWICHES $
(www.themainbar.com; 1944 Main St; sandwiches from $7; ⏱10am-4pm Mon-Sat; ✳) The Main Bar is a Sarasota classic, an old-school, booth-filled, diner-style deli founded by retired circus performers whose photos blanket the walls. They offer a ton of sandwiches, but – no kidding – order their 'famous' Italian, which instantly transports you to Brooklyn c 1958.

Bijou Cafe   FRENCH $$$
(941-366-8111; www.bijoucafe.net; 1287 1st St at Pineapple Ave; lunch $12-18, dinner $20-33; ⏱11am-2pm Mon-Fri, from 5pm nightly) When Sarasotans want a gourmet meal from locally sourced ingredients and an excellent wine before catching the opera, they pick this chef-owned fine-dining bistro across the street. Fresh seafood and French standards like steak *au poivre* are featured; the spicy shrimp piri piri is a signature dish.

Marina Jack's Restaurant — SEAFOOD $$$

(☑941-365-4232; www.marinajacks.com; 2 Marina Plaza; sandwiches $9-13, mains $25-34; ⊙11:30am-10pm) Anchoring the marina is this well-loved multilevel, multivenue eatery that offers something for everyone, but most especially that quintessential harbor-at-sunset ambience. Be serenaded by steel drums in the relaxed downstairs cafe and lounge, with expansive outdoor seating, tropical cocktails and an easy-on-the-wallet menu. The Bayfront dining room upstairs positions every formally laid table before curving, two-story windows and serves upscale surf-and-turf; make reservations.

Patrick's — AMERICAN $$

(www.patricksofsarasota.com; 1400 Main St; mains $9-15; ⊙11am-midnight) Martinis and fat, juicy burgers are Patrick's stock in trade. A sports bar for the business set, this is a low-key place for a reliable, easy meal downtown.

Morton's Gourmet Market — MARKET $

(www.mortonsmarket.com; 1924 S Osprey Ave; mains $4-10; ⊙8am-8pm Mon-Sat, 10am-6pm Sun) This chichi grocery store is a must-stop for Siesta Key–bound gourmands dreaming of that perfect beach picnic: simply partake of Morton's unusually wide selection of takeout salads, sandwiches, sushi and entrees. About 15 blocks south of downtown.

Farmers' Market — MARKET

(Lemon Ave & State St; ⊙7am-1pm Sat) One of the region's better farmers' markets.

LIDO KEY

Kilwin's — ICE CREAM $

(www.kilwins.com; 312 John Ringling Blvd; ice creams from $3.50; ⊙10am-11pm) Follow your nose to this St Armand's Circle institution and order fresh-from-the-griddle waffle cones stuffed with homemade ice cream.

Blue Dolphin — DINER $

(www.bluedolphincafe.com; 470 John Ringling Blvd; mains $7-10; ⊙7am-3pm) On St Armand's Circle, this small, casual diner is a go-to destination for a pre-beach breakfast or quick lunch.

SIESTA KEY

TOP CHOICE Broken Egg — BREAKFAST $

(www.thebrokenegg.com; 140 Avenida Messina; mains $7-14; ⊙7:30am-2:30pm; 🐾) Each morning, it feels like all of Siesta Key gathers on the outdoor patio of this diner-style restaurant for delicious skillet eggs, blintzes, ched-dary home fries and pancakes as big as hub-caps. Yet service is unfailingly upbeat and efficient, and the wait goes fast.

Lobster Pot — SEAFOOD $$$

(www.sarasota-lobsterpot.com; 5157 Ocean Blvd; lunch $9-15, dinner $16-45; ⊙11:30am-9pm Mon-Thu, to 9:30pm Fri & Sat, 5-9pm Sun only winter) At this charmingly unpretentious lobster shack, walls and ceilings are crammed with nautical hoo-ha, and tables are spread with red-and-white-checked oilcloth. So don't worry about making a mess as you crack open crustaceans and slurp bisque and chowder. Lunchtime lobster rolls are the bomb. No reservations; dinner waits can be long.

Ophelia's on the Bay — FUSION $$$

(☑941-349-2212; www.opheliasonthebay.net; 9105 Midnight Pass Rd; mains $27-34; ⊙5-10pm) On the harbor-side at the southern end of Siesta Key, Ophelia's is the island's top romantic spot. The water lapping the dock at your feet and the distant mangroves are a serene balm to the soul. The menu is all over the map, reaching around the globe for influences, but everything is finely prepared and stylishly presented. Reserve ahead.

Blasé Café & Martini Bar — ITALIAN $$

(☑941-349-9822; www.theblasecafe.com; 5253 Ocean Blvd; mains $15-23; ⊙3pm-2am) At the end of Siesta Village, Blasé combines the artful vibe of an urban wine bar with a seaside casual bistro. The menu of pastas and standard entrees is fine, but it tastes much better with a dry martini or generous pour of Cabernet. Shawl-draped tables and splashy contemporary paintings make this a hip alternative.

LONGBOAT KEY

Moore's Stone Crab — SEAFOOD $$$

(☑941-383-1748; www.mooresstonecrab.com; 800 Broadway; mains $15-30; ⊙11:30am-9:30pm) At the northern tip of Longboat Key, informal Moore's is a destination for one thing only: fresh, delectably sweet stone crab. They only serve it in season (October through March). It's an annual pilgrimage. Everything else is strictly standard.

🍷 Drinking

Why doesn't downtown Sarasota have a nightlife? In the evening, everyone is strolling St Armand's Circle or Ocean Blvd in Siesta Village, a five-block stretch of seaside eats and drinks that appeals equally to families, teens and Spring Break coeds. Siesta's warm, friendly scene doesn't get rowdy till late.

For events and the local scene, visit This Week in Sarasota (www.thisweekinsarasota .com).

Old Salty Dog   BAR
(www.theoldsaltydog.com; 1601 Ken Thompson Pkwy, City Island; mains $7-16; ⊙11am-9:30pm) At the City Island marina across from the Mote, Old Salty Dog is a perfect end to a day or start to an evening. Unwind with a brew and some above-average fish and chips on the breezy outdoor deck. A second location in Siesta Village lacks the ambience.

Gator Club   BAR
(www.thegatorclub.com; 1490 Main St; ⊙11am-2am) Downtown Sarasota doesn't offer much, but it does have the historic Gator Club, a two-story bar and nightclub with carved wooden bars, pressed-tin ceiling and an old-world scotch-and-cigar atmosphere. Live bands span all genres.

Siesta Key Oyster Bar   BAR
(www.skob.com; 5238 Ocean Blvd, Siesta Village; ⊙11am-midnight Sun-Thu, to 1:30am Fri & Sat) At SKOB, the tilting rafters are tacked with dollar bills – yes, it's that kind of place. Live music.

Beach Club   BAR
(www.beachclubsiestakey.com; 5151 Ocean Blvd, Siesta Village; ⊙11am-2am) Cavernous bar with pool tables, stage, great white shark and Sunday bikini contests. Live music.

Gilligan's Island Bar & Grill   BAR
(www.gilligansislandbar.net; 5253 Ocean Blvd, Siesta Village; ⊙11:30am-2am) Classic Florida thatched-roof tiki-bar vibe, with VW bus, outdoor courtyard and deadly fishbowl cocktails. Live music.

☆ Entertainment

Burns Court Cinema   CINEMA
(☑941-955-3456; 506 Burns Lane) This wee theater in an alleyway off Pineapple Ave presents independent and foreign films. It's run by the Sarasota Film Society (SFS; www .filmsociety.org), which screens over 40 of the year's best international films in November during the annual 10-day CINE-World Film Festival.

Asolo Repertory Theatre   THEATER
(☑941-351-8000; www.asolorep.org; 5555 N Tamiami Trail; tickets $15-50; ⊙Nov-Jul) Adjacent to the Ringling Estate, this lauded regional theater company is also an acting conservatory (in partnership with Florida State University). It presents a vibrant mix of commissioned works, classics and current Tony-winning dramas on two main stages. The Sarasota Ballet (www.sarasotaballet.org) also performs here.

Van Wezel Performing Arts Hall   PERFORMING ARTS
(☑941-953-3368, 800-826-9303; www.vanwezel .org; 777 N Tamiami Trail; tickets $25-80; ⊙Nov-May) This puce-colored, city-run arts hall hosts a full slate of crowd-pleasing favorites, from touring Broadway musicals to magicians, celebrities, modern dance, pops orchestras and more.

Players Theatre   THEATER
(☑941-365-2494; www.theplayers.org; 838 N Tamiami Trail; tickets from $18) This highly regarded nonprofit community theater emphasizes family fun. It stages both popular Broadway musicals and new plays and collaborations.

Sarasota Opera House   OPERA
(☑941-366-8450; www.sarasotaopera.org; 61 N Pineapple Ave; tickets $20-100; ⊙Feb-Mar) This elegant, 1000-seat Mediterranean Revival venue was built in 1926, and the two-month winter opera season is a serious affair. Otherwise, there are only occasional performances.

🛍 Shopping

In downtown Sarasota, Main St, Pineapple Ave and Palm Ave form the main shopping district, with lots of fun and trendy stores.

Towles Court Artist Colony   ART
(www.towlescourt.com; cnr Morrill & Adam Sts; ⊙noon-4pm Tue-Sat) A dozen or so hip galleries occupy quirky, parrot-colored bungalows in this artist colony. The most lively time to be here is the evening stroll on the third Friday of each month (6pm to 10pm). Otherwise, individual gallery hours can be, mmm, whimsical.

Book Bazaar/Parker's Books   BOOKS
(www.aparkers.com; 1488 Main St; ⊙10am-5pm Mon-Sat) Huge used bookstore perfect for cheap beach reading.

Circle Books   BOOKS
(www.circlebooks.net; 478 John Ringling Blvd, St Armand's Circle; ⊙10am-6pm Mon-Fri, 9am-9pm Sat, to 5pm Sun) Independent bookstore with a few international newspapers and excellent Florida section.

ⓘ Information

INTERNET ACCESS **Selby Public Library** (www.suncat.co.sarasota.fl.us; 1331 1st St; ⊙10am-8pm Mon-Thu, to 5pm Fri & Sat, 1-5pm

Sun) Gorgeous library, downtown location, free internet access.

MEDIA Sarasota Herald-Tribune (www .heraldtribune.com) The main daily owned by the *New York Times.*

MEDICAL SERVICES Sarasota Memorial Hospital (941-917-9000; www.smh.com; 1700 S Tamiami Trail; 24hr) The area's biggest hospital.

POST Post office (1661 Ringling Blvd at Pine Pl; 8am-5:30pm Mon-Fri, 9am-noon Sat)

TOURIST INFORMATION Sarasota Visitor Information Center (941-957-1877; www .sarasotafl.org; 701 N Tamiami Trail; 10am-5pm Mon-Sat;) Very friendly, tons of info, sells good maps.

Siesta Key Chamber of Commerce (941-349-3800; www.siestakeychamber.com; 5118 Ocean Blvd, Siesta Key; 9am-5pm Mon-Fri, to noon Sat) Tracks daily hotel availability and will help find a room. Good maps.

WEBSITES Arts and Cultural Alliance (www .sarasotaarts.org) All-encompassing event info.

Out in Sarasota (www.outinsarasota.com) Gay life and entertainment.

Simply Siesta Key (www.simplysiestakey.com)

Getting There & Around

Driving, Sarasota is roughly 60 miles south of Tampa and about 75 miles north of Fort Myers. The main roads into town are Tamiami Trail/US 41 and I-75.

Sarasota-Bradenton International Airport (SRQ; www.srq-airport.com; 6000 Airport Circle) Served by many major airlines. Go north on Hwy 41, and right on University Ave.

Greyhound (941-955-5735; www.greyhound .com; 575 N Washington Blvd) Connects Sarasota and Miami, Fort Myers and Tampa.

Sarasota County Area Transit (SCAT; 941-861-1234; www.scgov.net/SCAT; cnr 1st St & Lemon Ave; 6am-6:30pm Mon-Sat) Buses (75¢ per ride) have no transfers and very limited Sunday service.

Myakka River State Park

Florida's oldest resident – the 200-million-year-old American alligator – is the star of this 57-sq-mile **wildlife preserve** (941-361-6511; www.myakkariver.org; 13207 State Rd 72; per car $6; 8am-sunset). Between 500 and 1000 alligators make their home in Myakka's slow-moving river and its shallow, lily-filled lakes, and you can get up close and personal with these toothsome beasts via canoe, kayak and pontoon-style airboat. During mating season in April and May, the guttural love songs of the males ring out across the waters.

The extensive park offers much more besides: its hammocks, marshes, pine flatwoods and prairies are home to a great variety of wildlife, and 38 miles of trails criss-cross the terrain. Don't miss the easy, dramatic Canopy Trail. The park's seven paved miles, and various dirt roads, make excellent cycling, and bird-watchers can spot great egrets, flocks of white pelicans and blue herons.

In winter, airboat trips (adult/child $12/6) depart at 10am, 11:30am, 1pm and 2:30pm; call for summer times. Winter-only wildlife trams run at 1pm and 2:30pm and cost the same; do one tour, and get a half-price discount on the other.

Tours, kayak and bike rentals, the camp store, and the cafe and gift shop are at the **Myakka Outpost** (941-923-1120; rental canoes/bikes from $20/15; 9:30am-5pm Mon-Fri, 8:30am-5pm Sat & Sun). The cafe isn't bad, serving delicious, homemade gator stew and seafood gumbo.

The recommended, recently expanded **campground** (sites $26, cabins from $70) is prime during dry season, January to April; avoid rainy, buggy summer. The five amenity-rich cabins have kitchens, air-con and linens; book 11 months ahead, if possible, through Reserve America (www.reserveamerica .com).

To reach the park from Sarasota, take US 41 south to Hwy 72/Clark Rd and head east for about 14 miles; the park is about 9 miles east of I-75.

Venice

941 / POP 20,700

About the only resemblance Venice has to its Italian namesake is that it's an island in the sea. Venice has scenic, tan-sand beaches but is otherwise an extremely quiet seaside town that's most popular with retirees and families with young kids, who enjoy hunting for shark's teeth. It also appeals to budget-minded travelers looking for a low-key getaway – far from the condos and hard-drinking beach bars elsewhere. Here, entertainment pretty much begins and ends with saluting the tangerine sun's nightly descent into the shimmering ocean.

From US 41/Tamiami Trail, Venice Ave heads west directly to Venice Beach. About five blocks east of the beach, the main downtown commercial district is along W Venice Ave between US 41 and Harbor Dr.

The helpful **Venice Chamber of Commerce** (941-488-2236; www.venicechamber.com; 597 S Tamiami Trail; 8:30am-5pm Mon-Fri) provides good free maps.

Sights & Activities

All Venice-area beaches have free parking.

Venice Beach
BEACH

Where W Venice Ave dead-ends is a covered beach pavilion with restrooms and a snack bar. There's free yoga on the sand daily at 9am, and free acoustic music Saturday to Wednesday around 5pm. Sea turtles nest on Venice Beach from May to October.

Venice Pier
BEACH

Off Harbor Dr 1.5 miles south of W Venice Ave, this long, wide beach with a huge parking lot is the most popular, especially for sunset. Modest surf near the pier encourages boogie boarding; at the pier's base, Sharkey's provides food and drink.

Caspersen Beach
BEACH

Another 1.5 miles south of Venice Pier along Harbor Dr, Caspersen is famous for the fossilized prehistoric shark's teeth that wash up. Most teeth are the size of a fingernail, but occasional finger-long specimens are found. Its attractive, palmetto-backed sand, playground and paved bike path also make Caspersen popular; there are facilities but no concessions.

Nokomis Beach
BEACH

North of Venice on Casey Key, Nokomis is yet another attractive, low-key tan-sand beach. Its 'minimalist'-style beach pavilion is an intriguing architectural bauble; it has nice facilities but no concessions (bring lunch). Also, at sundown on Wednesday and Saturday nights things get genuinely groovy: the **Nokomis Beach Drum Circle** (www.nokomisbeachdrumcircle.com) gathers and its rhythm draws upwards of several hundred folks. To get to Nokomis Beach take US 41 N to Albee Rd W.

Warm Mineral Springs
SPA

(941-426-1692; www.warmmineralsprings.com; 12200 San Servando Ave; adult/child $20/10; 9am-5pm) Was this warm mineral spring the actual fountain of youth Ponce de León was hunting? So they say. And it's an appropriate fable for this Old Florida throwback. The spring's 87°F waters, with the highest mineral content of any in the US, have long been a favored health tonic by elderly Eastern Europeans. Today, a recent face-lift has freshened the whole place up. The refurbished spa, changing areas and vegetarian cafe, not to mention the free yoga, pilates and water-aerobics classes, are attracting a new generation of wellness fanatics. It's still not chic, but it sure feels nice. From US 41 east of North Port, go north 1 mile on Ortiz Blvd.

Sleeping

TOP CHOICE Inn at the Beach Resort
HOTEL $$$

(941-484-8471; www.innatthebeach.com; 725 W Venice Ave; r $225-350, ste $353-515;) Right across from the beach and a perfect choice for an extended stay, this well-managed hotel-style resort worries the details so you don't have to. Each room's attractive palette of cream yellow, burnt umber and sage avoids seaside cliches, and the fully functional kitchenettes are a pleasure to cook in. Everything is spotless and fresh, and excellent amenities include continental breakfast and complimentary water and snacks all day. Multinight stays get good discounts.

Venice Beach Villa
CONDO HOTEL $$$

(941-488-1580; www.venicebeachvillas.com; 501 W Venice Ave; r $150-250;) More homey and less polished, the 23 units in this condostyle hotel vary widely in size and layout. All are low-key seaside roosts, most with full kitchens for long stays; they only rent weekly in high season. If you don't need daily maid service, this is a relaxed, satisfying choice.

El Patio Hotel
HOTEL $$

(Valencia Hotel; 941-488-7702; 229 W Venice Ave; r $160;) Admittedly, the 16 2nd-floor suites in this historic building are awkwardly designed, old-fashioned and dowdy, with teensy bathrooms. But in high season, you can't beat the price or the location overlooking W Venice Ave downtown.

Eating & Drinking

Stroll W Venice Ave west of US 41 and you'll pass bakeries, an Irish pub, ice cream and other modest eats, along with all the boutiques and gift shops you need.

Robbi's Reef
SEAFOOD $$

(www.robbisreef.com; 775 Hwy 41 By-Pass S; mains $8-15; 11am-9pm Tue-Sat) This perfect simulacrum of a harbor seafood shack is incongruously in a strip mall a half mile south of Venice Ave. From the walls crammed with fisherman photos to the flagstone bar to the unpretentious, delicious cooking, you'd swear you were at the docks. Go figure. Fish tacos and Bayou Willy's pasta get high marks.

Snook Haven   SOUTHERN $$
(☏941-485-7221; www.snookhaven.com; 5000 E Venice Ave; mains $8-17; ◷9am-9pm Mon-Thu, 11am-9pm Fri & Sat, noon-5pm Sun) Snook Haven is a bona fide Old Florida landmark, a former fish camp on the Myakka River that's hardly changed in 50 years. Everyone eats at folding chairs and tables with plastic cutlery, while listening to old-timey jazz or hammer dulcimer bands. It's homespun fun; retirees can't get enough of it. Check the music schedule, and come enjoy some corn fritters, gator bites, fried okra, BBQ or catfish under Spanish moss–draped trees. Be warned, though: the banjo society meeting at 11am Thursday is a true SRO event. Come way early to hear 40 banjo players do their thing. Take E Venice Ave over 6 miles till it dead-ends as a dirt road.

Sharky's on the Pier   SEAFOOD $$
(☏941-488-1456; www.sharkeysonthepier.com; 1600 Harbor Dr S; mains $10-27; ◷11:30am-10pm, to midnight Fri & Sat) With the prime sunset spot at the Venice Fishing Pier, Sharkey's doesn't have to try too hard. It's a typical middle-of-the-road seafood restaurant with a long thatched-roof tiki bar and deck positioned for evening's magic moment.

Fort Myers

☏239 / POP 62,300

Nestled inland along the Caloosahatchee River, and separated from Fort Myers Beach by several miles of urban sprawl, the city of Fort Myers is often defined by what it's not: it's not an upscale, arty beach town like Sarasota or Naples, and it's not as urbanely sophisticated as Tampa or St Pete. While it isn't a city to base a trip around, it's worth making a trip to see, and it's striking distance from the region's top beaches.

In fact, after a recent face-lift, Fort Myers' historic district has become a quaint, bricklined centerpiece sprinkled with cool galleries and restaurants, notable theaters and lively bars. Fort Myers is best known as the city where Thomas Alva Edison built a winter home and laboratory in 1885, and Edison's well-cared-for estate still constitutes the primary reason folks peel themselves off the sand to visit town. Yet Fort Myers has an ever-increasing number of good reasons to linger.

Definitely pick up a city map at the visitor center, though: the city limits are expansive, to say the least.

⊙ Sights & Activities

Most of Fort Myers' sights are in a compact area near the US 41 bridge along the river. The historic district is a tidy, six-block grid of streets along 1st St between Broadway and Lee St, and extending to the riverfront.

Edison & Ford Winter Estates   MUSEUM
(☏239-334-7419; www.edisonfordwinterestates .org; 2350 McGregor Blvd; adult/child $20/11; ◷9am-5:30pm) Florida's snowbirds can be easy to mock, but not this pair. Thomas Edison built his winter home in 1885 and lived in Florida seasonally until his death in 1931. Edison's friend Henry Ford built his adjacent bungalow in 1916. Together, and sometimes side by side in **Edison's lab**, these two inventors, businessmen and neighbors changed our world.

The **museum** does a good job of presenting the overwhelming scope of Edison's achievements, which included 1093 patents for things like the lightbulb, the phonograph, wafflemakers, talking dolls, concrete and sprocketed celluloid film. Edison, Ford and Harvey Firestone were dedicated 'tin-can tourists' who enjoyed driving and camping across America together, and exhibits chronicle their journeys and how these fed their refinements of the automobile. Indeed, the main purpose of Edison's Fort Myers lab was to develop a domestic source of rubber (primarily using goldenrod plants) for auto manufacturing.

While it's possible to buy discounted tickets only for the museum and lab, don't forgo a self-guided audio tour of the estates, which won a 2008 national preservation award (guided tours are $5 extra). The rich botanical gardens and genteel homes very nearly glow, and are decked out with more historical goodies and period furniture. Grounds also include one of the largest banyan trees in the US.

FREE Six Mile Cypress
Slough Preserve   SWAMP
(☏239-533-7550; www.leeparks.org/sixmile, www .sloughpreserve.org; 7791 Penzance Blvd; parking per hr/day $1/5; ◷dawn-dusk) A 2000-acre woodland and wetland, or slough

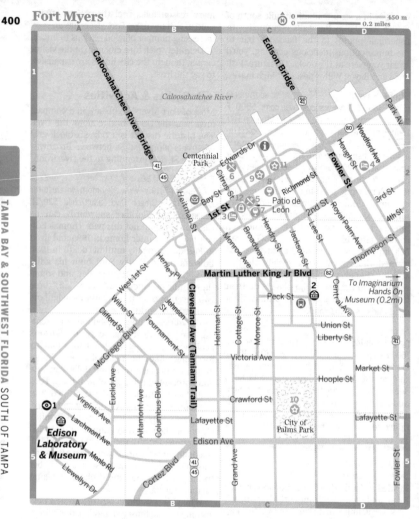

(pronounced 'slew'), this park is a great, easily accessible place to experience southwest Florida's flora and fauna. A 1.2-mile boardwalk trail is staffed by volunteers who help point out and explain the epiphytes, cypress knees, migrating birds, turtles and nesting alligators you'll find. Wildlife watchers should target the winter dry season, when animals concentrate around smaller ponds. However, the wet summer season is also dramatic: at its peak, the entire slough becomes a forested stream up to 3ft deep. The small **nature center** (⊙10am-4pm Tue-Sat, to 2pm Sun) has excellent displays; from

December to April, free guided walks are 9:30am and 1:30pm daily.

From downtown Fort Myers, go south on Cleveland Ave/US 41, east on Colonial Blvd/Hwy 884, then south for 3 miles on Ortiz Ave (which becomes Six Mile Cypress Pkwy).

Southwest Florida Museum of History   MUSEUM
(☎239-321-7430; www.swflmuseumofhistory.com; 2031 Jackson St; adult/child 3-18yr $9.50/5; ⊙10am-5pm Tue-Sat; ⊕) Crammed with cool artifacts, this museum leapfrogs from the giant sloths and woolly mammoths of the Pleistocene Era to the twisted props of

Fort Myers

downed WWII fighter jets in a veritable blink. Along the way, iron cannons and Calusa dugout canoes, a Cracker house and an iron lung provide vivid snapshots of Florida through the ages. If you have kids, get combo tickets with the Imaginarium.

Imaginarium Hands On Museum MUSEUM
(☑239-337-3332; www.imaginariumfortmyers.com; 2000 Cranford Ave; adult/child $12/8; ⊙10am-5pm Mon-Sat, noon-5pm Sun; ⊕) Principally for the 10-and-under set, this above-average interactive play space stands out for its reptile-rich animal lab (including baby gators and a bufo toad), an outdoor pond with gigantic carp and turtles to feed, and 3D movies (included with admission). Along with the more typical hands-on activities, it books first-rate traveling exhibits that make this worthy of an afternoon. It's on the corner of Cranford and Martin Luther King Jr Blvd.

FREE Lee County Manatee Park WILDLIFE SANCTUARY
(☑239-432-2038; www.leeparks.org; 10901 State Rd 80; parking per hr/day $1/5; ⊙park 8am-sunset year-round, visitor center 9am-4pm Nov-Mar, closed

summer) November through March, manatees flock up the Orange River to this warm-water discharge canal from the nearby power plant. The waterway is now a protected sanctuary, with a landscaped park and playground in addition to viewing platforms at water's edge, where manatees swim almost at arm's reach. **Calusa Blueway Outfitters** (☑239-481-4600; www.calusabluewayoutfitters .com) rents kayaks; reserve ahead whenever the VC is closed. The park is signed off Hwy 80, about 6.5 miles from downtown Fort Myers, and 1.5 miles east of I-75.

☞ Tours

Classic Air Ventures AIR TOUR
(☑941-505-9226; http://coastalbiplanetours.com; 605 Danley Dr; per 2 people $175-335; ⊙11am-5pm Mon-Sat Oct-May) At Page Field, off Cleveland Ave, just south of downtown Fort Myers, Classic Air operates restored 1940s open-cockpit biplanes (that's right, goggles, leather helmet and all). It offers four different flights from 20 to 60 minutes in length.

✯ Festivals & Events

Edison Festival of Light CULTURAL
(www.edisonfestival.org) For two weeks around Edison's birthday on February 11, Fort Myers is the place to be. Dozens of mostly free events include street fairs, antique-car shows, fun runs, music, numerous parades, and the best school-sponsored science fair you'll ever see. Everything culminates in the enormous Parade of Light.

🛏 Sleeping

Some of the area's best budget options are the midrange chain hotels that line S Cleveland Ave near the airports: try Days Inn, Comfort Inn, Holiday Inn, La Quinta and Homewood Suites. Otherwise, downtown Fort Myers has two good, if different, options.

Hotel Indigo HOTEL **$$**
(☑239-337-3446; www.hotelindigo.com/fortmyersfl; 1520 Broadway; r $170-200; ❄@🛜☁) Now anchoring the downtown historic district, this new-in-2009 boutique chain makes a fresh, attractive, reliable stay. The 67 designer-style rooms have powder-blue comforters, wall murals, a mix of wood floors and carpets, and snazzy glass-door showers. The kicker is the small rooftop pool and bar, with panoramic views of the scenic riverfront. All it lacks is self-parking; use the street or their valet ($14).

River District Youth Hostel HOSTEL **$**

(☎239-362-2799; http://riverdistrictyouthhostel.com; 1631 Hough St at 2nd St; per person r/dm $29/25) In a cozy house on the outside edge of the historic district, this hostel has just two rooms (one dorm, one private) that share one bathroom. Guests also share the pretty backyard and hot tub. It's plain but clean, well managed and feels like home.

Eating

Locals will tell you that 'Fort Misery' isn't very good for dining, but they sell it short. The historic downtown has attractive choices, and more are hidden within strip malls further out. The upscale Bell Tower Shops, at S Cleveland Ave and Cypress Lake Dr, has several.

TOP CHOICE Cantina Laredo MEXICAN **$$**

(☎239-415-4424; www.cantinalaredo.com; 5200 Big Pine Way, Bell Tower Shops; mains $12-23; ⊙11am-10pm Sun-Thu, noon-11pm Fri & Sat) Maybe it's the margarita talking, but this atmospheric Mexican chain does everything right, with sharp service, low, romantic lighting, top-shelf tequila, Mexican beer on tap, and guacamole made fresh tableside. Contemporary updates of standard Mexican entrees are well executed and delicious: the *camarones con Tocino* (bacon-wrapped, cheese-stuffed shrimp) and *poblano asado* (steak-wrapped poblano pepper) are superb.

La Trattoria Caffe Napoli ITALIAN, SPANISH **$$**

(☎239-931-0050; 12377 S Cleveland Ave; mains $17-25; ⊙11am-2:30pm & 5-10pm Mon-Fri, 5-10pm Sat) The illustrious Gloria was born in Cuba, grew up in Spain and studied cooking in Sweden, which partly explains her bilingual Spanish-Italian menu, which offers tapas and paella as well as veal scallopini and homemade gnocchi. Caesar salads and garlicky shrimp are winners. Black bistro chairs, red-and-yellow walls and Mexican-tile floors lend a romantic Spanish ambience. It's in an easy-to-miss strip mall, near Crystal Dr in Villas Plaza.

Spirits of Bacchus TAPAS **$$**

(www.spiritsofbacchus.com; 1406 Hendry St; small plates $7-12; ⊙from 4pm Mon-Fri, 6pm Sat, 1pm Sun) This stylish exposed-brick saloon is a favorite Fort Myers watering hole serving a range of fancy tapas, sandwiches and bar food, along with wine and cocktails. Nosh and slosh your way through an evening on the vine-wrapped patio.

Cafe Matisse CAFE **$**

(2236 1st St; mains $4-8; ⊙7am-9pm Mon-Fri, 8am-10pm Sat & Sun) In the heart of the historic district, this hip coffeehouse is a good place to start your morning, with a variety of eggs and lunch sandwiches.

 Drinking & Entertainment

The historic downtown, in and around 1st St, is plenty active come nightfall; definitely cruise the restaurants and bars in Patio de León, a courtyard off Hendry St near 1st St. The district becomes a veritable street party twice monthly: for the first-Friday Art Walk (www.fortmyersartwalk.com) and the third-Saturday Music Walk (www.fortmyersmusicwalk.com).

Bars

These bars have regular live music.

Indigo Room BAR

(☎239-332-0014; 2219 Main St; ⊙11am-2am Tue-Sat, 7pm-2am Sun & Mon) Landmark, quasi-punk dive bar on Patio de León.

Space 39 BAR

(www.space39.com; 39 Patio de León; ⊙4pm-2am) An art gallery–hip lounge with live jazz and snazzy cocktails.

Red Rock Saloon BAR

(☎239-689-8667; 2278 1st St; ⊙11am-2am) Unpretentious, friendly newcomer attracts young tat-and-biker crowd.

Theater

Arcade Theatre THEATER

(☎239-332-4488; www.floridarep.org; 2267 1st St; tickets $17-38; ⊙Oct-May) The beautifully renovated, intimate 1908 Arcade Theatre is home to the **Florida Repertory Theatre**, one of the best regional theaters in Florida. It produces popular comedies, musicals and recent Tony winners, like *God of Carnage*.

Davis Art Center PERFORMING ARTS

(☎239-333-1933; www.sbdac.com; 2301 1st St; ⊙Oct-Jun) This new-in-2010 performance space downtown produces an eclectic slate of drama, children's theater, dance, music and film. At night, a sculpture splashes the old bank facade with illuminated words.

Sports

March in Fort Myers means major-league baseball's spring training. **City of Palms Park** (2201 Edison Ave) is the spring-training field for baseball's hallowed **Boston Red Sox** (www.redsox.com). The **Minnesota Twins** (www.mntwins.com) play in Hammond Stadium at **Lee County Sports Complex** (14100 Six Mile Cypress Pkwy), just southwest of the intersection of Daniels Parkway and Six Mile Cypress Parkway. During the regular season, the Fort Myers Miracles (the Minnesota Twins' class A minor-league baseball team) play here.

🛍 Shopping

Franklin Shops ARTS & CRAFTS
(www.thefranklinshops.com; 2200 1st St; ⊙10am-6pm Mon-Thu, to 8pm Fri & Sat) Riding Fort Myers' upsurge in artsy cool, this gift store–gallery represents over 60 local artists and businesses, including Leoma Lovegrove and Bert's of Matlacha. Great for unusual, retro, only-in-southwest-Florida gifts.

ℹ Information

Greater Fort Myers Chamber of Commerce
(☑239-332-3624; www.fortmyers.org; cnr Lee St & Edwards Dr; ⊙9am-4:30pm Mon-Fri) Lots of info, good maps, and they'll help you find a room.

Lee Memorial Hospital (☑239-343-2000; www.leememorial.org; 2776 Cleveland Ave; ⊙24hr)

Library (http://library.leegov.com; 2050 Central Ave; ⊙9am-8pm Mon-Wed, to 6pm Thu, to 5pm Fri & Sat) Free internet access.

Post office (cnr Bay St & Monroe Ave)

ℹ Getting There & Around

A car is essential. US 41/S Cleveland Ave is the main north–south artery. From downtown, both Summerlin Rd/Hwy 869 and McGregor Blvd/Hwy 867 eventually merge and lead to Sanibel Island; they also connect with San Carlos Blvd/Hwy 865 to Fort Myers Beach.

Southwest Florida International Airport (RSW; http://flylcpa.com; 16000 Chamberlin Pkwy) I-75 exit 131/Daniels Parkway. It's also the main airport for nearby Naples.

Greyhound (www.greyhound.com; 2250 Peck St) Connects to Miami, Orlando and Tampa.

LeeTran (www.rideleetran.com; 2250 Widman Way; ride $1.25) Buses serve commuters, not tourists. Routes to Fort Myers Beach and Pine Island, but not to Sanibel or Captiva Islands.

Fort Myers Beach

☑239 / POP 6300

Like Clearwater Beach and St Pete Beach, Fort Myers Beach foments a party atmosphere year-round, and spring unfolds like one long-running street festival slash frater-

nity bash. And yet, situated on the 7-mile-long Estero Island, Fort Myers Beach has sand and space enough to accommodate all needs and ages. In the north, the so-called Times Sq area is a walkable concentration that verily epitomizes 'sun-bleached seaside party town': it offers a long pier, frosty tropical drinks, cheap T-shirts, fried seafood, melting ice cream, performing magicians and hordes of families, teens and coeds socializing along the water's edge.

Head south and the beachfront becomes more residential, less crowded and much quieter, yet it's lined with enough motels, condos and restaurants that your week could pass without ever needing to visit Times Sq. Plus it's less expensive than nearby Sanibel and Naples, which is why families often choose Fort Myers Beach as a base for regional visits. Well, that and 7 miles of gorgeous sand as soft and white as talcum powder.

On the mainland, about 2 miles north of the Sky Bridge, the **Greater Fort Myers Beach Chamber of Commerce** (☑239-454-7500; www.fortmyersbeachchamber.org; 17200 San Carlos Blvd; ⊙9am-5pm Mon-Fri, 10am-5pm Sat, 10am-3pm Sun) maintains a daily list of hotel vacancies, and it'll help you find a room. Narrow Estero Island itself has a single main drag, Estero Blvd, that runs the island's length, from Bowditch Point Park in the north to Lover's Key State Park. A red **LeeTran trolley** (www.rideleetran.com; fare 50¢; ⊙every 25min 6:30am-9pm) plies this route daily, and connects to Fort Myers buses at Summerlin Sq on the mainland. Trolleys make it easy to avoid driving on the island, though they still get caught in the annoying Times Sq traffic.

⊙ Sights & Activities

Fort Myers BEACH
Fort Myers Beach is long, long, long. The southern end is dominated by condos, with very little public access. The middle has a large number of end-of-road access points with tiny metered lots ($2 per hour); this is also low-key. The northern Times Sq area, right where the causeway dumps visitors, has large paid lots ($5 to $10 per day) and is typically packed and loud, with beach bars pumping out the music. Parasail and water-sport concessions congregate thickly here, and a bait house on the pier rents fishing rods.

Bowditch Point Park PARK, BEACH
At the island's northernmost tip, Bowditch is a favorite with families and picnickers.

The small parking lot fills up fast, so come early; there's a good snack bar, kayak and paddleboard rentals, a ping-pong table, expansive, shady picnic areas, and a sliver of sand that narrows around the tip.

A current beach-replenishment project, due for completion in summer 2012, will add a jetty at Bowditch and a park near the pier, and will, town planners hope, provide the island's northern stretch with an epic, 200ft-wide beach that will end their annual battles with erosion.

Lovers Key State Park BEACH
(☎239-463-4588; www.floridastateparks.org/lovers key; 8700 Estero Blvd; per car/bike $8/2; ⊙sunrise-sunset) In the mood for a good hike, bike or kayak, with a chance to spot manatees in spring and summer? Come to Lovers Key, just south (and over a bridge) from Estero Island. Canals and 2.6 miles of trails around inner islands provide head-clearing quietude and bird-watching. The long, narrow beach is excellent for shelling, but erosion can make it too slim to lay a towel at high tide. There're a snack bar, rental concessions and nice facilities; a tram shuttles between beach and parking lot.

⭐ Festivals & Events

Fort Myers Beach Shrimp Festival FOOD
(www.fortmyersbeachshrimpfestival.com) For two weekends in early March, Fort Myers celebrates bounteous local Gulf pink shrimp with parades, beauty queens, craft fairs and lots of cooking.

American Sandsculpting Championship Festival CULTURAL
(www.sandsculptingfestival.com) Four-day national sand-sculpting event, with amateur and pro divisions; street festival atmosphere during first weekend in November.

🛏 Sleeping

You pay extra to be within the Times Sq action. Stay mid-beach or in the south for quieter beaches.

TOP CHOICE Edison Beach House HOTEL $$$
(☎239-463-1530; www.edisonbeachhouse.com; 830 Estero Blvd; r $200-335; ❄🤙🏊🐾) Built in 2001, this all-suite hotel was designed smartly from the ground up and proudly maintains impeccable standards of cleanliness and upkeep. Attractive decor and rattan furniture are pleasing, but more sizable rooms are comfortable for longer stays and all frame perfect ocean views from nice balconies. Fully equipped kitchens are stocked with good-quality appliances; each room has a washer-dryer. It's beachside near the pier, and walkable to Times Sq.

TOP CHOICE Mango Street Inn B&B $$
(☎239-233-8542; www.mangostreetinn.com; 126 Mango St; r $145-165; ❄🤙🏊) Mango Street's affable husband-and-wife owners have created a winning seaside B&B: its eclectic, idiosyncratic decor is funky and memorable but relaxed enough to feel homey. The six rooms with full kitchens hug an interior courtyard with wood deck and pretty pergola. It's a short walk to the beach, with loaner bikes and beach gear. Most memorable, though, is the gourmet breakfast; Dan is a Cajun-trained chef who encourages guests' culinary efforts.

Beach Shell Inn MOTEL $$
(☎239-463-9193; www.beachshellinn.com; 2610 Estero Blvd; r $162-220; ❄🤙🏊) With one exception, decor is mostly standard-issue, blue-and-green seaside, but the 15 rooms at this well-managed, mid-island motel are notably clean and in good nick. All are carpeted, with flat-screen TVs; some have small efficiency kitchens. Then there's the retro bachelor pad with black-leather couch and mirror over the bed. Yowza. The kidney-shaped pool is appealing.

Dolphin Inn MOTEL $$
(☎239-463-6049; www.dolphininn.net; 6555 Estero Blvd; r $120-160; ❄@🤙🏊🐾) This vintage, Old Florida motel is best if you get one of the newly renovated rooms. Yet all sport no-fuss furniture and have full kitchens; the best are bayside, overlooking a scenic residential harbor where manatees play. Amenities include a sizable L-shaped pool, communal grills, loaner kayaks, DVD library and cheap bike rental. The personable owners create a friendly atmosphere.

Neptune RESORT $$$
(☎239-463-6141; www.theneptuneresort.com; 2310 Estero Blvd; r $220-310; ❄@🏊🐾) This beachside, 70-room resort lacks personality or warm fuzzies, but it's a reliable, full-service choice with top-notch amenities and cleanliness. Families can bunk comfortably; all rooms have good efficiency kitchens. Grounds include two pools, and it's walkable to Times Sq.

Eating & Drinking

Most of the restaurant and nightlife action is centered on Times Sq, which is rife with middling eateries and seafood joints, several with live-music bars that can become quite raucous after sunset.

Doc Ford's   SEAFOOD $$

(☑239-765-9660; www.docfords.com; 708 Fisherman's Wharf; mains $10-22; ☺11am-10pm, bar later) Part-owner Randy Wayne White once lived on the marina here, and he named this scenic wharf eatery after his beloved mystery-novel protagonist, marine biologist Doc Ford. The wood-sided building with spacious decks, big windows, and multiple bars emphasizes Floribbean flavors and a Latin American spice rack. The Yucatan shrimp and panko-crusted fish sandwich are highly recommended. It's on the mainland at the base of the causeway bridge.

Heavenly Biscuit   BREAKFAST $

(110 Mango St; items $3-8; ☺8am-noon Mon, 7:30am-2pm Tue-Sun) This unassuming shack offers two genuine delights: sumptuous fresh-baked buttermilk biscuits – overflowing with eggs, cheese and bacon – and delectable cinnamon rolls. Eat directly off the waxed paper on the tiny porch or get it to go; you can build a bigger breakfast with grits and home fries. It's nothing fancy or highbrow, just a simple thing done right.

Sandy Butler   ITALIAN $$$

(☑239-482-6765; www.sandybutler.com; 17650 San Carlos Blvd; mains $18-32; ☺market 10am-8pm, restaurant 11:30am-9pm, to 10pm Fri & Sat) The best grocery store and the most soothing and refined sit-down meal at Fort Myers Beach are actually inland 2.5 miles from the bridge. The Sandy Butler is both: on one side is a gourmet market with fresh fish and meats and tons of prepared foods for a delicious picnic. Attached but entirely separate, the airy, industrial-hip dining room specializes in contemporary Italian cuisine.

Beached Whale   SEAFOOD $$

(☑239-463-5505; www.thebeachedwhale.com; 1249 Estero Blvd; mains $10-18; ☺11am-2am) The breezy upstairs deck is a long-standing favorite for a reliable sunset meal with gulf views; go for either grilled seafood or sticky-sweet barbecue. An older crowd creates a friendly vibe in this unpretentious local watering hole, which has live music and gets more rowdy later in the evening.

Gulfshore Grill & the Cottage   SEAFOOD $$

(www.gulfshoregrill.com; 1270 Estero Blvd; mains $11-21; ☺8am-10pm, bar to 1:30am) Meals at this rambling, multilevel, beachside 'cottage' define average, but the menu is extensive, family-friendly and includes Caribbean and Mexican choices. It's more known for its bars, which take over after the dinner hour and draw a young, Spring Break crowd. Live music and DJs rock the sand almost nightly.

Top O'Mast Lounge   BAR

(1028 Estero Blvd; mains $8-15; ☺11am-2am) Exemplifying the quintessential drink first, think later approach to beach fun, Top O'Mast anchors the base of the pier in Times Sq. It's a landmark party institution that makes sure the beach throbs to some kind of music nightly. The Mexican restaurant across the courtyard serves meals here.

Pine Island & Matlacha

☑239 / POP 740

The tiny fishing village of Matlacha (pronounced mat-la-shay) straddles the drawbridge to Pine Island, and it provides a quirky window into local life. Along with unpretentious fresh seafood markets and restaurants, a collection of old fishing huts have been transformed into gift shops that sit like a clutch of chattering Day-Glo-painted tropical birds.

Matlacha makes a fun afternoon's diversion, but Pine Island is better known as a jumping-off point for all-day adventures among the region's tarpon-rich waterways and gorgeous barrier islands. Of these, Cayo Costa is rightly considered one of the jewels of the coast, a sweeping, undeveloped state park so lightly traveled you can feel like a *Lost* castaway. Most people visit Cayo Costa as a day trip, but it's possible to camp overnight. The 17-mile-long Pine Island, the region's largest, has no sandy beaches to call its own but offers relaxing, quiet lodgings for anglers, kayakers and romantics fleeing the tourist hordes.

Pine Island encompasses several communities but is known as a single entity. Due west of Matlacha is 'Pine Island Center,' a crossroads with a small amount of commerce; from here, take Stringfellow Rd north to reach more marinas with boat and fishing charters (at Pineland and Bokeelia) and several lodgings and restaurants. For more information, visit www.pineislandchamber .org and www.floridascreativecoast.com.

👁 Sights & Activities

TOP CHOICE Cayo Costa State Park · BEACH
(☎941-964-0375; www.floridastateparks.org/cayo costa; entrance $2, campsites $22, 4-person cabins $40; ⊙8am-sunset) Unspoiled and all natural, as slim as a supermodel and just as lovely, Cayo Costa Island is almost entirely preserved as a 2500-acre state park. While its pale, ash-colored sand may not be as fine as others, its idyllic, peaceful solitude and bathtub-warm azure waters are without peer. Bring a snorkel mask to help scour sandbars for shells and huge conchs – delightfully, many still house colorful occupants (who, by law, must be left there). Bike dirt roads to more-distant beaches, hike interior island trails, kayak mangroves. The ranger station near the dock sells water and firewood, and rents bikes and kayaks, but otherwise bring everything you need.

The 30-site campground is exposed and hot (thank 2004's Hurricane Charley, which knocked down the pines), with fire-pit grills, restrooms and showers, but sleeping on this beach is its own reward. Twelve plain cabins are essentially hard-sided tents, with bunk beds and vinyl-covered mattresses. January to April is best; book far in advance. By May, the heat and no-see-ums (biting midges) become unpleasant.

The only access is by boat, which doubles as a scenic nature-and-dolphin cruise. The park's official concessionare is Tropic Star (☎239-283-0015; www.tropicstarcruises.com; Jug Creek Marina, Bokeelia). Day-trip ferries to Cayo Costa ($25) take an hour one-way; a range of other options include stops at Cabbage Key for lunch (see p406). It also offers private water taxis ($150 per hour), which are much faster; other boat charters and water taxis are available at Pineland and Matlacha marinas.

Gulf Coast Kayak · KAYAKING
(☎239-283-1125; www.gulfcoastkayak.com; 4530 NW Pine Island Rd) In Matlacha, just past the drawbridge, Gulf Coast offers several kayak tours ($50 per person) in the wildlife-rich Matlacha Pass Aquatic Preserve. Or rent a canoe or kayak ($30 to $65) and paddle yourself. Want to kayak *to* Cayo Costa? Talk to them.

🛏 Sleeping

Beachhouse Lodge · LODGE $$
(☎239-283-4303; www.beachousefl; 7702 Bocilla Lane, Bokeelia; r $120, apt $150-200; ❇ 🛜 🐾) Tucked down a quiet lane, this wood-sided house has five rooms: four generous apartments with excellent, full-service kitchens (making it a joy to cook your catch) and one

---

CHEESEBURGER IN PARADISE: CABBAGE KEY INN

As all Parrotheads know, Jimmy Buffett's famous song 'Cheeseburger in Paradise' was allegedly inspired by a meal at the Cabbage Key Inn (☎239-283-2278; www.cabbagekey .com; r $100-140, cottages $160-415; ⊙7:30-9am, 11:30am-3pm & 6-8:30pm). Truth be told, the burger is only average, and it wouldn't be worth writing a song about if it weren't served on this 100-acre, mangrove-fringed key in the Gulf of Mexico, which somehow makes everything more special. Built atop a Calusa shell mound, and originally the 1938 home of writer Mary Roberts Rinehart, the inn has the romantic air of a secluded semitropical port for global wayfarers, one that receives ferry loads of tourists every lunchtime. The bar is certainly a sight: the walls are matted and spongy with perhaps $80,000 in signed $1 bills, including framed bills from ex-president Jimmy Carter and of course Mr Buffett. Bills flutter to the floor daily, which the inn collects, annually donating $10,000 to charity.

Staying in one of the inn's six rooms or seven cottages is definitely the best experience. Accommodations vary markedly; all are Old Florida atmospheric with pretty touches (Rinehart and Dollhouse are favorites), but they aren't resort-plush: no TVs, no DVDs, no pool, no swimming beach, no grills or fires, and wi-fi only in the restaurant. But you're not exactly marooned: the inn serves powerful cocktails and full dinner nightly ($16 to $29, and they'll cook your catch), but make reservations. Most people visit for lunch ($9 to $11); we'd recommend the blackened mahimahi with black beans and rice, but we know what you'll probably order.

To get here, Tropic Star (see p406) has ferries that include lunch at Cabbage Key, or you can rent your own boat or book a private water taxi on Pine Island, Matlacha or Captiva Island.

tiny 'hotel-style' room. Extremely clean and comfortably decorated, it feels like home in less than 24 hours.

Bokeelia Tarpon Inn
B&B **$$$**

(☎239-283-8961; www.tarponinn.com; 8421 Main St, Pine Island; r $200-300; ❄🛜) If you want a little more pampering, book one of the five rooms at this B&B on Pine Island's northern tip. Public spaces are gracious and relaxing, exuding a turn-of-the-century seaside-holiday mood. Rooms are crisply decorated, with hardwood floors, rattan bed frames and pretty quilts. Loaner bikes, kayaks and golf carts are offered. To ensure romance, small children are discouraged.

Bridge Water Inn
MOTEL **$$**

(☎239-283-2423; www.bridgewaterinn.com; 4331 Pine Island Rd, Matlacha; r $69-189; ❄🛜🚲) Built on a pier, this family-run angler's haven has five suites with kitchenettes and four standard motel rooms. All open onto a deck, so you can fish from your room. It's bright-painted and friendly, if decidedly plain inside.

✖ Eating

Several restaurants line Stringfellow Rd on Pine Island. Those below, and more, are in Matlacha on either side of the drawbridge.

TOP CHOICE Perfect Cup
BREAKFAST **$**

(☎239-283-4447; 4548 Pine Island Rd, Matlacha; mains $5-10; ⊙6am-3pm Mon-Sat, 7am-2pm Sun) A genuine local gathering place, Perfect Cup offers just that: a bottomless mug of flavorful house-roasted coffee ($2) to go with its top-quality diner-style fare: creative omelettes, French toast, pancakes. Judging by awards, its chowder can't be beat. The cozy, friendly atmosphere is the perfect start to a day.

Andy's Island Seafood
MARKET **$**

(www.andysislandseafood.com; 4330 Pine Island Rd, Matlacha; items $8-14; ⊙10am-6pm Mon-Sat, to 4pm Sun) This lime-green shack offers a great selection of fresh seafood to cook, as well as succulent grouper sandwiches, crab cakes and chowder for lunch. It's so popular you'll find Andy's lunch trucks popping up on other islands.

Sandy Hook Restaurant
SEAFOOD **$$**

(☎239-283-0113; www.sandyhookrestaurant.com; 4875 Pine Island Rd, Matlacha; mains $14-22; ⊙4-9pm Tue-Sat, noon-8pm Sun) Walls and ceilings are a humorous, nonsensical nautical free-for-all, windows offer soothing water views,

and the seafood preparations stick to safe, dependable, crowd-pleasing standards.

🛍 Shopping

Lovegrove Gallery
ARTS & CRAFTS

(www.leomalovegrove.com; 4637 Pine Island Rd, Matlacha; ⊙10am-6pm Mon-Sat, 11am-5pm Sun) If Matlacha is unexpectedly groovy for such a sun-faded fishing village, you can thank artist Leoma Lovegrove. Her gallery has transformed a fisherman's shack into a whimsical vision of tile mosaics and paintings, with a loopy 'Tropical Waterways Garden' in back. Now the whole block is a bona fide slice of roadside Americana, with unusual gift and craft shops. Don't miss it.

ℹ Getting There & Around

Pine Island is due west of North Fort Myers and is not accessible by public transportation. By car, take US 41 to Pine Island Rd (Hwy 78), and go west until you get there.

Sanibel & Captiva Islands

🕿239 / SANIBEL POP 6500 / CAPTIVA POP 580

As the saying goes, millionaires are people, too, and they like their beach getaways as much as anyone. But on the beautiful barrier islands of Sanibel and Captiva, it can be hard to tell if the bicycling vacationers have money and position or not. By preference and design, island life is informal and egalitarian, and riches are rarely flaunted. Even Captiva's mansions are hidden behind thick foliage and sport playful names like 'Seas the Day.' Whether for a few days or a few weeks, the islands make a genteel escape from balance sheets, status and traffic lights, of which there are none.

Development on Sanibel has been carefully managed: the northern half is almost entirely protected within the JN 'Ding' Darling National Wildlife Refuge. The southern edge has the sand, and while there are hotels and resorts aplenty, the beachfront is largely undeveloped and free of commercial-and-condo blight. Plus, public beach access is limited to a handful of parking lots, and these are spread out, so there is no crush of day-trippers in one place. There is no 'downtown.' On Sanibel, businesses and restaurants are spread leisurely along the inner-island corridor: Periwinkle Way, which becomes Sanibel-Captiva Rd. On Captiva, the tiny village is confined to a single street, Andy Rosse Lane.

Spend a day here, and the benefits are obvious. Spend a week, and it can seem like heaven. You will adapt quickly to the preferred mode of travel – the bike – and come to forget that not every Gulf island is so relaxing and gives gifts so freely, its bounty of jewel-like shells spread generously for anyone to take.

◉ Sights & Activities

The quality of shelling on Sanibel is so high dedicated hunters are identified by their hunchbacked 'Sanibel stoop.' However, if you're serious, buy a scoop net, get a shell guide from the visitor center, and peruse the blog www.iloveshelling.com. Gathering the perfect bagful is like coming home with pirate's treasure.

Beaches   BEACH
What you gain in shelling you lose in powdery white sand: beaches are excellent but the sand isn't as purely fine as it is elsewhere (like Siesta Key). Public-access beaches are located away from hotels, meaning that staying overnight allows private access to even less-crowded stretches. All the following beaches except Blind Pass have restrooms; none have concessions or snack bars. Parking is $2 per hour.

Bowman's Beach is far and away the most popular beach; extremely long, with an enormous parking lot, sparkling sand and facilities and a playground. Prominent 'No nude sunbathing' signs are meant to dissuade scofflaws from doing just that at the distant west end.

Modest-size parking lot limits access at Tarpon Bay Beach; the sand is not quite as good as Bowman. The same can be said for Gulfside City Park.

Lighthouse Beach is a modest lot, narrow beach. The historic metal lighthouse can't be entered; short nature trails lead around the point. Turner Beach & Blind Pass are very small lots on either side of Captiva Island bridge. Shellers favor these short stretches.

Captiva's main beach at its northern end, Alison Hagerup Beach has a frustratingly small lot; arrive *very* early. Nice sand ideally positioned for sunset.

JN 'Ding' Darling National
Wildlife Refuge   WILDLIFE RESERVE
(☑239-472-1100; www.fws.gov/dingdarling; Sanibel-Captiva Rd at MM 2; per car/cyclist $5/1; ⊙visitor center 9am-5pm, refuge 7am-7pm Sun-Thu) Named for cartoonist Jay Norwood 'Ding' Darling, an environmentalist who helped establish more than 300 sanctuaries across the USA, this 6300-acre refuge across northern Sanibel is home to an abundance of seabirds and wildlife, including alligators, night herons, red-shouldered hawks, spotted sandpipers, roseate spoonbills, pelicans and anhinga. The refuge's 5-mile Wildlife Drive provides easy access, but bring binoculars; flocks sometimes sit at expansive distances. Only a few very short walks lead into the mangroves. For the best, most intimate experience, canoe or kayak Tarpon Bay.

Don't miss the free educational center, with excellent exhibits on refuge life and Darling himself. Naturalist-narrated Wildlife Drive tram tours (☑239-472-8900; www.tarponbayexplorers.com; 900 Tarpon Bay; adult/child $13/8; ⊙Sat-Thu) depart from the visitor-center parking lot, usually on the hour from 10am to 4pm.

Bailey Matthews Shell Museum   MUSEUM
(☑239-395-2233; www.shellmuseum.org; 3075 Sanibel-Captiva Rd, Sanibel; adult/child 5-16yr $7/4; ⊙10am-5pm) Like a mermaid's jewelry box, this museum is dedicated to shells, yet it's much more than a covetous display of treasures. It's a crisply presented natural history of the sea, detailing the life and times of the bivalves, mollusks and other creatures who reside inside their calcium homes, as well as the role of these animals and shells in human culture, medicine and cuisine. Fascinating videos show living creatures. It's nearly a must after a day spent combing the beaches.

Sanibel Historical Village   HISTORIC SITE
(☑239-472-4648; www.sanibelmuseum.org; 950 Dunlop Rd, Sanibel; adult/child $5/free; ⊙10am-1pm Wed-Sat summer, to 4pm Wed-Sat winter) Well polished by the enthusiasm of local volunteers, this museum and collection of nine historic buildings preserves Sanibel's pioneer past. It's a piquant taste of the settlers' life, with general store, post office, cottage and more.

Sanibel Recreation Center   HEALTH & FITNESS
(☑239-472-0345; www.mysanibel.com; 3880 Sanibel-Captiva Rd, Sanibel; family/individual $20/12; ⊙6:30am-8pm Mon-Thu, to 6:30pm Fri, 8am-5pm Sat & Sun) Want resort amenities without paying resort prices? Frequent this pristine rec center. It has a lap pool, kids' pool with waterslide, extensive exercise room, four tennis courts and indoor game room, and all

classes are included in the day fee. Call for open-swim hours, which vary.

Billy's Rentals
BICYCLE RENTAL
(☎239-472-5248; www.billysrentals.com; 1470 Periwinkle Way, Sanibel; bikes per 2hr/day from $5/15; ☺8:30am-5pm) Nearly all of Sanibel's main roads are paralleled by paved bike paths; on Captiva, main roads have bike lanes. Bikes have preference at road crossings, and they scoot by auto backups and full parking lots at public beaches. So rent a bike and forget your worries. Billy's rents every type of wheeled contrivance, including joggers, tandems, surreys, scooters and more.

Tarpon Bay Explorers
KAYAKING
(☎239-472-8900; www.tarponbayexplorers.com; 900 Tarpon Bay Rd, Sanibel; ☺8am-6pm) Within the Darling refuge, this outfitter rents canoes and kayaks ($25 for two hours) for easy, self-guided paddles in Tarpon Bay, a perfect place for young paddlers. Guided kayak trips (adult/child $40/25) are also excellent, and they have a range of other trips. Reserve ahead or come early, as they book up.

'Tween Waters Marina
KAYAKING
(☎239-472-5161; www.tween-waters.com; 15951 Captiva Rd, Captiva; ☺7:30am-5:30pm) For a more-involved kayak, target Buck Key off Captiva. 'Tween Waters Marina, at the 'Tween Waters Inn, can set you up with rentals ($20 for two hours) and guided kayak tours ($40).

Tours

Boats and cruises are nearly as ubiquitous as shells on the islands. Sanibel Marina (☎239-472-2723; www.sanibelmarina.com; 634 N Yachtsman Dr) is the main small-boat harbor with a ton of boat rentals (from $125) and charters (from $350). On Captiva, McCarthy's Marina (www.mccarthysmarina.com; 11401 Andy Rosse Lane, Captiva) is where Captiva Cruises (☎239-472-5300; www.captivacruises.com) departs from. It offers everything from dolphin and sunset cruises (from $25) to various island excursions (from $35), like Cayo Costa and Cabbage Key.

Festivals & Events

Sanibel Music Festival
MUSIC
(www.sanibelmusicfestival.org) A classical- and chamber-music festival that draws international musicians for a month-long concert series every Tuesday and Saturday in March.

'Ding' Darling Days
CULTURAL
(www.dingdarlingsociety.org/dingdarlingdays. php) A week-long celebration of the wildlife refuge, with birding tours, workshops, guest speakers and tons more. A huge mid-October event.

Sanibel Luminary Fest
CULTURAL
One of Sanibel's signature events is this street fair the first weekend of December, when paper luminaries line the island's bike paths.

Sleeping

As elsewhere, low season sees a huge drop in rates. If you're interested in a one-week vacation rental, contact Sanibel & Captiva Accommodations (☎800-237-6004; www.sanibelaccom.com).

'Tween Waters Inn
RESORT $$$
(☎239-472-5161; www.tween-waters.com; 15951 Captiva Dr, Captiva; r $160-215, ste $220-405, cottages $265-445; ✳@🛜🐾) For great resort value and an ideal getaway location on Captiva, choose 'Tween Waters Inn. Building exteriors are sun-faded, and you should request one of the recently renovated rooms, which are pristine, attractive roosts with rattan furnishings, granite counters, rainfall showerheads and Tommy Bahama–style decor. Kitchenettes are up-to-date, and tidy little cottages are romantic. All hotel rooms have view balconies; those directly facing the Gulf are splendid. Families make good use of the big pool, tennis courts, full-service marina and spa. Multinight discounts are attractive.

Tarpon Tale Inn
MOTEL $$
(☎239-472-0939; www.tarpontale.com; 367 Periwinkle Way, Sanibel; r $150-260; ✳@🛜🐾) The five charming, tile-floored rooms evoke a bright, blue-and-white seaside mood; each has its own shady porch and tree-strung hammock. Two rooms have efficiencies and three have full kitchens. With communal hot tub and loaner bikes, it does a nice imitation of a B&B without the breakfast.

Blue Dolphin Cottages
MOTEL $$$
(☎239-472-1600; www.bluedolphincottages.com; 4227 W Gulf Dr, Sanibel; r $190-280; ✳🛜) On a secluded stretch of Gulf Dr, Blue Dolphin has 11 duplex rooms set within pretty gardens right on the beach. Most have full kitchens, and all have well-kept, easy-clean, standard seaside decor. Communal grills face the water, and continental breakfast is included.

Mitchell's Sandcastles   MOTEL $$$

(☎239-472-1282; www.mitchellssandcastles.com; 3951 W Gulf Dr; r $170-275; ❄@🖤🛎️🐾🐕🏊) Another getaway Gulf Dr choice is Mitchell's, also right on the beach. Its 25 rooms are strictly standard, but each has full kitchen and its own grill. The range of amenities appeals to families: small pool, tennis court, fitness center, and loaner kayaks and bikes, if you ever tire of the sand.

Sunshine Island Inn   MOTEL $$

(☎239-395-2500; www.sunshineislandinn.com; 642 E Gulf Dr; r $130-200; ❄@🖤🛎️🐾🏊) This low-key, friendly motel offers great value for families who want to get comfortable and aren't picky about decor. The five rooms are well kept and good sized but eclectically furnished; all have sliding doors opening directly onto the small pool. It's across the street from the beach but directly on the Sanibel River, with loaner kayaks.

🍴 Eating & Drinking

TOP CHOICE Sweet Melissa's Cafe   AMERICAN $$$

(☎239-472-1956; www.sweetmelissascafe.net; 1625 Periwinkle Way, Sanibel; tapas $11-14, mains $26-34; ⏱11:30am-2:30pm Mon-Fri, from 5pm nightly) From menu to mood, Sweet Melissa's offers well-balanced, relaxed refinement. Dishes are creative without trying too hard, and most mains can be served tapas size, which encourages experimenting. Try the shrimp with grits, seared scallops over curried cauliflower, grilled romaine and the refreshing watermelon salad. Service is attentive and the atmosphere upbeat.

Over Easy Cafe   BREAKFAST $$

(www.overeasycafesanibel.com; 630 Tarpon Rd at Periwinkle Way, Sanibel; mains $8-13; ⏱7am-2:30pm; 🐕) Despite Provence-style decor, the menu is strictly top-quality diner, with eggs every which way. Add fluffy pancakes, good coffee and friendly, efficient service, and this becomes Sanibel's go-to morning choice, so expect a wait. In summer, it also opens for dinner Tuesday to Saturday.

🌿 Mad Hatter Restaurant   AMERICAN $$$

(☎239-472-0033; www.madhatterrestaurant.com; 6467 Sanibel-Captiva Rd, Sanibel; mains $29-45; ⏱6-8:45pm) Vacationing Manhattan and Miami urbanites flock to what is widely regarded as Sanibel's best locavore gourmet restaurant. Contemporary seafood is the central focus, with creative appetizers like truffled oysters and a seafood martini, while mains emphasize bouillabaisse, crab cakes, pan-seared grouper and so on. As the name suggests, it's not stuffy, but it's for culinary mavens whose concern is quality, whatever the price.

Bubble Room   AMERICAN $$$

(www.bubbleroomrestaurant.com; 15001 Captiva Dr, Captiva; lunch $10-15, dinner $20-30; ⏱11:30am-3pm & 4:30-9pm; 🐕) All the creativity is on the walls at this Captiva classic; if you have kids, it's almost required. Unbelievable decor is a blender-ized, overwhelming riot of 1930s to 1950s memorabilia, a pastiche of superheroes, cartoon characters, movie stars, toy trains, bric-a-brac and Christmas. Entertaining servers in scout uniforms bring meals and desserts that, if nothing else, don't lack for size. No reservations, so expect waits.

Mucky Duck   PUB $$

(www.muckyduck.com; 11546 Andy Rosse Lane, Captiva; mains $10-25; ⏱11:30am-3pm & 5-9:30pm Mon-Sat) The unpretentious, shingle-roofed Mucky Duck is perfectly positioned for Captiva sunsets, and devoted locals jockey for beach chairs and picnic tables each evening. The extended menu offers more than just pub grub, with pasta, steak, chicken and seafood. Really, though, it's the friendly bar and toes-in-the-sand Gulf views that keep 'em coming.

Jacaranda   SEAFOOD $$$

(☎239-472-1771; www.jacarandaonsanibel.com; 1223 Periwinkle Way, Sanibel; mains $20-30; ⏱4-10pm, lounge to 12:30am) The restaurant menu is classic surf and turf, but the most fun is in the atmospheric lounge. Here, you can mix the less-expensive bar menu's seafood ($9 to $11) with the creative martinis and cocktails, while listening to live music nightly. After enough drinks, dancing is known to occur.

Gramma Dot's   SEAFOOD $$$

(☎239-472-8138; North Yachtsman Dr, Sanibel Marina; lunch $11-15, dinner $19-25; ⏱11:30am-8pm) Pull up a bar stool next to the charter-boat captains at this longtime Sanibel Marina favorite. Enjoy a no-fuss fried-oyster sandwich, mesquite-grilled grouper or the coconut shrimp, plus Caesar salad several ways. A great lunch stop.

Families with underage picky eaters should keep in mind these options:

Sanibel Bean   BREAKFAST $

(www.sanibelbean.com; 2240 Periwinkle Way, Sanibel; mains $5-9; ⏱7am-9pm; 🐕) Extensive cafe menu of quick, cheap eats.

RC Otter AMERICAN $$
(☎239-395-1142; 11506 Andy Rosse Lane, Captiva; mains $10-23; ☺8am-10pm; 👪) Midrange, family-focused choice; above-average kids' menu.

ℹ️ Information

Sanibel & Captiva Islands Chamber of Commerce (☎239-472-1080; www.sanibel-captiva .org; 1159 Causeway Rd, Sanibel; ☺9am-5pm; 📶) One of the more helpful VCs around; keeps an updated hotel-vacancy list with dedicated hotel hotline.

ℹ️ Getting There & Around

Driving is the only way to come. The Sanibel Causeway (Hwy 867) charges an entrance toll (cars/motorcycles $6/2). Sanibel is 12 miles long, and Captiva 5 miles, but low speed limits and traffic make them seem longer. The main drag is Periwinkle Way, which becomes Sanibel-Captiva Rd.

Naples

☎239 / POP 19,500

For upscale romance and the prettiest, most serene city beach in southwest Florida, come to Naples, the Gulf Coast's answer to Palm Beach or California's Marin County. As on Sanibel and Captiva Islands, development along the shoreline has been kept almost strictly residential. The soft white sand is backed only by narrow dunes and half-hidden, perfectly manicured mansions. More than that, though, Naples is a cultured, sophisticated town with a clear, adult sense of self. On the one hand, it is unabashedly stylish and privileged, a place where couture-wearing matrons clutching pocket dogs shop for organic vegetables. But it is also welcoming and fun-loving: families, teens, grandparents, middle-aged executives and smartly dressed young couples all mix and mingle as they stroll downtown's 5th Ave on a balmy evening, everyone queuing up eagerly for Kilwin's ice-cream cones just like anywhere else. Travelers sometimes complain that Naples is expensive, but it's equally true that you can spend as much elsewhere for a whole lot less.

👁 Sights & Activities

Downtown Naples is an easily negotiated grid of streets; all downtown parking (off-beach) is free. There are two primary retail corridors: the main one is 5th Ave between 9th St S/US 41 and W Lake Dr. Pretty, picnic-friendly Cambier Park is here, at 8th St S and 6th Ave S. The other retail district is along 3rd St S between Broad Ave S and 14th St S; this area, called 3rd St South Shops, forms the heart of Old Naples, where ogling mansions is its own pastime.

Naples Area Beaches BEACH
Free of commerce or even one concession stand, **Naples city beach** is a long, dreamy white strand that succeeds in feeling lively but rarely overcrowded, partly because the abundant parking access is spread out. From 7th Ave N to 17th Ave S, every dead end along Gulf Shore Blvd is a small lot with 10 to 15 spots of mixed resident and metered parking ($1.50 per hour); only park at meters or you'll be ticketed. The only true parking lot is near Naples Pier at 12th Ave S, which also has the only beachside restrooms. North of the city beach are three more public beach parks. **Lowdermilk Park** (cnr Banyan Blvd & Gulf Shore Blvd) has more delicious white sand, along with snack-bar pavilion, restrooms and showers, picnic area, playground and two volleyball courts. The large parking lot has relatively few meters for nonresidents. **Clam Pass County Park** (☺8am-sunset) is next to Naples Grand Beach Resort at the end of Seagate Dr from US 4. The resort runs both the water-sports rentals and the free tram that travels the half-mile boardwalk between the large parking lot ($8 per day) and the well-groomed white-sand beach, a favorite with families and young adults. The snack bar serves beer and cocktails. **Delnor-Wiggins Pass State Recreation Area** (11135 Gulf Shore Dr; per car/bike $6/2; ☺8am-sunset) is more of a locals' beach, with extended families crowding the grills. The sand isn't quite as nice, and there are no concessions or rentals, just restrooms and showers. Afternoon winds attract kiteboarders. Lots fill by 11am on high-season weekends. From US 41, take 111th Ave/Hwy 846.

TOP CHOICE **Naples Nature Center** NATURE CENTER
(☎239-262-0304; www.conservancy.org; 14th Ave N & Goodlette-Frank Rd; adult/child $10/5; ☺9am-4:30pm Mon-Sat) Already one of Florida's premier nature-conservancy and -advocacy nonprofits, the Conservancy of Southwest Florida is completing a $20-million renovation to create a LEED-certified campus that will make it an ecological leader. Its new Discovery Center will immerse visitors in southwest Florida environments,

from swamp to Gulf, and two-way mirrors will allow a rare peek into the avian nursery, where over 2000 injured wild birds are rehabilitated annually. With its permanent collection of raptors, animal presentations, films and naturalist-run boat rides, it's a must-visit destination for anyone interested in Florida's environment and its preservation. Call to confirm hours, which may vary until construction is completed.

Naples Museum of Art MUSEUM
(☏239-597-1900; www.thephil.org; 5833 Pelican Bay Blvd; adult/child $8/4; ☻10am-4pm Tue-Sat, noon-4pm Sun Oct-Jun) Next to the Philharmonic, this engaging, sophisticated art museum focuses on 20th-century modernism, particularly American abstract expressionism and Mexican art. One exhibit cleverly designs gallery rooms to match the times of the paintings they display, while the 'Mouse House' recreates Olga Hirshhorn's home, crammed with drawings and ephemera from 20th-century masters. Rotating exhibits emphasize contemporary artists and cutting-edge works. The museum also has some notable Chihuly glass.

Naples Zoo at Caribbean Gardens ZOO
(☏239-262-5409; www.napleszoo.com; 1590 Goodlette-Frank Rd; adult/child 3-12yr $20/13; ☻9am-5pm) Caribbean Gardens is an Old Florida attraction that's been updated into a modest zoo. Though it lacks some big-ticket species (like elephants and manatees), it has some interesting wrinkles, such as narrated boat rides in a lake to visit free-roaming, island-bound monkeys and bigger-than-usual outdoor-theater animal shows (11am and 3pm daily). All presentations are included.

Von Liebig Art Center GALLERY
(☏239-262-6517; www.naplesart.org; 585 Park St; adult/child $5/2; ☻10am-4pm Mon-Sat) In downtown's Cambier Park, this nonprofit community arts center has rotating exhibits in its small gallery and features local artists in its gift shop. Check the online calendar for Naples arts events, such as the Naples National in February.

Cambier Park PARK
(cnr 8th St S & 6th Ave S) Pretty, picnic-friendly park in the main retail corridor.

☝ Tours

Naples Trolley Tours TROLLEY TOUR
(www.naplestrolleytours.com; 1010 6th Ave S; adult/child 4-12yr $25/12.50; ☻9:30am-5:30pm)

Hop-on, hop-off narrated trolley tours make a 1¾-hour circuit through the city daily. They also do Segway tours.

✹ Festivals & Events

Spring to fall, the Old Naples district along 3rd St hosts a range of community events: music, art and a Saturday-morning farmers' market. See the online calendar at www.thirdstreetsouth.com.

🛏 Sleeping

Naples specializes in top-end lodgings, but an economical sleep can be had. A few are listed below, and a string of midrange chain hotels line US 41/Tamiami Trail south of Pine Ridge Rd: try Best Western, Ramada, Residence Inn and Courtyard Marriott. Quoted rates are for high season, but as elsewhere, stay outside February to mid-April and prices drop dramatically, often by half.

Lemon Tree Inn MOTEL $$
(☏239-262-1414; www.lemontreeinn.com; 250 9th St S at 3rd Ave S; r $130-200; ❄@☂☐🐾) Value for money is high at the Lemon Tree, where 34 clean and brightly decorated rooms (some with passable kitchenettes) form a U around pretty, intimate gardens. Screened porches, free lemonade and continental breakfast are nice, but most of all, treasure being walking distance to the 5th Ave corridor.

Cove Inn APARTMENTS $$$
(☏239-262-7161; www.coveinnnaples.com; 900 Broad Ave S; r $180-280; ❄@☂☐🐾) The individually owned condo units of this marina hotel are something of a gamble: most are surprisingly attractive, up-to-date, tile-floored, rattan-furnished rooms with peaceful harbor views. A few await 21st-century face-lifts and feel as tired as the building's bleached exterior. So request an updated unit and enjoy one of Naples' better values. Has a pool and three on-property restaurants.

Inn on 5th HOTEL $$$
(☏239-403-8777; www.innonfifth.com; 699 5th Ave S; r $320-500; ❄@☂☐) This well-polished, Mediterranean-style luxury hotel provides a redolent old-world flavor in its public rooms and an unbeatable location in the midst of 5th Ave. Stylish rooms are more corporate-perfect than historic-romantic, but who complains about pillow-top mattresses and glass-walled tile showers? Full-service amenities include a 2nd-floor heated pool, busi-

DETOUR: THE EVERGLADES

If you've traveled as far south as Naples, you really owe it to yourself to visit the Everglades. Heading west on the Tamiami Trail/Hwy 41, you can be in Everglades City in half an hour, Big Cypress in 45 minutes and Shark Valley in 75 minutes. For more on the big adventures awaiting at these places, see p137.

ness and fitness centers, and an indulgent spa. Free valet parking.

Bellasera Hotel
APARTMENTS $$$

(☎239-649-7333; www.bellaseranaples.com; 221 9th St S; r $250-450; ✻@🛜🏊🐾) Each of the 100 freshly furnished, spotless condo apartments in this extensive three-story complex evoke Tuscany with their sorrel, maroon and burnt-umber palette. Except for 10 studios, spacious suites have full kitchens and dining-living areas designed for families to spread out comfortably. The fantastic pool enjoys bar service from the restaurant. Walkable to 5th Ave.

Inn of Naples
HOTEL $$

(☎239-649-5500; www.innofnaples.com; 4055 Tamiami Trail N; r $140-150; ✻@🛜🏊🐾) With standard midrange chain decor and amenities, this hotel is a budget-friendly choice. Cleanliness and furnishings are reliably well kept, but a few dings and carpet snags show, and the location is 3 miles north of 5th Ave. Has a good pool, fitness center and laundry.

Naples Grande Beach Resort
RESORT $$$

(☎888-722-1267; www.naplesgranderesort.com; 475 Seagate Dr; r & ste $250-400; ✻@🛜🏊🐾) Just north of Naples, this high-end, full-service resort offers families everything, thus absolving you of the need to go anywhere else during your stay. Rooms are large and up to date, and Clam Pass beach is perfection. Rates add a $27 resort fee.

✗ Eating & Drinking

Naples has one of the region's friendliest downtown evening strolls; it's most appealing to families and snappily dressed, romance-minded couples. In high season, 5th Ave sidewalks are crowded till well past 10pm, and restaurant bars typically serve cocktails till midnight or 1am. More restaurants cluster on 3rd St S in Old Naples.

TOP CHOICE Cafe Lurcat
FUSION $$$

(☎239-213-3357; www.cafelurcat.com; 494 5th Ave; lunch $14-18, dinner $25-40; ⊙cafe 5-9:30pm Sun-Thu, to 10pm Fri & Sat, bar to 11pm or midnight nightly) Slip into your sexiest clothes for Naples' hippest, most stylish scene, really two places in one: the cafe upstairs has more formal dining beneath a vaulted ceiling with a Chagall-inspired mural. The trendy downstairs lounge features low leather banquettes, an under-lit glass bar and live jazz on weekends. The tapas menu is served in both, while the cafe adds an entree menu. The cuisine skillfully dips a ladle into the world's soup pot, serving eclectic, updated takes on Chinese BBQ, stroganoff, sea bass in miso and great salads.

TOP CHOICE IM Tapas
SPANISH $$$

(☎239-403-8272; http://imtapas.com; 965 4th Ave N; tapas $9-21; ⊙from 5:30pm) Off the beaten path in a strip mall, this simply decorated, romantic Spanish restaurant serves Madrid-worthy tapas. The mother-daughter team presents contemporary interpretations of classics like salt cod, Serrano ham, angula (baby eels), and shrimp with garlic, but even seemingly simple dishes like wild leeks are elegant and heavenly.

Captain Kirk's Stone Crabs & Fresh Seafood Market
MARKET $

(☎239-263-1976; 628 8th St S; sandwiches $9-11; ⊙9am-6pm Mon-Fri, to 5pm Sat, lunch to 3pm) For an easy, delicious lunch, come to this seafood market across from grassy Cambier Park. Its moist, flavorful grilled-grouper sandwich verily sets the Florida standard, but you can't go wrong with bisque or chowder. Get stone crab in season.

Campiello
ITALIAN $$

(☎239-435-1166; www.campiello.damico.com; 1177 3rd St S; lunch $14-22, dinner $15-40; ⊙11:30am-3pm & 5-10pm, to 10:30pm Fri & Sat) Campiello hits you with the perfect one-two combo: an attractive, umbrella-shaded patio for stylish alfresco dining along the 3rd St shopping corridor, and refined, top-quality Italian cuisine priced for all budgets. Go light with a wood-fired pizza or a house-made pasta, or tuck into rich versions of osso bucco or Kobe steak. Extensive wine list and live jazz on Wednesday to Saturday evenings. Make reservations; it's popular.

Chops City Grill
STEAKHOUSE $$$

(☎239-262-4677; www.chopscitygrill.com; 837 5th Ave S; mains $25-45; ⊙5-10pm) Naturally,

Naples dining wouldn't be complete without an upscale chophouse. Enjoy phonebook-thick steaks (with one side dish included), grilled fish and a raw bar within a dramatic, copper-columned dining room. Reserve ahead.

5th Ave Coffee Company BREAKFAST $
(☑239-261-5757; 599 5th Ave S; dishes $5-8; ☺7am-9pm Mon-Thu, to 10pm Fri & Sat, to 6pm Sun) Grab a national newspaper and an espresso, and join locals at a sidewalk table for a light breakfast or lunch and fresh-baked goods. A go-to choice for a quick meal.

Lindburgers BURGERS $
(☑239-262-1127; 330 9th St S; mains $7-10; ☺11am-9pm Mon-Sat) Oilcloth-covered tables and paper-towel rolls are good signs in a burger joint: these are load-'em-up, never-mind-the-mess burger creations. Choose from a dozen options, like Todd's Way, with fried egg, bacon and three cheeses. An unpretentious Naples institution.

Dock at Crayton Cove SEAFOOD $$$
(☑239-263-9940; www.dockcraytoncove.com; 845 12th Ave S; mains $12-28; ☺11am-9pm; 🐾) For Caribbean-influenced seafood and tropical cocktails in a lovely dockside setting. Good kids' menu and relaxed harbor atmosphere perfect for families.

Old Naples Pub PUB $$
(☑239-649-8200; www.naplespubs.com; 255 13th Ave S; mains $8-18; ☺11am-10pm Mon-Sat, noon-9pm Sun) Near 3rd St S, typical Irish-style pub for above-average bar meals and friendly pints.

Kilwin's ICE CREAM $
(☑239-261-9898; 743 5th Ave S; ice creams $4-8; ☺11am-10:30pm) Fresh-made waffle cones, handmade chocolates and other goodies.

🛍 Shopping

For upscale boutiques, trendy fashion, jewelry and other ritzy shopping, stroll Old Naples' **3rd St S Shops** (www.thirdstreetsouth .com) or wander 5th Ave S. For seaside trinkets, pink flamingos and 'Mommy needs a timeout' T-shirts, head to **Tin City** (www.tin -city.com; 1200 5th Ave S), a jaunty harborside tourist trap.

Farmers' Market MARKET
(cnr 3rd St S & Broad Ave; ☺7:30-11:30am Sat) At one of the region's best farmers' markets, you can find organic produce and lots of artisan products – bread, soaps, jams, woven baskets and more.

ℹ Information

Greater Naples Chamber of Commerce
(☑239-262-6141; www.napleschamber.org; 900 5th Ave S at 9th St S; ☺9am-5pm Mon-Sat; @) Will help with accommodations; good maps, internet access and acres of brochures.

Outdoor Concierge Desk (☑239-434-6533; www.thirdstreetsouth.com; 3rd St S btwn 12th Ave & 13th Ave S; ☺9am-5pm Mon-Fri, 10am-5pm Sun) What's in Old Naples? This friendly outdoor kiosk is glad you asked.

ℹ Getting There & Around

A car is essential and easy, with ample, free downtown parking. Naples is about 40 miles southwest of Fort Myers via I-75.

Collier Area Transit (CAT; www.colliergov.net; fare $1.50; ☺6am-7:30pm) Buses serve the greater Naples area.

Greyhound (☑239-774-5660; www.greyhound .com; 2669 Davis Blvd; ☺Mon-Sat) Connects Naples to Miami, Orlando and Tampa.

Corkscrew Swamp Sanctuary

The crown jewel in the **National Audubon Society's** (☑239-348-9151; www.corkscrew.audu bon.org; adult/child 6-18yr $10/4; ☺7am-5:30pm Oct–mid-Apr, 7am-7:30pm mid-Apr–Sep) sanctuary collection, this property provides an intimate exploration of six pristine native habitats, including sawgrass, slash pine and marsh, along a shady, 2.25-mile boardwalk trail. The centerpiece is North America's oldest virgin bald-cypress forest, with majestic specimens over 600 years old and 130ft tall. Abundant wildlife includes nesting alligators, night herons, endangered wood storks and trees full of ibis. However, two rare species, when spotted, make the news: the famed ghost orchid and the elusive Florida panther. Volunteers help point out wildlife, and signage is excellent; the visitor center (with exhibits and snack bar) rents binoculars ($3). Corkscrew is as good as the Everglades.

The preserve is northeast of Naples and southeast of Fort Myers; take I-75 exit 111 and head east on Hwy 846/Imokalee Rd to Sanctuary Rd; follow signs. Bring repellent for deer flies in late spring.

NORTH OF TAMPA

The Gulf Coast north of Tampa (and south of the Panhandle) is relatively quiet and often bypassed. As such, it preserves more of that oft-promised, hard-to-find 'Old Florida' atmosphere than most spots in modern-day Florida. For moss-draped river paddles, manatees and unabashed mermaid kitsch, this is the place.

Tarpon Springs

☎727 / POP 23,500

Once upon a time, Tarpon Springs was a sponging center, which attracted the Greek immigrants who made up so much of the town's culture from the early 1900s until the sponge died off in the 1940s. After new sponge beds were discovered in the 1980s, the boats and divers bustled once again. But today the sponge docks along Dodecanese Blvd are purely a gone-to-seed Old Florida tourist trap. There's ironic fun to be had in such things as the spectacularly dusty Spongeorama Museum and the sponge-diving exhibitions, though the middling Greek restaurants have lost much claim to authenticity.

A few surprises remain. For a real Greek bakery and some honey-saturated baklava while you walk, visit National Bakery (☎727-934-5934; 451 Athens St at Mill St). Also, while the historic downtown has fallen on hard times, the magnificent St Nicholas Church (www.epiphanycity.org; 36 N Pinellas Ave; ⊙10am-4pm) is a Greek Orthodox beauty featuring Czech stained glass. For more information, visit www.tarponspringschamber.org.

Weeki Wachee Springs

☎352 / POP 12

Were the 'City of Mermaids' ever to close up shop, a bit of Florida's soul would wink out forever. The 'city' of Weeki Wachee is almost entirely constituted by this state park (☎352-592-5656; www.weekiwachee.com; 6131 Commercial Way/US 19 at Hwy 50; adult/child 6-12yr $13/5; ⊙10am-3pm Mar, to 4pm Apr-Aug), and the park is almost entirely dedicated to the underwater mermaid show that has entertained families and the famous since 1947. Esther Williams, Danny Thomas and Elvis Presley have all sat in the glass-paneled underwater theater and watched as graceful, long-haired mermaids perform pirouettes and adagios in the all-natural spring while turtles and fish swim past, oblivious to the beauty. The three daily half-hour shows (at 11am, 12:30pm and 2:30pm) remain gleeful celebrations of nostalgic kitsch, particularly the mainstay, *The Little Mermaid*. While

there's no mystery to the trick – the mermaids hold air hoses as they swim, and gulp air as needed – there's an undeniable theatrical magic (and no little skill) to their smiling, effortless performances while swimming nonstop underwater. Little girls (and their mothers) will be delighted to know each show ends with a live mermaid photo op.

But wait, there's more! The park also offers animal shows, a sedate riverboat cruise and a modest, weekend-only water park (combined admission $26/12), plus picnic areas, that make for an afternoon's entertainment. Parking is free.

The spring itself – a 100ft hole that pumps about 170 million gallons of water daily – is actually the headwater of the crystal-clear Weeki Wachee River. Kayaking or canoeing this river is one of the region's best paddles. At the back of the Weeki Wachee parking lot, follow signs to Paddling Adventures (☎352-592-5666; kayak rentals $30-35; ⊙9am-3pm, last launch noon). The 7-mile route includes beach areas with good swimming and rope swings, plus you'll see lots of fish and even manatees in winter and spring. Trips take three to four hours, and include pickup service. Reserve a week ahead; they book up.

The springs are about 25 miles north of Tarpon Springs via US 19 and 80 miles northwest of Orlando via Hwy 50. It's about 45 minutes from Tampa via I-75 north to Hwy 50 west.

Homosassa Springs

☎352 / POP 13,800

Signed along US 19, Homosassa Springs Wildlife State Park (☎352-628-5343; www.floridastateparks.org/homosassasprings; adult/child 6-12yr $13/5; ⊙9am-5:30pm, last entrance 4pm) is essentially an old-school outdoor Florida animal encounter – aka, zoo – that features Florida's wealth of headliner species: American alligators, black bears, bobcats, whooping cranes, Florida panthers, tiny Key deer, eagles, hawks and – especially – manatees. Homosassa's highlight is an underwater observatory directly over the springs, where through glass windows you can gawk eyeball to eyeball with enormous schools of some 10,000 fish and ponderous manatees nibbling lettuce. Various animal presentations happen daily, but time your visit for the manatee program (11:30am, 1:30pm and 3:30pm). The park itself is a short, narrated boat ride from the visitor center.

Leave US 19 along Hwy 490/W Yulee Rd (just south of the park) and enter an Old Florida time warp, where live oaks dripping in Spanish moss curtain the roadway, which is dotted with local eateries and funky galleries. After about 3 miles, take a right on Cherokee Way and you'll come to MacRae's (☎352-628-2602; www.macraesofhomosassa.com; 5300 S Cherokee Way; r $85-125; ✳🖥🛈), a friendly motel, restaurant and marina that promises 'everything for the fisherman.' The 22 plain but clean rooms have fully stocked kitchens and faux log-cabin exteriors, and the adjacent marina supplies everything but the fish. Airboat tours, kayak rentals and fishing guides are also offered.

The park is about 20 miles north of Weeki Wachee, 65 miles north of Clearwater and 75 miles north of Tampa; US 19 north leads to the park entrance.

Crystal River

☎352 / POP 3100

Every winter, about 20% of Florida's Gulf Coast manatee population meanders into the 72°F, spring-fed waters of Kings Bay, near the town of Crystal River, and for this reason the bay is almost entirely protected within the Crystal River National Wildlife Refuge (☎352-563-2088; www.fws.gov/crystalriver; 1502 SE Kings Bay Dr; ⊙visitor center 8am-4pm Mon-Fri). Up to 560 of these gentle, endangered sea creatures have been counted in a single January day, and like any wildlife spectacle, this draws crowds of onlookers. Nearly 40 commercial operators offer rentals and guided tours of Kings Bay, via every type of nautical conveyance, and the chance to swim with wild manatees is a truly wondrous opportunity not to miss. However, whether visitors should be allowed to actively touch manatees is an ongoing controversy (which may lead to a prohibition against it).

The best place to begin is the refuge headquarters, which has tons of excellent information and a list of approved operators. There is no public viewing area on land to view manatees; the only access to the refuge is by boat. However, a new boardwalk is in the works. Also, though manatees live in Kings Bay year-round, the population dwindles to a few dozen in summer.

The following operators are recommended:

Port Hotel & Marina (☎352-795-7234; www.porthotelandmarina.com; 1610 SE Paradise Circle) Next to refuge HQ; rental kayaks ($35) and boats (from $20 per hour), plus guided snorkels ($42) and dives ($125).

Birds Underwater (☎352-563-2763; www.birdsunderwater.com; 320 NW Hwy 19) Long-time operator, with kayak rentals (from $30), snorkel tours ($35) and dives (from $100).

Nature Coast Kayak Tours (☎352-795-9877; www.naturecoastkayaktours.com; 8153 W Justin Lane) Smaller, kayak-only tours ($40) with Tracy Colson, a conservation-minded no-touch advocate.

The Panhandle

Best Places to Eat

» Ball Room Restaurant (p448)

» Indian Pass Raw Bar (p437)

» Dewey Destin's (p431)

» Joe Patti's (p427)

Best Places to Stay

» Wakulla Springs Lodge (p447)

» Island Hotel (p451)

» Coombs House Inn (p438)

» Hotel DeFuniak (p441)

» Hibiscus Coffee & Guesthouse (p433)

» Aunt Martha's Bed & Breakfast (p431)

Why Go?

Take all the things that are great about the Deep South – friendly people, the molasses-slow pace, oak-lined country roads, fried food galore – and add several hundred miles of sugar-white beaches, dozens of gin-clear natural springs, and all the fresh oysters you can suck down, and there you have it: the fantastic, highly underrated Florida Panhandle.

Kick up your heels on the Gulf Coast, whose luscious aqua waters will make you think you've landed in the Caribbean, gallery-hop in the urban centers of Pensacola or Tallahassee, fish the primeval river of Steinhatchee, hike the moss-shrouded trails of wildernesses like the Apalachicola National Forest, or, hey, suck down a few Jell-O shots with the Spring Breakers in Panama City Beach (we won't judge!).

Lovers of the offbeat will appreciate the Panhandle's quirky charms – billboards announcing the End of Times, roadside stands hawking alligator jerky, adorably retro mid-century motels. Consider it road trip heaven.

When to Go
Pensacola

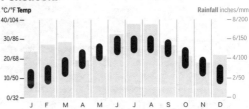

Mar & Apr Spring Breakers descend upon Pensacola and Panama City for weeks of frenzied partying.

May-Sep The weather is steamy and the beaches crowded with vacationing families.

Nov-Feb Chilly winter temps mean you'll have the region all to yourself.

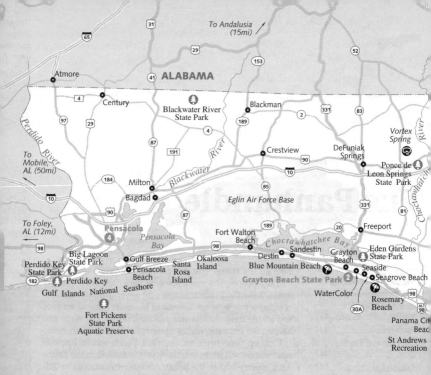

Panhandle Highlights

① Slurp down oysters at the venerable **Indian Pass Raw Bar** (p437), then stay for some line dancing on the porch

② Wander the windswept dunes and luminous gulf waters

of **Grayton Beach State Park** (p433), which has the region's most picturesque beach

③ Get a wildlife thrill on a guided river cruise at **Wakulla Springs State Park** (p447),

where mossy cypress trees and mangroves mingle with manatees, alligators and a slew of wading birds

④ Marvel at the **Blue Angels** (p421), the US Navy's flight

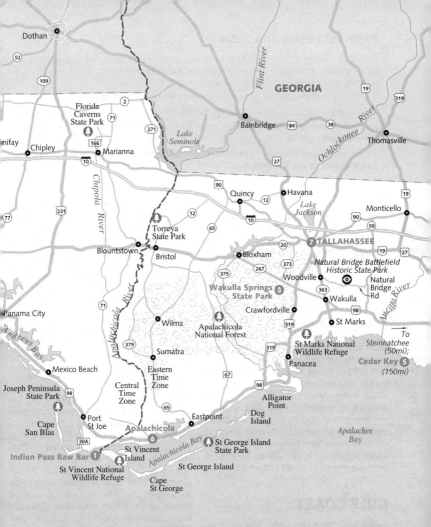

demonstration squad, in Pensacola

5 Go under the radar at **Cedar Key** (p450), an isolated, windswept island beloved by bikers and fishermen

6 Spend a romantic weekend browsing art galleries and sampling charming bistros in **Apalachicola** (p437), the Gulf's cutest small town

7 Groove to the blues at **Bradfordville Blues Club** (p446), just outside Tallahassee, with a blazing bonfire and sizzling music

PANHANDLE FOR CHILDREN

The down-to-earth Panhandle is one of Florida's most family-friendly regions, with laid-back beaches, aquariums, seaside fudge shops and fudge museums.

Some of our top picks for the junior set:

» Manning your own fighter jet at the Pensacola **Naval Air Station** (p423)

» Watching the dolphins frolic at the **Gulfarium** (p430)

» Shooting 'em up at the laser tag course at Panama City Beach's hyperstimulating **WonderWorks** (p435)

» Checking out cool, hands-on exhibits on dinosaurs or bugs or ships at the **Mary Brogan Museum of Art & Science** (p443)

History

The area that would become Tallahassee (meaning 'abandoned fields') was first inhabited by Native Americans of the Apalachee tribes, who cleared out and were felled by disease after the region was settled by Spaniards in 1539, with explorer Hernando De Soto leading the way. After the US Territory of Florida was founded in 1821, Tallahassee was chosen as the state capitol; a plantation economy soon developed – as did the city's reckless reputation, with frequent knife and gun fights leading to the formation of the city's police department.

A rail line linked Tallahassee with the gulf port in 1837, making it the commercial center of the region. And, by the late 1800s, cotton estates were snapped up by wealthy northerners, who turned them into hunting retreats. Eventually, environmentalists reacted against the man-versus-beast behavior of the hunters, which led to the establishment of groundbreaking ecological efforts in the region.

GULF COAST

Dubbed the 'Forgotten Coast' along its eastern half, the name is apt to describe the entire shoreline here – unless you're from the region and are already happily familiar with the Gulf Coast's magical beauty. That's not to say the beaches are always desolate (though they certainly are in the off-season), just that most folks tend to think of the southern portion of the state when conjuring images of Florida's famed beaches. But these northern, gulf-side spits are spectacular: with sand that's as soft and white as sugar, rolling dunes that resemble polished marble sculptures and clear, turquoise waters that'll make you wonder why you haven't been spending summers here all your life.

Alongside all the natural beauty are towns that burst with Southern charm – from the lure of Apalachicola's historic district to the odd perfection of the lovely planned community of Seaside, along with some insanely over-developed Spring Break destinations that may be best avoided, depending on your constitution. But whatever you're looking for, you will find your place in the sun.

Pensacola & Pensacola Beach

☑ 850 / POP 54,000

The Deep South meets Florida in Pensacola – quite literally. The Alabama border is just a few miles down the road, and the city has the small-town friendliness and sleepy pace of its Southern neighbor. But Pensacola (or P'Cola, as locals say), keeps it colorful with lively beaches, a thrumming military culture and a sultry, Spanish-style downtown.

Visitors to Pensacola come for the all-American blue collar vacation experience: snow-white beaches, jam-packed seafood restaurants, and bars where beer flows like water. During March and April, things reach fever pitch when hoards of students descend for the week-long bacchanalia known as 'Spring Break.' Beware.

Visitors less inclined toward tequila shots and wet T-shirt contests will appreciate the city's cultured, historical side. Since Pensacola's permanent settlement was established in 1698, flags belonging to Spain, France, Britain, the Confederacy and the US have flown over the city, often more than once, hence the city's nickname, 'City of Five Flags.' Traces of the past are visible today in the city's architecture and numerous historical sites and museums.

Downtown Pensacola, centered on Palafox St, sits just north of the waterfront. Southwest of downtown, the Pensacola Naval Air Station has trained pilots since WWII, and the base's airmen and airwomen are an intrinsic part of the city's culture. Across the Pensacola Bay Bridge from downtown is the mostly residential peninsula of Gulf Breeze; continue south over the Bob Sikes Bridge (toll $1) to Pensacola Beach, the destination for most of Pensacola's tourists. So why not toss your sunscreen and a novel in your beach bag, and head across the bridge to join them?

Sights & Activities

PENSACOLA

Historic Pensacola Village   HISTORIC BUILDINGS
(Map p424; www.historicpensacola.org; adult/child $6/3; 10am-4pm Tue-Sat, tours 11am, 1pm & 2:30pm) In a corner of downtown Pensacola, a handful of 19th-century buildings are maintained by West Florida Historic Preservation as a series of museums and exhibits. Admission includes a two-hour walking tour, leaving from **Tivoli House** (Map p424; 205 E Zaragoza St) and led by a period-costumed guide. You'll take in many district buildings such as **Lavalle House** (Map p424; 205 E Church St) and **Julee Cottage** (Map p424; 210 E Zaragoza St), the former home of freed slave Julee Paton. Included in Historic Pensacola Village are the **Museum of Commerce** (Map p424; 201 E Zaragoza St), the **Museum of Industry** (Map p424; 200 E Zaragoza St) and the **TT Wentworth Museum** (Map p424; 330 S Jefferson St; admission free; 10am-4pm), an elaborate 1907 yellow-brick Renaissance Revival building that was the original Pensacola City Hall. Across from the Plaza Ferdinand (where Florida was admitted into the US), the museum dominates the block with its wide eaves, red-tile roof and deep 2nd-story arcade. Quirky exhibits include a Coca-Cola room and a display about the ill-fated expeditions of the early Spanish explorers to the region.

Pensacola Museum of Art   MUSEUM
(Map p424; www.pensacolamuseumofart.org; 407 S Jefferson St; adult/child $5/free; 10am-5pm Tue-Fri, noon-5pm Sat) Interestingly housed in the city's old jail (1908), this lovely art museum features nearly 20 exhibits a year – anything from Rodin sculptures to the pop-art work of Jasper Johns. Its impressively growing collection, shown on a rotating basis, includes major 20th- and 21st-century artists across genres including Cubism, realism, pop art and folk art.

Pensacola Scenic Bluffs Highway & Bay Bluffs Park   SCENIC DRIVE
This 11-mile stretch of road, which winds around the precipice of the highest point along Florida's coastline, makes for a peaceful drive or (slightly difficult) bike ride. You'll see stunning views of Escambia Bay, and pass a notable crumbling brick chimney – part of the steam-power plant for the Hyer-Knowles lumber mill in the 1850s, which is

BLUE ANGELS

To maintain its profile after WWII, and to reinforce its recruitment drive, the US Navy gathered some of its most elite pilots to form the **Blue Angels** (www.blueangels.navy.mil), a flight demonstration squadron traveling to air shows around the country. The name caught on during the original team's trip to New York in 1946, when one of the pilots saw the name of the city's Blue Angel nightclub in the *New Yorker*.

These days performing for about 15 million people a year, 'the Blues' (never 'the Angels'), their C130 Hercules support aircraft named Fat Albert and their all-Marine support crew visit about 35 show sites a year. Six jets execute precision maneuvers, including death-defying rolls and loops, and two F/A-18s undertake solo flights; culminating in all six planes flying in trademark Delta formation.

Each of the Blues does a two-year tour of duty, staggered to rotate every two years. In addition to the six pilots (which always includes one Marine) is a narrator, who'll then move up through the ranks, and an events coordinator.

The Blues practice frequently (as would you if you were doing 500mph stunts in a quarter of a million dollars worth of aircraft): you can see take-off (a jet-assisted, near-vertical incline by way of rocket propellant) on Tuesday and Wednesday at 8:30am between March and November (weather permitting); Wednesday sessions are followed by pilot autographs. It's best to arrive between 7:30am and 8am. Bleachers are available for the first 1000 spectators; BYO coffee and lawn chairs. The viewing area is behind the National Museum of Naval Aviation parking lot.

THE PANHANDLE GULF COAST

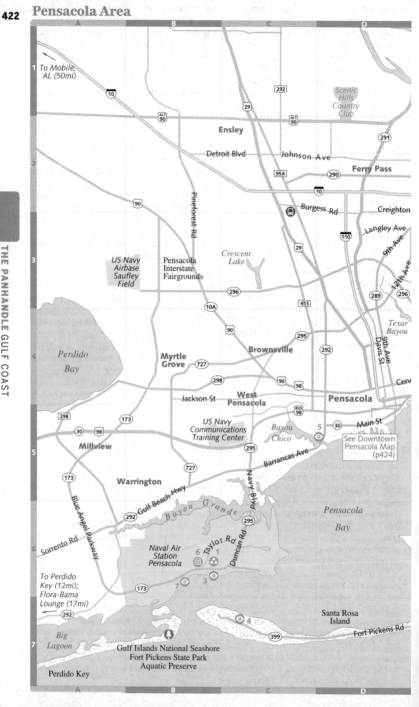

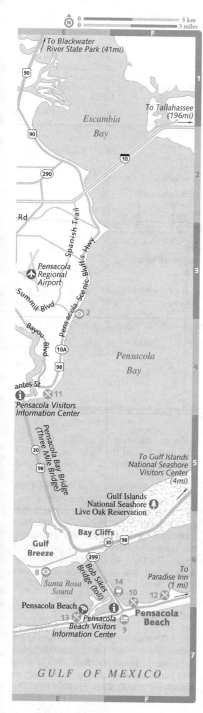

the only remnant of what was the first major industrial belt on the Gulf Coast. Also along here is beautiful **Bay Bluffs Park** (Map p422; Scenic Hwy), a 32-acre oasis of wooden boardwalks that lead you down along the side of the steep bluffs, through clutches of live oaks, pines, Florida rosemary and holly to the empty beach below.

NAVAL AIR STATION PENSACOLA
Every US WWII pilot was trained at the Naval Air Station Pensacola (NAS; Map p422), known as 'the cradle of naval aviation.' Today, some 6000 young aviators train here, and the base is a major part of Pensacola's social fabric. Southwest of downtown Pensacola, NAS has a number of interesting attractions for visitors. To get here, take Hwy 295 to the NAS entrance, south of the bridge at the end of Navy Blvd, across Bayou Grande. You'll be stopped at the gate for a security check of your car, so be sure to bring photo ID.

The base is also home to the Blue Angels (p421), the military's daredevil flight demonstration squadron – watch them zip overhead on Tuesday and Wednesday mornings between March and November.

TOP CHOICE National Museum of
Naval Aviation   MUSEUM
(Map p422; www.navalaviationmuseum.org; 1750 Radford Blvd; admission free; ⊙9am-5pm; 🖼) You

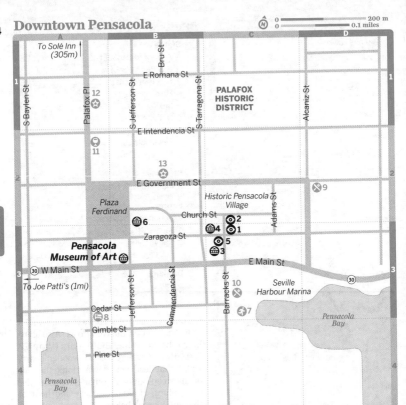

THE PANHANDLE GULF COAST

don't have to be an aviation geek to adore this 291,000-sq-ft museum, a genuine don't-miss. Suspended from the ceiling of the hangar-like space are dozens of aircraft from every historical era, from WWI biplanes to modern fighter jets. Upstairs, a series of exhibits recreate WWII scenes: the sickbay of an aircraft carrier, a Pacific Island navy base, a mock 1940s Pensacola street, complete with walk-in shops. Kids (and, uh, adults) will love climbing into the cockpits of various planes for a bit of fighter pilot role playing (Nnyyyyyyr! Pow!!!), or hopping into a genuine flight simulator ($5) for some just-like-real action. An IMAX cinema ($8.50) screens largely aviation-themed movies throughout the day.

For a more in-depth experience, join a guided tour. Tours depart 9:30am, 11am, 1pm and 2:30pm and are led by retired naval aviators, most of whom have served in some capacity and regale visitors with firsthand experiences of various aircrafts.

You can also hop on a shuttle for a free 20-minute tour of the flight line to see the planes being refinished in the restoration hangar.

Finally, take a break at the **Cubi Bar Cafe** (◷10:30am-3:30pm) in the museum, a precise recreation of the famous officers' club at Cubi Point in the Philippines, with over 1000 hand-carved Vietnam War–era squadron plaques brought over from the original venue. The Cubi serves perfectly good hot dogs, warm pita pilot wraps and salads (meals about $7), but is really as much an exhibit as the rest of the museum.

Fort Barrancas & Advanced Redoubt
FORTRESS

(Map p422; admission free; ◷9:30am-5pm winter, 8:30am-4pm summer) On a dramatic bluff overlooking Pensacola Bay, 19th-century Fort Barrancas was built by slaves atop an abandoned 18th-century Spanish fort. The fort, now part of the National Park Service,

Downtown Pensacola

has endless dark passageways to explore, but not much in the way of displays. A half mile away via a walking trail lie the ruins of Advanced Redoubt, a Civil War–era fort. Wander around on your own, or wait for one of the regularly scheduled ranger **tours** (2pm daily at Barrancas and 11am Saturday at Advanced Redoubt).

Pensacola Lighthouse   LIGHTHOUSE
(Map p422; adult/child $5/3; ☉10:30am-5:30pm Mon-Sat, 12:30-5:30pm Sun) Just down the street from Fort Barrancas, this 160ft, 1859 lighthouse is rumored to be haunted. So be on the lookout for ghosts of lighthouse keepers past as you climb the 177 steps and poke around the adjacent museum.

PENSACOLA BEACH
Distinctly separate from Pensacola itself, Pensacola Beach (Map p422) – known fondly by Southern visitors as the 'Redneck Riviera' – is a paradise of powdery white sand, gentle warm waters and a string of mellow beachfront hotels. The beach occupies nearly 8 miles of the 40-mile-long Santa Rosa barrier island, surrounded by the Santa Rosa Sound and Gulf of Mexico to the north and south,

and by the federally protected Gulf Islands National Seashore on either side. Though determined residents have protected much of the barrier island from development, there is change afoot, as several high-rise condos have recently created a bit of a Gulf Coast skyline.

The area is a major hub for local entertainment and special events, including Mardi Gras celebrations, a triathlon, wine tastings, a summer music series, parades and the annual Blue Angels air show in July, which is a local institution.

Gulf Islands National Seashore   PARK, BEACH
(Map p422; www.nps.gov/guis; 7-day pedestrian or cyclist admission $3, vehicle $8; ☉sunrise-sunset) Stretching 150 miles between West Ship Island, Mississippi, and Santa Rosa Island, Florida's section of this national seashore covers Perdido Key, two sections of Santa Rosa Island (extending to the NAS across the Fort Pickens State Park Aquatic Preserve) and a clip of coastline around Destin and Fort Walton Beach (p430).

In the Pensacola region, there are visitors centers at Fort Barrancas, Naval Live Oaks (a few miles east of Gulf Breeze) and Fort Pickens (about 10 miles west of Pensacola Beach). Head to the Naval Live Oaks area for more than 7.5 miles of hiking trails and a calm, family-friendly beach. The Fort Pickens area has miles of bone-white beaches – driving the road down the narrow island feels like driving through snow.

The Fort Pickens area's highlight is the pentagonal brick **Fort Pickens** (Map p422), begun in 1829, completed in 1834 and used until around the end of WWII. The fort, which was damaged by an accidental gunpowder explosion in 1899 and again by hurricanes throughout the 20th century, has a fascinatingly ruined quality. Bring a flashlight to explore the eerie, narrow mine tunnels.

Diving & Sailing   WATER SPORTS
The Oriskany CV/CVA 34 aircraft carrier, at approximately 900ft long and 150ft tall, was the largest vessel ever sunk as an artificial reef when it was submerged in 2007 off Pensacola Beach. Plenty of outfitters will gear you up and show you the way out, including **MBT Divers** (Map p422; ☎850-455-7702; www.mbtdivers.com; 3920 Barrancas Ave), offering two-tank Oriskany dives for $150, plus various other charters.

Conditions at Pensacola Bay are perfect for sailing. Beginners can take part in various sailing courses with **Lanier Sailing**

Academy (Map p424; ☑850-432-3199; www
.laniersail.com; 600 S Barracks St, Seville Harbour
Marina, slip number N1), or rent a Capri 22 for
$215 daily and take to the waters yourself.

UFO Spotting   VIEWPOINT

Maybe it's activity from the nearby Pensacola Naval Air Station, but this stretch of the
gulf has apparently had hundreds of UFO
sightings in the past few decades; **Shoreline Park** (Map p422; 700 Shoreline Dr) in Gulf
Breeze is a particular hot spot, where you're
likely to find local skywatchers (including members of the Mutual UFO Network,
which meets here regularly) with binoculars
and lawn chairs. Sightings have been reported right along the coast – it's as good a
reason as any to spread out a picnic or beach
blanket and gaze up at the stars.

🛏 Sleeping
PENSACOLA

You'll find plenty of budget and midrange
chains on N Palafox St in Pensacola. Hotels
with personality are a bit harder to come by.

Pensacola Victorian B&B   B&B $$

(☑850-434-2818, 800-370-8354; www.pensaco
lavictorian.com; 203 W Gregory St; r $85-125; ❀🤶)
This stately 1892 Queen Anne building was
built for a ship's captain whose son so loved
entertaining musicians that the Pensacola
Philharmonic Orchestra (now the Pensacola
Symphony) was founded as a result. Today
the warm and in-the-know owners, Chuck
and Barbara, lovingly maintain four restful
guest rooms – we especially like Suzanne's
Room, with its hardwood floors, blue toile
prints and clawfoot tub. It's about a mile
north of downtown Pensacola.

Solé Inn   MOTEL $

(off Map p424; ☑850-470-9298; www.soleinnand
suites.com; 200 N Palafox St; r $99; ❀🤶🏊) Just
north of downtown, this sleekly renovated
motel goes for a 1960s mod look, with black
and white color schemes, animal prints and
acrylic bubble lamps. Rooms are not huge,
but the price, location and general zaniness
of the place more than make up for lack of
space.

New World Inn   HOTEL $$

(Map p424; ☑850-432-4111; www.newworldland
ing.com; 600 S Palafox Pl; r from $109; ❀🤶) Well
located between downtown and the waterfront, this historic inn's 15 rooms are plush
and modern, if a bit bland in the manner of
a display home in an upscale suburban sub-

division (beige carpet, lots of earth tones).
Celebrities visiting Pensacola are usually put
up here – check out the array of signed head-
shots in the lobby.

PENSACOLA BEACH

There's a row of midrange and upmarket
chain hotels on the main strip near the
bridge – the Hilton's the most luxurious, the
Days Inn the cheapest.

Margaritaville Beach Hotel   HOTEL $$$

(Map p422; ☑850-916-9755; www.margaritaville
hotel.com; 165 Ft Pickens Rd; r $119-460; ❀🤶🏊)
Jimmy Buffett, he of the Hawaiian shirts
and 'Cheeseburger in Paradise' theme restaurant chain, is not exactly known for his
tastefulness. Yet this brand-new hotel is
extraordinarily, well...elegant. The 162 spacious rooms are done up in crisp whites
and aquas, with arty oversized photomurals
and huge flat-panel TVs. Downstairs, a sleek
grown-up crowd swans around the airy
lobby or sips cocktails by the swanky pool
area. Buffett's sister, a chef, is rumored to be
opening a restaurant next door.

Paradise Inn   MOTEL $$

(off Map p422; ☑850-932-2319; www.paradiseinn-pb
.com; 21 Via de Luna Dr; r winter & fall $69-150, spring
& summer $100-200; ❀🤶🏊) Just across the
road from the beach, this sherbet-colored motel is a lively, cheery place thanks to its popular bar and grill (early-to-bed types should ask
for rooms on the far side of the parking lot).
Rooms are small and clean, with tiled floors
and brightly painted walls. The pool is micro-
scopic, but that doesn't stop anyone!

Fort Pickens Campground   CAMPGROUND $

(☑850-934-2656; www.nps.gov/guis; Fort Pickens
entrance to Gulf Islands National Seashore; sites
$20; 🐕) Amid the windblown trees across
from the beach, these two pleasant campgrounds are popular with RV-ers, though
you'll see the odd tent or two. There are fire
pits, a bathhouse and a small camp store.
Leashed pets are OK.

🍴 Eating
PENSACOLA

S Palafox St has scads of bars and cafes with
outdoor seating. Many of Pensacola's more
popular restaurants have massive waits,
even on weeknights – go early, or plan to
hang out at the bar for an hour or so. Where
reservations are recommended, we've included phone numbers.

TOP CHOICE Joe Patti's SEAFOOD, SUSHI **$**

(off Map p424; www.joepattis.com; 534 South B St at Main St; ⏰7am-6pm Mon-Thu & Sat, to 7pm Fri) Don't leave Pensacola without a visit to this beloved seafood emporium, begun by Sicilian immigrant Joe Patti in the 1930s and now run by his descendants. Watch workers debone fish at long steel tables, google at row upon row of oysters, octopi, mullet and squid, or stock up on prepared picnic foods like shrimp salad or clam chowder. If you're hungry right now, pick up a fresh-from-the-boat spicy tuna roll at the in-house sushi bar. To complete the meal, grab wine and cheese from the connected emporium.

Dharma Blue INTERNATIONAL **$$**

(Map p424; ☎850-433-1275; www.dharmablue .com; 300 S Alcaniz St; mains $9-21; ⏰11am-4pm & 5-9:30pm Mon-Sat) A cozy pink cottage perched at the edge of a peaceful park, this friendly, eclectic eatery is considered by many locals to be the area's best restaurant. Choose a seat either outside on the fat porch – cooled by ceiling fans, marble-slab tables and plenty of hanging plants – or in the expansive dining room hung with bright local artwork, and order any of the delightful dishes. Lunch brings fried green tomato sandwiches, veggie stir-fry and daily quiches, while dinner dips into sushi, crab cake and duck breast territory. Monday means $2 off sushi rolls – expect crowds.

Fish House & Atlas Oyster House SEAFOOD **$$**

(Map p424; ☎Fish House 850-470-0003, Atlas Oyster 850-437-1961; www.goodgrits.com; 600 S Barracks St; mains $12-23; ⏰11am-late) In a huge multilevel building overlooking the harbor, these twin seafood restaurants are always packed with a mix of tourists, businesspeople and locals on date night. Fish House is slightly more upscale, with a dark wood interior and fish cooked every way (pecan-crusted, with mango salsa etc.). Atlas is best for oyster on the half shell and glasses of white wine on the porch. Both are known for their Grits a Ya Ya – spicy gulf shrimp, bacon and garlicky veggies over steaming gouda cheese grits. Weekend happy hours throb with crowds and live music.

McGuire's Irish Pub STEAKHOUSE **$$**

(600 E Gregory St; mains $11-30; ⏰11am-late) Promising 'feasting, imbibery and debauchery,' this barnlike spot is part restaurant, part bar, part faux Irish theme park. Animal heads deck the walls, while thousands of dollar bills adorn every other available surface. Steaks and burgers are the order of the day here – peer through a window to watch the beef aging in a special temperature-controlled room. Bring your patience – waits can top an hour – and don't expect to actually hear your dinner date. It's just east of downtown Pensacola – look for the green double-decker bus marking the spot.

Jerry's Drive-In AMERICAN **$**

(Map p422; 2815 E Cervantes St; mains $7-12; ⏰10am-10pm Mon-Fri, 7am-10pm Sat) Look for the pig sign outside of this roadhouse-meets-diner (not a drive-in, though it was when it opened in 1939), serving up fat omelettes, juicy burgers, milkshakes and plenty of daily specials under the kitschy neon signs. You'll rub elbows with serious regulars – the kind that get greeted by first name – especially at lunchtime, when the place gets packed.

THE PANHANDLE PENSACOLA & PENSACOLA BEACH

THE OIL SPILL

On April 20, 2010, 40 miles off the coast of Louisiana, a BP oil rig called Deepwater Horizon exploded, killing 11 workers and touching off one of the worst environmental disasters in American history. In the three months it took to stymie the gushing well, nearly 5 million barrels of crude oil were released into the Gulf of Mexico, poisoning sea life and causing inestimable harm to the fishing and tourism industries along the coasts of Texas, Louisiana, Mississippi, Alabama and Florida.

Though the globs of oil that once washed up on Gulf Coast beaches are now gone, the damage has been done: many coastal businesses did not survive the economic thrashing, and many tourists have remained wary of eating local seafood (though tests run by the National Oceanographic and Atmospheric Administration continue to show no sign of contaminants in fish and shrimp). Fortunately, as of 2011, the tourism economy seemed to be on the upswing again. But chat with any Gulf Coaster, and they'll tell you that the psychological scars still remain.

GAY PENSACOLA

Pensacola is a small, bright spot for gay culture in the Panhandle, an area not known for its progressive values. The last weekend in May, members of the LGBTQ community descend on the city for the annual **Gay Memorial Day** (www.memorialweekendpensacola.com), a three-day fiesta of DJ soirees, concerts, dances, all-night beach parties, drag-queen shows, you name it – all over town. Crowds reach as many as 50,000 – so book ahead!

The area's top gay club, **Emerald City** (www.emeraldcitypensacola.com; 406 E Wright St; cover $5-10; ⊙5pm-3am Wed-Sun, 9pm-3am Mon) pulls in a mixed, though male-heavy, crowd for dancing, drinks and Monday and Saturday drag shows. The adjacent video bar, Othersides, is a lower-key watering hole. Emerald City is a mile northeast of the center of downtown.

There's even a local LGBTQ community center, **Equality House** (317 N Spring St; ⊙10am-8pm Wed-Sat), which organizes film screenings, speakers and other community events. Equality House is less than a mile north of downtown on Spring St.

PENSACOLA BEACH

Peg Leg Pete's
SEAFOOD $$

(Map p422; www.peglegpetes.com; 1010 Ft Pickens Rd; mains $12-20; ⊙11am-late; 🛋) This once-humble beach shack has morphed into a massively popular, wildly overcrowded eatery/bar/gift shop. But Pete's still serves some of the best oysters on the beach – try 'em raw, or Cajun-spiced, or topped with crumbled Parmesan. Casual seafood dishes round out the menu, but the live music and pirate-themed decor are the real draws. If you don't mind a wait, dinner here is good, noisy fun.

Native Café
AMERICAN, CARIBBEAN $

(Map p422; www.thenativecafe.com; 45a Via de Luna Dr; mains $4-9; ⊙7:30am-3pm) This funky breakfast and lunch spot, 'owned and operated by friendly natives,' is a welcome addition to the fried-fish stretch. Try a shrimp po' boy, grilled chicken sandwich, fish tacos, rice and beans or seafood gumbo – or, for a cheap morning jumpstart, eggs Benedict or pancakes.

Hemingway's Island Grill
SEAFOOD, CARIBBEAN $$

(Map p422; 📞850-934-4747; www.hemingways islandgrill.com; 400 Quietwater Beach Rd; mains $13-30; ⊙11am-late) This airy restaurant is a favorite for more upscale dining, serving Key West-y cuisine (think seafood with rum glazes, lots of tropical fruit salsas) overlooking the bridge. Appropriate to its namesake, Hemingway's is big on booze – the mojito is considered the best in town.

🍷 Drinking & Entertainment

Pensacola's beach bars can have a bit of a Spring Break vibe (tequila shots, sozzled 21-year-olds); downtown offerings tend to be slightly more sophisticated. Most restaurants also have a bar scene. Check the *Pensacola News Journal*'s Friday 'Weekender' section for music listings.

TOP CHOICE Seville Quarter
BAR, CLUB

(Map p424; www.sevillequarter.com; 130 E Government St; ⊙11am-late) Taking up an entire city block, this massive entertainment complex contains seven separate eating, drinking and music venues, all tied together with a sort of HG Wells-ian 1890s vibe – gas lamps, blimps hanging from the ceiling, lots of brass and dark wood. Try Rosie O'Grady's for beer, peanuts and an old-school saloon feel, Lili Marlene's for karaoke, Fast Eddie's for pool, or Apple Annie's for courtyard seating and boozy fun.

McGuire's Irish Pub
PUB

(www.mcguiresirishpub.com; 600 E Gregory St; ⊙11am-late) More popular as a restaurant during dinner hours (see p427), this ginormous Irish theme park of a pub gets rowdy around 9pm. If you don't sing along with the live music, you'll find yourself up the ladder to kiss the moose. Don't try to pay for your drinks with one of the thousands of dollar bills hanging from the ceiling – a local recently found himself in the slammer that way!

Bamboo Willie's
BAR

(Map p422; www.bamboowillies.com; 400 Quietwater Beach Rd; ⊙11am-11pm, later on weekends) An open-air bar right on the boardwalk in Pensacola Beach, this is the spot to get twisted in a variety of ways, with signature frozen cocktails from the Bushwacker to the 190 Octane (don't ask – just drink).

Blazzues `JAZZ`
(Map p424; 200 S Palafox Pl; ⊙doors open around 6pm) Ignore the Miller Lite sign blazing in the window; this art deco-ish blues and jazz bar is actually quite the classy place – some nights more so than others (blues nights are sophisticated, '80s dance party nights not so much).

Saenger Theatre `THEATER, MUSIC`
(Map p424; ✆850-444-7686; www.pensacolasaen ger.com; 118 S Palafox Pl) This Spanish baroque beauty was reconstructed in 1925 using bricks from the Pensacola Opera House, which was destroyed in a 1916 hurricane. It's now home to a popular Broadway series, big-name concerts, as well as the **Pensacola Symphony Orchestra** (✆850-435-2533; www .pensacolasymphony.com) and **Pensacola Opera** (✆850-433-6737; www.pensacolaopera.com).

 Information

The daily is the *Pensacola News Journal*. National Public Radio (NPR) is at 88.1FM.

Pensacola Beach Visitors Information Center (Map p422; ✆850-932-1500; www .visitpensacolabeach.com; 735 Pensacola Beach Blvd) On the right as soon as you enter Pensacola Beach; this is a small place with some useful maps and brochures about goings on, road closures (due to storms) and anything else beach oriented.

Pensacola Visitors Information Center (Map p422; ✆850-434-1234, 800-874-1234; www .visitpensacola.com; 1401 E Gregory St; ⊙8am-5pm) At the foot of the Pensacola Bay Bridge, has a bounty of tourist information, knowledge-able staff and a free internet kiosk.

Public Library (200 W Gregory St; ⊙9am-8pm Tue-Thu, 9am-5pm Fri & Sat) Has free internet.

 Getting There & Around

Pensacola Regional Airport (Map p422; ✆850-436-5000; www.flypensacola.com) is served by many major airlines; it's 4 miles north-east of downtown off 9th Ave on Airport Blvd. A taxi costs about $15 to downtown and $28 to the beach. Try **Yellow Cab** (✆850-433-3333; www .yellowcabpensacola.com).

The **Greyhound station** (W Burgess Rd at Pensacola Blvd) is located north of the down-town area. **Escambia County Transit** (ECAT; www.goecat.com) has a limited bus service around Pensacola ($1.75 base fare); the compa-ny's free trolley connects downtown Pensacola and the beach between Memorial Day weekend and the end of September. The I-10 is the major east–west thoroughfare to catch the bus from; a number of buses pass down Palafox St.

Perdido Key
✆850

About 12 miles southwest of Pensacola, off Hwy 292 (which becomes Hwy 182), the easternmost Florida piece of the Gulf Is-lands National Seashore (p425) spans Perdi-do Key's crystalline waters. These dunes are home to the endangered Perdido Key beach mouse, which blends in well with the white-quartz sands here. There are two coastal state parks in the area: **Perdido Key State Park** (✆850-492-1595; 12301 Gulf Beach Hwy; admission per vehicle $3; ⊙8am-sunset) and, on the northern side of the lagoon, between Perdido Key and the mainland, **Big Lagoon**

THE PANHANDLE PERDIDO KEY

INTERSTATE MULLET TOSS

Every year in April, locals gather on both sides of the Florida/Alabama state line for a time-honored tradition: the mullet toss. The idea – apart from a very fine excuse for a party – is to see who can throw their (dead) mullet (an abundant local fish) the furthest across the border from Florida into Alabama. People have developed their own tech-niques: tail first, head first, or breaking its spine and bending it in half for better aerody-namics.

The mullet toss is organized by Perdido Key's **Flora-Bama Lounge, Package and Oyster Bar** (www.florabama.com; 17395 Perdido Key Dr; ⊙10am-10pm Mon-Thu, to late Fri-Sun), a legendary bar and roadhouse just east of the state line. Out-there events are a hallmark of the Flora-Bama – it also hosts the annual Polar Bear Dip (with a free drink if you brave the winter seas). Flora-Bama has tried to get mullet tossing into the *Guinness Book of World Records*, but its time hasn't come, yet.

Hurricane Ivan sadly did a number on the Flora-Bama, but after years of fundraising and beer-fueled rebuilding parties, the lounge rose again in April 2011. So if you miss the mullet toss, still do stop by for a rowdy night of live music, booze and a mean plate of fried pickles!

State Park (☎850-492-1595; 12301 Gulf Beach Hwy; admission per vehicle $6; ☉8am-sunset), with great crabbing in the lagoon's shallows. You'll find several free beach areas along the stretch of town, too.

The town of Perdido Key is centered not on hotels but condo resorts, all requiring multinight stays, and there are few restaurants or bars – the notable exception being the venerable Flora-Bama Lounge (p429). There are also a handful of seafood spots along the main drag. Visitors can stay in Pensacola, or three miles west in Orange Beach, Alabama.

Perdido Key runs right to the state line. From here, you can follow Hwy 182 straight into Alabama and take Hwy 59/US 90 north to connect with 1-10.

If you're arriving in Perdido Key on Hwy 182 from the west, welcome to Florida.

Destin & Fort Walton Beach

☎850 / DESTIN POP 12,600 / FORT WALTON BEACH POP 18,600

These twin resort towns – slightly calmer, smaller and less developed than Panama City Beach, but still more on the party-hearty and high-rise end of the scale than the Beaches of South Walton – offer more luminous waters and sugar-white sands, plus plenty of happenin' spots to eat, drink and be merry. Bountiful deep-sea fishing is also an entrenched part of the area's tradition, with an offshore shelf dropping to depths of 100ft about 10 miles off Destin's east pass, engendering its endearing claim as the 'world's luckiest fishing village' (back when it was still actually a village, and not the high-rise skyscape it has become since development took root). The area has a rich Native American history, a historic downtown, and beaches and family attractions punctuating its adjoining barrier island, Okaloosa Island.

Between the pair of towns, which bend around Choctawhatchee Bay like two crab claws, lies pristine beachfront owned by the US Air Force, whose largest base, Eglin, is in Fort Walton Beach.

◉ Sights

The beach is the biggest attraction here, followed closely by shopping at Silver Sands Outlets (www.silversandsoutlet.com).

Indian Temple Mound & Museum   ARCHAEOLOGICAL SITE
(admission free) One of the most sacred sites for local Native American culture to this day, the 17ft-tall, 223ft-wide ceremonial and political temple mound, built with 500,000 basket loads of earth and representing what is probably the largest prehistoric earthwork on the Gulf Coast, dates back to somewhere between AD 800 and 1500. On top of the mound you'll find a recreated temple housing a small exhibition center. Next door, the museum (139 Miracle Strip Parkway; adult/child $5/3; ☉noon-4:30pm Mon-Sat, from 10am Sun) offers an extensive overview of 12,000 years of Native American history, and houses flutes, ceramics and artifacts fashioned from stone, bone and shells, as well as a comprehensive research library.

Gulfarium   AQUARIUM
(www.gulfarium.com; 1010 Miracle Strip Parkway; adult/child $18.75/11; ☉9am-4pm, last admission 2hr before close; ☕) This marine show aquarium is more than 50 years old, making it the oldest attraction of its kind in the world. But it still inspires fresh excitement through its dolphin and sea-lion shows, great fun for kids.

US Air Force Armament Museum   MUSEUM
(100 Museum Dr, Eglin Air Force Base; admission free; ☉9:30am-4:30pm) As you approach this hangar-style museum, you'll see the aircrafts – which include an A-10A Warthog, an F-16A, a cool B-17 Flying Fortress and the SR-71A Blackbird reconnaissance (viz spy) plane – on the lawn outside the base's west gate. The exterior appears small, but inside are tons of weapons, a Warthog simulator and a terrifying F-105 Thunderchief missile, plus a detailed history of Eglin. Military buffs will dig the extensive weapons displays – check out those antique machine guns!

The museum is about 9 miles northeast of Fort Walton Beach; take Eglin Parkway (Hwy 85), and turn right on Nomad Way, which after 1.5 miles becomes Museum Dr – the museum is on your left.

🏃 Activities

Fishing, snorkeling, dolphin watching and party boat cruises are all popular activities in the area. In Destin, the shiny Harbor-Walk Village (www.harborwalkdestin.com) is a Disney-fied marina complex of shops, restaurants and nightclubs. Most of the area's tour operators have kiosks here. The Boardwalk (www.theboardwalkoi.com) on Okaloosa Island is another good place to scope out activities.

Southern Star
CRUISE

(☑850-837-7741; www.dolphin-sstar.com; Harborwalk Marina; adult/child $29/15.50; ☺4 tours per day Mon-Sat Jun-Aug) Bottlenose dolphins live year-round in the temperate waters of these parts; Southern Star is one of several companies offering dolphin cruises in hopes of spotting a few. The welcoming owner-operators will take you out on a two-hour cruise in a 76ft glass-bottom boat. Call for schedules in other months.

Water Sports
WATER SPORTS

Take advantage of the region's great diving with ScubaTech (☑850-837-2822; www.scubatechnwfl.com; 301 Hwy 98 E), where competent dive staff know the entire area from the bottom up. A four-hour, two-tank, 60ft to 90ft dive is $80 per person; snorkel trips are $30.

Waverunners, parasailing and boat rentals are plentiful, and you'll often find specials. Check out the HarborWalk Marina for operators. Just Chute Me (☑850-200-2260; www.parasaildestin.com; 404 Harbor Blvd, Destin) specializes in parasailing, with flights from $50.

HarborWalk Charters
FISHING

(www.harborwalkfishing.com; HarborWalk Marina, Destin; 4hr trip per person $100) Can accommodate groups of all sizes on its private fishing charters.

Okaloosa Island Pier
FISHING

(www.okaloosaislandpier.com; 1030 Miracle Strip Parkway E, Fort Walton Beach; walk-on $1, fishing adult/child $7.50/4.50; ☺24hr) Lit for night fishing and has rental gear available. No fishing license required. Rods rent for $7.

🛏 Sleeping

Chain hotels of all stripes line Hwy 98.

TOP CHOICE Aunt Martha's Bed & Breakfast
B&B $$

(☑850-243-6702; www.auntmarthasbedandbreakfast.com; 315 Shell Ave SE, Fort Walton Beach; r $105-115; ✹☎) Bill, a retired FBI agent, and Martha, a painter from an old Fort Walton family, run this charming inn overlooking the Intracoastal, a short walk from downtown. Elegant, unfussy rooms with big brass beds look out into the leafy branches of live oak trees. The lovely common area has a baby grand piano, well-stocked library and French doors that open onto a breezy veranda. Martha's Southern breakfasts – crawfish quiche, ham and cheese grits, stuffed French toast, you name it – are a veritable feast.

Henderson Park Inn
INN $$

(☑866-398-4432; www.hendersonparkinn.com; 2700 Old Hwy 98, Destin; r $139-389; ✹☎☎☎) This classy little shingled inn has 36 rooms done up in tasteful, if slightly dull, neutrals – beige carpet, high-end white linens, beachy prints. Thoughtful touches, like a Rocher chocolate on your pillow, make it feel exclusive. Breakfast, lunch, drinks and snacks are all included, making this a popular spot with honeymooners.

Henderson Beach State Park
CAMPGROUND $

(☑850-837-7550; www.floridastateparks.org; 17000 Emerald Coast Parkway/Hwy 98; sites $30, day use $6) This coastal paradise has 54 very private sites and good restrooms amid twisted scrub pines, with a 0.75-mile nature walk through the dune system. It's better suited to RVs than tents.

🍴 Eating

TOP CHOICE Dewey Destin's
SEAFOOD $$

(www.destinseafood.com; 202 Harbor Blvd, Destin; mains $8-20; ☺11am-late) Refreshingly human-scale compared to some of the corporate behemoth restaurants on Destin's main strip, this longtime local favorite serves up simple-but-delicious fried and steamed seafood platters and cool rum drinks in a crowded old beach shack decorated with vintage Florida photos.

Boathouse Oyster Bar
SEAFOOD $

(boathouseoysterbar.com; 228 Hwy 98 E; mains $3-13; ☺11am-late) What looks like a waterfront shed (because it is – there aren't even any restrooms inside) is the most happening little place in Destin, with live music from country to jazz and phenomenal Apalachicola oysters, crawfish and seafood gumbo.

Donut Hole
DINER, BAKERY $

(635 Harbor Blvd; mains $5-10; ☺24hr in season, slightly shorter hours in winter) Serving hearty egg breakfasts, perfect homemade buttermilk donuts, and gorgeous wedges of Key lime pie round the clock, this handsome wood diner is Americana at its finest.

Staff's Seafood Restaurant SEAFOOD, AMERICAN $$$

(☎850-243-3482; www.staffrestaurant.com; 24 Miracle Strip Parkway SE; mains $15-34; ☺5-10pm) Right near Aunt Martha's Bed & Breakfast, this character-laden 1913 warehouse with pressed metal ceilings and quirky antiques has been in Martha's family for over 90 years. It's renowned for its elegant home cooking – think seafood, veggies and home-baked bread – and for the free dessert you get with every full meal.

Seoul Garden Korean Restaurant KOREAN $$

(www.koreanfoodftwalton.com; 234 Miracle Strip Parkway SW; mains $10-20; ☺11am-8:30pm Mon-Sat, noon-7pm Sun) Short on atmosphere but long on flavor, this nondescript spot on the highway is a nice ethnic surprise in this land of seafood and burgers, with traditional Korean favorites like *bibimbop* and kimchi fried rice.

🍷 Drinking & Entertainment

HarborWalk Village and The Boardwalk on Okaloosa Island have plenty of nightlife, with busy, tourist-oriented pubs and restaurants overlooking the water.

AJ's/Club Bimini BAR, CLUB

(www.ajs-destin.com; 116 Harbor Blvd; ☺9pm-late) This tiki palace is dedicated to pleasure, with multiple tiers of dining and dancing. The bar also arranges daily sunset cruises on its luxury schooner.

ℹ Information

Servicing the area is the **Emerald Coast Visitors Welcome Center** (☎850-651-7131, 800-322-3319; www.destin-fwb.com; 1540 Miracle Strip Parkway; ☺8am-5pm Mon-Fri, 10am-4pm Sat & Sun). Additional info can be found online at the Destin Area Chamber of Commerce website (www.destinchamber.com), and at www.destin-ation.com.

ℹ Getting There & Around

Destin is about 45 miles west of Panama City Beach and about 47 miles east of Pensacola, along Hwy 98. The **Okaloosa Regional Airport** (www.flyvps.com) serves the Destin–Fort Walton area with direct services to many US cities, including Chicago and Tampa, with American Eagle, Vision, Delta, Continental and US Airways.

Okaloosa County Transit (www.rideoct.org) runs a shuttle service four times daily from 8am to 7pm Monday to Saturday in winter, and eight times daily from 8am to 10pm in summer (fares $1).

Beaches of South Walton

☑850

Sandwiched between Destin and Panama City along scenic Hwy 30A, this collection of 15 unincorporated communities makes up what is collectively known as Santa Rosa Beach, or the Beaches of South Walton. Each town has its own identity – some have a matchy-matchy country club vibe, while others are arty and funky. Many are master-planned, meaning they've been purpose built as resort towns, so all the architecture follows the same theme. All lie along an incredibly gorgeous stretch of Gulf front that's been dubbed the Emerald Coast.

Just driving the stretch of highway between the towns is a delight – peer between the fancy houses and condos for glimpses of rosy beachfront, or park the car to wander around boutiques and cafes. Highlights along the way include upscale Sandestin, hippie-ish Grayton Beach, the eerily picture-perfect village of Seaside, the whimsically named planned community of WaterColor, the Moroccan-themed Alys Beach, and the Dutch-inspired hamlet of Rosemary Beach.

Though it's a relatively short distance, allow at least 1½ hours to drive, even if you're not planning to stop, as speed limits are low, kids and cars plentiful and some views mesmerizing.

👁 Sights & Activities

Seaside VILLAGE

Spending an afternoon or night – or even a half hour – in this perfect, Necco Wafer–colored tiny town will make you feel like you've stumbled onto a movie set. Which, in fact, you will have done, as Seaside served as the on-location set for the 1998 movie *The Truman Show*, which was about an unwitting star in a popular reality TV show who lived in an annoyingly perfect place. And though the real place is pretty ideal – with street names like Cinderella Circle and Dreamland Heights – it's really not annoying. Famed and lauded as the country's first planned community, it was created in 1981 with input from a range of accomplished architects, and has been hailed as a model for New Urbanism. But instead of taking off as a year-round place to live, it has become an almost totally seasonal community, providing the second, summer homes for folks who live in other parts of the South.

If you come in the off-season (before April), it'll seem even more surreal than usual – if you go for an evening stroll, you may be the only one on the streets. In season, though, folks will be out in force, and really are incredibly friendly – in a genuine way. There's a hip book and music shop **Sundog Books** (www.sundogbooks; 89 Central Sq; ⊙9am-9pm), carrying great literature and very cool tracks, plus a handful of excellent eateries, art galleries and an absolutely gorgeous beach. The grassy town square is a great spot to just sit and people-watch – many days a group of vintage silver **Airstream trailers** forms a temporary food court in the center of town, selling everything from cupcakes to juices.

Grayton Beach State Park   PARK
(357 Main Park Rd, Santa Rosa Beach; vehicle $5) An 1133-acre stretch of marble-colored dunes rolling down to the water's edge, this state park's beauty is genuinely mind-blowing. The park sits nestled against the wealthy but down-to-earth community of Grayton Beach, home to the famed Red Bar (p434) and to the quirky **Dog Wall** – a mural on which locals paint portraits of their dogs. The park also contains the **Grayton Beach Nature Trail** (get a self-guiding tour at the gate), which runs from the east side of the parking lot through the dunes, magnolias and pine flatwoods and onto a boardwalk to a return trail along the beach. Locals flock here for nightly sunsets, and to wakeboard on the unique coastal dune lakes that shimmer across the sand from the gulf; you can even spend the night in the wilds, as you can camp in tents or cabins here.

Eden Gardens State Park   PARK
(181 Eden Garden Rd; entrance fee $4) Inland from 30A on a peninsula jutting into Choctawhatchee Bay, manicured gardens and lawns front the 1800s estate home of the Wesleys, a wealthy Florida timber family. The white-columned house was purchased and renovated in 1963 by Lois Maxon, who turned it into a mint-condition showcase for Louis XVI furniture and many other heirlooms and antiques. Today you can enjoy guided tours Monday to Thursday from 10am to 3pm for $3, or simply relax on the oak-lined grounds. There's a lovely picnic area by the water.

Cycling   CYCLING
You can explore the area along the 19-mile paved **Timpoochee trail**, which parallels scenic Hwy 30A; the 8-mile **Longleaf Pine**

Greenway hiking and cycling trail, paralleling Hwy 30A inland from just east of SR 395 to just before SR 393; and the **Eastern Lake trail**, which starts in Deer Lake State Park and links up with the western end of the Longleaf Pine Greenway, and also offers numerous loops. You can find a virtual bicycle tour, complete with maps and photos, on www.discover30A.com.

Simply cycling up and down the peaceful streets of each village is also a pleasant afternoon activity.

Big Daddy's (☑850-622-1165; www.bigdaddys rentals.com; Blue Mountain Beach) and **30-A Bike Rentals** (☑850-865-7433; www.30Abikerentals .net; Seagrove Beach) rent and deliver bikes starting at $20 a day.

🛌 Sleeping

You won't find chain hotels around these parts – accommodations are limited to rentals and a handful of intimate guesthouses. So book your rooms ahead of time, or plan on crashing in Destin or Panama City.

TOP CHOICE **Hibiscus Coffee & Guesthouse**   GUESTHOUSE $$
(☑850-231-2733; www.hibiscusflorida.com; 85 Defuniak St, Grayton Beach; r $130-250 Oct-Feb, $150-300 Mar-Sep; ❋⚂) This sweet little garden guesthouse, run by a patchouli-scented owner who doles out wonderful hugs, is tucked into a tree-studded corner of the oldest of the area's townships. Rooms and apartments are done up with tropical prints and funky folk paintings, like an arty friend's beach house. Anyone can enjoy multigrain pancakes or mango smoothies at the on-site **vegetarian cafe** (mains $4-9; ⊙7:30-11:30am), but it's included in the price for guests.

Pensione   BOUTIQUE HOTEL $$$
(☑850-231-1790; www.cottagerentalagency.com; 78 Main St, Rosemary Beach; r $180-210; ❋⚂) As its name suggests, this corner inn in downtown Rosemary Beach is more a European-style guesthouse than a hotel. There's no lobby, and the 11 guest rooms are quiet and individually decorated with simple, bright colors. For privacy lovers, it's hard to beat – if you want some conversation, drop by the lovely Italian restaurant on the ground floor for a glass of red.

Seagrove Villas Motel   MOTEL $$
(☑800-554-9522; 3040 30A, Seagrove; r $85-230, cottages $140-360; ❋⚂⚒) A relief from the cutesy-ness of nearby Seaside, this retro

THE PANHANDLE BEACHES OF SOUTH WALTON

motor lodge has big, clean, comfy rooms with dated green carpeting, and more up-scale cottage units with glassed-in porches.

✖ Eating & Drinking

Grayton Beach, Seaside and Rosemary Beach all have fun downtown areas with several restaurants and nightlife spots.

Bud & Alley's   AMERICAN $$$
(☎850-231-5900; www.budandalleys.com; Cinderella Circle, Seaside; mains $24-36; ⊙11:30am-3pm & 5:30pm-late) This landmark seafood restaurant, with dining room and rooftop tables that overlook the Gulf, is a seriously happening place to be – especially at sunset, when locals and visitors gather to cheer on the sky while enjoying cold beers and some of the excellent dishes, from seared halibut to grilled shrimp and grits. Weekends bring live world, jazz and funk music.

Red Bar   PUB $$
(www.theredbar.com; 70 Hotz Ave, Grayton Beach; dinner mains $13-21; ⊙11am-3pm & 5-10pm, bar open late) There's live jazz most nights at this funky, homey local's favorite, housed in the old general store and bringing in the friendly mobs, who either hunker down for beers or tuck into a small selection of well-prepared dishes, like crab cakes or shrimp-stuffed eggplant.

Fish Out of Water   SEAFOOD $$$
(☎850-534-5050; 34 Goldenrod Circle, WaterColor; mains $19-33; ⊙7-10:30am & 5:30-9pm, later on weekends) In the ritzy WaterColor resort, James Beard Award semifinalist chef Philip Krajeck works his creative magic on local bounty – Gulf triggerfish with pumpkin seeds, rock shrimp gnocchi, fresh Apalachicola oysters. The dining room, with its blown-glass sculptures and undulating walls, oozes understated good taste.

Bud & Alley's Taco Bar   MEXICAN $
(www.budandalleys.com; Cinderella Circle, Seaside; tacos $4-7; ⊙11am-late) A welcome addition to Seaside, this colorful, open-air joint, just steps from the water, presents authentic meat, seafood and veggie tacos, with all the fixings you'd find at a great roadside stand on the other side of the border.

Cowgirl Kitchen   TEX-MEX $
(www.cowgirlkitchen.com; 54 Main St, Rosemary Beach; mains $6-12; ⊙7am-9pm Tue-Sun, 5-7pm Mon; 🚗) A longtime favorite for casual Tex-Mex bites like burritos and spicy chicken salads, in the center of cute, walkable downtown Rosemary Beach.

❶ Information

The **Beaches of South Walton Tourist Center** (☑800-822-6877; www.beachesofsouthwalton.com; cnr Hwy 331 & Hwy 98; ⊙8am-4:30pm) is inland, between SR 283 and SR 83. There's also a bulletin board with tourist brochures on the eastern end of Seaside Town Sq.

A great web resource is www.discover30A.com, which is a constantly updated guide to beaches, shops, inns and eateries.

Panama City Beach
☑850 / POP 14,500

While much of the Panhandle's charms rely on its mellow 'Old Florida' roots, don't expect to find any of those vibes in Panama City Beach – an insanely overdeveloped gulf-front pocket that's in love with its recent transformation from an old-school resort to a mind-numbing, over-commercialized mob scene of condo-mania. New, architecturally dire high-rises – one less interesting than the next – now line the waterfront, with more outdoor malls, chain hotels and restaurants crowding in at every turn. And, from March to May, the place absolutely bonkers as a Spring Break destination, when students from 150 colleges east of the Mississippi roar into town to drink in the sun till they puke.

Luckily, despite the build-up in town, the beaches themselves are quite dazzling, with powder-fine sand and cerulean, crystal-clear waters that beckon fans of swimming, fishing and diving. The area is renowned as a wreck-diving site with dozens of natural, historic and artificial reefs attracting spectacular marine life. And the noisy, raucous family atmosphere that usually prevails (with the exception of Spring Break time) may make it a natural destination – for better or worse – for those traveling with young, hard-to-entertain kids.

◎ Sights & Activities

St Andrews State Recreation Area   PARK
(4607 State Park Lane; vehicle $8) A haven from the hurdy-gurdy of activity, this peaceful park spans 1260 acres graced with nature trails, swimming beaches and wildlife, including foxes, coyotes, snakes, alligators and seabirds. One of the best places to swim with children is the kiddie pool's 4ft-deep water near the jetties area (parents, no need to fear: gators live in freshwater; swimming areas are in the ocean). There's also excellent year-round waterfront camping, for both

tents and RVs, which costs $28 a night. You can still see the circular cannon platforms from when this area was used as a military reservation during WWII; look for them on the beach near the jetties.

The Camp Store (the first store you'll see as you enter the park) has an ATM and rents kayaks for $20 per half-day.

Just offshore, Shell Island has fantastic snorkeling. Buy tickets for the **Shell Island Shuttle** (www.shellislandshuttle.com; round-trip adult/child $15/7, snorkel package incl gear & transportation $22; ⊙9am-5pm, every half hr in summer, reduced schedule in winter) at the Pier Marketplace; there's a trolley service to the boat. Be aware that there are no facilities on the island, and there is no shade: wear a hat and plenty of sunscreen.

WonderWorks   MUSEUM
(www.wonderworkspcb.com; 9910 Front Beach Rd; adult/child $23/19, laser tag extra $3; ⊙9am-10pm Sun-Thu, to midnight Fri & Sat; 🖢) Designed to look like an upside-down building (complete with an upside-down lawn and palm trees), this wacky new interactive museum and fun center is impossible to miss – even if you want to! While hands-on exhibits like a spinning g-force bike, an obstacle climbing course and virtual reality soccer may give some grown-ups a migraine, kids will have a blast (literally, in the case of the laser tag maze!).

Museum of Man in the Sea   MUSEUM
(maninthesea.org; 17314 Panama City Beach Parkway; adult/child $5/free; ⊙10am-4pm Tue-Sun) Owned by the Institute of Diving, this museum takes a close look at the sport. Interactive exhibits let you crank up a Siebe pump, climb into a Beaver Mark IV submersible, check out models of the underwater laboratory Sealab III, and find out how diving bells really work. There's also a cool collection of old diving suits and a sea life–filled aquarium.

Ripley's Believe It or Not!   MUSEUM
(www.ripleyspanamacitybeach.com; 9907 Front Beach Rd; adult/child $15/10; ⊙10am-late; 🖢) Love it or hate it, the ubiquitous Ripley's is very Panama City Beach – loud, crowded, tacky-but-fun. In a building designed to look like a ship, the 'odditorium' features bizarro exhibits like a replica of the world's tallest man and an Amazonian shrunken head (believe it? Or not?). There's also laser tag, and an IMAX with seats that shake.

Gulf World Marine Park   AQUARIUM
(www.gulfworldmarinepark.com; 15412 Front Beach Rd; adult/child $27/17; ⊙9am-5pm, later in summer and holidays) Open since 1969, this well-loved aquarium is a good way to get up close to marine animals through its myriad shows and activities, like a stingray-petting pool, swim-with-dolphins program and California sea-lion show.

Diving   DIVING
Opportunities for wreck diving are excellent here; the area has earned its 'Wreck Capital of the South' nickname with more than a dozen boats offshore including a 441ft WWII Liberty ship and numerous tugs. There are more than 50 artificial reefs made from bridge spans, barges and a host of other sunken structures, as well as natural coral reefs. Visibility varies from 10ft to 80ft, averaging around 40ft. In winter, the average water temperature is 60°F, rising to 87°F in summer. Numerous dive companies offer packages; try **Dive Locker** (☎850-230-8006; www.divelocker.net; 106 Thomas Dr; ⊙8am-6pm Mon-Sat). A basic supervised dive is $90, gear included. Basic Open Water courses cost $285.

Pier Park   OUTLET MALL
(Front Beach Rd; ⊙10am-9pm Mon-Sat, noon-6pm Sun) Popular with families, this sprawling outdoor mall and entertainment zone has endless chain stores for clothing, accessories and snack foods, and several touristy restaurants and bars.

🛏 Sleeping

There are endless places to lay your head here – just don't expect to find small, tranquil places brimming with character (though many of the motels are family-owned). Look for the code words 'family-friendly' or 'families only' if you're looking to avoid Spring Breakers. Note also that rates vary dramatically between the quieter winter months and super-busy summers, and spike at various (and variable) times, such as Spring Break (March to May). For a complete guide to hotels and resorts, visit www.pcbeach.org.

Wisteria Inn   MOTEL $$
(☎850-234-0557; www.wisteria-inn.com; 20410 Front Beach Rd; r from $109; 🌬🐾🛁) Away from the maddening crowds, this sweet little 15-room motel advertizes itself as 'adults only' (kids 12 and older are OK) and discourages Spring Breakers. Rooms have a

bright, Caribbean theme, with tiled floors and personal touches like guest robes. Chat it up with other guests during daily poolside mimosa hours.

Marriott Bay Point Resort & Spa   HOTEL **$$**
(☑850-236-6000; www.marriottbaypoint.com; 4200 Marriott Dr; r $116-409; ❋☏☎) One of the most luxurious bases in PCB is this pleasantly appointed Marriott-run resort, featuring views of St Andrews Bay, two golf courses, Waverunner and kayak rentals, a lovely pool, four on-site restaurants and a full-service spa. Rooms are cushy, modern and airy.

Beachbreak by the Sea   MOTEL **$**
(☑850-234-3870, 800-346-4709; www.beachbreak bythesea.com; 15405 Front Beach Rd; d $79-169; ❋☎) A refreshing four-story spot in a sea of high-rises, this place offers basic motel-style rooms, a central beachfront location and continental breakfast, not to mention reasonable rates.

✖ Eating & Drinking

Waiting for a table at one of Panama City Beach's many massive restaurants is an endurance sport. Downtown Panama City has more low-key offerings.

Pineapple Willy's   CARIBBEAN, AMERICAN **$$**
(www.pwillys.com; 9875 S Thomas Dr; mains $15-22; ☺11am-late) This kitschy, casual place features its own sheltered wooden pier jutting over the sand, gulf-view dining and a fun bar. It's famed for its house special – slo' cooked Jack Daniels BBQ ribs by the pound and pound-and-a-half bucket load. The frozen margaritas and special Pineapple Willy cocktail – a potent potion of Myer's rum, pineapple juice and cream of coconut – are pretty popular, too.

Firefly   SEAFOOD **$$$**
(☑850-249-3359; www.fireflypcb.com; 535 Beckrich Rd; mains $22-36; ☺5-10pm) This uberatmospheric, low-lit fine dining establishment beckons diners with clever seafood dishes – salmon with ginger-soy and tempura-fried twin lobster tails – as well as meals of pasta, pork, lamb and beef. A cool lounge bar, designed to look like a fancy library, doles out tasty flavored martinis. It's good enough for the president – Obama ate here when he was in town in 2010.

Tootsie's Orchid Lounge   LIVE MUSIC
(www.tootsies.net; Pier Park; ☺10am-late) A sister to the legendary Nashville honky tonk of the same name, this Tootsie's may lack the dusty character of the original, but the non-stop live country music is still plenty boot stompin'.

ℹ Information

The **Panama City Beach Convention & Visitors Bureau** (☑850-233-5070, 800-722-3224; www .visitpanamacitybeach.com; 17001 Panama City Beach Parkway; ☺8am-5pm) has maps, as well as loads of information about the new developments in town. Another great source is the brand- new information office run by the **Panama City Beach Chamber of Commerce** (☑850-235-1159; www.pcbeach.org; 309 Richard Jackson Blvd; ☺9am-5pm Mon-Fri, 9am-2pm Sat), which has touch-screen kiosks with information on where to sleep, shop and play. The **Panama City Beach Public Library** (12500 Hutchison Blvd; ☺9am-6pm Mon-Wed, to 5pm Thu & Fri, to 4pm Sat) provides free internet access. The most convenient post office is at 420 Churchwell Dr.

ℹ Getting There & Around

The **Panama City-Bay County International Airport** (☑850-763-6751; www.iflybeaches .com; 6300 West Bay Pkwy) is served by Delta and Southwest, with daily nonstop flights to Orlando, Houston, Washington, DC and more.

There's a **Greyhound bus station** (917 Harrison Ave) in Panama City.

By car, Panama City Beach is almost halfway between Tallahassee (about 130 miles) and Pensacola (95 miles). Coming along the coast, Hwy 98 takes you into town; from I-10 take either Hwy 231 or Hwy 79 south.

The **Bay Town Trolley** (baytowntrolley.org; tickets $1.50) runs in Panama City Beach. The service continues to add stops to its coverage, but its schedule is still limited to Monday to Friday between 6am and 8pm.

Classic Rentals (☑850-235-1519; 13226 Front Beach Rd) rents scooters (half/full day $20/35) and old-school Harleys (half/full day $75/125).

Cape San Blas & Port St Joe

☑850 / POP 3500

Delicate Cape San Blas curls around St Joseph Bay at the southwestern end of the bulge in the Panhandle, starting on the mainland at Port St Joe and ending at its undeveloped, 10-mile-long tip with **St Joseph Peninsula State Park** (8899 Cape San Blas Rd; vehicle $6, camping $24, cabins $100; ☺8am-sunset). The sugar-sand beaches stretch for 2516

INDIAN PASS RAW BAR

On a desolate stretch of 30A just outside Port St Joe, this old wooden building might look like an abandoned general store. But look a little closer, and you'll see pickup trucks parked two deep in the back lot, and note the twang of guitar music coming from the porch. This, my friend, is the 82-year-old Indian Pass Raw Bar (☑850-227-1670; www .indianpassrawbar.com; 8391 Indian Pass Rd; mains $10-17; ☺noon-9pm Tue-Sat), one of the true classics of old Florida Gulf culture. Inside, grab a beer from the cooler (on the honor system) and take a seat at a crowded table (you may have to share). The menu, posted above the bar, is simple: oysters three ways (raw, steamed or baked with parmesan cheese), crab legs and a handful of shrimp dishes. Please, get the oysters – even if you think you don't like the salty bivalves, you'll be surprised at the sweetness of these guys, drawn just this morning from the waters of nearby Apalachicola. Stay for a slice of Key lime pie and impromptu line dancing on the porch.

acres along grassy, undulating dunes, edging wilderness trails and the 13-mile **Loggerhead Run Bike Path**, named for the turtles that inhabit the island, which is perfect for cyclists, joggers or bladers.

The state park is one of the most prized camping spots along the Gulf Coast, home to 119 sites in two separate developed grounds. You can stay in seclusion in just-renovated loft-style timber cabins with queen beds and walkways leading from your back door to the water (bring your own towels). At the peninsula's northern extremity, primitive camping is allowed in designated areas of the wilderness preserve in the park, a sojourning point for migratory birds and butterflies. You'll need to bring everything, including water and a camp stove, as no fires are allowed. Pets are not permitted anywhere in the park.

There is a lovely place to picnic right at the start of the cape, though – Salinas Park (Cape San Blas Rd), where you can stroll an over-dunes boardwalk, take a dip in the Gulf or just sit and enjoy the waterfront breezes before continuing on with your journey.

Across the bay, which has gentle rip- and current-free swimming, the town of Port St Joe was once known as 'sin city' for the casinos and bordellos that greeted seafarers. The Florida Constitution was originally drafted here in 1838, but scarlet fever and hurricanes combined to stymie its progression as one of Florida's boom towns. These days it's in something of a transition as industry, particularly paper mills, gives way to tourism, with a small historic district showing fledgling signs of renewal.

A really pleasant Panhandle overnight stop is the Port Inn (☑850-229-7678; www.port innfl.com; 501 Monument Ave (Hwy 98); r $65-165;

☀☎☒), with front-row seats of the sunsets over the bay. A timber porch with rocking chairs runs the full length of this lovely inn, which has bay-view rooms with sisal carpet, wicker furniture and sparkling bathrooms. The Thirsty Goat lounge bar is a nice, mellow spot to wind up your evening with a cold brew.

Apalachicola
☑850 / POP 2200

Slow, mellow and perfectly preserved, Apalachicola is one of the Gulf's most irresistible villages. Perched on the edge of a broad bay, the oak-shaded town combines an old-fashioned fishing-based economy with a new wave of bistros, art galleries, eclectic boutiques, and B&Bs in renovated old mansions. It's hugely popular as a romantic weekend getaway – stroll through the Historic District at sunset and you'll understand why. Don't even think of leaving without trying one of the area's famous oysters – Apalachicola Bay is one of the most famous producers of the tasty bivalves.

◉ Sights & Activities

The sights below – and 35 in total – are well marked on a chamber of commerce historic walking tour guide and map, available free from the chamber office and most B&Bs. Apalachicola's main drag is Ave E, and the entire Historic District is easily walked and is lined with interesting shops and restaurants.

Richard Bickel Photography   GALLERY
(www.richardbickelphotography.com; 81 Market St) Bickel, an internationally acclaimed photo-

journalist, has made a name for himself preserving the Apalachicola waterfront culture in images. His B&W photo books, *The Last Great Bay* and *Apalachicola River,* offer a moving portrait of the historic way of life here – and remind folks that, sadly, depending on the economy and environmental situation, it may not be long for this world.

John Gorrie State Museum　MUSEUM
(46 6th St; admission $2; ☉9am-5pm Thu-Sun) This tiny, old-fashioned museum commemorates one of Apalachicola's most famous sons, Dr John Gorrie (1803–55). We have Gorrie to thank for one of the South's most crucial and universally beloved inventions: air-conditioning (all together now: 'ahhhhhhh'). He developed an ice-making machine to keep yellow fever patients cool during an epidemic, but was unable to market it and died poor and unknown, unaware of how his invention laid the groundwork for modern refrigeration and A/C. Displays in the museum include a model of Dr Gorrie's invention, as well as exhibits on Apalachicola's local (and long-defunct) sponging and cotton-storage industries.

Raney House　HISTORIC BUILDING
(46 Ave F; tour free; ☉1-4pm Sun-Fri, 10am-4pm Sat) Just a few blocks from downtown, this 1838 Southern-style plantation home sits behind a white-picket fence and a facade of grand columns, and was the home of Harriet and David Raney, the latter a two-time mayor of the city. A small museum has some historical exhibits on the town.

Trinity Episcopal Church　CHURCH
(79 6th St) Just across the street from the Gorrie museum, this handsome church was built in New York State and cut into sections, which were shipped down the Atlantic coast and around the Keys before making their way to this spot where the church was reassembled in 1836.

Grady Market　MARKET
(www.jegrady.com; 76 Water St; ☉10am-5:30pm Mon-Sat) Built in the late 1880s and rebuilt after a fire in 1900, this hulking brick space was originally a ship's chandlery and general store, as well as the home of a French consulate installed to look after French nationals working in the shipping industry. Now it encompasses a sprawling market of antiques traders and local artists' galleries, including creative textile designs, funky clothing and works of sculpture, painting and nautical-type crafts.

Boating & Fishing Tours　BOATING, FISHING
Numerous companies offer wildlife-spotting tours, where alligators, wading birds and willowy trees are the main attractions. **Backwater Guide Service** (☎850-653-2820; www.backwaterguideservice.com; tours $175-350) and **Brownie's Guide Service** (☎850-653-5529; www.apalachicolaguide.com) both offer such sightseeing tours, which include easy hikes along nature trails, as well as fishing charters including bait, tackle and licenses, and the promise of snagging your own red fish or speckled trout for grilling. Call Brownie's for its current tour prices.

🛏 Sleeping

TOP CHOICE **Coombs House Inn**　B&B $$
(☎850-653-9199; www.coombshouseinn.com; 80 6th St; r $129-269; ✿❄) This stunning yellow Victorian inn was built in 1905 by lumber entrepreneur James N Coombs, a friend of Theodore Roosevelt who turned down both the vice presidency and the governorship of Florida. He probably didn't want to leave his elegant house, featuring black cypress wall paneling, nine fireplaces, a carved oak staircase, leaded glass windows and beadboard ceilings. The place was left vacant in the 1960s, when it spent years deteriorating until luxury-hotel designer Lynn Wilson and her airline executive husband Bill Spohrer discovered the property in the '80s, purchased it from surviving family members and brought it back to spectacular life, eventually adding an additional two buildings. Settle into one of the fabulous rooms and be sure to join the other guests for nightly wine socials in the dining room, the same room where a lavish breakfast is served each morning.

Gibson Inn　INN $$
(☎850-653-2191; www.gibsoninn.com; 51 Ave C; r $105-250; ✿) The first landmark you'll see if you're approaching town from the east on Hwy 98 is this grand gray timber inn. Built in 1907, it's got 30 old-fashioned, somewhat creaky rooms with flowered wallpaper and high antique beds. Ask for one of the sweeping 2nd-floor rooms that open onto the sprawling veranda, or, if you're game, request room 309 – it's reputedly haunted by Captain Woods, who had a romantic liaison with one of the Gibson sisters.

House of Tartts　GUESTHOUSE $$
(☎850-653-4687; www.houseoftartts.com; 50 Ave F; r $105-130, carriage house $195; ✿) With

creaky wooden floors, fireplaces and rustic log cabin-ish walls, this charmingly low-key guesthouse feels every bit of its 125-plus years. A shared kitchen and a lack of daily housekeeping make this seem more like staying at a friend's house than a B&B.

River Inn   INN $$
(☑850-653-8139; www.apalachicolariverinn.com; 123 Water St; r lower/upper $145/179; ❋🐾) Strung with Christmas lights that twinkle across Apalachicola Bay, this waterfront inn – more of an upscale motel, really – has lovely, old-fashioned rooms done up in romantic pinks and purples. Upper rooms have gorgeous water views, hence the price difference.

✗ Eating

The Historic District is packed with cute cafes and bistros; nightlife pretty much consists of watching the moon dance over the bay.

Papa Joe's Oyster Bar & Grill   SEAFOOD $$
(www.papajoesoysterbar.com; 301b Market St; mains $8-18; ⏱11:30am-10pm) Hunker down at this locals' favorite to sample daily harvested oysters that are shucked to order and served on the half shell, in po' boys (sandwiches), steamed or baked and then topped with savories from butter and parmesan cheese, to capers and feta. The menu is also stocked with seafood treasures like crab cakes, popcorn shrimp and stuffed flounder, not to mention steaks and pasta creations.

Tamara's Café Floridita   SOUTH AMERICAN $$$
(☑850-697-4111; www.tamarascafe.com; 17 Ave E; mains $15-28; ⏱8:30am-10pm) In the heart of the Historic District, Tamara's is the hottest table in town, especially on Wednesday tapas night. Spices influenced by Tamara's native Venezuela pack a punch in dishes like grilled herb pork chop with shrimp and scallops in creamy tomato-tarragon sauce. Her margarita chicken, sautéed in honey, tequila and lime glaze with scallops, is inspired.

Seafood Grill   SEAFOOD $
(100 Ave B; mains $9-14; ⏱11am-9pm Mon-Sat, to 4pm Sun) With waxed tablecloths, squeeze bottles of ketchup and walls covered with vintage signs, this casual seafood joint is nothin' fancy, and that's just fine. Stick with the basics: fried shrimp, burgers, fish sandwiches.

❶ Information

Apalachicola Bay Chamber of Commerce
(☑850-653-9419; www.apalachicolabay.org; 122 Commerce St; ⏱9am-5pm Mon-Fri) Offers loads of tourist information, downtown walking tour maps and helpful advice.

❶ Getting There & Around

Hwy 98 (which becomes Market St) brings you into town from either direction. Downtown is easily strollable, but you'll need a car to explore the greater area.

St Vincent Island & Around

Just a few minutes from Apalachicola but accessible only by boat lies pristine **St Vincent Island** (www.fws.gov/saintvincent). The island's pearly dunes reveal 5000-year-old geological records, while its pine forests and wetlands teem with endangered species like red wolves, sea turtles, bald eagles and peregrine falcons. Fishing's permitted on lakes except when bald eagles are nesting (generally in winter). For those sick of the high-rises and bikini-clad crowds of the Gulf beaches, it's the perfect getaway for a day of hiking and solitude. To get here, hop aboard the **St Vincent Shuttle Services** (☑850-229-1065; www.stvincentisland.com; adult/child $10/7), which can also take your bike (bike and passenger $20), or rent you one of theirs ($25, including boat trip).

On the mainland near Apalachicola's shrimping boat docks, the **St Vincent National Wildlife Refuge headquarters & visitors center** (www.fws.gov/saintvincent/; north end of Market St; admission free; ⏱10am-3:30pm Mon-Thu) has interactive exhibits and information.

Opposite the St Vincent National Wildlife Refuge headquarters, the **Apalachicola National Estuarine Research Reserve** (261 7th St; admission free; ⏱8am-5pm Mon-Fri) provides a great overview of its research site which encompasses over 246,000 acres in Apalachicola Bay, with giant aquariums here simulating different habitats. A half-mile boardwalk leads down to the river where you'll find a free telescope on a turret.

St George Island

☑850 / POP 300

Located just over a 4-mile causeway from Apalachicola's neighbor of Eastpoint, this 28-mile-long barrier island is home to white sandy beaches, bay forests, salt marshes and an inoffensive mix of summer homes and condos. It's a great place for shelling, kayaking, sailing or swimming. At the end of every

PANACEA

Barely a speck on the map between Apalachicola and Tallahassee, this bay-front hamlet, named after its supposedly medicinal springs, has two things to recommend it.

The first is **Posey's Dockside** (mains $4-15), a genuine off-the-beaten path cafe/roadhouse with excellent local oysters and live music on the dock overlooking undeveloped Dickerson Bay.

Gulf Specimen Marine Lab (www.gulfspecimen.org; adult/child $7.50/5; ⊙9am-5pm Mon-Fri, 10am-4pm Sat, noon-4pm Sun; ☷), a small, homemade-feeling aquarium, is the second highlight. The aquarium is lined with touch tanks of horseshoe crabs, starfish and rays – most of the animals are brought in by divers gathering specimens to send to biological research labs across the country. The owner, Jack Rudloe, is a fascinating autodidact who has modeled himself after Doc, the marine collector in John Steinbeck's novel *Cannery Row* – Rudloe maintained a correspondence with Steinbeck for years.

street on the island you'll find public beach access and, generally, plentiful parking. St George Island State Park sits at the island's northeastern point; Little St George Island lies southwest.

◉ Sights & Activities

St George Island State Park   PARK
(www.floridastateparks.org/stgeorgeisland; vehicle $6, camping $24) The island at its undeveloped best is found here, in the 9 miles of glorious beach and sand dunes that make up this pristine park. There is a 2.5-mile nature trail that offers exceptional birding, as willet, least terns, snowy plovers and black skimmers regularly nest here. Throughout the park, boardwalks lead to shell-sprinkled beaches, where the shallow waters are perfect for canoeing and kayaking, as well as fishing for flounder and whiting. You can camp here, too, at one of the 60 campsites on grounds featuring hookups and a playground, or at the Gap Point primitive campsites, accessible by boat or by hiking a 2.5-mile nature trail through pine forests and coastal scrub. Catch the amazing loggerhead sea turtles beginning in May, when they come ashore to dig nests and lay their eggs, yielding hatchlings that race into the Gulf.

St George Lighthouse   LIGHTHOUSE
(www.stgeorgelight.org; adult/child $5/3; ⊙10am-5pm Mon-Wed, Fri & Sat, noon-5pm Sun) Just across from the bridge as you drive onto the island, this handsome lighthouse was built in 1858 and painstakingly reconstructed in 2008 after collapsing into the sea due to erosion in 2005. Today you can climb the 92 steps to the top for glorious water views.

Journeys   TOURS, KAYAKING
(☎850-927-3259; www.sgislandjourneys.com; 240 E 3rd St) This outfitter leads boat and kayak tours (from $50), and also rents kayaks ($60 a day), sailboats ($100 a day) and catamarans ($275 a day), all ideal ways to make the voyage to Cape St George.

⮥ Sleeping & Eating

Most visitors to the island rent cottages; hotels are limited to the two options below. Eating options are also surprisingly limited – if you're day-tripping here, you may want to pack a picnic.

St George Inn   INN $$
(☎850-927-2903; www.stgeorgeinn.com; 135 Franklin Blvd; r $90-150; ❄︎☎︎☷) One of the few historic structures on an island lined with new condo development, this rambling clapboard inn has comfy-if-creaky rooms and numerous cozy sitting areas filled with dog-eared books.

Buccaneer Inn   MOTEL $$
(☎850-927-2585, 800-847-2091; www.buccinn. com; 160 W Gorrie Dr; r winter $60-115, summer $90-155; ❄︎☎︎☷) Right on the Gulf, rooms here are like those of a basic, design-challenged motel – dated green carpet, painted cinderblock walls. But all are clean, bright and surprisingly spacious, and some have kitchenettes.

Blue Parrot Oceanfront
Café   SEAFOOD, AMERICAN $$
(www.blueparrotcafe.net; 68 W Gorrie Dr; mains $10-25; ⊙11am-9pm) Out the back of this relaxed and breezy gulf-front cafe, locals sip rumrunners and down oversized po' boys or delicious crab crakes.

Getting There & Around

From the dock-lined town of Eastpoint on Hwy 98, 7 miles east of Apalachicola, follow the 4-mile-long causeway onto the island until Gulf Beach Dr, also known as Front Beach Dr, at the end. Turning left brings you to the state park; a right turn takes you toward Government Cut, which separates Little St George Island.

If you want to ditch the car, **Island Adventures** (850-927-3655; sgislandadventures.com; 105 E Gulf Beach Dr) rents bikes for just $10 a day.

Inland Panhandle

Though most of the attractions around here are indeed on the gulf, there are a couple of spots inland that are worth going out of your way for.

FLORIDA CAVERNS STATE PARK

Just over an hour from Tallahassee or Panama City, on Hwy 166, this 1300-acre park (camping reservations 800-326-3521; 3345 Caverns Rd; vehicle $5, cave tours adult/child $8/5, camping $20) on the Chipola River has fascinating caves unique to Florida. Eerie stalactites, stalagmites and flowstone (formed by water flowing over rock) fill the lighted caves, along with calcified shapes formed over the centuries as calcite has bubbled through the stone. You can take a 45-minute guided tour, available from 9am to 4pm daily, with a volunteer – who will surely mention the quirky (and slightly ridiculous) names they've come up with to describe the various formations, from 'wedding cake' to 'bacon.' Outside, the Blue Hole swimming area makes for a fun – if freezing – dip.

DEFUNIAK SPRINGS

Switzerland has one, and the Florida Panhandle has the other: the Walton County seat of DeFuniak Springs is home to one of just two almost perfectly round lakes in the world (the other is near Zurich). It's popularly thought that the lake was created by a meteorite crashing to Earth eons ago, but there's no final scientific word on its formation. Ringing the lake's approximately mile-long circumference along Circle Dr is the town's historic district, with 39 splendid Victorian buildings. Stroll around the lake, peruse the antiques shops downtown, peer at the old railroad car parked on Baldwin Ave – there's not much to do in this sleepy ol' town, and that's precisely its allure.

Fifteen minutes down the road, Ponce de Leon Springs State Park (2860 Ponce de Leon Springs Rd, Ponce de Leon; vehicle $4) has a glowingly clear aqua spring like something from a fairy tale, studded with knobby trees and surrounded by ladders for easy swimming access. Two short trails skirt the bank of a nearby blackwater creek.

If it's time in your travels for a rest, you may want to check into the utterly charming Hotel DeFuniak (850-892-4383; www.hoteldefuniak.com; 400 Nelson Ave; r from $89;), a 1920s downtown hotel with 12 atmospheric rooms done up with vintage telephones and pedestal sinks. Its restaurant, Bogey's (mains $10-26; 11am-2pm Tue-Fri, from 5pm Tue-Sat) has a menu of high-end classics (veal, shrimp scampi) and a wine-loving local clientele.

THE PANHANDLE INLAND PANHANDLE

WORTH A TRIP

VORTEX SPRING

Half an hour outside DeFuniak Springs in precisely the middle of nowhere exists something rather unexpected: Vortex Spring (850-836-4979; www.vortexspring.com), an inland scuba diving resort. On an 800-acre wooded property, the resort – which feels more like a summer camp for adults – surrounds a deep blue spring whose waters drop more than 110ft into a series of caverns. Divers come here for winter training, to master the tricky art of cave diving, or simply to enjoy diving in water clearer than any ocean. Though most come with pre-arranged groups, PADI-certified Vortex offers its own dive classes (beginner's Discover Dive $100, Open Water course from $350, two nitrox dives $250). Nondivers can swim in the springs or ride the zip line. Camping is $20, rustic cabins start at $50 and comfy lodge apartments start at $64. On weekends, an on-site restaurant becomes a hub of social activity – peel off your wetsuit and bust out your best brag-worthy diving tale. Day-trippers can hang out at the springs for $10.

DeFuniak Springs is 50 miles west of the Florida Caverns and Marianna along I-10; or 47 miles north of Destin on US 331.

fishing communities, freshwater springs, picturesque islands and the edges of the Apalachicola National Forest.

TALLAHASSEE & THE BIG BEND

Florida's gracious state capital, blanketed by moss-draped live oaks and infused with a blend of historic and university cultures, sits inland at the edge of what's known as the Big Bend region – a little-traveled arc of the Florida coastline that curves around the Gulf of Mexico. Within it, you'll find remote

Tallahassee

📞 850 / POP 172,500

Florida's capital, cradled between gently rising hills and beneath tree-canopied roadways, is a calm and gracious city, far more Southern, culturally speaking, than the majority of the state it administrates. Geographically it's closer to Atlanta than it is to Miami, and culturally, like Jacksonville, its citizens consider themselves Southern,

Tallahassee

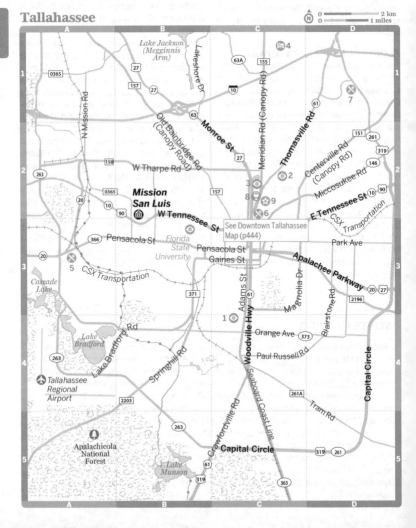

which is inversely the case the further south you travel. Despite the city's two major universities (Florida State and Florida Agricultural and Mechanical University) and its status as a government center, the pace here is slower than syrup and there's not much to detain a visitor for more than a day or two.

◉ Sights & Activities

Mary Brogan Museum of Art
& Science   MUSEUM
(Map p444; www.thebrogan.org; 350 S Duval St; adult/child $7.50/5; ☺10am-5pm Mon-Sat, 1-5pm Sun; ⏢) Affiliated with the Smithsonian, this museum is a hit with kids. It houses both a science center on the 1st and 2nd floors, and the Tallahassee art museum, mounting international exhibits, on the 3rd floor. It may seem like a strange marriage at first, but the museum does a great job of pointing out connections between left- and right-brained creations, with highlights including a living sea ecolab and a TV weather station, where kids can try their hands at forecasting.

FREE **Museum of Florida History**   MUSEUM
(Map p444; www.museumoffloridahistory.com; 500 S Bronough St; ☺9am-4:30pm Mon-Fri, 10am-4:30pm Sat, noon-4:30pm Sun) Though housed

HIDDEN GEM: SOUTHEASTERN REGIONAL BLACK ARCHIVES RESEARCH CENTER & MUSEUM

Universally referred to by its acronym, FAMU (fam-you), **Florida Agricultural & Mechanical University** (Map p442; www.famu.edu; 1500 Wahnish Way) was founded in 1887 as the State Normal College for Colored Students, with 15 students and two instructors. Today it's home to a population of about 10,000 students of all races, as well as the **Southeastern Regional Black Archives Research Center & Museum** (Map p442; Carnegie Library, cnr Martin Luther King Jr Blvd & Gamble St; admission free; ☺9am-5pm Mon-Fri). A forerunner in research on African American influence on US history and culture, the center and museum holds one of the country's largest collections of African American and African artifacts as well as a huge collection of papers, photographs, paintings and documents pertaining to black American life.

in a stark and off-putting modern building with no charm (it's a tie with the new Florida State Capitol for unattractiveness), this museum is filled with wonderful exhibits, tackling everything from Florida's Paleo-Indians, who inhabited these parts beginning at the end of the Ice Age, to Civil War times, Spanish shipwrecks in the Atlantic and the rise of 'Tin-Can Tourism,' when the middle-class traveler began hitting Florida in droves – driving south, camping out and eating dinner out of tin cans. You'll see a 1925 Model T, a 1911 Baker electric car, a reconstructed citrus packing house of the 1920s and the star attraction: a North American mastodon skeleton.

Mission San Luis   HISTORIC SITE
(Map p442; www.missionsanluis.org; 2020 W Mission Rd; adult/child $5/2; ☺10am-4pm Tue-Sun) In a lofty hilltop setting spanning 60 acres, the Mission San Luis is a trip back to the 17th century. The site of a Spanish and Native American mission settlement from 1656 to 1704, it was at one time the provincial capital under Spanish rule and home to up

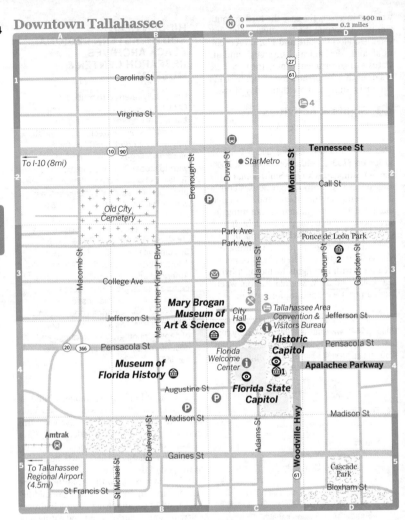

THE PANHANDLE TALLAHASSEE & THE BIG BEND

to 1500 residents. The entire mission has been wonderfully reconstructed – including the dramatic, soaring council house of the Apalachee village, which stands like a towering, light-filled tepee on the bucolic land. Free tours, led by knowledgeable interpreters, are available at the excellent visitor center, which also screens a short film.

FREE **Florida State Capitol**   VIEWPOINT
(New Capitol; Map p444; cnr Pensacola St & Duval St; ⊙8am-5pm Mon-Fri) It's stark, ugly and massively imposing, but the 22-story Florida State Capitol still deserves your

visit. That's mainly because of its top-floor observation deck, which affords wonderful 360-degree views of the city and its edge of rolling green hills that stretch to the horizon. In session, the Capitol is a hive of activity, with politicians, staffers and lobby groups buzzing in and around its honeycombed corridors.

FREE **Historic Capitol**   HISTORIC BUILDING
(Map p444; www.flhistoriccapitol.gov) Next door to the current state capitol is its far more charming 1902 predecessor, adorned by candy-striped awnings and topped with a repro-

Downtown Tallahassee

duction of the original glass dome, and as grand as its successor is uninviting. It now houses the **Florida Legislative Research Center & Museum** (Map p444; www.flrcm.com; 400 S Monroe St; admission free; ⊙9am-4:30pm Mon-Fri, 10am-4:30pm Sat, noon-4:30pm Sun & holidays), including a restored House of Representatives chamber and governors' reception area, plenty of governors' portraits, and exhibits on immigration, state development and the infamous 2000 US presidential election, with displays such as the equally infamous butterfly ballot, now enclosed in glass.

FREE **Knott House Museum** HISTORIC BUILDING (Map p444; www.museumoffloridahistory.com; 301 E Park Ave; ⊙gift shop 10am-4pm Mon-Sat, guided tours 1pm, 2pm & 3pm Wed-Fri, hourly 10am-3pm Sat) This stately, white columned 1843 house, affiliated with the history museum, is a quirky attraction. Occupied during the Civil War by Confederate and then Union troops before the Emancipation Proclamation was read here in 1865, it's otherwise known as 'the house that rhymes.' That's because in 1928 it was bought by politico William V Knott, whose poet wife, Luella, attached verses on the evils of drink to the many of the furnishings.

Tallahassee-St Marks
Historic Railroad State Trail RUNNING, CYCLING (admission free; ⊙8am-sunset) The ultimate treat for runners, skaters and cyclists, this trail has 16 miles of smooth pavement shooting due south to the gulf port town of St Marks and not a car or traffic light in sight. It's easy and

flat for all riders, sitting on a coastal plain and shaded at many points by canopies of gracious live oaks. (More experienced riders may opt for forest trails, like the rugged 7.5-mile **Munson Hills Loop trail**, navigating sand dunes and a towering pine forest.)

Rent bikes at **Great Bicycle Shop** (Map p442; ☑850-224-1240; www.greatbicycle.com; 1909 Thomasville Rd; bikes per 24hr $25).

Leon County Canopy Roads SCENIC DRIVES Tallahassee's famed oak- and moss-shrouded canopy roads make for lovely afternoon drives. Roads include Old St Augustine Rd, Centerville Rd, Meridian Rd, Miccosukee Rd and Old Bainbridge Rd.

🛏 Sleeping

With just a couple of charming exceptions, you'll find that Tallahassee's hotels are mostly midrange chains, clumped at exits along I-10 or along Monroe St, between I-10 and downtown. Be sure to book well ahead during the legislative session and football games, when prices peak.

Hotel Duval HOTEL $$ (Map p444; ☑850-224-6000; www.hotelduval .com; 415 N Monroe St; r from $119; 🅿🛜🏊) By far Tallahassee's slickest digs, this new 117-room hotel goes in for a neo-mod look, with bold leather headboards, plastic bubble chandeliers and funky animal prints. In-room computers with touch screens control everything from the TV to the air-conditioning. A rooftop bar and lounge is open until 2am most nights; Thursday evening sushi happy hour draws guests and townies alike. Shula's, a fancy chain steakhouse, is just off the lobby. The hotel's commitment to energy efficiency has earned it a Green Lodging designation.

Governor's Inn HOTEL $$ (Map p444; ☑850-681-6855; www.thegovinn.com; 209 S Adams St; r $129-149; 🅿🛜) When the state legislature's in session, politicians book up this discreet 41-room hotel, on a downtown pedestrian street. Rooms are classic and comfy, with striped wallpaper and soothing neutral tones. Exposed wood beams in the hallway, a testament to the hotel's past as a livery stable, add a touch of character. Beyond that, this is pretty much just a place to lay your head, with little lobby to speak of.

Little English Guesthouse B&B $$ (Map p442; ☑850-907-9777; www.littleenglish guesthouse.com; 737 Timberlane Rd; r $89-189;

(❋🛈) In a peaceful residential neighborhood 20 minutes from downtown Tallahassee, London-bred Tracey has turned her suburban house into a homey three-room B&B, complete with a friendly golden retriever. Rooms feel like staying at your Anglophile aunt's house, with beige carpet and coat-of-arms knickknacks.

✖ Eating

Catfish Pad
SEAFOOD $

(Map p442; www.catfishpad.com; 4229 W Pensacola St; mains $4-11; ◷11am-3pm & 5-9pm Mon-Sat) There's no doubt you're in the South at this home-style seafood joint, in a fluorescent-lit strip mall west of town. For 35 cents, you can get a fried mullet backbone – locals love to gnaw the bits of fish off the spiky bones. Or just go for a plate of cornmeal-battered catfish with a side of grits, chased down with a cup of sweet tea. Yum.

Reangthai
THAI $$

(Map p442; ☏850-386-7898; reangthai.com; 2740 Capital Circle NE; mains $13-20; ◷11am-2pm Tue-Fri, 5-10pm Mon-Sat) Thai food junkies (guilty as charged) proclaim Reangthai the real deal. Elegant, despite its strip mall setting, it serves the kind of spicy, fish saucey, explode-in-your-mouth cuisine so many American Thai restaurants shy away from. Try the larb appetizer, bursting with chili and fresh lime.

Kool Beanz Café
FUSION $$

(Map p442; ☏850-224-2466; www.koolbeanz-café.com; 921 Thomasville Rd; mains $16-23; ◷11am-2pm Mon-Fri, 5:30-10pm Mon-Sat, 10:30am-2pm Sun) It's got a corny name but a wonderfully eclectic and homey vibe – plus great, creative fare. The menu changes daily, but you can count on finding anything from hummus plates to jerk-spiced scallops to duck in blueberry-ginger sauce.

Andrew's Downtown
AMERICAN, ITALIAN $$

(Map p444; ☏850-222-3444; www.andrewsdowntown.com; 228 S Adams St; downstairs mains $9-13, upstairs mains $14-36; ◷downstairs 11:30am-10pm, upstairs 6-10pm Mon-Sat) Downtown's see-and-be-seen spot, politicians love this two-level restaurant – Capital Grill & Bar is a casual burgers-and-beer spot with indoor and outdoor seating, while Andrew's 228 (upstairs) is an upscale neo-Tuscan restaurant serving creative fare like pork chops with butternut squash orzo.

🍷 Drinking & Entertainment

Most of the frat bars are in and around Tennessee St between Copeland St and Dewey St. There are a few good options around town too. For a comprehensive guide to cultural events in town, such as lectures and art exhibits, be sure to visit the handy online calendar at www.morethanyouthought.com.

Bradfordville Blues Club
MUSIC

(☏850-906-0766; www.bradfordvilleblues.com; 7152 Moses Lane; tickets $15-20; ◷8pm-2am Fri & Sat) Don't be creeped out by the long drive down a quiet dirt road. You'll be glad you braved it when you arrive at the famed cinderblock building, where the friendly, old-time hippie hosts fired-up blues artists ranging from the known to the about-to-be. Torches and a raging bonfire light the yard, and the club's small tabletops bear painted portraits of blues greats from Bobby Rush to Gatemouth Brown. From the intersection of Thomasville Rd (Hwy 319) and I-10 (exit 301), head north on Thomasville Rd 4.5 miles; turn right onto Bradfordville Rd and follow it 3 miles then turn right onto Sam's Lane (there's a sign lit by a torch) and follow a bumpy, short dirt road. Veer left at the fork in the road; it's at the top of the hill.

Winery at the Red Bar
WINE BAR

(Map p442; www.thewinerytallahassee.com; 1122 Thomasville Rd) Located in the hip heart of Midtown, the sleek, low-lit Red Bar lounge features tons of wines by the glass, flight or bottle, plus a great selection of beers. Its winery, meanwhile, has homemade casks fermenting constantly, and offers a unique feature: you can speak with a wine crafter about your favorite *vino* qualities, and then wait six weeks for the vintage to be ready for drinking; the wine is made available for purchase as your own private label!

Waterworks
BAR

(Map p442; 1133 Thomasville Rd) This popular, gay-friendly place in Midtown has a Polynesian tiki-bar theme, and packs 'em in with nights of live jazz and Latin salsa, as well as rotating DJs.

🛈 Information

Florida Welcome Center (Map p444; ☏850-488-6167; www.flausa.com; cnr Pensacola St & Duval St; ◷8am-5pm Mon-Fri) In the new Florida State Capitol, this is a must-visit resource.

Leroy Collins Leon County Public Library (200 W Park Ave; ◷10am-9pm Mon-Thu, to

Half an hour from Tallahassee, these two charming villages make nice day trips from the capital. Quincy, nicknamed 'Cola-Cola Town,' struck it rich in the early 20th century by investing, en masse, in Coke stock. There's an original 1905 Coca-Cola mural on E Jefferson St, and 36 blocks of stunning historic homes built on the dividends of America's favorite soft drink. Havana, 12 miles down the road, is a former cigar-making town (hence the name) known for its antiques shops, which make for a pleasant afternoon of exploring. Most are concentrated around 2nd St, and most are only open Wednesday to Sunday.

If you find yourself here for the night, Quincy's 1843-built **Allison House Inn** (☑888-904-2511; www.allisonhouseinn.com; 215 North Madison St; r $85-155; P 🛜) has six peaceful, antique-y rooms downtown. A few blocks away, **McFarlin House Bed & Breakfast Inn** (☑850-875-2526; www.mcfarlinhouse.com; 305 E King St; r $99-249; P) is a turreted 1895 Queen Anne with nine museum-piece (if froofy) rooms, and a sweet communal deck.

6pm Fri, 10am-5pm Sat, 1-6pm Sun) Plenty of free online computers; enter the parking lot from Call St.

Post office (Map p444; 216 W College Ave) Close to the center.

Tallahassee Area Convention & Visitors Bureau (Map p444; ☑850-413-9200, 800-628-2866; www.visittallahassee.com; 106 E Jefferson St; ☺8am-5pm Mon-Fri) Runs the excellent Visitor Information Center, with brochures on walking and driving tours.

❶ Getting There & Around

Tallahassee is 98 miles from Panama City Beach, 135 miles to Jacksonville, 192 miles from Pensacola, 120 miles from Gainesville and 470 miles from Miami. The main access road is I-10; to reach the Gulf Coast, follow Hwy 319 south to Hwy 98.

The tiny **Tallahassee Regional Airport** (Map p442; ☑850-891-7800; www.talgov.com/airport) is served by a couple of major and several minor airlines. It's about 5 miles southwest of downtown, off Hwy 263. There's no public transport; some hotels have shuttles, but otherwise a taxi to downtown costs upwards of $20. Call **Yellow Cab** (☑850-580-8080).

The **Greyhound bus station** (Map p444; 112 W Tennessee St) is at the corner of Duval, opposite the downtown StarMetro transfer center.

StarMetro (Map p444; www.talgov.com/starmetro) is the local bus service around the greater Tallahassee area and has a main transfer point downtown on Tennessee St at Adams St. Fares are $1.25.

Around Tallahassee

You'll find historic sites, natural wonders and an abundance of antiquing opportunities in the fascinatingly diverse area surrounding Florida's capital.

WAKULLA SPRINGS STATE PARK
Glowing an otherworldly aqua and overhung with Spanish moss, the natural spring at the center of this 6000-acre **park** (www.floridastateparks.org/wakullasprings; 550 Wakulla Park Dr; vehicle $6) feels like something from the set of an exotic adventure movie – in fact, parts of the old Johnny Weismuller *Tarzan* movies were filmed here, as were parts of *The Creature from the Black Lagoon*. The spring, which gushes 1.2 billion gallons of water daily, is deep and ancient – in 1850, scientist Sarah Smith discovered the bones of an ancient mastodon at the bottom; since then the remains of at least nine other Ice Age mammals have been found.

If it's warm out, you can go for a swim in the deep, gin-clear waters, or dive off the elevated platform. But don't miss the chance to take a 40-minute guided **river cruise** (adult/child $8/5; ☺11am-3pm), which glide under moss-draped bald cypress trees and past an array of creatures, including precious manatees (usually in spring), massive alligators, tribes of red-bellied turtles and graceful wading birds, including anhingas, green herons and white ibises. On days when the spring is clear (and not after a storm, when the churned-up sludge ruins visibility), **glass-bottom boat tours** (adult/child $8/5; ☺11am-3pm) allow you to peer down the spring's 125ft depths. There are also various nature trails for strolling. Pick up a guide from the rangers or Wakulla Springs Lodge.

Time has stood still at the faded 1937 **Wakulla Springs Lodge** (☑850-224-5950; www.floridastateparks.org/wakullasprings; r $95-150), an immense (and immensely charming) Spanish-style building with an enormous faux stone fireplace in the lobby, an

THE PANHANDLE AROUND TALLAHASSEE

old-fashioned soda fountain in the gift shop, and an 11-foot stuffed gator called 'Old Joe' near the reception desk (he was killed by poachers in 1966 – the culprits remain at large). The 27 basic, slightly scruffy rooms have original marble floors, walk-in wardrobes and, blessedly, no TVs. The lodge is also ecofriendly, with low-flow toilets, energy-efficient lighting and landscaping that uses minimal water. The lodge's excellent **Ball Room Restaurant** (☑850-224-5950; mains $12-19; ◷7:30-10am, 11:30am-2pm & 6-8pm), named for financier Edward Ball who built the lodge, is a favorite dining spot with Tallahassee locals – try the fried chicken and the famous bean soup.

APALACHICOLA NATIONAL FOREST
☑850

The largest of Florida's three national forests, the **Apalachicola National Forest** (day-use areas $5; ◷8am-sunset) occupies almost 938 sq miles – more than half a million acres – of the Panhandle from just west of Tallahassee to the Apalachicola River. Made up of lowlands, pine, cypress hammocks and oaks, dozens of species call the area home including mink, gray and red foxes, coyotes, six bat species, beavers, red cockaded woodpeckers, alligators, Florida black bears and the elusive Florida panther. A total of 68.7 miles of the Florida National Scenic Trail extends through the forest, as well.

◉ Sights & Activities

Fort Gadsden Historic Site   HISTORIC SITE
In the west of the forest, this is the former location of an 1814-built British fort armed by African American and Native American soldiers, who the British armed and trained to defend against Spain's hold on Florida. The fort was blown to pieces two years later, killing more than 200 people, but its rebuilt fortification would later be used by Confederate troops. These days it's a green, serene picnic area, with an interpretive trail detailing its history. From Hwy 65, turn west on Forest Rd 129 then south on Forest Rd 129B.

Hiking & Cycling   OUTDOORS
On the eastern side of the forest is the 7.5-mile **Munson Hills Loop** bicycle trail, which spurs to the Tallahassee-St Marks Historic Railroad State Trail (p445). Experienced off-road cyclists can tackle this area made up of hammock, dunes, hills and brush, though its soft sand can make this a challenging route. If you run out of steam halfway through, take the Tall Pine Shortcut out of the trail,

roughly at the halfway point, for a total distance of 4.5 miles.

More than 6 miles of trails and boardwalks marked with interpretive signs wind past sinks and swamps in the **Leon Sinks Geological Area** (vehicle $3; ◷8am-sunset). Be sure to stay on the trails, as the karst (terrain affected by the underlying limestone bedrock dissolving) here is still evolving, and new sinkholes could appear anytime. One of the best viewing spots is the observation platform at Big Dismal Sink, where you'll see ferns, dogwoods and dozens of other lush plants descending its steep walls. The sinks are at the eastern end of the forest, just west of Hwy 319, about 10 miles south of Tallahassee.

Roughly 74 miles of the **Florida National Scenic Trail** (see p480) cuts a northwest-southeast swath through the forest. Prepare to get soaked if you opt for the Bradwell Bay Wilderness section, which involves some waist-deep swamp tramping. You can pick up the trail at the southeastern gateway, just east of Forest Rd 356 on Hwy 319; or the northwestern corner on Hwy 12.

Water Sports   WATER SPORTS
You can sunbathe on the white sandy shores or swim in the waters of **Silver Lake** (close to Tallahassee in the northeast of the forest on Forest Rd 370), **Wright Lake** (Forest Rd 379 in the southwest of the forest) and **Camel Lake** (off Hwy 12 in the northwest of the forest), all of which have facilities and picnic areas.

There are also plentiful opportunities for canoeing along the forest's rivers and waterways. Information on canoeing in the area and canoe rental is available from either ranger station, or visit the excellent website for **Florida Greenways and Trails** (www.dep.state.fl.us/gwt/guide), which has maps and updated lists of outfitters in the surrounding towns. Canoe rental costs around $25 to $35 per day.

Powerboats are allowed on the rivers, but not on the glassy lakes.

⌖ Sleeping

None of the campgrounds have hookups. For developed camping ($10), head to Camel Lake and Wright Lake, which have full bathrooms with hot showers, shelters and picnic tables.

Less-developed campgrounds ($4) with drinking water and vault toilets include Hickory Landing (from Sumatra, take Hwy

65 south; turn right on Forest Rd 101 and left on 101B), while primitive camping areas (drinking water but no toilets) include Wood Lake (from Sopchoppy, take Hwy 375 to Hwy 22 west, then take Hwy 340 south to Hwy 338).

ⓘ Information

The western half of the forest is controlled by the **Apalachicola Ranger Station** (☎850-643-2282; 11152 NW SR 20, Bristol), northwest of the forest near the intersection of Hwy 12 and 20, just south of Bristol. The eastern half is managed by the **Wakulla Ranger Station** (☎850-926-3561; 57 Taff Dr, Crawfordville), just off Hwy 319 behind the Winn Dixie in Crawfordville; the ranger stations operate together.

NATURAL BRIDGE BATTLEFIELD HISTORIC STATE PARK

Fifteen miles southeast of Tallahassee, this historic site (vehicle $3; ☉8am-sunset) is where a ragtag group of Confederate soldiers prevented Union troops from reaching Tallahassee in 1865. Today it's a peaceful picnic spot. In March costumed villagers and soldiers stage a battle reenactment, complete with a booming cannon. From Tallahassee, take Hwy 363 south to Natural Bridge Rd in Woodville.

Steinhatchee

☎352 / POP 1500

Talk about unexpected Florida! Steinhatchee (steen-hatch-ie) is an under-the-radar fisherman's haven that sits in a secret crevice of the Big Bend and beneath towering pines, mossy oaks and pink, juicy sunsets. The sleepy hamlet's claim to fame is its scallop season, which runs from July to early September and brings up to 1000 boats on its opening day to the otherwise peaceful waters of Dead Man's Bay. The season is kind of like a twisted Easter egg hunt, with locals and visitors taking a mesh bag, donning a snorkel and mask, and snatching up their own seafood as they swim. Locals will often clean your catch in exchange for half the meat.

🏃 Activities

Fishing & Water Sports   FISHING, WATER SPORTS
Depending on the season, cobia, sea trout, mackerel, tarpon and the famous scallops are plentiful.

For a guided fishing charter with locals who know the waters, try **Captain Tony Jackson** (☎386-294-2216; www.tjcharters.com)

or **Reel Song Charters** (☎352-895-7544; www.reelsongcharters.com), who specialize in inshore fishing for mackerel and trout. Trips cost from $400 per day for up to four people. For offshore fishing to hook snapper, **Booger Charters** (☎352-498-2705; www.boogercharters.com) guarantees that trips land fish or you don't have to pay. Booger Charters' offshore charter rates are $1095/1295 for 10/12 hours.

River Haven Marina & Motel (☎352-498-0709; www.riverhavenmarinaandmotel.com; 1110 Riverside Dr) rents a variety of fishing boats from $80 per half day and can put you in touch with fishing-charter guides. River Haven also rents kayaks (single/tandem per half-day $30/40, per day $50/60), including pickup and dropoff, which are great for exploring the myriad waterways.

For a full list of fishing guides, charter operators and boat rental services, check out www.steinhatcheeriver.info.

🛏 Sleeping & Eating

Steinhatchee Landing   RESORT $$$
(☎352-498-3513; www.steinhatcheelanding.com; 203 Ryland Circle; cottages $146-650; ❄☀♿🐾) This cute-as-a-button riverside resort community has one- through four-bedroom cottages clustered around a loop road, with a pool, country store, spa, and lusciously manicured grounds bursting with hibiscus and palms. Good for families.

Steinhatchee River Inn Motel   MOTEL $
(☎352-498-4049; 600 Riverside Dr; r from $79; ❄☀♿) This classic motel-style inn has decent-sized rooms and is close to the marina. Some rooms have kitchens, and all have TVs, coffeemakers, wi-fi and refrigerators.

Roy's   SEAFOOD $$
(www.roys-restaurant.com; 100 1st Ave; mains $10-23; ☉11am-9pm) Since 1969, Roy's, which sits overlooking the gulf, has been a favorite for seafood. The standard style is fried, but if you ask they'll serve it spiced and broiled, nestled up to sides that include heaping portions of grits, fries, baked potatoes and hushpuppies.

ⓘ Information

There's no visitor information center, but information is available online at www.steinhatchee.com, www.steinhatchee.info or from the marinas, motels and resort.

THE ROAD TO NOWHERE

In Jena, just east of Steinhatchee, turn south onto Rock Creek Cut Off Rd/ Hwy 361. Drive. Keep driving. Yep, keep driving. Eventually the road will turn to dirt, then back to rough, one-lane pavement. This is the Road to Nowhere, supposedly the former runway for drug smugglers' planes carrying loads of cocaine in from South America. Whatever its original purpose, the road now serves as an entryway into one of the most isolated and desolately beautiful stretches of Gulf Coast, passing through primeval forest and grassy savannah before ending, rather abruptly, at the edge of a vast and barren salt marsh. Watch out for snakes.

ℹ Getting There & Away

Coming from either the north or south, take Hwy 19 (also called Hwy 19/27 and Hwy 19/98) to the crossroads with a blinking light, then drive west on Hwy 51 to the end, about 12 miles.

Manatee Springs State Park

Between Cedar Key and Steinhatchee, this park (www.floridastateparks.org/manateesprings; 11650 NW 115th St; $6/vehicle; ⊙8am-sundown) is worth a stop, especially for a dip into the 72°F crystalline waters of the beautiful spring.

You can also scuba dive (bring your own gear and buddy, and register at the office) at the springhead, which gushes 117 million gallons of water per day, or canoe or kayak along the spring run (boat rentals $8 to $10 hourly). Scuba diving, canoeing and kayaking can be organized through the park office. On dry land – which is a uniquely spongy combo of sand and limestone shaded by tupelo, cypress and pine trees – there's an 8.5-mile-long hiking/cycling trail, the **North End Trail**, on your right as you enter the park. Camping ($20) is also available at 94 shady sites with picnic tables and ground grills. A highlight here is the wheelchair-accessible raised timber boardwalk that traces the narrow spring down to the Suwannee River as it flows to the gulf and out to sea.

Ranger programs include guided canoe journeys, moonlight hikes, nature walks and occasional covered-wagon rides. Contact the park office for details.

Cedar Key

☑352 / POP 950

Jutting 3 miles into the Gulf of Mexico, this windswept and isolated island has a bit of a wild frontier feel: an enchantingly ramshackle downtown of historic buildings, roadhouses with parking lots full of Harleys, long stretches of uninhabited bayou, meadows and bay. The otherworldly landscape sings with marshes that reflect candy-colored sunsets, and tiny hills offering sweeping island views. Cedar Key is just one of 100 islands (13 of which are part of the Cedar Keys National Wildlife Refuge) that make up this coastal community, which is gloriously abundant with wildlife and friendly, small-town vibes.

As the western terminus of the trans-Florida railroad in the late 1800s, Cedar Key was one of Florida's largest towns, second only to St Augustine. Its primary industry was wood (for Faber pencils), which eventually deforested the islands; a 1896 hurricane destroyed what was left. Consequently, the trees here are less than 100 years old. Aquaculture has recently revived the town's economy: spurred by government subsidies when net fishing was banned, it's now the largest clam farming region in the country.

◉ Sights & Activities

Cedar Keys National Wildlife Refuge   WILDLIFE RESERVE
(www.fws.gov/cedarkeys) Home to 250 species of bird (including ibises, pelicans, egrets, herons and double-crested cormorants), 10 species of reptile and one romantic lighthouse, the 13 islands in this refuge can only be reached by boat. The islands' interiors are generally closed to the public, but during daylight hours you can access most of the white-sand beaches, which provide great opportunities for both fishing and manatee viewing. Tidewater Tours (☑352-543-9523; www.tidewatertours.com) runs two-hour nature tours of the islands for $26, and rents pontoons and skiffs for solo exploration (from $60 for three hours) – be sure to time your visit to not get stuck on the mudflats.

Cedar Key Museum State Park   MUSEUM
(12231 SW 166th St; admission $2; ⊙10am-5pm Thu-Mon) This eclectic museum features the

historic house, remodeled to its 1902 state, of St Clair Whitman. A main player in both the pencil factory and the local fiber mill, he arrived in the area in 1882 and started collecting everything he saw: insects, butterflies, glass, sea glass, bottles and infinite varieties of seashells. After your visit, enjoy a bucolic walk on the surrounding nature trails.

Cedar Key Museum MUSEUM
(www.cedarkeymuseum.org; 609 2nd St; adult/child $1/50¢; ⊙1-4pm Sun-Fri, 11am-5pm Sat) Run by Cedar Key Historical Society, this small museum is worth a peek to check out its exhibits of Native American, Civil War and seafood industry artifacts, and especially for its extensive collection of Cedar Key historic photographs.

Kayaking KAYAKING
The waterways and estuaries in and around the refuge make for superb kayaking. Several companies operate ecotours, including **Kayak Cedar Keys** (☑352-543-9447; www.kayakcedarkeys.com; tours from $60), which also rents kayaks (from $30/50 per three hours/day) and can arrange to take you to offshore clam beds.

🛏 Sleeping & Eating

There are plenty of cute, family-run motels in the area. Dock St – a little spit of land jutting into the bay just across from downtown – is crowded with pubs and seafood restaurants, and takes on a raucous character on busy nights.

TOP CHOICE **Island Hotel** HOTEL $
(☑352-543-5111, 800-432-4640; www.islandhotel-cedarkey.com; 224 2nd St at B St; r $80-135; ❋🕏) A night in this old-fashioned, 1859 tabby shell and oak building will relax you for sure. Listed on the National Register of Historic Places, it has 10 simple and romantic rooms with original hand-cut wooden walls, a wraparound balcony with rocking chairs, a history of notable guests including John Muir and President Grover Cleveland and, by all reports, as many as 13 resident ghosts. It's also home to the island's fanciest restaurant, specializing in baked and sautéed fresh-caught seafood. Mains are $16 to $26 and it is open Tuesday to Sunday.

Faraway Inn MOTEL $$
(☑352-543-5330; www.farawayinn.com; cnr 3rd & G Sts; motel r from $70, cottages from $140; ❋🕏📶🐾) Overlooking a silent, glassy stretch

---

DETOUR: UPON THE SUWANNEE RIVER

Flowing 207 miles, the Suwannee River is immortalized by Stephen Foster in Florida's state song, 'Old Folks at Home.' Foster himself never set eyes on the river, but thought 'Suwannee' (or 'Swannee,' as his map apparently stated, hence his corruption of the spelling) sounded suitably Southern. As it happened he was right; the river winds through wild Spanish moss-draped countryside from the far north of the state to the Gulf of Mexico in the curve of the Big Bend. See it for yourself along the **Suwannee River Wilderness Trail** (www.suwanneeriver.com), which covers 169 miles of the river to the gulf, with nine 'hubs' – cabins – spaced one day's paddle apart. All are now open, though heavily booked, so reserve as early as possible. River camps along the banks of the trail are also in the pipeline.

The trail starts at the **Stephen Foster State Folk Cultural Center** (☑386-397-2733, 800-326-3521; vehicle $5, campsites $20, cabins $100; ⊙park 8am-sunset, museum & carillon 9am-5pm), north of White Springs. With lush green hills and monolithic live oak trees, the park has a museum of Florida history that you'd swear is a 19th-century plantation. The three-day Florida Folk Festival, a celebration of traditional Floridian music, crafts, food and culture, takes place here every Memorial Day weekend. Next door to the park, canoe rentals are available from **American Canoe Adventures** (☑386-397-1309; www.aca1.com; 10610 Bridge St, White Springs), which offers day trips ($35 to $60, depending on mileage and terrain), where you're transported upstream, then paddle down. Overnight canoe rentals are $25.

The **Suwannee River State Park** (☑386-362-2746; 20185 CR 132, Live Oak; vehicle $5, camping $22, cabins $100), at the confluence of the Withlacoochee and Suwannee Rivers, has Civil War fortifications. The five cabins sleep up to six people. The park is 13 miles west of Live Oak, just off US 90 – follow the signs.

of bay, this funky little motel complex has rooms and cottages decorated in driftwood art and bright colored prints. Guests chill on waterfront porch swings for mind-blowing sunsets.

Tony's SEAFOOD **$$**
(www.tonyschowder.com; 597 2nd St; mains $8-30; ⊙11am-8pm Sun-Thu, to 10pm Fri & Sat) Creamy, whole clam-studded clam chowder – Tony's claim to fame – is truly superlative, and a reason to visit this otherwise mediocre seafood restaurant in a downtown storefront.

Pickled Pelican SEAFOOD, PUB **$$**
(Dock St; mains $8-14; ⊙11am-8pm Mon-Thu, to 9pm Fri & Sat, to 4pm Sun; ▣) Probably the most popular of the Dock St eateries, this 2nd-floor pub specializes in beach-y bar food – fried pickles, burgers, fish sandwiches.

❶ Information

The **Cedar Keys Chamber of Commerce** (☑352-543-5600; www.cedarkey.org; 525 2nd St; ⊙10am-1pm Mon, Wed & Fri) offers local information. Across the street is the **post office** (518 2nd St; ⊙9am-5pm Mon-Fri, to 1pm Sat) and the **library** (460 2nd St; ⊙10am-4pm Mon, Wed & Thu, 4-8pm Tue, 10am-1pm Sat), which offers free internet access.

❶ Getting There & Around

There's no public transport to Cedar Key, but driving is easy: take Hwy 19/98 or I-75 to Hwy 24 and follow it southwest to the end.

You'll see locals zipping around in golf ('gulf') carts, which are perfect for traversing the little island; try **Cedar Key Gulf Kart Company** (☑352-543-5090; www.gulfkartcompany.com; cnr 1st St & A St; carts per 2hr/day from $22/55).

Understand Florida

Florida Today

House for Sale

Florida is a boom-and-bust place. People find something they can get rich with – oranges, real estate, tourism – and they ride it into the sky until nature, the stock market or their own exuberance sends them tumbling back to earth.

This truism is being keenly felt today as Florida tries to recover from a double whammy. First, there has been the national real-estate market collapse, which began in 2007 (sparked by banking's home-mortgage crisis). Among US states, Florida felt the effects first and hardest. As home prices tumbled, the construction industry tanked and growth essentially flatlined to its lowest point in 30 years. Foreclosures flooded the state, so that by 2010, 18% of Florida homes were vacant. Median home prices, meanwhile, tumbled to virtually half their 2006 value.

Without real estate, construction and population growth, Florida's economy has only one other main pillar: tourism. Yet this suffered a major blow following the April 2010 Deepwater Horizon oil spill in the Gulf of Mexico (the worst in US history). Even though only Panhandle beaches were touched by any oil, bad press and fear kept visitors away from Florida's entire Gulf Coast. Though impossible to calculate exactly, it's estimated Florida lost well over $3 billion in tourism-related spending.

By 2011 all Florida's Gulf beaches were clean of tar balls, and the state was sending out an urgent message to you, dear reader: please come back! (For more, see p427.)

Also, while real estate, construction, tourism and growth were again showing a pulse by 2011, it was insufficient to make up the estimated $3.6 billion shortfall in the state's $70 billion 2011 budget. How to bridge that gap – whether solely through budget cuts or by a combination of cuts and tax hikes – divided Florida's politics along now-predictable lines.

» Median home price 2006: $257,800

» Median home price 2010: $143,400

» Vacant homes 2010: 1.5 million

» Unemployment rate 2010: 11.5%

» Population growth 2006–07: +331,000

» Population growth 2008–09: -56,736

Major Media

Miami Herald (www.miami herald.com)

Orlando Sentinel (www.orlando sentinel.com)

St Petersburg Times (www .tampabay.com)

Tampa Tribune (www.tampatrib .com)

Florida Reads

Pilgrim in the Land of Alligators (Jeff Klinkenberg) Profiles of wacky Floridians.

Salvaging the Real Florida (Bill Belleville) Moving nature essays of a fragile landscape.

Paradise Screwed (Carl Hiaasen) *Miami Herald* columns of biting sarcasm and outrage.

The Orchid Thief (Susan Orlean) Yankee journalist loses her head in the swamp.

Weird Florida (Charlie Carlson) Too easy. Like shooting two-headed fish in a barrel.

belief systems
(% of population)

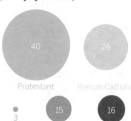

40
Protestant

26
Roman Catholic

3
Jewish

15
Others

16
Nonreligious

if Florida were 100 people

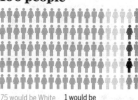

75 would be White
16 would be Black
2 would be Asian

1 would be Native American
6 would be other

*According to the US Census Bureau, Hispanics may be of any race so are included in applicable race categories.

A State Divided

Ever since the controversial 2000 Bush-Gore presidential election (see p463), Florida politics has been almost evenly divided between Republicans and Democrats. This held true in 2010, when the Tea Party–backed Republican Rick Scott won the governorship by a razor-thin margin of 1.15%, or 61,550 votes out of over 5.3 million cast.

Then within months of taking office, Governor Scott's statewide approval rating sank to 35% due to a series of actions: he refused to join a federal lawsuit to recover oil-spill-related losses; he scuttled a high-speed rail initiative between Orlando and Tampa; he enacted sweeping education reform that ended teacher tenure and tied pay to student test scores; and he vowed to balance the state budget through cuts alone.

Florida's mercurial political landscape has nationwide implications. Once again, most observers anticipate that the coming 2012 presidential election will be decided by Florida, which voted for President Obama by 50.9% in the 2008 election. However, the national Republican party, which is holding its 2012 nominating convention in Tampa, fervently hopes Governor Scott rallies, rather than alienates, state voters.

Other important issues galvanize residents – particularly the uncertain future of environmental programs like Florida Forever and Everglades restoration. Everything likely hinges on how fast Florida can sweep away the economic gray clouds. If history is a guide, a new boom must be just around the corner, ready to spark another frenzy of immigration, real estate and tourism, and once again brightening the outlook of the Sunshine State.

The *Miami Herald* publishes a separate Spanish-language version, *El Nuevo Herald* (www.elnuevo herald.com). This is more than a translation; it's different news aimed at Miami's Cuban and Latin citizens, and treats events in Cuba and Latin America with the same urgency English-language media give to Washington.

Florida on Film

Key Largo (1948) Bogart, Bacall.

Scarface (1983) Al Pacino.

The Birdcage (1996) Robin Williams, Nathan Lane as gay lovers.

Sunshine State (2002) Florida developers vs mermaid.

Adaptation (2002) Surreal adaption of *The Orchid Thief*.

Wild Etiquette

» When hiking, stay on the trail, pick up your trash.

» Never pick wildflowers, especially orchids.

» On beaches, never approach nesting sea turtles or hatchling runs. Adhere to nighttime lights-out policies when posted.

» When snorkeling or diving, never touch coral reefs.

» Never chase or feed wild dolphins or manatees; admire but don't touch.

» Never feed alligators; they bite.

History

Florida has the oldest recorded history of any US state, and it also might qualify as the most notorious and bizarre. Something about this swampy peninsula invites exaggeration and inflames desire, then gleefully bedevils those who pursue their visions. Just ask the Spanish. Possibly spurred by Cuban slave-trader tales of 'rejuvenating waters,' Ponce de León arrived in 1513 pursuing the legendary 'fountain of youth.' Under many guises, his mythic quest has plagued Florida ever since.

Spanish explorers also chased rumors of golden cities and claimed they saw mermaids, but they found no precious metals and what they encountered were manatees, not fish-tailed women. Yet only a fun-house mirror separates them from us: in Florida, mermaids perform daily, aging snowbirds flock for rejuvenation, Disney World promises a Magic Kingdom, manatees are a tourist attraction, and real-estate developers long ago discovered how to get gold from a swamp. Simply drain it.

Florida's modern history truly begins with the late-19th-century tycoons who dried the marshes, built railroads and resorts, and then ceaselessly promoted Florida as an 'emerald kingdom by southern seas.' They succeeded beyond their wildest dreams. Since then, each era has been marked by wild-eyed speculation inspiring great tides of immigration – from the 1920s real-estate mania to the 1950s orange boom to the 1960s Cuban exodus to the 1980s influx of Latin Americans – each inevitably followed by a crash: the Great Depression, race riots, cartel cocaine wars, 1992's Hurricane Andrew, and so on.

Today, Florida's boom-and-bust cycle continues. Whatever else, it makes for great storytelling.

Historic Resorts & Mansions

» Tampa Bay Hotel, Henry B Plant Museum, Tampa

» Hotel Ponce de León, St Augustine

» The Breakers, Palm Beach

» Whitehall Mansion, Flagler Museum, Palm Beach

» Biltmore Hotel, Coral Gables

First Inhabitants & Seminoles

Florida's original inhabitants never organized into large, cohesive tribes. For some 11,500 years, they remained split into numerous small

TIMELINE	10,000 BC	AD 500	1513
	After crossing the Bering Strait from Siberia some 50,000 years earlier, humans arrive in Florida, hunting mastodon and saber-toothed tigers, at the end of the last ice age.	Indigenous peoples settle in year-round villages and begin farming, cultivating the 'three sisters' of corn, beans and squash, plus pumpkins, lemons and sunflowers.	Ponce de León discovers Florida, landing south of Cape Canaveral, believing it an island. Since it's around Easter, he names it La Florida, 'The Flowery Land' or 'Feast of Flowers.'

chiefdoms or villages, becoming more settled and agricultural in the north and remaining more nomadic and warlike in the south.

The Apalachee in Florida's Panhandle developed the most complex agriculture-based society, but other tribes included the Timucua in northern Florida, the Tequesta along the central Atlantic Coast, and the fierce Calusa in southern Florida. Legends say it was a poison-tipped Calusa arrow that killed Ponce de León.

The most striking evidence of these early cultures is shell mounds or middens. Florida's ancestral peoples ate well, and their discarded shells reached 30ft high and themselves became the foundations of villages, as at Mound Key.

THE UNCONQUERED SEMINOLES

The US waged war on Florida's Seminoles three times. The First Seminole War, from 1817 to 1818, was instigated by Andrew Jackson, who ruthlessly attacked the Seminoles as punishment for sheltering runaway slaves and attacking US settlers.

Trouble was, Florida was controlled by Spain. After Jackson took over Pensacola, Spain protested this foreign military incursion, forcing Jackson to halt.

In 1830, 'Old Hickory,' now President Andrew Jackson, passed the Indian Removal Act, which aimed to move all Native Americans west of the Mississippi River. Some Seminoles agreed to give up their lands and move to reservations, but not all. In 1835 US troops arrived to enforce agreements, and Osceola, a Seminole leader, attacked an army detachment, triggering the Second Seminole War.

The war was fought guerrilla style by 2000 or so Seminoles in swamps and hammocks, and it's considered one of the most deadly and costly Indian wars in US history. In October 1837, Osceola was captured under a flag of truce and later died in captivity, but the Seminoles kept fighting. In 1842 the US finally called off its army, having spent $20 million and seen the deaths of 1500 US soldiers.

Thousands of Seminoles had been killed or marched to reservations, but hundreds survived and took refuge in the Everglades. In 1855 a US army survey team went looking for them, but the Seminoles killed them first. The resulting backlash turned into the Third Seminole War, which ended after Chief Billy Bowlegs was paid to go west in 1858.

But 200 to 300 Seminoles refused to sign a peace treaty and slipped away again into the Everglades. Technically, these Seminoles never surrendered and remain the only 'unconquered' Native American tribe.

In the 1910s, brutally impoverished, the Seminoles discovered that tourists would pay to watch them in their temporary camps, and soon 'Seminole villages' were a mainstay of Florida tourist attractions, often featuring alligator wrestling and Seminole 'weddings.'

In 1957, the US officially recognized the **Seminole Tribe** (www.semtribe.com), and in 1962, the **Miccosukee Tribe** (www.miccosukee.com). For more history, visit the Ah-Tah-Thi-Ki Museum (p147).

1539
Hernando de Soto arrives in Florida with 800 men, seeking rumored cities of gold. He fights Indians, camps near Tallahassee, but finding no precious metals, keeps marching west.

1565
Pedro Menéndez de Avilés founds St Augustine, which becomes the first permanent European settlement in the New World and is the oldest city in the continental US.

» Statue of Pedro Menéndez de Avilés, St Augustine (p328)

When the Spanish arrived in the 1500s, the indigenous population numbered perhaps 250,000. Over the next 200 years, European diseases killed 80% of them. The rest were killed by war or sold into slavery, so that by the mid-1700s, virtually none of Florida's original inhabitants were left.

However, as the 18th century unfolded, Creeks and other tribes from the north migrated into Florida, driven by or enlisted in the partisan European feuds for New World territory. These tribes intermingled and intermarried, and in the late 1700s they were joined by numerous runaway black slaves, whom they welcomed into their society.

At some point, these uncooperative, fugitive, mixed peoples occupying Florida's interior were dubbed 'Seminoles,' a corruption of the Spanish word *cimarrones,* meaning 'free people' or 'wild ones.' Defying European rule and ethnic category, they were soon considered too free for the newly independent United States, who brought war to them.

Five Flags: Florida Gets Passed Around

All Florida schoolchildren are taught that Florida has been ruled by five flags: those of Spain, France, Britain, the US and the Confederacy.

Spain claimed Florida in 1513 – when explorer Ponce de León arrived. Five more Spanish expeditions followed (and one French, raising its flag on the St Johns River), and nothing bore fruit until 1565, when St Augustine was settled. A malarial, easily pillaged outpost that produced little income, St Augustine truly succeeded at only one thing: spreading the Catholic religion. Spanish missionaries founded 31 missions across Florida, converting and educating Native Americans, occasionally with notable civility.

In 1698 Spain established a permanent military fort at Pensacola, which was thence variously captured and recaptured by the Spanish, French, English and North Americans for a century.

Spain found itself on the losing side of the 1754–63 French and Indian War, having backed France in its fight with England. Afterward, Spain bartered with the English, giving them Florida in return for the captured Havana. Almost immediately, the 3000 or so Spaniards in Florida gratefully boarded boats for Cuba.

The British held Florida for 20 years and did marginally well, producing indigo, rice, oranges and timber. But in 1783, as Britain and the US were tidying up accounts after the close of the American Revolution, Britain handed Florida back to Spain – which this time had supported the winning side, the US.

The second Spanish period, from 1783 to 1819, was marked by one colossal misjudgment. Spain needed settlers, and quickly, so it vigorously promoted immigration to Florida, but this backfired when, by 1810, those

Seminole & Indian Resources

» Ah-Tah-Thi-Ki Museum (www.ahtahthiki.com)
» The Museum (www.flamuseum.com)
» Heritage of the Ancient Ones (www.ancientnative.org)

1702	1776	1823	1835
In their ongoing struggle with Spain and France over New World colonies, the British burn St Augustine to the ground; two years later they destroy 13 Spanish missions in Florida.	The American Revolution begins, but Florida's two colonies don't rebel. They remain loyal to the British crown, and soon English Tories flood south into Florida to escape the fighting.	Tallahassee is established as Florida's territorial capital because it's halfway between Pensacola and St Augustine. Later attempts to move the state capital fail.	In attacks coordinated by Seminole leader Osceola, Seminoles destroy five sugar plantations on Christmas Day and soon after kill 100 US soldiers marching near Tampa, launching the Second Seminole War.

immigrants (mainly North American settlers) started demanding 'independence' from Spain. Within a decade, Spain threw up its hands. It gave Florida back to the US for cash in a treaty formalized in 1822. In 1845 Florida became the 27th state of the US, but in 16 short years, it would reconsider that relationship and raise its fifth flag.

From Civil War to Civil Rights

In 1838 the Florida territory was home to about 48,000 people, of whom 21,000 were black slaves. By 1860, 15 years after statehood, Florida's population was 140,000, of whom 40% were slaves, most of them working on highly profitable cotton plantations.

Thus, unsurprisingly, when Abraham Lincoln was elected president on an antislavery platform, Florida joined the Confederacy of southern states that seceded from the Union in 1861. During the ensuing Civil War, which lasted until 1865, only moderate fighting occurred in Florida.

Afterward, from 1865 to 1877, the US government imposed 'Reconstruction' on all ex-Confederate states. Reconstruction protected the rights of freed blacks, and led to 19 blacks becoming elected to Florida's state congress. Yet this radical social and political upheaval led to a furious backlash.

When federal troops finally left, Florida 'unreconstructed' in a hurry, adopting a series of Jim Crow laws that segregated and disenfranchised blacks in every sphere of life – in restaurants and parks, on beaches and buses – while a poll tax kept blacks and the poor from voting. From then until the 1950s, black field hands in turpentine camps and cane fields worked under a forced-labor 'peonage' system, in which they couldn't leave till their wages paid off their debts, which of course never happened.

The Ku Klux Klan thrived, its popularity peaking in the 1920s, when Florida led the country in lynchings. Racial hysteria and violence were commonplace; most infamously, a white mob razed the entire town of Rosewood in 1923.

In 1954 the US Supreme Court ended legal segregation in the US with Brown v Board of Education, but in 1957 Florida's Supreme Court rejected this decision, declaring it 'null and void.' This sparked protests but little change until 1964, when a series of race riots and demonstrations, some led by Martin Luther King Jr, rocked St Augustine and helped spur passage of the national Civil Rights Act of 1964.

More race riots blazed across Florida cities in 1967 and 1968, after which racial conflict eased as Florida belatedly and begrudgingly desegregated itself. Florida's racial wounds healed equally slowly – as

Alleged Fountains of Youth

» Fountain of Youth Archaeological Park, St Augustine

» De Leon Springs State Park, Deland

» Warm Mineral Springs, Venice

1845	1861	1912	1926
Florida is admitted to the Union as the 27th state. Since it is a slave state, its admission is balanced by that of Iowa, a free state.	Voting 62 to seven, Florida secedes from the US, raising its fifth flag, that of the Confederacy. Florida's farms and cattle provide vital Confederate supplies during the ensuing Civil War.	'Flagler's Folly,' Henry Flagler's 128-mile overseas railroad connecting the Florida Keys, reaches Key West. It's hailed as the 'Eighth Wonder of the World' but is destroyed by a 1935 hurricane.	A major hurricane flattens and floods South Florida. Nearly 400 people die, most drowning when Lake Okeechobee bursts its dike. Two years later, another hurricane kills 2000 people.

evidenced by more race riots in the early 1980s. Today, despite much progress and the fact that Florida is one of the nation's most ethnically diverse states, these wounds still haven't completely healed.

Draining Swamps & Laying Rail

By the middle of the 19th century, the top half of Florida was reasonably well explored, but South Florida was still an oozing, mosquito-plagued swamp. So, in the 1870s, Florida inaugurated its first building boom by adopting laissez-faire economic policies centered on three things: unrestricted private development, minimal taxes, and land grants for railroads.

In 10 years, from 1881 to 1891, Florida's railroad miles quintupled, from 550 to 2566. Most of this track crisscrossed northern and central Florida, where the people were, but one rail line went south to nowhere. In 1886, railroad magnate Henry Flagler started building a railroad down the coast on the spectacular gamble that once he built it, people would come.

In 1896 Flagler's line stopped at the squalid village of Fort Dallas, which incorporated as the city of Miami that same year. Then, people came, and kept coming, and Flagler is largely credited with founding every town from West Palm Beach to Miami.

It's hard to do justice to what happened next, but it was madness, pure and simple – far crazier than Ponce's dream of eternal waters. Why, all South Florida needed was to get rid of that pesky *swamp*, and then it really *would* be paradise: a land of eternal sunshine and profit.

In 1900 Governor Napoleon Bonaparte Broward, envisioning an 'Empire of the Everglades,' set in motion a frenzy of canal building. Over the next 70 years, some 1800 miles of canals and levees were etched across Florida's porous limestone. These earthworks drained about half the Everglades (about 1.5 million acres) below Lake Okeechobee, replacing it with farms, cattle ranches, orange groves, sugarcane and suburbs.

From 1920 to 1925 the South Florida land boom swept the nation. In 1915 Miami Beach was a sand bar; by 1925 it had 56 hotels, 178 apartment buildings and three golf courses. In 1920 Miami had one skyscraper; by 1925, 30 were under construction. In 1925 alone, 2.5 million people moved to Florida. Real-estate speculators sold undeveloped land, undredged land, and then just the airy paper promises of land. Everything went like hotcakes.

Then, two hurricanes struck, in 1926 and 1928, and the party ended. The coup de grâce was the October 1929 stock-market crash, which took everyone's money. Like the nation, Florida plunged into the Depression, though the state rode it out better than most due to New Deal public works, tourism, and a highly profitable foray into rumrunning.

Best Florida Histories

» *The New History of Florida,* Michael Gannon

» *The Everglades: River of Grass,* Marjory Stoneman Douglas

» *Dreamers, Schemers & Scalawags,* Stuart McIver

» *The Enduring Seminoles,* Patsy West

» *Miami Babylon,* Gerald Posner

1933–40	1935	1941–45	1942
New Deal public-works projects employ 40,000 Floridians and help save Florida from the Depression. Most notable construction project is the Overseas Hwy through the Keys, replacing Flagler's railroad.	'Swami of the Swamp' Dick Pope opens Cypress Gardens, the USA's first theme park, with water-ski stunts, topiary and Southern belles. Allegedly, this inspires Walt Disney to create California's Disneyland.	US enters WWII. Two million men and women receive basic training in South Florida. At one point, the army commanders 85% of Miami Beach hotels to house personnel.	From January to August, German U-boats sink over two dozen tankers and ships off Florida's coast. By war's end, Florida holds nearly 3000 German POWs in 15 labor camps.

Tin-Can Tourists, Retirees & a Big-Eared Mouse

For the record, tourism is Florida's number-one industry, and this doesn't count retirees – the tourists who never leave.

Tourism didn't become a force in Florida until the 1890s, when Flagler built his coastal railroad and his exclusive Miami Beach resorts. In the 1920s, middle-class 'tin-can tourists' arrived via the new Dixie Hwy – driving Model Ts, sleeping in campers and cooking their own food.

In the 1930s, to get those tourists spending, savvy promoters created the first 'theme parks': Cypress Gardens and Silver Springs. But it wasn't until after WWII that Florida tourism exploded. During the war, Miami

BLACK MARKET FLORIDA

In 1919, when the US passed the 18th Amendment – making liquor illegal and inaugurating Prohibition – bootleggers discovered something that previous generations of black slaves and Seminoles knew well: Florida is a good place to hide.

Almost immediately Florida became, as the saying went, 'wet as a frog,' and soon fleets of ships and airplanes were bringing in Cuban and Jamaican rum, to be hidden in coves and dispersed nationwide.

Interestingly, Florida rumrunning was conducted mostly by local 'mom-and-pop' operations, not the mob, despite the occasional vacationing mobster like Al Capone. In this way, Prohibition really drove home the benefits of a thriving black market. When times were good, as in the 1920s, all that (illicit) money got launder-...um...pumped into real estate, making the good times unbelievably great. When hard times hit in the 1930s, out-of-work farmers could still make bathtub gin and pay the bills. Because of this often-explicit understanding, Miami bars served drinks with impunity throughout the 1920s, and local police simply kept walking.

In the 1960s and '70s, the story was repeated with marijuana. Down-on-their-luck commercial fisherman made a mint smuggling plastic-wrapped bails of pot, and suddenly Florida was asking, 'Recession? What recession?' West Florida experienced a condo boom.

In the 1980s, cocaine became the drug of choice. But this time the smugglers were Colombian cartels, and they did business with a gun, not a handshake. Bloody shoot-outs on Miami streets shocked Floridians (and inspired the *Miami Vice* TV show), but it didn't slow the estimated $10-billion drug business – and did you notice Miami's new skyline? In the 1980s so much cash choked Miami banks that smuggling currency itself became an industry – along with smuggling out guns to Latin America and smuggling in rare birds, flowers, and Cuban cigars.

By the 1990s the cartels were finished and banking laws were stricter, but some still believed that smuggling remained Florida's number-one industry.

1946	1947	1961	1969
Frozen concentrated orange juice is invented. As the nation's top orange producer, this event leads to Florida's orange boom, giving birth to the orange millionaires of the '50s and '60s.	Everglades National Park is established, successfully culminating a 19-year effort, led by Ernest Coe and Marjorie Stoneman Douglas, to protect the Everglades from the harm done by dredging and draining.	Brigade 2506, a 1300-strong volunteer army, invades Cuba's Bay of Pigs on April 16. President Kennedy withholds air support, leading to Brigade 2506's immediate defeat and capture by Fidel Castro.	On July 16, *Apollo 11* lifts off from Cape Canaveral and lands on the moon, winning the space race with the Russians. Five more lunar-bound rockets take off through 1972.

was a major military training ground, and afterward, many of those GIs returned with their families to enjoy Florida's sandy beaches at leisure.

In addition, after the war, social security kicked in, and the nation's aging middle class migrated south to enjoy their first taste of retirement. As old folks will, they came slowly but steadily, at a rate of a thousand a week, till they numbered in the hundreds of thousands and then millions. Many came from the East Coast, and quite a few were Jewish: by 1960, Miami Beach was 80% Jewish, creating a famous ethnic enclave.

Then one day in 1963, so the story goes, Walt Disney flew over central Florida, spotted the intersection of I-4 and the Florida Turnpike, and said, 'That's it.' In secret, he bought 43 sq miles of Orlando-area wetlands. Afterward, like an expert alligator wrestler, Disney successfully negotiated with the state of Florida and was granted unprecedented and unique municipal powers to build his tourist mecca.

Exempt from a host of state laws and building codes, largely self-governing, Disney World opened in 1971. How big did it become? In 1950, Florida received 4.5 million tourists, not quite twice its population. By the 1980s, Disney alone was drawing 40 million visitors a year, or four times the state population.

Disney had the Midas touch. In the shadow of the Magic Kingdom, Florida's old-school attractions – Weeki Wachee, Seminole Village, Busch Gardens; all the places made famous through billboards and postcards – seemed hokey, small-time. The rules of tourism had changed forever.

> At the height of the industry in the 1940s, Florida's sugarcane fields produced one of every five teaspoons of sugar consumed in the US.

> After WWII, the advent of effective bug spray and affordable air-conditioning did more for Florida tourism than anything else. With these two technological advancements, Florida's subtropical climate was finally safe for delicate Yankee skin.

Viva Cuba Libre!

South Florida has often had a more intimate relationship with Cuba than with the rest of the US. Spain originally ruled Florida from Havana, and in the 20th century, so many Cuban exiles sought refuge in Miami, they dubbed it the 'Exile Capital.' Later, as immigration expanded, Miami simply became the 'Capital of Latin America.'

From 1868 to 1902, during Cuba's long struggle for independence from Spain, Cuban exiles settled in Key West and Tampa, giving birth to Ybor City and its cigar-rolling industry. After independence, many Cubans returned home, but the economic ties they'd forged remained. Then, in 1959, Fidel Castro's revolution (plotted partly in Miami hotels) overthrew the Batista dictatorship. This triggered a several-year exodus of over 600,000 Cubans to Miami, most of them white, wealthy, educated professionals.

In April 1961, Castro declared Cuba a Communist nation, setting the future course for US–Cuban relations. The next day, President Kennedy approved the ill-fated Bay of Pigs invasion, which failed to overthrow Castro, and in October 1962, Kennedy blockaded Cuba to protest the presence of Russian nuclear missiles. Khrushchev famously 'blinked'

1971

Walt Disney World in Orlando opens and around 10,000 people arrive on the first day. The park attracts 10 million visitors during its first year.

May 1980

In the McDuffie trial, white cops are acquitted of wrongdoing in the death of a black man, igniting racial tensions and Miami's Liberty City riots, killing 18 people.

» Children in the Mad Tea Party, Walt Disney World (p261)

and removed the missiles, but not before the US secretly agreed never to invade Cuba again.

None of this sat well with Miami's Cuban exiles, who agitated for the USA to free Cuba (chanting '*Viva Cuba libre*': long live free Cuba). Between 1960 and 1980, a million Cubans emigrated, or 10% of the island's population; by 1980, 60% of Miami was Cuban. Meanwhile, the USA and Cuba wielded immigration policies like cudgels to kneecap each other.

Unlike most immigrant groups, Cuban exiles disparaged assimilation (and sometimes the US), because the dream of return animated their lives. Miami became two parallel cities, Cuban and North American, that rarely spoke each other's language.

In the 1980s and 1990s, poorer immigrants flooded Miami from all over the Latin world – particularly El Salvador, Nicaragua, Mexico, Colombia, Venezuela, the Dominican Republic and Haiti. These groups did not always mix easily or embrace each other, but they found success in a city that already conducted business in Spanish. By the mid-1990s, South Florida was exporting $25 billion in goods to Latin America, and Miami's Cubans were more economically powerful than Cuba itself.

Today, Miami's Cubans are firmly entrenched, and the younger generation no longer considers itself exiles, but residents.

The Florida State Archives website (www.floridamemory.com) presents a fascinating collection of historical documents (a 1586 map of St Augustine, Civil War letters), plus oodles of great photos, both historic and modern.

Hurricanes, Elections & the Everglades

Florida has a habit of selling itself too well. The precarious foundation of its paradise was driven home in 1992, when Hurricane Andrew ripped across South Florida, leaving a wake of destruction that stunned the state and the nation. Plus, mounting evidence of rampant pollution – fish kills, dying mangroves, murky bays – appeared like the bill for a century of unchecked sprawl, population growth and industrial nonchalance.

Newcomers were trampling what they were coming for. From 1930 to 1980, Florida's population-growth rate was 564%. Florida had gone from the least-populated to the fourth-most-populated state, and its infrastructure was woefully inadequate, with too few police, overcrowded prisons, traffic jams, ugly strip malls, and some of the nation's worst schools.

It's all too easy to mock Florida for its bumbling 2000 presidential vote, but the HBO movie *Recount* (2008) doesn't. Instead, it cogently shows what happened and unearths the political grudges that shadowed an honest recount.

In particular, saving the Everglades became more than another environmental crusade. It was a moral test: would Florida really squander one of Earth's wonders over subdivisions and a quick buck? Remarkably, legislation was passed: the Florida Forever Act and the Comprehensive Everglades Restoration Plan were both signed into law in 2000.

Yet 2000 became even more emblematic of Florida's deeply divided self. That year's tight presidential election between Republican George W Bush and Democrat Al Gore hung on Florida's result. However, Florida's breathtakingly narrow vote in favor of Bush unraveled into a fiasco of

1980	1984	1992	1999
Castro declares the Cuban port of Mariel 'open'. The USA's ensuing Mariel Boatlift rescues 125,000 *Marielitos*, who face intense discrimination in Miami.	TV show *Miami Vice* debuts, combining music-video sensibilities, pastel fashions, blighted South Beach locations and cynical undercover cops battling gun-wielding Miami cocaine cartels.	On August 24, Hurricane Andrew devastates Dade County, leaving 41 people dead, over 200,000 homeless, and causing about $15.5 billion in damage.	On Thanksgiving, five-year-old Elián Gonzalez is rescued at sea, his Cuban mother having died en route. Despite wild protests by Miami's Cuban exiles, the US returns Elián to his father in Cuba.

'irregularities,' including defective ballots, wrongly purged voter rolls and mysterious election-day roadblocks. After months of legal challenges and partial recounts, Florida's vote was finally approved, but its reputation had been tarnished.

As the 21st century dawned, Florida's historic tensions – between its mantra of growth and development and the unsustainable demands that placed on society and nature, between its white Southern north and its multiethnic immigrant-rich south – seemed as entrenched and intractable as ever.

2000	2004	2008	2010
Before the presidential election, Florida mistakenly purges thousands of legitimate voters from rolls. George W Bush then narrowly defeats Al Gore by 537 votes in Florida to win the presidency.	Florida records its worst hurricane season ever, when four storms – Charley, Frances, Ivan and Jeanne – strike the state over two months, causing 130 deaths and $22 billion in damage.	Wanting greater influence in the Democratic presidential nomination, Florida moves up its primary to January. The Democratic party strips Florida of its delegates, so its votes don't count.	In the Gulf, *Deepwater Horizon*'s offshore oil spill becomes the worst in US history. Oil only affects Panhandle beaches, but Florida tourism plummets, with losses estimated at $3 billion.

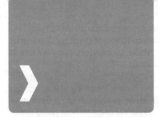

People & Culture

Florida's people and culture are a compelling mix of accents and rhythms, of pastel hues and Caribbean spices, of rebel yells and Latin hip-hop, of Jewish retirees and Miami Beach millionaires. Florida is, in a word, diverse. Like the prehistoric swamp at its heart, it is both fascinatingly complex and too watery to pin down, making for a very intriguing place to explore.

Portrait of a Peninsula

Pessimists contend that the state is so socially and culturally fractured that it will never have a coherent identity. Optimists, strangely enough, say nearly the same thing. Like an overpraised but insecure beauty queen, Florida is almost too popular for its own good, and it can never quite decide if the continual influx of newcomers and immigrants is its saving grace or what will eventually strain society to breaking point.

In terms of geography, Florida is a Southern state. Yet culturally, only Florida's northern half is truly of the South. The Panhandle, Jacksonville and the rural north welcome those who speak with that distinctive Southern drawl, serve sweet tea as a matter of course, and still remember the Civil War. Here, the stereotype of the Nascar-loving redneck with a Confederate-flag bumper sticker on a mud-splattered pickup truck remains the occasional reality.

But central Florida and the Tampa Bay area were a favored destination for Midwesterners, and here you often find a plainspoken, Protestant worker-bee sobriety. East Coast Yankees, once mocked as willing dupes for any old piece of swamp, have carved a definable presence in South Florida – such as in the Atlantic Coast's Jewish retirement communities, in callused, urban Miami, and in the sophisticated towns of the southern Gulf Coast.

Rural Florida, meanwhile, whether north or south, can still evoke America's western frontier. In the 19th century, after the West was won, Florida became one of the last places where pioneers could simply plant stakes and make a life. These pioneers became Florida's 'Crackers,' the poor rural farmers, cowhands and outlaws who traded life's comforts for independence on their terms. Sometimes any Florida pioneer is called a Cracker, but that's not quite right: the original Crackers scratched out a living in the backwoods (in the Keys, Crackers became Conchs). They were migrant field hands, not plantation owners, and with their lawless squatting, make-do creativity, vagrancy and carousing, they weren't regarded kindly by respectable townsfolk. But today, all native Floridians like to feel they too share that same streak of fierce, undomesticated self-reliance.

And yet, stand in parts of Miami and even Tampa, and you won't feel like you're in the US at all, but tropical Latin America. The air is filled with Spanish, the majority of people are Roman Catholic, and the politics of Cuba, Haiti or Colombia animate conversations.

Florida Stories: Conquistadors & Pioneers

» St Augustine

» Marjorie Kinnan Rawlings Historic State Park

» Stephen Foster State Folk Cultural Center

» Museum of Florida History, Tallahassee

» Tampa Bay History Center

» Historic Pensacola Village

'Crackers' got the name most likely for the cracking of the whips during cattle drives, though some say it was for the cracking of corn to make cornmeal, grits or moonshine. For a witty, affectionate look at what makes a Cracker, pick up *Cracker: The Cracker Culture in Florida History* by Dana Ste Claire.

Ultimately, Florida satisfies and defies expectations all at once, and is a study in contrasts. From Cuban lawyers to itinerant construction works, from fixed-income retirees to gay South Beach restaurateurs, it's one of the USA's more bizarre dinner parties come to life.

However, most residents do have something in common: in Florida, nearly everybody is from someplace else. Nearly everyone is a newcomer and, one and all, they wholeheartedly agree on two things: today's newcomers are going to ruin Florida, and wasn't it great to beat them here?

Immigrants & the Capital of Latin America

Like Texas and California, modern Florida has been largely redefined by successive waves of Hispanic immigrants from Latin America. What sets Florida apart is the teeming diversity of its Latinos and their self-sufficient, economically powerful, politicized, Spanish-speaking presence.

How pervasive is Spanish? One in four Floridians speak a language other than English at home, and three-quarters of these speak Spanish. Further, nearly half of these Spanish-speakers admit they don't speak English very well – because they don't need to. This is a sore point with some Anglo Floridians, perhaps because it's incontrovertible evidence that Florida's Latinos are enjoying America's capitalism without necessarily having to adopt its culture or language.

Florida's Cuban exile community (concentrated in Little Havana and Hialeah Park), who began arriving in Miami in the 1960s following Castro's Cuban revolution, created this from the start. Educated and wealthy, these Cubans ran their own businesses, published their own newspapers and developed a Spanish-speaking city within a city. Their success aggravated Florida's black population, who, at the moment the civil rights movement was opening the doors to economic opportunity, found themselves outmaneuvered for jobs by Hispanic newcomers.

Then Latinos kept arriving, nonstop, ranging from the very poorest to the wealthiest, and evincing the entire ethnic palette. In Miami they found a Spanish-speaking infrastructure to help them, while sometimes being shunned by the insular Cuban exiles who preceded them.

Today, every Latin American country is represented in South Florida. Nicaraguans arrived in the 1980s, fleeing war in their country, and now number over 100,000. Miami's Little Haiti is home to over 70,000 Haitians, the largest community in the US. There are 80,000 Brazilians, and large communities of Mexicans, Venezuelans, Colombians, Peruvians, Salvadorans, Jamaicans, Bahamians and more. This has led to significant in-migration around South Florida, as groups displace each other and shift to more fertile ground.

Profiles of Peoples

» *Voices of the Apalachicola* by Faith Eidse

» *Jews of South Florida* by Andrea Greenbaum

» *Cuban Miami* by Robert Levine and Moisés Asís

IMMIGRATION BY THE NUMBERS

For the last 70 years, the story of Florida has been population growth, which has been driven mostly by immigration. Before WWII, Florida was the least populated state (with under two million), and today it is the fourth most populated, with 18.8 million in 2010.

Florida's growth rate has been astonishing – it was 44% for the 1970s. While it's been steadily declining since, it was still over 17% for the 21st century's first decade, twice the national average. That equalled nearly three million new residents from 2000 to 2010.

Florida ranks fourth in the nation for the largest minority population (7.9 million), as well as for the largest number and percentage of foreign-born residents (3.5 million people, who make up 18%). In Miami, the foreign-born population exceeds 60%, which is easily tops among large US cities.

Finally, Florida is home to an estimated 700,000 illegal immigrants, and stemming this tide is currently a hot-button issue.

The children of Cuban exiles are now called YUCAs, 'young urban Cuban Americans,' while the next generation of Latinos has been dubbed Generation Ñ (pronounced enyey), embodying a hybrid culture. For instance, the traditional Cuban *quinceañera*, or *quince*, celebrating a girl's coming of age at 15, is still celebrated in Miami, but instead of a community-wide party, kids now plan trips. With each other, young Latinos slip seamlessly between English and Spanish, typically within the same sentence, reverting to English in front of Anglos and to Spanish or old-school Cuban in front of relatives.

Florida has also welcomed smaller waves of Asian immigrants from China, Indonesia, Thailand and Vietnam. And, of course, South Florida is famous for its Jewish immigrants, not all of whom are over 65 or even from the US. There is a distinctly Latin flavor to South Florida Judaism, as Cuban and Latin Jews have joined those from the US East Coast, Europe and Russia. Overall, Florida is home to 850,000 Jews, with two-thirds in the Greater Miami area.

Life in Florida

Let's get this out of the way first: Florida is indeed the nation's oldest state. It has the highest percentage of people over 65 (over 17%), which pulls the state's median age up to nearly 41, or four years higher than the national average. In fact, ever since WWII, South Florida has been 'God's waiting room' – the land of the retiree.

But the truth is, most immigrants to the state (whether from within the US or abroad) are aged 20 to 30, and they don't come for the early-bird buffet. They come because of Florida's historically low cost of living and its usually robust job and real-estate markets.

When times are good, what they find is that there are plenty of low- to midwage construction, tourist and service-sector jobs, and if they can buy one of those new-built condos or tract homes, they're money ahead, as Florida home values usually outpace the nation's. But in bad times when real estate falters (as most recently), home values plummet, construction jobs dry up and service-sector wages can't keep up with the bills. Thus, those 20- to 30-year-olds also leave the state in the highest numbers.

Florida's urban and rural divides are also pretty extreme. Urban sprawl, particularly around Miami, Orlando and Tampa, is universally loathed – because who likes traffic jams and cookie-cutter sameness? Yet it's nearly unavoidable: 80% of Floridians live within 10 miles of the coast because that's why everyone came – the beach.

So, along the peninsula's urbanized edges, everyone rubs up against each other: racial, ethnic and class tensions are a constant fact of life, but they have also calmed tremendously in recent decades. In general, tolerance (if not acceptance) of diversity is the norm, while tolerance of visitors is the rule. After all, they pay the bills.

But wilderness and rural life define much of interior and northern Florida: here, small working-class towns can be as white, old-fashioned and conservative as Miami is ethnic, gaudy and permissive. This is one reason why it's so hard to predict Florida elections, and why sometimes they turn on a handful of votes.

Floridians at Play

Floridians are passionate about sports. If you let them, they'll fervently talk baseball, football, basketball and Nascar through dinner, dessert and drinks on the porch.

For the majority of Floridians, college football is the true religion. Florida has three of the country's best collegiate teams – the University of Miami Hurricanes, the University of Florida Gators (in Gainesville) and

In *Dream State*, bawdy, gimlet-eyed journalist Diane Roberts weaves her family's biography with Florida's history to create a compelling, unique, hilarious masterpiece: Roberts is like the troublemaking cousin at Florida's family reunion, dishing the dirt everyone else is too polite to discuss.

When former *David Letterman* writer Rodney Rothman burned out, he decided to test drive 'retirement' in Boca Raton – at age 28. A good Jewish boy, Rothman crafts a very personal anthropological study of the unsentimental world of Florida retirees in *Early Bird: A Memoir of Premature Retirement*.

Florida real estate is a continual Ponzi scheme. For a heartfelt look at the human cost when the Florida real-estate market collapsed in 2007, read *Exiles in Eden* by Paul Reyes, a reporter who joined the family business of 'trashing out' foreclosed homes.

the Florida State University Seminoles (in Tallahassee). Between them, these teams have won nine national championships, but if anything, they are even more competitive with each other. It's hardly an exaggeration to say that beating each other is – at least for fans, who take deep pleasure in *hating* their rivals – almost more important than winning all the other games.

Florida also boasts three pro football teams: the Miami Dolphins, Tampa Bay Buccaneers and Jacksonville Jaguars. Florida has two pro basketball teams, the Orlando Magic and Miami Heat. The Stanley Cup–winning Tampa Bay Lightning is one of several pro and semipro hockey teams in the state, including the Miami-based Florida Panthers.

Major-league baseball's spring training creates a frenzy of excitement in March, when 13 pro teams practice across Southern Florida. These stadiums then host minor-league teams, while two pro teams are based here: the Florida Marlins (in Miami) and the Tampa Bay Rays (in St Petersburg).

Nascar originated among liquor bootleggers who needed fast cars to escape the law – and who later raced against each other. Fast outgrowing its Southern redneck roots to become popular across the US, Nascar is near and dear to Floridians and hosts regular events in Daytona.

Imported sports also flourish in South Florida. One is the dangerous Basque game of jai alai, which is popular with Miami's cigar-smoking wagering types. Another is cricket (see p95), thanks to the Miami region's large Jamaican and West Indian population.

Religion

Florida is not just another notch in the South's evangelical Bible belt. It's actually considerably more diverse religiously than its neighboring states.

In Florida, religious affiliations split less along urban/rural lines than along northern/southern ones. About 40% of Florida is Protestant, and about 25% of Protestants are Evangelicals, who tend to be supporters of the religious right. However, these conservative Protestants are much more concentrated in northern Florida, nearer their Southern neighbors.

CELEBRATING FLORIDA HERITAGE & CULTURE

Florida's diversity really comes alive in its many cultural festivals. Here are a handful worth planning a trip around. For more, see p21.

» **Zora Neale Hurston Festival of the Arts & Humanities** (www.zoranealehurston festival.com; Eatonville) For 20 years, Zora Neale Hurston's hometown has honored her with this African American cultural festival, culminating in a lively three-day street fair. Runs for one week in late January–early February.

» **Carnaval Miami** (www.carnavalmiami.com; Miami) The Calle Ocho festival in Little Havana, which runs for 9 days in early March, is the USA's biggest Hispanic street fair. There are domino tournaments, cooking contests, Latin-music concerts and more.

» **Florida Folk Festival** (www.floridastateparks.org/folkfest; White Springs) Since 1953 the Stephen Foster State Folk Cultural Center has held this enormous heritage festival, with hundreds of Florida musicians – from gospel singers to banjo pickers – plus storytellers and Seminole craft demonstrations. Held on Memorial Day weekend.

» **Miami Goombay Festival** (www.goombayfestivalcoconutgrove.com; Coconut Grove) One of the nation's largest black-culture festivals celebrates Miami's Bahamian immigrants with tons of Caribbean music, dancing and food. Held over four days in early June.

» **Barberville Jamboree** (www.pioneersettlement.org; Barberville) On the first weekend of November, the Pioneer Settlement for the Creative Arts hosts Florida's best pioneer-heritage festival, with folk music and authentic demonstrations of Cracker life.

The majority of the state's Roman Catholics (who make up 26%) and Jews (3%) live in South Florida. In South Florida, Jews make up 12% of the population, the second-highest percentage after the New York metro area. The high Catholic population reflects South Florida's wealth of Latin American immigrants.

South Florida also has a growing Muslim population, and it has a noticeable number of adherents of Santeria, a mix of West African and Catholic beliefs, and *vodou* (voodoo), mainly practiced by Haitians.

Further, about 16% of Floridians say that they have no religious affiliation. That doesn't mean they lack spiritual beliefs; it just means their beliefs don't fit census categories. For instance, one of Florida's most famous religious communities is **Cassadaga** (www.cassadaga.org), a home for Spiritualists for over 100 years.

Fine Art & Pink Flamingos

Florida has a well-earned reputation as a welcoming port for all manner of kitsch and low-brow entertainment. Florida invented the theme park and Spring Break, after all. It created swamp rock, *Miami Vice* and its own absurdist, black-comic semitropical crime noir. It has absolutely no problem embracing an injection-molded lawn ornament as a cultural icon, even if the plastic pink flamingo was invented by a Yankee (Don Featherstone). Immigrants are always welcome in Florida.

Yet this does Florida's arts an injustice. Should we dismiss Florida's contributions to high culture just because the colors are always sunshine bright, applied thick and fast, and invariably bleed into pink – from coral-pink gilded-age resorts to pastel art-deco hotels, from Christo's hot pink 'wrap' of Biscayne Bay islands to the saturated sunsets of the Highwaymen? At their best, Florida traditions are homegrown and humble – featuring self-taught painters, dance-happy musical fusions and novels about Cracker pioneers – and they vibrate with the surreal, mercurial truths of everyday life in this alligator-infested, hurricane-troubled peninsula.

> Florida's Division of Cultural Affairs (www.florida-arts.org) is a great resource for statewide arts organizations and agencies. Its Florida Artists Hall of Fame memorializes the Sunshine State's creative legacy.

Literature

Beginning in the 1930s, Florida cleared its throat and developed its own bona-fide literary voice, courtesy mainly of three writers. The most famous was Ernest Hemingway, who settled in Key West in 1928 to write, fish and drink, not necessarily in that order. 'Papa' wrote *For Whom the Bell Tolls* and *A Farewell to Arms* here, but he only set one novel in Florida, *To Have and Have Not* (1937), thus making his life more Floridian than his writing.

The honor of 'most Floridian writer' is generally bestowed on Marjorie Kinnan Rawlings, who lived in Cross Creek between Gainesville and Ocala. She turned her sympathetic, keen eye on Florida's pioneers – the Crackers who populated 'the invisible Florida' – and on the elemental beauty of the state's swampy wilderness. Her novel *The Yearling* (1938) won the Pulitzer Prize, and *Cross Creek* (1942) is a much-lauded autobiographical novel. Her original homestead is now a museum (p359).

> You can count among Florida's snowbirds some of the USA's best writers, like Robert Frost, Isaac Bashevis Singer and Annie Dillard, and every January the literati of the US hold court at the Annual Key West Literary Seminar.

Rounding out the trio is Zora Neale Hurston, an African-American writer who was born in all-black Eatonville, near Orlando. Hurston became a major figure in New York's Harlem renaissance of the 1930s, and her most famous novel, *Their Eyes Were Watching God* (1937), evokes the suffering of Florida's rural blacks, particularly women. In *Seraph on the Suwanee* (1948), Hurston portrays the marriage of two white Florida Crackers. Controversial in her time, Hurston died in obscurity and poverty.

Another famous window on Florida's pioneers is Patrick Smith's *A Land Remembered* (1984), a sprawling, multigenerational saga that highlights the Civil War. Meanwhile Peter Matthiessen's *Shadow Country* (2008) is an epic literary masterpiece. A trilogy revised into a single work, *Shadow Country* fictionalizes the true story of EJ Watson, a turn-of-the-century Everglades plume hunter who murdered his employees, and who in turn was murdered by the townsfolk.

Florida writing is perhaps most famous for its eccentric take on hard-boiled noir crime fiction. Carl Hiaasen almost singlehandedly defines the genre; his stories are hilarious bubbling gumbos of misfits and murderers, who collide in plots of thinly disguised environmentalism, in which the bad guys are developers and their true crimes are against nature. Some other popular names are Randy Wayne White, John D MacDonald, James Hall, and Tim Dorsey; for some recommended reads, see the boxed text below.

Florida's modern novelists tend to favor supernatural, even monstrously absurd Southern Gothic styles, none more so than Harry Crews; try *All We Need of Hell* (1987) and *Celebration* (1999). Two more cult favorites are *Ninety-two in the Shade* (1973) by Thomas McGaune and *Mile Zero* (1990) by Thomas Sanchez, both writerly, dreamlike Key West fantasies. Also don't miss Russell Banks' *Continental Drift* (1985), about the tragic intersection of a burned-out New Hampshire man and a Haitian woman in unforgiving Miami.

Most recently, Karen Russell's *Swamplandia!* (2011), about the travails of a family of alligator wrestlers, marries Hiaasen-style characters with swamp-drenched magical realism.

Naked Came the Manatee (1998) is a collaborative mystery novel by a constellation of famous Florida writers: Carl Hiaasen, Dave Barry, Elmore Leonard, James Hall, Edna Buchanan and more. It's like nibbling a delectable box of cyanide-laced chocolates.

FINE ART & PINK FLAMINGOS

Cinema & Television

Get this: Jacksonville almost became Hollywood. In the 1910s, Jacksonville had 30 production companies – far more than Hollywood – who were using its palm-tree-lined beaches as 'exotic' backdrops for 120 silent films. Yet, even as Laurel and Hardy were becoming famous in one-reeler

FLORIDA PULP

Florida mystery writers love to tickle the swampy underbelly of the Sunshine State. This list focuses on early novels of famous series. Grab one and hit the beach for another murderous day in paradise.

» *Rum Punch* (Elmore Leonard, 1992) Leonard is the undisputed master of intricate plots, crackling dialogue and terrific bad guys. Set in Miami, *Rum Punch* inspired Tarantino's movie *Jackie Brown*.

» *Double Whammy* (Carl Hiaasen, 1987) Hiaasen perfected his absurdist, black-comic rage in his second novel; you'll laugh till you cry. *Skinny Dip* and *Hoot* are also Hiaasen gems.

» *Girl in the Plain Brown Wrapper* (John D MacDonald, 1968) The godfather of Florida crime fiction introduces us to Travis McGee, who saves a girl from suicide and gets trouble as thanks.

» *Sanibel Flats* (Randy Wayne White, 1990) With crisp prose and tight plotting, White introduces his much-beloved 'retired' NSA agent/marine biologist Doc Ford.

» *Miami Blues* (Charles Willeford, 1984) Willeford first made it big with this addictive novel about a denture-wearing detective's chase after a quirky criminal.

» *Cold Case Squad* (Edna Buchanan, 2004) Miami police sergeant Craig Burch leads the cold-case squad after killers whose 'trails vanished long ago like footprints on a sea-washed beach.'

» *Torpedo Juice* (Tim Dorsey, 2005) Zany Serge A Storm only kills people who really deserve it – people who disrespect Florida – as he searches for love in the Keys.

» *Tropical Depression* (Laurence Shames, 1996) Shames is off-the-wall silly. Here, an inept Jersey bra magnate seeks to find himself in Key West. Yeah, right.

slapstick comedies, religiously conservative Jacksonville decided to run those wild movie types out of town. Then Florida's 1926 real-estate bust (and the talkies) killed what Florida moviemaking remained.

Still, it was a close call, and you can see why: Florida, like California, has always fostered dreams and fantasies. Only in Florida, they come to life as theme parks.

Actually, Hollywood has returned to Florida time and again to film both TV shows and movies, and Florida courts both. Some of the more notable popular films include the Marx Bros farce *Cocoanuts*, *Creature from the Black Lagoon* (filmed at Wakulla Springs), *The Truman Show* (filmed at Seaside), *Ulee's Gold*, *Donnie Brasco*, *Get Shorty*, *Hoot* and *Miami Blues*. See also Florida Today (p454).

Florida, as setting, has been a main character in a number of TV shows. In the 1960s, the most famous were *Flipper*, about a boy and his dolphin, and *I Dream of Jeannie*. Set in Cocoa Beach, *Jeannie* was Florida all over: an astronaut discovers a pinup-gorgeous female genie in a bottle, only she never quite fulfills his wishes like he wants.

In the 1980s, Miami was never the same after *Miami Vice* hit the air, a groundbreaking cop drama that made it OK to wear sport coats over T-shirts and which helped inspire the renovation of South Beach's then-dilapidated historic district. Today's popular *CSI: Miami* owes a debt to actor Don Johnson and *Miami Vice* it can never repay.

> The 1960 movie of Glendon Swarthout's novel *Where the Boys Are* is largely responsible for Spring Break as we know it today. It's a bawdy, cautionary coming-of-age tale about four Midwest coeds visiting Fort Lauderdale for sun, sand and sex.

Music

Florida's musical heritage is as rich and satisfyingly diverse as its cuisine. Folk and blues are deep-running currents in Florida music, and pioneers Ray Charles and Cannonball Adderley both hailed from the state. For folk, visit the **Spirit of the Suwannee Music Park** (www.musicliveshere.com), near Suwannee River State Park, while Tallahassee has a notable blues scene.

Florida's state song, 'Old Folks at Home,' was written by Stephen Foster in 1851. Best known for the refrain 'Waaaay down upon the Suwanee River...,' it is the lament of a displaced slave for the plantation. In recent decades, Florida has sought to modernize the lyrics, so that the song's sentimental paean to Old Florida is sanitized of racism, but some argue it should be retired nonetheless.

> Tampa is the home of both punk and 'death metal.'

Florida definitely knows how to rock. Bo Diddley, after helping define rock 'n' roll, settled near Gainesville for the second half of his life. Tom Petty, Lynyrd Skynyrd, and the Allman Brothers form Florida's holy rock trio, while Matchbox Twenty and Dashboard Confessional also got their start in Florida. And yet, the popular musician who most often defines Florida is Jimmy Buffett, whose heart lives in Key West, wherever his band may roam.

PERFORMING ARTS

Iconic American playwright Tennessee Williams called Key West home on and off for over 30 years, but Florida doesn't have much of a homegrown theater or dance tradition. However, several South Florida cities offer top-drawer performing arts and some spectacular stages.

Naturally, Miami leads the way. The Miami City Ballet, a Balanchine company, is one of the nation's largest. The statewide **Florida Dance Association** (www.floridadance association.org) promotes dance performances and education. Miami's showstopper is the Adrienne Arsht Center for the Performing Arts, but also don't miss the New World Center. Tampa and St Petersburg also have large, lauded performing-arts centers.

For good regional theater, head for Miami, Sarasota, Orlando and even Fort Myers.

Rap and hip-hop have flourished in Tampa and Miami, most notoriously with 2 Live Crew, while Orlando (by way of mogul and now jailbird Lou Pearlman) bestowed on the world the boy bands 'N Sync and Backstreet Boys.

Miami is a tasty mélange of Cuban salsa, Jamaican reggae, Dominican merengue, and Spanish flamenco, plus mambo, rumba, cha-cha, calypso and more. Gloria Estefan & the Miami Sound Machine launched a revival of Cuban music in the 1970s, when they mixed Latin beats with disco with 'Conga.' While disco has thankfully waned, Latin music has not; for a taste of hip-hop Miami-style, check out Los Primeros. The best times to see ensemble Cuban bands – often with up to 20 musicians and singers – is during celebrations like Carnaval Miami.

Architecture

Like its literature, Florida's architecture has some distinctive homegrown strains. These run from the old – the Spanish-colonial and Revival styles of St Augustine – to the aggressively modern, as in Miami and particularly South Beach.

At the turn of the century, Henry Flagler was instrumental in promoting a particularly Floridian Spanish-Moorish fantasia, which, as historian Michael Gannon writes, combined 'the stately architecture of Rome, the tiled rooftops of Spain, the dreamy beauty of Venice, [and] the tropical casualness of Algiers.' Prime examples are the monumental Hotel Ponce de León in St Augustine (now Flagler College), Whitehall Mansion in Palm Beach (now Flagler Museum) and Miami's awesome, George Merrick–designed Coral Gables.

Miami Beach got swept up in the art-deco movement in the 1920s and '30s (which Florida transformed into 'tropical deco'), and today it has the largest collection of art-deco buildings in the US. These languished until the mid-1980s, when their rounded corners and glass bricks were dusted off and spruced up with new coats of pastel-pink and aquamarine paint.

Florida's vernacular architecture is the oft-maligned 'Cracker house.' However, these pioneer homesteads were cleverly designed to maximize comfort in a pre-air-conditioning, subtropical climate. Raised off the ground, with windows and doors positioned for cross-ventilation, they had extrawide gables and porches for shade, and metal roofs reflecting the sun. They weren't pretty, but they worked. A great example is Marjorie Kinnan Rawlings' home in Cross Creek.

Two of the best film festivals in the US are the Miami International Film Festival (www.miamifilmfestival.com; March), a showcase for Latin cinema, and the up-and-coming Florida Film Festival (www.floridafilmfestival.com; April) in Orlando.

FINE ART & PINK FLAMINGOS

FILM FESTIVALS

THE FLORIDA HIGHWAYMEN

Beginning in the 1950s, about two dozen largely self-taught African-American painters made a modest living selling vivid, impressionistic 'Florida-scapes' on wood and Masonite for about $20 a pop. They sold these romantic visions of raw swamps and technicolor sunsets from the trunks of their cars along I-95 and A1A, a practice that eventually gave them their name.

The Highwaymen were mentored and encouraged by AE 'Beanie' Backus, a white artist and teacher in Fort Pierce. Considered the 'dean' of Florida landscape art, Beanie was also largely self-taught, often preferring the rough strokes of a palette knife over a brush. Backus and his contemporaries from the '50s and '60s are also referred to as the Indian River School, a reference to the famous Hudson River School of naturalist landscape painters.

Today, this outsider art is highly revered and collected. To learn more, pick up Gary Monroe's excellent book *The Highwaymen;* visit the **Highwaymen website** (www.highwaymenartist.com); and visit the **AE Backus Museum and Gallery** (www.backusgallery.com) in Fort Pierce.

Painting & Visual Arts

Florida has an affinity for modern art, and modern artists find Florida allows them to indulge their inner pink. In 1983, Bulgarian artist Christo 'wrapped' 11 islands in Biscayne Bay in flamingo-colored fabric, so that they floated in the water like giant discarded flowers, dwarfing the urban skyline.

Everyone loved it; it was so Miami.

But then so was Spencer Tunick when he posed 140 naked women on hot-pink rafts in the Sagamore hotel pool in 2007, and Roberto Behar and Rosario Marquardt when they plunked salmon-colored *The Living Room* in the Design District. Whatever the reasons, cartoon-hued silly-happy grandeur and exhibitionism seem Miami's calling cards. That certainly applies to Brazilian émigré Romero Britto, whose art graces several buildings, such as the Miami Children's Museum. Miami's prominence in the contemporary-art world was cemented in 2002, when the Art Basel festival arrived, and without question, Miami's gallery scene is unmatched outside of LA and Manhattan.

Some say Florida's affinity for bright colors started with the Florida Highwaymen and their vernacular, supersaturated Florida landscapes; see p473. Another famous self-taught folk artist was Earl Cunningham, sometimes nicknamed 'Grandpa Moses' for his naive portraits of a bygone Florida world.

And Florida does not lack for high-quality art museums. In addition to Miami, other notable cities are Fort Lauderdale, West Palm Beach, St Petersburg, Tampa, Sarasota, Naples and even Orlando.

Folk Art & Florida Funkiness

» Mennello Museum of American Folk Art, Orlando

» Richard Bickel Photography, Apalachicola

» Leoma Lovegrove Gallery, Matlacha

» Fort East Martello Museum & Gardens, Key West

A Florida Feast

Admittedly, as your road trip leaves Miami, Florida doesn't always fit the profile of a dining destination. You drive past strip mall after strip mall filled with nothing but bland corporate eateries and nondescript please-everyone restaurants. In beach towns, cooks can seem to have two loves, the deep fryer and the salt shaker. And just as often, Florida's residents and guests seem content: after a day of sun and sand, a dependable, affordable family-style meal pretty much hits the spot.

And yet, Florida offers as much culinary excellence and adventure as you'd like. Few places can boast its sublime fresh bounty from land and sea, and menus playfully nick influences from a hemisphere's worth of cultures: Southern, Creole, Cuban, Caribbean, and Central and South American, but also Jewish, Asian, Spanish and more. Gourmets can genuflect before celebrity chefs, while gourmands hunt Florida's bizarre delicacies, like boiled peanuts, frog's legs, snake and gator.

So try not to judge a book by its cover. Those tacky roadside shopping strips? Sometimes they hold the pearls you're looking for.

Destination Dining

Florida has a rich culinary heritage, but the state wasn't known as a place for good restaurants until the 1990s, when a wave of gourmet chefs transformed the Miami dining scene. They dedicated themselves to pleasing sophisticated urban palates by spicing up menus with South Florida's unique combination of Cuban, Caribbean and Latin American influences, which came to be dubbed Floribbean cuisine.

Today, Miami remains the epicenter of all things gourmet, and it has the greatest selection of ethnic cuisines, but the ripples have spread statewide. In big cities and anywhere moneyed tourists and snowbirds land, you will find upscale restaurants and skilled chefs plying their trade, often in contemporary dining rooms framing ocean views.

North of Miami and Miami Beach, Fort Lauderdale, Palm Beach and West Palm Beach offer the well-heeled foodie oodles of fun. Key West is, as in all things, more laid back, but its dining scene is notably stocked with creative-fusion cool.

The southern Gulf Coast is similarly satisfying: Tampa is riding the cusp of a culinary renaissance, with everything from Old World Iberian to locavore-inspired modern gastronomy. Skip south through the rich beach towns of Sarasota, Sanibel Island and Naples, and a memorable meal is a reservation away.

As you go north, robust Southern cuisine comes to dominate, and high-end dining favors classic Italian, French and seafood. Though lacking gourmet 'scenes', great choices are sprinkled in Orlando, Jacksonville, and Tallahassee. Along the Atlantic Coast, Amelia Island and St Augustine are foodie havens, and there's plenty of fresh, upscale seafood in Panhandle resort towns.

For pricing and tipping information, see p497.

For pricing and tipping information, see p497.

Florida Cookbooks

» *Cross Creek Cookery*, Marjorie Kinnan Rawlings

» *New World Cuisine*, Allen Susser

» *Miami Spice: The New Florida Cuisine,* Steve Raichlen

» *The Florida Cookbook: From Gulf Coast Gumbo to Key Lime Pie,* Jeanne Voltz and Caroline Stuart

» *Florida Bounty,* Eric and Sandra Jacobs

South Florida Food Blogs

» Jan Norris (www.jannorris.com)

» Mango & Lime (http://mangoandlime.net)

» Meatless Miami (www.meatlessmiami.com)

FLORIBBEAN CUISINE

Okay, somebody worked hard to come up with 'Floribbean' – a term for Florida's tantalizing gourmet mélange of just-caught seafood, tropical fruits and eye-watering peppers, all dressed up with some combination of Nicaraguan, Salvadoran, Caribbean, Haitian, Cajun, Cuban and even Southern influences. Some call it 'fusion,' 'Nuevo Latino,' 'New World,' 'nouvelle Floridian' or 'palm-tree cuisine,' and it could refer to anything from a ceviche of lime, conch, sweet peppers and scotch bonnets to grilled grouper with mango, *adobo* and fried plantains.

Bounty of the Sea

Florida has always fed itself from the sea, which lies within arm's reach of nearly every point. If it swims or crawls in the ocean, you can bet some enterprising local has shelled or scaled it, battered it, dropped it in a fryer and put it on a menu.

Grouper is far and away the most popular fish. Grouper sandwiches are to Florida what the cheesesteak is to Philadelphia or pizza to Manhattan – a defining, iconic dish, and the standard by which many places are measured. Hunting the perfect grilled or fried grouper sandwich is an obsessive Floridian quest, as is finding the creamiest bowl of chowder.

Of course, a huge range of other fish are offered. Other popular species include snapper (with dozens of varieties), mahimahi and catfish.

Florida really shines when it comes to crustaceans: try pink shrimp and rock shrimp, and don't miss soft-shell blue crab – Florida is the only place with blue-crab hatcheries, making them available fresh yearround. Winter (October to April) is the season for Florida spiny lobster and stone crab (out of season, both will be frozen). Florida lobster is all tail, without the large claws of its Maine cousin, and stone crab is heavenly sweet, served steamed with butter or the ubiquitous mustard sauce.

Finally, the Keys popularized conch (a giant sea snail); now fished out, most conch is from the Bahamas. From July to September, Steinhatchee is the place for fresh scallops, and in fall/winter, Apalachicola Bay produces 90% of Florida's small but flavorful oysters.

Cuban & Latin American Cuisine

Cuban food, once considered 'exotic,' is itself a mix of Caribbean, African and Latin American influences, and in Tampa and Miami, it's a staple of everyday life. Sidle up to a Cuban *loncheria* (snack bar) and order a *pan cubano:* a buttered, grilled baguette stuffed with ham, roast pork, cheese, mustard and pickles.

Integral to many Cuban dishes are *mojo* (a garlicky vinaigrette, sprinkled on sandwiches), *adobo* (a meat marinade of garlic, salt, cumin, oregano and sour orange juice) and *sofrito* (a stew-starter mix of garlic, onion and chili peppers). Main-course meats are typically accompanied by rice and beans and fried plantains.

With its large number of Central and Latin American immigrants, the Miami area offers plenty of authentic ethnic eateries. Seek out Haitian *griot* (marinated fried pork), Jamaican jerk chicken, Brazilian barbecue, Central American *gallo pinto* (red beans and rice) and Nicaraguan *tres leches* ('three milks' cake).

In the morning, try a Cuban coffee, also known as *café cubano* or *cortadito*. This hot shot of liquid gold is essentially sweetened espresso, while *café con leche* is just *café au lait* with a different accent: equal parts coffee and hot milk.

Another Cuban treat is *guarapo*, or fresh-squeezed sugarcane juice. Cuban snack bars serve the greenish liquid straight or poured over crushed

CUBAN BRANDS

In Miami, you can find classic Cuban brands that are no longer sold in Cuba itself – like Hatuey beer, La Llave coffee and Gilda crackers.

ice, and it's essential to an authentic mojito. It also sometimes finds its way into *batidos,* a milky, refreshing Latin American fruit smoothie.

Southern Cooking

The further north you travel, the more Southern the cooking, which makes up in fat what it may lack in refinement. 'Meat and three' is Southern restaurant lingo for a main meat – like fried chicken, catfish, barbecued ribs, chicken-fried steak or even chitlins (hog's intestines) – and three sides: perhaps some combination of hush puppies, cheese grits, cornbread, coleslaw, mashed potatoes, black-eyed peas, collard greens or buttery corn. End with pecan pie, and that's living. Po' boys are merely Southern hoagies, usually filled with fried nuggets of goodness.

Cracker cooking is Florida's rough-and-tumble variation on Southern cuisine, but with more reptiles and amphibians. And you'll find a good deal of Cajun and Creole as well, which mix in spicy gumbos and bisques from Louisiana's neighboring swamps.

Southern Floridian cooking is epitomized by writer Marjorie Kinnan Rawlings' famous cookbook *Cross Creek Cookery.* Near Rawlings' former home, the Yearling Restaurant (p359) is a good place to try Southern Floridian food.

Iced tea is so ubiquitous it's called the 'wine of the South,' but watch out for 'sweet tea,' which is an almost entirely different Southern drink – tea so sugary your eyes will cross.

If you love farmers' markets, visit www.florida -agriculture.com and click on 'Info for Consumers' and 'Community Farmers' Markets' to find a statewide list.

From Farm (& Grove) to Table

Florida has worked long and hard to become an agricultural powerhouse, and it's famous for its citrus. The state is the nation's largest producer of oranges, grapefruits, tangerines and limes, not to mention

---

FLORIDA SPECIALITIES

From north to south, here's a list of dishes strange and sublime, but 100% Florida; try not to leave without trying them at least once.

» **Boiled peanuts** In rural north Florida, they take green or immature peanuts and boil them until they're nice and mushy, sometimes spicing them up with Cajun or other seasonings. Sure, they feel weird in the mouth, but they're surprisingly addictive.

» **Tarpon Springs Greek salad** We don't know why, but in Tarpon Springs, Greek restaurants started hiding a dollop of potato salad inside a regulation Greek salad – now you can find this odd combination throughout central Florida.

» **Alligator** Alligator tastes like a cross between fish and pork. The meat comes from the tail, and is usually served as deep-fried nuggets, which overwhelms the delicate flavor and can make it chewy. Try it grilled. Most alligator is legally harvested on farms and is often sold in grocery stores. It's also healthier than chicken, with as much protein but half the fat, fewer calories and less cholesterol.

» **Frog's legs** Those who know say the 'best' legs come from the Everglades; definitely ask, since you want to avoid imported ones from India, which are smaller and disparaged as 'flavorless.'

» **Stone crabs** The first recycled crustacean: only one claw is taken from a stone crab – the rest is tossed back in the sea (the claw regrows in 12 to 18 months, and crabs plucked again are called 'retreads'). The claws are so perishable that they're always cooked before selling. October through April is less a 'season' than a stone-crab frenzy. Joe Weiss of Miami Beach is credited with starting it all.

» **Key lime pie** Key limes are yellow, and that's the color of an authentic Key lime pie, which is a custard of Key lime juice, sweetened condensed milk and egg yolks in a cracker crust, then topped with meringue. Avoid any slice that's green or stands ramrod straight.

mangoes and sugarcane. Scads of bananas, strawberries, coconuts, avocados (once called 'alligator pears'), and the gamut of tropical fruits and vegetables are also grown in Florida. The major agricultural region is around Lake Okeechobee, with field upon field, and grove upon grove, as far as the eye can see.

However, only relatively recently – with the advent of the USA's locavore, farm-to-table movement – has Florida started featuring vegetables in its cooking and promoting its freshness on the plate. Florida's regional highlights – its Southern and Latin American cuisines – do not usually emphasize greens or vegetarianism. But today, most restaurants with upscale or gourmet pretensions promote the local sources of their produce and offer appealing choices for vegetarians.

That said, old habits die hard. Outside Miami, dedicated vegetarian restaurants are few, and in many rural towns and standard eateries, vegetarians can be forced to choose among iceberg-lettuce salads and pastas.

One indigenous local delicacy is heart of palm, or 'swamp cabbage,' which has a delicate, sweet crunch. The heart of the sabal palm, Florida's state tree, it was a mainstay for Florida pioneers. Try it if you can find it served fresh (don't bother if it's canned; it's not from Florida).

Libations

Is it the heat or the humidity? With the exception of the occasional teetotalling dry town, Florida's embrace of liquor is prodigious, even epic.

Coinciding with modern refrigeration, frozen concentrated orange juice was invented in Florida in 1946: this popularized orange juice as a year-round drink and created a generation of 'orange millionaires.'

SUNSHINE STATE FOOD FESTIVALS

Many of Florida's food festivals have the tumultuous air of county fairs, with carnival rides, music, parades, beauty pageants and any number of wacky, only-in-Florida happenings.

Food Fest! by Joan Steinbacher is the definitive guide; her companion website (www.foodfestguide.com) lists festivals for the coming three months.

» **Everglades Seafood Festival** (www.evergladesseafoodfestival.com) Everglades City; three-day weekend, early February. Not just seafood, but gator, frog's legs and snakes, oh my!

» **Swamp Cabbage Festival** (www.swampcabbagefestival.org) La Belle; three-day weekend, late February. Armadillo races and crowning of the Miss Swamp Cabbage Queen.

» **Grant Seafood Festival** (www.grantseafoodfestival.com) Grant; two-day weekend, early March. This small Space Coast town throws one of Florida's biggest seafood parties.

» **Florida Strawberry Festival** (www.flstrawberryfestival.com) Plant City; 11 days, early March. Since 1930, over half a million folks come annually to pluck, eat and honor the mighty berry.

» **Carnaval Miami** (www.carnaval-miami.org) Miami; fortnight, early March. Negotiate drag queens and in-line skaters to reach the Cuban Calle Ocho food booths.

» **Isle of Eight Flags Shrimp Festival** (www.shrimpfestival.com) Amelia Island; three-day weekend, early May. Avast, you scurvy dog! Pirates invade for shrimp and a juried art show.

» **Palatka Blue Crab Festival** (www.bluecrabfestival.com) Palatka; four-day Memorial Day weekend. Hosts the state championship for chowder and gumbo. Yes, it's that good.

» **Florida Seafood Festival** (www.floridaseafoodfestival.com) Apalachicola; two days, early November. Stand way, way back at its signature oyster-shucking and -eating contests.

» **Ribfest** (www.ribfest.org) St Petersburg; three days, mid-November. Three words: ribs, rock, Harleys.

And as you ponder this legacy – from Prohibition-era rumrunners, Spring Break hedonists and drive-thru liquor stores to Ernest Hemingway and Jimmy Buffett – it can seem that quantity trumps quality most of the time.

Yet as with Florida's cuisine, so with its bars. Surely, Anheuser-Busch's Jacksonville brewery will never go out of business, but Tampa also boasts several handcrafted local microbreweries. Daytona's beaches may be littered with gallon-size hurricane glasses, but Miami mixologists hone their reputations with their designer takes on martinis and mojitos.

Indeed, Cuban bartenders became celebrities in the 1920s for what they did with all that sugarcane and citrus: the two classics are the Cuba *libre* (rum, lime and cola) and the mojito (rum, sugar, mint, lemon and club soda), traditionally served with *chicharrónes* (deep-fried pork rinds).

As for Hemingway, he favored piña coladas, lots of them. Jimmy Buffett memorialized the margarita – so that now every sweaty beach bar along the peninsula claims to make the 'best.' Welcome, good friends, to Margaritaville.

Edible Communities (www.edible communities .com) is a regional magazine series that celebrates and supports local, sustainable farming, culinary artisans and seasonal produce. It publishes editions (print and online) for Orlando and South Florida.

A FLORIDA FEAST

From Boots to Beaches

Florida doesn't have mountains, valleys, cliffs, big waves, churning rivers or snow.

What *does* Florida have?

Water, lots and lots of water – freshwater, saltwater, rainwater, springwater, swamp water. Florida's signature peninsula bends with over 1200 miles of coastline, which includes more than 660 miles of the best beaches in the US. For most visitors (and residents), that's all they need to know.

But consider: under the ocean is the largest coral-reef system in North America, while the peninsula is crisscrossed with 11,000 miles of lazy rivers and streams, ringed by more than 4500 islands, and dotted with some 7700 lakes and about 700 crystal springs bubbling up like Champagne. Florida is a bird-watcher's paradise and its prehistoric swamps and forests teem with Ice Age flora and dinosaur-era beasts.

In short, Florida doesn't have everything, but whether you swim, hike, bike, dive, paddle, surf or sail, you'll still agree that this surreal, watery landscape is one of the greatest shows on Earth.

Hiking & Camping

One thing Florida hikers never have to worry about is elevation gain. But the weather more than makes up for it. If your destination is South Florida, it's best to hike and camp from November through March. This is Florida's 'dry season,' when rain, temperatures, humidity and mosquitoes decrease to tolerable levels. In summer, hike before noon to avoid the midday heat and afternoon thundershowers.

Florida National Scenic Trail (FNST; www.floridatrail.org) is one of 11 national scenic trails and covers 1400 not-yet-contiguous miles. It runs north from the swamps of Big Cypress National Preserve; around Lake

---

Great Hiking & Camping Guides

» *30 Eco-Trips in Florida* (2005), Holly Ambrose

» *A Hiker's Guide to the Sunshine State* (2005), Sandra Friend

» *The Best in Tent Camping: Florida* (2010), John Malloy

TREAD LIGHTLY, EXPLORE SAFELY

These days, it should go without saying that any wilderness, even a swamp, is a fragile place. Practicing 'Leave No Trace' ethics (see www.lnt.org for comprehensive advice) boils down to staying on the trail, cleaning up your own mess, and observing nature rather than plucking or feeding it. See also A Kinder, Gentler Wilderness Encounter, p491.

As you enjoy Florida's natural bounty, take care of yourself, too. Carry lots of water – up to a gallon per person per day – and always be prepared for rain. Line backpacks with plastic bags, and carry rain gear and extra clothes for when (not if) you get soaked. Reid Tillery's *Surviving the Wilds of Florida* will help you do just that, while Tillery's website **Florida Adventuring** (www.floridaadventuring.com) covers backcountry essentials.

Okeechobee; through the Ocala National Forest; and then west to the Gulf Islands National Seashore near Pensacola. All the parks above are filled with great hikes.

Other prime hiking areas include the remote pine wilderness, karst terrain and limestone sinkholes of Apalachicola National Forest and Paynes Prairie Preserve State Park. Wekiwa Springs State Park rewards hikers, paddlers and snorkelers.

South Florida swamps tend to favor 1- to 2-mile boardwalk trails; these are excellent, and almost always wheelchair accessible. But to really explore the swamps, get in a kayak.

Prized camping spots include the shady riverside at Stephen Foster Folk Culture Center State Park; the Ocala National Forest; the Panhandle's St Joseph State Park; Myakka River State Park, and in the Florida Keys, Bahia Honda State Park.

For reservations, hiking organizations and statewide trail information, see p496.

Swimming & Springs

Florida's beaches are the best in the country, and incredibly diverse, so let's start with two questions: Do you prefer sunrise or sunset? Do you prefer surfing and boogie boarding or sunbathing and sandcastles? For sunrise and surfing, hit the bigger, east-facing waves of the Atlantic Coast; for sandcastles at sunset, choose the soporific, west-facing waters of the Gulf Coast.

Beyond that, your main concern is how close to or far from other people you want to be. With few exceptions, Florida's beaches are safe places to swim; the most dangerous surf will occur just before and after a storm. Also, stingrays in summer and occasional jellyfish can trouble swimmers (look for lifeguard-posted warnings).

Yet don't overlook Florida's lakes, rivers and springs. Taking a dip in one of Florida's 700 freshwater springs – each a goosebump-inducing 72°F and, when healthy, clear as glass – is unforgettable. There are too many to list, but good swimming destinations are the Suwannee River, the Ichetucknee River and Ponce de Leon Springs State Park.

Canoeing & Kayaking

To really experience Florida's swamps and rivers, its estuaries and inlets, its lagoons and barrier islands, you need a watercraft, preferably the kind you paddle. The intimate quiet of dipping among mangroves and startling alligators and ibis stirs wonder in the soul.

The winter 'dry' season is best for paddling. In summer, canoe near cool, freshwater springs and swimming beaches, because you'll be dreaming about them.

In terms of rivers, the 207-mile Suwannee River is quintessential Florida: a meandering, muddy ribbon (ideal for multiday trips) decorated with 60 clear blue springs that runs from Georgia's Okefenokee Swamp to the Gulf of Mexico. About 170 miles are an official wilderness trail (www.floridastateparks.org/wilderness; p451), and the section near Big Shoals State Park actually has some Class III rapids – woohoo!

Other unforgettable rivers include: the Atlantic Coast's 'Wild and Scenic' Loxahatchee River (p222); Orlando's 'Wild and Scenic' Wekiwa River (p244); and the Tampa region's placid Hillsborough River (p375) and the alligator-packed Myakka River (p397).

You'll tell your grandchildren about kayaking Everglades National Park (p137); Hell's Bay paddling trail is heavenly. The nearby 10,000 Islands are just as amazing, and nothing beats sleeping in the Everglades in a *chickee* (wooden platform above the waterline).

FROM BOOTS TO BEACHES

Wildlife-Watching Resources

» Florida Fish & Wildlife Conservation Commission (www.myfwc.com)

» Audubon of Florida (www.audubonofflorida.org)

» Great Florida Birding Trail (www.floridabirdingtrail.com)

» Florida Wildlife Viewing (www.floridawildlifeviewing.com)

PADDLING GUIDE

A great all-in-one paddling guide – with everything from the state's best water trails to nitty-gritty advice about weather, equipment and supplies – is *A Paddler's Guide to the Sunshine State* (2001) by Sandy Huff.

LIFE'S A BEACH

Florida's best beach? Why not ask us to choose a favorite child? It's impossible! Each beach has its own personality, its own wondrous qualities. But visitors do have to make decisions. For family-friendly beach towns, see p38. For boat-only, secluded islands, see p17. And for the best beaches by coastline, see below.

For a list based on 'science', consult Dr Beach (www.drbeach.org).

Best Gulf Coast Beaches

- » Siesta Key Beach (p391)
- » Fort DeSoto Park (p383)
- » Honeymoon Island State Park (p388)
- » Sanibel Island (p408)
- » Naples Beach (p411)
- » Fort Myers Beach (p403)

Best Atlantic Coast Beaches

- » Apollo Beach (p314)
- » Bahia Honda (p168)
- » Bill Baggs Cape Florida State Recreation Area (p84)
- » Fort Lauderdale (p190)
- » Lake Worth Beach (p206)
- » Hutchinson Island (p223)
- » Vero Beach (p316)

Best Panhandle Beaches

- » Grayton Beach State Park (p433)
- » St George Island State Park (p440)
- » Pensacola Beach (p425)

And don't forget the coasts. You'll kick yourself if you don't kayak Miami's Bill Baggs Cape Florida State Recreation Area; Tampa Bay's Caladesi Island; Sanibel Island's JN 'Ding' Darling National Wildlife Refuge; and the Big Bend's Cedar Key.

On Florida's Atlantic Coast, more mangroves, water birds, dolphins and manatees await at Canaveral National Seashore, particularly Mosquito Lagoon, and also seek out Indian River Lagoon. Big and Little Talbot Islands provide more intercoastal magic.

For paddling organizations, see p495.

Diving & Snorkeling

For diving and snorkeling, most already know about Florida's superlative coral reefs and wreck diving, but northern Florida is also the 'Cave Diving Capital of the US.' The peninsula's limestone has more holes than Swiss cheese, and most are burbling goblets of diamond-clear water.

Many spots line the Suwannee River: try Peacock Springs State Park (www.floridastateparks.org/peacocksprings), one of the continent's largest underwater cave systems; Troy Springs State Park (www.florida stateparks.org/troyspring); and Manatee Springs State Park. Another fun dive is Blue Spring State Park, near Orlando. Note that you need to be cavern certified to dive a spring (an open-water certification won't do), and solo diving is usually not allowed. But local dive shops can help with both (for dive organizations and resources, see p495). One place that offers certification courses is Vortex Spring (p441).

Every Florida spring has prime snorkeling. At times, the clarity of the water is disconcerting, as if you were floating on air; every creature and school of fish all the way to the bottom feels just out of reach, so that, as William Bartram once wrote, 'the trout swims by the very nose of the alligator and laughs in his face.'

If you prefer coral reefs teeming with rainbow-bright tropical fish, you're in luck...Florida has the continent's largest coral-reef system. The two best spots are John Pennekamp Coral Reef State Park and Biscayne National Park, but you won't be disappointed at Bahia Honda State Park.

Wreck diving in Florida is equally epic, and some are even accessible to snorkelers. So many Spanish galleons sank off the Emerald Coast, near Panama City Beach, that it's dubbed the 'Wreck Capital of the South'. But also check out wreck dives in Pensacola, Sebastian Inlet State Park, Troy Springs, Fort Lauderdale and Biscayne National Park.

Named for its abundant sea turtles, the Dry Tortugas are well worth the effort to reach them.

Biking

Florida is too flat for mountain biking, but there are plenty of off-road opportunities, along with hundreds of miles of paved trails for those who prefer to keep their ride clean. As with hiking, avoid biking in summer, unless you like getting hot and sweaty.

Top off-roading spots include **Big Shoals State Park** (www.floridastate parks.org/bigshoals), with 25 miles of trails along the Suwannee River, and Paynes Prairie Preserve State Park, with 20 miles of trails through its bizarre landscape. Also recommended are the Ocala National Forest and the Apalachicola National Forest, particularly the sandy Munson Hills Loop.

With so many paved biking trails, it's hard to choose. To dip among the Panhandle's sugar-sand beaches, take the 19-mile Timpoochee Trail, which parallels Hwy 30A. In Tallahassee, the 16-mile Tallahassee-St Marks Historic Railroad State Trail shoots you right to the Gulf. Both paved and off-road trails encircle Lake Okeechobee, which is a great way to take in the surrounding countryside. Two of the most unforgettable paved trails? Palm Beach's Lake Trail, aka the 'Trail of Conspicuous Consumption' for all the mansions and yachts, and the 15-mile Shark Valley Tram Road Trail, which pierces the Everglades' gator-infested saw-grass river.

GET YOUR BOARD ON

Ten-time world-champion surfer Kelly Slater is from Cocoa Beach, and four-time women's champion Lisa Anderson is from Ormond Beach. Both first learned how to carve in Space Coast waves, in the shadow of rockets, and Slater honed his aerials at Sebastian Inlet.

All of which is to say that while Florida's surf may be considered 'small' by Californian and Hawaiian standards, Florida's surfing community and history are not. Plus, Florida makes up in wave quantity what it may lack in wave size.

Nearly the entire Atlantic Coast has rideable waves, but the best spots are gathered along the Space Coast, which has surf lessons, rentals and popular competitions: shoot for Cocoa Beach, Indialantic, Sebastian Inlet and Playalinda Beach. However, you'll find tiny, longboard-friendly peelers from Fort Lauderdale down to Miami's South Beach.

Florida's northern Atlantic Coast is less attractive, partly due to chilly winter water, but consistent, 2ft to 3ft surf can be had at Daytona Beach; from Flagler Beach up to St Augustine; and around Amelia Island.

For more-involved overland adventures, do the Florida Keys Overland Heritage Trail, which mirrors the Keys Highway for 70 noncontiguous miles, and the urban-and-coastal Pinellas Trail, which runs 43 miles from St Petersburg to Tarpon Springs. For more biking advice, see p495.

Fishing

The world may contain seven seas, but there's only one Fishing Capital of the World: Florida. No, this isn't typically overwrought Floridian hype. Fishing here is the best the US offers, and for variety and abundance, nowhere else on the globe can claim an indisputable advantage.

In Florida's abundant rivers and lakes, largemouth bass are the main prize. Prime spots, with good access and facilities, are Lake Manatee State Park (www.floridastateparks.org/lakemanatee), south of St Petersburg; for fly-fishing, Myakka River State Park; and Jacksonville (www.jacksonvillefishing.com), which has charters to the St Johns River and Lake George for freshwater fishing and to the bay for ocean fishing, plus kayak fishing.

Near-shore saltwater fishing means redfish and mighty tarpon, snook, spotted seatrout and much more, up and down both coasts. The jetties at Sebastian Inlet are a mecca for shore anglers on the Atlantic Coast, while on the Gulf, Tampa's Skyway Fishing Pier is dubbed the world's longest fishing pier.

In the Keys, Bahia Honda and Old Seven Mile Bridge on Pigeon Key are other shore-fishing highlights.

However, as 'Papa' Hemingway would tell you, the real fishing is offshore, where majestic sailfish leap and thrash. Bluefish and mahimahi are other popular deep-water fish. For offshore charters, head for Stuart, Fort Lauderdale, Lauderdale-by-the-Sea, Destin, Steinhatchee, and Miami. The best strategy is to walk the harborside, talking with captains, until you find one who speaks to your experience and interests.

Note that you usually need a license to fish, and there are a slew of regulations about what you can catch; see p496 for fishing organizations and details.

Sailing

If you like the wind in your sails, Florida is your place. Miami is a sailing sweet spot, with plenty of marinas for renting or berthing your own boat – Key Biscayne is a particular gem. Fort Lauderdale is chock-full of boating options. In Key West, you can sail on a schooner with real cannons, though tour operators are plentiful throughout the Keys. To learn how to sail, check out Pensacola's Lanier Sailing Academy.

Golf

Fun fact: With more than 1250 courses (and counting), Florida has the most golf courses of any US state. Whether or not this is related to Florida's high number of wealthy retirees isn't known, but one thing is certain, if you want to tee up, you won't have to look far.

Golf courses are listed throughout this book, but towns that are notable for golf include Palm Beach, Naples, Fort Myers, Orlando, Jacksonville, Miami and St Augustine. Near St Augustine is the World Golf Hall of Fame.

For a comprehensive list of Florida courses, see Florida Golf (www.fgolf.com).

Florida mystery writer Randy Wayne White has created an angler's delight with the *Ultimate Tarpon Book* (2010), a celebration of Florida's legendary big-game fish, with 'contributions' from Hemingway, Teddy Roosevelt, Zane Grey and more.

Swamp Thing

Naturalist Marjory Stoneman Douglas called Florida 'a long pointed spoon' that is as 'familiar as the map of North America itself.' On that map, the shapely Floridian peninsula represents one of the most unique, ecologically diverse regions in the world.

It all began when, over millions of years, a thick layer of limestone was created as shells and bones drifted to the bottom of an ancient sea. As Earth's tectonic plates shifted, North America rose up, slipped away from Africa, and left an ocean between them. The bit of limestone that would become Florida settled just north of the Tropic of Cancer, and this confluence of porous rock and climate gave rise to a watery world of uncommon abundance – one that is threatening to be undone by human hands in the geological blink of an eye.

The Land

Florida is many things, but it's also flat as a pancake, or as Douglas says, like a spoon of freshwater resting delicately in a bowl of saltwater – a spongy brick of limestone hugged by the Atlantic Ocean and the Gulf of Mexico. The highest point, the Panhandle's Britton Hill, has to stretch to reach 350ft, which isn't half as tall as the buildings of downtown Miami. This makes Florida officially the nation's flattest state, despite being 22nd in total area with 58,560 sq miles.

However, over 4000 of those square miles are water; lakes pepper the map like bullet holes in a road sign. That shotgun-sized hole in the south is Lake Okeechobee, the second-largest freshwater lake in North America. Sounds impressive, but the bottom of the lake is only a few feet above sea level, and it's so shallow you can practically wade across.

Lake Okeechobee ever so gently floods the southern tip of the peninsula (or it wants to; canals divert much of the flow). From here, the land inclines about 6in every 6 miles until finally Florida can't keep its head above water anymore, petering out into the 10,000 Islands and the Florida Keys, which end with a flourish in the Gulf of Mexico. Key West, the last in the chain, is the southernmost point in the continental US.

What really sets Florida apart, though, is that it occupies a subtropical transition zone between northern temperate and southern tropical climates. This is key to the coast's florid coral-reef system, the largest in North America, and the key to Florida's attention-getting collection of surreal swamps, botanical oddities and monstrous critters. The Everglades gets the most press, and as an International Biosphere, World Heritage Site, and National Park, this 'river of grass' deserves it.

But the Panhandle's Apalachicola River basin has been called a 'Garden of Eden,' in which Ice Age plants survive in lost ravines, and where more species of amphibians and reptiles hop and slither than anywhere else in the US. The Indian River Lagoon estuary, stretching 156 miles along the Atlantic Coast, is the most diverse on the continent. And across north Florida, the pockmarked and honeycombed limestone (called karst terrain) holds the Florida Aquifer, which is fed solely by rain and which bubbles up like liquid diamonds in more than 700 freshwater springs.

Wildlife

With swamps full of gators, rivers full of snakes, manatees in mangroves, sea turtles on beaches, and giant flocks of seabirds taking wing at once, how is it, again, that a squeaky-voiced mouse became Florida's headliner?

Animals

Birds

Nearly 500 avian species have been documented in the state, including some of the world's most magnificent migratory waterbirds: ibis, egrets, great blue herons, white pelicans and whooping cranes. This makes Florida the ultimate birdwatcher's paradise.

Nearly 350 species spend time in the Everglades, the prime bird-watching spot in Florida. But you don't have to brave the swamp. Completed in 2006, the Great Florida Birding Trail (www.floridabirdingtrail. com) runs 2000 miles and includes nearly 500 bird-watching sites. Nine of these are 'gateway' sites, with staffed visitor centers and free 'loan' binoculars; see the website for downloadable guides and look for brown road signs when driving.

Among the largest birds, white pelicans arrive in winter (October to April), while brown pelicans, the only pelican to dive for its food, lives here year-round. To see the striking pale-pink roseate spoonbill, a member of the ibis family, visit JN 'Ding' Darling National Wildlife Refuge (p408), the wintering site for a third of the US roseate spoonbill population.

About 5000 nonmigratory sandhill cranes are joined by 25,000 migratory cousins each winter. White whooping cranes, at up to 5ft the tallest bird in North America, are nearly extinct; about 100 winter on Florida's Gulf Coast near Homosassa.

To learn about the incredible efforts to save the whooping crane, visit Operation Migration (www .operation migration.org), a nonprofit run by Bill Lishman, whose techniques inspired the film *Fly Away Home*. Another resource is www.bringback thecranes.org.

FLORIDA'S MANATEES

It's hard to believe Florida's West Indian manatees were ever mistaken for mermaids, but it's easy to see their attraction: these gentle, curious, colossal mammals are as sweetly lovable as 10ft, 1000lb teddy bears. Solitary and playful, they have been known to 'surf' waves, and every winter, from November to March, they migrate into the warmer waters of Florida's freshwater estuaries, rivers and springs. Like humans, manatees will die if trapped in 62°F water for 24 hours, and in winter Florida's eternally 72°F springs are balmy spas.

Florida residents for over 45 million years, these shy herbivores have absolutely no defenses except their size (they can reach 13ft and 3000lb), and they don't do much, spending most of each day resting and eating 10% of their body weight. Rarely moving faster than a languid saunter, manatees even reproduce slowly; females birth one calf every two to five years. The exception to their docility? Mating. Males are notorious for their aggressive sex drive.

Florida's manatees have been under some form of protection since 1893, and they were included in the first federal endangered species list in 1967. Manatees were once hunted for their meat, but today collisions with boats are a leading cause of manatee death, accounting for over 20% annually. Propeller scars are so ubiquitous among the living they are the chief identifying tool of scientists.

Population counts are notoriously difficult and unreliable, yet recent numbers are encouraging. A particularly cold 2010 winter yielded an all-time high count of 5060 manatees, exceeding the previous high by 1200.

Songbirds and raptors fill Florida skies, too. The state has over 1000 mated pairs of bald eagles, the most in the southern US, and peregrine falcons, which can dive up to 150mph, migrate through in spring and fall.

Land Mammals

Florida's most endangered mammal is the Florida panther. Before European contact, perhaps 1500 roamed the state. The first panther bounty ($5 a scalp) was passed in 1832, and over the next 130 years they were hunted relentlessly. Though hunting was stopped in 1958, it was too late for panthers to survive on their own. Without a captive breeding program, begun in 1991, the Florida panther would now be extinct and with only some 120 known to exist (for more, see p149), they're not out of the swamp yet.

You're not likely to see a panther, but black bears have recovered to a population of around 3000; as their forests diminish, bears are occasionally seen traipsing through suburbs in northern Florida.

Easy to find, white-tailed deer are a common species that troubles landscaping. Endemic to the Keys are Key deer, a Honey-I-Shrunk-the-Ungulate subspecies: less than 3ft tall and lighter than a 10-year-old boy, they live mostly on Big Pine Key (p168).

Marine Mammals

Florida's coastal waters are home to 21 species of dolphins and whales. By far the most common is the bottlenose dolphin, which is highly social, extremely intelligent and frequently encountered around the entire peninsula. Bottlenose dolphins are the species most often seen in captivity.

The North Atlantic population of about 300 right whales comes to winter calving grounds off the Atlantic Coast near Jacksonville (p339). These giant animals can be over 50ft long, and they are the most endangered species of whale.

Winter is also the season for manatees, which seek out Florida's warm-water springs and power-plant discharge canals beginning in November. These lovable, lumbering creatures are another iconic Florida species whose conservation both galvanizes and divides state residents. For more on manatees, see p151.

Reptiles & Amphibians

Boasting an estimated 184 species, Florida has the nation's largest collection of reptiles and amphibians, and unfortunately, it's growing. Uninvited guests add to the total regularly, many establishing themselves after being released by pet owners. Some of the more dangerous, problematic and invasive species include Burmese pythons, black and green iguanas and Nile monitor lizards.

The American alligator is Florida's poster species, and they are ubiquitous in Central and South Florida. See p488.

South Florida is also home to the only North American population of American crocodile. Florida's crocs number around 1500; they prefer saltwater, and to distinguish them from gators, check their smile – a croc's snout is more tapered and its teeth stick out.

Turtles, frogs and snakes love Florida, and nothing is cuter than watching bright skinks, lizards and anoles skittering over porches and sidewalks. Cute doesn't always describe the state's 44 species of snakes – though Floridian promoters emphasize that only six species are poisonous, and only four of those are common. Feel better? Of the baddies, three are rattlesnakes (diamondback, pygmy, canebrake), plus copperheads, cottonmouths and coral snakes. The diamondback is the biggest (up to 7ft), most aggressive and most dangerous. But rest assured, while cottonmouths live in and around water, most Florida water snakes are not cottonmouths. Whew!

SWAMP THING WILDLIFE

Naturalist Doug Alderson helped create the Big Bend Paddling Trail, and in his book *Waters Less Traveled* (2005) he describes his adventures: dodging pygmy rattlesnakes, meeting Shitty Bill, discussing Kemp's ridley turtles and pondering manatee farts.

KEEPERS OF THE EVERGLADES

Anyone who has dipped a paddle among the saw grass and hardwood hammocks of Everglades National Park wouldn't quibble with the American alligator's Florida sobriquet, 'Keepers of the Everglades.' With snout, eyeballs, and pebbled back so still they hardly ripple the water's surface, alligators have watched over the Glades for over 200 million years.

It's impossible to count Florida's wild alligators, but estimates are that 1.5 million lumber among the state's lakes, rivers and golf courses. No longer officially endangered, they remain protected because they resemble the still-endangered American crocodile. Alligator served in restaurants typically comes from licensed alligator farms, though since 1988, Florida has conducted an annual alligator harvest, open to nonresidents, that allows two alligators per person.

Alligators are alpha predators that keep the rest of the food chain in check, and their 'gator holes' become vital water cups in the dry season and during droughts, aiding the entire wetlands ecosystem. Alligators, which live for about 30 years, can grow up to 14ft long and weigh 1000lb.

A vocal courtship begins in April, and mating takes place in May and June. By late June, females begin laying nests of 30 to 45 eggs, which incubate for two months before hatching. On average, only four alligators per nest survive to adulthood.

Alligators hunt in water, often close to shore; typically, they run on land to flee, not to chase. In Florida, an estimated 15 to 20 nonfatal attacks on humans occur each year, and there have been 22 fatal attacks since 1948.

Some estimate an alligator's top short-distance land speed at 30mph, but it's a myth that you must zigzag to avoid them. The best advice is to run in a straight line as fast as your little legs can go.

Sea Turtles

Most sea-turtle nesting in the continental US occurs in Florida. Predominantly three species create over 80,000 nests annually, mostly on southern Atlantic Coast beaches but extending to all Gulf Coast beaches. Most are loggerhead, then far fewer green and leatherback, and historically hawksbill and Kemp's ridley as well; all five species are endangered or threatened. The leatherback is the largest, attaining 10ft and 2000lb.

During the May-to-October nesting season, sea turtles deposit from 80 to 120 eggs in each nest. The eggs incubate for about two months, and then the hatchlings emerge all at once and make for the ocean. Contrary to myth, hatchlings don't need the moon to find their way to the sea.

However, they can become hopelessly confused by artificial lights and noisy human audiences. For the best, least-disruptive experience, join a sanctioned turtle watch; for a list, visit www.myfwc.com/seaturtle, then click on 'Educational Information' and 'Where to View Sea Turtles.'

Visit the Florida Native Plant Society (www.fnps .org), a nonprofit conservation organization, for updates on preservation issues and invasive species and for a nice overview of Florida's native plants and ecosystems.

Plants

The diversity of the peninsula's flora, including over 4000 species of plants, is unmatched in the continental US. Florida contains the southern extent of temperate ecosystems and the northern extent of tropical ones, which blend and merge in a bewildering, fluid taxonomy of environments. Interestingly, most of the world at this latitude is a desert, which Florida definitely is not.

Wetlands & Swamps

It takes special kinds of plants to thrive in the humid, waterlogged, sometimes-salty marshes, sloughs, swales, seeps, basins, marl prairies and swamps of Florida, and several hundred specialized native plants evolved to do so. Much of the Everglades is dominated by vast expanses of saw grass, which is actually a sedge with fine toothlike edges that can reach 10ft high. South Florida is a symphony of sedges, grasses and rushes. These hardy water-tolerant species provide abundant seeds to feed birds and animals, protect fish in shallow water, and pad wetlands for birds and alligators.

The strangest plants are the submerged and immersed species that grow in, under and out of the water. Free-floating species include bladderwort and coontail, a species that lives, flowers and is pollinated entirely underwater. Florida's swamps are abundant with rooted plants with floating leaves, like the pretty American lotus, water lilies and spatterdock (if you love quaint names, you'll love Florida botany!). Another common immersed plant, bur marigolds, can paint whole prairies yellow.

Across Florida, whenever land rises just enough to create drier islands, tracts, hills and hillocks, dense tree-filled hammocks occur; ecological zones can shift as dramatically in 1ft in Florida as they do in a 1000ft elsewhere. These hammocks go by many names depending on location and type. Tropical hammocks typically mix tropical hardwoods and palms with semideciduous and evergreen trees like live oak.

Another dramatic, beautiful tree in Florida's swamps is the bald cypress, the most flood-tolerant tree. It can grow 150ft tall, with buttressed, wide trunks and roots with 'knees' that poke above the drenched soil. Cypress domes are a particular type of swamp, which arise when a watery depression occurs in a pine flatwood.

Audubon of Florida (www .audubonof florida.org) is perhaps Florida's leading conservation organization. It has tons of birding and ecological information, and it publishes *Florida Naturalist* magazine.

Forests, Scrubs & Flatwoods

Florida's northern forests, particularly in the Panhandle, are an epicenter of plant and animal biodiversity, just as much as its southern swamps. Here, the continent's temperate forests of hickory, elm, ash, maple, magnolia and locust trees combine with the various pine, gum and oak trees that are common throughout Florida along with the sawgrass, cypress and cabbage palms of southern Florida. The wet but temperate Apala-

GHOST HUNTERS

Florida has more species of orchids than any other state in the US, and orchids are themselves the largest family of flowering plants in the world, with perhaps 25,000 species. On the dial of botanical fascination, orchids rank highly, and the Florida orchid that inspires the most intense devotion is the rare ghost orchid.

This bizarre epiphytic flower has no leaves and usually only one bloom, which is of course deathly white with two long thin drooping petals that curl like a handlebar mustache. The ghost orchid is pollinated in the dead of night by the giant sphinx moth, which is the only insect with a proboscis long enough to reach down the ghost orchid's 5in-long nectar spur.

The exact locations of ghost orchids are kept secret for fear of poachers, who, as Susan Orlean's book *The Orchid Thief* makes clear, are a real threat to their survival. But the flower's general whereabouts are common knowledge: South Florida's approximately 2000 ghost orchids are almost all in Big Cypress National Preserve (p143) and Fakahatchee Strand Preserve State Park (www.floridastateparks.org/fakahatcheestrand). Of course, these parks are home to a great many other wild orchids, as are Everglades National Park (p137), Myakka River State Park (p397) and Corkscrew Swamp Sanctuary (p414).

To learn more, see Florida's Native Orchids (www.flnativeorchids.com) and Ghost Orchid Info (www.ghostorchid.info), and visit Sarasota's Selby Botanical Gardens (p392).

CARNIVOROUS PLANTS

chicola forest supports 40 kinds of trees and more insect species than scientists can count.

Central and northern Florida were once covered in longleaf and slash-pine forests, both prized for timber and pine gum. Today, due to logging, only 2% of old-growth longleaf forests remain. Faster-growing slash pine has now largely replaced longleaf pine in Florida's second-growth forests.

Scrubs are found throughout Florida; they are typically old dunes with well-drained sandy soil. In central Florida (along the Lake Wales Ridge), scrubs are the oldest plant communities, with the highest number of endemic and rare species. Sand pines, scrub oak, rosemary and lichens predominate.

Scrubs often blend into sandy pine flatwoods, which typically have a sparse longleaf or slash-pine overstory and an understory of grasses and/or saw palmetto. Saw palmetto is a vital Florida plant: its fruit is an important food for bears and deer (and an herbal medicine that some believe helps prevent cancer), it provides shelter for panthers and snakes, and its flower is an important source of honey. It's named for its sharp saw-toothed leaf stems.

Mangroves & Coastal Dunes

Where not shaved smooth by sand, southern Florida's coastline is often covered with a three-day stubble of mangroves. Mangroves are not a single species; the name refers to all tropical trees and shrubs that have adapted to loose wet soil, saltwater, and periodic root submergence. Mangroves have also developed 'live birth,' germinating their seeds while they're still attached to the parent tree. Of the over 50 species of mangroves worldwide, only three predominate in Florida: red, black and white. For more, see p166.

Mangroves play a vital role on the peninsula, and their destruction usually sets off a domino-effect of ecological damage. Mangroves 'stabilize' coastal land, trapping sand, silt and sediment. As this builds up, new land is created, which ironically strangles the mangroves themselves. Mangroves mitigate the storm surge and damaging winds of hurricanes, and they anchor tidal and estuary communities, providing vital wildlife habitats.

Coastal dunes are typically home to grasses and shrubs, saw palmetto and occasionally pines and cabbage palm (or sabal palm, the Florida state tree). Sea oats, with large plumes that trap wind-blown sand, are important for stabilizing dunes, while coastal hammocks welcome the wiggly gumbo-limbo tree, whose red peeling bark has earned it the nickname the 'tourist tree.'

In Florida, even the plants bite: the Panhandle has the most species of carnivorous plants in the US – a result of its nutrient-poor sandy soil.

National, State & Regional Parks

About 26% of Florida's land lies in public hands, which breaks down to three national forests, 11 national parks, 28 national wildlife refuges (including the first, Pelican Island), and 160 state parks. Attendance is up, with over 20 million folks visiting state parks annually, and Florida's state parks have twice been voted the nation's best.

Florida's parks are easy to explore. For more information, see From Boots to Beaches (p480) or the websites of the following organizations:

Florida State Parks (www.floridastateparks.org)

National Forests, Florida (www.fs.usda.gov/florida)

National Park Service (NPS; www.nps.gov)

National Wildlife Refuges, Florida (NWR; www.fws.gov/southeast/maps /fl.html)

Recreation.gov (www.recreation.gov) National lands campground reservations.

The Florida Fish & Wildlife Commission (www.myfwc.com) manages Florida's mostly undeveloped Wildlife Management Areas (WMA). The website is an excellent resource for wildlife-viewing, as well as boating, hunting, fishing and permits.

Environmental Issues

Florida's environmental problems are the inevitable result of its century-long love affair with land development, population growth and tourism, and addressing them is especially urgent given Florida's uniquely diverse natural world. These complex, intertwined environmental impacts include erosion of wetlands, depletion of the aquifer, rampant pollution (particularly of waters), invasive species, endangered species, and widespread habitat destruction. There is nary an acre of Florida that escapes concern.

The Florida chapter of the Nature Conservancy (www .nature.org) has been instrumental in the Florida Forever legislation. Check the web for updates and conservation issues.

In the last decade, Florida has enacted several significant conservation efforts. In 2000, the state passed the Florida Forever Act (www.support floridaforever.org), a 10-year, $3 billion conservation program that in 2008 was renewed for another 10 years. It also passed the multibillion-dollar Comprehensive Everglades Restoration Plan (CERP; www.everglades plan.org). For more on Everglades restoration, see p141.

Signs of progress can be encouraging. For instance, phosphorous levels in the Everglades have been seriously reduced, and the Kissimmee River is a model of restoration: within a few years of backfilling the canal

A KINDER, GENTLER WILDERNESS ENCOUNTER

While yesterday's glass-bottom boats and alligator wrestling have evolved into today's swamp-buggy rides and manatee encounters, the question remains: just because you can do something, does that mean you should? In Florida, everyone can be involved in protecting nature just by considering the best ways to experience it without harming it in the process.

For most activities, there isn't a single right answer; specific impacts are often debated. However, here are a few guidelines:

» **Airboats and swamp buggies** While airboats have a much lighter 'footprint' than big-wheeled buggies, both are motorized (and loud) and have far larger impacts than canoes for exploring wetlands. As a rule, nonmotorized activities are least damaging.

» **Dolphin encounters** Captive dolphins are typically rescued animals already acclimated to humans. For a consideration of dolphin swims, see p164. However, when encountering wild dolphins in the ocean, federal law makes it illegal to feed, pursue or touch them. Keep in mind that habituating any wild animal to humans can lead to the animal's death, since approaching humans often results in conflict and accidents (as with boats).

» **Manatee swims** When swimming near manatees, a federally protected endangered species, look but don't touch. 'Passive observation' is the standard. Harassment is a rampant problem that may lead to stricter 'no touch' legislation.

» **Feeding wild animals** In a word, don't. Friendly animals like deer and manatees may come to rely on human food (to their detriment), while feeding bears and alligators just encourages them to...hunt you.

» **Sea-turtle nesting sites** It's a federal crime to approach nesting sea turtles or hatchling runs. Most nesting beaches have warning signs and a nighttime 'lights out' policy. If you do encounter turtles on the beach, keep your distance and don't take flash photos.

» **Coral-reef etiquette** Coral polyps are living organisms and touching or breaking coral creates openings for infection and disease. To prevent reef damage, never touch the coral. It's that simple.

that had restricted its flow, the river's floodplain is again a humid marsh full of waterbirds and alligators. Also, in 2010 the state completed a purchase of 300 sq miles of Lake Okeechobee sugarcane fields from US Sugar, intending to convert them back to swamp. Along with plans to bridge 6.5 miles of the Tamiami Trail, the lake may once again water the Glades.

And yet, these efforts alone are insufficient to fix the sins of the past, and funding tends to dry up faster than an afternoon rainstorm in August. For instance, Governor Scott cut Florida Forever's 2010 funding entirely, and the program's future viability is now in question.

Lake Okeechobee, imprisoned by Hoover Dike since 1928, is full of toxic sludge which gets stirred up during hurricanes and causes 'red tides,' or algal blooms that kill fish. Red tides occur naturally, but they are also sparked by things like pollution and unnatural water flows.

Studies have found that half of the state's lakes and waterways are too polluted for fishing. Though industrial pollution has been curtailed, pollution from residential development (sewage, fertilizer runoff) more than compensates. This is distressing Florida's freshwater springs, which can turn murky with algae. Plus, as the groundwater gets pumped out to slake homeowners' thirsts, the springs are shrinking and the drying limestone honeycomb underfoot sometimes collapses, causing sinkholes that swallow cars and homes.

And residential development continues almost unabated. The Miami–Fort Lauderdale–West Palm Beach corridor (the USA's sixth-largest urban area) is, as developers say, 'built out,' so developers are targeting the Panhandle and central Florida. Projections for the next 50 years show unrelenting urban sprawl up and down both coasts and painted across central Florida.

Then there's the coming apocalypse: rising seas due to global warming. Here, the low-lying Florida Keys are a 'canary in a coalmine' that's being watched worldwide for impacts. In another century, some quip, South Florida's coastline could be a modern-day Atlantis, with its most expensive real estate underwater.

Great Nature Guides

» *The Living Gulf Coast* (2011), Charles Sobczak

» *Priceless Florida* (2004), Ellie Whitney, D Bruce Means & Anne Rudloe

» *Seashore Plants of South Florida & the Caribbean* (1994), David W Nellis

Survival Guide

Directory A–Z

Accommodations

Our reviews (and rates) use the following room types:

» single occupancy (s)
» double occupancy (d)
» room (r), same rate for one or two people
» dorm bed (dm)
» suite (ste)
» apartment (apt)

Unless otherwise noted, rates do not include breakfast, bathrooms are private and all lodging is open year-round.

Rates don't include taxes, which vary considerably between towns; in fact, hotels almost never include taxes and fees in their rate quotes, so always ask for the *total rate with tax*. Florida's sales tax is 6%, and some communities tack on more. States, cities and towns also usually levy taxes on hotel rooms, which can increase the final bill by 10% to 12%.

Throughout the book, quoted rates are usually 'high season' rates, unless rates are distinguished as winter/summer or high/low season. Note that 'high season' can mean summer *or* winter depending on the region; see destination chapters and p14 for general advice on seasons.

Our hotel price indicators refer to standard double rooms:

» $ less than $100
» $$ $100–200
» $$$ more than $200

These price indicators are guidelines only. Many places have certain rooms that cost above or below their standard rates, and seasonal/holiday fluctuations can see rates rise and fall dramatically, especially in Orlando and tourist beach towns. Specific advice for the best rates varies by region, and is included throughout: on the one hand, booking in advance for high-season tourist hotspots (like beaches and Orlando resorts) can be essential to ensure the room you want. On the other, inquiring at the last minute, or even same-day, can yield amazing discounts on any rooms still available.

For discounted rooms and last-minute deals, check the following websites:

» www.expedia.com
» www.hotels.com
» www.hotwire.com
» www.orbitz.com
» www.priceline.com
» www.travelocity.com

B&Bs & Inns

These accommodations vary from small, comfy houses with shared bathrooms (least expensive), to romantic, antique-filled historic homes and opulent mansions with private bath (most expensive). Those focusing on upscale romance may discourage children. Also, inns and B&Bs often require a minimum stay of two or three days on weekends and advance reservations. Always call ahead to confirm policies (regarding kids, pets, smoking) and bathroom arrangements.

Camping

Three types of campgrounds are available: undeveloped ($10 per night), public ($15 to $20) and privately owned ($25 and up). In general, Florida campgrounds are quite safe. Undeveloped campgrounds are just that (undeveloped), while most public campgrounds have toilets, showers and drinking water. Reserve state-park sites by calling ☎800-326-3521 or visiting www .reserveamerica.com.

Most privately owned campgrounds are geared to RVs (motor homes) but will also have a small section available for tent campers. Expect tons of amenities, like swimming pools, laundry facilities, convenience stores and bars. **Kampgrounds of America** (KOA; ☎406-248-7444; www.koa.com) is a national network of private campgrounds; their Kamping Kabins have air-con and kitchens.

Hostels

In most hostels, group dorms are segregated by sex and you'll be sharing a bathroom; occasionally alcohol is banned. About half the hostels throughout Florida are affiliated with **Hostelling International USA** (HI-USA; ☎301-495-1240; www. hiusa.org; 8401 Colesville Rd, Suite 600, Silver Spring, MD 20910). You don't have to be a member to stay, but you pay a slightly higher rate; you can join HI by phone, online or at most youth hostels. From the US, you can book many HI hostels through its toll-free **reservations service** (📞888-464-4872).

Florida has many independent hostels (www.hostels.com); most have comparable rates and conditions to HI hostels, and some are better.

Hotels

We have tried to highlight independently owned hotels in this guide, but in some towns, chain hotels are the best and sometimes the only option. The calling-card of chain hotels is reliability: acceptable cleanliness, unremarkable yet inoffensive decor, and a comfortable bed. TV, phone, air-conditioning, mini-refrigerator, microwave, hair dryer and safe are standard amenities in midrange chains. A recent trend, most evident in Miami and beach resorts, is chain-owned hotels striving for upscale boutique-style uniqueness in decor and feel.

High-end hotels – Ritz-Carlton in particular – overwhelm guests with services: valet parking, room service, newspaper delivery, dry cleaning, laundry, pools, health clubs, bars and other niceties. You'll find plenty of boutique and specialty hotels in places like Miami's South Beach and Palm Beach. While all large chain hotels have toll-free reservation numbers, you may find better savings by calling the hotel directly.

Chain-owned hotels include the following:
Hilton (📞800-445-8667; www.hilton.com)

Holiday Inn (📞888-465-4329; www.holidayinn.com)
Marriott (📞888-236-2427; www.marriott.com)
Radisson (📞888-201-1718; www.radisson.com)
Ritz-Carlton (📞800-542-8680; www.ritzcarlton.com)
Sheraton (📞800-325-3535; www.starwoodhotels.com/sheraton)

Motels

Budget and midrange motels remain prevalent in Florida; these 'drive-up rooms' are often near highway exits and along a town's main road. Many are still independently owned, and thus quality varies tremendously; some are much better inside than their exteriors suggest: ask to see a room first if you're unsure. Most strive for the same level of amenities and cleanliness as a budget chain hotel.

A motel's 'rack rates' can be more open to haggling, but not always. Demand is the final arbiter, though simply asking about any specials can sometimes inspire a discount.

Resorts

Florida resorts, much like Disney World, aim to be so all-encompassing you'll never need, or want, to leave. Included are all manner of fitness and sports facilities, pools, spas, restaurants and bars, and so on. Many also have on-site babysitting services. However, some also tack an extra 'resort fee' onto rates, so always ask.

Activities

For an introduction to all the things you can do in

Florida, turn to From Boots to Beaches (p480). This section focuses on the resources, websites, magazines and organizations that help you do all those things. For more information on Florida's national and state parks, see Swamp Thing (p490), which lists websites for the various governing bodies.

Biking

Note that the state organizations listed under Hiking also discuss biking trails. Florida law requires that all cyclists under 16 must wear a helmet (under 18 in national parks).
Bike Florida (www.bikeflorida.org) Nonprofit organization promoting safe cycling and organized rides, with good biking links.
Florida Bicycle Association (www.floridabicycle.org) Advocacy organization providing tons of advice, a statewide list of cycling clubs, and links to off-road cycling organizations, racing clubs, a touring calendar and more.

Canoeing & Kayaking

Water-trail and kayaking information is also provided by the Florida State Parks and the Greenways & Trails websites under Hiking & Camping. Here are more resources:
American Canoe Association (ACA; www.americancanoe.org) ACA publishes a newsletter, has a water-trails database and organizes courses.
Florida Professional Paddlesports Association (www.paddleflausa.com) Provides a list of affiliated member kayak outfitters.
Kayak Online (www.kayakonline.com) A good resource for kayak gear, with links to Florida outfitters.

Diving

Ocean diving in Florida requires an Open Water I certificate, and Florida has plenty of certification programs (with good weather,

DIRECTORY A–Z ACTIVITIES

BOOK YOUR STAY ONLINE

For more accommodations reviews by Lonely Planet authors, check out hotels.lonelyplanet.com/Florida. You'll find independent reviews, as well as recommendations on the best places to stay. Best of all, you can book online.

they take three days). To dive in freshwater springs, you need a separate cave-diving certification, and this is also offered throughout the state.

National Association for Underwater Instruction (NAUI; www.naui.org) Information on dive certifications and a list of NAUI-certified Florida dive instructors.

Professional Diving Instructors Corporation (PDIC; www.pdic-intl.com) Similar to NAUI, with its own list of PDIC-certified Florida dive instructors.

Fishing

Note that all nonresidents 16 and over need a fishing license to fish, and Florida offers several short-term licenses. There are lots of regulations about what and how much you can catch where; locals can give you details, but it doesn't hurt to review the Florida Fish & Wildlife Conservation Commission (FWC) website.

Florida Fish & Wildlife Conservation Commission (FWC; www.myfwc.com)

The official source for all fishing regulations and licenses (purchase online or by phone). Also has boating and hunting information.

Florida Fishing Capital of the World (www.visitflorida .com/fishing) State-run all-purpose fishing advice and information.

Florida Sportsman (www .floridasportsman.com) Get the lowdown on sport fishing, tournaments, charters, gear and detailed regional advice.

Hiking & Camping

For advice on low-impact hiking and camping, visit **Leave No Trace** (www.lnt.org). For a rich introduction to Florida trails, see **Florida Hikes** (www.floridahikes.com).

Florida Greenways & Trails (www.visitflorida.com /trails) The Florida Department of Environmental Protection has downloadable hiking, biking and kayaking trail descriptions.

Florida State Parks (www.floridastateparks.org) Comprehensive state-park

information and all cabin and camping reservations.

Florida Trail Association (www.floridatrail.org) Maintains the Florida National Scenic Trail (FNST); a wealth of online advice, descriptions and maps.

Florida Trails Network (www.floridatrailsnetwork.com) The state's main database of current and future trails.

Rails-to-Trails Conservancy (www.railstotrails.org) Converts abandoned railroad corridors into public biking and hiking trails; has a Florida chapter and reviews trails at www.traillink.com.

Recreation.gov (www .recreation.gov) Reserve camping at all national parks and forests.

For short hikes in national, state or regional parks, free park maps are perfectly adequate. Most outdoor stores and ranger stations sell good topographical (topo) maps. Or order them online:

US Geological Survey (USGS; ☑888-275-8747; www .store.usgs.gov)

Trails.com (www.trails.com) Create custom, downloadable topo maps.

National Geographic (www .nationalgeographic.com) Custom maps and GPS maps.

Surfing

Looking for lessons, surf reports or competitions? Start here:

Florida Surfing (www.florida surfing.com) Instructors, contests, webcams, weather, equipment, history: it's all here.

Florida Surfing Association (FSA; www.floridasurfing .org) Manages Florida's surf competitions; also runs the surf school at Jacksonville Beach.

Surfer (www.surfermag.com) *Surfer's* travel reports cover Florida and just about every break in the USA.

Surf Guru (www.surfguru .com) East Coast Florida surf reports.

PRACTICALITIES

» Florida has three major daily newspapers: *Miami Herald* (in Spanish, *El Nuevo Herald*), *Orlando Sentinal* and *St Petersburg Times*.

» Florida receives all the major US TV and cable networks. **Florida Smart** (www.floridasmart.com/news) lists them all by region.

» Video systems use the NTSC color TV standard, not compatible with the PAL system.

» Electrical voltage is 110/120V, 60 cycles.

» Distances are measured in feet, yards and miles; weights are tallied in ounces, pounds and tons.

» Florida bans smoking in all enclosed workplaces, including restaurants and shops, but excluding 'stand-alone' bars (that don't emphasize food) and designated hotel smoking rooms.

» Most of Florida is in the US eastern time zone: noon in Miami equals 9am in San Francisco and 5pm in London. West of the Apalachicola River, the Panhandle is in the US central time zone, one hour behind the rest of the state. During daylight-saving time, clocks 'spring forward' one hour in March and 'fall back' one hour in November.

Business Hours

Unless otherwise noted the standard business hours in this guide are as follows:

Banks 8:30am to 4:30pm Monday to Thursday, to 5:30pm Friday; sometimes 9am to 12:30pm Saturday.

Bars most bars 5pm to midnight; to 2am Friday and Saturday.

Businesses 9am to 5pm Monday to Friday.

Post offices 9am to 5pm Monday to Friday; sometimes 9am to noon Saturday.

Restaurants Breakfast 7am to 10:30am Monday to Friday; brunch 9am to 2pm Saturday; lunch 11:30am to 2:30pm Monday to Friday; dinner 5pm to 9:30pm, later Friday and Saturday.

Shops 10am to 6pm Monday to Saturday, noon to 5pm Sunday; shopping malls keep extended hours.

Discount Cards

For discounts to Orlando-area theme parks, see the Theme Park Trip Planner (p30). There are no Florida-specific discount cards. For Florida hotel deals, see discounter websites like **Priceline** (www.priceline.com) and **Roomsavers** (www.room savers.com). Florida is a *very* competitive tourist destination, so persistence usually pays dividends.

Being a member of certain groups also gives access to discounts (usually about 10%) at many hotels, museums and sights. Simply carry the appropriate ID.

Auto-club membership See the Transportation chapter (p508)

Students Any student ID is typically honored; international students might consider an **International Student Identity Card** (ISIC; www.isiccard.com).

Seniors Generally refers to those 65 and older, but sometimes those 60 and older. Join the **American Association of Retired Persons** (AARP; ☎888-687-2277; www.aarp.org) for more travel bargains.

Electricity

110V/60Hz

110V/60Hz

Food & Drink

In this book, price indicators apply to the typical dinner main course; they are as follows:

» $ less than $10
» $$ $10–20
» $$$ more than $20

For Miami and Orlando:
» $ less than $15
» $$ $15–30
» $$$ more than $30

As a rule, for good to excellent service, always tip 15% to 20% of the total bill.

Gay & Lesbian Travelers

Florida is not uniformly anything, and it's not uniformly embracing of gay life. The state is largely tolerant, particularly in major tourist destinations, beaches and cities, but this tolerance does not always extend into the more rural and Southern areas of northern Florida. However, where Florida does embrace gay life, it does so with a big flamboyant bear hug. Miami (p48) and South Beach (p52) are as 'out' as it's possible to be, with some massive gay festivals. Fort Lauderdale (p197), West Palm Beach (p213), and Key West (p183) have long supported vibrant gay communities. But notable gay scenes and communities also exist in Orlando (p251), Jacksonville (p343), and Pensacola (p428), and to far lesser degrees in Daytona Beach, Tampa, and Sarasota.

Good gay-and-lesbian resources:

Damron (www.damron.com) Publishes popular national guidebooks, including *Women's Traveller, Men's Travel Guide,* and *Damron Accommodations.*

Gay Yellow Network (www.gayyellow.com) City-based yellow-page listings including six Florida cities.

Out Traveler (www.outtra veler.com)

Purple Roofs (www.purple roofs.com) Lists queer accommodations, travel agencies and tours worldwide.

Health

Florida, and the USA generally, has a high level of hygiene, so infectious diseases are not generally a significant concern for most travelers. There are no required vaccines, and tap water is safe to drink. Despite Florida's plethora of intimidating wildlife, the main concerns for travelers are sunburn and mosquito bites – as well as arriving with adequate health insurance in case of accidents.

Animal & Spider Bites

Florida's critters can be cute, but they can also bite and sting. Here are a few to watch out for:

Alligators and snakes Neither attack humans unless startled or threatened. If you encounter them, simply back away. Florida has several venomous snakes, so always immediately seek treatment if bitten.

Jellyfish and stingrays Florida beaches can see both; avoid swimming when they are present (lifeguards often post warnings). Treat stings immediately; they hurt but aren't dangerous.

Spiders Florida is home to two venomous spiders – the black widow and the brown recluse. Seek immediate treatment if bitten by any spider.

Health Care

In general, if you have a medical emergency, go to the emergency room of the nearest hospital. If the problem isn't urgent, call a nearby hospital and ask for a referral to a local physician; this is usually cheaper than a trip to the emergency room. Standalone, for-profit urgent-care centers provide good service, but can be the most expensive option.

Pharmacies are abundantly supplied. However, some medications that are available over the counter in other countries require a prescription in the US. If you don't have insurance to cover the cost of prescriptions, these can be shockingly expensive.

Health Insurance

The US offers some of the finest health care in the world. The problem is that it can be prohibitively expensive. It's essential to purchase travel health insurance if your policy doesn't cover you when you're abroad.

Bring any medications you may need in their original containers, clearly labeled. A signed, dated letter from your physician that describes all of your medical conditions and medications (including generic names) is also a good idea.

If your health insurance does not cover you for medical expenses abroad, consider obtaining supplemental health or travel insurance. Find out in advance whether your insurance plan will make payments directly to the providers or if they will reimburse you later for any overseas health expenditures.

Infectious Diseases

In addition to more-common ailments, there are several infectious diseases that are unknown or uncommon outside North America. Most are acquired by mosquito or tick bites.

Giardiasis Also known as traveler's diarrhea. A parasitic infection of the small intestines, typically contracted by drinking feces-contaminated fresh water. Never drink untreated stream, lake or pond water. Easily treated with antibiotics.

HIV/AIDS HIV infection occurs in the US, as do all sexually transmitted diseases. Use a condom for all sexual encounters.

Lyme Disease Though more common in the US northeast than Florida, Lyme disease occurs here. It is transmitted by infected deer ticks, and is signaled by a bull's-eye rash at the bite and flulike symptoms. Treat promptly with antibiotics. Removing ticks within 36 hours can avoid infection.

Rabies Though rare, the rabies virus can be contracted from the bite of any infected animal; bats are most common, and their bites are not always obvious. If bitten by any animal, consult with a doctor, since rabies is fatal if untreated.

West Nile Virus Extremely rare in Florida, West Nile Virus is transmitted by culex mosquitoes. Most infections are mild or asymptomatic, but serious symptoms and even death can occur. There is no treatment for West Nile Virus. For the latest update on affected areas, see the **US Geological Survey disease maps** (http://diseasemaps.usgs.gov).

Internet Resources

There is a vast wealth of travel health advice on the internet. Two good sources:

World Health Organization (www.who.int/ith) The superb book *International Travel and Health* is available free online.

MD Travel Health (www.mdtravelhealth.com) Provides complete, updated and free travel health recommendations for every country.

Also, consult your government's travel health website before departure, if one is available:

Australia (www.smarttraveller.gov.au)
Canada (www.hc-sc.gc.ca/index-eng.php)
UK (www.fco.gov.uk/en/travel-and-living-abroad)
USA (wwwnc.cdc.gov/travel)

Insurance

It's expensive to get sick, crash a car or have things stolen from you in the US. Make sure to have adequate

Entering the Region

A passport is required for all foreign citizens. Unless eligible under the Visa Waiver Program (see below), foreign travelers must also have a tourist visa. To rent or drive a car, travelers from non-English-speaking countries should obtain an International Drivers Permit before arriving.

Travelers entering under the Visa Waiver Program must register with the US government's program **ESTA** (https://esta.cbp.dhs.gov) at least three days before arriving; earlier is better, since if denied, travelers must get a visa. Registration is valid for two years.

Upon arriving in the US, all foreign visitors must register in the US-Visit program, which entails having two index fingers scanned and a digital photo taken. For information on US-Visit, see the **Department of Homeland Security** (www.dhs.gov/us-visit).

Visas

All visitors should reconfirm entry requirements and visa guidelines before arriving. You can get visa information through www.usa.gov, but the **US State Department** (www.travel.state.gov) maintains the most comprehensive visa information, with lists of consulates and downloadable application forms. **US Citizenship & Immigration Services** (www.uscis.gov) mainly serves immigrants, not temporary visitors.

The **Visa Waiver Program** allows citizens of three dozen countries to enter the USA for stays of 90 days or less without first obtaining a US visa. See the ESTA website above for a current list. Under this program you must have a nonrefundable return ticket and 'e-passport' with digital chip. Passports issued/renewed before October 26, 2006, must be machine-readable.

Visitors who don't qualify for the Visa Waiver Program need a visa. Basic requirements are a valid passport, recent photo, travel details and often proof of financial stability. Students and adult males also must fill out supplemental travel documents.

The validity period for a US visitor visa depends on your home country. The length of time you'll be allowed to stay in the USA is determined by US officials at the port of entry. To stay longer than the date stamped on your passport, visit a local **USCIS** (☑800-375-5283; www.uscis.gov) office.

Customs

For a complete, up-to-date list of customs regulations, visit the website of **US Customs & Border Protection** (www.cbp.gov). Each visitor is allowed to bring into the US duty-free 1L of liquor (if you're 21 or older) and 200 cigarettes (if you're 18 or older) and up to $100 in gifts and purchases.

Embassies & Consulates

To find a US embassy in another country, visit the website of the **US Department of State** (www.usembassy.gov). Most foreign embassies in the US have their main consulates in Washington, DC, but some have representation in Miami. Except for the Italian consulate, the following consulates are all in Miami:

Australia (☑305-858-7633; http://australia.visahq.com; 2103 Coral Way, Suite 108)

Brazil (☑305-285-6200; www.brazilmiami.org; 80 SW 8th St, Suite 2600)

Canada (☑305-579-1600; www.canadainternational.gc.ca/miami; 200 S Biscayne Blvd, Suite 1600)

France (☑305-403-4150; www.consulfrance-miami.org; 1395 Brickell Ave, Suite 1050)

Germany (☑305-358-0290; www.germany.info; 100 N Biscayne Blvd, Suite 2200)

Italy (☑305-374-6322; www.consmiami.esteri.it/consolato_miami; 4000 Ponce de León, Suite 590, Coral Gables)

Mexico (☑786-268-4900; http://consulmex.sre.gob.mx/miami; 5975 SW 72nd St, Suite 302)

Netherlands (☑877-388-2443; http://miami.the-netherlands.org; 701 Brickell Ave, Suite 500)

UK (☑305-374-3500; http://ukinusa.fco.gov.uk/florida; 1001 Brickell Bay Dr, Suite 2800)

coverage before arriving. For car insurance see p508. To insure yourself for items that may be stolen from your car, consult your homeowner's (or renter's) insurance policy or consider investing in travel insurance.

Worldwide travel insurance is available at www.lonely planet.com/travel_services. You can buy, extend and claim online anytime – even if you're already on the road.

Internet Access

The USA and Florida are wired. Nearly every hotel and many restaurants and businesses offer high-speed internet access. In hotel listings, @ indicates a guest internet terminal and 🛜 indicates in-room wi-fi. With few exceptions, all hotels offer in-room plug-in and wi-fi in the lobby. Always ask about connection rates.

Most cafes offer inexpensive internet access, and most transportation stations and city parks are wi-fi hotspots. Public libraries provide free internet terminals, though sometimes you must get a temporary nonresident library card ($10). See destination Information sections.

For a list of wi-fi hotspots (plus tech and access info), visit **Wi-Fi Alliance** (www .wi-fi.org) and **Wi-Fi Free Spot** (www.wififreespot.com). If you bring a laptop from outside the USA, invest in a universal AC and plug adapter. Also, confirm that your modem card will work.

Legal Matters

In everyday matters, if you are stopped by the police, note that there is no system for paying traffic tickets or other fines on the spot. The patrol officer will explain your options to you; there is usually a 30-day period to pay fines by mail.

If you're arrested, you are allowed to remain silent,

though never walk away from an officer; you are entitled to have access to an attorney. The legal system presumes you're innocent until proven guilty. All persons who are arrested have the right to make one phone call. If you don't have a lawyer or family member to help you, call your embassy or consulate. The police will give you the number on request.

Drinking & Driving

Despite what you sometimes see, it's illegal to walk with an open alcoholic drink on the street. More importantly, don't drive with an 'open container'; any liquor in a car must be unopened or else stored in the trunk. If you're stopped while driving with an open container, police will treat you as if you were drinking and driving. Refusing a breathalyzer, urine or blood test is treated as if you'd taken the test and failed. A DUI (driving under the influence) conviction is a serious offense, subject to stiff fines and even imprisonment.

To purchase alcohol, you need to present a photo ID to prove your age.

Money

Prices quoted in this book are in US dollars ($). See Need to Know (p15) for exchange rates.

The ease and availability of ATMs have largely negated the need for traveler's checks. However, traveler's checks in US dollars are accepted like cash at most midrange and top-end businesses (but rarely at budget places). Personal checks not drawn on US banks are generally not accepted. Exchange foreign currency at international airports and most large banks in Miami, Orlando, Tampa and other Florida cities.

Major credit cards are widely accepted, and they are required for car rentals.

Most ATM withdrawals using out-of-state cards incur surcharges of $2 or so.

Tipping

Tipping is standard practice across America. In restaurants, for satisfactory to excellent service, tipping 15% to 20% of the bill is expected; less is okay at informal diners. Bartenders expect $1 per drink; café baristas a little change in the jar. Taxi drivers and hairdressers expect 10% to 15%. Skycaps at airports and porters at nice hotels expect $1 a bag or so. If you spend several nights in a hotel, it's polite to leave a few dollars for the cleaning staff.

Photography

All camera supplies (print and slide film, digital memory, camera batteries) are readily available in local drugstores, which also usually provide inexpensive film developing (including one-hour service) and burning photo CDs and DVDs.

Don't pack unprocessed film (including the roll in your camera) into checked luggage because exposure to high-powered X-ray equipment will cause it to fog. As an added precaution, 'hand check' film separately from carry-on bags at airport security checkpoints.

When photographing people, politeness is usually all that's needed (though street performers appreciate a tip).

For a primer on taking good shots, consult Lonely Planet's *Travel Photography*.

Post

The **US Postal Service** (USPS; ☎800-275-8777; www .usps.com) is reliable and inexpensive. For 1st-class mail sent and delivered within the USA, postage rates are 44¢ for letters up to 1oz (20¢ for each additional ounce) and 29¢ for standard-size postcards. International airmail rates for postcards and letters up to 1oz are 80¢ to Canada and Mexico, and 98¢ to other countries.

You can have mail sent to you c/o General Delivery at most big post offices (it's usually held for 30 days). Most hotels will also hold mail for incoming guests.

Public Holidays

For festivals and events, see Month by Month (p21). On the following national public holidays, banks, schools and government offices (including post offices) are closed, and transportation, museums and other services operate on a Sunday schedule. Many stores, however, maintain regular business hours. Holidays falling on a weekend are usually observed the following Monday.

New Year's Day January 1

Martin Luther King Jr Day Third Monday in January

Presidents Day Third Monday in February

Easter March or April

Memorial Day Last Monday in May

Independence Day July 4

Labor Day First Monday in September

Columbus Day Second Monday in October

Veterans Day November 11

Thanksgiving Fourth Thursday in November

Christmas Day December 25

Safe Travel

When it comes to crime, there is Miami, and there is the rest of Florida. As a rule, Miami suffers the same urban problems facing other major US cities such as New York and Los Angeles, but it is no worse than others. The rest of Florida tends to have

lower crime rates than the rest of the nation, but any tourist town is a magnet for petty theft and car break-ins.

If you need any kind of emergency assistance, such as police, ambulance or firefighters, call ☑911. This is a free call from any phone. For health matters see p498.

Hurricanes

Florida hurricane season extends from June through November, but the peak is September and October. Relatively speaking, very few Atlantic Ocean and Gulf of Mexico storms become hurricanes, and fewer still are accurate enough to hit Florida, but the devastation they wreak when they do can be enormous. Travelers should take all hurricane alerts, warnings and evacuation orders seriously.

Hurricanes are generally sighted well in advance, allowing time to prepare. When a hurricane threatens, listen to radio and TV news reports. For more information on storms and preparedness, contact the following:

National Weather Service (www.nws.noaa.gov)

Florida Emergency Hotline (☑800-342-3557) Updated storm warning information.

Florida Division of Emergency Management (www.floridadisaster.org) Hurricane preparedness.

Telephone

Always dial '1' before toll-free (☑800, 888 etc) and domestic long-distance numbers. Some toll-free numbers only work within the US. For local directory assistance, dial ☑411.

To make international calls from the US, dial ☑011 + country code + area code + number. For international operator assistance, dial ☑0. To call the US from abroad,

the international country code for the USA is ☑1.

Pay phones are readily found in major cities, but are becoming rarer. Local calls cost 50¢. Private prepaid phone cards are available from convenience stores, supermarkets and drug stores.

Most of the USA's mobile-phone systems are incompatible with the GSM 900/1800 standard used throughout Europe and Asia. Check with your service provider about using your phone in the US. In terms of coverage, Verizon has the most extensive network, but AT&T, Sprint and T-Mobile are decent. Cellular coverage is generally excellent, except in the Everglades and parts of rural northern Florida.

Tourist Information

Most Florida towns have some sort of tourist information center that provides local information; be aware that chambers of commerce typically only list chamber members, not all the town's hotels and businesses. This guide provides visitor center information throughout.

To order a packet of Florida information prior to coming, contact **Visit Florida** (www.visitflorida.com), and

GOVERNMENT TRAVEL ADVICE

» **Australia** (www.smarttraveller.gov.au)

» **Canada** (www.dfait-maeci.gc.ca)

» **Germany** (www.auswaertiges-amt.de)

» **New Zealand** (www.safetravel.govt.nz)

» **UK** (www.fco.gov.uk)

» **USA** (www.travel.state.gov)

also see the list of websites in Need to Know (p15).

Travelers with Disabilities

Because of the high number of senior residents in Florida, most public buildings are wheelchair accessible and have appropriate restroom facilities. Transportation services are generally accessible to all, and telephone companies provide relay operators for the hearing impaired. Many banks provide ATM instructions in Braille, curb ramps are common and many busy intersections have audible crossing signals.

A number of organizations specialize in the needs of disabled travelers:

Access-Able Travel Source (www.access-able.com) An excellent website with many links.

Flying Wheels Travel (☏507-451-5005; www.flyingwheelstravel.com) A full-service travel agency specializing in disabled travel.

Mobility International USA (www.miusa.org) Advises disabled travelers on mobility issues and runs an educational exchange program.

Travelin' Talk Network (www.travelintalk.net) Run by the same people as Access-Able Travel Source; a global network of service providers.

Volunteering

Volunteering can be a great way to break up a long trip, and it provides memorable opportunities to interact with locals and the land in ways you never would when just passing through.

Volunteer Florida (www.volunteerflorida.org), the primary state-run organization, coordinates volunteer centers across the state.

Though it's aimed at Floridians, casual visitors can find situations that match their time and interests.

Florida's state parks would not function without volunteers. Each park coordinates its own volunteers, and most also have the support of an all-volunteer 'friends' organization (officially called Citizen Support Organizations). Links and contact information are on the website of **Florida State Parks** (www.floridastateparks.org/getinvolved/volunteer.cfm).

Finally, **Habitat for Humanity** (www.habitat.org) does a ton of work in Florida, building homes and helping the homeless.

Women Travelers

Women traveling by themselves or in a group should encounter no particular problems unique to Florida. Indeed, there are a number of excellent resources to help traveling women.

The community resource **Journeywoman** (www.journeywoman.com) facilitates women exchanging travel tips, with links to resources. The Canadian government also publishes the useful, free, downloadable booklet *Her Own Way*; look under 'Publications' at www.voyage.gc.ca.

These two national advocacy groups might also be helpful:

National Organization for Women (NOW; ☏202-628-8669; www.now.org)

Planned Parenthood (☏800-230-7526; www.plannedparenthood.org) Offers referrals to medical clinics throughout the country.

In terms of safety issues, single women need to exhibit the same street smarts as any solo traveler, but they are sometimes more often the target of unwanted attention or harassment.

Some women like to carry a whistle, mace or cayenne-pepper spray in case of assault. These sprays are legal to carry and use in Florida, but only in self-defense. Federal law prohibits them being carried on planes.

If you are assaulted, it may be better to call a rape-crisis hotline before calling the **police** (☏911); telephone books have listings of local organizations, or contact the 24-hour **National Sexual Assault Hotline** (☏800-656-4673; www.rainn.org). Or, go straight to a hospital. Police can sometimes be insensitive with assault victims, while a rape-crisis center or hospital will advocate on behalf of victims and act as a link to other services, including the police.

Work

Seasonal service jobs in tourist beach towns and theme parks are common and often easy to get, if low-paying.

If you are a foreigner in the USA with a standard nonimmigrant visitors visa, you are expressly forbidden to take paid work in the USA and will be deported if you're caught working illegally. In addition, employers are required to establish the bona fides of their employees or face fines. In particular, southern Florida is notorious for large numbers of foreigners working illegally, and immigration officers are vigilant.

To work legally, foreigners need to apply for a work visa before leaving home. Student exchange visitors need a J1 visa, which the following organizations will help arrange:

American Institute for Foreign Study (AIFS; ☏866-906-2437; www.aifs.com)

BUNAC (☏020-7251-3472; www.bunac.org)

Camp America (☏020-7581-7373; www.campamerica.co.uk)

Council on International Educational Exchange (CIEE; ☎800-407-8839; www.ciee.org)

InterExchange (☎212-924-0446; www.interexchange.org) Camp and au-pair programs.

International Exchange Programs (IEP) Australia (☎1300-300-912; www.iep.org.au), New Zealand (☎0800-443-769; www.iep.org.nz)

For nonstudent jobs, temporary or permanent, you need to be sponsored by a US employer, who will arrange an H-category visa. These are not easy to obtain.

Transportation

GETTING THERE & AWAY

Nearly all international travelers to Florida arrive by air, while most US travelers prefer air or car. Getting to Florida by bus is a distant third option, and by train an even more distant fourth. Major regional hubs in Florida include Miami (p133), Fort Lauderdale (p197), Orlando (p288) and Tampa (p373).

Flights, tours and rail tickets can be booked online at www.lonelyplanet.com/bookings.

Air

Unless you live in or near Florida, flying to the region and then renting a car is the most time-efficient option.

Airports & Airlines

Whether you're coming from within the US or from abroad, the entire state is well-served by air.

Major airports:

Fort Lauderdale-Hollywood International Airport (FLL; www.broward.org/airport) Serves metro Fort Lauderdale and Broward County. It's about 30 miles north of Miami and is frequently a less-expensive alternative to Miami.

Miami International Airport (MIA; www.miami-airport.com) One of the state's two busiest international airports. It serves metro Miami, the Everglades and the Keys, and is a hub for American, Delta and US Airways.

Orlando International Airport (MCO; www.orlando airports.net) Handles more passengers than any other airport in Florida. Serves WDW, the Space Coast and the Orlando area.

Tampa International Airport (TPA; www.tampaairport.com) Serves the Tampa Bay and St Petersburg metro area.

Other airports with increased international traffic include Daytona Beach (DAB) and Jacksonville (JAX).

Most cities have airports and offer services to other US cities; these include Palm Beach (PBI; actually in West Palm Beach), Sarasota (SRQ), Tallahassee (TLH), Gainesville (GNV), Fort Myers (RSW), Pensacola (PNS) and Key West (EYW).

The following international airlines service Florida:

Aerolineas Argentinas (AR; www.aerolineas.com)
AeroMexico (AM; www.aeromexico.com)
Air Canada (AC; www.aircanada.com)
Air France (AF; www.airfrance.com)
Air Jamaica (JM; www.airjamaica.com)
Air New Zealand (NZ; www.airnewzealand.com)
Alitalia (AZ; www.alitalia.com)
Bahamas Air (UP; www.bahamasair.com)
British Airways (BA; www.britishairways.com)
Cayman Airways (KX; www.caymanairways.com)
El Al (LY; www.elal.com)
Iberia (IB; www.iberia.com)
KLM (KL; www.klm.com)
Lan (LA; www.lan.com)
Lufthansa (LH; www.lufthansa.com)
Qantas (QF; www.qantas.com)
Swiss International Airlines (LX; www.swiss.com)
Varig Brazilian Airlines (RG; www.varig.com)
Virgin Atlantic (VS; www.virgin-atlantic.com)

Tickets

There are no ticket-buying strategies unique to Florida. However, compare flights among the handful of major international airports, as rates can sometimes fluctuate widely between them, depending on season and demand. As anywhere, the keys to bargains are research, reserving early – at least three to four weeks in advance – and flexible timing. Booking midweek and off-season can net savings.

For a good overview of online ticket agencies, visit **Airinfo** (www.airinfo.travel), which lists travel agencies worldwide. Then visit these:
Cheap Tickets (www.cheaptickets.com)
Expedia (www.expedia.com)
Kayak (www.kayak.com)
Mobissimo (www.mobissimo.com)

Orbitz (www.orbitz.com)
Travelocity (www.travelocity
.com)
Travelzoo (www.travelzoo
.com)

Land

Bus

For bus trips, **Greyhound**
(☎800-231-2222; www.grey
hound.com) is the main long-
distance operator in the US.
It serves Florida from most
major cities. It also has the
only scheduled statewide
service. For more, see Getting Around (p506).

Standard long-distance
fares can be relatively
high: bargain airfares can
undercut buses on long-
distance routes; on shorter
routes, renting a car can
be cheaper. Nonetheless,
discounted (even half-price)
long-distance bus trips are
often available by purchas-
ing tickets online seven to 14
days in advance. Then, once
in Florida, you can rent a car
to get around. Inquire about
multiday passes.

Car & Motorcycle

Driving to Florida is easy;
there are no international
borders or entry issues.
Incorporating Florida into a
larger USA road trip is very
common, and having a car
while in Florida is often a
necessity.

Train

If you're coming from the
East Coast, **Amtrak** (☎800-
872-7245; www.amtrak.com)
makes a comfortable, af-
fordable option for getting
to Florida. Amtrak's *Silver
Service* (which includes
Silver Meteor and *Silver
Star* trains) runs between
New York and Miami, with
services that include Jack-
sonville, Orlando, Tampa,
West Palm Beach and Fort
Lauderdale, plus smaller
Florida towns in between.
Unfortunately, there is no
longer any direct service to

BUS FARES

Sample one-way fares (advance-purchase/standard
fares) between Miami and some major US cities:

CITY	FARE	DURATION (HR)	FREQUENCY (PER DAY)
Atlanta	$79/144	16-18	5-6
New Orleans	$136/149	23-24	3-4
New York City	$156/172	33-35	5-6
Washington, DC	$149/164	27-29	5-6

CAR TRAVEL TIMES

Sample distances and times from various points in the
US to Miami:

CITY	DISTANCE (MILES)	DURATION (HR)
Atlanta	660	10½
Chicago	1380	23
Los Angeles	2750	44
New York City	1280	22
Washington, DC	1050	17

TRAIN FARES

Sample one-way fares (from low to high season) and
durations from NYC to points in Florida:

FROM	TO	FARE	DURATION (HR)
New York City	Jacksonville	$125-210	18-20
New York City	Miami	$125-215	28-31
New York City	Orlando	$125-210	22-23
New York City	Tampa	$125-210	26

Florida from Los Angeles,
New Orleans, Chicago or the
Midwest. Trains from these
destinations connect to the
Silver Service route, but the
transfer adds a day or so to
your travel time.

Another option is Am-
trak's *Auto Train*, which is
designed to take you and
your car from the Wash-
ington, DC area and to the
Orlando area; this saves you
gas, the drive, and having

to pay for a rental car. The
Auto Train leaves daily from
Lorton, Virginia, and goes
only to Sanford, Florida. It
takes about 18 hours, leaving
in the afternoon and arriving the next morning. On
the *Auto Train*, you pay for
your passage, cabin and car
separately. Book tickets in
advance. Children, seniors
and military personnel receive discounts.

Sea

Florida is nearly completely surrounded by the ocean, and it's a major cruise-ship port. For more on cruises, see Cruises. Fort Lauderdale is the largest transatlantic harbor in the US, and adventurous types can always sign up as crew members for a chance to travel the high seas.

GETTING AROUND

Once you reach Florida, traveling by car is the best way of getting around – it allows you to reach areas not otherwise served by public transportation.

Air

The US airline industry is reliable, safe and serves Florida extremely well, both from the rest of the country and within Florida. However, the industry's continuing financial troubles have resulted in a series of high-profile mergers in recent years: Midwest joining Frontier; Orlando-based Air Tran merging into Southwest; and biggest of all, Continental merging with United.

In general, this has led to fewer flights, fuller airplanes, less perks, more fees and higher rates. Airport security screening procedures also keep evolving; allow extra time.

Air service between Florida's four main airports – Fort Lauderdale, Miami, Orlando and Tampa – is frequent and direct. Smaller destinations such as Key West, Fort Myers, Pensacola, Jacksonville, Tallahassee and West Palm Beach are served, but sometimes less often or directly.

Airlines in Florida

Domestic airlines operating in Florida:

American (AA; ☎800-433-7300; www.aa.com) Miami hub; service to and between major Florida cities.

Cape Air (9K; ☎866-227-3247; www.flycapeair.com) Convenient between Fort Myers and Key West.

Delta (DL; ☎800-221-1212; www.delta.com) International carrier serving the main Florida cities, plus flights from Miami to Orlando and Tampa.

Frontier (F9; ☎800-432-1359; www.frontierairlines.com) Flies to Tampa, Orlando and Fort Lauderdale from Denver, Minneapolis and Midwest.

JetBlue (JB; ☎800-538-2583; www.jetblue.com) Serves Orlando, Fort Lauderdale and smaller Florida cities from the East and West Coast.

Southwest (SW; ☎800-435-9792; www.southwest.com) Major budget carrier flying to and between Fort Lauderdale, Tampa, Fort Myers, Orlando and Jacksonville.

Spirit (NK; ☎800-772-7117; www.spiritair.com) Florida-based discount carrier serving Florida cities from East Coast US, Caribbean, and Central and South America.

United (UA; ☎800-864-8331; www.united.com) International flights to Orlando and Miami, plus domestic flights to and between the main Florida cities.

US Airways (US; ☎800-428-4322; www.usairways.com) Serves Florida from most of US.

Air Passes

International travelers who plan on doing a lot of flying, both in and out of the region, might consider buying an air pass. Air passes are available only to non-US citizens, and they must be purchased in conjunction with an international ticket. Conditions and cost structures can be complicated, but all include a certain number of domestic flights (from three to 10) that must be used within 60 days. Sometimes you must plan your itinerary in advance, but dates (and even destinations) can sometimes be left open. Talk with a travel agent to determine if an air pass would save you money based on your plans.

The two main airline alliances offering air passes are **Star Alliance** (www.staralliance.com) and **One World** (www.oneworld.com).

Bicycle

Regional bicycle touring is very popular. Flat countryside

CLIMATE CHANGE & TRAVEL

Every form of transport that relies on carbon-based fuel generates CO_2, the main cause of human-induced climate change. Modern travel is dependent on aeroplanes, which might use less fuel per kilometer per person than most cars but travel much greater distances. The altitude at which aircraft emit gases (including CO_2) and particles also contributes to their climate change impact. Many websites offer 'carbon calculators' that allow people to estimate the carbon emissions generated by their journey and, for those who wish to do so, to offset the impact of the greenhouse gases emitted with contributions to portfolios of climate-friendly initiatives throughout the world. Lonely Planet offsets the carbon footprint of all staff and author travel.

and scenic coastlines make for great itineraries. However, target winter to spring; summer is unbearably hot and humid for long-distance biking.

For more on biking routes and destinations, see From Boots to Beaches (p483). For Florida biking organizations, some of which organize bike tours, see the Directory (p495). Renting a bicycle is easy throughout Florida; see destination chapters.

Some other things to keep in mind:

Helmet laws Helmets are required for anyone aged 16 and younger. Adults are not required to wear helmets, but should.

Road rules Bikes must obey auto rules; ride on the right-hand side of the road, with traffic, not on sidewalks.

Transporting your bike to Florida Bikes are considered checked luggage on airplanes, but often must be boxed and fees can be high (over $200).

Theft Bring and use a sturdy lock (U-type is best). Theft is common, especially in Miami Beach.

For more information and assistance, visit these organizations:

Better World Club (www .betterworldclub.com) Offers a bicycle roadside-assistance program.

International Bicycle Fund (www.ibike.org) Comprehensive overview of bike regulations by airline and lots of advice.

League of American Bicyclists (www.bikeleague .org) General advice, plus lists of local bike clubs and repair shops.

Boat

Florida is a world center for two major types of boat transport: crewing aboard privately owned yachts, and the fast-growing cruise-ship industry.

Each coastal city has sightseeing boats that cruise harbors and coastlines. It really pays (in memories) to get out on the water. Water-taxi services along intracoastal waterways are a feature in Fort Lauderdale and around Sanibel Island and Pine Island on the Gulf.

Cruises

Florida is a huge destination and departure point for cruises of all kinds. Miami likes to brag that it's the 'cruise capital of the world,' and Walt Disney World runs its own **Disney Cruise Line** (☎800-951-3532; www.disney cruise.disney.go.com), which has a number of three- to seven-night cruises throughout the Caribbean, including to Disney's own private island, Castaway Cay. In Fort Lauderdale, also see the boxed texts Out *Titanic*-ing the *Titanic* (p192) and Bahamas Day Trips (p194).

For specials on other multinight and multiday cruises, see the following:

Cruise.com (www.cruise .com)

CruiseWeb (www.cruiseweb .com)

Vacations to Go (www .vacationstogo.com)

CruisesOnly (www.cruises only.com)

Florida's main ports:

Port Canaveral (www.port canaveral.com) On the Atlantic Coast near the Kennedy Space Center and giving Miami a run for its money.

Port Everglades (www.port everglades.net, www.fort -lauderdale-cruises.com) Near Fort Lauderdale, and the third-busiest Florida port.

Port of Miami (www.miami dade.gov/portofmiami) At the world's largest cruise-ship port, the most common trips offered are to the Bahamas, the Caribbean, Key West and Mexico.

Port of Tampa (www.tampa port.com) On the Gulf Coast, and rapidly gaining a foothold in the market.

Major cruise companies:
Carnival Cruise Lines (☎800-764-7419; www.carnival .com)
Norwegian Cruise Line (☎866-234-7350; www.ncl .com)
Royal Caribbean (☎866-562-7625; www.royalcaribbean .com)

Bus

The only statewide bus service is by **Greyhound** (☎800-231-2222; www.grey hound.com), which connects all major and midsized Florida cities, but not always smaller towns (even some popular beach towns). Regional or city-run buses cover their more limited areas much better; used together, these bus systems make travel by bus possible, but time-consuming.

Individual city sections in this book usually include the local bus and Greyhound station information. On Greyhound, it's always a bit cheaper to take the bus during the week than on the weekend. Also, fares for children are usually about half the adult fare (see p508 for fares).

Car & Motorcycle

By far the most convenient and popular way to travel around Florida is by car. While it's quite possible to avoid using a car on single-destination trips – to Miami, Orlando theme parks, or a self-contained beach resort – relying on public transit can be inconvenient for even limited regional touring. Even smaller tourist-friendly towns like Naples, Sarasota or St Augustine can be frustrating to negotiate without a car. Motorcycles are also popular

GREYHOUND FARES

To get you started, here are some round-trip Greyhound fares and travel times around Florida:

FROM	TO	FARE	DURATION (HR)
Daytona Beach	St Augustine	$25	1
Fort Lauderdale	Melbourne	$54	4
Jacksonville	Tallahassee	$51	3
Melbourne	Daytona Beach	$34	3½
Miami	Key West	$54	4½
Miami	Naples	$41	3
Panama City	Pensacola	$40	3
St Augustine	Jacksonville	$18	1
Naples	Tampa	$54	5
Tampa	Orlando	$32	2
Tallahassee	Panama City	$34	2½

in Florida, given the flat roads and warm weather (summer rain excepted).

Automobile Associations

The **American Automobile Association** (AAA; ☎800-874-7532; www.aaa.com) has reciprocal agreements with several international auto clubs (check with AAA and bring your membership card). For members, AAA offers travel insurance, tour books, diagnostic centers for used-car buyers and a greater number of regional offices, and it advocates politically for the auto industry.

An ecofriendly alternative is the **Better World Club** (☎866-238-1137; www .betterworldclub.com), which donates 1% of earnings to assist environmental cleanup, offers ecologically sensitive choices for services and advocates politically for environmental causes. Better World also has a roadside-assistance program for bicycles.

In both organizations, the central member benefit is 24-hour emergency roadside assistance anywhere in the USA. Both clubs also offer trip planning and free maps, travel-agency services, car insurance and a range of discounts (car rentals, hotels etc).

Driver's License

Foreign visitors can legally drive in the USA for up to 12 months with their home driver's license. However, getting an International Driving Permit (IDP) is recommended; this will have more credibility with US traffic police, especially if your home license doesn't have a photo or is in a foreign language. Your automobile association at home can issue an IDP, valid for one year, for a small fee. You must carry your home license together with the IDP. To drive a motorcycle, you need either a valid US state motorcycle license or an IDP specially endorsed for motorcycles.

Insurance

Don't put the key into the ignition if you don't have insurance, which is legally required, or else you risk financial ruin if there's an accident. If you already have auto insurance (even overseas), or if you buy travel insurance, make sure that the policy has adequate liability coverage for a rental car in Florida; it probably does, but check.

Rental-car companies will provide liability insurance, but most charge extra. Always ask. Rental companies almost never include collision-damage insurance for the vehicle. Instead, they offer an optional Collision Damage Waiver (CDW) or Loss Damage Waiver (LDW), usually with an initial deductible of $100 to $500. For an extra premium, you can usually get this deductible covered as well. However, most credit cards now offer collision-damage coverage for rental cars if you rent for 15 days or less and charge the total rental to your card. This is a good way to avoid paying extra fees to the rental company, but note that if there's an accident, you sometimes must pay the rental car company first and then seek reimbursement from the credit-card company. Check your credit-card policy. Paying extra for some or all of this insurance increases the cost of a rental car by as much as $10 to $30 a day.

Rental
CAR

Car rental is a very competitive business. Most rental companies require that you have a major credit card, that you be at least 25 years old and that you have a valid driver's license (your home license will do). Some national companies may rent to drivers between the ages of 21 and 24 for an additional charge. Those under 21 are usually not permitted to rent at all.

Good independent agencies are listed in this guide and by **Car Rental Express** (www.carrentalexpress.com), which rates and compares independent agencies in US cities; it's particularly useful for searching out cheaper long-term rentals.

National car-rental companies:

Alamo (www.alamo.com)

Avis (www.avis.com)

Budget (www.budget.com)

Dollar (www.dollar.com)

Enterprise (www.enterprise.com)

Hertz (www.hertz.com)

National (www.nationalcar.com)

Rent-a-Wreck (www.rentawreck.com)

Thrifty (www.thrifty.com)

Rental cars are readily available at all airport locations and many downtown city locations. With advance reservations for a small car, the daily rate with unlimited mileage is about $35 to $55, while typical weekly rates are $200 to $400, plus myriad taxes and fees. If you rent from a nonairport location, you save the exorbitant airport fees.

An alternative in Miami is **Zipcar** (www.zipcar.com), a car-sharing service that charges hourly/daily rental fees with free gas, insurance and limited mileage included; prepayment is required.

MOTORCYCLE

To straddle a Harley across Florida, contact **EagleRider** (☏888-900-9901; www.eaglerider.com), with offices in Daytona Beach, Fort Lauderdale, Miami, St Augustine and Orlando. It offers a wide range of models, which start at $150 a day, plus liability insurance. Adult riders (over 21) are not required by Florida law to wear a helmet, but you should.

MOTORHOME (RV)

Forget hotels. Drive your own. Touring Florida by recreational vehicle can be as low-key or as over-the-top as you wish.

After settling on the vehicle's size, consider the impact of gas prices, gas mileage, additional mileage costs, insurance and refundable deposits; these can add up quickly. Typically, RVs don't come with unlimited mileage, so estimate your mileage up front to calculate the true rental cost.

Cruise America (☏800-671-8042; www.cruiseamerica.com) The largest national RV-rental firm has offices across Florida.

Adventures on Wheels (☏800-943-3579; www.adventuresonwheels.com) Office in Miami.

Recreational Vehicle Rental Association (☏703-591-7130; www.rvra.org) A good resource for RV information and advice, and helps find rental locations.

Road Rules

If you're new to Florida or US roads, here are some basics:

» The maximum speed limit on interstates is 75mph, but that drops to 65mph and 55mph in urban areas. Pay attention to the posted signs. City street speed limits vary between 15mph and 45mph.

» Florida police officers are strict with speed-limit enforcement, and speeding tickets are expensive. If caught going over the speed limit by 10mph, the fine is $155.

» All passengers in a car must wear seat belts; the fine for not wearing a seat belt is $30. All children under three must be in a child safety seat.

» As in the rest of the US, drive on the right-hand side of the road. On highways, pass in the left-hand lane (but anxious drivers often pass wherever space allows).

» Right turns on a red light are permitted after a full stop. At four-way stop signs, the car that reaches the intersection first has right of way. In a tie, the car on the right has right of way.

Hitchhiking

Hitchhiking is never entirely safe in any country, and we don't recommend it. Travelers who decide to hitch should understand that they are taking a small but serious risk. You may not be able to identify the local rapist or murderer before you get into the vehicle. People who do choose to hitch will be safer if they go in pairs and let someone know where they are planning to go. Be sure to ask the driver where he or she is going rather than telling the person where you want to go.

Local Transportation

Bus

Local bus services are available in most cities; along the coasts, service typically connects downtown to at least one or two beach communities. Some cities (like Tampa and Jacksonville) have high-frequency trolleys circling downtown, while some coastal stretches are linked by seasonal trolleys that ferry beachgoers among towns (like between St Pete Beach and Clearwater).

Fares are between $1 and $2. Exact change upon boarding is usually required, though some buses take $1 bills. Transfers – slips of paper that will allow you to change buses – range from free to 25¢. Hours of operation differ from city to city, but generally buses run from approximately 6am to 10pm.

Metro

Walt Disney World has a monorail, and Tampa has an old-fashioned, one-line streetcar, but the only real metro systems are in and near Miami. In Miami, a driverless Metromover circles downtown and connects with Metrorail, which connects downtown north to Hialeah and south to Kendall.

Meanwhile, north of Miami, Hollywood, Fort Lauderdale and West Palm Beach (and the towns between them) are well connected by Tri-Rail's double-decker commuter trains. Tri-Rail runs all the way to Miami, but the full trip takes longer than driving.

Train

Amtrak (☎800-872-7245; www.amtrak.com) trains run between a number of Florida cities. As a way to get around Florida, Amtrak offers extremely limited service, and yet for certain specific trips its trains can be very easy and inexpensive. In essence, daily trains run between Jacksonville, Orlando and Miami, with one line branching off to Tampa. In addition, thruway motorcoach (or bus) service gets Amtrak passengers to Daytona Beach, St Petersburg and Fort Myers.

behind the scenes

SEND US YOUR FEEDBACK

We love to hear from travelers – your comments keep us on our toes and help make our books better. Our well-traveled team reads every word on what you loved or loathed about this book. Although we cannot reply individually to postal submissions, we always guarantee that your feedback goes straight to the appropriate authors, in time for the next edition. Each person who sends us information is thanked in the next edition – and the most useful submissions are rewarded with a free book.

Visit **lonelyplanet.com/contact** to submit your updates and suggestions or to ask for help. Our award-winning website also features inspirational travel stories, news and discussions.

Note: We may edit, reproduce and incorporate your comments in Lonely Planet products such as guidebooks, websites and digital products, so let us know if you don't want your comments reproduced or your name acknowledged. For a copy of our privacy policy visit lonelyplanet.com/privacy.

OUR READERS

Many thanks to the travelers who used the last edition and wrote to us with helpful hints, useful advice and interesting anecdotes:
Sue Atkinson, Jochen Beier, Fiona Blaker, Richard Cassem, Lori Ceier, Ilona de Jong, Monica Fernandez, Katrin Flatscher, Lothar Franke, Heike Grosse, Keith Hall, Nicola Hicks, Geoff Lindsey, Joern Luethje, Manuela Mayer, Peter Phillips, Kelly Prieto, Julia Ringma, Mike, MJ Shepherd, H Sutton, Jeff Taylor, Maarten Woestenburg, Andrea Wolfschaffner

AUTHOR THANKS
Jeff Campbell

Jennye, Jennifer, Adam and Emily – you made this the easiest update ever! Many thanks to friends Anne Higgins, Ali DeLargy, Kathleen Ogle, and Michelle Kratochvil (and Judi!) for passing on their Florida tips. To Darby's own James, Karen and son William: thanks for your companionship to Cayo Costa and great advice. As always, endless thanks to my children, Jackson and Miranda, and my wife, Deanna, for all their love and support, and for not minding my tan.

Jennifer Denniston

Huge thanks to Jennye, Alison, Brigitte and Jeff – I appreciate your kindness, patience, wisdom, guidance and sense of humor. Special thanks to my husband Rhawn, my daughters Anna and Harper, my mom and dad, and Marj Whitley – without you, I couldn't do what I do. You guys are amazing research assistants, and I can always count on you to help me balance the gypsy with the homebody mom.

Adam Karlin

Thanks: Anna Whitlow, Paula Nino, Jordan Melnick, Megan Harmon, the Paquet family, my Keys crew and every other Floridian who hooked it up. Big thanks to the Lonely Planet crew: Alison, Jennye Garibaldi, Jeff, Jennifer and Emily. Thanks to my grandmother, Rhoda Brickman, for getting me down to Florida in the first place, to my parents who always give me a place to write, and to Rachel for being Rachel.

Emily Matchar

A huge thanks to Jennye Garibaldi, Brigitte Ellemor and the rest of the LP team! Thanks to Debbie and Joel Shlian for showing me all the great spots in Boca and Delray, to Melanie Hibbert for your great Gainesville tips, and to Stacie Nagy and Co for your great Pensacola and Panhandle foodie advice. Thanks, as always, to Jamin Asay, my partner in travel and in life.

ACKNOWLEDGMENTS

512

Climate map data adapted from Peel MC, Finlayson BL & McMahon TA (2007) 'Updated World Map of the Köppen-Geiger Climate Classification', *Hydrology and Earth System Sciences*, 11, 163344.

Cover photograph: Lifeguard station, Miami, Grafenhain Gunter / 4CornersImages ©. Many of the images in this guide are available for licensing from Lonely Planet Images: www.lonelyplanetimages.com.

BEHIND THE SCENES

THIS BOOK

This 6th edition of Lonely Planet's Florida guidebook was written by Jeff Campbell, Jennifer Denniston, Adam Karlin and Emily Matchar. The previous edition was written by Jeff Campbell, Jennifer Denniston, Adam Karlin, Becca Blond, Beth Greenfield and Willy Volk. This guidebook was commissioned in Lonely Planet's Oakland office, and produced by the following:

Commissioning Editor Jennye Garibaldi

Coordinating Editor Charlotte Orr

Coordinating Cartographer Valeska Canas

Coordinating Layout Designer Yvonne Bischofberger, Wibowo Rusli

Managing Editor Brigitte Ellemor

Senior Editor Susan Paterson

Managing Cartographers Mark Griffiths, Alison Lyall

Managing Layout Designers Chris Girdler, Jane Hart

Assisting Editors Alice Barker, Jackey Coyle, Carly Hall, Briohny Hooper, Anne Mulvaney, Catherine Naghten, Charles Rawlings-Way, Sarah Koel

Assisting Cartographers Jane Chapman, Karusha Ganga, Valentina Kremenchutskaya, Jacqueline Nguyen, Sophie Reed

Cover Research Naomi Parker

Internal Image Research Sabrina Dalbesio

Thanks to Sasha Baskett, Ryan Evans, Heather Howard, Evan Jones, Trent Paton, Raphael Richards, Dianne Schallmeiner, Tasmin Waby McNaughtan, Gerard Walker

index

000 Map pages
000 Photo pages

how to use this book

These symbols will help you find the listings you want:

◉	Sights	☞	Tours	♟	Drinking
🏖	Beaches	🎉	Festivals & Events	☆	Entertainment
🏃	Activities	🛏	Sleeping	🛍	Shopping
🎓	Courses	✖	Eating	ℹ	Information/Transport

Look out for these icons:

TOP CHOICE — Our author's recommendation

FREE — No payment required

🌿 — A green or sustainable option

Our authors have nominated these places as demonstrating a strong commitment to sustainability – for example by supporting local communities and producers, operating in an environmentally friendly way, or supporting conservation projects.

These symbols give you the vital information for each listing:

☏	Telephone Numbers	🛜	Wi-Fi Access	🚌	Bus
⊘	Opening Hours	🏊	Swimming Pool	⛴	Ferry
Ⓟ	Parking	🥗	Vegetarian Selection	Ⓜ	Metro
⊘	Nonsmoking	📖	English-Language Menu	Ⓢ	Subway
❄	Air-Conditioning	👪	Family-Friendly	⊖	London Tube
@	Internet Access	🐾	Pet-Friendly	Ⓣ	Tram
				Ⓡ	Train

Reviews are organised by author preference.

Map Legend

Sights
- Beach
- Buddhist
- Castle
- Christian
- Hindu
- Islamic
- Jewish
- Monument
- Museum/Gallery
- Ruin
- Winery/Vineyard
- Zoo
- Other Sight

Activities, Courses & Tours
- Diving/Snorkelling
- Canoeing/Kayaking
- Skiing
- Surfing
- Swimming/Pool
- Walking
- Windsurfing
- Other Activity/Course/Tour

Sleeping
- Sleeping
- Camping

Eating
- Eating

Drinking
- Drinking
- Cafe

Entertainment
- Entertainment

Shopping
- Shopping

Information
- Post Office
- Tourist Information

Transport
- Airport
- Border Crossing
- Bus
- Cable Car/Funicular
- Cycling
- Ferry
- Metro
- Monorail
- Parking
- S-Bahn
- Taxi
- Train/Railway
- Tram
- Tube Station
- U-Bahn
- Other Transport

Routes
- Tollway
- Freeway
- Primary
- Secondary
- Tertiary
- Lane
- Unsealed Road
- Plaza/Mall
- Steps
- Tunnel
- Pedestrian Overpass
- Walking Tour
- Walking Tour Detour
- Path

Boundaries
- International
- State/Province
- Disputed
- Regional/Suburb
- Marine Park
- Cliff
- Wall

Population
- Capital (National)
- Capital (State/Province)
- City/Large Town
- Town/Village

Geographic
- Hut/Shelter
- Lighthouse
- Lookout
- Mountain/Volcano
- Oasis
- Park
- Pass
- Picnic Area
- Waterfall

Hydrography
- River/Creek
- Intermittent River
- Swamp/Mangrove
- Reef
- Canal
- Water
- Dry/Salt/Intermittent Lake
- Glacier

Areas
- Beach/Desert
- Cemetery (Christian)
- Cemetery (Other)
- Park/Forest
- Sportsground
- Sight (Building)
- Top Sight (Building)

OUR STORY

A beat-up old car, a few dollars in the pocket and a sense of adventure. In 1972 that's all Tony and Maureen Wheeler needed for the trip of a lifetime – across Europe and Asia overland to ~~~~~ at the end ~~~~ broke but ~~~~~~~~~ le writing and stapling ~~~~~~~~~~ ss *Asia on the Cheap*. ~~~~~~~~~~ Lonely Planet was born. ~~~~~~~~~~ lelbourne, London and

Oakla~~~~ ~~~~~~~~~~ hat 'a great guidebook
shou~~~

2-8-12

917.59
LONE

OU~~~~~~~~

Jeff Campbell

Coordinating Author, Tampa Bay & Southwest Florida, Understanding Florida Jeff Campbell is the great-grandson of Florida pioneers who cleared the pines, mined the phosphate and paved the roads in central Florida. As a child, he remembers winter nights driving with his grandfather through the orange groves to 'light the pots,' searching for alligators in the local lake and riding Space Mountain the year it opened. As an adult, he's been a travel writer for Lonely Planet since 2000. He was the coordinating author of *Florida 5*, as well as of *Southwest USA; Zion & Bryce Canyon National Parks; Hawaii; New York, Washington & Mid-Atlantic Trips;* and three editions of *USA*.

Read more about Jeff at:
lonelyplanet.com/members/jeffcampbell

Jennifer Denniston

Orlando & Walt Disney World, The Space Coast Jennifer caught the travel bug at age nine, when her parents took the family on a 10-week trip through Europe, and has since traveled independently across five continents. She and her husband, a geology professor, spend three or four months every year road-tripping with their daughters Anna (10) and Harper (8). They live in Iowa, where Jennifer earned her Masters degree in American Studies and taught writing at the University of Iowa. She has written for Lonely Planet for many years.

Read more about Jennifer at:
lonelyplanet.com/members/jenniferdenniston

Adam Karlin

Miami, The Everglades, Florida Keys & Key West Adam grew up, as so many Americans do, with grandparents in Florida, and fondly remembers many a December snowbirding in West Palm Beach. Later in life he worked as a reporter for the *Key West Citizen* before being hired by Lonely Planet to cover South Florida in all her myriad weirdness. Since then he's written or contributed to over two dozen guidebooks for the company, almost always in tropical places: the Southern USA, Caribbean, Africa and Southeast Asia. It's a living. Follow Adam at www.walkonfine.com.

Read more about Adam at:
lonelyplanet.com/members/adamkarlin

Emily Matchar

Southeast Florida, Northeast Florida, The Panhandle Like 99% of Americans, Emily's first experience with Florida was a childhood trip to Disney World, and she's been eagerly returning to the state ever since. As a native Southerner, she has a particular affinity with the Panhandle, where, on this past trip, she ate more fried oysters than is probably recommended. When she's not traipsing the globe, Emily lives in Chapel Hill, North Carolina and writes about culture, travel and food for a number of magazines and newspapers. She's contributed to more than a dozen Lonely Planet guidebooks.

Read more about Emily at:
lonelyplanet.com/members/emilymatchar

Published by Lonely Planet Publications Pty Ltd
ABN 36 005 607 983
6th edition – Jan 2012
ISBN 978 1 74179 576 9
© Lonely Planet 2012   Photographs © as indicated 2012
10 9 8 7 6 5 4 3 2 1
Printed in China